Corporate Financial
Reporting and Analysis
Text and Cases

The Robert N. Anthony/Willard J. Graham Series in Accounting

Corporate Financial Reporting and Analysis

Text and Cases

Third Edition

David F. Hawkins
Professor of Business Administration
Graduate School of Business Administration
Harvard University

1986

IRWIN
Homewood, Illinois   60430

To Barbara

HF5686
C7
H35
1986 b

PREFACE

This book is based on the very successful Analysis of Corporate Financial Reports course taught in the MBA program of the Harvard Graduate School of Business Administration. The course is based on the assumption that the students have at best a limited understanding of accounting and financial analysis. The thurst of the course is that published corporate financial statements can represent genuine managerial performance, or they can represent the illusion of performance. Investors who can tell the difference have a considerable advantage in making their investment decisions. Similarly, corporate managers who understand the relationship between corporate reporting and business policy, as well as how other managers can influence profits through the judicious use of alternative accounting practices, are more likely to succeed than their less knowledgeable competitors. Ignorance of the options, uncertainties, and ambiguities of the practices underlying the compilation of corporate financial statements can lead creditors to make poor credit decisions. On the other hand, unless those practicing public accountancy understand how investors use financial data, how to identify and interpret the motives of managers issuing financial reports, and the relationship between business-operating and financial-reporting decisions, they cannot satisfactorily fulfill their third-party responsibility to the issuers and users of corporate financial statements. In short, an intimate knowledge of the practices and subtleties of financial accounting and the ability to apply sound financial analysis techniques can be critical to the success of many of those who participate in our business system.

Today corporations have considerable leeway in how they report their financial condition and results of operations. Despite recent progress in eliminating undesirable reporting practices, many areas remain in which alternative practices are equally acceptable for reporting essentially identical business situations. The profits of the reporting company will vary depending on which alternative is used.

This book provides the reader with an understanding of the current state of financial reporting practices; the ways in which the corporate financial statements published in annual reports, prospectuses, and proxy statements influence our economic system; the significant consequences of these data for the people who depend on their credibility; and the methods by which competent statement users interpret the data contained in corporate financial reports. It is not a book on accounting methodology.

The subject matter is approached from a variety of points of view. First and foremost are the interests of those closest to the corporation, namely, the management publishing the financial statements, existing and potential stockholders, financial analysts using the statements for investment recommendations, the grantors of trade and commercial credit, and the independent certified public accountant responsible for expressing an opinion on the fairness of the statements issued by the management. Also covered are the interests of others in a number of different business negotiations and transactions where the use and interpretation of financial statements has assumed major proportions, such as the determination of rates in regulated industries; the purchase and sale of businesses; government investigation of prices and other practices of particular industries and individual enterprises; and how unions determine what to demand through collective bargaining.

Textual Material

The first two chapters of this book present background material and do not include cases. The purpose of Chapter 1 is to familiarize the reader with (1) some of the fundamental issues in corporate reporting and analysis and (2) some of the key institutions that influence corporate reporting and financial analysis standards and practices. Chapter 2 provides a historical background for putting into perspective these issues and the roles of the key institutions.

Each of the other chapters consists of text and selected case studies. The split of pages between text and cases is about even. Thus, unlike a number of other casebooks, there should be sufficient textual material in this book to satisfy the professional user seeking to gain a better understanding of fundamentals and current practices in the area of corporate financial reporting and analysis. Such readers might include corporate executives, bankers, financial analysts, and individual investors.

Uses of Financial Data

Every chapter includes some discussion of financial statement analysis and interpretation practices relevant to that chapter. In Part Four, however, three chapters are devoted exclusively to financial analysis topics. These three chapters cover the fundamentals of financial analysis that the reader will need to interpret the text and cases presented in later chapters.

A Clinical Approach

The case studies have been prepared as a basis for discussion of the topics covered in the related text. They have not been selected to present illustrations of either appropriate or inappropriate handling of financial reporting problems. To decide what is appropriate action is the purpose of the case discussion.

Most of the cases require a decision on the part of the student. Typically, the student is asked to assume a role with a real sense of the professional and personal involvement of top management responsible for issuing financial data to the public in a particular situation or of a statement user responsible for making recommendations based on the data. To make the management decision realistically, the student must identify the administrative burdens of the decision maker, the opportunities for creative action, and the manager's responsibilities. In particular, the student must be concerned with how financial reporting relates to other areas of top management concern, such as stockholder relations, the market price of the company's stock, dividend policy, capital structure, union wage demands, product pricing, and antitrust actions. The student must think through the implications for the company of actions that investors, the company's independent auditor, the regulatory authorities, and others might take as a result of the company's decision. In cases where the student is asked to apply financial analysis techniques directly to obtain insights into the reporting company, the student should relate these to stock valuation practices and theory and to debt rating considerations, as well as assume the responsibility of making a competent recommendation to others who must rely upon the analyst's recommendations. Seldom will there be a simple, easy answer to the problems posed.

Discussion of the case studies within a decision-making framework should give students an appreciation of:

1. The "real world" difficulties in resolving financial reporting and analysis issues.
2. The role of judgment in the selection of appropriate accounting practices and analytical techniques.
3. The evolutionary state of accounting principles and analysis practices.
4. The significance and limitations of financial accounting data for corporate decision-making purposes and security valuations.
5. The need for managers to involve themselves in the financial reporting process.
6. The vital communication function that financial reports have in our economic system.

7. The difficulties encountered in trying to develop an integrated statement of a basic theory of accounting that is both acceptable to accounting theoreticians and at the same time responsive to the subtleties of our complex economic system.
8. The relationship between the accounting systems and reports management uses for management control and financial reporting purposes.
9. The urgent need for the business, financial analysis, and accounting professions to develop a set of accounting principles that eliminate the differences in accounting practices not justified by different circumstances.

Reading Plan

The cases and chapters included in this book have been used in many undergraduate and graduate accounting and financial analysis courses at both the introductory and advanced levels. In each of these courses the order and manner in which the materials were used varied according to the student's prior background in the field and the instructor's course objectives. Consequently, it is unlikely that the materials included in this book could be put together in an order that would meet the needs of all readers and courses.

It is suggested that each reader skim the table of contents before reading the text and determine where to begin and in what order the chapters should be covered. For example, readers with limited or no prior understanding of financial accounting and financial analysis probably should read the chapters in the order presented. On the other hand a reader with considerable exposure at the introductory level might just skim the first eight chapters and begin reading seriously at Chapter 11.

Changing Accounting Principles

The accounting principles and disclosure rules upon which corporate financial reports are based are continually being revised by the Financial Accounting Standards Board and the Securities and Exchange Commission. One way to keep abreast of these changes is to read either *The Wall Street Journal* or the *New York Times*. Both of these newspapers cover proposed and actual changes in accounting principles. More complete but less timely coverage can be found in the various publications of the Financial Accounting Standards Board, the *Journal of Accountancy*, published by the American Institute of Certified Public Accountants, or the *Financial Executive* (*FE*), published by the Financial Executives Institute.

At the time this book went to press, the Financial Accounting Standards Board had either released proposed changes for public comment or was considering drafts of a number of future accounting principles changes.

Since each of these decisions will have important implications for the future, the reader is urged to follow the reports of the board's deliberations on a current basis. To help the reader put these proposed changes in their proper perspective, each is discussed in later chapters.

Acknowledgments

A number of people have helped in the preparation of this book and the Harvard Business School's financial accounting course, from which the book draws heavily. Walter Frese provided the pedagogical and corporate-reporting-philosophy foundation for both the book and the course upon which it is based. Two of my colleagues—Robert Madera and Mary Wehle—were responsible for many of the original course materials that were subsequently incorporated into the book. The difficult and frustrating task of controlling the manuscript in its many drafts was ably accomplished by Ms. Elisa Lusetti. My wife, Barbara, provided both the inspiration needed and the continuing support that was required to squeeze out of our busy family and professional lives the time needed to complete the manuscript. Professor Robert Anthony provided helpful editorial advice. I am grateful to all of these people and hope they will share with me a feeling of accomplishment and pride in this most recent outgrowth of the Harvard Business School's course in Analysis of Corporate Financial Reports. In addition, I wish to thank the President and Fellows of Harvard College for their permission to reproduce the case and textual materials copyrighted in their name, as well as Robert Sprouse, Richard Vancil, Walter Frese, Robert Anthony, Brandt Allen, Russell Nelson, Norman Bartczak, John Yeager, Andrew McCosh, John Shank, Regina Herzlinger, Ross Walker, T. F. Bradshaw, C. A. Bliss, and Derek Newton for allowing me to use or adapt cases originally prepared by them. Others who have been associated either directly or indirectly with the development of the cases in the book include the Financial Accounting Standards Board, J. T. Ball, Len Savoie, Ed Jepson, David Macey, Arnie Ludwick, Don Bryant, David Koenig, Bob McInnis, Jerry Brougher, Neil Churchill, Leslie Pearlman, Keith Butters, Dennis Frolin, Malcom P. McNair, and Robert Merriam. I am also grateful to the Dow Jones Company, *The Wall Street Journal*, and *Barrons* for permission to reprint materials from their publications.

David F. Hawkins

CONTENTS

Part Three
Role of Certified Public Accountants' Opinion in Corporate Reporting and Analysis

Part Four
Basic Financial Statement Analysis Techniques

10　Growth Analysis **260**

Business Policy, Marketing, and Financial Dimensions of Growth:
*Optimum Strategies. Market Share. Exceptions. Other Strategies.
Product Portfolio and Product Strategy. Financial Strategies.*
Sustainable Growth Rate Equations: *Actual versus Indicated. Sources
of Growth. Valuation Implications. Additive Version. Some
Refinements.* Earnings-per-Share Growth. Analysis of Income Change:
Real versus Nominal. Additional Analysis.

Part Five
Measurement and Analysis of Income

11　Recognition and Analysis of Income **335**

Recognition: *Revenue Recognition Methods. Services. Nonmonetary
Transactions. Right to Return. Product Financing Agreements.
Inappropriate Interest Rates. Accounting for Bad Debts. Direct Write-
Off Method. Bad Debt Estimation Method. Accounting Entities for Bad
Debt Estimation Method. Financial Statement Presentation. Warranties
and Service Guarantees. Realization Controversy.* Analytical
Considerations.

Specific Intangible Assets: *Patents. Copyrights. Franchises. Trademarks and Trade Names. Leasehold Improvements. Organization Costs. Intangible Development Costs. Computer Software. Role of Judgment. Profit Impact of Shift. Inappropriate Practices.* Financial Analysis.

19 Inventory Pricing and Analysis **646**

Inventory Pricing: *Periodic and Perpetual Inventory Systems. Pricing Bases. Cost or Market, Whichever Is Lower. Statement Presentation.* Inventory Analysis. Summary.

20 Analysis and Reporting of Intercorporate Investments and Business
Combinations **691**

Equity Investments: *Ownership Interests of Less than 20 Percent. Ownership Interests of More than 20 Percent. Changes in Ownership Percentages.* Business Combinations: Two Approaches: *Purchase Method. Pooling of Interests Method. Opinion No. 16, "Business Combinations." Conditions Requiring Pooling Treatment. The 90 Percent Test. Accounting Mechanics. Reporting Requirements. Disclosure of Poolings. Purchase Accounting.* Goodwill: *The Nature of Goodwill. "Negative Goodwill." Goodwill Tax Consideration. Continuing Controversy.* Financial Analysis.

PART ONE

Corporate Reporting and Analysis Environment

CHAPTER 1

Institutions, Issues, and Process

This chapter is concerned with the preparation and interpretation of corporate financial accounting statements issued by business enterprises when reporting to parties outside of the business. The function of accounting is to provide information about economic entities that could be useful in making economic decisions. Accounting includes several branches, such as financial or corporate accounting, managerial accounting, and governmental accounting. Corporate financial reports provide a continual history, expressed in money terms, of the economic resources and obligations of a business enterprise and of the economic activities that affect those resources and activities. These items and any changes in them are identified and measured in conformity with financial accounting principles that are generally accepted at the time the statements are prepared. The typical outputs of this process are the statement of financial position, the income statement, and the changes in financial position statement.

The management of the company publishing financial statements is responsible for their content. Many people mistakenly believe that the statements are the responsibility of the public accountant who audited them. A careful reading of the statement issued by the independent certified public accountant with audited financial statements shows it expresses only a personal opinion as to (1) the fairness of statements; (2) their degree of conformity with the recognized generally accepted accounting principles; and (3) the consistency of the accounting practices used with those followed in the previous accounting periods.

The adequacy of financial statements is judged in terms of the fairness and usefulness of the data provided to all of the interested parties. These are difficult standards to define, and there is considerable disagreement as to their definition. Nevertheless, a great number of financial accounting conventions, concepts, principles, and standards of disclosure have evolved and been supported by recognized accounting authorities. These authorities include the Financial Accounting Standards Board (FASB), the American

3

Institute of Certified Public Accountants (AICPA), and the Securities and Exchange Commission (SEC).

One of the early actions of the Securities and Exchange Commission was to rule that companies under its jurisdiction be audited by independent public accountants. Although the SEC was given the power to establish accounting rules by the Securities Exchange Acts of 1933–34, very early in its existence the commission made it known that it expected the private sector to assume the main part of this activity. With few exceptions, the accounting profession carried out this responsibility through the AICPA's Accounting Principle Board (APB) and its predecessor, the Committee on Accounting Procedure (CAP). However, in 1973 the accounting profession voluntarily gave up its central role in developing generally accepted accounting principles to a newly created independent private body called the Financial Accounting Standards Board. At that time, the SEC indicated that it would continue its policy of leaving the determination of accounting rules to a responsible body and that it would support the FASB in much the same way as it had worked with the AICPA's earlier rule-making bodies.

Accounting Principles Authorities

The AICPA's activities in the development of a formal statement of accounting principles began in 1938 when it formed a Committee on Accounting Procedure (CAP) to "narrow the areas of difference in corporate reporting" by gradually eliminating less desirable practices. Over a period of 20 years, the CAP issued 51 *Accounting Research Bulletins* (ARBs) indicating preferred treatments of various items and transactions. Although these bulletins were advisory rather than binding, they became highly influential. They were supported by the SEC and the stock exchanges and were observed by the profession generally.

Despite this progress, a feeling persisted, both within and without the profession, that too many alternative accounting principles, still regarded as "generally accepted," were applicable in similar circumstances. It was also recognized that changed business conditions—new forms of financing, new tax laws, and the evolution of more complex corporate structures—required a more rapid development of accounting principles than had been previously considered necessary.

The AICPA in 1959 therefore created a new body to succeed the CAP and to carry on its work in a broader and more intensive way. Between 1959 and 1973, this 18-member Accounting Principles Board (APB) of the AICPA was the leading authority on accounting principles for business. It issued 31 *Opinions.* The FASB, which became the leading authority in 1973 after the APB was disbanded, adopted the *Opinions.* So, until some specific action is taken by the FASB, the APB *Opinions* continue to dictate practices which constitute acceptable corporate reporting.

Financial Accounting Standards Board

The FASB consists of seven full-time members with specific terms of appointment from the fields of public accounting, industry, government, and education. They are selected by the trustees of the Financial Accounting Foundation (FAF). Assisting the board members is a full-time research staff, as well as individuals who are invited to join ad hoc task forces to resolve specific issues, and an appointed Financial Accounting Standards Advisory Council. This broadly representative advisory council meets periodically and advises the FASB on agenda topics and priorities, suggests members for task forces, and consults on numerous other technical and administrative matters.

The standard-setting process of the FASB begins with placing an accounting problem on the board's technical agenda. Next, a board member is assigned to prepare, with staff assistance, a preliminary definition of the problem and a bibliography of the significant literature on the subject. Once this step is completed, the problem is reviewed by the FASB and a task force is appointed to continue work on the project. The task force (consisting of at least one member of the board who serves as chairperson, members of the advisory council, and other persons with expertise in some aspects of the problem) is responsible for preparing a neutral and comprehensive discussion memorandum on the agenda item. This document outlines alternative solutions to the problem and the arguments and implications relative to each.

Upon completion of the required research and the discussion memorandum, the FASB initiates a procedure to establish financial accounting standards taking into consideration the interests and points of view of all concerned parties. This process begins with the issuance of a 60-day notice of a public hearing on the problem and the simultaneous publication of the discussion memorandum. At the public hearings, oral reports and written papers are solicited and presented. After the public hearing, a proposed *Statement of Financial Accounting Standards* is prepared. An affirmative vote of at least four of the seven members is required before a draft statement can be released to the public. Next, after a public comment exposure period of at least 60 days, the FASB reviews the exposure comments, and if the required four out of seven votes are obtained, it issues a final draft of its statement. Normally, the effective date of application of a *Statement of Financial Accounting Standards* will not be earlier than the beginning of the reporting entities' fiscal year commencing 90 days or more after the statement is issued.

Securities and Exchange Commission

The Securities and Exchange Commission is responsible for administering the Securities Acts of 1933 and 1934. These acts give the SEC the power to set accounting standards and to require specific kinds of financial disclosure by corporations covered by the acts. The commissioners are appointed by the president of the United States. The commission's budget is approved by Congress.

The Securities Act of 1933 deals primarily with the registration of securities in public offerings. Under this act, the SEC is concerned with the adequacy and validity of the information disclosed to investors in the registration statements filed with the commission by corporations and the prospectuses furnished to investors by sellers of securities. The commission does not pass judgment on the merits of the securities offered.

The Securities Exchange Act of 1934 regulates the trading in securities. This act requires among other things that corporations registered with the commission periodically file reports on their operations and conditions.

The SEC issues pronouncements on accounting matters which registered companies must adopt. These may set new disclosure requirements, state the SEC's interpretation of a specific accounting standard, or describe the SEC's response to a common accounting problem encountered during the review of filings by corporations. The releases are concerned more with disclosure problems than with setting accounting principles. The commission, through its office of chief accountant, maintains a close liaison with the FASB. The SEC exerts a strong influence on the FASB's decisions, since the FASB is powerless to enforce them if the SEC does not require corporations filing with it to follow a FASB proposal.

Cost Accounting Standards Board

During the 1970s, the now defunct Cost Accounting Standards Board (CASB) issued a number of cost accounting standards to be followed by defense contractors and subcontractors in accounting on a contract basis for government contracts. Its rules still have the force of law for government cost-reimbursement contract purposes, including those in many nondefense agencies. In recent years, efforts have been made in Congress to reactivate the CASB.

Government Accounting Standards Board

In 1984, the Government Accounting Standards Board (GASB) was established to set accounting standards for state and local governments. This board is supported by various state and local governments and government financial officers' associations. It is an independent body appointed by the Financial Accounting Foundation.

American Institute of Certified Public Accountants

The AICPA's Accounting Standards Executive Committee (AcSec) is the senior technical committee authorized to speak for the institute in the area of financial and cost accounting. The institute's Auditing Standards Committee (AuSec) performs a similar function in the field of auditing.

Periodically the AICPA publishes "Statements of Position" (SOPs) on accounting principles and procedures, and guides related to industry accounting and auditing. These pronouncements are advisory to the institute's members rather than authoritative. However, in areas not covered by FASB pronouncements, the FASB and SEC have indicated that the SOPs are useful guides and should be followed as long as they do not conflict with other existing official FASB pronouncements. Furthermore, beginning in 1979 the FASB has indicated that certain of these SOPs and guides are encompassed in the conventions, rules, and procedures referred to as "generally accepted accounting principles."

Basic Issues

Underlying much of the contemporary controversy over corporate financial reporting practices covered in this book are these basic issues:

1. What should be the objective and scope of the corporate reporting process?
2. Should corporate reports be reports prepared by management or reports on management prepared by some nonmanagement-related party?
3. Should the accounting principles on which corporate reports are based be derived from business practice, their validity resting upon their general acceptance; or should they be developed conceptually, in a manner analogous to the principles of Euclidean geometry?
4. Should accounting principles be *uniform* in their application or should they permit *flexibility* on the part of the person responsible for the financial reports to choose from equally acceptable alternatives for reporting essentially identical transactions?
5. Should financial reports reflect the changing purchasing power of the dollar and rising cost of replacing most assets?
6. To what extent should corporate income, resources, and obligations reflect their current value and the changes in their value?

How each of these questions is decided will have an important impact on the means by which we measure and communicate managerial performance to investors.

Financial Accounting's Objective

The basic purpose of financial accounting and financial statements is to provide timely, reliable quantitative financial information about a business enterprise. There is little argument about this general objective. However, the implementation of the objective in practice involves considerable controversy.

For example, such issues as the following arise: Should the corporate statements be prepared for a particular class of users, such as investors, or should the statements be more general in their purpose? Should the reader be assumed to be naive or knowledgeable in accounting? What data are useful for users? Should the burden of the financial communication be carried by footnote disclosure or the values shown on the face of the statements?

Management's Statements

Today, management has the responsibility for measuring and reporting its own performance. A number of critics of the present corporate reporting system believe it is unreasonable to expect management to fulfill this public reporting responsibility objectively. In their opinion, the pressures from stockholders to show a pattern of increasing annual earnings per share are so enormous that managers of companies in trouble find it hard to avoid puffing up their earnings through accounting policy decisions. Or, conversely, in periods when the public is critical of unusually high corporate profits, some believe management is tempted to use accounting decisions to understate its otherwise excessive profits. Therefore, in order to ensure that stockholders obtain an objective measure of managerial performance, the critics believe it is necessary to shift the responsibility for the reports to a disinterested third party, such as the independent public accountant.

Others believe that the application of responsible management judgment is most likely to lead to the selection of the most meaningful accounting principles in particular situations. This point of view attaches importance to each company's need to select accounting methods which best communicate its management's unique policies, objectives, and the factors guiding its decisions. Since few public accountants are trained to bring this perspective and understanding to the financial reporting process, it is argued that it can be accomplished best through the exercise of responsible management judgment.

Different Approaches

Most managers, public accountants, and others involved in the corporate financial reporting process are uneasy about the present differences and inconsistencies in the preparation and presentation of financial information to stockholders. There is little agreement on how to resolve these problems, however. The two principal alternative approaches implemented in practice are the case-by-case process and the conceptual method.

The advocates of the conceptual approach believe that if a consistent theory of financial accounting could be developed, it would resolve many of the current controversies. They view current accounting practices as a collection of mutually inconsistent principles and procedures which no systematic theory can describe. Therefore, they believe it is necessary to find a set of basic concepts for measuring and communicating the results of business operations. Although there is little agreement on method, the approach they advocate most frequently has been to identify some accounting axioms on which a theory of accounting can be constructed logically. Few recommendations resulting from this process have been adopted, principally because they have seemed impractical to most practicing accountants.

The case-by-case approach, with its heavy reliance on acceptance, aims to identify, from accounting practices evolved from actual business experience, those principles that are generally accepted. Advocates of this approach also believe that restraint is necessary in trying to impose unilaterally any one set of standards on the business community. Thus, the role of the standard setting body is viewed more as a catalyst than as a prescriber of standards. This approach is based on the belief that financial reporting cannot be fair until it has a high degree of acceptance and is consistent with the modes of thought and customs of all major segments of the business community.

Uniformity versus Flexibility

The board accounting issue of "uniformity versus flexibility" arose when an increasing number of thoughtful business executives, accountants, and members of the financial community became concerned over the difficulties involved in making meaningful comparisons of the financial reports of different companies. These problems arose because business executives could (and still can) choose between several equally authoritative accounting treatments to report to investors on such items as inventories and depreciation. The result? Profit figures vary depending on the alternative chosen.

Some claimed that the unform application of accounting principles to similar transactions would solve these inadequacies of accounting practice. Greater unformity would produce financial statements that are fair to all those who rely upon financial data. Without this standard for fairness, the supporters of uniformity predict a general lack of confidence in financial statements and an inevitable increase in governmental control over the accounting practices followed by industry.

The supporters of a more flexible approach caution against uniformity for its own sake. They argue that management must have some flexibility in choosing between accounting principles to reflect the variations in basic business policies and management attitudes toward risk which exist in actual business practice. The proponents of flexibility charge that it would be misleading to give these variations the appearance of comparability through a uniform accounting system.

The answer to the uniformity versus flexibility question is not simple. Specifically, if generally accepted accounting principles become too inflexible, business reporting could become unduly constricted. At the other extreme, if generally accepted accounting principles are too flexible, business reporting may degenerate into confusion and mistrust. Both are undesirable situations. Where to draw the line is the critical issue.

Changing Prices

Inflation reduces the purchasing power of the dollar and, for most companies, pushes up the cost of replacing their inventories, property, plant and equipment. Since the primary financial statements that companies issue do not reflect this economic reality, some believe that financial statements are potentially misleading. Others take the position that since users of financial statements seem content with the present statements, there is no need to change the current approach. The FASB has been responsive to both positions. Since 1979, it has required some 1500 large companies to issue in a supplemental disclosure format selected financial data that reflect the impact of inflation on the company. This controversy is discussed in Chapter 17.

Current Values

A fundamental controversy underlying much of the ferment over accounting practices is the question of whether or not accounting measurements should reflect the historical cost of an item or some measure of its current value. Much more will be said on this issue in Chapter 15.

Management's Role

The controversy over the basic issues discussed above raises another basic question: What is management's role in the development and statement of generally accepted accounting principles?

Despite the obvious reasons why accounting principles are of vital interest to management, management has historically played only a small part in the development and statement of generally accepted accounting principles. In the absence of management participation, the problems of financial reporting, which have a broad social impact, have had to be dealt with by the accounting profession.

The FASB has recognized the necessity of joint effort by appointing representatives from industry to the FASB and its advisory groups. The controversy over accounting practices has also alerted many managements to their share of responsibility in helping to set realistic and workable ground rules for financial reporting. The assistance and support of the business community are important, since ultimately the success or failure of the FASB will rest largely with business executives.

Management Accounting

This book focuses on *financial* accounting—the goal of which is to provide stockholders and other external parties with useful financial information about the company. Nearly all businesses have another closely related system of accounting to provide management with useful financial information for running the business. This is an internally oriented system known as *management* accounting.

A company's management accounting need not conform to the generally accepted accounting principles that govern its financial accounting. In practice, however, these two accounting systems are usually closely related. One of the principal functions of management accounting is to measure the performance of the various units of a company against a set of performance standards. These performance measures are selected to motivate unit managers to achieve these standards through actions that collectively will move the company toward the realization of its overall corporate objectives. Since generally accepted accounting principles will be used to measure the total corporate progress, there must be a link between the two systems. There is no sense in motivating unit managers to achieve results that look good for internal accounting purposes but poor if they are translated into external accounting terms. Also, if a company's rules for maintaining the internal and external systems are different, the company must maintain two sets of books to record its business transactions. This can be very expensive. Therefore, to reduce accounting costs, most companies collect and record their basic management accounting data according to financial accounting rules.

While most companies use essentially the same accounting principles for management and financial accounting purposes, a number of companies have explicitly decided not to adopt this practice. Their rationale is that adopting some of the company's external reporting practices internally might introduce an undesirable behavioral bias in the decisions of unit managers. This practice raises a disturbing question: How can a company justify the use of a generally accepted principle for external reporting if it is not useful for internal purposes, either because it motivates managers to follow undesirable operating policies, provides top management with misleading measures of performance, or fails to reflect the company's real progress and prospects?

Behavioral Implications

Research into the behavioral implications of management accounting and measurement systems has led some financial accounting authorities to conclude that generally accepted accounting principles can condition managers' decisions as well as measure their performance for external reporting purposes. Unfortunately, in the opinion of these researchers, this has not always led to desirable results.

A number of these external reporting principles have a built-in bias which in certain circumstances motivates managers to adopt them in preference to alternative principles that might reflect more accurately the operating results and financial condition of their company. In other situations, managers may justify the use of certain generally accepted accounting principles by adopting specific operating policies that are not necessarily the most appropriate to their needs.

The FASB and its predecessors have reduced the number of these behaviorally undesirable accounting principles, but some still persist. A number of people believe that the accounting and management professions should have the goal of eliminating these remaining objectionable practices and creating a set of generally accepted principles that will motivate managers to make sound economic and factual reporting decisions. If this is not possible, our corporate reporting system should at least not encourage managers to act against what appear to be the best interests of their stockholders and society.

Those who hold this view believe the FASB and others who now influence the definition of what constitutes acceptable corporate financial accounting practices must ask themselves when considering the appropriateness of an accounting principle:

1. What might this accounting principle or practice motivate managers to do in their own selfish interest?
2. Could this possible action obscure actual managerial performance, give the illusion of performance where none exists, or lead to unsound economic actions?

If the answer to any part of the second question is yes, and the probability that it will occur in even a few cases is reasonably high, then the use of the accounting practice should not be encouraged, even though it may be sound from the technical viewpoint of accounting theory.

National Economic Interests

One of the events that hastened the demise of the APB was congressional rejection of its recommendation that only one method be used to account for investment tax credit. In the opinion of some congressional leaders, the method proposed by the APB was at variance with the national economic goals and the government's programs to achieve these goals.

Briefly, the incident was as follows: The APB proposed that the profit gain from the investment tax credit should be spread over the life of the assets giving rise to the credit. Congress favored the alternative approach that would allow corporations to record the full credit in the year in which it was granted. Congress felt that this approach, which the APB had specifically rejected, would be a more positive incentive for business executives to invest in capital assets, which was the goal of the investment tax credit legislation. Accordingly, Congress wrote the stipulation that nobody could restrict the manner in which corporations accounted for the tax credit. Faced with this situation, the APB withdrew its recommendations.

This clash between the APB and Congress led to a debate as to whether or not private groups responsible for setting accounting standards should be responsive to the economic programs of the national government, even though this might lead to adoption of an accounting principle alternative that was not thought to represent the best accounting standard. Those favoring the view that accounting standards should not be at variance with national economic program goals believe that private regulatory bodies like the FASB must gain acceptance of their point of view from all interested parties, which includes the government, before issuing recommendations. Those who reject this argument believe that the role of the FASB is to set accounting standards which in its opinion represent the best accounting practice. Only in this way, it is claimed, can the level of corporate reporting be raised.

Market Efficiency and Accounting Data

Some of those involved in examining the behavior of security prices with respect to accounting data believe the acrimony that arose out of the investment tax credit incident described above was a needless controversy that arose because those involved in the dispute were ignorant of much of the so-called efficient markets research.

This research suggests to some that the stock market, as reflected in price behavior, acts as if it looks through the reported accounting numbers and arrives at market values taking into account that earnings are being generated by different methods. If this is so, it would not matter if companies use different accounting methods. The market would adjust the earnings of the company to reflect the company's economic reality.

Furthermore, this research indicates that the market is efficient. That is, security prices act as if they fully reflect all of the publicly available information, including financial statement data, and no investor can expect to use published information in such a way as to earn abnormal returns on his or her security portfolio. Consequently, for investors trying to outperform the market, it is of little value to know that different companies use different accounting practices, since this fact is already reflected in the relative values of securities.

As a consequence of these findings, some researchers have suggested that the FASB should be more concerned with the full disclosure of information rather than the measurement of transactions and accounting principles. Such an objective, it is claimed, would have led to very different behavior by the APB with respect to the investment tax accounting controversy.

The APB should have sought to achieve full and comprehensive disclosure of how corporations accounted for the investment tax credit, and either left the decision of how to account for it to each company or approved only the approach favored by Congress. Irrespective of the accounting principle decision, the goal should have been to give statement users adequate data to recompute the reporting company's profit according to the user's preferred method of investment tax credit accounting.

Four major implications of the efficient market research findings have been suggested for the FASB and other accounting standard setting bodies. The recommendations place more emphasis on a goal of adequate disclosure than on refining the profit calculation.

First, some reporting issues, like the investment tax credit, are trivial and can be resolved by adequate disclosures. In these cases, the differences in the accounting record between costs of alternative methods are not significant to the issuer of statements. Similarly, the cost to the statement user of adjusting profit data from one method to another is nominal. The solution to these accounting issues is simple: Report by one method, with sufficient footnote disclosure to convert to other methods. Then let the statement user decide on the relevance of these data.

Second, the publication of financial data should prevent abnormal returns from accruing to individuals with inside information. Therefore, in deciding disclosure issues, if there are no additional costs to the issuer, the presumption should be that the data in question should be disclosed. This would reduce any advantage that might accrue to insiders.

Third, the FASB, SEC, and Congress should become less concerned in their accounting reforms with protecting the naive or ignorant investor and its associated objective of attempting to reduce the complexities of modern corporations to the level of understanding of these individuals. Rather, the goal should be to educate investors to the fact that accounting data cannot be used to detect overvalued or undervalued securities and that the naive investor is best protected if there is full disclosure.

While making this recommendation, it is also recognized that competent financial analysis can give investors in publicly traded securities an advantage over those less diligent and perceptive in their examination of financial statements. This advantage, developed through superior analysis, is likely to be temporary as others reach the same conclusions, and these conclusions are reflected in the stock prices as a result of buy or sell decisions.

Fourth, accountants must stop acting as if they are the only supplier of information about the firm, since in an efficient market the value of a security may be the same under a variety of different accounting methods because the market is using alternative nonaccounting sources of information, such as security analysts' reports and data published in trade magazines. Thus, the FASB should seek as its objective to provide information to investors by the most economical means and to encourage the development of nonaccounting sources if these sources can convey the data more cheaply than the accounting statements.

The theory promoted by the efficient market researchers that accounting alternatives do not make a difference to *equity* market values is not accepted by all accounting and finance authorities. In the opinion of some, the research findings are very inconclusive. Also, this research does not consider the impact of accounting alternatives on trade creditors, bank loan officers, and other non-stock market users of accounting data.

Tax Accounting

The typical objective of corporate tax planning is to minimize the current tax liability and then to defer the payment of this liability to the government as long as possible. A firm's taxable income is established by two sets of accounting rules and conventions that impinge upon each other. One set is established by the Internal Revenue Service. The other set consists of generally accepted accounting principles.

In general, a firm's taxable income is determined by the accounting system (based on generally accepted accounting principles) that is used in the normal course of its business. However, the tax code allows companies to deviate from this practice in specific areas when calculating taxable income without having to change the corporate financial reports issued to stockholders. As a result, in such areas as fixed asset accounting, a company can maintain two sets of accounting data: one for determining the current tax payments to the government, another for preparing the statements for public reporting purposes. This is legal. However, it does create problems of how to account for current corporate income tax expenses in financial reports to stockholders. These will be discussed at considerable length in Chapter 14.

From time to time, somebody advocates closer, if not complete, agreement between the income figures determined for taxation and for financial reporting purposes. This position fails to recognize that the objectives of financial and tax accounting are different. Financial accounting's objective is to present fairly the results of operations and the financial condition of a company to its stockholders and other interested parties external to the firm, such as employees and creditors. Tax accounting's objective is to raise tax revenues and to carry out the government's economic, political, and social policies. For example, tax surcharges and investment credits are adopted to influence the growth of the economy. The tax provision permitting rapid amortization of certain pollution control facilities is an example of congressional concern with the ecological problem of pollution. In addition, some tax accounting practices are based on administrative practicalities. For example, a basic tax concept is that the timing of a tax liability should be influenced by when the taxpayer can most readily pay and the government can most readily collect. Clearly, this concept is at odds with the accrual concept of financial accounting, which says income should be recognized when it is earned.

In general, business has been unwilling to accept an accounting principle for financial reporting purposes that reduces financial income unless it produces a tax reduction. For example, many business executives oppose the amortization of goodwill (i.e., excess cost of assets acquired over their fair market value) for financial reporting purposes because it is not a deductible expense for determining income tax payments. Similarly, many believe that the inability to claim a tax deduction for employee stock options justifies a similar treatment for financial accounting purposes, despite the fact that many accounting authorities believe that stock options represent a form of compensation and should be charged to earnings. Thus, while it is often argued that because of their different objectives, tax and financial accounting should be kept separate, in practice tax accounting does influence financial accounting.

Social Cost and Human Resource Accounting

Some accountants have explored the possibility of extending the traditional role of accounting to include the measurement and disclosure of a corporation's social contribution. Other accountants have been experimenting with accounting systems and concepts that would communicate to management and interested outsiders better data on a corporation's investment in and utilization of human resources. Both of these activities have generated considerable controversy as to how appropriate it is for accountants to undertake such responsibilities, how relevant the data would be, what methods to use to measure costs and benefits, and what interest management and the public would have in the data generated.

The supporters of social cost accounting argue that business is only part of a larger social system. As the public increasingly accepts this view of society, it judges each social unit, such as a business, in terms of its contribution to the whole society. As a result, the public needs access to data that permits evaluation of a corporation in terms of both its income responsibility to shareholders and its contribution to society as a whole. It is logical and reasonable for social accounting proponents to argue that accounting, because of its interests in corporate measurements and disclosure, should assume a role of informing the public of the social-responsibility activities of corporations.

Accordingly, it is proposed, the presentation of corporate results needs to be expanded to incorporate measurements of the social costs and benefits of business activities. Such social costs and benefits might include the degree to which a company's operations add or reduce the pollution of the environment, enhance or destroy public properties, or utilize or contribute to society's resources. To the extent possible, these costs and benefits should be measured. At a minimum, however, they need to be identified, disclosed, and discussed in corporate reports and presented along with traditional accounting data so that the public can evaluate the net social contribution of corporations.

Those opposed to a social welfare accountability role for accounting reports believe that other vehicles are more appropriate for conveying these social welfare data. Others believe that since reliable social data cannot be obtained, any attempt to measure social costs and benefits is futile and potentially misleading. Still another view expressed by those opposing a social reporting role for accounting is that the profits of a firm that operates within the legal framework provide the all-inclusive criterion for evaluating its social performance.

Human resource accounting advocates believe that accounting communications currently do not deal adequately with one of a corporation's most important resources, namely, its human resources. These resources are developed at a considerable cost to corporations, and a corporation's policies for developing and acquiring employees may be vital to its success. Traditional accounting, however, treats expenditures to acquire, develop, and hold human resources as expenses rather than as assets; rarely identifies and discloses the extent of these expenditures; and makes no effort to evaluate the effectiveness or value of a corporation's human resources. Those interested in human resource accounting are experimenting with different financial and nonfinancial measurements and disclosures of corporate human resources with the goal of incorporating these data in accounting communications.

An Approach to Financial Reporting Decisions

The process of analyzing and resolving financial reporting problems is similar to that followed in other business decision-making situations, except that the decision maker must usually work within the constraints of generally accepted accounting principles. Typically, the business executive is faced with a problem which has more than one possible solution. The task is to choose the best possible course of action. This can be done intuitively or through careful, systematic consideration and weighing of the anticipated consequences, or through some combination of these two approaches. Whatever the approach used, the manager must eventually make a decision.

The evaluation of the alternative courses of action can be facilitated by developing "yardsticks" or criteria, weighted by their relative importance. For any particular problem, these criteria can be used to distinguish between acceptable and unacceptable solutions and to rank the acceptable solutions in a relative order of attractiveness.

In the case of financial reporting problems, the decision criteria are usually developed from an analysis of the company's overall objectives and the operating strategy to achieve those objectives. This is done by answering these questions: Given the company's objectives and operating plans, what characteristics must the financial reporting policy satisfy if it is to measure and communicate clearly the extent of the realization of these plans? What are the implications for the company's financial reporting policies of the characteristics of the company's particular operations, relations with external groups, competitors' policies and plans, industry, financial structure, and management? Answers to these questions require a detailed analysis of such areas as the company's operations and plans, the stock market's evaluation of similar companies, the company's business environment, and the public interest and regulatory requirements that may be relevant.

The identification and correct definition of the problem is a critical stage in the decision-making process. Unless this is done well, the decision maker may tackle the wrong issue or solve only part of the problem, which may produce a more unsatisfactory situation. In most acounting reports presented, at least part of the problem is fairly evident. How clearly and fully one is able to state the problem will depend in large part on the quality of the operating and environmental analysis described above.

Financial reporting problems usually involve the selection of accounting principles to handle a specific item. These problems involve at least five interrelated considerations:

1. Which generally accepted principles are the most appropriate?
2. How should the decision on this accounting policy application be communicated to the public?
3. As a result of this decision, what other adjustments, if any, must be made in the particular mix of generally accepted accounting principles that collectively constitute the company's financial reporting policy?
4. What operating or financial bias will this decision have on management's future business decisions or policies?
5. How will this decision contribute to the real or apparent achievement of management's objectives?

The third question on the above list recognizes that a company's earnings per share and financial image are the net result of applying accounting policy decisions to a variety of individual transactions. Therefore, a change in one part of this mix may necessitate changes in other parts to achieve the overall effect management is seeking.

The alternative solutions to financial reporting problems usually reflect a choice between generally accepted accounting principles. Therefore, to fully appraise and consider the full range of possible solutions in any particular situation, the decision maker must be familiar not only with accounting principles but also the conditions justifying the usage of particular generally accepted principles and the main theoretical arguments for and against each.

Once the criteria, the problem, and the possible solutions are identified, the decision maker must sift through the facts available to extract those that are relevant to the problem. Some of these facts are measurable and others are not, but all must be related to the possible solutions. When the advantages and disadvantages of each solution are clear, the decision maker must then use judgment to decide which one of the possible solutions has the greatest net advantage.

There is often no right answer to financial reporting problems, or even an answer to which everyone will agree. The decision maker must make the best decision with the facts available, knowing that two people may interpret or weigh the same facts differently and reach quite different conclusions. Decision making under these circumstances is a complicated and difficult task, fraught with uncertainty.

Financial Analysis

Management's primary role in external financial reporting is communicating information for the use of others. The FASB is conscious of this management responsibility as it formulates generally accepted accounting principles. In addition, the SEC's regulations and governing legislation hold management directly responsible under the threat of civil and criminal legal actions for its communication and disclosure of information. In the light of its responsibility, it is in management's self-interest to anticipate the uses others will make of financial statement data and the analytical techniques they will apply.

The general purpose financial reports issued by business enterprises are used for a variety of purposes by many individuals who have no direct involvement in the management of the reporting company. A dominant common interest of many of these external statement users is the ability of a business to generate future cash flows. Yet, the primary focus of the financial reports statement that they examine is information about the company's earnings and its components.

Financial statement analysis helps to bridge this gap between the financial accounting data provided and the users' cash flow interests. Financial statement techniques make it possible for statement users to penetrate the historical accrual accounting data and thus develop an understanding of an enterprise's past, present, and continuing ability to generate cash flows. This understanding is gained by applying techniques and standards that focus on evaluating management's operating and financial performance, identifying past cash receipts and payments, assessing the quality of a company's earnings, identifying "red flags" that suggest emerging problems, estimating the level of business and financial risk, measuring potential borrowing power, and confirming or rejecting earlier predictions or assessments.

Financial statements are prepared with knowledgeable statement users in mind. Consequently, skill in financial analysis is necessary to appreciate fully the content of financial statements and to use the data effectively for decision-making purposes in such diverse activities as granting credit, buying securities, negotiating mergers, extending trade credit, and conducting business research. The mechanical or arithmetic dimension of financial analysis is fairly simple and straightforward and not difficult to master. More difficult is developing the ability to interpret the significance of the quantitative and qualitative data that financial analysis generates in the form of ratios, trends, and quality assessments. This ability comes with experience, an understanding of the business being analyzed, a thorough knowledge of corporate financial reporting practices, and a full appreciation of the technical and business aspects of the purpose for which the analysis is being performed. In addition, the skillful analyst possesses such traits as ability to recognize irregularities, inquisitiveness, skepticism, diligence, and a willingness to consult with others with more specialized knowledge.

Given the importance of financial analysis in the interpretation of financial statement data, it is imperative that those who regulate corporate financial reporting, set the standards for corporate reports, issue financial statements, and use corporate reports have a thorough understanding of the tools, techniques, and processes encompassed by the field of financial statement analysis. To exercise authority in any of these aspects of corporate reporting without this competence would be irresponsible.

Challenges

It is important that those who set standards and those who issue and use financial statements individually and collectively work together to upgrade further our already high standards of corporate financial reporting. Each of these important parties in the corporate reporting process has a set of challenges to meet if this desirable state of affairs is to be achieved.

The challenge to those who define generally accepted accounting principles is to develop a set of principles that is sound in both a behavioral and a technical context. They should be behaviorally sound in that they:

1. Inhibit managers from taking undesirable operating actions to justify the adoption of an accounting alternative.
2. Inhibit the adoption of accounting practices by corporations to create the illusion of performance.

The traditional approach to defining generally accepted accounting principles has focused on technical considerations. Historically, this has been done well on a principle-by-principle basis. Today, the technical challenge is to ensure that accounting principles are consistent within a fundamental conceptual framework, such as the FASB's various *Statements of Financial Accounting Concepts.*

The financial reporting challenge to corporate managers is to issue financial statements that satisfy the legitimate information needs of responsible, knowledgeable statement users. This is a difficult task given the diversity of purposes for which accounting data are used. This challenge can be met if the reporting corporation's choice of accounting principles is appropriate for its circumstances and its disclosures are relevant, informative, and timely. Above all, managers must avoid letting the marginal firms set reporting standards and must resist the temptation during difficult times to adopt accounting practices that communicate an illusion of acceptable performance rather than the reality of the situation.

Statements users' financial accounting challenge is to participate actively in FASB deliberations, to maintain pressure on management to raise the standards of corporate reporting without being unreasonable and unresponsive to genuine corporate concerns, to exercise due professional care in the conduct of their statement analyses, to make informed decisions based in part on their analysis, and to faithfully communicate the results of their analyses to others.

CHAPTER 2

Development of Corporate Reporting Practices

From 19th-century traditions of corporate secrecy, American corporations have moved slowly toward more public and credible financial disclosure practices. This chapter examines the variety of political, technical, social, and economic pressures from the business community, the accounting profession, the government, and the public which have impelled this movement and governed its direction and tempo. An appreciation of this process is necessary to put our contemporary practices and problems into proper perspective. People with such a sense of history seem to be more closely in touch with reality and able to deal with change more creatively. The study of corporate reporting history also sharpens one's sense of when to introduce change and how long it may take.

As late as 1900, the amount of financial information presented to stockholders by the managers of most publicly owned American manufacturing corporations was meager. After 1900, the level and frequency of corporate financial disclosure by industrial management began to rise slowly and the credibility of its representations began to improve. These changes in the quality of the financial reporting practices of American manufacturing concerns have four principal causes: (1) gradual recognition by some managers of their public responsibility; (2) increasing criticism of corporate reporting practices by a number of influential groups and individuals outside of the management class; (3) direct federal government regulation, such as the Securities Acts of 1933 and 1934; and (4) the recognition by the American accounting profession, and acceptance by the business community, of some common accounting and reporting standards. Underlying and contributing to these forces for change have been a number of social, political, and economic factors such as the emergence of a large number of small investors, the evolution of big business, and the increasing willingness of the public to seek government action to reform undesirable commercial practices.

The development of financial analysis parallels the shift that began in the late 19th century in the management of business enterprises from the enterprise capitalists who practiced corporate secrecy to the professional managers and the financial institutions from which they obtained their capital. The managerial and creditor ratio analysis interests were different. Managerial analysis emphasized profitability measurements whereas the credit analysis focused on the company's ability to meet its financial obligations. In the early years, the credit analysis approach dominated the general development of ratio analysis. Later, as the public ownership of stock became more widespread and the role of professional investment advisers and managers grew, ratio analysis concerned with dividends payments and equity valuation evolved from the managerial and creditor analysis to meet the analytical needs of this new group of financial statement users.

Nineteenth Century

The modern reviewer of management financial reporting practices during the 19th century is immediately struck by the limited amount of information made public by manufacturing firms—even the larger ones with widespread public ownership. Not only was there inadequate financial disclosure, but some companies were irregular in the frequency with which they issued reports. For example, between 1897 and 1905, the Westinghouse Electric and Manufacturing Company neither published an annual financial report to its stockholders nor held an annual meeting.

This lack of financial information pertaining to manufacturing concerns was in contrast to the reporting practices of public utilities, insurance companies, banks, and railroads, whose activities (being more in the public service) were more closely regulated and more fully reported. Even here, however, practice varied in accordance with state requirements, and there were some notable nonreporters. For instance, in 1866, the treasurer of the Delaware, Lackawanna, and Western Rail Road Company, in response to a request for information from the New York Stock Exchange, replied simply: "The Delaware Lackawanna R.R. Co. make no reports and publish no statements and have done nothing of the sort for the last five years."

Before 1900, for the few publicly held manufacturing corporations in existence, it was possible for investors to obtain some information pertaining to the companies' capitalization, if not from management, from the standard financial sources such as *Hunt's Merchant's Magazine,* and later, the *Commercial and Financial Chronicle.* Less frequently was a simple balance sheet available and seldom were sales and profit figures released—an income statement showing sales less the major expense items was rare. In addition, few of these published financial facts were accompanied by either a company or independent auditors' certificate, since neither the theory nor practice of these procedures was common in America. The public had to rely upon management's integrity in determining if published financial information was reliable.

After 1890, a few of the newly created industrial combinations sometimes published more detailed financial statements. By modern standards, even in these cases, the amount of data released was sketchy. Companies such as American Tobacco, which issued the more detailed financial reports, usually did so because of enlightened managers or because of their heavy dependence on outside sources for capital.

Generally, as might be expected, the small and the closely held manufacturing corporations were the more secretive. Yet as late as 1900, there were some notoriously secretive managements among the large publicly traded corporations. This group included such companies as the American Tin Plate Company, a large publicly owned company, which controlled 95 percent of the tin-plate production in the United States and whose stock was traded on the New York and Chicago stock exchanges. It published in 1900 a balance sheet containing only four asset and five liability accounts.

Factors Contributing to Financial Secrecy

There were four principal reasons for corporate managers being so secretive with regard to their companies' financial affairs during most of the 19th century: (1) there was no tradition of publicity, for no one would have thought of asking individual proprietors, partners, or early family owners to divulge such information; (2) management believed the public had no right to information on these matters; (3) managers feared that by revealing financial information they would unwittingly assist their competitors; and (4) to many, the doctrine of *caveat emptor* seemed as applicable to buyers of securities as to purchasers of horses. For instance, during the testimony heard before the Industrial Commission in 1899, Henry O. Havemeyer, the president of American Sugar Refining Company, and commission member Thomas Phillips had the following exchange:

Phillips: You think, then, that when a corporation is chartered by the State, offers stock to the public, and is one in which the public is interested, that the public has no right to know what its earning power is or to subject them to any inspection whatever, that the people may not buy stock blindly?

Havemeyer: Yes; that is my theory. Let the buyer beware; that covers the whole business. You cannot wet-nurse people from the time they are born until the day they die. They have got to wade in and get stuck and that is the way men are educated and cultivated.

The testimony of another witness before the commission, Charles W. King, secretary and general manager of the New Jersey Corporations Agency,[1] illustrates another of the reasons for secrecy:

---

[1] The New Jersey Corporations Agency was formed in 1895 for the purpose of furnishing corporations chartered in New Jersey but operating out of state with the necessary facilities for complying with the state's liberal incorporation laws. Mr. King's office represented several hundred such corporations, including the Amalgamated Copper Company, the American Car and Foundry Company, the American Thread Company, the Pressed Steel Car Company, and the American Soda Fountain Company.

Livingston (commission member): Now, then, when the people ask for information, why not just give it? You say because it would be giving away your private business. Well, you did not think of that when you went to the public for your franchise, did you?

King: The public may not be your competitors, but you may have competitors, and in giving it to the public you would have to give it to your competitors.

These comments of Havemeyer and King represented in part an inheritance by late 19th-century management of a number of the attitudes of the owner-managers of the century's earlier industrial ventures. Ownership and management, if not the same persons, were closely related, and the owners were in continual personal touch with the affairs of the enterprise. Because there were few or no outside investors, there was little need for management to think about the problems of financial disclosure. Under these conditions a company's financial statements were considered private, just as were the financial affairs of any private citizen.

State corporation laws reflected this antipublicity sentiment of managers and their agents. By 1900, reports of some kind were required in 27 states. The remainder of the states required no report whatsoever.

About half the states provided for reports to stockholders. In general, these statutes merely specified that an "annual report" be provided the stockholders. Seldom were the contents of the report specified or a provision included to require the mailing of annual reports to those stockholders who were unable to attend the stockholders' meeting. To have imposed the burden of detailed public reports upon management would not have improved a state's chances of attracting incorporations—a lucrative business few states wished to discourage.

The accepted method of marketing new industrial securities also placed little pressure upon management for greater financial disclosure. During the 19th century, investors bought securities primarily on the basis of their confidence in the promoter or the investment banker offering the issue. In particular, investment bankers, it was widely believed, undertook searching investigations of all securities before they were offered to the public, only offered securities of investment quality, and practically guaranteed the security. Consequently, prospectuses offering new industrial securities seldom ran more than two pages and contained sketchy financial data. The first test of a security was the reliability of the investment bankers involved, not the financial conditions of the issuing company. Under these conditions, as long as companies paid their dividends, investors rarely needed, or demanded, financial statements.

Finally, the absence of a strong accounting profession and an established body of accounting theory in America contributed to the inadequacy of management's financial reports. Not only was there nondisclosure, but when information was released it was of dubious value, since different companies used different accounting concepts to measure and report similar transactions. For instance, the concept of depreciation was little understood. A number of firms made no provisions for depreciation. Some related depreciation expense to chances in appraised asset values. There were also several other areas where accounting practice was far from standardized and the use of different accounting practices created confusion—including the treatment of unusual charges and credits, the valuation of assets, and the consolidation of subsidiaries.

These accounting vagaries existed partly because little attention had been given in the United States to the logic of accounting. Prior to 1900, nearly all of the American textbooks pertaining to the subject were concerned principally with the rules of bookkeeping.

In addition, the function of public accountants and their reports was misunderstood. For a company to call in independent auditors to examine its books was often taken by the public as an indication of suspected fraud, irregularity, losses, and doubt regarding the reporting company's financial strength. Some managers regarded such action as a reflection on their integrity. Even as late as 1900, many business executives were still reluctant to call in an accountant, and many investigations by public accountants were made secretly, often at night and on Sundays. Consequently, it is not surprising that an English chartered accountant wrote of American practice before 1905: "the profession of accounting has hitherto been little understood in America." The accountant in the United States was little known, little recognized, little wanted; most accountants neither could nor desired to modify management's desire for corporate secrecy.

Toward the Securities Acts and Improved Disclosure, 1900–1933

Almost as soon as business became big, a number of people became disturbed by its growth in power and critical of its practices. It was argued by many, for instance, that the large combinations should be dissolved, since the very existence of these new and powerful industrial groups threatened the fundamental civil liberties and morality of American society.

One of the most popular remedies suggested to rectify this imbalance of power and to end the predatory methods of large corporations was improved corporate financial publicity. For example, in 1900, the Industrial Commission recommended to Congress:

> The larger corporations—the so-called trusts—should be required to publish annually a properly audited report, showing in reasonable detail their assets and liabilities, with profit or loss; such report and audit under oath to be subject to government inspection. The purpose of such publicity is to encourage competition when profits become excessive, thus protecting consumers against too high prices and to guard the interests of employees by a knowledge of the financial condition of the business in which they are employed.

The increasing number of investors, it was thought, would also be protected by improved corporate publicity. While little correlation between the issuance of informative reports and willingness on the part of investors to buy stock was noted, public opinion nevertheless was appalled by the stock market manipulations of many managements and promoters who sought to enrich themselves at the expense of their stockholders. According to one contemporary observer:

> The suppression and misstatement of facts by corporations have in recent years misled investors as well as speculators to buy shares in concerns financially unsound and on the verge of bankruptcy. To prevent the "watering" of stock or to find some method of furnishing investors a basis of judging the condition of companies has absorbed the attention of the "public mind" for some time. "Secrecy" was said to be the evil; nor is it to be wondered at that "publicity" was the remedy suggested. No one word has been more frequently upon the lips of the American public in the last three years [1900–1903] than "publicity."

These pre–World War I demands for fuller financial disclosure, both by the critics of big business and the public, were generally ignored by management. Few companies, for instance, followed United States Steel Corporation's declared policy of presenting full and definite financial information, which first found expression in the 35 pages of financial data contained in the company's annual report of 1902. In contrast, most managements did not seem to care about public opinion. They disregarded it. In fact, some companies which had previously published financial statements quit issuing financial reports altogether. For instance, in 1901, George Westinghouse, president of Westinghouse Electric and Manufacturing, said:

> If some should be surprised that more complete statements have not been previously submitted to them, it can only be said that the directors as well as the stockholders who own the largest amounts of stock have believed that, in view of the existing keen competition and the general attitude toward industrial enterprises, the interests of all would be served by avoiding, to as great an extent as possible, giving undue publicity to the affairs of the company.

While the pioneer critics of big business had little direct impact on management, they greatly influenced, nevertheless, those who later played important roles in increasing the federal government's control over business affairs. For instance, before World War I, among early advocates of greater publicity of corporate affairs, few became more widely read and respected than the future associate justice of the Supreme Court, Louis D. Brandeis. In 1913, Brandeis said: "Publicity is justly commended as a remedy for social and industrial diseases. Sunlight is said to be the best of disinfectants; electric light the most efficient policemen." Later in 1933, it was Mr. Frankfurter—surrogate for Justice Brandeis—in his visits with President Roosevelt, who argued for this approach to business regulation.

Following World War I and until the economic and stock market disasters of 1929, there was a shift in the American political, social, economic, and ethical climate. The nation became more prosperous, and the public grew weary and disillusioned with the crusades of the preceding progressive era. Business executives were regarded with a new respect. The public, instead of disapproving, now looked upon the large-scale efforts to rig the securities market by such market operators as Harry F. Sinclair, Percy A. Rockefeller, and Bernard E. Smith with breathless admiration.

Consequently, during the period 1918–29, the public appeal of the critics of business waned but did not disappear. In 1926, for instance, Professor William Z. Ripley of Harvard University created "quite a flutter in financial centers" when he proclaimed: "let the word go forth that the Federal Trade Commission is henceforth to address itself vigorously to the matter of adequate and intelligent corporate publicity, and taken in conjunction with the helpful agencies at work the thing is as good as done." Ripley was particularly disturbed by the "enigmatic" accounting practices which made possible financial "obfuscation" and "malfeasance." Another who spoke in the same vein was the young Adolph Berle, Jr., who, as part of his notion of the "social corporation," demanded as an expression of the public responsibility of management fuller disclosure of corporate affairs, particularly to investors.

As with that of their predecessors, the immediate impact of such critics as Ripley was almost nil; but after 1930, when the nation lay in economic disorder, business executives were more easily discredited. The public once again became sympathetic to the opinions of those critical of business and finance, and it was the critics' standards—not those of management—by which managers were finally judged.

Between 1900 and 1933, others more closely allied with management sought to raise the level of financial reporting, including the New York Stock Exchange, the Investment Bankers Association of America, and the public accounting profession. Of these private groups, the New York Stock Exchange was perhaps the leading influence in the promotion of adequate corporate disclosure. The exchange's direct influence, however, was limited to companies listed on the exchange. The influence of the Investment Bankers Association and the public accounting profession was severely curtailed by the unwillingness of much of their membership to act independently of management.

The New York Stock Exchange

As early as 1869, the New York Stock Exchange's Committee on Stock List adopted a policy that companies should agree that once listed on the exchange they would publish some form of an annual financial report. Few companies, however, agreed to observe this stipulation. In fact, it was not until the Kansas City (Missouri) Gas Company listing agreement of 1897 that the exchange extracted from a listed company a substantive promise to observe some minimum reporting requirements. Nevertheless, from 1910 onward, the exchange influenced improvements in financial reporting practices of listed companies.

Before 1900, so reluctant was the exchange to enforce its reporting requirements upon industrial management that in 1885 it created the so-called Unlisted Department. This department sought to grasp business then going to outside street markets where fewer restrictions were placed upon issuers. The companies whose stocks were traded by the Unlisted Department (mainly industrials) were not required to furnish the exchange with financial information relevant to the issue. Nevertheless, these shares were traded with regularly listed securities, unlisted stocks being distinguished on quotation sheets only by an asterisk. In this manner, such active stocks as those of Amalgamated Copper and the American Sugar Refining Companies were dealt in on the exchange for many years without the public having any information regarding their affairs. They were in effect conducted and maintained as "blind pools." Those in control were then enabled to use their information for speculative purposes.

In 1910, under growing threats of government regulation, the New York Stock Exchange abolished its Unlisted Department. Thereafter, over the next 20 years, the exchange's Committee on Stock List actively sought to improve the reporting practices of listed companies, particularly with respect to the frequency with which they published financial statements. For example, in 1916, General Motors Company agreed to publish semiannually a consolidated income statement and balance sheet. In 1924, Inland Steel Company modified its original listing agreement and agreed to issue a public statement of quarterly earnings.

In 1926, the NYSE officially recommended the publication of quarterly reports by all listed companies. Also, by this time, nearly all listed manufacturing companies had adopted the practice of issuing annual reports covered by an independent auditor's opinion certificate, a practice made mandatory by the exchange in 1933. Such progress was not easy, however, since as late as 1931 many an executive of a listed company held the exchange's suggested publicity requirements to be arbitrary and unreasonable.

The exchange's control, of course, was restricted only to those corporations which sought to list securities. The securities handled on the over-the-counter markets and the securities listed on the regional exchanges—Chicago, Boston, Pittsburgh—were not only beyond the New York Stock Exchange's control but were also subject to less rigorous requirements so as to attract local lesser corporations, more closely controlled and less susceptible to educational appeal. Yet, these were the very corporations where the most need for improved financial reporting existed.

The Investment Bankers Association of America

Between 1920 and 1927, the Investment Bankers Association of America on several occasions sought, through voluntary action of its membership, to standardize the information regarding industrial securities presented to the public, particularly that in prospectuses. The initial impetus for these reform efforts grew out of a desire on the part of some association members to protect investors, to protect legitimate investment bankers from the growing public resentment against the sellers of fraudulent securities, and to forestall federal and state governmental regulation of securities. Already, by 1920, some 20 states, alarmed by the prevalence of fraudulent stock promotions, had passed so-called blue-sky laws; and on the federal level, security bills had been placed before Congress in 1918, 1919, and 1921, respectively.

On at least six occasions between 1920 and 1928, the Investment Bankers Association issued reports setting forth recommended minimum standards for financial disclosure in prospectuses. In general, these reports, three of which were related to industrial companies, called for an "adequate" and "understandable" balance sheet with some comments on such items as inventory, working capital, and depreciation policy, as well as a presentation of earnings by years. In the case of holding companies, it was suggested that investors be provided with a consolidated balance sheet, a consolidated statement of earnings, and an income statement for the holding company.

Few of these recommendations were ever followed in practice by investment bankers or their corporate clients. The reasons for the failure of the association's voluntary reform program were many. A number of members of the association were indifferent with respect to these recommendations. Also, among those companies that issued securities, some of the bigger and better known companies objected to allowing financial information to go beyond the eyes of their investment bankers.

In addition, a number of investment bankers still preferred to follow the 19th-century practice of selling securities on the basis of the investment banker's reputation alone, rather than on the merits of the issue and issuer. As late as 1923, "confidence," one investment banker said, "was the bulwark in the relationship between the dealer and the client." Earlier, in 1918, another investment banker had stated, "The questions of brick and mortar and turnover and rate of profit and all the other fine points are secondary considerations." Other investment bankers relied upon the 19th-century custom of nondisclosure to justify the hiding of weakness in the dubious securities they offered.

Clearly, such attitudes as these were hardly likely to lead to universal voluntary acceptance among investment bankers of the association's suggestions regarding financial disclosure. Some investment bankers, it would seem, were just as desirous as their corporate clients of fostering financial secrecy.

The Accounting Profession

During the years 1900 to 1933, with the growing dependence of business on outside sources of capital, with the introduction of the income tax law in 1913, and with the passage of the excess profits tax in 1917, the accounting profession became an essential part of American business life. Credit granters came to depend upon financial statements as the basis for credit decisions, and complete and accurate accounting records became necessary for income tax purposes.

Throughout most of this 33-year period, the primary force among accountants for improved corporate financial disclosure came from three sources: educators, individual practitioners, and the American Institute of Accountants. Around 1900, because of a growing recognition of the importance of business in American life, universities added to their curricula business courses which included accounting as a primary subject. University professors began to probe behind accounting practice and explore its logic, and the first university department of accounting, as such, was established by New York University in 1900. For the first time in the United States, accounting education was rising above the level of bookkeeping, and an ideology for accounting technology was slowly developed.

Among business executives, perhaps a more influential group were the leading practitioners of the accounting profession. Such men as George O. May, A. Lowes Dickinson, and Robert H. Montgomery through their day-to-day contracts—literary and personal—with other accountants and business executives, sought to raise the level of industrial financial disclosure and hasten the adoption of sounder accounting practices. In general, these men, whose early training had been in England, believed that the disclosure standards included in the English Companies Acts should be adopted by American business executives. Later, the framers of the securities acts exhibited a similar belief when they based the disclosure philosophy underlying the Securities Act of 1933 on the existing English Company Law.

The genesis of the modern American Institute of Certified Public Accountants (American Institute of Accountants) and its work to raise the standards of the American accounting profession can be traced back to similar earlier attempts in Great Britain before 1880. In Great Britain, a vital and influential accounting profession had existed since about 1850. Beginning in the 1880s, a number of these British chartered accountants came to the United States, principally to audit the various British investments there. To these transplanted Britishers, the first steps necessary to improve the stature of accounting in the United States appeared to be the establishment of a nationwide society of accountants, along the lines of the Institute of Chartered Accountants in England and Wales.

The first organized body of professional accountants in the United States was formed in New York in 1886. Soon after, other state and national accounting bodies were founded. In 1905, the contending national organizations were united to form one principal organization: the American Association of Public Accountants. In 1916, the association was reorganized as the American Institute of Accountants.

The first attempt of the Institute to set some auditing and reporting standards came in 1917 when it joined with the Federal Trade Commission and the Federal Reserve Board in publishing *Uniform Accounting*, the most comprehensive and authoritative document related to corporate financial disclosure and balance sheet audits yet published in the United States. Over the years, the Federal Trade Commission, in the course of its investigation of business conditions, had become disturbed over the lack of uniformity in balance sheet audits and financial reports. As the very first step toward standardization of practices relating to the compiling and verifying of corporate reports, the Commission requested the Institute to prepare a memorandum on balance sheet audits.

The Institute's memorandum was eventually prepared by a committee under George O. May's direction, approved by the Federal Trade Commission, and given tentative endorsement by the Federal Reserve Board. This tentative document was then submitted to bankers throughout the country for their consideration and criticism. Later in 1917, the final draft of *Uniform Accounting* was published by the Federal Reserve Board. In 1918, it was reissued under the name, *Approved Methods for the Preparation of Balance Sheet Statements*. Subsequently, in 1929, it was revised by the Institute for the Federal Reserve Board, republished, and renamed *Verification of Financial Statements*.

Uniform Accounting and its later versions were widely distributed. The bulk of this document related to balance sheet audits. Its last three pages, however, presented suggested forms for comparative income statements and balance sheets. The model income statement provided for some 29 revenue and expense items. The asset side of the proposed balance sheet called for details under the following headings: cash, notes and accounts receivable (less provision for bad debts), inventories, other quick assets, securities, fixed assets (less reserves for depreciation), deferred charges, and other assets. The liability side of the balance sheet indicated detailed information should be presented under these headings: unsecured bills and notes, unsecured accounts, secured liabilities, other current liabilities, fixed liabilities, and net worth.

Despite their prestigious backers, the recommendations outlined in *Uniform Accounting* were not quickly adopted by corporations, bankers, or the accounting profession—chiefly because bankers, out of fear of driving away customers, refrained from insisting upon audited statements from their clients. Nevertheless, some progress was made.

Except for the recommendations pertaining to inventories and disclosure of asset values, few of the improvements found their way into public reports. Business executives in general believed that the standard form of financial statements outlined in the Federal Reserve Board's publication called for too much information and would be used to their detriment by competitors.

Encouraged by the publication of *Uniform Accounting*, the Institute directed its main educational efforts for the next nine years toward encouraging business executives to use balance sheet audits for credit purposes. By

1926, George O. May declared to the accounting profession that, among prominent industrial companies, the practice of having audits "had become almost universal." Now, he said, the time had come for the Institute to assume a larger responsibility and "render a higher service to the community." The new goal he proposed for the profession was the adoption by industrial corporations of the financial disclosure standards embodied in the English Companies Act. To achieve this end, he suggested that the Institute cooperate with "such bodies as the leading stock exchange, the investment bankers, and the commercial banks which grant credit." It was impractical, May believed, to consider bringing about improved corporate disclosure in the United States through direct legislation, as had happened in England.

During the next four years, the Institute undertook two cooperative efforts along the lines suggested by May. The first undertaking with the Investment Bankers Association of America in 1928 produced little. The second was much more fruitful. In 1930, with the long-standing urging of J. M. B. Hoxsey, the executive assistant on stock list of the New York Stock Exchange, and May, reinforced by the effects of the market crash of 1929, the Institute appointed a committee to cooperate with the exchange "in consideration of all problems which are of common interest to investors, exchanges, and accountants."

Hoxsey's concern was principally for the protection of investors, of whom there were some 10 million in 1930. "Accounting," Hoxsey told the Institute, "is a matter of convention, but it is questionable whether these conventions have kept pace with the changes in modern business conditions."

At Hoxsey's suggestion, the American Institute appointed a Special Committee on Cooperation with Stock Exchanges, with George O. May as chairman, to work with the New York Stock Exchange to explore the issues raised by Hoxsey. This undertaking was a significant development as it represented a change in outlook by the accounting profession. *Uniform Accounting* had been prepared with an institution concerned with the quality of credit and the recommendations contained therein made with the credit granter in mind; the new undertaking was with the New York Stock Exchange and the accounting problems were to be considered from the standpoint of those who traded in securities—that is, investors.

On September 22, 1932, the Institute's special committee submitted its report to the exchange's Committee Stock List. The report, which was published in 1933 under the title *Audits of Corporate Accounts,* listed four principal objectives the committee thought the exchange should "keep constantly in mind and do its best to gradually achieve." These goals were to bring about a better recognition by the public that balance sheets did not show present values of the assets and liabilities of corporations, to encourage the adoption of balance sheets which more clearly showed on what basis assets were valued, to emphasize the cardinal importance of the income account, and to make universal the usage by listed corporations of certain broad principles of accounting which had won fairly general acceptance. On this last point, the report warned the exchange against attempting "to restrict the right of corporations to select detailed methods of accounting deemed by them to be best adapted to the requirements of their business." In addition, the report suggested each listed corporation should submit to the exchange a clear and detailed statement of the accounting principles it observed when compiling financial statements.

This document, which was the most specific statement yet formulated on just how financial reports would be made more informative and reliable, was given warm approval by the Controllers Institute and the Investment Bankers Association. Taking a lead from the report's recommendations, on January 6, 1933, the exchange announced that henceforth corporations seeking listing must submit financial statements audited by independent public accountants and agree to have all future reports to stockholders similarly inspected. In addition, the scope of the audit was to be no less than that indicated in *Verification of Financial Statements*.

The accountants read the exchange's announcement with "a feeling of hearty gratification" according to Richardson, the editor of the *Journal of Accountancy*. Richardson had campaigned long and hard for such a listing requirement and hailed the announcement as probably the "most important forward step in the history of accounting within recent years."

Such joy was short-lived. Within six months, the envisioned role of the Committee on Stock List and that of the Institute's special committee in effect passed to a federal agency—first to the Federal Trade Commission and then to the Securities and Exchange Commission. In 1934, many accountants, including George O. May, believed that the profession might in the future "all too easily, find itself merely the ciphering agency for virtually unreviewable bureaucrats." To date, such has not been the case.

Management and Financial Disclosure

Between 1900 and 1933, the financial disclosure practice of industrial corporations improved somewhat. Nevertheless, despite such exceptions as United States Steel Corporation, Bethlehem Steel Corporation, and General Motors Company, the financial reporting practices lagged far behind the recommendations for greater and more useful corporate financial disclosure made by the New York Stock Exchange. Also, the numerous alternative accounting principles which had caused so much confusion during the late 19th century were still observed in practice.

As time passed, however, the statements of industrial corporations became more uniform as to the degree and form of disclosure. By 1933, most publicly owned manufacturing corporations were publishing annual reports containing fairly detailed balance sheets. Furthermore, in line with the shift of emphasis in common stock evaluation techniques from the balance sheet to the income statement, a sketchy income statement showing sales, several major expense items, and current profits was now usually included. Auditing by outside accountants was also common.

Yet some of the larger companies still refused to provide stockholders with written financial statements. For instance, the Singer Sewing Machine Company did not issue annual reports, information regarding the company's affairs being given orally at the annual stockholders' meetings. As late as 1927, the Royal Baking Powder Company had issued no financial statement whatsoever. In addition to the nonreporting companies, a number of large companies rendered their reports to the public well after the close of their fiscal year.

There were two basic reasons for management's slow progress in improving corporate financial reporting. First, managers did not consider public reports a matter of prime importance. Second, and more important, business executives were still inclined toward financial secrecy, principally because of their fear of assisting competitors.

Financial chicanery and business custom were also responsible for corporate secrecy. Unfortunately, there were still a few industrial directors and officers who practiced financial secrecy so as to profit in their stock market activities through the use of corporate information not available to others. While the motivation of management in such cases was clearly to deceive or mislead, in most instances of nondisclosure, it should be noted, corporate financial secrecy resulted primarily because it was simply a custom that had been handed down from generation to generation to tell as little as possible.

In addition, there were still few external restraints upon management's financial reporting practices. State corporation laws relating to corporate financial reports had not advanced much beyond the 19th-century stage. Federal law was still silent on industrial financial publicity, as it was assumed this was a state matter. Also, after 1914, public opinion was indifferent to the attempts to improve the financial reports of industrial companies. In particular, investors, the very group the reformers sought to protect, were usually satisfied with generalities and did not request detailed financial statistics.

Similarly, accounting practice placed few restrictions on industrial management. There was an inviting variety of alternatives approved by accountants and employed by business executives. For example, there still were many different theories of depreciation. No consensus yet existed as to the degree of ownership which warranted consolidation. Frequently, no distinction was made between operating income and other income. And a variety of methods pertaining to the recording of asset values persisted. Such accounting freedom unfortunately tempted a number of managements to inflate reported profits through questionable adjustments, which were seldom revealed to the public.

Finally, the reformers were powerless to force their proposed financial reporting standards upon industrial management. Business executives, in the absence of regulatory restraints, held the balance of power vis-à-vis the would-be reformers. The efforts of the Investment Bankers Association were thwarted by its own membership, and the accounting profession was not yet willing to be truly independent. Even the New York Stock Exchange was unable to enforce its authority upon the recalcitrant listed companies.

Thus, as late as the 1920s, industrial management could ignore with impunity the demands for improved financial disclosure. The economic depression of 1930, the subsequent shift in the public's attitude toward business, the election of Franklin D. Roosevelt as president in 1932, and the passage of the Securities Acts of 1933 and 1934 brought this situation to an end. Henceforth, for most publicly owned industrial companies, the Securities and Exchange Commission became the final arbiter in matters of financial disclosure, not management.

The Securities Act and Its Aftermath

On May 29, 1933, President Roosevelt requested Congress to enact a federal securities bill which would add "to the ancient rule of *caveat emptor,* the further doctrine, 'let the seller also beware.' " The president's bill proposed to put the burden of telling the whole truth on those connected with the sale of securities—corporate officers, investment bankers, and accountants. Congress responded to the president's request, and on May 27, 1933, Roosevelt signed into law the Securities Act—"an act to provide full and fair disclosure of the character of the securities sold in interstate and foreign commerce. . . ."

The Securities Act was originally administered by the Federal Trade Commission, but in 1934, the act was amended to provide for the creation of a special body—the Securities and Exchange Commission—to assume its administration. Specifically, the Securities and Exchange Commission's task was to regulate the degree of disclosure, financial and nonfinancial, associated with new public security offerings as well as to require reports from those companies whose securities were already traded on the public security markets. Furthermore, the commission was given broad statutory authority to state accounting rules for registered companies and to enforce them.

In line with its power to prescribe accounting practices, the SEC quickly standardized the format of required financial statements it received. More important, the commission issued, from time to time, a number of opinions on accounting principles to encourage the development of uniform standards and practices in major accounting questions.

These opinions, however, cover but a small number of accounting practices. In those cases where no opinion has been expressed by the commission, its policy is to accept a registrant's accounting practice "if the points involved are such that there is a substantial authoritative support," which in most instances has meant acceptance by the accounting profession. The commission will not permit registered companies to disclose information in their reports to stockholders which is different from that filed with the SEC.

Next, beginning in 1939 and continuing through 1958, the Committee on Accounting Procedure of the American Institute issued a series of 51 *Accounting Research Bulletins,* touching upon a number of accounting problems and procedures. The principal objective of the bulletins was "to narrow areas of difference and inconsistency in accounting practices, and to further the development and recognition of generally accepted accounting principles." Each bulletin's opinions and recommendations "would serve as criteria for determining the suitability of accounting practices reflected in financial statements and representations of commercial and industrial companies." The authority of the opinions set forth in these bulletins rested "upon their general acceptability" among accounts and business executives. In practice, however, the bulletins' authority has been greatly strengthened by the reliance placed upon them by the New York Stock Exchange and the Securities and Exchange Commission in determining the acceptability of any questionable accounting practice.

Today, the reports filed by corporations with the Securities and Exchange Commission and the national stock exchanges are perhaps the most comprehensive, reliable, and detailed financial statements available publicly anywhere in the world. The financial statements published in periodic reports to stockholders are almost as detailed.

In 1959, faced with the growing discontent over current financial reporting practices and the increasing demand for more uniformity in accounting principles, the American Institute of Certified Public Accountants[2] dissolved its Committee on Accounting Procedure, the group that issued the *Accounting Research Bulletins,* and created the Accounting Principles Board. This substitution was intended to intensify efforts toward defining accounting "principles." The APB was provided with both an administrative director and the services of a research staff (the Accounting Research Division).

During its existence, the APB issued 31 *Opinions* and a number of research studies. However, in the early 1970s, the APB came under increasing criticism for its slow progress in resolving the many outstanding accounting controversies. As noted in Chapter 1, in June 1973, the APB was dissolved and the Financial Accounting Standards Board took over the task of defining what constitutes generally accepted accounting principles.

Some predict that if the FASB cannot succeed in its task, it is quite possible that the government will promulgate accounting principles, as has been done in several European countries.

---

[2] The American Institute of Accountants was renamed the American Institute of Certified Public Accountants in 1957.

Summary: Evolving Standards and Lagging Practice

The financial disclosure practices of modern American industrial management have nearly all developed since 1933. Yet modern standards have sprung from an earlier reaction to the secrecy which surrounded the financial affairs of most 19th-century manufacturing firms. This reaction, which began around 1900, is the historical base upon which recent developments rest. Improvements in reporting practices came principally as the result of continuing pressure from individuals outside the managerial group for improved corporate publicity. This nonmanagement group included such diverse characters as the so-called critics of big business and leaders of the public accounting profession and set the evolving standards by which the public evaluated corporate financial disclosures. The tempo of these critics' activities varied directly with the public attitude toward business, increasing markedly during those periods when management had fallen from popular favor.

Persistently, management's financial reporting practices lagged far behind the externally set standards, since management favored corporate secrecy and the would-be reformers were powerless to force their recommendations upon managers. Eventually, because management generally had not voluntarily adjusted its financial reporting practices to society's evolving financial informational needs (as perceived by management's critics), amid the business disorder following the 1929 stock market collapse the federal government intervened in the field of corporate financial disclosure, in 1933.

Thereafter, some authoritative, but nevertheless permissive, accounting standards, were developed by the SEC, CAP, and APB. To comply with these new standards, industrial management rapidly improved its financial reporting practices in a number of areas. Yet, in the meantime, the demand by some for fuller, more reliable, and more comparable financial data has persisted. Whether or not it will be necessary to expand government authority in the area of corporate accounting practice will probably depend upon the acceptance by both management and its critics of the authority and contents of the pronouncements of the FASB, as well as the FASB's willingness and ability to resolve quickly the issues confronting it. In any case, the historical evaluation of acceptable standards of financial disclosure among American industrial firms is far from complete.

PART TWO

Corporate Reporting Fundamentals

CHAPTER 3

Basic Accounting Concepts

Corporate financial reporting does not rest on one generally accepted unified theory of accounting. Rather, financial accounting decisions reflect a number of basic conventions or concepts which are more or less commonly accepted as useful guides to selecting appropriate accounting policies. These conventions have grown out of the experiences of accountants and business executives in devising ways to measure and communicate the results of operations and the financial condition of corporations, as well as from the theoretical works of accounting scholars. In practice, accounting conventions seem to be utilitarian. Their acceptance stems from their usefulness to those making decisions that involve accounting data. This usefulness is determined by whether the convention is compatible with the legal, social, and economic conditions, needs, and concepts of the time. Clearly, as these factors change over time, so must accounting conventions.

Significance to Users

Those who use financial statements might be tempted to dismiss the subject matter covered in this chapter (and other chapters in this series on accounting fundamentals) as being primarily of interest to managers, accountants, and bookkeepers. This would be a mistake. Financial statements are presented on the assumption that the reader understands the basics of accounting and finance. Therefore, knowledge of corporate reporting fundamentals is required to be a literate reader of financial statements.

The basic accounting conventions and definitions determine the character and scope of the data used for statement analysis. Because no one set of conventions governs accounting, financial statements include amounts that are arrived at by a variety of valuation procedures based on cash, economic, financial, and accrual concepts of measurement. A statement user who does not appreciate the account data's valuation bases can easily misinterpret financial statements.

The amounts shown against accounts listed in financial statements indicate that some event with financial consequences met the definition of the accounting transaction. Statement users must be able to distinguish between financial consequences included and those not included in financial statements. A knowledge of basic accounting concepts is helpful in this regard. For example, a company may be involved in a lawsuit that might result in an adverse judgment. For most statement users, this is a significant event. Someone unfamiliar with accounting's liability definition might assume that a prudent company would recognize a liability for the amount of a possible adverse judgment. However, if no reasonable estimate of the judgment amount can be determined, the accounting definition of a liability requires that no liability be recorded. A statement user familiar with accounting definitions would be aware of this possibility. Such an analyst would ask: "Is a provision for damages included or not included in the liabilities?" and then diligently seek out the answer to the question.

Financial statement analysis is usually undertaken for a specific decision, such as buying a security, determining a bond rating, or valuing a company. Statement users have to be careful when they incorporate financial statement data in their analyses leading up to such decisions. Frequently, the conventions of accounting result in financial statement data that are actually irrelevant for these decisions although they may appear to be relevant. For example, the market value of the properties of a company being considered for potential acquisition is important economic data for determining an acquisition price. Market price data will not be found in financial statements. Yet, there is something that could be misinterpreted as data relevant to property valuation, namely, the net book value (original cost less accumulated depreciation) of the company's properties. A statement user who is ignorant of the historical cost convention may unwittingly use these accounting values for the more relevant economic values. One who is aware of accounting conventions is not likely to fall into the trap of thinking the accounting data are something other than what they intended to represent.

One of the purposes of financial analysis is to determine if the accounting conventions incorporated in a particular company's financial statements are reasonable reflections of the company's circumstances. Knowledge of the basic conventions is necessary to make an appropriate test. For example, an important accounting convention is "the going concern" assumption. Because a company issues financial statements with no indication that the auditors question the company's continued existence, analysts should not assume that the issuer will in fact be in existence in the near future. As we will see later, an important use of financial analysis is to ferret out companies approaching financial difficulties and possible bankruptcy on the basis of data contained in the company's most recent statements, which were issued on the going concern assumption.

Those who analyze financial statements should know when to seek assistance from others more expert in accounting. To know when to call on others, analysts must know their own limitations. This requires a conscious effort to determine the gaps and limits in one's knowledge of the substance and scope of the basic accounting conventions. You cannot identify what you do not understand well until you have a broad sense of the subject in which you are testing the limits and depth of your own understanding.

Basic Accounting Concepts

The most authoritative source of a conceptual framework for financial accounting and reporting is the five *Statements of Financial Accounting Concepts* published by the Financial Accounting Standard Board (FASB). The conceptual framework is a coherent system of interrelated objectives and fundamentals that is expected to lead to consistent standards for prescribing the nature, function, and limits of financial accounting and reporting. The conceptual framework cannot directly solve financial accounting and reporting problems, but its objectives and concepts can be used as problem-solving tools. The five statements are not designed to establish generally accepted accounting principles or standards. The board is expected to be the most direct beneficiary of the guidance provided by this set of statements.

This chapter briefly describes a number of basic conventions. Some may argue that certain conventions should be combined or dropped. Others might try to break the list into categories that distinguish between postulates and principles. Many of these proposals will have merit, but the purpose of this list is simply to cover the basic conventions that seem to be accepted to some degree in outstanding books on this subject and in basic concepts statements issued by such groups as the FASB and the American Accounting Association.

Each of these conventions is discussed in greater detail in later chapters that focus on the relevant conventions for each accounting principle. For example, Chapter 15, Fixed Asset Accounting and Analysis, includes an expanded discussion of the historical cost convention and some of the alternative approaches proposed by accounting theorists, business executives, and statement users.

Business Entity

The business entity convention is that financial statements refer to a business entity that is separate and distinct from its owners. What happens to its owners' affairs is irrelevant. The principal reason for this convention is that it defines the accountant's area of interest and sets limits on the possible objectives and contents of financial reports. Consequently, the analysis of business transactions involving costs and revenue is expressed in terms of the changes in a firm's financial condition. Similarly, the assets and liabilities devoted to business activities belong to that entity. Also, since business activity is carried on between particular firms, financial statements must clearly identify the specific companies involved. This separation of ownership and management also recognizes the fiduciary responsbility to the stockholders of those who manage the business.

The boundaries of the business entity are sometimes difficult to establish. Typically, the accountant defines these boundaries in terms of the firm's economic activities and administrative control rather than legal relationships. For example, consolidated financial statements often present the financial condition and results of operations of different entities with common ownership in a single set of statements, thus treating the various entities as a single economic unit, even though they consist of several legal entities. Here the accountant is trying to present useful statements that look beyond legal relationships to the underlying economic and managerial relationships. The legal considerations are relevant only insofar as they define or influence economic activities and managerial control.

An alternative approach is to define the boundaries of the accounting entity in terms of the economic interests of the statement users rather than the economic activities of the unit. In practice, accounting reports may reflect to some degree this concept of the entity.

The entity concept applies equally to incorporated, unincorporated, small, and big businesses. In the case of incorporated, widely held, and publicly owned companies, such as General Motors, it is not difficult to separate the affairs of the business and its owners. However, in the case of small unincorporated businesses where the owners exert day-to-day control and personal and business assets are intermingled, the definition of the business entity is more difficult for financial—as well as managerial—accounting purposes.

The entity concept recognizes the long-standing belief that management has a stewardship responsibility to owners. Owners entrust funds to management and management is expected to use these funds wisely. Periodically, management must report to the owners the results of management's actions. Financial statements are one of the principal means whereby management fulfills this reporting responsibility. In the case of owner-manager businesses, the stewardship responsibility is assumed principally because of the analytical value of distinguishing how well the owner-managers did as investors in contrast to managers.

Going Concern

Unless evidence suggests otherwise, those preparing accounting statements for a business entity assume it will continue operations into the foreseeable future. This convention reflects the normal expectation of management and investors. To avoid misleading readers of financial statements, the statements of business entities with limited lives must clearly indicate the terminal date and type of liquidation involved (i.e., receiver's statements, etc.). Otherwise, the reader will assume that the accounts are based on the presumption that the enterprise has an indefinitely long life.

Accounting emphasizes and reflects the continuing nature of business activity. For example, the accountant expects that in the normal course of business the company will receive the full value of most of its accounts receivable. Accordingly, these items are recorded at their face value, less some deductions for anticipated bad debts, rather than at current liquidation value. Similarly, expenditures for finished goods inventories are recorded as assets, since the accountant assumes the inventories will be disposed of later in the normal course of operations. The continuity assumption does not imply, however, that the future will be the same as the past.

The going concern convention leads to the corollary that individual financial statements are part of a continuous, interrelated series of statements. This further implies that data communicated are tentative.

Not all accounting theorists support the common interpretation of the continuity convention. One author claims that the continuity assumption underlying accounting is misleading since it is a prediction rather than an assumption. Another views the firm as being in a continual state of orderly liquidation.

Monetary

Accounting is a measurement process dealing only with events that can be measured in monetary terms. This convention reflects the fact that money is the common denominator used in business to measure the exchange value of goods, services, and capital. Obviously, financial statements should indicate the money unit used.

The monetary convention leads to one of the limitations of accounting. Accounting, for example, does not record or communicate factors such as the state of the president's health, the attitude of the labor force, or the relative advantage of competitive products. Consequently, the most important aspect of a business may not be reflected in the financial statements.

Another potential limitation of the monetary convention is that it fails to distinguish between the purchasing power of monetary units in different periods. This can become a significant problem in trying to interpret financial statements during periods of inflation. For example, expenses may include dollars spent currently as well as dollars spent in earlier periods when the dollar purchased more goods and serivces.

Accounting Period

For decision-making purposes, managers and investors need periodic "test readings" of the progress of their business. Accounting recognizes this and breaks the flow of business activity into a series of reporting or fiscal periods. These periods are usually 12 months in length. Most companies also issue quarterly or semiannual statements to stockholders. For management use, statements covering shorter periods such as a month or week may be prepared. Regardless of the length of the period, the statements must indicate the period covered.

The success of a business can be determined accurately only upon liquidation. Consequently, the periodic financial statements are at best estimates, subject to change as future events develop.

Breaking business activity into a series of discrete segments creates a number of accounting problems. For example, given the uncertainties surrounding the life of an asset and its scrap value, how should the cost of the asset be allocated to specific periods? How should the income and costs associated with long-term contracts covering several accounting periods be treated? Such questions must be resolved in the light of the particular circumstances. There is no easy, general solution. The accountant and business executive must rely upon their experience, knowledge, and judgment to arrive at the appropriate answer.

The timing of the accounting period will depend upon the nature of the business. For most companies, the accounting period runs from January 1 to December 31. Some companies use a different period, usually because their yearly business cycle does not conform to the calendar year. For example, the annual statements of department stores are more revealing if their fiscal period ends January 31. This is a time when inventories are low and the Christmas holiday selling peak is over.

Consistency

The consistency convention requires that similar transactions be reported in a consistent fashion from period to period. Clearly, comparison of interperiod results would be difficult if a company changed its depreciation policy each year. The consistency concept is not inflexible, however. Changes in accounting policies are appropriate when justified by changing circumstances.

Accountants place considerable emphasis on consistency. When expressing an audit opinion, the accountant notes whether or not the statements were prepared "on a basis consistent with that of the preceding year." If changes were made, the auditor notes these in the audit opinion and insists that the nature and impact of these changes be fully disclosed.

The consistency concept does not necessarily mean that accounting practices are uniform among affiliated business units or even within a single company. One unit may value inventory on the so-called LIFO basis, whereas another may use the FIFO basis. Simiarly, a single unit might use both methods to value different parts of its inventory. In either case, the policy should be disclosed and consistently followed.

The consistency concept does not imply uniformity in the treatment of particular items among different independent companies. Indeed, one characteristic of American accounting practice is the diversity of accounting methods among different companies, all of which meet the criterion of "generally accepted accounting principles."

Historical Cost

For accounting purposes, business transactions are normally measured in terms of the actual prices or costs at the time they were consummated. This convention applies to both the initial recording and subsequent reporting of transactions. While agreeing with the need to record historical costs initially, some influential accountants argue that accounting would be "more useful" if, under certain conditions, estimates of current and future values were substituted for historical costs. The extent to which cost and value should be reflected in the accounts is central to much of the current accounting controversy.

The market value of assets may change with time. Typically, accounting does not recognize these changes in value. The cost of assets shown on financial statements seldom reflects the assets' current market value. Some believe that the historical cost convention flows from the going concern concept, which implies that since the business is not going to sell its fixed assets as such, there is little point in revaluing assets to reflect current values. For practical reasons, the accountant prefers the reporting of actual original costs to less certain estimates, which are more difficult to verify. By using historical costs, the accountant's already difficult task is not further complicated by the need to keep additional records of changing market values.

There is little disagreement among theorists that accounting should record the original cost value of a transaction initially. However, not all believe that this value should be used to measure expenses, to determine income, or value assets over time. For example, one proposal is that fixed assets be reported at their replacement cost and that the expense related to their use be based on this value. Another suggestion is that appraisals of current market values ought to be the basis for recording asset values. A third alternative suggestion is that the current cash equivalent value be used. The proponents of these recommendations argue that the going concern assumption does not necessarily depend on historical costs as the basis for accounting measurement; appraisal or replacement costs may be determined in a more objective fashion than historical costs; and the data communicated to statement users is more useful for such purposes as valuing securities or appraising management's use of the firm's resources.

While accounting is still based on historical costs, these proposals are slowly beginning to influence corporate reporting. For example, the FASB now requires certain large companies to report supplemental data showing the effect of changing prices on their financial results.

In practice, there have been a number of modifications to the historical cost concept. For example, under special conditions inventory may be reported at market values if it is less than historical cost. Assets acquired for stock are recorded at the estimated market value of the stock exchanged. Mutual funds and some pension funds whose assets consist almost entirely of securities report the market value of their investments, taking the gain or loss into income at the end of each reporting period. Similarly, donated assets may be carried at their appraised value at the time of acquisition.

The definition of the content of cost, irrespective of whether the historical cost convention or one of the alternative proposals is used, poses some problems. Issues arise as to what cost elements should be included in the cost of assets created by the company rather than bought from outsiders. Or, if an asset is acquired through a swap, the value to be placed on the asset given up or received may be unclear.

Realization

For accounting purposes, revenue is realized during the period when services or goods are exchanged for a valuable consideration, or when the revenue amount can be verified with a reasonable degree of objectivity. In practice, no one test, such as sale or delivery, has proven satisfactory, given the diversity of industry's production, sale, and credit practices. Consequently, the timing of revenue realization ranges from the act of production, in the case of some mining operations, to the receipt of cash, in the case of some installment sales contracts. Clearly, the application of the realization concept depends upon the circumstances of each case.

Some authorities claim revenue is earned during the operations process, rather than, say, entirely at the time of sale. They argue that all activities related to production and sales contribute to the final product and, hence, to revenue. Accordingly, they state that accounting should recognize revenue in proportion to the costs accumulated to date of such activities. In practice, one method of accounting for long-term construction contracts over several accounting periods does this by permitting revenues to be recognized in the proportion the estimated progress bears to the total job, provided it is anticipated that the contract can be completed and the profit originally estimated can be obtained. In the absence of firm contracts or reasonable certainty as to the course of future events, accounting practice does not normally recognize revenue during production.

Some accounting theorists advocate that revenue should be recognized when asset values change from accretion, such as occurs when timber grows or whiskey ages. This view is similar to that proposed by the production supporters, but it does not require a transaction to occur before revenue is recognized. In contrast, accretion revenue would be recognized through the production process by comparing inventory values at different points in time. This view of revenue may be acceptable in economic theory, but it is generally rejected in accounting practice because of the difficulty in determining asset values prior to sales and the tentative nature of such figures.

Matching of Costs and Revenues

Accounting income or profit is the net result of the accountant's trying to match the related costs and revenues of one period. This process can be described as matching "effort and accomplishments," where costs measure effort and revenues measure the related accomplishments. Often this ideal cannot be achieved, since costs cannot be easily identified with specific current or anticipated revenues.

Matching costs and revenues may require deferring recognition of expenses and revenues to future periods. For example, cash may be spent today to obtain subscriptions to a magazine that will provide subscribers with copies for the next five years. In this case, the accountant will defer recognizing the cash outlay as an expense until the magazines are due and the expected revenues are earned. At this time, the costs and the revenues would be matched. In the meantime, however, the unexpired cost would be reported as an asset (i.e., capitalized). Whether or not costs should be deferred and, if deferred, over what time period are difficult questions to resolve in practice.

The matching process is usually achieved through application of the accrual method of accounting rather than the cash method. The cash method of accounting records cash receipts and disbursements and focuses on changes in the cash account. The accrual method seeks to measure changes in owner's equity during the accounting period. Revenues are realized from noncapital transactions that result in an increase in owner's equity. In contrast, expenses are expired costs which are associated with the period, or the period's revenues that decrease owner's equity. The difference between revenues and expenses is net income for the period. These changes in owner's equity may not necessarily result in changes in the cash account. For example, a $100 sale on credit will increase accounts receivable and owner's equity. The accrual method recognizes the fact that the service has been performed and a valuable asset created. If a cash method was being used, no record of the event would be made until the customer's $100 cash was received.

The accrual method also leads to the accounting practice of recognizing costs as expenses when they expire (i.e., lose their future benefit generation value) rather than when they are incurred. In addition, the accrual method requires that costs be recognized as incurred when the firm receives goods and services, even though the actual billing or payment date is sometime in the future.

Dual Aspect

The dual aspect convention recognizes that someone has a claim on all the resources owned by the business. The resources are called "assets." The creditors' claims against these assets are usually referred to as "liabilities." The owners' claims are called either "stockholders' equity," "owners' equity," or "proprietorship." Consequently, since the total assets of the business are claimed by somebody, it follows that:

$$\text{Assets} = \text{Liabilities} + \text{Stockholders' equity}$$

Assets represent probable future, measurable economic benefits which the reporting entity has acquired through a current or past transaction. Assets include such items as cash, inventories, and buildings. An asset can represent an expected future economic benefit for several reasons:

1. The asset may be used to acquire other assets. Cash is the principal example of an asset that derives its value from its purchasing power.
2. The asset represents a claim upon another entity for money—for example, accounts receivable, which are amounts owed to the company for credit sales.
3. The asset can be converted to cash or a money claim. Finished goods inventories that will be sold in the normal course of business are an example.
4. The asset has potential benefits, rights, or services which will result in the entity earning something from its use in some future accounting period. Such assets include items like buildings and raw materials.

The term *liabilities* may be defined as probable future sacrifices of measurable economic benefits arising from the entity's obligations to convey assets or perform services to a person, firm, or another organization at some time in the future. These obligations require future settlement and represent claims of a nonownership nature on the entity's assets. Accounts payable to trade creditors, bonds payable, and taxes payable are examples of liabilities.

Liabilities also include so-called deferred credits. These do not represent clear-cut claims on the entity. They result from the need to recognize some expenses currently in order to get a "proper" matching of costs and revenues. To offset the expense item, a reserve balance is reported as a liability. Examples of deferred credits are reserves set up currently for tax expenses that may or may not be paid in the future but which accounting standards require to be recognized now.

Stockholders' or owners' equity is thought to represent ownership interest in the entity. It is a residual item. It is the excess of the entity's total assets over its liabilities.

Clearly, the measurement of owners' equity in the accounting equation represents no problem once liabilities and assets have been defined and measured. The problem arises in describing the nature of this residual amount. Certainly, it is not the market value of the firm to the owners. Some of the principal theories as to the nature of ownership equity are discussed below.

The proprietary theory regards the proprietor as the focus of interest in the accounting equation. Assets are owned by the proprietor, and liabilities are the proprietor's obligations. The basic accounting equation is:

$$\text{Assets} - \text{Liabilities} = \text{Proprietorship interest.}$$

The proprietorship interest implies that liabilities are negative assets, since the proprietor is thought to own all of the assets and the goal of accounting is to determine the net value of these assets to the proprietor.

The entity theory regards the business entity as separate from the wealth and personalities of its owners. The business assets of the entity are the entity's assets, and against these assets are equity claims by creditors and owners, who are regarded as the principal beneficiaries of the business' activities. This view of the entity is probably a better description of the typical corporate-investor relationship than the proprietorship theory. The entity theory's basic accounting equation is:

$$\text{Assets} = \text{Equities}$$

The enterprise theory regards the business-owner relationship in a similar fashion to the entity theory, except that beneficiaries of business activities are not limited to creditors and owners. It regards the entity as being operated for the benefit of society as a whole. As a result, the capital contributed and earnings retained in a business are thought of as benefiting more than just the stockholders, since the capital may produce benefits for society. Thus, society has an interest in the so-called net worth of a company.

A few accounting authors argue that the traditional accounting equation should be changed to reflect current thinking in finance and business. One such approach suggests that contemporary financial accounting practice is becoming increasingly concerned with maintaining a continuing record of capital invested in an enterprise from the double perspective of both sources and uses of funds, with funds broadly defined as all financial resources. This focus, it is argued, is in line with modern financial theory and practice, which tends to view assets as funds invested within the business, and liabilities and net worth as financial resources obtained from sources external to the firm. As a result, the balance sheet can be regarded as a report, at an instant of time, of both the status of funds obtained from sources external to the business and the items in which these funds (and those generated by drawing down other assets) are invested. This point of view regards earnings retained in the business as stockholders' reinvested profits; as such they represent an external source of funds.

Those who support this point of view express the dual aspect of transactions in terms of sources and uses of funds. Since for each use of funds there must be a matching source and for each source a use, the basic accounting equation suggested is:

$$\text{Items in which capital is invested (assets)}$$
$$= \text{External sources of capital (equities)}$$

Accounting systems are designed to record events in terms of their influence on assets, liabilities, or owners' equity. Every event has a dual aspect. For example, assume Jane Smith invested $5,000 in a new business;

the accounting entry would recognize the $5,000 asset of the business and Jane Smith's claim upon this asset:

$$\text{Asset, } \$5,000 = \text{Stockholders' equity, } \$5,000$$

Now, if the company borrowed $1,000 from the bank, the firm's accounting statement would be:

Assets		Liabilities and Stockholders' Equity	
Cash	$6,000	Bank loan payable	$1,000
		Stockholders' equity	5,000
Total	$6,000	Total	$6,000

Cash has increased $1,000 and so has the bank loan payable account. Next, assume the business used $2,000 of its cash to acquire some inventory; the new statement would be:

Assets		Liabilities and Stockholders' Equity	
Cash	$4,000	Bank loan payable	$1,000
Inventory	2,000	Stockholders' equity	5,000
Total	$6,000	Total	$6,000

The cash account is reduced by $2,000 and the inventory balance increased by a similar sum. Thus, the double-entry system requires two entries for each event. Other systems are possible, but the double-entry system is the most widely used.

Reliability of Evidence

Accountants recording events rely as much as possible upon objective, verifiable documentary evidence, in contrast to the subjective judgments of a person who may be biased. Acceptable evidence includes such items as approved sales or purchase invoices. This desire to base decisions on objective evidence is one of the principal supports of the historical cost convention, although, as noted earlier, some of the proponents of alternative approaches believe these approaches can be objective also.

In practice, accountants do not apply the absolute standard of objective, verifiable evidence. Many major decisions, such as allocation of costs between periods, must be based on reasonable estimates after considering all the relevant facts. In many instances, it is not feasible for an auditor to verify the recording of every event. As a result, auditors base their opinions in large part upon an assessment of management's internal controls— the procedures adopted by management to safeguard assets, check the reliability and accuracy of data, and encourage adherence to operating policies and programs.

The definition of what constitutes an objective measurement is not a settled matter. At least four different approaches can be identified among accounting writers. One author defines an objective measurement as being impersonal and outside the mind of the person making the measurement. Another thinks of it as based on the consensus of qualified experts. A third considers a measurement objective if it is based on verifiable evidence. The fourth approach rates objectiveness in terms of the narrowness of the statistical dispersion around the mean measurement from results obtained by different measurers. The narrower the dispersion, the less subjective is the mean considered to be.

A convention closely related to the reliability convention is the standard proposed by some that accounting statements should be free from bias, meaning that the facts have been impartially determined and reported and contain no built-in bias.

Disclosure

The disclosure convention requires that accounting reports disclose enough information that they will not mislead careful readers reasonably well informed in financial matters. Special disclosure is made of unusual items, changes in expectations, significant contractual relations, and new activities. The disclosure can be in the body of the financial statements, the auditor's opinion, or the notes to the statements.

The disclosure convention has received increasing attention in recent years. For example, financial analysts have been pressing with some success for fuller disclosure of sales and profits by divisions and major product lines. It is anticipated that the pressure for fuller disclosure will continue. In general, while management has cooperated with these demands, it has refused to disclose information of a "competitive" nature. The question of what constitutes "competitive" information has yet to be settled, however.

Conservatism

The conservatism convention prescribes a degree of skepticism in assessing the prospects that incompleted transactions will be concluded successfully. In practice, this means that in deciding between two permissible accounting alternatives, some added weight should be given to whichever alternative leads to the lowest asset or highest liability figures and that more stringent requirements must be imposed for recognizing revenues and gains as components of earning than for recognizing expenses and losses.

If not carefully applied, this convention can lead to abuses that result in unnecessary or dishonest understatements. Also, by understating income in one period, income in another period may be overstated. Thus, the application of this convention requires considerable judgment, especially since auditors may be sued if they condone grossly misleading statements.

A number of accounting theorists reject conservatism as a legitimate accounting convention. In their opinion, it leads to a deliberate misstatement and as such has no place in accounting. They also believe that statement issuers should provide unbiased data so that statement users can evaluate the risks of, say, investing in the issuer company. If conservatism is applied, issuers offer their valuations of risk to substitute for the user's independent evaluation, which might have been different from the issuer's if unbiased data had been available to the user. Finally, they argue that the convention of conservatism is capricious in practice. There are no uniform approaches to its application.

Materiality

Accounting conventions apply only to material and significant items. Inconsequential items can be dealt with expediently. However, in applying this convention, care must be taken to ensure that the cumulative effect of a series of immaterial items does not materially alter the total statements. Whether or not an item is immaterial depends on judgment and the particular circumstances. One common test of materiality is: Would the decision of a reasonably well-informed user of the statements be altered if the item was treated differently? If the decision would change, the item is material.

Substance over Form

In order to reflect economic activities, accounting emphasizes the economic substance of events, even though the legal form may differ from the economic substance and suggest a different treatment.

Application

The application of these conventions in specific instances is left to the judgment of managers and their accountants. The relative importance of these conventions changes from decision to decision. Also, in any one instance, two or more conventions may be in conflict. The problem facing the accountant or business executive is to select those conventions most relevant to the facts of the situation and the particular needs of the principal users of the statements. Whether or not a convention leads to a feasible solution will also determine its relevance.

The conventions of accounting define the scope and character of information contained in financial statements. Rarely is the whole answer to an analytical question contained in the financial statements. Statement users should always be conscious of this fact. In most cases, data beyond the scope of the financial statement must be obtained to complete a competent analysis.

Omega Novelty Shop
Economic versus Accounting Concepts

Paul Stone submitted to the Research Division of an eastern business school the most recent annual profit and loss statement for his small retail novelty shop shown in Exhibit 1.

On writing to Mr. Stone for supplementary information, the division learned that of the net profit of $10,627.98 shown on his statement, Mr. Stone had withdrawn $4,500. He did not make a charge for his own services as manager, but up to a few years ago he had been employed in a similar capacity in another store at a salary of $10,400 a year. Mr. Stone stated that he owned his store building, which had a rental value of $3,900 a year. From the balance sheets submitted for this firm, the division computed the net worth of the business exclusive of real estate to be $98,677.98. Interest on this sum at 6 percent, which Mr. Stone stated to be the local rate on savings-type accounts, amounted to $5,920.68.

On the basis of these additional data, the division adjusted the profit and loss statement for the Stone store and sent it back as shown in Exhibit 2.

After receiving this adjusted profit and loss statement, Mr. Stone wrote the following letter to the division:

Dear Sirs:

I have received a copy of my most recent profit and loss statement as adjusted by you, and I am at a loss to understand some of the changes you have made.

For instance, the statement which I sent you showed a net profit of $10,627.98 but the copy which you have returned to me shows a net merchandising loss of $5,851.10. I notice that you have charged $10,400 as my salary. I do not draw any regular salary from the business, and since I am in business for myself I consider that I am not working for a salary but for profits. Also you have shown a rental expense of $3,900. Since I own the building, I consider that the item of rent is adequately taken care

This case was prepared by David F. Hawkins.
Copyright © 1985 by the President and Fellows of Harvard College
Harvard Business School case 186–110

EXHIBIT 1

OMEGA NOVELTY SHOP
Profit and Loss Statement

Gross sales	$104,850.48	
Less: Returns and allowances to customers	4,500.00	
Net sales		$100,350.48
Net inventory of merchandise at beginning of year	$ 50,258.79	
Plus: Purchases of merchandise at billed cost	74,762.67	
Inward freight, express, and parcel postage	428.61	
Gross cost of merchandise handled	$125,450.07	
Less: Cash discounts taken	1,276.95	
Net cost of merchandise handled	$124,173.12	
Less: Net inventory of merchandise at end of year	55,245.84	
Net cost of merchandise sold		68,927.28
Gross margin		$ 31,423.20
Expenses:		
Total salaries and wages	$ 9,480.39	
Advertising	1,702.56	
Boxes and wrappings	556.41	
Office supplies and postage	1,220.73	
Taxes, insurance, repairs, and depreciation of real estate	2,616.30	
Heat, light, and power	515.79	
Taxes	342.00	
Insurance	863.31	
Depreciation of store equipment	660.00	
Interest on borrowed capital	178.80	
Miscellaneous expense	1,533.63	
Income taxes	1,125.30	
Total expenses		20,795.22
Net profit		$ 10,627.98

of by the expenses incurred in connection with the building, such as taxes, insurance, and so on. Furthermore, you have shown an expense of $5,920.68 for interest on owned capital. I have worked hard to put this business in a position where I would not have to borrow money, but if I have to charge interest on my own capital, I do not see where I am any better off, according to your version of affairs, than if I were continually in debt to banks and wholesalers.

In short, it seems to me that your adjustment of my statement amounts merely to shifting money from one pocket to another and calling it salary, rent, or interest, as the case may be; whereas what I am really interested in is the profit that I make by being in business for myself rather than working for somebody else.

An explanation from you will be appreciated.

Yours very truly,

PAUL STONE

EXHIBIT 2

OMEGA NOVELTY SHOP
Profit and Loss Statement
Merchandise Statement

Gross sales	$104,850.48		
Less: Returns and allowances to customers	4,500.00		
Net sales		$100,350.48	100.00%
Net inventory of merchandise at beginning of year	$ 50,258.79		
Plus: Purchases of merchandise at billed cost	74,762.67		
Inward freight, express, and parcel postage	428.61		
Gross cost of merchandise handled	$125,450.07		
Less: Cash discounts taken	1,276.95		
Net cost of merchandise handled..................	$124,173.12		
Less: Net inventory of merchandise at end of year	55,245.84		
Net cost of merchandise sold		68,927.28	68.69
Gross margin		$ 31,423.20	31.31%

Expense Statement

Proprietor's salary	$ 10,400.00		9.92%
All other salaries and wages	9,480.39		9.45
Total salaries and wages	$ 19,880.39		19.37%
Advertising	1,702.56		1.70
Boxes and wrappings	556.41		0.55
Office supplies and postage	1,220.73		1.21
Rent	3,900.00		3.89
Heat, light, and power	515.79		0.51
Taxes	342.00		0.34
Insurance	863.31		0.86
Depreciation of store equipment	660.00		0.66
Interest on borrowed capital .... $ 178.80			
Interest on owned capital invested in the business 5,920.68			
Total interest	$ 6,099.48		6.08
Miscellaneous expense.........................	1,533.63		1.53
Total expenses		$ 37,274.30	36.70%

Net Gain (Loss) Statement

Net merchandising loss		$ 5,851.10	5.58%
Interest and rentals earned: Interest on owned capital invested in the business	$ 5,920.68		
Rent of owned store building $3,900.00			
Less: Expense on owned store building (taxes, insurance, repairs, depreciation, interest on mortgages) 2,616.30	1,283.70		
Total interest and rentals		7,204.38	
Net gain		$ 1,353.28	
Provision for federal and state income taxes	$ 1,125.30		
Withdrawals...................................	4,500.00	5,625.30	
Deficit for the year		$ (4,272.02)	

Questions

1. Did Mr. Stone make a profit from his novelty business during the current year? How much, if any? How may the difference between Mr. Stone's computation of profits and that of the Research Division be explained?

2. Was Mr. Stone a successful business executive?

3. Should Mr. Stone have sold his novelty business?

4. What were the incentives which motivated Mr. Stone?

CHAPTER 4

Basic Financial Statements

The typical corporate annual report to stockholders contains three basic statements: a statement of financial position, a statement of net income, and a statement of changes in financial position. Occasionally, a fourth statement showing the changes in owners' equity is also presented. These statements are presented on a comparative basis with previous years.

In practice, there are many variations in the titles, form, content, and coverage of these statements. For example, they may be for a parent company alone or for a consolidated entity representing the parent and its subsidiaries. Irrespective of their title or whether they are annual or interim statements, the function of these basic statements is to communicate useful quantitative information of a financial nature about a business to stockholders, creditors, and others interested in the reporting company's financial condition, results of operations, and cash flows.

Annual statements, in contrast to interim statements, are always covered by a certified public accountant's opinion. This chapter describes the purpose and content of the typical balance sheet and income statement and the basic bookkeeping debit-credit mechanisms used to record the transactions summarized by these statements. The statement of changes in owners' equity is discussed also. The chapter also expands upon some of the definitions and concepts discussed in the previous chapter. The statement of changes in financial position is covered in a later chapter.

Statement Analysis

Financial statement data are the raw material of financial analysis. A knowledge of the debit-credit mechanism for recording accounting data and the accepted formats for financial statements is important to those who analyze financial statement data.

Financial analysts must understand the debit-credit mechanism because the clue as to what is going on in a company is often revealed by the account that represents the other side of the transaction rather than by the account that is of direct interest. For example, a company's sales growth may be the primary focus of an analyst's interest. Sales may appear to be growing at a spectacular rate. Yet the "sales" account is only one part of the accounting transaction. The analyst who knows that the offsetting entry to sales is accounts receivable will instinctively look at this second account. By examining the accounts receivable, the analyst may discover the company's sales are growing because it is extending extremely generous credit terms to customers of doubtful credit quality. In the light of this finding, the analyst may not be very impressed with the company's sales growth rate.

Sometimes companies use the terms "debit" and "credit" in their reports to stockholders to describe the results of some event. Unless the statement user understands the technical application of these terms, the user may be misled. For example, a company's income tax obligation may change because of a modification to its accounting practices for tax purposes. In its discussion of this event, its management may note that the accounting change resulted in a "credit to taxes payable." A naive statement reader may believe a "credit" is a good event, meaning lower taxes. This would be a wrong conclusion, because in accounting jargon a credit to a liability account, such as taxes payable, means an increase in that account balance. A statement user who understood the debit-credit mechanism would interpret correctly management's accounting language.

A knowledge of bookkeeping is also helpful to statement users. It helps identify account balances that are dependent on management's estimates and judgments. These are the so-called adjusting entries, such as the charging of depreciation expense and the establishment of a bad debt reserve. These accounts are of particular interest to financial analysts because an irresponsible management may manipulate them to achieve a desired end result. For these accounts, the financial analyst must make a judgment as to whether management's assertions are reasonable. This is not an easy task, but it must be done. Otherwise, the financial analyst may be fooled by a dishonest management. To the extent that a statement user is unfamiliar with the adjusting entries required by bookkeeping to complete a set of financial statements, the likelihood of being misled by an unscrupulous management increases.

The format of the three basic financial statements has become fairly standard. Statement users should the familiar with this format and its common variations. This knowledge will help analysts to identify unusual features in financial statement presentations which might indicate a need for extra thoroughness in conducting the statement analysis. Familiarity with the standard formats can also expedite the location of required data and make the analytical process more efficient.

Statement Objectives

According to the FASB's *Statement of Accounting Concepts No. 1,* "Objectives of Financial Reporting by Business Enterprises," the objective of the three basic financial reports is to provide:

1. Information that is useful to present and potential investors and creditors and other users in making rational investment, credit and similar decisions. The information should be comprehensible to those who have a reasonable understanding of business and economic activities and are willing to study the information with reasonable diligence.
2. Information to help present and potential investors and creditors and other users in assessing the amounts, timing, and uncertainty of prospective cash receipts from dividends or interest and the proceeds from the sale, redemption, or maturity of securities or loans.
3. Information about the economic resources of an enterprise, the claims to those resources (obligations of the enterprise to transfer resources to other entities and owners' equity), and the effects of transactions, events, and circumstances that change resources and claims to those resources.
4. Information about how an enterprise obtains and spends cash, about its borrowings and repayment of borrowings, about its capital transactions (including cash dividends and other distributions of enterprise resources to owners), and about other factors that may affect an enterprise's liquidity or solvency.
5. Information about how management of an enterprise has discharged its stewardship responsibility to owners (stockholders) for the use of enterprise resources entrusted to management.
6. Explanations and interpretations to help users understand financial information provided.

For pragmatic reasons, these objectives are focused on information for investment and credit decisions. Relevance, reliability, and costliness are criteria that should be used in evaluating and selecting accounting information for disclosure.

General Requirements

All financial statements must carry the name of the reporting company, the dates of the period covered, and an indication of whether or not the statements and accompanying footnotes are audited. Unless otherwise indicated, it is presumed that the statements are for a going concern. However, as noted in the previous chapter, in practice, this assumption should not be accepted literally in all cases, since reporting companies' future prospects for survival over the long run vary greatly. In addition, companies under the jurisdiction of the Securities and Exchange Commission should not publish statements that differ from those required to be filed with the commission on an annual and interim basis.

Financial statements should present data that can be understood by users of the statements in a form and with terminology compatible with the users' range of understanding. In practice, this requirement assumes that users have some basic familiarity with the business activities of the reporting entity, the financial accounting process, and the technical language used in financial statements.

Another basic requirement is that the comparative statements issued by a company be truly comparable. This requires that (1) the format of the statements be identical, (2) the same items from the underlying accounting records are classified under the same captions, (3) the accounting principles followed in preparing the statements are not changed (or if so, that the changes and their effects are disclosed), (4) changes in the circumstances of the enterprise are disclosed, and (5) the comparative reporting periods are of equal length.

Other requirements include: the statements must be complete for the periods covered; the data must be communciated soon enough after the close of the accounting period to be useful to the statement users; the disclosure of all data relevant to the users' needs must be adequate; and a summary of the accounting principles adopted must be presented.

Statement of Financial Position

The statement of financial position, or balance sheet, purports to present data related to a company's financial condition as of a specific time, based on the conventions and generally accepted principles of accounting. Balance sheets for the current and prior accounting periods are shown for comparative purposes. The amounts shown on these statements are the balances at the date of the statement. Typically these amounts, except for monetary items such as cash, accounts receivable, and accounts payable balances, may have little financial significance. For example, inventory may be stated at a cost that does not come close to approximating the actual investment in the inventory. Similarly, the net asset value reported for plant and equipment may be only a small fraction of the cash value of the asset. This situation occurs because of the historical cost convention and the preoccupation of accounting with the measurement of income. As a result, in practice, the statement of financial position is increasingly regarded as a step between two income statements that shows what residual balances remain in the accounts after current income has been determined. Statement users are expressing concern that much of the data in financial position statements may be of little significance to investors seeking to analyze the financial status of a company.

Balance sheets do not all follow the same precise format or use the same account titles. However, within reasonable limits of flexibility, the items on a balance sheet are typically grouped in the following general categories:

Assets		**Liabilities and Owners' Equity**	
Current assets	xxx	Liabilities:	
Long-term investments	xxx	Current liabilities	xxx
Fixed assets	xxx	Long-term liabilities	xxx
Other assets (sometimes divided into noncurrent, prepaid and deferred charges, and intangible assets)	xxx	Other liabilities (sometimes divided into deferred credits and accumulated provisions)	xxx
		Total liabilities	xxx
		Owners' equity:	
		Capital stock	xxx
		Other paid-in capital	xxx
		Retained earnings	xxx
		Total owners' equity	xxx
		Total liabilities and	
Total assets	xxx	owners' equity	xxx

The totals of the amounts listed in each of three major categories of the statement of financial position conform to the basic accounting equation.

$$\text{Assets} = \text{Liabilities} + \text{Owners' equity}$$

Assets

Assets represent probable measurable future economic benefits to which the business holds the right and which have been acquired through a current or past transaction. These resources may be considered to have future economic benefits for a variety of different reasons. For example, some expenditures, such as capitalized[1] franchise acquisition expenditures, are called assets because they are expected to contribute to the generation of income in future accounting periods. Some assets, such as accounts receivable, represent resources that can readily be converted into cash. Other resources, such as the land owned by the business, are called assets because they represent valuable property rights. Irrespective of the principal criterion used to determine whether an item is an asset, assets are not typically carried at a value greater than either their original cost or their net realizable value, whichever is lower. Monetary assets such as cash, accounts receivable, and marketable securities are carried at the equivalent of the cash value expected to be realized in the normal course of business.

Illustration 4–1 presents the asset section of a major corporation's consolidated balance sheet. Assets are divided into four categories common

---

[1] An expenditure is said to be capitalized when it is recorded as an asset rather than an expense.

ILLUSTRATION 4-1

Asset Section of a Major Corporation's Consolidated Balance Sheet
December 31, 1985
(in thousands)

Assets

Current assets:

Cash	$ 39,274
U.S. government and other marketable securities, at lower of cost or market (quoted market value: $3,726,000)	3,722
Notes and accounts receivable (less estimated losses, $4,251,000)	165,288
Inventories	193,795
Prepayments and other current assets	9,979
Total current assets	$ 412,058

Investments:

Investments in jointly owned companies, at equity	$ 36,068
Investments in subsidiaries not consolidated, at cost or less	9,690
Other, at cost or less	9,739
Total investments	$ 55,497

Property:

Land, buildings, machinery, and equipment, etc. (at cost)	$1,199,489
Less: Accumulated depreciation and depletion	594,085
Net property	$ 605,404

Other assets:

Excess of cost of investments in consolidated subsidiaries over equities in net assets	$ 11,165
Deferred charges	10,629
Total other assets	$ 21,794
Total assets	$1,094,753

---

to many statements—current assets, investments, property, and other assets. Although they are not shown here, the notes to the statements provide additional information relevant to understanding the data in the asset section of the statement. For example, the method used to determine inventory values and the company's depreciation accounting policy were disclosed. This illustration will be used to explain briefly the nature of the assets accounts found on most balance sheets. A fuller explanation of these items is presented in subsequent chapters.

Current Assets

Current assets include cash and other assets that are reasonably expected to be realized in cash or sold or consumed during the normal operating cycle of the business, or within one year if the operating cycle is shorter than one year. The operating cycle can be represented as that period during which the series of events described in Illustration 4-2 occur in sequence.

ILLUSTRATION 4–2
Normal Operating Cycle Illustrated

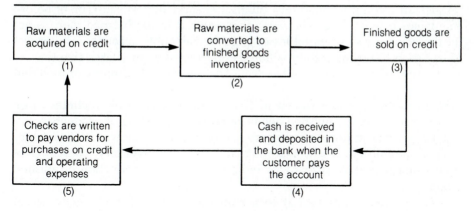

For most companies, the operating cycle is less than 12 months. However, there are some notable exceptions. For example, one large bowling equipment manufacturer sold bowling alley equipment in return for long-term notes with payment schedules ranging up to seven years. These notes receivable from customers were classified as a current asset on the grounds that the company's "normal operating cycle" was seven years, since it took that long to complete all of the events related to each sale. Other more common examples of industries with operating cycles longer than one year are the distilling and tobacco industries. Their inventories must age for a long period before being offered for sale. In other cases, such as land development companies, no distinction is made between current and noncurrent assets, since the period during which land is held for sale can be very long and the period over which the purchase price is paid by the buyer of the land even longer.

Current assets include cash, accounts receivable, marketable securities, and inventories. *Cash* is shown at its face value and includes cash on hand, undeposited checks at the date of the balance sheet, cash in banks, and checks in transit to banks. (Checks written by the company but not yet deposited and charged to the company's bank account are treated as if they had been deposited.)

Sometimes corporations invest surplus cash on a temporary basis in securities that can be readily sold under normal conditions. These *marketable securities* are held for investment purposes rather than to control the operations of the entity issuing the securities. Typically these securities, as in Illustration 4–1, are short-term obligations of the United States government. Marketable securities are presented at the lower of their cost or current market price. In addition, their current market value is shown parenthetically (i.e., in brackets next to the account).

Notes and accounts receivable represent the claims against customers generated by credit sales for amounts still due to the company. The balance of such an account includes only billings for services performed on or before the balance sheet date. The amount presented in the balance sheet is net of the company's estimated losses from uncollectible accounts. The procedures used to estimate these amounts are described in a later chapter.

Inventories include tangible items that will be sold directly or included in the production of items to be sold in the normal course of operations. The inventory account shown in Illustration 4–1 probably includes three types of inventory: a finished goods inventory, consisting of products ready for sale; a work in process inventory, consisting of products in various stages of production; and a raw materials and supplies inventory, consisting of items that will enter directly or indirectly into the production of finished goods.

Inventories are carried at cost, unless their utility is no longer as great as their cost. The so-called lower-of-cost-or-market rule to determine if the carrying value of inventories should be written down below cost is covered in a later chapter. This same chapter also discusses the alternative methods for determining the cost value of inventories shown on the balance sheet. These methods include the first-in, first-out method, which values the inventory on the balance sheet date using recent costs; and the last-in, first-out method, which uses old costs to value the asset inventory.

The current asset category may include other accounts which will be realized during the normal operating cycle. Examples are unbilled costs on construction contracts performed by contractors for customers, prepaid insurance and expenses where the benefits to be derived from the prepayment extend beyond the current accounting period, and tax refunds receivable. Even though they do not result in a conversion into cash, prepaid expenses are listed among current assets. This practice is followed because these expenditures are expected to be recovered in cash through sales during the operating cycle or the benefits from the expenditures are to be received during the operating cycle.

It is customary to list current assets in their descending order of liquidity. For example, in Illustration 4–1, cash is listed first, marketable securities next, and then accounts receivable. Marketable securities precede accounts receivable because, of the two items, marketable securities can more easily be turned into cash by management. For a similar reason, inventories are listed after accounts receivable but before prepayments.

Investments

Investments made in other companies are carried on the consolidated balance sheet as noncurrent items when the investing company's objective is one of control, affiliation, or some continuing business relationship with the company, and when the circumstances of the investment do not require the subsidiary to be consolidated. These investments may be common stock, debt securities, or long-term advances. It is not customary to state the market value of such noncurrent investments, since it is assumed there is no present intention to sell the securities. Depending on the circumstances, these securities may be carried at their original cost or at an amount equal to the investing company's original cost plus its proportional share of the subsidiary's retained earnings. This latter approach is called the equity method. Later chapters explain the cost and equity methods in greater detail.

Illustration 4–1 shows three types of long-term investments and their valuation basis: *investments in joint ventures*, valued according to the equity method; *investments in unconsolidated subsidiaries*, valued by the cost method at their original cost or less (these subsidiaries could be overseas subsidiaries in countries with unusual economic or political problems that limit the parent company's ability to influence their operations); and other miscellaneous long-term investments, shown at cost or less. Investments are shown at less than their original cost when there has been a loss in their value.

Property

Long-lived tangible assets, such as equipment acquired to produce goods for sale, are referred to as "fixed assets." Assets in this category are *land, buildings, machinery, equipment*, and any other long-lived tangible items used in the company's operations. Land is always stated at its original cost. The other assets are stated at their original cost less depreciation, rather than at their replacement value or current market value.

Depreciation represents the allocation of the cost of fixed assets due to use and obsolescence. An annual charge for depreciation is included in the expenses of current operations. The amount of this depreciation expense is related to the anticipated useful life of the asset, which may be computed on the basis of either expected years of service or actual use (i.e., hours of operation, units produced, etc.). The accumulated amount of depreciation expense related to the fixed assets still carried on the books of the company is presented on the balance sheet in an account called "accumulated depreciation."

A later chapter discusses the various depreciation methods in detail. The two principal approaches to depreciation are the straight-line and accelerated methods. Straight-line depreciation allocates the cost of a fixed asset, less any estimated salvage value, equally to operations over the life of the asset. Accelerated depreciation methods charge a greater proportion of an asset's total depreciation to operations during the early years of its life than during the latter years.

It is customary, as presented in Illustration 4–1 under the caption *property*, to show both the original cost and the depreciated book value of the fixed assets available for use in operations. The difference between these two amounts, accumulated depreciation, is shown as a deduction from the total original cost of the fixed assets to arrive at the net book value of the assets. This net book value, called "net property" in Illustration 4–1, seldom reflects the current market value of the asset. It is simply the balance left in the property accounts of the company's accounting records after deducting the related accumulated depreciation charges.

Illustration 4–1 refers to "accumulated depreciation and depletion." The term *depletion* relates to investments in natural resources, whereas the term *depreciation* is associated with plant and equipment investments. Depletion is the amount of a company's investment in natural resources that is charged to operations over the period during which these resources are extracted or exhausted. Accumulated depletion is the cumulative total of these charges related to the natural resource investments still available to the company for the generation of future revenues. Depletion is often charged on a units-of-production basis.

Other Assets

Items in the "other assets" category include intangible assets and deferred charges. Assets that fall into this category are patents, trademarks, copyrights, and franchises. To be recorded, these assets must be created or acquired through a business transaction. Intangible assets are carried at cost initially and then charged to operations in a systematic manner over their useful life. A later chapter covers the topic of intangible assets in greater detail.

Illustration 4–1 lists an *intangible asset* labeled "excess of cost of investments in consolidated subsidiaries over equities in net assets." The popular name for this item is "goodwill." It arises when a company purchases another company for a price in excess of the fair market value of its net assets. Goodwill, this difference between the purchase price and the net asset values acquired, must be charged to operations over a period of not more than 40 years. However, the actual period used varies greatly from company to company. The accounting for business acquisitions and goodwill is covered in a later chapter.

Deferred charges are similar to prepaid expenses, since both are payments or accruals recognized before the balance sheet date that properly should be charged to operations subsequent to that date. However, it is important to distinguish between them, since prepaid expenses are a current asset and deferred charges are assigned to the other-asset category. Prepaid expenses relate to amounts paid for services yet to be received, which are properly related to future revenues. In contrast, deferred charges represent amounts paid for services already received by the business but not yet charged to operations. For example, the prepayment of the premiums on a three-year insurance policy is a prepaid expense, since the insurance protection has yet to be received. In addition, since the benefit of the insurance is to be received over the next three years, it should be charged against income over this period. In contrast, preoperating expenditures for opening a new store that are expected to produce benefits beyond the current period may be considered a deferred charge, since the company has already received the preopening service. However, in order to determine income in accordance with the matching convention, the company has elected to hold off expensing this item until the future benefits are received.

Liabilities

Liabilities are probable, measurable, future economic sacrifices arising from the entity's obligations to convey assets or perform services to a person, firm, or other organization outside of the entity at some time in the future, plus deferred credits.

Liabilities include all claims of nonownership type against the business by outsiders. Stated another way, they represent the amounts owed to creditors. These obligations include such items as amounts due to vendors, bank loans payable, and debentures outstanding.

Liabilities represent claims against all assets, except where noted in the notes to the financial statements. Typically, where liabilities relate to specific assets, it is not acceptable to show the liability as a deduction from the asset. For example, the mortgage on a building is shown on the right-hand or liability side of the balance sheet and the asset "building" is listed on the left-hand side.

The accounting concept of liabilities is broader than liabilities in the popular sense of legal debts and obligations. The accounting concept includes certain deferred credits that do not involve a debtor-creditor relationship. For example, for accounting purposes, the seller's profit on a sale and leaseback transaction is not recognized in the income statement as a gain at the time of the sale. The preferred treatment is to list the profit as a deferred credit on the right-hand side of the balance sheet and allocate this amount to the income statement as a reduction to lease rentals over the life of the lease. This practice leads to a better matching of costs and revenues.

Illustration 4–3 presents an example of the right-hand side of a major corporation's consolidated balance sheet, the liabilities and owners' equity section. Taken together, Illustrations 4–1 and 4–3 comprise this company's entire balance sheet with the exception of the related notes.

Current Liabilities

Current liabilities are defined as (1) those liabilities that the company expects to satisfy with either assets classified as current in the same balance sheet or by creating of other current liabilities; (2) all obligations arising from operations directly related to the company's operating cycle; or (3) those

ILLUSTRATION 4–3

**Liability and Owners' Equity Section of a Major
Corporation's Consolidated Balance Sheet
December 31, 1985**
(in thousands)

Liabilities and Owners' Equity

Current liabilities:

Notes payable—banks	$ 59,504
Current maturities of long-term debt	7,953
Accounts payable and accruals	113,953
Domestic and foreign taxes on income	19,700
Total current liabilities	$ 201,110

Long-term debt:

11⅝% of sinking fund debentures	$ 125,000
10½% term loan	42,088
Other	26,666
Total long-term debt	$ 193,754

Deferred credits:

Deferred income tax	$ 36,186
Investment credit—unamortized balance	17,959
Other	1,793
Total deferred credits	$ 55,938

Accumulated provisions:

Product warranties	$ 10,356
Foreign operations	543
Total accumulated provisions	$ 10,899
Total liabilities	$ 461,701

Capital and retained earnings:

Cumulative preferred stock—authorized 5 million shares; no shares issued	—
Common stock—authorized, 50 million shares, par value $2.50 each; issued, 21,721,988 shares	$ 212,850
Earnings retained for use in the business	462,972
Less: Common stock in treasury, 1,245,420 shares at cost	(42,770)
Total capital and retained earnings	$ 633,052
Total liabilities and owners' equity	$1,094,753

liabilities expected to be satisfied during the following year. The one-year
rule is widely considered to be the cutoff between current and noncurrent
liabilities. However, if the enterprise's operating cycle is longer than 12
months, an exception is made to this rule and the operating cycle period
is used.

Current liabilities include the current portion (due within 12 months)
of notes payable to banks, amounts owed to trade creditors, wages earned
by employees but not paid to them, and funds received in advance for
services not yet rendered. The order of presentation followed in the current
liability section of Illustration 4–3 is typical of most balance sheets.

The captions of the various current liabilities listed in Illustration 4–3 are almost self-explanatory. *Notes payable to banks* represent the company's obligations to banks arising from short-term borrowing arrangements. The amount shown as the *current maturities on long-term debt* is a portion of the long-term debt's principal that must be repaid during the next 12 months. *Accounts payable* represent the claims of trade creditors for goods and services provided on an open account basis. If these trade obligations were evidenced by a note or similar written promise to pay, they would be included with notes payable. The *accruals* combined with the accounts payable in Illustration 4–3 are most probably items such as wages owed to employees or deposits owed to customers on returnable containers not yet returned. The taxes owed as of the balance sheet date that will be paid to various taxing authorities during the next 12 months are included in the obligations listed as *domestic and foreign taxes on income.*

Long-Term Liabilities

Long-term liabilities are all of an enterprise's noncurrent liabilities. They are often subdivided on the balance sheet into several different categories. For example, the long-term liabilities shown in Illustration 4–3 are presented in three groups—long-term debt, deferred credits, and accumulated provisions.

Long-term debt represents debt obligations of a company that will mature beyond one year's time. These obligations are recorded at their principal value. However, in the case of long-term debt, such as bonds and debentures issued at a discount or premium, the discount or premium is shown as an adjustment to the principal amount. In the case of bank loans, the principal value is the amount owed the banks. The current interest on these obligations is charged to operating income as the interest obligation is incurred. A later chapter discusses the accounting for long-term debt in greater detail.

Deferred Credits

Deferred credits are the opposite of deferred charges. They are unearned revenues, such as subscriptions collected in advance of providing the service; or deferred profits, such as the deferral or profit on a sale-and-leaseback transaction. Another important class of deferred credits results from charges required by generally accepted accounting principles to current or past income in advance of the actual expenditure or obligation being incurred, such as the deferred credit resulting from income tax allocation requirements (see below). Some deferred credits, such as subscriptions received in advance, are obligations; whereas others, such as deferred sale-and-leaseback profits, are not.

Illustration 4–3 shows two significant deferred credits: namely, the deferred income tax and the unamortized investment tax credit items. Both of these accounts and the controversy surrounding them are covered in a later chapter.

Deferred income tax represents the amount of the company's potential income tax obligation that the company has deferred from past periods to future periods by following different accounting practices for book and tax purposes. For example, deferred income tax arises in situations where a company uses straight-line depreciation for book purposes and accelerated depreciation for its tax returns. If the company's depreciable assets are new, this can result in a lower income for tax purposes than that reported to stockholders, since the depreciation charge for tax reporting purposes is bigger than the book depreciation expense. In such situations, the tax expense calculation for book purposes should be based on the profits before tax reported to stockholders, rather than the taxable income actually used to determine the company's current income tax payments. Thus, in the example, the company's current book tax expense will be greater than actual payments due to the government. The difference between the tax actually due and the book tax expense recognized is the addition to the deferred tax account. This amount is not a legal obligation like long-term debt. It simply results from the accounting requirement to reconcile book tax expenses recognized and actual taxes paid. Double-entry bookkeeping forces the recognition of this deferred tax item on the liability side of the balance sheet when the cumulative tax payments actually made or due to the government lag behind the cumulative tax expenses recognized for book purposes.

The federal government from time to time grants an *investment tax credit* for certain qualified investments in tangible property. This amount is deducted from the company's current tax bill. Some companies, for book purposes, recognize the full benefit of this reduction of taxes during the period in which the credit is granted. Other companies spread the tax expense reduction benefit over the life of the asset giving rise to the credit. This is the method adopted by the company in Illustration 4–3.

Accumulated Provisions

Accumulated provisions are estimates of future expenditures, asset impairments, or liabilities that have been accrued by a charge to income. Illustration 4–3 presents two examples of accumulated provisions.

The two examples of accumulated provisions shown in Illustration 4–3 are contingencies for future losses. In both cases, the estimated loss from the future contingencies has already been charged to income in anticipation of the event. The offsetting accounting entry was made to the related liability account. When the actual loss occurs, it will be charged to this liability account. Loss contingencies are discussed further in a later chapter.

Product warranties are obligations incurred in connection with the sale of goods or services that may require further performance by the seller after the sale has taken place. To record the correct profit from a sale, it is necessary to recognize as a current expense all of the past, current, and future costs associated with each sale at the time the sale revenue is recorded. Warranty obligations are future costs of current sales. Because of the uncertainty surrounding claims that may be made under warranties, warranty obligations fall within the definition of a contingency. The amount shown in Illustration 4–3 for this item should be a reasonable estimate of the probable future warranty costs associated with recorded sales.

The *provision for foreign operations* represents the recognition by management that they will probably sustain some identifiable losses overseas. The provision was set up by a charge to income. When the actual extent of the losses is known, they will be charged to the liability account. Any actual losses in excess of the amount set aside in the liability account will be charged to income directly.

Owners' Equity

Owners' equity represents the interest of the owners in an enterprise. It is the balance that remains after deducting the total liabilities of the enterprise from its total assets. For most companies, the residual owners' interest determined in this fashion bears little relationship to the actual market value of that interest. Two companies identical in all respects except for their accounting policies could show in their balance sheets very different values for their owners' equity. The company with the more conservative accounting practices would report the lower book value for owners' equity. Yet the market value of the two companies could be the same.

Illustration 4–3 presents the owners' equity for our example company under the caption "capital and retained earnings." Other terms used to describe the owners' equity are "net worth," "net assets," and "stockholders' equity." A later chapter covers equity capital transactions.

The *capital* section of the balance sheet lists (1) the amount and type of capital stock authorized, (2) the number of shares issued, (3) the net amount received by the company for the issued stock, and (4) the number of shares and acquisition costs of the company's own stock held by the company. Illustration 4–3 shows that the company's stockholders have authorized five million shares of preferred stock, but none have been issued. The authorized number of shares represents the maximum number of shares the company may sell under the terms of its charter. Thus, the principal source of company's capital from stock issues was the 21.7 million shares of $2.50 par-value common stock sold at various times for a total consideration of $212 million.

Rather than showing, as in Illustration 4–3, the value of the total consideration received from the issuance of common stock, a preferred approach is to value the common stock account at the par value of the securities issued. Then, if the company sells any of this stock for more than its par value, this excess is shown in an account labeled Capital Received in Excess of Par Value of Stock Issued. This account appears immediately below the common stock account.

The *retained earnings* account represents the balance of net income of the enterprise from the date of incorporation, after deducting distributions of dividends to shareholders. Translation gains and losses resulting from restating the local currency-denominated balance sheets of foreign subsidiaries into dollars may also be included in this account or as a separate line item. In addition, under some circumstances, such as when stock dividends are declared, transfers may be made from retained earnings to the capital stock accounts.

Data related to issued stock reacquired by the issuing company are presented in the treasury stock account. This stock is carried at its acquisition cost. It is always presented as a deduction from owners' equity. Accounting regards only the stock actually in the hands of the stockholders as outstanding stock.

Income Statement

The results of operations of a business for a period of time are presented in the income statement.[2] For comparative purposes, statements for the current and two preceding accounting periods are presented.

From the accounting system's point of view, the income statement is subordinate to the balance sheet. The income statement simply presents the details of the changes in the retained earnings balance sheet account due to profit-directed activities. In contrast to this accounting perspective, most users of financial statements regard the income statement as a more important source of information than the balance sheet because net income more directly influences equity stock prices and dividend payments.

Elements

The elements of a business's profit-directed operations and their net results can be represented by the equation:

$$\text{Revenues} - \text{Expenses} = \text{Net income (Net loss)}$$

The income statement presents the details of this expression in a commonly agreed upon format. Also included in the income statement are gains and losses arising from peripheral or incidental transactions that change the net assets of a company and are included in the determination of net income as required by generally accepted accounting principles.

Revenue (i.e., sales) is defined in *Concepts Statement No. 3* as:

---

[2] Common alternatives are: "statement of profit and loss," "statement of earnings," and "statement of operations."

Inflows or other enhancements of assets of an entity or settlements of its liabilities (or a combination of both) during a period from delivering or producing goods, rendering services, or other activities that constitute the entity's ongoing major or central operations.

Not all increases in assets or decreases in liabilities are included in revenue. For example, the receipt of cash from a bank loan does not result from profit-directed activities and does not change owners' equity. It is not revenue. This transaction increases an asset (cash) and a liability (bank loans payable). In contrast, a cash sale of inventory in the normal course of business is revenue. It increases the asset cash and changes the owners' equity account, Retained Earnings. If the goods are sold at a profit, Retained Earnings will increase by the after-tax amount of the profit.

Different concepts of revenue can be found in accounting theory. This diversity reflects the lack of common agreement as to the nature of revenue. One approach regards revenues as an inflow of assets derived from the sale of goods and rendering of services. An opposite concept, the so-called outflow approach, considers revenue to be goods and services created by a business that are transferred to customers.

Expenses are the goods and services of a business that are used in the process of creating revenues. In this process, the expenditures incurred for this business's goods and services are said to have expired. Some of these expenditures, like administrative costs, may be incurred and expire in the same accounting period. Others, like inventory, may be incurred in one period, held as unexpired costs on the balance sheet, and then expensed as expired costs in a later period when the inventory transfers to the customer.

Concepts Statement No. 3 defines expenses as:

Outflows or other using up of assets or incurrences of liabilities (or a combination of both) during a period from delivering or producing goods, rendering services, or carrying out other activities that constitute the entity's ongoing major or central operations.

Like revenues, expenses can only result from profit-directed activities that change owners' equity. The reduction of inventory as the result of a sale is an expense, since the net result of this operating transaction is a change in the owners' equity account, Retained Earnings. The purchase of inventory on credit is not an expense. It does not change owners' equity. The purchase increases the asset inventory and the liability trade payables.

Although the payment of dividends reduces owners' equity, it is not an expense. This transaction reduces cash and the owners' equity retained earnings account, but it is not a profit-directed activity. It is a distribution of capital.

Net Income. The FASB could not reach agreement among its members on a definition of "net income." Accordingly, in *Statement of Financial*

Accounting Concepts No. 5, "Recognition and Measurement in Financial Statement of Business Enterprises," it advanced two concepts related to income that encompassed all of the various net income concepts advocated by individual board members. These novel concepts were labeled "earnings" and "comprehensive income." According to *Concepts Statement No. 5:*

> Statements of earnings and of comprehensive income together reflect the extent to which and the ways in which the [owners'] equity increases or decreases from all sources other than transactions with owners during a period. . . .
>
> The concept of earnings . . . is similar to net income in present practice. . . .
>
> Earnings is a measure of entity performance during a period. It measures the extent to which asset inflows (revenues and gains) associated with cash-to-cash cycles substantially completed during the period exceed asset outflows (expenses and losses) associated, directly or indirectly, with the same cycles. . . .
>
> Comprehensive income is a broad measure of the effects of transactions and other events on an entity, comprising all recognized changes in equity (new assets) of the entity during a period from transactions and other events and circumstances except those resulting from investments by owners and distributions to owners.

The board's concept of earnings differs from the net income figure resulting from current practice. It excludes certain acounting adjustments to prior periods that are now included in net income. The board's conceptual framework includes these accounting adjustments in comprehensive income. Recognized holding gains and losses are also excluded from earnings and included in comprehensive income. The board expects practice will move toward its earnings concept through a gradual evolutionary process. A later chapter discusses the many problems associated with income recognition. Particular aspects of expense measurement are discussed in a number of different chapters.

Basic Conventions

Four basic conventions discussed in an earlier chapter influence the preparation of the income statement. These are the accrual concept, the accounting period concept, the realization concept, and the matching concept. Each will be reviewed here briefly.

The *accrual concept* relates revenues and expenses to changes in owners' equity, not cash. Statements prepared on this basis recognize and report the effects of transactions and other events on the assets and liabilities of a business in the time period to which they relate, rather than only when cash is received or paid. Accordingly, for example, wage expense is recognized when labor services are performed, not when the workers are paid.

The *accounting period* is the segment of time covered by the income statement. All events affecting income determination during this period should be measured and recorded in the company's accounting records and assigned to this period for income determination purposes. The accounting period is bounded by a beginning and ending balance sheet. The income statement relates to the changes in owners' equity from one balance sheet date to another due to profit-directed activities.

In practice, the *realization of recognition concept* is interpreted to mean that revenue is generally recognized when the following conditions are met: (1) the earnings process is complete or virtually complete; (2) an exchange has taken place; (3) the amount of income is determinable and its collection is reasonably assured; and (4) reasonable estimates can be made of related future costs. For example, interest revenue from loans to others is recognized as time passes, since that, assuming the borrower is solvent, is the critical event dictating the timing and amount of interest receivable.

The *matching concept* recognizes that some costs have a presumed direct association with specific revenues or time periods. This is a process of associating cause and effect. It is through this matching process that income is determined.

Expenditures and Expenses

A troublesome accounting problem is determination of whether a purchase results in an asset or an expense. An expenditure occurs whenever an asset or service is purchased. At the moment of the transaction, all expenditures for purchases can be thought to result in assets. These assets will then become expenses if they *(a)* are directly or indirectly related or associated with the revenue of the period or *(b)* suffer a loss during the period in their future revenue-generating capacity, such as in the case of assets destroyed by fire or patents carried as assets in prior periods that become worthless due to the development of a new technology.

Statement Format

A common order of items in the income statement is:

1. Revenues (sales for the period).
2. Cost of sales (the manufacturing or acquisition costs of the goods sold during the period).
3. Gross profit or margin (the difference between revenues and cost of sales; item 1 less item 2).
4. Operating expenses (the selling, administration, and general expenses associated with operating the company's principal business activity during the period).
5. Operating income (item 3 less item 4).
6. Nonoperating revenues (revenues derived from sources other than

operations during the period, such as interest on the temporary investment of excess cash).
7. Nonoperating expenses (expenses not directly related to the principal business activity and the financial cost of borrowed money).
8. Provision for taxes (the income tax expense, based on item 5 plus item 6 less item 7).
9. Income before extraordinary items (item 5 plus item 6 less item 7 and item 8).
10. Extraordinary items.[3] (These are infrequent, abnormal gains or losses that are clearly not related to the company's normal operations or business activities. These items are shown net of their tax effect.)
11. Net income (item 9 plus or minus item 10).[4]

An alternative form of income statement is shown in Illustration 4–4. This statement omits the gross and operating profit calculations. It is known as single-step statement. Each of the items on this statement will be discussed briefly.

ILLUSTRATION 4–4
Example: A Major Corporation's Single-Step Income Statement

Statement of Earnings
For the Year Ended December 31, 1985

Net sales	$1,962,487,755
Cost and expenses:	
Cost of products sold	$1,445,785,281
Selling, advertising, general, and administrative expenses	182,507,421
Interest and debt expense	7,581,233
	$1,635,873,925
Earnings before provision for taxes	$ 326,613,830
Provision for federal and state taxes on income	176,569,000
Net income	$ 150,044,830

The *net sales* figure represents the company's net sales during the calendar year 1985. It is derived by deducting from gross sales any sales returns, allowances, and discounts. The gross sales amount is the invoice price of the goods and services sold. Sales returns and allowances result from the

---

[3] A later chapter discusses extraordinary items.

[4] A more complicated statement is presented when a company makes a change in an accounting principle or discontinues a part of its operations. These more complicated statements are presented in a later chapter.

credit given to customers for sales returns or defective goods. Sales discounts are discounts granted to customers for prompt payment of amounts owed to the seller. Sometimes this item is shown as a sales expense rather than as a reduction of gross sales. Discounts from list price granted to members of the seller's trade do not enter into the accounting records. These sales are recorded as the actual invoice price.

Cost of products sold is the manufactured cost or, in the case of merchandising companies, the purchase price of the goods sold during the period. The manufactured cost includes the cost of direct labor, raw materials, and manufacturing overhead. The amount of cost of goods sold expense matched with current revenues will depend in large part on the company's inventory valuation practices, since any current expenditures for products not included in cost of products sold must be assigned to the inventory account.

Selling, general, and administrative expenses are all of the expenses incurred for these activities during the accounting period. Generally, these expenditures are not assumed to have a lasting value beyond the current period. Therefore, they are related directly to the current accounting period for income determination purposes.

Interest and debt expenses are financial charges. It is customary to segregate these items from operating expenses. This approach assumes that users of the statements wish (1) to identify and evaluate the cost of financing operations and (2) to determine whether or not management's return from operations is adequate, given the financing costs.

Earnings before provision for taxes are the basis for determining the company's tax expense. It should be remembered that this amount most likely will be different from the taxable income shown on the company's tax return. Two common reasons for this difference are that some cost items included in the income statement are not recognized for tax purposes, and that some revenue items recognized currently to determine book income are deferred to future periods for tax purposes.

Provisions for federal and state taxes on income will, for most companies, consist of two parts: the taxes actually payable based on the income shown in the current tax return and the taxes recognized for book purposes for which there is no current tax liability. This latter type of accounting expense is the source of the changes in deferred tax liability discussed earlier.

Net income is the final figure on the statement. It represents the net impact of profit-directed activities on owners' equity after considering all items of profit and loss recognized during the period.

Interrelationship

The items on the income statement and the balance sheet are interrelated. For example, when a credit sale is made, revenues and accounts receivable both increase. In addition, the sale causes finished goods inventory to decline and cost of goods sold to increase, and the increased tax expense related to the profit on the sale causes taxes payable to increase. Therefore, in order to gain a full appreciation of any item on one statement, it is necessary to examine also the related items on the other.

Changes in Owners' Equity

The income statement alone does not present all of the changes in owners' equity during an accounting period since it relates only to profit-directed activities. Therefore, to describe the changes due to capital additions and distributions, an additional statement or disclosure is sometimes required of the changes in owners' equity, which presents changes in both the retained earnings and the capital stock accounts.

The Retained Earnings account is the link between the net income figure and the owners' equity. The retained earnings balance at the end of the period is derived as follows:

1. Beginning retained earnings (the balance at the beginning of the accounting period).
2. Net income (shown in the income statement for the period—add to 1).
3. Dividends paid to common stockholders. (Subtract from sum of 1 and 2.)
4. Ending retained earnings (the amount appearing in the balance sheet at the end of the period—equal to item 1 plus item 2 less item 3).

Other Considerations

Notes to Financial Statements

Financial statements are inevitably accompanied by notes. These are an integral part of the statements and should be read before relying on the accounting figures. The functions of notes are:

1. To amplify the numerical data and descriptive captions presented on the face of the statements by giving such details as the requirements of bond indentures and the terms of lease agreements.
2. To present additional information on events that may subsequently affect the data reported, such as contingencies that may arise from outstanding legal suits or the future audit of current tax returns by the tax authorities.
3. To disclose events that have occurred subsequent to the balance sheet date that may materially affect the statement users' evaluation of the data presented but not require adjustment to the statements, such as an issue of debentures after the balance sheet date.
4. To identify the particular accounting methods used to prepare the

statements and the impact on key financial statistics of any changes in these methods.

5. To disclose commitments of an unusual nature, such as a major plant expansion.

Most companies include in their notes some details of their activities broken down by major lines of business and geographical areas. Typically, these line-of-business data are limited to a disclosure of segment sales, some form of earnings figure, and net assets.

Auditor's Report

The auditor's report accompanying financial statements should always be read in conjunction with the statements. It is important for anyone using the statements to know the auditor's appraisal of the statements.

Financial statements are the direct responsibility of the management and directors of the reporting company. Although the company's public auditor may assist and advise management in its preparation of the statements, management alone is responsible for their contents. Management is not compelled to follow the auditor's advice. However, the auditor does have a responsibility to state whether he or she agrees with the fariness of the financial presentation. In practice, it is this duty of the auditor to state exceptions that brings reluctant managements to accept auditors' recommendations in cases where differences of opinion exist between management and auditors. A later chapter discusses in greater detail the nature of the auditor's opinion and the basis for reaching this opinion.

Interim Statements

Most corporations publish condensed income statements for the quarter and the year to date on a comparative basis with the same periods during the previous year. Companies also present in their quarterly reports a condensed balance sheet as of the end of the quarter.

Considerable caution should be exercised when using quarterly statements, since:

1. Although it is common practice for companies to involve their auditors in the preparation of quarterly statements, quarterly statements are usually unaudited. Some managements in trouble take advantage of this to hide their problems from stockholders during the year in the hope that all can be made right by year-end.

2. Adjustments to data reported in earlier interim statements and decisions to change accounting methods are made usually during the fourth quarter. More data are available as year-end approaches; management has a better feel of whether or not it can reach its earnings goals as a result of operations; and lax accounting practices are turned

up by the auditor, who during this period is spending an increasing amount of time with the company conducting the audit examination related to the annual statements.

3. Comparisons of the current interim results with those of the same period during the prior year may not be entirely valid, because the structure of the business may be expanding and changing.

4. Annual predictions based on interim results may be misleading due to the seasonality of the business.

5. *APB Opinion No. 28* on interim statements may be interpreted differently by different managers as they apply it to their business. Despite these limitations, a number of authorities on stock price determinants believe interim results influence stock market price movements more than the information presented in annual statements.

Forecasts

Companies seldom include forecasts of sales and net income for future periods in their public reports.

Some accounting authorities advocate that annual reports should disclose in summary form the reporting companies' forecasted results for the next annual period. It is argued that these data would provide stockholders with a better basis for evaluating management's planning capabilities and how well management achieved its objectives for the reporting period. In addition, it would put the current results into better perspective.

The accounting profession has not encouraged this type of reporting because of the problems associated with auditing forecasts objectively. Managements have also been reluctant to publish these forward-looking data, considering forecast data to be competitive data that should not be revealed publicly. Also, management is concerned that a *failure* to achieve the forecast might lead to stockholder litigation.

However, under certain circumstances, the SEC encourages the publication of forecasts. The AICPA has published guidelines for preparing these forecasts and the auditor's role in communicating them to the public.

Summary of Financial Results

In addition to the financial statements covered by the auditor's opinion, annual reports typically include two sets of summary financial statistics. First, inside the front cover, and opposite the chief executive officer's letter to the stockholders that inevitably begins the text of the report, selected statistical data on a three-year comparative basis are shown, related to such items as current earnings per share, sales volume, dividends per share, return on investment, net income as percentage of sales, and the ratio of current assets to current liabilities. Second, usually following the notes to the financial statements, a 5- or 10-year statistical summary is presented. The basic data included in this summary are often similar to that covered in the statistical presentation at the beginning of the report. Additional statistics presented may include such data as the number of employees, the number of common shares outstanding, and the preferred dividends paid per share.

These statistical summaries are not covered by the auditor's opinion. However, for companies under the jurisdiction of the SEC, these disclosures should not be materially different from the data presented in the audited statements. The SEC also requires management to include an analysis of the current and past few years' results along with the summary of financial results. This presentation is known as the "Management Discussion and Analysis" (MD&A) section of the financial report.

Analysts should read the MD&A carefully. It contains management's views on the company's operation, liquidity, and ability to cope with inflation. Also presented are explanations of changes in circumstances and of unusual events and their consequences. The MD&A tends to follow a consistent format. Analysts should regard changes in its format as a red flag signaling a conscious decision by management to change the format, possibly to exclude or obscure some unfavorable information.

Text

Most annual reports include textual material describing the companies' activities, plans, and problems. A thorough reading of this material is essential for anyone trying to determine the significance of the communication contained in the financial statements.

Basic Accounting Mechanics

So far the effect of individual transactions in terms of their impact on the balance sheet and income statement have been discussed with little concern for accounting mechanics. This section presents a summary of the systematic procedures used by accountants to record and summarize transactions. These procedures are called bookkeeping. The objective of this material is to help the reader without prior accounting training learn how to reduce, in an efficient manner, a complex set of business facts to the comprehensible set of relationships expressed in financial statements.

Accounts

Accountants use a series of accounts to record transactions. These accounts correspond to the items shown on the financial statements. The simplest form of account, and the one we will use, is a T-account. The Cash account of a company using this format might look like this:

	Cash	
(Increases)		(Decreases)
Beginning balance at beginning of accounting period	100,000	3,000
	5,000	8,000
	20,000	40,000
	10,000	
	135,000	51,000
New beginning balance at end of accounting period	84,000	

All of the increases in cash are shown on one side. All of the decreases are recorded on the other. The new balance is determined by (1) adding all of the amounts listed on the increases and decreases side and (2) subtracting one total from the other.

Debit-Credit Mechanism

Each accounting transaction has two parts. This dual aspect convention, discussed in an earlier chapter, is reflected in the statement, "The payment by a customer of an accounts receivable increases cash and reduces accounts receivable." This statement uses layman's language to describe what occurred. The accountant would describe this transaction in terms of the debit-credit mechanism.

The accountant uses the term *debit* (Dr.) to describe that part of a transaction that

1. Increases an asset account.
2. Decreases a liability account.
3. Decreases an owners' equity account.
4. Decreases a revenue account.
5. Increases an expense account.

The term *credit* (Cr.) is used to describe that part of the transaction that

1. Decreases an asset account.
2. Increases a liability account.
3. Increases an owners' equity account.
4. Increases a revenue account.
5. Decreases an expense account.

The reader is encouraged to memorize these debit-credit rules rather than to try to determine their algebraic relationship to the basic accounting equation: Assets = Liabilities + Owners' equity.

Here are some examples of the debit-credit terminology used to describe transactions:

1. A company borrows $10,000 cash from the bank. The accounting effect of the transaction is:

   Dr. Cash 10,000
       Cr. Bank Notes Payable   10,000

2. The company repays the loan. The accountant would describe the transaction as:

   Dr. Bank Notes Payable 10,000
       Cr. Cash   10,000

The words *debit* and *credit* have no meaning in accounting other than the following: debit means the amount is entered on the left-hand side of the T-account; credit means the amount is entered on the right-hand side of the T-account. The words carry no moral judgment. Depending on the account involved, they can be "desirable" or "undesirable" from the company's point of view.

Illustration 4–5 shows the relationship between T-accounts and the debit-credit mechanism. The reader should note that because debit and credit are used to signify the left and right sides of the T-account, the side used to record an increase or a decrease depends on the account. For example, increases in assets are recorded on the left or debit side, whereas increases in liabilities are listed on the right or credit side.

ILLUSTRATION 4–5
Debit-Credit Rules

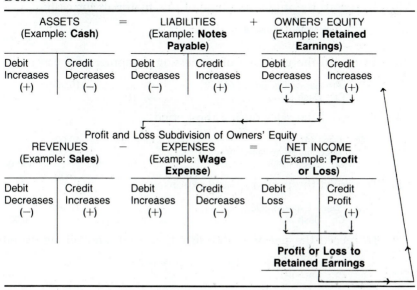

An Example

The following problem will be used to illustrate the steps in the process used to prepare financial statements.

Climax Industries, Inc., a new company started on January 1, 1985, sold at the beginning of the year 10,000 shares of common stock for $50,000. The company bought for cash $20,000 worth of raw materials and processing equipment worth $10,000. The equipment was expected to last 10 years. During the year, the company had sales of $45,000, of which $5,000 was still owed by customers at year-end; consumed $15,000 worth of raw materials; spent $10,000 cash on wages; and paid $5,000 cash for administration, rent, and selling activities. During the year, the company also bought $15,000 of raw materials for which it still owed $5,000 at the end of the year. Dividends of $2,000 were declared and paid at year-end. The company anticipates it will have no bad debts. Your assignment is to prepare an income statement for the period and a balance sheet as of the end of the year. (Disregard taxes.)

The first step is to *analyze* the transactions and record them in the debit-credit form. This is called *journalizing original entries.* It is purely mechanical. Here are the journal entries. To help you understand the debit-credit decision better, each account will be labeled *A* if it is an asset account, *L* if it is a liability account, and *OE* if it is an owners' equity account. For the purpose of this exercise, the revenue and expense accounts will be treated as subdivisions of owners' equity.

1. To record the sale of capital stock for cash:

   Dr. Cash *(A)* 50,000
        Cr. Capital Stock *(OE)*   50,000

2. To record the initial purchase of raw materials for cash:

   Dr. Raw Materials Inventory *(A)* 20,000
        Cr. Cash *(A)*   20,000

3. To record the purchase of processing equipment for cash:

   Dr. Processing Equipment *(A)* 10,000
        Cr. Cash *(A)*   10,000

4. To record the sales during the period:

   Dr. Cash *(A)* 40,000
        Accounts Receivable *(A)* 5,000
        Cr. Sales *(OE)*   45,000

5. To record the period's wage expense:

   Dr. Wage Expense *(OE)* 10,000
        Cr. Cash *(A)*   10,000

6. To record the period's administration, rent, and selling expense:

   Dr. Administration, Rent, and Selling Expense *(OE)* 5,000
        Cr. Cash *(A)*   5,000

7. To record the purchase of raw materials during the year:

```
Dr.  Raw Materials Inventory (A) ......................  15,000
     Cr.  Cash (A) ...................................              10,000
          Accounts Payable (L) ........................               5,000
```

8. To record dividend declaration and payment:

```
Dr.  Retained Earnings (OE) .........................   2,000
     Cr.  Cash (A) ...................................               2,000
```

9. To record the Raw Materials Inventory withdrawals during the year:[5]

```
Dr.  Raw Materials Expenses (OE) .....................  15,000
     Cr.  Raw Materials Inventory (A) ..................              15,000
```

10. To record the processing equipment's depreciation expense (see below for the debit-credit treatment of the "contra asset" account accumulated depreciation):

```
Dr.  Depreciation Expense (OE) .......................   1,000
     Cr.  Accumulated Depreciation (L) ................               1,000
```

This last journal entry is called an adjusting entry. There is no transaction with parties outside the entity to prompt the recording of the event or to determine the amounts. These entries are made at the end of the period. They are the adjustments to assets or liabilities previously recorded that are required to achieve a periodic matching of costs and revenues. Many of these entries require considerable judgment to determine the amounts involved. In this case, management estimated the equipment would last 10 years. Based on this estimate, one tenth of the asset's costs was expressed this year.

Using the scheme of T-accounts similar to those in Illustration 4–5, the next step is to *post* the journal entries to the appropriate T-accounts. The results of this process are shown in Illustration 4–6. The numbers beside each amount refer to the journal entries describing the transaction.

Illustration 4–6 shows the Accumulated Depreciation account under the "liabilities" caption. The debit-credit mechanism treats this account as a liability. However, for statement purposes it is shown as a deduction, or a contra account, to the asset "Processing Equipment."

The next step is to calculate the *ending balances* in the asset and liability accounts, *close out* the expense and revenue accounts to the net income account, and then close the balance in this account to retained earnings. Here are the required journal entries to reduce the revenue, expense, and net income accounts to zero:

---

[5] The ending inventory can be calculated as follows:

Beginning inventory ..	$20,000
Plus: Purchases	15,000
Less: Withdrawals	15,000
Ending inventory ..	$20,000

ILLUSTRATION 4–6
T-Accounts for Climax Industries, Inc., Example

ASSETS
Cash

+	−
50,000(1)	20,000(2)
40,000(4)	10,000(3)
	10,000(5)
	5,000(6)
	10,000(7)
	2,000(8)
	57,000
90,000	
33,000	

Raw Materials

+	−
20,000(2)	15,000(9)
15,000(7)	
35,000	15,000
20,000	

Processing Equipment

+	−
10,000(3)	0
10,000	

Accounts Receivable

+	−
5,000(4)	0
5,000	

LIABILITIES
Accounts Payable

−	+
0	5,000(7)
	5,000

Accumulated Depreciation*

−	+
0	1,000(10)
	1,000

OWNERS' EQUITY
Capital Stock

−	+
0	50,000(1)
	50,000

Retained Earnings

−	+
2,000(8)	14,000(13)
2,000	14,000
	12,000

Retained Earnings Subdivisions

REVENUES

−	+
	45,000(4)
45,000(11)	

EXPENSES

+	−
10,000 (5)	31,000(12)
5,000 (6)	
15,000 (9)	
1,000(10)	
31,000	31,000

= NET INCOME

−	+
31,000(12)	45,000(11)
14,000(13)	
45,000	45,000

* Contra asset account (i.e., reported as an offset to the asset account Processing Equipment).

11. To close the revenue account:

    Dr. Revenues 45,000
        Cr. Net Income   45,000

12. To close the expense account:

    Dr. Net income 31,000
        Cr. Expenses   31,000

13. To close the net income account:

    Dr. Net Income 14,000
        Cr. Retained Earnings   14,000

Now the statements can be prepared. Illustration 4–7 presents the company's income statement combined with a statement of changes in retained earnings. Illustration 4–8 presents the balance sheet of Climax Industries, Inc.

ILLUSTRATION 4–7

CLIMAX INDUSTRIES, INC.
Statement of Earnings and Changes in Retained Earnings
For the Year Ended December 31, 1985

Sales		$45,000
Cost of goods sold:		
Raw materials	$15,000	
Direct labor	10,000	
Manufacturing depreciation	1,000	26,000
Gross profit		$19,000
Selling, rent, and administration		5,000
Net income		$14,000
Less: Common stock dividends declared		2,000
Additions to income retained in the business		$12,000

ILLUSTRATION 4–8

CLIMAX INDUSTRIES, INC.
Statement of Financial Condition
December 31, 1985

Assets			**Liabilities and Owners' Equity**		
Current assets:			Current liabilities:		
Cash	$33,000		Accounts payable	$ 5,000	
Accounts receivable	5,000		Long-term liabilities	—	
Raw materials inventory	20,000		Total liabilities	$ 5,000	
Total current assets	$58,000				
			Owners' equity:		
Property (at cost):			Capital stock	$50,000	
Processing equipment..........	$10,000		Retained earnings	12,000	
Less: Accumulated depreciation	1,000		Total owners' equity	$62,000	
Net property	$ 9,000		Total liabilities and		
Total assets	$67,000		owners' equity	$67,000	

CASE 4-1

Ottoman Car Company
Preparation of Journal Entries, Balance Sheet, and Income Statement

Fred Ottoman was a fire truck salesman for many years, while Bill, his brother, worked as a book salesman for a major publishing house. Although they had done fairly well financially, they wanted to "be their own bosses," so they decided to go into business together.

They agreed that selling cars would be a good line for them to go into as both had been interested in sports cars for many years. Also, the small town in Ohio where they lived did not have any automobile dealerships. The nearest dealer was some 30 miles away.

After some searching, they chose a suitable site for their proposed operation. It was situated on a popular shopping street. A dilapidated building which had been condemned by the local authorities stood on the site.

At this point in time, the brothers decided to incorporate the business. The services of a lawyer were obtained to draw up the legal papers and to handle all aspects of the execution of the incorporation. The fee for this service was $400, and each of the brothers paid half of it.

Fred purchased 1,800 shares of the company's stock for $36,000, and Bill purchased 500 shares for $10,000. The payment for legal services was considered part of these investments, so the actual cash received was $45,600. Further purchases of the company's shares could be made only at the prevailing book value per share at the time of the purchase and only if both parties agreed to the transaction. If either brother wished at any time to sell his shares back to the company, this transaction would also be conducted at the prevailing book value of the shares. The brothers also agreed that they should each receive salaries of $12,000 per year at all times during which they were engaged in the company's business on a full-time basis. Both knew this amount was less than they could earn in

This case was prepared by Andrew McCosh (under the direction of David F. Hawkins).

Copyright © 1965 by the President and Fellows of Harvard College

Harvard Business School case 113–060 (Revised 1985)

other jobs, but they realized a small salary was needed at this time to ensure that the dealership could pay its bills on time.

On November 1, 1985, with the aid of a $20,000 bank loan and $16,000 of the company's money, Fred purchased the property which had been selected. The same day, he left his job to devote his full attention to the new enterprise.

First, Fred arranged to have the old building demolished. A cursory examination revealed there was nothing of any significance that could be salvaged, except for some building stone. Mr. Mahoney, the wrecker, agreed to clear the site for $3,500, provided he could have the stone. Otherwise, he would want $4,500. Fred was convinced he could get a better price for the stone, so he instructed Mr. Mahoney to clear the site and store the stone in a corner of it. This work was started immediately and completed before Christmas. Mr. Mahoney agreed to defer collection of payment until May 31, 1986.

In the meantime, Fred got in touch with a large automobile manufacturer, National Cars, Inc., who had previously indicated interest in the projected dealership. Fred asked National for financial help to construct the buildings needed to carry on business. National agreed to provide all the finances needed for the building through a loan repayable in 10 equal annual installments, provided Ottoman Cars sold only National models. The loan earned an interest rate of 10 percent per year, payable from April 1, 1986. The first repayment, including interest, would fall due on March 31, 1987.

On December 31, 1985, National Cars sent a check for $20,000 to get Ottoman Cars started. Fred deposited the check in the business's bank account. The remainder of the loan would be forthcoming when the building was completed.

Next, Fred arranged through a consulting architect for several construction companies to bid for the job. The lowest bidder was the Birkett and Snell Company. They agreed to construct the specified building for $62,000. On the advice of his architect, however, Fred Ottoman decided to accept the Holmes Brothers Construction Company bid of $70,000; the architect knew Birkett and Snell Company was less reliable than Holmes in meeting promised completion dates.

The construction was started immediately, Holmes promising completion by the end of March 1986. Progress payments on certificates from the architects were to be made at the end of January, the end of February, and the date of completion in amounts of $20,000, $20,000, and $30,000.

During the winter period, Fred tried to obtain some orders for cars, which he planned to deliver directly to customers from National's warehouse in Cleveland. Fred had some success with the model he had recently bought for himself. Between January 1 and March 30, Fred sold 17 of this model at an average cash cost to Ottoman Cars of $4,500. Nothing was paid to National for these cars during the period. These 17 sales realized $91,800, whereof $29,000, represented trade-in allowances, $56,000 in cash, and the rest was outstanding at March 30. Fred sold all the trade-in cars for $27,400 cash before March 30. Previously, Bill and Fred agreed that the latter should receive $20 for every new car sale as compensation for using his private car as a display model.

At the end of March, the building was completed. However, there was an additional charge of $1,200 for materials, which Ottoman had to pay according to the provisions of the building contract. At the same time, the architect's bill for $1,300 arrived.

Fred sent the progress payments to the builder as previously arranged, making the January payment with $20,000 of the company's money and the February payment with the National loan. On March 31, the last $30,000 progress payment and the $1,200 materials surcharge were paid. The $20,000 bank loan plus interest of $1,000 was repaid by check on March 30.

On March 30, Bill quit his job with the publishing house and joined Ottoman Cars on a full-time basis. At Bill's request, it was agreed that financial statements would be prepared, to allow the two brothers to see where they stood at the end of March. National Cars, Inc., asked that a portion of the amount of the dealership owed the manufacturers for cars be regarded as payment due to the dealership under the building contract, and Fred accepted this arrangement on behalf of Ottoman Cars. The two brothers agreed that they would invite Mr. William Hurley, an accountant who was a mutual friend of theirs, to prepare the accounts.

Questions

1. As Mr. Hurley, prepare journal entries to record the events that have taken place in the business up to March 31, 1986.

2. From these journal entries, prepare a balance sheet as of March 31, 1986, and an income statement for the period to that date.

3. Based on your financial statements, what is the value of each brother's equity in the company?

4. Prepare a statement showing the sources and uses of cash during the period from the formation of the business until March 31, 1986.

Peter Fuller

Determining Financial Reporting Policy and Preparation of Projected Financial Statements

Peter Fuller was the inventor of a metal hoseclamp for automobile hose connections. Having confidence in its commercial value, but owning no surplus funds of his own, he sought among his friends and acquaintances for the necessary capital to put it on the market. The proposition which he placed before possible associates was that a corporation should be formed with capital stock of $30,000, that he be given $16,000 par value of stock for his patent, and that the remaining $14,000 be sold for a sum as near par as possible.

The project looked attractive to a number of the individuals to whom the inventor presented it, but the most promising among them—a retired manufacturer—said he would be unwilling to invest his capital without knowing what uses were intended for the cash to be received from the proposed sale of stock. He suggested that the inventor determine the probable costs of experimentation and of special machinery, and prepare for him a statement of the estimated assets and liabilities of the proposed company when ready to begin actual operations. He also asked for a statement of the estimated transactions for the first year of production and sales operations, together with an analysis of the operating results indicated by those expectations. This information would be based on the studies the inventor had made of probable markets and costs of labor and materials. It would include a listing of resulting assets and liabilities; an analysis of expected sales, expenses, and profits; and an explanation of expected flow of cash over the course of the year.

After consulting the engineer who had aided him in constructing his patent models, Fuller drew up the following list of data relating to the

This case was prepared by David F. Hawkins.

Copyright © 1985 by the President and Fellows of Harvard College
Harvard Business School case 186–112

transactions of the proposed corporation during its period of organization and development.

1. Probable selling price of $14,000, par value of stock, $18,000.
2. Probable cost of incorporation and organization, $825, which includes estimated officers' salaries during developmental period.
3. Probable cost of developing special machinery, $13,000. This sum includes the cost of expert services, materials, rent of a small shop, and the cost of power, light, and miscellaneous expenditures.
4. Probable cost of raw material, $500, of which $300 is to be used in experimental production.

Fuller drew up the first of the statements desired by his prospective associate in the following manner:

**Probable Assets and Liabilities of the Proposed Company
When Ready to Begin Actual Operations**

Assets		Liabilities and Proprietorship	
Patent	$16,000	Capital stock at par	$30,000
Machinery	13,000	Plus: Premium on stock	4,000
Organization costs	825	Capital paid in	$34,000
Experimental costs	300		
Raw materials and supplies	200		
Cash..........................	3,675		
Total assets	$34,000	Total liabilities	$34,000

With this initial part of his assignment completed, the inventor set down the following estimates as a beginning step in furnishing the rest of the information desired.

1. Expected sales, $28,000, all to be received in cash by the end of the first year following completion of organization and initial experimentation.
2. Expected additional purchases of raw materials and supplies during the course of this operating year, all for cash, paid by end of year, $9,000.
3. Expected help from the banks during year—but loans, including $50 interest, to be repaid before close of year—$2,000.
4. Expected payroll and other cash expenses and manufacturing costs for the operating year, $14,000 (of which $3,000 is to be for selling and administrative expenses).
5. Expected inventory of raw materials and supplies at close of period, at cost, $1,800.
6. No inventory of unsold process or finished stock expected as of the end of the period. All goods to be sold "on special order"; none to be produced "for stock."
7. All experimental and organization costs, previously capitalized as essentially going concern assets or "valuations," to be charged against income of the operating year.

8. Estimated depreciation of machinery, $1,300, based on a 10-year life. (However, Fuller was aware of a plastic hoseclamp being developed by a major corporation that might make his product and the equipment used to produce it obsolete in about four years' time. If this occurred, Fuller thought that it might be possible to convert the special machinery into general-purpose equipment at a cost of several thousand dollars.)
9. Machinery maintenance, cash, $75.
10. New machinery and equipment to be purchased for cash, $1,000.
11. Profit distributions of net cash proceeds of sales, $3,000.

The above transaction data were for the most part cumulative totals, and should not be interpreted to mean that the events described were to take place in the precise order or sequence indicated.

Questions

1. Prepare the information wanted by the retired manufacturer.
2. What kind of a financial image do you think Fuller should present to the retired manufacturer? Do statements prepared according to Fuller's proposed accounting rules create this image? What changes would you make?

CHAPTER 5

Consolidated Financial Statements

Business executives, statement users, and accountants generally recognize that for a parent company with one or more subsidiaries, the presumption is that consolidated statements are more meaningful than separate statements. Consolidated financial statements present the financial position and operating results as if a parent company and its subsidiaries were a single company. The corporation owning a major portion (more than 50 percent) of the outstanding capital stock of another corporation is the parent, while the controlled corporation is the subsidiary. The parent and its subsidiaries are sometimes called affiliated companies. The term "affiliate" is also used for companies in which the parent's ownership interest is less than 50 percent.

The subject of accounting for intercorporate investments is covered in greater detail in Chapter 20, which discusses the accounting for nonconsolidated subsidiaries, joint ventures, equity interests between 20 and 50 percent, marketable securities, and business combinations. This chapter focuses on the nature of consolidated statements, the process followed in preparing them, and some considerations for financial analysis that arise from the nature of consolidated statements. The chapter on consolidated statements comes early in the book since most of the statements that the reader will use will probably be consolidated statements.

Since consolidated statements are most frequently used for financial statement analysis, analysts should be familiar with the consolidation rules and the four accounts that are peculiar to consolidated statements. In addition, statement users should be familiar with the advantages, limitations, and pitfalls of working with consolidated statements. These are discussed at the end of this chapter.

Consolidation Concepts and Practices

Consolidated statements treat parent and subsidiary corporations as a single economic unit, even though they are legally separate entities. Financial information is combined as if the corporations involved were merely departments or divisions of a larger corporation. The consolidating procedure cancels out on worksheets all offsetting reciprocal pairs of assets and liabilities, revenues and costs, and investment and equity accounts which appear on the statements of the affiliated corporations being consolidated. For example, a parent may lend its subsidiary $100,000. This will appear as a loan receivable on the parent's statements. It will be carried as a loan payable on the subsidiary's books. When the statements of the two companies are consolidated, these items will be eliminated. Similarly, all such transactions involving intercompany investments and gains and losses on intercompany transactions are reversed on the worksheets so that only events involving the economic unit and outside parties will show on the consolidated statements.

Consolidation Policy

At least two conditions should be present to justify consolidation: control and homogeneity of operations.

Control. In general, the parent must have currently, and expect to continue, ownership and management control over the subsidiary. For full consolidation, the parent company must have a minimum ownership in the subsidiary of more than 50 percent.

Irrespective of the degree of ownership control, however, managerial control is a prerequisite for consolidation. Managerial control is not considered adequate if the parent-subsidiary relationship is hampered or threatened by currency, dividend, legal, or political restrictions. Principally for these reasons, foreign subsidiaries may be excluded from consolidation when there are significant limitations or threats to the economic flexibility or the continuity of these operations. Also, the lack of managerial control justifies the nonconsolidation of bankrupt or insolvent subsidiaries.

Homogeneity. In earlier periods, it was believed that statements for a parent and its consolidated subsidiaries should represent a homogeneous economic unit. However, increasing corporate diversification has resulted in substantial relaxation of this requirement. So long as the parent retains control, nonhomogeneous subsidiaries may be and often are consolidated. Typically, however, manufacturing entities do not consolidate their financial subsidiaries, such as finance or insurance companies. These interests are reported on an equity basis.

The equity method is also used to report on statements of the parent company investments in companies that represent between 20 and 100 percent of the investee's common stock. Another use of the equity method is to report on consolidated statements investments of between 20 and 50 percent in the equity of affiliated companies.

The equity method limits effect of the investment in the subsidiary to one line of the parent company or the consolidated balance sheet and income statement. When the equity method is used, the reporting entity includes its share of the subsidiary's net income, after removing the effect of intercompany transactions, as a single line on the reporting entity's income statement. None of the subsidiary's revenue and expense amounts are combined with the reporting entity's revenue and expense items. Similarly, none of the subsidiary's balance sheet accounts are combined with the reporting entity's balance sheet accounts. The only effect of the equity method on the reporting entity's balance sheet is an entry to the investment in unconsolidated subsidiary asset account. This account reflects the cost of the investment in the subsidiary plus the reporting entity's share of the subsidiary's retained earnings since acquisition, again after all intercompany transactions have been eliminated. The equity method is discussed in greater detail later in this chapter, as well as in Chapter 20.

Disclosure

The parent company policy regarding consolidation is disclosed in notes to the financial statements, as in the following example.

> *Consolidation Principles.* The consolidated financial statements cover the accounts of all significant majority-owned subsidiaries, after including Acton Fire Insurance Company and other financial subsidiaries on an equity basis. Consolidated financial statements for Acton and combined financial statements for the other financial subsidiaries are included in support of the consolidated financial statements of the Corporation.
>
> Other investments are carried at cost, except investments in 20–50 percent-owned companies ($52,482,000 and $45,045,000 at December 31, 1985, and 1984, respectively) which are included on an equity basis.
>
> Intercompany transactions are eliminated in the consolidated financial statements.

Accounting Concepts Peculiar to Consolidated Statements

Most items appearing on consolidated financial statements are comparable to those found on statements of the individual corporations. Four items are peculiar to consolidated statements: minority interest, goodwill, consolidated net income, and consolidated retained earnings.

Minority Interest. Financial statements prepared for single corporations do not distinguish between the individuals or groups owning a single class of capital stock. In the case of consolidated statements, if the parent does not own 100 percent of the capital stock of a subsidiary, that part of ownership equity not owned by the parent is presented separately on the consolidated balance sheet and identified as minority interest. This practice conforms to the concept of preparing consolidated financial statements from the point of view of the parent company which exercises controlling ownership over its subsidiaries.

After total net income for the affiliated group is determined, a deduction is made for that part of the subsidiary's earnings applicable to the minority ownership. Thus, the minority interest shown on the consolidated balance sheet consists of a pro rata share of net worth based on capital contribution plus accumulated earnings less any dividends paid.

From the parent's point of view, some accountants argue that the minority interest has characteristics of a liability. Others claim it represents a separate class of equity. As a result, in practice "minority interest" is usually recorded between liabilities and ownership rather than being included in either category.

Goodwill. The intangible asset goodwill is recognized only when a going business is acquired through a purchase transaction at a price greater than the value of the acquired company's net assets.[1] When a parent acquires an interest in a subsidiary under these circumstances, this excess of investment over the market value of the net assets acquired is not separated on the parent's statements. It remains as an unidentified part of the parent's total investment in the subsidiary which is listed as an asset. On the parent's statements, the portion of the investment account representing goodwill is amortized against the parent's share of the subsidiary's net income recognized on the equity basis over a period not to exceed 40 years.

When the subsidiary and the parent are combined in consolidated statements, the parent's investment in the subsidiary is eliminated along with the parent's interest in the equity of the subsidiary. If the original purchase transaction created goodwill, the investment and equity amounts eliminated in consolidation will differ by the amount of the original goodwill less any goodwill amortized since the acquisition date. This goodwill balance is recorded on the consolidated statements as an asset. In addition, the current amount of goodwill amortized is included as a current expense of the consolidated entity.

Consolidated Net Income. Consolidated income statements present the total net income during the period for the affiliated group as if it were operating as a single corporation. To achieve this, all intercompany transactions giving rise to gains or losses are eliminated. Also, those earnings applicable to minority ownership are deducted from consolidated net income and included as part of minority interest. The resulting consolidated net income consists of parent company earnings, plus the parent's share of subsidiary earnings period, less goodwill amortized during the period and any intercompany transaction effects.

---

[1] The nature and handling of goodwill will be treated in greater detail in Chapter 20.

Consolidated Retained Earnings. Consolidated retained earnings include all of the retained earnings of the parent, plus the parent's share of the subsidiary's retained earnings from the date of acquisition, less any goodwill amortized and intercompany transactions effects. Of course, earnings applicable to the minority interest have been removed. Also, dividends paid by subsidiary companies to the parent have been eliminated, since they are merely transfers of cash within the consolidated entity.

Investment in Subsidiary

There are two methods—cost and equity—for recording a parent company's ownership interest in a subsidiary corporation. The use of the equity method is required if the investor company has "the ability to exercise significant influence over the operating and financial policies of the investee company." There is a presumption that ownership of 20 percent or more of the voting stock gives the investor this control. Typically, the equity method is used to account for subsidiary investments that are not fully consolidated.

Cost Method. Under the cost method, the original price paid for the subsidiary is recorded on the parent's records as the "investment in subsidiary." This original investment figure remains unchanged by the subsequent activities of the subsidiary. Neither subsequent profits nor losses of the subsidiary are given any recognition in the parent's accounts. However, any cash dividends received from the subsidiary are recorded as income at the time of receipt.

Equity Method. Under the equity method, initially, the acquisition price is recorded in the parent's books as "Investment in Subsidiary," as it is under the cost method. Subsequently, this investment account is increased by the parent's pro rata share of the subsidiary's additions to stockholders' equity (or decreased by reduction in stockholders' equity). The parent's share of the subsidiary's profits (or losses) are shown on the parent's books as being the parent's equity in the subsidiary's earnings and are included as a one line item in the parent's income statement at the close of each accounting period. The offsetting debit entry is to the investment account. Cash dividends received by the parent from the subsidiary are recorded as reductions to the investment account and increases in the cash account. Thus, the account labeled "Investment in Subsidiary (equity method)" reflects the original investment cost plus (or minus) the parent's share of changes in the subsidiary's retained earnings from the date of acquisition (i.e., profits minus dividends).

As noted above, when the equity method is used, any goodwill created must be amortized and the effect of intercompany transactions eliminated.

The equity method is not a valid substitute for full consolidation and should not be used to justify exclusion of a subsidiary when full consolidation is otherwise appropriate.

Consolidation Procedures

A number of alternative methods involving worksheets are used to accomplish consolidation. The act of consolidation occurs only on the worksheet used for assembling the consolidated data, not in the accounts or records of the parent or subsidiary corporations. Each parent and subsidiary's accounting records and financial statements is based upon the principle that each company is a separate legal entity.

None of the alternative worksheet procedures, or methods of recording ownership of subsidiaries prior to consolidation, has any distinguishing effect upon the final consolidated financial statements. The reader of the consolidated statements cannot determine which alternative was used.

Confusion in consolidating procedures is minimized if one bears in mind constantly that (1) consolidating, adjusting, and eliminating entries are never recorded in the accounts of the affiliated group and (2) each periodic or annual consolidation is made as if it were the initial consolidation.

A common procedure for preparing consolidated financial statements involves the following steps:

1. Arrange vertically in parallel columns on a worksheet the unconsolidated statements of the parent and of the subsidiaries to be consolidated, as shown in Illustration 5–1.

2. Make any preconsolidating adjustments necessary to bring consistency into the statements. For example, a worksheet adjustment would be required if an affiliate had forwarded cash to another affiliate in payment of a debt but the other affiliate had not yet received the cash as of the closing date. In this case, the statement of the affiliate to whom the cash was sent would be adjusted as if the cash had actually been received. All intercompany relationships such as these must be reconciled and brought into agreement before eliminations can be made. (The receipt of cash such as $10,000 for payment of accounts receivable by the parent from the subsidiary is shown as adjustment 1 in the illustration.)

3. Eliminate intercompany assets and liabilities. All debtor-creditor relationships between affiliates to be consolidated are offset on the worksheet. This is achieved by making worksheet entries which cancel the asset of one affiliate against the liability of another affiliate. The effect of these eliminations is reversal of transactions that created the intercompany assets and liabilities in the accounts of affiliates. For example, if a subsidiary borrowed $175,000 from its parent, the subsidiary would enter the transaction on its books by debiting Cash $175,000 and crediting Loans Payable $175,000. The parent's records will reflect an entry debiting Loans Receivable $175,000 and crediting Cash $175,000. On the consolidating worksheet the

ILLUSTRATION 5–1
Consolidation Working Papers (in thousands)

	Parent	Sub-sidiary	Adjustments Debits		Adjustments Credits		Con-solidated Statement
Assets							
Cash..........................	$ 400	$ 20	(1)	10			$ 430
Accounts receivable	700	125			(1)	10	815
Inventory	1,200	275					1,475
Investment in subsidiary	400				(5)	400	
Note due from subsidiary	175	—			(2)	175	—
Plant and equipment (net)	300	200					500
Goodwill.......................			(5)	240	(6)	30	210
Other assets	25	10					35
Total assets	$3,200	$630					$3,465
Liabilities							
Accounts payable	$ 200	$100					$ 300
Notes payable	400	30					430
Loans payable—bank	1,000	25					1,025
Loans payable—parent...........		175	(2)	175			—
Common stock	1,000	200	(4)	40			1,000
			(5)	160			
Retained earnings	600	100	(4)	20			650
			(5)	0			
Minority interest			(6)	30	(4)	60	60
Total liabilities	$3,200	$630					$3,465
Income Statement							
Sales	$1,200	$475	(3)	150			$1,525
Costs of goods sold	800	125			(3)	150	775
Gross margin	$ 400	$350					$ 750
Selling expense	$ 50	$ 75					$ 125
Operating expense	75	125	(7)	10*			210
Total expense..................	$ 125	$200					$ 335
Net income	$ 275	$150					$ 415

* Single entry (see text p. 103 for explanation).

eliminating entry will debit Loans Payable and credit Loans Receivable each for $175,000. (See adjustment 2.) This entry, involving accounts from the statements of different corporations, has the effect of reversing the entries made on the books of the affiliates, but no entries to Cash are necessary because assets and liabilities of all affiliates will be combined. As noted earlier, all eliminating entries are made only on the consolidating worksheets and are not entered in the accounts of the individual corporations.

4. Eliminate (or cancel out) any intercompany revenue against the appropriate costs or expenses. Adjustment 3 shows the entries reversing $150,000 of intercompany sales. This entry assumes none of the goods sold to the subsidiary are still in its inventory account.

5. Eliminate the effect of dividends declared by a corporation to another member of the affiliated group. (None shown in Illustration 5–1.)

6. Eliminate from the accounts all intercompany profits or losses which may be cumulatively included in asset accounts of the purchaser and in equity accounts of the seller. The gains or losses of prior periods of affiliation as well as those of the current period must be canceled.

Illustration 5–1 does not include an example of this kind of adjustment. If such an adjustment is required, however, it might be handled as follows: Assume the parent had sold three years earlier to its subsidiary a machine for $20,000, including the parent's $2,000 profit, and the subsidiary was depreciating this machine over 10 years, the adjustments would be:

a. To eliminate the profit on the intercompany sale from the gross carrying value of the assets of the subsidiary and the retained earnings of the parent:

Retained Earnings (parent)	2,000	
Plant and Equipment (sub)		2,000

b. To eliminate the depreciation expense based on the intercompany profit of $2,000 included in the subsidiary's fixed asset account. This requires $200 (or $2,000/10 years) to be deducted from this year's depreciation expense and an elimination from the subsidiary's retained earnings of $400 representing the last two years' depreciation charged by the subsidiary on the intercompany profits included in its asset base.

Accumulated Depreciation (sub)	600	
Depreciation Expense (sub)		200
Retained Earnings (sub)		400

7. Eliminate the investment account of the parent in those subsidiaries being consolidated and adjust those subsidiaries' equity accounts for any minority interests that may be present. The minority interest is equal to the minority stockholders' proportional share of the subsidiary's *current* net worth.

The computation of the minority interest is:

Minority interest (in subsidiary):		
Common stock	20% × $200 =	$40
Retained earnings	20% × $100 =	20
Minority interest		$60

The adjusting entries in Illustration 5–1 (number 4) are:

```
Common Stock (sub) ...........................................      40
Retained Earnings (sub) .......................................      20
    Minority Interest ..........................................         60
```

If the parent's investment in the subsidiary exceeded its proportional share of the subsidiary's equity capital and retained earnings accounts at the *acquisition date,* an adjustment will also be required to determine the goodwill amount on the consolidated statements. To illustrate, assume the $400 "investment in subsidiary" balance shown in Illustration 5–1 represents an 80 percent interest in the subsidiary's equity and the subsidiary's retained earnings were zero at the time the investment was made because prior to this time it had been the practice of the investee to pay out all of its profits in dividends. Also, assume that the asset and liability values on the subsidiaries' books approximate their fair market values.[2]

The goodwill at date of acquisition calculation is:

```
Investment (parent) ...................        $400
Common stock (sub), 80% × 200 ......  $160
Retained earnings (sub), 80% × $0 ....      0    160
    Goodwill .........................        $240
```

The adjusting entries in Illustration 5–1 (number 5) are:

```
Common Stock (sub) ...........................................      160
Retained Earnings (sub) .......................................        0
Goodwill .....................................................      240
    Investment in Subsidiary (parent) ............................         400
```

The goodwill account, if positive, is usually labeled descriptively as "excess of cost over net assets of acquired companies" and presented as an asset on the consolidated balance sheet. A negative balance is identified as "excess of net assets of acquired companies over cost." The amount of positive or negative goodwill is amoritzed as a charge against income over a period not to exceed 40 years.

In the case of Illustration 5–1, the amortization of the goodwill in the consolidated statement involves (1) a write-down of the goodwill asset by an amount equal to the sum of the annual charges to date, (2) an increase in the operating expense by the annual charge (and a decrease in profits by the amount of this charge), and (3) a decrease in retained earnings by the cumulative effect of the goodwill charges to profits. Thus, assuming a 24-year write-off period, the goodwill balance shown on Illustration 5–1 would be decreased by $30[(240/24) \times 3]$; retained earnings would decline by 30 (prior two-year charges plus current year charge); operating profits would decrease by 10 (current year charge); and operating expenses would increase by 10.

---

[2] Goodwill is computed after adjusting the acquired company's assets and liabilities to their fair market value.

The adjusting debit-credit entries to recognize goodwill amortization in Illustration 5–1 (number 6) are:

```
Dr.  Retained Earnings .........................................   30
     Cr.  Goodwill ...............................................        30
```

The above debit-credit procedure for handling goodwill is not technically correct. It was done in this fashion because Illustration 5–1 focuses on the consolidating process. The goodwill amortization adjusting entries should have been made to the parent's statements prior to consolidation by a $30 credit to investment in subsidiary, a $20 debit to retained earnings, and a $10 debit to operating expenses. Because this procedure was not followed, to achieve the correct consolidated income figure, a single-entry debiting operating expenses $10 must be made (number 7).

8. Combine all remaining statement amounts for all affiliates being considered. The balances can then be arranged in the traditional financial statement form, modified for the four concepts peculiar to consolidation described previously.

Consolidated Federal Income Tax Returns.   The choice of filing consolidated federal income tax returns by an affiliated group is completely independent of financial reporting practices. In general, domestic industrial corporations which are related by a minimum of 80 percent control (or have this degree of common ownership) may elect to report on a consolidated basis. The complex regulations governing the filing of consolidated returns provide for elimination of intercompany gains and losses and for offsetting profits of one affiliate against losses of another member of the group and, depending on the particular tax code in effect, intracorporate dividends.

Financial Analysis Considerations

Typically, consolidated statements provide those wishing to appraise a company's total performance and financial risk with much more relevant data than if the user had to work with the individual statements of the parent company and subsidiaries. In the latter case, the user would have no way to appraise the extent to which individual company statements were distorted by intercompany transactions. Simply combining the individual company reports would not suffice. The distortions would still exist. Consolidating statements eliminates this problem.

The underlying assumption that consolidated financial statements are more meaningful than separate statements for affiliated companies needs to be qualified. Since consolidated financial statements ignore the separate legal character of affiliated corporations, information concerning any of the individual companies included in the consolidated statements cannot be obtained from the statements. For example, creditors and investors cannot evaluate the profitability or financial condition of any single corporation within the group on the basis of the consolidated statements. The analyst is unable to identify the assets and liabilities of the consolidated group with any of the individual corporations. Similarly, the statements are of limited value to the minority stockholder interested in a subsidiary company.

In order to find information about the individual companies comprising the consolidated and unconsolidated company group, users should examine the notes to the consolidated statements where summary statements for significant unconsolidated entities may be presented, locate published copies of individual company reports with public minority stockholders, check credit reference services for data, and if regulated, obtain copies of the company reports from the regulatory authorities.

While using consolidated statements, it is wise to keep several points in mind. First, there may be restrictions on the ability of consolidated subsidiaries to pass cash up to the parent. This may occur if the subsidiary has borrowed money directly. If such restrictions exist, some of the consolidated cash flows might not be available for dividends or reinvestment in other subsidiaries. Restricted cash flow is less valuable than unrestricted cash flow.

Second, the parent may be obligated to maintain an unconsolidated subsidiary's capital ratios at specified levels. Since the unconsolidated subsidiary's balance sheet accounts are excluded from the consolidated statements, the consolidated entity's total financial risk may not be properly represented by the consolidated statements.

Third, the equity method includes the income of unconsolidated subsidiaries in the consolidated income, but none of the unconsolidated subsidiaries' sales, expenses, or balance sheet items are included in the consolidated statements. This can distort the significance of certain financial ratios. For example, if the unconsolidated subsidiaries' income is included in consolidated net income but their sales are excluded from consolidated sales, the ratio of consolidated net income to consolidated sales will overstate management's ability to generate profit from sales. Similarly, the level of financial safety indicated by the ratio of consolidated net income to consolidated net interest expense will be overstated, since the unconsolidated subsidiaries' interest expense is not included in the consolidated interest expense, but their income is included in consolidated income.

These distortions can be overcome in several ways. One is to exclude the income of unconsolidated subsidiaries from consolidated net income where its inclusion might lead to misleading impressions based on consolidated financial ratios. If the unconsolidated subsidiaries' net income is excluded from consolidated income, it may also be appropriate in some cases to exclude the asset investments in unconsolidated subsidiaries when calculating ratios that include consolidated total assets and owners' equity.

Another approach is to combine the unconsolidated subsidiaries' statements with the consolidated statements. This is the solution preferred by most financial analysts. A combined balance sheet can be generated by (1) eliminating from the consolidated balance sheet the asset investments in unconsolidated subsidiaries, (2) deducting the offsetting debt and equity amounts from the unconsolidated subsidiaries' balance sheets, and (3) adding the consolidated and unconsolidated entities' balance sheets together. Since the income of the unconsolidated subsidiaries is already included in consolidated income, a combined income statement can be created by simply adding the unconsolidated subsidiaries' revenues and expenses to the consolidated income statement. Any known intercompany transactions should also be eliminated.

Care must be exercised in using combined statements. Financial ratios may not make a lot of sense if an unconsolidated subsidiary's business is very different from the other businesses included in the combined statements. For example, operating ratios based on data in a combined income statement for a finance company and a manufacturing company would be meaningless. The revenue items are not compatible. In this case, however, a combined balance sheet might be very useful for assessing the combined company's level of financial risk, particularly if the finance subsidiary primarily finances the manufacturing company's accounts receivable.

The fourth point to keep in mind when using consolidated statement data for analysis purposes is that while the consolidated sales and expenses are not adjusted for any minority interests, minority net income is deducted from the total income of the affiliated companies before arriving at consolidated net income. This deduction is made to determine the net income available to the parent company stockholders. For a ratio analysis focusing on evaluating management's operating performance, such as measuring management's ability to generate profits from sales activities, the consolidated profit before the minority interest deduction is the appropriate figure. It reflects management operating activities and is not influenced by ownership arrangements.

Finally, when incorporating data from consolidated statements into a financial analysis, it is important to remember that equity income related to unconsolidated entities whose financial policies can be influenced by the parent company is more valuable than equity income related to uncontrolled investee companies. The element of influence gives the parent the ability to determine how the cash flows associated with the equity income will be used.

CASE 5-1

Company P and Subsidiary Company S
Preparation of Consolidated Statements

Company P purchased 80 percent of the outstanding capital stock of Company S from individual stockholders for $290,000 cash on January 1, 1982. On this date, the retained earnings of Company S were $30,000.

Company S was primarily, but not exclusively, engaged in marketing goods purchased from Company P. Though purchases from Company P during the year 1986 were 1.2 million, the inventory held by Company S at the beginning or the close of the year did not include any merchandise acquired from Company P. On December 31, 1986, the balance due to Company P for these intercompany purchases was $280,000.

All plant and equipment owned by Company S was acquired for cash from Company P on January 1, 1984, and has been depreciated on the basis of its estimated life of 10 years, using the straight-line method without salvage value. In 1984, Company P recorded a $50,000 profit on the sale of these fixed assets to its subsidiary.

A 10 percent cash dividend was declared and paid by Company S on its outstanding capital stock on July 1, 1986.

Financial statements of Company P and of Company S are presented in vertical form on the accompanying worksheet (Exhibit 1) to facilitate assembly of information for consolidated statements.

Questions

1. Complete the worksheet provided (or use any method you prefer) to assemble the information necessary for—
   a. A consolidated income statement.
   b. A consolidated retained earnings statement.
   c. A consolidated balance sheet.
2. Compare the financial condition of Company P on an unconsolidated basis with

---

This case was prepared by F. R. Madera (under the direction of David F. Hawkins).

Copyright © 1965 by the President and Fellows of Harvard College

Harvard Business School case 110–089 (Revised 1985)

EXHIBIT 1

COMPANY P AND SUBSIDIARY COMPANY S
Working Papers for Consolidated Statements
For the Year Ended December 31, 1986
(in thousands; parentheses indicate deductions)

	Company P	Company S	Adjustments and Eliminations Dr.	Cr.	Consolidated Statements
Income Statement					
Sales	$1,500	$ 1,800			
Cost of sales	(900)	(1,400)			
	$ 600	$ 400			
Depreciation	(40)	(20)			
Operating expenses	(440)	(290)			
Net income from operations	$ 120	$ 90			
Dividend income	24				
Minority net income					
Net income..........................	$ 144	$ 90			
Retained Earnings Statement					
Retained earnings, Jan. 1, 1986:					
Company P........................	$ 248				
Company S		$ 70			
Net income (as above)...............	144	90			
Dividends:					
Company P........................	(72)				
Company S		(30)			
Retained earnings,					
December 31, 1986	$ 320	$ 130			
Balance Sheet					
Cash	$ 110	$ 150			
Accounts receivable (net)	375	410			
Inventories	310	75			
Plant and equipment	885	200			
Less: Accumulated depreciation......	(265)	(60)			
Investment in Company S (at cost) ...	290				
Goodwill					
Total assets	$1,705	$ 775			
Accounts payable	$ 385	$ 345			
Minority interest					
Capital stock:					
Company P........................	1,000				
Company S		300			
Retained earnings (as above)	320	130			
Total liabilities	$1,705	$ 775			

that presented by the consolidated statements. Your comparison should include computations of—

a. Working capital (current assets − current liabilities).
b. Total assets.

    c. Long-term capital.

    d. Any ratios or relationships you think significant.

3. Compare the profitability of Company P on an unconsolidated basis with that shown by the consolidated statements.

4. How meaningful are consolidated statements to you as—
    a. A stockholder of Company P?
    b. A minority stockholder of Company S?

CASE 5-2

Mohawk Products, Incorporated
Determination of the Consolidated Entity

In 1933, Edwin Franklin, after inheriting a large fortune, established Mohawk Products, Inc., in Greensville, South Carolina, to manufacture textile products. Between 1933 and 1985, the company prospered and expanded to the point where it was one of the largest privately held companies in the nation. In 1985, its operations included two foreign and one domestic textile subsidiary, a real estate subsidiary, a finance subsidiary, an electronics subsidiary, a bank, and a farm equipment company. Mohawk Products or one of its subsidiaries established each of these companies and owned 100 percent of their outstanding common stock.

    In mid-1985, James Franklin, president and principal stockholder of Mohawk Products, learned that the FASB was considering a rule that would require investor companies to consolidate fully for financial reporting purposes all of the investee companies they "controlled." Mr. Franklin was concerned that this possible accounting development might hurt his plan to make a small public offering sometime in the next few years to a limited number of investors of some of his Mohawk Products common stock. Several members of the Franklin family thought a wider market holding of their stock would simplify the valuation of their holdings in the company for

---

This case was prepared by F. R. Madera (under the direction of David F. Hawkins).

Copyright © 1965 by the President and Fellows of Harvard College

Harvard Business School case 110–093 (Revised 1985)

estate tax purposes. In 1985, Mohawk had outstanding, and in the hands of the Franklin family, 1 million shares of common stock.

To date, for internal reporting purposes, Mohawk carried its subsidiaries on Mohawk's financial statement as an "investment in unconsolidated subsidiaries." The investment was valued according to the equity method. Mohawk had never prepared consolidated statements. James Franklin believed that he was better able to manage the group of companies by treating each company separately, rather than as a group or even part of a group of companies.

Mr. Franklin realized for the purposes of the stock offering he would have to present the company's financial statements on a consolidated basis. In addition, if the FASB decided to change consolidation accounting rules, he was not sure which subsidiaries he would have to consolidate.

In line with Edwin Franklin's often articulated belief that "every tub should stand on its own bottom," it had been Mohawk's practice to reinvest the earnings of its subsidiaries in the subsidiary creating the earnings, to minimize intercompany investment and operating transactions, and to satisfy the needs of Mohawk's stockholders for dividends from the current earnings of the parent. To date, the parent had never received dividends from its subsidiaries. For income tax purposes, the company submitted unconsolidated returns. Intercompany transactions were immaterial.

Textile Companies. Mohawk Products owned three subsidiaries in the textile area: Iroquois Woolens, Inc.; Bull Dog Linens Proprietary, Ltd.; and Mohawk Products (Australia), Ltd. Iroquois Woolens was formed in 1939 to manufacture blankets in Madison, Quebec. Bull Dog Linens, the company's British subsidiary, was created in 1953 to produce fine linen goods for the British and European markets. Bull Dog's two plants were located in Manchester and Liverpool. During recent years, repeated labor troubles had plagued Bull Dog Linens. The Australian subsidiary, Mohawk Products (Australia), was formed in 1976 to operate a small textile mill near Sydney, Australia.

Banking Company. In 1939, following the collapse of Greensville's two banks, Edwin Franklin created the Franklin Trust Company in Greensville. Since the Mohawk mill was the major company there, he saw an opportunity for Mohawk Products to make a profit by becoming the banker for its employees, their relatives, and the many local tradespeople who relied upon the mill and its employees for their livelihood. Over the years, new companies moved into the town and its population increased considerably. Throughout this period, the Franklin Trust was the town's only bank and its business expanded.

Since it had been founded, the Franklin Trust had held all of Mohawk's cash balances. However, it had never loaned money to its parent or its subsidiaries. This "no loan" practice followed Edwin Franklin's promise to the townspeople and the state's banking commission that the bank would avoid conflict-of-interest situations, such as lending money to its parent or any of its parent's subsidiaries. As a result, whenever Mohawk or its subsidiaries needed financing they obtained it from Franklin's correspondent bank in Atlanta.

Farm Equipment Company.   In 1937, Edwin Franklin's youngest daughter married John Atkins, the sales vice president for one of the largest farm equipment manufacturers in the country. As a wedding present, Mr. Franklin used Mohawk Products' cash to buy at a distress price the eastern franchise to distribute and sell the well-known Walpole farm equiment line. He made Atkins the president of the new company, Consolidated Farm Equipment, Inc. John Atkins quickly developed an effective system of subdistributors, and the company made progress, despite the unfavorable state of the farm economy.

In early 1939, the franchise became worthless when the Walpole Farm Equiment company went bankrupt. Aware of the growing threat of war in Europe, John Atkins bought the assets of Walpole at book value, with the expectation that in the event of war, Consolidated Farm Equipment could manufacture tanks and small arms profitably at the Walpole plants. Mohawk guaranteed the loans with which Consolidated Farm Equipment financed this acquisition. Accordingly, during World War II, Consolidated Farm Equipment manufactured farm equipment, tanks, and small arms, and its wartime profits were used to extinguish the loans obtained to buy Walpole.

Finance Company.   In early 1981, for tax, financial, and administrative reasons, Consolidated Farm Equipment created a wholly owned finance subsidiary, Consolidated Finance Corporation, to finance the company's credit sales to dealers. Beginning in 1980, Consolidated Farm Equipment began a major program to increase both the number of its dealers and their inventory levels. As part of this program, Consolidated Farm Equipment sold equipment to its dealers on extremely favorable credit terms. In turn, Consolidated Farm Equipment sold its dealers' accounts receivable at a discount to Consolidated Finance. As part of this arrangement, the banks lending to Consolidated Finance forced Consolidated Farm Equipment to agree to take back any dealer receivables falling in default.

Electronics Company.   In 1983, Mohawk bought a patent covering a new technique for manufacturing electronic interconnect systems. In order to exploit this patent, Mohawk established a new company called Transiton, Inc. Within six months, the company was in business and rapidly developed a market for its product. Unlike the other Mohawk subsidiaries, Transiton had yet to earn a profit.

Real Estate Company. For tax reasons, Transiton leased its building from Equity Real Estate Company, a wholly owned subsidiary of Mohawk. In 1985, the Equity Real Estate Company did not have any other business. Sometime in the future, however, James Franklin planned to extend Equity's activities in the real estate area to include some form of non-Mohawk business.

Exhibit 1 presents the profits after taxes of Mohawk Products and its subsidiaries for the period 1975–84, inclusive. Exhibit 2 shows condensed balance sheets for Mohawk Products and its subsidiaries as of December 31, 1983, and 1984, respectively.

EXHIBIT 1

MOHAWK PRODUCTS, INC.
Mohawk Products and Subsidiaries
Profits after Taxes, 1975–1984
(millions of dollars; 0 = less than $100,000)

	1984	1983	1982	1981	1980	1979	1978	1977	1976	1975
Mohawk Products	4.2	4.5	4.1	4.5	3.2	3.1	5.0	4.7	4.8	4.2
Iroquois Woolens	2.9	3.2	3.1	2.9	1.9	1.4	2.9	2.8	2.7	2.6
Franklin Trust	0.5	0.4	0.3	0.2	0.1	0.1	0.2	0.1	0.2	0.1
Consolidated Farm	2.8	2.9	3.9	1.9	(0.4)	(1.0)	3.4	3.7	3.6	2.4
Bull Dog Linens	(0.4)	(0.6)	0.4	0.7	0.6	0.4	0.5	0.4	0.1	0.1
Mohawk (Australia)	2.5	1.9	1.3	(0.6)	0.8	0.9	(0.4)			
Consolidated Finance	0.2	0.2	0.2	0.1						
Transiton	(0.6)	(1.5)								
Equity Real Estate	0.0	0.0								

Questions

1. Under the existing generally accepted accounting principles, what consolidation policy would Mr. Franklin have to adopt if he issued public statements for Mohawk Products? How would adopting these standards change Mohawk Products' financial statement? Give examples. What would be the principal differences between these statements and statements prepared using the FASB's possible change in consolidation accounting?

2. Assuming that you are not constrained by any generally accepted accounting principles, what subsidiaries do you think Mr. Franklin ought to include in the consolidated statements presented in the prospectus given to potential outside investors?

3. Do you think it makes sense for the FASB to issue a rule requiring consolidation of all controlled investee companies?

EXHIBIT 2

MOHAWK PRODUCTS, INC.
Condensed Balance Sheets
(millions of dollars; 0 = less than $100,000)

December 31, 1983

	Mohawk Products	Iroquois Woolens	Franklin Trust	Consolidated Farm	Bull Dog Linens	Mohawk (Australia)	Consolidated Finance	Transition	Equity Real Estate
Assets									
Cash	3.8	2.3	4.9	1.7	0.9	1.2	0.7	0.8	0.1
Accounts (loans) receivable	8.7	5.4	77.0	-0-	1.4	4.0	30.7	2.3	-0-
Investments in subsidiaries (equity method)	143.55	-0-	-0-	2.5	-0-	-0-	-0-	-0-	-0-
Other assets	81.3	69.2	10.2	48.4	7.1	12.5	2.3	6.8	3.2
Total assets	237.35	76.9	92.1	52.6	9.4	17.7	33.7	9.9	3.3
Equities									
Accounts payable (deposits)	5.7	5.8	81.2	3.1	1.3	2.0	-0-	2.1	-0-
Other current liabilities	8.7	2.7	2.3	3.6	0.7	1.8	0.7	4.3	0.3
Long-term debt	-0-	-0-	-0-	-0-	-0-	5.0	30.0	-0-	2.5
Capital stock*	50.0	10.0	3.5	8.5	4.0	5.0	2.5	5.0	0.5
Retained earnings	172.95	58.4	5.1	37.4	3.4	3.9	0.5	(1.5)	0.0
Total equities	237.35	76.9	92.1	52.6	9.4	17.7	33.7	9.9	3.3

December 31, 1984

Assets

Cash	4.2	2.1	5.2	1.4	0.7	1.3	0.6	0.7	0.1
Accounts (loans) receivable	9.2	5.2	76.9	-0-	1.5	4.3	32.3	2.4	-0-
Investment in subsidiaries (equity method)	150.98	-0-	-0-	2.5	-0-	-0-	-0-	-0-	-0-
Other assets	80.7	72.7	12.7	51.3	6.7	15.0	2.2	6.5	3.1
Total assets	245.08	80.0	94.8	55.2	8.9	20.6	35.1	9.6	3.2

Equities

Accounts payable (deposits)	4.9	6.2	83.3	2.7	1.4	2.3	-0-	3.7	-0-
Other current liabilities	7.7	2.5	2.4	3.8	0.5	1.9	0.7	3.0	0.2
Long-term debt	-0-	-0-	-0-	-0-	-0-	5.0	31.2	-0-	2.4
Capital stock*	50.0	10.0	3.5	8.5	4.0	5.0	2.5	5.0	0.5
Retained earnings	182.48	61.3	5.6	40.2	3.0	6.4	0.7	(2.1)	0.1
Total equities	245.08	80.0	94.8	55.2	8.9	20.6	35.1	9.6	3.2

* Original investment.

CHAPTER 6

Preparation and Analysis of Changes in Financial Position Statements

The statement of changes in financial position describes a company's uses and sources of financial resources during the accounting period. It is presented in a three-year comparative format in corporate financial reports along with the income and financial position statements. The statement of changes in financial position, or funds flow statement as it is commonly called, is a powerful analytical tool. It provides the following information:

1. The extent to which profit-directed activities created working capital and cash flow.
2. An explanation of the changes in the working capital position and cash balances from the previous accounting period.
3. The financial resources expended to acquire new assets, pay dividends, and repay debt.
4. The debt and equity sources of the financial resources used to pay dividends, acquire new assets, and repay debt.

These data are useful to statement users trying to appraise a company's financial policies, its ability to satisfy its financial obligations, and its capacity to finance growth. In addition, analysts find the structure of the funds flow statement a convenient format for thinking about, preparing, and presenting projections of a company's dividends, financial transactions, and investments. In some cases, a funds analysis can also help an analyst to comprehend the underlying economic reality of an income statement that involves complex, unusual, or liberal accounting practices.

Illustration 6–1 presents General Electric's three-year comparative funds flow statement published in its 1984 annual report. Its format focuses on explaining the changes in cash, marketable securities, and short-term debt. This is a preferred format, although many company's funds flow statements foot to changes in cash. This is a common and equally acceptable

116

ILLUSTRATION 6–1
General Electric Company

GENERAL ELECTRIC COMPANY AND CONSOLIDATED AFFILIATES
Statement of Changes in Financial Position
Funds Provided (Used)
For the Years ended December 31
(in millions)

	1984	1983	1982
Funds provided from operations:			
Net earnings	$ 2,280	$ 2,024	$ 1,817
Adjustments for items not representing current fund usage:			
Depreciation, depletion, and amortization	1,100	1,084	984
Earnings retained by nonconsolidated financial services affiliates	(330)	(55)	(42)
Income tax timing differences	(171)	4	139
All other operating items	11	34	36
Funds provided from operations	$ 2,890	$ 3,091	$ 2,934
Funds provided from (used for) changes in working capital:			
Decrease (increase) in inventories	$ (512)	$ (129)	$ 432
Decrease (increase) in current receivables	(260)	(509)	132
Increase (decrease) in current liabilities other than short-term borrowings	(112)	556	(447)
Net funds provided from (used for) working capital	$ (884)	$ (82)	$ 117
Total funds provided from operations and working capital	$ 2,006	$ 3,009	$ 3,051
Funds provided from (used in) investment transactions:			
Additions to property, plant, and equipment	$(2,488)	$(1,721)	$(1,608)
Dispositions of property, plant, and equipment	1,346	209	160
Additions to funds held for business development	(359)	(455)	—
Additional investments in nonconsolidated financial services affiliates	—	(228)	(166)
All other transactions—net	454	158	(377)
Net investment transactions	$(1,047)	$(2,037)	$(1,991)
Funds provided from (used in) financial transactions:			
Disposition of GE shares from treasury	$ 254	$ 238	$ 216
Purchase of GE shares for treasury	(284)	(319)	(222)
Increase in long-term borrowings	80	52	113
Decrease in long-term borrowings	(242)	(152)	(157)
Net financial transactions	$ (192)	$ (181)	$ (50)
Funds used for dividends declared	$ (930)	$ (852)	$ (760)
Net increase (decrease) in funds	$ (163)	$ (61)	$ (250)
Analysis of net change in funds:			
Increase (decrease) in cash and marketable securities	$ (132)	$ (82)	$ 116
Decrease (increase) in short-term borrowings	(31)	21)	134
Increase (decrease) in funds	$ (163)	$ (61)	$ (250)

presentation. Funds flow statements that focus on working capital changes, while popular in the past, are not encouraged today.

Nature of the Statement of Changes in Financial Position

Funds flow reporting can be distinguished from the other concepts of financial reporting. The funds flow statement shows changes in the firm's assets, liabilities, and equity accounts during a specified period of time. In contrast, the balance sheet presents the company's financial position at an instant of time. The income statement shows revenues, expenses, and profit for a period of time.

Causes for changes in the firm's financial position can be readily observed in a well-prepared funds flow statement. Funds flowing from operations, borrowing, sale of properties, and equity contributions are related to outflows for property acquisitions, dividends, and debt retirement. Answers are provided to such questions as: What happened to profits generated by operations? How was it possible for the firm to distribute dividends? What happened to money borrowed during the period? What caused the change in the working capital position? Why did the cash and marketable securities balance change?

Current Practice

The definition of funds and the statement format used in public corporate reports:

> The statement summarizing changes in financial position should be based on a broad concept embracing all changes in financial position. . . . The statement of each reporting entity should disclose all important aspects of its financing and investing activities regardless of whether cash or other elements of working capital are directly affected.

Using this definition of funds, sources and uses of financial resources or funds may be defined as:

Sources of Funds	Uses of Funds
Increases in liabilities	Decreases in liabilities
Increases in owners' equity	Decreases in owners' equity
Decreases in assets	Increases in assets

The above table of sources and uses of funds can be related to the debit-credit accounting process as follows: All of the sources of funds are credit entries, and all of the uses of funds are debit entries. If the above table was expanded to show revenues as a source of funds and expenses as a use of funds, this relationship of funds flow to the dual entry convention would be the same.

Definition of "Funds"

For analytical and accounting purposes, the term "funds flow analysis" can be defined in at least five different ways. These definitions, beginning with the narrowest and moving to the broadest, define funds flows as changes in (1) cash, (2) the sum of cash and marketable securities, (3) net monetary assets, (4) working capital, and (5) all financial resources. Each of these definitions leads to emphasis being placed on a different aspect of funds flow. The appropriateness of any definition will depend upon the particular circumstances of the firm and the purpose of the user of the statement.

Whether or not a particular accounting transaction is defined as a funds flow will depend on the definition of funds used. For example, the *declaration* of dividends changes a company's net monetary assets, net working capital, and "all financial resources." Thus, in a company that used a funds definition based on changes in any one of these items, this transaction would be regarded as a funds flow. If the company strictly adhered to a funds definition related to changes in cash or cash and marketable securities, this transaction would not be recorded as a funds flow, since it does not change either of these two asset accounts (only the liability and net worth accounts are changed).

These five definitions of funds are demonstrated below. The changes in financial position statements resulting from each definition will be based upon the simplified balance sheets and statement of retained earnings for the Carter Company shown in Illustration 6-2. As the various changes in financial position statements are developed, it must be remembered that each is based entirely upon the balance sheet and statement of retained earnings. That is, each statement must be considered independently, rather than as part of a continuing illustration.

Each funds statement begins with a section labeled *funds from operations,* which is defined as the sum of net income plus nonfund debits (expenses) minus nonfund credits (income) included in the determination of income. What constitutes a nonfund item depends on the definition of funds. For example, if *changes in* working capital is the funds definition (see below), changes in long term accounts receivable is deducted from income to calculate funds from operations since this item is a nonfund revenue source. Irrespective of the funds definition, nonfund expense items added back to net income are depreciation, amortization of intangible assets, and deferred taxes. Income recognized using the equity method in excess of dividends received from unconsolidated subsidiaries is a nonfund credit. It is deducted from net income to derive funds from operations.

1.   Funds Defined as Cash.   When funds are defined as cash, the increase in the cash account of $2 in Illustration 6-2 can be explained by a rearrangement of differences in the balance sheet accounts other than cash.

The handling of the investment in fixed assets is tricky in this case. The amount shown in the cash flow statement (Illustration 6-3) for "increase in fixed assets" is $8, not the $10 indicated in Illustration 6-2. The issuance

ILLUSTRATION 6–2

CARTER COMPANY
Balance Sheets
December 31, 1985, and 1986

	1985	1986	Difference
Assets			
Cash	$ 28	$ 30	$ 2
Marketable securities	10	15	5
Receivables	32	40	8
Inventories	40	35	(5)
Fixed assets (net)	130	140	10
Total assets	$240	$260	$20
Liabilities			
Current payables	$ 54	$ 47	$ (7)
Long-term debt	46	53	7
Capital stock	100	105	5
Retained earnings	40	55	15
Total liabilities	$240	$260	$20

CARTER COMPANY
Statement of Retained Earnings
For the Year Ended December 31, 1986

Balance, December 31, 1985	$40
Net income for the year	20
	$60
Less: Dividends paid on December 31, 1986	5
Balance, December 31, 1986	$55

Additional data: During 1986, depreciation of $8 was charged against operations, and long-term debt of $10 was issued for fixed assets in the same amount.

ILLUSTRATION 6–3

CARTER COMPANY
Cash Flow Statement
For the Year Ended December 31, 1986

Funds provided:		
From operations:		
Net income	$20	
Depreciation	8	$28
From decrease in inventories		5
From increase in capital stock		5
Total		$38
Funds applied:		
To increase in marketable securities	$ 5	
To increase in receivables	8	
To increase in fixed assets	8	
To decrease in current payables	7	
To decrease in long-term debt	3	
To payment of dividends	5	
Total		36
Net increase in funds (cash)		$ 2

of $10 of long-term debt for fixed assets is ignored in changes in cash statement, using the cash definition of funds in its most restricted sense, since it did not result in a change in cash. (See "additional data" note to Illustration 6–2.) If the $10 is deducted from both fixed assets in the 1986 balance sheet, fixed assets for 1985 and 1986 are $130. Since depreciation of $8 was charged during 1986, $8 of fixed assets requiring cash outlays must have been acquired in 1986.

Depreciation is added to net income to determine total funds provided from operations, since depreciation charges requiring no expenditure of cash were subtracted in the determination of net income.

It should be noted that in the Carter Company example, dividends were paid out on December 31, 1986. As a result, the cash account was reduced by $5 and the payment of dividends is a use of cash. If on the other hand, the company had simply declared a dividend of $5 but not paid it yet, the declaration of the dividend would not be a cash flow since the declaration of a dividend does not change the cash account's balance.

Cash flow statements can be very helpful in analyzing the liquidity of a firm, its ability to generate cash from operations, its debt coverage and capacity, and its dividend-paying ability. Typically, in analyzing cash flows it is useful to distinguish among those cash flows that are (1) recurring or one time, (2) not directly related to operations, (3) spasmodic, or (4) variable at management's discretion. Such distinctions are particularly useful when trying to predict future dividends. For example, a company that cannot create enough cash flow from operations to finance its growth may resort to borrowing from banks to pay its dividends. However, in some years the company may not borrow cash because it pays dividends with the cash receipts from the sale of fixed assets. An analysis that distinguishes the nature of a firm's cash flows would highlight these practices and raise questions in the analyst's mind as to the continuing ability of the company to maintain or raise dividends.

2. *Funds Defined as Cash and Marketable Securities.* Under this definition of funds, arrangement of balance sheet account changes other than cash and marketable securities will result in the funds flow statement shown in Illustration 6–4. This statement differs from the preceding illustration only in that marketable securities are considered as funds in addition to cash. The comments made previously about the difference between the declaration and payment of dividends on the cash flow statement shown in Illustration 6–3 apply also in this example.

Since marketable securities are for all practical purposes the equivalent of cash, the definition of funds as cash and marketable securities may be superior to the more limited cash definition for most analytical purposes that involve an analysis of cash.

3. *Funds Defined as Net Monetary Assets.* Under this alternative, funds are identified as net quick assets: that is, monetary assets, such as

ILLUSTRATION 6–4

CARTER COMPANY
Changes in Cash and Marketable Securities
For the Year Ended December 31, 1986

Funds provided:
From operations:

Net income	$20	
Depreciation	8	$28
From decrease in inventories		5
From increase in capital stock		5
Total		$38

Funds applied:

To increase in receivables	$ 8	
To increase in fixed assets	8	
To decrease in current payables	7	
To decrease in long-term debt	3	
To payment of dividends	5	
Total		31
Net increase in funds (cash and marketable securities)		$ 7

cash, marketable securities, and accounts receivable, less those short-term obligations, such as accounts payable, that require cash to extinguish them. For the Carter Company, the total of cash, marketable securities, and receivables reduced by current payables is $16 and $38 at the close of 1985 and 1986, respectively. This net increase in funds of $22 can be explained by the statement shown in Illustration 6–5.

Using the funds definition in Illustration 6–5, both the declaration and payment of a dividend would be a funds flow.

The net monetary asset definition of funds is considered by some to

ILLUSTRATION 6–5

CARTER COMPANY
Changes in Net Monetary Assets
For the Year Ended December 31, 1986

Funds provided:
From operations:

Net income	$20	
Depreciation	8	$28
From decrease in inventories		5
From increase in capital stock		5
Total		$38

Funds applied:

To increase in fixed assets	$ 8	
To decrease in long-term debt	3	
To payment of dividends	5	
Total		16
Net increase in funds (quick assets)		$22

ILLUSTRATION 6–6

CARTER COMPANY

December 31

	1985	1986	Difference
Current assets:			
Cash	$ 28	$ 30	$ 2
Marketable securities	10	15	5
Receivables	32	40	8
Inventories	40	35	(5)
	$110	$120	$10
Less: Current liabilities:			
Current payables	54	47	7
Working capital	$ 56	$ 73	$17

be superior to the cash flow definitions. These people believe that accounts receivable and accounts payable can be considered to represent in essence constructive receipts and payments of cash. As a result, they believe the broader net monetary asset definition to be more useful since it includes all of the cash-type fund movements.

4. *Funds Defined as Working Capital.* This definition of funds treats transactions that change working capital (current assets less current liabilities) as funds. The working capital of the Carter Company can be summarized as shown in Illustration 6–6.

Balance sheet changes that increase or decrease the working capital balance (current assets − current liabilities) are:

Increases	*Decreases*
Additions to current assets	Decreases in current assets
Decreases in current liabilities	Increases in current liabilities
(both debit entries)	(both credit entries)

Working capital is increased by the increases in cash, marketable securities, and receivables and the decrease in current payables. The reduction in inventory between 1985 and 1986 reduces working capital.

The changes in financial position statement is prepared by analyzing all noncurrent balance sheet accounts to explain the increase in working capital of $17, as shown in Illustration 6–7.

The working capital funds definition is popular. This definition is thought to have the advantages of presenting a clear picture of a company's general liquidity and of concentrating on the funds flow that resulted from long-term major transactions, rather than those that arose from the day-to-day operating cycle. The principal disadvantage of this definition is that it treats nonmonetary items, such as inventory and payments in advance, as being

ILLUSTRATION 6–7

CARTER COMPANY
Changes in Working Capital
For the Year Ended December 31, 1986

Funds provided:

From operations:

Net income	$20	
Depreciation	8	$28
From increase in capital stock		5
Total		$33

Funds applied:

To increase fixed assets	$ 8	
To decrease long-term debt	3	
To payment of dividends	5	
Total		16
Net increase in funds (working capital)		$17

Explanation of Changes in Working Capital

Increases (decreases):

Cash	$ 2
Marketable securities	5
Receivables	8
Inventories.......................	(5)
Current payables	(7)
Increase in working capital	$17

---

the same as cash, which they are not. In addition, this definition, if literally interpreted, may obscure major movements within the working capital accounts if only the net change in working capital is shown. In practice, this is not a major problem since the changes in working capital items are required to be shown in detail to explain the changes in working capital balance. Current practice discourages the use of this format for public reporting purposes.

5. Funds Defined as All Financial Resources. This concept of funds is required for general usage. When funds are defined in this broad manner, the preceding working capital concept of funds flow is extended to include all transactions involving financial resources even though working capital is not directly affected. For example, the Carter Company issued $10 long-term debt directly for fixed assets; current asset and liability accounts were not changed in any way. Statements of changes in financial position prepared under previous narrower definitions of funds deliberately excluded the effect of this transaction. Such omissions would obscure an important event in Carter's financial affairs. Therefore, the transaction should be recognized in the changes in financial position statement. In addition, the details of the working capital changes are shown if the all-financial resources definition is used. The statement resulting from application of this broadest concept of funds is shown in Illustration 6–8. Also, if the broad definition of funds

ILLUSTRATION 6–8

CARTER COMPANY
Changes in Financial Position
For the Year Ended December 31, 1986

Funds provided:

From operations:

Net income	$20	
Depreciation	8	$28
Decrease in inventories		5
Increase in capital stock		5
Increase in long-term debt		10
Total		$48

Funds applied:

Increase in receivables	$ 8
Decrease in current payables	7
Increase in fixed assets	18
Decrease in long-term debt	3
Payment of dividends	5
Increase in cash and marketable securities	$ 7

---

is used, it is desirable to show the net difference between the uses and sources of funds as a change in cash; although less desirable, the balancing amount can also be the changes in working capital.

The $10 increase in long-term debt is listed as a source of funds and the $3 retirement of long-term debt is included as an application of funds. As an alternative, these items might be netted and the resulting $7 increase would be included as a source of funds. Since the underlying objective of the funds flow statement is to provide useful information to the reader, the APB requires that all material information be presented in gross terms.

The increase in fixed assets is shown as $18. This is the $8 previously calculated using more restrictive funds definitions, plus the $10 purchased using long-term debt.

Statements of changes in financial position are provided in many forms. Often, the details of the changes in working capital or cash are not shown separately but are presented as in Illustration 6–9.

In each of the example statements, "funds from operations" was derived by adding the nonfund expense item (depreciation) back to net income. Other nonfund expenses besides depreciation include such charges as the amortization of goodwill, the write-off of other capitalized intangibles, and the deferred tax portion of the current book tax expense. Some nonfund credit items may be excluded from net income to derive the funds from operations figure. A common example of a nonfund credit is the equity in the earnings of unconsolidated subsidiaries or investee companies that are included in net income. In this case, only the dividends received from these companies is shown as a source of funds. The difference between the equity

ILLUSTRATION 6–9

CARTER COMPANY
Changes in Financial Position Statement
For the Year Ended December 31, 1986

Funds provided:
From operations:

Net income	$20	
Depreciation	8	$28
Increase in capital stock		5
Increase in long-term debt		10
Decrease in inventories		5
Total		$48

Funds applied:

Increase in fixed assets	$18
Decrease in long-term debt	3
Payment of dividends	5
Increase in receivables	8
Decrease in current payables	7
Increase in cash and marketable securities	7
Total	$48

method income figure and these dividends is backed out of net income as a nonfund credit.

Statement of Balance Sheet Changes

For a number of analytical purposes, a rough approach to funds flow analysis can be accomplished by summarizing increases and decreases in compara-

ILLUSTRATION 6–10

CARTER COMPANY
Changes in Financial Position Statement
For the Year Ended December 31, 1986

Funds provided:
Decreases in assets:

Inventories	$ 5

Increases in liabilities and owners' equity:

Long-term debt	7
Capital stock	5
Retained earnings	15
Total	$32

Funds applied:
Increases in assets:

Cash	$ 2
Marketable securities	5
Receivables	8
Fixed assets	10

Decreases in liabilities and owners' equity:

Current payables	7
Total	$32

tive balance sheet accounts without adjustments. Such a statement for the Carter Company might appear as shown in Illustration 6–10.

Statement Preparation

Appendix 6–A presents an example of how a funds statement can be prepared using accountants' working papers and the debit-credit mechanism. This methodology helps the preparer to keep track of the various adjustments and reduces the probability of errors.

Funds Analysis

Statement users who find the format of published funds statements unsatisfactory for their analytical purposes must recast the data into a more relevant format. These analytical formats emphasize the analyst's concerns, which often are:

1. To what extent is the company able to finance its projected growth in fixed assets with internally generated funds?
2. How dependent is the company on external sources of financing, such as borrowing and new equity?
3. Is this dependence on external financing detrimental or beneficial to the current stockholders' interests?
4. Is the company creating a liquidity, external financing, and self-financing profile that may lead to dividend increases or decreases?
5. Are temporary loans or other short-term liabilities being used to finance long-term investments?
6. What do the changes in the working capital accounts suggest relative to the company's funds needs or generation?
7. Is the company's growth rate outstripping its ability to create funds internally or from outside sources?
8. What has been the impact of inflation on the company's cash flows and liquidity?

The increasing use of the funds statement in an original or a restructured format reflects a growing awareness by statement users that reported net income can be a poor indicator of a company's ability to pay trade payables, declare dividends, finance growth, and repay debt. For example, for many years investors assumed that if a company's earnings were projected to rise, then dividends would also increase proportionately. However, during the above-average inflationary periods of the 1970s and early 1980s, dividends growth lagged behind earnings growth. This was due principally to the corporate liquidity squeeze caused by the rising rate of inflation driving up working capital investments and the cost of replacing assets consumed in the generation of income. This experience led analysts interested in predicting dividend growth and financial risk levels to the realization that a firm's dividend decisions involved management consideration of the company's ability to generate cash internally or through external financing in order to finance its operating cycle, capital expenditures, debt repayment obligations, and unexpected cash outflows. Clearly, the funds statement rather than the income statement provides more information relevant to dividend decisions when viewed in this context.

Total Cash Flow Format

The total cash flow funds statement format has emerged as one of the more popular analytical funds statement formats. Versions of it are now the preferred format for public reporting purposes also. The General Electric statement in Illustration 6–1 is based on the total cash flow format. Total cash flow analysis focuses on how well a company is able to finance its financial requirements from internally generated cash flow and the extent to which it is dependent on external fund sources to meet any cash shortfall. Illustration 6–11 illustrates this analytical format.

ILLUSTRATION 6–11
Total Cash Flow Analysis Format

	1986	1985
Funds from operations*	$145	$134
Increase (decrease) in accounts receivable	(30)	(21)
Increase (decrease) in inventory	27	(84)
Increase (decrease) in other current assets (excluding cash)	(1)	2
	$141	$ 31
(Increase) decrease in accounts payable	8	42
(Increase) decrease in other current liabilities (excluding current debt)	6	9
Cash generated from operating cycle	$155	$ 82
Capital expenditures	(65)	(73)
Other operating sources (uses)	1	5
Cash available for dividends before investments and external financing transaction	$ 91	$ 14
Dividend payments	(31)	(30)
Cash available for investments and external financing transactions	$ 60	$ (16)
Asset disposal	17	12
Investments	(12)	(36)
Cash available after investments and before external financing transactions	$ 65	$ (40)
Issuance of short-term notes payable	(91)	48
Issuance of long-term debt	86	12
Decrease in long-term debt	(35)	(26)
Equity capital transactions	1	(2)
Changes in cash and marketable securities	$ 26	$ (8)

* Net income plus nonfund expenses less nonfund revenues.

As its captions suggest, the total cash flow statement shown in Illustration 6–11 rearranges the data presented in published funds statements as follows:

1. First, the cash generated by the operating cycle is computed by adjusting the funds from operations figure for changes in the current asset and liability accounts (excluding cash, marketable securities, and debt). Account receivables or payables included in the long-term section of the balance sheet should be treated as current operating balances. This step in essence de-accrues the net income figure by backing out the unpaid expenses and uncollected receivables from current sales as well as recognizing that the opening period balance of payables and receivables had been paid and received in cash. The measure, after inventory adjustments, is the cash generated from the management of the firm's operating cycle resources. Short-term debt changes are excluded from this calculation since they are part of the external financing transactions prescribed later in the statement.

2. Next, capital expenditures and other operating uses and sources of cash are deducted from the operating cycle cash flow to measure the extent to which capital expenditures are funded with internally generated cash flow related to the operating cycle.

3. The next section of the statements focuses on the extent to which the company's cash after capital expenditures is available to fund dividend payments and, after payment of dividends, the firm's investments and external financing transactions.

4. The firm's investment-related uses and sources of funds are grouped together in the next section and deducted from the cash available for investments and external financing total to measure the net cash generated or used before considering external financial transactions.

5. The last portion of the total cash flow format summarizes the firm's various short- and long-term external financial transactions.

6. The final balancing line of the statement is the change in the cash and marketable securities accounts during the period covered by the statement.

The format of the total cash flow statement highlights the data needed by statement users to answer a number of important questions raised in many analyses. These are:

1. Are dividends being paid with internally generated cash or borrowings? Borrowing to pay dividends may in some cases be a sign of financial difficulties.

2. How close are net income and funds from operations to being realized in the form of cash? Profitable companies that have negative operating cycle cash flows may be using accounting gimmicks or

artificially boosting sales to create the illusion of success when, in fact, they have serious operating problems.

3. How is the company financing its long-term investments? The use of short-term debt to finance capital expenditures may expose the company to financial difficulties should short-term interest rates rise. Or, alternatively, if the company is using short-term debt because it thinks long-term interest rates may fall and this will provide an opportunity to refinance using long-term debt, it may get into trouble if long- and short-term rates both rise.

4. Is the company able to generate sufficient cash internally to finance its requirements? Overreliance on external financing may put the company in a precarious position if the capital markets encounter difficulties or develop a negative attitude toward the company.

Other Analytical Techniques

Funds statements when presented as simple balance sheet account changes may not fully explain all of a company's fund transactions. In these cases T accounts may be used to derive the missing amounts.

If a company has disposed of property plant and equipment, the change in the allowance for the depreciation account will be less than the annual depreciation expense. When these relationships exist, the analyst should attempt to identify the book value of the asset sold and determine whether or not the disposal resulted in a gain or loss. To illustrate the technique used to identify the book value of the assets sold, assume the following account balances and announced property transactions:

Beginning property account balance	$100
Closing property account balance	120
Announced purchases	30
Beginning allowance for depreciation balance	60
Ending allowance for depreciation balance	70
Depreciation expense	20

The first step in the analysis is to set up the T accounts for the fixed asset and allowance for depreciation accounts. Next, enter the known transactions. The plug figure needed on the credit side of the account to derive the ending fixed asset balance is the original cost of the asset removed from the account. Similarly, the plug figure on the debit side of the allowance for depreciation is the accumulated depreciation related to this asset. The net of these two plug figures is the asset's book value. Illustration 6–12 presents the T account analysis to derive the book value of an asset disposal using the above figures. Any gain or loss on the asset disposal should be reported in the income statement. Also, since losses on disposal are nonfund

ILLUSTRATION 6–12
Asset Disposal Book Value Calculation

Property Plant and Equipment				Allowance for Depreciation			
Debit		*Credit*		*Debit*		*Credit*	
Beginning balance	$100	Disposals (plug)	10	Reversals (plug)	10	Beginning balance	$60
Additions	30					Additions	20
Ending balance	$120					Ending balance	$70

Book Value Calculation	
Property, plant, and equipment credit	$10
Less allowance for depreciation debit	10
Book value of disposal	$ 0

items, they should also be reported as part of the funds from operations calculation.

Typically, the funds statements presented in interim reports are skimpy. The analyst should always expand these statements using the techniques described in this chapter.

Another occasion when T account analysis may be helpful is when the change in an intangible asset does not equal the amount expensed in the income statement. This occurs when an addition is made to the asset account. The amount added is the plug figure required to make the account's ending balance correct, after all of the known balances and transactions have been recorded in the T account.

T accounts can also be helpful in keeping track of the long-term debt related funds flows when transfers are made between the long-term debt and the current maturities on long-term debt accounts. When using T accounts to untangle these movements, remember (1) the transfer between the two accounts is not a cash item, and (2) the opening balance of the current maturities on long-term debt account should have been paid off during the annual period.

Cash Flow per Share

Some analysts and financial reporting services give considerable weight to a figure commonly called "cash flow per share," which is usually defined as net profit after taxes plus noncash expenses such as depreciation. Often, the impression is given that cash flow per share is superior to net income as a measure of management performance. In response to this point of view, the APB in *Opinion No. 3* stated:

> The amount of funds derived from operations cannot be considered as a substitute for or an improvement upon properly determined net income as a measure of results of operations and the consequent effect on financial

position. Misleading implications can result from isolated statistics in annual reports of "cash flow" which are not placed in proper perspective to net income figures and to a complete analysis of source and application of funds. "Cash flow" and related terms should not be used in annual reports in such a way that the significance of net income is impaired, and "cash earnings" or other terms with a similar connotation should be avoided. The board regards computations of "cash flow per share" as misleading since they ignore the impact of cash expenditures for renewal and replacement of facilities and tend to downgrade the significant economic statistic of "earnings per share."

Cash flow per share computed by adding nonfund expenses back to net income is not cash flow, since it does not recognize that revenues may be tied up in accounts receivable and some expenses not yet paid. It is a funds concept, not a cash flow value.

APPENDIX 6–A

Use of Working Papers for Preparation of Statement of Changes in Financial Position

It was noted earlier that the statements of changes in financial position could be prepared directly from the differences between balance sheet accounts at the beginning and close of the accounting period. Minimum analysis of account balances is ordinarily required to obtain the needed information. When the number of accounts is unusually great or when transactions are complex, it may be desirable to use working papers to assemble the information for the funds statement in an orderly manner.

The working paper for the changes in financial position statement of the Dexter Company is presented in Illustration 6–A–1, as an example of the procedure which might be used to eliminate inaccuracy and confusion. The broader financial resources definition of funds and the change in working capital format are used. The following additional information is offered to make the illustration more comprehensive. During the year, Dexter issued $12,000 in long-term notes payable for fixed assets, charged $5,000 of goodwill and $35,000 of depreciation to earnings, and received $10,000 for its capital stock with a par value of $8,000. Operations resulted in net income after taxes of $20,000, and dividends of $5,000 were declared and paid during 1986.

The working paper consists of five pairs of columns in which net changes in the balance sheet accounts are computed, adjusted if necessary, and classified to assemble information needed for preparation of the funds flow statement. In the first pair of columns, the balance sheet accounts at the beginning and close of the period are listed, and net changes during the year are extended into the second pair of columns. In the Adjustments columns, certain of the net changes are eliminated, combined, or separated into component items after considering the effect upon funds flow. New accounts are created in the lower part of the worksheet to handle reclassification or labeling of items for the funds flow statement. The noncurrent items explaining funds flow are extended into the Funds Applied and Funds Provided columns, while current assets and liabilities are extended into the

ILLUSTRATION 6-A-1

DEXTER COMPANY
Working Paper Changes in Financial Position Statement
For the Year Ended December 31, 1986
(in thousands of dollars)

Accounts	Balances, 1985	December 31, 1986	Net Changes Debit	Net Changes Credit	Adjustments Debit	Adjustments Credit	Funds Applied Debit	Funds Provided Credit	Working Capital Increases Debit	Working Capital Decreases Credit
Debit balances:										
Cash	50	60	10						10	
Marketable securities	20	25	5						5	
Receivables	71	65		6						6
Inventories	74	82	8						8	
Fixed assets	320	373	53		(3) 5	(6) 53				
Goodwill	5	—		5						
	540	605								
Credit balances:										
Accumulated depreciation	65	100		35	(4) 35					
Current payables	105	100	5						5	
Long-term notes payable	80	90		10	(5) 12	(7) 2				
Capital stock at par	180	188		8	(8) 8					
Other paid-in capital	20	22		2	(8) 2					
Retained earnings	90	105		15	(1) 20	(2) 5				
	540	605	81	81						
Funds provided by operations:										
Net income per income statement						(1) 20		60		
Add: Depreciation						(4) 35				
Add: Amortization of goodwill						(3) 5				
Funds applied to dividends					(2) 5		5			
Funds provided by long-term notes						(5) 12		12		
Funds applied to purchase fixed assets					(6) 53		53			
Funds applied to retirement of long-term notes					(7) 2		2			
Funds provided by sale of capital stock						(8) 10		10		
					142	142	60	82	28	6
Increase in working capital							22			22
							82	82	28	28

final pair of Working Capital columns. The computation of the balance "increase in working capital" in the fourth and fifth pairs of columns aids in proving mathematical accuracy of the worksheet.

The eight keyed adjustments of the worksheet are explained briefly:

1. Net income of $20,000 for the year is entered as the explanation for increased retained earnings.

2. Dividends of $5,000 required the expenditure of funds and caused a corresponding decrease in retained earnings.

3. Amortization of goodwill is recorded as a nonfund addition to income, as the charge did not result in a funds outflow.

4. Depreciation charged for the year of $35,000 (the amount of the increase in accumulated depreciation shown as a credit balance in 6–A–1) is recorded as an addition to net income to compute total funds derived from operations.

5. The $12,000 issue of long-term notes payable for fixed assets is recognized. In the strictest sense, working capital was not affected by this transaction. However, in order to present funds flow in a broader manner, the event is treated as though notes payable had been issued for cash which was immediately paid for fixed assets.

6. The acquisition of fixed assets for $53,000 is entered. (This amount includes $12,000 acquired by issuing long-term notes payable. See 5 above.)

7. Payment of long-term notes payable of $2,000 can be inferred from the net increase of $10,000 during the year and the effect of adjustment 5 above. The notes payable account increased by $10,000. However, we know that $12,000 of notes payable were issued. Therefore, $2,000 of notes payable were retired.

8. Proceeds from the sale of capital stock is identified on the working paper as a single item by bringing together the net increases in the capital stock and other paid-in capital accounts.

The worksheet should not be considered a substitute for the changes in financial position statement. It merely provides a means for assembling the information for the statement. The formal changes in financial position statement can be easily prepared from the amounts extended into the Funds Applied and Provided columns, as shown in Illustration 6–A–2.

The Dexter Company total cash flow statement shown in Illustration 6–A–3 is reconciled to the changes in cash and marketable securities balance ($15,000). This is in contrast to the working paper in Illustration 6–A–1 and funds statement shown in Illustration 6–A–2. They reconcile to the change in net working capital ($22,000).

A number of alternative forms of the funds flow working paper might be used instead of the particular columnar headings and procedures illustrated. For example, the entire working paper could be simplified significantly by omitting the first and last pairs of columns and using only net

ILLUSTRATION 6–A–2

DEXTER COMPANY
Changes in Financial Position
For the Year Ended December 31, 1986

Funds sources:

From operations:

Net income for the year	$20	
Depreciation and amortization of goodwill	40	$60
Increase in long-term debt		12
Sale of capital stock		10
Total		$82

Funds applications:

Dividends paid	$ 5
Purchase of capital equipment	53
Repayment of long-term debt	2
Increase in working capital	$22

Increases (decreases) in working capital:

Increase in cash	$10
Increase in marketable securities	5
Decrease in receivables	(6)
Increase in inventories	8
Decrease in payables	5
Increase in working capital	$22

ILLUSTRATION 6–A–3

DEXTER COMPANY
Changes in Financial Position
For the Year Ended December 31, 1986

Net income	$20
Adjustments for items not representing current fund usage:	
Depreciation and amortization of goodwill	40
Decrease in receivables	6
Increase in inventories	(8)
Decrease in payables	(5)
Cash generated from operating cycle	$53
Purchase of capital equipment	(53)
Dividends paid	(5)
Cash flow before external financing	$ (5)
Repayment of long-term debt	(2)
Increase in long-term debt	12
Sale of capital stock	10
Increase in cash and marketable securities	$15

---

changes in the noncurrent accounts along with the single balancing amount of the net increase (or decrease) in working capital. Simplifications of this type emphasize that statements of changes in financial position may ordinarily be prepared directly from comparative balance sheets with a minimum analysis of accounts.

CASE 6-1

Lakeland Airlines, Incorporated
Determination of Funds Flow Disclosure Policy

On January 15, 1984, the board of directors of Lakeland Airlines, Inc., was considering what the content and format of the statement of changes in financial position should be that the company intended to include in its 1983 annual report to stockholders. The directors believed the funds flow statement should greatly enhance the ability of stockholders to analyze the company's activities as well as provide management with a useful means of communication with stockholders.

The Company

Lakeland Airlines, Inc., was founded in 1952 by Mr. John Drew, a former military air transport pilot. Originally the airline's only aircraft, a Korean war surplus Douglas DC–3, operated between Philadelphia and a number of small towns in upper Pennsylvania. During the following years, as more and more cities built airports and existing feeder lines went out of business, the company acquired CAB approval to fly additional routes throughout the mid-Atlantic states. Then, following the deregulation of airlines, the company expanded its operation to include Ohio, West Virginia, Kentucky, and upper New York state.

Initially, Mr. Drew financed his expansion through the sale of common stock and convertible debentures to a number of the major industrial companies within the area serviced by his company. These companies bought Lakeland stock so that the cities where their plants were located would have reliable air service. In 1970, in order to finance the acquisition of a number of more modern aircraft, Lakeland offered some common shares to the public. This offering was well received and the securities were traded actively on the New York over-the-counter market. Subsequently, in 1975,

This case was prepared by F. R. Madera (under the direction of David F. Hawkins).

Copyright © 1965 by the President and Fellows of Harvard College

Harvard Business School case 110–095 (Revised 1985)

a larger common stock offering was made in order to finance the purchase of several small jet aircraft. As of December 31, 1983, Lakeland had over 2,500 stockholders, of which 25 were corporations in towns serviced by Lakeland.

Through its 31-year history, Lakeland had almost constantly been short of cash, principally because of its policy of using the most modern aircraft available for its type of business and the increasing investments required to service its expanding route system. Consequently, small dividends had been declared only twice, and the company had entered into a number of bank loans. While no stockholder had ever questioned the "no dividend–

EXHIBIT 1

LAKELAND AIRLINES, INC.
Income Statement
For the Year Ended December 31, 1983
(millions of dollars)

Operating revenue:	
Commercial revenue	$25.6
Federal subsidy	4.2
Total operating revenue	$29.8
Operating expense:	
Flying operations	$ 7.3
Direct maintenance, flight equipment	4.5
Depreciation, flight equipment*	1.0
Total direct expense	$12.8
Direct maintenance, ground equipment	$ 0.3
Maintenance burden	1.9
Passenger servicing	1.1
Aircraft servicing	2.9
Traffic servicing	3.4
Reservation and sales	2.9
General and administrative	1.5
Depreciation, ground equipment*	0.3
Development and preoperating costs	0.1
Total indirect expense	$14.4
Total operating expense	$27.2
Operating profit	$ 2.6
Nonoperating expense:	
Interest and amortization of debt expense	$ 0.3
All other expense (income)	(0.1)
Total nonoperating expense	$ 0.2
Net income before taxes and special item	$ 2.4
Provision for federal income taxes:*	
Current	$ 1.0
Deferred	0.1
Total income taxes	$ 1.1
Net earnings before special item	$ 1.3
Special item:	
Amortization of goodwill	0.1
Net earnings retained for the year	$ 1.2

---

* See Note D to Exhibit 2.

heavy bank loan" policy, Mr. Drew believed many of the stockholders did not really understand the company's financial policy.

In early 1983, Lakeland acquired the Pioneer Airlines, a major feeder line servicing parts of West Virginia, Ohio, and Kentucky. Lakeland exchanged shares with a market value of $2.5 million for the Pioneer plant, equipment, and routes. These assets were carried on Pioneer's books at $2 million. The excess of investment over these values was added to the Lakeland Goodwill account. The board intended to write this goodwill off as a special charge against income over a five-year period, beginning in 1983.

To bring the Pioneer service up to Lakeland's high standards of quality, two secondhand turboprop planes were added to the Pioneer fleet at a cost of $1.7 million. In order to finance this purchase, $1 million was borrowed from the Marine Merchants Bank, New York, and $0.7 million of stock was sold to several insurance companies. In the near future, Mr. Drew planned to replace these aircraft with small jets.

John Drew's ambition was to build Lakeland into a major airline before he retired in 1990. Therefore, he anticipated there would be more stock issues, more route acquisitions, more bank loans, and more equipment investments during the remaining years of his presidency.

Exhibits 1 and 2 present the 1983 financial statements management planned to include in the 1983 annual report to stockholders. The 1982 balance sheet is also shown in Exhibit 2.

Questions

1. Why should companies like Lakeland include a statement of changes in financial position in their annual report to stockholders?
2. Which definition of "funds" do you think Lakeland should adopt?
3. Construct the 1983 statement of changes in financial position that you believe Lakeland should present to its stockholders.
4. Prepare a one-paragraph interpretive comment explaining the significant flows indicated by your statement.

EXHIBIT 2

LAKELAND AIRLINES, INC.
Balance Sheets at December 31, 1983 and 1982
(millions of dollars)

Resources

	1983	1982
Current assets:		
Cash	$ 2.1	$ 0.8
Accounts receivable:		
U.S. government agencies	0.7	0.9
Airline traffic, less reserve	2.2	2.0
Other, less reserve	0.3	0.3
Inventories (Note A)	1.9	1.7
Prepaid expenses	0.3	0.2
Total current assets	$ 7.5	$ 5.9
Assets applied to aircraft order (Note B):		
Cash deposits, restricted	$ 0.0	$ 3.6
Deposits on aircraft and engines	4.3	0.5
Aircraft acquisition costs	0.4	0.3
Total	$ 4.7	$ 4.4
Operating property and equipment (at cost):		
Flight equipment (Notes B, C)	$13.5	$12.4
Ground property and equipment	2.0	1.7
Construction in progress	0.0	0.1
	$15.5	$14.2
Less: Amortization and depreciation provisions (Note D)	6.9	6.0
Net operating property and equipment	$ 8.6	$ 8.2

Liabilities and Shareholders' Equity

	1983	1982
Current liabilities:		
Equipment obligations (Note B)	$ 0.5	$ 0.3
Accounts payable and accrued expenses	3.6	4.0
Accrued taxes on income (Note D)	1.0	0.2
Unearned transportation revenue	0.2	0.1
Total current liabilities	$ 5.3	$ 4.6
Long-term debt (Note C):		
Equipment obligations	0.7	0.4
Subordinated notes and debentures	6.4	9.2
Total long-term debt	$ 7.1	$ 9.6
Future liabilities:		
Deferred income taxes (Note D)	0.4	0.3
Lease and purchase commitments (Notes B, E)	0.0	0.0
Total future liabilities	$ 0.4	$ 0.3
Shareholders' equity:		
Capital stock, common $1 par, authorized shares, 3 million; outstanding shares:		
1,770,142, less 57,220 in treasury	1.7	
1,143,906, less 57,220 in treasury		1.1
Additional paid-in capital	5.8	3.2
Retained earnings	1.6	0.4
Total shareholders' equity	$ 9.1	$ 4.7

EXHIBIT 2 *(concluded)*

Deferred charges:		
Development and preoperating costs	$ 0.3	
Discount and expense on debt	0.1	
Total deferred charges	$ 0.4	
Other assets:		
Investments and advances	$ 0.1	
Notes receivable:		
Officers, secured by capital stock	0.0	
Goodwill	0.4	
Capital stock expense	0.2	
Total other assets	$ 0.7	
Total resources	$21.9	

	$ 0.2	
	0.2	
	$ 0.4	
	$ 0.1	
	0.1	
	0.0	
	0.1	
	$ 0.3	
Total liabilities and shareholders' equity	$21.9	$19.2
		$19.2

A. Inventories. The company's inventories consist of operating supplies and aircraft expendable parts. These inventories are carried at cost less valuation reserves established to provide for estimated losses from obsolescence and deterioration.

B. Replacement of flight equipment. The company has signed contracts and letters of intent under which it will during 1984–87 sell or trade most of its present aircraft and will purchase fan-jet and turbo prop aircraft. Net cost of the new aircraft is estimated at $49 million. Under contractual agreements, the company has made payments aggregating $4.3 million in advance of delivery on its purchase of aircraft and fan-jet engines. Preacquisition costs, including financing expense, incurred for purpose of acquiring these aircraft have been capitalized.

C. Notes payable and long-term debt. Equipment obligations and subordinated notes and debentures mature in various amounts over a 14-year period ending 1997. Six of the company's aircraft are pledged to secure equipment notes. The company has a bank loan commitment for $6 million and an informal agreement to obtain loans aggregating as much as $34 million in connection with its acquisition of new aircraft.

D. Income taxes. Current income taxes are shown net after deducting allowable investment credits. Adjustments of relatively immaterial amounts have been made in deferred income taxes to reflect changes caused by various changes in the tax code. Deferred income tax liability results primarily from use of straight-line depreciation and amortization rates for statement purposes, while accelerated methods are used in computing deductions for current income taxes.

E. Lease commitments. The company's headquarters and primary maintenance plant, as well as facilities in communities served by Lakeland, are entirely leased. Terms of these leases and contracts vary from 30 days to 25 years. It is estimated that present commitments will require annual net payments of approximately $1.3 million.

PART THREE

Role of Certified Public Accountants' Opinion in Corporate Reporting and Analysis

CHAPTER 7

The Auditor's Opinion

The financial statements published by management are usually accompanied by a signed auditor's report. It means that a member of a licensed profession, who is morally bound to exercise competent independent judgment, has examined management's financial statements to the extent necessary and stakes his or her professional reputation upon the opinion that the financial statements present fairly the financial position and results of operations of the company. The criteria used to judge the professional competence of the audit are "generally accepted auditing standards." The criteria for forming an opinion on the fairness of the statements taken as a whole are "generally accepted accounting principles."

Thus, the auditor's report expresses professional opinion. For many years, it was customary for auditors to use the phrase "we hereby certify" in their reports on financial statements. Even today the term "auditor's certificate" is used interchangeably with "auditor's report." This unfortunate terminology may be partly responsible for the confusion as to the nature of the auditor's work. The professional auditor may well be certified by a state licensing board, but the auditor does not certify financial statements.

Almost all publicly owned businesses offer audited statements, because they are required by stock exchange regulations or federal or state laws or because management recognizes a responsibility to include auditors' opinions in its report to stockholders.

Statement users must rely heavily on the auditor's opinion certificate, since they cannot independently verify management's assertions, estimates, and judgments embodied in financial statements. Consequently, it is important that statement users know what an audit report does and does not mean, as well as the procedures used by auditors to reach their opinions on financial statements. Typically, auditors' opinions are helpful to statement users when they are prepared by competent auditors who feel a responsibility to those who must rely upon their work and management's representations. Occasionally, audit examinations are conducted by incompetent audi-

145

tors, and their opinions or "certificates" can be very misleading. To protect themselves against these auditors, experienced statement analysts seldom accept the auditor's opinion as sufficient assurance without first making their own assessment of the company's quality of earnings, management's accounting estimates and judgments, and reporting company's ability to meet maturing obligations. In addition, astute statement users are aware of corporate conditions that are likely to lead to financial statement fraud, which may be difficult for the auditor to detect during the audit examination. When they find these conditions, statement users must exercise extreme caution and not depend too much on the auditor's opinion.

The Auditing Profession

Two characteristics which make the professional auditor opinion on published financial statements useful are independence and competence. The role of the auditor will continue to be significant only to the extent that the public continues to attribute these two qualities to the profession of public acccountancy.

From the public's point of view, independence is perhaps the more important of the auditor's characteristics; certainly it is the more difficult for the auditor to achieve. A basic conflict arises because the client whose financial statements are examined pays for the auditor's services. To be independent, professional auditors must be prepared to give higher priority to their responsibilities to third-party readers of financial reports than to their continued services to a particular client. This attitude of public responsibility and service is an essential characteristic of a profession and distinguishes it from commerical enterprise. By achieving this sense of public responsibility, public accountants have earned the right to call auditing a profession.

Competence is the second characteristic which the auditor must achieve and maintain. Professional accountants offering services to the public must comply with the licensing restrictions of the states in which they practice. Public accountancy boards are appointed by the state governors to administer each state's public accounting regulations. Those who wish to become certified public accountants must pass an examination, given simultaneously by each state board, that is prepared and graded by the American Institute of Certified Public Accountants. Typically, candidates must meet qualifying requirements of citizenship, education, experience, and personal character. These licensing requirements protect the public interest by restricting the practice of pubic accountancy to those who have a demonstrated proficiency in accounting and its applications.

The American Institute of Certified Public Accountants is a national organization whose members are subject to a code of professional ethics adopted voluntarily and enforced by the group. Training and professional development programs are sponsored continually. The institute has, as the voice of the accounting profession, assumed the position of leadership in the development of auditing standards. Its publications include the *Journal of Accountancy, Statements on Auditing Standards, Guides, Statements of Position,* and many technical and professional books and pamphlets.

Auditors, as members of a profession, have a legal responsibility to their clients and to third parties who might be injured by shortcomings in an auditor's opinions. As a general rule, the client may recover damages from auditors who have been negligent in the performance of their examinations, and third parties may claim damages in case of auditor's fraud, negligence, or failure to adhere to professional standards.

The professional accountant offers services to the public in a number of areas related to financial reporting and management. Traditionally, the certified public accountant is best known as an auditor who reviews the accounting statements and records of business firms and renders an opinion on them. The work of the professional accountant also includes preparation of tax returns and counseling in related matters, installation of accounting systems, and management consulting services. The following comments are concerned only with auditing.

The Auditor's Report

The auditor's report is addressed to the directors and stockholders of the client corporation. It usually follows closely a standard form and language. A typical short-form report is presented in Illustration 7–1. Each word and

ILLUSTRATION 7–1

Report of Independent Certified Public Accountants

To Share Owners and Board of Directors of
General Electric Company

We have examined the statement of financial position of General Electric Company and consolidated affiliates as of December 31, 1984, and 1983, and the related statements of earnings and changes in financial position for each of the years in the three-year period ended December 31, 1984. Our examinations were made in accordance with generally accepted auditing standards and, accordingly, included such tests of the accounting records and such other auditing procedures as we considered necessary in the circumstances.

In our opinion, the aforementioned financial statements appearing on pages 26, 28, 30, and 38–49 present fairly the financial position of General Electric Company and consolidated affiliates at December 31, 1984, and 1983, and the results of their operations and the changes in their financial position for each of the years in the three-year period ended December 31, 1984, in conformity with generally accepted accounting principles applied on a consistent basis.

Peat, Marwick, Mitchell & Co.
345 Park Avenue, New York, N.Y. 10154

February 15, 1985

---

phrase in this report has been carefully chosen to describe concisely the examination and to state the opinion to which the examination has led.

The first paragraph of the standard short-form report is called the "scope paragraph" and emphasizes that the auditor's examination has conformed to "generally accepted auditing standards." Auditing standards are the criteria for measuring the quality of the auditor's performance in his or her engagements. The auditing standards generally accepted by the profession are:[1]

General Standards

1. The examination is to be performed by a person or persons having adequate technical training and proficiency as an auditor.
2. In all matters relating to the assignment an independence in mental attitude is to be maintained by the auditor or auditors.
3. Due professional care is to be exercised in the performance of the examination and the preparation of the report.

Standards of Field Work

1. The work is to be adequately planned and assistants, if any, are to be properly supervised.
2. There is to be a proper study and evaluation of the existing internal control as a basis for reliance thereon and for the determination of the resultant extent of the tests to which auditing procedures are to be restricted.
3. Sufficient competent evidential matter is to be obtained through inspection, observations, inquiries, and confirmations to afford a reasonable basis for an opinion regarding the financial statements under examination.

Standards of Reporting

1. The report shall state whether the financial statements are presented in accordance with generally accepted principles of accounting.
2. The report shall state whether such principles have been consistently observed in the current period in relation to the preceding period.
3. Informative disclosures in the financial statements are to be regarded as reasonably adequate unless otherwise stated in the report.
4. The report shall either contain an expression of opinion regarding the financial statements, taken as a whole, or an assertion to the effect that an opinion cannot be expressed. When an overall opinion cannot be expressed, the reasons therefore should be stated. In all cases where an auditor's name is associated with financial statements, the report should contain a clear-cut indication of the character

---

[1] These standards are explained in greater detail in the various *Statements on Auditing Standards* published by the American Institute of Certified Public Accountants.

of the auditor's examination, if any, and the degree of responsibility he or she is taking.

The second paragraph of the standard short form is called the "opinion paragraph." In a single sentence the auditor attests that the financial statements:

1. Present fairly the financial position and the results of operations.
2. Are in conformity with generally accepted accounting principles.
3. Are on a basis consistent with that of the prior year.

The phrase "present fairly" means that the opinion applies to the statements taken as a whole. The auditor does not imply that any single item on the statements is exact or precisely correct. Instead, the auditor attests that the statements as a whole are a complete disclosure and free from any material bias or misstatement.

"Generally accepted accounting principles" is perhaps the most debated phrase in the area of financial accounting. Though the term has been commonly used for many years, no single definition or listing of principles has been universally accepted by accounting theorists and practitioners.

The most authoritative enumeration of accounting principles has been published by the Financial Accounting Standards Board. Members of the AICPA are required to disclose departures from these principles in financial statements. Another authoritative source is the publications of the Securities and Exchange Commission.

The auditor's reference to "consistency" assures the reader that accounting procedures and statement presentation methods used for the current period do not vary from those of the comparative statements presented for previous years. This uniformity allows useful comparisons of financial position and operating results for successive periods.

The SEC requires the auditors of companies registered with the SEC to comment in situations when the client company has adopted a new accounting principle.

Forms of the Audit Report

The auditor's opinion can be expressed in four different forms: (1) an unqualified opinion, (2) a qualified opinion, (3) an adverse opinion, and (4) a disclaimer of opinion. The choice of the form of opinion and the language used in departures from the recommended short-form opinion are a part of the auditor's responsibility for applying informed judgment in all matters concerning the audit.

The auditor's standard short-form report presented earlier illustrated an unqualified opinion. The auditor made no reservations and stated no conditions precedent to the opinion about the fairness of management's financial statements. In most audit engagements, conditions which might lead to a restricted opinion can be eliminated by agreement between the auditor and the client to extend the auditing procedure or revise the financial statements.

The qualified opinion includes a statement indicting that the auditor is unable to express a full unqualified opinion. There are a number of reasons why this style of opinion might be appropriate. The client's unwillingness to permit some essential auditing procedure, such as confirming accounts receivable or observation of the taking of inventories, would require qualification of the auditor's opinion. The auditor's failure to agree with the propriety of an accounting method or a presentation on the financial statements would also result in a qualification. Phrases, including "except" or "exception," are usually inserted in either or both paragraphs of the short-form opinion together with a necessary explanation why the auditor used a qualified opinion. Occasionally, an opinion notes another type of qualification; the phrase "subject to," followed by an explanation of uncertainties about valuation or realization of assets or prediction of contingent liabilities, is used when the auditor has reservations regarding these items as represented by management but can neither reject nor accept management's accounting decision. In recent years, the use of the "subject to" opinion form has been discouraged by the AICPA.

An adverse opinion is a completely negative expression by the auditor about the fairness of the financial statements. If exceptions concerning fairness of presentation are so material that a qualified opinion would not be justified, the auditor must state in the opinion that the statements "do not present fairly" the financial position and results of operations. A separate paragraph inserted between the scope and opinion paragraphs of the short-form report presents the reasons for the adverse opinion. This type of report is rarely published; an engagement leading to an adverse opinion would probably be terminated prior to its completion.

The disclaimer of opinion is a pronouncement by the auditor that this auditor is unable to express any of the preceding three types of opinion on the financial statements. A disclaimer is used when the auditor has not obtained "sufficient competent evidential matter" to form an opinion on the fairness of the financial statements. The reasons for the use of the disclaimer, which must be fully disclosed, might include a serious limitation on the scope of the examination, the existence of unusual uncertainties concerning the amounts reported in the statements, or the possibility that the client's business may not continue.

Frequently, the auditor's examination results in a so-called long-form report. Management and creditors may find this type of report more useful for their purposes. It contains all the essential elements of the more familiar short form as well as supplementary information about the business entity, its financial position, and operations. The examining procedures used and the responsibility of the auditor are the same for both the short- and long-form reports.

Typically, the auditor's short-form report presented in annual reports to stockholders covers the comparative balance sheets, income statements, statements of retained earnings, funds flow statements, and the notes accompanying these statements. Other financial and nonfinancial information included elsewhere in the annual report is not usually covered by the auditor's opinion.

The Auditor's Work

Auditors use a variety of techniques to examine the financial statements of a company. The techniques applied in carrying out an "audit program" can be grouped into four categories: internal analysis, inspection, external communication, and analytical review. The specific auditing procedures used in any engagement will be determined by the relevance of the "Standards of Field Work" to the particular situation. As noted earlier, these standards relate to planning and supervision, evaluation of the internal control system, and evidential matter.

The Audit Plan

After appraisal of the company's situation, the auditor prepares an audit plan, which schedules audit procedures and indicates the extent to which they will be applied during the course of the audit. This formalized plan of audit procedures serves several vital needs. First, it enables the auditor to anticipate time and manning requirements. Second, it permits effective assignment of assistants and facilitates the coordination of their efforts. Third, the audit program serves as a master list of the audit procedures used for indexing of working papers prepared during the examination. Some audit firms have developed standard "checklist" programs to ensure that no essential procedure is omitted. Other firms insist that the auditor in charge prepare a program specifically for each engagement. In any event, each audit will require program modifications to fit the requirements of the investigation. The program is subject to constant revision as the audit progresses and new circumstances come to light during the examination. In this sense, the audit plan is not in final form until the entire audit is completed and the auditor's report has been drafted.

Since the audit is essentially an examination of the financial statements, it is logical that investigations of the financial accounts are, in general, accomplished in the order of their appearance on the balance sheet and on the income statement. However, the interrelationship of the accounts makes it impractical to audit any single segment of the client's operations without recognizing the effect upon other accounts. For example, the examination of accounts receivable will directly relate to cash receipts, income recognition, and finished goods shipments. Therefore, the audit proceeds by investigation of various areas of functional activity rather than of individual account balances.

Evaluation of Internal Controls

Early in the examination, the auditor must make a study of the organization's internal controls. The system of internal controls includes all measures instituted by management (1) to ensure accuracy and dependability of financial data, (2) to protect assets from improper or inefficient use, and (3) to control and evaluate operations.

The modern auditor is concerned with all administrative aspects of the business entity examined as well as its financial records and properties. The extent of the auditing procedures to be required by the auditor will depend almost entirely upon the adequacy of the system of internal controls. The evaluation of internal controls continues throughout the entire course of the audit. Financial and administrative procedures are investigated by inquiry and observation. Usually the results of this essential part of the examination are summarized in a separate report to management, together with recommendations for improved internal controls. The auditor's evaluation of internal controls is the basis for determining the reliability of the resulting financial statements. If the internal controls are weak, the amount of evidential matter the auditor requires to reach an opinion on the financial statements will be greater than if the internal controls are judged to be strong.

Auditing Procedures

A comprehensive view of auditing procedures would require detailed consideration of the many groups of accounts which make up the financial statements. For our purposes, auditing procedures might be classified by the types of investigative activities employed by the auditor: (1) internal analysis, (2) inspection, (3) external communication, and (4) analytical review. Each of these is considered briefly to describe the varied techniques the auditor uses to form an opinion of management's financial statements.

Testing and sampling are employed extensively throughout the audit procedure. It would be impractical (and probably impossible) for the auditor to examine and review all records and activities of a business entity. The auditor's judgment, supplemented to an increasing extent by scientific sampling methods, is the basis for determining testing procedures.

Internal Analysis. A major part of the auditor's time is devoted to an analysis of the company's internal financial records. Internal analysis to verify mathematical accuracy is minimized by the presence of effective internal controls. Many of the accounts are analyzed for an independent verification of changes and balances. For example, receivable and payable accounts may be analyzed and listed for subsequent investigation. Plant asset and security investment accounts are analyzed to show necessary details of balances. Supporting business documents such as purchase invoices, checks issued, and cash remittance receipts are traced and compared to the accounting entries. The client's employees may assist with clerical work, but the auditor's independence must be maintained by close supevision and verification.

Inspection.   Auditors make extensive visual inspections of their client's properties to satisfy themselves that assets are properly presented. Cash on hand is counted and securities are inspected for reconciliation with records. Physical inventories taken by the client's employees are observed by the auditor. Plant assets may be inspected at least to a limited extent. These inspections and observations must be coordinated with the client's business operations and with preparation of appropriate analyses of the financial accounts.

External Communication.   The auditor should communicate directly with individuals, businesses, and institutions having dealings with the audit client. These external communications or confirmations aid the auditor in verifying relationships independently of the client's records. Information is requested from outsiders only with the client's approval and cooperation. Confirmations might be obtained (1) from banks, to verify balances of cash on deposit and amounts of indebtedness; (2) from trade creditors; (3) from customers; (4) from corporate transfer agents and registrars; (5) from sinking fund trustees; (6) from public warehouses; and (7) from others, such as appraisers and attorneys. In addition, the auditor may use specialists to conform management's assertions that involve technical considerations beyond the auditor's competence. Typically, these direct communications with third parties produce highly credible evidence for the auditor in forming an independent opinion.

Analytical Review.   An analytical review of the relationships between data shown by the financial records and revealed during the audit examination adds significantly to the auditor's satisfaction with the resulting financial statements. It is in this general area that the ingenuity and imagination of the auditor become especially important. For example, comparisons of the client's current bad debt losses with those of prior periods and with those for other businesses in the industry provide insights into the adequacy of the client's current bad debt provisions. Analysis of changes in departmental gross profit, percentages, and inventory turnover may help substantiate the recorded income and inventory levels. Comparisons of income from securities with records of security ownership adds assurance that financial statements present consistent data. Property tax payments will corroborate property ownership.

Audit Committee

Corporations appoint audit committees of their board of directors. These committees consist of outside directors. Their function is to monitor the corporations' corporate reporting practices, review the work of the company's auditors as to audit scope and results, and watch over the quality and appropriateness of the company's internal controls. The widespread appointment of such committees has been viewed favorably on the ground that involving outside board members in the corporate reporting process should reduce some shortcomings of corporate reports prepared and published by management without board review.

Detecting Financial Statement Fraud

Auditors cannot be relied upon to detect every case of financial statement fraud. Neither can statement users expect to catch fraudulent statements that go undetected during an auditor's examination. The best protection for statement users is always to be alert to the possibility of statement fraud and to be aware of the conditions likely to encourage it. Then, when these conditions are encountered and an analysis of the company's statements produces an uneasy feeling on the part of the user that something is wrong, that statement user should begin to suspect statement fraud is a possibility and act accordingly.

In most cases of revealed financial statement fraud one or more of the following conditions existed:

- The chief executive officer managed by setting ambitious simple financial objectives, such as a compound earnings growth rate of 25 percent per year.
- The chief executive officer had a low regard for the financial and accounting functions.
- The nonmanagement members of the board of directors played a passive role in the board and company affairs.
- The management believed accounting choices and actions are a legitimate means to achieve the corporate goals.
- In the past the company had used questionable accounting that, while legitimate, nevertheless stretched the rules.
- The company had a rapid growth in earnings that was becoming harder to sustain because of internal weaknesses, market changes, or competitive developments.
- The company and its chief executive's future survival was very dependent on maintaining a high earnings growth rate.
- Management repeatedly issued optimistic statements about the company's future.

Statement users should not assume because the chief executive officer appears to be honest that everyone else in the organization is honest and therefore the probability of financial statement fraud is remote.

The chief executive officer is not always the individual responsible for committing the statement fraud. It can occur at lower levels in the organization, such as in the case of a factory manager responsible for sales shipping to nonexistent customers at year-end in order to meet an annual sales goal. Such action may go undetected because of weak internal controls and lax auditing.

To appreciate properly the significance of findings generated by financial statement analysis, the analyst must understand the business of the company whose statement is being analyzed. Auditors exercising due professional care are expected also to have a thorough understanding of the client's business. Statement users should be able to assume that this is the case, but it may be a dangerous assumption. Not all independent auditors have the required level of knowledge of their client's business. In these cases the audit plan is inevitably deficient. It is not responsive to the company circumstances. Also, the auditor tends to rely too much on management assurances as to estimates, judgments, and values incorporated in the financial statements. Under these circumstances management may be tempted to commit financial statement fraud. If this occurs, and the statement user acts on his or her analysis without a thorough understanding of the business, the statement user must share in part the blame for any adverse consequences of actions based on that analysis. Knowledge of the reporting company's business is a prerequisite for a competent analysis. It is also protection against becoming the victim of statement fraud.

Statement users should exercise extra caution with audit opinions issued by small certified public accounting firms. Financial statement fraud is more likely to occur when a company's statements are audited by a small local firm than when a major international accounting firm is involved. The smaller firm may not have the required audit skills and internal audit quality controls needed to detect fraud. On the other hand, an audit opinion from one of the major international accounting firms is not a guarantee that the statements are free from fraud. Whether the audit firm is big or small, audit opinions should be relied upon with caution. The best advice is to test the results of your analysis against your knowledge of the business and, if something seems troublesome, out of line with expectations, irregular, or not understandable, act accordingly. Do not wait to find out for sure if you are right or wrong. It may be too late by then.

Summary

Auditing procedures include an almost unlimited variety of investigations designed to help the auditor form an independent professional opinion on management's financial statements. This opinion is expressed in the audit report. In an unqualified report, the auditor states to management and owners that: (1) the auditor has completed an examination of the business in a manner required by the application of generally accepted auditing standards and (2) offers opinion, backed by competence and independence, that management's financial statements present fairly the entity's financial position and the results of its operation in accordance with generally accepted accounting practices. A competent audit generates financial data that statement users can rely upon with confidence. Unfortunately, in cases of auditor negligence this trust in the auditor's opinion can be misplaced and result in misleading conclusions. A statement user's best protection against incompetent audit opinions is a skeptical attitude that recognizes conditions where statement fraud may exist, a deep understanding of the statement issuer's business, and a thorough analysis of its financial statements.

CASE 7-1

Comet Service, Incorporated
Testing Internal Controls for Cash Receipts and Disbursements

Comet Service, Inc., was engaged in servicing and repairing elevator equipment. Maintenance service contracts were the major source of revenue. Substantial repair jobs furnished the remainder of the company's revenue. Annual sales were approximately $10 million, and there were about 150 men engaged in service and repair work.

The company had not been previously audited. Your public accounting firm has been engaged to make annual examinations. You have been assigned to review and test the cash receipts and disbursements procedures and to make suggestions for improvements where the internal accounting controls appear to be deficient.

The company's accounting staff consists of:

1. Cashier.
2. Assistant cashier, who also posted the detail accounts receivable ledger.
3. Bookkeeper.
4. Assistant bookkeeper.
5. Billing and job cost clerk.
6. Two general clerks—filing, general office work, incoming and outgoing mail.
7. Secretary.
8. Messenger.

The vice president, who is engaged mostly in the technical end of the business, is also the treasurer. You are favorably impressed with the caliber of the staff, who appear to carry out their duties efficiently. The accounting records are kept on a manual basis.

This case was prepared by David F. Hawkins.

Copyright © 1970 by the President and Fellows of Harvard College
Harvard Business School case 171–028

The following is a brief summary of the procedures as you have recorded them in your notes:

Cash Receipts

    a. All incoming remittances were received by check.

    b. Incoming mail was opened by one of the general clerks.

    c. Clerk prepared two adding machine tapes of checks as a means of control, one tape of checks accompanied by remittance advices and another of checks for which remittance advices were not received. On the latter tape, the clerk noted against each item the name of the customer for the information of the accounts receivable ledger clerk in posting collections. Tapes were delivered to the ledger clerk, who was also the assistant cashier.

    d. Clerk delivered checks to the cashier, who endorsed them, prepared bank deposit, agreed amount with tapes, and wrote up cash receipts entry, which was supported by the adding machine tapes and remittance advices received from customers.

    e. Bank deposit was taken to the bank by the assistant cashier.

Cash Disbursements

    a. Invoices were processed for payment by assistant bookkeeper; invoices were matched up with receiving reports (received directly from receiving department) and with copies of purchase orders as to quantity, description, and price; invoices were matched with freight and trucking charges (if any); mathematical accuracy of invoices was checked; work done was not initialed for by the assistant bookkeeper.

    b. On the 10th and 25th of the month (or on discount date), invoices were assembled by vendor and vouchered for payment by the assistant bookkeeper, who also kept the accounts payable ledger. Amounts vouchered were entered in the accounts payable ledger.

    c. The vouchers with documents attached were sent to the cashier, who prepared the checks and entered them in the cash disbursements book.

    d. Checks and vouchers with attached documents were sent by the cashier to the vice president–treasurer; he reviewed the vouchers and supports, initialed the vouchers, signed the checks (one signature only on checks), and sent them back to the cashier. The vouchers and supporting documents were not canceled with a dated paid stamp or by machine.

    e. As the recording of checks was time consuming, the cashier abbreviated somewhat by using initials only instead of full names for some companies (e.g., TCSI for Technical Control Systems, Inc.). Apparently, some of the larger suppliers emphasized intials on their invoices and letterheads, and they had no difficulty cashing checks prepared in this manner.

f. Upon occasion, a representative of the company was required to visit certain suppliers to expedite shipments of sorely needed material for jobs. For psychological reasons, it was decided that the request for early shipments would be aided by the presentation of a check in payment of past orders, and therefore certain checks were secured from the mail clerk before mailing.

g. No examination of endorsements on paid checks was made at any time by the cashier in making the monthly bank reconciliation.

Questions

1. On the basis of the foregoing information, what recommendations would you make for improvement in internal accounting controls over cash receipts and disbursements?

2. Based on your appraisal of the company's internal controls, what audit steps would you undertake to examine cash receipt and disbursements and related areas?

CASE 7-2

Eagle Brands, Incorporated
Audit Tests of Year-End Inventories When Physical Inventory Is Taken at an Interim Date

Eagle Brands, Inc., manufactured a line of small hand tools and machines. Your public accounting firm audited the company's books, and you have been assigned responsibility for the inventory items.

Eagle's perpetual inventory records were maintained for raw materials and finished goods, showing quantities and dollar amounts; general ledger control accounts were maintained for raw materials and finished goods. No work in process records were maintained, since the production time

This case was prepared by David F. Hawkins.

Copyright © 1970 by the President and Fellows of Harvard College
Harvard Business School case 171–029

of each of the company's lines was generally one day. The cost of raw materials put into process and productive labor was charged directly to the finished goods account.

Charges to the raw material perpetual records were made from vendors' invoices and receiving reports. Credits for materials put into production were based on material requisitions, priced at weighted average cost.

A lot (or production) order was issued for the manufacture of quantities to be produced of each type of tool or machine, and a requisition was prepared for the required amount of raw materials to produce the quantity of finished product ordered. Labor tickets prepared by shop workers showed lot order number, hours worked, and units processed. These time tickets were extended for labor charges by the cost clerk; the hours were agreed with time-clock cards. Daily production line inspection counts were made by the timekeeper of finished products, and the quantities were agreed by the cost clerk with the production reported by the shop workers. A summary by lot orders was made by the cost clerk of materials, labor charges, and quantities produced, and the totals were charged to the perpetual records of finished products. A new weighted average was computed each time a production order was completed, and this new average was used by the cost clerk to calculate the cost of the sales made under shipping reports.

Requisitions for additional raw materials to replace items spoiled in manufacture and an estimate of labor spent on the spoiled materials were charged to shop overhead (spoilage account), with an offsetting credit to finished goods.

Monthly trial balances of the perpetual stock records of raw materials and finished products were reconciled monthly by the bookkeeper with the general ledger control accounts. overhead was apportioned to inventory at year-end only (December 31), based on the relation of overhead for the year to direct labor costs for the year.

Because Eagle experienced heavy production demands during the month of December and business was relatively slow in late summer, a complete physical inventory was taken at September 30, after shutting down production and clearing all in-process work. Your accounting firm had generally found the inventory to be carefully taken and the perpetual records to be reasonably accurate. Shipping and receiving cutoffs were properly recorded. The physical inventory at the interim date was priced as follows:

1. Raw materials at the latest weighted average cost of purchases.
2. Finished goods at the latest weighted average cost per unit (material and labor only).

Question

Your audit tests have satisfactorily established the reasonableness of the company's inventory as at the interim date. What audit tests do you suggest to determine that the inventories in the company's financial statements at the year-end are reasonably stated?

CASE 7-3

Wiley International Oil
Confirmation of Accounts Receivable

Wiley International Oil Company, a medium-sized integrated oil company, maintained three large sales divisions in the United States and three small sales divisions outside the United States. In addition, a separate sales division in the head office handled all large special sales and direct refinery shipments.

Divisions in the United States sold both at retail and wholesale. Retail accounts receivable arose through sales on credit cards. There were some 115,000 active credit card accounts. There were about 30,000 wholesale accounts and 200 general sales (special and refinery shipment) accounts. The accounts receivable and annual sales by divisions are summarized below (all *dollar* amounts are in thousands):

| | Accounts Receivable | | | | Annual Sales | |
| | Retail | | Wholesale | | | |
	No. of Accounts	Amount	No. of Accounts	Amount	Retail	Wholesale
Divisions in United States:						
No. 1	50,000	$ 700	10,000	$2,500	$10,000	$20,000
No. 2	35,000	500	10,000	2,000	7,000	18,000
No. 3	30,000	450	8,000	1,500	5,000	15,000
Divisions outside United States:						
No. 4			800	250		3,000
No. 5			1,000	400		4,000
No. 6			200	100		1,000
Special division			200	3,000		35,000
Total	115,000	$1,650	30,200	$9,750	$22,000	$96,000

The company's system of internal accounting control at the three U.S. divisions was satisfactory, the accounting staff at each of the sales divisions being sufficiently large to permit adequate segregation of duties. The com-

This case was prepared by David F. Hawkins.

Copyright © 1970 by the President and Fellows of Harvard College
Harvard Business School case 171–030

pany maintained a staff of internal auditors at each of the U.S. divisions.

The number of employees at each of the sales divisions outside the United States was small, and a certain amount of overlapping of duties existed. The company auditors did not regularly visit these divisions, their last visit having been about five years ago.

The company used the cycle method of billing retail accounts; that is, the accounts were divided into five groups or cycles, the billings of which were staggered throughout the month, one cycle being billed every five days. Trial balances of past-due accounts only were run for each cycle immediately before the cycle billing, and current billings were entered on these trial balances in one amount to balance to the controls maintained for each cycle. The cycle controls were balanced monthly with the divisional ledger.

Wholesale accounts were kept on bookkeeping machines, from four to six machines being used at each U.S. division. The accounts were segregated by area, and separate controls were maintained for each marketing area, of which there were between 60 and 100 in each division.

The number of transactions in the special sales division was relatively small, and the internal accounting control was considered adequate. The company auditors did not examine the records of this division.

The company maintained a credit section at each of the sales divisions, and the head office credit department controlled and supervised the divisional credit sections and received for review copies of all divisional trial balances.

Early in the year, the chief internal auditor submitted his proposed program of circularization (confirmation) of accounts receivable as of an interim date and told you that it was similar to those of the past five years:

1. No work would be undertaken at any of the divisions outside the United States or at the special sales division.
2. Retail accounts: 100 accounts at each U.S. division would be circularized by use of the positive form of confirmation (i.e., the customer would be requested to confirm his balance shown in the confirmation letter, regardless of whether or not the balance was correct). The chief auditor explained that only a token number of retail accounts would be circularized because (1) the credit risk was well spread, (2) it was his experience that most replies were unsatisfactory because of cycle billing, and (3) he considered a test of a significant portion of the accounts to be impracticable.
3. Wholesale accounts: 5 percent of the wholesale accounts at each U.S. division would be circularized by use of the positive form. The chief auditor maintained records of the ledgers circularized each year, so that over a period of years all ledgers would be circularized. The ledgers which he selected each year included some from each of the bookkeepers.
4. Accounts written off: Twenty-five percent of the accounts written off in the preceding two years would be circularized. This work

would include examination of the credit files on accounts circularized.

5. Second requests would be mailed to all regular wholesale accounts failing to reply at the end of one month if such accounts had not then been paid in full. Second requests would not be mailed on accounts written off. Confirmation requests returned unclaimed would be remailed if another address could be determined.

6. All incoming mail for a period of 10 days would be opened and remittances received noted for subsequent tracing to individual accounts.

7. All postings to wholesale accounts for a two-day period would be checked.

8. A report summarizing the results of the circularization would be prepared and furnished to you for review. The internal auditors' working papers would also be made available to you.

Questions

1. The work of the internal auditors is considered satisfactory by the external auditor. On that basis, to what extent should the independent certified public accountant circularize accounts receivable in the examination for the year ending December 31?

2. In reviewing the work of the internal auditors, what points would you keep in mind?

3. Do you recognize any situations in the facts stated that might call for recommendations to Wiley? What might customers' replies disclose that could prove helpful to management?

CASE 7–4

Fairmuir Instrument Corporation
The Audit Opinion

Fairmuir Instrument Corporation sold a line of high-temperature measuring instruments (pyrometers). The principal users of the equipment were steel

This case was prepared by J. M. McInnis (under the direction of J. R. Yeager).

mills and various metal extraction companies, and Fairmuir's small sales force had concentrated almost exclusively on establishing good relations with these customers. Occasional inquiries and orders came from other sources, such as scientific laboratories, but the company had never actively solicited these markets.

The device in its present form had been developed and put into production in the late 1970s. Essentially it utilized principles which had been known for almost a hundred years, but until recently the accuracy attainable had fallen short of the requirements of modern industry. The company had introduced no new products until the last quarter of 1984. Effectively, the company had not faced any serious competition in its market area until 1980 and had maintained a stable sales level of around $3 million until that time.

During 1980, a competing product had been introduced to the market. Operating on completely different principles, this device performed substantially the same job as Fairmuir's product and gave similar levels of accuracy. The only major differences were in its useful life (five years) and its purchase price, each of which was about half of those of the Fairmuir product. The lower purchase price was a telling sales advantage, and Fairmuir's sales had suffered accordingly. Exhibit 1 gives some of the financial data of Fairmuir Instrument Corporation from 1980 through 1984.

By 1981, the management of Fairmuir realized that without a new product to bolster its faltering sales volume, the company was facing a serious predicament. They therefore began a search for an additional product which would be suited to the competences of the company. In 1982, they approached an inventor, who held patents for just such a product, with a view to buying the patents. After some negotiation, a mutually satisfactory price was reached, and, as part of the agreement, the inventor agreed to join the company and lead the additional development work which was required before a commercial product was ready for marketing.

On top of the cost of the patents and the development expenses, the company was faced with substantial start-up costs and investment in invento-

EXHIBIT 1

FAIRMUIR INSTRUMENT CORPORATION
Financial Data as of December 31
(dollar figures in thousands)

	Audited Results				Unaudited
	1980	1981	1982	1983	1984
Inventories related to pyrometers	791	806	909	805	627
Working capital	933	1,021	1,165	1,155	819
Net assets	1,889	1,965	1,995	1,926	1,549
Net sales of pyrometers	2,881	2,475	2,025	996	583
Other sales (net)	—	—	—	—	115
Net income (loss)	108	77	67	(91)	(376)

ries. The company's financial resources, already adversely affected by the lagging sales of pyrometers, were inadequate without an injection of fresh capital. The company's capital stock was closely held by members of top management and a few of their friends and family members. None of these people was willing to contribute any further capital.

Management believed that the recent poor operating results made it unwise to seek fresh equity capital at that time, and they therefore decided that a bank loan was the only feasible recourse. It did not prove an easy matter to find a bank willing to make the required loan, but eventually the capital was obtained from a bank. In extending the loan, the bank imposed several restrictions upon the management of Fairmuir, one of these being that a minimum working capital level of $800,000 should be maintained. By the end of 1984, with the sales of pyrometers still falling and the new product only just introduced to the market, the company was close to defaulting on the requirements of the working capital covenant.

In the 1984 audit, the public accountant was satisfied with all the accounts except for the valuation of the inventories related to pyrometers. Most of this inventory was in good condition and had been carefully handled and stored. A few items of purchased parts had become obsolete, and management had written them down. This represented an insignificant adjustment, however, and the bulk of the inventory was still reported on the company's books at cost. The auditor was not concerned about the physical condition of the inventory, but he had serious reservations as to the marketability of the product, and therefore the realization of the investment through profitable sales. In approaching management on this matter the auditor was aware that a large adjustment would throw the company into default on its loan covenant concerning working capital.

The auditor, Mr. Bill Adams, arranged a meeting with the president of Fairmuir Instrument Corporation, Mr. Tom Fairmuir, in order to discuss the 1984 financial statements. Part of the meeting is recorded below.

> **Mr. Adams:** Everything seems to be in fine order except for your valuation of inventories relating to pyrometers, Tom. Now we discussed this matter briefly a few days ago and you expressed the opinion that there would be no material loss of value in the inventories and that you would in fact be able to sell it all in the normal course of business. Since then I have examined your record of sales orders, and at present you have only $58,000 worth of open orders on your books, compared with $65,000 worth at the beginning of the year. Your billings by quarters for the past year were fairly stable: $149,000 first quarter, $136,000 second quarter, $141,000 third quarter, and $157,000 in the final quarter.
>
> I have also read several articles in trade publications, such as this one in *Steel Monthly*, which seem to indicate that your type of pyrometer is at a technical as well as an economic (in terms of purchase price) disadvantage.

Frankly, it appears to me that you are going to be left with a lot of inventory which will have to be marked down very significantly to sell it.

Mr. Fairmuir: Now hold it, Bill, things are not so bleak as that. In fact, we have plans for our pyrometers which will return the sales volume to its previous level, or close to it. Look at these letters, Bill. These are inquiries concerning substantial orders, and we have been receiving such inquiries at a greatly increased rate recently. If this continues, and I have no doubt that it will, and even half of them become firm orders, we shall be selling pyrometers in 1985 at twice the 1984 level.

You know we hired a new sales manager this year? Well, he has reorganized our sales force and is beginning to get results. At the same time, we have gone over our production process and reduced the manufacturing cost of our lines by some 10 percent. No doubt you noticed that our cost of goods figures, which have been stable at about 60 percent of selling price for several years, were lower for the past two or three months. We expect to improve on that further in 1985. Of course this gives us some price flexibility when we are faced with a competitive situation. So you see, I have good reason to predict better results in the future.

Mr. Adams: What exactly has the new sales manager done?

Mr. Fairmuir: He reorganized the sales territories and reassigned the salesmen so that we should get greater market penetration. He released a couple of the men who have clearly not been pulling their weight and hired a couple of bright young men to replace them. The main thing is that he has done wonders for the morale of the sales force.

In addition he has identified new markets and is helping the men to break into these markets.

Mr. Adams: Why don't we look at the prospects market by market, Tom? You had sales of only $62,000 to steel mills in 1984. It seems as if the steel mills market is almost defunct, wouldn't you agree?

Mr. Fairmuir: It has certainly declined. However, some of our men have built up a good relationship with their customers in the steel industry and we expect this to produce a certain loyalty. We should keep a small part of the business, say, billings of about $50,000 a year.

Then in the other metal extraction industries we know that our product has some distinct competitive advantages, such as its ruggedness and lower maintenance costs. With the new emphasis on selling, we expect that our customers will be well aware of these advantages, and the downward sales trend should be reversed this year. On this basis, we expect 1985's sales to this market to be at least $400,000 and to increase further in the future.

Mr. Adams: But look, Tom, that means an increase over this year's sales, bucking a strong downward trend. I can't base my opinion on your optimism, you know.

Mr. Fairmuir: Well, look at this market which we think has great potential—scientific laboratories. We are going to place advertisements in some of the engineering journals and pay direct sales calls to many of the labs in our market areas, those which do a lot of high-temperature work. We anticipate a yearly volume of $200,000 to $300,000 in this market.

And, finally, we have set up a contract with a representative in Washington to handle our line in government sales. He has already got some orders for us, and he seems certain that we can build up a stable volume of some $300,000 a year. Several government agencies are testing our product at the moment, including the Atomic Energy Commission. If we get our equipment specified for installation into government nuclear plants, we shall have a large continuing market.

Mr. Adams: So you expect sales of about $1 million this year, twice 1984's sales?

Mr. Fairmuir: No, not right away. But we are confident of substantially reversing the trend of recent years and eventually, say, in two years or so, building our sales up to at least $1.5 million for pyrometers. For 1985, we predict sales of about $800,000.

Mr. Adams: Well, look at this from my point of view. I have a professional responsibility to give an opinion on your company's financial statements and I cannot base my opinion on your predictions. I have to go on historic facts and reasonable expectations. The historic facts are that sales of pyrometers have been falling and you have only a small volume of open orders on your books.

You have a substantial inventory, the value of which can only be realized through the sale of pyrometers. Any other representation of these facts would mislead the reader of the statements.

Mr. Fairmuir: I agree with you on that, and in my opinion, we *will* realize the value of our inventory through normal sales. I could not contemplate a write-down in the value of the inventory. For one thing, it would not be right to do so since it would be misleading in valuing our assets. And for another, it could easily lead to a difficult situation with the bank and, at worst, lead to liquidation of the company. True, we have experienced a few bad years. But we are fighting back, and I am confident we shall save our pyrometer line. And also our new line will start to contribute to profits this coming year.

The discussion continued for some time and became fairly heated. Finally, Mr. Adams terminated the discussion in order to consider the question further. He arranged a meeting with Mr. Fairmuir for three days later, at which time the two men agreed they would come to a decision as to whether or not the value of the inventory should be written down. Mr. Adams was concerned as to what opinion he should issue on Fairmuir's financial statements of 1984.

Questions

1. What further steps should Mr. Adams take in preparing for the coming meeting with Mr. Fairmuir?

2. Putting yourself in Mr. Fairmuir's position, what steps would you take in preparing for the meeting? If Mr. Adams insists that the value of the inventory be written down, what would you do?

3. Do you think that the value of the inventory should be written down? If so, how should the adjustment be made?

4. If the inventory was not written down by management, how would you, as auditor, phrase your opinion if you believed a write-down was appropriate?

PART FOUR

Basic Financial Statement Analysis Techniques

_____

_____

_____

_____

_____

_____

CHAPTER 8

Basic Financial Ratio Analysis and Equity Valuation

The use of financial ratios to analyze financial statements provides an important basis for valuing securities and appraising managerial performance. The measure of a financial ratio's usefulness is how well it helps statement users to appraise the financial condition of a company and the effectiveness of its management in earning a return on its invested capital. This chapter introduces some of the basic concepts of financial ratio analysis and common stock valuation. A knowledge of these techniques is essential to appreciate fully the communication aspect of financial reports. The valuation of debt securities and its related financial analysis techniques are discussed in Chapter 21. In addition, many of the ratios discussed in this chapter are also covered in greater detail in chapters dealing with the specific focus of a ratio.

Financial Ratio Analysis

Financial ratios are tools for interpreting financial statements. They can provide insight into two important areas of management: the return on investment earned and the soundness of the company's financial position. This analytical technique compares certain related items in the financial statements in a meaningful manner. The analyst evaluates these results against the particular characteristics of the company and its industry. The astute analyst seldom expects answers from this process. Rather, the analyst hopes it will provide clues as to where to focus subsequent analysis that may involve such investigation techniques as company visits, supplier and customer interviews, library searches, and credit bureau report reviews.

Financial ratios fall into four classes: ratios appraising *liquidity*, ratios measuring *solvency*, ratios evaluating *funds management*, and ratios measuring *profitability*. The categories indicate that different ratios may be more helpful than others for particular purposes. Therefore, rather than

171

calculating ratios indiscriminately, the experienced analyst begins by considering the kinds of insights that will be helpful in understanding the problem faced. The analyst then calculates those ratios that best serve his or her purpose. To get the most meaningful results, the analyst compares these ratios over a period of several years against some standard; examines in depth major variations from this standard; and cross-checks the various ratios against each other.

The balance sheet and income statement of the Ampex Corporation, a retailing business, will be used to illustrate some of the more common ratios (see Illustrations 8–1 and 8–2).

Liquidity Ratios

A corporation's liquidity is measured by its ability to raise cash from all sources, such as bank credit, sale of redundant assets, and operations. Liquid-

ILLUSTRATION 8–1

AMPEX CORPORATION
Comparative Balance Sheets, December 31, 1985, and 1986
(in thousands of dollars)

	1986	*1985*
Assets		
Current assets:		
Cash	$ 20	$ 30
Accounts receivable (net)	95	95
Inventory	130	110
Total current assets	$245	$235
Fixed assets:		
Land	$ 10	$ 10
Building and equipment (net)	120	100
Total fixed assets (net)	$130	$110
Other assets:		
Goodwill and organization costs	$ 10	$ 10
Total assets	$385	$355
Liabilities and Stockholders' Equity		
Current liabilities:		
Accounts payable	$ 50	$ 40
Estimated income taxes payable	10	10
Total current liabilities	$ 60	$ 50
Fixed liabilities:		
Mortgage bonds, 10 percent	$ 50	$ 50
Total liabilities	$110	$100
Stockholders' equity:		
Convertible preferred stock, 5 percent	$ 20	$ 20
Common stock (10,000 shares outstanding)	50	50
Retained earnings	205	185
Total stockholders' equity	$275	$255
Total liabilities and stockholders' equity	$385	$355

ILLUSTRATION 8–2

AMPEX CORPORATION
Condensed Income Statement, 1986
(in thousands of dollars)

Gross sales	$1,516	100.66%
Less: Returns and allowances	10	0.66
Net sales	$1,506	100.00%
Less: Cost of goods sold	1,004	66.67
Gross profit	$ 502	33.33%
Operating expenses*	400	26.56
Operating profit	$ 102	6.77%
Interest	5	0.33
Profit before taxes	$ 97	6.44%
Income tax expense	47	3.12
Net income	$ 50	3.32%
Less: Preferred dividends	1	0.07
Common dividends	29	1.93
Change in retained earnings	$ 20	1.32%

* Includes lease rental costs of $30,000 and depreciation of $10,000.

ity ratios have a narrower focus. They help statement users appraise a company's ability to meet its current obligations using its cash and current assets. These ratios compare current liabilities, which are the obligations falling due in the next 12 months, and current assets, which typically provide the funds to extinguish these obligations. The difference between current assets and current liabilities is called "working capital." Ampex's 1986 year-end working capital is $185,000 ($245,000 − $60,000).

Current Ratio

$$\frac{\text{Current assets}}{\text{Current liabilities}} = \frac{\$245,000}{\$ 60,000} = 4.1$$

The meaningfulness of the current ratio as a measure of liquidity varies from company to company. Typically, it is assumed that the higher the ratio, the more protection the company has against liquidity problems. However, the ratio may be distorted by seasonal influences, slow-moving inventories built up out of proportion to market opportunities, or abnormal payment of accounts payable just prior to the balance sheet date. Also, the nature of some businesses is such that they have a steady, predictable cash inflow and outflow, and a low current ratio is appropriate for such a business.

Acid-Test or Quick Ratio

$$\frac{\text{Quick assets}}{\text{Current liabilities}} = \frac{\$115,000}{\$ 60,000} = 1.9$$

The acid-test or quick ratio measures the ability of a company to use its "near-cash" or quick assets to immediately extinguish its current liabilities.

Quick assets include those current assets that presumably can be quickly converted to cash at close to their book value. Such items are cash, stock investments, and accounts receivable. Like the working capital ratio, this ratio implies a liquidation approach and does not recognize the revolving nature of current assets and liabilities.

Solvency Ratios

Solvency ratios generate insight into a company's ability to meet long-term debt payment schedules. There are a number of ratios that compare stockholders' equity or operating profits to the amount and cost of funds provided by creditors. All of these ratios are designed to give some measure of the extent to which operating cash flows and asset values provide protection to creditors should a company incur losses.

Times Interest Earned

$$\frac{\text{Operating profit (before interest expense)}}{\text{Long-term debt interest}} = \frac{\$102,000}{\$\ 5,000} = 20.4 \text{ times}$$

This coverage ratio is calculated on a pre-tax basis, since bond interest is a tax deductible expense. The ratio in the example implies that operating profits cover interest payments 20 times. This indicates the extent to which operating profits can decline without impairing the company's ability to pay the interest on its long-term debt.

Some analysts prefer to use operating profit plus noncash charges as the numerator of this ratio. This modification indicates the ability of the company to cover its cash outflow for interest from its funds from operations. For example, the only so-called noncash charge in the Ampex income statement is depreciation; that is, no cash outflow results from incurring this expense. Adding the company's $10,000 depreciation expense to operating profit changes the numerator to $112,000 and increases the coverage to 22 times.

Coverage ratios can be computed for preferred stock dividends and other fixed charges, such as lease rentals. The *preferred-stock-dividend-coverage* ratio is calculated on an after-tax basis, since preferred stock dividends are not a tax deductible expense. For example, the Ampex preferred-stock-dividend-coverage ratio is:

$$\frac{\text{Net income}}{\text{Preferred stock dividends}} = \frac{\$50,000}{\$\ 1,000} = 50 \text{ times}$$

A coverage ratio for all of a company's fixed charges is called the *times-fixed-charges-earned* ratio. The denominator of this ratio includes such items as lease rentals, interest, and preferred dividends converted to a pre-tax basis. The numerator is operating profit before these charges. The times-fixed-charges-earned ratio for Ampex is:

$$\frac{\text{Operating profit before fixed charges}}{\text{Lease rentals, interest, preferred dividends}} = \frac{\$132,000}{\$ 34,000} = 3.9 \text{ times}$$

Sometimes depreciation is added to the numerator.

Debt-to-Equity Ratios. The relationship of borrowed funds to owner-ship funds is an important solvency ratio. Capital from debt and other cred-itor sources is more risky for a company than equity capital. Debt capital requires fixed interest payments on specific dates and eventual repayment. If payments to a company's creditors become overdue, the creditors can take legal action which may lead to the company being declared bankrupt. Ownership capital is less risky. Dividends are paid at the discretion of the directors, and there is no provision for repayment of capital to stockholders. It is generally assumed that the more ownership capital relative to debt a company has in its capital structure, the more likely it is that the company will be able to survive a downturn in business that may force other more financially leveraged companies into bankruptcy. An excessive amount of ownership capital relative to debt capital may not necessarily indicate sound management practices, however. Equity capital is typically more costly than debt capital. Also, the company may be forgoing opportunities "to trade on its equity," that is, borrow at a relatively low interest rate and earn a greater rate of return on these funds. The difference between these two rates can increase earnings per share without having to increase the number of common shares outstanding.

There are a number of debt-to-equity ratios. Four of the most common are:

$$\frac{\text{Total liabilities}}{\text{Total assets}} = \frac{\$110,000}{\$385,000} = 28.6\%, \text{ or } 0.286 \text{ to } 1$$

This ratio indicates the proportion of a company's total assets financed by short- and long-term credit sources.

$$\frac{\text{Long-term debt}}{\text{Capitalization}} = \frac{\$ 50,000}{\$325,000} = 15.4\%, \text{ or } 0.154 \text{ to } 1$$

This measure, which excludes current liabilities, reflects management's pol-icy on the mix of long-term funds obtained from ownership and nonowner-ship sources. The term "capitalization" includes all of a company's long-term debt and equity capital.

$$\frac{\text{Total liabilities}}{\text{Stockholders' equity}} = \frac{\$110,000}{\$275,000} = 40\%, \text{ or } 0.4 \text{ to } 1$$

This ratio is another way of measuring the relative mix of funds provided by owners and creditors.

$$\frac{\text{Total assets}}{\text{Stockholders' equity}} = \frac{\$385,000}{\$275,000} = 1.4$$

The *total leverage* ratio relates total assets to stockholders' equity. This ratio is an indication of the degree to which management has financed the company's asset investments with nonownership capital. A 1.4 ratio means that for every dollar of owners' equity, $0.40 of nonownership funds has been used to fund the company's assets.

Ampex appears to have an adequate cushion of ownership funds against losses from operations, decreases in the book value of assets, and downturns in future cash flows.

Funds Management Ratios

The financial situation of a company turns in large measure on how its investment in accounts receivable, inventories, and fixed assets is managed. As a business expands its sales, it is not uncommon to find that the associated expansion of these three items is so great that despite profitable operations the company is short of cash. In such situations, the management of vendor credit becomes critical. It is a source of capital which should expand along with the increased sales.

Receivables to Sales

$$\frac{\text{Accounts receivable (net)}}{\text{Net sales}} = \frac{\$\ \ \ 95,000}{\$1,506,000} = 6.3\%$$

In the absence of an aging of accounts receivable (classification of outstanding receivables by days since billing) or other detailed credit information, the receivables-to-sales ratio, computed over a number of years, can give a crude indication of the trend in a company's credit policy. In those cases where a company sells for cash and credit, only credit sales should be used in the denominator. Receivables include accounts receivable, trade receivables, and trade notes receivable. The rather low receivables-to-sales percentage for Ampex is indicative that this retailer's sales most probably include a high proportion of cash sales.

Average Collection Period

$$\frac{\text{Accounts receivable}}{\text{Net sales}} \times \text{Days in the annual period} = \text{Collection period}$$

$$6.3\% \times 365 \qquad\qquad\qquad = 23 \text{ days}$$

A two-step method to get the same result is:

1. Calculate the average daily sales:

$$\frac{\text{Net sales}}{\text{Days}} = \frac{\$1,506,000}{365} = \$4,126 \text{ per day}$$

2. Calculate the day's sales represented by receivables:

$$\frac{\text{Accounts receivable}}{\text{Net sales per day}} = \frac{\$95,000}{\$\ 4,126} = 23 \text{ days}$$

To appraise the quality of accounts receivable, the average collection period can be related to the typical credit terms of the company and its industry. A collection period substantially longer than either of these standards might indicate credit management problems, resulting in an increasing amount of funds being tied up in this asset. On the other hand, a significantly shorter collection period than is typical in the industry might mean that profitable sales to slower paying customers are being missed.

Average Accounts Payable Period

$$\frac{\text{Accounts payable}}{\text{Purchases}} = \frac{\$\ \ 50,000}{\$1,024,000} = 4.9\%$$

Similar tests can be made of accounts payable to see how well they are managed. In this case, the accounts payable are compared to the purchases for the period (cost of goods sold plus inventory changes). The two-step calculation of the average day's payables is made as follows:

1. Calculate the average daily purchases:

$$\frac{\text{Purchases}}{\text{Days}} = \frac{\$1,004,000 + \$20,000}{365} = \$2,805 \text{ per day}$$

2. Calculate the day's purchases represented by payables:

$$\frac{\text{Accounts payable}}{\text{Purchases per day}} = \frac{\$50,000}{\$\ 2,805} = 18 \text{ days}$$

The day's-payables ratio becomes meaningful when compared to the credit terms given by suppliers to the object company's industry. If a company's average day's payables is increasing, it may mean trade credit is being used increasingly as a source of funds. If the payables period is less than the average for the industry, it may indicate that management is not using this source of funds as much as is possible. If it is longer, it may mean the company is overdue on its payables and is using this source of funds beyond the normal trade limits.

Rarely is the purchases figure available to people outside of the company. Consequently, the analyst has to approximate this amount. In merchandising situations, like the Ampex illustration, estimating purchases is fairly straightforward since a retailer's inventory value and cost of goods sold is the price paid to suppliers for the goods. Therefore, a retailer's outside purchases is equal to its cost of goods sold figure, adjusted for inventory changes.

In manufacturing situations, estimating outside purchases is not such an easy task. The cost of goods sold expense includes direct labor, raw materials, and some manufacturing overheads. If the raw materials portion of the cost of goods sold and inventories figures are available, they can be used to calculate an approximation of the raw materials purchases, which in most cases represents the minimum level of purchases.

Another difficulty is that the accounts payable figure may include payables incurred for other than items included in cost of goods sold. As a result of this problem and the other measurement problems, this ratio is usually not regarded as a particularly reliable indicator of the use of trade credit.

Inventory Turnover

$$\frac{\text{Cost of sales}}{\text{Average inventory}} = \frac{\$1,004,000}{\$\ \ 120,000} = 8.4 \text{ times}$$

The inventory-turnover ratio indicates how fast inventory items move through a business. It is an indication of how well the funds invested in inventory are being managed. The analyst is interested in two items: the absolute size of the inventory in relation to the other fund needs of the company and the relationship of the inventory to the sales volume it supports. A decrease in the turnover rate indicates that the absolute size of the inventory relative to sales is increasing. This can be a warning signal, since funds may be tied up in this inventory beyond the level required by the sales volume, which may be rising or falling.

Average inventory is used in the denominator because the sales volume is generated over a 12-month period. The average inventory is obtained by adding the opening inventory and closing inventory balances and dividing the sum by two.

If the cost of goods sold figure is not available, an approximation of the inventory-turnover rate can be obtained by using the sales figure in the numerator. If profit margins have remained fairly steady, then this sales-to-average-inventory ratio can provide, over a period of years, an indication of inventory management trends.

By dividing the turnover rate into 365 days, the analyst can estimate the average length of time items spent in inventory:

$$\frac{365 \text{ days}}{\text{Inventory turnover}} = \frac{365}{8.4} = 43 \text{ days}$$

If the company uses the so-called last-in, first-out (LIFO) inventory valuation method, the inventory balance must be converted to its equivalent value based on either the first-in, first-out (FIFO) or average cost inventory valuation method. This is accomplished by adding the LIFO reserve to the FIFO inventory balance reported on the balance sheet. The LIFO reserve figure can be found in the inventory note accompanying the financial statements.

Asset Turnover

$$\frac{\text{Net sales}}{\text{Average assets}} = \frac{\$1,506,000}{\$\ 370,000} = 4.07 \text{ times}$$

The asset turnover ratio is an indicator of how efficiently management is using its investment in total assets to generate sales. High turnover rates suggest efficient asset management.

Fixed Asset Turnover

$$\frac{\text{Net sales}}{\text{Average net fixed assets}} = \frac{\$1,506,000}{\$\ 120,000} = 12.6 \text{ times}$$

A similar turnover ratio can also be calculated for fixed assets. It provides a crude measure of how well the investment in plant and equipment is being managed relative to the sales volume it supports. The usefulness of this measure is reduced considerably because book values seldom approximate market values or are comparable from company to company due to different depreciation policies.

Capital or Investment Turnover

$$\frac{\text{Net sales}}{\text{Average total capital}} = \frac{\$1,506,000}{\$\ 315,000} = 4.78 \text{ times}$$

A ratio similar to the inventory and asset turnover ratios can also be calculated for a firm's total capital investment.

Profitability Ratios

Analysts look at profits in two ways: first, as a percentage of net sales; second, as a return on the funds invested in the business.

Profit margin. Profit margins relative to net sales can be evaluated in a number of different ways.

a. Net income as a percentage of net sales measures the total operating and financial ability of management, since net profit after taxes includes all of the operating and financial costs of doing business:

$$\frac{\text{Net income}}{\text{Net sales}} = \frac{\$\ 50,000}{\$1,506,000} = 3.32\%$$

b. Pre-tax income as a percentage of net sales measures management's ability to generate profits before recognizing taxes related to those profits. This figure is of interest because changes in the tax code or actions by management that impact the company's tax rate can result in more or less of the pre-tax profits flowing down to net income.

$$\frac{\text{Pre-tax profit}}{\text{Net sales}} = \frac{\$ 97,000}{\$1,506,000} = 6.44\%$$

c. The ratio of net profit before taxes and interest to net sales is indicative of management's operating ability. Interest is excluded because it relates to financing policy rather than operation efficiency:

$$\frac{\text{Earnings before interest and taxes}}{\text{Net sales}} = \frac{\$ 102,000}{\$1,506,000} = 6.77\%$$

d. Gross profit (sales minus cost of sales) as a percentage of sales is an indication of the management's ability to mark up its products over their cost:

$$\frac{\text{Gross profit}}{\text{Net sales}} = \frac{\$ 502,000}{\$1,506,000} = 33.3\%$$

In addition to these ratios, it is often informative to express all of these expense items as a percentage of net sales (see Illustration 8–2). This is called a common-size statement. Common-size statements can also be prepared for balance sheets using total assets as the base.

Return on investment. The relationship between profitability and investment is considered the key ratio by many analysts. It provides a broad measure of management's operating and financial success. Several different return-on-investment ratios are commonly used.

a. *Pre-tax operating return on total assets*

$$\frac{\text{Profit before taxes and interest}}{\text{Average total assets}} = \frac{\$102,000}{\$370,000} = 27.6\%$$

This ratio gauges how well management has managed the total resources at its command, before consideration of taxes and credit costs. It focuses on the earning power of the assets and is not influenced by how they are financed. Average total assets is used as the denominator since profit is earned over a 12-month period.

b. *Return on total assets*

$$\frac{\text{Net income}}{\text{Average total assets}} = \frac{\$ 50,000}{\$370,000} = 13.5\%$$

This variation of (a) measures the return on total assets after recognition of taxes and financing costs.

c. *Return on total capital*

$$\frac{\text{Net income}}{\text{Average total capital}} = \frac{\$ 50,000}{\$315,000} = 15.9\%$$

Another ratio measuring return on investment equates investment with total long-term capital (equity capital plus long-term liabilities). This ratio indicates how well management has managed the permanent funds at its disposal. The ratio can be computed on a before- or after-tax basis. If interest is paid on long-term liabilities, then this amount is sometimes added to the net income figure, since it relates to the financial management of those items.

    d. Return on stockholders' equity

$$\frac{\text{Net income}}{\text{Average stockholders' equity}} = \frac{\$\ 50,000}{\$265,000} = 18.9\%$$

The return on net worth percentage measures the return on ownership capital after all taxes and interest payments. It is perhaps the most common return-on-investment figure published by financial services.

    e. Return on tangible net worth

$$\frac{\text{Net income}}{(\text{Average net worth} - \text{Average intangible assets})} = \frac{\$50,000}{(\$265,000 - \$10,000)}$$

$$= \quad 19.6\%$$

This modification of *(d)* measures the return on net worth less the intangible assets, such as goodwill and capitalized organization costs. The principal use of this ratio is to present a more conservative measure of the investment base than *(d)*. The $10,000 deduction from net worth in the above equation is Ampex's investment in goodwill.

Linking Ratios

Statement users can often gain greater insight into a company's returns on capital, assets, and net worth by linking together selected financial ratios.

    For example, how a company achieves its return on total capital can be explained in terms of its investment-turnover and net income ratios by using the following equation:

Investment turnover × After-tax profit margin = Return on capital

$$\frac{\text{Net sales}}{\text{Average total capital}} \times \frac{\text{Net income}}{\text{Net sales}} = \frac{\text{Net income}}{\text{Average total capital}}$$

$$4.78 \text{ times} \quad \times \quad 3.32\% \quad = \quad 15.9\%$$

This formula indicates that a business return on investment can be improved by increasing the sales volume per dollar of investment, by generating more profit per dollar of sales, or some mix of these two factors. Thus, the performance of a firm earning 2 percent on sales with an investment turnover of 10 can be equivalent to that of another company with a profit margin of 10 percent and an investment turnover of 2 times. Both have the same return on investment, 20 percent.

    A number of other ratios are closely related. For example, a greater appreciation of the relationship between profit rates, asset turnover, and return on total assets can be obtained as follows:

$$\text{After-tax profit margin} \times \text{Asset turnover} = \text{Return on total assets}$$

$$\frac{\text{Net income}}{\text{Net sales}} \times \frac{\text{Net sales}}{\text{Average total assets}} = \frac{\text{Net income}}{\text{Average total assets}}$$

$$3.32\% \qquad \times \qquad 4.07 \text{ times} \qquad = \qquad 13.5\%$$

An analysis of the causes of changes in the level and quality of the company's return on stockholders' equity can be facilitated by the use of the equation presented in Illustration 8–3, which incorporates the Ampex Corporation data and ratios. The average, rather than ending, stockholders' equity and total asset values are used to compute the total leverage ratio because the equation is being used to explain the variables contributing to the company's return on average stockholders' equity.

The only new ratio introduced in Illustration 8–3 is the so-called *tax retention* ratio, which measures the percentage of pre-tax profits retained by the company after payment of income taxes. This ratio is expressed as 1 minus the book tax rate, which is the percentage of the book tax expense to the pre-tax profits.

A similar set of ratios which have more meaning when examined together are the components of the current ratio. For example, an examination

ILLUSTRATION 8–3
Analysis of Ampex Corporation's Return on Stockholders' Equity

Pre-tax profit margin	×	Asset turnover ratio	×	Total leverage ratio	×	Tax retention rate	=	Return on stockholders' equity
$\dfrac{\text{Pre-tax profits}}{\text{Net sales}}$	×	$\dfrac{\text{Net sales}}{\text{Average assets}}$	×	$\dfrac{\text{Average assets}}{\text{Average stockholders' equity}}$	×	$(1 - \text{Tax rate})$	=	$\dfrac{\text{Net income}}{\text{Average stockholders' equity}}$
6.44%	×	4.07	×	1.40	×	.52	=	19.1%

Pre-tax return on assets
(6.44% × 4.07 = 26.2%)

Pre-tax return on stockholders' equity
(6.44% × 4.07 × 1.40 = 36.7%)

Return on stockholders' equity
(6.44% × 4.07 × 1.40 × .52 = 19.1%)

of the relationship between the inventory turnover period and the receivables and payables periods demonstrates how changes in these working capital items influence funds flow.

Common Stock Ratios

Buyers and sellers of common stocks use a number of ratios relating market values to earnings and dividends. The significance of these ratios is discussed in the Stock Valuation section of this chapter.

Earnings per Share.   The most straightforward computation of earnings per share is for companies with fairly simple capital structures, like Ampex. In these situations, the calculation is:

$$\frac{\text{(Net income} - \text{Preferred stock dividends)}}{\text{Average number of common shares outstanding}} = \frac{\$50,000 - \$1000}{10,000}$$

$$= \$4.90 \text{ per share}$$

Preferred stock dividends, if any, are deducted from net income before calculating earnings per share. The divisor is the weighted average number of shares determined by relating *(a)* the portion of time within a reporting period that a number of shares of a certain security has been outstanding to *(b)* the total time in that period.

The number of earnings-per-share figures a company may report will vary with the complexity of its capital structure and whether or not its net income calculation involves extraordinary items. The profit figure used by most analysts to compute earnings per share is the profit before extraordinary items, since this figure is thought to be more representative of a company's continuing income stream.

The term *net income per share* should be used only in those cases where the capital structure of the company is such that there are no potentially dilutive convertible securities, options, warrants, or other agreements providing for contingency issuances of common stock. The FASB's rules for computing earnings per share require that companies with complex capital structures present with equal prominence two types of earnings-per-share amounts on the face of the income statement: one, primary earnings per share; the other, fully diluted earnings per share. Primary earnings per share is the amount of earnings attributable to each share of common stock outstanding, including securities that are equivalent to common stock—such as convertible preferred stock with a relatively low dividend rate at issue. Fully diluted earnings per share is the amount of current earnings per share reflecting the maximum dilution that would result from conversions, exercises, and other contingent issues that individually, in the future, may decrease earnings per share and in the aggregate might have a dilutive effect. Because of the variety of earnings-per-share data possible in some situations, it is always dangerous to use these figures without insisting first on knowing which definition is being used.

The detailed rules for calculating earnings per share are covered in Chapter 13.

Typically, financial analysts eliminate nonrecurrent items from a single-year analysis of companies but include them in long-term analysis. In single-year analysis, financial analysts tend to want to know whether or not the current earnings are in line with the "normal" earnings of the company. Consequently, unusual items such as material refunds of overpaid taxes are excluded from these analyses.

In long-run analyses of historical data, financial analysts tend to include in income every profit and loss item, unless it is quite unrelated to normal operations. This practice recognizes that many of these so-called unusual items are elements of profit and loss that would have been included in income if the accounting period had been longer than, say, one year. In this latter case, the tax refund excluded from the single-year analysis would be included. An example of items typically excluded from long-term analyses would be gains from pension plan termination.

Price-Earnings Ratio. Assuming the average price for the Ampex stock is $40, the company's price-earnings ratio is:

$$\frac{\text{Market price per share}}{\text{Earnings per share}} = \frac{\$40.00}{\$\ 4.90} = 8.2$$

Since the stock market is responsive to anticipated earnings-per-share estimates, the price-earnings ratio is often quoted using the company's projected next year's earnings-per-share figure. Typically, the net income figure before extraordinary items is used to compute this ratio. Also, the potential shares issuable to holders of potentially dilutive securities is included in the earnings-per-share calculation.

The reciprocal of the price-earnings ratio gives the so-called *capitalization rate* applied by investors to the company's earnings per share:

$$\frac{\text{Earnings per share}}{\text{Market price per share}} = \frac{\$\ 4.90}{\$40.00} = 12.2\%$$

Dividend Yield. In situations where cash dividends have been increased at the last payment date, the current dividend rate converted to a yearly basis is sometimes used for the numerator:

$$\frac{\text{Cash dividends per share}}{\text{Price per share}} = \frac{\$\ 2.90}{\$40.00} = 7.3\%$$

Stock dividends are not included in this calculation. The *payout ratio* is the percentage of net income paid out in cash dividends:

$$\frac{\text{Cash dividends}}{\text{Net income}} = \frac{\$29.00}{\$50.00} = 58\%$$

Basis of Comparison

The results of financial ratio analysis take on real meaning when compared to a standard appropriate to the company's stage of development, seasonal pattern, and industry and management plans. The selection of a relevant standard is always difficult.

The management of a company can use its budgets as a basis of comparison. These are rarely available to the outside analyst. Therefore, the statement user must seek other sources. By comparing a company's current results as shown in its financial reports to similar data in past reports, the analyst can get some indication of how much "better" or "worse" things are compared to the past.

Important sources of average ratios for a particular industry are Dun & Bradstreet's *Modern Industry*, Moody's *Manual of Investment*, and Standard & Poor's *Corporation Records*. Another source of comparison bases are the publications of the various trade associations. Often, these publications report selected financial ratios for industries broken down by sales volume categories. These ratios can be used to highlight variations from the average company situation.

Another source of standards can be ratios computed from the data in the annual reports of individual companies in the same industry. This type of external comparison, when used with good judgment, can indicate the relative quality of the company's operating performance and funds management compared to its competitors.

Experienced analysts rarely rely on any one standard. They use several standards. They also look at a variety of related ratios and know from experience that they must have a good appreciation of the particular company's business before drawing conclusions based upon ratio analysis.

A Warning

Financial ratio analysis has many limitations which can mislead the unsophisticated analyst. To be a useful analytical tool it must be used wisely.

First, ratio analysis deals only with quantitative data. It does not look at qualitative factors such as management's ethical values, the quality of the management, or the workers' morale. These are important considerations which should be taken into account when evaluating a company.

Second, management can take certain short-run actions prior to the statement dates to influence the ratios. For example, a company with a better than 1:1 current ratio can improve this ratio by paying off current liabilities just prior to the balance sheet date.

Third, comparison of ratios between companies can be misleading because of differences in accounting practices in such areas as depreciation, income recognition, and intangible assets. For this reason, analysts often put companies on a comparable accounting basis before making ratio comparisons.

Fourth, different definitions of common ratios are used by different analysts. Often, two analysts' reports that include the same ratios for a particular company may give very different results.

Fifth, because accounting records are maintained in historical dollars, a change in the value of the dollar can distort the comparability of the ratios computed for different time periods. For instance, in periods of inflation the ratios comparing sales and net income to assets and equity may be biased upwards.

Sixth, a ratio standing alone has no significance. What constitutes an appropriate ratio for a company is determined by its industry, management strategy, and the state of the general economy. For example, meat packers have high inventory-turnover ratios and jewelry stores have low inventory-turnover ratios. To conclude one ratio is good and the other bad is a mistake. The ratios must be evaluated in their business context.

Finally, ratios based on published financial statements show relationships as they existed in the past. The analyst interested in the future should not be misled into believing that the past data necessarily reflect the current situation or future expectation.

Stock Valuation

The need to value equity securities arises in such situations as the pricing of new issues, the purchase or sale of securities, and the exchange of stock in mergers or reorganizations. An equity security's value may be a function of the value of the net assets its ownership controls and the projected income and dividend streams of the business issuing the security, its relative level of risk, or some combination of all of these factors. The approach to valuation used in any particular situation depends on the particular circumstances of the buyer and seller.

Asset Valuation

There are three basic asset valuation approaches: book value, reproduction value, and liquidation value.

The *book value* of a company's common stock is the difference between the accounting value assigned to its assets and the sum of the liabilities and preferred stock, if any. This amount divided by the number of shares outstanding gives the book value per share. A more conservative approach also eliminates the intangible assets, such as organization expense and bond discounts, from the total asset values shown on the books. The resulting amount is labeled "tangible book value."

The principal weakness of the book value approach is its dependence on the accounting policies of the company. Comparing the book value of different companies is therefore difficult. Some analysts try to overcome this problem by readjusting the accounting statements to some comparable basis. This is a difficult and potentially dangerous task, since putting all companies on the same accounting basis may obscure important differences among the companies.

Book value rarely approximates the market value of the owner's equity in a company or its assets, principally because of the accountant's use of the historical cost convention. Consequently, book values are usually appropriate only in appraising companies, such as mutual funds, whose assets are mostly liquid and reflect current market values.

Reproduction value is the cost of reproducing at current prices the physical assets of a going concern. The principal deficiency of this approach is that the value of a going business is typically more than the sum of its individual physical asset values, which can be appraised reasonably accurately. What value to assign the company's reputation and other intangible assets is much more difficult. This approach is sometimes used by governmental agencies as a basis for setting public utility rates and in valuation situations where physical assets are the principal asset of the company, such as in real estate businesses, where reproduction of the buildings would be the principal cost of going into business.

Liquidation value focuses on the resale value of assets, principally their scrap value. It usually sets the lower valuation limit. Typically, this approach values accounts receivable at no more than 75 percent of their face value, inventories at between 25 percent and 50 percent of their FIFO value, equipment at no more than 50 percent of its book value, and land and buildings at their net book value, adjusted for general inflation since acquisition.

Sometimes the liquidation value approach is used in conjunction with the earnings approach. In cases where a company is bought for its income potential but has excess assets, the excess assets can be valued without reference to the company's value based on earning power and then properly added to the earning power value of the company. This approach is called the "redundant asset method." Similarly, if the potential purchaser must acquire additional assets to maintain a company's earning power, the value of these additional assets can be subtracted from the value derived from the earnings approach.

Earnings-Based Valuation

The current value of a business is determined in many cases by the estimated future earnings it can produce, adjusted for the degree of risk the investor associates with realizing the earnings projections. In these situations, the stockholder values the income flow rather than the physical and intangible assets which give rise to this income. This concept is widely accepted, but it is not easy to apply.

There are two steps in the capitalization of earnings valuation method; first, future earnings available to stockholders must be estimated; and second, a capitalization rate must be selected to apply to this estimate.

Typically, the analyst bases the estimate of a company's future earnings on its average earnings for the last few years plus or minus some adjustment to reflect the analyst's feelings about the company's prospects over the next five or so years. Rather than trying to predict earnings for each of these future years, the analyst simply settles on an average earnings figure for this period or projects a smooth trend line. Adjustments to the historical pattern of earnings may reflect anticipated changes in the national economy, new product introductions, potential mergers, conversion to common stock of convertible senior securities, and other similar factors which influence earnings per share.

The capitalization rate is the price-earnings ratio upside down, expressed as a percentage. It reflects the rate at which the market is capitalizing the value of current earnings. For example, dividing an average earnings figure by a capitalization rate of 10 percent is equivalent to calculating the present value of a stream of equal annual earnings over a long period of time discounted at 10 percent. Similarly, a capitalization rate of 20 percent (equivalent to a price-earnings ratio of five times) divided into the average projected earnings gives a value which is the present value of an infinite equal earnings stream discounted at 20 percent. Clearly, earnings streams are not constant over time. However, because of the high degree of uncertainty as to what the actual earnings will be in any particular year, the analyst feels more comfortable simplifying the problem by using an average projected earnings estimate.

In most situations, the more certain the analyst is that the projected earnings will be realized, the lower the capitalization rate applied to those earnings. For example, in the case of a business with very stable earnings historically and the prospect of continued stable earnings, the analyst might use a capitalization rate of 7 percent. Assuming projected earnings were $5 per share, this rate would imply a market value of about $70 ($5/0.07 = $71.43). Similarly, the analyst valuing high-risk businesses can use either a conservative earnings forecast or a high capitalization rate. In the case of companies with outstanding growth potential, a very low capitalization rate is sometimes applied to the current earnings. In these cases, the rate can approach 1 percent.

The selection of the appropriate capitalization rate is very subjective. It is a function of the estimated risk associated with realizing the projected earnings stream and the willingness of the investor to bear this risk given the investor's financial condition and attitude toward risk bearing. For example, based upon earnings estimates, an analyst may decide a 15 percent capitalization rate is appropriate. However, an investor may decide this is too low, given the fact that if the company fails to reach its projected earnings, any stock losses will eliminate most of the investor's life savings. Consequently, the investor may demand a capitalization rate of 30 percent before undertaking this type of investment. One guide to appropriate capitalization rates is the price-earnings ratios range assigned by the market to the current earnings of particular industries or companies with characteristics similar to the company being valued.

Dividend-Based Valuation

Considerable controversy surrounds the role of cash dividends in security valuation. The capitalization of earnings approach assumes that a dollar of earnings is equally valuable to an investor whether it is paid out in dividends or retained for reinvestment in the company. In contrast, some investors maintain that the value of a security reflects the expected cash flow derived from owning it, which is its dividend payments. This approach capitalizes a stock's projected dividend payments stream rather than earnings to determine its value. Eventually, how the individual investor incorporates the dividend factor in the formula for stock valuation will depend on the investor's financial needs and resources and the company's earnings prospects relative to the investor's potential rate of return on dividends.

The capitalization rate also reflects other considerations: for example, the interest rate obtainable on alternative investments, such as government and corporate bonds and the capitalization rates of other stocks, the projected state of the economy, and the relative quality of the company's earnings. Typically, high capitalization rates are experienced in periods when interest rates on prime quality debt securities are high and the economy's prospects are dismal and uncertain. Low capitalization rates are often associated with the opposite circumstances.

Dividend Discount Models

Dividend discount models are discounted cash flow techniques used frequently to estimate a stock's theoretical value. These models are based on the premise that the price of a company's stock equals the present value of its future dividends discounted by the company's cost of capital. Making the assumption that future dividends will grow at a constant rate forever, the general dividend discount model can be represented by this simple expression known as the *constant dividend growth model:*

$$P_o = \frac{dps}{(K_e - g)}$$

where:

P_o = The current price of the stock.
dps = Next year's dividend per share.
g = The perpetuity growth rate in dividends per share.
K_e = The company's cost of equity capital.

The constant dividend growth model has several weaknesses. It makes the unrealistic assumption that dividends grow at a constant rate. Therefore, it cannot be used when a company pays no dividends or has an unstable dividend pattern. Also, it cannot be used when a company's cost of equity capital is less than its dividend growth rate. The model works best with companies that increase dividends at a steady rate.

The cost of equity term in the constant dividend growth model can be difficult to estimate. Of course, it can be estimated directly if the price of a stock reflects a dividend valuation approach. The company's cost of equity capital is impounded in the stock price and can be computed by rearranging the terms of the constant dividend growth model expression as follows:

$$K_e = \frac{dps}{P_o} + g$$

Therefore, the cost of equity capital is the dividend yield using next year's dividend (dps/P_o) plus the projected constant growth rate of dividends.

If the price of the common stock is not known, or the investor wants to test the actual price against an indicated price computed using the constant dividend growth model, the firm's cost of equity capital must be determined directly. The *capital asset pricing model* can be used for this purpose.

The capital asset pricing model is a theoretical representation of how financial markets price securities and thereby determine expected returns on capital investments. The model provides a method for quantifying risk and then translating that risk into an estimate of a company's cost of capital. The capital asset pricing model expression for making this determination is:

$$R_s = K_e = R_f + \beta_s (R_m - R_f)$$

where:

R_s = The stock's expected return.
K_e = The company's cost of equity capital (and the stock's expected return).
R_f = The risk-free rate of return.
β_s = The stock's beta.
R_m = The expected return on the stock market as a whole.

The rationale underlying the above expression and a fuller explanation of its terms is presented below.

The capital asset pricing model assumes that (1) a company's cost of equity capital is equivalent to its stock's expected return and (2) expected return on a stock (dividends plus price appreciation) is related to the risk associated with owning the stock. This positive relationship between risk and return of a stock can be represented by a simple equation which expresses the expected return on a risky security (R_s) as being equal to the risk-free rate (R_f)[1] plus a premium for risk.

$$R_s = R_f + \text{risk premium}$$

The capital asset pricing model divides a security's risk into two categories: unsystematic and systematic risk. Unsystematic risk is the portion of a security's total risk that is peculiar to the company. This risk can be diversified away by holding a sufficiently large and diverse portfolio of equities.[2] Systematic risk is that portion of a stock's total risk that is related to the movement of the stock market. It is an unavoidable risk that the stockholder cannot diversify away. This is the risk premium incorporated in the above equation. The higher a stock's market risk, the higher the expected returns. As far as the capital asset pricing model is concerned, systematic or market risk is the only thing that matters when trading off risk and expected return.

The most popular way of measuring systematic risk is the so-called beta (β) of a stock. It reflects the tendency of a stock's past return to move in parallel with the return of the stock market as a whole. A beta of 1.0 indicates that a stock's average systematic risk rose and fell at the same percentage as a broad market index. A beta above 1.0 indicates that a stock's systematic risk tended to rise and fall by a greater percentage than the market. Conversely, a beta of less than 1.0 indicates the stock's systematic risk was less sensitive to market changes. That is, if the level of the market's systematic risk dropped, the stock's return declined at a slower rate. Or, if the market index rose, its return rose slower. The betas of stocks, based on statistical analyses of the stocks' past variability relative to the market, are published in most security guides, such as *Value Line Investment Survey*.

Estimating the third variable in the above expected return equation, market return (R_m), is more difficult. Typically, investors assume that it is equal to the current risk-free rate (R_f) plus the historical risk premium $(R_m - R_f)$ for owning risky securities in a well-diversified or market portfolio. Studies covering long periods of time indicate that the risk premium fluctuates around an average of about 9 percent. Therefore, if the current return on a riskless government T bill is 7 percent, the expected market return is estimated to be about 16 percent. This would also be the expected return for a stock with a beta of 1.0.

---

[1] The risk-free rate is the return on a riskless investment, such as a Treasury bill or similar government security.

[2] Empirical studies have shown that unsystematic risk can be almost eliminated in portfolios of 30 to 40 randomly selected stocks.

To illustrate the expected return equation and its application in a dividend model and to answer the question "What is the stock's theoretical price (P_o)?" assume the following: The risk-free rate (R_f) is 7 percent. The market return (R_m) is 16 percent. The stock's beta (β) is 1.5, and its expected next year's dividend per share *(dps)* is $1. The dividend is projected to grow *(g)* at an annual constant rate of 10 percent.

First, use the capital asset pricing model to calculate the stock's expected return (K_e), which is also its assumed cost of equity capital (R_s).

$$K_e = R_s = R_f + \beta \ (R_m - R_f)$$

$$K_e = 20.5\% = 7\% + 1.5 \ (16\% - 7\%)$$

Next, use the dividend discount model and incorporate the issuing company's cost of equity capital (K_e) to compute its stock price (P_o).

$$P_o = \frac{dps}{(K_e - g)} = \frac{\$1.0}{(.205 - .10)} = \underline{\underline{\$8.95}}$$

Despite their shortcomings, investors use dividend discount and capital asset pricing models to estimate theoretical stock prices and the cost of equity.

Fair Market Value

If a stock is publicly traded, its current market price may not necessarily reflect a reasonable valuation. There are a number of reasons for this conclusion.

First, the market for many listed and unlisted stocks is "thin." That is, there are few prospective buyers or sellers. In these cases, the price of the stock can fluctuate significantly with only a small number of shares being traded.

Second, some stock prices are maintained at an artificial level by deliberate attempts to manipulate the price. A legal illustration of this practice is the price stabilization support that underwriters often give initially to new issues.

Third, the marketplace tends to exaggerate upward and downward stock price movements. Consequently, at the peaks and troughs of price swings, the market may not necessarily reflect reasonable values.

Finally, the market price of most stocks reflects transactions involving relatively small numbers of shares relative to the total shares outstanding. Often it is not appropriate to use these prices as a basis for valuing large blocks of shares. The price of a large block of shares may be at a discount from the current market, since dumping them on the open market might depress the price of the stock. However, if the sale gives the purchaser control of the company, the buyer may have to pay a premium for the stock.

These objections to current stock prices as a measure of value have led to the development of the "fair market" or "intrinsic" value method. This method tries to establish the price at which a security would trade in a free market between fully informed, rational buyers and sellers. As a result, the intrinsic value method looks at the valuation problem from the point of view of the buyer and seller, using some of the asset and capitalized earnings and dividend valuation techniques described earlier.

Comparative Value

Another approach to security valuation is to identify publicly traded companies comparable to the company being valued and then assign similar values to its securities. The comparable companies should be in the same business and have financial ratios similar to the company being valued.

Range of Values

The principal security valuation methods help set the range of possible values for a company's common stock. With the capitalization of earnings and intrinsic value methods, ratio analysis techniques can be helpful in getting a feel for a company's risk characteristics and the appropriateness of different capitalization rates. In any particular situation, the stock value actually settled upon will probably be based on an approach involving several of these methods, modified by the negotiating skills of the buyer and seller.

Efficient Markets

The efficient markets research referred to in earlier chapters has reached these following tentative conclusions that may be relevant to financial analysis and equity valuation: The major equity markets are efficient in that security prices typically reflect all of the publicly available accounting and nonaccounting data. Inside information gives the holder of it an advantage over other investors until it is used. Financial statement data are used in investment decisions. The market is able to "look through" most accounting differences to distinguish real economic changes from the apparent changes reported by using different accounting alternatives. Finally, in the long run the market reflects economic reality.

Efficient market researchers believe these preliminary findings may have a number of implications for the field of financial analysis. Since traditional analysis and its results are widely known, the value of known analytical tools must already be impounded in security prices. Therefore, if security analysis is to be beneficial, it must be helpful in predicting future results or have some novel quality. However, once these techniques become public, the advantages of the predictor and innovator will be quickly lost. Thus, the goal of the financial analyst is to convert publicly available information to "inside" information by the use of new and different analytical tools and to keep the findings secret. However, once the analyst acts on the insight, it becomes impounded in the market price of the relevant security.

Another finding suggested by the research into the role of accounting data in equity markets is that companies using the more liberal accounting practices tend to have the higher market risk, as measured by the volatility of a stock's price relative to some index of the volatility of the market as a whole. Since companies that have liberal accounting often have weak operating and financial characteristics, some believe this market activity reflects the underlying corporate economics rather than the accounting practices. This belief is consistent with the efficient market theories.

Finally, it should be noted that the research to date has not been able to show satisfactorily the relationship between accounting information, stock prices, and investment returns.

Critical Skill

An understanding of financial analysis is essential to those who use and issue corporate financial statements. Issuers who hope to use financial statements to influence others will be more likely to succeed if they know how statement users analyze financial data. On the other hand, financial statement users will be less likely to respond naively to financial data if they know how to analyze it correctly. Through research we are learning more each day about how statement users analyze financial statements and how the results of these analyses are used. Anyone interested in corporate financial reporting should follow these research efforts on a current basis, as today's knowledge in this area is fast being made obsolete.

The Case of the Unidentified U.S. Industries
Industry Ratio Characteristics

Despite variations in operational and financial policies and practices and in operating results between firms in the same industry, the nature of the industry has an important impact on the general patterns of the need for funds, the methods of meeting these needs, and the financial results of most firms in the industry. Presented in Exhibit 1 are balance sheets, in percentage form, and selected ratios drawn from the balance sheets and operating statements of 12 different firms in 12 different industries. Recognizing the fact of certain differences between firms in the same industry, each firm whose figures are summarized is broadly typical of those in its industry.

Question

See if you can identify the industry represented. Then, be prepared as best you can to explain the distinctive asset structures and ratios of each industry. The 12 firms are:

1. Basic chemical company.
2. Electric and gas utility.
3. Supermarket chain.
4. Maker of name-brand, quality men's apparel.
5. Meat-packer.
6. Retail jewelry chain (which leased its store properties).
7. Coal-carrying railroad.
8. Automobile manufacturer.
9. Large department store (which owns most of its store properties).
10. Advertising agency.

This case was prepared by R. C. Satchell (under the direction of Charles M. Williams).
Copyright © 1961 by the President and Fellows of Harvard College
Harvard Business School case 261–001 (Rev. 1971)

EXHIBIT 1
The Case of the Unidentified U.S. Industries

	A	B	C	D	E	F	G	H	I	J	K	L
Balance sheet percentages:												
Cash and marketable securities	4.0	7.6	5.1	15.7	4.1	0.5	8.5	4.3	3.2	5.4	17.0	38.6
Receivables	3.9	8.6	16.4	26.8	21.5	3.8	13.7	5.4	27.6	13.0	72.1	59.2
Inventories	—	24.9	11.0	23.2	61.0	2.2	22.7	39.3	49.2	—	—	—
Other current assets	0.9	3.5	—	1.2	0.2	2.6	1.6	2.4	1.6	2.5	0.8	—
Plant and equipment (net)	78.7	44.6	49.5	33.4	10.9	90.0	45.4	44.1	17.1	73.9	7.4	1.1
Other assets	12.5[a]	10.8[b]	18.0[c]	0.7	2.3	0.9	8.1[d]	4.5	1.3	5.2	2.7	1.1
Total assets	100.0	100.0	100.0	100.0	100.0	100.0	100.0	100.0	100.0	100.0	100.0	100.0
Notes payable	—	—	12.8	—	5.1	3.1	0.8	5.2	2.0	—	—	—
Accounts payable	2.9	23.9	5.3	29.3	12.6	2.6	10.0	25.3	10.5	8.3	50.3	84.4
Accrued taxes	2.6	3.6	1.9	1.4	6.6	1.4	2.7	2.4	3.1	—	—	—
Other current liabilities	0.6	4.9	5.7	—	1.2	2.6	12.0	10.4	5.8	7.7	2.6	1.6
Long-term debt	35.2	3.4	30.4	1.7	5.8	43.3	25.6	3.8	20.6	45.6	3.3	5.9
Other liabilities	3.8	6.4	—	1.6	1.0	1.8	7.5	8.2	—	10.9	1.0	—
Preferred stock	—	—	—	—	2.2	9.4	4.9	—	0.1	—	—	—
Capital stock and capital surplus	16.7	6.8	27.8	9.4	31.0	25.3	11.9	12.0	17.4	8.4	6.8	5.1
Retained earnings and surplus reserves	38.2	50.0	16.1	56.6	34.5	10.5	24.6	32.7	40.5	19.1	36.0	3.0
Total liabilities and stockholder equity	100.0	100.0	100.0	100.0	100.0	100.0	100.0	100.0	100.0	100.0	100.0	100.0
Selected ratios:												
Current assets/current liabilities	1.45	1.38	1.25	2.06	3.41	0.92	1.85	1.19	3.81	1.29	1.44	—
Cash, marketable securities, and receivables/current liabilities	0.96	0.50	1.20	1.32	1.62	0.44	0.33	0.22	1.44	1.13	1.24	—
Inventory turnover (×)	—	6.4×	6×	23×	2.1×	—	8.8×	12.8×	3.1×	—	—	—
Receivables collection period (days)	20	19	64	18	64	44	30	4	66	69	42	—
Total debt/total assets	0.412	0.356	0.565	0.339	0.313	0.530	0.510	0.471	0.420	0.619	0.663	0.918
Long-term debt/capitalization	0.403	0.055	0.425	0.025	0.078	0.490	0.382	0.078	0.262	0.628	0.090	0.191
Net sales/total assets	0.32	1.61	0.69	5.40	1.30	0.32	1.65	5.03	1.51	0.69	5.33	0.06
Net profits/total assets	0.052	0.059	0.057	0.080	0.085	0.048	0.077	0.056	0.065	0.026	0.081	0.008
Net profits/total net worth	0.102	0.105	0.137	0.121	0.124	0.107	0.211	0.125	0.112	0.095	0.240	0.112
Net profits/net sales	0.167	0.037	0.083	0.015	0.065	0.153	0.047	0.011	0.043	0.037	0.015	0.131

[a] Includes 10.1 percent of investments in affiliated companies.
[b] Includes 9.2 percent of investments in affiliated companies.
[c] Includes 14.4 percent of investments in affiliated companies.
[d] Includes 5.9 percent of investments in affiliated companies.

11. A major airline.
12. Commercial bank (fitted into the most nearly comparable balance sheet and ratio categories of the nonfinancial companies).

CASE 8-2

Union Investments, Inc.
Analysis of Financial Statements

In March 1985, Fred Aldrich, a summer trainee with the Union Investments, Inc., was called into the office of the head of the investment analysis section of the trust department. The following conversation took place:

> Fred, here are the 1984, 1983, and 1975 Basic Industries Company's financials (Exhibit 1) and a 10-year summary (Exhibit 2). Our trust department has owned this stock since the early 1970s. As you know, our portfolio people place a lot of emphasis on the quality of a company's earnings and the return on owners' equity in making stock selections. Well, they are worried. The 1984 Basic Industries annual report shows a decline in the return on owners' equity. Now, they want us to comment on the way that the company has achieved its return on equity over the last 10 years, starting with 1975. I would like you to prepare this analysis. I suggest you forget the strike years of 1979 and 1980. Also, concentrate on what happened in the 1983–84 period. I hope the analysis will include a direct comparison of the quality of the 1975 and 1984 returns on stockholders' equity and the other key financial ratios for these two years. Finally, you should know that the company has not changed its accounting policies and practices materially over the last decade.

This case was prepared by David F. Hawkins.
Copyright © 1976 by the President and Fellows of Harvard College
Harvard Business School case 177–067 (Rev. 1985)

EXHIBIT 1

BASIC INDUSTRIES COMPANY AND CONSOLIDATED AFFILIATES
Statement of Current and Retained Earnings (as reported)
For the Years 1984, 1983, and 1975
(in millions)

	1984	1983	1975
Sales of products and services to customers	$13,413.1	$11,575.3	$6,213.6
Operating costs:			
Employee compensation, including benefits	$ 5,223.0	$ 4,709.7	$2,440.8
Materials, supplies, services, and other costs	6,966.7	5,690.5	3,063.4
Depreciation	376.2	334.0	188.4
Taxes, except those on income	123.0	113.5	51.6
Increase in inventories during the year	(270.8)	(227.2)	(176.1)
	$12,418.1	$10,620.5	$5,568.1
Operating margin	$ 995.0	$ 954.8	$ 645.5
Other income	185.8	183.7	72.1
Interest and other financial charges	(180.1)	(126.9)	(27.4)
Earnings before income taxes and minority interest	$ 1,000.7	$ 1,011.6	$ 690.2
Provision for income taxes	(382.4)	(418.7)	(352.2)
Minority interest in earnings of consolidated affiliates	(10.2)	(7.8)	17.1
Net earnings applicable to common stock	$ 608.1	$ 585.1	$ 355.1
Dividends declared	(291.2)	(272.9)	(216.7)
Amount added to retained earnings	$ 316.9	$ 312.2	$ 138.4
Retained earnings at January 1	2,683.6	2,371.4	1,246.0
Retained earnings at December 31	$ 3,000.5	$ 2,683.6	$1,384.4

BASIC INDUSTRIES COMPANY AND CONSOLIDATED AFFILIATES
Statement of Financial Position (as reported)
December 31, 1984, 1983, 1975
(in millions)
Assets

	1984	1983	1975
Cash	$ 314.5	$ 296.8	$ 289.9
Marketable securities	57.3	25.3	353.3
Current receivables	2,593.8	2,177.1	1,062.5
Inventories	2,257.0	1,986.2	1,136.9
Current assets	$ 5,222.6	$ 4,485.4	$2,842.5
Investments	1,004.8	869.7	241.0
Plant and equipment	2,615.6	2,360.5	1,037.0
Other assets	526.1	608.6	180.0
Total assets	$ 9,369.1	$ 8,324.2	$4,300.0

EXHIBIT 1 *(concluded)*

	1984	1983	1975
Liabilities and Equity			
Short-term borrowings	$ 644.9	$ 665.2	$ 120.6
Accounts payable	696.0	673.5	376.2
Progress collections and price adjustments			
accrued	1,000.5	718.4	300.5
Dividends payable	72.8	72.7	58.7
Taxes accrued	337.2	310.0	318.3
Other costs and expenses accrued	1,128.1	1,052.6	392.6
Current liabilities	$ 3,879.5	$ 3,492.4	$1,566.9
Long-term borrowings	1,195.2	917.2	364.1
Other liabilities	518.9	492.1	221.0
Total liabilities	$ 5,593.6	$ 4,901.7	$2,152.0
Minority interest in equity of consolidated			
affiliates	$ 71.2	$ 50.1	$ 41.4
Preferred stock	—	—	—
Common stock	$ 465.2	$ 463.8	$ 455.8
Amounts received for stock in excess of			
par value	414.5	409.5	266.8
Retained earnings	3,000.5	2,683.6	1,384.4
	$ 3,880.2	$ 3,556.9	$2,107.0
Deduct common stock held in treasury	(175.9)	(184.5)	—
Total shareowners' equity	$ 3,704.3	$ 3,372.4	$2,107.0
Total liabilities and equity	$ 9,369.1	$ 8,324.2	$4,300.4

Basic Industries is a diversified multinational corporation with major shares of various electrical related markets.

Question

Complete the assignment given to Fred Aldrich.

EXHIBIT 2

BASIC INDUSTRIES COMPANY AND CONSOLIDATED AFFILIATES
Ten-Year Financial Highlights
As Reported in 1984
(dollar amounts in millions; per-share amounts in dollars)

	1984	1983	1982	1981	1980	1979	1978	1977	1976	1975
Summary of operations:										
Sales of products and services	$13,413.1	$11,575.3	$10,239.5	$9,425.3	$8,726.7	$8,448.0	$8,381.6	$7,741.2	$7,177.3	$6,213.6
Materials, engineering, and production costs	10,137.6	8,515.2	7,509.6	6,962.1	6,423.6	6,346.1	6,251.7	5,779.4	5,311.0	4,449.2
Selling, general, and administrative expenses	2,280.5	2,105.3	1,915.2	1,726.2	1,754.2	1,615.3	1,482.1	1,320.9	1,234.3	1,118.9
Operating costs	$12,418.1	$10,620.5	$ 9,424.8	$8,688.3	$8,177.8	$7,961.4	$7,733.8	$7,100.3	$6,545.3	$5,568.1
Operating margin	$ 995.0	$ 954.8	$ 814.7	$ 737.0	$ 548.9	$ 486.6	$ 647.8	$ 640.9	$ 632.0	$ 645.5
Other income	185.8	183.7	189.2	152.0	106.8	98.7	86.3	91.4	72.4	72.1
Interest and other financial charges	(180.1)	(126.9)	(106.7)	(96.9)	(101.4)	(78.1)	(70.5)	(62.9)	(39.9)	(27.4)
Earnings before income taxes and minority interest	$ 1,000.7	$ 1,011.6	$ 897.2	$ 792.1	$ 554.3	$ 507.2	$ 663.6	$ 669.4	$ 664.5	$ 690.2
Provision for income taxes	(382.4)	(418.7)	(364.1)	(317.1)	(220.6)	(231.5)	(312.3)	(320.5)	(347.4)	(352.2)
Minority interest	(10.2)	(7.8)	(3.1)	(3.2)	(5.2)	2.3	5.8	12.5	21.8	17.1
Net earnings	$ 608.1	$ 585.1	$ 530.0	$ 471.8	$ 328.5	$ 278.0	$ 357.1	$ 361.4	$ 338.9	$ 355.1
Earnings per common share	$ 3.34	$ 3.21	$ 2.91	$ 2.60	$ 1.81	$ 1.54	$ 1.98	$ 2.00	$ 1.88	$ 1.97
Dividends declared per common share	$ 1.60	$ 1.50	$ 1.40	$ 1.38	$ 1.30	$ 1.30	$ 1.30	$ 1.30	$ 1.30	$ 1.20
Earnings as a percentage of sales	4.5%	5.1%	5.2%	5.0%	3.8%	3.3%	4.3%	4.7%	4.7%	5.7%
Earned on shareowners' equity	17.2%	18.1%	18.0%	17.6%	13.2%	11.5%	15.4%	16.5%	16.2%	18.0%
Cash dividends declared	$ 291.2	$ 272.9	$ 254.8	$ 249.7	$ 235.4	$ 235.2	$ 234.8	$ 234.2	$ 234.6	$ 216.7
Shares outstanding—average (in thousands)	182,120	182,051	182,112	181,684	181,114	180,965	180,651	180,266	180,609	180,634
Shareowner accounts—average	547,000	537,000	536,000	523,000	529,000	520,000	530,000	529,000	530,000	521,000
Market price range per share	65–30	75⅞–55	73–58¼	66½–46½	47¼–30⅛	49⅛–37	50¼–40⅛	58–41¼	60–40	60⅛–45½
Price-earnings ratio range	19–9	24–17	25–20	26–18	26–17	32–24	25–20	29–21	32–21	31–23
Current assets	$ 5,222.6	$ 4,485.4	$ 3,979.3	$3,639.0	$3,334.8	$3,287.8	$3,311.1	$3,207.6	$3,013.0	$2,842.4
Current liabilities	3,879.5	3,492.4	2,869.7	2,840.4	2,650.3	2,366.7	2,104.3	1,977.4	1,883.2	1,566.8
Total assets	9,369.1	8,324.2	7,401.8	6,887.8	6,198.5	5,894.0	5,652.5	5,250.3	4,768.1	4,241.5
Shareowners' equity	3,704.3	3,372.4	3,084.6	2,801.8	2,553.6	2,426.5	2,402.1	2,245.3	2,128.1	2,048.1
Plant and equipment additions	$ 671.8	$ 598.6	$ 435.9	$ 553.1	$ 581.4	$ 530.6	$ 514.7	$ 561.7	$ 484.9	$ 332.9
Depreciation	376.2	334.0	314.3	273.6	334.7	351.3	300.1	280.4	233.6	188.4
Employees—average worldwide	404,000	388,000	369,000	363,000	397,000	410,000	396,000	385,000	376,000	333,000
—average U.S.	307,000	304,000	292,000	291,000	310,000	318,000	305,000	296,000	291,000	258,000

CASE 8-3

Quality Furniture Company
Financial Ratio Analysis

In March 1982, Mr. Richard Allan, an assistant credit analyst for the Quality Furniture Company, was concerned about changes in two of Quality's accounts in Minnesota—Lloyd's, Inc., of Minneapolis and The Emporium department store in St. Paul. He therefore brought the credit folders of these two customers to the attention of Mr. Watt Ralphson, the credit manager of Quality Furniture. The Quality Furniture Company had its headquarters in Wheeling, West Virginia, and manufactured high-quality home furniture for distribution to department stores, independent home furnishing retailers, and regional chains.

Lloyd's retailed quality home furnishings from four locations, one in the downtown section of Minneapolis and the others in nearby surburban areas. Sales were somewhat seasonal, with a slight downturn in the midsummer months and a slight upturn during the December holiday season. Lloyd's sales were approximately 75 percent for cash and 25 percent on six-month installment terms. Installment terms called for 25 percent down and the balance in equal monthly payments over a six-month period.

Lloyd's had been established in 1937 as a partnership and was incorporated in 1953. In June 1981, two of the four original partners sold their shares in the company to the two remaining owners.

Lloyd's had been a customer of Quality Furniture since 1939 and had previously handled its affairs in a most satisfactory manner. The Emporium was a comparatively new customer of Quality's, having established an account in 1973. A medium-sized department store in downtown St. Paul, The Emporium was well known for its extensive lines of home furnishings. Its account with Quality had been satisfactory through 1981.

Both accounts were sold on terms of 2 percent, 10, net 30, and although not discounting, had been paying invoices promptly until December 1981. Mr. Ralphson had previously established a $50,000 limit on Lloyd's and an $85,000 limit on The Emporium.

This case was prepared by Norman J. Bartczak.

Copyright © 1982 by the President and Fellows of Harvard College

Harvard Business School case 182–234

Quality Furniture advertised its lines nationally and attempted to maintain intensive coverage of trading areas by distributing through stores strategically located within a particular marketing area. Beginning in 1980, activity in the furniture market had become sufficiently spotty that quality of product and service were not the only bases for competition among manufacturers for outlets. Credit terms and financing of dealers became equally important; thus, the Quality Furniture Company, in Mr. Ralphson's words, was "backed into the position of supporting numerous customers in order to maintain adequate distribution for its products." This was made somewhat more difficult because of the credit squeeze, which had meant higher interest rates on money borrowed by Quality. During 1980, the prime rate had risen from 15.25 percent in January to 21.50 percent in December. The prime moderated somewhat during 1981 and closed the year at 15.75 percent. At the beginning of March 1982, the prime rate stood at 16.50 percent.

Because of this requirement for the extension of fairly liberal credit, Mr. Ralphson had adhered strictly to a policy of obtaining current reports on the financial status of customers. These reports, obtained as annual balance sheets and profit and loss statements for customers that were considered satisfactory risks, were supplied directly by the customers. Under certain circumstances, wherein Quality was working very closely with a particular customer who was trading actively on a small investment, Mr. Ralphson received quarterly and at times monthly statements in order "to keep on top" of the credit situation.

In early March 1982, Richard Allan received the annual reports of Lloyd's and The Emporium. After reviewing these statements and checking the accounts receivable ledger for both customers, Mr. Allan felt that the accounts should be reviewed by Mr. Ralphson. Accordingly, he furnished Mr. Ralphson with the information found in Exhibits 1 through 5.

When reviewing the accounts, Mr. Allan kept in mind that 1981 had not been a particularly good year for retail furniture stores. It was generally known that stores such as The Emporium, carrying low-priced furniture lines, were the first to suffer the declines which had come in the late summer and early fall. This situation was followed by signs of a relaxing demand for furniture of higher quality and higher price toward the end of 1981. The drop in volume and the subsequent price cutting hit the profit margins

EXHIBIT 1

<table>
<tr><td colspan="7" align="center">Aging of Quality Furniture's Accounts Receivable Balances
Owed by Lloyd's and The Emporium
As of March 31, 1982</td></tr>
<tr><td></td><td>*Prior*</td><td>*December*</td><td>*January*</td><td>*February*</td><td>*March*</td><td>*Totals*</td></tr>
<tr><td>Lloyd's ....</td><td>$ —</td><td>$34,819</td><td>$5,480</td><td>$21,146</td><td>$ 6,168</td><td>$ 67,613</td></tr>
<tr><td>The Emporium .....</td><td>$2,285*</td><td>$29,304</td><td>$6,153</td><td>$26,112</td><td>$54,749</td><td>$118,603</td></tr>
</table>

* Represents invoice on disputed shipment; customer claimed damaged merchandise.

of some retailers to such an extent that the losses in the latter part of the year in some cases equaled, or more than offset, profits gained in the earlier part of the year.

In the early months of 1982, the "softness" of the furniture business continued. Although there was no severe drop in the buying of furniture at the retail level, retail stores reduced orders of new lines and reorders of established lines in January, February, and March, because of a general feeling that there had been considerable "overbuying" by consumers which would result in a subsequent downturn in retail sales. Throughout the country, orders for shipment in March were down about 30 percent from February; February had itself shown a drop of about 10 percent from January. Thus, credit managers among furniture manufacturing concerns were placed in the unhappy position of trying to please sales managers who wanted to maintain volume, while they were aware that the shipment of

EXHIBIT 2

LLOYD'S, INC.
Balance Sheets as of January 31, 1980–1982
(dollars in thousands)

	1/31/80	1/31/81	1/31/82
Assets			
Cash	$ 85	$ 65	$ 50
Accounts receivable, net	1,385	1,565	1,610
Inventory	1,825	1,820	1,825
Total current assets	$3,295	$3,450	$3,485
Land	355	355	355
Buildings, fixtures, and equipment	1,355	1,370	1,575
Less: Accumulated depreciation	190	290	395
Net buildings, fixtures, and equipment	$1,165	$1,080	$1,180
Investments	65	65	65
Due from stockholders	—	215	290
Deferred charges	40	20	20
Total assets	$4,920	$5,185	$5,395
Liabilities and Net Worth			
Accounts payable	$ 865	$ 870	$ 925
Notes payable—employees	70	80	80
Estimated federal income tax	65	—	—
Current maturities on long-term debt	155	360	220
Miscellaneous accruals	220	205	65
Total current liabilities	$1,375	$1,515	$1,290
Notes payable—bank*	545	900	875
Mortgage notes payable	2,260	2,250	2,630
Preferred stock—5 percent noncumulative	190	190	190
Common stock	360	360	360
Additional paid-in capital	—	—	115
Retained earnings (deficit)	190	(30)	(65)
Total liabilities and net worth	$4,920	$5,185	$5,395

* Secured by pledged accounts receivable.

EXHIBIT 3

LLOYD'S, INC.
Income Statements
For Years Ending January 31, 1980–1982
(dollars in thousands)

	1/31/80	1/31/81	1/31/82
Gross sales	$11,720	$9,600	$9,160
Less: Returns and allowances	1,050	1,115	730
Net sales	$10,670	$8,485	$8,430
Cost of goods sold	6,460	5,125	5,100
Gross profit	$ 4,210	$3,360	$3,330
Operating expenses	3,570	3,090	3,045
Operating profit	$ 640	$ 270	$ 285
Other income	400	65	85
Net profit after other income	$ 1,040	$ 335	$ 370
Other deductions	290	345	405
Net profit (loss) before tax	$ 750	$ (10)	$ (35)
Income tax expense	345	—	—
Net profit (loss)	$ 405	$ (10)	$ (35)
Dividends paid	$ 210	$ 210	$ —

EXHIBIT 4

THE EMPORIUM
Balance Sheets
As of January 31, 1980–1982
(dollars in thousands)

	1/31/80	1/31/81	1/31/82
Assets			
Cash	$ 565	$ 740	$ 475
Notes and accounts receivable*	5,450	5,500	5,305
Inventory	5,480	5,370	4,925
Tax carryback claim	—	—	445
Total current assets	$11,495	$11,610	$11,150
Fixed assets, net	1,370	1,465	1,325
Leasehold improvements, net	3,480	3,590	3,460
Cash value life insurance	285	280	275
Investments	55	55	55
Notes receivable—officers and employees	105	110	140
Prepaid and deferred items	140	145	155
Total assets	$16,930	$17,255	$16,560
Liabilities and Net Worth			
Notes payable—Industrial Finance Corporation*	$ 5,380	$ 5,310	$ 4,300
Accounts payable	2,305	2,440	2,660
Miscellaneous accruals	630	590	680
Total current liabilities	$ 8,315	$ 8,340	$ 7,640
Common stock and additional paid-in capital	3,420	3,420	3,420
Retained earnings	5,195	5,495	5,500
Total liabilities and net worth	$16,930	$17,255	$16,560

* Receivables pledged to secure 30-day renewable notes to Industrial Finance Corporation.

EXHIBIT 5

THE EMPORIUM
Income Statements
For Years Ending January 31, 1980–1982
(dollars in thousands)

	1/31/80	1/31/81	1/31/82
Gross sales	$32,125	$31,265	$28,970
Less: Returns and allowances	2,925	2,870	2,215
Net sales	29,200	28,395	26,755
Cost of goods sold	18,105	17,850	18,385
Gross profit	11,095	10,545	8,370
Operating expenses	9,080	8,995	9,780
Operating profit (loss)	$ 2,015	$ 1,550	$ (1,410)
Adjustments:			
Elimination—reserves for inventory losses	—	—	870
Reduction—bad debt reserve	—	—	105
Tax carryback	—	—	445
Federal income tax	925	650	—
Net profit before dividends	$ 1,090	$ 900	$ 10
Dividends paid	725	600	5
Net profit to retained earnings	$ 365	$ 300	$ 5

furniture to customers who had already overextended their financial positions was potentially dangerous in such a period.

Questions

1. What do you think is happening at Lloyd's and The Emporium?
2. What financial ratios and questions raised in your analysis of the two companies' financial statements support your opinions?

CHAPTER 9

Quality of Earnings

"The company has high- (low-) quality earnings" is a common phrase used by statement analysts to describe a company's earnings. Most of those who use the phrase would predict that if two comparable companies in the same industry had the same projected earnings growth rate, the company with the higher "earnings quality" would have the higher price-to-earnings multiple. However, few of these same individuals would agree on a definition of "quality of earnings," use the concept in similar fashion, or undertake an analysis of earnings quality in the same way.

The phrase "earnings quality" and the related earnings quality analysis techniques are seldom encountered outside of the securities industry. The quality of earnings analysis enters in a variety of different ways into the stock evaluation process. Some investors use earnings quality as a gauge of management's bias toward conservatism. Others focus on the accounting quality of the *change* in earnings from one accounting period to another in order to appreciate the role played by accounting in the earnings change. Some examine earnings quality in order to assess what portion of earnings is potentially available in distributable cash; this last analysis reflects an investment interest in a company's present and potential dividend-paying practices. Still others use earnings quality as part of their assessment of the riskiness of a stock. Another use of quality of earnings analysis by those in and outside of the investment field is to identify accounting "red flags" which may suggest that the character of the company is changing, its accounting figures are potentially misleading, or extra care should be taken in analyzing its statements.

Quality of Earnings Characteristics

There is no generally accepted or common definition of the degrees of earnings quality or what constitutes high or low earnings quality. The partic-

206

ular way each analyst describes what quality of earnings means to him or her reflects the analyst's analytical objective and the analyst's feelings as to what earnings characteristics are relevant to this objective. Some of the phrases used by investors and security analysts to describe the character of high and low quality earnings are:

High-Quality Earnings Are:

1. Earnings determined by conservative accounting principles, such as LIFO and accelerated depreciation.
2. Earnings that are potentially distributable in cash.

3. Earnings that do not fluctuate far from their trend line.
4. Current and recent earnings that are good indicators of future earnings streams.
5. Earnings that relate to the ongoing fundamental business of the company.

6. Earnings that reflect a prudent, realistic view of the company's current and anticipated circumstances.
7. Earnings that are accompanied by a balance sheet that has no potential future surprises lurking in it, such as major intangible write-off.
8. Earnings that come from operations, not financial maneuvers that may in the future jeopardize the current stockholders' equity in the firm.
9. Earnings that are domestic in character.
10. Earnings that are understandable.

Low-Quality Earnings Are:

1. Earnings computed using liberal accounting principles, such as FIFO and straight-line depreciation.
2. Earnings that are far from being realized in a distributable cash form.
3. Earnings that are volatile over time.
4. Earnings that are not indicative of future earnings.
5. Earnings that are not repeatable and are derived from activities other than the company's basic business activity.
6. Earnings that do not come close to economic reality and are based on an optimistic view of the future.
7. Earnings that are based on a balance sheet presentation that overstates realizable assets.

8. Earnings that are mostly the result of questionable and slick financial deals.

9. Earnings that are primarily offshore.
10. Earnings that are accompanied by pages of notes which only a joint Ph.D. in accounting and Old English could understand.

ILLUSTRATION 9–1
Quality of Earnings Determinants

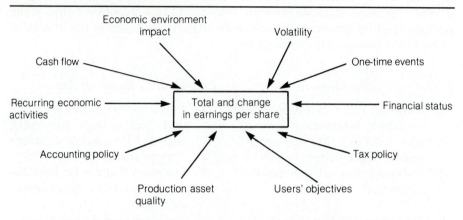

Much of the foregoing description of what constitutes high- and low-quality earnings suggests that the factors shown on Illustration 9–1 and their relationship to the absolute level and the annual change in earnings per share seem to be relevant.

High-quality earnings-per-share companies have these characteristics: (1) A consistent, conservative accounting policy that results in a prudent measurement of the company's financial condition and net income. (2) A pre-tax income stream that is derived from recurring, rather than onetime, transactions related to the basic business of the company. (3) Sales that quickly convert to cash after being recorded for accounting purposes. (4) A net income level and growth rate that is not dependent on a lowering of the tax rate through means which may be vulnerable to future tax code changes or place detrimental constraints on the company's use of the tax savings or deferrals. (5) A debt level that is appropriate for the business and a capital structure that has not been manipulated to produce earnings-per-share effects. (6) Earnings that are not materially inflated by unrealizable inflation or currency gains. (7) Earnings that are stable, predictable, and indicative of future earnings levels. (8) The fixed assets used in the generation of earnings are well maintained and up to date. (9) The income figure presented is relevant to the user's objective.

Low-quality earnings-per-share companies have the opposite characteristics.

When using the framework presented in Illustration 9–1, it is important to realize that there is no agreed-upon way that the various elements listed affect stock values. Also, there are no commonly agreed-upon standards to follow in rating the relative importance individually or collectively that the six elements bear on the quality assessment. Finally, the significance of the elements can change as the economy's prospects change and as the individual investor's preferences for risk shift.

The factors that enter into the quality of earnings assessment are similar to those used by analysts to quantify and classify the sources of the year-to-year changes in a company's earnings per share.

Financial and Operating Considerations

Earnings quality involves more than just income statement considerations. As indicated in Illustration 9-1, certain financial and operating characteristics can contribute to a higher or lower quality of earnings ratings.

A company's degree of operating leverage reflects the extent to which fixed costs are a part of the firm's total cost structure. The higher the percentage of fixed costs, the higher the degree of operating leverage and the greater are the potential earnings variations caused by changes in the level of sales. The more variable are the earnings of a company, the lower will be the quality rating of those earnings and the more risk associated with them by investors.

Also, as a company's variable costs as a percentage of sales decrease, it is harder to match expenses to revenues for income determination purposes because the relationship between revenues and the costs spent to generate revenues is not easy to establish. The tendency of companies with this cost structure is to capitalize expenditures rather than expense them when they experience operating problems. When this occurs, earnings quality declines.

Ratio and trend analysis may be helpful in evaluating operating-related earnings quality. For example, either an increase in fixed costs to total costs or a decline in the relationship of the percentage change in income from operations to percentage change in units sold might suggest higher fixed charges, greater potential earnings instability, and, hence, possibly lower quality earnings. In addition, any decreases in reported earnings to fixed charges may be regarded as an indicator of a potential lowering of earnings quality.

Adequate maintenance of capital assets is a key earnings quality rating factor. If capital assets are insufficiently maintained, earnings tend to be overstated in terms of the ability of a company to be competitive and maintain the efficiency of operations. Such earnings are considered to be of low quality.

Financial characteristics, such as financial leverage, liquidity position, and availability of financing, affect the quality of earnings ratings also. As financial leverage increases, it may become increasingly more difficult to obtain additional debt financing and when accomplished, it may be at a higher interest rate than the present debt. As the fixed interest expense increases, earnings have a tendency to be more volatile and, hence, of a lower quality.

Funds must be available for future growth, and the source of these funds bears directly on earnings quality. If a company is unable to finance its growth at reasonable and affordable costs, it may not be able to maintain its growth rate, and its earnings stability may be jeopardized.

Liquidity is a key factor in assessing a company's ability to meet its current obligations. Although liquidity may not bear directly on current reported earnings, a company that cannot meet its financial obligations will most likely have to resort to actions that will result in a greater level of uncertainty and risk being attached to future earnings. Also, earnings of nonfinancial institutions that include a high percentage of interest income are also considered to be low quality.

Industry

Industry analysis must be undertaken when looking at the quality of a company's earnings. Accounting and financial practices acceptable in one industry may not be so in another. For example, capitalization of interest on borrowings related to construction activities is acceptable to many investors in the utility field because future rates should reflect the recovery of this cost. In contrast, even though it is a generally accepted accounting principle requirement, interest on construction accounting is less acceptable in the industrial sector because the future recovery of the capitalized cost is less certain.

Political and environmental factors related to the industry also affect earnings quality. Typically, these factors are not controllable by management. For example, earnings from companies that operate in foreign countries with economic and political instability may be rated low quality because of the risk of nationalization and restrictions that the host country may place on earnings repatriation. Other government regulations such as price and wage controls may also adversely impact earnings stability and, hence, earnings quality.

Relationship to Earnings Multiples

An examination of the foregoing quality of earnings characterizations suggests why "the higher the quality of earnings, the higher the price-earnings multiple" prediction of those who used this phrase is not surprising. The first reason is purely mathematical. The others relate to the investor's investment goals and the variables considered relevant to these goals.

First, many of the characterizations, such as conservative accounting and realistic balance sheets, relate to accounting practices. With respect to these definitions, if two companies are similar in all respects, except that one uses more "liberal" accounting than the other, the one with the more "conservative" accounting will typically show lower earnings and a more prudent balance sheet. However, efficient market theory suggests that the stock market will see through the accounting differences and place a similar stock price value on the two companies. If this is so, then simple arithmetic dictates that the company with the more conservative lower earnings will have a higher total market value to earnings multiplier than the company with the more liberal higher earnings, since a smaller earnings figure will be divided into the market value that is common to the two firms.

Second, a number of the qualities attributed to high- or low-quality earnings relates to volatility and uncertainty. It is widely held that the stock market abhors uncertainty, and the typical expression of this sentiment is a low price-earnings multiple. Therefore, since high-quality earnings are associated with companies having highly predictable earnings with low volatility, experience suggests that earnings-oriented investors would tend to give such companies a higher price-earnings multiple than those companies with uncertain and volatile earning prospects.

Third, some of the characteristics of earnings quality seem to be related to the company's current potential dividend-paying ability or the closeness of the earnings figure to distributable cash which, besides being available for dividends, can be reinvested in the business to finance new assets or to reduce obligations. Again, it is not difficult to understand how those who have a dividend-oriented investment strategy might define earnings quality in these terms and assign higher earnings multiples to companies whose reported earnings closely reflect actual distributable cash.

Fourth, earnings quality seems to be defined by some as the closeness of the earnings to what is considered "economic reality." This is a very subjective assessment, but those who suggested this definition apparently feel capable of making it. Assuming that "economic reality" can be appraised, it is not surprising that higher quality earnings would be valued more than low-quality earnings which may be the result of accounting manipulations solely.

Finally, "understandability" is sometimes suggested as a criterion for judging the relative quality of an earnings figure or earnings history. Common sense suggests that confronted with two companies with identical earnings figures and earnings projections, the investor would value more highly the company with the earnings stream that lent itself more easily to a straightforward analysis and communication of results.

Red Flags

A common reason for examining the quality of a company's earnings is to detect "red flags" that may indicate changes in a company's fortunes which may or may not yet be reflected in the price of the company's stock or readily apparent from the key financial measures of performance or financial condition. Underlying this use of the quality of earnings concept is the belief that managers generally prefer to use conservative accounting, rely on regular operations to generate profits, and use outside debt financing prudently. As a management moves away from this ideal, the assumption is that the underlying condition of the company is such that the ideal cannot be realized. Of course, this approach recognizes that deviations from the ideal represent only red flags and not necessarily a declining or undesirable situation. Red flags identification is the beginning of an analysis, not the end.

A list of accounting quality-related red flags and the possible type of problems they may suggest are:

- An audit report that is unusually long; contains unusual wording; mentions material uncertainties; is dated later than is customary; or indicates a change in auditors. These red flags may indicate that management and their public accountants disagree over how certain transactions should be accounted for. Typically, this disagreement is over transactions that involve a high degree of uncertainty.
- Reductions of managed costs, such as advertising, in total or relative to sales. These costs are often reduced to help a company reach its profit goal. When this occurs, a question should be raised as to whether or not the long-run interests of the corporation are being endangered.
- Changes in accounting policies, accounting estimates, or the application of existing accounting policies toward a more liberal application. The accounting change may signal a change in the economics of the firm or simply be a change to create a higher earnings growth rate.
- An increase in accounts receivable that is out of line with the past experience. The company may be using credit to create sales in order to reach an earnings objective. These sales may be to higher credit risk customers, pulled into the current year from the next year or creating financial problems for the seller.
- Extension of trade payables that is out of line with past experience or longer than the normal trade credit period. Companies at balance sheet dates like to have their trade payables appear current.
- An unusual increase in intangible asset balances. The company may be capitalizing expenditures because income is insufficient to absorb the expenditures as expenses of the current period.
- Onetime sources of income, such as the sale of nonproductive assets like the company's headquarters buildings. The sale at a profit may be made to close the gap between actual and forecast profits.
- Decline in gross margin percentages. Price competition may be hurting the company, its costs may be out of control, or the company's product mix may be changing.
- Reduction of reserves by direct charges or reversals. The direct charges suggest that the contingency for which the reserve was created occurred or the company needs to reverse the reserve to create profits.

- Increase in borrowings. The company is having trouble financing its activities from internally generated funds.
- Increase in the deferred tax portion of the tax expense. The company may be making its accounting for public purposes more liberal, or the pre-tax profit for tax purposes may be falling, which may be a better measure of the company's actual performance trend.
- Increase in the unfunded pension liability reported in the notes or on the face of the balance sheet. The funding of pensions may be becoming more difficult, which suggests a cash flow problem.
- Low cash and marketable securities balances at year-end. The company may be using its cash to reduce payables so as to improve its current ratio on a one-shot basis.
- Peak short-term borrowings at year-end or at a time during the year that is different from the past. The company may have borrowed funds to support the use of credit to get sales up at year-end, or the nature of the business is changing from its traditional pattern.
- Slowdown of inventory turnover rate. Sales, inventory, or production problems may be developing.

Other Application and Measurement

In addition to its "red flag" usage, the quality of earnings concept is used in a variety of other ways. Some of those applications and a few of the efforts to measure earnings quality are discussed below.

Management Appraisal

One application involves a checklist of accounting policies to perform a penalty point by penalty point analysis of a company's accounting policies over the last three years. This formal system assigns penalty points to accounting policies that the analyst considers "liberal." For example, if a company uses straight-line depreciation, it receives one penalty point. The more penalty points a company accumulates, the lower its earnings quality. The penalty point scores are used to rank companies within their industry according to accounting quality, gain an understanding of the role of accounting in generating earnings, and the bias of management toward conservatism. This last application of the earnings concept is based on the hypothesis that the selection of accounting principles by management reflects in part the character of the management.

Relative Quality

The ranking of companies by their relative accounting practices quality is thought to be a useful exercise by some analysts. Those who use earnings quality in this manner believe that by keeping track of the relative earnings quality of the companies in an industry, you can detect changes in the relative earnings quality. Sometimes this may be a tip-off that the relative strengths of the companies are changing. Little in the way of formal research backs up this assertion, however.

Adjusted or Not Adjusted

Once they had identified the accounting rules used by management to determine earnings and the related balance sheet items, some analysts adjust the financial reports to conform to either the analyst's view of the appropriate accounting for the firm's circumstances or the accounting practices of the industry leader which often in practice has the most conservative accounting practices in the industry. The further the reported earnings are away from the adjusted earnings, depending on the direction, the lower or higher the earnings quality rating.

Most analysts, however, make no attempt to adjust the reported figures when valuing stocks. They make their adjustments to the price-earnings multiple if they believe earnings are over- or understated relative to some accounting standard of the analyst.

Volatility and Risk

One dimension of earnings quality is the volatility of earnings over time. Since lower volatility (i.e., a more stable earnings stream) implies less investment risk, low volatility is often associated with high-quality earnings.

Several simple statistical approaches used to measure the volatility and risk associated with a company's reported earnings are:

1. *Standard deviation:* This is a statistical term that measures variability of a set of observations from the mean of the distribution.

$$s = \sqrt{\frac{\Sigma(X - \bar{X})^2}{(n - 1)}}$$

where, for example, for a series of earnings figures:

X = Reported earnings for period t.
$\bar{X}$ = Average earnings (or mean).
n = Number of years.

The higher the standard deviation in earnings, the lower the earnings stability associated with the firm. Therefore, a high standard deviation may indicate lower quality of earnings.

2. *Coefficient of variation:* This is a measure of relative dispersion; it is used to determine the percentage deviation from the mean in a situation where the standard deviation could be misleading, i.e., where two different probability distributions may have the same standard deviation but different expected values or means.

$$v = \frac{s}{\bar{X}}$$

where:

s = Standard deviation.
$\bar{X}$ = Mean.

The coefficient of variation can be used to evaluate relative instability in earnings among companies. The higher the coefficient of variation in earnings of a company, the higher the risk associated with its earnings stream.

A Useful Tool

Those who evaluate earnings quality recognize that it is a subjective process, which at best can only be a crude evaluation technique. Also, they acknowledge that when assessing whether an earnings figure is "high," "acceptable," or "low" quality, the unique circumstances of the reporting company must be taken into account. In addition, they would agree that the quality of a company's earnings is only one factor to consider in the total investment quality appraisal of a stock. Nevertheless, those who try to evaluate earnings quality find it is a useful analytical tool, particularly when used for "red flag" identification purposes and as one of the rating factors in stock investment quality ratings schemes.

Westinghouse Electric Corporation
Quality of Earnings Analysis

On January 30, 1974, Westinghouse Electric Corporation reported net income for 1973 of $161.9 million or $1.82 a share. This represented a drop of 19 percent from net income of $198.7 million or $2.24 a share in 1972. Sales, however, were up 12 percent in 1973, to a record $5.7 billion from $5.1 billion.

The dramatic drop in earnings at Westinghouse came as somewhat of a surprise to Wall Street. Until late October 1973, most analysts were projecting 1973 earnings to exceed the record earnings reported by Westinghouse in 1972. Much of their optimism was based on statements by Westinghouse's chairman, D. C. Burnham, who had seen Westinghouse's sales double and its earnings quadruple in his 10 years as chief executive. As late as August 29, 1973, Mr. Burnham was expecting "a good year" for Westinghouse. At that time, analysts were projecting 1973 earnings for Westinghouse of between $2.35 and $2.50 a share.

During an August 29 interview, Mr. Burnham stated that he was "relatively satisfied with a growth of 10 percent a year" in sales. He added, however, "I'm not satisfied with our profit margin, which has been running around 4 percent. I think it should be 5 percent." Mr. Burnham indicated that the company would be "working very hard" in the third quarter in an effort to better the $49.7 million, or $0.55 per share earned in the third quarter of 1972.

On October 10, 1973, Westinghouse announced third-quarter earnings of $44.1 million or $0.50 per share. This was 11.3 percent less than third-quarter earnings in 1972. According to Mr. Burnham, most of the profit decline for the period could be attributed to Westinghouse's Power Systems Company where shipments of turbines and generators had lagged the entire year. Material shortages and production scheduling problems caused by

This case was prepared by Norman J. Bartczak.

delays in licensing new nuclear power stations were cited as the reason for the decline in shipments. However, according to John W. Simpson, president of Power Systems, "this is business which is only deferred and not lost." He expected that shipments would start to rebound during the fourth quarter. After Westinghouse's announcement of its third-quarter earnings, analysts pared their earnings projections for the year to be "flat," i.e., approximately the same as the $2.24 per share in 1972.

On December 20, 1973, Wall Street was again taken by surprise by Westinghouse. In a dramatic reversal from earlier optimism, Mr. Burnham announced that he expected Westinghouse's fourth-quarter net income to be "about half" 1972's $53.6 million or $0.61 per share, and profits to be down for the full year. He noted that the downward trend stemmed from "heavy losses" in four subsidiaries. Excluding the four loss operations, he added, 1973 results "would have exceeded" 1972's record net income.

Once again, analysts revised their estimates of Westinghouse's full year 1973 earnings, this time to between $1.80 and $1.85 per share. On January 30, 1974, Westinghouse announced 1973 earnings of $1.82 per share. Exhibits 1, 2, 3, and 4 present information concerning Westinghouse from various financial sources and from Westinghouse's 1972 and 1973 annual reports.

In an interview with *Forbes Magazine* published on February 15, 1974, Mr. Burnham and *Forbes* commented on Westinghouse's 1973 results, excerpts of which follow:

"We simply took on more projects than we had competent management to handle. What we didn't evaluate was the risk of a new business in a new location with a lot of new managers. And when things went wrong, we didn't control the costs . . . I will be riding herd a lot harder this year. I'm sure of that," says Burnham.

Westinghouse was clobbered especially hard in low-income housing, where it was dependent on government funding that eventually petered out. "In housing," says Burnham, "we've taken all the losses we know about on contracts not yet completed. In water control, we will sell some projects, drift out of some, stay in a few." In France, the management at its elevator company has been sacked and Burnham has tightened the auditing procedures.

All in all, Burnham expects some write-offs, but smaller ones, for 1974, and no bad surprises. Earnings for the year should be up slightly. Westinghouse has a good-sized lead over GE in orders for nuclear power plants, and its overall backlog, at $7.8 billion, is the biggest on record. "We've got the organization structure to grow with," Burnham says. "This year we'll do better than $6 billion sales"—a gain of nearly 20 percent.

By Burnham's own doing, Westinghouse's top executives, himself included, must step aside at age 60. That means that 1974 will be his last year on the corporate throne. He leaves no doubt that he intends to end his generally productive reign on a prosperous note. Which includes trying to get his stock up.

"I think," Don Burnham says, "that Wall Street doesn't look very far

EXHIBIT 1

WESTINGHOUSE ELECTRIC CORPORATION
Quarterly Income Statement Information
(dollars in millions, except per-share amounts)

	I	II	III	IV	Year
1972					
Sales	$1180.0	$1260.0	$1230.0	$1420.0	$5090.0
Net income	42.8	52.6	49.7	53.6	198.7
Earnings per share	$ 0.48	$ 0.60	$ 0.55	$ 0.61	$ 2.24
	I	II	III	IV	Year
1973:					
Sales	$1270.0	$1410.0	$1390.0	$1630.0	$5700.0
Net income	40.8	53.4	44.1	23.6	161.9
Earnings per share	$ 0.46	$ 0.60	$ 0.50	$ 0.26	$ 1.82

Quarterly Stock Price Information

	Daily Average Volume	High	Low	Close
1972:				
I	53,700	$48.25	$43.00	$47.75
II	40,100	54.875	47.75	50.75
III	61,900	52.50	38.375	42.50
IV	66,600	46.25	39.875	43.00
1973:				
I	61,300	47.375	35.25	38.125
II	56,400	38.375	31.125	35.00
III	50,400	38.875	31.375	36.75
IV	112,500	39.875	24.25	25.375

Selected Daily Stock Price Information

Date	Volume	High	Low	Close
8/28/73	29,000	$34.625	$34.25	$34.375
8/29/73	73,200	34.75	34.25	34.375
8/30/73	96,700	34.875	34.125	34.75
10/09/73	67,500	39.875	39.25	39.25
10/10/73	68,700	39.50	36.625	36.625
10/11/73	549,500	34.375	33.75	33.75
12/20/73	38,100	33.00	32.00	32.25
12/21/73	573,900	24.875	24.25	24.375
01/29/74	71,500	23.625	23.25	23.375
01/30/74	114,200	23.75	22.875	23.50
01/31/74	112,100	24.00	22.75	23.00
02/15/74	57,500	21.875	21.25	21.50
02/19/74	81,500	22.75	21.75	21.75

EXHIBIT 2

WESTINGHOUSE ELECTRIC CORPORATION
Ten-Year Summary: Selected Statistics—U.S. Economy and Westinghouse

	1973	1972	1971	1970	1969	1968	1967	1966	1965	1964
U.S. Economy										
Consumer price index (1967 = 100)	133.1	125.3	121.3	116.3	109.8	104.2	100.0	97.2	94.5	92.9
percent change	6.2	3.3	4.3	5.9	5.4	4.2	2.9	2.9	1.7	1.3
Gross national product (in billions of 1972 dollars)	$ 1235.0	1171.1	$ 1107.5	1075.3	$ 1078.8	1051.8	$ 1007.7	981.0	$ 925.9	$ 874.4
percent change (real)	5.5	5.7	3.0	(0.3)	2.6	4.4	2.7	5.9	5.9	5.3

Westinghouse Electric

	1973	1972	1971	1970	1969	1968	1967	1966	1965	1964
Per common share data:										
Earnings	$ 1.82	2.24	$ 2.08	1.53	$ 1.89	1.74	$ 1.60	1.55	$ 1.41	$ 1.02
Dividends	0.972	0.936	0.90	0.90	0.90	0.90	0.80	0.70	0.625	0.60
Book value	22.37	21.56	20.09	17.76	17.01	16.01	15.04	14.12	13.36	12.84
Stock price: high-low	$ 47–$24	55–$38	$ 49–$33	35–$27	$ 36–$27	40–$30	$ 40–$28	34–$20	$ 32–$29	$ 23–$15
Average annual P/E	18.9	20.6	21.0	20.9	16.3	20.5	19.4	17.2	18.4	17.9
Industry average P/E	18.7	20.3	20.4	18.2	21.7	23.3	25.0	23.6	24.4	27.7
S&P 425 average P/E	13.4	18.0	18.0	16.5	17.5	17.3	17.0	15.2	16.8	17.6
Common shares outstanding	88,320	88,300	83,603	82,219	81,418	79,005	77,875	77,177	75,516	74,560
Common stockholders	168	161	156	163	166	168	175	188	190	197
Employees	194	184	180	186	163	155	147	139	128	125

(data in thousands, except per share data; 1964–1969 financial position items and capital expenditures as reported: all other items adjusted for pooling of interests)

EXHIBIT 2 *(concluded)*

	1973	1972	1971	1970	1969	1968	1967	1966	1965	1964
Financial position:										
Current assets	$2,607,778	$2,172,488	$2,029,542	$2,041,477	$1,404,543	$1,352,900	$1,313,600	$1,280,500	$1,097,100	$1,042,300
Accounts receivable	1,308,232	1,016,191	950,149	911,467	720,630	688,800	564,725	472,263	438,257	434,783
Inventories	1,106,842	896,414	895,365	975,954	766,829	715,315	763,097	727,313	585,074	539,705
Total assets	4,407,665	3,843,291	3,537,851	3,358,167	2,477,612	2,271,400	2,075,300	1,931,600	1,711,500	1,606,600
Current liabilities	1,502,225	1,095,473	962,325	1,139,818	694,969	587,782	459,283	538,710	357,597	278,048
Accounts payable	405,307	351,045	297,235	288,296	132,631	131,090	126,921	143,291	102,663	92,656
Short-term debt and current maturities	475,301	208,346	182,070	431,061	228,311	149,700	66,000	143,900	15,000	15,000
Long-term debt	671,727	629,109	641,247	620,980	382,142	404,409	426,586	240,574	241,991	258,848
Stockholders' equity	1,996,137	1,930,119	1,776,818	1,487,417	1,389,330	1,276,574	1,189,409	1,103,089	1,037,918	983,951
Capital Expenditures	$ 202,414	$ 224,721	$ 200,018	$ 207,411	$ 173,700	$ 206,400	$ 145,400	$ 111,700	$ 73,000	$ 52,800
Income:										
Sales	$5,702,310	$5,086,621	$4,630,530	$4,313,410	$3,924,286	$3,664,050	$3,216,347	$2,851,396	$2,630,339	$2,486,843
Depreciation	115,161	103,240	90,913	87,015	76,944	73,000	63,641	65,442	69,019	65,895
Net income	161,928	198,667	175,256	126,999	154,920	139,052	125,874	121,371	108,314	77,868
Preferred dividends	1,158	1,158	1,158	1,158	1,191	1,410	1,510	1,541	1,548	1,548
Common dividends	$ 85,567	$ 81,966	$ 74,380	$ 71,748	$ 69,832	$ 68,937	$ 60,384	$ 51,936	$ 45,564	$ 43,509

EXHIBIT 3
Westinghouse Electric Corporation

<hr>

Westinghouse 1972 Annual Report: Letter to Stockholders

To Our Stockholders:

January 31, 1973

Again I can say, "It was the most successful year in Westinghouse history."

The company in 1972 achieved record sales for the 10th straight year, topping the $5 billion mark for the first time. We achieved record earnings despite some problems in the economy which prevented even better results. And while new marks were being set, Westinghouse was building a strong base for continued success in years ahead.

We invested nearly $225 million in new and improved plants and laboratories, adding 17 facilities in the United States and overseas. With 112 manufacturing plants in this country and 74 in 19 other countries of the world, Westinghouse is better prepared to serve the needs of customers and society than ever before. Our sales to countries outside the United States from both our domestic and worldwide facilities exceeded a billion dollars for the first time. This means your company is accelerating its drive to meet the needs of people in all parts of the world—and to build commercial success in so doing.

These things were achieved despite such problems in the economy as the delayed upturn in capital spending by industry, delays in licensing new electric power plants, and continued uncertainties in the minds of businessmen and consumers.

I am encouraged by the performance of our four operating companies. The Consumer Products Company showed improvement in sales and earnings which we expect will continue as a result of aggressive marketing of quality products and better cost control.

The Power Systems Company established another outstanding sales and earnings record. With the largest backlog of orders in its history and with exciting projects ahead—such as the lead role in building the nation's first large-scale fast-breeder nuclear power plant—Power Systems shows excellent prospects for strong performance throughout the decade of the 70s and beyond.

Record sales and backlogs also were achieved by the Industry and Defense Company in 1972. Improving business conditions and increased capital spending indicate a strong 1973 for this important Westinghouse business.

Higher TV and radio advertising expenditures helped provide a sales gain for our Broadcasting, Learning, and Leisure Time Company. This company also increased its participation in the leisure time market. At the same time, the learning business continued to pick up strength.

In January, our directors raised the quarterly dividend to 24.3 cents, consistent with the Phase 3 guideline of 4 percent.

For the future, the four operating companies will emphasize strategic planning which plots the Westinghouse course through the 70s and, in some cases, through the balance of this century. Backing up such planning is the continued support of research and development. We will increase research expenditures in 1973. Emphasis will also be placed on productivity improvement with capital expenditures for plants and equipment again at about the 1972 level.

Plans to keep Westinghouse moving with vigor in the future also involve organization. Early in 1972, we announced the "step-down-at-60" program which assures that the top seven positions in the company will be filled by competent young executives, and releases the talents and experience of the former top executives for programs of long-range significance to society and to Westinghouse.

The past 10 years have seen your company move into the mainstream of technological and social progress, encountering as it goes the problems which always accompany change. But solving people's problems is exactly where a company such as ours can make its greatest contribution to the good of mankind.

On the cover of this report are the words of Albert Einsten: "Concern for man himself and his fate must always form the chief interest of all technical endeavors." Westinghouse could find no better guideline for its future course.

D. C. Burnham
Chairman

EXHIBIT 4
Westinghouse Electric Corporation: Excerpts from Westinghouse's 1973 Annual Report

Review of 1973

While the steady growth in Westinghouse sales continued during 1973 and order backlogs reached a record of $7.8 billion, our earnings progress was interrupted by heavy losses in four subsidiaries, abnormally low scheduled shipments of turbine-generators, and continuing cost problems in our major appliance business. The result was a disappointing drop of 42 cents a share from 1972 earnings.

The losing subsidiaries, which are receiving close attention and undergoing vigorous corrective action, included operations engaged in low-income housing, water quality control, the direct mail-order and record club business, and our elevator company in France. After-tax losses from these four subsidiaries totaled $59 million, or 67 cents a share.

Steps have been taken to withdraw from the low-income and military housing business. Intensive assessment to determine the appropriate course of action with respect to the water quality control and the mail-order and record club businesses is continuing, and decisive action will be taken during 1974. The potential for successful operation of the French elevator subsidiary justifies further efforts to reach a profitable level.

Because these loss operations have had such a disproportionate effect on our overall results, we have instituted a tighter, centralized management system to prevent such areas of weakness from developing into major problems in the future. The division manager is still in charge of his operation, but our new, more sensitive system will help detect and solve problems more rapidly and effectively.

One of the 1973 problems was the low level of turbine-generator shipments. While incoming orders for generating equipment were at a record high, the effect of depressed order levels in several prior years resulted in relatively low shipments in 1973. Added production expense and investment to prepare for increased shipments ahead also reduced the profit contribution of the power generation group. We look for turbine-generator deliveries to improve moderately, starting in the second quarter of 1974. Urgent energy needs mean accelerated demand for generating equipment in the years ahead.

The Energy Crisis

The energy crisis is, of course, a major element in the business outlook. The greater requirement for electricity offers the electrical manufacturing industry a tremendous challenge and a great opportunity.

The need to turn from dependence on the scarce fuels—oil and natural gas—to the more abundant fuels—coal and uranium—means that the United States and all the developed nations must shift to an electric economy. Such a shift will make possible the cleanest, most efficient use of coal and nuclear fuel by first converting their energy to electricity.

Because the world's energy and environmental needs can only be met in the long run through such a shift to an electric economy, we have spelled out that fact on the cover of this report, and you will find its ramifications apparent in the following pages in which our operating companies assess the future. Its significance to Westinghouse can hardly be overestimated.

Record Nuclear Orders

Westinghouse results in 1973 gave indication of this bright future even though the year's earnings were disappointing. The Power Systems Company announced orders for 18 nuclear steam supply systems or nuclear power plants to bring our total above the 100 mark—more than have been sold by any other manufacturer. And the contract was signed under which we have been given lead responsibility for the nation's first fast breeder demonstration plant. The breeder reactor, which produces more nuclear fuel than it consumes, will provide a long-range answer to world energy needs.

For Power Systems, the tremendous significance of this world nuclear leadership was obscured perhaps by its short-range problem in turbine-generator shipments. I am confident, however, that we have in place an organization that is well positioned to take full advantage of the shift to an electric economy.

The vigorous markets for capital equipment and commercial and industrial construction were major factors in the strong sales and earnings performance achieved by our Industry and Defense Company. As factories strained to meet customer needs and sought to improve productivity, our industrial divisions found their products in great demand. In transportation, the growing need and federal support for rapid mass transit systems were reflected in many active customer nego-

EXHIBIT 4 *(continued)*

tiations. The BART system of San Francisco's bay area extended its service and is expected to be in full operation in 1974. Our experience in supplying the propulsion and automatic train-control systems for this pioneering venture puts us in good position to supply automated transit equipment which will be in great future demand.

Weakness in the housing market accentuated the problems of our subsidiary formed in 1968 in response to the urgent need for low-income and military housing. We stopped taking orders for such housing and sold the factory that had produced prefabricated housing modules. We are completing those housing jobs now on the books, but in the future will continue only our land development activity.

Productivity Improvement

The Consumer Products Company's principal problem in 1973 was the major appliance operation where our costs were too high for the prices in the marketplace. We are pursuing a vigorous productivity improvement program. Leading our consumer business were the lamp divisions which now must face the difficulties posed by some energy conservation programs which greatly exaggerate the energy to be saved by "turning off the lights." Lighting represents only about 1 percent of the nation's energy load. We need to encourage programs which both save energy and maintain acceptable lighting levels for efficiency and safety.

Television and radio advertising revenues increased and the Group W stations of our Broadcasting, Learning, and Leisure Time Company turned in good performances in both earnings and quality programming. The Westinghouse Learning Corporation was profitable for the second year in a row and now is set in a successful growth path.

The principal problems encountered by this company were in the direct-mail and record club business and the car rental operation, both of which lost money. These are being closely watched to determine if the corrective steps now being taken will produce the necessary improvement.

Worldwide Growth

Westinghouse continued to pursue a strong interest in world markets, convinced as we are that both manufacturing capability in other countries and exports from the United States are vital to the corporation's growth and prosperity. Our Consumer Products Company acquired a majority interest in Fabrelec, a major appliance firm in Spain; Power Systems established a strong minority interest in Framatome, a French nuclear equipment firm, and also in Eurofuel, a new French and Belgian nuclear fuel company.

Our board of directors held its first meeting outside the United States when, in September, it met in Brussels during a tour of Westinghouse European facilities. It was at this meeting that Dr. Marina v. N. Whitman, noted economist of the University of Pittsburgh, was elected to our board. In June, Richard R. Pivirotto, president of Associated Dry Goods Corporation, was elected to the board. On January 28, 1974, we learned with deep sorrow of the death of Dillon Anderson, an esteemed member of the board for two decades.

Although the energy crisis may have a direct effect on those divisions which use large amounts of plastics and gas, we are prepared to cope with these shortages so that production should be able to continue as planned, with few temporary disruptions.

To summarize 1973, although Westinghouse experienced a difficult time in several of its newer businesses, it moved ahead as planned in most of its basic operations whose prospects for both the near and long-term future have steadily brightened. Westinghouse management is confident that we can resume the progress that marked our past decade of profitable growth. We expect this progress to begin slowly in 1974 but to gain momentum as the year progresses.

I have asked the executives of our operating companies to give you an assessment of their businesses for the years immediately ahead in the pages which follow the financial section of this report.

D. C. Burnham
Chairman

January 30, 1974

EXHIBIT 4 *(continued)*

Financial Highlights

	1973	1972
Sales	$5,702,310,000	$5,086,621,000
Net income	161,928,000	198,667,000
Net income per common share	1.82	2.24
Dividends paid per common share	.972	.936
Average common shares outstanding during		
year	88,320,000	88,299,000
Dividends paid	86,725,000	83,124,000
Working capital at year-end	1,105,553,000	1,077,015,000
Expenditures for new and improved facilities	202,414,000	224,721,000
Depreciation	115,161,000	103,240,000

Westinghouse: Consolidated Statements of Income and Retained Earnings

	Year Ended December 31, 1973	Year Ended December 31, 1972
Income:		
Sales	$5,702,310,000	$5,086,621,000
Equity in income from nonconsolidated		
subsidiaries and affiliated companies	3,868,000	25,702,000
Other income	70,662,000	57,771,000
	$5,776,840,000	$5,170,094,000
Cost and expenses:		
Cost of sales	$4,423,557,000	$3,877,876,000
Distribution, administration, and general	868,706,000	783,116,000
Depreciation	115,161,000	103,240,000
Interest	76,940,000	56,699,000
Income taxes	127,236,000	147,167,000
Minority interest in net income of		
consolidated subsidiaries	3,312,000	3,329,000
	$5,614,912,000	$4,971,427,000
Net income	$ 161,928,000	$ 198,667,000
Net income per common share	$1.82	$2.24
Retained Earnings:		
Retained earnings at beginning of year	$1,145,711,000	$1,028,892,000
Plus:		
Net income	161,928,000	198,667,000
Pooling of interests adjustments	—	1,276,000
Less:		
Dividends paid on preferred stock	1,158,000	1,158,000
Dividends paid on common stock	85,567,000	81,966,000
Retained earnings at end of year	$1,220,914,000	$1,145,711,000

EXHIBIT 4 *(continued)*

Westinghouse: Consolidated Balance Sheet

	At December 31, 1973	At December 31, 1972
Assets		
Current assets:		
Cash and marketable securities	$ 129,289,000	$ 139,227,000
Customer receivables	1,308,232,000	1,016,191,000
Inventories	983,911,000	866,901,000
Prepaid and other current assets	186,346,000	150,169,000
Total current assets	$2,607,778,000	$2,172,488,000
Investments	185,935,000	183,706,000
Plant and equipment, net	1,324,913,000	1,213,390,000
Other assets	289,039,000	273,707,000
Total assets	$4,407,665,000	$3,843,291,000
Liabilities and Stockholders' Equity		
Current liabilities:		
Short-term loans and current portion of long-term debt	$ 475,301,000	$ 208,346,000
Accounts payable—trade	405,307,000	351,045,000
Accrued payrolls and payroll deductions	175,154,000	157,113,000
Income taxes currently payable	19,182,000	29,091,000
Deferred current income taxes	140,009,000	116,441,000
Other current liabilities	287,272,000	233,437,000
Total current liabilities	$1,502,225,000	$1,095,473,000
Noncurrent liabilities	87,131,000	81,101,000
Deferred noncurrent income taxes	80,955,000	42,187,000
Long-term debt	671,727,000	629,109,000
Minority interest	69,490,000	65,302,000
Stockholders' equity:		
Capital	775,223,000	784,408,000
Retained earnings	1,220,914,000	1,145,711,000
Total stockholders' equity	$1,996,137,000	$1,930,119,000
Total liabilities and stockholders' equity	$4,407,665,000	$3,843,291,000

EXHIBIT 4 *(continued)*

Westinghouse: Consolidated Statement of Changes in Financial Position

	Year Ended December 31, 1973	Year Ended December 31, 1972
Changes in Financial Position:		
Resources provided:		
Net income	$ 161,928,000	$ 198,667,000
Income charges (credits) not affecting working capital:		
Depreciation	115,161,000	103,240,000
Deferred income taxes	64,424,000	23,600,000
Minority interest in income of consolidated subsidiaries	3,312,000	3,329,000
Equity in income from non-consolidated subsidiaries and affiliated companies	(3,868,000)	(25,702,000)
Working capital provided by operations	$340,957,000	$303,134,000
Increase in long-term debt	69,185,000	27,913,000
Issuance of common stock to employees	26,278,000	29,825,000
Total resources provided	$ 436,420,000	$ 360,872,000
Resources applied:		
Expenditures for new and improved facilities	$ 202,414,000	$ 224,721,000
Dividend payments	86,725,000	83,124,000
Purchase of common stock for treasury	36,296,000	645,000
Reduction in long-term debt	26,567,000	40,051,000
Increase in investments	14,273,000	17,683,000
Other—net	41,607,000	10,529,000
Total resources applied	$ 407,882,000	$ 376,753,000
Net change in working capital	$ 28,538,000	$ (15,881,000)
Analysis of Changes in Working Capital:		
Increase (decrease) in working capital:		
Cash and marketable securities	$ (9,938,000)	$ 47,946,000
Customer receivables	292,041,000	66,042,000
Inventories....................................	117,010,000	3,937,000
Prepaid and other current assets	36,177,000	(658,000)
Short-term loans and current portion of long-term debt	(266,955,000)	(26,276,000)
Accounts payable—trade	(54,262,000)	(53,810,000)
Income taxes (including deferred income taxes) ...	(13,659,000)	(8,896,000)
All other current liabilities	(71,876,000)	(44,166,000)
Net change in working capital	$ 28,538,000	$ (15,881,000)

EXHIBIT 4 (*continued*)

Westinghouse: Consolidated Statement of Capital

	Cumulative Preferred Stock	Common Stock	Capital in Excess of Par Value	Treasury Stock at Cost	Total
Balance at January 1, 1972	$30,482,000	$272,642,000	$453,180,000	$ (8,378,000)	$747,926,000
Common stock issued:					
842,046 shares under stock option, employee stock, and savings and investment plans	—	2,631,000	27,194,000	—	29,825,000
377,109 shares for businesses acquired	—	1,179,000	5,741,000	—	6,920,000
65,384 shares acquired for treasury	—	—	—	(645,000)	(645,000)
4,470 treasury shares delivered for businesses acquired	—	—	85,000	143,000	228,000
Other—net	—	—	112,000	42,000	154,000
Balance at December 31, 1972	$30,482,000	$276,452,000	$486,312,000	$ (8,838,000)	$784,408,000
Common stock issued:					
210,118 shares under stock option, employee stock, and savings and investment plans	—	656,000	6,863,000	—	7,519,000
1,047,537 shares acquired for treasury	—	—	—	(36,296,000)	(36,296,000)
580,155 treasury shares delivered under stock option, employee stock, and savings and investment plans	—	—	(1,575,000)	20,334,000	18,759,000
Other—net	—	—	256,000	577,000	833,000
Balance at December 31, 1973	$30,482,000	$277,108,000	$491,856,000	$(24,223,000)	$775,223,000

EXHIBIT 4 *(continued)*

Cumulative preferred stock, par value $100, 3.8 percent Series B; authorized 374,846 shares at December 31, 1973, and 1972; 304,820 shares outstanding at December 31, 1973, and 1972.

Cumulative preference stock, without par value; 10 million shares authorized; none issued.

Common stock, par value $3.125; authorized 120 million shares at December 31, 1973, and 1972; issued 88,674,610 shares at December 31, 1973, and 88,464,492 shares at December 31, 1972.

Common stock held in treasury amounted to 798,453 shares at December 31, 1973, and 364,778 shares at December 31, 1972.

During 1973, a systematic plan for reacquisition of common stock of the corporation was begun. All the shares will be used to supply the various plans under which common stock is distributed to employees.

Westinghouse: Accounting Principles and Policies

The major accounting principles and policies followed by Westinghouse are presented below to assist the reader in evaluating the consolidated financial statements and other data in this report.

Principles of consolidation: The financial statements include the consolidation of all significant wholly and majority-owned subsidiaries except Westinghouse Credit Corporation and Urban Systems Development Corporation. The equity method of accounting is followed for nonconsolidated subsidiaries and for investments in significant affiliates (20 to 50 percent owned).

The assets and liabilities of non-U.S. subsidiaries are translated at current exchange rates except that plant and equipment are translated at rates in effect at dates of acquisition. Income and expense amounts, except depreciation, are translated at rates prevailing during the year. The effects of translation are included in net income except losses attributable to long-term debt are deferred and amortized over the term of the debt. Translation adjustments in the consolidated financial statements are not material.

Sales are recorded as products are shipped on substantially all contracts. The percentage-of-completion method is used only for nuclear steam supply system orders with durations generally in excess of five years and for certain construction projects where this method of accounting is consistent with industry practices.

In accordance with these practices, Long-Term Contracts in Process are stated at cost plus estimated profits recognized to date. Costs related to long-term contracts are also accumulated in Inventories, Recoverable Engineering, and Development Costs (Government Contracts), and Progress Payments to Subcontractors. In accordance with terms of the particular contracts, progress billings are made to customers and are shown in total as Progress Billing on Contracts. The amounts of long-term contracts in process do not exceed realizable value.

Inventories: The cost of the inventories of the consolidated companies is determined principally by the LIFO method. Inventories not on LIFO are valued at current standard costs, which approximate actual, or average cost. In accordance with the practice of the corporation and of the electrical manufacturing industry generally, inventories include items which are not realizable within one year.

Pension plans cover substantially all employees of the corporation. Benefits under the plans are being funded by the pension trust method. It is the policy of the corporation to fund each year the amount actuarially determined to be necessary to provide benefits earned during the year and to amortize prior service liability over a period of 30 years.

Depreciation on plant and equipment acquired since January 1, 1968, is provided for on the straight-line method based upon guideline lives. Plant and equipment acquired prior to 1968 is depreciated using accelerated methods. Accelerated depreciation methods using guideline lives, giving effect to the class life system for assets acquired since 1970, are used for federal income tax purposes.

Deferred income taxes are provided for timing differences between financial and tax reporting, principally related to long-term contracts in process, product guarantees, and depreciation.

Deferred federal income taxes are not provided on the undistributed earnings of certain subsidiaries (primarily located outside the United States) when such earnings have been indefinitely reinvested or will be remitted in the form of a tax-free liquidation.

Investment tax credit is recorded under the flow-through method of accounting as a reduction of the current provision for federal income taxes.

Research and development costs are recorded as expenses when incurred.

EXHIBIT 4 *(continued)*

Westinghouse: Financial Review

Sales and Income after Taxes
of the Westinghouse Companies (amounts in thousands of dollars)

	Year Ended December 31, 1973				Year Ended December 31, 1972			
	Sales		Income after Taxes		Sales		Income after Taxes	
	Amount	Percent	Amount	Percent	Amount	Percent	Amount	Percent
Power systems	$1,776,447	31%	$ 61,463	38%	$1,642,697	32%	$ 86,107	43%
Consumer products	905,377	16	3,082	2	875,220	17	6,466	3
Industry and defense:								
Industry	2,140,730	38	62,619	39	1,743,183	34	52,833	27
Defense	469,528	8	11,117	7	428,208	9	11,251	6
Broadcasting, Learning, and Leisure .								
Time	369,723	6	8,534	5	351,362	7	23,218	12
Other	40,505	0	15,113	9	45,951	1	18,792	9
Total	$5,702,310	100%	$161,928	100%	$5,086,621	100%	$198,667	100%

EXHIBIT 4 *(continued)*

Sales and income after Taxes are presented in the table above on the basis of the organization of the corporation. Income after taxes are determined by allocating income taxes to the companies based on the effective consolidated tax rate for the corporation and its subsidiaries. Net income from Westinghouse Credit Corporation is included in the Other category.

Business combinations: The corporation invested $17 million during 1973 in business combinations accounted for as purchases. The net assets and results of operations of these companies are not material.

No significant business combinations ac-counted for as poolings of interests were consummated during 1973.

During 1972, the corporation delivered 377,109 shares of previously unissued common stock to acquire Host Enterprises, Inc., an operator of resort hotels. This combination was recorded as a pooling of interests.

On August 31, 1972, all the outstanding stock of Linguaphone Institute, Ltd., a subsidiary of FAS International, Inc., was acquired in exchange for cash and notes of $9,975,000. Linguaphone conducts language instruction courses. Four other combinations were ac-counted for as purchases, one of which re-sulted in the issuance of 4,470 treasury shares.

Statement of Changes in Pension Assets

	1973	1972
Book value—beginning of year—at cost	$802,688,000	$762,908,000
Additions:		
Company contributions	60,376,000	48,733,000
Employee contributions	10,558,000	7,825,000
Income from investments	28,133,000	25,867,000
Net gain from disposal of assets	2,512,000	1,253,000
Other—net	(2,229,000)	1,034,000
	$ 99,350,000	$ 84,712,000
Deductions:		
Benefit payments	50,458,000	44,932,000
Book value—end of year—at cost	$851,580,000	$802,688,000
Market value	$838,661,000	$993,620,000

Pension expense was $60.4 million in 1973 and $48.7 million in 1972. No changes in actu-arial assumptions were made in either year. Unfunded prior service liability at December 31, 1972, was estimated at $444 million, of which $268 million represented unfunded vested benefits. Based upon the latest actuarial valuation which recognizes the increased pension benefits that became effective in 1973,

unfunded prior service liability approximates $579 million, of which $431 million represents unfunded vested benefits at December 31, 1973.

Various pension arrangements, which are normally supplemented by required government plans, are in effect for most non-U.S. subsidiary companies.

Income Taxes

	Year Ended December 31, 1973	Year Ended December 31, 1972
Income taxes currently payable:		
Federal	$ 25,445,000	$ 91,494,000
State	8,598,000	15,083,000
Non-U.S.	28,769,000	16,990,000
	$ 62,812,000	$123,567,000

EXHIBIT 4 *(continued)*

	Year Ended December 31, 1973	Year Ended December 31, 1972
Income taxes deferred:		
Federal	$ 54,932,000	$ 21,100,000
State	8,000,000	2,500,000
Non-U.S.	1,492,000	—
	$ 64,424,000	$ 23,600,000
Total	$127,236,000	$147,167,000

Deferred tax expense results from timing differences in the recognition of revenue and expense for tax and financial statement purposes. The source of these differences for the years 1973 and 1972, and the tax effect of each follow:

Income Taxes Deferred	1973	1972
Excess of tax over book depreciation	$32,840,000	$18,123,000
Difference between financial and tax reporting on long-term contracts in process	22,273,000	11,656,000
Provision for warranty costs not deductible for tax purposes until incurred	(2,422,000)	(8,583,000)
Other miscellaneous timing differences	11,733,000	2,404,000
Total	$64,424,000	$23,600,000

The reconciliation between the unadjusted federal statutory tax rate and the Westinghouse effective consolidated tax rate for 1973 follows:

Effective Consolidated Tax Rate	Amount	Effective Rate
Tax expense if based on unadjusted federal statutory tax rate	$140,388,000	48.0%
Increases (reductions) in taxes resulting from:		
Income of U.S. possessions companies exempt from tax, and income from a Domestic International Sales Corporation and a Western Hemisphere Trade Corporation, both of which are subject to reduced income tax rates	(22,925,000)	(7.8%)
Investment tax credit	(8,935,000)	(3.1%)
State and local income taxes ($16,598,000) less reduction in federal income tax	8,630,000	3.0%
Miscellaneous items	10,078,000	3.4%
Income taxes	$127,236,000	43.5%

Income taxes: The investment tax credit amounted to $8.9 million in 1973 and $11.1 million in 1972.

There are cumulative undistributed earnings of $180 million from certain subsidiaries which have been reinvested for an indefinite period of time and, therefore, no deferred federal taxes have been provided. (Author's note: Cumulative undistributed earnings were $120 million in 1972.) The federal income tax returns of the corporation and its wholly owned subsidiaries are closed through December 31, 1969, and it is believed that adequate provisions for taxes have been made through December 31, 1973.

Marketable securities ($17.3 million at December 31, 1973, and $17.2 million at December 31, 1972) are recorded at cost approximating market.

Customer receivables are net of doubtful account allowances of $34 million for 1973 and $23 million for 1972.

EXHIBIT 4 *(continued)*

Inventories

	1973	1972
Inventories—valued principally on LIFO method (Author's note: 58 percent valued on LIFO method)	$1,106,842,000	$ 896,414,000
Recoverable engineering and development costs (government contracts)	40,093,000	54,937,000
Long-term contracts in process	858,994,000	800,469,000
Progress payments to subcontractors	542,894,000	424,878,000
	$2,548,823,000	$2,176,698,000
Less: Progress billing on contracts	1,564,912,000	1,309,797,000
Total	$ 983,911,000	$ 866,901,000

* The excess of current cost (principally at current standards) over the cost of inventories valued on the LIFO basis was $163 million at December 31, 1973, and $152 million at December 31, 1972.

Investments include Westinghouse Credit Corporation and significant affiliates, valued at cost plus equity in undistributed earnings, and other securities at cost or less, not in excess of market value.

Other assets include goodwill of $91 million in 1973 and $85 million in 1972. Goodwill acquired prior to November 1, 1970, is not being amortized. Goodwill of $13.9 million at December 31, 1973, and $8.8 million at December 31, 1972, resulting from business combinations subsequent to November 1, 1970, remained to be amortized over the estimated period to be benefited, not to exceed 40 years.

Plant and Equipment, at Cost

	1973	1972
Land and buildings	$ 758,056,000	$ 702,671,000
Machinery and equipment	1,555,609,000	1,424,404,000
Construction in progress	99,486,000	92,005,000
	$2,413,151,000	$2,219,080,000
Less: Accumulated depreciation	1,088,238,000	1,005,690,000
Total	$1,324,913,000	$1,213,390,000

Short-term bank loans amounted to $450 million on December 31, 1973, and $184 million on December 31, 1972. These were the maximum amounts of borrowings outstanding during the respective years. The average aggregate short-term borrowings outstanding during 1973 totaled $280 million at a 9.5 percent approximate weighted average interest rate.

Credit arrangements include domestic bank lines of credit totaling $400 million at the prime commercial rate, $120 million short-term master notes under which the corporation may borrow at the 180-day commercial paper rate, and $238 million of credit available to subsidiaries principally outside the United States at the most favorable local rates. Of these lines, $297 million was unused at December 31, 1973, and $46 million was allocated to Urban Systems Development Corporation.

Compensating balance arrangements without contractual withdrawal restrictions exist between the corporation and the banks that provide the $400 million line of credit. Similar arrangements exist with banks which provide $195 million of credit lines for the Westinghouse Credit Corporation. These arrangements provide for balances ranging from 10 percent to 15 percent of the line of credit to assure future credit availability and for loans outstanding. The average balance of corporate funds identified for compensating balance purposes was $15 million during the year.

EXHIBIT 4 *(continued)*

Long-Term Debt

	Interest Rates	Year of Maturity	Amount	
			1973	1972
Debentures	3½%	1981	$105,000,000	$120,000,000
Debentures	5⅜%	1992	164,000,000	168,000,000
Debentures	8⅝%	1995	200,000,000	200,000,000
Other Debt	Various	Various	202,727,000	141,109,000
Total			$671,727,000	$629,109,000

Long-term debt: The 8⅝ percent indenture requires sinking fund deposits of $10 million annually beginning in 1976. Sinking fund deposits of $15 million annually through 1980 and $8 million annually through 1991 are being provided under the terms of the 3½ percent and the 5⅜ percent indentures, respectively.

Other debt is secured by various assets of wholly and majority-owned subsidiary companies and matures serially in various annual amounts through the year 2000. At December 31, 1973, this debt included $144 million of borrowings outside the U.S. with an average rate of 7.2 percent and $13 million of notes convertible into the corporation's common stock.

Long-term debt maturing in each of the following years is: 1974—$25.0 million; 1975—$38.2 million; 1976—$47.9 million; 1977—$52.0 million; and 1978—$76.8 million.

Stock Options

	1973		1972	
	Shares	Average Price Per Share	Shares	Average Price Per Share
Outstanding at beginning of year	767,500	$30.17	1,157,652	$28.77
Options substituted for outstanding options of Host Enterprises, Inc.	—	—	3,681	65.20
Exercised	(127,294)	22.72	(387,733)	26.29
Terminated	(46,400)	36.04	(6,100)	33.50
Outstanding and exercisable at end of year	593,806	$31.30	767,500	$30.17

Stock options outstanding conform to the requirements for "restricted stock options" or "qualified stock options" as defined in the Internal Revenue Code. The period of granting options under all plans has expired and the last options granted terminate in 1975.

(Author's note: Management Incentive Compensation Plan, as described in Form 10-K: Under Article XVI of the bylaws, as amended by the stockholders, a special committee of the board of directors is empowered to authorize the payment of additional compensation to executive and supervisory officers of the corporation and its subsidiaries for any year in which cash dividends of at least 25 cents per share on the corporation's common stock, par value $3.125 per share, are paid, in amounts which in the aggregate do not exceed 5 percent of the consolidated net income for that year before deducting taxes on income and before any provision for incentive payments under the bylaw plus any unused amounts that may be carried forward from previous years for which the full amount of payments permitted by the bylaw shall not have been made. Payments may be made in cash, in common stock of the corporation, or both. On awards payable in deferred installments in common stock, the bylaw authorizes the payment of amounts equivalent to the dividends which are paid during the period of deferment on a like number of outstanding shares. Such amounts equivalent to the dividends are used to purchase additional shares to be held for delivery on the same terms and conditions applicable to the other shares covered by the awards. Within the limits authorized by Article XVI, aggregate payments of

EXHIBIT 4 *(continued)*

$2,901,700 (including $876,200 for officers) and $7,129,650 (including $2,266,000 for officers) were approved for 1973 and 1972, respectively. A portion of the amount approved is contingently payable in two equal annual installments in cash, beginning in 1975 for 1973 amounts and in 1974 for 1972 amounts, and a portion is contingently payable in common stock purchased for this purpose in the open market.)

Lease commitments: Total rentals charged to operations amounted to $64 million in 1973 and $57 million in 1972.

Minimum annual rentals under noncancellable leases having an original term of more than one year are $34 million in 1974, $28 million in 1975, $24 million in 1976, $20 million in 1977, and $18 million in 1978. The average minimum annual rentals for the next three succeeding five-year periods are $12 million for years ending 1979–83, $6 million in 1984–88, and $2 million in 1989–93. The total liability for years ending after 1993 is approximately $5 million.

Litigation: Four operating subsidiaries of the American Electric Power Company filed suit in December, 1971, against the two major U.S. turbine manufacturers alleging practices in violation of the Sherman Act and claiming damages in an unspecified amount. Westinghouse denies all allegations of wrongdoing. No final decision is expected for several years and although litigation is always uncertain, based upon the present state of the law, management anticipates that the final result will be favorable to Westinghouse.

Contingencies: At December 31, 1973, the corporation was contingent guarantor of customers' notes sold to banks and other liabilities aggregating $154 million and of notes payable and other borrowings of nonconsolidated subsidiaries, principally Urban Systems Development Corporation and Half Moon Bay Properties, Inc., in the amount of $83 million.

Report of Independent Accountants

To the board of directors and stockholders of Westinghouse Electric Corporation:

In our opinion, the consolidated financial statements appearing on pages 4 through 13 and on page 16 present fairly the financial position of Westinghouse Electric Corporation and its subsidiaries at December 31, 1973, and 1972, the results of their operations and the changes in financial position for the years then ended, in conformity with generally accepted accounting principles consistently applied. Our examinations of these statements were made in accordance with generally accepted auditing standards and accordingly included such tests of the accounting records and such other auditing procedures as we considered necessary in the circumstances.

PRICE WATERHOUSE & CO.
Two Gateway Center
Pittsburgh, Pennsylvania 15222

January 21, 1974

Westinghouse Credit Corporation: Condensed Consolidated Financial Statements

Balance Sheet

	At December 31, 1973	At December 31, 1972
Cash	$ 6,020,000	$ 5,982,000
Receivables, less unearned finance charges and allowance for losses	1,021,376,000	855,940,000
Investments and other assets	21,976,000	3,939,000
Total assets	$1,049,372,000	$865,861,000
Short-term notes payable and other liabilities	$ 665,692,000	$550,606,000
Long-term debt	180,000,000	150,000,000
Subordinated debt	70,000,000	40,000,000
Subordinated debt due parent	26,800,000	40,100,000
Capital ($10 million contribution in 1973)	34,500,000	24,500,000
Retained earnings (1972 restated for accounting change, $1,778,000)	72,380,000	60,655,000
Total liabilities and stockholders' equity	$1,049,372,000	$865,861,000

EXHIBIT 4 *(concluded)*

Statement of Income

	Year Ended December 31, 1973	Year Ended December 31, 1972
Total earned income	$ 123,225,000	$ 95,496,000
Less:		
Operating expense	32,350,000	26,863,000
Interest	65,778,000	35,821,000
Income taxes	12,175,000	16,965,000
Equity in net losses of nonconsolidated subsidiaries	1,197,000	—
Net income	$ 11,725,000	$ 15,847,000

Statement of Changes in Financial Position

	Year Ended December 31, 1973	Year Ended December 31, 1972
Financial resources were provided by:		
Net income	$ 11,725,000	$ 15,847,000
Provision for losses on receivables	7,302,000	5,040,000
Increase in short-term notes payable	118,932,000	72,455,000
Increase in long-term debt	46,700,000	75,000,000
Capital contribution by parent	10,000,000	—
	$ 194,659,000	$168,342,000
Financial resources were used for:		
Increase in receivables, net of unearned finance charges	$ 166,318,000	$165,900,000
Receivables written off	6,420,000	2,640,000
Investment in nonconsolidated subsidiaries	17,507,000	—
Other net	4,414,000	(198,000)
	$ 194,659,000	$168,342,000

out. Our basic business doesn't look any different than before we had these problems. The problems only affect the short range. Wall Street reacts too much to short-range performance."

Company Operations (As of Early 1974)

Westinghouse was incorporated in Pennsylvania on April 9, 1872. As of February 1974, its principal business activity is the manufacture and sale of equipment and appliances for the generation, transmission, utilization, and control of electricity. It is generally regarded as the second largest producer of electrical equipment in the world, although its relative position varies as to particular products.

Included among the products of Westinghouse are practically all electrical and much related mechanical equipment required by power companies, railroads, city transit systems and industrial plants; steam and gas turbines; propulsion and electrical equipment for the United States Navy and the marine industry; electrical and electronic systems, instrumentation and other equipment for the aerospace industry; and consumer products. West-inghouse develops, designs, and furnishes nuclear power plant equipment and fuel for the generation of electricity. At December 31, 1973, it had 101 nuclear power plants operating, under construction, or on order. West-inghouse designs and manufactures offshore nuclear power plants through a joint venture with Tenneco, Inc. This joint venture, Offshore Power Systems, has accepted four orders amounting to about $1.5 billion at December 31, 1973, and the construction of the manufacturing facility for these plants at Jacksonville, Florida, has been authorized. Some products, such as motors and control devices, are used by other manufacturers as components for their products. Westinghouse has long been an important manufacturer of military products for the United States government.

Westinghouse supplies products to the construction industry and engages in conventional construction activities. It is also engaged in land development and sales, conventionally and federally financed real estate and housing development, and the operation and management of rental properties.

The Westinghouse Broadcasting Companies own and operate five television stations located in Baltimore, Boston, Philadelphia, Pittsburgh, and San Francisco, and seven radio stations located in Boston, Chicago, Fort Wayne, Los Angeles, New York, Philadelphia, and Pittsburgh.

Westinghouse Learning Corporation offers various educational services and materials to the nation's schools, sells language instruction courses, and develops and administers various training and management skill development programs. In the area of leisure time activities, Westinghouse subsidiaries bottle and distribute various soft drink brands in important market areas; manufacture, assemble, and sell wrist watches and other timepieces under the Longines, Wittnauer, Le Coultre, and Jubilee trade names; market and sell, principally by mail, musical recordings and various related items; lease and rent automobiles on both a direct basis and through franchisees in locations across the United States, in Canada, and in the Caribbean; and operate resort hotels.

Westinghouse Credit Corporation engages in the extension of credit in transactions secured by real or personal property or both and in leasing transactions including leverage leasing.

Westinghouse household appliances are sold to independent distributors and dealers through Major Appliance Sales, a sales organization of Westinghouse. The other products manufactured by Westinghouse are, in general, sold to customers through main and branch offices of other sales organizations of Westinghouse and, in certain cases, through independent distributors and dealers. As a service to customers, Westinghouse maintains plants and other facilities for the maintenance and repair of equipment and appliances of its own manufacture and equipment manufactured by others.

Westinghouse is engaged in the distribution outside the United States of electrical and other products, primarily those manufactured by Westinghouse. Such distribution is accomplished through a wholly owned subsidiary and through company representatives and independent distributors. Westinghouse also has a number of subsidiaries outside the United States, the majority of which are engaged in the manufacture and sale of electrical generation, transmission, utilization and control equipment, and consumer products.

Westinghouse is subject to a high degree of competition (including price, services, warranty, and product performance) for sales of heavy equipment, primarily from large companies and for sales of household appliances and smaller types of equipment from both large and numerous small competitors.

Top Management

Westinghouse is internally organized into four "company-like" units; (1) Consumer Products Company; (2) Industry and Defense Company; (3) Broadcasting, Learning, and Leisure Time Company; and (4) Power Systems Company. Each of the units is headed by a president who reports to the chairman and chief executive officer. As of December 31, 1973, the principal executive officers of Westinghouse are:

1. D. C. Burnham, chairman and chief executive officer. Age 58. Mr. Burnham has served as chief executive of Westinghouse since his election as president and a director in 1963 and chairman in 1969. He joined Westinghouse in 1954 as vice president, manufacturing. Mr. Burnham owns 77,089 shares of Westinghouse's common stock.

2. Marshall K. Evans, vice chairman—planning. Age 56. Mr. Evans joined Westinghouse in 1943. He was elected a director in 1966 and reelected to a four-year term in 1973. Mr. Evans was named vice chairman—planning in 1969, and as such is Westinghouse's top planning executive, responsible for the staff functions of management services, engineering and development, manufacturing, research, and marketing. He owns 20,709 shares of Westinghouse's common stock.

3. George L. Wilcox, vice chairman—corporate affairs. Age 58. Mr. Wilcox joined Westinghouse in 1942. He was appointed vice chairman—corporate affairs in 1969. His responsibilities include finance, personnel, public affairs, investor relations, law, and the World Regions organization. Mr. Wilcox was elected a director in 1965 and reelected to a four-year term as director in 1970. He owns 52,495 shares of Westinghouse's common stock.

4. Charles E. Hammond, executive vice president and president, Consumer Products Company. Age 52. Mr. Hammond joined Westinghouse in 1946. In 1969, he was appointed president, Consumer Prod-

ucts Company. Mr. Hammond owns 23,109 shares of Westinghouse's common stock.

5. Robert E. Kirby, executive vice president and president, Industry and Defense Company. Age 55. Mr. Kirby joined Westinghouse in 1946. He was elected to Westinghouse's board of directors in 1966 and appointed president, Industry and Defense Company, in 1969. He owns 51,906 shares of Westinghouse's common stock.

6. John W. Simpson, executive vice president and president, Power Systems Company. Age 59. Mr. Simpson joined Westinghouse in 1937. Currently he heads the Power Systems Company, composed of 21 divisions which supply equipment for the electric utility industry. Mr. Simpson owns 29,478 shares of Westinghouse common stock.

7. Donald H. McGannon, executive vice president and president, Broadcasting, Learning, and Leisure Time Company. Age 53.

Remuneration

The table below sets forth the direct remuneration for 1973 of the highest-paid officers and directors whose aggregate direct remuneration from Westinghouse and its subsidiaries on an accrual basis exceeded $40,000, and of the officers and directors as a group.

| | | 1973 Incentive Compensation | | |
	Salary*	Current	Deferred	Total†
D. C. Burnham	$ 251,250	$ 30,000	$ 30,000	$ 311,250
Marhsall K. Evans	155,250	17,500	17,500	190,250
George L. Wilcox	173,997	17,500	17,500	208,997
Charles E. Hammond	136,494	12,500	12,500	161,494
R. E. Kirby	187,497	25,000	25,000	237,497
John W. Simpson	181,242	35,000	35,000	251,242
80 officers and directors as a group	$5,412,503	$487,600	$388,600	$6,288,703

* Salary includes all direct remuneration except incentive compensation.
† Excluding estimated annual benefits under pension plans.

Questions

1. How do you assess the quality of the company's $1.82 earnings per share for 1973?

2. What signs do you see in the Westinghouse financial data that this company may or may not be experiencing difficulties?

3. At the time the financial data presented in this case was published, the economy was already experiencing a high rate of inflation. How well do you think Westinghouse will be able to cope with this inflation?

CASE 9-2

General Electric Company
Quality of Earnings Analysis

In late February 1974, the Portfolio Committee for the Edgebrook Company was to meet to review the blue chip stocks in its portfolio. Edgebrook was a small midwestern investment service. Its main clients were moderately wealthy individuals looking for a "safe" return on their investment. Edgebrook managed funds for approximately 100 clients, each having a minimum investment of $50,000.

On February 27, 1974, Allan Rashba, an Edgebrook portfolio officer, met with his staff assistant, Peter Baker, to plan the analysis of General Electric Company (GE). GE had been in Edgebrook's portfolio since 1964. As with other blue chip stocks, GE was reviewed only once a year to decide if it should be continued to be held in Edgebrook's portfolio. Mr. Rashba's comments follow:

> Peter, it has been a little over one year since Reg Jones became chairman and chief executive officer of GE. He appears to be following up on the strategic planning system instituted by his predecessor, Fred Borch. In particular, like Fred Borch, Reg Jones has consistently emphasized the link between GE's strategic planning and its returns on assets and equity. My file contains comments by Mr. Jones in this regard [see Exhibit 1]. I want you to keep that in mind when reviewing GE this year. Both their return on assets and their return on equity stayed the same even though GE achieved record earnings in 1973. Here's a copy of GE's 1973 annual report [see Exhibit 2]. Let me know what you think of the quality of GE's 1973 earnings. I'd be concerned if the record earnings in 1973 were due to a "relaxing" of GE's earnings quality.

Company Background (as of early 1974)

General Electric, from the time of its incorporation in 1892, has been primarily engaged in developing, manufacturing, and marketing a wide variety

---

This case was prepared by Norman J. Bartczak.

Copyright © 1982 by the President and Fellows of Harvard College
Harvard Business School case 182–243

of products used in the generation, transmission, distribution, control, and utilization of electricity and related technologies. GE is generally regarded as the largest and one of the most diversified producers of electrical equipment, although its relative position as to individual products varies considerably.

Top Management

General Electric has pioneered the concept of management decentralization. Its management views GE's various businesses as "strategic business

---

EXHIBIT 1
Excerpts from Presentation by Reginald H. Jones, President,
to the Investment Analysts Society of Chicago, November 30, 1972

General Electric's Performance and Prospects

Gentlemen, it's a pleasure to visit the Investment Analysts Society of Chicago. This is the first meeting with a group of analysts since my election as president of the General Electric Company a few months ago. But as some of you may recall, Greg Sheehan and I had many occasions to visit with the analysts during my stint as the company's chief financial officer, and I've kept in touch from that point on. So I look forward to this discussion, in part because I enjoy talking with analysts, and in part because our message is, I think, a good one. General Electric is a very exciting place to be these days.

EXCITING TIMES AT GE—Part of the excitement, of course, is simply the glow of better times after a few years of adversity. In the middle and late 60s, we were engaged in three major business ventures that ate up tremendous amounts of money—computers, nuclear energy, and commercial jets. Now those difficulties are essentially behind us. Three years ago, we suffered our first companywide strike in 26 years and, I hope, our last one. That seemed to be our point of turnaround. . . .

So these are exciting times at General Electric. But the real excitement stems not from the achievements of the past, but from the enormous vistas that open out in front of us and a sense that, with our new strategic planning process, we are learning how to allocate our resources to the right places, at the right time, for optimum growth and profitability—and at the same time, contain our risks. If there's one thing I'm interested in, it's a healthy return on assets.

GAMESMANSHIP VERSUS SOLID PLANNING—Many companies claim they do strategic planning, but the process may or may not be anything more than intuitive wheeling and dealing by the top man. The strategy of the conglomerates—trading high P/E for low P/E shares, or making acquisitions with "play money"—registered instant gains in earnings per share, but investors at last see through that rather frothy game. Other companies have temporarily increased earnings per share simply by optimistic bookkeeping—capitalizing expenses and so on—but analysts have learned to examine the balance sheet to determine the quality of earnings. And our studies of the Fortune 500 over the last decade showed that many of them boosted earnings per share by increasing investment through retained earnings and borrowings. Returns on investment steadily declined, but on the face of it, earnings per share were enhanced and share owners seemed to be satisfied.

As we closed the decade, there were some interesting developments. The intensive investment in facilities drained liquidity. Many, particularly the conglomerates, found their debt burdens oppressive. Both the government and the accounting profession began to tighten up bookkeeping practices. It became apparent that the game of expediency had caught up with itself. Good luck and unique inventions will always play a role, but for large companies the only path to solid, high-quality growth in earnings is through rigorous analysis, entrepreneurial business planning, and selectivity in the allocation of resources. Hard work, frankly.

EXHIBIT 2
General Electric Company Edited 1973 Annual Report

1973 Financial highlights

(Dollar amounts in millions; per-share amounts in dollars)

Summary of operating results	1973	1972
Sales of products and services	$11,575	$10,239
Operating costs		
Employee compensation, including benefits	4,710	4,168
Materials, supplies, services and all other operating costs	5,910	5,256
	10,620	9,424
Operating margin	955	815
Other income	184	189
Interest and other financial charges	(127)	(107)
Earnings before income taxes and minority interest	1,012	897
Provision for income taxes	(419)	(364)
Minority interest	(8)	(3)
Net earnings	$ 585	$ 530
Earnings per common share	$3.21	$2.91
Dividends declared per common share	$1.50	$1.40
Earned on share owners' equity	18.1%	18.0%

Operating results by major categories	Sales		Net earnings		Earnings as a percentage of sales	
	1973	1972	1973	1972	1973	1972
Industrial Power Equipment	$ 2,477	$ 2,249	$118	$120	4.8%	5.3%
Consumer	3,097	2,782	149	144	4.8	5.2
Industrial Components and Systems	3,728	3,158	186	160	5.0	5.1
Aerospace	1,611	1,514	39	27	2.4	1.8
International	2,318	1,830	151	99	6.5	5.4
General Electric Credit Corporation	—	—	42	41	—	—
Corporate eliminations & unallocated items	(1,656)	(1,294)	(100)	(61)	—	—
Total Company	$11,575	$10,239	$585	$530	5.1	5.2

Sales and net earnings by major category throughout this Report include intercategory transactions. To the extent that sales and earnings are recognized in more than one category, appropriate elimination is made at corporate level. Net earnings for each major category are after allocation of corporate items such as expenses of headquarters personnel, corporate research and development, interest and other financial charges and income as well as income taxes. Unless otherwise indicated by the context, the terms "General Electric" and "Company" are used on the basis of consolidation described on page 30.

EXHIBIT 2 *(continued)*

The Chairman comments:

"In 1973, General Electric moved to new highs in earnings, sales and orders. The new 'energy economics' resulting from shortages in fossil fuels enhances growth opportunities for the electrical industry by favoring a stronger shift to electrical technologies—particularly nuclear—to meet world energy needs."

General Electric people achieved a strong performance in 1973.

Earnings of $585 million, or $3.21 per share, amounted to a 10% gain. This fourth consecutive year of increased earnings was realized in the face of substantial inflation and other uncertainties.

The 1973 gain was achieved without help from "inventory profits," since the LIFO (last in, first out) method of accounting for U.S. inventories results in conservative valuation of these assets during inflationary periods. Our 1973 LIFO provision of $126 million was four times the $31-million provision in 1972.

Moreover, only three cents of 1973 per-share earnings came from sales of our holdings in Honeywell stock, compared with 11 cents in 1972—the result of our reduced sales of these shares in a year of generally depressed stock market conditions.

These adverse factors were more than offset by improved operating income from the sales of our products and services.

Sales billed rose 13% above the 1972 volume to an $11.6 billion total. Gains by the Company's business sectors in 1973 were led by international operations, supported both by our greatest year ever in exports from the U.S. and improved results from many overseas affiliates.

Industrial operations substantially improved their performance on the strength of a resurgence in sales of producer goods, together with high levels of sales of man-made materials, industrial components, medical systems and computer information services.

We further increased the levels of shipments of industrial power equipment, both for power generation and delivery—an essential contribution to helping our utility customers meet the needs for more electric power.

Demands for GE consumer goods were very strong, requiring production at virtually full capacity throughout most of the year.

Despite higher interest costs, the General Electric Credit Corporation was able to achieve a 1973 earnings performance about equal to 1972's exceptional level.

And a strong performance by commercial aircraft engine operations gave a welcome lift to the aerospace sector.

Another record-breaking year in orders built our orders backlog to a new high exceeding $14 billion, up 25% from the 1972 year-end backlog. We expect to deliver about one-third of these orders in 1974, with the other two-thirds applying to our billing in 1975 and subsequent years.

Dividends declared for share owners were increased to $1.50 a share for 1973 as the result of the Board of Directors' decision in September to raise the quarterly dividend rate. The new current rate of $1.60 per share annually amounts to a 14% increase over the previous $1.40 rate.

Completion of 37-month labor union contracts in mid-1973 provides both for employee progress and for sustained production through June 1976.

The shape of the U.S. and world economies in 1974 will obviously be influenced by the duration and intensity of the Mid-East oil embargo. Prospects for at least the year's first half have already been dimmed—both by the physical disruptions imposed by fuel shortages and by their psychological impact on consumers.

In our view, however, the basic economy of the U.S. remains strong. An easing of the embargo by mid-year could alleviate the adverse effects to some degree and

EXHIBIT 2 *(continued)*

stimulate a period of recovery in the last half of 1974.

The energy challenge has several special facets of meaning for General Electric.

One critical aspect is the need to conserve the fuel available to us in order to minimize the impact on our services to customers and on our employment levels. With GE people joining wholeheartedly and resourcefully in a Company-wide energy utilization and conservation program, our present expectation is that we can avoid any substantial disruption to our operations because of energy shortages.

The need to conserve energy applies to electricity, even though only about 17% of U.S. electric power is generated using oil as a fuel. Consequently, we are striving to be sources of practical ideas for saving electricity. We are also emphasizing greater efficiencies in our products and technologies in order to conserve energy.

Long-term, the new "energy economics" resulting from shortages in fossil fuels enhances growth opportunities for the electrical industry by favoring a stronger shift to electrical technologies to meet world energy needs. Electricity has the great virtue of delivering clean power from the full range of fuel sources. Most importantly, electric power generation can be based on nuclear fuels which provide the best solution from the standpoint of environmental impact, economics and independence from foreign sources of supply. While we continue to pursue energy research on many fronts, the light water reactor, such as the BWR developed by General Electric, offers a sound, tested alternative to fossil fuels for the decades ahead.

Another source of confidence for us is the continued development of a strategic planning system that provides a strong discipline for differentiating the allocation of resources—that is, investing most heavily in areas of business that we identify as offering the greatest leverage for earnings growth, while minimizing our investments in sectors we see as growing more slowly or remaining static.

In view of these favorable factors and opportunities for greater service to society, management throughout the Company has accepted the challenge to achieve, over time, the sustained improvement in earnings that will distinguish General Electric as an outstanding growth enterprise.

This Annual Report takes new steps in share owner communications. One is its increased financial content, aiming at supplying investors with more meaningful financial information, short of disclosures that would benefit our competitors. The other step is to include reports by the chairmen of the committees established by the Board to appraise and enhance the performance of management in five key result areas. The change gives appropriate recognition to the Board's active and dedicated performance in the share owners' interest. Since each of the committees is chaired by a Director who is not a Company employee, the change also emphasizes the independent perspective these committees provide in assuring that the great resources of General Electric are applied wisely and responsibly to the larger interests of society as a whole.

Reginald H. Jones

Chairman of the Board and Chief Executive Officer
February 15, 1974

EXHIBIT 2 *(continued)*

Statement of Current and Retained Earnings

General Electric Company and consolidated affiliates   *(In millions)*

For the year	1973	1972
Sales of products and services to customers . .	$11,575.3	$10,239.5
Operating costs		
Employee compensation, including benefits . . .	4,709.7	4,168.4
Materials, supplies, services and other costs . . .	5,690.5	4,973.1
Depreciation	334.0	314.3
Taxes, except those on income	113.5	116.3
Increase in inventories during the year	(227.2)	(147.3)
	10,620.5	9,424.8
Operating margin	954.8	814.7
Other income	183.7	189.2
Interest and other financial charges	(126.9)	(106.7)
Earnings before income taxes & minority interest .	1,011.6	897.2
Provision for income taxes	(418.7)	(364.1)
Minority interest in earnings of consolidated affiliates	(7.8)	(3.1)
Net earnings applicable to common stock . . .	585.1	530.0
Dividends declared	(272.9)	(254.8)
Amount added to retained earnings	312.2	275.2
Retained earnings at January 1	2,371.4	2,096.2
Retained earnings at December 31	$ 2,683.6	$ 2,371.4
Earnings per common share *(In dollars)*	$3.21	$2.91
Dividends declared per common share *(In dollars)*	$1.50	$1.40

EXHIBIT 2 *(continued)*

Statement of Financial Position

General Electric Company and consolidated affiliates   *(In millions)*

December 31	1973	1972
Assets		
Cash	$ 296.8	$ 267.0
Marketable securities	25.3	27.3
Current receivables	2,177.1	1,926.0
Inventories	1,986.2	1,759.0
Current assets	4,485.4	3,979.3
Investments	869.7	754.9
Plant and equipment	2,360.5	2,136.6
Other assets	608.6	531.0
Total assets	$8,324.2	$7,401.8
Liabilities and equity		
Short-term borrowings	$ 665.2	$ 439.4
Accounts payable	673.5	558.1
Progress collections and price adjustments accrued	718.4	624.2
Dividehds payable	72.7	63.7
Taxes accrued	310.0	308.6
Other costs and expenses accrued	1,052.6	875.7
Current liabilities	3,492.4	2,869.7
Long-term borrowings	917.2	947.3
Other liabilities	492.1	456.8
Total liabilities	4,901.7	4,273.8
Minority interest in equity of		
consolidated affiliates	50.1	43.4
Preferred stock	—	—
Common stock	463.8	463.1
Amounts received for stock in excess of par value .	409.5	396.6
Retained earnings	2,683.6	2,371.4
	3,556.9	3,231.1
Deduct common stock held in treasury	(184.5)	(146.5)
Total share owners' equity	3,372.4	3,084.6
Total liabilities and equity	$8,324.2	$7,401.8

EXHIBIT 2 *(continued)*

Statement of Changes in Financial Position

General Electric Company and consolidated affiliates   *(In millions)*

	For the year	1973	1972
Source of funds			
From operations:			
Net earnings		$ 585.1	$ 530.0
Depreciation		334.0	314.3
Income tax timing differences		—	(23.8)
Earnings of the Credit Corporation less dividends paid		(10.7)	(8.1)
		908.4	812.4
Major domestic long-term borrowings		—	125.0
Overseas Capital Corporation long-term borrowings		17.1	50.8
Increase in other long-term borrowings—net . . .		2.0	5.3
Newly-issued common stock		11.7	13.4
Total source of funds		939.2	1,006.9
Application of funds			
Plant and equipment additions		598.6	435.9
Dividends declared		272.9	254.8
Investments		114.8	40.6
Reduction in major domestic long-term borrowings		31.5	17.2
Reduction in Overseas Capital Corporation long-term borrowings		17.7	3.9
Other—net		20.3	(56.5)
Total application of funds		1,055.8	695.9
Net increase (decrease) in working capital . . .		$ (116.6)	$ 311.0
Analysis of changes in working capital			
Cash and marketable securities		$ 27.8	$ 8.3
Current receivables		251.1	184.7
Inventories		227.2	147.3
Short-term borrowings		(225.8)	130.4
Other payables		(396.9)	(159.7)
Net increase (decrease) in working capital . . .		$ (116.6)	$ 311.0

EXHIBIT 2 *(continued)*

1973 Financial Summary

This summary comments on significant items in the consolidated financial statements on pages 31, 32 and 33, generally in the same order as they appear in those statements.

The information contained in this summary, in the opinion of management, substantially conforms with or exceeds the information supplied in the annual financial statements constituting part of the report (commonly called the "10-K Report") submitted to the Securities and Exchange Commission. The few exceptions, considered non-substantive, are noted as appropriate in the following text. A reproduction of the following statements and summary is filed with that agency.

As an aid in evaluating the data in this Financial Summary, significant accounting and reporting principles and policies followed by General Electric are printed in blue.

Consolidated financial statements and accompanying schedules in this Report include a consolidation of the accounts of the Parent—General Electric Company— and those of all majority-owned affiliates (except finance affiliates since their operations are not similar to those of the consolidated group). All significant items relating to transactions between Parent and affiliated companies are eliminated from consolidated statements. Sales and net earnings attributable to each of the Company's major categories are summarized on page 3.

Except for fixed assets and accumulated depreciation, assets and liabilities of foreign affiliates are translated into U.S. dollars at year-end exchange rates, and income and expense items are translated at average rates prevailing during the year. Fixed assets and accumulated depreciation are translated at rates in effect at dates of acquisition of the assets. The net effect of translation gains and losses is included as other costs in current year operations. Translation losses for 1973 and 1972 were $3.5 million and $4.2 million respectively.

Net earnings include the net income of finance affiliates and the consolidated group's share of earnings of associated companies which are not consolidated but in which the group owns 20% or more of the voting stock.

During 1973, net earnings amounted to $585.1 million compared with prior year earnings of $530.0 million. Earnings per common share were $3.21 in 1973 compared with $2.91 in 1972. Fully diluted earnings per common share, which would result from the potential exercise or conversion of

such items as stock options and convertible debt outstanding, were $3.18 in 1973 and $2.87 in 1972.

Sales of products and services to customers are reported in operating results only as title to products passes to the customer and as services are performed as contracted.

Sales in 1973 totaled $11,575.3 million, an increase of 13% over the 1972 level.

Costs are classified in the statement of current earnings according to the principal types of costs incurred. Operating costs, excluding interest and income taxes, classified as they will be reported to the Securities and Exchange Commission, were: cost of goods sold of $8,515.2 million in 1973 and $7,509.6 million in 1972; and selling, general and administrative expenses of $2,105.3 million in 1973 and $1,915.2 million in 1972. Supplemental details required by the SEC are shown in the table below.

Supplemental Cost Details		*(In millions)*
	1973	**1972**
Company funded research and development using National Science Foundation definitions	$330.7	$303.2
Maintenance and repairs	319.6	270.4
Social security taxes	225.8	167.5
Advertising and sales promotion	170.5	149.0
Rent	86.6	71.5

Employee compensation, including the cost of employee benefits, amounted to $4,709.7 million in 1973. During the year, agreements were reached with various labor unions as described earlier in this Report.

General Electric Company and its affiliates have a number of pension plans, the total cost of which was $135.5 million in 1973 and $107.6 million in 1972. The most significant of these plans is the General Electric Pension Plan in which substantially all employees in the United States who have completed one year of service with the Company are participating and the obligations of which are funded through the General Electric Pension Trust. Financial statements of the Trust appear at right.

Investments of the Pension Trust are carried at amortized cost plus a programmed portion of unrealized appreciation in the common stock portfolio. This accounting recognizes the long-term nature of pension obligations by stressing long-term market trends.

The funding program uses 6% as the estimated rate of future income which includes provision for the systematic

EXHIBIT 2 (continued)

recognition of the unrealized appreciation in the common stock portfolio. This program has the objective of recognizing appreciation which, when added to cost, will result in a common stock book value approximating 80% of market value (consistent with Armed Services Procurement Regulations).

The actual earnings of the Trust, including the programmed recognition of appreciation, as a percentage of book value of the portfolio were 6.5% for 1973 and 6.6% for 1972.

Unfunded liabilities of the Trust are being amortized over a 20-year period and are estimated to be $474 million at December 31, 1973 based on book value of Trust assets compared with $323 million at the end of 1972. These amounts included unfunded vested liability of $377 million at December 31, 1973 and $239 million at December 31, 1972. The estimated market value exceeded book value of Trust assets by $309 million and $693 million at the end of 1973 and 1972 respectively.

Effective July 1, 1973, a supplementary pension plan was approved by the Company's Board of Directors, the purpose of which is to ensure that the pension benefits of long-service professional and managerial employees, when combined with their social security benefits, bear a reasonable relationship to their final average earnings. Obligations of this pension supplement are not funded. Current service costs and amortization of past service costs over a period of 20 years are being charged to operations currently. Cost for the partial year 1973 was $2.0 million.

Depreciation amounted to $334.0 million in 1973 and $314.3 million in 1972.

An accelerated depreciation method, based principally on a sum-of-the-years digits formula, is used to depreciate plant and equipment in the United States purchased in 1961 and subsequently. Assets purchased prior to 1961, and most assets outside the United States, are depreciated on a straight-line basis. Special depreciation is provided where equipment may be subject to abnormal economic conditions or obsolescence.

Taxes, except those on income, totaled $113.5 million in 1973 and $116.3 million in 1972. These taxes were mainly franchise and property taxes. They exclude social security taxes, which are included with employee benefits.

Other income amounted to $183.7 million in 1973, a decrease of $5.5 million from 1972. Significant items included in other income are shown below.

General Electric Pension Trust	(In millions)	
Operating statement	**1973**	**1972**
Total assets at January 1	$2,267.1	$2,071.8
Company contributions	125.9	102.2
Employee contributions	38.6	32.3
	164.5	134.5
Dividends, interest and sundry income	111.4	101.8
Common stock appreciation: Realized	34.2	44.8
Unrealized portion recognized	34.4	21.3
	68.6	66.1
Pensions paid	(115.6)	(107.1)
Total assets at December 31	$2,496.0	$2,267.1
Financial position—December 31		
Short-term investments	$ 51.3	$ 180.3
U.S. Government obligations and guarantees	56.0	60.1
Corporate bonds and notes	344.8	348.7
Real estate and mortgages	410.7	397.6
Common stocks & convertibles	1,530.6	1,211.1
Total investments	2,393.4	2,197.8
Other assets—net	102.6	69.3
Total assets	$2,496.0	$2,267.1
Funded liabilities: Liability to pensioners	$ 874.9	$ 799.9
Liability for pensions to participants not yet retired	1,621.1	1,467.2
Total funded liabilities	$2,496.0	$2,267.1

Other Income	(In millions)	
	1973	**1972**
Net earnings of the Credit Corporation	$41.7	$41.1
Income from:		
Customer financing	32.4	26.8
Royalty and technical agreements	36.9	30.2
Marketable securities and bank deposits	17.7	19.1
Other investments	31.6	31.8
Sale of Honeywell stock	7.8	29.5
Other sundry income	15.6	10.7
	$183.7	$189.2

Net earnings of General Electric Credit Corporation were $41.7 million in 1973, about the same as in 1972. Condensed financial statements for the Credit Corporation appear on page 37.

In view of depressed stock market conditions during 1973, the Company sold only 168,000 shares of Honeywell common stock as compared with 370,000 shares sold during 1972. Capital gains (using average cost) from these sales were $7.8 million and $29.5 million respectively ($5.5 million and $20.7 million after taxes).

EXHIBIT 2 *(continued)*

Interest and other financial charges increased to $126.9 million in 1973 from $106.7 million in 1972 primarily because of higher short-term borrowing rates. Amounts applicable to principal items of long-term borrowings were $58.3 million in 1973 and $52.5 million in 1972.

Provision for income taxes amounted to $418.7 million in 1973. Details of this amount are shown on page 36.

Provision for income taxes generally is computed using the comprehensive interperiod tax allocation method and is based on the income and costs included in the earnings statement shown on page 31.

Amounts of income taxes shown as payable are determined by applicable statutes and government regulations. Timing differences result from the fact that under applicable statutes and regulations some items of income and cost are not recognized in the same time period as good accounting practice requires them to be recorded. The cumulative net effect of such items is that earnings on which tax payments were required have been higher than earnings reported in the Company's Annual Reports. Accordingly, a deferred-tax asset has been established to record the reduction of future tax payments. Principal items applicable to U.S. Federal income taxes, and their effect on taxes payable are shown on page 36. Individual timing differences reflected in foreign income taxes were not significant.

Provision has been made for Federal income taxes to be paid on that portion of the undistributed earnings of affiliates expected to be remitted to the Parent. Undistributed earnings of affiliates intended to be reinvested indefinitely in the affiliates totaled $328 million at the end of 1973 and $252 million at the end of 1972.

U.S. Federal income tax returns of the Parent have been settled through 1964.

The Company follows the practice of amortizing the investment credit to income over the life of the underlying facilities rather than in the year in which facilities are placed in service. Investment credit amounted to $23.6 million in 1973 compared with $20.4 million in the prior year. In 1973 $10.6 million was added to net earnings compared with $8.3 million in 1972. At the end of 1973, the amount still deferred and to be included in net eanings in future years was $72.8 million. If the Company had "flowed through" the investment credit, this amount would have been included in earnings during 1973 and prior years.

Provision for income taxes amounted to 41.4% of income before taxes. Items accounting for the principal portion of the difference of 6.6 points between that rate and the 48.0%

Provision for income taxes	1973	*(In millions)* 1972
U. S. Federal income taxes:		
Estimated amount payable	$321.2	$315.3
Effect of timing differences	0.4	(21.0)
Investment credit deferred—net	13.0	12.1
	334.6	306.4
Foreign income taxes:		
Estimated amount payable	71.4	48.1
Effect of timing differences	(0.4)	(2.8)
	71.0	45.3
Other (principally state and local income taxes)	13.1	12.4
	$418.7	$364.1

Effect of timing differences on U. S. Federal income taxes		*(In millions)*
Increase (decrease) in provision for income taxes	1973	1972
Tax over book depreciation	$ 12.1	$ 2.3
Undistributed earnings of affiliates	6.7	12.3
Margin on installment sales	1.1	(6.1)
Provision for:		
Warranties	(7.7)	(19.6)
Other costs and expenses	(2.4)	(5.9)
Other—net	(9.4)	(4.0)
	$ 0.4	$ (21.0)

U.S. Federal ordinary income tax rate were the effect of consolidated affiliates, 2.5 points; inclusion of the earnings of the Credit Corporation in before-tax income on an "after-tax" basis, 2.0 points; investment credit, 1.0 points; and lower taxes on capital gains, 0.3 points.

Minority interest in earnings of consolidated affiliates represents the interest which other share owners have in net earnings and losses of consolidated affiliates not wholly owned by the Company.

Cash and marketable securities totaled $322.1 million at the end of 1973, an increase of $27.8 million from the end of 1972. Time deposits and certificates of deposit aggregated $134.4 million at December 31, 1973 and $113.7 million at December 31, 1972. Deposits restricted as to usage and withdrawal or used as partial compensation for short-term borrowing arrangements were not material.

Marketable securities are carried at the lower of amortized

EXHIBIT 2 *(continued)*

cost or market value. Carrying value was substantially the same as market value.

Current receivables, less allowance for losses, totaled $2,177.1 million at December 31, 1973 as shown in the table below. The increase of $251.1 million, or 13% during the year, was due principally to the increase in sales in 1973. Other current receivables include the current portion of advances to suppliers and similar items not directly arising from sales of goods and services. Long-term receivables, less allowance for losses, are reported under other assets. Supplemental information on sources of charges and credits to allowance for losses is included in the Form 10-K Report.

Current receivables		(In millions)
December 31	1973	1972
Customers' accounts and notes	$1,996.4	$1,784.1
Nonconsolidated affiliates	0.5	0.6
Other	238.7	192.4
	2,235.6	1,977.1
Less allowance for losses	(58.5)	(51.1)
	$2,177.1	$1,926.0

Inventories are summarized below, and at the end of 1973 were $1,986.2 million compared with $1,759.0 million at December 31, 1972 and $1,611.7 million at January 1, 1972. About 84% of total inventories are in the United States and substantially all of these are valued on a last-in, first-out (LIFO) basis. Substantially all of those outside the United States are valued on a first-in, first-out (FIFO) basis Such valuations are not in excess of market and are based on cost, exclusive of certain indirect manufacturing expenses and profits on sales between the Parent and affiliated companies. The LIFO basis values inventories conservatively during inflationary times, and on a FIFO basis the year-end 1973 inventories would have been $429.7 million in excess of this valuation. This excess increased $125.6 million during 1973 and $31.3 million during 1972.

Inventories		(In millions)
December 31	1973	1972
Raw materials and work in process	$1,276.1	$1,097.2
Finished goods	604.6	573.8
Unbilled shipments	105.5	88.0
	$1,986.2	$1,759.0

Working capital (current assets less current liabilities) totaled $993.0 million, a decrease of $116.6 million during 1973. The statement on page 33 provides a summary of major sources and applications of funds as well as an analysis of changes in working capital.

Investments amounted to $869.7 million at the end of 1973 as shown below.

Investments		(In millions)
December 31	1973	1972
Nonconsolidated finance affiliates	$327.4	$277.6
Honeywell Inc. and Honeywell Information Systems Inc.	154.6	167.3
Associated companies	68.1	47.7
Miscellaneous investments	331.7	274.6
	881.8	767.2
Less allowance for losses	(12.1)	(12.3)
	$869.7	$754.9

Investments in nonconsolidated finance affiliates are carried at equity plus advances. Advances to these affiliates aggregated $0.7 million at the end of 1973 compared with a 1972 year-end balance of $15.8 million.

Investment in General Electric Credit Corporation, a wholly-owned nonconsolidated finance affiliate, amounted to $321.4 million at the end of 1973 and $275.8 million at the end of 1972. Condensed financial statements for the General Electric Credit Corporation and its consolidated affiliates are shown at right. Copies of their 1973 Annual Report may be obtained by writing to General Electric Credit Corporation, P.O. Box 8300, Stamford, Conn. 06904.

Investments in the common stock of Honeywell Inc. and Honeywell Information Systems Inc. (HIS), a subsidiary of Honeywell, are recorded at appraised fair value as of date of acquisition, October 1, 1970, when the information systems equipment business was transferred to HIS. The appraised fair value recognized such factors as the size of the holdings, the various requirements and restrictions on the timing of the sale or other disposition of the securities, as well as the uncertainty of future events.

At December 31, 1973, General Electric held 1,612,432 shares of Honeywell common stock compared with 1,780,432 shares at December 31, 1972. Reflecting generally depressed market conditions, the shares on hand at the end of 1973 would have been valued at $113.1 million using the December 31 closing price. The market value of the shares on hand at year-end 1972 would have been $245.7 million. In addition, General Electric continued to hold an 18½% ownership in HIS.

EXHIBIT 2 *(continued)*

As commented upon under Other Income, on page 35, General Electric sold 168,000 shares of Honeywell common stock in 1973 and 370,000 in 1972. Cumulative sales through the end of 1973 were 913,000 shares.

During 1975 through 1980, Honeywell has the option to purchase from General Electric, and General Electric has the option to require Honeywell to purchase, General Electric's interest in HIS. Payment would be in Honeywell common stock. General Electric has agreed that if the U.S. Attorney General so requests, it shall, prior to the end of 1980, exercise its option to require Honeywell to purchase General Electric's interest in HIS. General Electric has committed to the U.S. Department of Justice to dispose of current holdings of Honeywell common stock in stages by June 30, 1978, and all other shares of Honeywell common stock received for

General Electric's interest in HIS by December 31, 1980.

A voting trust has been established in which General Electric must deposit all shares of Honeywell common stock received as part of these transactions.

Investments in associated companies which are not consolidated but in which the Company owns 20% or more of the voting stock are valued by the equity method.

Miscellaneous investments are valued at cost. On December 31, 1973, the estimated realizable value of these investments was approximately $405 million, an increase of $35 million during the year.

Plant and equipment represents the original cost of land, buildings and equipment less estimated cost consumed by wear and obsolescence. Plant additions were substantially greater in 1973 than in 1972 principally due to major additions to capacity in the Industrial Components and Systems category. Details of plant and equipment and accumulated depreciation are shown in the table below. Additions, dispositions, provisions for depreciation and other changes in plant and equipment, analyzed by major classes, are included in the 10-K Report. Expenditures for maintenance and repairs are charged to operations as incurred.

General Electric Credit Corporation *(In millions)*

Financial position

	December 31	1973	1972
Cash and marketable securities		$ 141.4	$ 120.9
Receivables		3,835.0	3,032.1
Deferred income		(396.7)	(313.8)
Allowance for losses		(76.7)	(70.0)
Net receivables		3,361.6	2,648.3
Other assets		27.0	20.3
Total assets		$3,530.0	$2,789.5
Notes payable:			
Due within one year		$1,756.2	$1,271.6
Long-term—senior		760.8	738.1
—subordinated		254.8	205.5
Other liabilities		437.5	314.3
Total liabilities		3,209.3	2,529.5
Capital stock		160.0	110.0
Retained earnings		160.7	150.0
Equity		320.7	260.0
Total liabilities and equity		$3,530.0	$2,789.5

Current and retained earnings

	For the year	1973	1972
Earned income		$ 406.4	$ 319.8
Expenses:			
Operating and administrative		117.0	102.0
Interest and discount		190.3	108.5
Provision for receivable losses		28.1	35.9
Provision for income taxes		29.3	32.3
		364.7	278.7
Net earnings		41.7	41.1
Deduct dividends		(31.0)	(33.0)
Retained earnings at January 1		150.0	141.9
Retained earnings at December 31		$ 160.7	$ 150.0

Plant and equipment *(In millions)*

	1973	1972
Major classes at December 31:		
Land and improvements	$ 104.4	$ 103.0
Buildings, structures and related equipment	1,445.9	1,347.5
Machinery and equipment	3,138.5	2,828.2
Leasehold costs and plant under construction	231.0	170.5
	$4,919.8	$4,449.2
Cost at January 1	$4,449.2	$4,134.2
Additions	598.6	435.9
Dispositions	(128.0)	(120.9)
Cost at December 31	$4,919.8	$4,449.2
Accumulated depreciation		
Balance at January 1	$2,312.6	$2,108.5
Current year provision	334.0	314.3
Dispositions	(95.8)	(107.6)
Other changes	8.5	(2.6)
Balance at December 31	$2,559.3	$2,312.6
Plant and equipment less depreciation at December 31	$2,360.5	$2,136.6

Other assets, less allowance for losses of $15.1 million ($16.5 million at December 31, 1972), totaled $608.6 million at December 31, 1973. Principal items comprising these bal-

EXHIBIT 2 *(continued)*

ances are shown below.

Deferred income taxes applicable to current assets and liabilities were $97.8 million and $94.1 million at the end of 1973 and 1972 respectively.

Research and development expenditures, except those specified as recoverable engineering costs on Government contracts, are charged to operations as incurred. Expenditures of Company funds for research and development are shown on page 34.

Licenses and other intangibles acquired after October 1970 are being amortized over appropriate periods of time.

Other assets		*(In millions)*	
December 31		**1973**	**1972**
Long-term receivables		$173.4	$133.9
Customer financing		141.2	117.4
Deferred income taxes		131.0	130.5
Recoverable engineering costs on Government contracts		61.3	67.3
Deferred charges		32.4	23.5
Licenses and other intangibles—net		30.9	30.7
Other		38.4	27.7
		$608.6	$531.0

Short-term borrowings, those due within one year, totaled $665.2 million at the end of 1973, compared with $439.4 million at the end of the previous year. A summary of these borrowings at year-end 1973 and 1972, and the applicable average interest rate at December 31, 1973, is shown in the tabulation below.

The average balance of short-term borrowings, excluding the current portion of long-term debt, during 1973 was $594.7 million (calculated by averaging all month-end balances for the year). The maximum balance included in this calculation was $775.1 million at the end of November 1973. The aver-

Short-term borrowings		*(In millions)*	
December 31		**1973**	**1972**
Banks			
Parent (average rate at 12/31/73—9.68%)		$ 99.0	$ 56.0
Consolidated affiliates (average rate at 12/31/73—11.87%)		158.7	115.6
Notes with Trust Departments (average rate at 12/31/73—7.93%)		215.8	215.9
Holders of commercial paper (average rate at 12/31/73—9.71%)		124.3	—
Other, including current portion of long-term debt		67.4	51.9
		$665.2	$439.4

age interest rate for the year 1973 was 9.9%, representing total short-term interest expense divided by the average balance outstanding.

Parent bank borrowings are principally from U.S. sources. Bank borrowings of affiliated companies, most of which are foreign, are primarily from sources outside the U.S.

Although the total unused credit available to the Company through banks and commercial credit markets is not readily quantifiable, informal credit lines in excess of $750 million had been extended by approximately 135 U.S. banks at year-end 1973.

Accounts payable at December 31, 1973 and 1972 are shown below.

Accounts payable		*(In millions)*	
December 31		**1973**	**1972**
Trade		$583.4	$489.3
Collected for the account of others		67.0	60.1
Nonconsolidated affiliates		23.1	8.7
		$673.5	$558.1

Other costs and expenses accrued at the end of 1973 included compensation and benefit costs accrued of $385.6 million and interest expense accrued of $22.6 million. At the end of 1972, compensation and benefit costs accrued were $339.9 million and interest expense accrued was $19.5 million. The remaining costs and expenses accrued included liabilities for items such as replacements under guarantees and allowances to customers.

Long-term borrowings amounted to $917.2 million at December 31, 1973, compared with $947.3 million at the end of 1972 as summarized at upper right.

General Electric Company 6¼% Debentures are due in 1979.

General Electric Company 7½% Debentures are due in 1996. Sinking fund payments are required beginning in 1977.

General Electric Company 5.30% Debentures are due in 1992. In accordance with sinking fund requirements, debentures having a face value of $10.0 million, and reacquired at a cost of $8.1 million, were retired in 1973. Debentures outstanding at the end of 1973 amounted to $160.8 million after deduction of reacquired debentures with a face value of $29.2 million held in treasury for 1974 and future sinking fund requirements.

General Electric Company 5¾% Notes are due in 1991. At December 31, 1973, $106.2 million was classified as long-

EXHIBIT 2 *(continued)*

Long-term borrowings			*(In millions)*
	December 31	**1973**	**1972**
General Electric Company:			
6¼ % Debentures		$125.0	$125.0
7½ % Debentures		200.0	200.0
5.30% Debentures		160.8	171.9
5¾ % Notes		106.2	112.5
3½ % Debentures		84.3	98.4
General Electric Overseas Capital Corporation		181.4	182.0
Other		59.5	57.5
		$917.2	$947.3

term and $6.3 million was classified as short-term. Notes having a value of $6.3 million were retired during 1973 in accordance with prepayment provisions.

General Electric Company 3½ % Debentures are due in 1976. Debentures having a face value of $16.1 million, and reacquired at a cost of $13.0 million, were retired during 1973 in accordance with sinking fund provisions. Debentures outstanding at the end of 1973 amounted to $84.3 million after deduction of reacquired debentures with a face value of $28.8 million held in treasury for future sinking fund requirements.

Borrowings of General Electric Overseas Capital Corporation (a wholly-owned consolidated affiliate) are unconditionally guaranteed by General Electric as to payment of principal, premium, if any, and interest. This Corporation primarily assists in financing capital requirements of foreign companies in which General Electric has equity interest. The borrowings include the Corporation's 4¼ % Guaranteed Bonds due in 1985 in the aggregate principal amount of $50.0 million. The bonds are convertible through November 1975 into General Electric common stock at $65.50 a share. Sinking fund payments on any 1985 bonds not converted are required beginning in 1976. Also included are the Corporation's 4¼ % Guaranteed Debentures due in 1987 in the amount of $50.0 million and convertible from June 15, 1973 to June 15, 1987 into Company common stock at $80.75 a share. During 1973, the Corporation issued 5½ % Sterling/Dollar Guaranteed Loan Stock due in 1993 in the amount of £3.6 million ($8.3 million), convertible from October 1976 into General Electric common stock at $73.50 a share.

Other long-term borrowings were largely borrowings by foreign affiliates with various interest rates and maturities.

Long-term borrowing maturities during the next five years, including the portion classified as current, are $42.0 million in 1974, $43.7 million in 1975, $132.3 million in 1976, $33.4 million in 1977 and $31.3 million in 1978. These amounts are

after deducting reacquired debentures held in the treasury for sinking fund requirements.

Additional miscellaneous details pertaining to long-term borrowings are available in the 10-K Report.

Other liabilities were $492.1 million at December 31, 1973 compared with $456.8 million at December 31, 1972 and included such items as the deferred investment tax credit, the noncurrent portion of the allowance for replacements under guarantees, deferred incentive compensation, and other miscellaneous employee plans costs. Supplemental information is included in the 10-K Report.

Preferred stock, $1.00 par value, up to a total of 2,000,000 shares has been authorized by the share owners. No preferred shares have been issued.

Common stock, $2.50 par value, up to a total of 210,000,000 shares has been authorized by the share owners. Shares issued and outstanding at the end of the last two years are shown below. The number of new shares issued varies between periods depending principally on the requirements of employee plans and the timing of deliveries of shares under the provisions of those plans.

Common stock issued and outstanding		
	1973	**1972**
Shares issued at January 1	185,243,848	184,936,318
New shares issued:		
Stock option plans	274,409	296,002
Savings and Security Program	—	11,528
Shares issued at December 31	185,518,257	185,243,848
Deduct shares held in treasury	(3,370,759)	(2,895,999)
Shares outstanding at December 31	182,147,498	182,347,849

Common stock held in treasury for various corporate purposes totaled $184.5 million at the close of 1973. The comparable amount at the end of 1972 was $146.5 million. Purchases during 1973 totaled 1,698,126 shares including 344,826 at current market prices from employees who acquired them through employee plans other than stock option plans. Other purchases were primarily through regular transactions in the security markets.

Treasury stock dispositions are shown in the table at the upper right. During 1973, the General Electric Company delivered 105,000 shares in connection with the acquisition of Midwest Electric Products Inc.

EXHIBIT 2 *(continued)*

Dispositions of treasury shares	1973	1972
Employee savings plans	1,011,101	876,231
Incentive compensation plans	107,216	94,515
Business combinations	105,000	—
Conversion of Overseas Capital Corporation 1985 bonds	—	151
Other	49	28
	1,223,366	970,925

Included in common stock held in treasury for the deferred compensation provisions of incentive compensation plans were 1,222,422 shares at December 31, 1973 and 1,151,053 shares at December 31, 1972. These shares are recorded at market value at the time of allotment. The liability is recorded under other liabilities.

The remaining common stock held in treasury is carried at cost, $127.7 million at the end of 1973 and $96.1 million at the end of 1972. These shares are held for future corporate requirements including 1,500,931 shares for possible conversion of General Electric Overseas Capital Corporation convertible indebtedness described under long-term borrowings, for distributions under employee savings plans and for incentive compensation awards.

Amounts in excess of par value received for stock increased $12.9 million during 1973 which resulted from amounts received for newly-issued shares in excess of par value of $11.1 million, and net gains from treasury stock transactions of $1.8 million. During 1972, there was an increase of $27.8 million which resulted from amounts received for newly-issued shares in excess of par value of $12.6 million and net gains from treasury stock transactions of $15.2 million.

Incentive compensation plans provide incentive for outstanding performance to over 3,000 key employees. Allotments made in 1973 for services performed in 1972 aggregated $27.8 million. Allotments made in 1972 for services performed in 1971 totaled $24.0 million.

Retained earnings at year-end 1973 included approximately $169.6 million representing the excess of earnings of General Electric Credit Corporation over dividends received from this affiliate since its formation. In addition, retained earnings have been reduced by $0.6 million, which represents the change in equity in associated companies since acquisition. At the end of 1972, these amounts were $158.9 million and $1.5 million respectively.

EXHIBIT 2 *(continued)*

Incentive compensation plans provide incentive for outstanding performance to over 3,000 key employees. Allotments made in 1973 for services performed in 1972 aggregated $27.8 million. Allotments made in 1972 for services performed in 1971 totaled $24.0 million.

The company's Incentive Compensation Plan and Stock Option Plans are administered by the Management Development and Compensation Committee of the board of directors. No present directors, except Messrs. Jones, Dance, Parker, and Weiss (who are not members of that committee) are eligible to participate in these plans or in the company's pension plans.

The company's Incentive Compensation Plan was approved by the share owners at their meeting in 1967 by 98.3 percent of the shares voting thereon. The plan authorizes the board of directors to appropriate to an incentive compensation fund each year an amount based on the net consolidated earnings of the company and all affiliates whose accounts are consolidated in the company's annual report. The maximum amount that may be appropriated for this fund in any year is 10 percent of the excess of the net consolidated earnings, as defined in the plan, over 5 percent of the average consolidated capital investment, as defined in the plan. The determination of this maximum amount is made by the Independent Certified Public Accountants and reported to the board of directors.

Allotments of incentive compensation may be made in such amounts and to such eligible employees as the Management Development and Compensation Committee of the board of directors may determine. Eligible employees are such key employees (including officers) in managerial and other important positions in the company and consolidated affiliates as are specified by that committee.

In 1973, allotments (including the deferred portions thereof) totaling $27,784,689 were made to 3,218 employees of the company and its consolidated affiliates for services performed in 1972, including allotments totaling $7,677,000 made to 99 officers and directors of the company as a group. The only directors who received allotments were Messrs. Jones, Dance, Parker, and Weiss.

Allotments are paid as soon as practicable after the date of allotment, except that part or all of the allotments are or may be payable on a deferred basis in annual installments following the end of the participant's employment. In the case of officers, a portion of each allotment, subject to certain aggregate career limits, is mandatorily deferred and may be forfeited if the company determines that such officer has engaged in activity which is harmful to the interest of the company either during or after termination of service.

Deferred allotments are credited in shares of General Electric common stock, valued at the closing price of the stock on the New York Stock Exchange on the last business day prior to the date of allotment. Participants are also credited (since 1965 in shares of General Electric common stock) with the equivalent of dividends on such shares when dividends are declared on the company's outstanding stock. Prior to 1965, such dividend equivalents were credited in cash. Beginning with deferred allotments granted in 1968, dividend equivalents are credited (also in shares of General Electric common stock) on shares representing dividend equivalents which have accumulated on such allotments.

The board of directors of the company may amend, suspend, or terminate the plan except as to any allotment previously made. However, no amendment may be made which would increase the maximum amount that may be appropriated to the incentive compensation fund for any year without prior approval of the share owners.

EXHIBIT 2 *(continued)*

The Stock Option and Stock Appreciation Rights Plan, approved by share owners in 1973 by 96.5% of the votes cast, as well as previous plans under which options remain outstanding, provided continuing incentive for more than 500 employees. Option price under these plans is the full market value of General Electric common stock on date of grant. Therefore, participants in the plans do not benefit unless the stock's market price rises, thus benefiting all share owners. Also, an employee can only exercise his option to the extent that annual installments have matured, normally, over a period of nine years. Thus the plans encourage managers and professional employees to have the long-term entrepreneurial interest that will benefit all share owners. Details of the 1973 Plan were included in the 1973 Proxy Statement.

A summary of stock option transactions during the last two years is shown below. At the end of 1973, there were 2,500,000 shares reserved for the 1973 Plan, and 2,123,266 shares covered by outstanding options granted under prior plans, for a total of 4,623,266 shares. Of this total amount, 803,209 shares were subject to exercisable options, 1,875,-022 shares were under options not yet exercisable and 1,-945,035 shares were available for granting options in the future. The number of shares available for granting options at the end of 1972 was 160,365; however, no options against these shares were granted and their availability was terminated May 1, 1973. Further details on stock options are available in the 10-K Report.

Stock Options	Shares subject to option	Average per share	
		Option price	Market price
Balance at Dec. 31, 1971	2,388,931	$45.70	$62.62
Options granted	475,286	67.62	67.62
Options exercised	(297,244)	42.71	65.79
Options terminated	(90,062)	45.52	—
Balance at Dec. 31, 1972	2,476,911	50.27	72.88
Options granted	554,965	64.75	64.75
Options exercised	(273,569)	42.84	63.69
Options terminated	(80,076)	52.50	—
Balance at Dec. 31, 1973	2,678,231	53.96	63.00

Lease commitments and contingent liabilities, consisting of guarantees, pending litigation, taxes and other claims, in the opinion of management, are not considered to be material in relation to the financial position of the Company.

Report of Independent Certified Public Accountants

To the Share Owners and Board of Directors of General Electric Company

We have examined the statements of financial position of General Electric Company and consolidated affiliates as of December 31, 1973 and 1972, and the related statements of current and retained earnings and changes in financial position for the years then ended. Our examination was made in accordance with generally accepted auditing standards, and accordingly included such tests of the accounting records and such other auditing procedures as we considered necessary in the circumstances.

In our opinion, the aforementioned financial statements present fairly the financial position of General Electric Company and consolidated affiliates at December 31, 1973 and 1972, and the results of their operations and the changes in their financial position for the years then ended, in conformity with generally accepted accounting principles applied on a consistent basis.

Peat, Marwick, Mitchell & Co.

Peat, Marwick, Mitchell & Co.
345 Park Avenue, New York, N.Y. 10022
February 15, 1974

EXHIBIT 2 *(concluded)*

Ten year summary

(Dollar amounts in millions; per-share amounts in dollars)

On worldwide basis of consolidation	1973	1972	1971	1970	1969	1968	1967	1966	1965	1964
Sales of products and services	$11,575.3	$10,239.5	$9,425.3	$8,726.7	$8,448.0	$8,381.6	$7,741.2	$7,177.3	$6,213.6	$5,319.2
Employee compensation, materials and all other operating costs	10,620.5	9,424.8	8,688.3	8,177.8	7,961.4	7,733.8	7,100.3	6,545.3	5,568.1	4,930.6
Operating margin	954.8	814.7	737.0	548.9	486.6	647.8	640.9	632.0	645.5	388.6
Other income	183.7	189.2	152.0	106.8	98.7	86.3	91.4	72.4	72.1	69.9
Interest and other financial charges	(126.9)	(106.7)	(96.9)	(101.4)	(78.1)	(70.5)	(62.9)	(39.9)	(27.4)	(21.2)
Earnings before income taxes & minority interest	1,011.6	897.2	792.1	554.3	507.2	663.6	669.4	664.5	690.2	437.3
Provision for income taxes	(418.7)	(364.1)	(317.1)	(220.6)	(231.5)	(312.3)	(320.5)	(347.4)	(352.2)	(233.8)
Minority interest	(7.8)	(3.1)	(3.2)	(5.2)	2.3	5.8	12.5	21.8	17.1	16.1
Net earnings	585.1	530.0	471.8	328.5	278.0	357.1	361.4	338.9	355.1	219.6
Earnings per common share *(a)*	3.21	2.91	2.60	1.81	1.54	1.98	2.00	1.88	1.97	1.22
Dividends declared per common share *(a)*	1.50	1.40	1.38	1.30	1.30	1.30	1.30	1.30	1.20	1.10
Earnings as a percentage of sales	5.1%	5.2%	5.0%	3.8%	3.3%	4.3%	4.7%	4.7%	5.7%	4.1%
Earned on share owners' equity	18.1%	18.0%	17.6%	13.2%	11.5%	15.4%	16.5%	16.2%	18.0%	11.7%
Book value per share	$ 18.35	$ 16.92	$ 15.38	$ 14.67	$ 14.05	$ 13.60	$ 12.83	$ 12.12	$ 11.56	$ 10.55
Cash dividends declared	$ 272.9	$ 254.8	$ 249.7	$ 235.4	$ 235.2	$ 234.8	$ 234.2	$ 234.6	$ 216.7	$ 197.7
Shares outstanding—average *(In thousands) (a)*	182,051	182,112	181,684	181,114	180,965	180,651	180,266	180,609	180,634	179,833
Share owner accounts—average	537,000	536,000	523,000	529,000	520,000	530,000	529,000	530,000	521,000	516,000
Market price range per share *(a) (b)*	75⅞-55	73-58¼	66½-46½	47¼-30⅛	49⅛-37	50¼-40⅛	58-41¼	60-40	60⅛-45½	46¾-39⅜
Price/earnings ratio range	24-17	25-20	26-18	26-17	32-24	25-20	29-21	32-21	31-23	39-32
Average annual price/earnings ratio	19.5	22.6	22.6	21.2	28.4	22.7	24.2	27.1	27.0	32.9
Current assets	$4,485.4	$3,979.3	$3,639.0	$3,334.8	$3,287.8	$3,311.1	$3,207.6	$3,013.0	$2,842.4	$2,543.8
Current liabilities	3,492.4	2,869.7	2,840.4	2,650.3	2,366.7	2,104.3	1,977.4	1,883.2	1,566.8	1,338.9
Total assets	8,324.2	7,401.8	6,887.8	6,198.5	5,894.0	5,652.5	5,250.3	4,768.1	4,241.5	3,788.2
Share owners' equity	3,372.4	3,084.6	2,801.8	2,553.6	2,426.5	2,402.1	2,245.3	2,128.1	2,048.1	1,896.4
Short-term debt	665.2	439.4	569.8	658.1	340.7	280.6	266.9	236.3	120.6	1.5
Long-term debt	917.2	947.3	787.3	573.5	673.3	749.1	724.1	476.6	364.1	191.9
Plant and equipment additions	$ 598.6	$ 435.9	$ 553.1	$ 581.4	$ 530.3	$ 514.7	$ 561.7	$ 484.9	$ 332.9	$ 237.7
Depreciation	334.0	314.3	273.6	334.7	351.3	300.1	280.4	233.6	188.4	170.3
Inventories	1,986.2	1,759.0	1,611.7	1,555.3	1,590.7	1,482.1	1,450.7	1,473.0	1,136.9	820.8
Employees—average worldwide	388,000	369,000	363,000	397,000	410,000	396,000	385,000	376,000	333,000	308,000
—average U.S.	304,000	292,000	291,000	310,000	318,000	305,000	296,000	291,000	258,000	243,000

(a) Amounts have been adjusted for the two-for-one stock split in April 1971.

(b) Represents high and low market price on New York Stock Exchange for each year.

units (SBUs)." The businesses are internally organized into 10 major operational groups, each headed by a vice president who operates with a great deal of autonomy.

As of December 31, 1973, the principal executive officers of GE are:

1. Reginald H. Jones, chairman of the board and chief executive officer. Age 56. Mr. Jones joined General Electric in 1939. In 1968, he was elected vice president—finance; in 1970, a senior vice president; and in 1972, he was successively elected vice chairman, president, and chairman and chief executive officer. Mr. Jones owns 23,546 shares of GE's common stock.

2. Walter D. Dance, vice chairman of the board and executive officer. Age 56. Mr. Dance joined GE in 1948. Most of his career at GE has been spent in the Appliance and Television Group. He was elected a director in 1971 and in 1972 was named an executive officer and elected vice chairman of the board. Mr. Dance owns 12,869 shares of GE's common stock.

3. Jack S. Parker, vice chairman of the board and executive officer. Age 55. Mr. Parker joined GE in 1950. His primary association has been with the Aerospace and Defense Group. In 1968, Mr. Parker was named an executive officer and elected a director and vice chairman of the board. He owns 31,452 shares of GE's common stock.

4. Herman L. Weiss, vice chairman of the board and executive officer. Age 57. Mr. Weiss joined GE in 1959. He became group executive of the Consumer Products Group in 1962. In 1968, Mr. Weiss was named an executive officer and elected a director and vice chairman of the board. He owns 38,758 shares of GE's common stock.

Questions

1. Identify those areas where General Electric and Westinghouse (see case 9–1) follow different accounting policies. How do you rate General Electric's earnings quality?

2. As best you can, restate General Electric's 1973 pre-tax earnings, net income, and earnings per share using Westinghouse's accounting practices and policies. If you cannot quantify an item, identify the direction in which it will affect General Electric's income.

3. What is the significance of your restatement and the differences in the two companies' accounting practices for investors interested in the stock of General Electric and Westinghouse? The following data may be helpful in answering this question:

	General Electric	Westinghouse
Average price earnings ratio 1969–73	22.9x	19.5x
Average price earnings ratio 1973	19.5x	18.9x
1973 Beta	1.05	1.10

Both companies were considered to have similar growth prospects.

CHAPTER 10

Growth Analysis

A corporation's value is determined in large part by its projected sales, earnings, and dividend growth rates, which in turn are a function of its projected industry growth rate, competitive position, and corporate strategy. Growth analysis examines the interrelationships and influence of these variables on corporate growth records in order to project growth trends and to identify possible changes in the character of corporations.

Because of the importance of corporate growth rates to corporate success and valuation, the growth rate of a corporation's sales, profits, and dividends is a major focus of many financial statement analyses: Investors are interested because of the close relationship between equity stock values and the projected growth rate and the expected volatility of earnings and dividends. Creditors examine past growth records in order to predict the future level of funding required to finance changes in accounts receivables, inventories, and productive assets. Corporations scrutinize growth rates of themselves and their rivals in order to ascertain how well they are doing on a comparative basis, to detect potential weaknesses in their competitors, and to predict future competitive behavior.

Typically, the analysis of growth characteristics and growth rates involves three major steps: First, a quantitative measurement of the rate of growth of the variables being examined. This quantification may range from a simple index number series to a complex mathematical equation describing the growth pattern inherent in the data. Second, the identification of the various sources of the growth. This phase involves both quantitative and qualitative assessments of the sources of growth as well as an analysis of the relationship of these various sources to each other, the operating and financial characteristics of the firm, and the external environment during the period under review. Third, the use of the preceding analyses in combination with other data, such as projected industry growth rates or managements' announced capital expansion plant, to forecast future levels of growth and to speculate on the possible financial and operating consequences of the projected growth rates.

Appendix 10–A presents some common quantitative approaches to the description and measurement of growth rates.

Business Policy, Marketing, and Financial Dimensions of Growth

Given its market share and industry growth rate, business policy studies indicate that a company can optimize its market value if it adopts certain pricing strategies, cost structures, financing practices, and dividend policies. An understanding of these optimum strategies should help analysts to appreciate better the significance of the historical, comparative, and projected financial statement statistics developed by their analysis of growth situations. For example, in some instances the financial analysis may indicate that the company has adopted the optimum strategy for its circumstances. This revelation may explain why the trends and ratios are what they are. It may provide also some clues as to what the future strategy of the company might be, which would, in turn, imply certain trends and ratios. Alternatively, the analysis might indicate that the optimum strategy is not being followed. This could raise questions as to why the optimum strategy is not being followed, which may result in the identification of some unique characteristics of the company that suggest the theoretical best strategy is not appropriate. Or, if the company indeed is following a suboptimizing strategy, a knowledge of the theoretical consequences of this action may improve the analyst's ability to forecast the consequences of the actual strategy.

Optimum Strategies

A corporation's optimum operating and financing strategy is in large measure determined by the growth rate or its industry or product lines and its market share. One model for optimum strategies using four market share–industry growth rate combinations is presented below. These optimum strategies are based on the premise that the company with the largest market share is its industry's low cost producer.

High Market Share–High Industry Growth Rate. A company in this situation should be seeking to consolidate its market share before the industry growth rate slows down as the market matures. During the high growth–consolidation phase, the company with the largest market share may be able to generate enormous cash flows because of its market position. However, it will also consume cash in large amounts. In fact, it is suggested that unless the company's return on assets is at least equal to the industry unit growth rate plus the rate of inflation, it will need to raise cash from external sources if it wishes to retain its market share. As a result, since such a high return is often difficult to achieve, companies in this situation nearly always employ high levels of financial leverage, sell equity frequently, and pay nominal dividends.

Super industry growth rates do not last forever. As the growth rate subsides, the cash requirements to finance growth subside also. If the company can maintain its high market share during this growth slowdown phase, it should be able to earn high profit levels relative to its smaller competitors and generate an excess cash flow, which can be used to improve liquidity, reduce debt, and increase dividends or finance new growth opportunities.

The stock market value of these companies during their super growth phase is based on the expectation that as growth slows down, the company will pay substantial dividends from its excess cash flow. Unfortunately, in practice this does not always occur. All too often a management, seeing its company's growth rate declining, tries to maintain the old level by investing in expensive, futile marketing programs to further increase market share; diversifies into industries that it does not understand; or spends huge sums on research in the vain hope of finding the next super growth product or technology.

High Market Share–Mature Industry With Low Growth Rate. A company in this position usually has a return on assets that is greater than its industry growth rate. Therefore, it is able to generate excess cash, reduce its borrowings, buy back its stock, and pay dividends without impairing its market share and growth potential.

Those with the highest market share may try to use their borrowing capacity to finance programs to increase their market share and to raise their return on equity. However, there is a point where it becomes so expensive to increase market share that the investment cannot be justified by the potential rewards.

Low Market Share–Low Industry Growth Rate. Companies in this situation are candidates for liquidation, since any profits earned must be reinvested to maintain market share in a situation which promises little future growth. Liquidation could be achieved through sale or by letting the company's market share deteriorate over time and paying out dividends to stockholders from the profits and funds freed by asset reductions.

Low Market Share–New Industry With Potentially High Growth Rate. Companies in this position have very uncertain futures and an enormous need for cash. Permanent market shares have not yet been established and the fight for share requires considerable investment, since everyone wants to end up with the dominant share. Also, since the industry has a high growth potential, capital must be invested to keep up with the projected growth rate. If a company cannot acquire a strong market position and keep up with the industry's growth rate, a company should consider withdrawing from the industry.

Market Share

A company's market share is an important determinant of how a company responds to and is affected by its industry's growth rate. As market share increases, profit margins tend to increase rapidly, purchases-to-sales ratios decrease, and marketing costs to sales decrease. Studies show that in some industries, for example, manufacturing costs fall to 70 percent of what they were before each time cumulative production experience doubles. This means that the most rapidly falling costs belong to the fastest growing companies in the industry, which are those who are improving their market share.

Once a position of cost leadership is gained, the leading firm has a powerful financial advantage, since it has the highest profit margin, the greatest debt capacity, and best ability to either pay dividends or fund additional growth. However, to achieve this position, considerable cash must be invested in financing growth. If a substantial cash flow is unavailable to the company from operations, it may be wiser to attempt penetration deeper into high growth markets unless the management is willing to take on the additional risks that accompany the high levels of financial leverage that are needed to finance the cash deficit.

Once the rate of growth slows for a market share leader, its market share can be maintained with little debt and generous dividend payments. This is the payoff for gaining market share. However, the market share strategy must be started before the industry growth slows down. Thus, market share strategy must be of prime importance in the super growth period of a growth industry company.

Exceptions

While it is generally true that on the average, companies with high market shares have higher pre-tax returns on investment than do firms with lower market shares and that low market share companies face serious business obstacles when competing with high-share companies, there are some low market share companies that are notable exceptions to these observations. These exceptions are companies that have formed the best fit between the opportunities in the competitive environment and the company's particular strengths, skills, and resources. Typically, low-share companies that are able to find the fit best and earning high returns on investment are those that think small, have an outstanding chief executive leadership whose influence pervades the entire organization, use research funds selectively and efficiently, carefully segment their markets, and most importantly, exploit those segments where the company has a comparative advantage.

This market segmentation may be by stages of production, manufacturing policies, prices, products, customers, and services.

Other Strategies

Corporations can pursue a variety of strategies with a domestic or multinational scope beyond those discussed to date. Some companies follow niche strategies where they seek to develop a specialty product or market position which others, for one reason or another, do not duplicate. When successful, this strategy can generate high rates of return and strong positive cash flows. Other companies may be locked into a business because the exit barriers, such as loss on disposal of assets or management pride, are high. Their strategy may be to liquidate the business through operations. Conversely, some companies are protected because their industry's entry barriers are high. These companies may adopt strategies designed to exploit this advantage. Private label strategies are pursued by others. These companies manufacture products that others will sell under their own label. This strategy's key to success is extremely low manufacturing costs and fast response to customer needs. Another strategy followed by some companies is to make the company attractive to potential buyers. For example, a company courting leverage buyout proposals, whereby a buyer finances the acquisition primarily with borrowing secured by the company's own assets and debt capacity, may build up substantial cash balances, eliminate all of its debt, and focus on developing those businesses with persistent cash flows.

Product Portfolio and Product Strategy

The foregoing discussion of corporate growth strategy and its financial implications applies equally well to individual product growth strategy. Individual products go through life cycles from introduction to maturity to withdrawal; have market share positions; and have rates of growth that can vary over their life cycle from very high to actual decline. In any company, these product life cycles overlap each other, and together the product lines represent a portfolio of products with varying market shares and growth rates.

Illustration 10–1 uses a market share, product growth rate grid to show the desired life cycle path of a product. A new product starts out in the "wildcat" quadrant. At this stage, its future is uncertain and it consumes far more cash than it generates. If the product fails to move into the "star" quadrant, it should be discontinued as it will drop into the "cash trap" quadrant and needlessly consume corporate assets without any future promise of an adequate return.

Ideally, new products should move into the "star" quadrant. Typically, these products are not consumers of cash and have high potentials for future cash generation once the market growth rate begins to slow down and

ILLUSTRATION 10–1
Product Life Cycle Grid

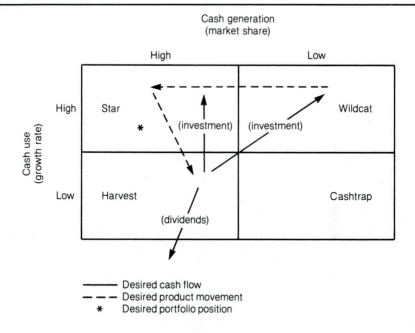

Desired cash flow
Desired product movement
* Desired portfolio position

the "star" product shifts to the "harvest" quadrant. During this mature stage, the product is a net cash generator.

The product portfolio should be managed so as to maximize the company's internal cash flow and debt capacity, which should be used to make investments in potential growth areas. Thus, the "harvest" products' superior cash flow should finance the cash needs of the "wildcat" and "star" products (this desired cash flow pattern is depicted in Illustration 10–1). If successful, the net result is the postponement of corporate maturity and the maintenance or decline of the corporate growth rate. Ideally, a corporation's product portfolio should place the corporation as a whole somewhere close to the "star"—"harvest" boundary in Illustration 10–1.

Illustration 10–1 could also be used as a graphic description of the industry growth rate–market share corporate strategy formulation framework. (See growth rate–market share axis on Illustration 10–1.)

Financial Strategies

A company's capital structure and dividend policies are an integral part of its market share, product portfolio strategy. For example, a company may set market share and growth rate objectives but be unable to finance the attainment of these objectives from internally generated funds after payment of dividends. In this case, some of the choices that the company may consider to finance the strategy are: issue new equity, borrow capital, reduce dividends, or some combination of these choices. Alternatively, the company may consider adopting less ambitious market objectives that are consistent with its existing and potential financial resources.

The key to whether or not a company may consider alternatives to its present financial policies or modify its market objectives is the relationship between the projected corporate growth rate, return on stockholders' equity, and the company's profit retention rate, which is 1 minus the company's dividend payout ratio. If the return on equity times the profit retention rate is lower than the corporate growth rate objectives, the growth rate objectives may have to be lowered or the company's financial policies changed in such a way as to raise the needed capital from external sources.

Four illustrations are presented below to show the relationship between financial policy, return on owners' equity, dividend policy, and a company's potential growth rate. The first example is the base case. It represents a company that has no liabilities (i.e., assets = owners' equity); retains all of its profits; has a return on assets of 10 percent; and a sales-to-asset turnover ratio of 2 times. The second situation is the same as the base case, except that the company has liabilities equal to its owners' equity (i.e., assets = 2 × owners' equity). It is assumed that liabilities have a zero interest cost, such as would be the case if trade credit and progress payments from customers are used. The third situation is the same as the second, except the company pays out 50 percent of its profits on dividends. The last illustration is the same as the base case, except that the company sells equity at the beginning of year 3 equal to the year's beginning equity.

The following data on Illustration 10–2, the base case, show that a company can grow as fast as its return on equity if all of its profits are reinvested.

ILLUSTRATION 10–2
Base Case

	Year 1	Year 2	Year 3
Sales (2 × assets)	2,000	2,200	2,420
Profit (10% of assets)	100	110	121
Dividends	—	—	—
Retained earnings addition	100	110	121
Total assets	1,000	1,100	1,210
Equity	1,000	1,100	1,210
Liabilities	—	—	—
Return on assets	10%	10%	10%
Total leverage (assets/equity)	1×	1×	1×
Return on equity*	10%	10%	10%
Profit retention rate†	100%	100%	100%
Profit growth rate	—	10%	10%
Sales growth rate	—	10%	10%

* Return on assets × Total leverage.
† (Profit − Dividends)/Profit.

ILLUSTRATION 10–3
Liabilities Equal Equity

	Year 1	Year 2	Year 3
Sales (2 × assets)	4,000	4,800	5,760
Profit (10% of assets)	200	240	288
Dividends	—	—	—
Retained earnings addition	200	240	288
Total assets	2,000	2,400	2,880
Equity	1,000	1,200	1,440
Liabilities	1,000	1,200	1,440
Return on assets	10%	10%	10%
Total leverage (assets/equity)	2×	2×	2×
Return on equity*	20%	20%	20%
Profit retention rate†	100%	100%	100%
Profit growth rate	—	20%	20%
Sales growth rate	—	20%	20%

* Return on assets × Total leverage.
† (Profit − Dividends)/Profit.

As illustrated, if a constant asset turnover ratio is assumed, the sales growth is the same as the profit growth rate. Both are 10 percent per year. Thus, if this company's industry was growing at, say, 20 percent per year, under the conditions outlined below, the company's market share would decline if other companies were able to finance growth at better than the industry's growth rate.

Illustration 10–3 illustrates the influence of financial leverage on the potential sales level and growth rate of sales and profits. The total leverage ratio of 2 times illustrated in Illustration 10–3 raises the return on equity to 20 percent. Since no dividends are paid, the potential growth rate in sales and profits for this company is now 20 percent per year. If the industry growth rate is 20 percent, the addition of the liabilities will permit this company to keep pace with the industry growth rate. Also, compared to the base case, the company's potential sales volume has doubled with the addition of the liability capital, if it can maintain its asset turnover ratio.

The situation illustrated in Illustration 10–4 is the same as in Illustration 10–3 except that the company has a profit retention rate of 50 percent, since it pays out half of its profits in dividends. In this case, the company still has a return on equity of 20 percent but its profit and growth rate falls back to 10 percent. Given a 20 percent industry growth rate, if this company maintained its dividend payout policy and its 20 percent return on equity, it would lose market share.

Illustration 10–5 is based on the same assumptions as the base case illustrated in Illustration 10–2—no dividends and a total leverage ratio of 1, except that new equity equal to the owners' equity is sold at the beginning of year 3. As shown in Illustration 10–5, the company's sales and profit growth rate is 10 percent, except in the year when the new equity is raised. In year 3, the sales and profit growth rate jumps to 100 percent. However,

ILLUSTRATION 10–4
Liabilities Equal Equity and 50 Percent Dividend Payout Policy

	Year 1	Year 2	Year 3
Sales (2 × assets)	4,000	4,400	4,800
Profit (10% of assets)	200	220	240
Dividends	100	110	120
Retained earnings addition	100	110	120
Total assets	2,000	2,220	2,400
Equity	1,000	1,100	1,200
Liabilities	1,000	1,100	1,200
Return on assets	10%	10%	10%
Total leverage (assets/equity liabilities)	2×	2×	2×
Return on equity*	20%	20%	20%
Profit retention rate†	50%	50%	50%
Profit growth rate	—	10%	10%
Sales growth rate	—	10%	10%

    * Return on assets × Total leverage.
    † (Profit − Dividends)/Profit.

ILLUSTRATION 10–5
Base Case with New Equity Issued in Year 2

	Year 1	Year 2	Year 3	Year 4
Sales (2 × assets)	2,000	2,200	4,400	4,840
Profit (10% of assets)	100	110	220	242
Dividends	—	—	—	—
Retained earnings addition	100	110	220	242
Total assets	1,000	1,100	2,200	2,420
Equity	1,000	1,100	2,200	2,420
Liabilities	—	—	—	—
Return on assets	10%	10%	10%	10%
Total leverage (assets/equity)	1×	1×	1×	1×
Return on equity*	10%	10%	10%	10%
Profit retention rate†	100%	100%	100%	100%
Profit growth rate	—	10%	100%	10%
Sales growth rate	—	10%	100%	10%

    * Return on assets × Total leverage.
    † (Profit − Dividends)/Profit.

in year 4, the growth rate drops back to 10 percent. The addition of equity doubled the company's potential sales volume but did not change its potential growth rate beyond the year of the equity addition. Hence, it would be a mistake to project future growth based upon the sales and profit growth recorded in year 3. A better indicator would have been year 3's return on equity (10 percent) times year 3's profit retention rate (100 percent), which is 10 percent.

Sustainable Growth Rate Equations

Historical and pro forma growth rate analyses can be summarized through the use of a convenient mathematical expression known as the "sustainable growth rate equation." This equation is based upon the facts illustrated in Illustrations 10–3 through 10–5; namely, if a company does not issue new equity, its potential maximum earnings growth rate will be a function of its rate of return on equity and dividend payout policy.

For example, assume that a company had earnings of $10 million during the year just ended; a net worth of $100 million at the beginning of that year; and a permanent dividend payout policy of 50 percent. Thus, during the year just ended, the company earned 10 percent on its beginning net worth; retained $5 million of earnings, and ended the year with an equity of $105 million. If the past year's 10 percent return on beginning equity is repeated during the next year, the company's earnings will grow to $10.5 million, i.e., 10 percent of this year's beginning net worth of $105 million. This 5 percent earnings growth rate will be repeated annually as long as the company continues to earn 10 percent on each year's beginning net worth and pays out 50 percent of its earnings in dividends.

The relationship between future earnings growth, return on beginning equity, and dividend payout policy described in this example is captured in more general terms in the sustainable growth rate equation.

$$g = ROE \times \left(1 - \frac{D}{E}\right)$$

where:

g = Annual net income growth rate or sustainable growth rate.

ROE = Rate of return on beginning-of-year net worth, including preferred stock.

$\dfrac{D}{E}$ = Dividends payout ratio, i.e., annual common and preferred dividends (D) divided by annual earnings (E).

$\left(1 - \dfrac{D}{E}\right)$ = Earnings retention rate, i.e., $1 -$ the dividend payout ratio.

By observation, it can be seen from the above equation that a future earnings growth rate cannot be greater than a company's return on beginning equity, i.e., $g = ROE$, when dividends are zero. In addition, should a company wish to maintain a given earnings growth rate, it can do so by a variety of combinations of payout ratio and return on equity levels. For example, should the company in the above example find that its projected return on beginning equity had slipped to, say 8 percent, it would have to adjust its payout ratio downward to 37.5 percent if it wished to maintain its 5 percent earnings growth rate in the future [$.08 \times (1 - .375) = .05$].

If the sustainable growth rate equation is further reduced from the form presented above, the sustainable growth rate is equal to the annual change in retained earnings divided by the year's beginning net worth:

$$g = \frac{E\left(1 - \dfrac{D}{E}\right)}{OE} = \frac{\Delta RE}{OE}$$

where:

g = Sustainable growth rate.
E = Annual earnings.
D = Annual dividends.
ΔRE = Change in retained earnings during the year.
OE = Net worth at beginning of the year.

Actual versus Indicated

In practice, a company's actual earnings growth rate may differ for at least four reasons from the rate indicated by the sustainable growth rate calculation. The first two reasons are fairly obvious: the actual return on equity and the actual payout ratio may differ from the ones used in the equation. The other two reasons require some explanation.

The sustainable growth rate is a maximum potential rate of growth. If a company's industry is growing slower than the company's potential growth rate and the company cannot increase its market share, then the industry growth rate becomes the sustainable growth rate.

Also, as noted earlier, the sustainable growth rate computation assumes a company's only source of new equity is retained earnings. If new equity is sold, then a company's earnings in the year in which the equity is sold will be derived from both the equity retained in the prior year and the new capital. This can result in a one-year earnings growth that is greater than the original projected growth rate.

Sources of Growth

Because of the key role of the return on equity, the sustainable growth rate analysis is expanded in practice to include those variables that influence a company's return on equity. This expansion reflects the fact that a company can change its return on equity and, hence, its earnings growth rate, by changing its:

- Pre-tax profit margin on sales.
- Asset turnover ratio.
- Financial leverage ratio.
- Tax rate.

The basic equation or model that is used to describe the relationship of these variables to return on equity is:

$$\frac{\text{Pre-tax profit}}{\text{Sales}} \times \frac{\text{Sales}}{\text{Assets}} \times \frac{\text{Assets}}{\text{Equity}} \times (1 - \text{Tax rate}) = \frac{\text{Net income}}{\text{Equity}}$$

or

Pre-tax margin $\times$ Turnover $\times$ Leverage $\times$ Tax retention = Return on equity

This equation is the well-known DuPont formula. In the financial analysts' application of this equation, the elements of each component are examined in minute detail. These analyses, however, are typically summarized by the basic DuPont equation because of its explanatory power.

The output of the DuPont equation is return on equity. To illustrate the DuPont model, assume: A company has $4 million pre-tax profit; a $40 million volume sales; total assets of $20 million; total liabilities of $10 million; a beginning-of-year owners' equity of $10 million; and a 50 percent income tax rate. The company's return on equity is 20 percent. This return can be analyzed as follows:

$$\frac{\text{Pre-tax profit}}{\text{Sales}} \times \frac{\text{Sales}}{\text{Assets}} \times \frac{\text{Assets}}{\text{Equity}} \times (1 - \text{Tax rate}) = \text{Return on equity}$$

or

$$\frac{\$\,4,000,000}{\$40,000,000} \times \frac{\$40,000,000}{\$20,000,000} \times \frac{\$20,000,000}{\$10,000,000} \times (1 - .50) = .20$$

Thus, from an examination of the above equation the analysts can state that the company was able to achieve its 20 percent return on equity because it had:

1. A 10 percent pre-tax profit margin $\left(\dfrac{\$\,4,000,000}{\$40,000,000} = .10\right)$.

2. An asset turnover ratio of 2 times $\left(\dfrac{\$40,000,000}{\$20,000,000} = 2 \text{ times}\right)$.

3. A total leverage ratio of 2 times $\left(\dfrac{\$20,000,000}{\$10,000,000} = 2 \text{ times}\right)$.

4. A tax retention rate of 50 percent $(1 - .50 = .50)$.

Additional explanation can be generated by combining some of these observations. For example, the pre-tax profit margin (10 percent) times the asset turnover ratio (2 times) is the pre-tax return on assets, 20 percent $(.10 \times 2)$. Going one step further, this pre-tax return on assets (20 percent) can be multiplied by the total leverage ratio (2 times) to get the company's pre-tax return on owners' equity, which is 40 percent $(.2 \times 2)$. Finally, the pre-tax return on owners' equity can be multiplied by the tax retention rate (50 percent), which is the percentage of profits retained after paying taxes, to get the company's after-tax return on equity of 20 percent $(.4 \times .5)$.

A company's return on equity is a common element in both the DuPont equation and the sustainable growth rate equations. Therefore, the two equations can be combined and the sources of earnings growth explained in the expanded equation as follows:

$$\frac{\text{Pre-tax profit}}{\text{Sales}} \times \frac{\text{Sales}}{\text{Assets}} \times \frac{\text{Assets}}{\text{Equity}} \times (1 - \text{Tax rate}) \times (1 - \text{Payout}) = g$$

or

Pre-tax margin × Turnover × Leverage × Tax retention
$$\times \text{ Profit retention} = \text{Sustainable growth}$$

Thus, since the company in the above illustration did not pay dividends, the explanation outlined above as to how the company achieved its 20 percent return on equity is the same as for its potential for a 20 percent increase in earnings. If the company had a 25 percent dividend payout ratio, the growth rate indicated by the above equation would have been 15 percent per year. In this case, the only added consideration for explaining the earnings growth would be the payout ratio of 25 percent (or a profit retention ratio of 75 percent).

Up to this point, we have discussed sustainable growth rate primarily in terms of sustainable *earnings* growth rates. However, it should be noted that the g computed is also the sustainable growth rate for *dividends,* since the payout ratio is assumed to remain constant. This means that dividends will grow at the same rate as earnings.

If a company maintains the same ratios for the variables in the growth equation from one period to another, its assets, liabilities, owner's equity, sales, profits, and dividends will all grow at the indicated sustainable growth rate. However, if the ratio level of any of the variables change, the actual growth rate of the variables will be different from the indicated growth rate at the beginning of the year, even if at the end of the year the sustainable growth rate figure is unchanged.

Valuation Implications

The linking of the DuPont model to the sustainable growth rate equation through their common element, return on equity, results in a much more powerful analytical equation for those interested in growth analysis than the sustainable growth rate equation standing alone. The sustainable growth rate equation indicates what the potential growth rate might be, but it says nothing about the risks associated with this indicated growth rate. The marrying of this equation to the DuPont model provides some perspective on how the growth was achieved and, in doing so, gives some perspective on the risk associated with the growth rate.

The expanded equation can be broken down into two parts—those ratios that relate to operations and those that relate to financial considerations. The "operating" ratios are sales turnover and gross margins. Those interested in growth analysis typically like to see a company's growth and return on investment coming from the operations areas since it relates to the ongoing economic activity of the company. In contrast, growth derived from the use of financial means such as debt, tax rate management and dividend policy, is less desirable since there is a limit to how much leverage and tax rate management can be used to achieve growth. Also, these sources of equity returns and growth depend on groups outside the company—the bankers and government. In addition, more leverage increases the risk of earnings volatility. In general, an increasing reliance on these financial ways to achieve a higher return on equity suggests a lowering of the quality of the returns on equity and a potentially more uncertain or volatile growth rate.

Additive Version

The basic sustainable growth rate equation can be restated to indicate the additive effect on the growth rate of the operating income rate of return on assets, the use of debt leverage, preferred stock leverage, the requirement to replace the depreciable assets, the company's tax rate, and its profit retention policy. The following equation on Illustration 10–6 shows the additive effect of these variables on the sustainable growth rate of the net income available to common stockholders, which is the growth rate of the net income after deducting preferred dividends.[1]

Terms 4, 5, and 6 of the Illustration 10–6 equation shows the pre-tax influence on the growth rate of income available to common stockholders of the operating income return on assets, which equals operating income

---

[1] Preferred stock is an equity stock and as such is part of net worth, which is the sum of preferred stock capital, common stock capital, and retained earnings. Up to this point, the growth rate equations have treated preferred stock as part of net worth and the preferred dividends as part of the dividends used to compute the dividend payout ratio. Thus, the return on equity computation includes preferred stock in the denominator; the payout ratio is the relationship of preferred and common dividends to net income; and the sustainable growth rate is the rate of growth of the net income shown on the income statement, which is the net income available to both preferred and common stockholders. Except for utilities, preferred stock is generally not an important source of capital. So, for most companies the growth in net income is essentially the same as the growth of net income available to common stockholders. An alternative approach, which is illustrated in the additive equation, is to treat preferred stock as if it were a debtlike security and to focus on the growth rate of net income available to the common stockholder. In this approach, it is assumed that the preferred stock capital will be leveraged relative to the earnings retained at the preferred stock leverage ratio, just as the debt is assumed to be leveraged by the addition to retained earnings by the debt leverage ratio used to compute the sustainable growth rate. In contrast, in the approach used earlier, which treated preferred stock as part of equity, the preferred stock capital was not assumed to change when earnings are retained.

If you wish to use the additive equation treating preferred stock as a part of equity, the following adjustments should be made: the payout ratio should include preferred stock dividends in the dividend figure and the reported net income should be the denominator; the equity figure should include preferred stock capital; and the preferred stock leverage term omitted.

ILLUSTRATION 10–6
Additive Version of Growth Equation

$$g_c = \left(1 - \frac{D_c}{I_c}\right)(1-t)\left[\frac{I_o}{A}\right] + \frac{d}{E_c}\left(\frac{I_o}{A} - i_d\right) + \frac{P}{E_c}\left(\frac{I_o}{A} - i_p\right) - \frac{X_d}{E_c}\right] = \frac{\Delta E_c}{E_c}$$

(1)	(2)	(3)	(4)	(5)	(6)	(7)
Growth rate of net income available to common equity holders.	Income available to common equity holders; retention rate impact on g_c.	Tax retention rate influence on g_c.	Operating income return on assets contribution to g_c.	Debt leverage contribution to g_c.	Preferred stock leverage contribution to g_c.	Reinvestment to replace depreciable assets consumed as measured by depreciation expense influence on g_c.

All before taxes (4 through 7).

After-tax income available to common equity holders return on total common equity capital (3 through 7).

where:

g_c = Sustainable growth rate of net income available to common equity holders.
D_c = Common stock dividends.
I_c = Income available to common stockholders (net income − preferred dividends).
t = Corporate tax rate (tax expenses ÷ profit before taxes).
A = Total assets.
d = Total short- and long-term interest-bearing debt.
E_c = Common stockholder's equity (net worth − preferred stock capital).
I_o = Operating income (profit before taxes + depreciation + interest).
i_d = Debt interest rate.
P = Preferred stock capital.
i_p = Before-tax equivalent of preferred stock yield at issue or pre-tax equivalent of preferred stock dividend divided by preferred stock book value at issue. (Pre-tax preferred stock dividend = Preferred stock dividend × Tax retention rate.)
X_d = Depreciation expense.

before depreciation, interest, and income taxes divided by total assets, debt leverage, and preferred stock leverage. The last term of the equation (term 7) reflects the fact that earnings must be reinvested to maintain existing levels of plant and equipment. If the pre-tax income available to common stockholders is to grow, the sum of terms 4, 5, and 6 must be greater than term 7. The term 3 of the equation, the corporate tax retention rate, converts the portion of the expression to its right (terms 4 through 7) to an after-tax basis. The lower the tax rate, the higher the potential g_c. The term 2 of the equation, the net income to common shareholders' retention rate, reflects the fact that it is the net income to common stockholders that is reinvested in the business that is the source of capital for financing future growth. Thus, the lower the common dividends, the greater is the capital retained and, in turn, the greater is the sustainable growth figure.

Some Refinements

In practice, there are a number of minor refinements in special cases to the DuPont portion of the expanded equation.

Some users of the expanded equation preferred to use long-term capital, rather than total liabilities, in the turnover and leverage ratios on the grounds that they are interested in how a company uses its "permanent" capital. If capital is defined as long-term liabilities and owners' equity, the ratios used in the DuPont equation are:

$$\text{Turnover} = \frac{\text{Sales}}{\text{Capital}}$$

$$\text{Leverage} = \frac{\text{Capital}}{\text{Owners' equity}}$$

A few analysts use the pre-tax income plus interest charges, rather than income before income taxes, as the numerator in the margin ratio. When a company's interest charges are large relative to pre-tax income, these analysts are interested in what is described as "pure" operating margin figure and a "pure" return on assets ratio. The ratios to adjust the DuPont equation are:

$$\text{Pre-tax margin} = \frac{(\text{Pre-tax income} + \text{Interest})}{\text{Sales}}$$

$$\text{Return on assets} = \frac{(\text{Pre-tax income} + \text{Interest})}{\text{Assets}}$$

To convert the pre-tax margin before interest deduction to the margin based on the reported pre-tax income figure, the following ratio has to be inserted into the expanded equation after the pre-tax before interest margin:

$$\begin{array}{l}\text{Ratio to adjust pre-tax before} \\ \text{interest margin to pre-tax margin}\end{array} = \frac{\text{Pre-tax income}}{(\text{Pre-tax income} + \text{Interest})}$$

Minority income is recorded as a deduction before pre-tax income is determined. If minority income is significant relative to pre-tax income, some analysts use pre-tax income before minority interest to compute their pre-tax margin ratio. Their conversion ratio is pre-tax income divided by pre-tax income before minority interest. No asset adjustment is necessary since pre-tax income before minority income relates to the total assets as presented.

If "other income" or "income from equity investments" is a significant percentage of net income before taxes, some analysts might make adjustments to the expanded equation in order to appraise pre-tax margins and returns on productive assets before considering these revenue items. Productive assets are total assets less investment assets.

Technically, the sustainable growth rate equation should be based on the return on equity at the beginning of the year. However, many analysts use the end-of-year equity to compute the return on equity figure that is used in the sustainable growth rate equation. The following equation can be used to convert an end-of-year equity-based growth rate to a beginning-of-year equity basis:

$$\frac{\text{Sustainable}}{\text{growth rate}} = \frac{\text{Return on year-end equity} \times (1 - \text{Payout ratio})}{1 - [(\text{Return on year-end equity} \times (1 - \text{Payout ratio})]}$$

Earnings-Per-Share Growth

Management frequently adopts earnings-per-share growth objectives. The attainment of this objective is influenced by the linkage between debt policy, payout ratio, market-determined interest rates, and returns on new investments. In order to understand the relationship of these variables to earnings-per-share growth, sometimes the sustainable growth equation is recast to focus on the analysis of earnings-per-share growth.

The following growth equation is a common earnings-per-share form of the sustainable growth rate equation. It is based on the assumption that next year's earnings per share will be equal to this year's earnings per share plus the profits on both the earnings retained and the incremental debt made possible by the retained earnings, after deducting the cost of the incremental debt:

$$eps_{t+1} = eps_t + eps(b)(r) + eps_t(b)\ (D/E)(r - i)$$

where:

b = Proportion of earnings retained ($1 -$ dividend payout ratio).
r = After-tax rate of return on incremental asset investment.
D/E = Debt to equity ratio (at book).
i = After-tax interest rate.

To illustrate, assume that this year's earnings per share is $2, the company pays out 50 percent of its profits in dividends; the after-tax rate of return on incremental asset investments is 10 percent; the debt to equity ratio is 2 times; and the after-tax cost of debt is 5 percent. Using the above equation, next year's earnings-per-share should be $2.20:

$$\underbrace{\$2.20} = \underbrace{\$2.00} + \underbrace{\$2.00(.5)(.10)} + \underbrace{\$2.00(.5)(2)(.10 - .05)}$$

Next year's = This year's + Incremental profit + Incremental profit on
eps   eps   on earnings retained   incremental debt

This basic equation can be rearranged and the rate of growth in earnings per share *(g)* can be calculated directly as follows:

$$g = br + (b)(D/E)(r - i)$$

Alternatively, if the analyst wished to compute the profit retention rate need to reach a specific earnings-per-share growth rate, the equation is:

$$b = \frac{g}{[r + D/E(r - i)]}$$

A slightly different version of the DuPont equation that focuses on earnings per share and the operating and financial factors that contributed to the results achieved is presented in Illustration 10–7. The shares outstanding in the last variable, book value per share, should be the number of shares used to compute the company's earnings per share, which could be either the primary or fully diluted earnings-per-share figure. For example, if the primary earnings-per-share figure is being explained, the weighted average of the common shares outstanding and common share equivalents should be used. In addition, any adjustments to the net income figure that are required to conform to *APB No. 15's* adjustment rules should be made to this reported net income. For example, if a convertible debt issue is classified as a common stock equivalent, the after-tax equivalent of this issue's interest should be added back to net income (see Chapter 13). (If material, the same income adjustments should be made to the other earnings-per-share equation presented above.)

Analysis of Income Change

In contrast to the growth equation analyses previously discussed, which focus on the operating and financial causes of the *rate of growth,* growth analysis also involves accounting for the sources of a company *dollar growth in earnings.* This dollar-oriented analysis develops answers to the question: "What accounted for the dollar change in earnings from one period to another?" The answer to this question is presented frequently in terms of the dollar contribution to the change in earnings of these six variables:

- Accounting.
- Environment.
- Infrequent and/or unusual transactions.

ILLUSTRATION 10–7
Earnings-Per-Share Version of DuPont Equation

$$
\frac{\text{Profit before interest and taxes}}{\text{Sales}} \times \frac{\text{Sales}}{\text{Assets}} \times \left(\frac{\text{Profit before taxes}}{\text{Profit before interest and taxes}} \middle/ \frac{\text{Net worth*}}{\text{Total assets}} \right) \times \left(\frac{\text{Profit after preferred dividends}}{\text{Profit after taxes}} \middle/ \frac{\text{Common equity}}{\text{Net worth}} \right) \times \frac{\text{Profit after taxes}}{\text{Profit before taxes}} \times \frac{\text{Common equity}}{\text{Shares outstanding}} = \frac{\text{Profit available for common equity owners}}{\text{Shares outstanding}}
$$

Pre-tax margin × turnover ×   Leverage   × tax retention × Book value per share = Earnings per share

* Net Worth = Common equity plus preferred stocks, if any.

- Tax rate.
- Capital structure.
- Operations.

An accounting source of earnings change may arise from a change in an accounting principle estimate or the way in which a principle is implemented. For example, a decision to use longer depreciation lives in the current period could be a source of earnings growth over the prior period, since the prior period's income will be based on the old depreciation lives schedule. The "Accounting Changes" notes to financial statements usually identifies and gives the dollar value of these sources of earnings change.

Environmental sources of earnings change include all of those domestic and international economic changes that influence earnings, other than interest rates. Typically these are: changes in the business cycle of the economy and/or the industries of the company, shifts in foreign exchange rates, and changes in the rate of inflation. It is difficult to relate net income changes to changes in the business cycle and/or the industries of a company. Often, the analyst has to be content to make such statements as: "Income improved due to an improvement in the economy." However, no matter how crude the final figure related to this source of earnings change, the analyst should try to gauge the relative significance of this influence. The impact on earnings of shifts in foreign exhange rates are reported in the notes. This figure relates to the balance sheet related gain or loss. In addition, the impact of the exchange rate shift on the translated foreign currency profits of the foreign income sources must also be estimated. In the case of inventories of LIFO companies, the impact of inflation is captured in the size of the LIFO reserve adjustment to cost of goods sold. FIFO companies do not make such a debit or credit to income. In this case, this missing debit or credit is the inventory-inflation source of profit change. The extent of the impact on profit changes of using historical cost depreciation in periods of inflation may be crudely estimated by computing how much the historical depreciation of a company falls short of its replacement cost depreciation.

Infrequent and/or unusual transactions may occur in one period and not another and as such are a source of earnings change. Examples of such transactions are extraordinary items and infrequent or unusual items included in income before extraordinary items, such as write-down of inventories or the gain on the sale of equipment.

Tax rate sources of earnings change are usually reflected directly in a change in the tax rate between two periods. The current income before taxes times the prior period's tax rate less the net income reported for the current period measures this influence. The tax expense note should provide clues as to what caused the company's book tax rate to change.

Capital structure derived changes in income include such transactions as: the conversion of debt securities to common stock, which changes the interest charged to income, and the reacquisition and extinguishment of debt securities, which changes the interest expense and may generate a gain or loss on the transaction.

Operating sources of income changes are those changes that can be identified with the basic ongoing business of the company. These include such sources of income change as market share shifts, changes in the cost structure, different product mixes, and new product price schedules.

Real versus Nominal

Most financial trend data is expensed in nominal dollars. Nominal dollars reflect the purchasing power of the period. These data are not adjusted for changes in the purchasing power of the dollar during the period covered. It may be useful, particularly in high inflation rate periods or when data spanning more than five years is being examined, to adjust the nominal data for price level changes. Chapter 17 discusses the various techniques for converting nominal dollar financial data to a real or price level adjusted basis.

Additional Analysis

This chapter has focused on the analysis and measurement of corporate growth, particularly sales, income, and dividend growth. The first task of the analyst is to identify the company strategy being followed, the consequences of this strategy, and assess whether or not it is the best one for the company. In approaching this task the analyst should remember that most businesses do not have the advantage of a high market share, they must devise a specific strategy that leads to their best performance irrespective of their position. The market share–industry growth rate classification scheme may be helpful in performing the analysis, but because it represents such a high level of abstraction, it should not be substituted for a precise, specific, and far-ranging description of the company's strategy. This statement should define the markets in which a business competes, the products that it sells, their performance and price characteristics, and the way in which they are produced, sold, and financed.

The analyses described in the chapter focus on explaining the rate of growth or the change in dollar levels of the growth variable being examined. These may be helpful in understanding both the strategy and its success. However, to fully appreciate the impact of growth on a company, additional detailed financial analyses should be undertaken of the key variables that (1) contribute to growth, such as capital structure changes, and (2) are influenced by growth, such as working capital needs. In addition, business segment data should not be neglected. It may provide important insights into product strategy, which is the central focus of most business strategies.

APPENDIX 10-A

Growth Analysis

Measurement of Growth

There are a variety of different ways to describe and measure growth of some variable, such as sales or profits, over a period of time. Some of the more common approaches are presented briefly below.

Index Numbers

Simple index numbers express the relative changes in a variable over time relative to a base value, which is expressed as 100.

A simple index number is computed from a single series of data which extends over a period of time. One time period is designated as the base, and the item for this base is taken as 100. The other data items in the series are then expressed as percentages of this base. Illustration 10-A-1 illustrates the steps involved in constructing a simple index number series (choosing a base period, dividing each item by the base figure, and multiplying the result by 100).

Index numbers are useful in measuring changes in growth over a period of time relative to the base. As seen from Illustration 10-A-1, Company A's sales in 1985 are 269 percent of sales in 1980 as compared to Company B's 165 percent change in sales from 1980 to 1985. To express the percentage change in sales in any period, take the index number of that period relative to the index in the period being compared. To illustrate, the increase in

ILLUSTRATION 10-A-1
Simple Index Numbers: Sales of Company A and Company B, 1980-1985

Year	Sales in Millions of Dollars		1970 = 100	
	Company A	Company B	Company A	Company B
1970....	40.0	395	100	100
1971....	51.3	402	128	102
1972....	64.7	479	162	121
1973....	89.3	501	223	127
1974....	99.2	549	248	139
1975....	107.4	650	269	165

ILLUSTRATION 10–A–2
Sales 1980–1985

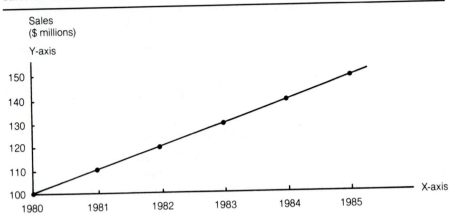

sales for Company A from 1983 to 1984 is 11.2 percent (248 ÷ 223 = 1.112). Other advantages include comparison of changes in series of data that may be expressed in a variety of units and description of typical seasonal or cyclical business patterns.

Arithmetic versus Compound Growth Rate

Growth rate may also be measured by plotting observations on a simple graph. In Illustration 10–A–2, annual sales that start at $100 million in 1980 and rise by $10 million for the next five years are plotted along the vertical or Y-axis against time expressed in years along the horizontal or X-axis.

Caution must be used in calculating growth rate from a simple graph such as the one in Illustration 10–A–2. Using the arithmetic process will produce a different result than when the compounding process is used. In the arithmetic process, to measure the rate of change when the figure is a straight line as in Illustration 10–A–2, the slope of the line must be calculated. This slope represents the change in Y (i.e., rate of growth) per unit change in X. Thus, for any two years on the straight line in Illustration 10–A–2, this ratio or slope would be 10; that is, for every year on the X-axis, sales in millions of dollars are measured on the Y-axis grow by 10. This rate is constant.

The compounding process works differently. Let us assume we want to find the compound growth rate in sales over the five-year period 1980–85. The end value in 1985 of $150 million is equal to the beginning value in 1980 of $100 million times a growth factor $(1 + g)^n$, where g is a growth rate (equivalent to an interest rate) and n represents the number of time periods involved. The following equation can be used to calculate g:

$$S_n = S_0(1 + g)^n$$

where:

S_n = End sales amount.
S_o = Beginning sales amount.
g = Growth rate (or interest rate).
n = Number of time periods involved.

There are tables that may be used to aid in the calculation of the compounding rate. (See Table A at the end of this book for the present value table.) Using the table and the data given in Illustration 10–A–2, we can calculate g in the following way. First, since the tables are present value tables, the above equation should be stated in terms of the beginning amount S_o.

$$S_o = S_n(PVIF)$$

where:

$PVIF$ = Present value interest factor.

Then, by substituting the data given (S_o = $100 million, S_n = $150 million, n = 5 years), find the time period in the left column of Table A (5) and move right until the value .667 S_o/S_n) is reached. Reading up from the approximate position of .667 on the table, we find the rate to be 8.5 percent. This may be substituted in the original equation.

Averages

Another basic tool used to measure the annual growth rate of a series of data, such as sales, is the average of the series. Some of the most common averages used are the arithmetic mean, median, mode, and moving average.

The *mean* of a series of values is the sum of the variables divided by the number of values. The formula $\bar{X} = \Sigma X/n$ is used to determine the mean from a series of data where:

$\bar{X}$ (read "X bar") = Mean of the variable X.
Σ = "Sum of."
n = Number of values.

For example, the mean of the series 10, 17, 27, 34, 50 would be 138 ÷ 5 = 27.6.

When the values to be averaged are of differing degrees of importance, they may be weighted by multiplying each value by a numerical weight based on its relative importance. The total is then divided by the sum of the weights, and the result is termed a *weighted mean*.

The *median* of a set of data is the middle value in order of size if there is an odd number of observations or the mean of the two middle values if the number of observations is even. The median may be more reliable than the mean in samples where extreme deviations occur.

ILLUSTRATION 10-A-3
Three-Month Moving Average

Time Period	Percent Growth Rate for Each Time Period	Three Month Total for Calculation Purposes	Average for Three Months
$t_0 - t_1$	2.0		3.00
$t_1 - t_2$	4.0	9.0	3.83
$t_2 - t_3$	3.0	11.5	3.67
$t_3 - t_4$	4.5	11.0	4.33
$t_4 - t_5$	3.5	13.0	5.17
$t_5 - t_6$	5.0	15.5	7.00
$t_6 - t_7$	7.0	21.0	7.33
$t_7 - t_8$	9.0	22.0	8.67
$t_8 - t_9$	6.0	26.0	9.17
$t_9 - t_{10}$	11.0	27.5	
$t_{10} - t_{11}$	10.5		

The *mode* is that value which occurs most often or around which there is the greatest degree of clustering. The mode is used when a problem specifically requires the most common value as an average.

A *moving average* is simply an average for a specified period of time, moved up a unit at a time, and the oldest unit included in the average dropped. For example, a three-month moving average is a three-month average moved up a month at a time and the data for the oldest month in the preceding three months dropped. A moving average can be calculated to include high and low seasonal months or business cycles during the year. To do so, one might use a 12-month moving average. Seasonal influences can thus cancel each other out and what remains is the smoothed trend or cycle. In this way, seasonal influences may cancel out while the trend remains. Since this is an average, however, there is no data for the beginning and ending period, which can make prediction of future trends difficult. An example of a three-month moving average is shown in Illustration 10-A-3.

Dispersion

When measuring growth rates over time, it is useful to consider the range of the values so as to put the growth rate into perspective. *Dispersion* is the term used to define this range or variation of a set of values, and the purpose of measuring dispersion is to try to determine the nature and cause of the variation in order to be able to control the variation.

Frequently distribution charts may be used to summarize and present data that will be useful in measuring dispersion. The histogram is one useful approach to presenting a frequency distribution. It is a set of vertical bars whose areas are proportional to the frequencies presented. The height of each bar shows the frequency per unit width. The tallest bar represents the modal class which has the greatest frequency of occurrence. On either side, the bars get smaller, which shows that the farther the figure is

ILLUSTRATION 10–A–4
Histogram: Sales in Millions of Dollars for 350 Companies

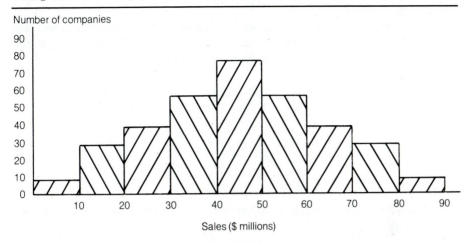

Number of companies

Sales ($ millions)

from the modal class, the smaller is the frequency of occurrence. Illustration 10–A–4 shows a histogram.

A smooth curve can be drawn to approximate the frequency distribution for a population of continuous data. Thus, a frequency is provided for every value on the X axis rather than just one value per class interval as in a histogram. If a smooth curve were drawn over the data in Illustration 10–A–4 to show a general nature of the distribution, we would most likely have a normal or bell-shaped curve as in Illustration 10–A–5. The area under any part of the curve corresponds to the number of values in that range.

Dispersion is the scatter or variation of a set of values, and the following are measures of dispersion: the range, the quartile deviation, the mean deviation, and the standard deviation. The measurements are all particularly useful when looking at an array of growth rates, for example, in attempting

ILLUSTRATION 10–A–5
Normal Bell-Shaped Curve for a Population of Continuous Data

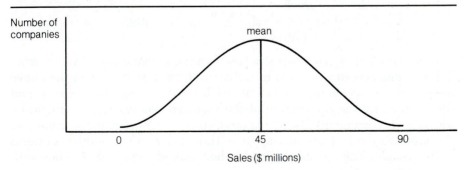

Number of companies

mean

Sales ($ millions)

to determine how variable a particular company's growth may be within an industry, or how variable a particular year's growth may have been for a single company.

The *range* is simply the difference between the largest and smallest values of a variable. The range can be unreliable and misleading if the two extremes are erratic and no indication is given of the intervening values.

The *quartiles* are the three points which divide a frequency distribution into four relatively equal parts. The quartile range $Q_3 - Q_1$ includes the middle half of the items, and the quartile deviation, Q, half this range, is as follows:

$$Q = \frac{Q_3 - Q_1)}{2}$$

where:

Q_1 separates lowest valued quarter of total number of values from the second quarter.

Q_2, usually the median, separates the second quarter from the third quarter.

Q_3 separates the third quarter from the top quarter.

Quartiles are commonly used as measures of dispersion in reporting operating statistics of companies in a particular industry.

The *mean* or *average deviation* is the mean of the absolute deviations of all the values in a distribution from a central point, usually the arithmetic mean or the median. It is a simple measure of variability. It takes every item into account and is less affected by extreme deviations than the range.

The formula for the mean deviation (measured from the arithmetic mean) is:

$$MD = \frac{\Sigma|X - \bar{X}|}{n}$$

where:

MD = Mean deviation.

$|\ |$ = Means that the signs of the values of X are ignored (absolute values are used).

$X - \bar{X}$ = Deviations of any value X from the arithmetic mean $\bar{X}$.

n = Number of values.

The *standard deviation* is also based on the deviation of all values from $\bar{X}$ but is much better adapted to further statistical analysis than the above measures of dispersion. It is calculated by first finding the variance and then extracting the square root of the variance. The variance is found by squaring the deviations of each value from the arithmetic mean, summing the squares, dividing the sum by $(n - 1)$, where n is the number of items in the sample. The formula below has been found to provide the best estimate of the standard deviation:

$$v = \frac{\Sigma(X - \bar{X})^2}{n - 1} \qquad s = \sqrt{\frac{\Sigma(X - \bar{X})^2}{n - 1}}$$

where:

v = Variance.

s = Standard deviation.

$(X - \bar{X})$ = Deviation of any value X from the arithmetic mean $\bar{X}$.

$\Sigma(X - \bar{X})^2$ = Sum of the squared deviations.

n = Number of items in the sample.

In the frequency distribution, the midpoint of each class is used to represent every value in that class. The above formula then becomes:

$$s = \sqrt{\frac{\Sigma f(X - \bar{X})^2}{n - 1}}$$

where:

$(X - \bar{X})$ = Deviation of the class midpoint X from the mean $\bar{X}$.

f = Frequency in that class.

Using the data from Illustration 10–A–4, the histogram, and approximating a mean $\bar{X}$ of $45 million, we can calculate the standard deviation as in Illustration 10–A–6:

ILLUSTRATION 10–A–6
Computation of Standard Deviation $\bar{X} = 45$

Sales in Millions of Dollars (Class Midpoint) X	Number of Companies (Frequency) f	Absolute Deviation from Mean Millions of Dollars) $(X - \bar{X})$	$(X - \bar{X})^2$	$f(X - \bar{X})^2$
5	5	40	1,600	8,000
15	25	30	900	22,500
25	40	20	400	16,000
35	65	10	100	6,500
45	80	0	0	0
55	65	10	100	6,500
65	45	20	400	18,000
75	15	30	900	13,500
85	10	40	1,600	16,000
Total	350			107,000

$$s = \sqrt{\frac{107,000}{350 - 1}} = \sqrt{\frac{107,000}{349}} = \sqrt{306.59} = 17.51$$

The standard deviation is a measure of dispersion about the mean in a sample. In this case, the 17.51 is equal to one standard deviation. What this means is that typically in a normal distribution, the proportion of items falling within one, two, or three standard deviations of the mean are as follows:

$\bar{X} \pm 1$ standard deviation (s) includes 68.27 percent of the items

$\bar{X} \pm 2$ standard deviation (s) includes 95.45 percent of the items

$\bar{X} \mp 3$ standard deviation (s) includes 99.73 percent of the items

where:

$\bar{X}$ = mean.

$\pm$ = plus or minus.

Graphs and Ratio Charts

Graphs and charts may also be used to show changes in data for purposes of growth rate calculation and projection. Caution must be used in charting and graphing material, however. Arithmetic scales show absolute changes in data but do not show the relative or percentage changes, which are often of more importance. Ratio charts show ratios in their true proportion. Equal ratios or percentages cover equal spaces on the vertical scale. This type of scale is preferable to the arithmetic scale when the relative changes in two series of data are being compared.

A ratio chart is plotted on semilogarithmic paper as opposed to arithmetic graph paper. In a semilog chart, the natural numbers are plotted on the vertical scale at distances from the bottom line that are proportional to their logarithms. The horizontal axis shows time on the usual arithmetic scale. Illustrations 10–A–7 and 10–A–8, respectively, show sales plotted against time for two companies: one is an arithmetic scale and the other is a ratio scale on semilogarithmic paper. On the arithmetic graph (Illustration 10–A–7), the larger company, Company B, appears to be growing at an increasingly faster rate than Company A. However, when plotted on the semilog graph (Illustration 10–A–8), the curves are parallel, which means that the rate of growth for both companies is precisely the same.

On a ratio scale, data series of disparate size or those not expressed in the same units may be compared because the slopes of the curves register percentage changes which may be compared. The slope of a line on a ratio chart indicates the percentage change between two points of time. Thus, when comparing two curves or sets of data, relative growth can be determined by comparing their slopes. A curve sloping downward represents a decreasing percentage growth rate; a straight line represents a constant growth rate; and a curve sloping upward represents an increasing growth rate, as do the curves in Illustration 10–A–8. On an arithmetic scale, the growth of the larger one would always be emphasized. This is clearly illustrated in Illustration 10–A–7. By using ratio charts, analysts can determine whether past growth rates are being maintained and can project historical trends to forecast future growth.

Regression Analysis and Correlation

In looking at a company's statistical data and growth rates, it is often useful to be able to estimate the degree of closeness with which two or more

ILLUSTRATION 10–A–7
Arithmetic Graph Sales 1980–1987, Company A and Company B

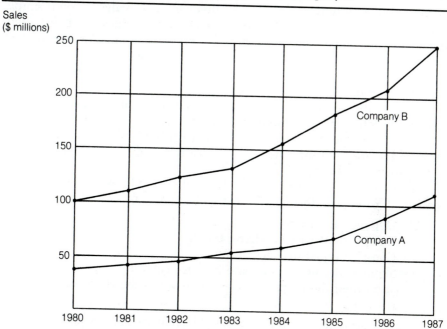

ILLUSTRATION 10–A–8
Semilog Graph Sales 1980–1987, Company A and Company B

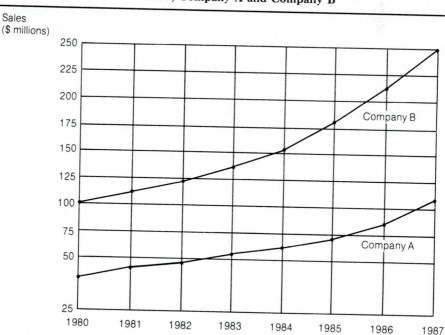

variables are associated and to be able to measure the average amount of change in one variable associated with a unit increase in the value of another variable. When only two variables are involved, the analysis used is simple regression or correlation. When more than two variables are being used, the process is called multiple regression or correlation. For purposes of this note, only simple regression analysis will be discussed.

Caution must be used, however, when measuring correlation between variables. Because two variables are correlated does not imply that one is the cause of the other. Generally, if two variables X and Y are correlated, any of the following statements might be correct: (1) X causes Y; (2) Y causes X; (3) X and Y influence each other continuously or intermittently; (4) X and Y are both influenced by a third factor Z; or (5) the correlation is due simply to chance.

The most simple way to express the relationship between two variables is a straight line. The formula for a straight line is $Y = a + bX$, where

$Y =$ Dependent variable (here, growth rate).

$X =$ Independent variable (here, time).

$a =$ Constant equal to Y when $X = 0$.

$b =$ Slope of the line or increase in Y for each unit increase in X; it is also called the regression coefficient when the regression equation is linear.

On a scatter diagram, the regression line may be determined by estimation, since the predicted value of Y is roughly the average of the observations, or by the least squares method. Using the least squares method will give the best possible fit to the data involved; that is, will best estimate the total observations. It is called least squares method because it minimizes the sum of the squared deviations from the line more than any other straight line would do. (The deviations below the regression line should be equal to those above, which means that their total value should be zero.) These deviations are vertical measures along the Y-axis. The straight line passes through the overall mean of the data.

To find the values of a and b in the equation $Y = a + bX$, use the following equation, where $n =$ number of pairs of data in the sample.

$$a = \frac{\Sigma Y}{n} - \frac{b\Sigma X}{n} = \bar{Y} - b\bar{X}$$

$$b = \Sigma(X - \bar{X})(Y - \bar{Y})\Sigma(X - \bar{X})^2$$

where

$$\bar{X} = \frac{\Sigma X}{n}$$

$$\bar{Y} = \frac{\Sigma Y}{n}$$

Illustration 10–A–9 shows these computations, using the data from Illustration 10–A–3. The method is simplified in trend analysis by choosing an

ILLUSTRATION 10–A–9
Arithmetic Straight Line Fitted by Least Squares

Time Period	Sales in Millions of Dollars Y	Periods from Beginning X	$(X - \bar{X})$	$(Y - \bar{X})$	$(X - \bar{X})(Y - \bar{Y})$	$(X - \bar{X})^2$
$t_0 - t_1$	2.0	0	−5	−3.95	19.75	25
$t_1 - t_2$	4.0	1	−4	−1.95	7.8	16
$t_2 - t_3$	3.0	2	−3	−2.95	8.85	9
$t_3 - t_4$	4.5	3	−2	1.45	−2.90	4
$t_4 - t_5$	3.5	4	−1	2.45	−2.45	1
$t_5 - t_6$	5.0	5	0	0.95	0	0
$t_6 - t_7$	7.0	6	1	1.05	1.05	1
$t_7 - t_8$	9.0	7	2	3.05	6.10	4
$t_8 - t_9$	6.0	8	3	0.05	0.10	9
$t_9 - t_{10}$	11.0	9	4	5.05	20.20	16
$t_{10} - t_{11}$	10.5	10	5	4.55	22.75	25
Sum..........	65.5	55	0	9.75	81.25	110

$$\bar{X} = \frac{55}{11} = 5$$

$$\bar{Y} = \frac{65.5}{11} = 5.95$$

$$b = \frac{81.25}{110} = 0.739$$

$$a = 5.95 - (0.739)(5.0)$$
$$= 2.255$$

Therefore $Y = 2.255 + 0.739X$

odd number of time periods and placing the X origin at the midpoint in time. In this way, the negative X values cancel out the positive so that the sum of all Xs = 0. Thus, the time variable is measured as a deviation from its mean. The constant a is the arithmetic mean of the series and b becomes a simple ratio.

Using any two time periods and calculating Y for each, a straight line can be drawn through the data arrayed on a graph that best approximates the given data.

Thus, the regression line gives an estimate of Y for any value X and the regression coefficient b gives the average change in Y for a unit change in X. There is a measure called the coefficient of determination (r^2) which is a relative measure of the relationship between two variables and ranges from 0 (no correlation) to 1 (perfect correlation). It may be defined as the proportion of the total variance in the dependent variable (Y) which is explained by the independent variable (X).

Curvilinear Regression

Sometimes the situation may call for a curved relationship rather than a straight line; or a curve may actually fit the data better than a straight line. Visual inspection of a scatter diagram can usually determine this. In this case, a curvilinear measure of regression should be used rather than the straight-line method. A regression curve may be fit by drawing a free-hand curve or estimate, fitting a parabola by least squares, or by transforming the available data into logarithms or other functions and then fitting a linear equation to these functions. Choosing the functional form of the equation is the key to fitting a mathematical curve.

Forecasting and Probability Distributions

Up to this point, the various mathematical and statistical tools described have been used to analyze historical performance and trends. Regression and correlation have been considered merely as descriptions of the relationship between variables. Managers, investors, and analysts, however, are usually interested in the results of such measures to be able to control future variation or to predict new values of the dependent variable from the original available data.

Future growth rate may be projected using some of the above-mentioned statistical tools in the following ways: 1) index numbers may be projected relative to a chosen base period using historical data, and from these projections, percentage changes in sales, growth, or whatever is being measured may be predicted; 2) arithmetic and/or compound growth rate analysis using the straight line method as in Illustration 10–A–2 may be used to predict future sales levels and growth rates; 3) averages may be used primarily to summarize historical data but are often used as a base for or starting point for further statistical analysis for purposes of projection; 4) dispersion analysis becomes useful for computation of standard deviation which is then used in future projection analysis; 5) graphs and ratio charts are useful in illustrating historical trends from which future predictions may be made visually; and finally 6) regression analysis is used to estimate historical data to fit a straight line from which future trends may be projected.

ILLUSTRATION 10–A–10
Probability Distribution

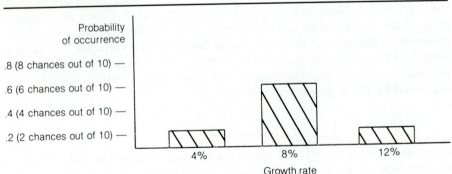

Probability
of occurrence

.8 (8 chances out of 10) —

.6 (6 chances out of 10) —

.4 (4 chances out of 10) —

.2 (2 chances out of 10) —

4%   8%   12%

Growth rate

ILLUSTRATION 10-A-11
Calculating the Expected Value of a
Probability Distribution

Probability of Occurrence ×	Growth Rate =	Expected Value
0.2	4%	.8%
0.6	8%	4.8%
0.2	12%	2.4%
Sum 1.0	Expected value = 8%	

One of the ways in which future growth rate may be estimated using the statistical measures described is through the use of a probability distribution, which is similar to a frequency distribution. A probability of occurrence must be assigned to each possible growth rate figure in the array to be used. The probabilities may be based on historical data or the estimates of a competent person. A simple distribution may look like the one in Illustration 10–A–10. Growth rate is plotted on the X-axis, and a probability of occurrence is assigned to each possible outcome. The sum of the probabilities must equal one (i.e., $.2 + .6 + .2 = 1$).

The expected value or mean of the distribution is found by multiplying each outcome by its probability and summing as in Illustration 10–A–11. The equation for expected value is:

$$\bar{X} = \sum_{t=1}^{n} (G_t P_t)$$

where:

G_t = Growth rate associated with time period t.
P_t = Probability of occurrence of the tth outcome.
$\bar{X}$ = Expected value or weighted average of the possible outcomes, weighted by the probability of each occurring.

For example, using the data from Illustration 10–A–11, there are three occurrences or time periods n, the respective growth rates G_t are 4 percent, 8 percent, and 12 percent, and the probability of each occurring P_t is .2, .6, and .2, respectively (i.e., 2 chances out of 10, 6 chances out of 10, etc.). The growth rates weighted by their respective probabilities are then summed as in Illustration 10–A–11, and the result is the expected value X. Since there is an unlimited number of possibilities, and not merely three as shown above, the distribution would be a continuous curve. Let us assume that the distribution is "normal," that is, the curve is bell shaped (see Illustration 10–A–12). The tighter the curve, that is, the closer the end points are to the mean, the less we expect the actual growth rate to be from the expected growth rate. The standard deviation is used as a measure of the tightness of a probability distribution. Thus, the smaller the standard deviation, the tighter is the probability distribution and the closer those

ILLUSTRATION 10–A–12
Normal Distribution—Bell-Shaped Curve

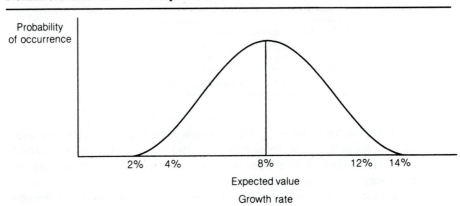

projecting expect the actual growth rate will be to the expected value in the distribution.

The standard deviation for a probability distribution is defined as:

$$s = \sqrt{\sum_{t=1}^{n} (\bar{X} - X_t)^2\, P(X_t)}$$

where:

$$s = \text{Standard deviation.}$$
$$(\bar{X} - X_t) = \text{Deviation from the mean.}$$
$$P(X_t) = \text{Probability of any occurrence.}$$

The above formula is for a probability distribution where the random variable (usually represented as the X-axis) has distinct values and no intermediate values. This may be contrasted to a distribution which has continuous values over a range.

Using the set of growth rates from Illustration 10–A–11 and the above formula, the standard deviation can be calculated as in Illustration 10–A–13.

ILLUSTRATION 10–A–13
Calculation of Standard Deviation for a Probability Distribution, (figures in percentages)

$\bar{X}$	$-$	X_t	$=$	$(\bar{X} - X_t)$	$(\bar{X} - X_t)^2$	$(\bar{X} - X_t)^2 P(X_t)$
8		4		4	16	$16(.2) = 3.2$
8		8		0	0	$0(.6) = 0$
8		12		−4	16	$16(.2) = \underline{3.2}$
						$6.4 = \text{sum}$

$$\sqrt{6.4} = 2.53 = \text{Standard deviation}$$

Projecting this value onto the normal bell-shaped distribution, the actual observed value will fall within the following ranges:

± one standard deviation	68.27 percent of the time
± two standard deviations	95.45 percent of the time
± three standard deviations	99.73 percent of the time

For example, in Illustration 10–A–12, we expect that the actual observed growth rate should fall between 5.47 percent and 10.53 percent, over 68.27 percent of the time.

Sometimes two different probability distributions can have the same standard deviation but different expected values or means. The percentage deviation from the mean of one distribution may be much higher or lower than that of the other. To determine this percentage deviation from the mean in a situation where the standard deviation may be misleading, or where the absolute measures of dispersion are not comparable because two different sets of data are expressed in different units, we use a measure of relative dispersion called the coefficient of variation. This measure is obtained by dividing the standard deviation s by the expected mean $\bar{X}$.

$$v = \frac{s}{\bar{X}} = \text{Coefficient of variation}$$

The coefficient of variation is thus a relative measure of the relationship between two variables. The smaller the number, the tighter, or less variable to the mean, is that probability distribution.

The prediction of future growth may require that the analyst determine the probability that a certain growth rate will occur. To do this, one must calculate the area under the curve (in a normal distribution).[1] Assume the expected growth rate to be 8 percent as in the above examples and the standard deviation to be 2.53 percent as calculated in Illustration 10–A–13. For purposes of illustration, let us find the probability that the growth rate of the firm being studied will be between 10.5 percent and 12 percent.

First, we must standardize the distribution using the Z variable, which represents the number of standard deviations from the mean of our outcome of interest.

$$Z = \frac{X - \bar{X}}{s}$$

where:

Z = Number of standard deviations from the mean.
X = Outcome of interest (growth rate).
$\bar{X}$ = Expected mean.
s = Standard deviation.

---

[1] A normal distribution assumes symmetry around the mean.

TABLE 10–A–1
Growth Analysis

Area Under the Normal Curve

$Z = \chi/\sigma$	.00	.01	.02	.03	.04	.05	.06	.07	.08	.09
0.0 ...	.0000	.0040	.0080	.0120	.0160	.0199	.0239	.0279	.0319	.0359
0.1 ...	.0398	.0438	.0478	.0517	.0557	.0596	.0636	.0675	.0714	0.753
0.2 ...	.0793	.0832	.0871	.0910	.0948	.0987	.1026	.1064	.1103	.1141
0.3 ...	.1179	.1217	.1255	.1293	.1331	.1368	.1406	.1443	.1480	.1517
0.4 ...	.1554	.1591	.1628	.1664	.1700	.1736	.1772	.1808	.1844	.1879
0.5 ...	.1915	.1950	.1985	.2019	.2054	.2088	.2123	.2157	.2190	.2224
0.6 ...	.2257	.2291	.2324	.2357	.2389	.2422	.2454	.2486	.2518	.2549
0.7 ...	.2580	.2612	.2642	.2673	.2704	.2734	.2764	.2794	.2823	.2852
0.8 ...	.2881	.2910	.2939	.2967	.2995	.3023	.3051	.3078	.3106	.3133
0.9 ...	.3159	.3186	.3212	.3238	.3264	.3289	.3315	.3340	.3365	.3389
1.0 ...	.3413	.3438	.3461	.3485	.3508	.3531	.3554	.3577	.3599	.3621
1.1 ...	.3643	.3665	.3686	.3708	.3729	.3749	.3770	.3790	.3810	.3830
1.2 ...	.3849	.3869	.3888	.3907	.3925	.3944	.3962	.3980	.3997	.4015
1.3 ...	.4032	.4049	.4066	.4082	.4099	.4115	.4131	.4147	.4162	.4177
1.4 ...	.4192	.4207	.4222	.4236	.4251	.4265	.4279	.4292	.4306	.4319
1.5 ...	.4332	.4345	.4357	.4370	.4382	.4394	.4406	.4418	.4429	.4441
1.6 ...	.4452	.4463	.4474	.4484	.4495	.4505	.4515	.4525	.4535	.4545
1.7 ...	.4554	.4564	.4573	.4582	.4591	.4599	.4608	.4616	.4625	.4633
1.8 ...	.4641	.4649	.4656	.4664	.4671	.4678	.4686	.4693	.4699	.4706
1.9 ...	.4713	.4719	.4726	.4732	.4738	.4744	.4750	.4756	.4761	.4767
2.0 ...	.4772	.4778	.4783	.4788	.4793	.4798	.4803	.4808	.4812	.4817
2.1 ...	.4821	.4826	.4830	.4834	.4838	.4842	.4846	.4850	.4854	.4857
2.2 ...	.4861	.4864	.4868	.4871	.4875	.4878	.4881	.4884	.4887	.4890
2.3 ...	.4893	.4896	.4898	.4901	.4904	.4906	.4909	.4911	.4913	.4916
2.4 ...	.4918	.4920	.4922	.4925	.4927	.4929	.4931	.4932	.4934	.4936
2.5 ...	.4938	.4940	.4941	.4943	.4945	.4946	.4948	.4949	.4951	.4952
2.6 ...	.4953	.4955	.4956	.4957	.4959	.4960	.4961	.4962	.4963	.4964
2.7 ...	.4965	.4966	.4967	.4968	.4969	.4970	.4971	.4972	.4973	.4974
2.8 ...	.4974	.4975	.4976	.4977	.4977	.4978	.4979	.4979	.4980	.4981
2.9 ...	.4981	.4982	.4982	.4983	.4984	.4984	.4985	.4985	.4986	.4986
3.0 ...	.49865	.4987	.4987	.4988	.4988	.4989	.4989	.4989	.4990	.4990
3.1 ...	.49903	.4991	.4991	.4991	.4992	.4992	.4992	.4992	.4993	.4993
3.2 ...	.4993129	.4993	.4994	.4994	.4994	.4994	.4994	.4995	.4995	.4995
3.3 ...	.4995166	.4995	.4995	.4996	.4996	.4996	.4996	.4996	.4996	.4997
3.4 ...	.4996631	.4997	.4997	.4997	.4997	.4997	.4997	.4997	.4998	.4998
3.5 ...	.4997674	.4998	.4998	.4998	.4998	.4998	.4998	.4998	.4998	.4998
3.6 ...	.4998409	.4998	.4999	.4999	.4999	.4999	.4999	.4999	.4999	.4999
3.7 ...	.4998922	.4999	.4999	.4999	.4999	.4999	.4999	.4999	.4999	.4999
3.8 ...	.4999277	.4999	.4999	.4999	.4999	.4999	.4999	.5000	.5000	.5000
3.9 ...	.4999519	.5000	.5000	.5000	.5000	.5000	.5000	.5000	.5000	.5000
4.0 ...	.4999683									
4.5 ...	.4999966									
5.0 ...	.4999997133									

SOURCE: Spurr and Bonini, *Statistical Analysis for Business Decisions* (Homewood, Ill.: Richard D. Irwin, 1973).

We already know that the probability of the growth rate falling between 5.4 percent and 10.53 percent is 68.2 percent since this is within one standard deviation from the mean of 8 percent. Thus, the probability of the rate falling between 8 percent and 10.53 percent is 34.14 percent (68.27/2). We now need to find the probability of the actual growth rate falling between 8 percent and 12 percent.

$$Z = \frac{12\% - 8\%}{2.53\%} = \frac{4\%}{2.53\%} = 1.58$$

Once we have determined the value of Z, the number of standard deviations from the mean of our outcome of interest, we must use a table for the area under the nominal curve (see Table 10–A–1). Each item in the table is that proportion of the total area under a normal curve which lies under the segment between the mean and Z value (Z standard deviations from the mean).

For example, for our Z value of 1.58, find 1.5 in the left column and move right horizontally to the .08 column. The area is .4429. Since we know the area between 8 percent and 10.5 percent (rounded) is .3414 (half of 68.27 percent), we must subtract that from .4429.

$$.4429 - .3414 = .1015$$

This means that the probability of the growth rate falling between 8.0 percent and 10.5 percent is 34.14 percent; between 8 percent and 12 percent is 44.29 percent; and finally, between our values of interest 10.5 percent and 12 percent, it is 10.15 percent.

Time Series Analysis

The tools of regression analysis may be used on monthly or yearly data, but caution must be used. Time series are probability samples and are subject to trends, cycles, and seasonality as well as to purely random movements. Extreme highs and lows may influence the regression line and, hence, distort the results. Time series analysis usually consists of the following steps: fitting a secular trend curve, measuring seasonal variation, and analyzing cyclical-irregular residuals. Secular trend is measured to appraise recent trends, for long-term forecasting, and to eliminate trends due to isolate cycles. A trend curve is fit by using graphic methods or the method of least squares to fit a mathematical curve. Seasonal variation is measured in much the same way as the secular trend component, while cyclical and irregular movements are usually treated as a residual in combined form.

There is a wide variety of statistical tools, measurements, and techniques to present and to analyze historical data and to project and predict the future. In the prediction of future data, it is important that past trends be correctly presented and estimated and that regression lines, for example, when used, fit the observed data as closely as possible. However, as noted above, the results can be misleading. In general, the more historical observations that are available, the better will be the total picture of historical trend as well as the better will be the mathematical projections.

CASE 10–1

Potter Lumber Company, Inc.
Projecting Growth Consequences

Following a rapid growth in its business during the preceding several years, the Potter Lumber Company in the spring of 1983 anticipated a further substantial increase in sales. In order to finance this increase and at the same time to continue taking purchase discounts, the company sought an additional bank loan of $200,000. The company had already borrowed $50,000 from the Sutter National Bank, that amount being the maximum which that bank would lend to any borrower. It was necessary, therefore, to go elsewhere for additional credit. Through a personal friend who was well acquainted with one of the officers of a large metropolitan bank, the First City National Bank, Mr. Potter, the sole owner of the Potter Lumber Company, Inc., obtained an introduction to the officer and presented his request. The credit department of the First City National Bank made its usual investigation of the company for the information of the loan officers.

The Potter Lumber Company was founded in 1973 as a partnership of Mr. Potter and Mr. Henry Smith, a brother-in-law of Mr. Potter. Six years later on January 1, 1980, Mr. Potter bought out Mr. Smith's interest and incorporated the business.

The business was located in a suburb of a large midwestern city. Land and a siding were leased from a railroad. Terms of the lease permitted cancellation by either party upon 30 days' notice. Two removable sheet metal storage buildings had been erected by the company. Operations were limited to the wholesale distribution of plywood, mouldings, and sash and door products to small contractors in the local area. Credit terms of 1 percent 30, net 60 days on open account were usually offered customers.

Sales volume had been built up largely on the basis of aggressive price competition, made possible through careful control of costs and operating expenses and by quantity purchases of materials at substantial discounts, generous credit terms, and a high inventory service level. Almost all of

This case was prepared by David F. Hawkins.

the mouldings and sash and door products, which amounted to 40 percent and 20 percent of sales, respectively, were used for repair work. About 55 percent of total sales were made from March through August. No sales representatives were employed, orders being taken exclusively over the telephone. Comparative operating statements for the years 1980 through 1982 and for the three months ending March 31, 1983, are given in Exhibit 1.

Mr. Potter was an energetic man, 39 years of age, who worked long hours on the job, taking care not only of management but also performing a large amount of the clerical work. Help was afforded by an assistant who, in the words of the investigator of the First City National Bank, "has been doing and can do about everything that Mr. Potter does in the organization."

Mr. Potter had adopted the practice of paying union dues and all social security taxes for his employees; in adition, bonuses were distributed to them at the end of each year. In 1982, the bonus amounted to 40 percent of annual wages. Mr. Potter was planning to sell stock to certain employees.

As a part of its customary investigation the First City National Bank

EXHIBIT 1

POTTER LUMBER COMPANY, INC.
Income Statements
For the Year Ending December 31, 1980
through 1982, and
For the Three Months Ending March 31, 1983
(in thousands)

	1980	1981	1982	First Quarter 1983†
Net sales	$1,481	$1,830	$2,358	$ 621
Cost of goods sold:				
Beginning inventory	222	194	368	409
Plus: Purchases	1,222	1,748	2,102	$ 632
	$1,444	$1,942	$2,470	$1,041
Less: Ending inventory	194	368	409	497
Cost of goods sold	$1,250	$1,574	$2,061	$ 544
Gross profit	$ 231	$ 256	$ 297	$ 77
Operating expenses	75	109	146	41
Net operating profit	$ 156	$ 147	$ 151	$ 36
Plus: Purchase discounts	9	9	11	1
	$ 165	$ 156	$ 162	$ 37
Less: Customer discounts	33	42	57	15
Profit before taxes	$ 132	$ 114	$ 105	$ 22
Tax expense*	57	48	44	9‡
Net income	$ 75	$ 66	$ 61	$ 13
Less: Dividends	–0–	–0–	20	5
Profits retained in the business	$ 75	$ 66	$ 41	$ 8

  * Twenty-two percent on total taxable income plus 26 percent on taxable income over $25,000. Taxes are payable in the following year.
  † In the first quarter of 1982, net sales were $504,000 and profit before taxes was $25,000.
  ‡ Based on estimated tax expense percentage for the year.

sent inquiries concerning Mr. Potter to a number of firms which had business dealings with him. The manager of one of his large suppliers, the Cotter Company, wrote in answer:

> The conservative operation of his business appeals to us. He has not wasted his money in disproportionate plant investment. His operating expenses are as low as they could possibly be. He has personal control over every feature of his business and he possesses sound judgment and a willingness to work harder than anyone I have ever known. This, with a good personality, gives him an excellent turnover, and from my personal experience in watching him work, I know that he keeps close check on his own credits.

All of the other trade letters received by the bank bore out the statements quoted above.

EXHIBIT 2

POTTER LUMBER COMPANY, INC.
Statement of Financial Position
As of December 31, 1980 through 1982
And as of March 31, 1983
(in thousands)

	December 31,			March 31,
	1980	1981	1982	1983
Assets				
Cash	$ 3	$ 3	$ 3	$ 4
Accounts receivable (net)	114	153	230	256
Inventory	194	$368	409	497
Total current assets	$311	$524	$642	$757
Property (less accumulated depreciation)	$ 22	$ 23	$ 25	$ 24
Deferred charges	5	6	10	8
Total assets	$338	$553	$677	$789
Liabilities				
Taxes payable	$ 57	$ 48	$ 44	$ 9
Notes payable—bank	–0–	–0–	43	50
Notes payable—trade	–0–	–0–	–0–	47
Notes payable—employees	–0–	–0–	–0–	10†
Accounts payable	115	298	350	421
Notes payable—Smith	48	–0–	–0–	–0–
Accruals	5	8	–0–	4
Total current liabilities	$225	$354	$437	$541
Owners' Equity				
Capital stock	$ 38	$ 58	$ 58	$ 58
Retained earnings	75	141	182	190
Total owners' equity	$113	$199	$239	$247
Total liabilities and owners' equity	$338	$553	$677	$789

* Includes $10,000 assigned to Cotter Company.
† For bonuses.

In addition to the ownership of his lumber business, Mr. Potter held jointly with his wife an equity in their home, mortgaged for $22,000, and which cost $40,000 to build in 1967. He also held a $50,000 life insurance policy, payable to Mrs. Potter. Mrs. Potter owned independently a half interest in a home worth about $48,000.

The bank gave particular attention to the debt position and current ratio of the business. It noted the ready market for the company's products at all times and the fact that sales prospects were particularly favorable. The bank's auditor reported," It is estimated volume may be somewhere near $2.9 million in 1983." The rate of inventory turnover was high, and losses on bad debts in past years had been quite small. Comparative balance sheets as of December 31, 1980 through 1982, are given in Exhibit 2. A detailed balance sheet drawn up for the bank as of March 31, 1983, is also presented in Exhibit 2.

The bank learned, through inquiry of another lumber company, that the usual terms of purchase in the trade were 2 percent 10, net 30 days after arrival.

Mr. Potter hoped to use the additional bank loan to pay off his debts to his trade creditors, earn the 2 percent purchase discount, and expand his business.

Questions

1. What is Mr. Potter's business strategy? How does he plan to make sales, keep his costs as low as possible, and use his capital?

2. How successful has Mr. Potter been in achieving his strategy? The following ratios might be useful in answering this question: Percentage increase in sales by years; percentage change in net income by years; annual net income divided by average net worth (one half of the sum of beginning net worth plus ending net worth); and profit as a percentage of sales.

3. How have the financial and operating characteristics of Mr. Potter's business changed over the periods covered by the financial statements presented in the exhibits?

4. How has Mr. Potter financed his business in recent years?

5. What has Mr. Potter done with the financial resources he has obtained?

6. Would you give Mr. Potter the additional loan he requests? *Hint:* If you forecast his December 31, 1983, annual balance sheet, you will have no problem answering this question. The preceeding ratios you computed in questions 2 and 3 can be used for this purpose. You should forecast every account in the balance sheet, except the Notes Payable—Bank account. This account balance will be the number that makes the assets equal to the sum of the liabilities and owners' equity.

7. What changes do you recommend Mr. Potter make in his operating and financial strategy? How might your suggestions change his financial needs and return on stockholders' equity (annual net income divided by average owners' equity)?

CASE 10-2

Baxter Travenol Laboratories, Inc.
Analysis of Growth

Baxter Travenol had always fascinated Jim Donaldson, director of research for the Commonwealth Group, a large investment advisory firm. Baxter had shown extraordinary earnings-per-share growth since 1954. As stated in Baxter's 1979 annual report, "We believe that, despite individual years' fluctuations, Baxter Travenol's 25-year, 21 percent compounded growth rate in earnings per share is an extraordinary record, unmatched by any *Fortune 500* company. We are proud of this accomplishment, and believe that our momentum positions us well for the future." Jim recalled that in early 1973, when he recommended purchase of Baxter for Commonwealth's portfolio, Baxter's 1972 annual report had carried a similar message (see Exhibit 1).

In recent years, however, Jim had been noticing a slowdown in the overall growth of the medical supplies industry. Indeed, in early 1981 Michael LeConey, a well-respected medical supplies industry analyst, had just issued a report in which he concluded, "I believe that this group's past superior performance has ended." Other analysts had expressed similar views about the medical supplies industry as a whole. Jim wondered how Baxter Travenol, a leading medical supplies company, would fare in this environment. As such, he decided to review Baxter extensively for the first time since Commonwealth had added Baxter's stock to its portfolio in early 1973. For his review, Jim felt it important to focus on how Baxter had grown in the past and how Baxter was likely to grow in the future. Also, he was interested in how Baxter would fund its growth. (Exhibit 2 shows Baxter's major sources of external financing prior to 1980 and a Statement of Additional Contributed Capital for the 1970s.)

This case was prepared by S. Krishnamurti (under the direction of Norman J. Bartczak).

Copyright © 1981 by the President and Fellows of Harvard College

Harvard Business School case 182–072 (Rev. 4/83)

EXHIBIT 1
Baxter Travenol Laborabories, Inc.

Chairman's Letter: Baxter 1972 Annual Report

To our shareholders:

In 1972, Baxter again extended its record of consecutive improvements in annual results. The yearly increases were the 18th in a row for earnings per share and the 17th in a row for sales.

Sales advanced 15 percent, from 1971's $242.1 million to $278.8 million. Earnings per share before extraordinary items rose 13 percent, from 68 cents to 77 cents. These improvements were especially noteworthy as gains over the sizable increases of 1971, which were influenced by the temporary withdrawal of a major competitor from the intravenous solutions market. Despite the competitor's reentry, 1972 unit sales of hospital solutions increased over 1971.

The International, Artificial Organs, Hyland, and Aminco divisions made especially strong contributions to 1972 increases.

Acceptance of the new line of intravenous solutions in Viaflex® plastic containers continued to grow rapidly. First marketed only some two years ago, the Viaflex line was accounting for more than half of our solution sales by the end of 1972. Viaflex products, which have significant convenience features as well as important medical advantages, are now essentially competitive in price with solutions in glass bottles.

Other recent product developments which were well received included: the Ultra-Flow® II artificial kidney coil, an improvement over earlier models; the Silicath™ catheter, a silicone elastomer catheter; medical examination and surgeons' gloves which carry unique design features; Hemofil® antihemophilic product, which benefited in increased production and 35 percent reduction in per-unit prices from a raw materials yield breakthrough; and Travase ointment, which helps dissolve and remove dead tissue from wounds.

Among 1972 product introductions was the RSP® clear canister module version of the artificial kidney machine. This unit permits continuous visual observation of the dialyzing fluid, is light in weight, and is especially useful in home treatment. The Wallerstein division introduced Fromase® milk clotting enzyme used in making cheese. Successively shorter supplies of rennet, which comes from calves' stomachs and has traditionally been used for this function, have stimulated cheese industry interest in a satisfactory substitute.

Baxter continued to intensify its commitment to development of new products and to increase its capacity to supply growing markets. Research expenditures were $14.0 million, compared to $12.5 million in 1971. Capital expenditures of $40.8 million brought the total for the last four years to $129.6 million.

Management changes in 1972 included these: William A. Jennett was elected executive vice president; Robert K. Ausman, M.D., was elected vice president—clinical research; Jack L. Barcus, vice president—engineering; and Richard L. McIntire, vice president—corporate development. McIntire was succeeded as president and chief executive officer of the American Instrument division by W. Donald Finn. In early 1973, Vernon R. Loucks, Jr., was elected senior vice president; James L. Katz, vice president—finance; and R. Douglas Petrie succeeded Loucks as president of the Baxter/Travenol division.

Earnings per common share/5 years

Adjusted for 2 for 1 stock splits in 1966, 1967, 1969
PERCENT INCREASE (over two-year base period).

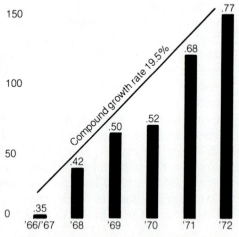

***Consistency in growth**—Whether viewed for the last 5, 10, or 15 years, the compound growth rate for Baxter's earnings per share has consistently clustered around the 20 percent level. Expressed in other terms, this means that Baxter's earnings per share have doubled, on the average, in less than every four years.*

EXHIBIT 1 *(continued)*

Earnings per common share/10 years

Adjusted for 2 for 1 stock splits in 1966, 1967, 1969
PERCENT INCREASE (over two-year base period)

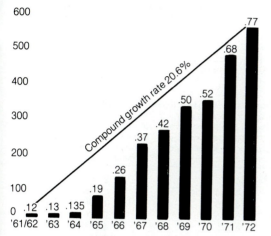

Earnings per common share/15 years

Adjusted for 2 for 1 stock splits in 1959, 1961, 1966, 1967, 1969
PERCENT INCREASE (over two-year base period)

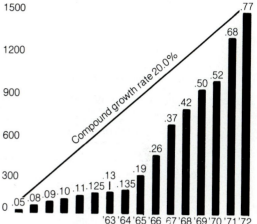

A major Baxter goal over the years has been consistent growth. In our field, growth can mean increasing contributions to the resources of medical practice, and to improved patient care. For our employees, growth can mean added career security and opportunity. For our shareholders, growth can mean continuing appreciation of the value of their equity. We continue in our commitment to sustained growth as a major corporate objective.

William B. Graham
Chairman of the Board and Chief Executive Officer

Background Information

In 1953, when William Graham took over as chairman and chief executive officer, Baxter Travenol had sales of $12 million and earnings per share of $0.03. Under Mr. Graham's leadership, the company experienced rapid and consistent growth. In 1971, Baxter Travenol became a *Fortune 500* company (1971 rank = 494; 1979 rank = 252). In 1972, Baxter became a charter member of the so-called "nifty-fifty," one of the top 50 New York Stock Exchange companies ranked by P/E ratio. By the end of 1980, Baxter Travenol's sales had grown to $1.37 billion and earnings per share had grown to $3.72. Although the medical supplies industry as a whole also grew very rapidly in the 1960s and 1970s, Baxter's growth was generally considered to have consistently exceeded the 15 percent compound annual growth rate of the industry.

EXHIBIT 2
Baxter Travenol Laboratories, Inc.:
Major Sources of External Financing and Comparative Market Information

I. External Financing

A. Subordinated Convertible Debentures

Date of Issue	Amount (in millions)	Coupon	Conversion Price	Most Recent Years' EPS	Due Date
1. 03/16/67	$ 25	4.000%	$17.250	$0.35	03/01/87
2. 03/05/70*	60	4.750%	38.500	0.50	03/01/90*
3. 11/09/71	55	4.375%	38.000	0.52	11/01/91
4. 03/17/76	100	4.750%	46.875	1.44	01/01/01

* Converted on June 12, 1975.

B. Statement of Additional Contributed Capital (in thousands of dollars)

Year	1. Excess of capital of pooled company over par value of common and preferred stock issued.	2. Excess of proceeds over par value of common stock sold to officers and employees under stock option and stock purchase plans.	3. Excess of principal amount of convertible subordinated debentures over par value of common stock issued in exchange, net of expenses.
1970	$ —	$4,072	$ 2,757
1971	25,290	4,444	2,715
1972	—	4,966	1,098
1973	—	5,495	2,276
1974	3,482	4,772	4,388
1975	1,321	5,168	58,136
1976	621	6,743	2,057
1977	4,870	6,100	1,404
1978	6,380	7,710	531
1979	7,168	8,628	216
1980	8,145	9,412	4,571

II. Market Information

	1971	1972	1973	1974	1975	1976	1977	1978	1979	1980
A. P/E Range										
1. Baxter	58–38	73–46	65–43	40–20	36–22	25–18	18–12	18–12	15–11	15–10
2. Abbott	50–32	31–22	24–14	15–8	17–9	17–12	14–10	16–10	15–10	16–10
3. Industry	51–30	53–36	44–30	33–18	26–17	22–16	16–12	16–11	14–10	16–9
4. S&P 500	20–14	21–15	17–10	13–7	13–8	12–9	10–8	9–7	8–6	10–6
B. EPS										
1. Baxter	$0.68	$0.77	$0.95	$1.22	$1.44	$1.85	$2.27	$2.73	$3.29	$3.72
2. Abbott	$0.21	$0.36	$0.42	$0.70	$0.64	$0.82	$0.99	$1.24	$1.49	$1.73
C. Price Range										
1. Baxter	39–26	56–36	62–41	49–24	51–32	46–33	41–28	50–33	40–35	57–36
2. Abbott	11–7	11–8	10–6	8–4	11–6	14–9	14–10	20–13	22–15	29–17
D. Beta										
1. Baxter	NA	NA	NA	NA	1.25	1.25	1.25	1.25	1.20	1.10
2. Abbott	NA	NA	NA	NA	1.05	1.10	1.15	1.15	1.15	1.15

The industry is dominated by six companies.[1] It is marked by high entry barriers in part caused by government regulations on quality and the proprietary nature of its major products. In the beginning of the 1970s, following

---

[1] Abbott Laboratories; American Hospital Supply; C. R. Bard; Baxter Travenol; Becton, Dickinson; and Johnson & Johnson.

a well-publicized Abbott Laboratories recall, the Food and Drug Administration (FDA) expanded its regulatory power over the industry. Where before the FDA control was primarily on the end product, subsequent to the recall the FDA pressured the industry to adopt "good manufacturing practices." In 1976, "good manufacturing and laboratory practices" were enacted into law. This regulatory action gave the FDA control over not only the product but also the process. As a result, medical supplies companies had to invest considerable sums on capital equipment for quality control.

Another entry barrier to the medical supplies industry arises from the proprietary nature of many of the products. Companies within the industry try to carve out "niches" in which they dominate. As such, hospitals and other institutions become accustomed to using the products of particular manufacturers. The equipment and techniques associated with the products are often sufficiently different to preclude easy substitution of one manufacturer's product with another's. Indeed, one of the FDA's major concerns in recalling Abbott Laboratories' intravenous (IV) solutions in 1971 was insuring that the medical institutions had replacements on hand from other makers. At that time, Abbott held 45 percent of the IV market.

In late 1973, Robert Bruce, a senior analyst with H. C. Wainwright & Company, summarized these industry factors and their potential impact:

> The basic trend I see occurring over the next five years is that the overseas market is going to be increasingly more important, while the domestic area, by and large, is going to be much more regulated by the government than it was before. Firms which are commodity-oriented, if you will, may not fare nearly as well as those companies that have proprietary interests in certain areas.
>
> In companies such as Baxter Laboratories, for example, although part of its product line is of a commodity nature, most of its product line is of a "specialized" nature. And I see those companies that have strong R&D effects as having the ability to move into emerging areas and stay ahead of the pack.
>
> In other words, while many commodity areas might not offer above-average growth, newer areas are emerging, and companies with strong R&D and marketing most likely will be able to move into those areas and thus offset to some degree the expected slowing growth pattern in the commodity lines.

In addition to different product-market strategies, companies in the medical supplies industry often follow different operating strategies. For example, American Hospital Supply manufactures only a fraction of the 80,000 items it sells. Baxter, on the other hand, manufactures almost all of its products. In addition, Baxter has followed a strategy of minimizing its effective tax rate to a greater extent than have its competitors. (Exhibit 3 provides comparative industry information.)

EXHIBIT 3
Baxter Travenol Laboratories, Inc.

Implied (Sustainable) Growth Rate Analysis

Note: Assets = Average assets
Equity = Average equity

Year	Pre-tax Margin	Asset Turnover	Pre-tax ROA	Total Leverage	Tax Retention Rate	Return on Equity	Profit Retention Rate	Implied Growth Rate
Baxter Laboratories								
1959	11.50	1.55	17.80	1.91	0.548	18.60	0.720	13.20
1960	10.00	1.49	14.90	1.54	0.633	14.50	0.625	10.40
1961	9.70	1.37	13.30	1.77	0.693	16.30	0.649	10.30
1962	9.40	1.22	11.50	2.11	0.714	17.30	0.659	10.50
1963	8.30	1.12	9.30	2.17	0.732	14.80	0.631	9.30
1964	7.80	1.05	8.20	2.31	0.734	13.90	0.605	8.40
1965	8.60	1.11	9.50	2.36	0.746	16.80	0.692	12.10
1966	11.30	1.14	12.90	2.00	0.723	18.70	0.737	13.80
1967	11.40	1.13	12.80	2.02	0.737	19.10	0.782	15.60
1968	11.80	0.95	11.30	2.29	0.732	18.90	0.785	14.80
1969	11.30	0.92	10.30	2.10	0.719	15.60	0.807	12.60
1970	9.60	0.81	7.80	2.05	0.794	12.70	0.802	10.20
1971	10.10	0.77	7.80	2.17	0.781	13.20	0.830	11.00
1972	9.77	0.71	6.94	2.16	0.814	12.20	0.825	10.07
1973	9.91	0.76	7.53	2.24	0.791	13.34	0.837	11.17
1974	9.71	0.83	8.06	2.28	0.802	14.74	0.857	12.63
1975	9.86	0.88	8.68	2.00	0.800	13.88	0.865	12.01
1976	12.39	0.90	11.15	1.87	0.715	14.91	0.882	13.15
1977	12.80	0.94	12.03	1.88	0.695	15.72	0.874	13.74
1978	11.86	0.96	11.39	1.85	0.770	16.23	0.853	13.84
1979	11.69	0.98	11.61	1.81	0.803	16.76	0.848	14.21
1980	11.62	1.02	11.81	1.72	0.804	16.29	0.828	13.49
Abbott Laboratories								
1971	7.30	1.02	7.45	1.71	0.70	8.91	0.35	3.12
1972	11.50	1.04	11.96	1.79	0.66	14.13	0.62	8.76
1973	11.10	1.03	11.44	1.95	0.67	14.95	0.65	9.72
1974	10.40	1.03	10.71	2.16	0.69	15.97	0.68	10.86
1975	10.90	1.08	11.77	2.25	0.69	18.28	0.72	13.16
1976	12.70	1.08	13.72	2.03	0.67	18.66	0.73	13.62
1977	14.70	1.07	15.73	1.87	0.64	18.82	0.72	13.55
1978	16.20	1.07	17.33	1.88	0.64	20.86	0.71	14.81
1979	16.40	1.06	17.38	1.91	0.65	21.58	0.68	14.68
1980	16.60	1.08	17.93	1.97	0.64	22.60	0.67	15.14
Industry								
1971	12.00	1.23	14.76	1.58	0.57	13.29	0.70	9.30
1972	12.90	1.23	15.87	1.58	0.57	14.29	0.74	10.57
1973	12.90	1.27	16.38	1.63	0.57	15.22	0.76	11.57
1974	11.60	1.29	14.96	1.71	0.59	15.10	0.75	11.32
1975	11.50	1.31	15.07	1.69	0.61	15.53	0.76	11.80
1976	12.40	1.31	16.24	1.64	0.59	15.72	0.75	11.79
1977	12.80	1.32	16.90	1.64	0.59	16.35	0.72	11.77
1978	12.80	1.34	17.15	1.66	0.61	17.37	0.71	12.33
1979	12.40	1.37	16.99	1.67	0.64	18.16	0.71	12.89
1980	12.40	1.36	16.86	1.67	0.63	17.74	0.70	12.42

EXHIBIT 3 *(concluded)*

Year	Pre-tax Margin	Asset Turnover	Pre-tax ROA	Total Leverage	Tax Retention Rate	Return on Equity	Profit Retention Rate	Implied Growth Rate
			S&P 500					
1971	10.50	0.70	7.35	2.80	0.56	11.52	0.48	5.53
1972	11.00	0.70	7.70	2.83	0.56	12.20	0.52	6.35
1973	11.70	0.73	8.54	2.97	0.56	14.21	0.60	8.52
1974	11.30	0.79	8.93	3.14	0.51	14.30	0.60	8.58
1975	10.20	0.76	7.75	3.20	0.50	12.40	0.56	6.95
1976	10.70	0.80	8.56	3.17	0.53	14.38	0.60	8.63
1977	10.60	0.81	8.59	3.19	0.53	14.52	0.58	8.42
1978	10.50	0.82	8.61	3.27	0.54	15.20	0.59	8.97
1979	10.50	0.85	8.93	3.35	0.56	16.74	0.62	10.38
1980	9.20	0.86	7.91	3.40	0.56	15.06	0.58	8.74

Baxter's Position in 1980

International sales account for 35 percent of Baxter's total sales. Baxter's primary product line is hospital solutions, with approximately 42 percent of its total sales coming from the hospital solutions segment. Its only principal competitor in this area is Abbott Labs. By 1980, Baxter's share of the U.S. hospital solutions market was 40 percent, and Abbott's was 35 percent. In the early 1980s, the entire hospital solutions market was expected to grow at 15 percent per year, down from the 25 to 30 percent rate of the 1970s.

Baxter's next important product line is blood therapy equipment, accounting for 22 percent of Baxter's sales in 1980. While total market share percentages are not readily available, Baxter is considered the dominant firm in the blood therapy equipment sector. For example, in the $60 million blood container industry in the United States, it was estimated that Baxter accounted for 97 percent of the market. Baxter's other product lines in which it holds a significant market share are renal and urological products and medical care products.

In February 1980, Baxter's chairman and chief executive officer, William Graham, and its president and chief operating officer, Vernon Loucks, Jr., made a joint presentation to The New York Society of Security Analysts. Under Bill Graham, presentations to security analysts had become a regular part of Baxter's financial relations policy. The theme of the February presentation was "Momentum for Future Growth," and it highlighted Baxter's accomplishments as well as Baxter's strategy for the future. (Exhibit 4 provides excerpts from the presentation.)

In early May 1980, William Graham, 68, relinquished his position of chief executive officer to Vernon Loucks, Jr., 45. It was generally believed that Mr. Graham had been grooming Mr. Loucks as his successor, and the

EXHIBIT 4
Baxter Travenol Laboratories, Inc.:
Excerpts from Presentation by William B. Graham, Chairman and Chief Executive Officer, and Vernon R. Loucks, Jr., President and Chief Operating Officer before the New York Society of Security Analysts, February 21, 1980

Momentum for Future Growth

Mr. Graham: It has now been more than 20 years since I first appeared before this New York Society. This is my seventh appearance here . . . and even may be a record. It's great to be here today to renew acquaintances with a lot of old friends.

Today, I want to detail our recent operating results, and then focus on our vision of what's ahead for Baxter Travenol.

1979 WAS A VERY GOOD YEAR FOR THE COMPANY, MARKING THE 25TH CONSECUTIVE YEAR IN WHICH BAXTER TRAVENOL ACHIEVED AN EARNINGS-PER-SHARE GAIN. DURING THIS PERIOD, EARNINGS PER SHARE HAVE COMPOUNDED AT A RATE OF APPROXIMATELY 21 PERCENT.

We believe this is a record unmatched by any other *Fortune 500* company. I take particular pride, personally, in the fact that 1979 was my 26th complete year as chief executive officer. We've achieved this earnings-per-share record despite individual years when our growth ranged from a low of 4 percent to more than 40 percent. There have been variations over these 25 years, though recently earnings per share have been more consistent.

The overall consistency is shown by breaking out our performance in 5, 10, 15, 20, and 25-year periods. During each of these periods, our compound growth in earnings per share varies only between 20 percent and 24 percent. For the most recent five-year period, the compound growth in earnings per share was 24 percent.

Sales over 24 years have been up every year, and have grown at a 21 percent compound rate.

With this, let's move to 1979. Sales for the year grew at an overall rate of 19%. A 13 percent sales gain was registered by domestic operations, while international sales increased 30 percent.

Net earnings increased to $111 million, or $3.29 per share, a 21 percent increase over 1978. This is a point at which I hope you'll forgive me for a little nostalgia. In remembering my early years as chief executive officer at Baxter Travenol, a quarter of a century ago, we struggled awfully hard to earn $1 million, let alone $111 million.

During 1979, we had some unusual items in the third and fourth quarters that were reflected in pre-tax as well as after-tax earnings. In the third quarter, we recognized a net gain equal to 15 cents per common share due to the disposition of fixed assets, which was primarily our building in Costa Mesa, California; and the tax relief resulting from a change in a United Kingdom law in August. The fourth quarter results included expense items equal to 12 cents per common share reflecting the termination of our joint venture with the American Red Cross, a provision for the reorganization of our Vicra Division, and a Puerto Rican tax provision. The Puerto Rican project represented a lot of difficult negotiating in which we worked out what we think was a very attractive total package, with a December 31, 1979, deadline on filing for tax exemption changes and conversions.

After adjusting for these unusual items, our earnings per share were up to $3.26, or 19 percent, instead of 21 percent. You should treat this $3.26 as a more appropriate base for making 1980 earnings estimates.

We are very proud of our performance during the year, particularly in such a challenging economic environment.

Having reviewed 1979's operating results, let me provide some perspective by reviewing our performance over the last five years. Sales over that period have grown at a compound rate of 21 percent, with domestic sales up 19 percent, and international sales up 24 percent.

Net earnings increased at a compound rate of 25 percent over this five-year period. This growth helps explain why the cash flow increased from $63 million in 1975 to $150 million in 1979. As a result, we provided a greater portion of our funding requirements from internal sources. Given the current environment of high interest rates, our ability to rely increasingly on funds generated from our operations continues to be a high priority. One of the areas in which we concentrate our funding is capital expenditures.

Baxter Travenol has had an ongoing commitment to expanding and modernizing operating facilities. Capital expenditures moved up to a level of $104 million by the end of 1979, with spending in the range of $105–110 million planned for 1980. I should point out, however, that while capital expenditures have shown healthy increases each year, our plant, property, and equipment, as a percentage

EXHIBIT 4 *(continued)*

of sales, has steadily decreased. I think this is indicative of our being able to more effectively leverage our expenditures for fixed assets.

Research and development also has moved up steadily during the last five years. Many of you have heard me say repeatedly that R&D is the lifeblood of our business.

WE REMAIN COMMITTED TO A STRONG R&D PROGRAM. WE EXPECT TO SPEND APPROXIMATELY $58 MILLION ON R&D IN 1980, AN INCREASE OF ABOUT 23 PERCENT OVER 1979.

Return on equity also has moved up steadily over the last five years, to 16.7 percent in 1979. We're particularly pleased to note that, while return on equity has improved, we have at the same time reduced our financial leverage. Total debt, including subordinated debentures, long-term leases, short-term and long-term debt, was 32.6 percent of total capital at year-end 1979. We believe this relationship of debt to equity reflects a capital structure appropriate to our current operations.

Dividends demonstrate another positive trend. On Feburary 11, we announced a 29 percent increase in our quarterly dividend, bringing it to the annual rate of 64 cents per share. Dividends have increased for 23 consecutive years and, over the last five years, have grown at a compound rate of approximately 27 percent.

Let's focus now on Baxter Travenol's future. We have been a premier growth company for the last quarter century, and I imagine many of you wonder where the growth will come from in the years ahead.

The health care market overall will continue to afford attractive growth opportunities. As we see it, four significant factors will contribute to that growth:

1. INCREASES IN HOSPITAL ADMISSIONS AND SURGICAL PROCEDURES. This trend reflects the continued population growth resulting, in part, from longer life expectancies.

2. DEVELOPMENT OF NEW PRODUCTS. With the increased sophistication of medical care, the needs and, in turn, the opportunities for new products in this field have grown apace. The development of new products in related health care fields has, therefore, provided significant growth to the market overall. As examples, our own pioneer work in the intravenous solution field was followed by the Fenwal developments of plastic containers for blood componentry. Baxter Travenol also was first to commercially market an antihemophilic factor. Other important

examples of new products are the first commercial artificial kidney, which we introduced in the mid-1950s, and the bubble oxygenator for heart-lung bypass surgery that followed shortly thereafter. More recently, Baxter Travenol has played a leading role in the development of the new dialysis technique, CAPD.

3. DEMAND TO UPGRADE EXISTING PRODUCTS. As medical technology becomes more advanced, there is a continuing demand to upgrade existing products. This phenomenon has been a significant contributor to Baxter Travenol's growth. For example, from the basic glass IV container we developed a more sophisticated plastic Viaflex (R) container and then, in turn, the Mini-Bag (TM) underfilled container; the coil dialyzer led to the capillary flow dialyzer; and the bubble oxygenator evolved into the membrane oxygenator.

4. BROADENED WORLD MARKETS. Raising the standard of medical care is a high priority worldwide. Recently, expenditures for medical care have increased by 7 percent to 15 percent in international markets. With this increasing sophistication comes the opportunity for Baxter Travenol to add product lines in markets in which we are already established, and to develop additional markets for our products in geographical areas where they have not been previously available.

So as we see it, the potential is there. The question is, what portion can Baxter Travenol carve out within our markets? Here to present some thoughts on the subject is Vern Loucks, our president and chief operating officer.

Mr. Loucks: I'd like to focus on some of our major markets and our strategies for each.

Baxter Travenol has meant a great deal to the market for intravenous solutions. We've led the way toward a revolution in IV solution delivery systems since the domestic introduction in 1971 of our flexible plastic Viaflex containers. With this Viaflex container as the core of our IV line, we've developed related products, such as underfilled Mini-Bag containers for intermittent drug therapy, Travasol (R) amino acid solutions for total parenteral nutrition (TPN), pour bottles for the cleansing of surgical lesions, and administration sets with flow control devices that provide for both the filtration and precise administration of IV fluid.

During 1979, we expanded our line of IV solutions and now offer 105 different therapeutic formulations in Viaflex con-

EXHIBIT 4 *(concluded)*

tainers. This is more than twice the number of formulations than any of our competitors offer in plastic containers.

OUR GROWTH STRATEGY FOR IVs IS TO DEVELOP SPECIALTY PRODUCTS FOR SEGMENTS WITHIN MAJOR MARKETS THAT ARE CAPABLE OF GROWING FASTER THAN THE OVERALL MARKET.

[EDITOR'S NOTE: The next portion of Mr. Loucks's presentation, dealing with a rather technical review of Baxter's products, has been omitted.]

* * * * *

Let's talk a little bit about international operations. We think our position abroad sets Baxter Travenol apart from other major domestic competitors.

WE'VE HAD A STRONG, ONGOING COMMITMENT TO ESTABLISHING AN INFRASTRUCTURE FOR INTERNATIONAL OPERATIONS, WHICH WE BELIEVE CANNOT BE MATCHED.

Our philosophy internationally emphasizes local manufacturing, local research and development, and direct marketing. Today, we have 20 manufacturing facilities outside the United States, including three recent plant additions—in Japan, France, and Singapore. We now manufacture products in 17 countries, and we market in more than 90. Approximately 37 percent of Baxter Travenol's sales were made in international markets during 1979. The compound growth rate of international sales over the past five years of 24 percent, versus 21 percent for the company as a whole, clearly indicates that our worldwide commitment to providing therapeutic medical care products is serving us well.

We continue to see very attractive international growth as countries commit increasing amounts of their resources to medical care. For 25 years, our major corporate thrust has been to achieve and maintain positions of product leadership in selected domestic markets because the United States has consistently led in technological development. Now, with our multinational infrastructure, we're well positioned to offer these products selectively and systematically as other countries narrow their technological gap with the United States. . . .

Our continued ability to establish market leadership worldwide will provide additional momentum for future growth, which will continue to distinguish Baxter Travenol. Specifically, 1980 looks like another good year, and I think we are well positioned for continued growth in the years beyond.

EXHIBIT 5
Excerpts from Baxter's 1980 Annual Report

Financial Summary (in millions of dollars, except per-share data)

For the Year	1980	1979	Percent Change
Net sales	$1,374.4	$1,191.2	+15%
Net income	$ 128.4	$ 111.9	+15%
Earnings per common share:			
Primary	$ 3.72	$ 3.29	+13%
Fully diluted	3.40	$ 3.02	+13%
Dividends per common share	$ .64	$ .50	+28%
Research and development expenses	$ 57.2	$ 47.0	+22%
Capital expenditures	$ 118.6	$ 103.7	+14%
At Year-End			
Total assets	$1,412.6	$1,290.9	+9%
Total debt	$ 349.5	$ 350.6	—
Stockholders' equity	$ 852.6	$ 723.5	+18%

EXHIBIT 5 *(continued)*

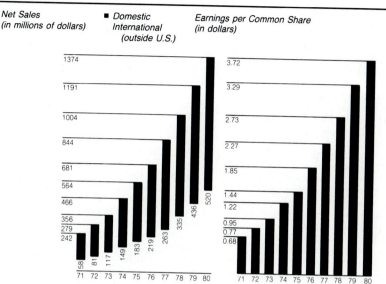

Net Sales
(in millions of dollars)

■ Domestic
International
(outside U.S.)

Earnings per Common Share
(in dollars)

To our stockholders:

1980 was another year of accomplishment for Baxter Travenol. We began the 80s with record earnings, completing the 26th consecutive year in which an increase was achieved in earnings per share. We are very proud, especially in these troubled economic times, to maintain such a consistent record of success for our stockholders.

Sales increased again for the 25th consecutive year, reaching $1.37 billion, a 15 percent increase over 1979. Net income increased 15 percent to $128.4 million. Earnings per share increased 13 percent from $3.29 to $3.72. Sustained, profitable growth remains one of the primary goals for management during the 1980s.

Contribution to our 1980 sales performance was well balanced across our medical care product classes. International sales increased 19 percent to $520.1 million. Domestic sales rose 13 percent to $854.3 million.

Newer products contributing to results included: AUTOPLEX™ injection, for hemophiliacs who have developed inhibitors to antihemophilic factor; intravenous gamma globulin, for patients requiring infection protection; TRAVASORB™ enteral nutrition products for malnourished patients; high concentration dextrose solutions in underfilled VIAFLEX® plastic containers, used in the administration of parenteral nutrition products; premixed potassium chloride solutions in VIAFLEX plastic

containers for drug additive therapy; respiratory therapy products for patients with breathing difficulties; and the CS-3000™ separator, a programmable instrument for blood cell separation. All of these products achieved excellent market acceptance and are expected to show significant growth during 1981.

Particularly gratifying to us in 1980 was the enthusiastic patient response to the new self-administered technique known as continuous ambulatory peritoneal dialysis (CAPD). During the year there was a threefold increase in kidney patients on this new and substantially lower cost method of dialysis. Currently, there are more than 5,000 patients around the world leading more normal, active lives using Baxter Travenol's CAPD products.

Research and development continues to be one of our highest priorities. Expenditures for 1980 were $57.2 million, an increase of 22 percent over the previous year.

We continued extensive work on manufacturing process development, cost improvement, automation, and product redesign. These efforts applied to large scale production are the most effective means to combat the impact of inflation and competitive pricing pressures. In the future, we expect significant support from these endeavors in strengthening our gross profit margin.

During the year, Baxter Travenol also increased its presence and investments around the world. A joint venture was established in Yugoslavia. Major additions to production ca-

EXHIBIT 5 *(continued)*

pacity were made at North Cove. North Carolina; Cleveland, Mississippi; Glendale, California; Eaton, Ohio; and Carolina, Puerto Rico. Expansions also were made in Belgium, Brazil, Colombia, Ireland, Mexico, and Canada. Capital expenditures were $118.6 million for the year, an increase of 14 percent over 1979.

1980 was also a year of change. At the annual meeting in May, Vernon R. Loucks, Jr., president and chief operating officer, was elected president and chief executive officer. William B. Graham continues as chairman of the board. The experience and depth of our management permitted a smooth transition. At the same time, however, the occasion offered an opportunity for reflection, reassessment, and planning of new management initiatives. Out of this ongoing process have come the initial directions and priorities for management in the decade ahead.

To adjust to world economic conditions of high inflation and high interest rates, we emphasized asset management, employee productivity, and operating expense control in 1980. While sales increased 15 percent for the year, the growth in inventory was limited to less than 2 percent. Sales per employee increased 19 percent as the total number of employees decreased from 33,176 at year-end 1979 to 32,232 at year-end 1980. Operating expenses, excluding research and development, decreased as a percentage of sales from 23.3 percent to 22.5 percent.

Although it will take several years to realize the full potential of these programs, the overall financial strength of the company showed definite improvements in 1980. Improved cash flow from operations has provided greater opportunity to enter the financial markets only when attractive to the company. The company's total debt at year-end 1980 remained relatively unchanged. We restructured the components of debt with a substantial shift from variable to fixed rate borrowings, which provided a degree of stability in this high interest rate environment. While the average interest rate on total debt

at year-end 1980 increased by less than .5 percent, the cost of domestic debt actually declined by more than .5 percent to an average rate that was just under 7 percent.

The Internal Revenue Service completed its examination of our tax returns for the years 1973 through 1976. As part of the settlement for these years, an agreement was reached on intercompany pricing relating to our Puerto Rican operations. This settlement had an immaterial impact on earnings and should facilitate the examination of tax years 1977 and 1978.

In addition to the change in chief executive officer, other management changes included the election of Wilbur H. Gantz to executive vice president and the naming of Thomas W. Hodson as treasurer. Notable retirements included those of former senior vice presidents Dr. Leonard G. Ginger, who for many years headed the company's research and development efforts, and Edward J. Nawoj, who was instrumental in expansion of the company's manufacturing operations over several decades. In February 1981, Victor M. G. Chaltiel was elected to the post of group vice president.

As the decade of the 80s unfolds and we enter our 50th year, we are excited about Baxter Travenol's potential. The challenges facing American industry are likely to remain, but we are confident that we have the the proper blend of skilled personnel, strategies and programs to continue the company's record of outstanding performance.

William B. Graham
Chairman of the Board

Vernon R. Loucks, Jr.
President and Chief Executive Officer

Management's Discussion and Analysis of Financial Condition and Results of Operations

The company's goal of sustained earnings growth was achieved in 1980. These results extend the company's record of profitable growth to 26 consecutive years.

The rate of growth in 1980 was reduced by inflationary, recessionary and competitive pressures on a world wide basis. These factors are likely to persist in 1981, making the task

of achieving the company's historical earnings growth rate a continuing challenge to management.

The company is continuing to capitalize on the strength of its market leadership, manufacturing expertise, new product innovations, and management, which should enable it to sustain profitable growth and increase

EXHIBIT 5 *(continued)*

its financial strength despite the unsettled state of the world's economy. However, factors such as inflationary pressures, governmental budgetary constraints, competitive pricing pressures, and worldwide regulatory limitations make the extent of the company's growth subject to a degree of uncertainty.

Liquidity and Capital Resources

During 1980, increased emphasis on asset management programs enabled the company to generate more prouctive yields from the resources employed. Control of asset growth resulted in a higher ratio of sales per average dollar of assets as sales increased 15.4 percent while assets grew 9.4 percent.

Current assets were up $50.8 million or 6.7 percent during the year while working capital increased 20.7 percent to $535.8 million. Accounts receivable were up $36.6 million, or approximately 15.1 percent while inventories increased only 1.4 percent to a $466.9 million level. Accounts payable showed a decrease of 10.2 percent to $69.5 million as the inventory management and expense control programs contributed to lower purchasing requirements.

Net property, plant, and equipment increased 11.9 percent to $560.7 million as the company continued to add capacity to meet increased sales demand and to enhance manufacturing efficiency which resulted in cost improvements. The ratios below summarize the changes in asset utilization during the three years ended December 31.

	1980	1979	1978
Sales/Average dollar of net property, plant, and equipment	$2.59	$2.52	$2.42
Sales/Average dollar of assets ..	$1.02	$ .98	$ .96

The effectiveness of the asset management programs was also manifested in the company's capital structure which showed a proportionately lower reliance on debt to support operations. An increasing share of the capitalization has come from internally generated funds. At year-end 1980, total debt represented 29.1 percent of capitalization as compared to 32.6 percent one year ago and 35.1 percent in 1978. Management believes that the current level of debt allows considerable flexibility to increase financial leverage should strategic business opportunities warrant such action.

Independent corporate debt rating agencies have given the Company an "A" rating for senior long-term debt issues and their highest rating for short-term commercial paper borrowings. This recognition of the strong financial condition of the company and its demonstrated ability to generate stable cash flows in various economic climates allow borrowing at favorable rates. Although increasingly able to fund its operations internally, the company's ability to obtain favorably priced external financing increases its flexibility.

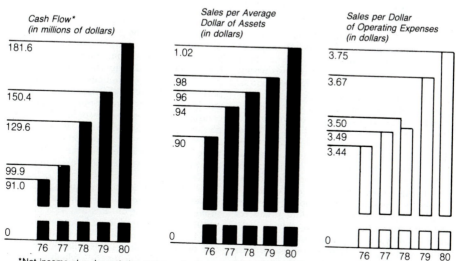

Cash Flow*
(in millions of dollars)

181.6
150.4
129.6
99.9
91.0
0
76 77 78 79 80

Sales per Average Dollar of Assets
(in dollars)

1.02
.98
.96
.94
.90
0
76 77 78 79 80

Sales per Dollar of Operating Expenses
(in dollars)

3.75
3.67
3.50
3.49
3.44
0
76 77 78 79 80

*Net income plus depreciation and amortization, and deferred income taxes.

EXHIBIT 5 (continued)

During 1980, $50 million of the short-term debt outstanding at December 31, 1979, was refinanced with a three-year term loan. The 12 percent maximum interest rate on this loan is attractive compared with the current rate environment. The 1978 and 1980 plans adopted by the company to repatriate earnings from subsidiaries operating in Puerto Rico helped to reduce commercial paper debt. As part of the 1980 plan, additional earnings will be repatriated in 1981 and 1982. The company has no intention to repatriate other earnings from these subsidiaries prior to liquidation unless such earnings may be distributed free of tax.

During 1980, the company considered further reducing its short-term borrowings through the sale of long-term debentures, but because of financial market conditions and favorable internal cash flows, the company refrained from issuing the debentures.

The company's convertible subordinated debentures represent 43.5 percent of total debt. These debentures bear interest at fixed rates averaging 4.6%, well below current market rates. The existence of this attractive fixed rate financing helps to moderate the effect of interest rate fluctuations.

When external financing is necessary to support international growth, the financing is often obtained in local currencies to reduce foreign currency exposure or interest expense.

During 1981, the company expects capital expenditures to be in the $125 million range, the majority of which is not committed by contractual agreements at this time. It is expected that these expenditures will be largely financed through internally generated funds.

Results of Operations

The company's overall increase in net sales during the past three years reflects sales growth in each of the product classes within the Medical Care Segment. The decrease in the Instrumentation and Other Segment primarily reflects divestitures of various industrial products. The company estimates that most of its sales growth in 1980 and 1979 was attributable to increases in physical volume and improved product mix. Increases in physical volume reflect growing demand for recently introduced products in addition to normal market growth, improved market shares in selected areas, and penetration of new markets. Increases in average selling prices for the company's products on a worldwide basis have had only a minor impact on sales growth during recent years. Efforts to improve pricing, as yet, have not significantly impacted

sales due to continued competitive pressures and the contractual nature of much of the company's business. Most of these contracts either have terms of one year or permit annual price increases. As these contracts are renewed or reach an anniversary date, realization of price increases should improve.

Sales by Product Classes (in millions of dollars)

	1980	1979	1978
Medical Care Segment:			
Parenteral Products	$ 549.6	$ 474.9	$ 409.4
Blood therapy products	345.2	311.7	239.9
Renal and urological products	267.6	221.9	179.3
Other medical care products	202.5	170.7	145.5
Total Medical Care Segment	$1,364.9	$1,179.2	$ 974.1
Instrumentation and Other Segment	9.5	12.0	30.1
Total net sales	$1,374.4	$1,191.2	$1,004.2

Sales in international markets increased 19.2 percent in 1980 and 30.3 percent in 1979. A major factor contributing to these increases is the rising standard of medical care worldwide. The company has added new products in markets in which it is already established, and has developed new markets for products in other geographical areas. However, the company is experiencing considerable pressure in the form of government-funded health care budget reductions and inventory control programs as recessionary conditions continue to deepen in certain foreign countries. Competitive pricing pressures are also being experienced overseas, especially in hemodialysis and therapeutic blood fractions.

Domestic sales posted a 13.2 percent increase in 1980 as compared to 12.8 percent growth in 1979. The growth in domestic sales is primarily due to market growth, continued product line expansion, improved mix, and the introduction of important new products, such as fluids for continuous and ambulatory peritoneal dialysis, AUTOPLEX™ injection (an anti-inhibitor coagulant complex), high concentration dextrose solutions in VIAFLEX® plastic containers, radioimmunoassay diagnostic tests, and cell separation products. Competitive pricing pressures continue to affect a significant portion of products sold in domestic markets.

Although the amount of gross profit increased in each year as sales increased, gross profit as a percent of sales was 41.3 percent in 1980, as compared to 42.3 percent in 1979 and 43.7 percent in 1978. The decline in the rate of gross profit reflects inflationary pressures on manufacturing costs which were not

EXHIBIT 5 *(continued)*

fully offset by price increase realizations and cost improvement programs. A smaller factor contributing to the margin decline was the impact of reduced production levels during the second half of 1980, related to significant improvements in materials management systems that enabled the company to reduce the growth in inventory investments. It is expected than inflation will continue to exert pressure on gross margins in 1981, which the company will respond to through aggressive programs to improve sales mix, production costs, and price increases. Supplementary data on the effects of changing prices appears in Note O of notes to the consolidated financial statements.

As a result of the company's sales growth, operating income increased $21.3 million, an increase of 11.8 percent in 1980 as compared to an 18.4 percent increase in 1979. These increases were less than the sales growth rates, primarily because of reduced gross profit margins. Operating income was 14.6 percent of net sales in 1980 as compared to 15.1 percent in 1979 and 1978. Operating expense increases overall have remained below the rate of sales growth despite significant increases in research and development spending.

In 1980, interest expense increased 25.9 percent to $40.9 million, as compared to an increase of 33.6 percent in 1979. These increases reflect higher average rates on borrowings which were 10.6 percent in 1980, 8.8 percent in 1979, and 6.9 percent in 1978. The company's cash flow from operations has been increasing steadily, and as a result, the proportion of debt to total capitalization has declined.

Sundry includes many nonrecurring items which in the aggregate are immaterial. In 1979, such items represented a gain on the sale of a facility, less costs associated with reorganization of several divisions, the abandonment of certain fixed assets, and termination of the company's involvement in a joint venture with the American National Red Cross.

The after-tax effect of foreign currency fluctuations, including those which enter into the determination of operating income, amounted to a gain of $6.2 million in 1980 as compared to a gain of $5.4 million in 1979 and $0.4 million in 1978.

The vertical integration of the company's international operations helps minimize the impact of dramatic fluctuations in foreign exchange rates. Actions that the company takes in an attempt to reduce risk include the financing of facilities through foreign currency borrowings, the timing of currency flows, forward foreign currency contracts, and asset-management programs.

BAXTER TRAVENOL LABORATORIES, INC., AND SUBSIDIARIES
Consolidated Statements of Income
(in thousands of dollars, except per-share data)

	Year Ended December 31		
	1980	1979	1978
Net sales	$1,374,384	$1,191,193	$1,004,196
Cost of goods sold	806,400	686,858	565,062
Gross profit	567,984	504,335	439,134
Marketing and administrative expenses	309,581	277,470	246,782
Research and development expenses	57,202	46,953	40,390
Total operating expenses	366,783	324,423	287,172
Operating income	201,201	179,912	151,962
Interest expense	40,852	32,439	24,277
Other expense, net	661	8,167	8,579
Income before income tax expense	159,688	139,306	119,106
Income tax expense	31,288	27,398	27,423
Net income	$ 128,400	$ 111,908	$ 91,683
Earnings per common share:			
Primary	$3.72	$3.29	$2.73
Fully diluted	$3.40	$3.02	$2.52
Average number of common shares outstanding (in thousands)	34,522	34,008	33,552

See accompanying notes to consolidated financial statements.

EXHIBIT 5 *(continued)*

BAXTER TRAVENOL LABORATORIES, INC., AND SUBSIDIARIES
Consolidated Balance Sheets
(in thousands of dollars, except per-share data)

	December 31	
	1980	**1979**
Assets		
Current assets:		
Cash	$ 11,784	$ 12,900
Certificates of deposit	8,397	3,712
Marketable securities, at cost, which approximates market	1,830	878
Accounts receivable, principally trade, less allowance for doubtful accounts of $4,492 in 1980 and $4,271 in 1979	278,446	241,829
Inventories:	274,044	244,224
Finished products	87,240	96,745
Work in process	105,595	119,241
Raw materials	466,879	460,210
Total inventories	38,204	35,162
Prepaid expenses and sundry deposits	$ 805,540	$ 754,691
Total current assets		
Property, plant, and equipment:		
Land	$ 11,396	$ 10,901
Buildings and leasehold improvements	270,542	238,834
Machinery and other equipment	415,088	343,957
Construction in process........	55,333	66,417
Property, plant, and equipment, at cost	752,359	660,109
Less: Accumulated depreciation and amortization	191,669	159,133
Net property, plant, and equipment........	$ 560,690	$ 500,976
Other assets	$ 46,408	$ 35,261
Total assets........	$1,412,638	$1,290,928
Liabilities and Stockholders' Equity		
Current liabilities:		
Notes payable to banks	$ 54,502	$ 35,477
Commercial paper	4,665	64,910
Current maturities of notes payable and lease obligations........	17,611	9,757
Accounts payable, trade	69,543	77,412
Accrued liabilities	90,827	97,677
Income taxes	32,619	25,435
Total current liabilities	$ 269,767	$ 310,668
Long-term notes payable and lease obligations	120,641	83,613
Deferred income taxes and other deferred credits	17,526	16,275
Convertible subordinated debentures	152,098	156,862
Stockholders' equity:		
Convertible preferred stock, first series, authorized 500,000 shares; issued and outstanding 64,683 shares in 1980 and 76,703 shares in 1979	$ 65	$ 77
Common stock, $1 par value, authorized 100 million shares; issued 34,858,525 shares in 1980 and 34,249,949 shares in 1979	34,859	34,250
Additional contributed capital	231,802	209,404
Retained earnings	586,016	479,782
Less: Common stock in treasury, at cost, 2,852 shares in 1980 and 93 shares in 1979	136	3
Total stockholders' equity	$ 852,606	$ 723,510
Total liabilities and stockholders' equity........	$1,412,638	$1,290,928

See accompanying notes to consolidated financial statements.

EXHIBIT 5 *(continued)*

BAXTER TRAVENOL LABORATORIES, INC., AND SUBSIDIARIES
Consolidated Statements of Stockholders' Equity
(in thousands of dollars, except per-share data)

	Year Ended December 31		
	1980	1979	1978
Convertible preferred stock:			
Balance, beginning of year	$ 77	$ 101	$ 105
Sale of convertible preferred stock under stock purchase plan	25	—	—
Conversion of convertible preferred stock	(37)	(24)	(4)
Balance, end of year	$ 65	$ 77	$ 101
Common stock:			
Balance, beginning of year	$ 34,250	$ 33,771	$ 33,315
Sale of common stock, principally under stock option and stock purchase plans	236	252	260
Conversion of convertible subordinated debentures and convertible preferred stock, net of related expenses	189	37	33
Par value of common stock contributed to the employees' profit sharing trusts, 184,155, 189,589, and 162,976 shares in 1980, 1979, and 1978, respectively	184	190	163
Balance, end of year	$ 34,859	$ 34,250	$ 33,771
Additional contributed capital:			
Balance, beginning of year	$209,404	$193,392	$178,771
Sale of common stock and convertible preferred stock, principally under stock option and stock purchase plans	9,412	8,628	7,710
Conversion of convertible subordinated debentures, net of related expenses	4,571	216	531
Excess of market over par value of common stock contributed to the employees' profit sharing trusts	8,415	7,168	6,380
Balance, end of year	$231,802	$209,404	$193,392
Retained earnings:			
Balance, beginning of year	$479,782	$384,967	$306,777
Net income for the year	128,400	111,908	91,683
Cash dividends declared on common stock— $.64 per share in 1980, $.50 per share in 1979, and $.40 per share in 1978	(22,111)	(17,039)	(13,442)
Cash dividends declared on convertible preferred stock—$.71 per share in 1980, $.59 per share in 1979, and $.49 per share in 1978	(55)	(54)	(51)
Balance, end of year	$586,016	$479,782	$384,967
Treasury stock, at cost:			
Balance, beginning of year	$ 3	—	—
Treasury stock purchased	136	3	—
Treasury stock contributed to the employees' profit sharing trusts	(3)	—	—
Balance, end of year	$ 136	$ 3	—
Total stockholders' equity	$852,606	$723,510	$612,231

See accompanying notes to consolidated financial statements.

EXHIBIT 5 *(continued)*

BAXTER TRAVENOL LABORATORIES, INC., AND SUBSIDIARIES
Consolidated Statements of Changes in Financial Position
(in thousands of dollars)

	Year Ended December 31		
	1980	1979	1978
Sources of working capital:			
Net income	$128,400	$111,908	$ 91,683
Depreciation and amortization	51,203	40,963	31,857
Deferred income taxes	2,042	(2,516)	6,079
Working capital provided from operations	$181,645	$150,355	$129,619
Proceeds from sale of common stock, principally under stock option and stock purchase plans	8,152	8,254	7,255
Common stock issued upon conversion of convertible subordinated debentures and convertible preferred stock, net of related expenses	4,760	253	564
Dispositions of property, plant, and equipment	6,604	12,386	1,613
Increase in long-term notes payable and lease obligations	58,110	36,911	21,758
Market value of common stock contributed to employees' profit sharing trusts	8,602	7,358	6,543
Total sources of working capital	$267,873	$215,517	$167,352
Applications of working capital:			
Additions to property, plant, and equipment	118,645	103,654	90,057
Payments on long-term notes payable and lease obligations	21,082	8,465	21,116
Conversion and redemption of convertible subordinated debentures and convertible preferred stock	4,801	254	567
Dividends declared	22,166	17,093	13,493
Other, net	9,429	13,350	13,995
Total applications of working capital	$176,123	$142,816	$139,228
Increase in working capital	$ 91,750	$ 72,701	$ 28,124
Changes in working capital, increase (decrease):			
Cash	$ (1,116)	$ 704	$ 6,221
Certificates of deposit	4,685	1,372	(52,908)
Marketable securities	952	(760)	(5,638)
Accounts receivable	36,617	28,092	41,845
Inventories	6,669	63,068	86,932
Prepaid expenses and sundry deposits	3,042	5,463	16,691
Notes payable to banks	(19,025)	5,161	(30,328)
Commercial paper	60,245	10,090	(13,500)
Current maturities of notes payable and lease obligations	(7,854)	(6,168)	(1,631)
Accounts payable, trade	7,869	564	(16,813)
Accrued liabilities	6,850	(22,326)	(13,299)
Income taxes	(7,184)	(12,559)	10,552
Increase in working capital	91,750	72,701	28,124
Working capital at beginning of year	444,023	371,322	343,198
Working capital at end of year	$535,773	$444,023	$371,322

See accompanying notes to consolidated financial statements.

EXHIBIT 5 *(continued)*

Notes to Consolidated Financial Statements

Note A: Summary of significant accounting policies

The summary of significant accounting policies is presented to assist the reader in understanding and evaluating the consolidated financial statements. These policies are in accordance with generally accepted accounting principles, and have been followed consistently in all material respects.

Basis of consolidation: The consolidated financial statements include the accounts of Baxter Travenol Laboratories, Inc., and its subsidiaries ("the company"). The International and Puerto Rican operations, except for the Canadian subsidiary, have been included in the consolidated financial statements on the basis of fiscal years ended November 30.

Inventories: Inventories are stated at the lower of cost (principally, first-in, first-out method) or market. Market for raw materials is based on replacement costs and for other inventory classifications on net realizable value. Appropriate consideration is given to deterioration, obsolescence, and other factors in evaluating net realizable value.

Property, plant, and equipment: Property, plant, and equipment are stated at cost. Depreciation and amortization are provided for financial reporting purposes principally on the straight-line method over the estimated useful lives of the individual assets or over the terms of the related leases if shorter. For tax purposes, the straight-line and accelerated methods of depreciation are used.

Intangible assets: Intangible assets include the excess of the consideration paid for companies in purchase transactions over the net assets of such companies. This excess is included in Other Assets and is being amortized on a straight-line basis over periods not exceeding 40 years.

Purchased patents, which are included in Other Assets, are amortized on a straight-line basis over their legal or commercial lives, whichever is shorter. Costs of internally developed patents and patent applications filed by the company are charged to expense as incurred.

Plant start-up costs: Start-up costs related to production facilities are capitalized until such time as the facility achieves a normal activity level, or six months after start-up; whichever occurs first. Subsequently, such costs, which are included in Other Assets, are amortized over 36 months on a straight-line basis.

Income taxes: United States federal income taxes are not provided on undistributed earnings of foreign subsidiaries, as it is intended that such earnings remain permanently invested in those companies. Investment tax credits are recognized as a reduction of income tax expense in the year in which the related assets are placed in service.

Note B: Accrued liabilities

Accrued liabilities consisted of the following at December 31, 1980, and 1979 (in thousands of dollars):

	1980	1979
Salaries, wages, and other compensation	$17,974	$22,384
Property, payroll, and other taxes	12,840	16,268
Other	60,013	59,025
Total	$90,827	$97,677

Note C: Profit sharing and retirement plans

The company and certain of its subsidiaries have contributory profit sharing plans covering the majority of employees. The plans provide for annual contributions equal to a minimum of 6 percent of consolidated net income before the contribution, administrative charges, and income tax expense. Upon retirement, a participant may receive the full value of his account as monthly retirement income payments or, at the discretion of the administration committee, as a lump sum payment or an annuity.

The company and certain of its subsidiaries also have pension and retirement plans for certain employees who are not covered by profit sharing plans.

Note D: Income taxes

The United States federal income tax returns of the company through December 31, 1976, have been examined and cleared by the Internal Revenue Service (IRS). In February 1981, an agreement was reached with the IRS for years 1973 through 1976 relating to intercompany pricing on sales by subsidiaries operating in Puerto Rico under tax incentive grants. This agreement had an immaterial impact on earnings. The IRS has also issued a Technical Advice Memorandum agreeing with the company's treatment of the 1974 liquidation of an operating subsidiary in Puerto Rico as tax free. The returns for 1977 and 1978 are presently under examination. In the opinion of management, based upon the 1973–76 agreement, adequate provision has been made for 1977, 1978, and subsequent years not yet examined.

EXHIBIT 5 *(continued)*

The effective income tax rate applicable to consolidated income is less than the "statutory" U.S. federal income tax rate for the following reasons:

	Percent of Pre-Tax Income		
	1980	1979	1978
Effective tax rate	19.6%	19.7%	23.0%
Tax-exempt operations	24.4	26.2	24.6
Investment tax credits	3.5	4.5	2.8
United Kingdom stock relief ..	1.8	2.3	—
Higher effective foreign tax rates	(1.4)	(7.4)	(1.2)
Other factors, including state and local taxes	(1.9)	0.7	(1.2)
"Statutory" U.S. tax rate ..	46.0%	46.0%	48.0%

In 1968, 1974, 1977, and 1978, the company liquidated subsidiaries which had been operating in Puerto Rico under tax exemptions granted by the Commonwealth of Puerto Rico. The retained earnings of these subsidiaries were returned to the company without payment of U.S. federal income taxes under present law which permits the tax-free liquidation of domestic subsidiaries. In connection with the 1978 liquidations, the company entered into an agreement with the Commonwealth of Puerto Rico to avail itself of certain tax benefits provided under Puerto Rican law. This agreement required the repatriation of a portion of earnings of other subsidiaries operating in Puerto Rico and the payment of Puerto Rican taxes which were included in 1978 income tax expense.

In 1980, the company entered into agreements with the Commonwealth of Puerto Rico pursuant to which two of its currently effective tax exemptions and six of its exceptions under which operations have not yet begun were converted into partial tax exemptions under the 1978 Industrial Incentives Act. As a result, the exemption periods were extended for 10 years and the exemptions were otherwise modified. Appropriate taxes are currently being provided on earnings of the converted companies. In connection with the agreements, the company adopted a plan under which certain of its Puerto Rican operating subsidiaries paid dividends equal to their retained earnings (less certain amounts required to be invested in Puerto Rico) accumulated through 1979 and all exempt subsidiaries currently in operation in Puerto Rico will pay dividends equal to all such earnings accumulated during 1980 and 1981. In accordance with the plan, adequate taxes have been provided in 1980 and 1979 on such dividends.

A provision will be made in 1981 for the anticipated tax on dividends to be paid from earnings of that year under the plan.

Without consideration of the 10-year extensions referred to above, subsidiaries of the company now manufacturing in Puerto Rico hold exemptions expiring on various dates between 1985 and 2004.

The U.S. 1976 Tax Reform Act provides for the tax-free repatriation of the earnings of these subsidiaries; however, the Commonwealth of Puerto Rico would assess a tax of up to 10 percent in the event of repatriation of earnings prior to liquidation. The company, except as described above, has no further plans to repatriate earnings prior to liquidation unless such earnings may otherwise be distributed free of tax.

The earnings of one subsidiary operating in Ireland are 100 percent tax exempt until July 1987, and those of a second subsidiary are tax exempt through 1990. Thereafter, earnings of both subsidiaries are expected to be subject to taxes at rates not exceeding 10 percent until 2000.

Tax savings attributable to tax-exempt operations in aggregate and per-share amounts were $38,974,000 ($1.13), $36,505,000 ($1.07), and $29,373,000 ($.88) in 1980, 1979, and 1978, respectively.

The United Kingdom (U.K.) stock relief factor relates to a 1979 change in the U.K. tax law. Under this change, deferred income taxes may become permanent tax savings. Consequently, income tax expense has been reduced by $3,002,000 and $3,187,000 in 1980 and 1979, respectively, representing the company's current estimate of its future permanent tax savings.

Since the company plans to reinvest unremitted earnings of foreign subsidiaries, even though immaterial amounts may be repatriated from time to time, no additional provision for U.S. federal income taxes is required. U.S. federal income taxes, net of available tax credits, on unremitted earnings would be approximately $20 million, $22 million, and $16 million at December 31, 1980, 1979, and 1978, respectively.

Income before income tax expense by category is as follows (in thousands of dollars):

	1980	1979	1978
Domestic, including Puerto Rico	$137,365	$102,181	$ 83,531
Foreign	22,323	37,125	35,575
Income before income tax expense	$159,688	$139,306	$119,106

EXHIBIT 5 *(continued)*

Income tax expense in analyzed by category and by income statement classification as follows (in thousands of dollars):

	1980	1979*	1978*
Current:			
Domestic			
Federal	$13,469	$ 7,293	$10,235
State and local, including			
Puerto Rico	7,846	5,777	3,106
Foreign	7,931	16,844	8,003
Current income tax expense	29,246	29,914	21,344
Deferred:			
Domestic	1,304	(4,353)	825
Foreign	738	1,837	5,254
Deferred income tax expense	2,042	(2,516)	6,079
Income tax expense	$31,288	$27,398	$27,423

* Reflects reclassifications to conform to 1980 presentation.

The following factors comprise the components of deferred income tax expense (in thousands of dollars):

	1980	1979	1978
Accelerated depreciation	$ 3,689	$ 3,484	$3,464
Foreign exchange	(1,731)	139	1,279
United Kingdom stock relief .	(2,616)	(3,187)	—
Other timing differences	2,700	(2,952)	1,336
Deferred income tax expense	$ 2,042	$(2,516)	$6,079

The deferred income tax liability was $17,067,000 and $15,563,000 at December 31, 1980, and 1979, respectively.

Note E: Short-term credit agreements

At December 31, 1980, the company had domestic bank credit arrangements, generally at prime rates, totaling $152 million including $45 million for domestic and multicurrency revolving credit agreements. These revolving credit agreements expire at various dates through 1986. The commitment fee cost for these revolving agreements averages .25 percent per annum on the daily unborrowed amount. All or any part of these revolving credit agreements and the bank credit lines may be canceled by the company at any time. The company has arrangements with certain banks to compensate them for credit lines (including revolving credit agreements) on a compensating balance or fee in lieu of balance basis. Fees average .08 percent per annum of total lines, and balances aggregate $7,010,000; such balances also compensate the banks for other banking services performed for the company. There are no legal restrictions on the company's use of the funds. As of December 31, 1980, there were no borrowings under $150,800,000 of these lines and revolving credit agreements. Such lines and agreements support commercial paper borrowings.

During February 1981, the company reduced its domestic bank credit arrangements from $152 million to $111 million, with domestic and multicurrency revolving credit agreements representing $15 million of the total.

The company has also arranged additional short-term credit agreements aggregating approximately $179,294,000 in support of its international operations. At year-end 1980, approximately $101,790,000 remained in unused credit under these agreements.

Note F: Long-term notes payable and lease obligations

Long-term notes payable and lease obligations consisted of the following at December 31, 1980, and 1979 (in thousands of dollars):

	1980	1979
Notes payable:		
Bank note due February 1983, interest rate at prime, except limited to 15¼ percent during the first six months; minimum of 9 percent, maximum of 12 percent for the remaining 30 months	$ 50,000	$ —
10.375 percent bank note due October 1981	10,000	10,000
International short-term borrowings expected to be refinanced, denominated in foreign currencies, interest rates from 6 percent to 22 percent at December 31, 1980, supported by revolving credit agreements expiring through January 1986	29,004	31,700
Miscellaneous notes due 1981 through 1994, interest rates from 6 percent to 27 percent at December 31, 1980	27,146	26,846
Capitalized lease obligations, payments extend to 2008, interest rates from (10 percent to 16 percent at December 31, 1980	22,102	24,824
Total	$138,252	$93,370
Less current portion	17,611	9,757
Long-term portion	$120,641	$83,613

The current portion of capitalized lease obligations was $2,127,000 and $2,115,000 at December 31, 1980, and 1979, respectively.

Aggregate maturities, exclusive of capitalized lease obligations and amounts intended to be refinanced under long-term agreements,

EXHIBIT 5 (continued)

1981 to 1985, are as follows: 1981—$15,-484,000; 1982—$10,968,000; 1983—$55,-354,000; 1984—$1,097,000; 1985—$767,000.

The company leases warehouses, offices, transportation equipment, and data processing equipment under operating leases expiring at various times. Most of the operating leases contain options that allow the company to renew its lease at the then fair rental value.

Future minimum lease payments, including interest, by year and in the aggregate, under capital leases and noncancellable operating leases, consisted of the following at December 31, 1980 (in thousands of dollars):

	Capital Leases	Operating Leases
1981	$ 3,497	$24,658
1982	3,411	12,969
1983	3,145	9,121
1984	3,068	5,702
1985	2,711	4,092
Thereafter	17,865	21,864
Future minimum lease payments	33,697	$78,406
Less amounts representing interest	11,595	
Present value of net minimum lease payments	$22,102	

Total rent expense for all operating leases was $34,094,000, $23,823,000, and $17,812,000 in 1980, 1979, and 1978, respectively.

Property recorded under capital leases includes the following amounts (in thousands of dollars):

	1980	1979
Land	$ 30	$ 30
Buildings and leasehold improvements	28,474	29,563
Machinery and other equipment	4,649	4,693
Capitalized leased property	33,153	34,286
Less: Accumulated amortization	9,728	8,631
Net capitalized leased property	$23,425	$25,655

Note G: Convertible subordinated debentures
Convertible subordinated debentures consisted of the following at December 31, 1980, and 1979 (in thousands of dollars):

	1980	1979
4 percent, due 1987	$ 1,173	$ 2,023
4⅜ percent, due 1991	51,011	54,839
4¾ percent, due 2001	99,914	$100,000
Total	$152,098	$156,862

The convertible subordinated debentures are convertible into shares of common stock (with antidilution provisions) at the following rates: 4 percent—$17.25; 4⅜ percent—$38.00; 4¾ percent—$46.875. Sinking fund requirements to retire 50 percent of the 4 percent and 4¾ percent and 75 percent of the 4¾ percent original issues commenced in 1977 and will end in 2000. Under the indentures, conversions prior to these dates satisfy the scheduled requirements. Accordingly, no payments were required in 1980 and 1979, and amounts due annually 1981 to 1985, are as follows: 1981—none; 1982—$1,511,000; 1983—$2,750,000; 1984—$2,750,000; 1985—$2,-750,000.

Note H: Preference and convertible preferred stocks
The stockholders have authorized the issuance of 1 million shares of no par value preference stock; no shares have been issued. The preference stock can be issued in series with varying terms as determined by the board of directors.

Baxter/Travenol International Capital Corporation ("International"), a wholly owned subsidiary of Baxter Travenol Laboratories, Inc. ("Baxter"), was formed to assist in financing the operations of Baxter outside the United States and Canada. The convertible preferred stock of International, first series, is nonvoting; convertible share for share into Baxter common stock (subject to antidilution adjustments); entitled to receive semiannual cumulative dividends of $.07 more than the dividends paid during the preceding six months on the equivalent Baxter common stock; and, upon liquidation of International, entitled to receive Baxter common stock on a share for share basis (subject to antidilution adjustments). During 1980, 1979, and 1978, 36,610 shares, 23,845, and 4,320 shares, respectively, were converted into Baxter common stock.

Note I: Common stock
The company has employees' stock purchase plans under which the sale of its common

EXHIBIT 5 *(continued)*

stock has been authorized. Stock purchase transactions for the three years ended December 31, 1980, are summarized below:

	Shares Subscribed For		
	1980	1979	1978
Beginning balance	150,900	192,740	300,535
Additional subscriptions	200,790	120,280	119,015
Issued	(168,975)	(162,120)	(226,810)
Ending balance	182,715	150,900	192,740
Purchase price per share	$24.49–47.71	$24.44–42.13	$24.44–42.13

The company has three stock option plans: The Qualified Stock Option Plan of 1973 and the Nonqualified Stock Option Plans of 1973 and 1977. All outstanding options under these plans have been granted at 100 percent of market value on the dates of grant. Stock option transactions for the three years ended December 31, 1980, are summarized below:

	Option Shares		
	1980	1979	1978
Outstanding, beginning of year	353,839	390,858	422,493
Granted	148,110	107,825	93,160
Exercised	(64,500)	(39,582)	(25,186)
Canceled	(31,271)	(105,262)	(99,609)
Outstanding, end of year	406,178	353,839	390,858
Option price per share:			
Exercised ..	$29.38–42.38	$25.31–41.75	$29.38–44.44
Outstanding, end of year	$29.44–48.88	$29.38–46.94	25.31–43.63

At December 31, 1980, 173,290 option shares were exercisable.

The 1977 plan also provides for the discretionary grant of stock appreciation rights in conjunction with the options which allow the holder to receive an amount, in cash and/or stock, equal to the difference between the cur-

rent market value of a share of stock and the option price of such share of stock. Under this plan, when options and stock appreciation rights are granted in tandem, the exercise of one cancels the other. Stock appreciation rights transactions for the three years ended December 31, 1980, are summarized below:

	Rights		
	1980	1979	1978
Outstanding, beginning of year	57,500	28,250	—
Granted	49,000	33,250	30,250
Exercised	(2,750)	—	—
Canceled	(6,250)	(4,000)	(2,000)
Outstanding, end of year	97,500	57,500	28,250
Right price per share:			
Exercised ..	$40.13	—	—
Outstanding, end of year	$39.00–44.13	$39.00–40.13	$40.13

At December 31, 1980, 22,000 rights were exercisable.

At December 31, 1980, 4,793,136 shares of the company's common stock were reserved as follows:

Convertible subordinated debentures	3,542,564
Convertible preferred stock	165,093
Stock purchase plans	227,977
Stock option plans	857,502
Total shares reserved	4,793,136

Note J: Industry segments

The company operates in two industry segments: the major segment is Medical Care and the minor segment is Instrumentation and Other. The Medical Care Segment of the business has accounted for 99 percent, 99 percent, and 97 percent of consolidated net sales in 1980, 1979, and 1978, respectively.

Note K: Operations by geographic area

Financial information by geographic area for 1980, 1979, 1978, is summarized as follows (in thousands of dollars):

EXHIBIT 5 (continued)

	United States			Europe			Other International		
	1980	1979	1978	1980	1979	1978	1980	1979	1978
Net sales, trade	$ 888,086	$780,065	$685,826	$324,957	$278,341	$206,466	$161,341	$132,787	$111,904
Inter-area sales	112,049	99,261	74,531	25,715	21,404	18,382	10,664	12,135	6,827
Total net sales	$1,000,135	$879,326	$760,357	$350,672	$299,745	$224,848	$172,005	$144,922	$118,731
Operating income before corporate expense	$ 179,211	$150,365	$123,927	$ 29,076	$ 41,866	$ 33,084	$ 14,853	$ 8,840	$ 11,693
Identifiable assets	$ 928,619	$867,961	$810,400	$294,978	$277,303	$202,022	$163,015	$121,949	$ 94,627

Consolidated

	1980			1979			1978		
	Subtotal	Eliminations	Total	Subtotal	Eliminations	Total	Subtotal	Eliminations	Total
Net sales, trade	$1,374,384	$ —	$1,374,384	$1,191,193	$ —	$1,191,193	$1,004,196	$ —	$1,004,196
Inter-area sales	148,428	(148,428)	—	132,800	(132,800)	—	99,740	(99,740)	—
Total net sales	$1,522,812	$(148,428)	$1,374,384	$1,323,993	$(132,800)	$1,191,193	$1,103,936	$(99,740)	$1,004,196
Operating income before corporate expenses	$ 223,140	$ (1,185)	$ 221,955	$ 201,071	$ (2,497)	$ 198,574	$ 168,704	$ 626	$ 169,330
Corporate expenses			20,754			18,662			17,368
Operating income			201,201			179,912			151,962
Interest and other expenses, net			41,513			40,606			32,856
Income before income tax expense			$ 159,688			$ 139,306			$ 119,106
Identifiable assets	$1,386,612	$ (11,521)	$1,375,091	$1,267,213	$ (8,670)	$1,258,543	$1,107,049	$ (8,515)	$1,098,534
Corporate assets			37,547			32,385			31,103
Total assets at year-end			$1,412,638			$1,290,928			$1,129,637

EXHIBIT 5 *(continued)*

Transactions between areas are accounted for at arm's length prices. Identifiable assets are those assets associated with operations in each geographic area. Corporate assets are principally cash, certificates of deposit, marketable securities, and corporate property and equipment.

Foreign sales (including U.S. export sales) and net assets (including advances from the company and its subsidiaries) of all consolidated foregin subsidiaries and branches located outside the U.S., its territories, and possessions were as follows (in thousands of dollars):

	1980	1979	1978
Foreign sales	$520,134	$436,412	$335,027
Foreign net assets at year-end	$256,198	$199,783	$163,933

Note L: Interest expense and other expense, net

Interest expense and other expense, net for the three years ended December 31, 1980, are summarized as follows (in thousands of dollars):

	1980	1979	1978
Interest expense:			
Interest cost accrued	$42,906	$32,939	$25,303
Less interest capitalized	2,054	$ 500	1,026
Net interest expense	$40,852	$32,439	$24,277
Other (income) or expense:			
Interest income	$ (2,468)	$ (2,347)	$ (3,782)
Contributions to employees' profit sharing trusts	10,209	8,904	7,608
Sundry, net	(7,080)	1,610	4,753
Other expense, net ..	$ 661	$ 8,167	$ 8,579

The net after-tax effect of foreign currency fluctuations included in the Consolidated Statements of Income, including amounts which enter into the determination of operating income, were gains of $6,178,000, $5,432,000, and $423,000 in 1980, 1979, and 1978, respectively.

Note M: Litigation

The company is a defendant in a number of lawsuits. Based upon the advice of counsel, management believes that note of these cases will have a material effect upon the company's conduct of its business or its financial position.

Note N: Earnings per share

Primary earnings per share of common stock are computed by dividing the net income applicable to common stock by the weighted average number of shares of common stock outstanding during the year. Common stock equivalents do not have a materially dilutive effect and are not recognized in the computation of primary earnings per share. Fully diluted earnings per share of common stock are computed using (1) the weighted average number of shares of common stock and common stock equivalents outstanding during the year, (2) shares of common stock issuable upon conversion of convertible subordinated debentures and preferred stock, and (3) the dilutive effect of outstanding stock options and stock purchase plans. The fully diluted computation also adds back to income applicable to common stock the preferred stock dividends, interest on convertible subordinated debentures, and eliminates the related profit sharing contribution and income tax expense.

Note O: Supplementary data on changing prices (unaudited)

Supplementary statement of income adjusted for changing prices for the year ended December 31, 1980 (in millions of dollars):

	As Reported in the Primary Financial Statements	Adjusted for General Inflation (Constant Dollars)	Adjusted for Changes in Specific Prices (Current Costs)
Net sales	$1,374.4	$1,374.4	$1,374.4
Cost of goods sold, excluding depreciation	771.6	828.3	784.0
Other operating expenses, excluding depreciation	357.4	357.4	357.4
Depreciation expense	44.2	60.8	63.5
Interest and other expenses, net	41.5	41.5	41.5
Total costs and expenses	1,214.7	1,288.0	1,246.4
Income before income tax expense	159.7	86.4	128.0
Income tax expense	31.3	31.3	31.3
Net income	$ 128.4	$ 55.1	$ 96.7
Gain from decline in purchasing power of net amounts owed		$ 32.9	$ 32.9

EXHIBIT 5 (continued)

Five-year comparison of selected supplementary financial data adjusted for effects of changing prices (in millions of average 1980 dollars):

counting control. This system is designed to provide reasonable assurance that assets are safeguarded and transactions are executed in accordance with management's authorization

		1980	1979	1978	1977	1976
Net sales	Historical	$ 1,374.4	$ 1,191.2	$ 1,004.2	$ 844.4	$ 681.4
	Constant 1980 dollars	$ 1,374.4	$ 1,352.0	$ 1,268.3	$ 1,148.4	$ 986.7
Net income	Historical	$ 128.4	$ 111.9	$ 91.7	$ 75.1	$ 60.4
	Constant 1980 dollars	$ 55.1	$ 57.3			
	Current costs	$ 96.7	$ 105.8			
Earnings per common share	Historical	$ 3.72	$ 3.29	$ 2.73	$ 2.27	$ 1.85
	Constant 1980 dollars	$ 1.60	$ 1.69			
	Current costs	$ 2.80	$ 3.11			
Cash dividends declared per common share	Historical	$ .640	$ .500	$ .400	$ .285	$ .218
	Constant 1980 dollars	$ .640	$ .568	$ .505	$ .388	$ .316
Net assets at year-end	Historical	$ 852.6	$ 723.5	$ 612.2	$ 519.0	$ 440.5
	Constant 1980 dollars	$ 1,041.0	$ 973.3			
	Current costs	$ 1,068.7	$ 1,007.1			
Gain from decline in purchasing power of net amounts owed		$ 32.9	$ 39.8			
Market price per common share at year-end	Historical	$ 52.875	$ 47.500	$ 41.000	$ 38.000	$ 40.500
	Constant 1980 dollars	$ 50.496	$ 51.015	$ 49.856	$ 50.388	$ 57.348
Average consumer price index		246.8	217.4	195.4	181.5	170.5

At December 31, 1980, the current cost of inventory was $469 million and the current cost of property, plant, and equipment, net of accumulated depreciation and amortization was $821.5 million. During 1980, the company's estimated increase in specific prices (current costs) of inventories, property, plant, and equipment held during the year was approximately $90.5 million or $54.4 million less than expected when measured by applying the annual rate of change in the CPI to the average current costs balances of these assets.

Management's Responsibilities for Financial Reporting

The consolidated balance sheets of Baxter Travenol Laboratories, Inc., and Subsidiaries as of December 31, 1980, and 1979, and the related consolidated statements of income, stockholders' equity, and changes in financial position for each of the three years ended December 31, 1980, have been prepared by management which is responsible for their integrity and objectivity. The statements have been prepared in conformity with generally accepted accounting principles appropriate in the circumstances, and include some amounts that are based upon management's best estimates and judgments. The financial information contained elsewhere in this annual report is consistent with that contained in the financial statements.

In meeting its responsibility for the integrity of the financial statements, management relies on the company's system of internal ac-

and recorded properly. The concept of reasonable assurance is based on the recognition that there are inherent limitations in all systems of internal accounting control, and that the cost of such systems should not exceed the benefits to be derived. A professional staff of corporate auditors reviews the accounting practices, systems control, and compliance therewith.

In connection with their annual audit, independent certified public accountants perform examinations in accordance with generally accepted auditing standards, which include a review of the system of internal accounting control and assurance that the financial statements are fairly presented.

The board of directors, through its audit committee composed solely of nonemployee directors, reviews the company's financial reporting and accounting practices. The independent certified public accountants and corporate auditors meet regularly with and have access to this committee with or without management present to discuss the results of their audit work.

Baxter Travenol Laboratories, Inc.

Auditors' Report

Board of Directors and Stockholders
Baxter Travenol Laboratories, Inc.

We have examined the consolidated balance sheets of Baxter Travenol Laboratories,

EXHIBIT 5 (continued)

BAXTER TRAVENOL LABORATORIES, INC., AND SUBSIDIARIES
Eleven-Year Summary of Selected Financial Data
(in thousands of dollars, except per-share data)

	1980	1979	1978	1977	1976	1975	1974	1973	1972	1971	1970
Operations:											
Net sales	$1,374,384	1,191,193	1,004,196	844,446	681,364	564,085	466,284	355,974	278,841	242,146	187,606
Gross profit	$ 567,984	504,335	439,134	371,567	298,731	234,478	194,682	149,936	120,174	107,614	83,741
Marketing and administrative expenses	$ 309,581	277,470	246,782	294,826	164,546	135,840	109,089	90,074	73,922	64,746	52,066
Research and development expenses	$ 57,202	46,953	40,390	37,123	33,809	26,839	21,385	17,572	13,977	12,517	10,065
Operating income	$ 201,201	179,912	151,962	129,618	100,376	71,799	64,208	42,290	32,275	30,351	21,610
Interest expense	$ 40,852	32,439	24,277	17,509	15,960	14,213	18,546	10,700	7,178	6,142	4,743
Income before income tax expense	$ 159,688	139,306	119,106	108,089	84,454	55,591	45,274	35,274	27,244	24,484	18,059
Net income	$ 128,400	111,908	91,683	75,120	60,395	44,472	36,288	27,889	22,183	19,116*	14,343
Financial position:											
Working capital	$ 535,773	444,023	371,322	343,198	311,333	223,901	213,982	196,542	181,939	186,619	118,779
Net property, plant, and equipment	$ 560,690	500,976	445,223	383,754	337,060	290,114	248,681	207,220	153,827	125,073	97,818
Total assets	$1,412,638	1,290,928	1,129,637	964,189	837,247	685,006	594,932	525,602	412,573	368,554	259,161
Long-term debt	$ 272,739	240,475	212,259	212,180	209,676	146,823	201,598	186,609	147,992	148,726	95,802
Total debt	$ 349,517	350,619	331,486	285,948	276,983	208,471	240,437	227,099	171,642	156,903	105,399
Stockholders' equity	$ 852,606	723,510	612,231	518,968	440,479	373,766	267,531	224,771	193,374	168,252	121,333
Share data:											
Primary earnings per share	$ 3.72	3.29	2.73	2.27	1.85	1.44	1.22	.95	.77	.68*	.52
Fully diluted earnings per share	$ 3.40	3.02	2.52	2.10	1.74	1.37	1.16	.92	.74	.66*	.51
Dividends per common share	$ .64	.50	.40	.285	.2175	.195	.175	.155	.135	.111	.103
Average number of common shares outstanding (in thousands)	34,522	34,008	33,552	33,072	32,644	30,872	29,682	29,171	28,789	27,952	27,472
Other data:											
Capital expenditures	$ 118,645	103,654	90,057	83,776	71,474	61,014	64,713	65,089	40,771	35,165	22,898
Depreciation and amortization	$ 51,203	40,963	31,857	26,890	24,060	20,492	16,764	12,698	9,874	7,558	5,600
Employees at year end	32,232	33,176	31,936	29,935	24,761	25,684	19,668	18,483	13,392	12,325	10,950
Sales per employee (in dollars)	$ 42,840	35,905	31,444	28,209	27,518	21,963	23,708	19,260	20,821	19,647	17,133
Statistics:											
Gross profit margin	41.3%	42.3	43.7	44.0	43.8	41.6	41.8	42.1	43.1	44.4	44.6
Operating expenses as a percent of sales	26.7%	27.2	28.6	28.7	29.1	28.8	28.0	30.2	31.5	31.9	33.1
Operating income as a percent of sales	14.6%	15.1	15.1	15.3	14.7	12.7	13.8	11.9	11.6	12.5	11.5
Net income as a percent of sales	9.3%	9.4	9.1	8.9	8.9	7.9	7.8	7.8	8.0	7.9*	7.6
Debt as a percent of capitalization	29.1%	32.6	35.1	35.5	38.6	35.8	47.3	50.3	47.0	48.3	46.5
Return on average common equity	18.3%	16.7	16.2	15.7	14.8	13.9	14.7	13.3	12.2	13.2*	12.8

* Before effect of extraordinary expense of $.03 per share.

EXHIBIT 5 *(continued)*

Inc., and Subsidiaries as of December 31, 1980, and 1979, and the related consolidated statements of income, stockholders' equity, and changes in financial position for each of the three years ended December 31, 1980. Our examinations were made in accordance with generally accepted auditing standards, and accordingly included such tests of the accounting records and such other auditing procedures as we considered necessary in the circumstances.

In our opinion, the financial statements referred to above present fairly the consolidated financial position of Baxter Travenol Laboratories, Inc., and Subsidiaries at December 31, 1980, and 1979, and the consolidated results of their operations and changes in their financial position for each of the three years ended December 31, 1980, in conformity with generally accepted accounting principles applied on a consistent basis.

Alexander Grant & Company

Chicago, Illinois
February 11, 1981

Market for the Company's Common Stock and Related Security Holder Matters

Baxter Travenol Laboratories, Inc., common stock is listed on the New York, Midwest, and Pacific Coast Stock Exchanges, on The Stock Exchange in London, and on the Swiss stock exchanges of Zurich, Basle, and Geneva. The principal market on which the company's common stock is traded is the New York Stock Exchange. The high and low sales prices on such exchange and dividends per share in each quarter of 1980 and 1979 were as follows:

| | 1980 | | 1979 | | Dividends per share | |
	High	Low	High	Low	1980	1979
First quarter .	$47¾	$35¾	$43⅞	$35⅜	$.16	$.125
Second quarter .	47	38⅞	43⅛	37⅛	.16	.125
Third quarter .	55⅜	44⅛	48¼	41½	.16	.125
Fourth quarter .	58⅜	45½	49½	42¼	.16	.125
					$.64	$ .50

At February 17, 1981, there were approximately 27,100 holders of record. Certain of the company's debt agreements contain limitations on the payment of dividends. However, under the most restrictive convenants of these agreements, at December 31, 1980, all retained earnings of the company were available for payment of dividends.

EXHIBIT 5 (*concluded*)

Quarterly Financial Results
(in thousands of dollars, except per share data)

| | Net Sales | | Gross Profit | | Net Income | | Earnings per Share | | | |
| | | | | | | | Primary | | Fully Diluted | |
	1980	1979	1980	1979	1980	1979	1980	1979	1980	1979
First quarter	$ 313,053	$ 274,898	$135,522	$117,685	$ 30,444	$ 25,700	$ .89	$ .76	$ .82	$ .70
Second quarter	337,729	296,471	138,491	124,038	33,145	29,224	.96	.86	.87	.79
Third quarter	345,317	292,363	142,791	126,646	31,785	32,200	.92	.95	.84	.86
Fourth quarter	378,285	327,461	151,180	135,966	33,046	24,784	.96	.72	.87	.67
Total year	$1,374,384	$1,191,193	587,984	$504,335	$128,400	$111,908	$3.72	$3.29	$3.40	$3.02

transition had been widely anticipated. Mr. Graham maintained his position as chairman of the board.

As Baxter's new chief executive officer, Mr. Loucks stated that he did not anticipate a major reshuffling or reorganization of Baxter. He was quoted as saying, "You look for reasons to change, but if things go as well as they are, there really aren't any reasons. We've had 25 years of growth in excess of 20 percent. The company has the very firm stamp of Mr. Graham on it. That's a tough act to follow." He added, however, that he did expect "to manage in a different style." To some Baxter observers, this was interpreted as signaling a change from the "take the hill" style of Bill Graham to a "let's take the hill" approach. Exhibit 5 provides excerpts from Baxter's 1980 annual report, covering the first half year of Vernon Loucks's tenure as chief executive officer.

Questions

1. Complete Jim Donaldson's review of Baxter. What was Baxter's strategy in 1972? Has it achieved that strategy?

2. While Baxter has shown very high growth and consistent earnings growth, its stock price has not performed very well. How can you explain this anomaly? You should consider (a) the relationship between Baxter's earnings-per-share growth and the quality of its earnings and (b) the relationship between Baxter's book-value-per-share growth and its sustainable growth rate.

3. What is Baxter's strategy for the 1980s as characterized by Bill Graham? By Vernon Loucks? How would you rate Baxter's growth prospects for the future?

PART FIVE

Measurement and Analysis of Income

CHAPTER 11

Recognition and Analysis of Income

The determination of net income involves relating revenues, expenses, gains, and losses to appropriate accounting periods to capture the financial effects of actual and anticipated transactions, events, and circumstances whose financial effects are recognizable, measurable, and relevant to measuring business income or loss. This is a difficult managerial task. It requires allocating the activities of a continuing business into arbitrary time periods which rarely coincide with the periods during which the various activities of the total business are started and completed. Determining if management's measurement of periodic income is a fair, reasonable, reliable reflection of a business's economic realities and prospects is a principal analytical task of statement readers, since periodic income figures are central to the purposes of most analytical reviews.

This chapter focuses on the timing of income or revenue recognition and one of the key elements of the net income measurement process, namely, the simultaneous matching of specific revenues, when they are recognized, with expenses that relate directly or jointly to the same transaction or events. Other elements of the net income measurement process are covered in later chapters.

Statement users wishing to understand the income recognition practices of specific industries should refer to the numerous AICPA *Statements of Positions* and *Industry Accounting Guides* that discuss the specialized accounting principles and practices of various industries. Many of these publications have been reissued with modifications by the FASB as official statements. This procedure is important to CPAs. It elevates the AICPA publications from being mere reference documents to an authoritative source for determining what accounting practices constitute generally accepted accounting principles under rule 203 of the AICPA Rules of Conduct. This rule specifies what pronouncements a CPA may regard as authoritative when expressing an opinion as to whether or not financial statements are in accordance with generally accepted accounting principles.

Recognition

Two conditions must be met before revenue and gains can be recognized. These two prerequisites are labeled *(a)* realized or realizable and *(b)* earned, with sometimes one and sometimes the other being the more important. *Concepts Statement No. 5* states:

> Revenues and gains generally are not recognized until realized or realizable.[1] Revenues and gains are realized when products (goods or services), merchandise, or other assets are exchanged for cash or claims for cash. Revenues and gains are realizable when related assets received or held are readily converted to known amounts of cash or claims to cash.
>
> Revenues are not recognized until earned. . . . Revenues are considered to have been earned when the entity has substantially accomplished what it must do to be entitled to the benefits represented by the revenues.

No one accounting rule or practice covers all revenue recognition situations. Nevertheless, an analysis of revenue recognition practices seems to indicate that revenue is typically recognized when the event that reduces the risk of ultimately receiving a determinable amount of revenue is reduced to a minimum level considered prudent by those issuing and using financial statements. This point in the earnings process is referred to as the critical event. Depending on the circumstances, the critical event can be anywhere in the chain of business events from production through the receipt of cash from the sale of goods or services, and, in some cases, to the fulfilling of warranty obligations. Determining this critical event in novel situations can require expert management judgment which must be exercised in the light of a thorough, objective analysis of the particular circumstances and the generally accepted accounting principles applicable to analogous situations.

There can be disagreement as to the nature of the critical event and what is prudent. As a result, recognition rules, even for very compatible exchanges within industries, can vary. For example, some computer companies recognize in current income all shipments made prior to midnight on the last day of the accounting period that are billable to customers within the next 30 days. Other computer companies use the midnight cutoff, but include in the current period all shipments that will be installed in the next 14 days. Still others use the midnight cutoff criterion coupled with a requirement that all of the paperwork related to the shipment be materially completed.

While the generation of net income in most situations seems to turn on the timing of revenue recognition, the final measurement of net income

---

[1] *Concepts Statement No. 5* uses these terms in a more restrictive sense than the accounting realization convention discussed in earlier chapters notes. In those chapters, which reflect the collective thinking of the FASB and many other accounting authorities, the term *realization* is used as a synonym for *recognition*. This is the more common use of that term among businessmen, financial analysts, and practicing accountants.

must also include a consideration of the past, current, and estimated future costs related to the revenue recognized. In practice, management appears to tolerate slightly more uncertainty in the recognition of costs than it does in the case of revenues. However, if the total amount of revenue from a transaction is certain and the eventual costs of obtaining the revenue are fairly uncertain, the revenue should be deferred and held back from the income statement until the costs are more certain. To do otherwise might be misleading and imprudent. Again, this is a management decision, involving responsible and careful consideration of the particular facts.

Revenue Recognition Methods

The recognition of income varies from the time of production, in the case of certain mining operations, to the actual receipt of cash, in some installment sale situations. These variations fall into seven revenue recognition categories:

1. Recognition at the time services are rendered or goods are shipped (i.e., sales method).
2. Recognition at the time the sale price is collected (i.e., installment sales method).
3. Recognition at the time the product is completed, but before delivery (i.e., production method).
4. Recognition proportionally over the performance of a long-term contract (i.e., percentage-of-completion method).
5. Recognition at the completion of a long-term contract (i.e., completed contract method).
6. Recognition after the buyer's cumulative cash payments exceed the seller's total costs (i.e., cost recovery method).
7. Recognition at time of delivery if the sale is made and cash is received prior to delivery or production (delivery method).

Sales. The time of sale is the most common revenue recognition method. Typically, the act of invoicing, accompanied by delivery or consignment to a common carrier, is considered to constitute a sale for accounting purposes, rather than the legal criterion of title passing. In recognition of the fact that the cash eventually received from sales will fall short of the invoiced sales, a number of estimated deductions are made directly from the sales. These include: allowance for returns, warranty or service guarantees, and cash discounts. Allowances for bad debts are usually reported as an expense rather than a revenue deduction. Also, cash discounts for prompt payment are sometimes deducted from a customer's account at the time of sale, and then any discounts not taken are reported as a separate revenue item.

Installment Sales. An installment sale involves a down payment and a specified series of payments over time. Depending on the circumstances, the gross profit from such sales can be recognized in one of two ways: at the time of sale, or proportionally as the cash payments are received. This latter approach is known as the installment method. Many retailers use the installment method for calculating tax payments while recognizing the income at the time of sale for accounting purposes. This practice is consistent with *Opinion No. 10,* which says that installment sales should ordinarily be accounted for by the sale method, with appropriate provision for uncollectible accounts. The *Opinion* is very emphatic that "unless the circumstances are such that the collection of the sale price is not reasonably assured," the installment method of recognizing income is not acceptable for financial reporting purposes.

Cost Recovery. The cost recovery method is seldom used. This method does not recognize any gross profit from the sale until the cumulative total of the payments received equals the cost of the item sold. *FASB Statement No. 5,* "Accounting for contingencies," indicates that it is used only where receivables are collectible over an extended period of time and, because of the terms of the transaction or other conditions, there is no reasonable basis for estimating the degree of collectibility. In situations where the cost recovery method is used, some managements may shift to the installment method to recognize the unrecorded income when the debtor has made sufficient payments to assure management that the future payments are collectible. In this situation, other managements may decide to recognize all of the deferred income, even though not all of the cost is recovered.

Production. In some industries, the sale or the collection of cash is not the critical event in the recognition of income. For example, in the case of a number of extractive industries, there is a market that stands ready to take their product at a going firm price. The company has merely to make the decision as to when and where it will convert its inventory of products into a sale. For such companies, production is the critical event in the recognition of income.

Long-Term Contracts. There are two methods for recognizing income from contracts covering a long period of time: the *completed contract method* and the *percentage-of-completion* method. Both of these methods are acceptable for federal income tax purposes, and it is possible to use one method for calculating income tax payments and the other for measuring accounting profit.

APB Opinion No. 45, "Long-Term Construction-Type Contracts," sets forth the first authoritative guidelines for long-term contract accounting. Many believed this *Opinion* presented the two methods of long-term contract accounting as free choice alternatives. Later the AICPA in SOP

81-1, "Accounting for Performance and Certain Production-Type Contracts," took a position that in effect eliminated this choice. SOP 81-1 also stated that percentage-of-completion was the preferable method and that persuasive evidence to the contrary was necessary to overcome this presumption. The FASB supported this position in *Statement No. 56*.

According to the AICPA, the percentage-of-completion method is the preferable accounting policy for long-term contracts in circumstances in which reasonably dependable estimates can be made and in which all the following conditions exist:

1. Contracts executed by the parties include provisions that clearly specify the enforceable rights regarding goods and services to be provided and received by the parties, the consideration to be exchanged, and the manner and terms of settlement.
2. The buyer can be expected to satisfy his or her obligation under the contract.
3. The contractor can be expected to perform his or her contractual obligation.

The percentage-of-completion method recognizes income as the work on the contract progresses. The income recognized is the percentage of estimated total income.

1. That incurred costs to date bear to estimated total costs after giving effect on costs to complete based upon most recent information; or
2. That may be indicated by such other measures of progress toward completion as may be appropriate having due regard to work performed.

Under this method, current assets may include costs and recognized income not yet billed, with respect to certain contracts; and liabilities, in most cases current liabilities, may include billings in excess of costs and recognized income with respect to other contracts.

When the current estimate of total contract costs indicates a loss, in most circumstances provision should be made for this loss on the entire contract. If there is a close relationship between profitable and unprofitable contracts, such as in the case of contracts which are parts of the same project, the group may be treated as a unit in determining the necessity for a provision for loss.

There are two principal advantages to the percentage-of-completion method. First, periodic income is recognized currently rather than irregularly as contracts are completed. Second, the status of the uncompleted contracts is provided through the current estimates of costs to complete or of progress toward completion.

The principal disadvantage of the percentage-of-completion method is that in order to accrue current income, it is necessary to make estimates of ultimate costs. Typically, these are subject to the uncertainties frequently inherent in long-term contracts.

The completed contract method recognizes income only when the contact is completed or substantially so. Accordingly, costs of contracts in process and current billings are accumulated, but there are no interim charges or credits to income other than provisions for losses. A contract may be regarded as substantially completed if remaining costs are not significant in amount.

When the completed contract method is used, it may be appropriate to allocate general and administrative expenses to contract costs rather than to periodic income. This may result in a better matching of costs and revenues than would result from treating such expenses as period costs, particularly in years when no contracts were completed. It is not so important, however, when the contractor is engaged in numerous projects, and in such circumstances it may be preferable to charge those expenses as incurred to periodic income. In any case, there should be no excessive deferring of overhead costs, such as might occur if total overhead was assigned to abnormally few or abnormally small contracts in process.

Although the completed contract method does not permit the recording of any income prior to completion, provision should be made for expected losses in accordance with the well-established practice of making provision for foreseeable losses. If there is a close relationship between profitable and unprofitable contracts, such as in the case of contracts which are parts of the same project, the group may be treated as a unit in determining the necessity for a provision for losses.

When the completed contract method is used, an excess of accumulated costs over related billings should be shown in the balance sheet as a current asset, and an excess of accumulated billings over related costs should be shown among the liabilities, in most cases as a current liability. If costs exceed billings in some contracts, and billings exceed costs on others, the contracts should ordinarily be segregated so that the figures on the asset side include only those contracts on which costs exceed billings, and those on the liability side include only those on which billings exceed costs. It is suggested that the asset item be described as "costs of uncompleted contracts in excess of related billings" rather than as "inventory" or "work in process," and that the item on the liability side be described as "billings on uncompleted contracts in excess of related costs."

The principal advantage of the completed contract method is that it is based on final results rather than on estimates for unperformed work which may involve unforeseen costs and possible losses.

The principal disadvantage of this method is that it does not reflect current performance when the period of any contract extends beyond more than one accounting period. Under these circumstances, it may result in an irregular pattern of income recognition.

Interim billings should not be used as a basis for recognizing income, since considerations other than those acceptable as a basis for the recognition of income frequently enter into the determination of the timing and the amounts of interim billings.

Services

Income from services is recognized during the period in which the service is rendered. For example, in the case of services such as providing the use of money or facilities to others, the interest or rent income is accrued and included in income as the services are provided over time.

Because services cannot be stored, they must be marketed before they are provided. If these activities involve substantial outlays, some portion of the revenue from the sale of services may be attributed to marketing costs. For instance, leasing companies spend a considerable sum on selling and negotiating leasing contracts before any receipts are received from lease agreements. For a number of years, in order to cover these costs, many leasing companies at the time of the lease agreement was signed recognized for income determination purposes some portion of the lease rental receipts before they were received. Currently, the preferred practice is to spread these costs over the life of the lease.

Nonmonetary Transactions

Typically, business sale transactions involve the exchange of cash or other monetary assets or liabilities for nonmonetary assets or services.[2] The monetary element of such exchanges generally provides an objective basis for measuring the cost of the goods and services received by an enterprise as well as the gain or loss on the business.

However, some business transactions do not involve monetary items, such as when a company exchanges inventory for equipment. Since there is no monetary element in the transaction, the determination of the value to assign to the nonmonetary asset transferred, or the amount of gain or loss on the transaction, is not clear. *Opinion No. 29* sets forth the accounting for such reciprocal nonmonetary assets by a company for which no assets are received in exchange, such as in the case of a payment of dividends in kind rather than cash. Transactions of this kind are called nonmonetary transactions.

In general, the accounting for nonmonetary transactions should be based on the fair values of the assets or services involved which is the same basis as that used in transactions that involve monetary elements. The fair value of a nonmonetary asset transferred to or from a business in a nonmonetary transaction can be determined in a number of ways. These include (1) refer-

---

[2] Monetary assets and liabilities are assets and liabilities whose amounts are fixed in terms of units of currency by contract or otherwise, such as cash and notes payable.

ence to the estimated realizable values in cash transactions involving the same or similar assets; (2) quoted market prices for the same or similar assets; (3) independent appraisals; and (4) management estimates, if adequate evidence to support the estimate is available. If one of the parties to the nonmonetary transaction could have elected to receive cash rather than a nonmonetary asset, then the amount of cash that might have been received could be considered as evidence of the fair value of the nonmonetary asset.

There are certain modifications to the general principle laid out in *Opinion No. 29*. For example, if the fair value of the nonmonetary assets transferred cannot be determined within reasonable limits, then the transaction should be recorded at the book value of the assets transferred. Another exception occurs when the exchange is not essentially the culmination of an earnings process. In this case, the accounting for its transaction should be based on the book value (after reduction, if appropriate, for an impairment of value) of the nonmonetary asset relinquished.

The APB defined two types of nonmonetary exchange transactions that do not culminate an earnings process:

1. An exchange of a product or property held for sale in the ordinary course of business for a product or property to be sold in the same line of business to facilitate sales to customers other than the parties to the exchange.
2. An exchange of a productive asset not held for sale in the ordinary course of business for a similar productive asset or an equivalent interest in the same or similar productive asset.[3]

An exchange of nonmonetary assets that qualified for being recorded at the asset's book value may sometimes include a monetary consideration. *Opinion No. 29* described the appropriate accounting for such transactions:

> The recipient of the monetary consideration has realized gain on the exchange to the extent that the amount of the monetary receipt exceeds a proportionate share of the recorded amount of the asset surrendered. The portion of the cost applicable to the realized amount should be based on the ratio of the monetary consideration to the total consideration received (monetary consideration plus the estimated fair value of the nonmonetary asset received); or, if more clearly evident, the fair value of the nonmonetary asset transferred. The board further believes that the entity paying the monetary consideration should not recognize any gain on a transaction that is not the culmination of an earnings process but should record the asset received as the amount of the monetary consideration paid plus the recorded amount of the nonmonetary asset surrendered. If a loss is indicated by the terms of a transaction described in this paragraph

---

[3] The *Opinion* defines a productive asset as an asset held for or used in the production of goods or services by the enterprise. Productive assets include an investment in another entity if the investment is accounted for by the equity method but exclude an investment not accounted for by that method. Similar productive assets are productive assets that are of the same general type, perform the same function, or are employed in the same line of business.

or is not the culmination of an earnings process, the entire indicated loss on the exchange should be recognized.

Sometimes corporations distribute nonmonetary assets to owners in a spin-off or some other form of reorganization or liquidation. The accounting for nonreciprocal transfers of this kind should be based on the recorded amount of the asset distributed. Other nonreciprocal transfers of nonmonetary assets to owners should be accounted for at fair value if the distributing entity could have realized this value in an outright sale at or near the time of distribution. If this circumstance cannot be met, book values must be used to value the transaction.

Right to Return

Products sold with a buyer's right-to-return privilege should only be recorded as sales with appropriate accruals for expected returns or losses when all of these conditions set forth in *FASB Statement No. 48*, "Revenue Recognition When Right of Return Exists," are met:

1. The seller's price to the buyer is substantially fixed as determinable at the date of sale.
2. The buyer has paid the seller, or the buyer is obligated to pay the seller and the obligation is not contingent on resale of the product.
3. The buyer's obligation to the seller would not be changed in the event of theft or physical destruction or damage of the product.
4. The buyer acquiring the product for resale has economic substance apart from that provided by the seller.
5. The seller does not have significant obligations for future performance to directly bring about resale of the product by the buyer.
6. The amount of future returns can be reasonably estimated.

Sales revenue and cost of sales that are not recognized because these conditions are not met can be recognized when either the return privilege expires or the conditions are met.

Product Financing Agreements

Sometimes companies attempt to generate sales revenue through transactions that in essence agree to repurchase the buyer's unsold inventory at a price equal to the original sale price plus carrying and financing costs. The FASB in *Statement No. 49*, "Accounting for Product Financing Arrangements," required that such transactions be accounted for as borrowing rather than sales.

Inappropriate Interest Rates

Sometimes the seller of property, goods, or services may receive in exchange a note with a face value that does not reasonably represent the present value of the consideration given or received in the exchange. This situation may arise if the note is noninterest bearing or has a stated interest rate which is different from the rate of interest appropriate for the debt at the date of the transaction. Unless in these circumstances the note is recorded at its present value rather than the stated amount, the sales price and profit to the seller and cost to the buyer are misstated, and interest income and interest expense in subsequent periods are also misstated.[4]

Opinion No. 21, "Interest on Receivables and Payables," sets forth the appropriate accounting in these cases. It requires that the receivable or payable be recorded on the balance sheet at its face value with an adjustment to arrive at its discounted value. Then, the interest income or expense is the market rate, which is the interest actually received or paid plus a portion of the adjustment amount shown on the balance sheet.

Accounting for Bad Debts

Revenues are ordinarily accounted for at the time a transaction is completed, with appropriate provision for uncollectible amounts. This section presents alternative procedures used by businesses in recognizing and reporting losses from uncollectible receivables.

Every enterprise extending credit to customers sustains some losses from bad debts. An account receivable becomes a bad debt when all reasonable expectation of collection is exhausted. The amounts of bad debt loss to the business firm will depend upon such factors as the type of customer served, policies regarding investigative procedures prior to granting credit, and policies employed in the collection of receivables. In spite of efforts to minimize these losses, it is impossible to predict customer payments with certainty, and some accounts will remain uncollectible. Bad debt losses can be avoided only if a firm receives payment in cash at the time of sale.

There are two basic reasons for recognizing bad debt losses in the financial records. First, the determination of net income based upon the proper matching of revenue and expense must include these unavoidable losses. Second, the valuation of receivables in the balance sheet requires consideration of these losses to present a realistic estimate of the anticipated funds that will flow from the collection of receivables.

Accounting for bad debt losses can be accomplished by either of two methods: (1) the direct write-off method or (2) the bad debt estimation method. For federal income tax purposes, the deduction for bad debt expense can be determined by either of these two methods. In fact, one method can be used for financial reporting purposes while the other method is used for income tax purposes. However, for practical reasons, the method adopted by a business for tax or book purposes is usually used for both purposes.

---

[4] The present value amount is the future cash payments required by the note discounted at the appropriate market interest rate.

Direct Write-Off Method

The direct write-off method of accounting for bad debt expense ignores the possibility of any bad debt loss until individual accounts receivable prove to be uncollectible. No advance provision is made for doubtful accounts. Under this method, the bad debt expense represents the amount of receivables which have actually become uncollectible during the operating period.

When an account receivable is considered uncollectible, the following entry is made:

```
Dr.  Bad Debt Expense .................................................  xxx
     Cr.   Accounts Receivable (customer A) ...........................        xxx
```

This entry has the effect of charging an asset account (Accounts Receivable) directly to an expense account (Bad Debt Expense) and gives this method its descriptive name.

If subsequent events prove that an account previously written off can be collected, the entry required to reinstate the receivable is:

```
Dr.  Accounts Receivable (customer A) ................................  xxx
     Cr.   Bad Debts Recovered (or Bad Debt Expense) ..................        xxx
```

At the close of the accounting period, bad debts recovered must be recognized as revenue while bad debts expense is deducted in the determination of net income. Alternatively, recoveries and expenses might be netted.

The direct write-off method has two severe limitations. First, the bad debt expense may be deducted from the revenue of an accounting period subsequent to the original sale. Hence, it fails to properly match income and expense of a particular operating period. Second, current assets in the balance sheet may be overstated, since no recognition is given to the probable uncollectibility of some part of the receivables. For these reasons, the direct write-off method is not widely used by businesses of significant size. However, its simplicity makes it a popular method among very small businesses.

Also, in those cases where a reasonable estimate of the anticipated bad debts cannot be made, *FASB Statement No. 5* requires that the direct write-off method be used.

Bad Debt Estimation Method

Matching of revenue and expense and a realistic valuation of accounts receivables is achieved by including an estimate of bad debt expense in the financial statements.[5] The estimated amount of bad debt losses which will eventually result from sales of an accounting period is treated as an expense of the period. That part of the estimated loss which cannot be identified with

---

[5] This method is sometimes called the "reserve" method. However, preferred modern terminology disapproves of the reserve label previously given to the accumulated estimate of uncollectibility.

particular receivables is deducted from total receivables on the balance sheet to show the expected amount to be collected eventually.

The special feature of the bad debt estimation method is the creation of the asset valuation account deducted from receivables. This contra-asset account, called Allowance for Doubtful (or Uncollectible) Accounts, is increased as estimated bad debt expense is recorded and decreased by recognition of actual bad debt losses.

There are several different approaches to the estimation of bad debt expense. Bad debt losses for a business enterprise can usually be estimated with a high degree of accuracy based upon its own experience of actual bad debt losses over a period of time or upon the experience of similar businesses. For estimating purposes, this experience can be related on a percentage basis to (1) sales for a period of operations or (2) the amount of receivables at the close of the operating period. Either of these approaches will, over a period of time, theoretically result in proper charges to income and proper valuation of receivables.

Percentage of Sales.   The estimate for bad debt losses may be expressed as a percentage of sales. For example, historical experience might indicate that actual bad debt losses averaged 2 percent of sales. This rate for estimating bad debt losses might be applied in successive operating periods until actual experience suggests that the rate be adjusted upward or downward to achieve greater accuracy. Frequently, the rate is determined on the basis of a sales figure adjusted by eliminating cash sales and sales returns, in recognition that bad debts result only from net credit sales to customers.

Percentage of Receivables.   The estimate for bad debt losses may be expressed as a percentage of receivables at the close of an accounting period. For example, prior experience might indicate that on the average, 5 percent of the balance of receivables subsequently proves uncollectible. In each operating period, sufficient bad debt expense might be charged to maintain the Allowance for Doubtful Accounts at 5 percent of receivables until actual experience requires revision of this rate.

To obtain greater accuracy in estimating uncollectibility, an analysis grouping accounts receivable by "age" from date of sale may be prepared. Since older accounts are more likely to be uncollectible, separate consideration of each group of accounts might suggest that the provision for uncollectibility should be equal, for example, to 1 percent of receivables 0 to 30 days old, 3 percent of receivables 31 to 60 days old, and 5 percent of receivables over 60 days old.

Accounting Entities for Bad Debt Estimation Method

The following accounting entries are typically required to handle estimated and actual bad debt losses under the estimation method.

1. To record estimated bad debt expense:

    Dr. Bad Debt Expense xxx
    Cr. Allowance for Doubtful Accounts xxx

    This entry is usually made only at the close of the accounting period immediately before financial statements are prepared. The amount of the entry will be either (1) the amount of bad debt expense computed as a percentage of sales or (2) the amount necessary to bring the Allowance for Doubtful Accounts to a computed percentage of receivables.

2. To write off an account determined to be uncollectible:

    Dr. Allowance for Doubtful Accounts xxx
    Cr. Accounts Receivable (customer A) xxx

    In this entry, specific uncollectible receivables are identified with the bad debt expense previously recognized on an estimated basis.

3. To recognize collectibility of a receivable previously written off:

    Dr. Accounts Receivable (customer A) xxx
    Cr. Allowance for Doubtful Accounts xxx

    This entry will reflect the amount expected to be collected from the customer. Reinstatement of the receivable previously written off is accomplished so that a complete history of dealings with customers is maintained in the accounts receivable records. The actual collections on the reinstated account will then be recorded as though the account had never been written off.

Financial Statement Presentation

Bad debt expense recorded on the basis of an estimate is reported as an expense on the income statement. Usually this expense is classified as selling expense or as administrative expense, depending upon where the firm assigns responsibility for the granting of credit.

The allowance for doubtful accounts is subtracted from the total of the related receivables in the current asset section of the balance sheet. This net amount presents the expected cash proceeds from subsequent collection of the receivables.

FASB Statement No. 5 requires that the bad debt estimation method be used when the amount of the anticipated bad debts can be reasonably estimated.

Warranties and Service Guarantees

Some merchandise is sold with a warranty against defects or a service guarantee, which when fulfilled usually involves the expenditure of labor and materials rather than cash. These items are similar to bad debts in that the future expense and accompanying liability are unknown at the time of sale. Therefore, initially, they must be estimated. If the amount of the future warranty cost can be reasonably estimated, *FASB Statement No. 5* requires that future warranty costs be recorded at the time a sale is made. If a reasonable estimate cannot be made, the warranty costs must be recognized as they are actually incurred in future accounting periods.

The accounting for warranty or service guarantees is analogous to bad debt accounting. The estimated expense is recognized at the time of the sale and an offsetting liability is established. This liability is then reduced when the cost of the guarantee or warranty is paid. Sometimes the estimated costs are shown as a revenue offset instead of an expense.

Realization Controversy

Accounting practice has relied heavily on the realization principle as a guide to recognizing income. With the exceptions discussed earlier, this principle states that income generally arises at the point of sale. A number of accounting authors do not accept this concept and its related practices as an essential feature of accounting. They claim it lacks analytical precision. Also, it is in more or less continual conflict with the going concern convention, which places emphasis on the continuity and whole process of business activity. In contrast, the realization principle places undue emphasis on the act of selling, which is only one point in a company's total economic activity.

The critics of the realization concept believe the proper function of accounting is measurement of the resources of specific entities and of changes in these resources. These changes are attributable to the whole process of business activity. Accordingly, the principles of accounting should be directed toward fulfilling this function. In the critics' opinion, changes in resources (income) should be classified among the amounts attributable to:

1. Price level changes which lead to restatement of capital, but not to revenues and expenses.
2. Changes in the current value of assets beyond the effect of price level changes.
3. The recognition through sales and other operating-related transfers of net realizable value which leads to revenue or gain.
4. Other causes, such as the accretion or discovery of previously unknown natural resources.

This approach requires the use of price level accounting and current values of assets rather than the presently more accepted historical cost principle.

The supporters of the realization principle argue that it is difficult to determine the fairness and reasonableness of appraisals which seek to restate plant and equipment in terms of current values. They cite as evidence the disillusionment of investors from the experiences of the 1920s, when companies wrote up asset values only to have to write them down again during the 1930s. Those who argue for the realization concept do so principally on its demonstrated practical utility. In addition, they believe it is not prudent to recognize gains before they are realized.

Analytical Considerations

Evaluation of operating cash flows and periodic net income is a critical part of most financial analyses. To complete this analytical task competently requires a thorough understanding of how a company generates and recognizes revenues, since operating revenues are the principal source of positive gross cash flow for most companies, and the accounting revenue recognition rules adopted by management determine in large part the timing and measurement of net income.

The most important fact to remember always when analyzing revenues and their related profits is that revenues, other than cash sales, are recorded typically using the accrual accounting bookkeeping entry:

```
Dr.  Accounts Receivable .........................................  xxx
     Cr.  Sales ...................................................      xxx
```

If the analyst keeps this bookkeeping entry in mind, the analyst will never fall into the trap of thinking the flow of revenues and their related profits recorded by accountants are cash flows. As the above entry indicates, the offsetting entry to record a sale is to accounts receivable, which is one step away from cash. Until the cash is received, the company has to continue financing the cost of the item sold. If the receivable is due well into the future, this could be expensive. Also, if the customer's credit is weak, the anticipated cash payment may never be received.

Analysts should never assume that a company is healthy because its accounting revenues and profits appear to be robust. This could be an illusion. The sales could be accounting fictions that do not have future beneficial cash flow consequences.

Usually, an accounts receivable aging and total cash flow analysis will uncover these situations. In carrying out these analyses it is important to track down off-balance-sheet financing and recording of receivables and revenues. If the analyst does not consider these items, his or her total cash flow analysis will be limited to consolidated financial statement cash flow, revenues, and income data, and these data may not capture the whole story. For example, the consolidated data will not capture fully off-balance-sheet transactions, such as sales of receivables to wholly owned finance subsidiaries or guaranteeing customer borrowings to pay off payables due the guarantor, that may be used to boost consolidated cash flow and income.

Understanding how a business actually generates sales and ultimately collects cash is fundamental to revenue and income analysis. It is the actual business transactions, not their accounting representations, that generate the cash flows that determine this economic value of individual assets and of the business as a whole. Financial analysis is a tool that helps statement users penetrate the accounting data to develop insights into these actual flows and to determine the appropriateness of the company's revenue and income recognition rules, given the company's underlying cash flow generating process.

An analyst concerned with revenues is usually trying to understand the market share, seasonal, and cyclical pattern of a company's cash flow from sales as well as possible future trends in this pattern. While statement analysis can be used to track past flows and make statement projections of possible future flows, the analyst must go beyond financial statement data to develop an appreciation of the underlying business factors that determine actual cash flows. This requires an understanding of the nature of a company's products as well as who buys them, why they are bought, where they are bought, how they are bought, and when they are bought. This knowledge can be used to determine the company's critical marketing, distribution, and product development success factors, which in turn are useful for focusing analytical attention on how well the company is executing those actions that are key to the generation of revenues and operating cash flows. This company-specific knowledge will also help the analyst to appreciate the impact on cash flows and revenues of seasonality, economic cycles, exchange rate shifts, inflation, new regulations, changing customer purchasing patterns, and competitive behavior. This understanding should be used to explain the results of the financial analysis of past financial statement data and to project cash flows and revenues based on an environmental, business, and financial analysis appreciation of the determinants of the company's revenues and cash flows.

An understanding of a business's earnings process is necessary to appraise the appropriateness of management's selection of revenue recognition rules. To make a proper earnings quality appraisal, the analyst must be familiar with the details of the company's recognition rules, the nature of the possible alternative rules rejected, and the range of income recognition methods in the company's industry. The two key questions are: Is management's designation of the "critical act" appropriate, and are the recognition methods consistent with this designation?

Analysts should form their own judgments as to what constitutes this critical act. Sometimes they will find conservative managers designating the critical act as one occurring much later in the earnings process than those designated by other managers in their industry or even the analyst's selection. Typically these conservative companies are not a problem. The companies to worry about are those that seem to be prematurely recognizing income relative to the generally acknowledged leading companies in the industry and the analysts's designated critical act. Because the timing of revenue recognition is so influential in the measurement of net income, such liberal recognition practices carry a heavy negative weighting in assessing earnings quality. They are also a red flag suggesting that other aggressive accounting practices may be followed. In addition, early recognition of income can precipitate later adverse earnings reports because subsequent unanticipated events may lead to related accounts receivable being written off as the costs to complete the earnings process rise unexpectedly or the receivables prove to be uncollectible.

When income is recognized before the earnings process is completed, provision must be made for some future costs or revenue adjustments, to reflect the nature of the earnings process yet to be completed. These costs, such as warranty expense, and revenue adjustments, such as provisions for returns and allowances, are based on management estimates. Analysts should check these estimates carefully, as managers tend to overstate these items in highly profitable years and understate them in times of difficulty. Adjustments to gross sales as a percentage of net or gross sales should always be calculated. Similarly, the revenue-related expenses based on management estimates should be tracked as a percentage of net sales. In both cases, the question should be asked: Does this percentage figure make sense given the circumstances?

Statement readers should be aware of the various actions management can take in the short run to pump revenues up to hide a deteriorating situation. These include accelerating work on contracts accounted for by the percentage-of-completion method; advancing the shipping date of goods not originally due to be received by the customer until a later period in return for not requiring payment until after the original payment date; overloading the channels of distribution; guaranteeing customer financing so that customers can place an order they normally might defer because of funding problems; and swapping sales with firms in similar difficulties. In reality, shipments generated in these ways are little more than shipping inventories to someone else's warehouse and calling it a sale.

Normally, these actions are hard to detect. The best indicator of these dubious sales-boosting maneuvers is unusual changes in the inventory and accounts receivable levels relative to sales. For example, if receivables rise faster than sales in one quarter and there is no discernible reason for this relationship, sales may have been pulled into that quarter from future periods or goods sold to questionably creditworthy customers. Similarly, if the prior quarter's reports indicate excessive inventories and these excess inventories apparently disappear in the current quarter, sales-boosting tactics that have little lasting value may have been engaged in to move the excessive inventories and to cover up indications of poor production controls and planning.

Analysts focusing on revenues should always look at the liability side of the balance sheet. It is where deferred revenues and income are presented. This is an important source of revenue information because under some circumstances the recognition of income may be deferred to the future, even though the company has already received cash or a note from the transaction. This occurs, for example, when a magazine sells subscriptions or an asset is sold on an installment basis to buyers who may have difficulty making the payments. These deferred revenue and income items can be an important source of future revenues and income and should be traced over time to see how management uses them for balance sheet, funds flow, and earnings management purposes.

Southern Land Company
Cash Flow and Income Recognition

In late 1982, the three members of the audit committee of the Southern
Land Company were considering whether or not they should approve the
proposal presented by management for the recognition of a substantial gain
that would arise from the sale of the company's thematic recreation park
in Miami. The management wished to recognize all of the profit at the
time of the sale as ordinary income. However, at least one member of
the audit committee believed that income should be recognized in some
appropriate way over the buyer's payment period. Another member of
the committee thought that possibly the gain should be shown as an extraordinary item.

The company's CPA firm backed management's position.

Southern Company

Southern Company owned large real estate holdings in the Southwest, California, and Hawaii. The company also operated two thematic recreation
parks in Louisville and Miami. The Louisville park, which was operated
under a management contract, had been sold by Southern in the previous
year to a group of private investors. The sale of the Miami park was to be
a similar deal.

Southern Company was controlled by the Cleveland Corporation, a
widely diversified conglomerate. Cleveland owned 90 percent of the Southern equity. The other 10 percent was publicly held.

Although it was not generally realized by the public, at the time of
the Southern sale of its Miami property the Cleveland Corporation was
close to bankruptcy. For 1982, the company's management expected Cleveland to report an operating loss of some $25 million, before the profits of

This case was prepared by David F. Hawkins.

Copyright © 1975 by the President and Fellows of Harvard College
Harvard Business School case 176–080 (Rev. 1985)

the Miami park sale were included in Cleveland's consolidated income statement. In addition, the company's consolidated tax return would show a substantial loss.

In 1981, the Southern Company reported sales of $117 million and a net income of $27.4 million.

The Miami Sale

In late 1982, a limited partnership of 152 individuals (Partnership No. 1) was formed to acquire Southern's Miami park. These partners contributed $5.95 million to the limited partnership. These funds were used to acquire the Miami park. Immediately after the purchase, the limited partnership transferred the property to another partnership (Partnership No. 2) in which a new Southern subsidiary became the general partner for a contribution of $1,000. Partnership No. 1 was a limited partner in Partnership No. 2. Therefore, the new Southern subsidiary became the sole and exclusive manager of the business of Partnership No. 2.

The $5.95 million of Partnership No. 1 was distributed as follows: $1.5 million as a down payment for the Miami park; $3.93 million for the prepayment of interest; $416,000 to the underwriter for his commission; and the remainder to the partnership for working capital.

The selling price for the Miami park and a 10-year agreement by Southern not to compete was set at $40 million. This price was established through negotiations between Southern and Realty Appraisers, a Texan realty firm. Partnership No. 1 did not participate in these negotiations.

At the time of the proposed sale, the gross book value of the Miami park as reported on Southern's balance sheet was $14.2 million. The related accumulated depreciation reserve was $4.9 million, and the net book value was $9.3 million.

The $40 million purchase price was allocated by the buyer as follows: land, $5 million; buildings and improvements and personal property, $25 million; the covenant not to compete, $8 million; and goodwill, $2 million.

Partnership No. 1 was to pay for the park as follows: $1.5 million cash and a 6.5 percent note for $38.5 million. (At the time, the prime borrowing rate was well over 10 percent.) The agreement did not require any principal payments for the first three years. Thereafter, for the next 32 years equal principal and interest payments of about $2.3 million annually were required to liquidate the note. In addition, should Partnership No. 1 default on the note, Southern's sole recourse was to recover the park. Neither of the partnerships nor any of the partners individually was liable for the payment of the note or for any deficiency if the property was foreclosed.

In the future, all of the park's depreciation losses, tax credits, and amortization charges were to be allocated to the partners of Partnership No. 1.

For its part in the negotiations to set the selling price of the park, Realty Appraisers were paid $1.2 million in cash plus a $750,000 promissory note. In addition, Realty Appraisers was the sole owner of Realty Interstate, the underwriters of Partnership No. 1. An underwriting commission of $416,000 was paid to Realty Interstate.

The Louisville Sale

Previously, on December 31, 1981, Southern had sold to a group of wealthy individuals all of the property and equipment at its Louisville park for $23 million. This sale resulted in a gain of $4.8 million. Upon completion of the sale the purchaser contributed the park to a limited partnership in which a Southern subsidiary was the general partner and operator. As partial consideration of the sale, Southern received a 7 percent $21 million mortgage note secured by the park. The note was payable in annual principal installments of $700,000 beginning in March 1988.

The 1981 financial statements of Southern reported the $4.8 million gain as a discontinued business income item.

Subsequently, the company changed its policy toward amusement parks from one of constructing and operating parks to one of constructing, developing, selling, and operating parks. Management believed this change in company policy would require that the 1981 sale be reclassified in the comparative 1981 statement included in the 1982 annual report as an ordinary item rather than as a discontinued business item.

Question

What is the appropriate accounting for the gain on the Miami sale?

CASE 11-2

Ravenwood Oil Corporation
Carved-Out Oil and Gas Production Contracts

The Ravenwood Oil Corporation was formed in 1977 by a group of Denver business executives to engage in oil exploration in the western part of the

This case was prepared by F. R. Madera under the direction of David F. Hawkins.
Copyright © 1965 by the Presidents and Fellows of Harvard College
Harvard Business School case 110–088 (Rev. 1985)

United States. Its operations included exploration, development, and production activities in scattered areas from Texas to Canada and west to California. More than one half of the 4 million shares of common stock authorized by its Delaware charter were issued to the incorporation and about 750 investors through public offerings.

This case deals with the accounting methods used by the corporation to report *profits* from the sales of carved-out oil and gas production payments in 1984, 1985, and 1986.

To obtain funds for exploration or other purposes, the owner of a producing oil property may sell carved-out oil production payments. In exchange for an immediate payment in cash, the purchaser of the carved-out oil production payment receives the right to a certain amount of money to be paid from a specified percentage of the oil produced from an existing producing property. For example, Ravenwood, as an owner of oil properties, might sell to an investor for $100,000 cash the right to receive up to $125,000 from the proceeds of 20 percent of the oil produced from one of its producing properties. Ravenwood would continue to operate the property and bear

EXHIBIT 1

RAVENWOOD OIL CORPORATION
Balance Sheets at December 31
(in thousands)

	1985	1984
Assets		
Cash	$ 262	$ 178
Receivables (net)	1,852	1,838
Materials and supplies (at cost)	158	162
Other current assets	98	44
Total current assets	$ 2,370	$ 2,222
Net property	6,846	6,640
Undeveloped leases	1,644	1,214
Other assets	137	114
Total assets	$10,997	$10,190
Liabilities and Stockholders' Equity		
Accounts payable	$ 306	$ 496
Notes payable	520	2,468
Accrued expenses	430	88
Total current liabilities	$ 1,256	$ 3,052
Long-term notes payable	2,980	1,886
Total liabilities	$ 4,236	$ 4,938
Stockholders' equity:		
Common stock (par value $1)	$ 2,428	$ 2,396
Paid-in surplus	2,748	2,274
Retained earnings	1,585	582
Total stockholders' equity	$ 6,761	$ 5,252
Total liabilities and stockholders' equity	$10,997	$10,190

EXHIBIT 2

RAVENWOOD OIL CORPORATION
Income Statements for the Year Ended December 31
(in thousands)

	1985	1984
Income:		
Sales of oil and gas	$4,775	$4,228
Operating costs and expenses:		
Lease operations	$ 752	$ 864
Production and ad valorem taxes	234	216
Administrative and general	470	464
Interest on long-term debt	126	144
Other interest	26	14
Miscellaneous	4	2
	$1,612	$1,704
Other costs:		
Intangible development costs	$ 728	$ 716
Dry holes and abandonments	102	166
Depreciation and depletion	1,012	1,034
Released or expired interests	318	116
	$2,160	$2,032
Total costs and expenses	$3,772	$3,736
Net income	$1,003	$ 492

all costs of producing the oil. The transaction is considered a sale of the oil under the ground; no liability for repayment is created by such sale. As the owner of the oil, the purchaser of the oil payment will receive the proceeds from the sale of the oil directly from the buyer of the crude oil. The excess of the oil payment over the cash paid by the investor indicates the risk assumed by the investor regarding the certainty that production will be sufficient to satisfy the payment. Typically, the level of risk assumed by the buyer of this carved-out oil payment is low.

Initially, Ravenwood's operations had been a disappointment to the incorporators. Between 1977 and 1983, irregular profits and losses had been reported, and at the close of 1983 retained earnings were $90,000.

Operations in 1984 and 1985 resulted in profits of $492,000 and $1,003,000, respectively, however (see Exhibits 1 and 2). Profits from carved-out oil payments sold but not satisfied by production before year-end were $116,000 in 1984 and $1,360,000 in 1985. These amounts had been recognized as income at the time of sale and were included in the sales of oil and gas reported in those years, after making adequate provision for estimated future production costs. All oil payments were satisfied by production within 12 months following the sale of the oil payment.

On April 10, 1986, after the 1985 annual statements were issued to stockholders but before interim statements for the first quarter of 1986 were prepared, the company changed its methods of accounting for the profits from the sale of carved-out oil production payments. Effective January 1, 1986, all such profits were to be deferred until the oil and gas was produced.

Operations for the year 1986 resulted in a net loss of $275,000 exclusive of any consideration of profits from sales of oil production payments. By December 31, 1986, all oil payments sold in previous years had been satisfied by oil production. The single carved-out oil production payment sold in 1986 resulted in a profit of $255,000, but no oil was produced from this property in 1986.

To date, the company had not declared any dividends.

Questions

(NOTE: Ignore the income tax considerations in your answers.)

1. What net income would Ravenwood report in 1986 if the accounting method used previously had been continued?
2. What is the net income for each of the years 1984, 1985, and 1986 under the newly adopted method of deferring profits from sales of carved-out oil production payments until production takes place?
3. What are the earnings per share in each of the three years under:
   a. The accounting method originally used?
   b. The newly adopted accounting method?
4. What reasons can you suggest for adoption of the new accounting method?
5. How do you think Ravenwood should report its profits from sales of carved-out oil production payments? Why?

CASE 11-3

Lectro-Magic Company
Accounting for Bad Debt and Warranty Service Costs

The Lectro-Magic Company was incorporated in Ohio, in April 1982, to produce and sell a new line of small electrical appliances. Organizational

This case was prepared by F. R. Madera under the direction of David F. Hawkins.
Copyright © 1965 by the President and Fellows of Harvard College
Harvard Business School case 110–108 (Rev. 1985)

leadership for Lectro-Magic was provided by Roger Wiswell, who left his position as district sales manager for a national electrical appliance firm. Reluctant to accept a promotion requiring transfer to the West Coast, Wiswell had for more than a year been alert to an opportunity to use his abilities in a smaller firm in the Cleveland area.

In mid-1981, Wiswell was introduced to a young electrical engineer who had developed a miniature power unit around which he designed a number of unusual and effective small appliances. After a six-month investigation of product marketability and anticipated costs, the two decided to pool their resources to produce and market the line.

The limited financial resources of the promoters were supplemented by investments of four mutual friends. These investors were not interested in direct participation in the management of the enterprise. However, all six planned to serve as the firm's board of directors. After the corporate charter was granted by the state of Ohio, 100,000 of the 500,000 authorized $1 par value shares of capital stock were issued to the six incorporators at $3 per share. Roger Wiswell was elected president of the new corporation.

Several tentative agreements made prior to incorporation were now formalized by contracts. The corporation agreed to pay a 5 percent royalty, based on the selling price of appliances, to the engineer-inventor in return for exclusive rights to the use of his patents. Two small electrical and metal stamping firms agreed to manufacture and assemble the appliances at prices subject to periodic revision based upon negotiation.

Early in the planning stages of the venture, the principal promoters agreed that the mechanical nature of the products would require extensive servicing after sale in order to gain customer acceptability. Therefore, from the outset, all appliances were sold with a two-year warranty. Lectro-Magic was to provide unlimited service and repairs for this period without charge to the ultimate purchaser. Only transportation costs were paid by appliance owners under this liberal service policy. The manufacturer who contracted to produce the electrical components agreed to provide the required service and repairs for Lectro-Magic under a cost-plus arrangement.

By October 1982, Lectro-Magic's operations were well under way. Sizable expenditures for promotion and introduction of the product line resulted in almost immediate customer acceptance. During the balance of the year, efforts were concentrated upon marketing activities in a selected six-state area.

From the beginning, the firm's accounting and related clerical activities were supervised by a competent but inexperienced young accountant. His attention had been entirely directed toward establishing procedures and records for control of cash, inventories, accounts receivable, and accounts payable. Since Wiswell's time was taken by more pressing matters, accounting and reporting practices were given little consideration by him beyond the selection of a calendar-year closing date.

Early in January 1983, the company accountant prepared a balance sheet at December 31, 1982, and an income statement covering 1982 operations. These statements are shown in the first columns of Exhibits 1 and 2. All accounts payable and accruals of monetary liabilities had been recorded. Cash, receivables, and inventories had been carefully reconciled. A net loss from operations had been expected during this initial period, and no income tax liability was anticipated.

Several events in January 1983 brought President Wiswell's attention directly to accounting matters. These related to bad debts and warranty service costs.

During the year 1981, bad debt losses had not been anticipated. Shipments had been made to retailer customers after cursory reference to a publication of a credit reporting service. In January, however, Lectro-Magic was notified that a customer owing $4,000 had been declared bankrupt. There was little prospect of even a partial recovery of the unpaid balance.

In a review of the warranty service contract, Wiswell noted that costs to the end of 1982 had exceeded earlier projections. The costs taken into account in pricing the company's line were estimated to be 12 percent of the total sales price. These service costs were expected to be incurred as

---

EXHIBIT 1

LECTRO-MAGIC COMPANY
Balance Sheets at December 31
(in thousands)

	1982 (actual)	1983 (estimated)
Assets		
Current assets:		
Cash	$125	$201
Accounts receivable	70	125
Inventories	30	151
Total current assets	$225	$477
Plant and equipment	$213	$213
Less: Accumulated depreciation	4	12
Net book value	$209	$201
Total assets	$434	$678
Liabilities and Equity		
Current liabilities:		
Accounts payable	$137	$235
Taxes payable	—	45
Other accruals	13	35
Total current liabilities	$150	$315
Stockholders' equity:		
Capital stock	$100	$100
Other paid-in capital	200	200
Retained earnings	(16)	63
Total stockholders' equity	$284	$363
Total liabilities and equity	$434	$678

EXHIBIT 2

LECTRO-MAGIC COMPANY
Income Statements
For the Years 1982 and 1983
(in thousands)

	1982 (actual)	1983 (estimated)
Sales	$200	$600
Cost of sales:		
Production costs	$100	$300
Royalties	10	30
Total	$110	$330
Gross profit	$ 90	$270
Expenses:		
Warranty service costs	$ 6	$ 24
Selling expenses	16	48
General and administration	24	50
Bad debts	—	4
Promotional expenses	60	20
Total	$106	$146
Net income before taxes	$ (16)	$124
Provision for income taxes*	—	52
Net income after taxes	$ (16)	$ 72

* Federal income tax rates on corporations for 1982 and 1983 were: the normal tax rate of 22 percent on all taxable income, plus a surtax of 26 percent on taxable income over $25,000. (This does not include a special surtax imposed in 1982–83, which should not be considered in computation.)

follows: 2 percent in the year of sale, 6 percent in the succeeding year, and 4 percent in the second year following sale. Wiswell noted, however, that a number of minor changes made in product design late in 1982 were expected to reduce the need for repairs and service from these projected levels.

While conferring with the company's legal counsel late in January, Wiswell was reminded that Lectro-Magic's federal income tax return would be due on March 15, 1983. The attorney suggested that it might be wise to retain a certified public accountant to make an audit of the firm's operations and prepare the income tax returns. He noted that accounting methods used by taxpayers in initial periods must generally be continued in subsequent periods unless prior permission for change is obtained within 90 days after the beginning of the taxable year. In addition, borrowing or security offerings to finance possible expansion would probably require financial statements with an independent accountant's opinion.

Immediately after returning to his office, Wiswell asked the company's accountant to prepare estimated statements for the year 1983 based upon projections of sales, costs, and expenses. These estimated statements appear in the second columns of Exhibits 1 and 2.

Mr. Wiswell planned to spend the evening studying the actual 1982 and estimated 1983 financial statements.

Questions

1. How, if at all, should the company's financial statements reflect—
   a. Warranty service costs?
   b. Bad debt expense?
2. What other areas of financial reporting should be considered by management?
3. Using available information and any assumptions you choose to make, recast 1982 statements and 1983 estimates to reflect fairly the financial position and the results of operations.

CASE 11-4

D.C. Contracting, Inc.
Long-Term Contract Accounting

Introduction

On March 7, 1977, the board of directors of D.C. Contracting, Inc., (D.C.) approved a proposal from Citibank N.A. whereby Citibank would be D.C.'s agent bank on a two-bank, $5 million reducing revolving credit agreement having a maturity of seven years, and D.C.'s lead bank on a contemplated two-bank, $6 million line of credit.

On March 30, 1977, D.C. signed the reducing revolving credit agreement with Citibank N.A. and First Pennsylvania Bank N.A. (the "banks"). Citibank and First Pennsylvania also established lines of credit in favor of D.C. not to exceed $4 million and $2 million respectively, bearing interest in Citibank's base rate (important terms of the agreement are provided in Exhibit 1). The total provided by the banks aggregates $11 million and is available on an unsecured basis to D.C. and its subsidiaries for working capital needs. This arrangement replaced D.C.'s $5 million unsecured line of credit with Provident National Bank of Philadelphia, of which $4 million was available for general working capital purposes and the remaining $1

This case was prepared by Norman J. Bartczak.

EXHIBIT 1

D.C. Contracting, Inc.: Significant Terms of D.C.'s March 30, 1977, Credit Agreement with Citibank N.A. and First Pennsylvania Bank N.A.

Bank Credit Decision. D.C. represents and warrants that the balance sheets of D.C. and its subsidiaries as at March 31, 1976, and the related statements of income, retained earnings, and changes in financial position for the fiscal year then ended, copies of which have been furnished to each of the banks, fairly present the financial condition of D.C. and its subsidiaries as at such date and the results of operations of D.C. and its subsidiaries for the period ended on such date, all in accordance with generally accepted accounting principles consistently applied, and since March 31, 1976, there has been no material adverse change in such condition or operations.

Each bank acknowledges that it has, independently and based on the financial statements referred to above and such other documents and information as it has deemed appropriate, made its own credit analysis and decision to enter into this agreement. Each bank also acknowledges that it will, independently and based on such documents and information as it shall deem appropriate at the time, continue to make its own credit decisions in taking or not taking action under this agreement.

Working Capital Covenant. D.C. and its subsidiaries shall maintain:

(i) An excess of consolidated current assets over consolidated current liabilities (excluding deferred income taxes) of not less than $22 million to and including March 31, 1977, rising in $500,000 increments each year thereafter to a maximum of $25.5 million after March 31, 1983.

(ii) A ratio of consolidated current assets to consolidated current liabilities of not less than 1.3 to 1.0.

(iii) A ratio of consolidated current assets to consolidated current liabilities (excluding deferred income taxes) of not less than 2.7 to 1.0.

Net Worth Covenant. D.C. and its subsidiaries shall maintain an excess of consolidated total tangible assets over consolidated total liabilities of not less than $14 million to and including March 31, 1977. The excess shall increase by $1 million increments each annual period after March 31, 1977, to a maximum of $21 million after March 31, 1983.

Dividend Restriction. D.C. and its subsidiaries will not, without the written consent of the banks, declare and pay cash dividends to its stockholders, except for those declared out of 66⅔ percent of net income of D.C. and its subsidiaries arising after March 31, 1977, and within the 12-month period immediately preceding the date of computation and computed on a cumulative consolidated basis. This provision is applicable to the next quarterly cash dividend scheduled to be paid in August 1977. It is not applicable to the dividend declared prior to the signing of the agreement, namely the 16 cents per share dividend declared February 5, 1977, and payable May 25, 1977, to stockholders of record April 26, 1977.

Debt Covenant. D.C. and its subsidiaries will not, without the written consent of the banks, create or suffer to exist any debt maturing in excess of one year from the date of determination, if immediately after giving effect to such debt and the receipt and application of any proceeds thereof, the ratio of the aggregate amount of such debt of D.C. and its subsidiaries, on a consolidated basis, to *(x)* the total tangible assets less *(y)* total liabilities would be greater than 1.0 to 1.0.

---

million was available on a short-term, specific transactional basis, at the discretion of Provident National.

On March 31, 1977, D.C. borrowed $5 million at 6½ percent per annum under the reducing revolving credit agreement.

Company Background

D.C. Contracting was founded in 1915 by David Caldwell, a District of Columbia electrician. Mr. Caldwell's reputation for efficiently providing electrical construction for business, institutions, and other large structures brought him success in the new industry of electrical contracting.

D.C. became a public company in 1968, and since 1968 it has experienced rapid growth. As of early 1977, D.C. has become one of the United States's largest electrical construction and contracting firms participating in all sectors of construction other than single-family housing. In fiscal 1976, contract income was $110 million. D.C. is active in the following business sectors: public and institutional construction; industrial plant construction, expansion and modernization; commercial construction of all kinds; public utility plant and distribution facilities; and space and military projects.

During the last five fiscal years, the approximate percentage of D.C.'s gross contract income attributable to the various categories of its business were as follows:

	Fiscal Year Ended March 31				
Category	1972	1973	1974	1975	1976
Public and institutional	23%	43%	40%	39%	40%
Industrial	28	11	14	19	22
Commercial	30	15	15	21	20
Utilities	17	27	27	14	14
Space and military	2	4	4	7	4
Total	100%	100%	100%	100%	100%

D.C.'s business is performed under contracts obtained by competitive bidding or by negotiations based on plans and specifications submitted by the owner or general contractor. It employs more than 2,600 people and operates 19 branches in the continental United States and 2 branches overseas.

Types of Contracts

Although the terms of individual contracts may vary substantially, D.C.'s business is generally performed under two basic types of contracts:

Fixed Price Contracts. The greater share of D.C.'s work is done pursuant to contracts where it receives a fixed sum for the project or a fixed amount per unit of work performed, which is intended to cover D.C.'s costs and overhead and to return a profit.

Cost Plus Contracts. To a lesser extent, and generally in cases where final plans and specifications for the work are not available to establish a fixed price bid, D.C. contracts on a cost plus basis. Under these contracts it is reimbursed for its costs, and receives a fee which may be a fixed amount or a percentage of cost.

Fixed price contracts generally involve greater risks for D.C. but also have greater potential profit margins. Cost plus contracts customarily insulate it from the risk of cost increases. For the five years ended March 31, 1976, the percentages of contract income derived from fixed price contracts were 83 percent in 1972, 84 percent in 1973, 74 percent in 1974, 75 percent in 1975, and 85 percent in 1976. The balance of contract income in each year was derived from cost plus contracts.

Practically all of D.C.'s business is obtained by competitive bidding or negotiation based on plans and specifications submitted to it by the owner or general contractor. Competitive bidding generally is limited to contractors which have qualified for inclusion on the customer's bid list. Such qualifications depends on, among other things, the contractor's financial responsibility, its ability to perform the work, and its record of on-time completions. Standard company estimating procedures are followed for submitting a fixed contract price or fixed unit price. Where the plans and specifications are not sufficiently definitive to permit reliable estimates, the cost plus contract is utilized with the fee portion negotiated or bid to the customer. D.C. assumes the risk of losses on contracts if its cost estimates prove to be incorrect. In addition, contract specifications may be inaccurate or projects may be deferred or delayed by customers or other contractors, in which case additional costs and expenses may be incurred by D.C. for which it must seek recourse through negotiation or litigation. When the customer requests, D.C. furnishes surety bonds for the performance of its work and the payment of its suppliers and personnel. D.C. has never defaulted on a contract nor required its surety company to complete a project or perform any obligation to a customer.

Operations

While D.C. generally contracts for its own account, it has participated in joint ventures with other electrical contractors, where the joint venture enters into a subcontract with the general contractor. It generally acts as manager of these joint ventures, for which it receives a management fee. It has also participated in joint ventures with building contractors in other trades, where the joint venture acts as the general contractor. These joint ventures have been principally in connection with the construction of automated bulk mail facilities for the United States Postal Service. As a participant in a joint venture, D.C. is jointly and severally obligated with each of its joint venturers for the performance of the joint venture's contract with the customer. D.C. has recently reduced its participation in joint ventures with building contractors in other trades.

Under almost all of D.C.'s contracts, payment is made by the general contractor or owner monthly, or sometimes more frequently, based upon the percentage or stage of completion of the job. Usually a percentage of the amount which is due is retained by the general contractor or owner until completion and acceptance of the project.

No material part of the business of D.C. is seasonal. Due to its diversity in the various sectors of the construction industry, it has not experienced cyclical variations in its total contract income even though sectors of the construction business are cyclical. Major fixed price contracts generally require 18 to 30 months to complete.

Domestic.   D.C. conducts its business in the continental United States through 19 branch offices. The following table sets forth the approximate percentages of gross contract income by geographical region during the last five fiscal years:

Region	Fiscal Year Ended March 31				
	1972	1973	1974	1975	1976
Mid-Atlantic	27%	27%	26%	32%	30%
Southern	26	29	31	31	26
Midwestern	20	20	18	14	21
Northeastern	27	24	25	22	20
Western	—	—	—	1	3
Total	100%	100%	100%	100%	100%

International.   D.C. International Corporation was incorporated as a wholly owned subsidiary in August 1974 to engage in contracting activities in foreign countries. Its contract income for the fiscal year ended March 31, 1975, was $853,000, of which $653,000 was attributable to one materials supply contract which is substantially completed and on which D.C. realized a nominal profit. The general and administrative expenses of this subsidiary, including the cost of bids during the start-up period, accounted for its loss after tax benefit of $582,000 ($.43 per share) in that fiscal year. Activities prior to April 1, 1975, were not significant.

D.C. expects that international operations will become a material part of its business. It is intended that operations will be conducted primarily in developing nations and difficult climates and, accordingly, weather conditions, actions of foreign governments, fluctuations in local currencies, transportation difficulties, shortages of labor or materials, civil strife, and other factors may subject D.C. to more substantial risks of loss than those present in its domestic activities. A guaranty of performance is generally required under fixed price contracts, both domestic and foreign. While domestic contracts traditionally call for surety bonds issued against the general credit of D.C., foreign contracts often require a financial guaranty by a bank in the foreign country backed by a letter of credit which may involve a deposit of collateral in addition to the general credit of D.C.

A substantial amount of overseas work was awarded to D.C. late in the fourth quarter of fiscal 1976 consisting mainly of two contracts, one for approximately $22 million with a United States general contractor for the U.S. Corps of Engineers for construction of housing, water wells, medical support facilities, and hospital air conditioning in Saudi Arabia. D.C.'s contract covers the electrical, mechanical, and utilities work involved in the project which is being constructed for, and funded by, the Saudi Arabian government. The guaranty of D.C.'s performance was furnished by surety bonds. The other major foreign contract involves the construction of a hotel in El Salvador.

Competition

D.C. is one of the four largest electrical contractors in the United States, based on published contract awards. (Fischbach & Moore is D.C.'s largest competitor with 1976 fiscal year contract income of $611 million). The electrical contracting industry is characterized by intense competition. D.C. competes with many large and small firms, both union and nonunion, as well as with certain large general contractors which have their own electrical contracting capability. Competition for large contracts and contracts with respect to specialized electrical installations, while limited to fewer concerns (including D.C.), is still active.

Management and Ownership

Executive Officers

Name, Age	Position	Current Rate of Remuneration
Edward P. Johnson, Sr., Age 77	Chairman of the board, chief executive officer, joined D.C. in 1935	$150,200
J. A. Martin, Age 65	President, chief operating officer, joined D.C. in 1939	$126,200
Nicholas J. Grady, Age 65	Executive vice president, chief administrative officer, joined D.C. in 1954	$102,200
Edward P. Johnson, Jr., Age 46	Senior vice president, International, joined D.C. in 1955	$ 66,200
R. A. Clay, Age 34	Vice president—finance, treasurer, joined D.C. in 1969	Less than $50,000
Joseph J. McCarthy, Age 60	Secretary, general counsel, joined D.C. in 1966	$ 49,200

Board of Directors

Name	Occupation	Director Since	Common Shares Beneficially Owned
Edward P. Johnson, Sr.	Chairman and chief executive officer of D.C.	1939	218,283
John A. Martin	President and chief operating officer of D.C.	1956	188,515
Joseph J. McCarthy	Secretary and general counsel of D.C.	1967	3,736
Arthur S. Friedman	Member, Tanner & Friedman, P.C., Attorneys at Law	1968	6,754
Nicholas J. Grady	Executive vice president and chief administrative officer of D.C.	1970	5,089
Edward P. Johnson, Jr.	Senior vice president, International of D.C.	1972	144,729
Francis Lyman Hine	Chairman and director of Meta-Glas Systems Corp.; vice president and director, National Glass Plastics Corp.	1973	0

Principal Shareholders and Sale of Shares

On July 27, 1976, D.C. offered to sell 400,000 shares of common stock. The offering came to market at $9 per share and consisted of 140,000 new shares and 260,000 shares from selling shareholders. The following table, from the offering prospectus, sets forth certain information with respect to the selling shareholders and D.C.'s principal shareholders:

Name	Owned as of May 31, 1976 (1) No. of Shares	Owned as of May 31, 1976 (1) Percentage of Outstanding	No. of Shares to be Sold	To be Owned after the Offering No. of Shares	To be Owned after the Offering Percentage of Outstanding
Edward P. Johnson, Sr.	302,283	22%	84,000	218,283	15%
John A. Martin	272,515	20%	84,000	188,515	13%
Trust Company Bank, Edward P. Johnson, Jr., and Arthur S. Friedman, as trustees under trust agreement dated July 5, 1968	228,739	17%	84,000	144,729	10%
Joseph J. McCarthy	5,736	—	2,000	3,736	—
Richard L. Senior III	3,841	—	2,000	1,841	—
James K. Shannon	6,306	—	2,000	4,306	—
Robert H. Shepherd	3,841	—	2,000	1,841	—

The actual number of new shares sold to the public was 155,000. The net proceeds to D.C. of the sale were $1,256,900.

Financial Information

Disagreement on Accounting Matter. On March 7, 1977 (the same day on which D.C. approved Citibank's proposal), D.C.'s board of directors engaged Richard A. Eisner & Company as the independent accounting firm to conduct the audit of D.C.'s financial statements for the fiscal year ending March 31, 1977. Eisner was engaged in place of Arthur Young & Company who audited D.C.'s financial statements initially for the fiscal year ended March 31, 1969, and each fiscal year thereafter, through and including the fiscal year ended March 31, 1976.

On March 22, 1977, D.C. filed a Form 8-K "Current Report" with the Securities and Exchange Commission reporting a disagreement between D.C. and Arthur Young & Company (its former accountants) as to the application of D.C.'s percentage-of-completion method of accounting on a foreign contract in the third quarter ended December 31, 1976. Details of the disagreement are provided in Exhibit 2.

Quarterly Information

D.C. CONTRACTING, INC.
Quarterly Data
(dollars in thousands, except per-share amounts)

Fiscal 1977	I 6/30/76	II 9/30/76	III 12/31/76	IV 3/31/77
Contract income	$29,514	$34,478	$32,025	NA*
Net income	650	735	863	NA
Net income per share	.48	.50	.57	NA
Dividends per share	.14	.15	.16	$ .16
Market price: High	9.75	9.75	11.125	12.25
Low	7.75	8.25	8.50	10.00

Fiscal 1976	I 6/30/75	II 9/30/75	III 12/31/75	IV 3/31/76
Contract income	$23,700	$26,441	$28,599	$31,171
Net income	539	565	552	807
Net income per share	.40	.41	.40	.60
Dividends per share	.11	.12	.12	.12
Market price: High	6.875	9.00	7.375	8.50
Low	5.25	6.625	6.375	6.50

Fiscal 1975	I 6/30/74	II 9/30/74	III 12/31/74	IV 3/31/75
Contract income	$20,900	$22,226	$26,443	$26,467
Net income	485	523	541	598
Net income per share	.35	.38	.40	.43
Dividends per share	.075	.075	.10	.10
Market price: High	5.25	4.875	4.875	6.375
Low	4.375	4.00	3.75	4.50

* Not available on 3/31/77.

Recent Financial Statements. A condensed version of D.C.'s 1976 annual report and fiscal 1977 third quarter (12/31/76) 10-Q (financial report to the SEC) are provided in Exhibit 4.

EXHIBIT 2
D.C. Contracting, Inc.: Excerpts from Form 8-K, "Current Report," Filed with the Securities and Exchange Commission on March 22, 1977

D.C. engaged Arthur Young & Company to perform limited reviews in accordance with the provisions of *Statement on Auditing Standards No. 10*, with reporting by them to the company's board of directors. In connection with such reviews for the three-month periods ended September 30, 1976, and December 31, 1976, there was disagreement relating to the recognition of a material amount of income under a foreign fixed price contract. In these respective three-month periods contract costs included and contract profit, based on costs incurred to date to total estimated costs, was recognized on (i) the costs of materials shipped overseas which were on the project site but not yet installed, (ii) the costs of materials which were in transit to the project site, and (iii) the cost of expendable capital equipment purchased for the project and included in the original estimate of total contract costs. The question of including such costs first arose in November 1976 with respect to the second quarter ended September 30, 1976, and was resolved to Arthur Young & Company's satisfaction with D.C. excluding the applicable costs in question. However, D.C. maintained the correctness of its accounting procedures for review in the then current quarter ending December 31, 1976.

As a result of the review for the quarter ended December 31, 1976, Arthur Young & Company expressed the opinion that D.C., in respect of the specific foreign contract, should not recognize income on the basis of the relationship of incurred costs to date to estimated total costs since, in their view, the unusually high costs of materials and the relatively limited installation effort created an imbalance in the "incurred costs" which did not reflect a fair basis for determination of the percentage of completion of the contract, for which the major installation effort is not scheduled until subsequent to March 31, 1977.

They recommended that, in the specific case of the contract in question, performance could more properly be reflected by determining percentage of completion on the basis of the relationship of labor hours expended to date to total estimated labor hours. They suggested that an approximately equivalent result would be obtained were income to be recognized on a "cost incurred" basis by excluding from such costs all materials not at the job site, by including as costs only the proportionate periodic depreciation applicable to capital assets to be utilized during the life of

the contract, and by recognizing 50 percent of the anticipated contract profit relative to the costs of materials delivered to the job site but not yet installed.

Arthur Young & Company, in a meeting with the board of directors on February 5, 1977, informed D.C. that should the presently known fact pattern relating to the specific contract in question remain unchanged, they would not be able to express an unqualified opinion on the March 31, 1977, consolidated financial statements since, in their opinion, the accounting which D.C. proposed to follow during such fiscal year for the recognition of profit on that contract is not in accordance with generally accepted accounting principles. That opinion was reaffirmed by letter dated February 14, 1977, to the chairman of the board of directors.

D.C. has not made the adjustments requested by Arthur Young & Company since, in its opinion, the adjustments are inconsistent with the substance of the transaction. It was anticipated that the purchase of materials and shipment to the foreign project site would be required before installation efforts could commence. The costs of the materials, delivery, and freight have been established by fixed price contracts with suppliers obtained by D.C. To exclude the requested portion of the incurred costs would, in D.C.'s opinion, be a departure from the procedure by which D.C. recognizes income and in its opinion would not result in a more meaningful allocation of income to the fiscal periods involved. Independent accounting opinion from Richard A. Eisner & Company has been obtained concurring with D.C.'s accounting treatment.

Arthur Young & Company's reports on the financial statements for the fiscal years ended March 31, 1975, and 1976 did not contain any adverse opinion or disclaimer of opinion or qualifications as to uncertainty, audit scope, or accounting principles.

[Case writer's note: Below is a copy of Arthur Young & Company's opinion on D.C.'s financial statements as issued in conjunction with the common stock issue by D.C. in 1976.]

Report of Certified Public Accountants

The Board of Directors
D.C. Contracting, Inc.

We have examined the accompanying consolidated balance sheet of D.C. Contracting,

EXHIBIT 2 *(concluded)*

Inc., at March 31, 1976, and the related consolidated statements of income, stockholders' equity, and changes in financial position for the five years then ended. Our examination was made in accordance with generally accepted auditing standards, and accordingly included such tests of the accounting records and such other auditing procedures as we considered necessary in the circumstances.

In our opinion, the statements mentioned above present fairly the consolidated financial position of D.C. Contracting, Inc., at March 31, 1976, and the consolidated results of oper-

ations and changes in financial position for the five years then ended, in conformity with generally accepted accounting principles applied on a consistent basis during the period.

Arthur Young & Company

Washington, D.C.
May 27, 1976

EXHIBIT 3
D.C. Contracting, Inc.: July 7, 1976, Report to Shareholders from D.C. Management in 1976 Annual Report

To Our Stockholders

D.C. Contracting set new records in earnings and volume in fiscal 1976. That performance, accompanied by a record backlog at year-end, was achieved in a period when the nation's overall construction industry continued to be beset by recession.

Contract income reached $109.9 million, up 14 percent (of which one fourth of the increase was due to the acquisition of Amelco Electric Company, Inc.) from last year's record of $96 million. Earnings per share increased to $1.81, up 16 percent from $1.56. Net income compared with last year was $2,463,000 to $2,147,000, an increase of 15 percent.

Backlog of $100 million as we began fiscal 1977 was 37 percent ahead of last year's record $73 million.

Cash dividends totaled $.47, an increase of 34 percent from the previous year. This reflects the policy of the board to declare quarterly cash dividends in relation to D.C.'s earnings, financial condition, and other factors.

Even as the country began to throw off the most troublesome of the recent recessions and real activity such as industrial production and employment began to move up, the construction industry this year remained depressed.

Nationally, construction expenditures in 1975 fell 9 percent from the previous year to $123.5 billion. Real unit volume decreased even more, considering an approximate 8 percent industry inflation factor. In the private sector, cautious attitudes discouraged new

capital investment. In the public sector, the problems of New York City and other cities had a negative impact on raising funds for construction programs. As a result, competition intensified for fewer available jobs.

D.C. did well in this environment for a number of reasons. The company continued to obtain contracts for projects of increasing size and complexity. Gains in contract income were recorded in energy/utilities, environmental controls work, water treatment, public transit, and the institutional sectors. These types of projects required major commitments of resources that tended to limit the number of qualified bidders.

The mix of our contracts also contributed to our growth and stability. As major joint venture projects, begun a few years ago, were completed, they were more than balanced by new joint venture projects and subcontracts for the company's own account.

Market recognition of D.C.'s technical capabilities and management experience benefited us.

Productivity gains by the company kept job costs under control. The depressed state of the construction industry, generally, made ample supplies of materials and skilled workers available, which resulted in good job movement.

Another factor in our improved performance was the contribution to profit from the new branches. New domestic branches opened since fiscal year 1973 have helped to contribute to our return on stockholders' equity as well as to our contract volume and backlog. Expansion has given us additional

EXHIBIT 3 *(concluded)*

geographic diversity by providing new centers for business in the West, Midwest, and Northeast in addition to our traditional presence in the Middle Atlantic States and the South. At this time, we have 19 domestic branches operating, including the New Orleans branch recently opened in the South.

D.C.'s contract income shows growing regional diversity for the past five years.

In international operations, D.C. International Corporation, a wholly owned subsidiary, received a major contract for overseas construction late in the fourth quarter. This subsidiary, created in August 1974, should begin to make a contribution to profit during the present fiscal year.

Current Year

For D.C. to date in fiscal 1977, business has been good based on contracts awarded. Major contract awards have been made for energy projects, environmental pollution and waste water treatment control facilities, and industrial expansion and renovation. We have recently received a contract in commercial construction involving a major office structure. In the public sector, while government activity has increased, projects for the most part are of limited size. Nevertheless, as the economic recovery continues and the New York City "ripple effect" subsides, capital may be easier to come by and delayed institutional projects could be rescheduled.

The U.S. Department of Commerce forecasts a better year for construction expenditures in 1976. D.C. should benefit from this improved domestic construction industry outlook in fiscal 1977.

Overseas, the race by the nonindustrial nations to achieve self-sufficiency through industrialization and to raise living standards in line with those of the established industrial nations offers excellent opportunities for this company.

D.C. of course must continue to be able to operate at efficient costs and to maintain standards of performance as we grow and extend our operations around the country and the world. This is not an easy task. However, our selectivity in the projects we undertake and the contractors we work with remain the keystone of our operating policy. In addition, we intend to continue tight controls over every aspect of our business, wherever it may be.

Financial Condition

The company's financial position at year-end was strong. Dividends were increased again for the current fiscal year by the board of directors. The quarterly dividend payable August 25, 1976, to stockholders of record July 26, 1976, goes from 12 cents in the preceding quarter to 14 cents per common share.

Edward R. Johnson, Sr.
Chairman

John A. Martin
President

EXHIBIT 4
D.C. Contracting, Inc.: Condensed Version of D.C. Contracting Fiscal 1976 Annual Report and 1976 Third-Quarter Report

D.C. CONTRACTING, INC.
Consolidated Statement of Income and Retained Earnings
Five Years Ended March 31, 1976, and Nine Months Ended December 31, 1975, and 1976
(dollars in thousands)

	Year Ended March 31					(Unaudited) Nine Months Ended December 31	
	1972	*1973*	*1974*	*1975*(g)	*1976*(h)	*1975*	*1976*
Contract income (a)	$63,433	$70,489	$79,187	$96,036	$109,911	$78,710	$96,017
Costs and expenses (a) (b) (c) (d):							
Direct contract	55,131	60,247	68,205	83,197	92,311	66,164	81,047
General and administrative	5,927	6,727	7,171	8,243	11,649	8,857	9,922
Depreciation	464	396	347	377	515	355	444
Minority interests in profit of consolidated joint ventures	—	—	—	—	289	—	418
	$61,521	$67,370	$75,723	$91,817	$104,764	$75,375	$91,831
	$ 1,911	$ 3,119	$ 3,465	$ 4,219	$ 5,148	$ 3,334	$ 4,186
Interest income (expense), net......................	(89)	(78)	(13)	253	(18)	48	(113)
Income before income taxes and extraordinary charge	$ 1,822	$ 3,041	$ 3,451	$ 4,472	$ 5,130	$ 3,383	$ 4,073
Provision for income taxes (e):							
Current	—	—	95	30	87	—	—
Deferred	900	1,555	1,686	2,295	2,580	1,727	1,822
	$ 900	$ 1,555	$ 1,781	$ 2,325	$ 2,667	$ 1,727	$ 1,822
Income before extraordinary charge	$ 922	$ 1,486	$ 1,670	$ 2,147	$ 2,463	$ 1,656	$ 2,251
Extraordinary charge (f)	(395)	—	—	—	—	—	—
Net income	$ 528	$ 1,486	$ 1,670	$ 2,147	$ 2,463	$ 1,656	$ 2,251
Retained earnings— beginning of year	$ 2,312	$ 2,484	$ 3,730	$ 5,123	$ 6,790	$ 6,790	$ 8,612
Stock dividends	(356)	(240)	—	—	—	—	—
Cash dividends	—	—	(277)	(481)	(641)	(477)	(662)
Retained earnings—end of year	$ 2,484	$ 3,730	$ 5,123	$ 6,790	$ 8,612	$ 7,968	$10,201
Per share of common stock (i):							
Income before extraordinary charge	$.66	$1.06	$1.20	$1.56	$1.81	$1.21	$1.55
Extraordinary charge (f)	(.28)	—	—	—	—	—	—
Net income	$.38	$1.06	$1.20	$1.56	$1.81	$1.21	$1.55
Cash dividends	$ —	$ —	$ .20	$ .35	$ .47	$ .35	$ .45
Shares of stock used to calculate earnings per share of common stock (i)	1,396,489	1,397,071	1,386,405	1,376,980	1,363,541	1,363,882	1,451,874

See accompanying notes.

EXHIBIT 4 *(continued)*

D.C. CONTRACTING, INC.
Notes to Consolidated Statement of Income

(a) The consolidated statement of income includes the company's proportionate share of the operations of joint ventures in which it does not have a majority share (generally 20 percent to 50 percent) as follows:

benefits reflect the inclusion of certain amounts in the extraordinary charge which are taxable at capital gain rates.

(g) The outstanding capital stock of D.C. Midwest, Inc. (formerly Amelco Electric Co.,

	Year Ended March 31				
	1972	*1973*	*1974*	*1975*	*1976*
Contract income	$11,167,000	$15,227,000	$17,654,000	$21,737,000	$14,484,000
Direct contract costs ...	9,676,000	13,712,000	15,208,000	18,434,000	11,822,000
Equity in joint venture income	$ 1,491,000	$ 1,515,000	$ 2,446,000	$ 3,303,000	$ 2,662,000

(b) Pension expense was approximately $1,700,000, $1,900,000, $2,375,000, $3,126,-000, and $4,088,000 for the years ended March 31, 1972, 1973, 1974, 1975, and 1976, respectively, for employees covered by union pension plans and, commencing in 1974, for salaried employees under a company plan.

(c) The amounts of bonuses and profit sharing costs under an informal discretionary plan were $288,000, $364,000, $677,000, $519,000, and $634,000 for the years ended March 31, 1972, 1973, 1974, 1975, and 1976, respectively.

(d) The provision for doubtful accounts was $82,000, $404,000, $59,000, $117,000, and $10,000 in 1972, 1973, 1974, 1975, and 1976, respectively.

(e) The provisions for income taxes exceed the amount of tax determined by applying the U.S. federal statutory income tax rate to income before income taxes, principally due to the inclusion of state income taxes in the provision. State income taxes included in the provision for income taxes are $36,000 for 1972, $181,000 for 1973, $242,000 for 1974, $325,000 for 1975, and $437,000 for 1976, including $95,000, $30,000, and $87,000 classified as current income tax expense in 1974, 1975, and 1976, respectively. See Note *(f)* with respect to 1972.

(f) In March 1972, the company disposed of its interest related to a partnership which was the owner of a building in Norfolk, Virginia. The net loss of $395,000, after related tax benefits of $555,000, is shown as an extraordinary charge in the consolidated statement of income for the year ended March 31, 1972, and includes the company's share of net loss of $125,000 after related taxes, from operations of the building. The allocated tax

Inc.) was acquired by D.C. Contracting, Inc., as of January 31, 1975, for cash and notes of $573,000 in a transaction accounted for as a purchase. If D.C. Midwest had been combined for the entire year ended March 31, 1975, contract income and net income on a pro forma basis, using D.C. Midwest's year ended September 30, 1974, would have been $107,848,000 and $1,261,000 ($.92 per share), respectively. D.C. Midwest had contract income of $2,830,000 for its six months ended March 31, 1975, and a net loss of $835,000. The net loss includes a $950,000 charge to operations prior to its acquisition as a result of D.C. Midwest's former parent having provided guaranty of performance on a joint venture entered into in 1972.

(h) D.C. International Corporation, incorporated in August 1974, engages in contracting activities outside the United States and through May 1976 has been awarded several significant contracts. For fiscal 1976, D.C. International's contract income was $853,000 and its loss, after tax benefit, was $582,000 ($.43 per share). Activities prior to fiscal 1976 were not significant.

(i) Net income per share of common stock has been computed on the basis of the weighted average number of shares outstanding during the periods, including applicable equivalent shares under the stock option plan, adjusted for the 5 percent stock dividend in 1972 and the 3 percent stock dividend in 1973. Warrants to purchase 20,079 shares, which expired in August 1974, were not considered as common stock equivalents since such treatment would be antidilutive for the years ended March 31, 1972, 1973, and 1974. Certain other options were not considered as common stock equivalents since they would

EXHIBIT 4 *(continued)*

be antidilutive or have an immaterial effect on net income per share.

(j) The amounts of material and supplies inventory were $314,000, $463,000, $473,000, $573,000, $1,085,000, and $813,000 at March 31, 1971, 1972, 1973, 1974, 1975, and 1976, respectively.

D.C. CONTRACTING, INC.
Consolidated Balance Sheets
March 31, 1975, March 31, 1976, and December 31, 1975 and 1976
(dollars in thousands)

	March 31, 1975	March 31, 1976	(Unaudited) December 31, 1975	(Unaudited) December 31, 1976
Assets				
Current assets:				
Cash	$ 3,116	$ 4,447	$ 3,220	$ 3,888
Contract receivables, including unbilled retainage due after one year (Note 1)	17,673	23,213	18,748	28,942
Less: Allowance for doubtful accounts	490	490	490	590
Net contract receivables	$17,183	$22,723	$18,258	$28,352
Equity in unconsolidated joint ventures (Note 6)	3,726	3,945	5,503	5,444
Material and supplies inventory	1,085	813	689	726
Other	293	178	151	159
Total current assets	$25,403	$32,106	$27,821	$38,569
Property and equipment, at cost:				
Land and buildings	1,486	1,922	1,922	2,477
Furniture, machinery, and equipment	4,484	5,162	5,025	5,591
	$ 5,970	$ 7,084	$ 6,947	$ 8,068
Less: Accumulated depreciation	3,491	3,912	3,938	4,311
Net property and equipment	$ 2,479	$ 3,172	$ 3,009	$ 3,757
Other assets	449	621	560	1,229
Total assets	$28,330	$35,899	$31,390	$43,555
Liabilities and Stockholders' Equity				
Current liabilities:				
Note payable to bank (Note 5)	$ 970	$ 1,000	$ 1,000	$ 4,000
Accounts payable	4,855	6,168	4,919	7,180
Accrued liabilities	1,495	1,743	240	922
Advance payments on uncompleted contracts	1,131	2,349	2,517	1,752
Installment obligation	250	300	300	300
Minority interest in consolidated joint ventures	—	289	150	407
Total current liabilities before deferred income taxes	$ 8,701	$11,849	$ 9,126	$14,561
Deferred income taxes (Note 4)	9,270	11,710	10,997	12,527
Total current liabilities	$17,971	$23,559	$20,123	$27,088
Noncurrent liabilities:				
Accrued deferred compensation	230	342	272	459
Mortgages payable, generally over a 25-year period	53	424	53	479
Other (primarily noncurrent deferred income taxes)	300	—	—	1,094
Total noncurrent liabilities	$ 583	$ 766	$ 325	$ 2,032

EXHIBIT 4 (continued)

	March 31, 1975	March 31, 1976	(Unaudited) December 31, 1975	(Unaudited) December 31, 1976
Stockholders' equity (Note 7):				
Common stock, $.50 par value; 1,399,782 shares issued at March 31, 1975, and 1976, and December 31, 1975, 1,554,782 shares issued at December 31, 1976	700	700	700	777
Capital in excess of par value	2,470	2,464	2,464	3,640
Retained earnings (Note 6)	6,790	8,612	7,968	10,201
	$ 9,960	$11,775	$11,132	$14,619
Less: Cost of shares of common stock in treasury; 35,616 shares at March 31, 1975, 37,696 at March 31, 1976, and 35,796 shares at December 31, 1975, 34,571 shares at December 31, 1976	183	202	190	183
Total stockholders' equity	$ 9,777	$11,574	$10,942	$14,435
Total liabilities and stockholders' equity	$28,330	$35,899	$31,390	$43,555

See accompanying notes.

D.C. CONTRACTING, INC.
Consolidated Statement of Changes in Financial Position
Five Years Ended March 31, 1976 and Nine Months Ended December 31, 1975, and 1976
(dollars in thousands)

	Year Ended March 31					(Unaudited) Nine Months Ended December 31	
	1972	1973	1974	1975	1976	1975	1976
Source:							
Income before extraordinary charge	$ 922	$1,486	$1,670	$2,147	$2,463	$1,656	$2,251
Charges against income not involving working capital in the current period:							
Depreciation	464	396	347	377	515	355	444
Deferred compensation	—	—	76	93	113	—	—
Other	20	—	—	—	—	—	—
Working capital provided from operations, excluding extraordinary charge	$ 1,407	$1,882	$2,094	$2,617	$3,090	$ 2,011	$2,695
Working capital provided from extraordinary charge (net extraordinary charge—$395,000; charges not involving the use of working capital—$552,000)	127	—	—	—	—	—	1,266
Increase in long-term debt	2,000	1,000	—	355	400	—	1,272
Proceeds from sale of common stock ...	—	—	—	—	—	—	—
Proceeds from disposal of interests related to real estate partnership	2,525	—	—	—	18	—	—
Exercise of stock options	—	—	—	—	—	—	—
Disposition of property and equipment	18	26	33	8	34	—	—
Sale of treasury stock	18	—	—	—	—	—	—
Decrease in other assets	—	111	—	—	—	—	—
	$ 6,096	$3,019	$2,126	$2,981	$3,542	$ 2,011	$5,233

EXHIBIT 4 *(continued)*

	Year Ended March 31					(Unaudited) Nine Months Ended December 31	
	1972	1973	1974	1975	1976	1975	1976
Application:							
Cash dividends	—	—	$ 277	$ 481	$ 641	$ 477	$ 662
Property and equipment	$ 168	$ 318	345	1,749	1,241	884	1,028
Reduction in long-term liabilities	1,549	910	575	2	329	258	—
Purchase of treasury stock	—	63	30	90	43	—	—
Investment and long-term receivables	980	—	—	—	—	—	—
Increase in other assets	2	—	119	136	173	126	609
	$ 2,697	1,291	$1,346	$2,458	$2,427	$ 1,745	$2,299
Increase in working capital	$ 3,398	$1,728	$ 780	$ 523	$1,116	$ 266	$2,934
Changes in components of working capital:							
Increase (decrease) current assets:							
Cash	$ 554	$ 858	$1,027	$ 193	$1,332	$ 104	$ (559)
Contract receivables	(2,277)	1,727	1,005	4,624	5,540	1,075	5,629
Equity in unconsolidated joint ventures	1,294	(18)	1,142	656	219	1,777	1,499
Material and supplies inventory	149	10	100	512	(272)	(396)	(87)
Other	184	(137)	138	18	(115)	(142)	(19)
	$ (96)	$2,441	$3,412	$6,002	$6,704	$ 2,418	$6,463
Increase (decrease) in current liabilities:							
Notes payable to banks	$(1,900)	$ (500)	—	$ 970	$ 30	$ 30	$3,000
Accounts payable	(1,445)	109	$ 271	1,638	1,313	64	1,012
Accrued liabilities	144	(752)	720	(174)	248	(1,255)	(821)
Advance payments on uncompleted contracts	(639)	52	282	544	1,218	1,386	(597)
Installment obligation	—	—	—	250	50	50	—
Long-term debt due within one year	1	272	(291)	—	—	—	—
Minority interests in consolidated joint ventures	—	—	—	—	289	150	118
Deferred income taxes	345	1,532	1,648	2,251	2,440	1,727	817
	$(3,494)	$ 713	$2,631	$5,480	$5,588	$ 2,152	$3,529
Increase in working capital	$ 3,398	$1,728	$ 780	$ 523	$1,116	$ 266	$2,934

See accompanying notes.

D.C. CONTRACTING, INC.
Notes to Consolidated Financial Statements
March 31, 1975, March 31, 1976, and December 31, 1976

1. Summary of Significant Accounting Policies

Consolidation—The consolidated financial statements, from which appropriate eliminations have been made for intercompany transactions, include the accounts of D.C. Contracting, Inc., its wholly owned subsidiaries, D.C. Midwest, Inc. (formerly Amelco Electric Company, Inc.) and D.C. International Corporation; and joint ventures in which the company has a majority share. Other joint ventures (in which the company's share is generally 20 percent to 50 percent are accounted for on the equity method and contract income and costs and expenses in the consolidated statement of income include the company's proportionate share of these items from such ventures.

Accounting for contracts—Income from contracts, including joint venture contracts, is recorded on the percentage-of-completion method utilizing engineering estimates when experience is sufficient to project final results with reasonable accuracy. Under this method, there is included in income that proportion of the total contract price which the cost of

EXHIBIT 4 (continued)

the work completed bears to the total estimated cost of each contract. When a loss is anticipated on a contract, the entire amount of the estimated loss is provided for in the current period. Contract receivables have been adjusted by the following amounts to reflect income on the percentage-of-completion method:

Pensions—There is a noncontributory pension plan for salaried employees and also defined contributions are made to pension plans for employees covered under union agreements. There is no liability for past service costs for employees under the union plans. Pension costs for the salaried employees' plan are accrued and funded currently,

At March 31

1972	1973	1974	1975	1976
$(193,000)	$211,000	$(594,000)	$(341,000)	$(2,260,000)

Pursuant to industry practice, unbilled contract retainage is classified as a current asset, and approximately $2.2 million relates to contracts with anticipated completion dates after March 31, 1977. The following amounts of unbilled retainage are included in contract receivables:

including amortization of past service costs over 30 years.

2. Acquisition

See Note (g) to Consolidated Statement of Income for the acquisition of D.C. Midwest,

At March 31

1972	1973	1974	1975	1976
$2,923,000	$3,204,000	$3,404,000	$4,862,000	$6,841,000

Income from contracts is determined for federal and state income tax purposes under the completed contract method. Deferred income taxes, arising principally from the difference in contract accounting for book and tax purposes, relate to items included in current assets and accordingly are classified as a current liability.

Material and supplies inventory—Inventory is stated at the lower of cost, determined on the first-in, first-out method, or market.

Depreciation, amortization, and maintenance and repairs—Depreciation is determined principally on the straight-line basis, over estimated useful lives of 25 to 40 years for buildings and 3 to 10 years for furniture, machinery, and equipment.

The cost of ordinary maintenance and repairs and minor renewals of property and equipment are charged to income. Major replacements or renewals are capitalized and the items replaced are retired.

Upon sale or retirement of property and equipment, the cost and accumulated depreciation are removed from the respective accounts and any gain or loss is included in income for the year.

Investment credit—Investment tax credits which have not been material in amount are applied as a reduction of income taxes on the flow-through method.

Inc. (formerly Amelco Electric Company, Inc.) as of January 31, 1975.

3. Foreign Operations

See Note (h) to Consolidated Statement of Income for information with respect to foreign operations.

4. Income Taxes

On the basis of its tax returns, the company has net operating loss carryforwards at March 31, 1976, of approximately $2.2 million. These carryforwards, resulting from the difference in contract accounting for book and tax purposes (see Note 1), are available to reduce taxable income generally during fiscal years ending through March 31, 1981.

In addition, there are preacquisition operating loss carryforwards for tax purposes of approximately $1 million attributable to D.C. Midwest which can be used only against its separate taxable income and which generally expire ratably over fiscal years ending in 1978. Approximately $430,000 of such operating losses have been recognized by D.C. Midwest since date of acquisition for financial accounting purposes resulting in a tax benefit of $215,000, which has been credited in consolidation to the cost of property and equipment at date of acquisition of D.C. Midwest.

EXHIBIT 4 *(concluded)*

Based upon anticipated future activities, the company estimates the cash outlay for income taxes in 1977 will exceed income tax expense in that year by approximately $2.5 million. Such excess has been estimated on assumptions as to future events which are expected to result in future recognition for tax purposes of gross profits from completion of contracts which have been previously recognized for financial accounting purposes on the percentage-of-completion basis.

In fiscal year 1977, the company formed a Domestic International Sales Corporation ("DISC"). In accordance with the provisions of the Internal Revenue Code, taxes of approximately $133,000 are not currently payable, all of which are attributable to fiscal 1977 (through the nine months ended December 31, 1976,) operations. Since the company does not intend to act in such a manner as to terminate this tax deferral, no provision has been made in the accompanying financial statements for such taxes.

5. Note Payable to Bank

This consists of borrowings under a $4 million unsecured line of credit with a bank, entered into in May 1975, of which $3 million is available for general working capital purposes and the remaining $1 million is available on a short-term, specific transactional basis at the discretion of the bank. Additionally, a $300,000 limit is available under the line to be used for letters of credit issued on behalf of the company's subsidiary, D.C. International Corporation. Outstanding letters of credit under this provision reduce the amount available under the working capital portion

the bank in an amount deemed sufficient by the bank; such amount has not been defined in terms of dollars or percentage of credit in use or available.

The approximate average daily amount of borrowings under the line of credit was $1,872,000, the maximum amount of borrowings at the end of any month was $3,533,000 and the weighted average interest rate was 7.5 percent.

6. Unconsolidated Joint Ventures

Condensed combined balance sheet data for these joint ventures are shown below at March 31, 1976:

Assets, principally current, including $1,250,000 unbilled receivables	$13,555,000
Current liabilities	3,822,000
Total venture equity (Company share—$3,945,000)	$ 9,733,000

At March 31, 1976, retained earnings of the company include undistributed joint venture income, less applicable income taxes, from these ventures of approximately $1,050,000.

See Note *(a)* to Consolidated Statement of Income for the company's proportionate share of the operations of these ventures.

[Notes 7 and 8 omitted.]

9. Renegotiation

Certain of the company's contracts are subject to the Renegotiation Act of 1951. In the opinion of management, no excess profits have been realized.

10. Supplementary Income Statement Information

	Year Ended March 31				
	1972	1973	1974	1975	1976
Taxes, other than income:					
Payroll	$1,186,000	$1,502,000	$1,983,000	$2,266,000	$3,141,000
Other	103,000	110,000	115,000	141,000	201,000
Total	$1,289,000	$1,612,000	$2,098,000	$2,407,000	$3,342,000

of the line. The line bears interest at a rate equal to the bank's published "prime" rate. There is no formal compensating balance arrangement with the bank, but it is understood that the company will maintain balances at

Maintenance and repairs, depreciation, rents, and advertising costs were not individually in excess of 1 percent of total contract income. There were no royalties or amortization of intangible assets during the periods.

Questions

1. Before beginning your analysis of the company's long-term contract accounting and the company's financial statement data, try to understand the kind of company D.C. Contracting is and the nature of the industry in which it operates. What are the key success factors in this industry? How do companies in this industry earn a profit?

2. What is the company's strategy? How successful does management believe D.C. Contracting has been in the past? In the future?

3. Do the financial statements reflect management's views?

4. How liquid is D.C. Contracting? How do you rate the quality of its earnings? Does the company's funds flow statement reflect your views? Would an alternative format capture your perception of the company's liquidity and earnings quality?

5. Would you be willing to increase D.C. Contracting's line of credit from $5 to $11 million? Why?

CASE 11-5

A. T. Bliss and Company, Inc.
Revenue Recognition

On Monday, February 7, 1983, the following article appeared in *The Wall Street Journal:*

A. T. Bliss Holders Found That Friday Wasn't Very Blissful
Solar-Heater Concern's Shares Plunged in Heated Trading on 'Sell Order' and Rumors

By Jim Montgomery

Staff Reporter of *The Wall Street Journal*

For A. T. Bliss and Company shareholders, Friday was anything but blissful.

Shares in the distributor of solar waterheat- ing systems caught fire in over-the-counter trading, ignited by a broker's "sell" recommendations and rumors. One of them, untrue,

---

was that this newspaper was preparing a "blistering" article about Bliss, to run in today's editions.

By day's end, 371,340 shares had changed hands at wildly gyrating prices, plunging to $15 bid in the morning—down more than 50 percent from $30.50 late Thursday—then recovering to $26 about midafternoon before declining to $24.375 late Friday.

Bliss shares peaked January 20 at $38.75 bid. That was shortly after the company, based in Pompano Beach, Florida, estimated that earnings tripled in 1982. Through 1982's first nine months, the shares fluctuated between $4.125 and $8.875.

At its nadir, Friday's price drop wiped out $58.1 million of the market value of the 3.75 million shares outstanding, reducing their aggregate value to $56.3 million from $114.4 million Thursday.

The shares' market value of $87.7 million late Friday reflected a one-day fall of 23 percent.

And Bliss's president, Edward J. Roy, whose own holding of 1 million shares represents about 27 percent of the total, was furious. He aimed his sharpest words at First of Michigan Corporation, a regional brokerage house in Detroit that he said issued a "sell order" to its 26 branch offices a few minutes after trading ended Thursday.

He said everything happened because First of Michigan "decided to take a profit and acted in a very unprofessional manner. The manner in which they conducted themselves was reprehensible." He also conceded there had been "a personality conflict between myself" and a First of Michigan official, but declined to elaborate.

First of Michigan officials couldn't be reached for comment.

Mr. Roy estimated that First of Michigan held "more than half a million shares" of Bliss for its customers who, on the basis of an earlier "buy" recommendation from the brokerage firm, "were very heavy in the stock in the $5 and $6 range."

He said that First of Michigan sold many of those shares in Friday's frantic market— when volume shot five times ahead of the previous day—and added: "A broker makes a living on commissions from buying and selling."

The executive said most calls he got from holders Friday and Saturday expressed "puzzlement" over the "sell" order.

He claimed that other callers were, like him, "irate over the way First of Michigan treated its customers and contributed to a disorderly market." In the end, he said "First of Michigan hurt its customers and hurt itself. The market will recover. Just watch it on Monday."

Though repeated efforts to reach First of Michigan officials were unsuccessful, an analyst for the firm said Friday that it changed its recommendation on Bliss shares to "sell" because it doesn't see any indication "that solar tax credits will be extended beyond 1985" and it believes that the Internal Revenue Service "may be taking a dimmer view of solar tax shelters."

Mr. Roy disputed that view. "Our information," he said, "is that solar tax credits stand a chance not only of being extended to 1986, but also of being increased." If the credits aren't extended, he said, "it would hurt us, but it wouldn't put us out of business."[1]

Concerning rumors about A. T. Bliss, the above article specifically points out that, "One of them, untrue, was that this newspaper was preparing a 'blistering' article about Bliss, to run in today's editions." While *The Wall Street Journal* did not run such an article on February 7, the *Journal's* weekly counterpart *Barron's National Business and Financial Weekly*[2] did run an article critical of A. T. Bliss and its accounting practices in its February 7, 1983, edition (see Exhibit 3 for a reproduction of the article). Subsequently, *Barron's* carried two more articles critical of A. T. Bliss in its February 21 and February 28, 1983, editions, respectively (see Exhibits 4 and 3 for reproductions of these articles).

---

[1] Reprinted by permission of *The Wall Street Journal.* Copyright © Dow Jones & Company, Inc. (1983). All rights reserved.

[2] Dow Jones & Co., Inc., publishes both *The Wall Street Journal* and *Barron's.*

EXHIBIT 1
A. T. Bliss and Company, Inc.: Special Situation Report

June 25, 1982

price (OTC–ATBL)	5¾–5⅞
Price range 1981–1982	8¼–3⅛

Earnings per share
(Year-end Dec. 31)*

1979	$0.22
1980	$0.61
1981	$1.28
1982 estimated	$2.50
1983 estimated	$4.20

* Adjusted for a 3-for-2 stock split effective August 31, 1981.

Summary and Recommendation

Through shrewd and innovative marketing tactics, A. T. Bliss has emerged as perhaps the leading company involved in solar energy. Its sales and leasing program enables Florida homeowners to receive the benefits of solar hot water heating systems without making the costly capital expenditures necessary to purchase the system outright. The current severe recession has made consumers even more price-conscious, and the Bliss plan enables homeowners to save nearly 75 percent on hot water costs over the first two years of the plan and at least 50 percent subsequently. These savings incentives have spurred brisk demand for the Solar-Bliss™ hot water systems, which are currently being leased out at the rate of 500 a month. Each system sold (to a limited partnership which then enters into an agreement with Bliss's leasing agent) produces gross sales for Bliss of $3,600. At the same time, Bliss's complex but highly efficient operating structure results in extremely high profit margins—32 percent on gross sales in 1981 and an estimated 40 percent and 41 percent in 1982 and 1983, respectively.

We regard these shares at current price levels as deeply undervalued relative to the company's outstanding sales and earnings growth potential over the next few years. On this score, we suggest purchase of the stock by growth-oriented investors seeking superior capital gains potential. Currently the stock is trading at a mere 2.3 times our 1982 earnings-per-share estimate and a minuscule 1.3 times our 1983 estimate.

A Marketing System Patterned after CATV

A. T. Bliss's approach to solar hot water systems is fashioned after the cable television industry. If individual homeowners were required to purchase a share of the transmission lines, satellite, home equipment, etc., the cost would be prohibitive, and the cable TV industry as we know it today would be nonexistent. Instead, by selling the equipment to third-party interests, cable TV becomes affordable to homeowners who do not actually own the system but instead pay a modest monthly rental and maintenance fee.

Bliss's marketing plan is similar. It sells the solar hot water systems to a limited partnership which is interested in short-term tax credits and long-term rental income. The system is then leased to Florida homeowners whose hot water costs are reduced by about 75 percent for the first two years and by at least 50 percent per month thereafter. Hence, Bliss is able to offer consumers an affordable solar hot water system and an attractive alternative to electrically heated water, the only other type available to Florida residents.

Because Forida is regarded as the premier solar hot water state, the Bliss system is marketed exclusively in that area. Besides its abundant sunshine, Florida is burdened with one of the nation's highest electricity rates, with residential rates in recent years increasing more rapidly than in any other state. For example, from an average residential electric utility rate per 1,000 kwh of $18.90 in 1970, the Florida homeowner is currently paying a punishing $70 (approx.), on average, per 1,000 kwh. Moreover, no relief is in sight; Florida residential electricity rates are expected to continue to escalate at an above-average pace.

Modus Operandi

Bliss's intricate operating structure is fashioned to provide Florida homeowners an economical alternative to electric hot water heating and at the same time enable Bliss to achieve exceptionally high profit margins. Bliss has virtually no overhead and incurs no research and development expenditures. The following details Bliss's method of operation.

Equinox Solar, Inc.

Formed in May 1980 with the aid of Bliss, which purchased 50 percent of Equinox's outstanding common shares, Hialeah, Florida-based Equinox Solar in August 1980 sold 3

EXHIBIT 1 *(continued)*

million common shares at 25 cents each without the aid of an underwriter. Of the 9 million Equinox shares currently outstanding (OTC–EQIX–½–⅝), Bliss owns 33.3 percent, which has a current market value of about $1.5 million.

As Bliss's manufacturing affiliate, Equinox produces the solar flat plate collectors and the solar fluid handling modules used for the hot water heating. It also supplies to Bliss under private label the hot water system. The complete manufacturing cost of the entire system is about $900. Bliss owns no patents.

The high-quality Bliss solar panel had the highest BTU rating in its class of 100 in a May 1980 performance efficiency test conducted by the Florida Solar Energy Center, a respected solar research entity operated by the State of Florida. Bliss's collector was also tested under various weather conditions by the Metropolitan Dade County Authority and approved for use there.

Solar water heating is a mature technology and no major advances are anticipated. The first solar hot water heating system on record was in France in 1872, and some systems have been functioning in southern Florida for at least 50 years.

While the solar energy industry is quite competitive stateside, only about 25 companies derive as much as half of their total revenues from the sale of solar products. The electric solar heater retrofit market is the most attractive segment of the solar market, since the hot water heater can account for as much as 60 percent of an average family's electric bill. It is especially attractive in Florida where electricity costs have increased as much as 270 percent since January 1969.

The Solar-Bliss™ hot water system consists of a collector, valves, pumps, temperature sensors, control units, and auxiliary heating equipment.

Incorporating a black-coated copper "absorber plate" and copper tubing which is connected to the residence's water tank, the collector, placed on the homeowner's roof, converts radiant solar energy into heat. Valves, pumps, temperature sensors, and control units help circulate the water through the copper tubing and the collector. As the sun's rays are collected, the water is heated.

Although in sun-rich Florida solar energy is able to supply about 90 percent of a family's hot water needs, the Bliss system includes a conventionally powered backup system for periods of exceptionally inclement weather or unusually high demand.

Aqua-Solar Associates

Bliss sells its solar hot water systems for $3,600 each to Aqua-Solar Associates, a limited partnership which offers interests in the partnership (in $150,000 and $75,000 units) to individuals seeking tax benefits. As the general partner of the limited partnership, Bliss has unlimited liability for the partnership. If the partnership is unable to pay for the equipment, the general partner is required to do so.

A management agreement is then entered into between Aqua-Solar and Nationwide Power Corporation, which markets and leases the systems to homeowners and is responsible for the installation, maintenance, and insurance of the systems.

Two federal tax credits are important to the limited partnership. Besides the regular investment tax credit of 10 percent, an energy tax credit of 15 percent is available. The energy tax credit will expire December 31, 1985, unless extended. Since the tax shelter effect is the salable feature of the solar hot water system, significant negative changes in investment and solar energy tax credits could obviously adversely impact Bliss's sales and earnings and would necessitate a change in marketing strategy.

However, recent legislative changes regarding solar energy have been favorable. For instance, the Economic Recovery Tax Act of 1981 excluded solar equipment from the new "at risk" provisions applicable to property eligible for investment tax credits. The "at risk" provision states that in order to take 100 percent depreciation and 100 percent of the investment tax credit for the purchased property, the payment must be made in cash or with full recourse negotiable notes. Exclusion from the "at risk" provision means that solar energy equipment may be purchased largely with nonrecourse notes without sacrificing the tax credits.

Bliss requires a 50 percent and 40 percent down payment from investors purchasing the $75,000 and $150,000 units, respectively, with the balance payable on a 10-year, 9 percent per annum interest-bearing note. The equipment sold is considered collateral for the note and may be repossessed by Bliss in the event of default by the purchaser. About 90 percent of the total sales contracts signed in 1981 involved recourse notes and the balance was nonrecourse notes.

Over the past three years, Bliss has extended the following terms on purchases of the equipment.

EXHIBIT 1 *(continued)*

TABLE 1

	1981	1980	1979
Down payment	25%	25%	20%
6% interest payable over 30 years	–0–	–0–	80%
7½% interest payable over 15 years	–0–	75%	–0–
9% interest payable over 10 years	75%	–0–	–0–
	100%	100%	100%

As can be gleaned from Table 1, there has been a trend towards more favorable terms for Bliss, with down payment requirements and interest rates increasing and with note maturities shortening. This will continue to have a salutary effect on Bliss's profits.

Prior to 1982, Bliss sold its solar systems directly to individual purchasers. On October 28, 1980, the SEC commenced an investigation to determine if Bliss had been and were offering for sale and selling securities contrary to the provisions of the Securities Act of 1933 and the Securities and Exchange Act of 1934. In essence, the SEC wanted to determine if Bliss's marketing method at the time constituted the sale of property or the sale of a security. (In 1982, Bliss began marketing its solar equipment strictly to limited partnerships through a qualified offering.) Bliss was informed by the Miami Branch office of the SEC in January 1982 that the branch had completed its investigation and that a recommendation to the commission was forthcoming seeking authority to negotiate a settlement with Bliss or to institute proceedings against Bliss based on the conclusions drawn from the investigation. At this time, Bliss is unable to predict the outcome of the proceedings and settlement negotiations. However, the company's counsel has been advised by a number of independent certified accountants that the company's financial statements for 1981 and for prior years as stated in the 1981 annual report and 10-K conform with generally accepted accounting principles. As of this time, the SEC has not indicated whether it approves or disapproves Bliss's current reporting procedures and marketing methods which were drawn up strictly to the guidelines of SEC rule 146 and were reviewed by a special outside SEC council.

At the time of executing a contract and receiving the cash down payment, Bliss recognizes a sale, records all costs of the sale, and establishes an allowance for doubtful collections and reduction of the long-term notes receivable to present value due to lower than prevailing interest rates. For example, upon execution of a $75,000 contract, Bliss would immediately record $75,000 in revenues, although only 50 percent of that amount, or $37,500, would initially actually be collected in cash. From the $37,500 balance to be collected in 10-year, 9 percent per annum notes, a 40 percent allowance (reserve) is taken. This allowance includes, first, an adjustment to present value for lower than prevailing interest rates. Bliss discounts the difference between the current 20-year Treasury notes rate and its own 9 percent rate, and this amount appears on the income statement as a deduction from gross revenues to arrive at a net revenue figure. This discount (which is actually deducted from the face of the note) is amortized and picked up as income over the life of the note.

The allowance also includes a reserve for doubtful collections, considered an operating expense. Before 1982, Bliss had been taking a very conservative 50 percent reserve for the reduction of long-term notes receivable to present value due to lower than prevailing interest rates and for possible bad accounts. However, based on its experience of the prior three years—virtually no bad debts—Bliss recently decided to lower its reserve to 40 percent. This should have a significant positive impact on 1982 earnings. As the notes are paid off, the reserves will be reversed—cash will be debited and the notes receivable and reserve accounts will be credited. As a result of its conservative allowance policy, Bliss has a sizable amount of unrealized profits.

Because Bliss sells its solar equipment to investors seeking a tax shelter, its sales and earnings are subject to seasonal biases. More specifically, about 50 percent of Bliss's sales are recorded in the fourth quarter.

Nationwide Power Corporation

With seven offices located in central and southern Florida, Lakeland-based Nationwide Power Corporation, as Bliss's exclusive leasing agent, installs and maintains the Solar-Bliss™ hot water heating systems. As a property manager, Nationwide leases the equipment for the limited partnership in return for a percentage of the gross revenues.

A privately held Florida corporation formed in June 1980, Nationwide now has about 6,000 homes under lease and is currently adding to this figure at the rate of about 500 a month. Bliss's goal is to reach an average monthly installation rate of 1,000 in 1983.

EXHIBIT 1 *(continued)*

Prior to 1982, Bliss was paying Nationwide a promotional fee of $500 per system leased, but this fee was recently eliminated entirely. This too will have a positive impact on 1982 earnings.

Although Nationwide plans to gradually expand its offices into northern Florida, it has no immediate plans to market the system outside of the state. Florida is regarded as an exceptionally attractive market for solar hot water heating because of ideal weather conditions, a relatively dense population, and the very high cost of the alternative energy source (in this case, electricity).

Despite Nationwide's indicated rapid expansion, there appears to be no imminent danger of saturation. Indeed, current demographics suggest a limited penetration thus far and ample potential for further growth.

It is estimated that 2.5 million single-family Florida homes are currently qualified candidates for solar hot water heating (based on a research study by Solar Engineering magazine, six of the top seven domestic solar markets are in Florida). Moreover, in Bliss's current marketing area, there are about 87,000 new homes coming on stream each year, or nearly 15 times Nationwide's current annual installment rate. Meanwhile, Bliss's unique marketing approach should continue to keep its competitors at bay.

Nationwide currently operates offices in South Dade, North Dade, Broward, West Palm Beach, Tampa, Lakeland, and Orlando, Florida, and each office has the *capability* of installing 150 units a month.

Of these locations, five are included in the top nationally ranked metropolitan areas for solar hot water heating. Over the next half year, Nationwide plans to open new offices in Daytona, Ft. Meyers, Ft. Pierce, Melborne, and Sarasota, Florida.

Bliss has the option to purchase 3 million common shares of Nationwide Power after July 2, 1983, but before July 2, 1986, at a price of $1 million, payable in cash or common stock of A. T. Bliss and calculated at the market price at the date of payment. Nationwide is expected to be brought public within the next year.

The Homeowner

As part of the agreement with Nationwide, the homeowner enters into a two-year plan and pays an initial charge of $478.80 to cover labor installation expenses and costs of certain parts of the solar water heating system not leased. At the end of the two-year period, the homeowner has the option of either having the system removed at no additional cost or to lease the system at a modest monthly rate which would be no more than 50 percent of what the electric utility would charge to heat the water. In the event that the homeowner decides to discontinue use of the solar hot water system at the end of the initial two-year contract, Bliss is obligated to guarantee performance of Nationwide in leasing the equipment. While none of the contracts have yet reached the renewal date, a recent survey of the company's customers revealed that 95 percent were satisfied with the system, suggesting that the vast majority would choose to lease the system following the initial two-year trial period.

Including a federal tax credit of 40 percent or $191.52 for installation, parts, and labor, the homeowner's effective cost for the initial two-year period averages $11.97 per month, which compares very favorably with the average $45 monthly charge to heat water electrically in Bliss's marketing area. The homeowner receives no tax credits after the first two years, i.e., during the lease period.

For the initial charge of $478.80 covering the first two years, Bliss offers the homeowners three alternative payment schedules:

a. The amount may be paid off in one lump sum. To encourage upfront cash payments, Bliss offers the homeowner 90-days' free use of the equipment.

b. The amount may be paid off in four steps: $28.80 down and $150 a month for three months.

c. Homeowners may choose to pay the amount in monthly installments with an effective 18 percent annual rate of interest.

For the homeowner, the Nationwide plan provides solar hot water heating sans the substantial initial capital investment required to purchase a system outright. To wit, in most states because there is a higher retail markup on the system, the initial cash outlay necessary to purchase a new system is typically $3,000–$5,000. In Florida, because of a highly competitive solar water heater market and because the state does not provide a solar tax credit (44 states currently provide a solar income tax credit), there is a smaller markup and the initial cash outlay is a bit less—about $2,500. By leasing the system from Nationwide, the homeowner, as noted, needs only to put down $478.80.

EXHIBIT 1 *(continued)*

Once the solar system is installed, the savings are substantial vis-à-vis the costs required to heat the same water electrically. Moreover, as Florida electric utility rates continue to increase, as expected, the Nationwide plan would become even more attractive to homeowners.

Because of Florida's dynamic population growth rate, most of the state's electric public utilities have insatiable capital outlay demands, which should lead to consistent rate hikes.

Consider the situation of Florida Power & Light (FPL) which serves eastern and southern Florida and is a major factor in the bulk of Nationwide's current marketing areas:

1. It is estimated that FPL's capital outlays in the 1981–85 period would be a staggering $4.2 billion.
2. Its fuel costs are increasing rapidly. In 1981, FPL's fuel and purchased power costs soared 41 percent, a much steeper rise than the 29 percent increase in revenues, and another hefty increase in its fuel and purchased power costs is anticipated for 1982.
3. FPL's own cost of capital is increasing. In early June, the company sold $100 million of long-term bonds with an onerous 16.4 percent rate of interest.
4. Because of its huge capital outlay needs and its own increasing expenses, additional rate relief should be necessary. Along these lines, in April FPL filed for a $281 million rate increase and an interim $65.9 million increase which, if approved in full, would raise the current average residential bill a hefty 14 percent to $71.58 a month from $62.87.

Financial Position

Bliss's long-term debt was as follows:

Table 2

December 31	1981	1980	1979
Mortgage payable, 11½%	$ 296,967	$296,967	$300,000
Notes payable, 6%	—	—	198,600
Notes payable, 9%	2,336,250	—	—
	$2,633,217	$296,967	$498,600
Less: Amounts due within one year	10,830	5,671	79,000
Total	$2,622,387	$291,296	$419,600

The mortgage debt is payable in monthly installments based on a 20-year amortization period with a balloon payment at the end of 7½ years.

The 9 percent notes payable are due to Equinox Solar, Inc., in 1983. However, it is likely that at least one half of the amount due will be prepaid in 1982.

Since Bliss reports its sales on the installment basis, a provision is made for deferred income taxes. This amounted to $650,000 in 1979, $1,837,000 in 1980, and $2,967,000 in 1981.

Recent Results

For the year ended December 31, 1981, a sharp increase in the number of Solar-Bliss™ systems sold (to about 3,900 from around 2,100 in 1980) and a notable improvement in the profit margin to an unusually high 31.6 percent from 24.7 percent spurred strong sales and earnings growth. Gross revenues increased 66 percent to $15,424,723 from $9,316,394. Net income jumped 117 percent to $4,878,353 from $2,304,627. Earnings per share (adjusted for a 3-for-2 stock split effective August 31, 1981), on about a 1 percent increase in outstanding shares, increased 110 percent to $1.28 per share from $0.61 in 1980. A portion of the 1981 income gain is due to $781,000 of investment tax and energy tax credits earned on the equipment owned by Bliss and leased to outside parties.

For the three-month period ended March 31, typically the company's weakest quarter, Bliss recorded gross revenues of $607,714, compared to $217,497 for the same period last year. Net income totaled $95,335 or 2 cents a share versus $94,789 or 2 cents. This excludes an extraordinary gain of $205,000 (net of taxes) or 6 cents a share in the 1982 quarter resulting from the company's sale of 4 million shares of Jiffy Industries, Inc. (OTC–JIFY–½–⅝) to Edward Roy, Bliss's president, for a total consideration of $500,000.

The bulk of the first quarter's income was derived from interest income on Bliss's rapidly growing portfolio of notes receivable.

Forecast

For 1982 and 1983, we foresee substantial increases in Bliss's sales and earnings. Since Bliss has virtually no overhead, it is able to attain an exceptionally high profit margin on gross sales. In 1981, the margin was about 32

EXHIBIT 1 *(continued)*

percent. For both 1982 and 1983, several factors should propel margins sharply higher. First, this year the $500 per unit promotional fee to Nationwide has been eliminated. Secondly, also in 1982, Bliss lowered its allowance for the reduction of long-term notes receivable to present value due to lower than prevailing interest rates and for doubtful accounts to 40 percent from 50 percent. Thirdly, Bliss in both 1982 and 1983 will garner sharply higher interest income due to the rapidly growing size of its receivables portfolio and the higher rates collected by Bliss on the notes. Fourthly, Bliss will experience increased income from discount on notes. Finally, we expect Bliss in 1982 to prepay at least half of the 9 percent, $2.3 million note due to Equinox Solar. This would reduce interest expense and produce higher margins in 1983. We anticipate Bliss to earn 40 percent and 41 percent on gross sales in 1982 and 1983, respectively.

As noted above, Nationwide has been leasing the solar hot water systems at the rate of 500 a month or an annual pace of 6,000

units. However, Bliss has recently been pressing Nationwide to increase its lease rate, and this effort could bear fruit with an acceleration of lease agreements in the final half of 1982. For all of 1982, we conservatively estimate Nationwide to lease about 6,000 units and, assuming a perfect parity between the units leased by Nationwide and the units bought by the limited partnership, this would result in 1982 revenues from sales of $21.6 million. To this amount we add other revenues of $2.0 million and $400,000 for interest income and income from discount on notes, respectively, to produce gross revenues of $24 million. Deducting $3 million for adjustment to present value of lower than prevailing interest rates results in net revenues of $21 million. From this we subtract $11.4 million cost of sales, operating expenses, and provision for income taxes to arrive at estimated net income of $9.6 million or $2.50 a share.

For 1983, Bliss's goal is to lease the solar units at about a 12,000 annual rate. We consider a 10,000 annual rate or about 835 a month a more likely scenario. This would pro-

TABLE 3
Worksheet*

Year-End December 31	1982 Estimates	1983 Estimates
Units sold	6,000	10,000
Price per unit.....................	× $3,600	× $3,600
Revenues from sales..............	$ 21,600,000	$ 36,000,000
Additional revenues:		
Interest income	2,000,000	3,000,000
Income for discount on notes	400,000	1,000,000
	2,400,000	4,000,000
Gross revenues	24,000,000	40,000,000
Adjustment to present value for lower than prevailing interest rates	(3,000,000)	(5,000,000)
Net revenues.....................	21,000,000	35,000,000
Cost of sales and operating expenses and provision for income taxes using 40% (1982) and 41% (1983) profit margins on gross revenues	(11,400,000)	(18,600,000)
Net income	$ 9,600,000	$ 16,400,000
Shares outstanding	3,850,000	3,900,000
Earnings per share................	$2.50	$4.20

* Assuming perfect parity per year between units sold and units leased.

EXHIBIT 1 *(concluded)*

duce gross revenues of about $40 million, of which we feel $16.4 million or $4.20 per share would flow to net income.

Based on these projections, we regard the shares of A. T. Bliss as deeply undervalued at current quoted prices. Consequently, we suggest purchase of the stock by growth-oriented investors seeking superior capital gains potential and able to assume a moderate degree of risk. First of Michigan Corporation makes a market in the stock. There are cur- *rently about 3.8 million shares outstanding, of which about 1.5 million are in actual float.*

James J. Leonard
Investment Research
June 25, 1982
Additional information available upon request.

EXHIBIT 2
A. T. Bliss and Company, Inc.: Follow-Up Report

11/11/82 price (ATBL–OTC)	18¼–18⅜
Price range 1982	18⅜–4⅛
Earnings per share*:	
1979...........................	$0.22
1980...........................	$0.61
1981...........................	$1.28
1982 estimated	$3.00
1983 estimated	$4.50
Indicated dividend	–0–
P/E ratio	9.4

* Excludes extraordinary gains.

Summary and Recommendation

Pompano Beach, Florida-based A. T. Bliss has emerged as perhaps the leading company involved in solar energy. Its sole product, solar hot water heating systems, is marketed in Florida where electricity rates are among the highest in the nation. Bliss's solar systems are produced by Equinox Solar (30 percent owned) and are sold to a limited partnership which offers interests to investors seeking short-term tax benefits and long-term rental income.

When the solar systems are sold to the limited partnership for $3,600 a unit, Bliss books the entire $3,600 as revenues. Bliss requires a 25 percent ($900) down payment, about equal to *its* cost of the equipment. The receivable (75 percent) is financed at 9 percent, payable in monthly installments. Against the receivable, Bliss charges about 40 percent to various reserves.

Due to Florida's relatively high electric rates, solar hot water heating is an extremely attractive alternative to conventional water heating. Bliss's solar system, marketed by Nationwide Power Corporation, Bliss's authorized leasing agent, reduces the cost of the hot water for Florida homeowners by at least 50 percent. These savings incentives have spurred brisk demand for the solar systems, with Nationwide Power currently leasing the units at a rate of about 10,000 a year (gross), up sharply from a 3,000–4,000 rate earlier in the year.

The acceleration of installations should propel 1982 revenues and earnings to record levels. We have raised our 1982 gross revenues estimate to $29 million from $24 million and our earnings estimate to $3.00 per share from $2.50. Our 1983 estimates have been boosted to $43 million from $40 million for gross revenues and to $4.50 from $4.20 for earnings per share. In light of the sharp increase in the stock price from our original recommendation, we have reduced our recommendation from a buy to a hold. First of Michigan Corporation makes a market in the stock.

Expansion Plans

Florida is such a fertile area for solar hot water heating, Bliss has no *immediate* plans to expand outside that state. Besides its abundant sunshine, Florida has one of the highest electricity rates in the nation. With a Bliss solar water heater installed, the homeowner's hot water costs total a mere $11.97 per month, which compares very favorably with the state's average *electric* hot water cost of $45 a month for a family of four.

In addition to the sizable solar water heat-

EXHIBIT 2 *(concluded)*

ing retrofit market currently existing in Florida, substantial sales potential exists with the 80,000 or so new single-family homes coming on stream each year.

Nationwide currently operates seven Florida-based offices with five new offices scheduled for opening in 1983 and 12 planned for 1984. Current plans call for expansion into northern Florida no later than early 1984, and possible expansion into other nearby states, such as Georgia, North Carolina, and South Carolina, around 1985.

The SEC Investigation

Since our original research report on A. T. Bliss (dated 6/25/82), there have been no new developments regarding the SEC investigation. Prior to 1982, Bliss had sold the solar equipment directly to individual investors, but the SEC objected to the company's form of accounting for the transactions. Bliss's president, Ed Roy, notes that the SEC investigation of its pre-1982 marketing practices is apparently still open, but that Bliss has not recently heard from the SEC and that there have been no new developments.

The Equinox Solar Holdings

One overlooked development regarding A. T. Bliss is its Equinox Solar (OTC–EQIX–2¼) holdings. At the time we wrote the original Bliss research report, the Equinox stock was trading at ½ and Bliss's holdings of Equinox was valued at $1.5 million. With the Equinox stock currently being quoted at 2¼, Bliss's holdings of Equinox is now valued at $6.75 million, representing an increase in the value of Bliss's holdings in Equinox since our original report of $5.25 million or $1.40 per Bliss share.

EXHIBIT 3

Up & Down Wall Street
By Alan Abelson
Barron's, February 7, 1983

Ignorance is bliss. At least as far as A. T. Bliss is concerned. And that's one Bliss you may be ignorant of. That felicitous name belongs to a Pompano Beach, Florida, company which distributes solar hot water heating systems. Its shares are traded over the counter, and while neither the company nor its works have yet become household names, its stock has done right well. Since 79, when they first were publicly traded, the shares have gone from as close to nothing as you can get (⅛) to over 30. Then suddenly last Friday, they fell to 15 before meeting a few friends on the Street and recovering to a bit above 23.

The NASD held up trading in the shares Friday so that an announcement could be made. What was announced was a rather bemused statement by the company on why its stock took gas (terrible indignity for a solar stock). Bliss bristled that it knew of "no undisclosed corporate developments which would change or impact the financial condition of the company." However, it allowed as it was aware of "a Street recommendation to sell." Street schmeet, Bliss added, it was sticking to its forecast of $6.50 a share this year, up from $4.70.

The source of the sell recommendation also went public in short order. A regional broker, First Michigan Corporation, owned up to having undergone a change of heart on Bliss Thursday night. Reason: "We see no indication that solar tax credits will be extended beyond 1985," and even more frightening, "the IRS may be taking a dimmer view of solar tax shelters." That was enough to send scads of investors (or whatever you want to call them) rushing to come in out of the sun.

With the aid of Kate Welling, we ran a cursory check on Bliss and found that tax credits and tax shelters are not the only clouds on its horizon. For on closer inspection, that exponential growth in sales and earnings Bliss has been blithely racking up doesn't seem to hold water. Last year alone, both reported sales and earnings more than tripled. But there's a small hitch: roughly 75 percent of the revenues on the company's books are really 10-year notes. Those I-owe-yous were issued by limited partnerships that, in turn, lease the equipment to customers—ordinary people like you and me—who agree to keep the units they've leased for only two years. Bliss's sole security on the notes is the solar heating equipment installed in houses across southern Florida.

EXHIBIT 3 *(concluded)*

We'll boil it all down for you: Bliss takes in a huge chunk of revenues, on which it reports earnings, from 10-year notes issued by groups of rich folks who have formed limited partnerships for tax purposes. The rich folks have leased the equipment to homeowners who have agreed to keep it in their houses for two years. And that's all. If the homeowner fails to renew, the partnerships must take the hit; on the other hand, if the partnerships break up—who pays the many years' balance on the notes? You need an especially sunny view of life to think that this arrangement is the equivalent of getting money in the till as soon as something is sold or a service rendered. It's mostly bookkeeping profits, money that, as they say in southern Florida, you can't buy a beer with.*

Up & Down Wall Street
By Alan Abelson
Barron's, February 28, 1983

Last week, you may recall, Michael Brody wrote a great piece about A. T. Bliss and its corporate kin, Jiffy Industries—both run by a chap named Ed Roy. Michael pointed out that the extraordinary earnings record of Bliss (and, by extension, the extraordinary performance of its stock) owed not a little to tax-shelter purchases of Bliss's solar heating equipment and the interesting way Bliss had of accounting for the income from such purchases.

Now, Michael reports another exciting episode in the Bliss saga. Seemingly aware that tax shelters are a seasonal phenomenon occurring late every year, Mr. Roy, in accordance with standard management operating procedures recommended by the Harvard Business School, furloughed his stable of salesmen who had been pushing Bliss's solar equipment and the tax shelters to buy it. Most accepted the sad news with a wan smile and a shrug, but one particularly aggrieved fellow, claiming he had not been paid a fairly considerable sum due him in bonus money, threatened to tell all (whatever that might be) to the SEC.

Well, before you can say, "Cheez it, the cops!" that obstreperous gent found himself in the local hoosegow, courtesy of Mr. Roy, charged with attempted extortion (the collar was made as the check was changing hands). Michael's conversation with some of the gendarmes led him to believe that the constable is not overjoyed at being party to what appears to be merely a corporate family squabble. The ex-salesman, now breathing the bracing air of freedom, thanks to the institution of bail, refuses to say what information he had in mind to take to the SEC. But several government agencies, including that oft-napping watchdog, reportedly are sniffing about Bliss.*

EXHIBIT 4
Burning Daylight

The Story Behind Some Overheated Solar Energy Stocks
By Michael Brody

Why are the solar energy stocks so hot? As even the most cursory observer of the investment scene knows, the surest way to scatter a crowd in Wall Street these days is to mention the word "energy." It seems like ancient history, but in fact a scant three years ago energy was all the rage and shares of companies with even the remotest connection with the sun or the wind, to say nothing of oil and gas, were bid up feverishly. But then a funny thing happened to the price of crude on its way to $100 a barrel.

The global glut of petroleum has turned the oil patch into a disaster area and drowned

EXHIBIT 4 *(continued)*

the hopes of coal, nuclear, and most of the "alternative" energy sources. But unlike their fossil fuel counterparts, beginning last fall, the solar shares have been enjoying a remarkable revival in speculative esteem.

Thus a host of little over-the-counter stocks bearing a solar label have scored absolutely sizzling gains in recent months, leaving even this roaring bull market in their wake. What triggered the rally in this rather far-out sector were earnings, actual or prospective. Not that the country suddenly decided to go solar. No, rather, producers of solar panels benefited from a burst of tax shelter deals. More specifically, investors bought the solar equipment made by these companies and got the special 15 percent federal tax credit on solar hardware: they then leased the panels and such back to homeowners or commercial and industrial users.

In fact, upfront payments by tax shelter purchasers enabled some little companies to show big gains in earnings. Case in point: American Solar King, which reported net of $2.24 million in the quarter ended January 31 versus $27,000 last year. American Solar's stock has been a smashing winner—but so, for that matter, have the shares of companies that can only boast expectations—not the earnings themselves. Besicorp Group, for one; Servamatic Solar Systems, for another. But the most spectacular showing was staged by a pair of little outfits in Pompano Beach, Florida, both the handiwork of local entrepreneur and tax shelter promoter Ed Roy. Roy has been busily building a corporate empire out of solar panels and outdoor toilets for construction sites, and is now branching out, imaginatively, into solar-powered sewage treatment plants.

A couple of Roy's hot numbers are A. T. Bliss, which sells solar equipment to tax shelter investors, and its manufacturing satellite, Equinox Solar. The action of the Bliss shares were bliss, indeed, to their holders, rising from $3 last year to over $40 by the end of January. During the same stretch, the smaller Equinox scored a rather impressive gain, too—over 1,000 percent, from $7/16$ to $5^7/16$.

The perfervid performances of these two were exceeded only by that of another of Roy's companies, Jiffy Industries (formerly Jiffy Johns), which for most of its corporate existence leased out portable privies for construction sites. Jiffy was tabbed by Chase Econometrics as the top-gaining stock in the United States last year, appreciating an incredible 1,660 percent, to $16.50 from 94 cents (ad-

justed for a one-for-five reverse stock split at midyear), and trading as high as $20 recently.

Bliss found itself unexpectedly in the speculative spotlight early this month. A regional brokerage house that had recommended the stock last year put out a "sell" signal. The switch by First of Michigan sent Bliss's shares reeling, to $15 from over $30 on the morning of Friday, February 4. The NASD hurriedly halted trading, whistled up some official comment, and the stock subsequently recovered to around $23. That same day, in sympathy, Jiffy sold off to around $14 from $19, before meeting support. (Bliss, now carried on the NASDAQ National Market list, closed last week at $18 bid; Jiffy, carried on the supplemental list, was quoted at $14.25 bid.)

President Ed Roy, who owns about a third of Bliss's outstanding stock, denounced First of Michigan for acting "in a very unprofessional manner" and claimed that selling by the Detroit brokerage firm's customers represented most of the 371,000 shares traded in that hectic session. Analyst Jim Leonard replies that his firm unloaded only about 20,000 shares on behalf of clients, that Friday; the bulk of the 400,000-odd shares First of Michigan had held for customers, Leonard says, were sold earlier as the stock went into orbit. Repeating his forecast of $6.50 a share in profits this year, up from $4.74 reported for 1982 and $1.28 for 1981, Roy scoffed at First of Michigan's caution that solar tax credits, which have powered the company's tax shelter sales, are in danger of being phased out by Washington after 1985. And, last Friday, after Bliss's stock slipped again to $15.75, Roy announced he would buy stock himself through a charitable foundation he controls, forcing the price back up to $18.

As noted two weeks ago in these pages (Up & Down Wall Street, February 7), regardless of what may or may not be happening in the back rooms of Congressional tax committees, a close look at the nature and quality of Bliss's reported earnings might well cool off a good many investors' enthusiasm. And quite possibly, the same holds true for other red-hot "tax-advantaged" solar leasing operations that have caught the speculative fancy.

Bliss's operating structure is somewhat complicated, but its business is simple enough: leasing solar-powered hot water heaters to homeowners in return for a monthly rental fee. The equipment is bought by Bliss from its manufacturing subsidiary, Equinox Solar, for about $900, and leased to homeowners

EXHIBIT 4 (continued)

through another subsidiary, Nationwide Power Corporation. The homeowner pays $479 to begin with, to cover installation and use of the equipment for the first two years. After that, his monthly rent (currently about $20), according to Bliss, will not exceed half of what his local utility bill would run for a conventional water heater.

If Bliss retained ownership of the equipment, the rentals would hardly provide the sort of spectacular earnings reported for 1982 and forecast for 1983. This is where the tax angle comes in. Bliss, which buys the solar equipment from Equinox for $900 or so, resells it to a tax shelter partnership, Aqua-Solar Associates, for $3,600. Rather a substantial mark-up, since the same Equinox system can be bought from a local Miami dealer for about $1,800. But the tax shelter partners, who invest in units of $150,000, are putting up only $900 in cash for each system—an amount that just meets the actual cost to Bliss of buying the equipment from Equinox. The remaining $2,700, or three quarters of the purchase price, is covered by a 10-year note, bearing interest at 9 percent and amortized in 10 annual payments of $421 each, due every December.

What makes the deal seem more attractive to tax shelter purchasers than the usual equipment leasing arrangement—computers, machinery, or whatever—is the 15 percent federal tax credit on solar investments. Once the equipment is in service, the tax partnership is promised not only a 10 percent investment tax credit but also a 15 percent solar tax credit; that means, in effect, the investor receives an immediate payback of his $900. Of the $479 shelled out by the homeowner, a quarter goes to the leasing subsidiary. Nationwide Power, which also gets a percentage of future rental payments on the unit. The other 75 percent goes to the partnership, which enjoys a five-year accelerated depreciation on the equipment as well, and the lion's share of future rental income.

For its part, Bliss, as noted, takes in $900 in cash, plus 10 equal annual payments each December, of $421. But what Bliss reports as income in the year the tax shelter investment is made is the full $3,600 paid by Aqua-Solar Associates for the equipment, even though three quarters of that is paper. Bliss does take a 40 percent reserve against these "revenues," to hedge against both the lower-than-market rate on the notes and the possibility that those annual payments might not be collected.

(Taxes on the "earnings" are, of course, deferred until they are actually received.)

According to Bliss, roughly 7,000 solar heating systems were installed under earlier tax shelter programs, while 6,000 more are being installed or waiting to be leased, on behalf of the 1982 year-end Aqua-Solar partnerships. Owing to the seasonal nature of tax shelter sales (generally a year-end rush), no new partnerships are likely to be formed until late this year.

Thus, Bliss's net revenues after purchase and leasing of the solar equipment boils down essentially to the year-end payment of $421 it receives for each collector in place. Take off something for salaries and overhead (both admirably low; the operation appears to be run on a shoestring), as well as for lower payments on many of the earlier systems, plus provision for current income taxes, divide by 3.8 million shares outstanding, and *cash* earnings for 1982 and 1983 work out to something around 30 cents and 67 cents, respectively— somewhat short of Bliss's reported $4.74 and predicted $6.50.

Earnings distortions aside, Bliss's "third-party financing" set-up is an eyebrow raiser on other scores. In the first place, Nationwide, which estimated last year that it would be leasing out 1,000 solar heating systems a month by end of 1982, has not come close to that target. The company claims a current monthly rate of 800, but according to informed onlookers, the actual installation rate is 500–600 a month. A hefty backlog of units purchased by the tax shelter partnerships is sitting in warehouses waiting to be leased. And Bliss, which formerly guaranteed to its tax shelter investors the success of Nationwide's leasing efforts, no longer does so.

Secondly, although the shelter is designed to assure significant benefits during the first five years of tax credits and accelerated depreciation write-offs, the investment would require 8 to 10 percent annual rises in electricity rates (and thus rental rates on the solar equipment) to pay off for investors once those tax advantages are exhausted. Slumping oil and coal prices are already making that scenario increasingly unlikely, forcing Bliss to abandon plans to boost the price of the Equinox solar units to $4,000 from $3,600.

If those increases in rentals fail to materialize, investors might be strongly tempted to dissolve their partnerships and stop making payments on the notes after the first five years. The obligations are supposed to be full re-

EXHIBIT 4 *(continued)*

course paper. But Bliss Treasurer Reinhard Mueller acknowledges that the equipment does supposedly provide full collateral. Further, he observes that if the question of legal action against a dissolved tax shelter partnership to recover the remaining principal value of the note ever came up, "whether we actually would proceed against the partner is not necessarily [certain] . . . we probably would have to take a look at it at that time, make a decision about what's best for the company."

Paradoxically, if electric rates and equipment rentals soar, that would sharply enhance the likelihood of homeowners opting out of their lease after the first two years and *buying* a home system instead. (Indeed, at present prices, it makes no sense for anyone to lease a solar heating system rather than buying one and taking advantage of the tax credits. But, as Bliss President Ed Roy notes, the firm's customers "aren't very savvy people." Nationwide's apparent difficulties in getting the systems leased, however, suggest that customers are wising up fast.)

Finally, the quadruple mark-up that Bliss puts on the cost of the Equinox system before selling it to the tax shelter partnership, tax lawyers say, is likely to upset the IRS. If the system is available through retail distributors for as little as $1,800, the IRS may decide that the rental income from the system (as against the tax benefits of ownership) justifies a valuation no higher than that and disallow the rest of the price as qualifying for tax credits and accelerated depreciation. The rest of the investor's $3,600 would have to be treated as a payment for leasing, servicing, and other management services, which could be written off only on a straight-line basis over the life of the agreement. Such a ruling would wreck the entire scheme, since there would no longer be any way that the investor could get his money back.

Bliss holds a one-third interest in Equinox Solar, the manufacturing subsidiary; it has an option on a controlling stake in Nationwide Power, the leasing subsidiary, at a bargain-basement price. While such holdings have appreciated considerably in value on paper, the fortunes of these operations are tied inextricably to that of Bliss itself.

Bliss's 20 percent interest in Jiffy consists of 604,000 shares, purchased at a cost of 5 cents a share (adjusted for a one-for-five reverse split last year), and now valued at $14.25 a share or so. Jiffy is expanding beyond leasing portable privies for construction sites and out-door events to the production and sale to tax shelter investors of solar-powered treatment plants for converting human waste into fertilizer. (Jiffy already manufactures its own portable fiber glass privies and chemical sanitary tanks, and also owns two earlier ventures of Roy's: a comic book publisher and a small motel chain.)

Bliss almost didn't hold on to its stake in Jiffy. According to Roy, analysts in love with Bliss's solar business couldn't understand its connection with an "outhouse outfit," prompting Roy to offer to personally buy Bliss's shares in Jiffy. The suggested price was 62½ cents each for 800,000 shares (adjusted for the reverse split). By last summer, however, when the shareholders were supposed to weigh the offer, Roy, wearing his hat as president of Jiffy Industries, had announced the firm's new solar-powered waste treatment process (which subsequently received a patent and regulatory approval); Jiffy's share price had soared, and it was clear that it was in Bliss's best interest to retain its position. So Roy withdrew his bid.

Since Jiffy declared earnings of 3 cents a share for the fiscal year ending July 31, 1982, the stock—which has been as high as 20—obviously isn't selling on immediate earnings. What has excited investors is hope for its new solar-powered sewage treatment business—which, once again, is being packaged for sale to tax shelter investors. Three plants have been built and sold to limited partnerships for $10 million; Roy plans to build and sell two or three more before July 31, and 10 to 20 in the next fiscal year.

Florida, where Bliss and Jiffy operate, has a massive urban sewage disposal problem, in part because of the Environmental Protection Agency's restrictions on both river and ocean dumping and incineration of untreated sewage. Fertilizer prices, however, are going through the floor, and no matter how cheaply a solar-powered heat-treatment plant works, the economics remain problematic.

Once again, the tax shelter investors are laying out 25 percent cash upfront, which they get back immediately in the form of investment and solar energy tax credits; the remaining $7.5 million is covered by a note at 9 percent, in this case amortized in five equal annual installments, so that the plant is fully paid for by the time all of the accelerated depreciation has been taken. A 35 percent reserve is being set up against the principal of the note; but of the $10 million sale price,

EXHIBIT 4 *(concluded)*

$7.3 million will be reported as 1983 revenues, even though only $2.5 million of the sum will be in cash.

Will the IRS uphold the economic valuation for tax credit purposes of Bliss's and Jiffy's solar systems? Will Congress renew the solar tax credit in 1985? The answers are crucial to the future of both Bliss and Jiffy. And they're highly uncertain. One thing for sure: companies can't pay dividends out of phantom profits.*

Throughout this period, A. T. Bliss's stock price continued to plummet downward. From January 3, 1983, until January 14, 1983, Bliss's shares traded between $24.00 and $31.25 bid on average daily volume of 49,400 shares. From January 17, 1983, until January 28, 1983, Bliss's shares traded between $32.25 and $38.75 bid on average daily volume of 79,500 shares. During the month of February 1983, Bliss's shares traded as follows:

Date	Volume	Bid Prices* High	Low	Close
02/01/83	42,000	$ NA	$ NA	$33.75
02/02/83	32,600	NA	NA	33.25
02/03/83	68,000	NA	NA	30.50
02/04/83	371,300	NA	NA	23.375
02/07/83	250,100	NA	NA	20.25
02/08/83	202,400	23.75	20.50	21.50
02/09/83	103,200	22.75	21.00	22.75
02/10/83	112,900	24.00	22.25	22.75
02/11/83	115,400	23.25	20.50	21.50
02/14/83	39,500	22.50	21.25	22.00
02/15/83	48,000	22.50	21.50	22.00
02/16/83	69,200	22.25	20.00	20.00
02/17/83	208,200	20.50	17.00	17.375
02/18/83	171,300	20.00	15.75	18.00
02/21/83		HOLIDAY		
02/22/83	334,100	16.25	11.50	12.00
02/23/83	393,100	13.00	9.875	12.50
02/24/83	181,400	14.00	12.75	13.75
02/25/83	82,600	14.875	13.75	13.75
02/28/83	91,100	13.75	11.50	11.75

* A. T. Bliss and Company, along with 15 other companies, were added to the NASDAQ National Market list of securities on February 8, 1983. While other over-the-counter stocks have market quotations disseminated by dealers, the 100 national market stocks are subject to last-sale reporting and trading volume tallies through the day. Prior to February 8, "High-Low" prices for Bliss were not readily available.

On March 2 and 3, Bliss's stock traded heavily, 152,700 and 159,200 shares respectively, and closed at $16.25 bid on March 3. On March 4, 1983, Bliss and its president, Edward J. Roy, filed suit against Dow Jones

& Company (publisher of *Barron's*), Alan Abelson, and Michael Brody (authors of the articles critical of Bliss). According to the complaint:

> This action seeks actual damages in excess of $60 million and punitive damages in the amount of $30 million for libelous statements published by defendants in the February 7, 21, and 28, 1983, issues of *Barron's National Business and Financial Weekly* ("*Barron's*"). Disregarding the standards of care and accuracy in investigating and reporting financial and business news, *Barron's* published gross inaccuracies, distortions, and falsehoods concerning the accounting practices, business prospects, and the integrity of management of A. T. Bliss and Company ("Bliss"), in particular its president, Edward J. Roy. Among other things, defendants misrepresented and falsely characterized the accounting practices of Bliss as the basis for "phantom profits," when in fact those accounting practices conform precisely with generally accepted accounting principles. As a result of defendants' libelous statements, the quoted value of Bliss's outstanding common stock declined an aggregate amount exceeding $40 million. In addition, defendants attributed to Bliss's president statements not made by him which, by virtue of their falsehood, cast Bliss and its president in an unfavorable light in their relations with Bliss's customers and shareholders. After publication of the initial libelous article, defendants were alerted that their criticism of plaintiffs was inaccurate and unfounded. Instead of correcting their errors, defendants recklessly and maliciously repeated the libel in two successive articles.

In support of its position, Bliss issued (1) a Management Statement (Exhibit 5) which rebutted the *Barron's* articles; (2) a letter (Exhibit 6) from its independent auditor; and (3) a letter (Exhibit 7) to *Barron's* from an accounting firm which took issue with Mr. Abelson's comments regarding A. T. Bliss.

Ray Shaw, president of Dow Jones, called the action "a classic nuisance suit aimed at stifling objective reporting on matters of keen interest to investors. The suit has absolutely no merit; *Barron's* and its editors will be vigorously defended."

Throughout March 1983, Bliss's stock continued in the doldrums. It closed at $13.25 bid on trading of 26,500 shares on March 31, 1983.

EXHIBIT 5
Bliss Management Statement

This report does not attempt to address every misstatement and innuendo contained in the series of articles. As we are entering into litigation against *Barron's*, this will be the only statement made by A. T. Bliss and Company, Inc.

The major areas of concern that we will address here are:

a. *The price of the equipment:*
A. T. Bliss provides a total package to its customers for approximately $3,600, not just solar water heating equipment. Comparable solar water heating systems range from $2,000 to $5,000 per system. Bliss's package price does, in fact, fall within that

EXHIBIT 5 *(continued)*

range. Included in the package is not only the primary solar water heating equipment, but also long-term financing at favorable interest rates, a management contract with a reputable leasing company (Nationwide Power Corporation) who leases, installs, maintains, and collects monthly rental fees, and other professional services including legal, accounting, and engineering.

b. *Accounting principles:*
The financial statements of A. T. Bliss and Company, Inc., have been prepared in accordance with generally accepted accounting principles and are certified as conforming thereto by a firm of certified public accountants and favorably reviewed by the Florida State Board of Accountancy as part of its normal peer review.

A. T. Bliss receives payment for its sales in cash and notes, usually a minimum of 25 percent in cash at the time the sale is made and the balance of 75 percent in long-term installment notes. These are full recourse notes signed by, as *Barron's* calls them, "rich folks," and fully collateralized by the equipment. Bliss has never had a default on any note. This method of reporting revenue is prescribed by *Accounting Principles Bulletin No. 43 (APB No. 43)*. It would *not* be proper to report as revenue the cash only and ignore the notes receivable.

A similar example might be a sale of a $10,000 car by General Motors financed through GMAC for $7,000 with a $3,000 down payment. General Motors had a $10,000 sale, not a $3,000 sale.

We do not know the source of *Barron's* calculations here, nor how they arrived at the $.30 or $.67 earnings per share, respectively, but we do suspect that the American Institute of Certified Public Accountants would take issue with *Barron's* results. The company and its certified public accountants have no choice but to follow the accounting rules laid down by the American Institute of CPAs or other accounting authorities.

As an example of the faultiness of *Barron's* calculations, you might consider that on December 31, 1982, A. T. Bliss had a portfolio of notes receivable of $43 million, which will produce interest income (paid in cash) for the year 1983 of $1.30 per share. This would not take into account any additional equipment

sales or gains on sales from our investment portfolio.

c. *Inventory backlog:*
Nationwide Power Corporation currently installs over 600 systems per month, a rate that has steadily increased since the company's inception. There are currently 7,000 systems available for installation. It is scheduled that these systems will be installed by September or October of this year, in time for A. T. Bliss's fourth quarter, which is historically the peak sales season, accounting for 80 percent of Bliss's business.

d. *Renewal of energy tax credits:*
The energy tax credit does not expire until January 1, 1986. Our information is that a bill will be introduced in Congress this year extending the energy tax credit through 1990 and expanding the credit from its current rate of 15 percent to 25 percent.

A good parallel analogy is the "temporary" 10 percent investment tax credit which is now over 20 years old.

The energy tax credit helps Bliss's sales, but is by no means crucial to the company's survival. The underlying value of the Bliss program is that it provides the homeowners hot water at half the cost of the local utility.

e. *Oil glut:*
It is true that the limited partners expect increases in electric rates in order to produce substantial profits in later years. What is not true is that slumping oil and coal prices have made the scenario unlikely. The oil glut of the last two years has not produced a decrease in electric rates. Based on authoritative sources, such as *The Kiplinger Washington Letter* of October 8, 1982, no such decrease is expected in the near future.

If we look at the components of the average residential electric bill, we can see the potential impact of a decrease in oil prices. Florida Power & Light, which services a large number of Nationwide's customers, spends 32 percent of the average residential kilowatt hour rate on fuel oil, therefore 68 percent of the bill is composed of other costs, such as wages, generating plants, transmission facilities, taxes, etc. This is particularly evident in fast growing areas requiring construction of new facilities. If oil costs decrease by 20 percent, it would take an increase of only 10 per-

EXHIBIT 5 *(concluded)*

cent in the other costs to keep rates from decreasing at all.

Without going into the detailed costs or operating problems of electric utilities, the long-term trend of electric rates appears to be going up. The limited partners are astute businessmen, generally represented by CPAs and tax attorneys, and understand the risks and are willing to invest their money for potential future rewards.

f. Last, but not least, A. T. Bliss and Company, Inc., and Ed Roy, its president, take the strongest exception to the false attribution to Mr. Roy of the quote concerning the astuteness of the firm's customers. "We feel that the finest people in the world are our customers and shareholders."

EXHIBIT 6

ETUE, WARDLAW AND COMPANY, P.A.
Certified Public Accountants
2513 North Andrews Avenue
Fort Lauderdale, Florida 33311

Mr. Reinhard Mueller
A. T. Bliss and Company, Inc.
1300 N. Andrews Avenue Extension
Pompano Beach, FL 33060

September 6, 1982

Dear Reinhard,

First, I want to thank you and Ed for allowing our firm to use A. T. Bliss and Company, Inc., for a "peer review" or quality control review of the 1981 financial statements and workpapers.

Mr. Don Piersal of the Fort Lauderdale office of the Department of Professional Regulations, Board of Accountancy, together with Miss Susan Missal, CPA, met with me on July 26, 1982, to discuss the review approach. Subsequent to that date, Miss Missal reviewed the entire workpaper file, the financial statements, and the notes to the statements.

Her review was performed to determine whether or not I had conformed with generally accepted auditing standards as published by the AICPA, incorporated into the laws of the state of Florida and enforced by the Board of Accountancy thereof.

In Miss Missal's opinion, the audit performed by our firm was very good. She did call to my attention a few minor items that in no way detracted from the "fair presentation" of information in the statements, nor affected the truthfulness of those representations.

In my opinion, our firm came through with "colors flying high." Naturally, I was more than pleased with the results of the quality control review.

For your information, the report is a matter of public record, on file at the D.P.R.'s offices in Tallahassee, Florida.

Again, thank you for your cooperation.

Yours truly,

James E. Etue
Certified Public Accountant
JEE:le

EXHIBIT 7

ALLEN & MEYER
Certified Public Accountants
(A Professional Corporation)

February 8, 1983

Mr. Alan Abelson
Barron's
22 Cortlandt Street
New York, N.Y. 10007

RE: A. T. Bliss & Company, Inc.
February 7, 1983

Dear Mr. Abelson:

I read with keen interest your comments in your "Up & Down Wall Street" column in the February 7, 1983, issue of *Barron's*. I had the opportunity to review in depth a limited partnership, Aqua-Solar Associates, sponsored by A. T. Bliss and Company, Inc., since I had several clients interested in investing in it.

Coincidentally I reached the same gnawing question that you posed, namely, ". . . if the partnership breaks up—who pays the many years' balance on the notes?" However, my answer was 180 degrees out of phase with yours. Each limited partner ("rich folks" in your column) signs a promissory note (a copy of the note is attached), which is payable over 10 years. You do not have to be a Rhodes scholar to see that there are not many defenses if Aqua-Solar Associates or their assigns makes demand on the limited partner. I was most uncomfortable with the deal because each investor was personally liable on a $112,500 note for a 10-year period.

It is rare that a potential investor in a tax shelter deal has the opportunity to see through "glass pockets" to the inner workings of the promoter. In the case of Aqua-Solar Associates, all the companies that deal with the partnership are public companies (A. T. Bliss and Company, Inc.; Equinox Solar, Inc., and Nationwide Power Corporation). My recommendation to my clients was that the more risk-free investment appeared to be the ownership of A. T. Bliss and Company, Inc., common stock because Bliss held full recourse notes from each limited partner (the "rich folks") and all of the notes were collateralized by the equipment sold. Think about it. Which side of the deal would you prefer to be on—the limited partner's side or Bliss's side? I, for one, would rather be on the side of the assets and positive cash flow.

From a revenue recognition standpoint, generally accepted accounting principals (GAAP) dictates that revenue be recognized "when a sale in the ordinary course of business is effected, unless circumstances are such that the collection of the sale price is not reasonably assured." (Source: *APB No. 43*, chap. 1A, par. 1.) Furthermore "the installment method of recognizing revenue is not acceptable" and "revenues should ordinarily be accounted for at the time a transaction is completed, with appropriate provision for uncollectible accounts." (Source: *APB No. 10*, par. 12.)

It seems to me as a CPA that if the financial statements are audited by a CPA firm and your hypothesis would prevail, then the CPA firm could be charged with negligence and the door opened for a nice fat malpractice suit. This is substantial support that the earnings are not "bookkeeping profits," but earnings that are "fairly presented in conformity with generally accepted accounting principles" as the auditor's opinion probably reads.

I hope that I have given some insight into another possible answer to the same gnawing question that you posed in your column.

Very truly yours,

CEA/mb

bec: A. T. Bliss

Charles E. Allen III
Certified Public Accountant

Company Information

The following June 25, 1982, "buy" recommendation (Exhibit 1) of First Michigan Corporation provides a detailed description of the operations of A. T. Bliss. On June 25, 1982, Bliss's stock closed at $5.625 bid.

A subsequent November 11, 1982, "hold" recommendation (Exhibit 2) from First Michigan updates its outlook for A. T. Bliss. On November 11, 1982, Bliss's stock closed at $19.625 bid. On December 31, 1982, it closed at $26.50 bid. On Thursday evening, February 3, 1983, First Michigan issued a two-sentence internal "sell" order to its 26 branches for A. T. Bliss stock which preceded the "free-fall" in Bliss's share price. On February 7, 1983, Bliss issued its 1982 Annual Report to Shareholders (Exhibit 8).

EXHIBIT 8
A. T. Bliss and Company, Inc., Annual Report

President's Letter: Helping America Achieve Energy Independence

To our Shareholders:

Nineteen hundred and eighty-two was a year of growing and strengthening at A. T. Bliss and Company, Inc. I am proud to report that your company was among the top 20 performing stocks in the nation—a positive reflection of the marketplace's analysis of company operations.

Year in Review:

We have surpassed our earnings projections for the fourth year in a row. Your company showed an after-tax net income of $18,103,575 on gross revenues of $41,085,583. Earnings per share for 1982 were $4.74 with an average of 3,823,044 shares outstanding.

Comparatively, the after-tax net income in 1981 was $4,878,000 on gross revenues of $15,425,000. Earnings per share were $1.28 last year with an average of 3,817,454 shares outstanding.

Bliss Foundation

The Bliss Foundation has been created to assist in the support and education of gifted orphaned children from all over the world. President Reagan's guidelines concerning corporate charitable contributions suggest that 2 percent of corporate pre-tax earnings be donated to charity. We at Bliss have committed 5 percent of our pre-tax earnings to the Bliss Foundation to attain our goal.

The first major commitment of funds is to build and operate a live-in school in Mount Dora, Florida. The school is projected to be open in September 1983. It is our belief that this method will produce the greatest possible impact in proportion to the relatively few persons or dollars involved.

Portfolio Investments:

Your company invests in equity growth situations as a normal part of its business.

The net asset value of our investment portfolio fluctuates with the market, but currently is worth approximately $50 million. This represents approximately $13 per share before tax considerations. Gains on the bulk of our investments are taxed at the corporate long-term capital gains rate.

Two of the companies whose stock is held in our portfolio, Jiffy Industries, Inc., (JIFY) and Equinox Solar, Inc. (EQIX), were also among the top 20 performing stocks on the over-the-counter market last year.

Financial Projections

We believe that the heart of A. T. Bliss and Company—the limited partnership investment program—will achieve a wider acceptance and understanding in the financial community over the next year. The market for investment programs which provide long-term income, capital gains, and short-term tax advantages are vast and still growing.

We therefore confidently project our earnings per share to be $6.50 in fiscal 1983. We project our net income to be $24.8 million and gross revenues to be $65 million.

We are the leader in the solar energy industry and are determined to maintain our position. Our fifth year will be a milestone in your company's history.

EXHIBIT 8 *(continued)*

1983 Goals

In 1983, we plan to diversify management of your company by increasing the number of directors on our board. We have begun searching for qualified persons outside of A. T. Bliss to expand our management board and advise us on continuing our rapid growth.

We will continue our close analysis of emerging growth industries to supplement our securities portfolio. The program is an extremely important part of your company's business and financial information is constantly updated so that we may achieve the most benefit from these emerging equity growth situations.

We will continue to work with our exclusive authorized leasing agent, Nationwide Power Corporation, over the next year to expand their leasing program. This will not only be accomplished by increasing the areas of Florida served, but by moving into other geographic regions of the country as well. Nationwide Power Corporation is currently conduct-

ing market research in several areas to determine their economic viability for domestic solar hot water.

We intend to continue to further the understanding and awareness of A. T. Bliss by working closely with the financial community. We also intend to work vigorously with the Solar Energy Industries Association in Washington towards the extension and expansion of the energy tax credit plan in 1986.

In conclusion, I would like to take this opportunity to thank you, our shareholders, for your valued support and interest.

Yours sincerely,

Edward J. Roy
President

Financial Highlights

	Year Ended December 31				
	1983 Projections	1982	1981	1980	1979
For the period:					
Gross revenues	$65,000,000	$41,085,583	$15,424,723	$9,316,394	$3,715,803
Net income	24,800,000	18,103,575	4,878,353	2,304,627	735,284
Earnings per share	$6.50	$4.74	$1.28	$ .61	$ .22
Number of solar water heating systems sold	14,000	9,000	3,900	2,380	990
At end of period:					
Working capital	$ 9,200,000	$ 868,301	$ 1,435,046	$ 485,590	$ 154,163
Notes receivable (at face amount)	79,800,000	43,296,613	19,856,079	9,542,118	2,957,053
Total amount of reserves	27,000,000	15,916,150	8,356,568	4,771,059	1,774,240
Market value of investments	(No estimate)	52,840,000	2,475,000	1,867,914	—
Total assets	96,000,000	51,179,447	17,900,316	7,501,113	2,317,541
Long-term debt	9,660,000	5,361,847	2,622,387	291,296	419,600
Shareholders' equity	52,200,000	27,383,029	8,010,955	3,106,911	752,284
Shares outstanding	3,828,633	3,828,633	3,817,454	3,802,500	3,765,000

Quarterly Stock Price Range (Bid)

	1982		1981		1980		1979	
	High	Low	High	Low	High	Low	High	Low
January–March	6½	4⅛	4¼	3⅛	1⅝	⅝	³⁄₃₂	¹⁄₁₆
April–June	6⅞	5	8⅜	4	1½	1½	³⁄₃₂	¹⁄₁₆
July–September	9⅝	6	8⅝	4⅜	3	2⅛	³⁄₁₆	³⁄₃₂
October–December	28½	8⅛	7⅛	4⅝	3¾	2⅝	³⁄₁₆	³⁄₃₂

EXHIBIT 8 *(continued)*

A. T. Bliss and Company, Inc.: Balance Sheet

	December 31		
Assets	*1982*	*1981*	*1980*
Current assets:			
Cash..................................	$ 6,073,670	$ 1,786,290	$ 538,424
Receivables	1,313,207	1,358,415	1,433,794
Inventories, at cost	—	103,315	129,278
Total current assets	$ 7,386,877	$ 3,248,020	$2,101,496
Noncurrent assets:			
Notes receivable, noncurrent portion, net of allowance of $15,916,150 in 1982, $8,356,568 in 1981, and $4,771,059 in 1980...............................	$26,398,050	$10,868,944	$4,792,173
Investments in related companies:			
Investment, at cost (market value $52,840,000 in 1982, $2,475,000 in 1981, and $1,867,914 in 1980)	$13,164,347	$ 299,000	$ 212,914
Property and equipment:			
Land	$ 50,000	$ 50,000	$ 50,000
Building	311,100	311,100	310,000
Equipment	233,226	88,143	64,793
Leased equipment	4,080,250	3,115,000	—
Total	$ 4,674,576	$ 3,564,243	$ 424,793
Less: Accumulated depreciation	444,403	79,891	30,263
Total property and equipment	$ 4,230,173	$ 3,484,352	$ 394,530
Total assets	$51,179,447	$17,900,316	$7,501,113

This bar projection is not an integral part of the auditor's report.

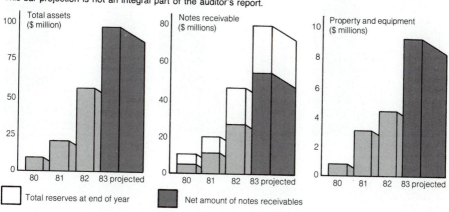

The notes to financial statements are an integral part of the financial statement.

EXHIBIT 8 *(continued)*

	December 31		
	1982	1981	1980
Liabilities and Shareholders' Equity			
Current liabilities:			
Accounts payable and accrued expenses— related parties and other	$ 1,935,259	$ 1,020,613	$ 754,204
Notes payable—officers and other	1,682,500	—	—
Due Nationwide Power Corporation	343,192	781,531	856,031
Income taxes payable	1,185,000	—	—
Current portion of long-term debt	1,372,625	10,830	5,671
Total current liabilities	$ 6,518,576	$ 1,812,974	$1,615,906
Long-term debt, related parties and other	$ 5,361,842	$ 2,622,387	$ 291,296
Deferred income taxes	11,916,000	5,454,000	2,487,000
Shareholders' equity:			
Capital stock, common, par value $.01 per share			
Authorized 6 million shares			
Issued and outstanding:			
1982 3,828,633 shares	$ 38,286		
1981 3,817,454 shares		$ 38,175	
1980 3,802,500 shares			$ 25,350
Capital in excess of par value	1,343,321	74,933	62,067
Retained earnings	26,001,422	7,897,847	3,019,494
Total shareholders' equity	$27,383,029	$ 8,010,955	$3,106,911
Total liabilities and shareholders' equity	$51,179,447	$17,900,316	$7,501,113

This bar projection is not an integral part of the auditor's report.

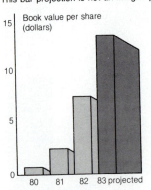

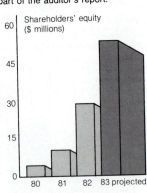

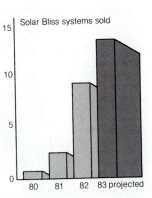

EXHIBIT 8 *(continued)*

A. T. Bliss and Company, Inc.: Statement of Income for the Years Ended

	December 31		
	1982	*1981*	*1980*
Gross revenues	$41,085,583	$15,424,723	$9,316,394
Adjustment to present value for lower than prevailing interest rates	2,746,782	1,873,334	2,996,819
Net revenues	$38,338,801	$13,551,389	$6,319,575
Cost of sales and operating expenses	12,588,226	5,706,036	2,177,948
Income before income taxes	$25,750,575	$ 7,845,353	$4,141,627
Provision for income taxes:			
Current..............................	1,185,000	—	—
Deferred	6,462,000	2,967,000	1,837,000
Net income	$18,103,575	$ 4,878,353	$2,304,627
Retained earnings, beginning of year	7,897,847	3,019,494	714,867
Retained earnings, end of year	$26,001,422	$ 7,897,847	$3,019,494
Average number of shares outstanding	3,823,044	3,817,454	3,783,750
Earnings per share	$4.74	$1.28	$ .61

This bar projection is not an integral part of the auditor's report.

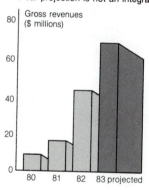

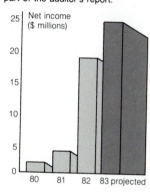

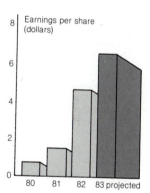

EXHIBIT 8 *(continued)*

A. T. Bliss and Company, Inc. Statement of Changes in Financial Position for the Years Ended

	December 31		
	1982	*1981*	*1980*
Sources of working capital:			
From operations:			
Net income	$18,103,575	$ 4,878,353	$2,304,627
Deferred income taxes	6,462,000	2,967,000	1,837,000
Depreciation	364,512	49,628	23,726
Total	$24,930,087	$ 7,894,981	$4,165,353
Sales of common stock	2,025,999	25,691	50,000
Increase in long-term debt	5,361,842	2,336,250	—
Total sources	$32,317,928	$10,256,922	$4,215,353
Uses of working capital:			
Purchase of property and equipment	$ 1,110,333	$ 3,139,450	$ 11,814
Purchase of common stock	757,500		
Increase in noncurrent notes receivable	15,529,106	6,076,771	3,530,894
Investments	12,865,347	86,086	212,914
Payments on long-term debt	2,622,387	5,159	128,304
Total uses	$32,884,673	9,307,466	$3,883,926
Increase (decrease) in working capital	$ (566,745)	$ 949,456	$ 331,427
Changes in components of working capital:			
Increase (decrease) in current assets:			
Cash	$ 4,287,380	$ 1,247,866	$ 264,931
Receivables	(45,208)	(75,379)	1,060,977
Inventories	(103,315)	(25,963)	125,768
Total	$ 4,138,857	$ 1,146,524	$1,451,676
Increase (decrease) in current liabilities:			
Note payable	$ 1,682,500	$ —	$ (87,000)
Accounts payable	914,646	266,409	424,547
Increase in amount due Nationwide Power Corporation	(438,339)	(74,500)	856,031
Income tax payable	1,185,000	—	
Current portion of long-term debt	1,361,795	5,159	(73,329)
Total	$ 4,705,602	$ 197,068	$1,120,249
Increase (decrease) in working capital	$ (566,745)	$ 949,456	$ 331,427

This bar projection is not an integral part of the auditor's report.

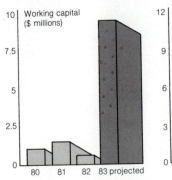
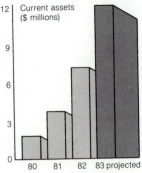
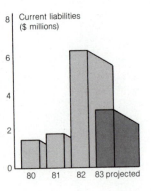

EXHIBIT 8 *(continued)*

Auditor's Report

ETUE, WARDLAW AND COMPANY, P.A.
Certified Public Accountants
2513 North Andrews Avenue
Fort Lauderdale, Florida, 33311

Board of Directors and Stockholders
A. T. Bliss and Company, Inc.
1300 N. Andrews Extension
Pompano Beach, FL 33060

Gentlemen:

We have examined the balance sheets of A. T. Bliss and Company, Inc., as of December 31, 1982, 1981, and 1980 and the related statements of income, retained earnings, and changes in financial position for the years then ended. Our examination was made in accordance with generally accepted auditing standards and, accordingly, included such tests of the accounting records and such other auditing procedures as we considered necessary in the circumstances.

In our opinion, the financial statements referred to above present fairly the financial position of A. T. Bliss and Company, Inc., as of December 31, 1982, 1981, and 1980, and the results of its operations and the changes in financial position for the years then ended, in conformity with generally accepted accounting principles on a basis consistent with the previous years.

Etue, Wardlaw and Company, P.A.
February 7, 1983

A. T. Bliss and Company, Inc.:
Notes to Financial Statements
NOTE 1: Summary of Significant Accounting Policies and History

The company was incorporated in 1969 under the laws of the commonwealth of Massachusetts as the successor to a business dating back to 1876. It ceased all activities in 1972 and remained inactive until 1978, when it acquired Classic Adventures, Inc., a distributor of art and manuscripts. Classic Adventures, Inc., was sold for $1,000 in 1979 and its results, which were immaterial, have been excluded from these statements.

The unaudited financial position of the company for the preceeding two years was as follows:

	December 31	
	1978	1977
Assets	$ –0–	$ –0–
Liabilities	–0–	–0–
Stockholders' equity:		
Common stock, par value $.01 per share		
Issued and outstanding 2 million shares	20,000	20,000
Capital in excess of par value	417	417
Retained earnings (deficit)	(20,417)	(20,417)
Total stockholders' equity	$ –0–	$ –0–
Sales for the year ended	$ –0–	$ –0–

During 1979, the company entered its present business of manufacturing and distributing its Solar-Bliss™ Water Heating Systems. The company sells its product for cash and long-term notes and has in years prior to 1981 offered deferred payment terms on portions of the down payment. It recognizes the sale at the time of executing contracts and receiving a cash down payment. It records all costs of sales and establishes an allowance for doubtful collections and reduction of the long-term notes receivable to present values due to lower than prevailing interest rates. The company has in the past assisted its customers at their request in obtaining leases for the Solar Bliss Water Heating Systems and, in connection therewith, has guaranteed the performance of such leases prior to 1982.

In 1982, the company changed its selling method to organizing limited partnerships with the company serving as general partner and then sells the partnership units to limited partners. The partnership in turn purchases the equipment from the company and leases it to individual homeowners, employing Nationwide Power Corporation as property management and leasing agent.

The company has made substantial investments in other companies, and intends to do so in the future. The criteria for selection in-

EXHIBIT 8 *(continued)*

clude management and superior growth potential. The purpose is to increase the company's portfolio of investments, effective utilization of cash resources, as well as substantial capital gain potential. Gains or losses are recognized at the time of sale and are included in gross revenues.

The company's financial statements are presented on the accrual basis. The statements include the results of A. T. Bliss and Company, Inc. (a Florida corporation), a wholly owned subsidiary. All intercompany transactions have been eliminated.

Property and equipment are recorded at cost. Depreciation is booked at both straight-line and accelerated methods, with useful lives assigned as follows:

Building	30 years
Equipment	7 to 15 years
Leased Equipment	10 years

Investments are accounted for under the equity method for those companies in which the stock ownership equals 20 percent or more or where the company exercises significant influence due to concentration of purchases or common management. The equity method used consists of cost plus increase in the company's share in the equity since date of acquisition. Unrelated investments are carried at the lower of cost or market.

The statement of Income for the year 1980 has been reclassified to conform to the presentation of the 1981 and 1982 results. Specifically, originally reported results for 1980 did not distinguish between allowances for less than prevailing interest rates and allowances for doubtful collections. Both allowances had been included in operating expenses, whereas the 1981 and 1982 presentations reflect the allowance for less than prevailing interest rates as a reduction from gross revenues to arrive at net revenues. Therefore, the amount reported in 1980 as "total revenues" is equal to the 1981 and 1982 item "gross revenues." The reclassification of 1980 did not result in any change in net income, earnings per share, or shareholders' equity.

NOTE 2: Receivables

The company's receivables consisted of the following:

	1982	1981	1980
Accounts receivable	$ 330,794	$ 727,848	$ 1,454,908
Notes receivable, 6% interest, payable in monthly installments over 30 years	2,533,460	2,570,190	2,920,518
Notes receivable, 7½% interest, payable in monthly installments over 15 years with interest only payable during the first seven years	6,474,600	6,474,600	6,621,600
Notes receivable, 9% interest, payable in monthly installments over 10 years	9,830,901	10,357,789	—
Notes receivable, 9% interest, payable in monthly installments over 20 years	8,807,212	453,500	—
Notes receivable from Aqua-Solar Associates, Ltd., 9% interest, payable in semiannual installments over 20 years	15,600,000	—	—
Notes receivable, 12% interest, payable on demand	50,440	—	—
Total	$43,627,407	$20,583,927	$10,997,026
Less: Adjustment to present value for lower than prevailing interest rates	7,853,569	5,186,487	3,468,291
Less: Allowance for doubtful collections and obligations under lease guarantees..........................	8,062,581	3,170,081	1,302,768
	$27,711,257	$12,227,359	$6,225,967
Less: Current portion, net of applicable portion of allowances	1,313,207	1,358,415	1,433,794
Noncurrent receivables	$26,398,050	$10,868,944	$ 4,792,173

EXHIBIT 8 *(continued)*

The 1982 notes receivables include non-recourse notes of $5,520,297. Also included are notes from Aqua-Solar Associates ($15.6 million) and Nationwide Power Corporation ($7,608,570), who are related parties and described in more detail in Note 7. All the above recourse and nonrecourse notes are collateralized by equipment sold by the company as described in the underlying security agreements.

In addition, the note from Aqua-Solar Associates is secured by the assignment of full recourse notes owed by the Limited Partners to Aqua-Solar Associates totaling $17,662,500.

In 1979, 1980, and 1981, the company guaranteed the performance of the lease agreements with Nationwide Power Corporation. Such leases are for initial periods of five or seven years and include a provision that

the amount of the outstanding note obligation. The amount of contingent liability appears to be negligible due to available recourse to the proceeds from the leased equipment.

The company has provided allowances against the carrying values of its notes receivable portfolio for the following purposes:

1. Allowances for less than prevailing interest rates. This allowance is deducted from gross revenues and is amortized over the life of the notes.
2. Allowances for doubtful collections and obligations under lease guarantees. This allowance has been charged to operations.

The charges and credits to the allowance made during the years ended December 31, 1982, 1981, and 1980 were as follows:

	1982	1981	1980
Balance, beginning of year	$ 8,356,568	$4,771,059	$1,774,240
Additions to allowance:			
Deducted from gross revenues	3,132,500	1,999,122	2,416,850
Charged to operations	4,957,500	1,951,680	623,728
Amortization of previously			
established allowance	(385,718)	(125,788)	(43,759)
Portion of allowance no longer required			
due to cancellation of notes	(144,700)	(239,505)	–0–
Balance, end of year	$15,916,150	$8,356,568	$4,771,059

the owner of the equipment may require Nationwide Power Corporation to purchase the equipment at the end of the lease period for

NOTE 3: Investments

Investments consist of the following:

	1982	1981	1980
Related companies, reported on equity basis:			
Equinox Solar, Inc.	$ 95,732	$ 97,000	$ 45,000
Jiffy Industries, Inc.			
Investment	733,010	102,000	48,000
Advance	—	—	119,914
Nationwide Power Corporation	2,420,000	100,000	—
Sunshine Power Corporation	1,000,000	—	—
Aqua-Solar Associates	94,047	—	—
Jiffy Partners '82, Ltd.	8,621,558	—	—
	$12,964,347	$299,000	$212,914
Unrelated companies, reported on cost basis:			
Lasercraft	200,000	—	—
Total	$13,164,347	$299,000	$212,914

EXHIBIT 8 (continued)

A summary of combined financial information of related companies accounted for by the equity method for the years 1982, 1981, and 1980 is as follows:

year amortization period with a balloon payment at the end of 7½ years.

The mortgage balance including accrued interest have been paid in full in January 1983

	December 31 1982	(Unaudited) December 31 1981	December 31 1980
Total assets	$94,362,012	$6,185,877	$1,844,302
Total liabilities	43,883,550	3,743,028	966,038
Net assets	$50,478,462	$2,442,849	$ 878,264
A. T. Bliss and Company, Inc., share of net assets	$12,696,073	$ 911,002	$ 316,611
Net sales	$24,284,873	$6,034,586	$ 681,113
Net income	6,832,540	305,683	55,000
A. T. Bliss and Company, Inc., share of net income	$ 2,012,905	$ 106,000	$ 23,000

Additional information as of December 31, 1982, is presented in the following schedule. For transactions during the year with related parties, see Note 7:

and are therefore included in the amounts due within one year.

The 9 percent note payable of $6,437,500 is owed to Jiffy Partners '82, Ltd., and is pay-

	Percent Owner- ship	Quoted Bid Price per Share	Approxi- mate Market Value
Equinox Solar, Inc. 1,315,000 shares (EQIX)	14.6	$ 3.81	$ 5,010,000
Jiffy Industries, Inc. 604,000 (JIFY)	15.1	16.50	9,966,000
Nationwide Power Corporation 3 million shares	49.1	9.25	27,750,000
Sunshine Power Corporation 200,000 shares	5.7	6.00	1,200,000
LaserCraft 200,000 shares	—	1.00	200,000
Aqua-Solar Associates	1.0	—	94,000
Jiffy Partners '82, Ltd.	86.9	—	8,620,000
Total			$52,840,000

The market value of investments which do not have a publicly quoted bid price has been determined by the company's board of directors. The shares of common stock of related companies are considered restricted stock and would require a registration statement or an exemption from registration prior to any sale on the open market.

NOTE 4: Long-Term Debt

The company's long-term debt consisted of the following:

able in five annual installments of $1,655,083 including interest and principal. The note payments are expected to be paid out of the annual partnership distributions of Jiffy Part-

	1982	1981	1980
Mortgage payable 11½%	$ 296,967	$ 296,967	$296,967
Note payable 9%	6,437,500	—	—
Notes payable 9%	—	2,336,250	—
Total	$6,734,467	$2,633,217	$296,967
Less amounts due within one year	1,372,625	10,830	5,671
Total	$5,361,842	$2,622,387	$291,296

The mortgage payable is secured by the real estate owned by the company. It is payable in monthly installments based on a 20-

ners '82, Ltd., however the principal portion of the first installment has been included in the amounts due within one year.

EXHIBIT 8 *(continued)*

NOTE 5: Income Taxes

Income taxes are accounted for under the flow-through method. For income tax purposes, the company reports its sales on the installment basis. The resulting timing differences are shown as deferred income taxes, none of which are due within the next 12 months. Investment and energy tax credits are treated as a reduction of income taxes in the year the assets giving rise to the credits are placed in service.

The provision for income taxes for financial statement purposes differs from the statutory federal income tax rates as follows:

Equinox Solar, Inc., is a manufacturer of solar water heating systems and related items. A. T. Bliss and Company, Inc., owns 1,315,000 shares of Equinox Solar, Inc., common stock, or approximately 14.6 percent of the total outstanding. During the year 1982, the company made product purchases in its normal course of business from Equinox Solar, Inc., of approximately $3,725,000 of which $1,338,567 was owed as of December 31, 1982, and included in accounts payable.

Nationwide Power Corporation is a leasing company headquartered in Lakeland, Florida. A. T. Bliss and Company, Inc., owns 3 million shares of common stock, or approximately

	1982	1981	1980
Statutory U.S. tax rate	46.0%	46.0%	46.0%
Investment and energy tax credits	(9.6)	(10.1)	—
Equity in earnings of affiliates	(3.6)	(.6)	(.3)
Tax rate differences as on capital gains	(3.0)	—	—
State taxes and other	(.1)	2.5	(1.3)
Effective tax rate	29.7%	37.8%	44.4%

The sources of timing differences giving rise to deferred income taxes were as follows:

49.1 percent of the total outstanding. During the year 1982, Nationwide power Corporation

	1982	1981	1980
Revenue reported on installment basis	$6,227,150	$2,764,000	$1,837,000
Excess of tax over book depreciation	234,850	203,000	—
Total deferred tax expense	$6,462,000	$2,967,000	$1,837,000

It is the policy of the company to reinvest the equity in undistributed earnings of affiliates indefinitely, therefore no income tax has been accrued on the $2,012,905 included in 1982 income. If such earnings were to be remitted to Bliss, the resulting income tax liability would be $138,900.

NOTE 6: Earnings per Share

Earnings per share is based on the weighed average number of shares in the year. There is no dilutive effect on income per share.

NOTE 7: Related Party Transactions

During its ordinary course of business, A. T. Bliss and Company, Inc., transacts business with several parties, who are considered related parties by virtue of common management, common stock ownership, or economic control. Management believes that in all cases, transactions have been made on the same terms and conditions as would have been made under identical circumstances with unrelated parties. Transactions with companies who could be considered to be related were as follows:

purchased solar water heating systems for $10,150,000 from the company and as part of that purchase owes a note in the amount of $7,608,570 at 9 percent interest payable in monthly installments over a 20-year period. This transaction conforms to terms that have been offered in 1982 to unrelated parties.

Nationwide Power Corporation also leases equipment from customers of A. T. Bliss and Company, Inc. In years prior to 1982, the company guaranteed the performance of such leases and it makes payments of promotional assistance, which totaled $1,193,000 for the year 1980, $1,943,500 for the year 1981, and $2,035,000 for the year 1982. Nationwide Power Corporation also leases equipment from A. T. Bliss and Company, Inc., and during the year 1982, paid approximately $86,000 in rents to the company.

Aqua-Solar Associates is a Limited Partnership of which A. T. Pliss and Company, Inc., is the general partner and owns 1 percent of the capital. During the year 1982, Aqua-Solar Associates purchased 5,684 domestic solar water heating systems at a total cost of $20,841,352, of which $15.6 million is owed

EXHIBIT 8 *(continued)*

as of December 31, 1982, in the form of a 20-year, 9 percent interest note payable in semiannual installments including principal and interest. The note is secured by a lien on the equipment as well as the assignment of subscription notes from the Limited Partners totaling $17,662,500. Aqua-Solar was organized to own these systems and lease them to individual homeowners, employing Nationwide Power Corporation as its property and leasing agent. As general partner, A. T. Bliss and Company, Inc., has received a $5,000 syndication fee in 1982 and will receive a general partner fee of $20,000 annually in future years.

Jiffy Partners '82, Ltd., is a limited partnership, of which Jiffy Industries, Inc., is the general partner. A. T. Bliss and Company, Inc., owns 604,000 shares of Jiffy Industries, Inc., or 15.1 percent of the total outstanding. It is also related to Jiffy Industries, Inc., through common management. During the year 1982, the company purchased limited partnership units totaling $8,650,000, of which $6,437,500 was owed to the partnership on December 31, 1982. The note for the balance is due in five annual installments at 9 percent interest and is expected to be paid out of future distributions from the partnership. These units, representing 86.9 percent of the total capital, were purchased from Jiffy Partners '82, Ltd., on the same basis as those offered to and purchased by unrelated parties.

During 1982, officers of the company and an officer of a related company loaned $2,257,500 to the company for working capital. The company issued notes, payable upon demand, bearing interest at 12 percent per annum. At December 31, 1982, $1,682,500 was the balance outstanding on these notes, all of which was repaid in January 1983.

NOTE 8: Contingencies

In the summer of 1980, the staff of the Securities and Exchange Commission commenced inquiries of A. T. Bliss and Company, Inc. Pursuant to an order directing a private investigation by the Securities and Exchange Commission dated October 28, 1980, the staff of the commission commenced an investigation to determine if A. T. Bliss and Company, Inc., and others had been and were offering for sale and selling securities contrary to the provisions of the Securities Act of 1933 and the Securities and Exchange Act of 1934 and rules promulgated thereunder.

In January 1982, counsel to A. T. Bliss and Company, Inc., was informed by the Miami Branch Office that it had concluded the investigation and that it was going to submit a recommendation to the commission seeking authority to enter into negotiations to settle the proposed proceedings and seeking authority to institute injunctive proceedings against A. T. Bliss and Company, Inc., and certain of its principals based upon conclusions reached as a result of the above referenced investigation. Contrary to the opinion reached by the company based upon information directed to the company's counsel by the staff of the Miami Branch Office in January 1982, the staff has subsequently advised that their investigation is not concluded and in January 1983 reaffirmed that it was going to submit a recommendation to the commission as previously described. At this time, A. T. Bliss and Company, Inc., is unable to predict the outcome of the proceedings and settlement negotiations.

The company in its usual course of business offers limited partnership interests in a majority of the states. Varying securities laws, their complexity, and frequent changes might result in isolated cases of alleged noncompliance, none of which would have a material impact on the financial condition of the company.

Management's Discussion and Analysis of Financial Condition and Results of Operations

Results of Operations

The company's gross revenues have increased substantially over the past three years, with the year ending December 31, 1982, producing a 166 percent increase over the prior year. The following schedule shows the individual items included in the company's gross revenues for the past three years:

EXHIBIT 8 *(continued)*

	1982	1981	1980
Sales of equipment	$32,857,302	$14,431,103	$8,931,000
Gross profit on sales of securities	4,417,090	—	—
Equity in earnings of affiliates	2,012,905	106,000	23,000
Interest, rents, and other income	1,798,286	887,620	362,394
Total revenues	$44,085,583	$15,424,723	$9,316,394

Sales of equipment continues strong as customers become more aware of the economic viability of solar energy compared to the cost of electric energy produced from fossil fuels.

The demand for equipment continues to benefit from various incentives by the federal and state governments. The Congress of the United States through the 1978 Energy Tax Act created an energy investment tax credit for purchasers of certain alternative energy equipment, which was extended by the 1980 act. In the case of solar energy equipment, the energy tax credit was increased from 10 percent to 15 percent of the purchase cost. Such credits are an important factor in the decision of the company's customers to purchase such equipment. The Economic Recovery Tax Act of 1981 continued the favorable treatment afforded to alternative energy property, more specifically, by excluding solar equipment from the new "at-risk" provision applicable to property eligible for the investment tax credit.

The company also assists its purchasers, if requested, to obtain leases for the equipment as well as maintenance and accounting services. In this respect, the company acts strictly as a referral service to its customers without compensation and without further equity interest in such services. The company maintains a continuing relationship with Nationwide Power Corporation, an independent leasing company, which was appointed the company's authorized leasing representative. In that capacity, the company, in order to induce its customers to purchase the company's equipment, has guaranteed to its customers the performance of the leases entered into between them and Nationwide Power Corporation prior to 1982.

In 1982, the company redirected its marketing efforts towards the organization of limited partnerships, who would own the equipment and lease it to homeowners, utilizing the services of Nationwide Power Corporation as property management agent. The company, as general partner for the partnership, offers the partnership units to individual investors. Such partnership units typically sell for $150,000 each, payable in cash and full recourse notes.

Interest income has shown steady substantial increases each year due to the increase in the amount of notes receivable owned from prior years' equipment sales.

The company also invests in other emerging growth companies, including those affiliated through common management or business transactions. The company includes in gross revenues its share in the earnings of such affiliates, which have shown substantial increases over the last three years, reflecting both the increased size of the company's investments, as well as increased sales and earnings of those affiliates. Nineteen eighty-two was the first year in which the company sold securities from its portfolio, producing a gross profit on such sales of $4,417,090, which has been included in gross revenues. Management expects such sales to continue in the future, producing on a recurring basis both revenues and net profits. The expectation of future results is supported by the fact that the approximate value of the investments at December 31, 1982, totaled $52,840,000, which includes approximately $39,675,000 in presently unrealized profits.

Gross revenues are reduced to net revenues due to an allowance for less than prevailing interest rates. This allowance is established to discount notes given by the company in accordance with its standard terms of sale at a rate of 9 percent simple interest, to a present value based on prevailing interest rates at the time of sale. The general decline in interest rates during the second half of 1982 has also resulted in a substantial decrease in this allowance, which has the direct result of increasing the company's income for the period.

Cost of sales and operating expenses increased in a direct relationship to the company's sales of equipment; however, they de-

EXHIBIT 8 *(concluded)*

creased as a percentage of gross revenues due to the growing proportion of revenue items not requiring any operating expenses or costs of sales.

The effect of the increases in gross revenues and decreases in interest rates for 1982 as well as the growth and revenue items not burdened by cost or operating expenses was an increase in net income of 271 percent to $18,103,575 from $4,878,353 for 1981.

Liquidity and Capital Resources

The company's standard terms of sale include a down payment and a substantial part of the sale price in the form of long-term notes. In each case, the equipment sold is pledged as security for the note and, in the case of nonpayment by the purchaser, the underlying equipment may be repossessed by the company. For income tax purposes, these notes are reported on the installment basis, which results in a deferral of a portion of the federal income taxes until such time as the principal portion of the note is collected.

The change in the method of sale from outright sales of equipment to the organization of limited partnerships during 1982 has resulted in a shift of equipment sales from the midyear period to the last quarter of 1982. This shifting of the timing of sale increased the demand on the company's capital resources, which was met through short-term loans to the company by officers of the company, all of which have been repaid in January of 1983. Management anticipates additional security sales from its portfolio in early 1983, which should eliminate the need for any future borrowings.

Management anticipates additional future investments, which will depend on available opportunities as well as available liquidity and therefore cannot presently be predicted with any degree of accuracy.

Board of Directors and Executive Officers

Edward J. Roy: President and director, age 39, Mr. Roy, a resident of Lincoln, New Hampshire, is president of the company and also chairman of the board. He has a degree in business administration from Boston University majoring in financial management. He is also president and chairman of the board of Jiffy Industries, Inc., (NASDAQ:JIFY) a publicly traded company, active in the field of solar powered municipal and septic waste treatment plants, and also president and chairman of the board of Sunshine Power Corporation, a publicly traded company currently engaged in research and development of photovoltaic solar energy. Mr. Roy currently owns 1 million (26 percent) of A. T. Bliss's common shares [1,232,325 shares (32.3 percent) at the end of 1981].

Reinhard P. Mueller: Treasurer and director, age 49, a resident of Fort Lauderdale, Florida, is a certified public accountant. He left his accounting practice to join A. T. Bliss and Company, Inc. He has served as chief financial officer of several public companies and also was a partner in a major national accounting firm. Mr. Mueller is also treasurer and a director of Sunshine Power Corporation. He currently owns 137,500 (4 percent) of A. T. Bliss's common shares [262,500 shares (6.9 percent) at the end of 1981].

Carolyn J. Civit: Secretary and director, age 34, a resident of Boca Raton, Florida, received a degree from the University of London. Prior to her joining the company, Ms. Civit was a principal in a marine communications company in Central America.

No executive officer or director has received remuneration, either cash, cash equivalent, or contingent, nor do they have any options to purchase stock, participation in health or medical reimbursement plans, nor is there any proposed remuneration pursuant to an existing plan or arrangement, except: commencing January 1, 1981, Mr. Mueller has received remuneration of $24,000 per year, and commencing January 1, 1982, Carolyn J. Civit received remuneration of $1,000 per quarter through June 30, 1982, and $2,000 per quarter through December 31, 1982, as and for serving as a director. In addition, Ms. Civit also received a salary of $15,600 per annum as secretary of the company.

Questions

1. Describe the corporate, financial, cash flow, and product relationships between the various parties involved in manufacturing, financing, sale, installation, maintenance, and use of Bliss solar systems.

2. How should A. T. Bliss account for its solar system sales?

3. What is your reaction to the inclusion of projections in the A. T. Bliss annual report?

4. Would you buy A. T. Bliss shares on April 12, 1983? To help you make your decision, here is some share price information on the following Bliss shareholdings:

Company	Shares Owned by Bliss	Bid Prices			
		12/31/82	01/31/83	02/28/83	4/12/83
Equinox Solax, Inc.	1,315,000	$ 3.81	$ 5.06	$ 2.19	$ 2.25
Jiffy Industries	604,000	16.50	19.25	12.25	12.00
Nationwide Power Corporation ..	3,000,000	9.25 ⎤	no readily available quotes		
Sunshine Power Corporation	200,000	6.00 ⎦			
Laser Craft	200,000	1.00	2.19	1.56	1.38
Aqua-Solar Associates	1% of capital	⎡ not publicly quoted; market value			
Jiffy Partners.................	86.9% of capital	determined by Bliss's board of directors; see case for valuations as of 12/31/82 ⎦			

CHAPTER 12

Reporting and Evaluation of Unusual Items, Discontinued Operations, and Accounting Changes

One of accounting's oldest and most persistent controversies is how unusual gains or losses, the effects of an accounting change, and a decision to discontinue part of a company's operations should enter into the determination of periodic net income.

Income statements are used by financial analysts to measure past corporate performance and as a basis for estimating future performance and assessing future cash flow prospects. Therefore, what items are included or omitted in the income statement, where in the statement these items are presented, and management's discretion in deciding these questions are all important to statement users. Like managers and accountants, statement users have a diverse range of opinions as to how the current accounting for unusual items, discontinued operations, and accounting changes should be interpreted and used for their purposes, as well as what is the best accounting format for reporting these items.

Unusual gains or losses include such diverse events as the sale of a plant, the loss of property from a hurricane, a onetime payment as a result of successful litigation, and the settlement of a prior year's tax liability for an unexpectedly higher or lower amount than anticipated. Some of these items are designated as unusual operating items and others are labeled "extraordinary" items. The *discontinuance of a business segment* accounting problem arises when, for example, a company sells a division or closes down a segment of its business. *Accounting changes* include decisions to switch from one accounting principle to another, such as a change from accelerated to straight-line depreciation, and revisions of accounting estimates, such as the extension of depreciation lives from 10 to 12 years.

APB Opinion No. 30 is the most authoritative guide to the accounting for extraordinary, unusual, and infrequently occurring events and transactions. It also covers the accounting for discontinued operations. *APB Opinion*

No. 20 is the principal source of accounting authority on accounting changes. In addition, a number of other APB *Opinions* and FASB *Statements* touch on these accounting issues.

Future developments in the accounting for unusual and extraordinary items, discontinued operations, and accounting changes may be influenced by the FASB's *Statement of Financial Accounting Concepts No. 5*, "Recognition and Measurement in Financial Statements of Business Enterprises." This final publication of the FASB's conceptual framework project introduced two new concepts, *earnings* and *comprehensive income*, which could lead to a different approach to presenting revenues, expenses, gains, and losses in financial statements. *Opinions No. 30 and 20* do not rest on this conceptual framework. These *Opinions'* conclusions flow from the APB's attempt to resolve the differences between two older competing concepts of income—the so-called current operating performance and all-inclusive concepts.

Current Presentation

Much of the controversy over how to account for unusual and extraordinary items, discontinued operations, and accounting changes involves the question of where in the income statement these items should be recorded and presented. The current income statement format for presenting these items is shown in Illustration 12–1.

Two Points of View

The format shown in Illustration 12–1 reflects an evolution in accounting for net income toward the "all-inclusive" concept of the income statement. Others argue that "current operating performance" is preferable. Those

ILLUSTRATION 12–1
Statement of Income Format

Revenues		$100
Expenses		80
Gain from unusual sources		(3)
Income from continuing operations		$ 23
Loss on discontinued operations:		
Income from operating discontinued segment......................	$10	
Loss on disposal of discontinued segment	12	2
Income before extraordinary items and effect		
of a change in accounting principles.............................		$ 21
Extraordinary loss	$ 6	
Cummulative effect on prior years of a change		
in accounting principles	2	8
Net income		$ 13

holding the extreme version of this point of view would include only the revenue and expense items shown in Illustration 12–1 in net income. All of the other items would be treated as adjustments to owners' equity.

The major arguments for the all-inclusive concept are:

1. The annual income statements taken for the life of an enterprise should, when added together, represent total net income.
2. Omitting certain items from the income statements invites statement manipulation and income smoothing.
3. It is simple to prepare and leads to borderline cases being treated in a consistent manner by all companies.
4. Past income statements are of limited value in forecasting future results. Therefore, the inclusion of unusual and extraordinary items in income does not diminish their predictive value to statement users.
5. Including all items in income protects statement users against overlooking material extraordinary items.
6. If all items are included in income statements, users can use their judgment to decide which items should be omitted.

The major arguments of those favoring the current operating performance concept are:

1. Including unusual items in current income may be so distorting as to lead to unsound judgments with respect to the current earnings performance of a company.
2. It leads to an income figure that is more representative of what a company is able to earn from its usual or typical operations.
3. Not all statement users are trained to eliminate distorting extraordinary and unusual items included in an income figure determined using the all-inclusive concept.
4. Management and their independent accountants are in a better position than statement users to decide which distorting items should be excluded from income.
5. Comparisons with the income of prior years and other comparisons are easier.

To date, the FASB, SEC, and APB recommendations primarily reflect the all-inclusive point of view. The current operating performance concept has also been accepted in part, since the recommendations of these three bodies have provided for an identification of the nonrecurring and unusual items in the income statement.

Extraordinary Items, Unusual Events, and Prior Period Adjustments

APB Opinion No. 30 concluded that all items of profit and loss should be included in the determination of net income, with the exception of items which are essentially adjustments to the results reported in prior periods. In addition, the APB recommended that extraordinary items, net of their related tax effect, should be segregated from the operating-related results in the income statement.

Opinion No. 30 adopted the point of view that an event or transaction should be presumed to be a usual and ordinary activity or event for the reporting entity unless the evidence clearly justifies its classification as an extraordinary item. *Opinion No. 30* defines an extraordinary item as an event or transaction that is both unusual and infrequent. It defines these qualities as follows:

   a. Unusual nature—the underlying event or transaction should possess a high degree of abnormality and be of a type clearly unrelated to, or only incidentally related to, the ordinary and typical activities of the entity, taking into account the environment in which the entity operates.
   b. Infrequency of occurrence—the underlying event or transaction should be of a type that would not reasonably be expected to recur in the foreseeable future, taking into account the environment in which the entity operates.

Since the environment in which the reporting company operates must be taken into account, judgment is required to determine whether or not an item is extraordinary. For example, an event or transaction may be unusual in nature for one entity but not for another, because of differences in their respective industries, locations, or extent of government regulation. Similarly, because the probabilities of an unusual occurrence differ in different environments, a specific transaction of one company may not meet the *Opinion's* definition of infrequency of occurrence, whereas a similar transaction of another company might. The fact that an unusual or infrequent event is beyond the control of management or significant financially does not automatically make it extraordinary.

The APB anticipated that extraordinary items would be rare. Gains or losses directly resulting from a major casualty or an expropriation are examples of extraordinary items cited in the *Opinion.*[1]

The *Opinion* specifically noted that the following gains and losses should *not* be reported as extraordinary items, because they are usual in nature and may be expected to recur as a consequence of customary continuing business activities:

   1. Write-down or write-off of receivables, inventories, equipment leased to others, deferred costs, or other intangible assets.

---

[1] Any portion of the losses from such events which would have resulted from a proper valuation of assets on a going concern basis should be excluded from the extraordinary item.

2. Gains or losses from exchange or translation of foreign currencies, including those relating to major devaluation and revaluations.
3. Gains or losses on disposal of a segment of a business.
4. Other gains or losses from sale or abandonment of property, plant, or equipment used in the business.
5. Effects of a strike, including those against competitors and major suppliers.
6. Adjustment of accruals on long-term contracts.

Extraordinary items and prior year adjustments are reported in comparative statements, as shown in Illustration 12–2. It is important to note in Illustration 12–2 that (1) the earnings-per-share calculation is made for both the "income before extraordinary items" and "net income" amounts; (2) the earnings-per-share data are shown on the face of the income statement; and (3) the earnings-per-share amount for the extraordinary items and prior period adjustments are disclosed.

Immaterial extraordinary items may be included in the net income without the extraordinary item label. *Opinion No. 30* discussed materiality as it related to extraordinary items as follows:

> The effect of an extraordinary event or transaction should be classified separately in the income statement if it is material in relation to income before extraordinary items or to the trend of annual earnings before extraordinary items, or is material by other appropriate criteria. Items should be considered individually and not in the aggregate in determining whether

ILLUSTRATION 12–2
Illustrative Comparative Statement Presentation (amounts, except per-share figures, in thousands)

	1986	1985
Income before extraordinary items	$10,130	$ 7,990
Extraordinary items, net of applicable income taxes		
of $1,880,000 in 1986 and $500,000 in 1985	(2,040)	(1,280)
Net income	$ 8,090	$ 6,710
Retained earnings at beginning of year:		
As previously reported..................................	$28,840	$25,110
Adjustments..	(3,160)	(1,760)
As restated	$25,680	$23,350
	$33,770	$30,060
Cash dividends on common stock, $0.75 per share	4,380	4,380
Retained earnings at end of year	$29,390	$25,680
Per share of common stock:		
Income from ordinary operations.........................	$1.73	$1.37
Extraordinary items, net of tax	(0.34)	(0.22)
Net income	$1.39	$1.15

an extraordinary event or transaction is material. However, the effects of a series of related transactions arising from a single specific and identifiable event or plan of action that otherwise meets the two (extraordinary item) criteria should be aggregated to determine materiality.

Unusual Events and Transactions

One of the potential major criticisms of *Opinion No. 30* is that many material transactions or events that are of an unusual nature or infrequent occurrence, but not both, may be included in the determination of income before extraordinary items. In the opinion of some statement users this requirement may obscure the profits from the continuing underlying business operations of the business, which is a figure many believe is very relevant to appraising the future prospects of a company. To counter this criticism, *Opinion No. 30* required that such transactions or events should be reported as a separate component of income from continuing operations on the face of the statement, or, alternatively, disclosed in the notes of the statement. These items should not be reported net of taxes.

Prior Period Adjustment

The APB believed that prior period adjustments were rare in modern business. The FASB in *Statement No. 16,* "Prior Period Adjustments," required, with two exceptions, that all items of profit and loss recognized during a period, including accruals of estimated losses from loss contingencies, be included in the determination of net income of the period. The two prior period adjustments excepted were corrections of errors in the financial statement of a prior period discovered subsequent to their issuance, and adjustments from realization of income tax benefits of preacquisition operating loss carry forwards of purchased subsidiaries.

APB Appraisal

The APB believed its approach to reporting net income had the following advantages and disadvantages:

> The principal advantages are: *(a)* inclusion of all operating items related to the current period, with segregation and disclosure of the extraordinary items; *(b)* a reporting of current income from operations free from distortions resulting from material items directly related to prior periods; and *(c)* proper retroactive reflection in comparative financial statements of material adjustments relating directly to prior periods. . . . [The principal disadvantages are] *(a)* occasional revision of previously reported net income for prior periods to reflect subsequently recorded material items directly related thereto; *(b)* difficulty in segregating extraordinary items and items related to prior periods; and *(c)* the possibility that disclosures regarding

adjustments of opening balances in retained earnings or of net income of prior periods will be overlooked by the reader.

No Solution

Opinion No. 30 is regarded by many accounting authorities as being an inappropriate or inadequate solution to the unusual and extraordinary items accounting problem. Some believe the whole idea of trying to label some items as extraordinary and others as ordinary is unworkable. What is needed, these critics claim, is a separate identification of abnormal, unusual, or infrequent items. Others believe the extraordinary item criteria are subjective and arbitrary. And, as indicated earlier, some believe the *Opinion* blurs the presentation of operating income. This, it is claimed, confuses statement users, particularly as the statement format implies that only ordinary events and transactions are included in income before extraordinary items. Still others feel that an event or transaction takes on the character of being extraordinary if it combines infrequency of occurrence with abnormality of scale.

As this debate on the proper way to measure business income continues, one fact becomes clearer every day; namely, that determinations of periodic income will always be an imprecise measure of performance involving subjective human judgment. Also, those who seek to refine its computations, as well as those who rely on net income figures, would be well advised to reflect upon the words of the late Robert Frost: "No figure has ever caught the whole thing."

Discontinuance or Disposal of a Business Segment

Opinion No. 30 set forth accounting rules for discontinued business operations, whether by sale or abandonment. For the purposes of the *Opinion,* a discontinued operation was defined as the operations of a segment of a business that has been sold, abandoned, spun off, or otherwise disposed of or, although still operating, is the subject of a formal plan for disposal. A segment of business is a component of an entity whose activities represent a separate major line of business or class of customer. A segment may be in the form of a subsidiary, a division, or a department. It may also be a joint venture or nonsubsidiary investee, provided the entities are clearly distinguishable operationally and physically from the investor entity.

Opinion No. 30 concluded that the results from continuing operations should be reported separately from discontinued operations, and that any gain or loss from disposal of a segment of a business should be reported in conjunction with the related results of discontinued operations and not as an extraordinary item. Accordingly, operations of a segment that has been or will be discontinued should be reported separately on a net of tax basis as a component of income before extraordinary items and the cumulative effect of accounting changes (if applicable) in the following manner:

Income from continuing operations before income taxes	$5,000	
Provision for income taxes	2,000	
Income from continuing operations		$3,000
Discontinued operations:		
Income (loss) from operations of discontinued Division A		
less applicable income taxes of $500	$ 500	
Loss on disposal of division A including provision		
of $300 for operating losses during phase-out period		
(less applicable income taxes of $100)	400	100
		$2,900

In addition, the statement of prior periods should be restated to disclose the results of operations of the disposed segment, less applicable income taxes, as a separate component of income before extraordinary items.

The measurement date of the gain or loss from a disposal of a business segment is the date when the management with the authority to approve the action commits itself to a formal plan to dispose of the segment. If a loss is anticipated on the disposal, the anticipated loss should be provided for in the accounting period that includes the measurement date. If a gain is expected, it should be recognized when it is realized, which ordinarily is the time of the disposal. Should the plan of disposal be expected to be carried out over several accounting periods, any estimated income or losses from the projected operations of the segment during these periods should be considered at the measurement date in determining the anticipated gain or loss.

All expected losses from future operations between the measurement and disposal date should be included in the gain or loss computation. If income is projected during this period, it should be included in the computation up to the amount of any projected losses. Income in excess of the projected losses should be recognized when realized. In addition to any projected income or losses from operating the segment, the gain or loss from disposal should include only those costs and expenses subsequent to the measurement date that are directly associated with the decision to dispose of the segment, such as severance pay and employee relocation expenses. Finally, should the estimate of the disposal loss included in the measurement date period later prove faulty, the revised estimates of the loss should be included in the determination of income in the period of the revised estimate.

Accounting Principle, Estimate, and Entity Changes

The net income and financial condition of a company may change from one period to another because of accounting changes. This will affect the usefulness of historical data for trend analysis. It may also obscure poor managerial performance. Therefore, users of financial statements must be aware of (1) how changes in accounting are reflected in financial statements, and (2) when and how to adjust accounting data to make the presentation comparable from one period to another.

The treatment of accounting changes is determined primarily by *Opinion No. 20* "Accounting Changes." The *Opinion* covers: (1) changes in accounting principles, (2) changes in accounting estimates, and (3) reporting a change in the definition of the entity issuing the financial statements. These are considered to be accounting changes. In addition, the *Opinion* deals with reporting corrections of errors in previously issued financial statements, which is not considered to be an accounting change, however.

In general, *Opinion No. 20* requires that:

1. The cumulative effect of an accounting principle change is reported in the period of the change.
2. Changes in accounting estimates are accounted for prospectively.
3. Changes in the reporting entity require the restatement of all prior period statements presented to conform to the new reporting entity.
4. A correction of an error in the previously issued financial statement is reported as a prior period adjustment.

Opinion No. 20 and several subsequent FASB *Statements* contain exceptions to the general rule for accounting principle changes. These exceptions will be discussed after the review of the general rules.

Principle Changes

A change in accounting principle comes with the adoption of a generally accepted accounting principle that is different from the one used previously to report a particular kind of transaction. The *Opinion* notes that an accounting principle change includes not only changes in accounting principles and practices but also changes in the method of applying them.

Common examples of an accounting change include a shift from accelerated to straight-line depreciation and a change from reporting income on an installment basis to the sale method.

A characteristic of these changes is that each involves a choice between two or more generally accepted accounting principles.

A change in accounting principles does not occur when:

1. An accounting principle is adopted initially in recognition of events or transactions occurring for the first time or which were previously immaterial.
2. An adoption or modification of an accounting principle is required by a change that is clearly different in the substance of events or transactions from those previously occurring.

Whenever an accounting principle is changed, the statements of the period in which the change is made must include (1) the current annual charge or credit for the item according to the new principle as an element of operating income, and (2) an adjustment to the current period's net income equal to the cumulative effect on the period's beginning retained earnings of applying the new accounting principle retroactively. This cumulative amount, which is the difference between the recomputed amount and the amount originally recorded, is shown after extraordinary items. In addition, pro forma net income figures, based upon a retroactive adjustment of the prior periods' statements to reflect the new principle, should be included for each period presented in the statements. Thus, the current comparative statement presents both actual and pro forma results.

Cumulative Effect. The cumulative effect of changing to a new accounting principle is shown in the income statement between the captions "extraordinary items" and "net income," but it should not be considered as an extraordinary item. This item is shown net of its related tax effect.

In addition, both the gross amount and the per-share amount of the effect of an accounting principle change must be disclosed. The per-share data on the face of the statement should also include the per-share amount of the cumulative effect of the accounting change.

The data for prior periods included in the comparative statements are not adjusted for the accounting change. It is the same as stated previously in the prior years' annual reports.

Pro Forma Effects. In addition to the current period's actual net income (including the cumulative effect) shown on the face of the statements, income before extraordinary items and net income on a pro forma basis, computed as if the newly adopted accounting principle had been applied to all periods presented, should be disclosed. These data should also be on a per-share basis.

In addition to the direct effects of the change, the pro forma income figure should include adjustments for any nondiscretionary items that are based on either income before taxes or net income. Such nondiscretionary items may be profit sharing expenses or royalties based on income. In these cases, if the accounting principle change resulted in a different income figure than reported previously, these income-based expense items would automatically be different. In computing the pro forma data, all related tax effects should be recognized.

Disclosure is required of the adjustments made to prior years' income before extraordinary items and net income to determine the pro forma amounts. In addition, if only an income statement for the current period is presented, the actual and pro forma amounts for the current and immediately preceding periods should be disclosed.

Which Income Number? Users of financial statements should base their evaluation of a company on both the net income and pro forma net income figures. Of the two, however, the pro forma figures are usually the better indicator of future earnings, since the current year's net income figure includes the one time cumulative debit or credit and the prior year's net income was determined using the old accounting method. The footnote related to these presentations should always be examined since it will explain (1) the nature and effect of the accounting principle change and (2) the computation of the pro forma figures. There is no requirement that this footnote disclosure be repeated in subsequent periods.

ILLUSTRATION 12–3
Reporting an Accounting Principle Change

	1986	1985
Income before extraordinary item and cumulative effect of a change in accounting principle	$1,200,000	$1,100,00
Extraordinary item (description)	(35,000)	100,000
Cumulative effect on prior years (to December 31, 1985) of changing to a different depreciation method (Note A)	125,000	
Net income	$1,290,000	$1,200,000
Per-share amounts:		
Earnings per common share—assuming no dilution:		
Income before extraordinary item and cumulative effect of a change in accounting principle	$1.20	$1.10
Extraordinary item	(0.04)	0.10
Cumulative effect on prior years (to December 31, 1985) of changing to a different depreciation method	0.13	
Net income	$1.29	$1.20
Earnings per common share—assuming full dilution:		
Income before extraordinary item and cumulative effect of a change in accounting principle	$1.11	$1.02
Extraordinary item	(0.03)	0.09
Cumulative effect on prior years (to December 31, 1985) of changing to a different depreciation method	0.11	
Net income	$1.19	$1.11
Pro forma amounts assuming the new depreciation method is applied retroactively:		
Income before extraordinary item	$1,200,000	$1,113,500
Earnings per common share—assuming no dilution	$1.20	$1.11
Earnings per common share—assuming full dilution	$1.11	$1.04
Net income	$1,165,000	$1,213,500
Earnings per common share—assuming no dilution	$1.17	$1.21
Earnings per common share—assuming full dilution	$1.08	$1.13

Note A: *Change in Depreciation Method for Plant Equipment.* Depreciation of plant equipment has been computed by the straight-line method in 1986. Depreciation of plant equipment in prior years, beginning in 1954, was computed by the sum-of-the-years'-digits method. The new method of depreciation was adopted to recognize . . . (state justification for change of depreciation method) . . . and has been applied retroactively to equipment acquisitions of prior years. The effect of the change in 1986 was to increase income before extraordinary item by approximately $10,000 (or one cent per share). The adjustment of $125,000 (after reduction for income taxes of $125,000) to apply retroactively the new method is included in income of 1986. The pro forma amounts shown on the income statement have been adjusted for the effect of retroactive application on depreciation, the change in provisions for incentive compensation which would have been made had the new method been in effect, and related income taxes.

Illustration 12–3 presents the recommended way to report a change in accounting principles in a two-year comparative statement. If statements for more than two years are presented, the same format is used.

The situation assumed in Illustration 12–3 is: The ABC Company decided in 1986 to adopt the straight-line method of depreciation for plant equipment. The straight-line method will be used for new acquisitions as well as for previously acquired plant equipment for which depreciation has been provided on the accelerated method.

This illustration further assumes that the direct effects are limited to the effect on depreciation and related income tax provisions and that the direct effect on inventories is not material. The pro forma amounts have been adjusted for the hypothetical effects of the change in the provisions for incentive compensation. The per-share amounts are computed assuming that 1 million shares of common stock are issued and outstanding, that 100,000 additional shares would be issued if all outstanding bonds (which are not common stock equivalents) are converted, and that the annual interest expense, less taxes, for the convertible bonds is $25,000. Other data assumed for this illustration are:

Year	Excess of Accelerated Depreciation Over Straight-Line Depreciation	Effects of Change	
		Direct, Less Tax Effect	Pro Forma (after adjustment for incentive compensation)
Prior to 1982	$ 20,000	$ 10,000	$ 9,000
1982	80,000	40,000	36,000
1983	70,000	35,000	31,500
1984	50,000	25,000	22,500
1985	30,000	15,000	13,500
Total at beginning of 1986	$250,000	$125,000	$112,500

Amortization Method Changes. Long-lived assets are charged to income through a process which, depending on the type of asset involved, is called depreciation, depletion, or amortization (all of which are referred to as amortization in this chapter). Sometimes changes are made in the amortization method for classes of similar identifiable assets. In such cases, if the new method is adopted for all newly acquired assets of a particular class (and the old method is used for the previously recorded asset in that class), there is no need to adjust income figures shown on the face of the statements. That is, no cumulative effect is included and no pro forma data are presented. Such data are presented only if the new method of amortization is applied to the previously recorded assets.

When an amortization method change is not applied to previously recorded assets, the nature of the change and its effects on income and related per-share data should be disclosed.

Amounts Not Determinable. If it is impossible to compute the cumulative effect on beginning retained earnings, the effect on the change on the current period's results should be disclosed. In addition, an explanation should be given for omitting the cumulative effect and the pro forma amounts.

If the pro forma amounts cannot be determined for individual prior periods, the cumulative effect should nevertheless be computed and included in an adjustment to current income. The reason for not showing the pro forma amounts should be explained.

Special Retroactive Restatements. Restatement of all prior periods presented to reflect the retroactive application of a newly adopted accounting principle is required by *Opinion No. 20* in three special cases. These are:

1. A change from the LIFO method of inventory pricing to another method.
2. A change in the method of accounting for long-term construction-type contracts.
3. A change to or from the full cost method of accounting, which is used in the extractive industries.

The APB gave no reason for these special cases beyond saying, "Certain changes in accounting principles are such that the advantages of retroactive treatment in prior period reports outweigh the disadvantages."

Restatement is achieved by:

a. Including in each statement for the periods presented an amount based upon the new principle. This replaces the amount determined by the old method in all periods preceding the current one.
b. Adjusting each period's beginning retained earnings for the cumulative effect of the change up to that point in time.

Subsequently, the FASB added more special cases to the APB's list of accounting principle changes that must be reported on a retroactive restatement basis. These were all situations where a company must change its accounting principles to conform to certain new FASB *Statements.* The FASB permitted these exceptions to the cumulative effect accounting method because it believed "the prior period adjustment method will provide the most useful information."

Interim Statements. If an accounting principle change is made in the first interim period of a fiscal year, the cumulative effect of the change should be included in the first period's statement. Accounting changes of this type made during the accounting year should be presented as if the change had been made in the first interim period of the year. That is, the current period should not include the cumulative effect. However, the year-to-date figures and first interim period should be restated to include the cumulative effect of the change. All interim periods subsequent to the first period of the fiscal year should be restated to conform to this restatement.

Justification. If a new accounting principle is adopted, the change must be justified on the ground that it is preferable. Periodically, the FASB issues *Statements* specifying that certain specialized accounting and reporting principles contained in AICPA *Statements of Position* and *Guides* on accounting and auditing matters are preferable accounting principles solely for justifying an accounting change as required by *Opinion No. 20*. The burden of justifying other changes rests with the entity proposing the change.

The nature, effect on income, and justification for an accounting change should be disclosed in the footnotes to the statements of the period in which the change is made. In addition, similar data related to accounting changes must be filed with the SEC along with a letter from the company's auditor stating that the new principle is preferable to the old one.

Consistency. Financial reporting presumes that once an accounting principle is selected, it will be applied consistently from one period to another to account for similar events and transactions. This makes statements comparable and enhances their usefulness and intelligibility.

Changes in Accounting Estimates

The preparation of financial statements requires estimating the effects of future events, such as the life of a piece of equipment or the amount of future warranty expenses related to current sales. Since the future cannot be predicted accurately, it is desirable that accounting estimates be revised as more experience is acquired or additional information is obtained.

Sometimes it is difficult to distinguish between a change in the accounting principle and a change in an accounting estimate. For example, a company may decide to write off all of its deferred plant preoperating costs immediately, because it now seems unlikely that the related plant will become a profitable commercial venture. Thus, the new accounting method is adopted in part because the estimate of the investment's future benefits has changed. The principle and estimate changes are inseparable. Changes of this type are considered to be changes in estimates for the purposes of applying *Opinion No. 20*.

Prospective Treatment. *Opinion No. 20* requires that the effect of a change in accounting estimate be recorded prospectively in financial statements. That is, the estimate change should be accounted for in (a) the period of the change if the change affects that period only; or (b) the period of the change and future periods if the change affects both. The statements of prior periods must not be restated on a direct or pro forma basis to reflect accounting estimate changes.[2]

Disclosure. The effects on income before extraordinary items, on net income, and on related share amounts of an estimate change that affects future periods should be disclosed. Unless the information is material, disclosure is not necessary of estimates made each period in the ordinary course of accounting for such items as uncollectible accounts or inventory obsolescence.

Changes in the Entity

A change in the reporting entity occurs when the definition of the reporting entity with its group of companies represented in the current period's statement is different from the entity represented in the immediately prior period's statement. This situation results from *(a)* presenting consolidated or combined statements in place of individual company statements; or *(b)* changing the specific subsidiaries in the group of companies for which consolidated or combined financial statements are presented.

Changes in the reporting entity should be made by restating the financial statements of all prior periods presented in order to provide the financial information of all periods for the new reporting entity. A later chapter describes the accounting for change in the reporting entity due to a business combination.

The nature, the effect on income figures and related share amounts, and the reasons for a change in the reporting entity should be disclosed for all periods presented. Subsequent statements need not repeat this disclosure.

Correction of an Error

Errors in financial statements result from mathematical mistakes, mistakes in the application of an accounting principle, or oversight or misuse of facts that existed at the time the statements were prepared. (In contrast, a change in estimate results from new information or subsequent developments which provided better insight or improved judgment.) A change to a generally accepted accounting principle from one that is not generally accepted is considered to be a correction of an error.

An error in the statement of a prior period discovered subsequent to its issue should be reported as a prior period adjustment. That is, the beginning retained earnings of each period presented should be adjusted for

---

[2] The only exception occurs when the change meets all the conditions for a prior period adjustment.

the error. If the error relates to any of the income figures presented, these should be adjusted for the related amount of the error.

The nature of the error and its effect on the statements should be disclosed in the period in which the error was discovered and corrected. Future statements need not repeat this disclosure.

Requirements

The basis for *materiality* determinations is defined for the purposes of *Opinion No. 20* as being any effect of a change, or the combined effect of changes, that materially affect *(a)* income before extraordinary items and net income or *(b)* the trend of earnings.

This latter basis for determining materiality is a shift from past practices. It conforms more closely to the investor's interest in statements. Investors focus on both net income and the change in income from one period to another. Items that are immaterial relative to total income may be very relevant when compared to the amount of change in income from the prior period.

More recently, the *FASB Statement of Financial Accounting Concepts No. 2*, "Qualitative Characteristics of Accounting Information," defined material as: "The magnitude of an omission or misstatement of accounting information that, in the light of surrounding circumstances, makes it probable that the judgment of a reasonable person relying on the information would have been changed or influenced by the omission or misstatement."

A change that does not materially affect the current status, but is reasonably certain to have material effects on later periods, should be disclosed in the period of change.

Historical summaries of financial information, such as the selected five-year balance sheet and income statement items included in annual reports, should be prepared in the same manner as prescribed by *Opinion No. 20* for the primary financial statements and their related pro forma data. In particular, the cumulative effect included in the income of the period of change should be shown separately along with any net income and related share amounts for that period.

Accounting changes made in anticipation of an *initial public distribution of stock* are exempt from the requirements of *Opinion No. 20*. Typically, closely held private companies follow different accounting practices than they would use if they were publicly held. Since these old practices are likely to be discontinued once the initial public distribution is made, the APB believed it would be more useful to investors for such companies to adopt their new accounting principles and estimates retroactively in connection with initial public stock offerings.

This exemption is available only once. It is also available only when a company first issues its financial statements for any one of the following purposes: *(a)* obtaining additional equity capital from investors; *(b)* affecting a business combination; or *(c)* registering securities.

When a company uses this exemption, full disclosure of the nature of the changes and their justification is required.

Different Viewpoints

The proper reporting of accounting changes was a very difficult issue for the APB to resolve. Among the differing viewpoints they considered were:

1. The same accounting principle should be used for the current and past periods. The use of different principles in different periods may result in misinterpretation of earnings trends and other analytical data that are based on comparisons. Accordingly, restatement of prior period data should be required.

2. The financial statements of prior periods were prepared under the conditions prevailing at the time. To restate these statements might suggest either (a) the conditions were different, which they were not; or (b) the accountant made a mistake, which he or she did not. Therefore, restating the financial results of prior periods may dilute the public confidence in corporate reports and confuse the user of these statements.

3. It is sometimes impossible or very difficult to restate past statements since adequate information may not be available. This can occur when a company shifts from a completed contract method to a percentage of completion method. Consequently, restatement as a general requirement may not be feasible in all cases.

4. Restatement may be required in some cases because the assumptions made about the data might be erroneous if restatement was not required. For example, if a company switched from the LIFO method to the FIFO method, without restatement, the statement user might assume the ending LIFO inventory of the prior period was the beginning inventory of the current FIFO inventory. To avoid this kind of problem, restatement of earlier periods is required in some cases.

5. Unless the cumulative effect of the change is charged to current income, an accounting change could result in material revenue and expense amounts never being charged to income.

Six out of 18 members of the APB dissented to *Opinion No. 20*. Some of the objections voiced by these dissenters were:

1. The APB in most of its *Opinions* had urged retroactive application of its recommendations. This *Opinion* should have been consistent with these earlier recommendations.

2. The cumulative effects applicable to earlier periods should not be included in the determination of current income as it is not related to current revenues or events.

3. Because retroactive restatement is generally prohibited by the

Opinion, it precludes the adoption of preferable accounting in prior periods and impairs the compatibility of statements.

4. Income and expense items should be included in financial statements once, but neither more nor less than once. This can be done only if newly adopted principles are applied prospectively.

5. The pro forma presentation of past years cannot properly report the results of those years. The operating results themselves have an influence on nonaccounting operating decisions, such as pricing. Therefore, arithmetically reconstructing prior years to reflect accounting principle changes cannot reflect how things might have been given these results.

6. The APB's solution (i.e., cumulative pro forma data, special retroactive restatements, and prospective treatment of estimate changes) is an arbitrary compromise that lacks logical coherence and any supportable rationale. As a result, it will contribute to the confusion of statements users.

In contrast to these views, some believe that the inclusion of the cumulative effect in the current income statement is a clear signal to statement users that an accounting principle change has occurred. They also believe the *Opinion* is consistent with the objective of giving statement users a more realistic perspective regarding the judgments which underlie annual income determination.

Financial Analysis

The typical issue that confronts statement users when they encounter unusual items, discontinued operations, and accounting change situations is whether these items should be included or excluded from their financial ratios, cash flow, and earnings quality assessments that include a profit component. While the resolution of this issue depends upon the company's circumstances and the objective of the financial analysis, some general practices have evolved. These are described below.

In most cases, unusual items that qualify for extraordinary item accounting treatment are excluded from current appraisals of management performance and earnings projections based on current and past statements. These exclusions are justified by management's inability to control the event giving rise to the extraordinary items and the nonrecurring, unusual, and unexpected nature of the item. In contrast, cash flow effect, if any, of an extraordinary item is always included in analyses of a company's cash flow. Extraordinary items have cash flow benefits and disadvantages that can impact the total current and anticipated resources of a company, its ability to meet financial commitments, and the value of its stock. Standing alone, extraordinary items are usually excluded from earnings quality assessments. If a company reports extraordinary items frequently or has the potential to report them frequently, however, this characteristic is regarded as a negative earnings quality consideration. The earnings surprise aspect of extraordinary items merits this rating, irrespective of whether the company reports extraordinary gains or losses.

Unusual events not classified as extraordinary items for accounting purposes are often excluded from single-year appraisals of management, but are nearly always included in long-term management performance evaluations and earnings projections based on past earnings data. This treatment reflects the operating nature of the item and also the fact that by recording an unusual operating item, management is indicating that prior period operating results may have been over- or understated in the light of current knowledge. Like extraordinary items, the cash flow effect of unusual nonextraordinary items is always included in cash flow appraisals. Unusual items giving rise to losses are usually considered to be a negative quality-of-earnings factor. It indicates the company's earlier earnings may have been overstated, and the same bias may still be present in current and prospective earnings. Unusual gains leave the opposite impression. While this may seem to suggest they should be regarded as a positive factor, they are not, primarily because statement users generally don't like positive or negative surprises. Furthermore, unusual gains may be a red flag signaling that management is realizing gains in an attempt to mask declining operating earnings.

Income from continuing operations is used by most statement users to predict future income levels, since by definition any income or losses reported for discontinued operations is not expected to continue once the operation responsible is discontinued in future periods. While following this practice, statement users should always be mindful that some so-called discontinued operations have continued to operate over many accounting periods beyond the announcement date of management's intention to discontinue them. Because of this experience and management's responsibility to manage the operation until discontinued, the results of discontinued operations are usually included in current appraisals of management until the discontinued operation is in fact discontinued. Since discontinued operations impact cash flows, they are included in cash flow analysis. Discontinued operations involving losses are regarded as a negative earnings quality factor until discontinued. Discontinued operations involving potential gains are normally treated like one time income sources and as such are regarded as a low-quality source of earnings.

The effects of accounting changes are usually excluded from management appraisals in the year of change, since the accounting change typically has little, if any, economic substance. However, most statement users seem to use the actual reported income for the prechange year as well as the change year in making earnings projections based on past earnings data. Their rationale is that since management often makes accounting changes to maintain past earnings trends, the trend line rather than actual earnings is the more important piece of data for projection purposes. Also, in the future, to maintain historical growth rates management will continue to make accounting changes that cannot be predicted in the current period.

While past periods are not usually restated for prediction purposes, statement users ought to restate past earnings to the new accounting basis to understand why it was not used in the past. Projecting the restated data can also be helpful in understanding some future implications of the accounting change.

Since accounting changes are usually made only for reporting purposes and not for tax reporting, they typically do not have any cash flow effect. Therefore, they often do not enter into cash flow analyses.

In most cases, accounting changes result in lower quality earnings, since the shift is from a conservative to a more liberal accounting method. Since most companies making accounting changes retain their tax method, which is usually a more conservative approach than their book method, statement users often examine the deferred tax effect of the differences between the tax and the new and old book methods to get a sense of dollar effect of the shift away from conservatism.

Finally, the reported dollar effect of retaining the old accounting method should always be identified in both the year of change and the following year. In most instances, the reason for the change is higher profits or an improved balance sheet ratio, rather than the reason stated to meet the *Opinion No. 20* accounting change criteria.

For analysis purposes, extraordinary items, unusual gains, and discontinued business profits are usually excluded from those ratios incorporating profits that are designed to measure a company's ability to sustain a level of performance over time, such as debt coverage ratios and measures of return on capital. The inclusion of these items is thought to distort future profits implied by the current measurement, and, in the case of gains, to overstate current performance. Unusual and (if the discontinued business is still being operated) discontinued business losses are usually included in these ratios. This practice reflects the conservative bias of prudent analysts. Since accounting changes seldom have any economic or cash flow substance, care must be taken not to interpret ratios incorporating the profit figures inflated by the accounting change as indicators of an improved situation.

Quality Products, Incorporated
Accounting for Discontinued Operations and Unusual and Infrequent Events Business School case 9–177–082.

In April 1975, David Strange, president, Quality Products, Inc. (QPI), said: "We believe it is clearly in the best interests of stockholders to discontinue QPI's feed business, to sell the assets of the Feed Division, and release capital funds for operations that offer greater opportunities for profit and growth." In late May, the company's audit committee met to review the accounting issues facing the QPI top management as a result of the decision to discontinue the Feed Division.

In addition, the audit committee planned to review at this meeting the accounting for several other major events that had occurred during the last quarter of the company's fiscal year. These were: the write-off of a foreign subsidiary's inventories as a result of a new government regulation banning the use of a certain food preservative; the decision of management to extend the depreciation life of some domestic depreciable assets; the out-of-court settlement of a claim against the company; an uninsured loss arising from the destruction by a tornado of a major QPI grain storage facility in Kansas; and the gain on the sale of land acquired in the late 1950s for possible future plant sites.

The Company

In 1975, QPI was a large convenience foods manufacturer with diversified interests in specialty chemicals, electronics, materials testing equipment, and related fields. Sales for the fiscal year ended May 31, 1974, exceeded $575 million and net earnings after taxes were almost $13 million for the same period. (See Exhibit 1 and 2 for financial statements.) The company's operations included more than 50 flour mills, terminal elevators, flour and

---

This case was prepared by David F. Hawkins.

Copyright © 1976 by the President and Fellows of Harvard College
Harvard Business School case 177–082 (Rev. 1985)

EXHIBIT 1

QUALITY PRODUCTS, INC.
Consolidated Balance Sheet at May 31
(in thousands)

	1974	1973
Assets		
Cash	$ 12,541	$ 15,211
Accounts receivable (net)	44,825	42,515
Inventories	69,513	55,879
Total current assets	$126,879	$113,605
Sundry costs chargeable to future periods	8,767	7,268
Land, buildings, and equipment (net)	124,780	121,048
Miscellaneous assets	2,816	2,790
Goodwill, patents, trade names, and other intangibles	4,646	3,970
Total assets	$267,888	$248,681
Liabilities and Equity		
Notes payable	$ 7,250	—
Accounts payable and accrued expenses	29,611	$ 22,597
Accrued taxes	12,833	12,513
Thirft accounts of officers and employees	3,665	3,539
Dividends payable	277	277
Total current liabilities	$ 53,636	$ 38,926
Long-term debt	45,444	45,200
Reserves for self-insurance, price declines, and other purposes	4,837	4,959
Total liabilities	$103,917	$ 89,085
Stockholders' equity:		
Preferred stock, 5% cumulative	$ 22,147	$ 22,147
Common stock	46,276	45,123
Retained earnings	95,787	92,658
Treasury stock (deduct)	(239)	(332)
Total stockholders' equity	$163,971	$159,596
Total liabilities and equity	$267,888	$248,681

food packaging plants, and chemical and electronic installations throughout the United States and in a number of foreign countries.

QPI was incorporated in 1936 to acquire several grain-handling and milling firms in the midwest. Numerous acquisitions in related areas were made in the years following. During its early years, the company was essentially a holding company; but in 1945, most of the subsidiary corporations were dissolved and the firm became an operating company. Rapid expansion followed as the company integrated vertically and developed brand-name consumer goods including breakfast cereals, cake mixes, and similar products based upon its basic milling activities. Livestock feed products were an integral part of operations throughout most of the company's history.

Increased competition and declining profit margins for food manufacturers caused QPI to seek more rapid growth by diversification into chemicals,

EXHIBIT 2

QUALITY PRODUCTS, INC.
Consolidated Income Statement for the Fiscal Year Ended May 31
(in thousands)

	1974	1973
Sales of products and services	$575,512	$537,818
Costs:		
Costs of products and services sold, exclusive of items shown below	$431,060	$405,256
Depreciation	8,427	7,681
Interest	2,989	2,502
Contribution to employees' retirement plan	2,779	2,435
Selling, general, and administrative expenses	105,966	97,582
Federal taxes on income	11,459	10,847
Total costs	$562,680	$526,303
Earnings for the year	$ 12,832	$ 11,515

electronics, oil-seed processing, and for a short time into small household appliances. Sales increased only modestly in the 1960s and profits moved erratically. QPI found itself competing for sales in industries that were dominated by large companies and where, again, margins were very low or even nonexistent. This was the case for a number of years in the company's Feed Division.

The company also sought to reach wider markets on an international scale. In 1962, productive and marketing facilities were constructed in Canada for several food products. In the early 1960s, acquisitions were made in Central and South America, in Pakistan, and in Europe. Most of these international ventures were wholly owned subsidiaries, but a few were joint enterprises with firms in foreign nations. The nature of these foreign operations varied from food product marketing and raw material processing to electronic activities.

The company's 1974 sales volume was distributed among the major segments of the company as follows: consumer foods, $260 million; flour, $161 million; feed, $78 million; specialty products, $28 million; chemicals, $15 million; and electronics, $33 million.

Change in Management and Company Policy

In December 1974, several important changes were made in the QPI top management. David Strange, who had come to the company from a top management position in the food industry, was named president. Several new vice presidents and divisional managers were also announced about this time.

The change in management was followed by a change in corporate policy directed toward improved profitability and growth through concentration in the areas of convenience foods and specialty chemicals. Early in 1975, in response to a stockholder's question, "Where is the company's profit potential?" management published its succinct answer in QPI *News*, a quarterly publication directed to stockholders: "Our combined chemical and electronics business was still less than 10 percent of total sales in the last fiscal year. We expect growth in these areas, but our greatest profit potential is in packaged convenience food products." A large consumer foods research facility was completed, and expenditures for research and development and for advertising were increased markedly. Management believed that development and marketing of new convenience food products would bring the desired higher sales and wider profit margins.

All areas of the company's activities were reorganized to conform to this new policy. For example, several further changes were made in the organization and personnel of the company's Electronic Group, which had been created a year earlier to combine all electronic, mechanical, aerospace, and related operations into a single unit. In line with these changes, management was considering the discontinuance of several of its electronic operations at a later date.

Decision to Liquidate the Feed Division

For several years, the entire operation of the Feed Division of QPI had been under study. Management could not see any means of changing operations to make a satisfactory return on investment in the future, despite efforts to build needed volume in the highly competitive, low-margin feed industry through extensive expansion into poultry, broiler, and turkey growing operations. Prices of broilers and turkeys during most of the 1975 fiscal year were below the costs of production. In addition, many direct feed customers, suffering from the same depressed prices, were unable to buy in normal volumes and some could not meet their financial obligations. Increasing bad debt losses from uncollectible receivables added to the company's operating losses in this area.

Feed Division operating losses had been substantial for several prior years, and losses for the fiscal year to end May 31, 1975, were expected to be $5 million before tax credits of $2.3 million.[1] Total company sales and profits were expected to be significantly lower than those reported in the 1974 fiscal year.

The decision to begin liquidation of the Feed Division was made and announced in April 1975. An orderly withdrawal extending over a two- or three-year period was planned. During this period, all plant facilities

---

[1] The estimated operating losses of the division between the measurement date April 1975 and May 31, 1975, included in this amount were $1 million before a tax credit of nearly $500,000.

of the division were to be sold. Operations were to be continued into the 1976 fiscal accounting period, but only to honor existing firm contracts which were to require several months for completion. The 900 or more employees were to be transferred and absorbed into other QPI operations or to be terminated with benefits in line with existing company policies.

Reporting the Feed Division Liquidation to Stockholders

The controller was asked by the audit committee to prepare a projection of the amounts involved in the Feed Division liquidation. This report did not include the 1975, $5 million pre-tax operating loss of the division. His report was submitted to the QPI audit committee in late May. The controller's projections were made to May 31, 1975, and gave recognition to the operations and partial liquidation transactions that were expected to occur both prior to and after that date. A summary of his detailed report is shown in Exhibit 3.

The analysis pointed out that neither the timing nor the method of reporting the liquidation in the annual report to stockholders would have any effect upon income tax reporting. The estimated total book loss of more

EXHIBIT 3

QUALITY PRODUCTS, INC.
Projection of Estimated Costs and Losses Arising from
Feed Division Liquidation as of May 31, 1975

Accounts receivable charged off between measurement date (April 1975) and end of fiscal year	$5,110,461	
Less: Bad debt allowance provided from operations to date	3,644,536	
	$1,465,925	
Estimated future additional uncollectible receivables	570,000	$ 2,035,925
Losses and write-down of land, building, and equipment: Recorded between measurement date and end of fiscal year	$1,465,425	
Estimated additional losses in future dispositions	6,867,608	8,333,033
Costs and expenses related to discontinuance of operations: Incurred between measurement date and end of fiscal year	$2,294,559	
Estimated future liquidation costs, including fiscal year 1976 operation to satisfy existing contracts............	2,803,073	5,097,632
Total		$15,466,590
Less income tax credits*		11,027,752
Total after income tax credits		$ 4,438,838

---

* Income tax credits will be claimed against actual tax liability when expenses are incurred or when properties are sold. Loss carryover provisions in the tax law will provide full benefit of losses not used currently. Tax credits include benefit of write-off of feed division goodwill not carried on books as an asset. This goodwill resulting from acquisitions of feed companies in earlier years was written off the books, but a deduction for income taxes was not allowable until liquidation of feed operations.

than $15 million was significantly reduced by computed tax benefits, to a projected net loss of $4,438,838.

The loss on liquidation was significant in amount in comparison to both net income and financial size.

Over a period of several years, QPI had accumulated "reserves for self-insurance, price declines, and other purposes" by charges to retained earnings. These reserves totaled $4,836,654 on the consolidated balance sheet at May 31, 1974, of which $2,855,786 applied to the Feed Division. This amount would no longer be required after liquidation of the division. The controller's analysis of estimated losses in Exhibit 3 was before possible credits from these reserves.

Other Agenda Items

In addition to the Feed Division liquidation accounting issue, the audit committee had to consider five other accounting items on its agenda.

In early March 1975, after several years of litigation, the French courts upheld a government ban on the use in food products of certain preservatives that were thought to cause cancer. This ruling required the company to destroy all of its existing inventories containing the banned preservatives and recall all of the affected products from the marketplace. The estimated cost of this action was $500,000 after tax credits. It was expected that the recall program would be completed by May 31, 1975. In addition, it was anticipated that in the near future other Common Market governments might follow the lead of the French government. To avoid any possible trouble in these other Common Market countries, QPI had stopped using the banned preservative in all of the other Common Market countries. The estimated after tax cost of reformulation and testing associated with the switch in preservatives was $300,000. The after tax legal and other costs incurred in contesting the government's ban were $500,000 in 1974 and $75,000 in 1975.

During the fourth quarter of fiscal year 1975, the QPI management decided to use a 13-year depreciation life for a certain class of equipment used extensively in the company's food operations. Previously, this class of equipment had been depreciated on a 10-year basis. This decision applied only to equipment purchased after March 1, 1975. This decision increased the fourth-quarter after-tax profits by $200,000 over what they would have been if a 10-year life had been used.

In April 1975, QPI reached an out-of-court settlement with a consumer protection group which had brought a class action against the company on behalf of a number of individuals who claimed a QPI product had been injurious to their health. This action which had been in litigation since 1970 was settled for an after-tax cost of $250,000. Originally, the plaintiffs for the class had sought $100 million in damages. Since the company could not reasonably estimate what their ultimate loss might have been from this claim, no provisions for this possible loss had been made in prior years. In addition, QPI did not have a general litigation loss reserve, since the company believed its industrial and general insurance covered most of the expected types of claims that might be made against the company. This $250,000 settlement was not covered by insurance.

In the fourth quarter of fiscal 1975, an unseasonal and unusually severe tornado destroyed the QPI central grain facility in Kansas. The company estimated that its after-tax loss from this catastrophe was $135,000 more than QPI would recover from its facilities insurance claim.

Soon after the new management took over control of the company, it conducted a survey to identify redundant and surplus assets that might be sold to raise funds to finance the company's operations. Among the assets identified as potential candidates for sale were several pieces of industrial land purchased in the early 1950s as possible factory or distribution center sites. After several months of trying, QPI sold two of these sites in May 1975 for an after-tax gain of $750,000.

During the prior three quarters of fiscal year 1975, the company had not reported any extraordinary items, discontinued operations, or accounting changes in its interim financial statements.

Some Considerations

The terms of the sizable long-term promissory note indebtedness of QPI placed a restriction upon the payment of dividends to common stockholders. In general, the dividends paid or declared after May 31, 1964, could not exceed 85 percent of consolidated net earnings since that date. At May 31, 1974, $30,411,380 of retained earnings was free of this restriction.

Management was very much aware of its position in the competitive environment in which it operated. Selected information for several firms in the milling and consumer foods industries is shown in Exhibit 4.

In mid-April 1975, the market price of QPI's common stock had dropped to $28 after being in the middle $30s in the last few months of 1974. Although sales for the six months ended November 30, 1974, had exceeded those of the corresponding period for the previous year, earnings per share had declined to $0.55 from $0.75 for the same period. At the end of the third quarter of fiscal year 1975, market analysts were anticipating that earnings for the year ending May 31, 1975, would just cover the $1.20 annual dividend and that in the longer run the stock price would recover to the 1974 levels.

Perhaps the most important single factor considered by management in choosing the method of reporting Feed Division liquidation losses was the anticipated effect upon stockholder and prospective investor attitudes toward the company. Throughout its entire history, QPI had maintained an ideal relationship with its stockholders, and the new management would not consider any reporting alternative which stockholders would be likely to interpret as improper or uninformative. Management was aware that

EXHIBIT 4
Selected Industry Data*

	Sales†	Net Income after Taxes*	Earnings per Sales Dollar	Earnings per Share	Dividends per Share	Price Range High	Low
Quality Products:							
1970	$ 527,701	$12,235	2.3%	$1.63	$1.00	$ 23	$19
1971	529,820	14,694	2.8	1.98	1.00	30	20
1972	545,998	16,817	3.1	2.26	1.00	38	30
1973	537,818	11,515	2.1	1.46	1.15	34	24
1974	575,512	12,832	2.2	1.63	1.20	39	31
Processors United:							
1970	$ 331,362	$ 4,006	1.2%	$2.02	$1.25	$ 22	$20
1971	350,610	5,641	1.6	2.90	1.25	37	21
1972	359,657	7,913	2.2	3.70	1.25	50	37
1973	373,818	6,541	1.8	3.03	1.40	47	32
1974	384,962	7,911	2.1	3.62	1.40	77	44
Parker Foods:							
1970	$ 438,261	$14,569	3.3%	$2.28	$0.80	$ 31	$23
1971	493,527	17,468	3.5	2.71	1.00	52	25
1972	530,571	17,784	3.4	2.74	1.20	52	42
1973	527,816	18,915	3.6	2.76	1.20	45	39
1974	581,042	19,908	3.4	3.03	1.35	45	39
National Foods:							
1970	$ 971,334	$42,399	4.4%	$1.81	$1.95	$ 25	$20
1971	1,008,897	48,397	4.8	1.99	2.00	40	24
1972	1,052,964	54,145	5.1	2.21	2.30	54	37
1973	1,087,076	61,071	5.6	2.48	2.60	75	62
1974	1,160,177	66,821	5.8	2.69	2.10	108	69
Consumer Products:							
1970	$1,432,319	$44,058	3.1%	$3.18	$1.80	$ 39	$33
1971	1,451,245	45,544	3.1	3.27	1.80	50	38
1972	1,605,725	49,362	3.1	3.51	1.95	54	46
1973	1,667,176	50,667	3.0	3.59	2.00	66	45
1974	1,790,834	50,211	2.8	3.51	2.00	79	59

* Fiscal year endings for the companies are: Quality Products and Processors United Company, May 31; Parker Foods Company, September 30; National Foods, Inc., March 31; and consumer Products Corporation, December 31.

† In thousands. All data adjusted for stock splits and dividends.

the amount of net income reported for the fiscal year ending May 31, 1975, might have an effect upon the market price of the company's common stock. Not only was there a concern to preserve the position of present stockholders, but there was a strong possibility that in the near future, additional issues of common might be offered to facilitate further acquisitions for expansion in the area of convenience foods. Management was therefore anxious to avoid any reporting practice which might have a significant, continuing adverse effect upon its relations in the stockholder and financial communities.

Questions

1. How should the liquidation of the Feed Division be reflected in the company's financial statements?

2. How should the company account for the other items on the audit committee's agenda?

3. Assume that the QPI's 1975 profit after taxes before considering the "other agenda items" on the audit committee's agenda will be $9.5 million, prepare the company's 1975 income statement, starting with the line "Income from continuing operations." The $9.5 million includes the estimated 1975 operating losses of the Feed Division, but not the items included in Exhibit 3.

4. How do you think existing and potential investors might react to the 1975 income statement treatment of the items on the audit committee's agenda?

CHAPTER 13

Computing and Analyzing Earnings per Share

The concept of earnings per share can range from being simple to complex, depending on a company's capital structure. The periodic earnings per share of a company with a simple capital structure is determined by dividing net income for the period by the weighted average number of its common shares outstanding during the period. The resulting figure represents the common stockholders' equity in the company's net income. For companies with complex capital structures, the earnings-per-share computation requires some adjustments to net income and the weighted number of shares outstanding to reflect preferred dividends and potential dilution by convertible securities, warrants, and options. The resulting earnings per share is a statistical representation of common stockholders' equity in net income after allowing for potential dilution of that interest by securities that are substantially equivalent to common stock or could have claims on net income either directly or through the right to acquire common stock under certain conditions.[1] In addition, depending on its capital structure, a company may present two earnings-per-share figures: "primary" and "fully diluted" earnings per share. If the company's earnings computation involves extraordinary items, each of these two earnings-per-share figures will also be presented for both the "income before extraordinary items" and "net income" amounts.

Earnings-per-share data are the key financial statistics for most statement users. They should know how these data are computed and their usefulness and limitations. Earnings-per-share data can be very useful, together with other data, in evaluating management's past performance and predicting future earnings potential. However, overreliance on published earnings-per-share figures has several pitfalls. First, the earnings-per-share data tend

---

[1] It is important to note that the adjustments in complex capital structure situations are made for the sole purpose of calculating earnings per share. Neither the net income figure shown on the income statement nor the actual number of shares outstanding is affected by these adjustments.

to be accepted without examining the details of the income statement. This can lead to misleading inferences. Second, the emphasis on a single share-earnings figure tends to shift the attention of statement users and investors away from the enterprise's total operations and financial condition.

The accounting rules for computing earnings per share are primarily presented in *APB Opinion No. 15* and its various amendments. *Statement No. 21* exempted nonpublic enterprises from the requirement in *Opinion No. 15* to publish earnings-per-share data.

Dual Presentation: A Summary

After trying unsuccessfully for many years to deemphasize the significance of earnings per share in accounting reports, the APB switched its position and required these data to be displayed on the earnings statement. The factors contributing to this decision were: *(a)* the widespread use of these data; *(b)* the importance people attached to them; *(c)* the apparently misleading use of this figure by certain companies to boost their stock prices by issuing securities with common stock characteristics which did not enter into the earnings-per-share calculation; *(d)* the increasing use of warrants and convertible securities which had the potential effect of diluting earnings per share; and *(e)* the apparent unwillingness of other accounting authorities to deal forcefully with the inconsistencies, confusion, and abuses in this area.

The APB required that companies present a primary earnings-per-share computation that would take into consideration all of a company's common stock and common stock equivalents. It also stated that when this primary earnings-per-share calculation was subject to future potential dilution from the conversion of senior securities, a second earnings-per-share figure should be published showing the full effect of this dilution. Henceforth, companies with complex capital structures had to present with equal prominence on the face of the income statement the company's primary earnings-per-share and fully diluted earnings-per-share amounts.

Primary earnings per share are the amount of net income attributable to each share of outstanding common stock and common stock equivalent. A common stock equivalent is any security which, because of its terms or the circumstances under which it was *issued,* is in substance equivalent to common stock.

Fully diluted earnings per share is the amount of current earnings per share reflecting the maximum dilution that would result from conversion of convertible securities and exercise of warrants and options that individually would decrease earnings per share and in the aggregate would have had a dilutive effect. All such issuances are assumed to have taken place at the beginning of the period (or at the time of issuance of the convertible security, if later).

The term "earnings per common share" should be used without qualifying language *only* when *no* potentially dilutive convertible securities, options, warrants, or other agreements providing for contingent issuances of common stock are outstanding. In all other cases, qualifying language (such as the word "primary") must be used with the term "earnings per share."

Finally, even if some securities are regarded as common stock equivalents, they should not be included in the computation of primary or fully diluted earnings per share if their inclusion will have the effect of increasing the earnings per share or decreasing the loss per share otherwise computed. This effect is referred to as being "antidilutive."

Opinion No. 15 is a very controversial opinion. Several prominent accounting authors have described it as reading like an episode from *Alice in Wonderland*. Some of its critics believe the APB should never have issued the *Opinion*, since the subject matter is one of financial analysis, not accounting principles. Others disagree with the novel concepts and methods introduced in this *Opinion* and the prominence it gives to the earnings-per-share figure in income statements. Still others believe that the *Opinion's* recommendations are inconsistent and do not reflect the ways investors calculate and use earnings-per-share data.

Analysts' Preference

Because the fully diluted earnings-per-share calculation reduces the earnings per share of a company to the lowest figure possible, a number of analysts tend to use this figure in preference to primary earnings per share. In addition, some analysts claim that the fully diluted data are more indicative of a company's future earnings-per-share potential. However, a number of analysts believe the APB's definition of common stock equivalents is arbitrary and has little practical justification. Hence, they consider the resulting earnings-per-share data meaningless for the purpose of predicting long-term market values. They prefer to use other approaches to valuation, such as dividend and cash flow models.

Legal Considerations

The requirements for calculating earnings per share presented in *Opinion No. 15* do not change in any way the legal rights of the various security holders. Thus, the long-term capital section of the balance sheet still reflects the legal relationships between the various classes of securities. Also, the interest expense related to convertible debt shown as an expense in the computation of net income remains unchanged regardless of how the related debt securities are treated for earnings-per-share calculation purposes.

Opinion No. 15

Opinion No. 15 sets forth some general standards and specific methods for (1) computing earnings per share in a consistent manner and (2) presenting these data in a meaningful way in reports to stockholders.

Opinion No. 15 concluded that the extent of the earnings-per-share data shown on the face of the income statement and the captions used should vary with the complexity of the company's capital structure. Accordingly, the *Opinion* distinguished between companies with simple and complex capital structures. The primary and fully diluted earnings-per-share share concepts introduced by the *Opinion* apply only to companies with complex capital structures.

Simple Capital Structures

In the case of companies with relatively simple capital structures, a single presentation of earnings per share is appropriate. Such cases include companies whose capital stock consists only of common stock and includes none or very few other securities, options, or warrants that upon conversion could materially dilute earnings per share.

Three Percent Test

The so-called 3 percent test is used to determine if a company should make a dual presentation. The required reporting of earnings-per-share data depends on the materiality of the dilution produced by securities enabling their holders to obtain common stock in the future. If aggregate dilution from all such securities is less than 3 percent of earnings per common share outstanding, it is not considered material and need not be reported for either primary or fully diluted earnings per share. Thus, if both the primary and fully diluted amounts are more than 97 percent of earnings per common share outstanding, earnings per share may be based on only common shares outstanding.

The 3 percent provision applies to fully diluted earnings per share compared to earnings per common share outstanding, not compared to primary earnings per share. Antidilutive securities should be excluded in computing aggregate dilution. An antidilutive security is a security which, when included in the earnings-per-share calculation, would result in an increase in the amount reported as earnings per share, or a decrease in the amount reported as net loss per share. A dilutive security has the opposite effect on earnings per share.

The 3 percent provision also applies to the reporting of any other earnings-per-share information, such as supplementary data.

Aggregate dilution of less than 3 percent generally should be reported when it is anticipated that earnings-per-share data for the period that the provision applies might subsequently be included in a comparative income statement in which the following period reflects dilution of 3 percent or more. Otherwise, dilution in the following period would appear greater than it was in fact.

Illustration

Illustration 13–1 presents the disclosure of earnings-per-share data for a company with a simple capital structure. (This and subsequent illustrations assume that *Opinion No. 15* was effective for all periods covered.) The numbers of shares assumed for Illustration 13–1 are as follows:

	1986	1985
Common stock outstanding:		
Beginning of year	3,300,000	3,300,000
End of year	3,300,000	3,300,000
Issued or acquired during year	None	None
Common stock reserved under employee stock options granted	7,200	7,200
Weighted average number of shares	3,300,000	3,300,000

The shares issuable under employee stock options are excluded from the weighted average number of shares on the assumption that their effect is not dilutive (i.e., that is, less than 3 percent).

In Illustration 13–1, the claims on current income such as dividends, senior securities such as nonconvertible preferred stock, or other securities that have preferential rights and are not a common stock or common stock equivalent should be deducted from net income and income before extraordinary items before computing earnings per share. Dividends on cumulative preferred stock should be deducted from net income or loss irrespective of whether or not they are earned. If the claims of senior securities are payable only if earned, then the amount deducted should be limited to the extent income is available therefor.

Complex Capital Structures

Corporations with complex capital structures are required to present two types of earnings-per-share data with equal prominence on the face of the

ILLUSTRATION 13–1
Examples of Disclosure of Earnings per Share, Simple Capital Structure Conclusion of Income Statement (in thousands, except per-share data)

	1986	1985
Income before extraordinary item	$ 9,150	$7,650
Extraordinary gain, less applicable income taxes	900	—
Net income	$10,050	$7,650
Earnings per common share:		
Income before extraordinary item	$2.77	$2.32
Extraordinary item	0.28	—
Net income	$3.05	$2.32

income statement. If a company had no common stock equivalents, *Opinion No. 15* suggested that it use the titles:

"Earnings per common share, assuming no dilution."
"Earnings per common share, assuming full dilution."

If common stock equivalents are present, the titles are to read approximately as follows (exact titles were not prescribed in the *Opinion*):

"Earnings per common and common equivalent share."
"Earnings per common and common equivalent share, assuming full dilution."

In practice, the terms "primary earnings per share" and "fully diluted earnings per share" have been adopted extensively.

At Issue

The APB concluded that the determination of whether or not a convertible security is a common stock equivalent should be made at the time of issuance, and that as long as the security is outstanding it retains this status. The tests for determining a convertible stock's status as set forth in *Statement No. 85*, an amendment to *Opinion No. 15*, are:

> A convertible security shall be considered a common stock equivalent if, at the time of issuance[2] it has an effective yield of less than 66⅔ percent of the then-current average Aa corporate bond yield.[3] The effective yield shall be based on the security's stated annual interest or dividend payments, any original issuance premium or discount, and any call premium or discount and shall be the lowest of the yield to maturity and the yields to all call dates. The computation of effective yield does not include considerations of put options or changing conversion rates.

Fully Diluted Earnings per Share

The purpose of the fully diluted earnings-per-share presentation is to indicate on a prospective basis the maximum potential dilution of current earnings per share. Securities whose conversion, exercise, or other contingent

---

[2] This is generally the date when agreement as to terms has been reached and announced, even though such agreement is subject to certain further actions, such as directors' or stockholders' approval.

[3] If the security was sold as issued outside of the United States, the most comparable yield in the foreign country should be used.

issuance would have an antidilutive effect are excluded from this computation.

Full diluted earnings-per-share data are required to be shown on the face of the income statement for each period presented

> if shares of common stock (a) were issued during the period on conversions, exercises, etc., or (b) were contingently issuable at the close of any period presented and if primary earnings per share for such period would have taken place at the beginning of the period or would have been reduced had such contingent issuances taken place at the beginning of the period. The above contingencies may result from the existence of (a) senior stock or debt which is convertible into common shares, but is not a common stock equivalent, (b) options or warrants, or (c) agreements for the issuance of common shares upon the satisfaction of certain conditions (for example, the attainment of specified higher levels of earnings following a business combination). The computation should be based on the assumption that all such issued and issuable shares were outstanding from the beginning of the period (or from the time the contingency arose, if after the beginning of the period). Previously reported fully diluted earnings-per-share amounts should not be retroactively adjusted for subsequent conversions of subsequent changes in the market prices of the common stock.

Net Income Adjustments: Convertible Securities

The concept of earnings per share contained in *Opinion No. 15* requires certain adjustments, for the earnings-per-share calculation *only*, of a company's profit after taxes for interest expense and preferred dividends. This is necessary to reflect the fact that the reporting company's net income before and after preferred dividends includes payments that are deducted in arriving at these figures, but which would be avoided if the securities giving rise to adjustments were converted as is assumed in the earnings-per-share calculations.

Two possible approaches were considered by the APB to handle interest charges and preferred dividends applicable to the common stock, namely, the "if-converted" and the "two-class" methods of computation. The if-converted method computes earnings-per-share data on the assumption that convertible securities are converted at the beginning of the earliest period reported (or at time of issuance, if later). The two-class method computes primary earnings per share by treating common stock equivalents as though they were common stocks with different dividend rates.

Opinion No. 15 expressed a preference for the if-converted method in the case of most convertible securities. The *Opinion* described these two methods and their application:

> The "if-converted" method recognizes the fact that the holders of convertible securities cannot share in distributions of earnings applicable to the common stock unless they relinquish their right to senior distributions. Conversion is assumed, and earnings applicable to common stock and com-

mon stock equivalents are determined before distributions to holders of these securities.

The "if-converted" method also recognizes the fact that a convertible issue can participate in earnings, through dividends or interest, either as a senior security or as a common stock, but not both. The two-class method (see below) does not recognize this limitation and may attribute to common stock an amount of earnings per share less than if the convertible security had actually been converted. The amount of earnings per share on common stock as computed under the two-class method is affected by the amount of dividends declared on the common stock. . . .

Although the two-class method is considered inappropriate with respect to [most convertible securities] . . . its use may be necessary in the case of participating securities and two-class common stock. This is the case, for example, when these securities are not convertible into common stock.

Under the two-class method, common stock equivalents are treated as common stock with a dividend rate different from the dividend rate on the common stock and, therefore, conversion of convertible securities is not assumed. No use of proceeds is assumed. Distributions to holders of senior securities, common stock equivalents, and common stock are first deducted from net income. The remaining amount (the undistributed earnings) is divided by the total of common shares and common share equivalents. Per-share distributions to the common stockholders are added to this per-share amount to arrive at primary earnings per share.

Computation Examples

To illustrate the recalculations of earnings per share as required by *Opinion No. 15,* assume the ABC Company had a net income of $90,000 after interest and taxes paid at a 50 percent rate, but before preferred dividends of $40,000; paid a dividend of $0.30 per common share; and had the following long-term capital structure:

Convertible 12 percent bonds (convertible into 100,000 common shares)	$ 500,000
Convertible 10 percent preferred stock (convertible into 50,000 common shares)	400,000
Common stock (250,000 shares authorized, 50,000 outstanding)	2,000,000

The if-converted method recommended by *Opinion No. 15* is initially used in these examples.

First, assume that the ABC Company has a simple capital structure. That is, the yield at issue of *neither* the convertible bonds *nor* the convertible preferred was such as to require these securities to be classified as common stock equivalents. The computation of the ABC Company's "earnings per share, assuming no dilution," according to *Opinion No. 15,* is:

$$\text{Earnings per share} \atop \text{assuming no dilution} = \frac{\text{Net proft after taxes} - \text{Preferred dividends}}{\text{Weighted average number of common}}\atop \text{stock outstanding}$$

$$= \frac{\$90,000 - \$40,000}{50,000 \text{ shares}}$$

$$= \$1 \text{ per share}$$

Now, assume that the convertible preferred stock, but *not* the convertible debt, was classified at issue as a common stock equivalent. This would give the ABC Company a complex capital structure. As a result, the computation of the company's primary earnings per share (or earnings per common and common equivalent shares) is:

$$\text{Primary earnings} \atop \text{per share} = \frac{\text{Profit after taxes before preferred dividends}}{\text{Common stock outstanding}}\atop \text{+ Common stock equivalent of preferred stock}$$

$$= \frac{\$90,000}{(50,000 + 50,000) \text{ shares}}$$

$$= \$0.90 \text{ per share}$$

This calculation reflects the fact that if the convertible preferred stock were converted, the need to pay preferred dividends would be eliminated.

Continuing with the same ABC Company complex capital example, the company's fully diluted earnings per share (or earnings per common and common equivalent share, assuming full dilution) is calculated as follows:

$$\text{Fully diluted} \atop \text{earnings per share} = \frac{\begin{matrix}\text{Profits after taxes} \\ \text{before} \\ \text{preferred dividends}\end{matrix} + \begin{matrix}\text{After-tax equivalent} \\ \text{of convertible} \\ \text{debt interest}\end{matrix}}{\begin{matrix}\text{Common shares} \\ \text{outstanding}\end{matrix} + \begin{matrix}\text{Common stock equivalent} \\ \text{of convertible preferred} \\ \text{stock plus common stock} \\ \text{potentially issuable to} \\ \text{convertible debt holders}\end{matrix}}$$

$$= \frac{\$90,000 + \$30,000}{(50,000 + 50,000 + 100,000) \text{ shares}}$$

$$= \frac{\$120,000}{200,000 \text{ shares}}$$

$$= \$0.60 \text{ per share}$$

This last calculation reflects the elimination of the preferred dividends and the interest cost after the assumed conversion of the convertible preferred and debt issues.

Two-Class Method

The two-class method of computing primary earnings per share treats common stock equivalents as though they were common stock with different dividend rates from that of the common stock. It incorporates an earnings base that reflects (1) the fact that the common stock equivalent (convertible preferred in the ABC Company complex capital example) has a disproportionate preference to earnings relative to the common stock and (2) the actual amounts were paid to the holders of these common stock equivalents based on the stock's actual relationship, preference, and privileges. Accordingly, the following calculation is based on the assumption that amounts already paid to the common stock equivalent holders cannot logically be attributed to any other security during the current period.

To illustrate the application of the two-class method for *nonconvertible* securities, assume that a corporation had 5,000 shares of $100 par value nonconvertible preferred stock and 10,000 shares of $50 par value common stock outstanding during 1986 and had a net income of $65,000. The preferred stock is entitled to a noncumulative annual dividend of $5 per share before any dividend is paid on common. After common has been paid a dividend of $2 per share, the preferred stock then participates in any additional dividends on a 40:60 per-share ratio with common. That is, after preferred and common have been paid dividends of $5 and $2 per share respectively, preferred participates in any additional dividends at a rate of two thirds of the additional amount paid to common on a per-share basis. Also assume that for 1986, preferred shareholders have been paid $27,000 (or $5.40 per share), and common shareholders have been paid $26,000 (or $2.60 per share).

Under the two-class method for *nonconvertible* securities, earnings per share for 1986 would be computed as follows:

Net income		$65,000
Less dividends paid:		
Preferred	$27,000	
Common	26,000	53,000
Undistributed 1986 earnings . . .		$12,000

Allocation of undistributed earnings:

$$\underline{\text{5,000 preferred shares}} \qquad \underline{\text{10,000 common shares}}$$

$$\frac{0.4}{2,000} \times \qquad + \frac{0.6}{6,000} \times \qquad = 8,000 \text{ "equivalent shares"}$$

$$\frac{2,000}{8,000} \times \$12,000 = \$3,000 \qquad \frac{6,000}{8,000} \times \$12,000 = \$9,000$$

$$\frac{\$3,000}{5,000} = \$0.60 \text{ per share} \qquad \frac{\$\ 9,000}{10,000} = \$0.90 \text{ per share}$$

Earnings per share:

	Preferred	Common
Distributed earnings	$5.40	$2.60
Undistributed earnings	0.60	0.90
	$6.00	$3.50

The two-class method is rarely appropriate for convertible and other participating securities, and may be applied only if it results in greater dilution than would result from using the if-converted method.

To illustrate the application of the two-class method for a *convertible* security, assume the company has 30,000 shares of Class A common stock (the ordinary common) and 10,000 shares of Class B common stock outstanding during 1986, and a net income of $160,000. Each share of Class B is convertible into two shares of Class A. The Class B is entitled to an annual dividend of $4 per share. After Class A has been paid a dividend of $2 per share, Class B then participates equally on a per-share basis with any additional dividends paid per share to Class A stockholders. For 1986, the Class B shareholders have been paid $75,000 (or $2.50 per share), and the Class B shareholders have been paid $45,000 (or $4.50 per share).

Under the if-converted method (assume Class B is converted), the earnings per share are:

$$\frac{\$160,000}{50,000 \text{ shares}} = \$3.20 \text{ per share}$$

Under the two-class method for convertible securities, the earnings-per-share calculation is:

Net income		$160,000
Less dividends paid:		
Class A common	$75,000	
Class B common	45,000	120,000
Undistributed 1986 earnings....		$ 40,000

Allocation of undistributed earnings:

$$\frac{\$40,000}{50,000 \text{ shares}} = .80 \text{ per share}$$

$$2(.80) = \$1.60 \text{ per Class B share}$$

Earnings-per-share amounts:

	Class A	Class B
Distributed earnings	$2.50	$4.50
Undistributed earnings	.80	1.60
Totals	$3.30	$6.10

The two-class method would not be used in this case, since it does not result in greater dilution than the if-converted method.

Because of the great variety of features which participating and two-class common stock securities have in practice, *Opinion No. 15* did not set detailed specific guidelines for determining when they should be considered common stock equivalents. Rather, it stated simply:

> Dividend participation does not per se make a security a common stock equivalent. A determination of the status of one of these securities should be based on an analysis of all the characteristics of the security including the ability to share in the earnings potential of the issuing corporation on substantially the same basis as the common stock.

Treasury Stock Method

Opinion No. 15 regards options, warrants, and similar arrangements as common stock equivalents at all times. Typically, whatever value these arrangements have is derived from their right to obtain common stock at a specific price during a specified time period. Accordingly, the *Opinion* maintains that primary earnings per share should reflect the assumption that these securities have been exercised.

The earnings-per-share effect of such securities is computed by the "treasury stock" method. This approach assumes (1) that the warrants and options are exercised at the beginning of the period (or at time of issuance, if later), and (2) that any proceeds received by the issuing company are used to purchase its common stock, up to 20 percent of the outstanding stock, at an average market price during the period.[4] If funds from assumed exercises of options and warrants are still available after this 20 percent limit is reached, their assumed application must follow specific rules outlined in paragraph 38 of the *Opinion* (see below). These computations should not, however, reflect the exercise or conversion of any security if the effects

---

[4] For example, if a corporation has 10,000 warrants outstanding exercisable at $54 and the average market price of the common stock during the reporting period is $60, the $540,000 which would be realized from exercise of the warrants and issuance of 10,000 shares would be an amount sufficient to acquire 9,000 shares; thus, 1,000 shares would be added to the outstanding common shares in computing primary earnings per share for the period.

on earnings per share are antidilutive, except as indicated in paragraph 38 of the *Opinion*.

As a practice, the APB recommended that the assumed exercise not be reflected in primary earnings-per-share data until the market price of the common stock obtainable had been in excess of the exercise price for substantially all of three consecutive months,[5] ending with the last month of the period to which earnings-per-share data relate.

This is a onetime test. Exercise need not be assumed for the computations until the test has been met in a particular quarter. However, once the test is met, the average market price would be computed thereafter, unless the market prices are clearly antidilutive.

The test applies for both primary and full diluted computations. But after the test has once been met, an ending market price which is above the exercise price is used for the fully diluted computations if it would result in more dilution than the average market price for the period.

Previously reported earnings-per-share amounts should not be adjusted retroactively in the case of options and warrants as a result of subsequent changes in market prices of common stock.

The APB recognized that the funds obtained by issuers from the exercise of options and warrants are used in many ways, with a wide variety of results that cannot be anticipated. Application of the treasury stock method in earnings-per-share computations is not based on an assumption that the funds will or could actually be used in that manner implied by this method. Nevertheless, the APB believed its assumed use of funds represented a practical approach to reflecting the dilutive effect that would result from the issuance of common stock under option and warrant agreements at an effective price below the current market price.

The APB concluded, however, that the treasury stock method can be inappropriate, or should be modified, in certain cases. For example, some warrants contain provisions that permit, or require, the tendering of debt (usually at face amount) or other securities of the issuer in payment for all or a portion of the exercise price. The terms of some debt securities issued with warrants require that the proceeds of the exercise of the related warrants be applied toward retirement of the debt. Also, some convertible securities require cash payments upon conversion and are, therefore, considered to be the equivalent of warrants. In all of these cases, the if-converted methods should be applied as if retirement or conversion of the securities had occurred and as if the excess proceeds, if any, had been applied to the purchase of common stock under the treasury stock method. However, exercise of the options and warrants should not be reflected in the primary

---

[5] The *Opinion* does not define "substantially all." Presumably, 11 weeks would be substantially all of a 13-week quarter. Therefore, the computation would be made for any quarter after the market price has once been above the exercise price for any 11 weeks during a quarter.

earnings-per-share computation unless (a) the market price of the related common stock exceeds the exercise price or (b) the security which may be (or must be) tendered is selling at a price below that at which it may be tendered under the option or warrant agreement and the resulting discount is sufficient to establish an effective exercise price below the market price of the common stock that can be obtained upon exercise. Similar treatment should be followed for preferred stock bearing similar provisions or other securities having conversion options permitting payment of cash for a more favorable conversion rate from the standpoint of the investor.

The methods described above should be used to compute fully diluted earnings per share also if dilution results from outstanding options and warrants. However, to reflect maximum potential dilution, the market price at the close of the period reported upon should be used to determine the number of shares assumed to have been repurchased if this market price is higher than the average price used in computing primary earnings per share. Common shares issued on exercise of options or warrants during each period should also be included in fully diluted earnings per share from the beginning of the period, or from date of issuance of the options or warrants if later. In addition, the computation for the portion of the period prior to the date of exercise should be based on market prices of the common stock when exercised.

Finally, the number of incremental shares computed using the treasury stock method for any accounting period are assumed to be outstanding only for that period.

Computation Example

To illustrate the computation of primary and fully diluted earnings per share using the treasury stock method, assume the following data:

Net income for year	$2,000,000
Shares outstanding	1,000,000
Warrants and options to purchase equivalent shares (outstanding for full years)	100,000
Exercise price per share	$15
Average price	$20
Year-end market price	$25

Then primary earnings per share would be computed as:

$$\left(\frac{\$20 - \$15}{\$20}\right) \times 100,000 = 25,000 \text{ incremental shares}$$

$$\frac{\$2,000,000}{1,000,000 + 25,000} = \$1.95$$

Fully diluted earnings per share would be:

$$\left(\frac{\$25 - \$15}{\$20}\right) \times 100,000 = 40,000 \text{ incremental shares}$$

$$\frac{\$2,000,000}{1,000,000 + 40,000} = \$1.92$$

The fully diluted computation uses the year-end market price, since it leads to greater dilution.

Paragraph 38: Twenty Percent Test

The treasury stock method's assumed use of proceeds from options and warrants may not adequately reflect potential dilution when options and warrants to acquire a substantial number of common shares are outstanding. Accordingly, the APB concluded in paragraph 38 of *Opinion No. 15:*

> If the number of shares of common stock obtainable upon exercise of outstanding options and warrants in the aggregate exceeds 20 percent of the number of common shares outstanding at the end of the period for which the computation is being made, the treasury stock method should be modified in determining the dilutive effect of the options and warrants upon earnings-per-share data. In these circumstances, all the options and warrants should be assumed to have been exercised and the aggregate proceeds therefrom to have been applied in two steps:
>
> a. As if the funds obtained were first applied to the repurchase of outstanding common shares at the average market price during the period, but not to exceed 20 percent of the outstanding shares; and then
>
> b. As if the balance of the funds were applied first to reduce any short-term or long-term borrowings and any remaining funds were invested in U.S. government securities or commercial paper, with appropriate recognition of any income tax effect.
>
> The results of steps *(a)* and *(b)* of the computation (whether dilutive or antidilutive) should be aggregated and, if the net effect is dilutive, should enter into the earnings-per-share computation.

Illustration 13–2 demonstrates the application of paragraph 38. Case 2 in the illustration shows a dilutive effect despite a market price below exercise price.

Weighted Average Computations

The divisor for the earnings-per-share calculation should be the weighted average number of outstanding common shares and common share equivalents, if any, during each period presented.

This number is determined by relating *(a)* the portion of time within a reporting period that a particular number of shares of a certain security has been outstanding to *(b)* the total time in that period. Thus, for example, if 100 shares of a certain security were outstanding during the first quarter

ILLUSTRATION 13–2
Application of Paragraph 38

	Case 1	Case 2
Assumptions:		
Net income for year	$ 4,000,000	$ 2,000,000
Common shares outstanding	3,000,000	3,000,000
Options and warrants outstanding to purchase		
equivalent shares	1,000,000	1,000,000
20% limitation on assumed repurchase	600,000	600,000
Exercise price per share	$ 15	$ 15
Average and year-end market value		
per common share to be used	$ 20	$ 12
Computations:		
Application of assumed proceeds ($15 million):		
Toward repurchase of outstanding common shares at		
applicable market value	$12,000,000	$ 7,200,000
Reduction of debt	3,000,000	7,800,000
	$15,000,000	$15,000,000
Adjustment of net income:		
Actual net income	$ 4,000,000	$ 2,000,000
Interest reduction (6%) less 50% tax effect	90,000	234,000
Adjusted net income (A)	$ 4,090,000	$ 2,234,000
Adjustment of shares outstanding:		
Actual outstanding....................................	3,000,000	3,000,000
Net additional shares issuable (1,000,000 − 600,000)	400,000	400,000
Adjusted shares outstanding (B)	3,400,000	3,400,000
Earnings per share:		
Before adjustment.....................................	$1.33	$0.67
After adjustment (A ÷ B)	$1.20	$0.66

of a fiscal year and 300 shares were outstanding during the balance of the year, the weighted average number of outstanding shares would be 250, i.e. (100 + 300 + 300 + 300) divided by 4. The use of a weighted average is necessary so that the effect of changes in the number of shares outstanding is related to the operations during the portion of the accounting period affected.

If the company reacquires its shares, these shares should be excluded from the weighted average calculation from the date of their acquisition.

Computations of earnings-per-share data should give retroactive recognition in all periods presented to changes in the capital structure due to stock splits, stock dividends, or reverse stock splits. If the capital structure is changed by such events after the close of the period but before the completion of the financial report, the per-share calculations for the period should be based on the current capitalization. This presumes that the reader's primary interest is related to the current capitalization.

When a business is acquired for stock, the transaction can be accounted for as either a purchase or a pooling of interests, depending on the particular circumstances. When a business combination is accounted for as a purchase, the new shares should be included in the computation of earnings per share only from the acquisition date. In the case of a pooling of interests, the computation should be based on the aggregate of the weighted average outstanding shares of the merged business, adjusted to the equivalent shares of the surviving business for all periods presented. These computations reflect the difference in accounting for income under the two methods of accounting for business combinations. (In a purchase, the income of the purchaser includes the income of the purchased company only from the date of acquisition. In a pooling of interests, the net incomes of the two companies are combined for all periods presented.)

Using the treasury stock method to include options and warrants in the per-share calculations can complicate the computation of the various quarterly, year-to-date, and annual earnings-per-share figures. The following paragraphs set forth some of the rules that apply to the computation of these per-share figures when options and warrants are outstanding.

Dilutive options or warrants which are issued or which expire or are canceled during a period are reflected in both primary and fully diluted earnings-per-share computations for the time they were outstanding during the period. The common stock equivalent shares to be considered enter earnings-per-share computations as part of the weighted average number of shares.

A "period" is the time for which net income is reported and earnings per share are computed. However, when the treasury stock method or any method requiring computation of an average market price is used and the reporting period is longer than three months, a separate computation is made for each three-month period.

A weighted average of shares is computed on the basis of average market prices during each three months included in the reporting period. Thus, if the period being reported upon is six months, nine months, or one year, a weighted average of shares is computed for each quarter. The weighted averages for all quarters are then added together, and the resulting total is divided by the number of quarters to determine the weighted average for the period.

When the ending market price of common stock is higher than the average market price for the period, the ending market price is used for the fully diluted computation to reflect maximum potential dilution. The use of different market prices for primary and fully diluted earnings-per-share computations naturally results in different numbers of shares for the two computations. The use of a higher ending market price for fully diluted computations may also result in the assumption of exercise for fully diluted earnings per share but not for primary earnings per share. Year-to-date computations for fully diluted earnings per share may also be more complex when market prices of common stock increase and then decrease during the year, since the share computation is then made two ways and the greater number of shares is used in computing year-to-date fully diluted earnings per share.

Common stock issued upon the exercise of options or warrants is included in the weighted average of outstanding shares from the exercise date. The treasury stock method is applied for exercised options or warrants from the beginning of the period to the exercise date. For primary earnings per share, the computation for the period prior to exercise is based on the average market price of common stock during the period the exercised options or warrants were outstanding (if the result is dilutive). Incremental shares are weighted for the period the options or warrants were outstanding, and shares issued are weighted for the period the shares were outstanding. For fully diluted earnings per share, however, the computation for the period prior to exercise is based on the market price of common stock when the options or warrants were exercised regardless of whether the result is dilutive or antidilutive. Incremental shares are weighted for the period the options or warrants were outstanding, and shares issued are weighted for the period the shares are outstanding.

No retroactive adjustment or restatement of previously reported earnings-per-share data is made if there is a change in the incremental number of shares determined by applying the treasury stock method. Computations for each quarter or other periods are independent. Earnings-per-share data should not be restated retroactively or adjusted currently to obtain quarterly (or other period) amounts to equal the amount computed for the year to date. As a result, the total of four quarters' earnings per share may not equal the earnings per share for the year when market prices change and the treasury stock method is applied.

Stock Appreciation Rights

Stock appreciation rights are awards entitling employees to receive over time cash, stock, or a combination of cash and stock in an amount equivalent to any increase in the market value of a stated number of shares of the employer's stock over a stated price. The employee does not own the stock.

During the unexercised rights period, the employer recognizes a compensation expense for the change in the values of the rights. This expense is allocated to the current and future periods. The difference between the stated grant price and the actual exercised price is a tax deductible expense for the employer. The influence of stock appreciation rights on earnings-per-share data is presented below.

If the employee is to receive the stock appreciation rights compensation in the form of stock, rather than cash, the potential shares issuable are common stock equivalents and as such should be included in the earnings-per-share calculations using the treasury stock method.

FASB Interpretation No. 31 specifies that the exercise proceeds used in applying this method is the sum of the cash to be received on exercise, the amount of measurable compensation ascribed to future services not yet charged to expense, and the amount of any related tax benefits beyond those recognized for financial reporting purposes that are yet to be credited to capital.

The dilutive effect for primary earnings-per-share determination is computed using the average aggregate compensation and average market price of the stock for the period.

For computing fully diluted earnings per share, the more dilutive is used of either: the market price and aggregate compensation at the close of the period or the average market price and average aggregate compensation for that period.

To illustrate a one-year application of the treasury stock method to stock appreciation rights, assume stock appreciation rights are granted January 1, 1985. The expiration date is December 13, 1995. The employee's rights are vested 100 percent at the end of four years. One thousand shares are under option at a grant price of $10 per share, which is also the quoted market price at the grant date. The rights are payable in stock at no cash cost to the employee. There is no tax windfall, since the employer's deduction of compensation equals the compensation recognized for financial accounting purposes. The quoted market price on December 31, 1985, is $11 per share. The average share price for the year is $10.50.

First, the compensation for 1984 is computed:

Year-End Market Price	Aggregate Compensation (1)	Compensation Accrued (2)	Exercise Proceeds (3)
$11	$1,000	$250	$750

1. Option shares (1,000) times $1 ($11 market price less $10 grant price).
2. Aggregate compensation ($1,000) divided by 4 to reflect four-year vesting period.
3. Unaccrued compensation in this example ($1,000 − $250).

Next, the incremental number of shares to be included in primary earnings per share is calculated as follows:

Shares Issuable (1)	Treasury Shares Assumed Repurchased (2)	Incremental Shares (3)
47	35	12

1. Average aggregate compensation ($500 = $1,000/2) divided by average market price ($10.50).
2. Average exercise proceeds ($750/2) divided by average market price ($10.50).
3. Shares issuable (47) less treasury shares assumed repurchased (35).

Finally, the incremental shares for determining fully diluted earnings per share is computed as follows:

Shares Issuable (1)	Treasury Shares Assumed Repurchased (2)	Incremental Shares (3)
90	68	22

1. Year-end aggregate compensation ($1,000) divided by market price as of year-end ($11). Year-end values are used since they are more dilutive than average values.
2. Year-end exercise proceeds ($750) divided by market price at year-end ($11).
3. Shares issuable (90) less treasury shares assumed repurchased (68).

If the employee has the option to receive stock or cash, the presumption should be made that the employee will elect to receive stock.

Contingent Issues

Some agreements call for the further issuance of shares either directly or from the company's escrow accounts contingent on such conditions as the attainment of specific earnings levels. Such contingent issuable shares should be considered as outstanding in both the primary and fully diluted earnings computations if the conditions for their issuance are currently being attained. If these conditions are not being met, they should be included only in the fully diluted earnings calculation.

The number of shares contingently issuable may depend on some future market price of the stock. In such cases, the current earnings-per-share computations should use the number of shares that would be issuable based on the market price of the stock at the close of the period. If the number of shares issued or contingently issuable changes subsequently because of market price changes, the earnings per share reported for prior periods should be restated. A similar approach should be used if the number of shares contingently issuable is dependent on both future earnings and future stock prices.

Securities of Subsidiaries

In some cases, warrants, options, or securities issued by subsidiaries must be considered as common stock equivalents when computing consolidated and parent company earnings per share that reflect the subsidiary's results of operations through consolidation or the use of the equity method. Circumstances requiring this approach and the appropriate rule to follow in reporting consolidated or parent company earnings include:

a. Certain of the subsidiary's securities are common stock equivalents in relation to its own common stock.

In this case, the earnings per share should include the portion of the subsidiary's income that would be applicable to the consolidated group based on its holdings and the subsidiary's primary earnings per share.

b. Other of the subsidiary's convertible securities, although not common stock equivalents in relation to its own common stock, would enter into the computation of its fully diluted earnings per share.

Under these conditions, only the portion of the subsidiary's income that would be applicable to the consolidated group based on its holdings and the fully diluted earnings per share of the subsidiary should be included in consolidated and parent company fully diluted earnings per share.

c. The subsidiary's securities are convertible into the parent company's common stock.

Such securities should be considered as issued and treated the same way as the related parent stock in the computation of primary and fully diluted earnings per share.

d. The subsidiary issues options and warrants to purchase the parent company's common stock.

These rights should be considered as common stock equivalents by the parent company.

Further Requirements

The complexity of the earnings-per-share calculations requires additional disclosures to explain *(a)* the pertinent rights and privileges of the various securities outstanding and *(b)* the assumptions and adjustments made to calculate primary and fully diluted earnings per share. The disclosure of rights and privileges should include dividends and liquidation preferences, participation rights, call prices and dates, conversion or exercise prices or rates and pertinent dates, sinking fund requirements, and unusual voting rights.

The disclosure of how the earnings-per-share amounts were obtained should not be shown in such a manner as to imply that an earnings-per-share amount which ignores the effect of common stock equivalents constitutes an acceptable presentation of primary earnings per share. In addition, earnings-per-share data are required to be presented for all periods covered by the statement of income or summary of earnings. If it is necessary to restate previous periods' income, the prior periods' earnings-per-share data must also be restated.

Dividends-per-share presentations in comparative statements should reflect the actual dividends declared during the appropriate period adjusted for any subsequent stock splits or dividends. Following a pooling of interests, the dividends-per-share presentation for periods prior to the pooling creates a problem. In these cases, the typical practice is to disclose the dividends declared per share by the principal constituent.

Conflicting Viewpoints

Opinion No. 15 has been criticized widely. In fact, the *Opinion* was not wholeheartedly endorsed by 8 of the 18 members of the APB. The principal reservations of these eight APB members as well as the viewpoints of others who have objected to *Opinion No. 15,* are:

1. The required dual presentation of earnings per share dignifies one figure above all others. This practice runs counter to the profession's position that fair presentation of financial condition and results of operations is achieved by the whole presentation, not by the specific location of any item. Accordingly, the *Opinion* should not be so specific on the location of the dual presentation of earnings per share.

2. The determination of common stock equivalence is a subjective one which cannot be accommodated within prescribed formulas or mathematical rules. This determination, however, does begin with the one factually determinable figure of earnings per actual outstanding common share. It does not serve the interests of meaningful disclosure to deny corporations the right to report this one factually determined figure on the face of the income statement as a basis for investor pro forma per-share calculations. Given this figure as a base, plus adequate disclosure of information related to capital structure that falls within the present bounds of fair disclosure, the calculation of pro forma common stock equivalence should be left to the investor to do in whatever way best serves the investor's purpose. Accounting should not preempt the investor's judgment.

3. Investors have a right to view the primary earnings-per-share data as a realistic attribution of the earnings of the issuer to the various complex elements of its capital structure based on current economic realities—not those existing years earlier, when securities were issued. In addition, the at-issue test disregards the fact that both the issuers and holders of newly issued convertible securities that are not classified as common stock equivalents at issue recognize the possibility that as the value of the underlying common stock increases, the convertible features will become increasingly significant. Therefore, the common stock equivalent concept should have validity at issuance and subsequently.

4. The use of one effective yield test for determining whether or not convertible securities are common stock equivalents does not differentiate among types of security issued and the credit standing of the issuers.

5. It is erroneous to attribute earnings to securities that do not currently, and may never, share in those earnings, particularly when part or all of

those earnings may have already been distributed to others as dividends. Furthermore, until convertible securities are converted, the common stockholders are in control of earnings distributions. Therefore, to show an amount per share which assumes conversion is improper.

6. It is potentially baffling to investors that convertible debt is debt in the statement of earnings but is common stock equivalent in the statement of earnings per share, and that dividends per share are based on the actual number of shares outstanding while earnings per share are based on a different and larger number of shares. Others go further and claim that the source of potential confusion is that there is no such category as "common stock equivalent" in reality and the concept involves assumptions and intricate determinations resulting in figures of questionable meaning that are more confusing than enlightening.

7. The market parity method to determine the common stock equivalence of securities has been supported by some. This approach compares a convertible security's market value with its conversion value. If the two values are substantially equivalent and in excess of redemption price, the convertible security is considered to be a common stock equivalent. The advantage of this method as compared with the investment value test, which requires an estimate of investment value, is that it uses amounts that are readily available and ascertainable.

8. Financial statements should be consistent with the method used to determine earnings per share. Accordingly, the convertible debt considered to be the equivalent of common stock should be classified in the balance sheet in a combined section with common stock under a caption such as "equity of common stockholders and holders of common stock equivalents." In the income statement, the interest paid on common stock equivalents should be shown as a distribution of income with a caption such as "distributions to holders of common stock equivalents."

9. Similarly, it is considered inconsistent and misleading by some that the income of subsidiaries reflected in consolidated and parent company statements disregards the existence of the subsidiary's common stock equivalents, whereas the earnings-per-share calculation reflects these securities.

10. The requirement that options and warrants whose exercise price is at or above the market price of related common stock be taken into account in the computation of primary earnings per share destroys the usefulness of the dual presentation of primary and fully diluted earnings per share. It fails to disclose the magnitude of the contingency arising from the outstanding warrants and options. The requirement is also inconsistent with the determination of the status of convertible securities at time of issuance only, since it apparently recognizes that market conditions subsequent to issuance can determine the status of a security.

11. The 20 percent limitation on the use of the treasury stock method of applying proceeds from the assumed exercise of options and warrants is arbitrary and unsupported.

12. It is inconsistent, in computing fully diluted earnings per share, to measure potential dilution by the treasury stock method in the case of most warrants and to assume conversion in the case of convertible securities. This inconsistency results in recognizing potential dilution attributable to all convertible securities and at the same time, through the use of the treasury stock method, understating or not recognizing potential dilution attributable to warrants.

13. The treasury stock method is unsatisfactory, and other methods are preferable. One alternative proposed is that the number of equivalent shares be computed by reference to the relationship between the market value of the option or warrant and the market value of the related common stock. With this method, options and warrants have an impact on earnings per share whenever they have a market value, not only when the market price of the related common stock exceeds the exercise price, as the treasury stock method prescribes.

14. Some argue that the treasury stock method is improper since it *(a)* fails to recognize dilution unless the market price of the common stock exceeds the exercise price, and *(b)* assumes substantial blocks of treasury stock can be acquired without influencing the current market price, which is based on actual current trades.

15. There are preferable approaches to the use of funds assumed to be received from the exercise of outstanding warrants and options. Other uses proposed include the application of these funds to *(a)* reduce short- or long-term borrowings, *(b)* invest in government obligations or commercial paper, *(c)* invest in operations of the issuer, or *(d)* fulfill other corporate purposes.

16. The inclusion of stock issuable in connection with a business combination on a purely contingent basis should not be included in the computation of primary earnings per share if its issuance is wholly dependent upon the future movement of market prices. As a general practice, it is unsound for the determination of earnings to depend on the fluctuations of security prices, since it makes earnings per share a function of market price movements. The earnings per share should affect market price, and not vice versa.

17. Finally, there are some who claim that no matter how long accounting rulemakers labor to solve the problems associated with computing earnings per share, no real progress will be made until a sounder definition of net income is developed.

Financial Analysis

Inexperienced statement users and equity investors tend to focus on the earnings-per-share statistics too much. This is a mistake. These summary data do not capture the whole story of a company's financial condition, results of operation, and cash flows. While the earnings-per-share data have some significance to equity investors, it is always wise to remember that it is only one of many pieces of data presented in financial statements that bear on the value of securities and the measurement of management's performance. These other data must be analyzed carefully in order to put the earnings-per-share data in its proper perspective.

Statement users should be aware of the following observations when using earnings-per-share data:

a. The same number of shares do not enter into the dividend-per-share and earnings-per-share calculations. Therefore the earnings-per-share figure should not be divided into the dividend-per-share figure to compute payout ratios. Dividends per share is based on actual shares outstanding, whereas earnings per share may include all or some of *Opinion No. 15's* adjustments to its actual number of shares outstanding.

b. *Opinion No. 15's* at-issue rule can lock a convertible security into being a common stock equivalent for accounting purposes throughout its life. Subsequent to issue, interest rates may decline to the point that the securities market no longer regards the security as being a common stock equivalent. In these cases, the reported earnings-per-share figure will be out of line with reality and lose some of its usefulness for equity valuation purposes.

c. Earnings-per-share figures are seldom comparable when comparing companies because of differences in accounting, the probability that common stock equivalents and potentially dilutive shares will be actually turned into common shares, and levels of financial risk.

d. Despite the framers of *Opinion No. 15's* wish to make the determination of earnings per share independent of equity price movements, the application of the treasury stock method does make a company's earnings per share dependent in part on the company's common stock price. This reduces the value of the earnings-per-share figures of such companies for determining appropriate common stock valuations since an element of circular reasoning is introduced.

Fully diluted earnings-per-share data are used for most purposes where earnings-per-share figures are relevant. This is conservative. However, it can be misleading if it does not represent the current reality or expectations for the securities entering into the earnings-per-share calculation. Accordingly, experienced analysts always identify the impact of common stock equivalents and potentially dilutive securities in the earnings-per-share calculations, check the current market status of the key securities leading to adjustments, and, if they believe the market and accounting views of these securities differ, the analyst readjusts the earnings-per-share figures accordingly.

CASE 13-1

General Power Corporation*
Weighted Average Number of Shares

The General Power Corporation had 25,000 shares of common stock outstanding during a year and also had granted options which resulted in the following incremental shares, computed using the treasury stock method: 500 in the first quarter; none in the second quarter, because they would have been antidilutive; 1,400 in the third quarter; and 1,000 in the fourth quarter.

Question

Compute the weighted average of shares for computing the company's annual primary earnings per share.

CASE 13-2

Wiley Company†
Calculating Incremental Stock Issues

The Wiley Company has 100,000 common shares outstanding, and 10,000 warrants outstanding which are exercisable at $20 per share to obtain 10,000

* This case was prepared by David F. Hawkins.

Copyright © 1970 by the President and Fellows of Harvard College Harvard Business School case 171–190 (Rev. 1985)

† This case was prepared by David F. Hawkins.

Copyright © 1970 by the President and Fellows of Harvard College Harvard Business School case 171–191 (Rev. 1985) common shares. Assume also the following market prices per share of common stock during a three-year period:

	Year 1		Year 2		Year 3	
Quarter	Average	Ending	Average	Ending	Average	Ending
1	$18*	$22	$24	$25	$20	$18
2	20*	21	22	21	18	22
3	22	19	20	19	24	21
4	24	23	18	17	22	25

* Assume market prices had been more than $20 for substantially all of a previous quarter.

Questions

1. Compute the number of incremental shares related to the warrants to be included in each quarter's calculation of (a) primary earnings per share and (b) diluted earnings per share.

2. Compute the number of incremental shares included in the year-to-date weighted average for calculating (a) primary earnings per share and (b) fully diluted earnings per share.

CASE 13-3

The Thomas Company
Calculation of Earnings per Share Business School case 9-171-189.

The Thomas Company was located in Boston, Massachusetts. Its stock was traded in the local over-the-counter market. Trading seldom reached a thou-

This case was prepared by David F. Hawkins.

sand shares a day. Certain data related to the company's earnings, capital structure, and security prices are presented below:

Market Price of Common Stock. The market price of the common stock was as follows:

	1986	1985	1984
Average price:			
First quarter	$50	$45	$40
Second quarter	60	52	41
Third quarter	70	50	40
Fourth quarter	70	50	45
December 31 closing price	72	51	44

Cash Dividends. Cash dividends of $0.125 per common share were declared and paid for each quarter of 1984 and 1985. Cash dividends of $0.25 per common share were declared and paid for each quarter of 1986.

Convertible Debentures. Nine percent convertible debentures with a principal amount of $10 million due in 2004 were sold for cash at a price of $100 in the last quarter of 1984. Each $100 debenture was convertible into two shares of common stock. No debentures were converted during 1984 or 1985. The entire issue was converted at the beginning of the third quarter of 1986 because the issue was called by the company. The Aa corporate bond rate was 12 percent on the issue date.

Convertible Preferred Stock. At the beginning of the second quarter of 1985, 600,000 shares of convertible preferred stock were issued for assets in a purchase transaction. The annual dividend on each share of this convertible preferred stock was $0.20. Each share was convertible into one share of common stock. This convertible stock has a market value of $53 at the time of issuance, and the Aa corporate bond rate was 11 percent.

Holders of 500,000 shares of this convertible preferred stock converted their preferred stock into common stock during 1986. (Assume even conversion throughout the year.)

Warrants. Warrants to buy 500,000 shares of common stock at $60 per share for a period of five years were issued along with the convertible preferred stock mentioned above. No warrants have been exercised.

Common Stock. The number of shares of common stock outstanding was as follows (in thousands):

	1986	1985
Beginning of year	3,300	3,300
Conversion of preferred stock	500	—
Conversion of debentures	200	—
End of year	4,000	3,300

Net Income. The 1985 and 1986 net income before dividends on preferred stock was (in thousands):

1985:	Net income	$10,300
1986:	Income before extraordinary item	12,900
	Net income	13,800

Federal and state taxes in 1985 were 48 percent; in 1986 they were 52.8 percent.

Questions

1. Compute the company's primary and fully diluted earnings per share for 1986 and 1985.

2. Starting with the "income before extraordinary item" line of the comparative 1986 and 1985 statements, complete the remaining portion of the bottom of the income statement for presentation in the company's annual report. (The last line should disclose the company's net income per share, assuming full dilution.)

3. Prepare the footnote to accompany the per-share data presented in the 1986 income statement.

4. Does paragraph 38 of *Opinion No. 15* apply in this case?

PART SIX

Asset and Expense Reporting and Analysis

CHAPTER 14

Income Tax Expense Determination and Analysis

Income taxes are an expense of doing business and should be allocated to income and other accounts in the same fashion as other expenses. However, a number of companies report items of income and expense for income tax purposes on a basis different from that followed for financial reporting to stockholders and creditors. This raises a fundamental accounting question: Should the annual income tax expense reported in the published income statement be based on the taxable income reported to the Internal Revenue Service on the company's tax return for that year or some other amount?

The income tax data included in financial statements can be very useful to statement users. These data provide an alternative measure of corporate profits that is typically determined by more conservative accounting practices than those used to determine book income. The detailed notes to these statements explaining the elements of the deferred tax expense and the reasons why the company's tax rate and the statutory rate differ can provide insights into the quality of a company's earnings; they can also reveal possible accounting manipulations, identify the contribution of tax rate management to the levels and change in reported earnings; facilitate the deaccrual of income to a cash basis, and help readers estimate the effect of changes in its tax code on the company's earnings and cash flows.

The accounting for investment-type tax credits is covered in Chapter 15.

Origins of the Problem

The income tax allocation controversy is a direct outgrowth of the federal government's increasing use of income taxes as a positive or negative stimulus to the economy. The use of taxes as a stimulus takes a variety of forms:

1. "Across-the-board" stimulus, in the form of general changes in the tax rate.
2. Specific modifications to the continuing rules of determining taxable income, such as exemptions of certain revenues from taxable income.
3. Changes in the pattern of payment of the tax liability.
4. Changes in the timing of recognizing taxable revenues or tax deductible expenses.

There is general agreement that it is appropriate to reflect the effects of the changes specified above in the first two categories directly in the income statement during the period in which they occur. Such changes are, by law and regulation, directly relatable to items entering currently into the determination of income subject to tax.

The third type of stimulus—changes in the pattern of tax payments—affects a company's cash flow rather than income pattern. The delay in the payment of the tax increases the taxes payable liability account, and as such represents a source of funds. The eventual payment, which draws down the cash account, is a use of funds. The size of the tax expense is unaffected. To the extent that corporate tax payments are moving closer to a pay-as-you-go basis, an important source of funds from delayed tax payments is being taken away from business executives.

The tax allocation accounting issue arises when the government employs the fourth category of stimulus; that is, it allows a different timing pattern for revenues and expenses on tax returns from that employed in the financial accounting reports.

Permanent and Timing Differences

Differences between the income reported in the financial statement and that reported on the tax return may be either (1) permanent or (2) related to timing differences. *Permanent* differences arise from specific statutory concessions or exclusions of the tax code. For example, expenses required for financial reporting, such as premiums on officers' life insurance or amortization of goodwill, may not be deducted in the computation of taxable income.

Timing differences arise from the recognition in the financial reports and tax returns of income and expense in different periods. For example, a retailer may be required under *Opinion No. 10* to use in its published financial reports the accrual method, which recognizes income from installment sales at the time of sale. For tax purposes, however, the retailer may elect to use the installment method, which recognizes the profit from the sale proportionately as the installment debt is paid. Another common example of timing differences is the use of straight-line depreciation in financial reports but accelerated depreciation in tax returns.

There are four general types of timing differences. The individual transactions giving rise to these timing differences originate in one period and reverse themselves in subsequent periods:

1. Revenues are included in taxable income later than in pre-tax accounting income, as in the installment sales example.
2. Expenses are deducted later in determining taxable income than in determining financial statement income, as in the case of warranty costs, which are deductible from taxable income only when incurred.
3. Revenues are included earlier in taxable income than in pre-tax accounting income. For example, rent payments received in advance may be reported when received for tax determination, but in later periods when earned for financial reporting purposes.
4. Expenses or losses are deducted in determining taxable income earlier than in determining pre-tax book income, such as in the case of store-opening expenses that may be deducted immediately on a tax return, but amortized in the financial statements over several years.

The major accounting problem arising from the timing differences is the method of recognizing the tax effects of timing differences. Permanent differences between pre-tax accounting income and taxable income present no problem, since, under applicable tax laws and regulations, current differences are not offset by corresponding differences in later periods.

Timing differences which reverse or turn around in later periods result in an equivalent reversal of the tax effects. Often the impact of the reversal of these differences is indefinitely postponed as similar new transactions balance out the reversal. A basic question develops as to whether the tax effect of timing differences should be recognized in view of the possibility of indefinitely postponing the actual payment of the tax.

Different Approaches

A number of widely different solutions, each with strong support, have been proposed for handling this timing problem. One concept is that the income tax expense of a period should equal the tax payable for the period. Advocates of this "flow-through" method argue that there is no tax liability created until a later period; thus, there is no need to create an additional tax expense applicable to the current book pre-tax income.

Others argue for the "deferred" method of reporting the income tax expense. This point of view holds that the tax expense reported in the financial statements should be the same as if the book profit were the profit actually reported for tax purposes. Any difference between this tax calculation and the tax currently due to the Internal Revenue Service is recorded as a potential tax liability labeled "deferred tax liability."[1] Prior to any new FASB tax accounting rules, *Opinion No. 11* requires this approach.

The FASB favors the "liability" method. Under this approach, deferred tax expenses are computed using tax rates expected to be in effect when the timing differences reverse. Also existing deferred tax balances are adjusted when tax rates change or future tax rate changes become known. Both the deferred and the liability methods are referred to as being "comprehensive tax allocation" approaches.

Other less widely supported approaches have been suggested, such as the "partial allocation" method which would recognize in the determination of current income only those taxes deferred that are reasonably certain to be paid during, say, the next three to five years. Another approach, the so-called net-of-tax form of presentation, accepts interperiod tax allocation, but would include deferred taxes as an element of the valuation of the asset and liability giving rise to the tax deferral.

Example

The problem of recognizing timing differences is illustrated in the following example. In early January 1986, retailer Smith sold a TV set for $360 on an installment sale basis. The installment sales contract called for no down payment and 36 payments of $10 per month plus interest on the unpaid balance. The retailer's gross margin was 20 percent of the sales price. (The interest and any carrying charges related to the installment payments can be ignored in this discussion.)

According to *Accounting Principles Board Opinion No. 10,* the retailer must use the so-called accrual method to record the transaction *on his books* rather than the installment method, since the circumstances of the sale were such that the collection of the sales price was reasonably assured. Therefore, Smith must recognize the full pre-tax profit of $72 at the time of the sale. If he had been able to use the installment approach, he would have shown a $2 before-tax profit at the time each $10 installment payment was received. The timing of the pre-tax profit recognition under the two methods is compared in Illustration 14–1.

First-Year Taxes

For calculating his tax payments, however, retailer Smith still has the option of using either the accrual or the installment method. If Smith decides to conserve his cash and use the installment method for tax purposes, he creates a tax deferral situation: he has recorded on his books the full $72 profit at

---

[1] If a company's taxable income reported to the IRS is greater than its book profits before taxes and the difference is due to timing differences, a "deferred tax asset" results.

ILLUSTRATION 14–1
Accrual versus Installment
Treatment of Pre-tax Profit

	Accrual	Installment
1986	$72	$24
1987	—	24
1988	—	24
Total	$72	$72

the time of the sale, but for tax purposes he defers the actual payment of taxes on this profit until the time the installments are collected.

The after-tax profit consequences of using the accrual method for book purposes and the installment basis for tax purposes would depend on whether Smith uses the flow-through treatment for handling the tax deferral or the comprehensive allocation method. (Of course, in practice Smith would be required to use a comprehensive tax allocation approach in this situation. The purpose of this illustration is to show the differences between the flow-through and comprehensive approaches to tax expense accounting.)

The flow-through approach records for book purposes the current year's tax payment actually shown on the retailer's tax return. If we assume a 50 percent tax rate, its application in this case would lead to the incremental effect on profits shown in Illustration 14–2.

Given the pre-tax profit of $72 on the company's books in the year of sale and no anticipated future tax rate changes, both the deferred and liability comprehensive allocation approaches lead to a book profit of $36 after taxes. This treatment puts the profit effect of the installment sale on the same basis as an equivalent cash sale. The difference between the $36 tax expense shown on the books and the actual tax of $12 paid to the Internal Revenue Service in 1986 is set up as a deferred tax account of $24 on the liability side of the balance sheet. This account is reduced incrementally each subsequent year by the amount of taxes paid on the profit from the

ILLUSTRATION 14–2
Flow-Through Tax Accounting
Illustrated

	Pre-tax Profit	Tax*	Net Profit
1986	$ 72	$12	$ 60
1987	—	12	(12)
1988	—	12	(12)
Total	$ 72	$36	$ 36

* 50 percent of the 20 percent profit included in the installments collected.

installment payments received during that year. So, in this example, the deferred tax account would be reduced by $12 each year over the remaining two-year installment payment period. The income statement is not affected by these subsequent tax payments or installment collections.

The accounting entries for the tax effect would be:

Comprehensive Allocation

Year 1:

Dr. Tax Expense	36	
Cr. Taxes Payable		12
Deferred Tax Liability		24

Years 2 and 3:

Dr. Deferred Tax Liability	12	
Cr. Taxes Payable		12

Flow-Through

Year 1:

Dr. Tax Expense	12	
Cr. Taxes Payable		12

Years 2 and 3:

Dr. Tax Expense	12	
Cr. Taxes Payable		12

A comparison of the results obtained from the flow-through and the comprehensive allocation methods, when Smith uses different book and tax income recognition timing, is shown in Illustration 14–3. (The cash flow effect of this sale depends upon whether the retailer sells for cash or on an installment basis and upon the method he uses in his tax return to recognize the profit from the sale. The financial accounting handling of the deferred taxes, if any, does not change his cash flow.)

ILLUSTRATION 14–3
Flow-Through versus Comprehensive Tax Accounting: After-Tax Book Profits

	Flow-Through	Comprehensive	Differential
1986	$ 60	$36	$ 24
1987	(12)	—	(12)
1988	(12)	—	(12)
Total	$ 36	$36	$ 0

Second-Year Taxes

In addition to realizing a first-year profit differential of $24, the flow-through approach provides an opportunity to offset the $12 reduction in second-year profits (see Illustration 14–3). Smith can accomplish this by making a similar $360 TV set installment sale in 1987. Again, the after-tax profit differential between the flow-through and comprehensive allocation treatment would be $24. But he would offset this amount with the second-year $12 profit reduction associated with the 1986 sale. So the net differential in the second year would be $12. This effect is shown in Illustration 14–4.

ILLUSTRATION 14–4
Flow-Through versus Comprehensive Tax
Accounting: After-Tax Book Profits

	Flow-Through	Comprehensive	Differential
1986	$ 60	$36	$24
1987	48	36	12
1988	(24)	—	(24)
1989	(12)	—	(12)
Total	$ 72	$72	$ 0

The liability method would give results different from the deferred method if in 1986 it was known that the tax rates for 1987 and 1988 would be 40 percent. In this case the 1986 deferred tax expense is $31.20 ($12 plus 40% of $48). The accounting entry is:

```
Dr.  Tax Expense .................  $31.20
     Cr.  Taxes Payable ............        12.00 (50% of $24)
          Deferred Tax Liability ......        19.20 (40% of $48)
```

If the retailer in the second example is using the comprehensive allocation approach and the tax rate is projected to stay at 50%, the deferred tax item appearing on the balance sheet at the end of the first year would be $24. This deferral would rise to $36 at the end of the second year (the $24 difference between the tax payment recognized by the second-year sale handled on an accrual versus an installment basis, less the $12 reduction for taxes related to the first-year sale's actual tax payments made during the second year). If Smith sells one $360 TV set each year on a three-year installment sale basis, his deferred tax will remain at $36. If he increases his installment sales volume, the deferred tax item will increase. It is this so-called permanent deferral that the partial allocation advocates claim should be included in earnings.

ILLUSTRATION 14–5
Flow-Through versus Comprehensive Tax
Accounting: After-Tax Book Profits

	Flow-Through	Comprehensive	Differential
1986	$(12)	$12	$(24)
1987	24	12	12
1988	24	12	12
Total	$ 36	$ 36	$ 0

So far we have looked only at recognizing the full book profits at the time of sale. Let us go back to the original one-TV-set sale and lay aside for a moment the APB's earlier accrual basis decision for recording installment sales for book purposes. If Smith, the retailer in this example, had handled his installment sale in a way exactly opposite to the previously assumed method—that is, if he reported the sale on an accrual basis for tax purposes and on an installment basis for book purposes—the sale would have had the after-tax effect on book profits shown in Illustration 14–5. The first-year pre-tax profits on the installment method are $24, and the taxable income on the accrual method reported to the government is $72. In years 2 and 3, the book pre-tax profit is $24 each year. There is no profit reported on the tax return since it was all recognized in year 1. In Illustration 14–5, if comprehensive allocation is applied, the deferred tax item will show up on the asset side of the balance sheet, since the first-year profit recorded for taxes would be greater than the profit recorded for financial accounting purposes. In a sense, the company has overpaid, or prepaid, some taxes.

Points of View

Those supporting comprehensive allocation approaches tend to believe that net income principally measures how effectively management has added to the capital of the business through its operations that utilize the capital already invested in the enterprise. Management's exercise of the privilege the income tax code afforded to postpone taxes does not, in their opinion, constitute improved operating performance, no matter how long the prospect of continuing the tax postponement. They view tax postponement as providing an opportunity to perform better in the future because of being able to conserve current funds for use in the business.

Consequently, they maintain that this funds retention benefit should be reflected in terms of a favorable capital "funds flow," rather than in terms of an immediate increase in income from operations, as proposed by the partial allocators. Furthermore, the income benefits flowing from the deferral of tax payments should be reflected in income only as management earns profits by reducing financial charges or improving operations, through using the funds retained effectively.

Many comprehensive tax advocates feel that a standard that recognizes income as earned only through "honest-to-goodness" operating efficiency is vital to maintaining any semblance of integrity in the earnings figures as a measure of performance. For example, it has been noted that a retailer who sells on the installment basis using flow-through tax accounting with increasing sales would show higher profits than another retailer with identical sales who sells for cash. To achieve this result, the credit sales would be recorded on the accrual basis for book purposes and the installment basis for tax purposes. Obviously, any accounting procedure that permits higher after-tax gross margin profits from credit sales than from cash sales is undesirable.

In contrast to the comprehensive allocation supporter's views, advocates of the flow-through method would recognize as taxes only those amounts immediately payable based upon current tax returns. They believe that only the current taxes are a legal liability and that to recognize future taxes results in undesirable income normalization. Further, since in the case of many companies tax deferrals are not likely to be paid in the foreseeable future, continuing a tax deferral policy of deferring taxes may result in an ever-increasing amount on the liabilities side of the balance sheet which does not represent a legally enforceable claim against the corporation.

In reply, comprehensive allocation proponents who advocate the deferred method note that the accounting convention that profits result from matching revenues with their related costs requires tax expense to be recorded in the same accounting period as that in which the related revenue and expense items are recognized for book purposes. Given this approach, when there is a timing difference between the recognition and payment of taxes, the logic of the debit-credit mechanism requires a deferred balance to be placed on the appropriate side of the balance sheet. Thus, in this typical case, a credit entry to offset the debit to tax expense is made to the liability account, deferred taxes. This liability item, they argue, is only a "residual" entry, and as such should not be expected to have all of the usual characteristics of a liability.

The comprehensive allocation proponents who support the liability method argue that deferred tax assets and liabilities meet FASB *Concepts Statement No. 3*'s asset and liability definitions. Therefore, these items rightfully belong on the balance sheet and their values should be adjusted from time to time to reflect known changes in tax rates.

Advocates of comprehensive allocation further argue that the fact that reversal of timing differences may be more than offset by new timing differences does not alter the fact that the reversals do occur, and may be readily identified as to their tax effect. Accounting principles, they state, cannot be predicated on a reliance that these offsets will continue. They therefore conclude that the fact that the tax effects of two transactions happen to go in opposite directions does not invalidate the necessity of recognizing separately the tax effects of the transactions as they occur.

In the view of many managers supporters of comprehensive allocation have failed to develop an adequate explanation of the deferred tax item on the balance sheet, and the method has been subjected to continuing criticism. Business executives have been concerned that users of financial statements might include deferred tax credits as debt in the debt-to-equity or the working capital ratios, despite the fact that these deferrals do not have the characteristics of debt. This apprehension has made it difficult for many to see how comprehensive allocation produces fairer, more useful results than partial allocation.

Present Value Approach

Some accounting commentators have proposed that certain long-term tax allocation accounts be presented on a present value basis. Laying aside the practical difficulties of determining the discount rate and period, advocates of this proposal claim it reflects the correct accounting theory approach to liabilities and is consistent with conventional accounting theory related to long-term debts.

The advocates of the nondiscounting approach believe their point of view reflects the emphasis business executives place on the amount of funds obtained currently from tax deferrals rather than on the amount owed. Using this approach, they argue, there is no need to determine and report the deferrals on a discounted basis. It is of little interest and relevance. Consequently, in their opinion, the practice which does not report discounted deferred taxes is correct.

The APB and FASB reject the present value approach to measuring deferred tax expenses and balance sheet values.

Rate Changes

The appropriate handling of changes in the corporate income tax rate which occur after the establishment of the original tax deferrals on the balance sheet presents a thorny problem. *Opinion No. 11*'s solution was to adopt the deferred method. Under this approach, there is no adjustment to deferred tax accounts for subsequent rate or for code changes. The liability method adjusts these balances for code changes.

Public Utilities

A number of public utilities subject to rate-making processes have elected to use acclerated depreciation on their income tax returns and straight-line depreciation on their reports to stockholders. In these circumstances, some regulatory commissions have permitted the public utility neither to record deferred taxes in their accounts nor include deferred taxes as an allowable cost for rate-making purposes.[2] In these cases, most of the affected public utilities follow flow-through accounting for reporting their current tax expense to stockholders. This creates several problems for public accountants: Should an unqualified opinion be given on financial statements that do not provide for deferred taxes? What constitutes full and fair disclosure when flow-through accounting is used?

In *Statement No. 71*, "Accounting for the Effects of Certain Types of Regulation," the FASB concluded that when a regulator does not include the income tax effect of certain transactions in allowable costs in the period in which the transactions are reported, but includes income taxes related to those transactions in allowable costs in the period in which these taxes become payable, flow-through tax accounting is permissible.

Loss Carryback and Carryforward Credits

Where an operating loss for income tax calculation purposes occurs, a corporation may offset the loss against the taxable income of the preceding years to the extent that the entire loss is offset. (The number of years varies depending on the current tax code in effect.) This is accomplished by filing amended tax returns for the prior years. The difference between tax liability on the amended and original returns can be claimed by the corporation as a tax refund.

If taxable income during the previous qualifying years is less than the current year's loss, the unabsorbed portion of the current year's loss may be carried forward to reduce taxable income. (Again, the number of years depends on the current tax code in effect.) Where two loss years occur, the amount of the first loss is offset in full before the second loss is matched retroactively or prospectively against taxable income.

The carryback and carryforward provisions of the tax code create an accounting problem, since the realization of the benefits of the loss carried forward generally is not assured in the loss periods. The issue is: Should the tax reductions resulting from the carryforwards be included in net income for the year in which the tax benefit is realized, or should they be applied to the prior year in which the losses occurred, as a partial recovery of such losses?

The accounting rules are:

1. The tax effects of any realizable loss carrybacks should be recognized in the determination of net income of the loss periods. The tax

---

[2] In a regulated industry, the price of the product is determined by a formula which permits the utility to recover from its operating revenues its operating costs plus a fair return on the cost or fair market value of property used in the public service.

loss carryback and the related tax refund claims are measurable and realizable in the current period.

2. The tax effects of loss carryforwards should not be recognized until they are realized, since realization of the tax benefits of the loss periods is dependent on future income.[3]

3. Disclosure should be made of the amounts of any loss carryforwards not recognized in the loss period and the expiration date of such carryforwards.

Statement Presentation

Deferred taxes are part of the tax expense recognized in the determination of current income. Therefore, the portion of taxes deferred should not be included in stockholders' equity. This practice is supported by the FASB and the SEC, even though some accounting authors and many business executives argue that the portion of income taxes deferred indefinitely should be considered as part of the stockholders' equity.

Despite the fact that deferred taxes do not represent receivables or payables in the traditional sense, they should nevertheless be presented in a manner that is consistent with the customary distinction between current and noncurrent items. The general rule is that deferred taxes should be classified in the balance sheet in the same manner as the related assets and liabilities giving rise to the deferred taxes. For example, that portion of deferred taxes arising from the use of different plant depreciation methods should be classified as a long-term liability. This corresponds to the plant's classification as a long-term asset.

The components of the tax expense shown on the current income statement should be disclosed by the following categories:

1. Taxes estimated to be payable currently.
2. Tax effects of timing differences.
3. Tax effects of operating losses.

These amounts should be allocated to (a) income before extraordinary items and (b) extraordinary items.

The FASB does not favor the notion of "indefinite reversals," which are timing differences that may or may not reverse at the discretion of management. A common example is the reinvestment overseas of earnings of foreign subsidiaries to avoid paying U.S. taxes that would be due if the profits were remitted to the United States. Until new FASB rules are issued nonaccrual of the potential U.S. taxes in these situations is permitted.

---

[3] Under the APB's rules in certain unusual circumstances, the loss carryforward tax benefit could be recognized in the loss period when future realization of these benefits was assured beyond any reasonable doubt at the time the loss carryforwards arise.

Financial Analysis

The tax expense note accompanying the financial statement should always be carefully analyzed by statement users. It can be a valuable source of information. Statement users should always note the following:

1. The percentage deferred taxes are of the total tax expense. A high percentage suggests liberal book accounting is being used, income is being recorded that may not be realized as cash until a much later period, or the company is relying on tax-shelter schemes to protect its income from taxes.

2. The percentage book tax expenses are of the book pre-tax income and the dollar contribution to the change in earnings attributable to the change in the book tax rate. A reduction in the book tax rate and/or a high contribution of tax savings due to a change in income tax rate may indicate that management is becoming more reliant on tax rate management as a source of net income. A low tax rate might indicate the company is vulnerable to tax code changes or its earnings are in low tax rate environments that might have restrictions on the use of profits earned in those locations. Low tax rates are generally considered low-quality earnings sources and a possible red flag. In making these calculations, equity-method income should be excluded. It can distort the tax rate percentage as it is included in pre-tax profits on an after-tax basis.

3. Unusual changes in the tax effect of individual timing difference items. A significant change may indicate a change in the level of activity related to the item or a shift in book or tax accounting methods and estimates.

4. The company's past policy toward accruing potential U.S. taxes on overseas earnings: The nonaccrual of potential U.S. taxes that would be due on repatriated foreign earnings could expose the company to a tax expense charge in a later period when the previously recorded overseas profits are repatriated.

5. The current portion of the tax expense: This figure is indicative of the level of profits reported to taxing authorities.

6. Onetime tax savings and sources of tax savings that are vulnerable to tax code changes: The contribution of these items to net income might be nonrecurring and as such should be regarded as a low-quality earnings source.

7. Capital gains: Tax rate reduction attributable to capital gains might indicate that the company is selling assets at a gain to cover a decline in operating earnings.

How deferred taxes should be regarded in financial analyses is a controversial topic. Some analysts argue that, in most cases, deferred tax liabilities are equivalent to permanent equity capital and should be lumped with owners' equity when computing debt-to-equity ratios. Others with this same view go even further. They would exclude deferred tax expenses from income in computing return on equity. In making this calculation, these individuals, for some unexplained reason, do not add the deferred tax liability back to owners' equity. This is a mistake. Another approach followed by some analysts is to exclude deferred tax liabilities from total calculations when computing debt-to-equity ratios. This approach is often used for debt covenant purposes. Many analysts, while recognizing that deferred tax liabilities are not the equivalent of debt and deferred tax expenses are not like most other expense items that must be paid in cash, accept the deferred-tax-accounting liability and expense classification for financial ratio purposes. This latter approach is generally followed when computing margin and return on investment ratio for management performance evaluation purposes. It is based on the belief that normalized earnings figures are better indicators of management performance over time than, say, income based on flow-through tax accounting. In contrast, in most financial structure analysis, all or some portion of the deferred tax liability is usually excluded from liabilities and/or included in equity. This treatment reflects the widespread acceptance among statement users of the quasi-equity nature of most deferred tax liabilities.

Franklin Stores, Incorporated
Accounting for Income Tax Expense

In June 1985, the board of directors of Franklin Stores, Inc., a large chain of discount stores, approved a recommendation from the company's president, Joe Franklin, that Franklin Stores offer its customers the opportunity to purchase goods on an installment sales basis. Prior to this time, all of Franklin Stores' sales had been on a cash or credit card basis.

As part of this decision, the board had to consider a recommendation concerning the accounting treatment of the installment sales made by Peter Lewis, the company's financial vice president. Lewis recommended that Franklin account for its installment sales by the installment sales method for tax purposes. That is, the profit from the sale would be recognized as collections were made from the customer, or when the installment sales contract was sold to a finance company. He claimed that this method would defer the payment of income taxes arising from the sales and, thus, help the company's cash position. He likened the deferred taxes to an "interest-free loan from the government."

Lewis told the board that generally accepted accounting principles required Franklin to adopt the sales or accrual method for public reporting purposes, however. The sale method, he said, recognized the profit on the transaction at the time the goods giving rise to the installment sales contract were sold. Business School case 9-110-110. Revised 1985.

Following Lewis's recommendation, the board approved the use of the installment method for tax purposes. However, several directors asked Lewis to explain the nature of the deferred tax account created by the use of the installment method for the calculation of income taxes and the sale method for determining profit in the financial reporting to stockholders.

Several other directors questioned the appropriateness of using the sale method for book purposes, since the company had no prior experience

This case was prepared by F. R. Madera under the direction of David F. Hawkins.
Copyright © 1965 by the President and Fellows of Harvard College
Harvard Business School case 110-110 (rev. 1985)

on which to base its estimate of the collections from installment sales. Excerpts from this conversation are presented later in the case.

Franklin Stores, Inc.

Franklin Stores, Inc., was founded in 1967 by Joe Franklin, his brother William, and Peter Lewis to sell television sets at a deeply discounted price on a cash-and-carry basis. The company's merchandising policy was an instant success—so much so that customers began to ask the store to obtain other appliances for them at a discount. As a result of these requests, the founders decided to expand their business to include a full line of household appliances. By 1975, the company was the largest retailer of appliances in its market area.

In 1978, the founders decided to expand their operations to include other cities. Accordingly, during the next five years they established new Franklin Stores in three cities. Also during this same period, Franklin stores expanded its operations to include records, home furnishings, musical instruments, toys, and a variety of other goods. This expansion was financed by a large public stock offering. Eventually, Mr. Franklin hoped to have Franklin Stores in every major city of the nation.

Beginning in the early 1980s, the company began to experience greater competition from other discount stores and department stores. The competing discount stores cut heavily into Franklin's sales by improving their store layouts, installing more attractive displays, and granting liberal credit terms. The department stores became more competitive by lowering their prices to meet the discounted items, offering better service on the goods sold, and granting more liberal and varied credit terms.

These industry trends forced Franklin in 1985 to adopt an installment sales plan. The plan was a fairly simple one: Customers could purchase merchandise by paying as little as 10 percent of the purchase price at the time of purchase and then paying the outstanding balance over the next 12, 24, or 36 months in equal installments. A service charge of 2 percent of the outstanding balance was charged each month. Under this plan, Franklin continued to hold title (reduced by the buyer's equity as established by payments) to the merchandise until the final payment. Before customers could use the installment plan, they were checked out by the company's credit bureau to see if they were able to comply with the terms of the installment sales contract.

June Board Meeting

After the decisions concerning installment sales were made, the following discussion related to deferred taxes occurred at the June board of directors meeting.

Lewis: Let me begin by saying that whenever you report items of income and expense for income tax purposes on a basis different from that followed for financial accounting purposes, the provision for the income tax expense does not represent the taxes actually paid, but the taxes properly allocated to the profit shown in the income statement.

Let me illustrate this problem with an example: Suppose we sold a freezer unit for $800 on August 1, 1985. The customer paid $80 down and agreed to pay $720 in equal installments over the next 36 months. Furthermore, let us assume the freezer cost us $600. So, we made $200 on the sale. As a percentage of the sales price, this represents a 25 percent gross margin.

Now here's how we'd account for the sale using the installment method.

On August 1, we'd record the sale, the creation of an installment receivable, and the initial down payment thus:

Installment Receivable	800	
Inventory[1]		600
Deferred Gross Profit on Installment Sales		200

Cash	80	
Installment Receivable		80

Now, on September 1 and monthly thereafter for 36 months as the payments are received, the following entries will be made:

Cash	20	
Installment Receivables		20

Of course, there'd be an entry recognizing the service charge, but for the purposes of this example let's not worry about it.

Next, at the close of the fiscal year during which the sale was made, we'd recognize the profit on the collections. Here's the journal entry:

Deferred Gross Profit on Installment Sales	40	
Recognized Gross Profit on Installment Sales		40

The $40 is the sum of the payments received times the percentage gross margin on the sale: that is, $160 × 25 percent.

Now the entries for the same transaction are . . . [Lewis went on to explain the accounting for the accrual method and to demonstrate how the deferral and actual taxes were calculated].

Small [*director, retired business executive*]: That was an excellent explanation. However, I still don't understand why we have to provide for deferred taxes.

Lewis: Well, it is the generally accepted way to handle such situations by business executives and the public accounting profession. In fact, the general principle of income tax allocation is required by the FASB.

Small: Oh, yes. I recall you mentioned that at our last meeting when you told us about some possible new rules in this area. Nevertheless, I think we ought to have some good business reasons for following this deferred tax method. Irrespective of how much authority such statements may have among accountants, I don't see why we should blindly follow them.

---

[1] Franklin Stores, Inc., maintained perpetual inventory records.

Franklin: You may have a good point there, but I think we have no alternative. I have another question for Peter: Where is this deferred tax item carried on the balance sheet?

Lewis: It ought to be reported as a current liability, since the installment receivables giving rise to the deferred taxes are classified as current-assets. The SEC insists upon this approach for registered companies.

Small: It seems silly to carry as a current liability an item that will in aggregate never be paid. Are there some alternative ways?

Lewis: No. However, in the past people have proposed the following: first, as a deduction from the related asset; second, below current liabilities, but above long-term debt; and finally, below long-term debt, but above stockholders' equity.

Murphy [director, president of utility company]: At one time, many years ago, didn't American Electric Power Company try to show as part of net worth the deferred taxes arising from using different depreciation policies for tax and book purposes?

Lewis: Yes. They claimed it was part of the stockholders' equity. However, the Securities and Exchange Commission issued a "Statement of Administrative Policy" stating they considered classifying the deferred tax liability as part of common stock equity was misleading for financial statement purposes. The AICPA also issued a similar pronouncement. After discussions with the SEC and AICPA, a compromise was reached. The item was placed by this utility between net worth and long-term debt. In addition, all parties agreed the amount was to be considered as neither long-term debt nor common stock equity.

Franklin: Clearly, this question of the location of deferred taxes on the balance sheet is of some importance, since it will have a direct impact on our financial ratios. I think we ought to direct the executive committee to look further into this deferred tax business and make a recommendation as to how we should explain it and its impact on earnings and balance sheet ratios over the next few years to our stockholders. Are there any other questions related to this topic that you want the executive committee to consider?

Peterson [vice president, public relations]: Yes, as I said earlier when the recommendation was first made, I'm not at all convinced we ought to use the sales method in published statements for installment sales. Now, after listening to this discussion of deferred taxes, I'm even less convinced. It seems to me that we can avoid this whole deferred tax business by using the installment method in our published statements. And, unlike Peter, I happen to think the installment method does match costs and revenues. In my opinion, when we make an installment sale, we don't make a profit until at least about 80 percent of the monthly collections are made. In previous discussions with Peter, he tells me that GAAP requires that we should use the sales method. However, we are new at the installment sales business, and without any track record to guide us in estimating the probability of collections, I think we ought to be very conservative in recognizing income.

Franklin: Any other items for the executive committee?

Small: Yes, Peter's example was very helpful, but it dealt with only one sale. As I see it, our installment sales volume is going to continue growing over the years, and I'm curious just how big this deferred tax account is going to be in say, 1988. Are we talking of $1 million or $10 million?

Lewis: I'll get that figure to you by the next board meeting.

Lorenz: I'd like to know what our auditors say about this. Also, do they think we should indicate in the annual report what we estimate the present value of this liability to be?

Franklin: Of course, we have been discussing this matter with our auditors. In fact, it's clear to me now that I made a mistake by not asking Frank Towle [the audit partner in charge of the Franklin Stores account] to come to this meeting. I'll make sure he comes to the next executive committee meeting, however. . . .

Questions

1. Complete the freezer example Peter Lewis presented to the board. What are the accounting entries for the installment sale, using the accrual and the installment methods? Assuming a 50 percent income tax rate, what will be the related actual tax payments for 1985, 1986, 1987, and 1988? What will be the deferred tax accounting entries during these years?

2. The following projections of Franklin Stores' operations are available (all amounts are millions of dollars):

	Sales			Cash Collected on Installment Receivables	Selling and General Expense
	Install-ment	Cash	Total		
1985	$ 8	$20	$28	$ 2.8	$4.2
1986	18	22	40	9.5	6.0
1987	24	26	50	18.2	7.5
1988	30	30	60	24.1	9.0

Assuming a constant 25 percent gross margin and a 50 percent income tax rate, and ignoring service charges, compute the amounts of net income after taxes, income taxes payable, deferred gross profit on installment sales, and deferred income taxes at the close of each year, 1985 through 1988, under each of these alternatives:

a. The accrual method is used for financial reporting and for income tax purposes.

b. The installment method is used for financial reporting and for income tax purposes.

c. The accrual method is used for financial reporting, and the installment method is used for income tax purposes.

3. How would your answers to question 2 change if in 1985 it was announced that the tax rate would be lowered to 40 percent in 1986. (Use the liability method.)

4. How would you explain the deferred tax items on the balance sheet and income statement to the stockholders?

5. Should Franklin use the installment or accrual method in its public financial statements? Why?

6. Which net income figure is more relevant for valuing the Franklin Stores common stock? The net income computed on a comprehensive tax allocation basis or a flow-through basis? Using the accrual or installment sale basis?

7. Describe how classifying the installment sale related deferred tax liability as a current liability, a long-term liability, a portion of owners' equity, or an item between long-term liabilities and owners' equity might change Franklin Stores' various financial ratios. Where do you believe this deferred tax liability should be presented on the balance sheet?

CASE 14–2

American Manufacturing Company
Accounting for Losses Carried Forward

In the first few paragraphs of his letter to stockholders in the September 30, 1985 annual report, the new president of American Manufacturing Company, Peter C. Scully, outlined the company's situation:

> We began in June 1985 to take decisive action that will place this company in the forefront of American industry. Included in these actions are steps to face financial reality, build a new management team, reorganize along decentralized lines, market new products, and negotiate new ventures. . . .
>
> Sales totaled $767 million in 1985, compared with the company's sales volume of $821 million in 1984. The net loss reported for 1985 is $54 million, divided into (1) $22 million from regular operations, (2) $19 million identified as new charges and reserves, and (3) $13 million from unusual

---

This case was prepared by David F. Hawkins.

nonrecurring charges. As explained in Note 6 to the financial statements, in 1985 the company changed its method of computing depreciation and extended the application of tax allocation accounting procedures. These changes had the effect of reducing the net loss for the year by $8.9 million. In 1984, net income totaled $5 million. . . .

Our 1985 operating results were adversely affected by reduced sales and unusual expenses involving costs and reserves related to closing down unprofitable plants for optimum utilization of manufacturing space and cutting out slow-moving inventory not associated with profitable product lines. . . .

The 1985 income statement presented in the 1985 annual report is shown in Exhibit 1. Notes 3 and 6 read as follows:

NOTE 3: *Special Reserves and Income Taxes.* During the last quarter of 1985, a major change took place in the company's management. The new management made an extensive study of the company's operations, products, and markets. This study resulted in changes in company philosophy and policies relating to organization, products and production facilities, marketing, and relations with dealers and customers. The company has estimated that implementation of these policy changes will result in substantial costs and losses for *(a)* parts replacement, warranty costs, repossession

EXHIBIT 1

AMERICAN MANUFACTURING COMPANY
State of Income (Loss)
American Manufacturing Company and Consolidated Subsidiaries

	Year Ended September 30	
	1985	*1984*
Sales and other income:		
Sales	$767,313,100	$821,764,535
Discounts, interest earned, and other income	11,152,147	6,428,597
Income of finance subsidiaries	9,901,233	6,893,641
	$788,366,480	$835,086,773
Costs and expenses:		
Materials, plant payrolls, and services (Note 3)	$703,041,018	$689,225,155
Depreciation (Note 6)	16,024,167	18,713,666
Selling, general, and administrative expense (Note 3)	131,352,862	100,216,572
Discount and interest on receivables sold to finance subsidiaries	21,662,133	11,158,812
Other interest expense	9,380,927	9,590,531
	$881,461,107	$828,904,736
Income (loss) before income taxes and unusual charges	$ (93,094,627)	$ 6,182,037
Unusual charges, (Note 3)	(28,494,304)	—
Federal and Canadian income taxes (Notes 3 and 6)	66,999,211	(1,180,200)
Net income (loss) for the year	$ (54,589,720)	$ 5,001,837

losses, and price allowances; and *(b)* relocation and discontinuance of facilities and products. Provisions were recorded in the last quarter of 1985 to establish special reserves totaling $68,754,410 for these anticipated costs and losses. Of this amount, $28,494,304 (equivalent to $13,437,093 net of taxes), associated with relocation and discontinuance of products and facilities, is shown as an unusual charge in the consolidated statement of income (loss). The remaining provisions, totaling $40,260,106, were charged to sales ($5,627,178); materials, plant payroll, and services ($28,190,928); and selling, general, and administrative expenses ($6,442,000).

Although the costs and losses to be charged to the special reserves cannot be finally determined at the present time, management believes, based on the company's extensive studies and evaluations which were reviewed in depth by the independent auditors, that the provisions recorded in 1985 represent a fair and reasonable determination of the amounts required.

The net loss for the year has been determined after giving recognition to income taxes recoverable ($14,345,721) from carryback to prior years of operating losses and to estimated future tax benefits ($50,900,000) of unused losses, including $6,836,276 relating to an accounting change described in Note 6 to the financial statements. The amounts recoverable from carryback to prior years are included in current assets in the consolidated balance sheet, together with 1985 tax refunds receivable of $3,970,000 and estimated future income tax benefits of $17,303,304 relating primarily to normal book-tax timing differences applicable to amounts included in current assets and liabilities. The realization of estimated future income tax benefits which total $60,275,704 is dependent upon the company's ability to generate future taxable income. This amount is included in the financial statements because, in the opinion of management, the realization of such tax benefits is assured beyond any reasonable doubt.

The company has unrecorded investment tax credit carryforwards of $6,098,722, applicable to the years 1979 through 1985, which may be used to reduced income taxes payable in future years.

NOTE 6: Accounting Changes. The company has adopted, for financial reporting purposes, the straight-line method of computing depreciation for substantially all plants and equipment. These fixed assets were previously depreciated on an accelerated basis. This change, effective October 1, 1984, reduced depreciation expense by $4,505,109 and decreased the net loss by $2,126,411, equal to $0.21 per common share.

In 1985, the company extended the application of tax allocation accounting procedures to certain overseas reserve accounts to comply fully with tax accounting requirements as now interpreted by the current management. The extension of these procedures decreased the net loss by $6,836,276, equal to $0.66 per common share.

Shortly after the company issued its 1985 annual report, an article entitled "A Bit of Rouge for American" appeared in *Business Magazine*. It stated:

The accounting that appears in annual reports sometimes serves a cosmetic purpose—it is there not so much to inform stockholders as to help management keep them happy, or at least quiet, by touching up blemishes and brightening beauty spots. When a company is not doing well, and at the same time is trying to fend off unwanted merger, the cosmeticians of accountancy can sometimes perform wonders—even when they are limited to shades of red. Quite a number of companies in this year's directory used bookkeeping devices of various kinds to brighten their results. But one of the country's oldest companies, American Manufacturing, outdid them all at the rouge pot.

As 1985 ended, long-suffering American found itself with some conflicting needs and desires. It presumably wanted to put the best possible face on 1985 results in order to maintain stockholder support in a bitter battle against a hostile takeover by Consolidated Industries. But the new president of American, Peter C. Scully, who took office June 1, wanted to write off at once the tremendous charges associated with past mistakes and thereby turn the company around. To do that, he had to slap stockholders with some very bad news just when Consolidated's onslaught was hotting up.

American resolved this conflict with some intricate accounting that let it accept Scully's write-off while minimizing the bad news that had to be reported to stockholders. The published results were still pretty dismal: on sales of $767,313,100, the company reported a loss of $54,589,720. That was, however, a whole lot better than the $121,588, 931 that the company *actually* lost last year.

To understand how an actual loss of $122 million can become a reported loss of $55 million requires some comprehension of tax accounting. It is well known, of course, that a corporate dollar earned is roughly 50 cents lost to the tax collector. The converse is also true, i.e., a dollar lost is 50 cents earned. American simply claimed a credit on its profit and loss statement for the taxes that it saved by achieving a loss. The company said, in effect: "If Uncle Sam deserves his slice of profits, he also deserves his slice of the losses. We cannot be said to have lost $122 million when we thereby hung on to something over $60 million in taxes that we otherwise would have had to pay." Recently, the SEC took a dim view of Aetna Life Insurance picking up future anticipated tax credits in current income. It is reported that the SEC is looking closely at American's similar ploy. American may be one of the last companies to take advantage of the tax loss carryforward rule loophole. It is rumored the FASB is going to disallow this practice when it issues its new tax accounting rules later this year.

American had deducted from its operating loss of $93,094,627 "federal, state and Canadian income taxes" of $66,999,211. Part of this was provided by a loss carry-back of $14,345,721, effectively refunding taxes paid in 1982, 1983, and 1984. The remainder was supplied by potential carry-forward benefits. The company listed as a current asset "income tax refunds and future income tax benefits" of $35,619,025, and an additional asset, between current and long-term assets "estimated future income tax benefits" of $42,972,400 (see Exhibit 2).

EXHIBIT 2

AMERICAN MANUFACTURING COMPANY
Statement of Financial Position

	September 30	
	1985	1984
Assets		
Current assets:		
Cash	$ 23,483,905	$ 32,778,384
Receivables, less reserves of $16,171,800 and $12,990,000, respectively	126,836,883	125,835,967
Inventories, at lower of approximate cost (10% valued at LIFO) or market, less progress payments of $14,286,644 and $13,816,887, respectively	234,115,066	231,107,182
Income tax refunds and future income tax benefits (Note 3)	35,619,025	21,590,000
Other current assets	3,997,779	4,496,240
Total current assets	$424,052,658	$415,807,773
Estimated future income tax benefits (Note 3)	42,972,400	—
Investments and other assets:		
Investment in finance subsidiaries, at equity, in net assets	$ 53,498,936	$ 46,594,803
Investment in other subsidiaries, at cost, less reserves (Note 1)	18,524,117	23,748,137
Intangible assets arising from acquisition (Note 2)	7,389,935	7,389,935
Other investments, assets, and deferred charges (Note 5)	6,366,775	5,244,786
	$ 85,779,763	$ 82,977,661
Plants and equipment at cost:		
Land and buildings	$110,168,287	$103,163,467
Machinery and equipment	190,005,484	180,635,390
Tools and fixtures	32,212,797	29,925,202
Furniture and fixtures	7,136,070	6,391,647
	$339,522,638	$320,115,706
Accumulated depreciation and amortization (Note 6)	186,714,838	178,989,166
	$152,807,800	$141,126,540
	$705,612,621	$639,911,974
Liabilities and Equity		
Current liabilities:		
Notes payable and current maturities of long-term debt	$106,382,295	$ 50,797,500
Accounts payable and payrolls	68,970,051	69,978,681
Federal, state, and Canadian income taxes	883,458	4,072,998
Reserves for completion of contracts and product corrections and current portion of special reserves	69,486,985	12,611,115
Other current liabilities	20,606,507	19,237,153
Total current liabilities	$266,329,296	$156,697,447

EXHIBIT 2 *(Concluded)*

	September 30	
	1985	*1984*
Special reserves (Note 3):		
Estimated costs of parts replacement, warranty costs, repossession losses, and price allowances	$ 40,260,106	—
Estimated costs and losses associated with relocation and discontinuance of facilities and products	28,494,304	—
	$ 68,754,410	—
Less: Amount included in current liabilities	48,000,000	—
	$ 20,754,410	—
Long-term debt (Note 4):		
Notes payable	$ 66,000,000	$ 69,000,000
Sinking fund debentures	45,000,000	45,000,000
Other long-term debt	3,361,924	4,228,487
	$114,361,924	$118,228,487
Deferred income taxes	—	$ 1,449,260
Shareowners' equity (Notes 5 and 9):		
Preferred stock, $100 par value, 500,000 shares authorized,134,594 shares, 4.20% cumulative convertible series outstanding in 1984	—	13,459,400
Common stock, $10 par value, 12.5 million shares authorized, 10,410,292 and 9,881,481 shares outstanding after deducting 42,869 and 82,869 shares held in treasury, respectively	$104,102,920	98,814,810
Capital in excess of par value of capital stock	122,548,752	113,198,182
Earnings retained	77,515,319	138,064,388
Total shareowners' equity	$304,166,991	$363,536,780
	$705,612,621	$639,911,974

Opinion No. 11 states:

If operating losses are carried backwards to earlier periods under provisions of the tax law, the tax effects of the loss carry*backs* are included in the results of operations of the loss period, since realization is assured. If operating losses are carried forward under provisions of the tax law, the tax effects usually are not recognized in the accounts until the periods of realization, since realization of the benefits of the loss carry*forwards* generally is not assured in the loss periods. The only exception to that practice occurs in unusual circumstances when realization is assured beyond any reasonable doubt in the loss periods. Under an alternative view, however, the tax effects of loss carry*forwards* would be recognized in the loss periods unless specific reasons exist to question their realization.

The auditor's opinion on the 1985 financial statements read:

As explained in Note 3 to the financial statements, in the last quarter of 1985, the company recorded substantial amounts associated with (a) reserves for anticipated costs and losses and (b) estimated income tax benefits expected to be realized in the future. Although these reserves and anticipated tax benefits reflect the best current judgment of the company's management, we cannot determine at this time the amounts of costs and losses which ultimately will be charged against the reserves, and the amounts of future tax benefits which ultimately will be charged against the reserves, and the amounts of future tax benefits which ultimately will be realized.

In our opinion, subject to the effect of any adjustments which may result from ultimate determination of the matters referred to in the preceding paragraph, the accompanying consolidated financial statements examined by us present fairly the financial position of American Manufacturing Company and its subsidiaries at September 30, 1985, and the results of their operations for the year, in conformity with generally accepted accounting principles applied on a basis consistent with that of the preceding year, except for the changes in accounting for depreciation and income taxes as explained in Note 6 to the financial statements.

The fiscal year 1986 first quarter earnings were projected by security analysts to be $11.7 million, less a provision for taxes, for a net profit of $5.1 million. The tax carryforward benefit had been taken completely in 1985 for book purposes. Hence, it was not available for 1986. In contrast, the actual tax payment credit benefits could only be realized as future profits were reported for tax purposes.

Questions

1. Appraise the current and prospective corporate implications of the corporate reporting decisions discussed in the American case.

2. Comment on the appropriateness of these decisions from the point of view of "fairness" and "generally accepted accounting principles."

3. What is your appraisal of the comments included in the Business Magazine article?

4. What is your evaluation of the auditor's opinion?

5. Complete the following matrix using the data in the case:

	Before Tax	Tax Effects (in millions)	After Tax Effects
Operating loss before special reserves	$	$	$
Special reserves			
Unusual charges			
Total loss	$	$	$ 54.6

What added insights into American's condition and accounting practices does the above analysis provide?

CHAPTER 15

Fixed Asset Accounting and Analysis

A company's fixed assets include all of its physical assets with a life of more than one year that are used in operations but are not intended for sale as such in the ordinary course of business. Fixed assets can be classified in three different categories: (1) those subject to depreciation, such as plant and equipment; (2) those subject to depletion, such as natural resources; and (3) those not subject to depreciation or depletion, such as land. Fixed assets are normally carried at their original cost less any accumulated depreciation or depletion. Depreciation is the process of allocating the cost of fixed assets over the useful life of the asset so as to match the cost of an asset with the benefits it creates, and depletion is the process whereby the cost of wasting assets is matched with the revenues generated by the asset. The allocation of the cost of fixed assets to the income statement to determine periodic income is covered in Chapter 16. This chapter focuses on the measurement of investments in fixed assets.

Fixed assets are shown on the balance sheet as follows:

Fixed assets:
Plant and equipment (original cost) xxxx
　　Less: Allowance for depreciation xxxx
　　　　Net plant and equipment xxxx

Ordinarily, no mention is made of a fixed asset's market value. However, the FASB does require certain companies to indicate the current cost of their productive assets in their supplemental inflation data disclosures.

Statement users should pay close attention to the fixed asset accounting employed by the companies they analyze. The net book value of plant and equipment is a major determinant of many companies' book value (assets less liabilities), which is a key value often used in equity valuation appraisal and debt covenants. The condition of a company's plant may determine in large measure its cost structure and ability to improve its capital and employee productivity. The values assigned to fixed assets influence periodic income since they are the basis for future depreciation and depletion charges. Management decisions to capitalize or not capitalize fixed-asset-related expenditures can influence current profits. Finally, management can improve or depress current profits by lowering or raising the level of maintenance expenditures required to maintain the company's fixed assets.

Capitalization Criteria

Considerable judgment is sometimes required to determine whether or not an expenditure related to fixed assets should be capitalized or expensed as incurred. Generally, those fixed-asset-related expenditures are capitalized whose usefulness is expected to extend over several accounting periods, expand the usefulness of a fixed asset, or extend its useful life. Conversely, expenditures should be expensed when they neither extend the useful life of a fixed asset beyond the original estimates nor generate benefits beyond the current accounting period. Companies usually establish minimum cost limits below which all fixed-asset-related expenditures are expensed, even if they might otherwise be properly capitalized. The minimum amount selected should be set at a point which still results in fair financial reporting without placing an unreasonable burden on the accounting system.

Cost Basis

Unless otherwise indicated, the cost of a purchased fixed asset is the price paid for the asset plus all of the costs incidental to acquisition, installation, and preparation for use. Care must be applied to assure the inclusion of all material identifiable elements of cost, such as purchasing, testing, and similar items.

Fixed assets may be acquired by manufacture or by exchange. The cost of assets manufactured for use in the business generally includes the materials, labor, and manufacturing overhead directly related to the construction. How much, if any, of the general factory overhead is included in the construction cost depends on whether or not the plant constructing the asset is operating at or below capacity.

When the plant is operating at or near capacity, the use of the scarce productive facilities to construct an asset for internal use reduces the opportunity to produce regular items for sale. Because of this lost profit opportunity, a fair share of general manufacturing overhead is typically charged to an asset construction project, thereby relieving the income statement of costs that, in the absence of the construction, would have generated some offsetting revenue.

When below-capacity utilization conditions exist, it is debatable whether a fair portion of general manufacturing overhead should be charged to the cost of assets constructed for a company's own use. The arguments for charging a portion of general manufacturing overhead include: *(a)* the current loss from idle capacity will be overstated unless a cost for idle capacity used for construction is capitalized; *(b)* the construction will have future benefits, so all costs related to acquiring these benefits should be deferred; and *(c)* the construction project should be treated the same as regular products, which are charged with general overhead.

The principal arguments opposing this point of view are: *(a)* the cost of the asset should not include general overhead costs that would still have been incurred in the absence of the construction; *(b)* the general overhead was probably not considered as a relevant cost in making the decision to construct the asset for the company's own use, since the costs would be incurred irrespective of whether or not the asset was constructed; *(c)* when part of the general overhead is capitalized, the resulting increase in current income will be due to construction rather than the production of salable goods; and *(d)* it is more conservative not to capitalize general overhead.

Increasingly, the practice of charging general overhead to fixed assets constructed for a company's own use, on the same basis and at the same rate as regular goods produced for sale, is being adopted without regard to the prevailing capacity conditions. This trend reflects a movement away from conservatism for its own sake and a growing concern for proper allocation of costs to reduce distortions of periodic income due to undervaluation of assets.

Assets manufactured for a company's own use may cost less than their purchase price. This saving should not be recorded as profit at the time the asset is completed, since profits result from the use of assets, not their acquisition. The advantage of the saving will accrue to the company over the life of the asset through lower depreciation charges than would have been incurred if the asset had been purchased.

Assets costing more to construct than their purchase price are sometimes recorded at their purchase price in the interests of conservatism. The difference between construction cost and purchase price is charged to income upon completion of the asset.

The cost of a nonmonetary asset, such as a building, acquired in exchange for another nonmonetary asset is the fair value of the asset surrendered to obtain it, and a gain or loss should be recognized on the exchange if the exchange is essentially the culmination of an earnings process. However, if the exchange is not the culmination of an earnings process, the accounting for an exchange of nonmonetary assets between an enterprise and another entity should be based on the book value of the asset relinquished with no gain or loss recognized on the exchange.

Trade-in allowances on exchanged assets are often greater than their market value. Consequently, the use of trade-in allowances to value a newly acquired asset may have misleading results, through an overstatement of its cost and subsequent depreciation charges. Caution must be exercised in trade-in situations, since assets acquired through exchanges should not be recorded at a price greater than would have been paid in the absence of a trade-in.

The interest cost on funds financing construction must be capitalized as part of the fixed asset cost. *Statement No. 34* established the standards for capitalizing interest costs as part of the historical cost of acquiring certain assets. Examples of the types of assets covered include assets intended for the enterprise's own use (such as facilities) or assets intended for sale or lease that are constructed as discrete projects (such as ships or real estate projects). This statement states:

> To qualify for interest capitalization, assets must require a period of time to get them ready for their intended use. . . . Interest cannot be capitalized for inventories that are routinely manufactured or otherwise produced in large quantities on a repetitive basis.
>
> The interest cost eligible for capitalization shall be the interest cost recognized on borrowings and other obligations. The amount capitalized is to be an allocation of the interest cost incurred during the period required to complete the asset. The interest rate for capitalization purposes is to be based on the rates of the enterprise's outstanding borrowings.
>
> If the enterprise associates a specific new borrowing with the asset, it may apply the rate on the borrowings to the appropriate portion of the expenditures for the asset. A weighted average of the rates on other borrowings is to be applied to expenditures not covered by specific new borrowings. Judgment is required in identifying the borrowings on which the average rate is based.

In the 1982 Tax Act, Congress expanded the prior law requiring certain taxpayers to capitalize interest and real property taxes incurred during construction to all corporations other than those constructing residential real estate.

Donated assets should be recorded at their fair market value.

Expenditures Subsequent to Acquisition and Use

After a fixed asset is acquired and put into use, a number of expenditures related to its subsequent utilization may be incurred. The manager must decide whether or not these expenditures should be capitalized as part of the asset cost or expensed as incurred. The general practice is to capitalize those expenditures that will generate future benefits beyond those originally estimated at the time the asset was acquired. However, if there is substantial uncertainty as to whether the benefits will ever be realized, such expenditures are charged to current income. Also, all expenditures related to fixed assets that are necessary to realize the benefits originally projected are expensed.

Repairs and Maintenance

Maintenance and repair costs are incurred to maintain assets in a satisfactory operating condition. When these expenditures are ordinary and recurring, they are expensed. Significant expenditures made for repairs which lead to an increase in the asset's economic life or its efficiency beyond the original estimates should be charged to the allowance for depreciation. This effectively raises the asset's book value. In addition, the asset's depreciable rate should also be changed to reflect the new use, life, and residual value expectations. Extraordinary expenditures for repairs that do not prolong an asset's economic life or improve its efficiency probably represent the cost of neglected upkeep of the asset, and as such should be charged to income as incurred.

Repairs made to restore assets damaged by fire, flood, or similar events should be charged to loss from casualty up to the amount needed to restore the asset to its condition before the damage. Expenditures beyond this amount should be treated like any other expenditure that prolongs the economic life of an asset.

When some assets are acquired, it is anticipated that unusually heavy maintenance costs, such as repainting, may be incurred at different points during their lives. In these situations, some managers establish an Allowance for Repairs and Maintenance account to avoid unusually large charges against income. This practice, which is permissible, charges income with a predetermined periodic maintenance expense based upon management's estimate of the total ordinary and unusual maintenance costs over the asset's life. The credit entry is to the liability account, Repairs and Maintenance Allowance. When the actual expenditures for the anticipated maintenance are incurred, the allowance account is charged with this amount. Since the allowance represents a future charge to current assets, it is sometimes treated as a current liability. In other cases, it is reported as a contra account to fixed assets, along with the allowance for depreciation account. Credit balances are deducted from original cost in determining book value. Debit balances are regarded as temporary additions, and as such increase book value. For income tax purposes, only the actual expenditures for maintenance are deductible. Therefore, the establishment of an allowance usually has deferred tax accounting implications also.

Betterments, Improvements, and Additions

Expenditures for betterments and improvements, such as replacing wooden beams with steel girders, usually result in an increase in an asset's economic life or usefulness. As such, these expenditures are properly capitalized and subsequently charged to the related asset's allowance for depreciation. Also, the asset's depreciation rate should be redetermined to reflect the economic consequences of the expenditure. Minor expenditures for betterments and improvements are typically expensed as incurred.

Additions to existing assets, such as a new wing to a plant, represent capital expenditures and as such should be recorded at their full acquisition cost just like the original investment in fixed assets.

Land

Land is a nondepreciable asset. Its life is assumed to be indefinitely long. Land should be shown separately on the balance sheet.

The cost of land includes the purchase price, all costs incidental to the purchase, and the costs of permanent improvements, such as clearing and draining. Expenditures made for improvements with a limited life, such as sidewalks and fencing, should be recorded in a separate account, Land Improvements, and written off over their useful lives.

If land is held for speculative purposes, it should be captioned appropriately and reported separately from the land used for productive facilities. The carrying costs of such land can be capitalized, since the land is producing no income and the eventual gain or loss on the sale of the land is the difference between the selling price and the purchase price plus carrying charges. For income tax purposes, the carrying charges can be either capitalized or deducted as incurred.

Wasting Assets

Mineral deposits and other natural resources that are physically exhausted through extraction and are irreplaceable are called "wasting assets." Until extracted, such assets are classified as fixed assets. The cost of land containing wasting assets should be allocated between the residual value of the land and the depletable natural resource. If the natural resource is discovered after the purchase of the land, it is acceptable to reallocate the original cost in a similar way.

Companies in the business of exploiting wasting assets on a continuing basis incur exploration costs to replace their exhausted assets. These exploration costs can be either expensed or capitalized. Because of the great uncertainty associated with exploration in the extractive industries, the typical practice is to capitalize only those costs identifiable with the discovery and development of productive properties and expense the rest as incurred.

There are two basic approaches to the capitalization of discovery and development costs. These are commonly called the "full cost" and "field cost," or "successful efforts," methods. In practice, these methods are applied in a variety of different ways.

The field cost method assigns the costs of discovery and development to specific fields of wasting assets, such as a specific oil or gas field in Oklahoma. If the exploration and development activities related to that field are unsuccessful, the costs are expensed. If the field proves to be successful, the costs are capitalized and written off against the production of the field on a units of production basis. If the costs exceed the value of the field's reserves, the costs are capitalized only to the extent they can be recovered from the sale of the reserves. Should a field be abandoned, any capitalized costs are written off immediately.

The full cost method assigns costs of discovery and development to regions of activity, such as the North American continent. These regions may include one or more fields in which the company is active. The full cost method follows the same capitalization-expense rules as the field method. However, since the area for measuring reserves is now a larger region, the costs of discovery and development in unsuccessful fields can be lumped together with the costs of successful efforts and written off against the total region's production.

Historical Costs and Accountability

The general practice of recording fixed assets at cost can lead to situations where adherence to the cost principle may conflict with management accountability for the use of the assets. In some rare cases where this conflict arises, it is permissible to depart from the cost principle. In most cases, however, it is not permissible. *Opinion No. 6* discussed the accounting for appreciation:

> The board is of the opinion that property, plant, and equipment should not be written up by an entity to reflect appraisal, market, or current values which are above cost to the entity. This statement is not intended to change accounting practices followed in connection with quasi-reorganizations or reorganizations. This statement may not apply to foreign operations under unusual conditions such as serious inflation or currency devaluation. However, when the accounts of a company with foreign operations are translated into United States currency for consolidation, such write-ups normally are eliminated. Whenever appreciation has been recorded on the books, income should be charged with depreciation computed on the written up amounts.

Alternative Measurement Proposals

Historical cost is the only accepted base for measuring plant and equipment and related depreciation charges in published financial statements. A number of other approaches have been proposed by accounting authors. These include: making the carrying value of assets more responsive to their current market values, adjusting the historical cost base to reflect general price level changes, and the use of replacement costs as the basis for calculating annual depreciation charges.

Those who oppose the use of historical costs to value fixed assets do so principally on the ground that it does not, in their opinion, lead to useful financial statements. For many years, supporters of alternative approaches to the historical cost convention did not challenge the objectivity and feasibility of historical costs in comparison with other, alternative methods for measurement of fixed assets. In recent years, however, these two qualities have been increasingly questioned.

The proponents of historical cost argue that it is a useful basis and part of the discipline of management in that it holds management responsible for the funds invested in fixed assets. Also, the users of financial reports are fully aware that historical costs do not represent value but merely unexpired costs. The weight of convention, experience, and acceptance is clearly on the side of historical costs; therefore, it is argued, the burden of proving any alternative basis more useful rests with those who oppose the use of historical costs to measure assets.

The essence of the price-level and market value approaches often proposed as alternatives to the historical cost method can be illustrated as follows. A farmer's sole asset is land purchased 15 years ago for $8,000. The current appraisal of the land's market value is $300,000. During the 15 years the farmer held the land, general price levels doubled.

A historical cost statement for this farmer would show assets of $8,000 and net worth of $8,000 (other items excluded). If price-level adjustments were made, the statement would show assets of $16,000 and a similar amount for net worth. The $16,000 is the current purchasing power equivalent of the original $8,000 ($8,000 × 200 percent inflation). If market values were used, the statements would show assets at $300,000 and net worth at $300,000, which would consist of $8,000 original investment and $292,000 appreciation by reason of holding the land in a rising market. If the price-level and market value approaches were combined, the assets would remain the same, but net worth would now consist of the $8,000 original investment, the $8,000 price-level gain, and the $284,000 appreciation in the market value of the land after adjusting for general price-level changes.

General price-level adjustment (constant dollar accounting) attempts to state historical costs incurred in different years in terms of a common monetary unit of equivalent purchasing power. It is not a valuation method. It simply adjusts nominal dollars spent or received in different periods to a common purchasing power equivalent. In countries with rapidly rising price levels, it is common practice to adjust the historical acquisition costs of fixed assets for general price-level changes. This results in a measurement of fixed assets and their related depreciation charges in terms of the general purchasing power invested and expiring. Under conditions of rapid inflation, few question the wisdom of this practice. However, for many years, it was argued that the annual rate of inflation in the United States had not been high enough to justify converting the historical costs invested in assets during prior years to equivalent dollars having the same purchasing power. In 1979, the FASB, after a period of above-average inflation, decided that general-price-level-adjusted statements may be more meaningful than historical-cost-based statements and required certain larger companies to provide supplemental disclosure of their price-level-adjusted data. Later, in

1985, the FASB rescinded this requirement to publish data adjusted for changes in the general price level. Price change accounting and recent developments in this area are covered in greater detail in Chapter 17.

The case for the market value method of asset valuation is expressed as follows. Assets are recorded at cost initially, because this is the economic measure of their potential service value. After acquisition, the accounting goal should continue to be to express the economic value of this service potential. This is difficult to measure directly, but the current market price others are willing to pay for similar assets approximates this value in most cases. Therefore, to the extent that market values are available, they should be used to measure fixed asset carrying values and their subsequent consumption in the production of goods and services. Property values are more useful than historical costs to managers and stockholders because market values determine the collateral value of property for borrowing purposes, fix liability for property taxes, establish the basis for insurance, and reflect the amount an owner might expect to realize upon sale of the property.

The principal objection to market value is that it is often difficult to determine objectively. The proponents of market value answer this argument by indicating that the notion of market value has some important qualifications. For example, the fair determination of market values should be recognized only when the disparity between market value and cost is likely to prevail for a fairly long period. Furthermore, the market value of an asset should be recognized only on the basis of reliable evidence. The notion of market value probably has little relevance to nonstandardized equipment or special fixed assets for which no readily available market exists. Historical costs must suffice in these cases.

The market value approach has significant implications for the income statement. Market value advocates claim that management continually faces the alternative of using or disposing of assets. Income statements based on historical cost do not show how well management has appraised this alternative, since in no way is the "cost" of the alternative forgone included in the statements. In a case where the market value of an asset is greater than its historical cost, historical-cost-based depreciation leads to an overstatement of the incremental benefit gained by using rather than selling, since the book depreciation basis is understated. The reverse is true when the market value is less than the book value. It is claimed that market-value-based depreciation would overcome this weakness. The incremental benefit of continuing to use the asset would be determined after a depreciation charge based on the "cost" of the income forgone by not disposing of the asset.

There is a difference of opinion among market value supporters as to how changes in the carrying value of the assets should be recorded. Some would treat the increases or decreases in stockholders' equity in much the same way as appraisal adjustments are recorded. Others propose including the changes as part of the income determination.

The replacement cost approach advocates carrying assets at the cost of reproducing equivalent property, not identical property (as some critics of replacement cost assume). This approach is based on a concept of income which recognizes no profit until depreciation charges have provided adequately for the eventual cost of replacing the capacity represented in existing assets with an asset of more modern design. Based on this theory, traditional depreciation, which recovers original cost from revenues, fails to provide adequately for future replacement in periods of rising replacement costs, and so leads to an overstatement of distributable profits. As a result, excessive dividends, wages, and income taxes may be paid, to the detriment of the company's ability to maintain its current level of capacity.

The replacement cost approach is usually implemented by multiplying an asset's original cost by a price index specifically related to the changing cost of the asset involved. Sometimes a further adjustment is made to this figure to reflect technological changes since the date of the original asset's acquisition. The result approximates the replacement cost of an asset's equivalent capacity derived through an appraisal. Such price indexes are available and widely accepted for specific categories of assets. The replacement cost proponents argue that their method has the advantage of the objectivity associated with recording the original cost of the asset at acquisition, as well as minimizing the role of judgment in subsequent revaluations. Thus, the net result of their approach, they argue, is a more useful income figure without any sacrifice in objectivity.

In *Statement No. 33*, the FASB required certain companies to report the current cost of their property, plant, and equipment. This valuation approach is similar in many respects to the replacement cost concept. The FASB defined current cost as "the current cost of acquiring the same service potential (indicated by operating costs and physical output capacity) as embodied by the asset owned." The service potential (or future economic benefit) of an asset is its capacity to provide services or benefits to the company using the asset.

Investment Tax Credit

To encourage investment in productive assets, Congress from time to time has allowed taxpayers a direct credit against income taxes payable of up to a specified percentage of the acquisition cost of certain tangible property used in business operations.

To illustrate the calculation of the straight 8 percent investment tax credit, assume a qualified piece of machinery with a 10-year life and zero salvage is purchased for $200,000. The company's profits before taxes, but after depreciation, on all other items except the new machinery is $1,320,000. Therefore, the company's taxable income is:

Profit after all depreciation, but before taxes
 and depreciation on new equipment $1,320,000
Less: Depreciation on new machinery ($200,000 × 0.10)....   20,000
Taxable income $1,300,000

The effect of the purchase and an 8 percent tax credit on the company's tax payment is:

Income taxes before investment credit (46 percent
 of taxable income) .... $ 598,000
Less: Investment credit ($200,000 × 0.08)   16,000
Tax payment due .... $ 582,000

It is important to note that the investment tax credit is a direct reduction of the tax otherwise payable.

The granting of investment tax credits created a serious accounting problem. Although most people agreed that the credit was a factor which influenced the determination of net income, they could not agree on how the credit increased income.[1]

A number of business executives and accountants support the flow-through method for handling the credit. Under this method, the investment tax credit is considered as being in substance a selective reduction in taxes which otherwise would have been payable and which are related to the taxable income of the year in which the credit is granted. This approach considers the credit as related to taxable income rather than to the cost of using assets. Also, since the credit is not relatable to, or dependent on, future revenues, the flow-through advocates maintained that the credit is earned during the period in which it was obtained.

Supporters of the deferral approach believe that the investment tax credit should be put on the balance sheet as deferred income and reflected in earnings as a separately identifiable item as the related asset is used and depreciated. They reject the flow-through approach, principally on the ground that the credit does not enhance the integrity of the earnings figure if earnings can be increased simply by buying an asset.

To illustrate the effect of these different approaches to handling the investment credit, assume that the Hampton Company bought a new piece of equipment costing $100,000. The expected life of the equipment was 10 years. Consequently, the company qualified to receive an investment

---

[1] It was argued by some that the credit was in effect a subsidy by way of a contribution to capital and, hence, should be so recorded directly as an increase in owners' equity. This position was not considered by the Accounting Principles Board, since it ran counter to the widespread belief that the credit increased income.

tax credit of $8,000. Handling the credit on a flow-through basis would improve after-tax profits by the full $8,000 in the year of purchase, but by only $800 on a deferral basis. In both cases, the cash flow would be the same. However, use of the flow-through method would boost the Hampton Company's after-tax profits by $7,200 over the deferral method amount. Adoption of the deferral method would result in future profits being $800 more annually for the next nine years than if the flow-through method had been adopted.

The accounting for the 8 percent investment tax credit in the above example is:

a. Flow-through method:

Dr. Taxes Payable	8,000	
Cr. Tax Expense		8,000

b. Deferral method—year 1:

Dr. Taxes Payable	8,000	
Cr. Tax Expense		800
Deferred Investment Tax Credit		7,200

Deferral method—years 2 through 10:

Dr. Deferred Investment Tax Credit	800	
Cr. Tax Expense		800

While expressing a preference for the deferral approach, the APB in *Opinion No. 4* approved the use of both the flow-through and deferral methods. In practice, the flow-through approach is the more popular of the two methods. Irrespective of the method elected, it is important to remember that the cash flow effect is the same.

If a company has earned investment tax credits that for some reason cannot be recognized for tax purposes, these should be disclosed in the notes. Unused tax credits can be carried forward for 15 years.

In mid-1985, the Treasury Department proposed discontinuance of the investment tax credit.

Analysis of Fixed Assets

Companies usually file more information on their various fixed asset balances, additions, subtractions, and lives, as well as maintenance costs, with the SEC in their 10-Ks than they disclose in annual reports. These SEC filings are essential for a thorough analysis of a company's fixed assets. With these data, statement users should attempt to appraise the competitive quality of the company's fixed assets. Indications that a company's fixed assets may be becoming less competitive are:

a. Lengthening of the average age of the company's plant and equipment, suggested by a drop-off in nominal or inflation-adjusted capital expenditures for plant and equipment and an increasing estimate of the plant and equipment's average age in years, determined by dividing the accumulated depreciation balance by the current year's depreciation expense.

b. Failure to maintain plant and equipment, indicated by a decline in maintenance expenditures relative to gross plant.

c. Uncompetitive facilities and equipment, suggested by an excess of annual current cost depreciation over annual capital expenditures.

It is difficult to establish absolute standards to evaluate the results of fixed asset studies. The analyst must make judgments on the relative results of fixed asset studies of companies in the same industry, the object company's own trend data, and management's description of its business strategy and the role of fixed assets in that strategy.

To understand in depth the quality of a company's earnings, the details of the fixed asset accounts should be analyzed to detect any gains or losses from the disposition of fixed assets. Losses may suggest the company is underdepreciating its assets, with the result that earnings from operations are overstated. A gain on the sale of an asset may appear in the details of the fixed asset accounts but be reported simply as other income in the income statement. The unwary reader relying solely on the income statement presentation might miss this onetime source of income and thus overestimate the company's income from operations.

Brazos Printing Company
Problems in Fixed Asset Transactions

The Brazos Printing Company was founded as a one-man job printing firm in a small southwestern town. Shortly after its founding, the owner decided to concentrate on one specialty line of printing. Because of a high degree of technical proficiency, the company experienced a rapid growth.

However, the company suffered from a competitive disadvantage in that the major market for this specialized output was in a metropolitan area over 300 miles away from the company's plant. For this reason, the owner 12 years later decided to move nearer his primary market. He also decided to expand and modernize his facilities at the time of the move. After some investigation, an attractive site was found in a suburb of his primary market, and the move was made.

A balance sheet prepared prior to the move is shown in Exhibit 1. The transactions that arose from this move are described in the following paragraphs.

1. The land at the old site together with the building thereon was sold for $35,000. The land had originally cost $5,000. The building appeared on the company's books at a cost of $76,000, and a depreciation allowance of $45,000 had been accumulated on it.

2. Certain equipment was sold for $4,500 cash. This equipment appeared on the books at a cost of $16,700 less accumulated depreciation of $9,700.

3. New bindery equipment was purchased. The invoice cost of this equipment was $20,000. A 2 percent cash discount was taken by the Brazos Company, so that only $19,600 was actually paid to the seller. The Brazos Company also paid $80 to a trucker to have this equipment delivered.

This case was prepared by J. Brougher under the direction of Robert N. Anthony.

Copyright © 1953 by the President and Fellows of Harvard College

Harvard Business School case 154–001 (Rev. 1985)

EXHIBIT 1

BRAZOS PRINTING COMPANY
Condensed Balance Sheet
Assets

Current assets:		
Cash		$ 91,242
Other current assets		69,720
Total current assets		$160,962
Fixed assets:		
Land		5,000
Buildings	$76,000	
Less: Accumulated depreciation	45,000	31,000
Equipment	$65,822	
Less: Accumulated depreciation	42,340	23,482
Total assets		$220,444

Equities

Current liabilities	$ 41,346
Common stock	100,000
Retained earnings	79,098
Total equities	$220,444

Installation of this equipment was made by Brazos workmen, who worked a total of 40 hours. These men received $1.50 per hour in wages, but their time was ordinarily charged to printing jobs at $4 per hour, the difference representing an allowance for overhead ($2.10) and profit ($0.40).

4. The city to which the company moved furnished the land on which the new plant was built as a gift. The land had an appraised value of $20,000; the appraisal had been made recently by a qualified appraiser. The company would pay property taxes on its assessed value, which was $15,000.

5. The Brazos Company paid $4,000 to have an old building on the gift plot of land torn down. (The value of this building was not included in the appraised or assessed values named above.) In addition, the company paid $2,000 to have permanent drainage facilities installed on the new land.

6. A new strip caster with an invoice cost of $4,500 was purchased. The company paid $3,000 cash and received a trade-in allowance of $1,500 on a used strip caster. The used strip caster could have been sold outright for not more than $1,200. It had cost $3,000 new, and accumulated depreciation on it was $1,200.

7. The company erected a building at the new site for $90,000. Of this amount, $70,000 was borrowed on a mortgage.

8. After the equipment had been moved to the new plant, but before operations began there, extensive repairs and replacement of parts were

made on a large paper cutter. The cost of this work was $1,100. Prior to this time, no more than $100 had been spent in any one year on the maintenance of this paper cutter.

9. Trucking and other costs associated with moving equipment to the new location and installing it there were $1,400. In addition, Brazos Company employees worked an estimated 120 hours on that part of the move that related to equipment.

10. During the moving operation, a piece of equipment costing $3,000 was dropped and damaged; $400 was spent to repair it. Mr. Timken believed, however, that the salvage value of this equipment had been reduced to $200. Up until that time, the equipment was being depreciated at $240 per year, representing a 10 percent rate after deduction of estimated salvage of $600. Accumulated depreciation was $960.

Questions

1. Analyze the effect of these transactions on the items in the balance sheet.
2. In your opinion, should the transactions which affect net worth in the case be accounted for in the profit and loss account or carried directly to retained earnings? If in the profit and loss account, where should these items appear in the profit and loss statement?

CHAPTER 16

Depreciation Accounting and Analysis

The term depreciation, as used in accounting, refers to the process of allocating the cost of a depreciable tangible fixed asset to the accounting periods covered during its expected useful life. Some of the difficulties encountered by financial statement users in connection with depreciation result from failure to recognize the meaning of the term in this accounting sense. Outside the area of accounting, depreciation is generally used to denote a reduction in the value of property; misunderstandings are caused by attempts to substitute this concept for the more specialized accounting definition.

Depreciation was defined by the American Institute of Certified Public Accountants in its *Accounting Terminology Bulletin No. 1:*

> *Depreciation accounting* is a system of accounting which aims to distribute the cost or other basic value of tangible capital assets, less salvage (if any), over the estimated useful life of the unit (which may be a group of assets) in a systematic and rational manner. It is a process of allocation, not of valuation.
>
> *Depreciation for the year* is the portion of the total charge under such a system that is allocated to the year. Depreciation can be distinguished from other terms with specialized meanings used by accountants to describe asset cost allocation procedures. Depreciation is concerned with charging the cost of man-made fixed assets to operations (and not with determination of asset values for the balance sheet). Depletion refers to cost allocations for natural resources such as oil and mineral deposits. Amortization relates to cost allocations for intangible assets such as patents and leaseholds. The use of the term depreciation should also be avoided in connection with valuation procedures for securities and inventories.

A good grasp of the nature of depreciation is important to statement users since depreciation enters into a number of common statement analysis ratios and techniques. For example:

1. Depreciation is added back along with other items to net income to derive funds from operations and cash flow from the operating cycle.
2. Capital expenditures are related to historical cost and current cost depreciation to judge the adequacy of a company's capital expenditure program.
3. The gross depreciable asset original cost balance is divided by the annual depreciation expense to determine the average depreciable life of a firm's plant and equipment.
4. The accumulated depreciation account is divided by the annual depreciation expense to estimate the average age of a company's plant and equipment.
5. Depreciation is an element of both the cost of goods sold and the general, administration, and selling expense items; as such it influences gross margin and operating profit percentages.
6. A company's book and tax depreciation accounting choices influence its deferred tax balances, tax payments, and earnings quality.

Computing Depreciation

Depreciation expense for a period of operations can be determined by a variety of means, all of which satisfy the general requirements of consistency and reasonableness. Depreciation accounting requires the application of judgment in four areas: (1) determination of the cost of the asset depreciated (covered in Chapter 15), (2) estimation of the useful life of the asset, (3) estimation of the salvage value at the end of expected useful life, and (4) selection of a method of computing periodic depreciation charges.

Estimating the Useful Life of Fixed Assets

The estimated useful life of most fixed assets is expressed in terms of a period of calendar time. For example, a time basis for determining depreciation charges is suitable for general-purpose assets such as buildings. The useful life of an asset might be expressed in units other than time, however. For instance, the life of a motor vehicle could be estimated as 100,000 miles, while the life of a unit of specialized machinery could be estimated as 200,000 units of output or as 5,000 operating hours.

The estimated life of an asset should be the period during which it is of use to the business. Thus, the estimate should take into account such factors as the use of the asset, anticipated obsolescence, planned maintenance, and replacement policy. The period of useful life may be less than the entire physical life of the asset. For example, machinery with an expected physical life of 10 years under normal conditions will have a useful life for depreciation purposes of 6 years if company policy is to trade or dispose of such assets after 6 years or if technological improvements are expected to make the machine obsolete in 6 years.

Salvage value of fixed assets represents estimated realizable value at the end of this useful life. This may be the scrap or junk proceeds, cash sale proceeds, or trade-in value, depending upon the company's disposition and replacement policies.

Depreciable cost is determined by subtracting salvage value from the cost of the fixed asset. This depreciable cost is the amount allocated to the operating periods over the asset's useful life.

Depreciation Methods

Any depreciation method which results in a logical, systematic, and consistent allocation of depreciable cost is acceptable for financial accounting purposes. The procedures most commonly used are based upon straight-line, declining-balance, sum-of-the-years'-digits, and units-of-production (or service-life) depreciation methods. The commonly used depreciation methods are illustrated and discussed separately below. Several rarely used and comparatively complex depreciation methods which take into account the imputed earning power of investments in fixed assets will not be discussed. This group includes the annuity and sinking fund methods.

Straight-Line Depreciation

The most simple method of computing depreciation is the straight-line method. For purposes of illustration, a machine with a cost of $6,000 and estimated salvage value of $1,000 at the end of its expected five-year useful life is assumed. Depreciation expense for one year is computed thus:

Cost of machinery $6,000
Less: Estimated salvage value 1,000
Depreciable cost $5,000

$$\frac{\text{Depreciable cost}}{\text{Estimated life}} = \text{Depreciation expense}$$

$$\frac{\$5,000}{5 \text{ years}} = \$1,000 \text{ per year}$$

The straight-line method's strongest appeal is its simplicity. Until accelerated depreciation methods were permitted for income tax purposes, this method was used almost universally. Objections to the straight-line method center on the allocation of equal amounts of depreciation to each period of useful life. Identical amounts are charged in the first year for use of a new and efficient machine and in the later years as the worn machine nears the salvage market.

Accelerated Depreciation

Accelerated depreciation methods provide relatively larger depreciation charges in the early years of an asset's estimated life and diminishing charges in later years. The double-declining-balance method and the sum-of-the-years'-digits methods are the two best-known methods.

Double-declining-balance depreciation for each year is computed by multiplying the asset cost less accumulated depreciation by twice the straight-line rate expressed as a decimal fraction. Using the earlier example—machinery with a cost of $6,000 and a five-year estimated useful life, which is equal to 20 percent per year—depreciation is computed as follows:

First year:	$6,000 × 0.40	$2,400
Second year:	($6,000 − $2,400) × 0.40	1,440
Third year:	($6,000 − $3,840) × 0.40	864
Fourth year:	($6,000 − $4,704) × 0.40	518
Fifth year:	($6,000 − $5,222) × 0.40	311
Total		$5,533

Note that estimated salvage value is not used directly in these computations, even though the asset has salvage value. Since the double-declining-balance procedure will not depreciate the asset to zero cost at the end of the estimated useful life, the residual balance provides an amount in lieu of salvage value. Ordinarily, however, depreciation is not continued beyond the point where net depreciated cost equals a reasonable salvage value. Also, it is common practice to switch from double-declining-balance depreciation to straight-line depreciation over the remaining life of an asset when the annual depreciation charge falls below what the charge would have been if straight-line depreciation had been used on the remaining cost of the asset.

Sum-of-the-years'-digits depreciation for the year is computed by multiplying the depreciable cost of the asset by a fraction based upon the years' digits. The years' digits are added to obtain the denominator (1 + 2 + 3 + 4 + 5 = 15), and the numerator for each successive year is the number of the year in reverse order.

The formula for determining the sum-of-the-years' digits is:

$$SYD = n \left(\frac{n+1}{2} \right)$$

Again using the facts for the illustration of straight-line depreciation, annual depreciation computed by the sum-of-the-years'-digits method would be:

First year:	$5,000 × 5/15......	$1,667
Second year:	$5,000 × 4/15......	1,333
Third year:	$5,000 × 3/15......	1,000
Fourth year:	$5,000 × 2/15......	667
Fifth year:	$5,000 × 1/15......	333
Total		$5,000

Accelerated depreciation methods provide larger depreciation charges against operations during the early years of asset life, when the asset's new efficient condition contributes to greater earnings capacity. Further, the increasing maintenance and repair costs in the later years of asset use tend to complement the reducing depreciation charges, thereby equalizing the total cost of machine usage. Therefore, it is claimed that accelerated depreciation methods more properly match income and expense than does the straight-line method.

Units-of-Production Depreciation

The units-of-production depreciation method is based upon an estimated useful life in terms of units of output, instead of a calendar time period. Units-of-production (or service-life) methods are appropriate in those cases where the useful life of the depreciable asset can be directly related to its productive activity.

Under the units-of-production method, depreciation is determined by multiplying the actual units of output of the fixed asset for the operating period by a computed unit depreciation rate. This rate is calculated by dividing the depreciable cost by the total estimated life of the asset expressed in units of output. A $6,000 machine is estimated to have a $1,000 salvage value after producing 100,000 units of output. The depreciation rate for the machine is:

$$\frac{\$5,000}{100,000 \text{ units}} = \$0.05 \text{ per unit}$$

And, the depreciation charge for a year in which 25,000 units are produced with this machine is $1,250 (25,000 units × $0.05 per unit).

The units-of-production depreciation method relates fixed asset cost directly to usage. It is argued that this method best matches depreciation costs and revenues. However, the life of an asset is not necessarily more accurately estimated in units of output than in terms of time. Further, this depreciation method requires a record of the output of individual assets, which may not be readily available without significant additional effort and cost.

A hybrid straight-line and production method is sometimes used by companies in cyclical businesses. The straight-line portion is treated as a period cost and is the minimum depreciation charge. In addition, when production increases beyond a "normal" operating level, an additional depreciation charge is made to reflect the use of assets which are idle at normal production levels.

Accounting for Depreciation

Regardless of the method chosen for computing depreciation, the accounting entry required to record depreciation applicable to a period of operation is:

```
Dr.  Depreciation Expense ..........................................  XXX
      Cr.  Accumulated Depreciation ...................................        XXX
```

In addition, both account titles should indicate the type of fixed assets involved, that is, buildings, machinery, office equipment, and so on. This aids in proper handling of the accounts in the financial statements.

Depreciation expense can be listed in the income statement as a single item or according to the nature of the fixed asset giving rise to the depreciation. Depreciation expense on factory machinery can be included in factory overhead, while depreciation on office equipment can be included among the administrative expenses.

Accumulated Depreciation (sometimes called Allowance for Depreciation) is deducted from the related fixed asset account on the balance sheet. This account's credit balance increases as assets are depreciated in successive accounting periods. Of course, the allocation of fixed asset cost could be accomplished by crediting the amount of depreciation directly to the fixed asset accounts. This procedure is not recommended because it merges the cost of the fixed asset with estimated depreciation charges, and the users of financial statements would be denied information about fixed asset investment and depreciation policies.

Depreciation charges are continued systematically until the asset is disposed of or until the asset is depreciated to its salvage value. Fully depreciated assets remaining in service may or may not be carried in the accounts until disposition. From time to time, significant changes in a company's circumstances may require a switch from one depreciation method to another.

Group Depreciation

Depreciation is frequently computed for a group of assets owned by a business. In preceding illustrations, it was assumed that depreciation was calculated separately for each fixed asset; such procedures are called unit methods. If the asset units can be grouped together in some general category, such as machinery, delivery equipment, or office equipment, it may be desirable to compute depreciation for the total of each group. This practice minimizes detailed analyses and computations. Also, errors in estimates of useful life and salvage value tend to balance out for the group. Estimated useful life is established for the entire group of assets, and depreciation is computed on the basis of weighted average or composite rates.

Both unit and group methods will theoretically achieve the same results of charging fixed asset costs to operations during the period of expected useful life.

Depreciation and Federal Income Tax

Federal income tax laws recognize depreciation as an expense in the computation of taxable income. There is no requirement that the same depreciation methods be used for both tax and financial reporting purposes. It is not uncommon for a business to adopt an accelerated depreciation method for tax purposes while using the straight-line depreciation method for financial reporting. Material differences in annual depreciation charges under this procedure will require appropriate deferred tax accounting in the financial statements.

Depreciation Schedule Revisions

Depreciation schedules are based upon management's best estimate of the future utilization of an asset at the time it is acquired. During the life of the asset, these estimates may prove to be improper due to circumstances that indicate the asset's useful life or the disposal value, or both, should be revised. Under these conditions, the approach specified in *Opinion No. 20* is to leave the book value as it is and alter the rate of future depreciation charges.[1] The changes are made prospectively, not retroactively.

For example, assume a company depreciating an $11,000 asset on a straight-line basis over 10 years decided after 5 years that the asset's remaining useful life was only going to be 2 years rather than 5. In addition, the previous $1,000 estimate of the salvage value was now thought to be erroneous. The new salvage value was estimated to be zero. The prior depreciation schedule was $1,000 per year ([$11,000 − $1,000] ÷ 10). Therefore, after five years, the book value of the asset would be $6,000 ($11,000 − [5 × $1,000]). Before the change in the estimated life and salvage value, the annual depreciation charge over each of the next five years would have been $1,000. Now, based on the revised estimates, the annual depreciation charge over the next two years will be $3,000 per year ([$6,000 − $0] ÷ 2).

Depreciation Method Changes

In recent years, a number of companies have changed their depreciation method. Typically, the shift has been from an accelerated to a straight-

---

[1] Chapter 12 discusses the accounting for changes in accounting estimates and policies in greater detail.

line depreciation method. A company may adopt the new accounting method for depreciable assets bought after a specific date, usually the beginning of the fiscal year in which the accounting change is initiated, or for all of its existing depreciable assets. In *Opinion No. 20*, the APB recommended that when a company changes its depreciation accounting policy for all of its depreciable assets, the change should be recognized by including in the net income for the period of the change the cumulative effect, based on a retroactive computation, of changing to the new depreciation principle.

Additions

For depreciation purposes, an addition to fixed assets should be depreciated over its own economic life or that of the original asset, whichever is shorter.

Donated Assets

Fixed assets donated to a company on a conditional basis raise a difficult issue: Should income be charged with depreciation on such assets before full title is obtained? Since the company does not own the asset, it can be argued that depreciation should not be charged. On the other hand, the economic life of an asset is not dependent on who owns it. Therefore, if depreciation is not charged until title is obtained, the full depreciation charge must be applied to the economic life of the asset remaining after this event. This practice, which relates depreciation to ownership rather than the period of use, results in a misleading variation of income charges during two similar operating periods. Therefore, it is argued, the depreciation for such assets should be charged to operations during the full period of use.

Asset Write-Downs

Should it become clear to a company that it cannot recover through sale or productive use its remaining investment in a fixed asset, the asset should be written down to its net realizable value and current income charged with the write-down amount.

Written-Up Assets

The writing up of assets is not a generally acceptable practice. However, *Opinion No. 6* indicated that it may happen under certain circumstances in the accounts of foreign subsidiaries. *Opinion No. 6* indicates that when appreciation is entered on the books, the company is obligated to make periodic depreciation charges that are consistent with the increased valuation rather than the historical cost basis.

Accounting for Retirements

The accounting for asset retirement is fairly straightforward. At the time an asset is retired, its original cost is credited to the appropriate asset account and the related accumulated depreciation is charged to the accumulated depreciation account. Any gain or loss on the retirement after adjusting for the cost of removal and disposition should be recognized as a gain or loss in the period of disposition.

To illustrate, assume the Cleveland Company purchased a piece of equipment for $100,000. After two years, the company sold the equipment for $50,000. At the time of the sale, the asset's book value was $60,000 and the related accumulated depreciation was $40,000.

The entries to record the purchase are:

Dr.	Machinery	100,000	
	Cr. Cash		100,000

The entries to record the subsequent sale are:

Dr.	Cash	50,000	
	Accumulated Depreciation	40,000	
	Loss on Sale of Machinery	10,000	
	Cr. Machinery		100,000

If the group method of depreciation had been in use, there would have been no loss and Accumulated Depreciation would have been reduced by $50,000.

Capital Investment Decisions

Some fault current depreciation accounting on the ground that it does not lead to a measurement of return on investment which matches the economic concept of return on investment used by many companies in making asset investment decisions.

To illustrate, assume a company approves a proposed investment of $1,000, which is estimated to earn $250 *cash* per year after taxes for five years and therefore is expected to earn 8 percent on the amount, at risk, as indicated by Illustration 16–1. The economic return on this investment is 8 percent, since the investor's principal is recovered over the life of the investment and each year the investor receives an 8 percent return on the principal balance outstanding.

Assuming a straight-line depreciation method, this investment will be reported for financial accounting purposes as shown in Illustration 16–2. From this illustration, it is clear that the financial reports in no year show a return of 8 percent. This problem is eliminated if the periodic cost-based depreciation of an asset is shown as the difference between the present value of the related future service benefits at the beginning and end of the accounting period discounted by the internal rate of return calculated

ILLUSTRATION 16–1

Year	Total Earnings (a)	Return at 8 Percent on Investment Outstanding (b)	Balance Capital Recovery (c) = (a) − (b)	Investment Outstanding End of Year (d)
0	—	—	—	$1,000
1	$250	$80	$170	830
2	250	66	184	646
3	250	52	198	448
4	250	36	214	234
5	250	19	231	3*

* Due to rounding.

ILLUSTRATION 16–2

Year	Gross Assets	Average Net Assets*	Net† Income	Computed Return On Gross	Computed Return On Net
1	$1,000	$900	$50	5%	5.5%
2	1,000	700	50	5	7.1
3	1,000	500	50	5	10.0
4	1,000	300	50	5	16.7
5	1,000	100	50	5	50.0

* Beginning and ending book values divided by 2.
† Cash earnings, $250, minus depreciation, $200. Income taxes are included in the calculation of net earnings.

in the purchase decision analysis.[2] In practice, it is difficult to measure the future service benefits accurately enough to apply this approach with confidence, so managers resort to using the various depreciation methods discussed above.

Depletion

Depletion is the process of allocating the cost of an investment in natural resources through systematic charges to income as the supply of the physical asset is reduced in the course of operations, after making provision for the residual value of the land remaining after the valuable resource is exhausted.

There are two depletion methods: the production method and percentage method. The production method is acceptable for accounting purposes, whereas the percentage method is not. It is used in certain circumstances for computing income tax payments, however.

The production method establishes the depletion rate by dividing the cost of the depletable asset by the best available estimate of the number

---

[2] The internal rate of return is the discount rate that reduces the present value of the future benefits to the present value of the investment.

of recoverable units. The unit costs are then charged to income as the units are extracted and sold. The unit can be the marketing unit (ounces of silver) or the extractive unit (tons of ore), although the marketing unit is preferred. It is permissible to adjust the depletion rate when it becomes apparent that the estimate of recoverable units used to compute the unit cost is no longer the best available estimate.

To illustrate the cost-based depletion method, assume a coal mine containing an estimated profitable output of 10 million tons of coal is developed to the point of exploitation at a cost of $1 million. Furthermore, during the first year of operations, 500,000 tons of coal are mined and 450,000 tons are sold. The depletion unit charge is the total development cost divided by the estimated profitable output, or 10 cents per ton, that is, $1 million/ 10 million tons. The total depletion charged to the inventory in the first operating year is $50,000, that is, total production (500,000 tons) times the depletion unit cost ($0.10). The depletion charged to income as cost of goods sold during this period is $45,000, that is, total production sold (450,000 tons) times the depletion unit cost of ($0.10). Consequently, $5,000 of the year's depletion charge is still lodged in the inventory account.

Depletion differs from depreciation in several respects: depletion charges relate to the actual physical exhaustion of an asset, and as such are directly included in inventory costs as production occurs. In contrast, depreciation recognizes the service exhaustion of an asset and is allocated to periodic income, except for depreciation related to manufacturing facilities, which is included in inventory costs on an allocated basis.

The percentage or statutory method, which is permissible for some tax purposes, computes depletion as a fixed percentage of the gross income from the property. The percentage varies according to the type of product extracted. The cost method is also permissible for determining income tax payments. Companies are not obliged to use the same depletion method for book and tax purposes. Over the years, Congress has eliminated or reduced the use of percentage depletion for tax purposes for many oil- and gas-producing companies.

Inflation Adjustments

Statement No. 33, amended requires certain large companies to present depreciation expense on a current cost basis. This and other supplemental inflation-adjusted disclosures are discussed in greater detail in Chapter 17.

Depreciation Decisions

The accounting criteria for choosing one depreciation method rather than another in any particular situation are fuzzy.

The decision to use one of the depreciation methods over another should be made on the basis of a close examination of the asset's characteristics and the way management viewed these characteristics in its investment decision. Empirical and theoretical evidence suggests that most productive assets tend to become less and less valuable over time. Maintenance costs rise and the quality and length of the asset's service potential declines. Also, as technological advances are made, the quality of the existing equipment declines relative to alternative more modern equipment, even though quality does not deteriorate absolutely. Based on this evidence, it is believed by some that productive equipment depreciates on an accelerated basis in most cases, rather than, as was thought for a long time, on a straight-line basis. Similar studies indicate straight-line depreciation is a reasonable approximation of the depreciation rate of buildings and plant structures.

When an asset is utilized in a project whose future success is more uncertain than the typical situation, some managements believe it is prudent to use accelerated depreciation. Others object to this practice on the ground that the project is more likely to be viewed as unsuccessful because the high depreciation charges will lower profits in the early years. Thus, the action taken to reflect the excessive risk involved would contribute to the worst fears of management being realized.

More often than not, depreciation accounting is used as an instrument of management's financial reporting policy. Management selects the depreciation method or mix of methods that contributes to the desired financial results it hopes to achieve over time. For example, in some cases, accelerated depreciation methods have been used to hold earnings down and conserve funds by reducing stockholder pressure to increase dividend distributions. It also provides an argument against pay increases. In other situations, straight-line depreciation has been utilized to smooth earnings. In times of depressed profits, some companies have switched from accelerated to straight-line depreciation to boost earnings with the hope that this will maintain the market price of the company's stock. The choice of service life can be used in a similar way to further the achievement of management's financial objectives.

The different nature of assets argues for retaining the present wide range of permissible depreciation methods. However, the apparent use of depreciation as a tool of financial policy, and the difficulty in practice of determining which method is the most appropriate for any given asset, have led some to conclude that depreciation methods should be standardized for similar categories of assets.

Analytical Considerations

Depreciation is a difficult item for analysts to deal with since depreciation accounting practices can vary considerably from company to company, are influenced by management judgments, and can be used to manipulate income. Faced with this situation, some statement analysts would prefer to exclude the distorting effect of depreciation from income when comparing the earnings performance of companies. This is a mistake. Depreciation is a cost of doing business and must be recovered like any other cost in order to earn a profit. Also, many of the differences between company depreciation accounting practices do reflect genuine differences in the nature of the companies' assets and their economic circumstances which justify, if not demand, different approaches to depreciation accounting.

Some financial analysts have claimed in the case of appreciating assets, such as real estate properties, that depreciation should not be charged against income. They argue that these assets are gaining value, not losing value. This point of view misses the cost allocation character of accounting depreciation, which has nothing to do with value. Also, it assumes assets appreciate forever. This is imprudent and does not reflect actual experience, which clearly indicates physical assets have definite lives and are subject to wear, tear, and exhaustion.

Depreciable asset accounting practices should be scrutinized carefully in earnings quality assessments and income generation analyses. For example, a switch in depreciation method from accelerated to straight-line usually indicates that a company has trouble maintaining its earnings at a level high enough to support its former conservative approach to depreciation accounting. Another red flag indicating earnings problems and low-quality earnings is the use of unrealistically long depreciation lives. A depreciation red flag that can appear in profit analysis is a declining depreciation to sales ratio. This may indicate management is "milking" the company by not reinvesting in new assets and thereby not maintaining the operating quality of its plants and equipment. This practice is known as "riding down" the depreciation curve because as more assets become fully depreciated, the level of depreciation to sales falls at an increasing rate. This usually results in the company becoming uncompetitive. Finally, in profit analysis, the depreciable asset-related expense maintenance should be tracked relative to sales or total product costs (cost of goods sold plus change in inventory). Management may attempt to push profits up by cutting back on maintenance. This is another red flag indicating profitability problems and, if continued, can lead to operating difficulties.

Some statement users prefer to measure profits after adjusting depreciation for inflation. This approach to profit measurement and the role of inflation-adjusted depreciation on statement analysis is discussed in Chapter 17. In times of above-average inflation rates, these inflation-adjusted data may produce more meaningful insights into how well a company is coping with inflation than the historical-cost-based depreciation data.

Union Carbide Corporation
Fixed Asset Related Accounting Changes

Founded in 1917, the Union Carbide Corporation (UCC) was by 1979 an industrial behemoth with 171,000 shareholders and sales exceeding $9 billion. It was the second largest chemical producer in the United States and was ranked among the 25 largest U.S. corporations. Its industrial products included ethylene glycol, polyethylene (20 percent of the U.S market), oxygen ferroalloys, tungsten, and graphite electrodes; its consumer products included Eveready batteries, Prestone antifreeze, Glad wraps and bags, and Simoniz waxes. Union Carbide operated in 37 countries, and foreign sales accounted for 30 percent of total sales.

In January 1977, William S. Sneath was appointed chairman and chief executive officer. Sneath, who rose through the financial ranks, had many years of service with UCC. Known as a "coldly objective manager with an uncanny ability to detect evasions,"[1] Sneath immediately began a drastic reorganization and divestiture program to eliminate marginal activities and enhance longer term earnings. In 1977 and 1978, Union Carbide withdrew from 12 businesses that employed more than $435 million in net assets, but returned only .6 percent on those assets. Capital spending for 1977 was reduced to $805 million in 1977 and $985 million in 1978. By 1979, most divestitures had been made. In addition, managerial ranks were trimmed by a combination of early retirements and performance-related firings. By 1979, the company had reduced its ranks of managers by 1,250, which resulted in savings of approximately $50 million in annual salaries and benefits.

During this period, the price of a share of UCC dropped from a 1976 high of 76¾ to a 1978 low of 33⅝. (See Exhibit 1 for market and economic

This case was prepared by Lynne O. Cabot under the direction of Regina E. Herzlinger.
Copyright © 1981 by the President and Fellows of Harvard College
Harvard Business School case 181–099 (Rev. 10/83)

[1] Jeffrey A. Tannenbaum, "Slimming Down," *The Wall Street Journal*, January 3, 1979, p. 1.

EXHIBIT 1
Union Carbide Corporation

UNION CARBIDE CORPORATION AND CONSOLIDATED SUBSIDIARIES
Ten-Year Summary
(millions of dollars, except per-share figures)

	1979	*1978*	*1977*	*1976*	*1975*	*1974*	*1973*	*1972*	*1971*	*1970*
For the year:										
Net sales	**$9,176.5**	$7,869.7	$7,036.1	$6,345.7	$5,665.0	$5,320.1	$3,938.8	$3,261.3	$3,037.5	$3,026.3
Deductions (additions):										
Cost of sales	**6,490.7**	5,580.4	4,930.6	4,337.2	3,839.3	3,497.9	2,575.9	2,137.1	2,016.4	2,002.9
Research and development	**160.8**	155.9	155.8	142.4	120.2	94.2	76.8	69.6	78.3	78.0
Selling, administrative, and other expenses	**1,052.6**	942.9	860.2	756.1	638.7	531.3	426.2	376.8	368.7	360.3
Depreciation	**469.7**	416.6	358.8	301.0	269.8	248.3	245.2	245.2	229.3	236.4
Interest on long-term and short-term debt	**161.3**	159.3	149.1	120.2	100.2	69.8	60.6	56.1	60.9	58.5
Other income—net	**42.1**	(12.4)	(12.9)	(37.7)	(48.7)	(25.6)	(0.5)	(10.3)	(7.3)	(6.7)
Income before provision for income taxes	**799.3**	627.0	594.5	726.5	745.5	904.2	554.6	386.8	291.2	296.9
Provision for income taxes	**251.4**	205.5	178.8	266.4	343.2	375.4	245.0	164.3	126.9	130.4
Income of consolidated companies	**547.9**	421.5	415.7	460.1	402.3	528.8	309.6	222.5	164.3	166.5
Less: Minority share of income	**25.0**	32.5	31.6	27.9	28.4	30.7	25.0	17.8	15.7	13.3
Plus: UCC share of income of companies carried at equity	**33.3**	5.3	1.0	9.0	7.8	27.0	12.6	3.5	4.4	4.1
Income before extraordinary items	**556.2**	394.3	385.1	441.2	381.7	525.1	297.2	208.2	153.0	157.3
Extraordinary items	**—**	—	—	—	—	—	—	(2.2)	(0.2)	—
Net income	**556.2**	394.3	385.1	441.2	381.7	525.1	297.2	206.0	152.8	157.3
Net income per share	**8.47**	6.09	6.05	7.15	6.23	8.61	4.89	3.40	2.52	2.60
Dividends	**190.1**	181.2	178.4	153.8	146.9	132.6	126.1	121.3	121.1	121.0
Dividends per share	**2.90**	2.80	2.80	2.50	2.40	2.175	2.075	2.00	2.00	2.00
Capital expenditures	**831.3**	687.8	805.4	964.5	862.2	516.6	288.7	243.9	335.2	393.7
Market price range per share:										
High	**44½**	43¼	62⅜	76¾	66½	46	51¾	52	50⅜	40½
Low	**34**	33⅝	40	55⅝	40⅛	31¾	29¼	41⅞	38⅝	29½

EXHIBIT 1 (*continued*)

	1979	1978	1977	1976	1975	1974	1973	1972	1971	1970
At year-end:										
Working capital	2,070.4	1,621.3	1,645.2	1,663.2	1,654.4	1,347.0	1,205.0	997.3	870.7	789.3
Total assets	8,802.6	7,866.2	7,423.2	6,621.6	5,740.8	4,879.2	4,163.4	3,711.3	3,546.3	3,563.8
Total capitalization	6,316.8	5,794.1	5,603.3	5,087.4	4,411.5	3,773.0	3,344.3	3,091.5	3,020.5	3,070.1
UCC stockholders' equity	4,042.5	3,638.5	3,407.0	3,055.1	2,748.0	2,502.4	2,106.4	1,929.4	1,839.3	1,804.6
Equity per share	61.06	55.92	52.79	49.45	44.80	41.01	34.60	31.77	30.37	29.84
Other data:										
Current ratio (at year-end)	2.2	2.0	2.2	2.3	2.5	2.2	2.5	2.6	2.6	2.2
Total debt as percent of total capitalization (at year-end)	31.4	32.3	34.5	36.3	33.8	29.3	32.6	33.2	34.9	38.2
Net income as percent of:										
Sales	6.1	5.0	5.5	7.0	6.7	9.9	7.5	6.3	5.0	5.2
UCC stockholders' equity (average)	14.5	11.2	11.9	15.2	14.5	22.8	14.7	10.9	8.4	8.8
Net income plus minority share of income as percent of total capitalization (average)	9.6	7.5	7.8	9.9	10.0	15.6	10.0	7.3	5.5	5.7
Dividends as percent of net income	34.2	46.0	46.3	34.9	38.5	25.3	42.4	58.9	79.3	76.9
Shares outstanding (thousands; at year-end)	66,206	65,065	64,533	61,787	61,336	61,016	60,868	60,732	60,568	60,479
Number of employees (at year-end)	115,763	113,371	113,669	113,118	106,475	109,566	109,417	98,114	99,181	102,144

Net income per share is based on weighted average number of shares outstanding during the year.
Total debt consists of short-term debt, long-term debt, and current installments of long-term debt.
Total capitalization consists of total debt plus minority stockholders' equity in consolidated subsidiaries and UCC stockholders' equity.

EXHIBIT 1 *(continued)*

Data for Other Chemical Companies

Company	Earnings per Share		Average Price/Earnings Multiple		Beta Coefficient (NYSE Composite Index)	
	1979	1978	1979	1978	1979	1978
Allied Chemical	.20	4.25	205	8.6	1.05	1.10
American Cyanamid	3.52	3.26	7.8	8.4	1.05	1.05
Celanese	9.52	7.61	4.6	5.3	.90	1.00
Diamond Shamrock	3.37	3.26	7.0	7.7	1.15	1.10
Dow Chemical	4.33	3.16	6.5	8.2	1.25	1.15
DuPont	6.42	5.39	6.7	7.3	1.05	1.10
W. R. Grace	5.02	4.23	6.2	6.4	.95	1.10
Hercules, Inc.	3.89	2.36	5.0	6.6	1.15	1.05
Monsanto	9.11	8.29	5.8	6.2	1.05	1.15
Rohm and Haas	7.39	4.30	5.5	7.8	1.15	1.10
Stauffer Chemical	3.10	2.88	6.8	7.1	1.00	1.05
Union Carbide	8.47	6.09	4.6	6.4	1.05	1.10
Composite for industry			6.9	7.8		

EXHIBIT 1 (*concluded*)

Union Carbide

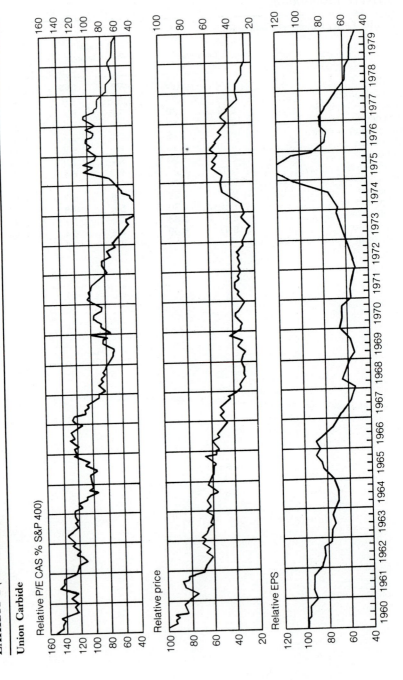

data on Union Carbide and its major competitors.) In addition, the company's bond rating was downgraded by Standard & Poor's from AA to AA−.

Exhibit 2 shows Union Carbide financial statements for the year 1979 as they appeared in its annual report. In the same annual report, the company announced its intention of making three accounting changes in its future annual reports. In January 1980, Mr. William S. Gray, Jr., vice president and chief financial officer, explained these changes and the reasons for adopting them to a group of New York security analysts. The changes he described were:

1. Extension of the Life of Fixed Assets for Depreciation Purposes

We will increase the average useful lives of our assets for depreciation purposes approximately 35 percent, from 14 to 19 years. Why? Essentially it relates directly to our strategic planning process, showing the differentiation of our businesses under the portfolio concept. We can assign lives which are appropriate to those businesses, which business managers understand.

EXHIBIT 2
Union Carbide Corporation

UNION CARBIDE CORPORATION AND SUBSIDIARIES
Year Ended December 31
(millions of dollars, except per-share figures)

	1979	1978
Net sales	$9,176.5	$7,869.7
Deductions (additions):		
Cost of sales	6,490.7	5,580.4
Research and development	160.8	155.9
Selling, administrative, and other expenses	1,052.6	942.9
Depreciation	469.7	416.6
Interest on long-term and short-term debt	161.3	159.3
Other income—net	42.1	(12.4)
Income before provision for income taxes	$ 799.3	$ 627.0
Provision for income taxes	251.4	205.5
Income of consolidated companies	$ 547.9	$ 421.5
Less: Minority stockholders' share of income	25.0	32.5
Plus: UCC share of income of companies carried at equity	33.3	5.3
Net income	$ 556.2	$ 394.3
Retained earnings at January 1*	3,120.3	2,904.8
	$3,676.5	$3,299.1
Dividends declared	190.1	181.2
Retained earnings at December 31	$3,486.4	$3,117.9
Per share:		
Net income†	$8.47	$6.09
Dividends declared	$2.90	$2.80

* After adjustment for a credit of $2.4 million in 1979 for companies with which business combinations were effected on a pooling of interests basis ($0.3 million charge in 1978).
† Based on 65,673,908 shares (64,738,610 shares in 1978), the weighted average number of shares outstanding during the year.

EXHIBIT 2 (continued)

UNION CARBIDE CORPORATION AND SUBSIDIARIES
At December 31
(millions of dollars)

	1979	1978
Assets		
Cash	$ 115.7	$ 109.1
Time deposits and short-term marketable securities	333.3	174.6
	$ 449.0	$ 283.7
Notes and accounts receivable	1,433.3	1,258.6
Inventories:		
Raw materials and supplies	498.8	436.5
Work in process	445.6	396.2
Finished goods	829.2	708.4
	$1,773.6	$1,541.1
Prepaid expenses	155.3	154.3
Total current assets	$3,811.2	$3,237.7
Property, plant, and equipment	8,729.5	8,050.1
Less: Accumulated depreciation	4,271.2	3,931.2
Net fixed assets	$4,458.3	$4,118.9
Companies carried at equity	213.1	178.2
Other investments and advances	107.1	113.1
Total investments and advances	$ 320.2	$ 291.3
Other assets	212.9	218.3
Total assets	$8,802.6	$7,866.2

	1979	1978
Liabilties and Stockholders' Equity		
Accounts payable	$ 528.0	$ 433.8
Short-term debt	155.6	338.2
Payments due within one year on long-term debt	51.9	53.6
Accrued income and other taxes	239.4	220.0
Other accrued liabilities	765.9	570.8
Total current liabilities	$1,740.8	$1,616.4
Long-term debt	1,773.1	1,482.5
Deferred credits	952.5	847.5
Minority stockholders' equity in consolidated subsidiaries	293.7	281.3
UCC stockholders' equity:		
Common stock:		
Authorized—90 million shares		
Issued—66,292,649 shares (65,165,069 shares in 1978)	557.1	521.7
Retained earnings	3,486.4	3,117.9
	$4,043.5	$3,639.6
Less: Treasury stock, at cost—87,090 shares (99,846 shares in 1978)	1.0	1.1
Total UCC stockholders' equity	$4,042.5	$3,638.5
Total liabilities and stockholders' equity	$8,802.6	$7,866.2
Cash and time deposits and short-term marketable securities at beginning of year	$ 283.7	$ 323.1

EXHIBIT 2 *(continued)*

UNION CARBIDE CORPORATION AND SUBSIDIARIES
Year Ended December 31
(millions of dollars)

	1979	*1978*
Funds provided by:		
Net income	**556.2**	394.3
Noncash charges to net income:		
Depreciation	**469.7**	416.6
Deferred income taxes	**104.0**	85.7
Other noncash charges—net	**(5.6)**	27.6
Total funds from operations	**$1,124.3**	$ 924.2
Long-term debt:		
New borrowings	**370.4**	39.8
Reductions	**(80.1)**	(43.3)
Increase (decrease) in short-term debt and current portion of long-term debt	**(184.3)**	156.6
Increase in common stock	**35.5**	18.7
Total funds from financing	**$ 141.5**	$ 171.8
European ethylene derivatives businesses sold:		
Net fixed assets	—	267.5
Other assets—net	—	101.7
Long- and short-term debt assumed by purchaser	—	(217.9)
Net assets sold	—	151.3
Reductions of net fixed assets	**22.9**	23.7
Decrease (increase) in investments and other assets	**7.1**	(18.2)
Increase in payables and accruals	**290.8**	221.0
Other—net	**7.3**	(40.0)
Total funds from other sources	**$ 328.1**	$ 337.8
Total funds provided	**$1,593.9**	$1,433.8
Funds used for:		
Dividends	**190.1**	181.2
Capital expenditures	**831.3**	687.8
Net fixed assets of Gulf Coast Olefins Company, an affiliate consolidated in 1978	—	296.9
Increase in notes and accounts receivable	**174.7**	224.2
Increase in inventories	**232.5**	83.1
Total funds used	**$1,428.6**	$1,473.2
Net increase (decrease) in funds	**$ 165.3**	$ (39.4)
Cash and time deposits and short-term marketable securities at end of year	**$ 449.0**	$ 283.7

Major changes in financial position resulting from significant acquisitions and divestments are reported separately in this statement. See note 3, "Significant Transactions," for further details. Amounts reported for the changes in asset and liability accounts are exclusive of changes in account balances resulting from the sale of consolidated European ethylene derivatives businesses.

The Notes to Financial Statements are an integral part of this statement.

EXHIBIT 2 *(continued)*

(millions of dollars)

Sales

Industry segments:	1979	1978	1977	1976	1975
Chemicals and plastics	$3,348	$2,908	$2,787	$2,571	$2,183
Gases and related products	1,432	1,263	1,104	987	885
Metals and carbons	1,772	1,416	1,243	1,151	1,088
Batteries: Home and automotive products	1,599	1,356	1,196	1,052	1,036
Specialty products	1,026	927	706	585	473
Total UCC consolidated	$9,177	$7,870	$7,036	$6,346	$5,665

Geographic segments:	1979	1978	1977	1976	1975
United States and Puerto Rico	$6,395	$5,336	$4,789	$4,253	$3,726
Africa and Middle East	105	85	75	48	48
Canada	531	426	366	381	369
Europe	959	1,011	929	910	819
Far East	597	478	406	355	315
Latin America	590	534	471	399	388
International operations	$2,782	$2,534	$2,247	$2,093	$1,939
Total UCC consolidated	$9,177	$7,870	$7,036	$6,346	$5,665

Operating Profit

Industry segments:	1979	1978	1977	1976	1975
Chemicals and plastics	$ 396	$309	$285	$395	$290
Gases and related products	158	167	149	153	137
Metals and carbons	267	166	202	202	220
Batteries: Home and automotive products	195	178	146	113	157
Specialty products	56	48	48	47	56
Total UCC consolidated	$1,072	$868	$830	$910	$860

Geographic segments:	1979	1978	1977	1976	1975
United States and Puerto Rico	$ 754	$626	$619	$669	$609
Africa and Middle East	13	10	9	9	4
Canada	74	30	58	50	53
Europe	108	67	15	80	98
Far East	82	60	45	41	35
Latin America	41	75	84	61	61
International operations	$ 318	$242	$211	$241	$251
Total UCC consolidated	$1,072	$868	$830	$910	$860

(millions of dollars)

Identifiable Assets

Industry segments:	1979	1978	1977
Chemicals and plastics	$3,463	$3,232	$3,114
Gases and related products	1,362	1,254	1,122
Metals and carbons	1,577	1,433	1,442
Batteries: Home and automotive products	907	777	672
Specialty products	955	768	669
Intersegment eliminations	(68)	(56)	(55)
Total identifiable assets	$8,196	$7,408	$6,964

Geographic segments:	1979	1978	1977
United States and Puerto Rico	$5,884	$5,344	$4,770
Africa and Middle East	124	107	90
Canada	615	566	520
Europe	833	726	1,096
Far East	459	372	271
Latin America	486	471	385
International operations	$2,517	$2,242	$2,362
Intersegment eliminations	(205)	(178)	(168)
Total identifiable assets	$8,196	$7,408	$6,964

EXHIBIT 2 *(continued)*

Notes to Segment Data

Sales of chemicals in each of the years 1975–79 were $1,482, $1,664, $1,824, $1,969, and $2,286 million, respectively. Sales of plastics were $701, $907, $963, $939, and $1,062 million, respectively.

Sales as presented are to unaffiliated customers. Transfers between segments were as follows:

(millions of dollars)	1979	1978	1977
From chemicals and plastics	$ 224	$ 186	$ 184
From other industry segments	51	37	34
Total between segments	$ 275	$ 223	$ 218
From United States and Puerto Rico	$ 437	$ 358	$ 320
From other geographic segments	136	96	59
Total between segments	$ 573	$ 454	$ 379

Products are transferred between segments on a basis intended to represent the approximate market value of the products.

The following table reconciles total identifiable assets to the consolidated financial statements:

(millions of dollars)	1979	1978	1977
Total identifiable assets	$8,196	$7,408	$6,964
Investments and advances	320	291	268
Corporate assets	287	167	191
Total UCC consolidated	$8,803	$7,866	$7,423

In 1978, assets shown for Chemicals and Plastics and for United States and Puerto Rico include $322 million representing identifiable assets of Gulf Coast Olefins Company, an affiliate consolidated in 1978. In 1977, assets shown in Europe include $363 million representing identifiable assets of European ethylene derivatives businesses, reported principally under the Chemicals and Plastics industry segment, that were sold in 1978.

Withdrawal from the imaging system hardware business in 1979 resulted in a net charge of $24.3 million included in operating profit of the Specialty Products and United States and Puerto Rico segments.

Sale of consolidated European ethylene derivatives businesses in 1978, resulting in a gain of $52.9 million, is included in operating profit of the Chemicals and Plastics and Europe segments.

Sale of the calendered rigid vinyl products business in 1977, resulting in a gain of $9.8 million, is included in operating profit of the Specialty Products and the United States and Puerto Rico segments.

A write-off in 1976 due to abandonment of plans to produce disposable diapers, resulting in a net charge of $14.7 million, is included in operating profit of the Batteries: Home and Automotive Products and United States and Puerto Rico segments.

Sale of the flexible vinyl film business in 1976, resulting in a gain of $8.1 million, is included in operating profit of the Specialty Products and United States and Puerto Rico segments.

Shutdown in 1975 of facilities at Whiting, Indiana, resulted in a net charge of $11.0 million to operating profit of the Chemicals and Plastics and United States and Puerto Rico segments.

International operations amounts reported do not include results of international companies carried at equity.

Notes to Financial Statements

1. Summary of Significant Accounting Policies

Principles of consolidation—The consolidated financial statements include the assets, liabilities, revenues, and expenses of all significant subsidiaries except Ucar Capital Corporation, which is carried at equity in net assets. All significant intercompany transactions have been eliminated in consolidation. Investments in significant companies 20 to 50 percent owned are carried at equity in net assets, and Union Carbide's share of their earnings is included in income. Other investments are carried generally at cost or less.

EXHIBIT 2 *(continued)*

Marketable securities—Marketable securities are carried at the lower of cost or market.

Inventories—Inventory values, which do not include depreciation, are stated at cost or market, whichever is lower. Cost is determined generally on the last-in, first-out (LIFO) method for U.S. companies and for certain subsidiaries operating outside the United States. Generally, the average cost method is used by all other subsidiaries.

Approximately 63 percent of inventory amounts before application of the LIFO method at December 31, 1979 (65 percent at December 31, 1978) have been valued on the LIFO basis. It is estimated that if these inventories had been valued at current costs, inventories would have been approximately $786 million and $655 million higher than reported at December 31, 1979, and December 31, 1978, respectively.

Fixed assets and depreciation—Fixed assets are carried at cost. Expenditures for replacements are capitalized and the replaced items are retired. Maintenance and repairs are charged to operations. Gains and losses from the sale of property are included in income.

Depreciation is calculated on a straight-line basis utilizing generally 1962 U.S. Internal Revenue Service guideline lives. The corporation and its subsidiaries use other depreciation methods (generally accelerated) for tax purposes where appropriate.

Patents, trademarks, and goodwill—Amounts paid for purchased patents and for securities of newly acquired subsidiaries in excess of the fair value of the net assets of such subsidiaries have been charged to patents, trademarks, and goodwill. The portion of such amounts determined to be attributable to patents is amortized over their remaining lives and the balance is amortized over the estimated period of benefit, but not more than 40 years.

Research and development—Research and development costs are charged to expense as incurred. Depreciation expense applicable to research and development facilities and equipment is included in depreciation in the income statement ($10.4 million in 1979 and $8.1 million in 1978).

Income taxes—Provision has been made for deferred income taxes where differences exist between the period in which transactions, principally relating to depreciation, affect taxable income and the period in which they enter into the determination of income in the financial statements.

The investment tax credit is deferred and amortized over the average depreciable life of fixed assets by reductions in the provision for income taxes. Benefits from energy tax credits are included currently in net income.

Retirement program—The corporation's contribution to the U.S. retirement program in each year is based on the recommendation of an independent actuarial firm using the entry age normal method. Accrued costs are funded for all employees age 25 and over, with unfunded prior service costs being amortized over 30 years except for experience gains and losses occurring after 1975 and adjustments to retirees' benefits which are amortized over 15 years. An investment income assumption of 6 percent is used for actuarial purposes.

Program costs of consolidated international subsidiaries are accounted for substantially on an accrual basis.

Net income per share—Net income per share is based on the weighted average number of shares of common stock outstanding in each year. There would have been no material dilutive effect on net income per share for 1979 or 1978 if convertible securities had been converted and if outstanding stock options had been exercised.

2. *Ucar Capital Corporation*

Ucar Capital Corporation (Capital), a wholly owned finance subsidiary, purchases without recourse certain customer obligations from Union Carbide at a discount sufficient to yield earnings of not less than one and one half times its fixed charges. In the consolidated statement of income and retained earnings, Capital's income before income taxes, which amounted to $8.5 million in 1979 and 1978, is included in Other Income—Net, as a reduction of discount expense, and the related income tax is included in Provision for Income Taxes.

The average effective interest rate on Capital's borrowings, which consist of $100 million of 15-year notes due 1992 and $100 million of 5-year notes due 1982, was 8.4 percent in 1979 and 1978.

Additional financial information relating to Capital is presented below:

	December 31	
(millions of dollars)	**1979**	*1978*
Total assets	**$ 251.6**	$ 250.1
Less: Total liabilities ..	**203.8**	206.9
Net assets	**$ 47.8**	$ 43.2

EXHIBIT 2 *(continued)*

3. Significant Transactions

In October 1978, the corporation purchased the remaining interest in Gulf Coast Olefins Company (GCOC), whose principal asset is an olefins unit at Taft, Louisiana, thereby increasing its interest in GCOC to 100 percent. Concurrently, GCOC retired its long-term debt of $292 million with funds provided by Union Carbide.

Also in 1978, the corporation sold its consolidated European ethylene derivatives businesses for net proceeds of $176 million plus assumptions by the purchaser of $217.9 million in long- and short-term debt. In the con-

gains and losses, resulted in a charge to Other Income—Net of $36.8 million ($51.4 million in 1978). The effect, after adjustments for taxes on exchange gains and losses, for minority interests, and for currency adjustments of companies carried at equity, was to decrease net income in 1979 by $29.3 million ($59.1 million in 1978).

5. International Operations

The following is a financial summary of consolidated international subsidiaries and international companies carried at equity:

(millions of dollars)	December 31, 1979		December 31, 1978	
	Consolidated Subsidiaries	Companies Carried at Equity	Consolidated Subsidiaries*	Companies Carried at Equity
Total assets	$2,690.2	$ 963.6	$2,407.0	$ 784.2
Less: Total liabilities	1,288.8	632.6	1,166.3	523.4
Net assets	$1,401.4	$ 331.0	$1,240.7	$ 260.8
UCC equity	$1,139.5	$ 151.8	$ 991.1	$ 121.5
Net sales	$2,782.1	$ 920.0†	$2,533.8	$ 602.7†
Net income	$ 168.3	$ 69.4	$ 106.4	$ 14.7
UCC share	$ 145.7	$ 32.0	$ 76.4	$ 9.1

* Net sales includes $314.6 million representing sales of European ethylene derivatives businesses that were sold in 1978, and net income and UCC share include a loss of $31.8 million for these operations. Net income and UCC share also include a gain of $24.7 million from the sale of these businesses. See note 3.

† Exclusive of $77.5 million net sales to UCC and its consolidated subsidiaries in 1979 ($78.1 million in 1978).

solidated statement of income and retained earnings, net sales for 1978 includes $314.6 million and net income includes a loss of $31.8 million for these European operations. This sale resulted in a gain of $52.9 million ($24.7 million after tax, or $0.38 per share) which is included in Other Income—Net in 1978.

6. Segment Information

Summaries of industry and geographic segment data are included. Amounts for 1979 and 1978 included in the summaries are incorporated by reference as part of this note.

Capital expenditures and depreciation by industry segment are as follows:

(millions of dollars)	Capital Expenditures		Depreciation	
	1979	1978	1979	1978
Chemicals and plastics	$ 324	$ 267	$ 218	$ 191
Gases and related products	227	183	101	88
Metals and carbons	102	77	75	65
Batteries: Home and automotive products	91	78	36	30
Specialty products	87	75	40	36

4. Foreign Currency Adjustment

In 1979, translation of balance sheet accounts carried in foreign currencies, and exchange

The following is a reconciliation of segment operating profit to the consolidated financial statements:

(millions of dollars)	1979	1978
Total segment operating profit	$1,072	$ 868
Less: General corporate expenses—net	112	82
Interest on long-term and short-term debt	161	159
Income before provision for income taxes	$ 799	$ 627

EXHIBIT 2 *(continued)*

7. *Other Income—Net*

The following is an analysis of Other Income—
Net:

(millions of dollars)	1979	1978
Investment income (principally from short-term investments)	$ 39.1	$ 30.7
Foreign currency adjustments	(36.8)	(51.4)
Net discount expense on sales of customer obligations to Ucar Capital Corporation	(17.0)	(17.0)
Charges related to the sale of a mineral production payment	(11.6)	(11.6)
Sales and disposals of businesses and other assets*	(21.1)	54.4
Other	5.3	7.3
	$ (42.1)	$ 12.4

* Includes for 1979 a charge of $24.3 million ($13.1 million after tax, or $0.20 per share) resulting from withdrawal from the corporation imaging systems hardware business. Includes for 1978 a gain of $52.9 million ($24.7 million after tax, or $0.38 per share) from sale of the corporation's consolidated European ethylene derivatives businesses.

8. *Supplementary Balance Sheet Detail*

(millions of dollars)	December 31 1979	1978
Notes and accounts receivable:		
Trade	$1,334.4	$1,159.1
Other	128.1	120.5
	$1,462.5	$1,279.6
Less: Allowance for doubtful accounts	29.2	21.0
	$1,433.3	$1,258.6
Fixed assets:		
Land and improvements	$ 489.1	$ 464.8
Buildings	911.0	854.8
Machinery and equipment	6,646.6	6,242.0
Construction in progress and other	682.8	488.5
	$8,729.5	$8,050.1
Other assets:		
Deferred charges	$ 72.7	$ 70.4
Long-term receivables	47.6	57.7
Patents, trademarks, and goodwill	92.6	90.2
	$ 212.9	$ 218.3
Deferred credits:		
Income taxes*	$ 491.1	$ 399.4
Investment tax credit	217.9	195.2
Mineral production payment	68.6	91.4
Deferred revenue from sales of certain customer obligations to Ucar Capital Corporation	122.9	123.0
Other	52.0	38.5
	$ 952.5	$ 847.5

* Deferred income taxes related to current items are included in accrued income and other taxes in the amount of $61.4 million in 1979 ($80.3 million in 1978).

EXHIBIT 2 *(continued)*

12. Capital Stock

At December 31, 1979, and 1978, there were 10 million shares of preferred stock ($1 par value) authorized and unissued. Issued shares of common stock ($1 par value) include 31,818 shares at December 31, 1979 (46,418 shares at December 31, 1978) held by the corporation as collateral under employee stock purchase contracts executed under the corporation's previous stock option plans. The amount to be paid under these contracts, $0.8 million at December 31, 1979 ($1.1 million at December 31, 1978), has been deducted from common stock.

Issuances of shares of common stock were as follows:

tion and its consolidated subsidiaries have various purchase commitments for materials and supplies incident to the ordinary conduct of business; and commitments to several companies, in which the corporation has investments, for working capital or supplies and for product support. The commitments are, in the aggregate, not expected to have a material adverse effect on the consolidated financial position of the corporation.

In the normal course of business, the corporation and its consolidated subsidiaries are involved in a number of legal proceedings and claims with both private and governmental parties. These cover a wide range of matters, including trade regulation, product liability,

	1979	1978
Dividend reinvestment and stock purchase plan:		
Issued at 95% of market price for dividend reinvestments	620,139	173,457
Issued at market price for optional cash payments	97,400	69,961
Purchased at market price by the trustee under the savings plan for employees	200,803	228,013
Issued under employee stock option plans	2,100	—
Issued in business combination transactions	207,138	—
	1,127,580	471,431

13. Retirement Program

The retirement program of Union Carbide Corporation covers substantially all U.S. employees and certain employees in other countries. Various arrangements for providing retirement benefits are maintained by consolidated international subsidiaries. Total program costs for 1979 amount to $172.6 million ($157.5 million in 1978), of which $148.0 million ($133.8 million in 1978) related to the U.S. Retirement Program.

At January 1, 1979, the date of the latest actuarial valuation, the computed value of benefits vested with U.S. and internationally assigned employees exceeded the carrying value of plan assets by approximately $167 million. At September 30, 1979, the estimated corresponding amount was approximately $133 million.

The estimated amount necessary to provide for all unfunded prior service costs was approximately $896 million at September 30, 1979.

14. Commitments and Contingencies

At December 31, 1979, the cost of completing authorized construction projects is estimated at $1.3 billion. A portion of this amount is covered by firm commitments. Also, the corpora-

utility regulation, federal regulatory proceedings, patents, trademarks, contracts, and taxes. In some of these cases, the remedies that may be sought or damages claimed are substantial. In the opinion of counsel, the outcome of the legal proceedings and claims are not expected to have a material adverse effect on the consolidated financial position of the corporation. Should any losses be sustained, in excess of provisions therefor, they will be charged to income in the future.

15. Supplementary Data on Changing Prices (Unaudited)

Management's Overview. Management believes that constant dollar/current cost information is very significant in today's inflationary economy. Historical measures of profit are deceptive because of rapidly changing prices. While the current cost data is subjective, it provides a reasonable approximation of the margin between Union Carbide's current revenues and the current costs of goods consumed and services utilized. This margin is less than under traditional measures of income based on historical costs. The reduction in net income results from the higher levels of depreciation and cost of sales under constant dollar/current cost concepts.

EXHIBIT 2 *(continued)*

Of particular concern is the higher proportion of income absorbed by income taxes in the data adjusted for the impact of inflation. The effective tax burden is shown to be approximately 25 percent greater than on a historical cost basis. The data emphasizes the critical need for national monetary and fiscal policies designed to provide adequate returns to stockholders and capital for future business growth which, in turn, will mean increased productivity and employment.

Following are additional comments pertaining to the supplementary data presented. Net sales for 1979 were $9,176.5 million.

Net sales for 1975, expressed at their equivalent in average 1979 dollars amounted to $7,650.6 million. The average annual sales growth rate in constant dollars from 1975 to 1979 was 5 percent, compared with 13 percent on an historical cost basis.

The excess of increase in general price level over increase in specific prices of $505.2 million is the result of a significant difference between the Consumer Price Index for all Urban Consumers and the rate of increase in construction costs experienced by the corporation during the year.

		Year Ended December 31, 1979	
(millions of dollars)	At Historical Cost	Adjusted for General Inflation (Average 1979 Dollars)	Adjusted for Changes in Specific Prices (Current Costs)
Summary Statement of Income Adjusted for Changing Prices			
Net sales	$ 9,176.5	$ 9,176.5	$ 9,176.5
Cost of sales	6,490.7	6,631.4	6,632.5
Depreciation	469.7	490.4	487.8
Other operating expense—net	1,247.2	1,247.2	1,247.2
Interest expense	161.3	161.3	161.3
Provision for income taxes	251.4*	251.4*	251.4*
Net income	$ 556.2	$ 394.8	$ 396.3
Net income per share	$ 8.47	$ 6.01	$ 6.03
Gain due to decline in purchasing power of net monetary liabilities		$ 263.9	$ 263.9
Effect of increase in general price level of inventories and property, plant, and equipment held during the year			$ 992.5
Increase in specific prices (current cost)			487.3
Excess of increase in general price level over increase in specific prices			$ 505.2
Summary Balance Sheet Data Adjusted for Changing Prices			
Inventories	$ 1,773.6	$ 2,138.0	$ 2,559.1
Property, plant, and equipment, net of accumulated depreciation	4,458.3	5,832.9	5,732.4
UCC stockholders' equity	4,042.5	5,781.5	6,102.1

* In accordance with *Statement No. 33,* no adjustment has been made to the provision for income taxes. As a result, the effective tax rate for 1979 rises from 31.4 percent of a historical cost basis to 39.4 percent and 39.3 percent, respectively, in the average 1979 dollar and current cost calculations.

EXHIBIT 2 (continued)

	1979	1978	1977	1976	1975
Five-Year Comparisons					
Net sales:					
At historical cost	**$9,176.5**	$7,869.7	$7,036.1	$6,345.7	$5,665.0
In average 1979 dollars		8,767.8	8,439.4	8,102.4	7,650.6
Dividends per share:					
At historical cost	**2.90**	2.80	2.80	2.50	2.40
In average 1979 dollars	**2.90**	3.12	3.36	3.19	3.24
Market price per share (at year-end):					
At historical cost	**42.00**	34.00	41.25	61.88	61.13
In average 1979 dollars	**39.70**	36.32	47.97	77.06	79.92
Average consumer price index .	**217.7**	195.4	181.5	170.5	161.2

Valuation of Current Costs. Current cost values presented in the supplementary data were determined as follows:

Inventories and cost of sales—Cost of sales, determined for historical cost purposes on the last-in, first-out (LIFO) method for U.S. companies and for certain subsidiaries operating outside the United States, have been adjusted to reflect current material, labor, and overhead costs. If the LIFO method had not been utilized in the primary financial statements, the impact on cost of sales would have been significantly greater.

Property, plant, and equipment—The current cost of property, plant, and equipment is defined by *Statement No. 33* as the current cost of acquiring the same service potential embodied by the asset owned. If follows that the current cost of an asset will be directly affected by the differences between its operating costs and the operating costs of a technologically superior asset that has become available. Therefore, the estimated current cost of property, plant, and equipment was calculated by application of indices, adjusted for technological change, to historical costs of assets. Indices appropriate to domestic operations were selected on the basis of applicability to major business segment facilities. For foreign property, plant, and equipment calculations, indices utilized were selected based on major country/company operations. Adjustments for technology change based on representative facilities were extended to related asset groups before incorporation into the indices ultimately utilized.

Land—Real current costs of individual properties can be determined only by actual sale. Land values have been based on estimates of current cost.

Depreciation—Historical depreciation expense is calculated on a straight-line basis generally utilizing 1962 U.S. Internal Revenue Service guideline lives. These shortened lives have the effect of accelerating depreciation charges and tend to provide some allowance for inflation. The extension of historical costs of property, plant, and equipment by constant dollar or current cost indices and the use of guideline lives to arrive at inflation adjusted depreciation would overstate the effects of inflation. Consequently, for purposes of *Statement No. 33*, revised estimated useful lives have been used for calculating depreciation. Beginning in 1980, these revised lives will also be reflected in historical costs reported in Union Carbide's primary financial statements.

Report of Independent Certified Public Accountants

To The Stockholders and Board of Directors of Union Carbide Corporation

We have examined the accompanying consolidated financial statements (pages 24 through 34) of Union Carbide Corporation and subsidiaries as of December 31, 1979, and 1978, and the 10-year summary (page 21). Our examinations were made in accordance with generally accepted auditing standards and, accordingly, included such tests of the accounting records and such other auditing proce-

EXHIBIT 2 *(concluded)*

dures as we considered necessary in the circumstances.

In our opinion, the accompanying consolidated financial statements present fairly the financial position of Union Carbide Corporation and subsidiaries at December 31, 1979, and 1978, and the results of their operations and the changes in their financial position for the years then ended, in conformity with generally accepted accounting principles applied on a consistent basis. Also, in our opinion, the

10-year summary presents fairly the financial information included therein.

Main, Hurdman & Cranston
Certified Public Accountants
280 Park Avenue
New York, N.Y.
February 13, 1980

From the standpoint of the income statement, we believe it will provide a better matching of depreciation with the revenue-producing capability of assets. We have a number of fully depreciated assets which throw off no depreciation against continuing revenue from those facilities, and this does not provide a proper relationship. With respect to the balance sheet, it will more properly reflect the book value over the life of the asset. Finally, these lives will be much more compatible with the asset lives used by our competitors.

UCC has been on the straight-line method since 1967. We would just as soon stay with it. Certainly, it's easy to understand, calculate, and forecast, particularly for business people, who tend to carry cost in their heads. We think it makes sense to have the same depreciable cost over the life of the asset. There's also less potential for year-to-year fluctuation of cost and earnings, both at the corporate and business levels. And finally, it is the method used by most of our competitiors. In a Price Waterhouse compendium of 40 chemical companies in the industry, 85 percent of that group is on the straight-line method. We are aware of the exception of Dow and Du Pont, [but] we believe that the trend is toward straight line. In the last dozen years, Celanese, Allied, and Monsanto have all moved to the straight-line method.

For the estimated impact of the change, we have shown 1979 for reference purposes; we're doing this prospectively in 1980. In 1980, we believe our previous asset lives would have produced around $495 million in depreciation; the estimated useful lives will produce about $325 million, with a

TABLE 1

Estimated Impact of Changes in Life of Fixed Assets
(dollars in millions except per share)

	1979	1980
Guideline lives—straight line	$474	$495
Estimated useful lives—straight line	319	325
Change—depreciation	−$155	−$170
Change—EPS	+$1.28	+$1.37

decrease in depreciation—an increase in income—of $170 million, which, by the time we get to the bottom line after tax, will produce appoximately $1.37 in earnings per share. (See Table 1.)

2. Flow-Through of the Investment Tax Credit (ITC)

Were we to increase the depreciable lives, we would have to increase the amortizable life of the investment tax credit so that this would spread it out even further. As for the disadvantages of the deferred method, we believe that the most serious problem is that the deferred earnings are eroded by inflation over time. Also, the retained earnings are understated, and the deferred method is not used by most of our competitors. In the chemical 40-company study, 76 percent of the companies are using the flow-through method, and in industry generally, 87 percent are using the flow-through method—clearly the preferred method in use today. Why did we adopt the flow-through method? With inflation, the earnings impact of ITC is most favorable in the first year allowed. As we defer and hang up these credits in the balance sheet, inflation erodes that deferred credit over time, so that it means less and less to us as we bring it back into the profit and loss statement. And the regular ITC rate is now permanent. Also, the impact on earnings will be consistent with cash flow—it will be one less item of book-tax reconciliation in the statement of financial position. We estimate that the flow-through method will produce a credit of $52 million in 1980; the deferred method would have produced $35 million. The result is an increase in the tax credit of $17 million for 1980, totaling $.26 in earnings per share. We believe the comparable number in 1979 would be around $.21 earnings per share. (See Table 2.)

Over the years, we have been deferring and amortizing this item, so that at the end of 1979 there's approximately $214 million left on our balance sheet which needs to find its way down to retained earnings. Under the accounting rules, we will handle this by making a onetime, nonrecurring entry in the first quarter of this year, bringing $3.22 through our income statement to retained earnings.

3. Capitalization of Interest

Effective January 1, 1980, *FASB 34* requires the capitalization of interest cost during construction, and it's permitted in 1979. The interest cost must be capitalized and amortized over the depreciable life of the asset. The amount of interest capitalized cannot exceed the actual interest cost in-

TABLE 2

Estimated Impact of Changes in the Investment Tax Credit (dollars in millions except per share)

	1979	*1980*
Flow-through method	$41	$52
Deferred method	27	35
Change—ITC	+$14	+$17
Change—EPS	+$.21	+$.26
Deferred ITC at 12/31/79		+$214
Nonrecurring impact EPS 1980		$3.22

curred in the period. There's no impact for tax purposes. As a result, there will be no change in cash flow.

What we'll actually do is capitalize interest cost for major capital projects. In 1980, that will have the effect of approximately $20 million, or $.30 per share. The comparable number for 1979 would be $14 million, or about $.22 a share. There is no change in cash flow, no tax effect.

Summary of Proposed Accounting Changes

So the net earnings will be affected by an increase of an estimated $1.93. In the first quarter, we'll bring the deferred prior cumulative investment tax credit through the income statement, through net income to retained earnings, so that the overall effect for the year at the bottom, bottom line will be an estimated $5.15. The $1.93 kind of number will continue to occur from here out—somewhere in the range of $2 a share in earnings will be added in the future.

Response to the Changes

One analyst noted, "Perhaps the strangest element of the Carbide changes is that they contradict the most recent U.S. Treasury position that depreciable lives in the chemical industry *are shortening.*" (See Table 3.)

The Treasury's Asset Depreciation Range (ADR) system gives companies the option of using, *for tax depreciation,* useful lives that lie within a stipulated range. There are over 100 "classes" of assets in the ADR system. It appears that about 60 percent of Carbide's assets fall into Class 28.0, Manufacture of Chemicals. Until recently, the life for assets in Class 28.0 was set at 11 years. However, since ADR uses a "range" of lives, the shortest life allowable was actually nine years. In mid-1979, the Treasury *shortened* the Class 28.0 life to 9.5 years, with a minimum of 7.5 years.

The Treasury continuously reexamines and revises the class lives given to different industries under the ADR system. The revisions are made on the basis of forecasts of anticipated average lives of new equipment. Treasury staff members monitor equipment purchases of companies and make actual plant visitations.

When queried, Treasury officials who work on the ADR system were unable to explain the apparent contradiction between their conclusion that the depreciable lives of chemical equipment should be shortened and Car-

TABLE 3
Total Life Span of Plant and Equipment

	Cyanamid	Dow	Du Pont	Union Carbide
1976	17.2 years	18.5 years	20.5 years	20.9 years
1977	17.3	18.6	20.4	21.9
1978	17.7	20.3	21.0	21.7
1979	16.4	14.3	14.0	18.6

SOURCE: William C. Norby, Duff & Phelps, Inc., "Accounting For Financial Analysis," *Financial Analysts Journal,* March–April 1980, p. 19.

bide's that they should be lengthened. Some chemical company executives suggested that the Treasury conclusions were politically motivated, being part of an administration attempt to improve capital investment. Treasury officials, however, denied that contention, pointing out that recent ADR revisions included both shortening and lengthening of lives.[2]

On the other hand, there is some evidence of excessive short asset lives in UCC's case. Bear Stearns and Company estimated the $1 to $1.7 billion of UCC's fixed assets were already fully depreciated. These assets are still being used.

Publicity regarding the accounting changes was not widespread. However, the financial press reacted with skepticism in its reporting of the changes and their potential effect on earnings. *The Wall Street Journal* introduced its coverage with this headline: "Carbide's Changes in Its Accounting to Boost 1980 Profit."[3] In its financial section, *The New York Times* waited to report the accounting changes until UCC's first-quarter earnings announcement. Under the headline, "Profit Up Threefold at Union Carbide," the *Times* reported that "accounting changes contributed to a more than threefold increase in earnings in the first quarter."[4]

Under the headline, "Union Carbide's Paper Boom," *Business Week* devoted two pages to the accounting changes. Noting that the changes

TABLE 4
How Union Carbide's Accounting Changes Will Boost Its 1980 Earnings

	Net Income (millions of dollars)
Estimated income before changes*	$481
Additions from accounting changes:	
Longer life for equipment lowers depreciation charge	92
Capitalizing construction financing defers some interest cost to future	20
1980 investment tax credit flow-through cuts income tax	17
Income before extraordinary gain	610
Flow-through of unamortized prior year tax credits produces onetime gain	214
Estimated income after changes	824

* Based on mid-range of analysts' projections.
SOURCE: "Union Carbide's Paper Boom," *Business Week,* February 18, 1980, p. 103.

---

[2] Lee J. Seidler, *Accounting Issues* (New York: Bear Stearns & Company, January 28, 1980, p. 5.

[3] "Carbide's Changes in Its Accounting to Boost 1980 Profit," *The Wall Street Journal,* January 25, 1980, p. 14.

[4] "Profit Up Threefold at Union Carbide," *The New York Times,* April 24, 1980, section IV, p. 4.

would qualify as news based solely on the "sheer magnitude of numbers" involved, *Business Week* reported that the changes "will add $129 million to Carbide's regular earnings for 1980" and have the potential effect of raising profits reported to shareholders 25 percent above previous projections. Table 4 details that *Business Week* estimate.[5]

Questions

1. Why do you think Union Carbide changed its depreciation and other fixed asset related accounting policies?

2. How do you rate the quality of Union Carbide's earnings?

3. What can you learn from Union Carbide's financial statements about the way Mr. Sneath has managed the company and its future prospects?

---

[5] "Union Carbide's Paper Boom," *Business Week* February 18, 1980, p. 103.

CHAPTER 17

Inflation Accounting and Analysis

Inflation is a condition of overall rising prices. At some point, the rate of price increases requires that business performance, resources, and obligations be measured by other than the historical cost method to avoid distortions caused by the general inflation rate and the changes in specific prices paid for physical resources.

In the United States, inflation accounting is governed by *FASB Statement No. 33*, "Financial Reporting and Changing Prices," as amended in 1985. This *Statement* requires certain large, publicly held companies to supplement their annual primary financial statements with information about the effect of changing prices on income from continuing operations and selected assets and their related expenses. While *Statement No. 33* is generally regarded as dealing with accounting during periods of inflation, it applies equally well to periods of deflation, when price levels are falling.

Inflation-adjusted statements are very useful for evaluating how well a company is coping with inflation. By applying standard techniques in financial analysis to price-change data presented in these statements, the statement user can determine how well a company is doing in real terms. This view of a company during periods of inflation helps the statement user to avoid falling into inflation's trap of thinking the company is doing better than it is in reality.

Measures of Inflation

Economists measure inflation by selecting a sample of goods and services representative of the economy and recording their price movements. Each item in the sample is weighted by its relative importance, measured by its volume of sales in relation to the sales of all items. Next, a base year is selected and the index number 100 is assigned to represent that year's composite price. The sample's composite price index for subsequent years can then be compiled and compared with the base year to measure changes in the price-level index.

The Consumer Price Index (CPI), prepared monthly by the Bureau of Labor Statistics of the U.S. Department of Labor, is a widely used indicator of general price-level changes in the United States. The base year for this index is 1967. The index is a weighted average of the prices paid for a variety of consumer products in various regions of the United States. Consumer price indexes are also computed for different segments of the population. For example, there is an index for the goods and services consumed by urban dwellers (CPI–U). The general CPI is often used in escalator clauses in wage and lease contracts.

A broader measure of changes in the overall level of prices is the Implicit Price Deflator for the Gross National Product (GNP). It is calculated by dividing GNP in current prices by GNP in constant prices. This index, published by the Office of Business Economics of the U.S. Department of Commerce, is used to translate the GNP from nominal prices to constant prices.

Another commonly used price index is the Wholesale Price Index, compiled by the Bureau of Labor Statistics. It measures price changes in primary producers' markets. Because of its limited coverage, this index is not considered a good measure of inflation.

The CPI and the GNP Implicit Price Deflator often show different rates of inflation for the same period. These differences have led to controversy over which index is the more reliable measurement. The Implicit Price Deflator reflects broader price changes than the CPI, since it includes a wider range of goods and services. Apparently, however, it is less sensitive to short-run price changes.

The principal virtue of the CPI is that it is more easily understood by the general public. The principal criticism of it is that it does not adequately take into account changes in product quality. Nevertheless, quality is not ignored, and over the years, this index has generally proved to be a reasonable measure of the general rate of inflation.

In addition to the indexes that measure general shifts in prices, government agencies and private companies publish a number of indexes that measure the changes in the prices of specific items, such as construction, services, durables, electrical motors, and steel wire.

Business Considerations

During periods of high inflation, businessmen try to offset inflationary cost increases by raising prices and improving productivity. In addition, they try to improve their asset and investment turnover ratios, because inflated prices usually result in lower liquidity, higher investments in working capital, and higher interest costs.

Purchasing Power

In time of inflation, businessmen also try to minimize, if not eliminate, purchasing power losses on their monetary assets. The ways to do this are well known to business executives. The problem is to achieve them in practice.

Cash, accounts receivable, and similar monetary assets are all exposed to purchasing power losses in an inflationary economy. For example, a $10,000 check deposited in a bank on January 1 and left there for 12 months would buy fewer goods on December 31 if prices rose 10 percent during the year. Similarly, accounts and loans receivable held during the period would lose purchasing power.

Conversely, accounts payable, long-term debt, and similar monetary liabilities are exposed to purchasing power gains. If a liability is paid with dollars (or other currency) that have less purchasing power than those obtained by incurring the liability, a company is better off.

Consequently, most business executives during inflationary times seek to maintain a net monetary liability balance (i.e., monetary liabilities in excess of monetary assets), or at least operate at the minimum net monetary asset balance possible.

To the extent feasible, managers shift their resources from monetary to physical assets, such as inventory, plant, or equipment. They assume that raw materials and finished goods inventories are protected against inflation as long as the selling prices of finished goods keep pace with the rate of inflation. Similarly, fixed assets are protected to the extent that their resale or replacement value rises with inflation and their cost of replacement is recovered through increases in the prices of the goods and services produced with them.

Performance Measurement

During periods of high inflation, financial measures of business performance expressed in nominal dollars (that is, actual dollars of the period) may give the impression that a business is doing better than it really is. To avoid being misled by these potentially illusory measurements, businesses have found it essential to keep track of their results in "real" terms by eliminating the effects of inflation on the cash flows and values incorporated in the nominal accounting measurements.

Three kinds of accounting adjustments are used. These are the so-called current cost, constant dollar, and current cost/constant dollar adjustments.

Adjustments

Current cost adjustments to historical cost financial statements restate the historical costs of inventory and productive assets on hand and consumed to their current or specific cost equivalent. This approach to measuring performance tries to avoid the overstatement of profits that can result from including so-called "inventory and underdepreciation profits" in income. These amounts are the difference between the historical cost values and what it costs currently to replace the inventory sold or the asset giving rise to depreciation. If the prices of these items are rising, a portion of profits equivalent to the difference between the replacement cost and the historical cost of inventories and plant and equipment consumed during the account period must be reinvested in the business to maintain its physical inventories and productive capacity. If this portion of profits is distributed as dividends or used to reduce debt, the company's inventories and production capacity may shrink unless alternative funding is available.

Adjusting the historical cost carrying amounts of inventory and productive assets to a current cost basis inevitably changes the carrying amount of total assets. To even both sides of the balance sheet, owners' equity is also adjusted by an amount equal to the net current cost adjustment to assets.

To illustrate the current cost approach to income measurement, assume a company's historical cost statements report profits before taxes of $3,000 on sales of $12,000, after charging $3,000 to cost of goods sold, $2,000 to depreciation, and $4,000 to other costs. The company's tax rate is 50 percent. After analyzing the changes in the specific prices of the company's inventory, management decides that the current cost of the inventory sold was 10 percent higher than its historical cost at the time of sale. On the basis of another analysis, management concludes that the current cost of the assets giving rise to depreciation has risen since they were acquired, making the current cost depreciation of these assets $1,000 higher than the $2,000 charged in the historical cost. (How this determination is made will be discussed later.) The current cost method does not require restatement of sales and other costs. The company's historical cost and current cost income statements are compared in Illustration 17–1.

The businessman's current cost view of performance assumes that a business does not earn a profit until it has earned enough to cover the

ILLUSTRATION 17–1

	Historical Cost Income Statement	Current Cost Adjustments	Current Cost Income Statement
Sales	$12,000		$12,000
Cost of sales	3,000	+$ 300	3,300
Gross margin	$ 9,000		$ 8,700
Depreciation	2,000	+$1,000	3,000
Other costs	4,000		4,000
Profit before taxes	$ 3,000		$ 1,800
Taxes	1,500		1,500*
Net income	$ 1,500		$ 300

* Since the current cost step-up in costs is not tax deductible, the tax expense is based on the historical cost pre-tax profit.

current cost of replacing the assets consumed in the generation of income during the period.

Constant dollar adjustments[1] eliminate the effect of general inflation by restating dollar results or the dollar value of transactions occurring in different periods to a constant dollar or equivalent-purchasing-power basis. These adjustments are made to avoid treating dollars representing different purchasing power outflows and inflows to the business as being equivalent.

To illustrate the constant dollar approach, assume a company's sales in nominal dollars grew 10 percent, from $5 million to $5.5 million, during the last two years. If the inflation rate during this period was 20 percent, an astute businessman, knowing that the dollar was losing purchasing power, would restate the sales figures to a constant dollar or equivalent purchasing power basis to measure the real change in sales. To achieve this, the manager would first select one of the two years as a base against which the other's nominal sales purchasing power equivalent will be measured. Next, if the most recent year were selected, the prior year's sales would be adjusted to their base year purchasing power equivalent. In this example, that would be $6 million ($5 million $\times$ $^{120}\!/_{100}$).

When both years' sales are expressed in constant dollars, the real sales trend of the company becomes apparent. It is down 8.3 percent, from $6 million to $5.5 million. This trend reflects the fact that the 5.5 million nominal sales dollars earned during the most recent year would have bought 8.3 percent fewer goods and services during the current year than the prior year's actual nominal $5 million sales dollars bought during the prior year. This general purchasing power comparison of sales reflects a financial point of view that believes sales do not grow in real terms unless the growth rate of nominal sales exceeds the general rate of inflation.

The constant dollar approach to measuring performance during inflationary periods is based on the managerial concept that a profit is not earned until the purchasing power invested in owners' equity is preserved. As we will see later, to remeasure profits in constant dollars requires adjusting many accounts besides sales.

Current cost/constant dollar adjustments are the third kind of modifica-

---

[1] *Statement No. 33* uses the term *historical cost/nominal cost statements* to identify statements based on historical costs that have not been adjusted in any way for changing prices. The primary financial statements are prepared on this basis. In this chapter, these statements are referred to simply as historical cost statements. Primary statements adjusted for general price level changes are referred to by *Statement No. 33* as historical cost/constant dollar statements. The condensed form "constant dollar statements" is used in this chapter to refer to historical cost statements adjusted for general purchasing power changes. *Statement No. 33* adopted the term *constant dollar* accounting to describe the method prescribed for restating financial data for changes in the general price level. Subsequently, in *Statement No. 70*, "Financial Reporting and Changing Prices: Foreign Currency Translation," the term *constant dollar* was superseded by the term *constant purchasing power.* This change in terminology was necessary to accommodate reporting by enterprises for which the U.S. dollar is not the functional currency (see Chapter 25). As noted earlier, in this chapter and elsewhere, the more familiar term *constant dollar*, rather than *constant purchasing power*, is used.

tion businessmen make to historical cost financial measurements during periods of high inflation. As its name implies, this method combines the current cost and constant dollar approaches. It is used to restate comparative current cost statements to a constant dollar basis. This is done by selecting one of the current cost statements as the equivalent purchasing power base and then adjusting each item in the other current cost statements to that base.

For example, assume current cost income statements for the last three years are presented, the inflation rate has been 10 percent per year over the period, and the most recent statement is selected as the purchasing power equivalent base. To adjust the current-cost statement for the most recent prior year to a current year's constant dollar equivalent, one would multiply each item in the statement by 1.1, the rate of inflation between the two years (1.1 × 1.0). Similarly, the statement items for the year two years prior would be multiplied by 1.21 (1.1 × 1.1 × 1.0).

The current cost/constant dollar approach to measuring real performance reflects the belief of some businessmen that a business does not increase its real profits unless its change in current cost profits exceeds the general rate of inflation.

Internal Measurements

Most U.S. managers do not use inflation accounting for internal management purposes. Among those few companies adjusting internal financial statements for changing prices, the current cost approach to measuring managerial performance is preferred, primarily because it reflects the specific inventory and productive asset cost inflation managers must cope with in their particular businesses. Also, in most situations it is relatively easy to apply.

The constant dollar approach may be used if the current cost method is not applicable, as is true for financial institutions that have few physical assets, or is difficult to apply, as would be true for a timber company with millions of acres of land to value. Other managers prefer the constant dollar method because they think it gives a more comprehensive picture than the current cost approach of the impact of inflation on their company's resources, obligations, and operations.

The current cost/constant dollar approach is the least popular of the three, primarily because it is not well understood. Those few companies that use this method believe it is superior to the other two approaches because it reflects, over time, the effects of both specific and general price changes on their businesses.

Irrespective of which method they use, those companies that use price-change data internally believe it helps managers think in real terms, and this in turn leads to better inflation management practices.

Accounting Requirements

In the United States, all companies' primary financial statements are prepared initially in terms of historical costs. These statements assume that the local currency is a constant unit of measure. Inasmuch as the amounts shown in the statements result from many transactions occurring at different times, however, their purchasing power equivalents will not be the same if inflation has occurred over the recording period. Also, the expenses charged for the consumption of inventories and productive assets may not reflect current replacement costs.

In countries with extreme inflation, it is generally agreed that it is desirable to restate historical cost based statements to some basis that reflects the impact on the reporting company of specific price changes and general inflation. In the United States, however, until the late 1970s inflation rates had been relatively low, and there was little support for proposals that financial statements be restated to reflect changing prices. As a result, the practice was not to adjust statements, although a few companies did voluntarily publish supplemental statements showing the impact of inflation on their businesses.

The above-average inflation during the late 1970s changed the situation. In 1979, the FASB in *Statement No. 33* required certain large, publicly traded companies[2] to publish supplementary financial-statement data adjusted for changes in the purchasing power of the dollar as measured by changes in the Consumer Price Index for All Urban Consumers (CPI–U) and in the specific prices of the company's inventories and productive assets.

Statement No. 33 was experimental. In 1985, the FASB reviewed this experiment and decided in *Statement No. 82* to amend *Statement No. 33* by dropping the general requirement to adjust supplemental statements for general purchasing power changes for those companies that present current cost/constant dollar supplement statements. The amended version retained the board's earlier approval of the acceptability of using constant dollar statements as substitutes for current cost statements in the following specialized asset industries: timberlands and timber-growing, income-producing real estate, motion pictures, and oil and gas. In other industries, the amended *Statement No. 33* permits constant dollar accounting to be substituted for current cost accounting if there is no material difference between the two methods. In *Statement No. 82*, the FASB indicated it would review its current cost/constant dollar disclosure requirements and,

---

[2] Companies whose total assets amount to more than $1 billion (after deducting accumulated depreciation), or whose inventories and property, plant, equipment, land, and other natural resources and capitalized leasehold interests in aggregate amount to more than $125 million (before deducting accumulated depreciation, depletion, and amortization).

ILLUSTRATION 17–2
General Electric's 1984 Annual Report, Note 24

24. Effect of Changing Prices (Unaudited)

In the "adjusted for" column in the table at right, restatements are made to (1) cost of goods sold for the current cost of replacing inventories, (2) depreciation for the current cost of plant and equipment, and (3) unusual items for current cost of assets sold as evidenced by the sales proceeds. GE's 1979 and 1980 annual reports included technical information about methodology used in preparing these data and may be obtained from Corporate Investor Communications at the address on page 57.

Restatements of cost of goods sold are relatively small because of GE's extensive use of LIFO inventory accounting and the relatively low rate of inflation in 1984. However, restatements of depreciation expense to current levels are relatively large, reflecting the cumulative effect of price increases over a number of years since the assets were acquired. Similarly, the restatement of 1984 unusual items reflects the cumulative increase in current cost of assets sold since they were acquired.

Trends in these adjusted data over time, excluding unusual items, may be at least as useful in understanding inflation's impact as are the data for a single year. The table below presents selected data adjusted for inflation for the past five years.

Effect of Changing Prices for the Year Ended December 31, 1984

(in millions)	As Reported	Adjusted for Current Costs (a)
Sales of products and services to customers ..	$27,947	$27,947
Cost of goods sold	19,460	19,560
Selling, general, and administrative expense .	4,542	4,542
Depreciation, depletion, and amortization	1,100	1,386
Operating costs	$25,102	$25,488
Operating margin	$ 2,845	$ 2,459
Other income	989	989
Interest and other financial charges	(333)	(333)
Earnings before unusual items	$ 3,501	$ 3,115
Unusual items	(145)	(762)
Earnings before income taxes	$ 3,356	$ 2,353
Provision for income taxes	(1,065)	(1,065)
Minority interest	(11)	(9)
Net earnings	$ 2,280	$ 1,279
Earnings per share (in dollars)	$ 5.03	$ 2.82
Share owners' equity at December 31	$12,573	$15,774

(a) In dollars of average 1984 purchasing power.

Selected Financial Data Adjusted for the Effect of Changing Prices in Dollars of Average 1984 Purchasing Power

(dollar amounts in millions; per-share amounts in dollars)	1984	1983	1982	1981	1980
Sales	$27,947	$27,949	$28,524	$31,110	$31,469
Current cost information:					
Net earnings before unusual items (a)	1,896	1,609	1,269	1,330	1,262
Net earnings per share before unusual items (a)	4.18	3.54	2.80	2.92	2.77
Share owners' equity at December 31	15,774	16,043	16,025	16,090	16,281
Excess of increase in general price level over increases in specific GE price levels (b)	547	592	584	803	246
Other:					
Purchasing power loss on net monetary items	112	84	52	96	249
Dividends per share	2.05	1.96	1.80	1.79	1.87
Market price per share at December 31	56	60	51	31	38
Average consumer price index (CPI-U; 1967 = 100)	311.1	298.4	289.1	272.4	246.8

(a) Unusual items affected current cost earnings in 1984 only. Net earnings and net earnings per share including unusual items in 1984 were $1,279 million and $2.82, respectively.

(b) At December 31, 1984, in end-of-year dollars, the current cost of inventory was $5,704 million and of property, plant, and equipment was $9,095 million. In dollars of average 1984 purchasing power, the increase that might have been expected from general inflation was more than the increase in specific GE current costs by the amount shown. A similar pattern is shown in the other years.

at a later date, issue a new statement combining all of its pronouncements related to *Statement No. 33.*

Statement No. 33 Amended.   With the exceptions noted above, *Statement No. 33,* as amended, requires certain publicly traded companies to make supplemental current year and five-year disclosures of the effect of restating selected items included in their primary annual statements for changes in their specific prices, using constant dollar/current cost accounting.

The FASB believes that these disclosures are relevant to those making investment, credit, and similar decisions requiring assessments of future cash flows, enterprise performance, erosion of operating capability, and loss of general purchasing power.

The price-change disclosures for each of the five most recent years required by the amended *Statement No. 33* include:

1.   Income and current cost income per share from continuing operations.
2.   Net assets at fiscal year-end stated on a current cost basis.
3.   Increases or decreases in the current cost amounts of inventory and property, plant, and equipment, net of inflation.
4.   Purchasing power gain or loss on net monetary items.
5.   Cash dividends per share and market price per common share at fiscal year-end, both adjusted for changes in the general purchasing power of the dollar.

Statement No. 33, as amended, also requires that the current period's historical cost and current cost income statements be presented in a comparable format. Typically, the amounts listed in the current cost income statement are identical to the amounts reported in the company's primary financial statements except for cost of goods sold and depreciation, which are computed on a current cost basis.

Illustration 17–2 presents a typical presentation in an annual report of price-change data.

Current Cost Restatement

Current cost accounting measures inventories, property, plant, and equipment and the associated expenses at their current cost or lower recoverable amount at the balance sheet date or at the date of use or sale.

Inventory

The current cost of inventory depends on the type of inventory involved. The current cost of purchased inventory is the current cost of purchasing the goods concerned. The current cost of manufactured inventory is the current cost of the resources, including allocated overheads, required to produce the inventory items.

In practice, companies using LIFO inventory accounting assume that the current cost of goods sold is equivalent to their LIFO-based cost-of-goods-sold figure, and the current cost of inventories on hand is equivalent to their FIFO value. This FIFO amount is estimated by adding back the so-called LIFO reserve to the LIFO inventory value.

Companies using FIFO inventory accounting often assume that their inventory's FIFO cost is equivalent to its current cost. FIFO companies have to adjust their historical cost based cost-of-goods-sold figures to a current cost basis. Typically, this means an upward adjustment. If the current cost of the inventory items is falling, however, the current cost of goods sold will be lower than its historical cost FIFO equivalent.

Property, Plant, and Equipment

The current cost of property, plant, and equipment is the current cost of acquiring the service potential embodied in the owned asset. The service potential of an asset is equivalent to the estimated purchase price of a new improved asset minus an allowance for the operating disadvantages of the asset owned (higher operating costs or lower output potential) and an allowance for depreciation, calculated according to an acceptable accounting method. For public reporting purposes, fully depreciated assets are not adjusted to reflect their current costs. Also, in most circumstances, the current cost of owned assets must be reported whether or not the company intends to replace them.

Two alternative, less complicated methods for estimating the current cost of owned assets are very frequently used. One is to estimate the purchase price of an asset of the same age and in the same condition as the asset owned. The other is to estimate the purchase price of a similar new asset minus an allowance for depreciation, calculated according to an acceptable accounting method.

Current Cost Measurement

The approach chosen to measure current cost should fit the situation, taking account of the availability and reliability of the evidence. Typically, the measurement approaches used can be divided into two categories: direct pricing methods, such as using current vendor invoices, and methods using indexes. Most companies seem to prefer a sample index approach similar to the one illustrated in the following example.

Illustration 17–3 shows the calculation of 1984 and 1985 current cost and current cost depreciation for a company's plant. To calculate the 1984 and 1985 current cost for a building bought in 1983 for $10 million, assume the following: The building's straight-line depreciation is 5 percent per year.

ILLUSTRATION 17–3
Current Cost Calculation Example (dollars in millions)

a. **Current Cost Depreciation**

Year	Historical Cost (Gross)	×	Construction Index	×	Depreciation Rate	=	Current Cost Depreciation
1984	$10.0	×	110	×	.05	=	$.55
1985	$10.0	×	(110 × 115)	×	.05	=	$.63

b. **Current Cost**

Year	Current Cost (Gross)	×	Undepreciated Percentage	=	Current Cost
1984	$11.0*	×	95%	=	$10.45
1985	$12.65†	×	90%	=	$11.39

* $10 × 1.1.
† $10 × 1.1 × 1.1.

A reliable construction index indicates that the cost of constructing a similar building increased 10 percent in 1984 and 15 percent in 1985. In Illustration 17–3, the 1985 current cost of the building ($11.39 million) does not equal its 1985 gross current cost ($12.65 million) minus the sum of the 1984 and 1985 current cost depreciation ($1.18 million), because, unlike in the original cost minus accumulated depreciation approach to measuring a depreciable asset's net historical cost book value, the current cost of a depreciable asset is calculated directly each year.

Income Tax Effect

Current cost accounting is not allowed for tax purposes. For public current cost reporting purposes, therefore, the current cost tax is based on the historical cost taxable income. Consequently, a company's excess of current cost expenses over its historical cost expenses reduces net income by the same amount of the adjustment. Where current cost income is greater than historical cost income, the reverse is true.

The FASB believed no provision for taxes related to the difference between current cost and historical cost profits was desirable. The board believed this approach reduced the complexity of its current cost requirements and reflected the actual impact of inflation on companies. Not everyone agreed with this decision. Many commentators on the board's proposal favored some form of income tax allocation for current cost accounting purposes.

Constant Dollar Restatement

The restatement for general-price-level changes required to generate constant dollar statements of equivalent purchasing power is a statistical procedure independent of other accounting principles and procedures.

The general rule for restating is to multiply the historical cost figure by the price-level index at the time chosen to measure constant dollar equivalents divided by the price-level index at the time of the transaction. For example, assume the decision is made to restate historical cost data to constant end-of-year dollars, a $1,000 sale takes place on January 1, and the price-level index rises steadily from 100 to 110 between then and the end of the fiscal period on December 31. The end-of-year purchasing power or constant dollar equivalent of this sale is $1,100 ($1,000 × 110/100). If the average level of inflation for the year is selected as the constant dollar or purchasing power equivalent to which sales are to be adjusted, then the mid-year or average-for-the-year constant dollar equivalent of the sale is $1,050 ($1,000 × 105/110).

For the purpose of restating the balance sheet in constant dollars, all items are classified as either monetary or nonmonetary. This distinction is important, since inflation affects the two classes differently. Monetary items are those normally carried in the accounts at current cash values, such as cash, accounts receivable, accounts payable, and long-term debt.[3] The remaining, nonmonetary items include inventories, plant and equipment, and capital stock.

The purchasing power of monetary items changes during periods of changing prices. Monetary assets held during periods of inflation lose purchasing power, whereas holding monetary liabilities leads to a gain in purchasing power. One of the principal objectives of restatement is to measure this net gain or loss.

Monetary items held at the balance sheet date do not need to be restated if the balance sheet date is also the time selected to measure purchasing power equivalents. They are automatically stated in constant dollars. Alternatively, if the average for the year-end dollar were selected for this restatement basis, these year-end balances would have to be restated to their mid-year purchasing power equivalents. Similarly, monetary items reported in earlier period balance sheets would have to be restated to their base-period equivalent. The Cruzeiro Corporation example presented in Appendix 17–A demonstrates this restatement process and the calculation of monetary gains and losses.

Nonmonetary items are restated to the current equivalent of the purchasing power expended or received at the time they were recorded originally in the company's books. This is done by multiplying the item's historical-dollar cost by the price-level index at the time selected to measure constant dollar equivalents divided by the price-level index at the time of

---

[3] *Statement No. 33* defines a monetary asset as money, or a claim to receive a sum of money, the amount of which is fixed or determined without reference to future prices of specific goods or resources. A monetary liability is defined as an obligation to pay a sum of money the amount of which is fixed or determinable without reference to future prices of specific goods or services. *Statement No. 33* includes an extensive list of accounts classified as either monetary and nonmonetary for the guidance of statement preparers.

the original transaction. The difference in the amounts shown for nonmonetary assets on the historical cost based statements and the constant dollar statements is due entirely to a change in the measuring unit from historical cost to constant dollars. No actual profit or loss results from this process. The adjustment simply restates the original dollars involved in the transaction in terms of the constant dollars' purchasing power equivalent. Restatement of nonmonetary items is also illustrated in Appendix 17–A.

Common Requirements

Statement No. 33 applies the same depreciation method and recoverable amounts standards to both constant dollar and current cost restatement.

Statement No. 33 assumes that depreciation methods, estimates of useful lives and salvage values of assets will be the same for the purposes of current cost, constant dollar and historical cost accounting. If the methods and estimates used in the primary historical cost statements have been chosen partly to allow for expected price changes, however, different methods might be used for the purposes of current cost and constant dollar accounting. This situation may arise when a company uses accelerated depreciation or short lived asset depreciation periods aggressively in the primary statements.

Recoverable amount means the current worth of the net cash expected to be recovered from the use or sale of an asset. If the recoverable amount for a group of assets or assets used individually is materially and permanently lower than their historical cost when expressed in constant dollars or current cost, the recoverable amount is used in price-change accounting as the asset value and for the expenses associated with its use or sale.

Current Cost/Constant Dollar Restatement

Current cost statement values are expressed in nominal dollars. As a result, during periods of inflation, comparative current cost statements unadjusted for changing general price levels are not comparable. The dollar values in the statements reflect different purchasing power. In this respect, they have the same weakness as comparative historical cost statements during periods of changing prices. *Statement No. 33* recognized this deficiency. It required comparative nominal dollar current cost statements to be restated to a common purchasing power equivalent using the current cost/constant dollar method.

The restatement of comparative current cost statements to a common purchasing power equivalent is a simple procedure. The most recent statement period is usually selected as the purchasing power base to which the earlier comparative statements are restated. Next, the earlier current cost statements are restated to their base period purchasing power equivalent by multiplying each item in the statements by the rate of inflation between the statement period and the base period.

ILLUSTRATION 17–4
Current Cost/Constant Dollar Income Statement Restatement Example (in millions)

	1984			1985		1986
	Current Cost/ Nominal Cost		Current Cost/ Constant Dollar	Current Cost/ Nominal Cost	Current Cost/ Constant Dollar	Current Cost/ Nominal Cost
Sales	$100 × 1.21* =		$121	$120 × 1.1 =	$133	$120
Cost of sales	80 × 1.21	=	97	96 × 1.1 =	106	106
	$ 20		$ 24	$ 24	$ 27	$ 24
Taxes	15 × 1.21 =		18	18 × 1.1 =	20	18
Net income	$ 5		$ 6	$ 6	$ 7	$ 6

* (1.10 × 1.10).

Illustration 17–4 shows how current cost income statements are restated to a current cost/constant dollar basis. The assumed general rate of inflation during the period covered by the illustration is 10 percent per year. The 1984 and 1985 current cost statements are restated to their 1986 purchasing power equivalent simply by multiplying the statement amounts by the rate of inflation from the period covered by the statement to the base period. The 1986 current cost/nominal cost does not need to be restated since it is the base period statement. The same procedure is used to restate comparative current cost/nominal cost balance sheets to a current cost/constant dollar basis.

Other Disclosures

Statement No. 33, as amended, requires that a company adjust its reported dividends per share for the most recent five years by the general rate of inflation. These inflation-adjusted values are simply the nominal values restated to a common purchasing power equivalent, which is usually the dollar of the current statement year.

Statement No. 33 also requires disclosure of the annual increases and decreases net of inflation in the current cost amounts of inventory and property, plant, and equipment. This disclosure is intended to tell statement users whether changes in the current cost of these assets also represent a net increase or decrease in purchasing power.

A comparison of the 1985 and 1986 nominal and general-inflation-adjusted current cost statements highlights the advantage of current cost/ constant dollar statements for evaluating corporate performance over time. The 1985 and 1986 current cost/nominal cost statements indicate that 1985 and 1986 profits were the same ($6 million). In contrast, the current cost/ constant dollar statements for the same two years indicate that the base period's 1986 profits ($6 million) declined from their real 1985 level ($7 million). This real profit decline reflects the fact that the 1985 nominal current cost profits of $6 million were equivalent to more purchasing power than the 1986 base period's $6 million profit.

In addition, *Statement No. 33* requires disclosure of the annual CPI–U for each year included in the supplementary price-change presentation.

Real Analysis

As might be expected, the usefulness of inflation-adjusted statements increases significantly during periods of high inflation. Typically, the inflation-adjusted data prepared using the current cost/constant dollar method are the most useful if growth rates are important to an analysis. If a single year is the focus of attention, current cost data are preferred.

Not every company publishes inflation-adjusted data. In these cases, statement users must develop their own estimated inflation-adjusted statements from the data in the company's historical cost statements. This can be done by using the constant dollar method, illustrated in Appendix 17–A, and estimates of the company's average fixed-asset and inventory ages.

The average age of a fixed asset can be estimated by dividing the most recent period's annual depreciation expense into the accumulated historical cost depreciation balance. For example, if the annual depreciation expense is $5 million and accumulated depreciation expense is $50 million, the estimated average age of the plant is 10 years. If the general rate of inflation had been 300 percent over the last 10 years, the estimated constant dollar equivalent of the $5 million historical cost depreciation expense would be $15 million ($5 million $\times$ 3.0).

The estimated age of an inventory is its turnover period divided by 2. For example, if a company's inventory turns over every six months (a turnover ratio of 2), the average age of its inventory is three months. If the year-end dollar is the purchasing power base, the ending inventory will have to be restated for the inflation during the last three months of the year.

The estimated constant dollar statements users are able to develop using the method in Appendix 17–A and asset-age approximations will be crude, but will be the best that can be achieved under the circumstances.

The principal value of price-change financial-statement data for statement users is that it allows them to determine how well companies are coping with inflation. These statements not only show the absolute real values of the various balances, they also provide inflation-adjusted data to compute the significant financial ratios, such as return on investment, dividend payout, and net income percentage, as well as the growth rates of net income, sales, and dividends per share. For evaluation purposes, these real ratio values and growth rates should be compared with the company's performance during periods of low inflation and the most recent real ratio values and growth rates of comparable companies.

How to deal with net monetary gains or losses in financial analysis is a controversial topic. Some statement users evaluating a company's ability to cope with inflation include net monetary gains and losses in price-change adjusted income. They believe that net monetary losses should be included in income because they represent a measurable loss to stockholders. Also, they believe that including in income interest earned on monetary assets, without recognizing the purchasing-power losses on these assets that the inflation component of the interest is supposed to compensate creditors for incurring, leads to an overstatement of income. With respect to monetary gains, it is argued that they benefit the stockholders. Also, they should be included in the income of net borrowers to offset the high interest rates creditors charge to compensate for the purchasing power losses on their loans. Charging the debtor with the high interest rates and failing to give the debtor credit for a net purchasing power gain ignores, it is claimed, the economic reality of the situation.

Those who do not include net monetary gains or losses in price-change income argue that these are noncash items and, as such, do not improve a company's ability to cope with inflation. Furthermore, to include net monetary gains in income is potentially misleading. As an example, they cite the near-bankrupt company with excessive debt that may appear to be profitable simply because of its large monetary gains.

Irrespective of how net monetary gains and losses are treated for purposes of income management and financial analysis, statement users should not ignore them. A large purchasing power loss on a net monetary assets position that is not recovered through interest income or product pricing is usually a good indication that a company is having problems coping with inflation. Similarly, a large net monetary loss on a negative monetary asset position not offset by low interest expenses is an indicator of potential coping difficulties.

During periods of high inflation, the cost of productive assets may rise beyond the ability of some companies to finance replacement of their obsolete and worn-out assets. These companies may show high nominal profits because their depreciation charges are low in relation to their inflating revenue, but in reality they are falling behind their competitors by not buying more advanced, cost-effective productive assets.

Three simple ratios can be used to gauge whether a company is replacing its productive assets. The ratio of historical cost depreciation to accumulated historical cost depreciation can be used to approximate the average age in years of a company's depreciable assets. If this period is lengthening, the company may be slowing down its asset replacement. The ratio of historical cost depreciation to current cost depreciation and the ratio of capital expenditures for productive depreciable assets to current cost depreciation can also be used for this purpose. In both cases, a ratio of less than 1 may indicate inadequate asset-replacement expenditures.

Illiquidity is a major financial and operating problem for most corporations during prolonged periods of high inflation. This occurs because customers slow down payments, vendors demand faster payment, the costs of doing business often rise faster than selling prices increase, inventory investments rise, and the cost of credit increases significantly. Simple ratios, such as accounts receivables to sales, inventory turnover, payables to purchases, gross margin to sales, and fixed charges to operating income before fixed charges, using both nominal dollar and current cost statement data, can be employed to develop an understanding of a company's liquidity trends. In addition, comparative total cash flow statements can be very rewarding. These will show how well a company is able to finance its operations and asset replacements out of current operating cash flows, as well as the extent to which it is relying on outside financing. A trend toward increased reliance on expensive outside financing, coupled with a slowdown in productive depreciable asset replacement, should be interpreted as a sign of increasing inability to cope with inflation.

Controversy

There are three major points of view on how much primary financial statements in the United States should be restated to reflect changing prices. These are: no restatement, limited restatement, and complete restatement, including monetary gains and losses.

No Restatement

Those advocating no restatement argue that despite the inflationary problems of the 1970s, inflation in the United States has typically been mild, and thus, has not led to any gross misstatements of income in most years. In addition, they believe that price-change-adjusted statements would be confusing to the users of financial statements. Other arguments include: (a) Price-level adjustments are not acceptable for determining income tax liability. (b) There is no practical, easy way to make reliable current cost adjustments. Constant dollars seldom reflect a company's more relevant specific or current costs. The cost principle is easily understood, and has proved a useful convention in practice. (c) Business executives would not adopt price-change accounting that resulted in lower profits unless they were public utilities seeking to prove that their reported unadjusted cost-based income was overstated for rate-making decisions. (d) There is little demand for price-change-adjusted statements by investors, bankers, or creditors.

Limited Restatement

The proponents of limited price-change adjustments support restatement of only the inventory, cost-of-goods-sold, fixed-asset, and depreciation accounts. Generally, these people are sympathetic to the "no restatement" point of view. They feel, however, that limited restatement might demonstrate to the taxation authorities the extent to which income taxes confiscate capital in times of inflation. Other advantages claimed for limited restatement are that it will provide management with current cost data for financial decisions as well as indicate to stockholders whether a company's financial policy is designed to prevent an impairment of capital by price-level changes. The limited restatement advocates also believe their approach avoids confusing readers of financial statements with the notion of losses and gains on monetary items.

Complete Restatement

The complete restatement supporters claim their approach is necessary to avoid having net income measured partly in historical costs and partly in current costs, which might result from limited restatement. Also, they believe widespread adoption of their proposal would better increase the chances of some income tax relief. More important, however, they argue that matching revenues and expenses in dollars of equivalent purchasing power and showing all balance sheet items in similar dollars would be more useful for measuring performance and judging the effectiveness of financial policies. In addition, the complete restatement proponents claim that the cumulative effect of inflation in the United States over the life of most long-lived assets and liabilities has been far from "mild," and that the notion of gains and losses on monetary items is well understood by most users of financial statements.

Controversial Method

To the extent that one approach to price-change accounting is favored over the other, current cost accounting tends to have more support than constant dollar accounting, but it is nevertheless a very controversial accounting method. Many who oppose current cost accounting do so because they see it as a major step toward current value accounting, which they oppose. Some claim current cost accounting is subjective and open to income manipulation and as such can lead to unreliable and misleading income figures. Others believe that current cost calculations fail to capture management's options when replacing assets.

Despite the many criticisms of price-change accounting, in 1985 the FASB decided to retain *Statement No. 33*'s required current cost supplemental disclosures. This was done in the belief that should the U.S. economy once again experience high rates of inflation, statement users and business management would be well served by having price-change-adjusted data readily available.

APPENDIX 17–A

Cruzeiro Corporation Example

The unadjusted statements in local currency (LC$) of the Cruzeiro Corporation, a Latin American company in a highly inflationary economy, are presented in Illustrations 17–A–1 and 17–A–2. They will be used to illustrate the full range of techniques for adjusting for general-price-level changes. This same approach would be used by a U.S. corporation preparing constant dollar statements. The general approach would also be used by a statement user trying to recast a company's historical cost statements to a price-change basis.

The following price index for the period 1975–85 reflects the changes in the government's year-end wholesale price index. To speed up the restatement of past years to 1985 purchasing power equivalents, the index has been restated to show 1985 as the base year (1.0 = base period). This restatement is achieved by dividing the price-level index for 1985 by the price-level index for the past year. For example, the price-level index for 1985 (1252) divided by the price-level index for 1984 (864) gives a factor of 1.45.

ILLUSTRATION 17–A–1

CRUZEIRO CORPORATION
Comparative Balance Sheets
As of December 31, 1984, and 1985

Assets	1984	1985	Liabilities	1984	1985
Cash	LC$ 10	LC$ 20	Accounts payable	LC$ 60	LC$ 92
Accounts receivable	100	150	**Stockholders' Equity**		
Inventory	120	185			
Plant and equipment			Common stock	200	200
(at cost)	260	280	Retained earnings	118	205
Less: Accumulated			Total liabilities and		
depreciation	(112)	(138)	stockholders' equity	LC$378	LC$497
Total assets	LC$ 378	LC$ 497			

571

ILLUSTRATION 17-A-2

CRUZEIRO CORPORATION
1985 Income Statement

Sales	LC$900
Cost of goods sold	690
Gross margin	LC$210
Depreciation	26
Other expenses	97
Net income	LC$ 87

These factors will be used to adjust the company's statements to a common purchasing power equivalent.

December		Price Index	Factor
1985		1252.0	1.00
1984		864.1	1.45
1983		566.5	2.21
1982		420.1	2.98
1981		309.9	4.04
1980		228.5	5.48
1979		220.0	5.69
1978		174.9	7.16
1977		150.3	8.33
1976		123.2	10.16
1975		100.0	12.52

The price-level factors for the last four months of 1984 and 1985 are:

	1984	1985
September	1.63	1.17
October...........	1.57	1.13
November	1.50	1.06
December	1.45	1.00

The company's unadjusted balance sheet at the beginning (December 31, 1984) and at the end (December 31, 1985) of calendar year 1985 are not comparable, because the units of measurement in these balances are local currency of different dates and therefore of different purchasing power. To make these balance sheets comparable, we must adjust them to a common unit of measurement, namely, the local currency as of December 31, 1985.

Monetary assets and liabilities at the end of 1985 are already stated in local currency purchasing power at the closing balance sheet date. The monetary assets and liabilities at the beginning of the year must be restated in year-end local currency, however, so that they may be compared with year-end balance sheet figures. The restatement of December 31, 1984,

ILLUSTRATION 17–A–3
Net Monetary Assets

	Before Adjustment	Factor	After Adjustment
Cash	LC$ 10	1.45	LC$ 14
Receivables	100	1.45	145
Accounts payable	(60)	1.45	(87)
Net monetary assets	LC$ 50		LC$ 72

monetary assets and liabilities is shown in Illustration 17–A–3. The adjustment factor of 1.45 is based on the 45 percent increase in the general price level that occurred between December 31, 1984, and December 31, 1985.

The company's inventories are stated at their local currency cost at time of purchase. To make the beginning and year-end inventory figures comparable, it is necessary to restate them in end-of-year local currency. Assuming that inventories are valued by the first-in, first-out (FIFO) method and that they represent purchases made during the last months of each year, their restatement to the December 31, 1985, price level is accomplished as shown in Illustration 17–A–4. The adjustment factors applied are based on increases in the price level from the date of purchase to December 31, 1985, as shown by the monthly price-level index.

Typically, the greatest distortion due to inflation is found in the property, plant, and equipment accounts. To adjust the property accounts and the related reserves for depreciation to the end-of-year price level, it is necessary first to analyze the accounts by dates of acquisition. In this example, we

ILLUSTRATION 17–A–4
Inventories

	Before Adjustment	Adjustment Factor	After Adjustment
December 31, 1984, Balance			
Purchases:			
October 1984	LC$ 30	1.57	LC$ 47
November 1984	40	1.50	60
December 1984	50	1.45	73
Year-end inventory	LC$120		LC$180
December 31, 1985, Balance			
Purchases:			
September 1985	LC$ 25	1.17	LC$ 29
October 1985	45	1.13	51
November 1985	55	1.06	58
December 1985	60	1.00	60
Year-end inventory	LC$185		LC$198

ILLUSTRATION 17–A–5
Plant and Equipment

	Before Adjustment		Adjustment Factor	After Adjustment	
	Cost	Depr.		Cost	Depr.
December 31, 1984, Balance					
Investments:					
1979	LC$180	LC$ 90	5.69	LC$1,024	LC$512
1980	50	20	5.48	274	110
1983	20	2	2.21	44	4
1984	10	—	1.45	14	4
Plant and equipment	LC$260	LC$112		LC$1,356	LC$626
December 31, 1985, Balance					
Investments:					
1979	LC$180	LC$108	5.69	LC$1,024	LC$614
1980	50	25	5.48	274	137
1983	20	4	2.21	44	9
1984	10	1	1.45	14	1
1985	20	—	1.45	20	—
Plant and equipment	LC$280	LC$138		LC$1,376	LC$761

will assume all acquisitions were made at year-end for cash. The appropriate restatement factors are then applied to the cost and reserve balances as shown in Illustration 17–A–5. Combining the above price-level adjustments with these calculations, the adjusted balance sheets are shown in Illustration 17–A–6.

ILLUSTRATION 17–A–6

CRUZEIRO CORPORATION
Comparative Balance Sheets
December 31, 1984, and 1985

	Before Adjustment		After Adjustment	
	1984	1985	1984	1985
Cash	LC$ 10	LC$ 20	LC$ 14	LC$ 20
Accounts receivable	100	150	145	150
Accounts payable	(60)	(92)	(87)	(92)
Net monetary assets	50	78	72	78
Inventory	120	185	180	198
Plant and equipment (at cost)	260	280	1,356	1,376
Less: Accumulated depreciation	(112)	(138)	(626)	(761)
Stockholders' equity	LC$ 318	LC$ 405	LC$ 982	LC$ 891
Reconciliation of stockholders' equity, beginning of year	—	LC$ 318	—	LC$ 902
Net income	—	87	—	(91)*
End of year	—	LC$ 405	—	LC$ 891

* Assume for the moment that this is a balancing figure. Derivation and proof are presented in Illustration 17–A–8.

In addition, the 1985 cost of goods sold must be restated to year-end December 31, 1985, local currency:

	Before Adjustment	Adjustment Factor	After Adjustment
Opening inventory	LC$ 120	(See Ill. 17–A–4)	LC$ 180
Purchases	755	1.255	925
Closing inventory	(185)	(See Ill. 17–A–4)	(198)
Cost of goods sold	LC$ 690		LC$ 907

To simplify our calculations, purchases are assumed to be made evenly throughout the year. They have been adjusted by the average adjustment factor for the year: $(1.45 + 1)/2 = 1.225$.

For the sake of convenience, 1985 sales and other expenses are also adjusted by the average adjustment factor for the year (this implicitly assumes these items were also evenly distributed throughout the year):

	Before Adjustment	Adjustment Factor	After Adjustment
Sales	LC$900	1.225	LC$1,103
Other expenses	97	1.225	119

To adjust the 1985 income statement to year-end 1985 local currency, we need to restate the 1985 depreciation expense. Using the adjusted data determined above, the 1985 depreciation expense is:

	Before Adjustment	After Adjustment
Cost of plant and equipment at December 31, 1985 (see Ill. 17–A–5)	LC$280	LC$1,376
Less: December 31, 1985, addition not depreciated...........................	20	20
Total	LC$260	LC$1,356
1985 depreciation (at 10% rate)	LC$ 26	LC$ 135

To complete the adjustment of the financial statements to common year-end local currency, it is necessary to calculate the loss for the year on the monetary items and to restate each item in the conventional income statement.

Monetary assets (such as cash, receivables, and deposits) and liabilities (such as bank loans and accounts payable) are stated in fixed local currency amounts. As the price level rises, monetary assets lose purchasing power,

ILLUSTRATION 17–A–7
Exposure to Inflation

	Balance	
	Beginning of Year	End of Year
Cash	LC\$ 10	LC\$ 20
Receivables	100	150
Accounts payable	(60)	(92)
Add: Cash used to acquire property on December 31, 1985	—	20
	LC\$ 50	LC\$ 98
Average exposure, $\dfrac{50 + 98}{2}$	LC\$ 74	
Loss on exposure to 45% inflation, 74 × 0.45	LC\$ 33	

and liabilities become payable in local currency of decreasing purchasing power. The excess of monetary assets over liabilities represents the "exposure to inflation." The inflation loss may be computed on the basis of the average "exposure to inflation," as shown in Illustration 17–A–7.

The income statement before and after the price-level adjustments explained above is summarized in Illustration 17–A–8. In this example, the results of operations reported in accordance with generally accepted accounting principles indicated a profit, but a loss after general price-level adjustments. In addition, the balance sheet financial ratios are significantly different before and after the general-price-level adjustments are made.

ILLUSTRATION 17–A–8
1985 Income Statement

	Before Adjustment	After Adjustment
Sales	LC\$900	LC\$1,103
Cost of goods sold	690	907
Gross margin	LC\$210	LC\$ 196
Depreciation	26	135
Other expenses	97	119
Loss on net monetary assets	—	33
Net income (loss)	LC\$ 87	LC\$ (91)

CASE 17-1

Holden Corporation
Calculating the Effect of Price-Level Changes

The Holden Corporation was a two-year-old merchandising firm. During this period, the price-level index changed as follows:

Opening of business	150
First year, average	160
First year, end	175
Second year, average	190
Second year, end	200

The company business was such that all of its revenues and expenses were earned or incurred fairly evenly throughout the year. The only exceptions to this generalization were depreciation and that portion of the merchandise sold represented by the beginning inventory. Inventory was priced on a first-in, first-out basis. Dividends were declared and paid at the end of each year.

The company's plant and equipment was acquired on the first day of business and at the end of the first year. All of the plant and equipment was depreciated on a straight-line basis over a 10-year life. The land on which the plant was located was held under a long-term lease agreement.

At the beginning of the company's second year, management paid off in cash $50,000 of the company's $350,000 long-term liabilities. The remaining $300,000 was converted to capital stock.

Exhibit 1 presents the company's income statements on a historical basis for each of its first two years of operations. Exhibit 2 shows the unadjusted statement of retained earnings for the same periods. Holden's balance sheets at the opening of business and at the end of each year's operations are presented in Exhibit 3.

This case was prepared by David F. Hawkins.

Copyright © 1968 by the President and Fellows of Harvard College
Harvard Business School case 112–004 (Rev. 1985)

EXHIBIT 1

HOLDEN CORPORATION
Comparative Income Statement—Historical Basis
(in thousands)

	Year 1	Year 2
Sales	$800	$1,000
Operating expenses:		
Cost of goods sold	$470	$ 600
Depreciation	30	40
Other expenses (including income tax)	280	300
Total operating expenses	$780	$ 940
Net profit from operations	$ 20	$ 60

EXHIBIT 2

HOLDEN CORPORATION
Comparative Statement of Retained Earnings—Historical Basis
(in thousands)

	Year 1	Year 2
Retained earnings, beginning of year	—	$15
Net profit from operations	$20	60
Total	$20	$75
Dividends to stockholders	5	10
Retained earnings, end of year	$15	$65

EXHIBIT 3

HOLDEN CORPORATION
Comparative Balance Sheet—Historical Basis
(in thousands)

	Opening of Business	End of Year 1	End of Year 2
Assets			
Cash, receivables, and other monetary items	$200	$195	$235
Inventories	250	300	200
Plant and equipment	300	400	400
Less: Accumulated depreciation	—	(30)	(70)
Total assets	$750	$865	$765
Liabilities and Stockholders' Equity			
Liabilities:			
Current liabilities	$100	$200	$100
Long-term liabilities	350	350	—
Total liabilities	$450	$550	$100
Stockholders' equity:			
Capital stock	$300	$300	$600
Retained earnings	—	15	65
Total stockholders' equity	$300	$315	$665
Total liabilities and stockholders' equity	$750	$865	$765

At the end of the second year's operations, the management wanted the company's statements restated in current dollars to determine whether or not the company had experienced a monetary gain or loss to date. Management also wanted to know how much of this accumulated gain or loss related to the second year of operations.

Question

Restate the company's statements for its first two years' operations in current dollars. (Note: If you are using the Cruzeiro Corporation example as a guide, the example does not include long-term liabilities whereas the Holden Corporation case does.)

CASE 17-2

General Motors
Real Performance Analysis

John Grant, a financial analyst for a major investment advisory service, had been assigned the task of using the data in the company's 1982 annual report (1) to assess General Motors' ability to cope with inflation, and (2) to measure the impact of inflation on the company's financial results. Presented below are excerpts from the 1982 annual report that John Grant found relevant to his assignment.

Chairman's Letters

Mr. R. B. Smith, chairman, in his 1982 letter to the stockholders, noted:

> The year 1982 was another year of mixed economic results. While both inflation and interest rates declined significantly, the long-sought upturn in economic activity did not occur. As a result, industry deliveries of passenger cars and trucks declined for the third straight year. Nevertheless, Gen-

---

eral Motors continued to gain in many important areas. Despite the drop in volume, our profits improved, reflecting determined efforts in cost control. In addition, we achieved significantly better quality in our products through improvements in the manufacturing of existing products and in the design of new products. Importantly, 1982 marked a new beginning in our relations with our employees as we negotiated a new labor agreement, far in advance of the expiration of the old agreement. These and other gains more than offset the discouraging economic conditions so that 1982 was a year of progress and of improved prospects for General Motors.

GM's worldwide factory sales of 6.2 million cars and trucks were down about 8 percent from 1981, and GM's factory sales of 4.0 million units in the United States were off 12 percent from 1981. However, due to the improvement in efficiency of the operating units and the profitability of its financing and insurance operations (General Motors Acceptance Corporation and Motors Insurance Corporation), the corporation closed out 1982 with earnings well above 1981 earnings, despite the lower factory unit volume. Similarly, 1981 profit was earned on a unit volume which was 5 percent lower than that attained in 1980 when General Motors sustained a loss.

Maintaining profitability in all four quarters, GM closed out 1982 with earnings of $962.7 million, or $3.09 per share of common stock. This is an improvement of $629.3 million, or $2.02 per share, over 1981. The two-year improvement since 1980 is $1,725.2 million, or $5.74 per share, with volume 857,000 units lower.

Substantial as this progress has been, 1982 earnings were only 1.6 percent of sales. Better than the 0.5 percent return on sales in 1981, it nonetheless is far below the level of capital generation needed to operate the business successfully over the long term.

Still, General Motors has continued to pay a modest dividend while meeting the enormous demands for capital funds for the corporation's product and facility programs. On the surface, it might appear prudent to pull back from such extensive investments during difficult economic times, but commitment to a more competitive stance in today's global automotive market could not wait for the return of more normal times. Thus, in the context of the times, payment of a dividend—even at the 60-cents-per-share rate maintained since the second quarter of 1980—reflects a strong and abiding commitment to the stockholders of General Motors. It also reflects the confidence of your board of directors in GM's present strength and future prospects.

General Motors' overall improvement made in the last two years is a measure of the leaner, tougher—and better—corporation we are building. Granted, this process is not complete; indeed, the work of creating and rebuilding must always go on. But we are confident that in continuing to face our management responsibilities squarely, we can control what your corporation must become. We will continue to be unrelenting in the pursuit of cost reduction, unwavering in our insistence on improved product quality necessary to customer satisfaction, and untiring in building on a new spirit of cooperation among all GM people.

Slower growth of our costs following renegotiation of labor contracts

EXHIBIT 1
General Motors

HIGHLIGHTS

(dollars in millions except per-share and hourly amounts)	1982	1981	1980
Sales of all products:			
United States operations:			
Automotive products	$ 47,391.2	$ 48,803.5	$42,812.0
Nonautomotive products	2,138.9	3,233.1	3,456.9
Defense and space	793.8	716.9	655.6
Total United States operations	$ 50,323.9	$ 52,753.5	$46,924.5
Canadian operations	7,972.6	8,846.4	8,094.7
Overseas operations	12,212.8	11,870.5	12,111.1
Elimination of interarea sales	(10,483.7)	(10,771.9)	(9,401.8)
Total	$ 60,025.6	$ 62,698.5	$57,728.5
Worldwide automotive products	$ 56,676.8	$ 58,384.6	$53,173.0
Worldwide nonautomotive products	$ 3,348.8	$ 4,313.9	$ 4,555.5
Worldwide factory sales of cars and trucks (units in thousands)	6,244	6,762	7,101
Net income (loss):			
Amount	$ 962.7	$ 333.4	$ (762.5)
As a percent of sales	1.6%	0.5%	(1.3%)
As a percent of stockholders' equity	5.3%	1.9%	(4.3%)
Earnings (loss) per share of common stock	$3.09	$1.07	($2.65)
Dividends per share of common stock	$2.40	$2.40	$2.95
Taxes:			
United States, foreign, and other income taxes (credit)	$ (252.2)	$ (123.1)	$ (385.3)
Other taxes (principally payroll and property taxes)	2,470.3	2,505.5	2,248.8
Total	$ 2,218.1	$ 2,382.4	$ 1,863.5
Taxes per share of common stock	$7.22	$7.97	$6.37
Investment as of December 31:			
Cash and marketable securities	$ 3,126.2	$ 1,320.7	$ 3,715.2
Working capital	$ 1,658.1	$ 1,158.8	$ 3,212.1
Stockholders' equity	$ 18,287.1	$ 17,721.1	$17,814.6
Book value per share of common stock	$57.64	$57.21	$58.82
Number of stockholders as of December 31 (in thousands)	1,050	1,138	1,191
Worldwide employment*:			
Average number of employees (in thousands)	657	741	746
Total payrolls	$ 17,043.8	$ 19,257.0	$17,799.0
Payrolls as a percent of sales	28.4%	30.7%	30.8%
Total cost of an hour worked—U.S. hourly employees	$21.50	$19.80	$18.45
Property:			
Real estate, plants, and equipment—Expenditures	$ 3,611.1	$ 6,563.3	$ 5,160.5
—Depreciation	$ 2,403.0	$ 1,837.3	$ 1,458.1
Special tools—Expenditures	$ 2,601.0	$ 3,178.1	$ 2,600.0
—Amortization	$ 2,147.5	$ 2,568.9	$ 2,719.6
Total expenditures	$ 6,212.1	$ 9,741.4	$ 7,760.5

* Includes financing and insurance subsidiaries.

and improved operating efficiencies were principal factors permitting us to reduce or hold prices on more than half of our 1983 passenger car lineup in the United States.

Other Data

Additional inflation-related data Grant found useful in the 1982 annual report are included in Exhibits 1 through 5. These Exhibits present the following data:

Exhibit 1: Selected "highlights" showing financial, unit sales, and other data for the period 1980–82.

Exhibit 2: Statement of consolidated income, 1980–82.

Exhibit 3: Consolidated balance sheet as of December 31, 1982, and 1981.

Exhibit 4: Significant accounting policies.

Exhibit 5: Management's discussion of the effects of inflation on the company's financial data and a comparison of selected data adjusted for effects of changing prices.

EXHIBIT 2
General Motors

Statement of Consolidated Income
For the Years Ended December 31, 1982, 1981, and 1980
(dollars in millions except per-share amounts)

	1982	1981	1980
Net sales	$60,025.6	$62,698.5	$57,728.5
Costs and Expenses:			
Cost of sales and other operating charges, exclusive of items listed below	$51,548.3	$55,185.2	$52,099.8
Selling, general, and administrative expenses	2,964.9	2,715.0	2,636.7
Depreciation of real estate, plants, and equipment	2,403.0	1,837.3	1,458.1
Amortization of special tools	2,147.5	2,568.9	2,719.6
Total costs and expenses	$59,063.7	$62,306.4	$58,914.2
Operating income (loss)	961.9	392.1	(1,185.7)
Other income less income deductions—net	476.3	367.7	348.7
Interest expense	(1,415.4)	(897.9)	(531.9)
Income (loss) before income taxes	$ 22.8	$ (138.1)	$ (1,368.9)
United States, foreign, and other income taxes (credit)	(252.2)	(123.1)	(385.3)
Income (loss) after income taxes	$ 275.0	$ (15.0)	$ (983.6)
Equity in earnings of nonconsolidated subsidiaries and associates (dividends received amounted to $412.7 in 1982, $189.7 in 1981, and $116.8 in 1980)	687.7	348.4	221.1
Net income (loss)	$ 962.7	$ 333.4	$ (762.5)
Dividends on preferred stocks	12.9	12.9	12.9
Earnings (loss) on common stock	$ 949.8	$ 320.5	$ (775.4)
Average number of shares of common stock outstanding (in millions)	307.4	299.1	202.4
Earnings (loss) per share of common stock	$3.09	$1.07	($2.65)

EXHIBIT 3
General Motors

Consolidated Balance Sheet
December 31, 1982, and 1981
(dollars in millions except per-share amounts)

	1982	1981
Assets		
Current assets:		
Cash	$ 279.6	$ 204.1
United States government and other marketable securities and time deposits—at cost, which approximates market of $2,835.5 and $1,086.3	2,846.6	1,116.6
Total cash and marketable securities	$ 3,126.2	$ 1,320.7
Accounts and notes receivable (including GMAC and its subsidiaries—$312.0 and $636.2)—less allowances	2,864.5	3,643.3
Inventories (less allowances)	6,184.2	7,222.7
Prepaid expenses and deferred income taxes	1,868.2	1,527.1
Total current assets	$14,043.1	$13,713.8
Equity in net assets of nonconsolidated subsidiaries and associates (principally GMAC and its subsidiaries)	4,231.1	3,369.5
Other investments and miscellaneous assets—at cost (less allowances) . . .	1,550.0	1,783.5
Common stock held for the incentive program	35.2	71.5
Property:		
Real estate, plants, and equipment—at cost	37,687.2	34,811.5
Less: Accumulated depreciation	18,148.9	16,317.4
Net real estate, plants, and equipment	19,538.8	18,494.1
Special tools—at cost (less amortization)	2,000.1	1,546.6
Total property	$21,538.4	$20,040.7
Total assets	$41,397.8	$38,979.0
Liabilities and Stockholders' Equity		
Current liabilities:		
Accounts payable (principally trade)	$ 3,600.7	$ 3,699.7
Loans payable (principally overseas)	1,182.5	1,727.8
Accrued liabilities	7,601.8	7,127.5
Total current liabilities	$12,385.0	$12,555.0
Long-term debt	4,452.0	3,801.1
Capitalized leases	203.1	242.9
Other liabilities (including GMAC and its subsidiaries—$876.0 and $424.0) . .	4,259.8	3,092.7
Deferred credits (including investment tax credits—$1,158.7 and $1,111.1) .	1,720.8	1,566.2
Stockholders' equity:		
Preferred stocks ($5.00 series, $183.6; $3.75 series, $100.0)	283.6	283.6
Common stock (issued, 312,363,657 and 304,804,228 shares)	520.6	508.0
Capital surplus (principally additional paid-in capital)	1,930.4	1,589.5
Net income retained for use in the business	15,552.5	15,340.0
Total stockholders' equity	$18,287.1	$17,721.1
Total liabilities and stockholders' equity	$41,397.8	$38,979.0

EXHIBIT 4
General Motors

Significant Accounting Policies

Principles of Consolidation

The consolidated financial statements include the accounts of the corporation and all domestic and foreign subsidiaries which are more than 50 percent owned and engaged principally in manufacturing or wholesale marketing of General Motors products. General Motors' share of earnings or losses of nonconsolidated subsidiaries and of associates in which at least 20 percent of the voting securities is owned is generally included in consolidated income under the equity method of accounting.

Income Taxes

Investment tax credits are deferred and amortized over the lives of the related assets. The tax effects of timing differences between pretax accounting income and taxable income (principally related to depreciation, sales, and product allowances, undistributed earnings of subsidiaries and associates, and benefit plans expense) are deferred. Provisions are made for estimated United States and foreign taxes, less available tax credits and deductions, which may be incurred on remittance of the corporation's share of subsidiaries' undistributed earnings less those deemed to be permanently reinvested. Possible taxes beyond those provided would not be material.

Inventories

Inventories are stated generally at cost, which is not in excess of market. The cost of substantially all domestic inventories was determined by the last-in, first-out (LIFO) method. If the first-in, first-out (FIFO) method of inventory valuation had been used by the corporation for U.S. inventories, it is estimated they would be $1,886.0 million higher at December 31, 1982, compared with $2,077.1 million higher at December 31, 1981. As a result of decreases in unit sales and actions taken to reduce inventories, certain LIFO inventory quantities carried at lower costs prevailing in prior years, as compared with the costs of current purchases, were liquidated in 1982, 1981, and 1980. These inventory adjustments favorably affected income (loss) before income taxes by approximately $305.0 million, $89.2 million, and $259.2 million in the respective years. The cost of inventories outside the United States was determined generally by the FIFO or the average cost method.

Major Classes of Inventories (dollars in millions)	1982	1981
Productive material, work in process, and supplies	$3,774.4	$4,561.5
Finished product, service parts, etc.	2,409.8	2,661.2
Total	$6,184.2	$7,222.7

Depreciation and Amortization

Depreciation is provided on groups of property using, with minor exceptions, an accelerated method which accumulates depreciation of approximately two thirds of the depreciable cost during the first half of the estimated lives of the property.

Expenditures for special tools are amortized, with the amortization applied directly to the asset account, over short periods of time because the utility value of the tools is radically affected by frequent changes in the design of the functional components and appearance of the product. Replacement of special tools for reasons other than changes in products is charged directly to cost of sales.

Pension Program

The corporation and its subsidiaries have several pension plans covering substantially all of their employees, including certain employees in foreign countries. Benefits under the plans are generally related to an employee's length of service, wages and salaries, and, where applicable, contributions. The costs of these plans are determined on the basis of actuarial cost methods and include amortization of prior service cost over periods not in excess of 30 years from the later of October 1, 1979, or the date such costs are established. With the exception of certain overseas subsidiaries, pension costs accrued are funded within the limitations set by the Employee Retirement Income Security Act.

Product-Related Expenses

Expenditures for advertising and sales promotion and for other product-related expenses are charged to costs and expenses as incurred; provisions for estimated costs related to product warranty are made at the time the products are sold.

Expenditures for research and development are charged to expenses as incurred and amounted to $2,175.1 million in 1982, $2,249.6 million in 1981, and $2,224.5 million in 1980.

EXHIBIT 4 *(concluded)*

Foreign Exchange

Exchange and translation activity included in net income in 1982, 1981, and 1980 amounted to gains of $348.4 million, $226.2 million, and $164.6 million, respectively. *Statement of Financial Accounting Standards No. 8,* "Accounting for the Translation of Foreign Currency Transactions and Foreign Currency Financial Statements," was applied throughout the three-year period.

Interest Cost

Total interest cost incurred in 1982, 1981, and 1980 amounted to $1,544.6 million, $995.2 million, and $567.1 million, respectively, of which $129.2 million, $97.3 million, and $35.2 million related to certain real estate, plants, and equipment acquired in those years was capitalized.

EXHIBIT 5
General Motors

Effects of Inflation on Financial Data

Inflation remains the nemesis of the orderly conduct of business. Its adverse ramifications are dramatized when the effects of inflation are taken into account in the evaluation of comparative financial results.

The accompanying schedules display the basic historical cost financial data adjusted for general inflation (constant dollar) and also for changes in specific prices (current cost) for use in such evaluation. The schedules are intended to help readers of financial data assess results in the following specific areas:

a. The erosion of general purchasing power.
b. Enterprise performance.
c. The erosion of operating capability.
d. Future cash flows.

In reviewing these schedules, the following comments may be of assistance in understanding the reasons for the different "income" amounts and the uses of the data.

Financial Statements—Historical Cost Method

The objective of financial statements, and the primary purpose of accounting, is to furnish, to the fullest extent practicable, objective, quantifiable summaries of the results of financial transactions to those who need or wish to judge management's ability to manage. The data are prepared by management and audited by the independent public accountants.

The present accounting system in general use in the United States and the financial statements prepared by major companies from that system were never intended to be measures of relative economic value, but instead are basically a history of transactions which

have occurred and by which current and potential investors and creditors can evaluate their expectations. There are many subjective, analytical, and economic factors which must be taken into consideration when evaluating a company. Those factors cannot be quantified objectively. Just as the financial statements cannot present in reasonable, objective, quantifiable form all of the data necessary to evaluate a business, they also should not be expected to furnish all the data needed to evaluate the effects of inflation on a company.

Data Adjusted for General Inflation— Constant Dollar Method

Financial reporting is, of necessity, stated in dollars. It is generally recognized that the purchasing power of a dollar has deteriorated in recent years, and the costs of raw materials and other items as well as wage rates have increased and can be expected to increase further in the future. It is not as generally recognized, however, that profit dollars also are subject to the same degree of reduction in purchasing power. Far too much attention is given to the absolute level of profits rather than the relationship of profits to other factors in the business and to the general price level. For example, as shown in Schedule A, adjusting the annual amount of sales and net income (loss) to a constant 1967 dollar base, using the U.S. Bureau of Labor Statistics' Consumer Price Index for Urban Consumers (CPI-U), demonstrates that constant dollar profits have not changed in recent years in line with the changes in sales volume. This is reflected in the general decline in the net income (loss) as a percent of sales over that period as well

EXHIBIT 5 *(continued)*

as the decrease in the dividends paid in terms of constant dollars of purchasing power.

The constant dollar income statement contains only two basic adjustments. Most importantly, the provision for depreciation and amortization is recalculated. Historical dollar accounting understates the economic cost of property (including special tools) consumed in production because the depreciation and amortization charges are based on the original dollar cost of assets acquired over a period of years. Constant dollar depreciation and amortization restates such expense based on asset values adjusted to reflect increases in the CPI–U subsequent to acquisition or construction of the related property. In addition to recalculating depreciation and amortization expense, cost of sales is adjusted to reflect changes in the CPI–U for the portion of inventories not stated on the last-in, first-out (LIFO) basis in the conventional financial statements. Other items of income and expense are not adjusted because they generally reflect transactions that took place in 1982 and, therefore, were recorded in average 1982 dollars.

Data Adjusted for Changes in Specific Prices—Current Cost Method

Another manner in which to analyze the effects of inflation on financial data (and thus the business) is by adjusting the historical cost data to the current costs for the major balance sheet items which have been accumulated through the accounting system over a period of years and which thus reflect different prices for the same commodities and services.

The purpose of this type of restatement is to furnish estimates of the effects of price increases for replacement of inventories and property on the potential future net income of the business and thus assess the probability of future cash flows. Although these data may be useful for this purpose, they do not reflect specific plans for the replacement of property. A more meaningful estimate of the effects of such costs on future earnings is the estimated level of future capital expenditures which is set forth in the Financial Review: Management's Discussion and Analysis.[1]

Summary

In the accompanying schedules, the effects of the application of the preceding methods on the last five years' and the current year's operations are summarized. Under both the constant dollar and the current cost methods, the net income of General Motors is lower (or the net loss is higher) than that determined under the historical cost method. This means that business, as well as individuals, is affected by inflation and that the purchasing power of business dollars also has declined. In addition, the costs of maintaining the productive capacity, as reflected in the current cost data (and estimate of future capital expenditures), have increased, and thus management must seek ways to cope with the effects of inflation through accounting methods such as the LIFO method of inventory valuation, which matches current costs with current revenues, and through accelerated methods of depreciation.

Another significant adjustment is the restatement of stockholders' equity—the investment base. The adjustment for general inflation puts all the expenditures for these items on a consistent purchasing power basis—the average 1967 dollar. This adjustment decreases the historical stockholders' equity, as represented by net assets in Schedule A, of about $18.3 billion at December 31, 1982, to a constant dollar basis of $10.1 billion. In other words, the $18.3 billion represented in the financial statements has only $10.1 billion of purchasing power expressed in 1967 dollars. The net assets adjusted for specific prices, as shown in Schedule A, amounted to $9.8 billion at December 31, 1982. This is $0.3 billion lower than that shown on a constant dollar basis due to the fact that the CPI–U index is not accelerating as rapidly as the indices of specific prices applicable to General Motors.

Finally, it must be emphasized that there is a continuing need for national monetary and fiscal policies designed to control inflation and to provide adequate capital for future business growth which, in turn, will mean increased productivity and employment.

---

[1] Management anticipated that total capital expenditures would approximate $6 billion in 1983. It was also stated that it is the corporation's policy to distribute from current earnings such amounts as the outlook and the indicated capital needs of the business permits. In this regard, management noted, a strong capital position must be maintained in order to meet the substantial level of capital expenditures in the years ahead. The current quarterly dividend rate of $0.60 per share of common stock reflects the need, during the current period of low earnings, to conserve funds for such expenditures.

EXHIBIT 5 (continued)

Schedule A

Comparison of Selected Data Adjusted for Effects of Changing Prices
(dollars in millions except per-share amounts)

Historical cost data adjusted for general inflation (constant dollar) and changes in specific prices (current cost). (A)

	1982	1981	1980	1979	1978
Net sales—as reported	$60,025.6	$62,698.5	$57,728.5	$66,311.2	$63,221.1
—in constant 1967 dollars	20,762.9	23,017.1	23,390.8	30,501.9	32,354.7
Net income (loss)—as reported	$ 962.7	$ 333.4	$ (762.5)	$ 2,892.7	$ 3,508.0
—in constant 1967 dollars	(38.9)(B)	(305.8)	(1,023.8)	817.0	1,384.5
—in current cost 1967 dollars	71.7 (B)	(252.8)	(829.5)	829.5	—
Earnings (loss) per share of common stock					
—as reported	$3.09	$1.07	$(2.65)	$10.04	$12.24
—in constant 1967 dollars	(0.14)(B)	(1.04)	(3.52)	2.83	4.83
—in current cost 1967 dollars	0.22 (B)	(0.86)	(2.86)	2.87	—
Dividends per share of common stock—as reported	$2.40	$2.40	$2.95	$5.30	$6.00
—in constant 1967 dollars	0.83	0.88	1.20	2.44	3.07
Net income (loss) as a percent of sales					
—as reported	1.6%	0.5%	(1.3)%	4.4%	5.5%
—in constant 1967 dollars	(0.2)	(1.3)	(4.4)	2.7	4.3
—in current cost 1967 dollars	0.3	(1.1)	(3.5)	2.7	—
Net income (loss) as a percent of stockholders' equity					
—as reported	5.3%	1.9%	(4.3)%	15.1%	20.0%
—in constant 1967 dollars	(0.4)	(3.0)	(9.4)	6.7	11.2
—in current cost 1967 dollars	0.7	(2.4)	(7.3)	6.4	—
Net assets at year-end—as reported	$18,287.1	$17,721.1	$17,814.6	$19,179.3	$17,569.9
—in constant 1967 dollars	10,153.9	10,247.2	10,887.6	12,163.4	12,351.3
—in current cost 1967 dollars	9,818.3	10,450.9	11,377.2	12,982.7	—
Unrealized gain from decline in purchasing power of dollars of net amounts owed	$ 130.5	$ 241.3	$ 182.3	$ 83.8	—
Excess of increase in general price level over increase in specific prices of inventory and property	$ 861.2	$ 619.0	$ 689.2	$ 221.8	—
Market price per common share at year-end					
—unadjusted	$62.38	$38.50	$45.00	$50.00	$53.75
—in constant 1967 dollars	21.58	14.13	18.23	23.00	27.51
Average consumer price index	289.1	272.4	246.8	217.4	195.4

(A) Adjusted data have been determined by applying the Consumer Price Index—Urban to the data with 1967 (CPI=100) as the base year. Depreciation has been determined on a straight-line basis for this calculation.

(B) These amounts will differ from those shown from constant dollar and current cost in Schedule B because a different base year (1982) has been used in Schedule B in order to illustrate the effect of changing prices in an alternative form.

EXHIBIT 5 (*concluded*)

Schedule B

Schedule of Income Adjusted for Changing Prices
For the Year Ended December 31, 1982
(dollars in millions except per-share amounts)

	As Reported in the Financial Statements (Historical Cost)	Adjusted for General Inflation (1982 Constant Dollar)	Adjusted for Changes in Specific Prices (1982 Current Cost)
Net sales	$60,025.6	$60,025.6	$60,025.6
Cost of sales	51,548.3	52,339.7	51,915.1
Depreciation and amortization expense	4,550.5	4,833.5	4,939.1
Other operating and nonoperating items—net	3,216.3	3,216.3	3,216.3
United States and other income taxes (credit)	(252.2)	(252.2)	(252.2)
Total costs and expenses	59,062.9	60,137.3	59,818.3
Net income (loss)	$ 962.7	$ (111.7)(A)	$ 207.3(A)
Earnings (loss) per share of common stock	$3.09	($0.41)(A)	$0.63(A)
Unrealized gain from decline in purchasing power of dollars of net amounts owed		$ 377.4	$ 377.4
Excess of increase in general price level over increase in specific prices of inventory and property			$ 2,490.1(B)

(A) These amounts will differ from those shown for constant dollar and current cost in Schedule A because a different base year (1967) has been used in Schedule A in order to illustrate the effect of changing prices in an alternative form.

(B) At December 31, 1982, current cost of inventory was $8,070.2 million and current cost of property (including special tools), net of accumulated depreciation and amortization, was $29,750.1 million. The current cost of property owned and the related depreciation and amortization expense were calculated by applying (1) selected producer price indices to historical book values of machinery and equipment and (2) the Marshall Valuation Service index to buildings, and the use of assessed values for land.

Questions

1. Explain the differences between General Motors' historical cost, constant dollar, and current cost financial results.

2. Why do you think General Motors selected 1967 for the base year in Schedule A and 1982 in Schedule B?

3. Why did General Motors use straight-line depreciation for the price-change calculations?

4. How should General Motors measure its periodic income during periods of inflation? Should it use historical cost, constant dollar, or current cost? Should purchasing power and "holding gain" be included or excluded? Would your answer change if you were measuring the trend in income?

5. How do General Motors' key financial ratios and measurements change when calculated on a price-change basis? Are these price-change-based ratios and measurements more useful for statement users than the comparable historical cost data?

6. How well is General Motors coping with inflation? What actions has management taken to mitigate the adverse effects of inflation? How has the company used inflation to its advantage?

7. What are the major points Grant should include in his report?

CHAPTER 18

Intangible Asset Accounting and Analysis

Intangible assets are expenditures for special rights, privileges, or competitive advantages which offer the prospect of increased revenues or earnings. They include expenditures for franchises, patents, and similar items that exist only on paper, but nevertheless can reasonably be expected to contribute to earnings beyond the current accounting period.

People often think that expenditures for intangibles, because of their nonphysical character, are less qualified to be shown as assets than physical assets. This is incorrect, since accounting regards an asset as an economic quantum. Whether or not it is represented in a physical form is incidental to the issue of whether or not an expenditure with potential future income benefits should be capitalized. The principal reason for associating asset quanta with specific physical or intangible items is to make explicit the kinds of resources in which management has invested the firm's funds.

Accounting for intangible assets raises the same kinds of troublesome questions encountered in accounting for tangible long-lived assets. What should be the asset's carrying cost? How should the asset cost be charged to income under normal business conditions? How should a substantial and permanent decline in the value of the asset be reflected in the financial statements?

Solving these problems in practice is complicated by the special characteristics of an intangible asset: its lack of physical qualities makes evidence of its existence elusive, its value is often difficult to estimate, and its useful life may be indeterminable. If the intangible asset is purchased, identifiable, and can be given a reasonably descriptive name, such as a patent, the task is somewhat easier than if the intangible is an unidentifiable acquisition, such as goodwill, or an internally developed asset. In the case of identifiable purchased intangibles, there is less uncertainty because a specific sum has usually been paid and the buyer has an idea of the future benefits that should flow from the acquired asset.

590

A number of managements and accountants believe conservatism should govern the accounting for intangibles. They adopt the general presumption that intangible asset costs should be written off as incurred or, if capitalized, amortized over a relatively short period of time. Increasingly, however, there is a growing belief that conservatism alone is not sufficient justification for eliminating a valid business asset from the accounts. Rather, the goal of accountancy should be to provide as accurate a record of costs and cost expiration as possible.

A business may acquire intangible assets from others or develop them itself. In theory, the accounting for these intangible items should be the same. In practice, however, acquired identifiable and unidentifiable intangible assets are recorded as assets and amortized over two or more accounting periods. In contrast, internally developed intangibles are typically expensed as incurred, rather than capitalized.

The practice of expensing as incurred the costs of internally generated intangibles is often justified on the ground that it is difficult to determine what future benefits might result from expenditures for a potential intangible as they are being made. Also, in companies that are continually making expenditures for internally developed intangibles, management considers this to be a regular, recurring expense of doing business and, hence, properly charged to income as incurred. In addition, it is sometimes difficult to determine the specific costs related to developing an intangible asset. Under these circumstances, the usual course of action is to expense the costs as incurred, on the ground that costs should be recorded as assets only when they can be specifically identified with an item being capitalized.

Statement Users

Statement users attempting to evaluate expenditures for intangibles find themselves confronted by the following dilemma. If management expenses these costs as incurred is it understating current income? On the other hand, if management capitalizes these costs as assets, is current income overstated? Typically, because the ultimate recoverability of expenditures for internally generated intangibles is difficult to determine, statement users prefer that these costs be expensed as incurred. If an intangible is acquired through a purchase transaction and has a history of revenues and profits, statement users are more willing to accept the capitalization of the expenditure as long as management is prepared to amortize the intangible's cost over a relatively short period of time. These attitudes, which are at variance with accounting theory, are the product of an accumulation of unpleasant investor experiences with companies that capitalized intangibles, reported profits, and then suddenly announced that the capitalized intangibles were worthless and had to be written off against income. This in turn led to losses for investors. These same experiences have led prudent statement users to be wary of companies that capitalize intangibles; they associate the capitalization of intangible assets with low earnings quality and label this practice an accounting "red flag."

Authoritative Sources

APB Opinion No. 17, "Intangible Assets," and *FASB Statement No. 2,* "Accounting for Research and Development Costs," are the basic authoritative statements dealing with intangible assets.

Opinion No. 17

Opinion No. 17 requires that a company record as assets at the date of acquisition the costs of intangible assets acquired from others. However, the costs of internally developing, maintaining, or restoring intangible assets should be expensed as incurred if these assets are not specifically identifiable, have indeterminate lives, and relate to the enterprise as a whole.

The cost of an acquired asset is the amount of cash distributed, the fair value of other assets exchanged, the present value of amounts to be paid for liabilities incurred, or the fair value of stock issued. If intangible assets are acquired as part of a group of assets, then the cost of the identifiable assets, both tangible and intangible, should be based on their individual fair values. The difference between these costs and the total assets cost should be assigned to the unidentifiable intangible assets acquired. A later note will describe in greater detail the process for assigning the purchase price of an acquired company to the individual assets and liabilities acquired.

The cost of an intangible asset should be amortized by systematic charges to income over the period expected to benefit from the asset. However, the amortization period must not exceed 40 years. If the expected life of the intangible asset is more, the 40-year write-off period must be used, not an arbitrary shorter period. *Opinion No. 17* states that the period of amortization should be determined after a consideration of these factors:

1. Legal, regulatory, or contractual provisions may limit the maximum useful life.
2. Provisions for renewal or extension may alter a specified limit on useful life.
3. Effects of obsolescence, demand, competition, and other economic factors may reduce a useful life.
4. A useful life may parallel the service life expectancies of individuals or groups of employees.
5. Expected actions of competitors and others may restrict present competitive advantages.
6. An apparently unlimited useful life may in fact be indefinite, and benefits cannot be reasonably projected.
7. An intangible asset may be a composite of many individual factors with varying effective lives.

The APB concluded that the straight-line method of amortization should be applied to intangible assets, unless another systematic amortization method can be demonstrated to be more appropriate.

Statement No. 2

Statement No. 2 requires that all research and development costs be charged to expenses when incurred. The statement defined research and development as follows:

a. *Research* is planned search or critical investigation aimed at discovery of new knowledge with the hope that such knowledge will be useful in developing a new product or service or a new process or technique or in bringing about a significant improvement to an existing product or process.

b. *Development* is the translation of research findings or other knowledge into a plan or design for a new product or process or for a significant improvement to an existing product or process whether intended for sale or use. It includes the conceptual formulation, design, and testing of product alternatives, construction of prototypes, and operation of pilot plants. It does not include routine or periodic alterations to existing products, production lines, manufacturing processes, and other ongoing operations even though those alterations may represent improvements and it does not include market research or market testing activities.

This statement does not apply to the prospecting, acquisition of mineral rights, exploration, drilling, mining, and related mineral development activities that are unique to the extractive industries. However, it does apply to the research and development activities of the extractive industries that are comparable to those undertaken by other enterprises. The cost of contract research and development conducted for others is also excluded from this *Statement*.

Statement No. 2 listed the following activities that typically would be included in research and development.

1. Laboratory research aimed at discovery of new knowledge.
2. Searching for applications of new research findings or other knowledge.
3. Conceptual formulation and design of possible product or process alternatives.
4. Testing in search for or evaluation of product or process alternatives.
5. Modification of the formulation or design of a product or process.
6. Design, construction, and testing of preproduction prototypes and models.
7. Design of tools, jigs, molds, and dies involving new technology.

8. Design, construction, and operation of a pilot plant that is not of a scale economically feasible to the enterprise for commercial production.
9. Engineering activity required to advance the design of a product to the point that it meets specific functional and economic requirements and is ready for manufacture.

The costs of materials, equipment, or facilities that are acquired or constructed for a particular research and development project that have no other alternative future use should be expensed as research and development costs at the time the costs are incurred. If the materials, equipment, or facilities have alternative future uses in research and development or other projects, the expenditures should be capitalized as tangible assets at the time they are acquired or constructed. The portion of cost consumed in research and development activities should be expensed as the assets are used for this purpose. These same rules apply to intangible assets that have been acquired or constructed and are used in research and development.

Salary, wages, and other related costs of personnel engaged in research and development activities are research and development costs and must be expensed as incurred. Also included in research and development costs are the services performed by others in connection with research and development activities. The research and development costs should include a reasonable allocation of indirect costs. However, general and administrative costs that have little relationship to research and development should not be classified as research and development costs.

The FASB reached the conclusion that research and development costs should be expensed as incurred because:

1. There is normally a high degree of uncertainty about the future benefits of individual research and development projects.
2. There is a lack of causal relationship between expenditures for research and development and the benefits received.
3. The capitalization of research and development costs is not useful in assessing the earnings potential of a company or the variability of this earnings potential.

Statement No. 2 requires that the total research and development cost charged to income in each period be disclosed in the notes for each period for which an income statement is presented.

Research and Development Arrangements

A popular tax shelter arrangement for individuals is to form a partnership to fund research and development arrangements with corporations wishing to develop new products. The partnership funds the research and development, which the corporation conducts and is reimbursed for under a contractual arrangement. The company records contract revenue, and the partnership reports losses for tax purposes. If the research and development is successful, the company buys the results from the partnership and records an intangible asset. This purchased intangible asset is then written off over an appropriate period.

FASB Statement No. 68 states that a company performing research and development under a funding arrangement must determine whether it is obligated to perform only contractual research and development for others, or is otherwise obligated. To the extent that the company is obligated to repay the partnership, it must record a liability and charge research and development costs to expense as incurred.

Income Tax Treatment

Intangible property which definitely has a limited life and is used in the business or production of income can either be written off as incurred or capitalized and amortized for tax purposes. However, these items cannot be amortized using the declining-balance or sum-of-the-years'-digit methods. Goodwill, trade names, and other intangibles with indefinite useful lives cannot be amortized for tax purposes, although certain organization costs can be amortized against taxable income.

If a company accounts for its intangibles differently for book and tax purposes, deferred tax accounting must be used. The exceptions to this rule are those intangibles, such as purchased goodwill, with indefinite lives that cannot be deducted as expenses for tax purposes but must be amortized over a 40-year period for book purposes. In these situations, there is a permanent timing difference between book and tax accounting. So, no deferred tax item is recognized. As a result, for financial reporting purposes the pre-tax charge is not reduced by a deferred tax credit in the determination of net income.

Specific Intangible Assets

Patents

Patents are granted by the United States Patent Office. They give holders the exclusive rights to control their invention for a period of 17 years. The actual period of control may be extended by obtaining additional patents on improvements to the original item. Patent rights may be sold or granted to others on a royalty basis.

The cost of an internally generated patent usually includes legal fees, patent fees, costs of models and drawings, and related experimental and development costs that can reasonably be identified with the patent. Since the registration of a patent is no guarantee of protection, it is usually necessary to defend the patent in court tests. Accordingly, the costs of successful court tests are generally included in the costs of the patent. When litigation is unsuccessful, the costs of litigation and the other costs of the affected patent should be written off immediately.

In the case of successful litigation, the costs of the patent should be amortized over the useful economic life of the patent. Because of technological or market obsolescence, this period is typically shorter than the patent's legal life. However, if a patent's effective economic life can be extended by an additional patent, it is permissible to write off the unamortized balance of the cost of the old patent over the economic life of the new one.

The classification of patent amortization charge depends on the nature of the patent. For instance, patents related to manufacturing activities are charged to manufacturing expenses.

Copyrights

A copyright gives its owner the exclusive right to sell literature, music, and other works of art. The costs of obtaining a copyright are nominal. Therefore, the cost is often written off as incurred. However, the cost of a purchased copyright may be substantial. The common practice is to write off such costs against the income from the first printing or its equivalent.

Franchises

A franchise may be either perpetual, revocable at the option of the grantor, or limited in life. The costs of a franchise include fees paid to the grantor and legal and other expenditures incurred in obtaining the franchise. When the franchise is perpetual, these costs should be amortized over 40 years. If the franchise is for a specific period of time, the franchise costs should be systematically amortized over the franchise period or 40 years, whichever is the shorter. The costs of revocable franchises, in the absence of a specific time limit on the life of the franchise, are usually accounted for as perpetual franchises, although some accounting authorities believe it is prudent to amortize the costs of such franchises over a relatively short period of time.

Trademarks and Trade Names

Trademarks, trade names, and distinctive symbols, labels, and designs used to differentiate products and brands can be protected from infringement by registering them with the United States Patent Office. Proof of prior and continuous use is required to retain the right to the trade name or trademarks registered. Protection of trademarks and names that cannot be registered can be sought through common law.

The cost of a trademark includes legal fees associated with successful litigation, registry fees, and all developmental expenditures that can be reasonably associated with the trademark. The cost of a purchased trademark is its purchase price.

As long as they are used continuously, trademarks have an unlimited life. Therefore, they can be written off over a 40-year period. However, in practice, their costs are often amortized rapidly, since the economic life of a trademark depends on the tastes of consumers.

Leasehold Improvements

Lessees often make alterations or improvements to the property they are leasing. At the end of the lease, such leasehold improvements revert to the lessor. Therefore, the lessee only has the right to use his improvements during the period of this lease. Consequently, leasehold improvements are amortized over the remaining life of the lease or their useful life, whichever is shorter.

Organization Costs

Organization costs include incorporation fees, legal fees, promotion expenditures, and similar costs associated with the initial organization of a company. These costs benefit the corporation during its entire life, which for accounting purposes can be considered to be unlimited, and as such written off over a 40-year period. Others agree that initial organization costs should be capitalized to avoid starting a business with a deficit, but argue that these costs should be amortized rapidly, since they have no ultimate disposal value. Hence, they should be written off against income before the ultimate income created by the business enterprise is determined. Others justify rapid amortization on the ground of conservatism.

Intangible Development Costs

In the oil and gas industry, all drilling costs, excluding the pipe and equipment used to complete a well, are classified as intangible development costs. Other intangible costs include drill site preparation, roads to the location, grading, logging (electrical well surveys conducted with special downhole instruments), perforating, cementing, and formation stimulation. Such costs are classified as being intangible since they do not give rise to an asset with physical substance or salvage value.

Some companies expense these costs as incurred. Increasingly, the prevalent practice is to capitalize these costs and amortize them over the life of the related productive wells. Most companies expense these costs as incurred for tax purposes.

Those companies deducting their intangible development costs as incurred for accounting purposes do so to be conservative or to conform with their treatment of these expenditures for tax purposes, even though this is not necessary to qualify the cost for tax deductibility. Others write these costs off as incurred since they believe that the annual charges approximate the amortization charges that would be recognized if a capitalization policy had been followed in earlier years.

In the opinion of many, capitalization of intangible development costs results in a proper matching of costs and revenues, since these costs are very similar in nature to capital expenditures. A few companies capitalize all of their intangible development costs on the premise that unsuccessful development activities are a necessary part of finding successful wells. The total pooled costs are then written off over the life of the productive wells. However, the more common practice is to capitalize only those intangible development costs associated with wells that appear productive. Intangible development costs for dry holes are expensed as exploration costs in the year the well is abandoned.

Some oil and gas companies capitalize all of their costs of discovering and developing oil or gas reserves. This method, which capitalizes dry hole costs, is called "full costing." In contrast, the "successful efforts" method capitalizes only those discovery and development costs related to a specific field where oil or gas reserves have been discovered.

Capitalizing intangible development costs in the accounting records and expensing them for tax purposes creates a timing difference which requires the application of interperiod tax allocation.

Computer Software

FASB Interpretation No. 6 discusses the applicability of *Statement No. 2* to computer software developed to be sold as software or as part of a product or process. It classifies software development costs incurred for conceptual formulation or the translation of knowledge into a design as research and development costs. Other costs, including those incurred for programming and testing software, are research and development costs when incurred in the search for or the evaluation of product or process alternatives or in the design of a preproduction model. On the other hand, costs for programming and testing are not research and development costs when incurred, for example, in routine or other ongoing efforts to improve an existing product or adapt a product to a particular customer's need.

In 1985, the FASB decided that the costs of software testing and coding following the completion of a working model or detailed program design must be capitalized when (1) the software product was to be sold, leased, or incorporated in hardware to be sold or leased; and (2) it was anticipated the capitalized costs were recoverable. The capitalized amounts must be amortized over the recovery period.

Role of Judgment

The appropriate accounting for intangible assets is very dependent on the particular circumstances of each situation, perhaps more so than in any other area of accounting. Seldom does an exhaustive analysis of the facts lead to a clear-cut answer. Therefore, selecting the best approach usually requires the exercise of management judgment.

The public accountant faces the same judgmental situation in deciding what form the opinion statement will take. Sometimes the auditor's problem is aggravated when the auditor is not fully satisfied with management's treatment of the item, but is not absolutely convinced that the preferred alternative treatment is the only possible answer. In these situations, the public accountant usually resorts to a "subject to" type of opinion. This warns the reader of the statement that the auditor has some reservations about management's handling of the intangible but feels management's position has merit. Of course, if management's treatment seems inappropriate and management insists on keeping that approach, the auditor will issue a more drastic form of opinion, or may even terminate the audit arrangement.

Businesses change over time, and often their past accounting practices and estimates become inappropriate for their new conditions. This is particularly true of accounting for intangibles. However, it is seldom clear at what precise point in time a change in accounting policy or estimate is justified. Again, responsible management judgment must be exercised. Unfortunately, in most cases changes in accounting for intangibles are made long after the events justifying a change have occurred. Also, a decline in profitability is often the event that appears to prompt the decision to change accounting methods. Changes under these circumstances inevitably raise questions about the integrity of management's statements.

Profit Impact of Shift

It is important to note that when a management changes from expensing to capitalizing the cost of an internally generated intangible, the favorable impact on profit may spread well beyond the year of the change. While there are many possible variations of this impact, depending on the direction and size of the annual expenditures, the following simple example presented in Illustration 18–1 should be sufficient to illustrate the point:

> The Viking Chemical Company has a very stable business. The management plans to continue its practice of spending $1 million per year to purchase patents over the next 10 years. In 1985, the company changed its accounting for purchased patents from expensing as acquired to capitalization and amortization over five years.

What will be the impact on profits of this decision over the next five years? Illustration 18–1 supplies the answer.

Inappropriate Practices

It is often difficult to determine whether or not an intangible asset expenditure will be recovered out of future revenues. Typically, this problem of

ILLUSTRATION 18–1
Profit Impact Illustration (in thousands)

	Old Policy: Expense Patents as Purchased 1985	New Policy: Capitalize Patents and Amortize over Five Years					
		1985	1986	1987	1988	1989	1990
Profits before taxes and patent expenses	$4,000	$4,000	$4,000	$4,000	$4,000	$4,000	$4,000
Patent expenses	1,000	200	400	600	800	1,000	1,000
	$3,000	$3,800	$3,600	$3,400	$3,200	$3,000	$3,000
Income taxes (50%)	1,500	1,900	1,800	1,700	1,600	1,500	1,500
Net profit after taxes and all charges	$1,500	$1,900	$1,800	$1,700	$1,600	$1,500	$1,500
Annual profit improvement	—	400	300	200	100	—	—
Deferred patent asset (balance sheet item)	—	800	1,400	1,800	2,000	2,000	2,000

uncertainty is resolved on the basis of conservatism, by expensing the cost as incurred. In the case of many well-established companies run by responsible managers, this treatment is often followed unnecessarily. This can result in an improper matching of costs and revenues and the omission of a valid business asset from the balance sheet. On the other hand, marginal firms often resort to capitalizing intangible asset costs of dubious future value in order to boost earnings. Thus, in practice, the inappropriate treatment is the one most often adopted.

Financial Analysis

Capitalized intangible expenditures purport to represent current and past investments that are expected to generate future revenues and whose ultimate recoverability has been established. Independently verifying this claim presents a difficult challenge to statement analysts, since it is nearly impossible to tell from past and current financial statement data how much the capitalized costs might be recovered and how appropriate the related amortization practices will be. The differences between different companies' applications of the intangible asset accounting rules are also hard to detect.

Because of these difficulties, statement users often rely on the independent auditor's opinion as to whether management's intangible asset accounting decisions are appropriate. This can be a mistake. The independent auditor, who may not fully understand the nature of the item involved, may be relying heavily on management representations that the accounting is appropriate. In these cases, the auditor's opinion provides little protection for statement users from unscrupulous managers. To protect themselves against inept auditing of intangibles, statement users must develop their own estimates of the probability that the capitalized costs will be recovered.

This requires an assessment of the financial, market, and technological feasibility of the product, claim, or concept represented by the intangible asset and of management's commitment to recovering the capitalized amounts. Typically, this assessment requires data beyond that presented in the financial statements, such as the relevant reports by security analysts, pertinent articles in trade journals, and interviews with people knowledgeable in the particular area. In making this assessment, it is prudent to be skeptical and remember that strong companies prefer to expense as incurred rather than capitalize expenditures for intangibles.

Outlined below are a few financial statement analysis hints. Frankly, they will not be all that helpful. The key to understanding how appropriately a company has applied the intangible asset accounting rules is to have a thorough knowledge of the company's products, product development skills, technological capabilities, and competitive environment. In the end, these are the factors that will determine whether or not a company's intangible asset accounting practices are sound.

The first analytical problem facing statement users is figuring out how much was spent during the accounting period on capitalized intangible assets. To compute the actual intangible asset cash expenditures in any one period, the analyst must add the change in the deferred costs to the deferred costs amortized in the period. Two suggested financial analysis techniques are:

a. Keep track of the periodic capitalized intangible expenditures. An unusual increase in the balance may be a red flag signaling capitalization of costs beyond that permitted by the rules, or it may be the result of increased intangible asset acquisition and development activities. Seek more information.

b. Watch the percentage of amortized intangible asset costs relative to sales. A decline in this percentage may indicate stretching of the amortization period or a growing reliance on old products, ideas, patents, or rights.

In making the above calculations, one should keep in mind that not all intangible assets are developed internally. Intangible assets can be purchased from others. So, acquisition expenditures should be considered when evaluating trends in the ratios and balances described above.

Bitter experience has taught statement users to be wary of capitalized intangible assets. Some of the more troublesome aspects of capitalizing expenditures for intangibles are:

1. Capitalization may remove the discipline of expensing, which forces management to question the value of the incremental expenditures for intangible assets since they will depress current profits. Capitalizing rather than expensing as incurred can lead to overfunding of unsound projects long after they should have been terminated. Unfortunately, since earnings

are not adversely impacted currently by imprudent funding, statement readers may fail to detect the poor management decision early enough to avert a disappointing earnings surprise when the capitalized balances are written off in a lump sum.

2. Application of the intangible asset accounting rules requires considerable judgment on the part of managers, who may be tempted to stretch the rules when their companies experience difficult times by including in the capitalized balances costs that do not legitimately belong in the account and extending the amortization period by overestimating potential revenues. Outsiders seldom see though this maneuver in time to avoid unpleasant surprises.

3. When faced with a decision between internally developing or purchasing an intangible asset, some managers may lean toward the purchase alternative because it will be easier to justify capitalizing the cost of purchased intangibles. Sometimes, the desire to avoid lowering current profits by expensing as incurred the cost of internally developed intangible assets may lead to management's overpaying for the purchased intangible asset. This in turn may make future recoverability of the cost more difficult. Overpayment is hard to detect directly from an examination of financial statements.

4. Capitalization of intangible asset expenditures can encourage optimism on the part of managers and statement users. Capitalizing an expenditure signals that the expenditure is thought to be recoverable in the future. This signal can lead managers and statement users to focus too much on the expected benefits and to downplay, or even forget, that there may be many hazardous competitive and technological steps that must be accomplished in the meantime. Capitalization is not synonymous with accomplishment. Statement readers who accept management's capitalization practices are well advised to remember this fact. To forget it can be costly.

Logic suggests that it is just as misleading to expense as incurred investments in intangible assets with a high probability of generating future benefits as it is to capitalize expenditures for intangible assets that are unlikely to produce future benefits. When statement users encounter a company that expenses as incurred its expenditures for intangible assets that it considers quite likely to produce future benefits, this practice should be considered a significant factor favoring a high-quality earnings rating for the company. In addition, since the anticipated future benefits will not be burdened by the amortization of prior period capitalized expenditures, the company's chances of being profitable in the future are enhanced.

CASE 18-1

Comserv Corporation
Accounting for Software Development Costs

In June 1983, Richard Daly, chairman of Comserv Corporation, a small computer software firm, reflected on the rationale behind his firm's decision to capitalize the costs of developing new software products:

> I believe it is very important for Comserv to be able to capitalize software development costs. We are producing assets—software that will bring in revenues in future periods—and for a fair picture of how we're doing, the costs of producing the assets must be matched against the revenues they produce. We do this by capitalizing the costs and amortizing them over a multiyear period.
>
> These software development investments are necessary for Comserv to grow, and even to survive. Forcing us to expense these costs would discourage us from investing as much as we should because our earnings would be severely penalized. I know we have some critics who are concerned about the risk of putting poor quality assets on the balance sheet, but I think the risk is minimal because we have good controls over our development expenditures.

Background of Comserv Corporation

Comserv was founded in 1968 in Minneapolis, Minnesota, initially to provide data processing services to local businesses. In the early 1970s, the company started developing software for its clients, and by 1982, it had grown to be the largest independent supplier of software products for the manufacturing industry, with annual sales in excess of $23 million.[1] (See financial information in Exhibits 1 and 2.)

As shown in Figure 1, the bulk of Comserv's revenues was derived

---

This case was prepared by Carolyn Bitetti (under the direction of Kenneth A. Merchant).

Copyright © 1984 by the President and Fellows of Harvard College

Harvard Business School case 184–084

[1] Software refers generally to the instructions and routines used to operate and control computer hardware. Software is entered into computer memory via the terminal keyboard, disks, tapes, or other media.

EXHIBIT 1

COMSERV CORPORATION
Consolidated Statement of Operations
(in thousands, except per share information)

	Year Ended December 31					
	1982	1981	1980	1979	1978	1977
Revenues	$23,407	$17,667	$10,704	$6,493	$4,257	$3,084
Operating costs	7,011	5,727	3,527	2,571	1,726	1,424
Selling expenses	8,014	5,635	3,623	1,723	1,046	693
General and administrative expenses	4,714	2,884	1,423	772	477	343
Amortization of computer software and educational courseware construction costs	1,743	720	470	314	318	199
Total costs and expenses	21,482	14,966	9,043	5,380	3,567	2,659
Operating income	1,925	2,701	1,661	1,113	690	425
Income before taxes and extraordinary item	2,067	3,628	1,441	916	538	302
Income before extraordinary item	1,644	2,213	903	516	315	238
Net income	1,644	2,213	903	516	315	291
Earnings per common share:						
Primary	$ .49	$ .71	$ .45	$ .35	$ .23	$ .23
Fully diluted	$ .49	$ .71	$ .42	$ .30	$ .22	$ .23

EXHIBIT 2

COMSERV CORPORATION
Selected Consolidated Balance Sheet Data
(in thousands)

	Year Ended December 31					
	1982	1981	1980	1979	1978	1977
Working capital	$ 9,491	$ 9,348	$ 2,327	$ 954	$ 64	$ 22
Capitalized software and coursework construction costs	15,283	7,790	4,258	2,899	2,005	1,456
Less: Accumulated amortization	3,937	2,194	1,473	1,075	761	443
	11,346	5,596	2,785	1,824	1,244	1,013
Total assets	51,587	25,870	11,130	6,244	3,843	2,702
Long-term debt (including current portion)	21,897	1,638	345	1,768	974	848
Redeemable preferred stock	—	—	—	200	200	—
Common stockholders' equity	18,418	16,721	6,505	2,074	1,495	1,187

from a family of software products called Advanced Manufacturing, Accounting, and Production System (AMAPS). AMAPS was designed to assist manufacturers in planning, scheduling, monitoring, and controlling their operations. It was comprised of a number of modules which could be purchased separately or in combinations, and it could be adapted to meet specific customer and industry requirements.

FIGURE 1

	1982 Revenue (in thousands)	Percent of Total
Software products (AMAPS)	$14,996	64%
Educational products/services	3,319	14
Professional services	2,905	12
Data processing	2,187	9
	$23,407	100%

Exhibit 3 presents an overview of the modules included in the AMAPS mainframe product (i.e., designed for large computers), most of which were fully developed by 1982. The AMAPS mainframe product was very successful. Datapro Research[2] rated AMAPS as the top mainframe-based manufacturing software package in both 1981 and 1982.

Training and professional support was provided to customers who pur-

EXHIBIT 3
Comserv Corporation

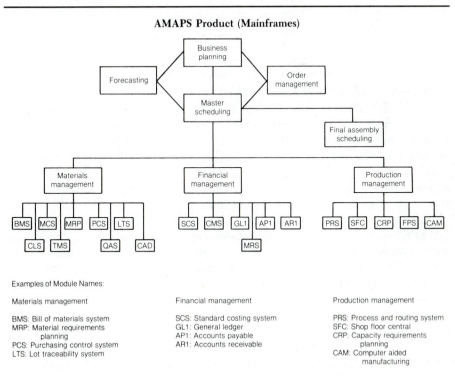

AMAPS Product (Mainframes)

Examples of Module Names:

Materials management

BMS: Bill of materials system
MRP: Material requirements
    planning
PCS: Purchasing control system
LTS: Lot traceability system

Financial management

SCS: Standard costing system
GL1: General ledger
AP1: Accounts payable
AR1: Accounts receivable

Production management

PRS: Process and routing system
SFC: Shop floor central
CRP: Capacity requirements
    planning
CAM: Computer aided
    manufacturing

[2] A software research and publishing subsidiary of McGraw-Hill.

chased AMAPS. Comserv had developed a variety of educational tools, including courses, workshops, videotapes, and workbooks; some of the offerings covered topics not directly related to Comserv software and were being offered to customers who had not bought AMAPS. The Professional Services staff was available to assist customers in implementing AMAPs and in utilizing the system to its full potential.

Comserv's original product—processing information on Comserv computers, primarily for small businesses—had become progressively less important. As shown in Figure 1, this service generated less than 10 percent of total 1982 revenues.

Customers purchased a 99-year license to use AMAPS software, and by the end of 1982, AMAPS had been installed in approximately 300 large manufacturing companies (e.g., Bausch & Lomb, Gillette, Plough, Warner-Lambert), all of which had IBM or IBM-compatible mainframes. A typical module cost $30,000 to $50,000 and if all the modules were purchased, the total price was approximately $500,000. A typical mainframe customer contract might total around $340,000, including professional services, educational services, and maintenance, as follows:

	In thousands
Software license	$220
Professional services	60
Educational services	40
Maintenance contract	20
Total	$345

Comserv was expanding its product offerings in several directions. Some new AMAPS modules were being planned or in development, and new AMAPS versions were in various stages of development. A minicomputer version, called AMAPS 3000, was just being offered to prospective clients, primarily smaller manufacturers ($25–75 million in sales) (see Exhibit 4); a version called AMAPS–G was being developed for government contractors; and a version called AMAPS–Q was being developed for use with remote terminals at manufacturing work stations.

Comserv was also expanding into international markets. Initially, AMAPS was licensed to foreign subsidiaries of existing clients, but in the early 1980s, offices were opened in Dublin, London, and Toronto to sell to non-U.S. corporations. International sales were expected to grow from approximately 13 percent of total revenues in 1982, possibly to 25 percent by the mid-1980s.

Organization

Comserv was organized functionally, with separate groups responsible for product construction, sales, marketing, and development of new products

EXHIBIT 4
Comserv Corporation

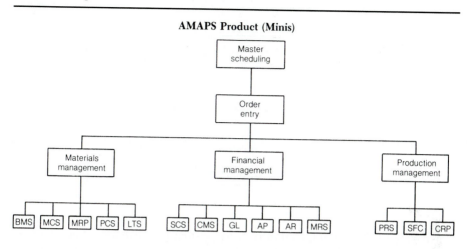

AMAPS Product (Minis)

(see Exhibit 5). Reporting to the vice president in charge of software construction were product line managers, responsible for development of specific mainframe products and minicomputer products (see Exhibit 6).

Performance Evaluation

Comserv provided annual bonuses to key employees. The bonus opportunity was approximately 30 percent of salary. Part of the bonus was based on the individual's grade level and overall company profitability. Another part

EXHIBIT 5
Comserv Corporation

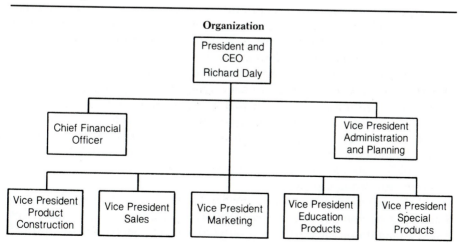

Organization

EXHIBIT 6
Comserv Corporation

Partial Organization Chart for Product Construction Group

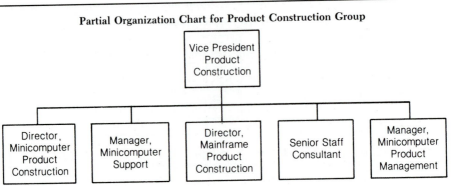

was based on the accomplishment of individual performance objectives set by each employee. For a product manager, these objectives might be based on objectives such as completing projects on time and within budget.

Gradually, Comserv was being transformed into a product-line organization with decision-making authority being delegated from top management to the product-line managers. The monthly financial reporting package included income statements for each product line, but this information was not yet being used to evaluate the product-line managers' performances. As the organization evolved, it was expected that greater importance would be placed on measurement of financial performance, with return on assets a key financial indicator.

The Decision to Capitalize Software Development Costs

Product improvement and new product development were large expenditure areas for Comserv, and both were vital to the company's continuing success. In 1982, Comserv spent $7.5 million (approximately 33 percent of revenues) on product development.

Comserv chose to capitalize expenditures related to the construction of computer software and educational coursework. Construction costs were defined as those incurred "to enhance, improve and adapt" existing products. This would include, for example, the costs of adding a purchasing module to AMAPS, adding an additional report to the existing material control module, or adapting AMAPS to a new type of computer. It would not include costs incurred before production was started, such as market research and product planning.

The capitalized costs were amortized over a four- to six-year period depending on the expected useful life of the product. For example, the AMAPS mainframe software was amortized over six years, while the AMAPS minicomputer software and the educational coursework were amortized over four years.

The rationale for capitalizing these costs was based partly on the belief that software development expenditures produce assets (software), and the costs of developing these assets should be matched against the future economic benefits that they will generate. Chairman Richard Daly explained:

> Matching expenses with revenues is a basic accounting principle, and when you violate this principle, you ought to look real hard at the reasons why. I think you'll get into trouble sooner or later. For instance, every company that expenses software construction costs is really reporting inflated margins.
>
> Take a look at the accounting definition of assets (shown in Exhibit 7). Our software meets those criteria. We are not speculating; we are building products which we are pretty sure we will be able to sell. If we were spending money developing new modeling techniques or using a new data base technology, then we'd expense it; that would be R&D. If we were going to spend $5 million building a system for the banking industry, we'd expense that too because we haven't demonstrated any capability in that area. But with the bulk of the products we are developing, there is no breakthrough in technology, and we have a demonstrated ability to develop marketable products.
>
> Take, for example, our purchasing module. It was built over an 18-month period, cost $735,000, and was delivered in the first quarter of 1981 to a backlog of $1.4 million within our existing account base. Cumulative reve-

EXHIBIT 7
Comserv Corporation

FASB Definition of Assets

Assets

.019   Assets are probable future economic benefits obtained or controlled by a particular entity as a result of past transactions or events.

Characteristics of Assets of Business Enterprises

.20   An asset has three essential characterisitcs: *(a)* it embodies a probable future benefit that involves a capacity, singly or in combination with other assets, to contribute directly or indirectly to future net cash inflows, *(b)* a particular enterprise can obtain the benefit and control others' access to it, and *(c)* the transaction or other event giving rise to the enterprise's right to or control of the benefit has already occurred. Assets commonly have other features that help identify them—for ex-

ample, assets may be acquired at a cost and they may be tangible, exchangeable, or legally enforceable. However, those features are not essential characteristics of assets. Their absence, by itself, is not sufficient to preclude an item's qualifying as an asset. That is, assets may be acquired without cost, they may be intangible, and although not exchangeable they may be usable by the enterprise in producing or distributing other goods or services. Similarly, although the ability of an enterprise to obtain benefit from an asset and to control others' access to it generally rests on a foundation of legal rights, legal enforceability of a claim to the benefit is not a prerequisite for a benefit to qualify as an asset if its receipt by the enterprise is otherwise probable.

SOURCE: FASB, *Statement of Financial Accounting Concepts No. 3*, "Elements of Financial Statements of Business Enterprises," paragraphs 19–20.
Copyright © by Financial Accounting Standards Board, High Ridge Park, Stamford, Connecticut 06905, U.S.A. Reprinted with permission. Copies of the complete document are available from the FASB.

nues from that module are at least five times that now. We've got a big client base out there that's waiting for our products.

Sure, there is some risk in what we do. How do you really know that the new products are going to produce revenue? We've had some minor write-offs. We developed some financial modules and then discovered that large companies don't buy financials; they have their own. So we had a small write-off, even though that work helped us develop the financial moduls for our minicomputer version of AMAPS. We also had to take some write-offs on a multiplant module we were working on, some of which seemed redundant when we announced AMAPS–Q. After a lot of discussion among ourselves and with our auditors, we settled on a number—$350,000— which I feel is very conservative (i.e., on the high side). But these are very minor in comparison with the total.

Mr. Daly went on to argue that expensing software development costs would cause Comserv to reduce its development expenditures:

If you look at our history, and specifically at our software development expenditures as a percentage of revenue, you'll see that it has gone up very dramatically as we've been able to bring more money into the company and staff up. It was around 10 percent in the early years, but last year it was about 32 percent. It just wouldn't be possible to expense all that. An analyst would look at our financial statements and say: "If you had expensed all that, you'd have lost a lot of money." My reply to that is: "If we had had to expense it, we wouldn't have spent it."

Tom Johnson (controller) elaborated on the same point:

There's no question that if Comserv were required to expense all software development, the expenditures would be discouraged. The discouragement wouldn't come from lower levels (i.e., from product proposal levels), it would come from the top. There is quite a bit of pressure to keep the levels of earnings up. We have to keep the level of investment such that we can still report adequate earnings.

Product Approval Process

A primary objection of those opposed to capitalization of software development expenditures was that is raised the risk of carrying assets of questionable value on the balance sheet. Mr. Daly agreed that this risk existed, but he felt that it could be limited with good management controls over development expenditures:

As soon as you start capitalizing something (it's not only true of software), then it can be a rat hole. You know, you can put a lot of stuff on your balance sheet. For example, if revenue for the Professional Services Group is down, one could theoretically move some of their expenses into the software construction area and hide it. There's a lot of exposure there, so you have to have good control, and I think that the companies that expense [software development costs] are saying to themselves: "We can't control it."

To control expenditures for software and educational coursework development, Comserv established what was called the product approval process. This process required the review and approval of every development project at each of a series of checkpoints by a seven-member Product Steering Committee (PSC). Included on the PSC were the vice presidents in charge of marketing, sales, product construction, product development, and business and systems planning.

The product approval process tracked each project from the early conceptual stages through the time the product was finally placed on the market. The initial idea could be described in the form of a formal product description and plan, or just in the form of a brief statement. If the PSC was willing to allow a project past the first stage, then a Business Plan was prepared. It included a complete description of the product, the targeted market, expected competition, projected revenues and costs for a five-year period (rough estimates), and whether or not the company had the in-house expertise to develop and support the project. Approximately 70% of the projects which reach the stage of being presented in a Business Plan obtained final approval.

If the Business Plan was approved, a specific review date was established, usually between 30 to 90 days in the future. At this and other review dates that would be established if the project continued to be funded, the PSC examined the progress being made, the expenditures to date, and the technical and market risk.

Comserv management felt that the product approval process provided a good, thorough review of development expenditures. The only problem was felt to be the delays sometimes imposed. Phillip Logan (Vice President—Product Construction) commented:

> The product approval process can get in the way sometimes. Sometimes I have to put a development team on hold status while we're waiting for approvals. The earliest it turns around is a week, but it can often be about 2 to 3 weeks by the time the PSC reviews the Business Plan. The most significant delays occur when all the people aren't around, or when the PSC asks for more information.

The Capitalization Issue and the SEC

In June 1983, the SEC[3] issued a temporary ban (SEC File No. S7–968) against companies switching from expensing to capitalizing software development costs until the accountants were able to establish a consistent set of rules. The FASB[4] was waiting for recommendations from a task force formed by the AICPA[5] and ADAPSO.[6]

---

[3] Securities and Exchange Commission.

[4] Financial Accounting Standards Board.

[5] American Institute of Certified Public Accountants.

[6] Association of Data Processing Service Organizations.

Richard Daly commented on what might happen if the FASB or the SEC eventually ruled against capitalization.

> If we lose this argument, I think it will be very bad for the software industry. The immediate reaction will be to reduce the size of our development expenditures.
>
> There are a few other things we could do to try to get around the problem, but none of them are what I would call satisfactory. We could try to obtain up-front payments from customers to fund a project. We're just starting to do some of this now, not for funding reasons, but to get some customer input into our development processes. We might be able to expand this procedure, but the customers have to be very cooperative. We could buy our software from outside parties because the accountants let us depreciate purchased assets. But I personally think that any company in our industry that goes out and buys a product is exposing itself to an even larger risk of write-offs because both the initial marketing and the ongoing support are very difficult. This is particularly true for companies with an integrated product line like ours. Finally, we could enter into R&D partnerships, as that keeps the investment off the balance sheet entirely. When the development is done, what is bought becomes an asset, or if you're obligated to a stream of royalty payments, it's essentially the same as amortization costs. But there are two problems. First, most of the stuff done in our industry is not R&D, and when the IRS takes a good look at it, they're going to disallow the tax benefits those R&D partnerships have generated. And second, it's very expensive financing, about three times as expensive as normal financing.

Tom Johnson (controller) reflected on the same issue:

> Richard Daly had the vision that Comserv really needed capitalization in order to operate in a realistic manner. Capitalization makes it possible for us to take a longer range view of what we're doing. We're not making the shortsighted investment decisions that some companies which expense software development are making; those companies are looking more toward short-term results. Overall, I think capitalization would be good for most firms in our industry.
>
> This has nothing to do with liberal versus conservative accounting, as I think Comserv's accounting is generally conservative. Take the area of revenue recognition, for example. A lot of companies recognize revenue at the time they sign the contract. We wait until we ship the product and get an acknowledgement from the customer that it has been received. Some people don't consider it conservative to capitalize software development, but this is one of those cases where other qualities of accounting numbers are more important than conservatism.

CASE 18-2

ASK Computer Systems, Inc.

Robert Riopel, vice president of finance and administration of ASK Computer Systems, Inc., was a proponent of the view that software development costs should be expensed, rather than capitalized:

> The current controversy over capitalization of software development costs focuses on the superficial issue concerning possible differences between software development and R&D. This reminds me of the phrase: "A rose by any other name . . ."
>
> For two reasons, I think software development, like R&D, should be expensed. One is to improve consistency among reporting companies. The other is to improve decision making, as expensing probably causes more thought to go into the allocation of resources.

Background of ASK

ASK, headquartered in Los Altos, California, was a leading independent producer of manufacturing and financial management software. The company was founded in 1974 and had grown rapidly—1983 revenues were over $39 million (see Exhibit 1). In October 1981, ASK made an $8.8 million stock offering and became a publicly held company. Finances were strong; the company had very little debt.

ASK's major product was an integrated group of six software modules called the Manufacturing Management Information System (MANMAN). These modules included the following:

- Manufacturing Management System (e.g., scheduling, material requirements planning).
- Order Management/Accounts Receivable System.
- Accounts Payable System.
- General Ledger System.
- Fixed Assets System.
- SERVICEMAN (service contract job reporting).

This case was prepared by Carolyn Bitetti (under the direction of Kenneth A. Merchant).
Copyright © 1983 by the President and Fellows of Harvard College
Harvard Business School case 184–037

EXHIBIT 1
ASK Computer Systems, Inc.

Financial Data

*Selected Financial Data**
(in thousands, except per-share data)

Five-Year Summary	1983	1982	1981	1980	1979
Year ended June 30:					
Net revenue	$39,388	$24,871	$13,361	$ 8,326	$ 2,775
Gross margin	20,389	12,234	6,716	3,707	1,215
Product development	3,422	2,229	1,270	438	335
Selling, general, and administrative	11,759	6,317	2,773	1,446	466
Operating income	5,208	3,688	2,673	1,823	414
Interest income	1,451	1,157	173	165	30
Income taxes	2,754	2,150	1,265	993	207
Net income	3,905	2,695	1,581	995	237
Earnings per share	.35	.27	.19	.13	.03
Dividends per share	—	—	—	—	—
Weighted average shares outstanding	11,080	10,096	8,381	7,501	7,501
At June 30:					
Working capital	$21,724	$11,743	$ 2,155	$ 1,086	$ 281
Total assets	38,902	20,803	6,990	3,566	1,376
Total long-term debt	1,004	21	29	—	—
Shareholders' equity	28,808	14,604	3,033	1,310	315

Unaudited Quarterly Results	First Quarter	Second Quarter	Third Quarter	Fourth Quarter
Fiscal 1983:				
Net revenue	$ 7,095	$ 8,654	$10,980	$12,659
Operating income	1,006	1,073	1,412	1,717
Net income	822	841	1,087	1,155
Earnings per share	.08	.08	.09	.10
Weighted average shares outstanding	10,531	10,658	11,554	11,578
Fiscal 1982:				
Net revenue	$ 5,248	$ 5,647	$ 6,684	$ 7,292
Operating income	932	808	1,002	946
Net income	556	652	766	721
Earnings per share	.07	.06	.07	.07
Weighted average shares outstanding	8,767	10,536	10,536	10,545

* Restated for an acquisition and two-for-one stock split.
SOURCE: ASK Computer Systems, Inc., Fiscal Year 1983 Annual Report.

The software programs comprising MANMAN were designed to assist manufacturers in running their operations more effectively and efficiently. ASK also offered a business graphics product, called GRAFMAN, and a report generator package which could be used in conjunction with MANMAN. To support these software products, ASK provided installation assistance, user education, and software assistance.

ASK usually provided its customers "turnkey" systems which included computer hardware and software. The software could be licensed separately, however, or accessed through an online service offered by the company

(ASKNET). ASK's software products were designed for use primarily with Hewlett-Packard minicomputers, but they could be adapted for use with other types of minicomputers.

Product Development

As with most other software companies, ASK's largest area of investment was for improvement of existing products and development of new products. ASK had consistently spent about 9 percent of its revenues on product development, and the size of these investments had increased sharply as the company had grown. As noted in a December 1982 prospectus:

> Product development increased 157 percent in fiscal 1981 and 53% in fiscal 1982, for a total increase of over $1 million from fiscal 1980. This increase reflects the company's expanding development efforts, including adapting its software for Digital Equipment Corporation's VAX computer system, developing new software packages, and enhancing existing products.

In terms of dollars, product development expenditures were $2.2 million in 1982 and $3.4 million in 1983.

ASK's Policy of Expensing Software Development Costs

ASK's policy was to expense software development expenditures as incurred. Mr. Riopel (vice president—finance and administration) was convinced that this policy was correct. He felt that software development costs should be considered the same as research and development costs in other industries and should not be accorded special accounting treatment. (U.S. accounting rules required that all research and development expenditures be expensed as incurred. Exhibit 2 presents excerpts from *FASB Statement No. 2* which sets the rules for accounting for research and development expenditures. Exhibit 3 presents excerpts from the FASB interpretation of *Statement No. 2* as it applies to software development costs.)

Some proponents of capitalization of software development expenditures argued that most software development did not require working with new technologies, and expenditures made for software development were, therefore, low-risk investments. This suggested that these expenditures should be capitalized and amortized in order to match the costs of development with the revenues the products would generate. Mr. Riopel agreed that the risk was often low, but he disputed the conclusion drawn from this point:

> There is no doubt that many, if not most, software development projects will result in an acceptable return on investment. That is not the issue. Most R&D is also product development, not basic research, and this is true in both *Fortune* 500 and high-technology start-up firms.

EXHIBIT 2
ASK Computer Systems, Inc.

Excerpts from Accounting Standard for Research and Development Costs

1. This statement establishes standards of financial accounting and reporting for research and development costs with the objectives of reducing the number of alternative accounting and reporting practices presently followed and providing useful financial information about research and development costs.

8. For purposes of this statement, research and development is defined as follows:

a. *Research* is planned search or critical investigation aimed at discovery of new knowledge with the hope that such knowledge will be useful in developing a new product or service (hereinafter "product") or a new process or technique (hereinafter "process") or in bringing about a significant improvement to an existing product or process.

b. *Development* is the translation of re-

search findings or other knowledge into a plan or design for a new product or process or for a significant improvement to an existing product or process whether intended for sale or use. It includes the conceptual formulation, design, and testing of product alternatives, construction of prototypes, and operation of pilot plants. It does not include routine or periodic alterations to existing products, production lines, manufacturing processes, and other ongoing operations even though those alterations may represent improvements, and it does not include market research or market testing activities.

12. All research and development costs encompassed by this statement shall be charged to expense when incurred.

SOURCE: Financial Accounting Standards Board, *Statement of Financial Accounting Standards No. 2,* "Accounting for Research and Development Costs" (October 1974). Copyright © by Financial Accounting Standards Board, High Ridge Park, Stamford, Connecticut 06905, U.S.A. Reprinted with permission. Copies of the complete document are available from the FASB.

The issue is whether criteria can be developed that provide reasonable assurance that different firms and their accountants will treat similar situations similarly, that development projects with uncertain future benefits are not inappropriately capitalized, and that firms cannot manipulate earnings in a significant way by their decision to capitalize or not capitalize certain projects. One of the reasons leading to *FASB Statement No. 2* was the subjectivity involved in evaluating the technical, marketing, and administrative risks of products being developed, and the resulting inconsistency in reporting results of operations. Before generally accepted accounting principles are changed to capitalize internally developed research and development (software or otherwise), far more definitive requirements than those currently proposed are required to assure consistent and verifiable treatment.

Supporters of capitalization also maintained that expensing development expenditures caused software developers' most important assets (i.e., software products) not to be reflected on their balance sheets. Mr. Riopel agreed with this point but did not think it caused problems great enough to warrant capitalization of software development expenditures.

It is a valid statement that balance sheets do not accurately reflect the current value of many companies' most important assets. But an appropriate question is, for example, whether a computer program is a more important

EXHIBIT 3
ASK Computer Systems, Inc.

Excerpts from FASB Interpretation of Applicability of Accounting
Standard on Research and Development Costs to Computer Software

1. The FASB has been asked to explain the applicability of *FASB Statement No. 2,* "Accounting for Research and Development Costs," to costs incurred to obtain or develop computer software.

7. *Development of software as a product or process to be sold, leased, or otherwise marketed.* Accounting for the cost of developing software for others under a contractual arrangement is beyond the scope of *Statement No. 2,* because paragraph 2 of the *Statement* indicates that this is part of accounting for contracts in general. On the other hand, if the development of software is undertaken to create a new or significantly improved product or process without any contractual arrangement, costs incurred for *conceptual formulation or the translation of knowledge into a design* would be research and development costs (see paragraph 8 of *Statement No. 2*). Other costs, including those incurred for programming and testing software, are research and development costs when incurred in the search for or the evaluation of product or process alternatives or in the design of a preproduction model. On the other hand, costs for programming and testing are *not* research and development costs when incurred, for example, in routine or other ongoing efforts to improve an existing product or adapt a product to a particular requirement or customer's need.

8. *Development of software to be used in research and development activities.* Developing or significantly improving a product or process that is intended to be sold, leased, or otherwise marketed to others is a research and development activity. Similarly, developing or significantly improving a process whose output is a product that is intended to be sold, leased, or otherwise marketed to others is a research and development activity. Costs incurred by an enterprise in developing computer software internally for use in its research and development activities are research and development costs and, therefore, shall be charged to expense when incurred. This includes costs incurred during all phases of software development because all of those costs are incurred in a research and development activity.

SOURCE: *FASB Interpretation No. 6,* "Applicability of *FASB Statement No. 2,* to Computer Software," (February 1975). Copyright © by Financial Accounting Standards Board, High Ridge Park, Stamford, Connecticut 06905, U.S.A. Reprinted with permission. Copies of the complete document are available from the FASB.

asset to a software company than a blueprint is to the computer manufacturer—no doubt most hardware manufacturers would give a resounding "no." A similar rationale could be used to argue for reflecting the current value of real property on many balance sheets. This problem is not unique to software developers.

It is true that the differences between manufacturing and software companies result in different ratios (e.g., return on assets), but the financial community seems fully capable of understanding and dealing with these differences. I don't mean to suggest that assets are not understated on balance sheets, but I think the problems caused are secondary to the difficulty in developing criteria for capitalization and formulae for amortization that increase, rather than lessen, the confidence level placed on financial statements.

A final argument of the proponents of capitalization was that requiring expensing of software development expenditures would tend to constrain investment because of the adverse effect on current period profitability.

Mr. Riopel also agreed with this point, but he thought this was an advantage of expensing.

> My feeling is that profit and loss constraints contribute to better decision making. Managers facing an immediate negative impact on the bottom line will probably take more care, and use more stringent criteria, in evaluating expenditure proposals. I'd hate to see ASK change its policy to allow capitalization of software expenditures. It would make my job of controlling the quality of our investments much more difficult.

CASE 18-3

SafeCard Services, Inc.
Accounting for Marketing Costs

On June 30, 1981, *The Wall Street Journal* reported that SafeCard Services, Inc., had filed a $30 million lawsuit in federal district court accusing a number of defendants of trying to ruin its business. Among the 10 defendants were Dow Jones, Inc., publisher of *Barron's* and *The Wall Street Journal;* Alan Abelson, managing editor of *Barron's* and author of the weekly column "Up and Down Wall Street"; and Steven Anreder, assistant managing editor of *Barron's* and assistant on the column. SafeCard accused the defendants of conspiring to "destroy the business" of SafeCard by "disseminating publicly and privately misleading information."

In replying to the suit, Robert M. Bleiberg, editor and publisher of *Barron's,* described it as "baseless." As reported in *The Wall Street Journal* (July 1, 1981), Mr. Bleiberg noted that *Barron's* had run three articles on SafeCard in the past three years and that a fourth article, written by Abra-

---

This case was prepared by Norman J. Bartczak.

ham J. Briloff, "an acknowledged authority in the field," would be "running in our pages as soon as possible." [The article by Professor Briloff appeared in the July 6, 1981, issue of *Barron's,* in which he expressed a number of misgivings regarding SafeCard's accounting.] According to Mr. Bleiberg: "In our view, it's no coincidence that the suit was filed last Friday (June 26, 1981), just four days after (Mr.) Briloff, as part of his preparation for the article, met with top executives of SafeCard and their lawyer and auditor." He added: "It's equally significant that the company recently filed an offering of one million shares of common stock, almost half of the proceeds of which will go to the two principal officers, Peter and Steven Halmos. This is the latest in a series of efforts by the company to discourage *Barron's* from commenting on SafeCard."

Mr. Bleiberg concluded by stating that "From the outset, our sole purpose was to enlighten our readers and give them a better insight into the company's workings. The allegations against us have been made up out of whole cloth. They are baseless and clearly aimed at suppressing fair comment. As in the past, we will vigorously defend our right to print the truth."

SafeCard Services

SafeCard Services, Inc., was founded in 1969 by two brothers, Peter A. Halmos and Steven J. Halmos, to provide a credit card loss notification service to cardholders and card issuers. This service, now referred to as the Hot-Line Credit Card Loss Notification ("Hot-Line") program, provides credit cardholders with a notification system for lost or stolen credit cards and other services. It is also designed to assist card issuers in minimizing losses from unauthorized use in excess of the $50 maximum for which cardholders may become liable. SafeCard has subsequently developed other consumer "continuity service" programs which, along with the Hot-Line service, are described in more detail below.

Hot-Line Service

The Hot-Line service is SafeCard's original program and has been its principal source of revenues and earnings. Under this program, a subscriber's credit cards may be registered with SafeCard's operations center where the information concerning the subscriber's credit cards is stored. In the event that a subscriber's credit cards are reported lost or stolen, SafeCard retrieves, or, if the cards have not been previously registered, obtains, the information necessary to notify credit card issuers of the loss.

In addition to loss notification services, the Hot-Line program includes: (1) requests for the replacement of lost cards; (2) issuance of fraud-deterrent stickers to be affixed to all credit cards; (3) notification to card issuers of address changes by the cardholder; and (4) issuance of an emergency medical card containing a microfilm history of certain medical facts provided by the subscriber. Also, upon request, SafeCard will wire a $100 cash advance to an eligible subscriber who suffers a loss of credit cards when more than 100 miles from home and/or send airplane tickets (which must be repaid within 30 days) to stranded subscribers. Other services available are a nationwide toll-free message service (similar to an answering service) and a lost key return service.

For the five years ended October 31, 1980, Hot-Line provided substantially all of SafeCard's direct mail marketing revenues and operating profits, i.e., such revenues less the cost of service programs, Hot-Line provided approximately $13 million, or 85 percent, and approximately $9 million, or 79 percent, of such revenues during the fiscal year ended October 31, 1980, and the six-month period ended April 30, 1981, respectively. As of June 1, 1981, Hot-Line had a subscriber base of approximately 3.5 million persons, of which 2.0 million are "retail" participants and 1.5 million are "wholesale" participants, i.e., wholesale participants participate through membership in associations which contract with SafeCard (see Marketing section).

Date Reminder Service

The Date Reminder Service ("Date-Reminder") provides to subscribers by mail a monthly computer-generated reminder which lists personal dates and events registered by the subscriber in addition to standard holidays. Subscribers may add as many dates and events as desired either by mail or by calling SafeCard's toll-free 24-hour-a-day operations center. Date-Reminder includes either a large, plastic-laminated wall calendar or a personal Almanac Appointment Book.

Revenues from Date-Reminder became material for the first time during fiscal 1980. For fiscal 1980 and the six months ended April 30, 1981, direct mail marketing revenues from Date-Reminder were approximately $1.5 million, or 10 percent, and approximately $2.2 million, or 19 percent, respectively, of such revenues. As of June 1, 1981, Date-Reminder had a subscriber base of approximately 1.4 million persons.

Reference Service

In 1980, SafeCard obtained the exclusive direct mail marketing rights for the credit card industry for the annual hardcover editions of the *Guinness Book of World Records* and *The World Almanac and Book of Facts.* Each contract requires minimum annual purchases by SafeCard in order to maintain its exclusivity rights. SafeCard provides these books annually to subscribers as part of its reference service. In addition, subscribers may call, toll-free, for information contained in the *Guinness Book of World Records* and *The World Almanac and Book of Facts.* SafeCard commenced the marketing of this service in February 1981. Through mid-1981, SafeCard shipped approximately 400,000 books. Also, through mid-1981, the contribution of the reference service has not been material to SafeCard's revenues.

Home Protection and Mini-File Services

National Home Protection Association ("Home Protection") provides for the registration and annual updating of a subscriber's personal property for insurance or police purposes in the event of loss, theft, or destruction. This service includes: (1) the cataloging of all valuable property in the subscriber's home through reports to SafeCard on property inventory forms furnished by SafeCard; (2) the assignment of registration numbers for such property; (3) theft-deterrent stickers indicating that property has been registered; and (4) burglar warning decals which offer a $500 reward payable by SafeCard for information leading to the arrest and conviction of any person committing a burglary in the subscriber's home. Revenues from Home Protection have not been material to SafeCard through mid-1981.

SafeCard recently augmented the Home Protection service to include the Mini-File Household Organizer ("Mini-File"), a home record-keeping file for household, tax, insurance, and other personal records. The Mini-File is shipped to subscribers annually along with the current edition of an income tax guide such as J. K. Lasser's *Your Income Tax*. SafeCard announced an expanded marketing program for the Mini-File service planned for late fall 1981. It anticipates charging an annual fee of between $15 and $19 for the newly augmented Home Protection service.

Marketing

SafeCard's programs are marketed under contracts with credit card issuers by direct mail to holders of credit cards. The programs provide for continuity of membership through annual renewals, with resultant savings to SafeCard in solicitation costs.

Typically, the Hot-Line service is offered as a six-month free trial. Credit cardholders who accept the free trial are informed by SafeCard in the fifth month of the trial period that, should they desire, they can cancel the Hot-Line service via a toll-free call to SafeCard or by mail. Otherwise, they are automatically billed $12 for the succeeding 12 months' service (fee in effect at mid-1981; the Hot-Line fee has been $12 since Hot-Line's inception six years ago). The fee is usually charged on the credit cardholder's monthly credit card bill (to be paid in the month subsequent to the end of the free trial period). In the past few years, a typical Hot-Line mailing, offering the initial six months of free service, has generated a 2 to 5 percent positive response rate, e.g., in a mailing to 100,000 people, between 2,000 to 5,000 accept the six-month free trial; but see page 622 for response rates by type of mailing). Approximately 65 percent of these respondents subsequently become paying subscribers in the first year. After the first year, the renewal rate has historically run at about 80 percent. SafeCard's management estimates that after the third renewal year, the renewal rate is higher than 80 percent.

SafeCard's other continuity service programs are usually offered on the basis of the first year free (except for a nominal charge for postage and handling; $2.99 in mid-1981). After the first year, the customer cost (in effect mid-1981) for: (1) the Date Reminder service is $9.95 plus postage; (2) the *Guinness Book of World Records* reference service is $11.95 plus postage; and (3) *The World Almanac and Book of Facts* is $9.95 plus postage. Response and renewal rates for these programs are estimated and/or expected to be similar to those for the Hot-Line service. However, unlike the Hot-Line programs, these continuity service programs provide, albeit as a premium, an actual *physical* product to customers, e.g. a calendar, appointment book, reference book, almanac. As a result, the direct acquisition costs for these programs are greater than the acquisition costs for the Hot-Line service. For example, one analyst estimated that the physical product cost of acquiring a subscriber to *The World Almanac* is approximately $4 (excluding postage and handling).

SafeCard's marketing efforts include direct mail ("solo") solicitation of credit cardholders (estimated by outside analysts to be 80 percent of all mailings in 1980) and billing inserts ("inserts").[1] In solo mailings, SafeCard provides, in addition to the solicitation brochure, a descriptive letter and other marketing materials, including a postage paid return subscription card. In a solo mailing, SafeCard bears all postage costs. Each solo mailing must be approved by the credit card issuer and is generally mailed in envelopes bearing the credit card issuer's name and logo.

SafeCard also designs advertising for its services for insertion in the monthly billing statements of a credit card issuer. Inserts have the advantage of low cost to SafeCard because postage is paid by the credit card issuer. Typically, these inserts are subject to prior approval of the credit card issuer. Due to the comparatively low cost of inserts and the limitation on the number of inserts which may be placed in any single billing statement, there is intense competition for insert space.

The average cost of solo mailings is $130 to $165 per thousand solicitations, as compared with $13 to $30 per thousand solicitations for inserts. However, there are significant advantages with solo mailings, the most important of which is significantly higher response rates (estimated at 3 percent to 5 percent versus 2 percent to 2½ percent for inserts). Moreover, solo mailings may be sent to all cardholders, whereas inserts are mailed to cardholders who have made a purchase during the previous billing period and are therefore receiving a statement.

SafeCard disclosed that, during *calendar-year* 1980, it incurred approxi-

---

[1] In mid-1981, SafeCard established a telephone marketing division to follow up mail solicitations by telephone.

mately $13 million of direct mail marketing costs in connection with the mailing of about 102 million pieces of direct mail advertising. This represents a significant increase from the roughly 35 million pieces of direct mail marketing advertising mailed in calendar 1979, 40 million pieces in calendar 1978, and 8 million pieces in calendar 1977. In mid-1981, SafeCard stated that it expected to incur approximately $25 million of direct mail advertising costs through the end of calendar 1982.

SafeCard has contractual ("retail") arrangements with various credit card issuers, including 12 major oil companies such as Atlantic Richfield Company and Gulf Oil Corporation, over 20 retail department stores such as J. C. Penney Company, Inc., units of Allied Stores Corporation, and Sears, Roebuck and Co. (through a Sears licensee), and over 45 banks and other credit card issuers such as National Car Rental System, Inc., and The Firestone Tire & Rubber Company. SafeCard also has subcontracting ("wholesale") arrangements with Exxon Travel Club, Inc., Shell Motorist Club, Inc., ARCO Travel Club, and the Amoco Traveler. The profitability to SafeCard of the retail programs is much greater than the wholesale programs.

SafeCard's marketing contracts with credit card issuers generally have a one-year term and provide for automatic annual renewals thereafter unless canceled by either party, subject to the fulfillment of certain specified contractual obligations. These contracts generally provide for (1) mailings of SafeCard's sales brochures to cardholders; (2) billing of membership fees by the card issuers; and (3) payment to the card issuers of commissions and service charges which are negotiated with each credit card issuer (for retail programs, commissions are estimated by outside analysts to range from 20 to 25 percent of SafeCard's fee to its customers). Authorization for each mailing of SafeCard's sales brochures must generally be separately obtained by SafeCard from the card issuer. SafeCard's ability to obtain these separate approvals for additional solicitations is important and is dependent on many factors, including: (1) the profitability to the credit card issuer of past solicitations; (2) the efficiency of SafeCard's customer servicing; and (3) competition for the limited advertising space which may be provided by any one issuer.

During fiscal 1980 and the six-month period ended April 30, 1981, aggregate subscriptions obtained through contracts with Shell Oil Company, Gulf Oil Corporation, Atlantic Richfield Company, Union Oil Company of California, and Mobil Corporation provided approximately 72 percent and 58 percent, respectively, of SafeCard's total direct mail marketing revenues.

In May 1981, SafeCard executed certain agreements with Citicorp Credit Services, Inc., a subsidiary of Citicorp. These agreements provide, among other things, for SafeCard: (1) to acquire the customer base of Citicorp's "Protection Plus," a credit card loss notification service similar to SafeCard's Hot-Line program; (2) to continue promoting the Protection Plus service as previously operated by Citicorp; and (3) to use the name Protection Plus. At the time of these agreements, Protection Plus had approximately

200,000 subscribers. SafeCard announced its intention to commence direct mail and telephone solicitations for Protection Plus to Citicorp's MasterCard and VISA credit cardholders in July 1981.

In June 1981, SafeCard executed an agreement with VISA International, licensor of the VISA credit card, providing for credit card loss notification services to all VISA Travelers Cheque customers who lose their travelers checks and credit cards. The credit card notification service is provided by VISA at no cost to the customer; VISA compensates SafeCard on a per incident basis. Details as to the compensation schedule are not available.

Competition and Regulation

As of mid-1981, it is estimated that there exist 600 million credit cards in the United States held by between 80 to 100 million people. Through its contracts with major credit card issuers, SafeCard is believed to have access to roughly 70 percent of this market. SafeCard's share of the lost credit card notification market is estimated to be about 50 percent. One of its principal competitors in this market is Credit Card Services Corporation (CCSC), a privately owned company based in Alexandria, Virginia. (CCSC is also named as a defendant in the SafeCard suit filed in June 1981). Because CCSC is privately owned, no comparative information on their financial performance is publicly available. Other privately owned national and regional firms also compete with SafeCard, some of which are believed to have substantially greater resources than SafeCard. Competition in securing contracts with the issuers of credit cards is based on: (1) the quality and reliability of the services; (2) the marketing expertise and capability of the firm supplying the services; and (3) the compensation paid to the credit card issuer.

Direct mail marketing is subject to the general regulatory jurisdiction of the Federal Trade Commission (FTC), which is empowered to establish regulations, investigate complaints, and institute administrative proceedings with respect to direct mail selling practices, advertising, and delivery of services and products. In addition, various states have laws and regulations which relate to SafeCard's direct mail marketing programs. SafeCard's direct mail marketing activities are similar to those followed by its competitors and comply with applicable laws and regulations.

Unrelated Activity

Farm Fresh Shrimp Corporation ("Farm Fresh") was incorporated by Peter A. Halmos and Steven J. Halmos in December 1973. Farm Fresh stemmed from Peter Halmos's MBA thesis on oceanography. In July 1976, the Halmos brothers sold their 65 percent interest in Farm Fresh to SafeCard for $10. SafeCard subsequently raised its ownership interest in 1976 to 82 percent through a purchase of newly issued shares directly from Farm Fresh for $75. SafeCard continues to own 82 percent of Farm Fresh.

Farm Fresh has developed a "factory production concept" for captive mating, spawning, feeding, and rearing of the giant Malaysian prawn, a freshwater crustacean which resembles shrimp in both appearance and taste. SafeCard has applied for various patents on this process, two of which have been recently granted. SafeCard recently discontinued a small-scale pilot project which it had operated since 1975 because of its belief that a prototype has been developed to the point where it can now be applied on a large scale commerical basis. SafeCard intends to develop a multiphase product testing and marketing program for shrimp and shrimp-based products. As of mid-1981, no revenues have been realized from Farm Fresh, and SafeCard does not anticipate any in the near term. All research and development costs associated with Farm Fresh have been expensed as incurred.

Ownership

SafeCard went public with an initial stock offering of 150,000 shares of common stock at $3 per share (1.2 million shares at $0.375 adjusted for two-for-one stock splits in June 1978, October 1980, and May 1981). In November 1977, it issued 200,000 more common shares at $20 per share (1.6 million shares at $2.50 adjusted for two-for-one stock splits in June 1978, October 1980, and May 1981). In late June 1981, SafeCard proposed to offer 1 million shares of common stock representing: (1) 500,000 new shares offered by SafeCard; (2) 217,500 secondary shares offered by Peter A. Halmos, chairman, chief executive officer, and secretary of SafeCard; Peter Halmos owns 20.6 percent of SafeCard's outstanding shares as of mid-1981; his ownership interest would be reduced to 15.0 percent after the offering; (3) 217,500 secondary shares offered by Steven J. Halmos, president and chief operating officer of SafeCard; Steven Halmos owns 15.3% of Safe-Card's outstanding shares as of mid-1981; his ownership interest would be reduced to 10.1 percent after the offering; (4) 65,000 secondary shares offered by Messrs. Richard W. Nixon and James L. D. Roser, directors of SafeCard; they own approximately 5.6 percent of SafeCard's outstanding shares as of mid-1981; their ownership interest would be reduced to approximately 4.0% after the offering. As of June 1, 1981, SafeCard has 5,188,800 shares outstanding (as adjusted for the 100 percent stock dividend paid May 20, 1981) of which approximately 40 percent is beneficially owned by the officers and directors (12 persons) of SafeCard. Their beneficial ownership would be reduced to roughly 28 percent after the offering.

Financial Analysis

In March 1981, two large New York brokerage firms issued purchase recommendations for SafeCard's common stock. At that time, SafeCard's stock was trading at about $14 per share (adjusted for all stock splits through

July 1981). The advisory firms cited SafeCard's exceptional growth potential as one of the reasons for their recommendations. One firm noted that "we believe that SafeCard Services can sustain a 40 percent growth rate over the next several years." The two investment companies estimated SafeCard's 1981 revenues at between $23.5 and $24.5 million and 1982 revenues of $35.0 million, respectively. Net income was projected at 4.5 to 5.0 million in 1981 and $6.5 million in 1982.

However, another large New York brokerage firm was not as enthusiastic about SafeCard. One of its analysts (named as a defendant in the SafeCard suit) cautioned its clients not to buy SafeCard's stock, citing the negative comments about SafeCard in a number of *Barron's* articles (see below) as well as his own negative points. Nevertheless, on June 15, 1981, SafeCard's stock reached a yearly high of $24.75 bid in the over-the-counter market.

Barron's Articles

During the period June 1978 through July 1981, *Barron's National Business and Financial Weekly* carried four separate stories concerning SafeCard Services, Inc. In general, the four pieces all questioned SafeCard's marketing and/or accounting practices. The first three stories appeared in *Barron's* weekly column "Up and Down Wall Street," written by Alan Abelson, *Barron's* managing editor. The fourth and most recent article ran in the July 6, 1981, issue of *Barron's* and was written by Professor Abraham J. Briloff.

Apart from being regarded as an expert accountant, Professor Briloff is considered by many to be one of the foremost critics of accounting and the accounting profession. Through his books *Unaccountable Accounting, More Debits than Credits*, and *The Truth about Corporate Accounting*, Dr. Briloff has taken companies and accounting firms to task for allegedly allowing the public to be misled by companies' accounting policies.

At the 1976 congressional "Metcalf Hearings" concerning proposed government regulation of the accounting profession, Professor Briloff provided expert testimony critical of accounting and accountants. He has also been a regular contributor to *Barron's*, as well as other academic and business journals, in which his articles have primarily focused on the shortcomings of specific companies' accounting practices.

Professor Briloff's analyses have not been ignored by the stock market. In an article entitled "In Defense of Fundamental Investment Analysis," published in the January/February 1975 issue of the *Financial Analysts Journal*, Leopold Bernstein noted "sharp declines" in the prices of companies criticized by Briloff. In a more rigorous academic study, published in the spring 1979 issue of the *Journal of Accounting Research*, Professor George Foster used a version of the capital asset pricing model to examine the risk-adjusted security market reaction to companies criticized by Briloff.

Professor Foster studied articles published by Briloff between 1968 and 1976, most of which appeared in *Barron's*, and all of which were based on publicly available information. Professor Foster concluded that "companies whose accounting practices are criticized by Briloff appear, on average, to suffer an immediate drop in price of approximately 8 percent. Using a 30-trading-day postannouncement period, this drop is a permanent one."

In his article on SafeCard, Professor Briloff focused his attention on footnote 3 of SafeCard's 1980 annual report. According to Professor Briloff, "the key to SafeCard's accounting is spelled out in . . . footnote 3." The following excerpts from the July 6, 1981, *Barron's* article summarize Dr. Briloff's analysis:

> The effect of this accounting approach [i.e., as described in footnote 3] is graphically evident in SafeCard's balance sheet. Capitalized marketing costs amounted to $7.3 million on October 31, 1978, and $20.4 million on October 31, 1980. On April 30, 1981, the total—which includes prepaid direct marketing costs, carried among current assets, and deferred direct marketing costs—stood at $25 million.

*   *   *   *   *   *

> My main misgivings with SafeCard's accounting center on those escalating cost deferrals.

*   *   *   *   *   *

> As a general rule, cost deferrals are comprehensible to the extent that they seek to match costs with revenues. But—and in SafeCard's case, this is a very big but—as the company's footnote suggests, SafeCard is matching most costs not only against revenues but also against extended expectations. And this is where the concern and its auditors, as I see it, part company with proper accounting.

*   *   *   *   *   *

> I maintain that the company, in fact, is engaged in accounting no-nos. When queried by me, the company's management and its auditors responded by asserting that they were following the "matching process," i.e., the matching of costs against related revenues. As I suggested, this is fine, up to a point. But SafeCard, I submit, is carrying this concept to an extreme.

> Thus, it is matching increased costs not only against revenues presumed to have been derived from those outlays, but also, as noted, those expected to be derived in the future. Trouble is, the latter is expected to be derived over as much as a decade through renewals, which may or may not materialize and which make little, if any, allowance for heightened competition or changing technology. And here is where I contend that SafeCard's management and auditors have departed from a fair application of generally accepted accounting principles, with a consequent distortion of the company's financial statements.

*   *   *   *   *   *

> Starting with fiscal 1980, a new wrinkle was introduced into SafeCard's accounting. Specifically, SafeCard stretched the amortization period of its Hot-Line deferred costs from a 3 to a 10-year period.

*   *   *   *   *   *

Especially noteworthy is the dynamics of the switch-over. The impact grows from quarter to quarter, because with each succeeding quarter, yet another quarter, at a reduced amortization rate, is picked up (and a quarter of the older three-year schedule is dropped). Then, too, the 10-year schedule applies to bigger amounts of expenditures, so that the effect of the stretch-out is compounded. And let the reader be forewarned: the quarterly impact on the 1981 earnings will be even greater, and as a consequence, the comparison with prior years will be more questionable.

By way of conclusion, I quote from a recent statement of Donald Kirk, chairman of the Financial Accounting Standards Board: "A primary objective of financial reporting is to provide information that helps investors, creditors, and others assess the amounts, timing, and uncertainty of prospective net cash inflows to an enterprise. Earnings information is certainly useful in assessing an enterprise's present and continuing ability to generate favorable cash flows, but it doesn't tell the whole story." SafeCard Services is very much a case in point.

The weeks surrounding the Briloff article were periods of significant volatility and downward pressure on SafeCard's stock price. After reaching

EXHIBIT 1
SafeCard Services, Inc.

SafeCard Services, Incorporated, Market Information
The daily share volume, closing bid quotations, and P/E ratios surrounding the mid-1981 events affecting SafeCard are presented below:

Period (day ending) 1981:	Share Volume	Closing Bid	P/E*
June 15	26,900	$24.75	42
16	9,000	23.50	40
17	4,900	23.25	40
18	41,900	20.50	35
19	13,000	20.50	35
22	11,400	20.75	35
23	10,200	21.50	37
24	4,800	21.50	37
25	15,400	22.25	38
26	15,300	22.00	38
29	27,800	20.75	35
30	26,200	19.00	32
July 1	24,100	16.75	29
2	27,500	15.50	26
6	50,300	14.50	25
7	38,600	16.00	27
8	33,100	16.00	27
9	6,300	16.00	27
10	4,600	16.00	27

NOTE: The traditional sources, i.e., Value Line, Merrill Lynch, etc., for betas have not computed a beta for SafeCard. Prior to November 1977, SafeCard's stock traded on a very limited basis and was not readily quoted. Beta is normally computed from at least 60 months of stock price data.
* P/E ratio is based on latest reported annual earnings.

EXHIBIT 2
SafeCard Services, Inc.

SafeCard Services, Incorporated, Management Remuneration

The following table sets forth information concerning remuneration paid or accrued by SafeCard during the fiscal year ended October 31, 1980, to the four most highly compensated executive officers of SafeCard, each of whose aggregate remuneration exceeded $50,000, and the aggregate remuneration paid or accrued to all directors and officers as a group:

Name of Individual or Group	Capacity in which Served	Salaries, Commissions, and Bonuses
Peter A. Halmos	Chairman of the board, chief executive officer, and secretary	$ 250,000*
Steven J. Halmos	President and chief operating officer	250,000*
Vince W. Harmann	Senior vice president	297,346†
Joanne J. Seehousen	Executive vice president	63,415
All officers and directors as a group (11 persons)		1,045,196‡

---

* SafeCard does not pay salaries directly to Peter A. Halmos or Steven J. Halmos, but instead pays a management fee for their services to Halmos & Company, Inc., which Messrs. Halmos control. In March 1979, SafeCard entered into a two-year management agreement with Halmos & Company, Inc., for the services of both officers. This agreement has been extended to March 1983. Pursuant to this management agreement, Peter A. Halmos and Steven J. Halmos each received in fiscal 1980, and will receive in each of the next two years, an annual base management fee of $75,000 plus a maximum bonus of $175,000 based upon a percentage of SafeCard revenues. The annual bonuses for fiscal 1980 were paid during fiscal 1980.

† SafeCard does not pay a salary to Vince W. Harmann, but instead pays commissions to Vince W. Harmann Associates, Inc., a marketing consulting company of which Mr. Harmann is the sole shareholder. The commissions are based upon revenues derived from certain marketing programs, net of certain costs and adjustments, and represent remuneration for Mr. Harmann's development and continuing assistance with such programs. Mr. Harmann is responsible for all costs incurred by his company in connection with his duties with SafeCard.

‡ Excludes approximately $9,000 paid as fees to a director for consulting services not related to his duties as a director of SafeCard.

---

a yearly high of $24.75 bid on June 15, 1981, SafeCard's stock price began a steady decline. On June 29, 1981, the Monday following the June 26 filing of the SafeCard suit, its stock closed at $20.75 bid, down $1.25 from the previous trading session. On July 1, 1981, the date of *Barron's* publisher's reply to the SafeCard suit, its stock closed at $16.75 bid, down $2.25 from the previous day. On Monday July 6, 1981, the first trading day after the appearance of the Briloff article in *Barron's*, SafeCard's stock closed at $14.50 bid, down $1.00 from the last trading session.

Exhibit 1 provides more detailed market information regarding Safe-Card. Exhibit 2 gives information concerning SafeCard's management. Exhibit 3 is SafeCard's second quarter (fiscal 1981) financial statements to shareholders (issued on June 12, 1981). Exhibit 4 is a combined version of SafeCard's 1980 annual report to shareholders and form 10-K.

The firm's CPA, Alexander Grant & Company, issued a "clean opinion" dated December 12, 1980, following its examination of the 1980 financial statements.

EXHIBIT 3
SafeCard Services, Inc.

SafeCard Services, Incorporated, Financial Statements to Shareholders for Fiscal Second Quarter 1981

Consolidated Income Statement
(in thousands)

	Three Months Ended April 30		Six Months Ended April 30	
	1981	*1980*	*1981*	*1980*
Revenues:				
Sales of service programs	$6,193	$3,508	$11,446	$6,616
Other	476	212	805	492
Net revenue	$6,669	$3,720	$12,251	$7,108
Operating costs and expenses:				
Cost of service programs	3,420	1,702	6,312	3,214
General and administrative	748	485	1,414	1,063
Other expenses	6	64	36	121
Total expenses	$4,174	$2,251	$ 7,762	$4,398
Earnings before income taxes	$2,495	$1,469	$ 4,489	$2,710
Income taxes:				
Currently payable	—	—	—	—
Deferred	1,215	715	2,187	1,320
Total income taxes	$1,215	$ 715	$ 2,187	$1,320
Net earnings	$1,280	$ 754	$ 2,302	$1,390
Earnings per common share	$0.24	$0.15	$0.43	$0.27
Weighted average common shares (adjusted for May 1981 stock split)	5,312	5,199	5,304	5,199

Consolidated Balance Sheet
(in thousands)

Assets	4/30/81	10/31/80	4/30/80
Current assets:			
Cash and certificates of deposit	$10,133	$ 7,111	$ 5,490
Short-term investments—at cost	2	3	3
Accounts receivable	1,572	6,588	2,440
Prepaid direct marketing costs	9,758	8,976	6,841
Total current assets	$21,465	$22,678	$14,774
Property, equipment, and leasehold improvements—net	662	616	560
Deferred charges and other:			
Deferred direct marketing costs	15,240	11,362	8,146
Other assets	36	36	33
	$15,276	$11,398	$ 8,179
Total assets	$37,403	$34,693	$23,513
Liabilities and Stockholders' Equity			
Current liabilities:			
Accounts payable	$ 622	$ 1,803	$ 408
Accrued expenses	54	123	222
Allowance for cancellations	3,590	4,734	2,038
Total current liabilities excluding deferred credits	$ 4,266	$ 6,660	$ 2,668

EXHIBIT 3 *(concluded)*

	4/30/81	10/31/80	4/30/80
Deferred credits:			
Customers' advance payments	10,685	10,070	5,974
Deferred income taxes	1,483	1,185	1,290
Total liabilities	$16,434	$17,915	$ 9,932
Deferred income taxes	7,388	5,499	3,956
Stockholders' equity:			
Common stock.........................	26	26	13
Additional paid-in capital	3,851	3,851	3,865
Retained earnings	9,715	7,413	5,747
	$13,592	$11,290	$ 9,625
Less: 4,000 treasury shares	(11)	(11)	—
Total stockholders' equity	$13,581	$11,279	$ 9,625
Total liabilities and stockholders' equity	$37,403	$34,693	$23,513

Exhibit 4
SafeCard Services, Inc.

Excerpts from SafeCard Services, Incorporated, 1980
Annual Report and 10-K
Financial Highlights
Years Ended October 31
(in thousands, except earnings per share)

	1980	1979	1978	1977	1976
Net revenue	$16,137	$12,499	$ 8,327	$4,699	$1,225
Operating costs and expenses	10,323	$ 8,795	$ 5,792	3,079	697
Earnings before taxes and extraordinary credit	$ 5,814	$ 3,704	$ 2,535	$1,620	$ 528
Income taxes	2,758	1,745	1,174	795	264
Earnings before extraordinary credit	$ 3,056	$ 1,959	$ 1,361	$ 825	$264
Extraordinary credit	—	—	—	—	52
Net earnings	$ 3,056	$ 1,959	$ 1,361	$ 825	$ 316
Net earnings per share*	$1.17	$.76	$.54	$.46	$.18
Weighted average number of common and common equivalent shares*	2,609	2,584	2,534	1,792	1,790
Total assets	$34,693	$19,577	$14,080	$4,114	$1,747
Net worth	$11,279	$ 8,154	$ 6,195	$1,288	$ 464
Long-term debt	$ 0	$ 0	$ 0	0	$ 0
Working capital	$ 4,763	$ 5,143	$3,778	$ 144	$ 110
Retained earnings	$ 7,413	$ 4,357	$ 2,397	$1,037	$ 212

SafeCard had approximately 85 and 74 full-time employees at October 31, 1980, and October 31, 1979, respectively. The number of shareholders at October 31, 1980, and October 31, 1979, was approximately 640 and 1,400, respectively.

The per-share figures and common stock outstanding figures *do not* reflect the two-for-one stock split of May 20, 1981. The annual report was issued five months before this split.

* Adjusted for the stock splits in the form of 100 percent dividends paid September 23, 1980, and June 23, 1978.

EXHIBIT 4 *(continued)*

Message to Shareholders

1980 was a good year.

Revenue and income increased substantially for the sixth straight record year. Please carefully review the financial statements included in this report.

SafeCard is established as the country's premier direct mail marketer and operator of continuity consumer service programs . . . recurring services including replaceable products for which consumers pay annually.

New customer enrollments are the target of SafeCard's marketing efforts. Last year, solicitations for new customer enrollments reached the milestone of 100 million pieces of direct mail advertising. This marketing investment of approximately $13 million was financed totally from cash flow.

To make certain that SafeCard's excellent customer service capability is maintained, the company is moving into an expanded operations facility which is equipped to accommodate the anticipated growth in the company's business volume.

We are pleased with SafeCard's progress, but not satisfied. We are working hard to maintain—and accelerate—SafeCard's growth.

Sincerely,

Peter A. Halmos,
Chairman

Steven J. Halmos,
President

Introduction

SafeCard is a unique marketing organization strategically positioned in the rapidly growing mail order and credit card industries.

Mail order, the fastest growing segment of retailing, represents a $35–$40 billion industry that has grown at an average annual rate of 15 percent over the past five years. By combining the use of credit cards and toll-free telephone lines, nonstore shopping by mail becomes even more convenient than in the past. The convenience of mail order, the rising number of employed women creating more dual-income families and/or single-person households, as well as time-saving advantages, are expected to dramatically increase the direct-to-consumer marketing business.

To date, SafeCard has targeted its direct-to-consumer marketing activities to credit card users through the sponsorship of many of the largest credit card companies in the United States. Through these credit card companies, SafeCard's potential audience of customers is estimated to be approximately 75 million credit card users.

SafeCard's mailings are made to the credit card customers of sponsoring credit card issuers in a variety of formats: enclosures with monthly credit card statements, direct mail, and others. Last year, SafeCard joined a select handful of companies, whose volume exceeded 100 million pieces of mail.

As the premier direct-to-consumer marketer and operator of continuity service programs (that is, programs which include ongoing annual renewals), SafeCard is well positioned to expand the number and scope of its marketing activities. While the Hot-Line credit card protection system contributed practically all of SafeCard's 1980 revenue the Date Reminder Service Program (which includes the DateMinder Calendar and/or Almanac Appointment Book) has been very well received and should produce an estimated $8 million in revenue by 1982. Marketing of the *Guinness Book of World Records* and *The World Almanac and Book of Facts* Reference Service programs commenced recently and is anticipated to be a meaningful source of revenue by 1983. The Reference Service is a telephone source of the data contained in these extraordinarily popular publications and is envisioned to be a source of up-to-date information such as new world records and important facts as they occur. SafeCard has the exclusive direct mail marketing rights to the hardcover editions of the *Guinness Book of World Records* and *The World Almanac and Book of Facts* in the credit card industry.

SafeCard has demonstrated the in-house capability to develop new marketing programs to meet the constantly changing interests of consumers. The variety of SafeCard's service programs and the nationwide market for such programs now enables the company to explore new mass-marketing methods. Whereas direct mail marketing has been SafeCard's sole means of advertising, other customer solicitation methods such as print media (newspapers, magazines), television, and radio appear to offer exciting long-term potential.

EXHIBIT 4 *(continued)*

As a nationwide direct-to-consumer marketing organization having a variety of proprietary continuity service programs, Safe-Card appears strategically positioned for continuing growth.

Hot-Line Credit Card Bureau of America . . .

. . . the nation's leading credit card loss notification service. Credit card holders register their credit cards with SafeCard for confidential protection. In the event of credit card loss or theft, customers may call SafeCard's toll-free telephone number 24 hours a day, report the loss/theft, and request that notifications be flashed to all indicated credit card companies. A variety of other credit card and convenience related services are also included. Hot-Line continues to enjoy great popularity in a national market of an estimated 100 million credit card users.

The Date Reminder Service Program with the Almanac Appointment Book . . .

. . . in just three years has grown to more than 700,000 enrollments for the 1981 edition. Each fall, enrolling customers receive, along with the Date Reminder Service, a 7¼″ × 9½″ deluxe annual Almanac Appointment Book. In addition to a diary section, each annual edition contains a variety of useful information to make it a valuable addition to home or office. The Date Reminder Service allows customers to register important dates and events (such as birthdays, anniversaries, etc.) which SafeCard stores in its computer system. On a regular basis, customers receive a computer-printed reminder of each registered event. Since customers may add or delete reminder dates at any time by simply calling SafeCard's toll-free telephone number, the program has become popular in a very short period of time.

The Date Reminder Service Program with the DateMinder Calendar . . .

. . . like the Almanac Appointment Book Program, has grown to more than 600,000 enrollments for the 1981 edition in just three years. In addition to the Date Reminder Service (explained with Appointment Book), enrolling customers receive annual editions of the 24″ × 37″ plastic-laminated Date-Minder wall calendar. It comes complete with a special marker for easy writing-on and wiping-off of notations on the plastic surface, as well as a variety of related materials. The customer even has a choice of either a vertical or horizontal format printed on opposite sides of the calendar, each offering one convenient place for noting activities for an entire year at a glance.

Reference Service with the Guinness Book of World Records/The World Almanac and Book of Facts . . .

. . . one of SafeCard's newest continuity service programs. Each year, enrolling customer's receive, along with the Reference Service, the latest annual hardcover edition of *The Guinness Book of World Records* and/or *The World Almanac and Book of Facts.* These very popular publications contain many thousands of records and facts from sports, science, nature, and entertainment, as well as little-known phenomena. The Reference Service not only puts all this information at a subscriber's fingertips via SafeCard's toll-free telephone lines, but is envisioned to be a source of up-to-date information as facts or events change.

Farm Fresh Shrimp Corporation

Farm Fresh's shrimp reproduction and cultivation research has been completed. The efficiency of Farm Fresh's technology appears to be far ahead of competing methods. However, Farm Fresh's shrimp yield is composed of small size shrimp of approximately three inches in length.

Today's market conditions favor larger size shrimp. For this reason, marketing of shrimp in the form of shrimp products appears to offer greater profit potential for Farm Fresh (at this time) than producing shrimp. The business plan for Farm Fresh is to develop processed shrimp products and implement a market testing program. Accordingly, emphasis on the marketing of shrimp products has created changes in the management and priorities of Farm Fresh.

Conventional methods of shrimp boat harvesting of the oceans appear outdated and inefficient. The cost of the fuel, labor, and equipment used in searching the oceans for a limited natural shrimp population should eventually force a reallocation of these resources to more efficient uses. To the contrary, Farm Fresh's technology: (1) is factory production . . . as opposed to "farming" or searching for shrimp with boats; (2) creates a renewable resource . . . rather than depleting the natural shrimp population, Farm Fresh reproduces "baby" shrimp at a rate estimated to be 125,000 times more efficient than nature; and

EXHIBIT 4 *(continued)*

(3) is production efficient . . . use of energy, labor, and land is minimal as contrasted to competing methods such that inflation should have a comparatively limited impact on Farm Fresh's future variable costs of production.

Market Prices

The high, low, and closing bid quotations of SafeCard's common stock traded in the over-the-counter market through December 31, 1980, are as follows (adjusted for the stock splits in the form of 100 percent dividends paid September 23, 1980, and June 23, 1978).

Period (quarter ending)	High	Bid Low	Close
1978: January 31	$6.00	$4.875	$5.25
April 30	$8.56	$5.31	$8.125
July 31............	$15.25	$3.25	$9.125
October 31	$9.50	$4.75	$4.75
1979: January 31	$6.875	$4.875	$6.75
April 30	$8.00	$5.875	$7.375
July 31............	$7.375	$2.81	$6.25
October 31	$7.25	$4.625	$6.00
1980: January 31	$7.375	$5.75	$7.00
April 30	$7.125	$4.375	$4.875
July 31............	$7.125	$4.75	$7.00
October 31	$17.25	$7.00	$15.25
December 31, 1980			$16.50

SAFECARD SERVICES, INCORPORATED, AND SUBSIDIARY
Consolidated Statements of Earnings

			Years Ended October 31		
	1980	1979	1978	1977	1976
			(in thousands, except per-share data)		
Revenues:					
Direct mail marketing revenues—net (note A3):					
Sales of service programs	$ 15,261	$ 9,965	$ 5,206	$ 2,641	$ 1,163
Sales of merchandise	39	1,910	2,792	1,839	—
Interest and other income...........	837	624	329	219	62
Net revenue recognized	$ 16,137	$ 12,499	$ 8,327	$ 4,699	$ 1,225
Operating costs and expenses:					
Costs of service programs (note A3)	7,846	5,073	2,211	1,124	531
Costs of merchandise (note A3)	15	2,039	2,664	1,592	—
General and administrative expenses	2,245	1,467	785	277	138
Other expenses (note A5)	217	216	132	86	28
	$ 10,323	$ 8,795	$ 5,792	$ 3,079	$ 697
Earnings before taxes and extraordinary credit	$ 5,814	$ 3,704	$ 2,535	$ 1,620	$ 528
Income taxes: (notes A4 and C)					
Current	—	—	—	—	—
Deferred	$ 2,758	$ 1,745	$ 1,174	$ 795	$ 264
	$ 2,758	$ 1,745	$ 1,174	$ 795	$ 264
Earnings before extraordinary credit...........................	$ 3,056	$ 1,959	$ 1,361	$ 825	$ 264
Extraordinary credit—reduction of deferred income taxes arising from effect of prior years' accounting losses	—	—	—	—	$ 52
Net earnings	$ 3,056	$ 1,959	$ 1,361	$ 825	$ 316
Earnings per share (note F):					
Earnings before extraordinary credit...........................	$ 1.17	$ .76	$ .54	$ .46	$ .15
Extraordinary credit	—	—	—	—	.03
Net earnings	$ 1.17	$ .76	$ .54	$ .46	$ .18
Weighted average number of common and common equivalent shares (note F)	2,608,944	2,583,694	2,533,692	1,791,600	1,789,600

Note references refer to the notes to the financial statements included elsewhere herein.

EXHIBIT 4 *(continued)*

SAFECARD SERVICES, INCORPORATED, AND SUBSIDIARY
Consolidated Balance Sheets
October 31
(in thousands)

	1980	1979	1978
Assets			
Current assets:			
Cash, consisting substantially of certificates of deposit	$ 7,111	$ 7,171	$ 3,861
Short-term investments—at cost which approximates market	3	3	3
Accounts receivable, less allowances (note A3)	6,588	2,285	2,544
Prepaid direct marketing costs (note A3)	8,976	4,813	3,370
Total	$22,678	$14,272	$ 9,778
Property, equipment, and leasehold improvements— at cost, less accumulated depreciation and amortization (notes A2 and B)	617	403	372
Deferred charges and other:			
Deferred direct marketing costs (note A3)	11,363	4,868	3,875
Other assets	35	34	54
	$11,398	$ 4,902	$ 3,929
Total assets	$34,693	$19,577	$14,079
Liabilities and Stockholders' Equity			
Current liabilities:			
Accounts payable	$ 1,803	$ 661	$ 337
Accrued expenses	123	8	87
Allowance for cancellations (note A3)	4,734	1,573	1,113
Total current liabilities, excluding deferred credits	$ 6,660	$ 2,242	$ 1,537
Deferred credits:			
Customers' advance payments (note A3)	10,070	5,255	4,166
Deferred income taxes (note A4 and C)	1,185	1,632	297
Total	$17,915	$ 9,129	$ 6,000
Deferred income taxes (notes A4 and C)	5,499	2,294	1,884
Commitments and contingencies (notes D and G)	—	—	—
Stockholders' equity (notes E and H):			
Common stock—authorized, 5 million shares of $.01 par value; issued and outstanding 2,596,400 shares in 1980 and 1,291,800 in 1979 and 1978	26	13	13
Additional paid-in capital	3,852	3,785	3,785
	$ 3,878	$ 3,798	$ 3,798
Retained earnings	7,412	4,356	2,397
	$11,290	$ 8,154	$ 6,195
Less: Cost of 2,000 common shares in treasury	(11)	—	—
	$11,279	$ 8,154	$ 6,195
Total liabilities and stockholders' equity	$34,693	$19,577	$14,079

EXHIBIT 4 *(continued)*

SAFECARD SERVICES, INCORPORATED, AND SUBSIDIARY
Consolidated Statements of Changes in Financial Position
Years Ended October 31
(in thousands)

	1980	1979	1978
Sources of working capital:			
From operations:			
Net earnings	$ 3,056	$ 1,959	$ 1,361
Charges to earnings not using working capital:			
Depreciation and amortization (note A2)	172	141	95
Issuance of common shares in litigation settlement	80	—	—
Deferred income taxes (note A4 and C)	3,205	410	1,277
Working capital provided from operations	$ 6,513	$ 2,510	$ 2,733
Sale of property and equipment	—	—	4
Proceeds from sale of common stock through public offering	—	—	3,624
Proceeds from sale of common stock under stock option plan	—	—	65
	$ 6,513	$ 2,510	$ 6,425
Applications of working capital:			
Additions to property, equipment, and leasehold improvements	$ 386	$ 171	$ 234
Direct marketing costs	6,494	993	2,396
Other assets	2	(20)	20
Purchase of common shares for treasury	11	—	—
Expenses of public offering	—	—	142
	$ 6,893	$ 1,144	$ 2,792
Increase (decrease) in working capital	$ (380)	$ 1,366	$ 3,634
Changes in components of working capital:			
Increase (decrease) in current assets:			
Cash and certificates of deposit	$ (60)	$ 3,309	$ 3,132
Short-term investments	—	—	(12)
Accounts receivable	4,303	(258)	2,195
Prepaid direct marketing costs	4,163	1,443	2,100
	$ 8,406	$ 4,494	$ 7,415
(Increase) decrease in current liabilities:			
Accounts payable and accrued expenses	$(1,257)	$ (245)	$ 178
Notes payable to officer	—	—	10
Allowance for cancellations	(3,161)	(460)	(996)
Customers' advance payments	(4,815)	(1,088)	(3,076)
Deferred income taxes	447	(1,335)	103
	$(8,786)	$(3,128)	$(3,781)
Increase (decrease) in working capital	$ (380)	$ 1,366	$ 3,634

EXHIBIT 4 *(continued)*

SAFECARD SERVICES, INCORPORATED, AND SUBSIDIARY
Consolidated Statements of Stockholders' Equity
Years Ended October 31, 1980, 1979, and 1978
(in thousands)

	Common Stock	Additional Paid-In Capital	Retained Earnings	Common Stock in Treasury	Total
Balance at November 1, 1977	$ 3	$ 248	$1,037	$ —	$ 1,287
Net earnings for the year	—	—	1,361	—	1,361
Exercise of options	1	64	—	—	65
Shares issued through public offering ..	2	3,480	—	—	3,482
Stock split in the form of a 100% dividend	7	(7)	—	—	—
Balance at October 31, 1978	$13	$3,785	$2,397	$ —	$ 6,195
Net earnings for the year	—	—	1,959	—	1,959
Balance at October 31, 1979	$13	$3,785	$4,356	—	$ 8,154
Net earnings for the year	—	—	3,056	—	3,056
Shares issued in settlement of litigation	—	80	—	—	80
Purchase of 4,000 common shares for treasury	—	—	—	$(11)	(11)
Stock split in the form of a 100% dividend	13	(13)	—	—	—
Balance at October 31, 1980	$26	$3,852	$7,412	$(11)	$11,279

The accompanying notes are an integral part of these statements.

SAFECARD SERVICES, INCORPORATED, AND SUBSIDIARY
Notes to Consolidated Financial Statements
October 31, 1980, 1979, and 1978

Note A—Summary of Accounting Policies
The company is engaged in the mass direct mail marketing of consumer service programs, and through its 82 percent-owned subsidiary is developing technology for the production of a species of shrimp under controlled conditions. Operations of the subsidiary are not significant.

1. Principles of Consolidation

The consolidated financial statements include the accounts of the company and its subsidiary, Farm Fresh Shrimp Corporation, since the date of acquisition. Intercompany accounts and transactions have been eliminated in consolidation.

2. Plant, Equipment, and Leasehold Improvements

Depreciation and amortization are provided for in amounts sufficient to relate the cost of depreciable assets to operations over their estimated service lives or, in the case of certain leasehold improvements, the lives of the respective leases, whichever is shorter. The straight-line method is used for both financial statement and income tax reporting purposes. Maintenance, repairs, and minor renewals are charged to operations as incurred. Improvements and major renewals of major facilities are capitalized. Upon sale or disposition of properties, the asset account is relieved of the cost and the accumulated depreciation account is charged with depreciation taken prior to the sale and any resultant gain or loss is credited or charged to earnings.

3. Income Recognition—Direct Mail Marketing

a. Services. The company receives an advance payment from customers who subscribe to its services. The subscription period and advance payment is generally for the ensuing 12-month period, multiyear subscriptions not being material. Accordingly, these advance payments, less an appropriate provision for cancellations, are deferred and amortized over the subscription period. Commissions

EXHIBIT 4 *(continued)*

paid in connection with such revenues are also deferred and amortized over the same 12-month period. Most customers enroll for a 12-month period; however, based upon the company's experience, the majority of customers renew their subscription for additional years beyond the initial 12-month enrollment period. Accordingly, marketing costs directly related to these customers are deferred and amortized over the anticipated benefit period, generally 3 to 10 years, principally on a declining balance basis, depending upon the depth of experience that the company has had with each of its programs. All amounts deferred are continually monitored, and if required, are adjusted when the future benefit period is shorter than anticipated.

In 1980, the company began amortizing costs in connection with new customers of its Hot-Line program, its longest established program, over a 10-year period on the declining balance method, which anticipates a customer renewal rate of not less than 75 percent to better match these costs with the related income benefit period. Under this method, it

marketing test costs, and other direct costs incurred in connection with these sales were charged to operations in the month sales were recognized. Other indirect costs were charged to operations as incurred.

4. Income Taxes

The company capitalizes certain direct marketing costs for financial reporting purposes, whereas these costs are deducted as incurred for income tax reporting purposes. Accordingly, deferred taxes have been provided on the timing differences resulting therefrom.

5. Research and Development Costs

Research and development costs of Farm Fresh Shrimp Corporation are charged to expense in the period incurred. The amounts charged to Other Expenses were approximately $215,000 both in 1980 and 1979, and $195,000 in 1978.

Note B—Property, Equipment, and Leasehold Improvements

Property, equipment, and leasehold improvements are as follows:

Category	Estimated Useful Life	1980	1979	1978
Furniture and fixtures	5–8 years	$ 670,000	$353,000	$247,000
Transportation equipment	3 years	166,000	112,000	60,000
Leasehold improvements—office (note G)	5 years	83,000	77,000	67,000
Leasehold improvements—hatchery . . .	life of lease	154,000	154,000	154,000
		$1,073,000	$696,000	$528,000
Less: Accumulated depreciation and amortization		456,000	293,000	156,000
		$ 617,000	$403,000	$372,000

is anticipated that approximately 80 percent of the costs would be amortized in five years. Prior to 1980, these costs were being amortized over a three-year period in a manner which approximated the declining balance method. No change in the estimated benefit period was made for those deferred costs for which amortization had begun prior to 1980. The effect on the results of operations of the change in 1980 was not material.

b. Merchandise. In 1980, the company eliminated merchandise sales and all company programs now being marketed are service based. However, in 1979 the company did sell merchandise and its merchandise sales and related cost of merchandise were recognized in the month in which the product was billed; shipment to customers in most cases was being made directly by the supplier. Commissions,

Note C—Income Taxes

Deferred income taxes represent amounts payable in future years as a result of certain timing differences, after giving effect to loss carryforwards and tax credits available. The principal differences in timing involve *(a)* marketing costs deducted for tax purposes but deferred over periods of benefit for financial statement purposes, and *(b)* service billings recorded prior to 1976 as income for tax purposes as to which the Internal Revenue Service has permitted the change over a 6-year period to conform to the company's method of recognition over a 12-month period of service. At October 31, 1980, and 1979, the company had available for tax purposes net operating losses of approximately $5,940,000 and

EXHIBIT 4 *(continued)*

$1.6 million, respectively. In addition, at October 31, 1980, and 1979, the company had investment tax credits of approximately $60,000 through 1987 and $35,000 through 1986, respectively, all of which have been utilized in reducing deferred taxes.

The components of deferred taxes are as follows:

	1980	1979	1978
Deferred marketing costs	$ 5,190,000	$1,186,000	$ 2,231,000
Utilization of net operating losses	(2,407,000)	569,000	(1,044,000)
Other	(25,000)	(10,000)	(13,000)
	$ 2,758,000	$1,745,000	$ 1,174,000

Note D—Commitments and Contingencies

The company does not pay salaries to two of its officers, but instead pays a fee for their services under a two-year management agreement ending March 1981 to a company controlled by these two officers. Each officer receives an aggregate annual base fee of $75,000 plus a bonus of 2 percent of the corporation's net revenue recognized from direct mail programs up to a maximum of $125,000 and $175,000 each in fiscal years 1979 and 1980, respectively. Also, see note G for lease of facilities from these officers.

As part of the acquisition of Farm Fresh, the company has agreed to pay dividends to the minority stockholders of Farm Fresh in any year in which the net earnings of Farm Fresh exceed $200,000. None have been required through October 31, 1980.

The company has arrangements to pay commissions in connection with its direct mail marketing programs. Certain of these arrangements are with a related party (note G.)

The company has written agreements with a few large credit card issuers which account for a large percentage of its direct mail marketing revenues. The company would be adversely affected if any of these agreements were to be terminated.

Note E—Common Stock and Stock Options

In September 1980, the board of directors declared a stock split in the form of a 100 percent dividend to be paid on October 23, 1980, to stockholders on record on October 9, 1980. The shares and exercise prices described below have been adjusted to reflect all stock distributions.

The nonqualified stock option plan established in 1979 for key employees (not directors) owning less than 5 percent of the company's common stock provides for granting of options for not more than 26,000 shares of common stock at fair market value at the time options are granted. The options have a term of five years, but become void at the time of termination of employment. Under this plan, options to purchase 12,000 shares of common stock at $4.625 per share ($55,500 in aggregate) were granted during 1979. During 1980, the optionees personally and unconditionally obligated themselves to pay the exercise price of the options within the term of the options. Options to purchase 5,500 shares at $4.75 per share ($26,125 in aggregate) and 1,500 shares at $5.125 per share ($7,687.50 in aggregate) were granted during 1980. Options issued during 1980 contain the additional restriction which states that shares issued upon exercise of options must be returned to the company with the exercise price being refunded to the employee if termination of employment occurs within three years of the date of grant of the options.

In June 1980, stock options to purchase 2,000 shares of common stock at fair market value were granted to a former officer of Safe-Card for his development and continuing assistance with certain marketing programs (see note G), at which time the former officer personally and unconditionally obligated himself to pay the exercise price of the options within the five-year term of the options.

In June 1977, the company, upon advise of counsel, believed that options for 52,000 shares of common stock issued under the 1969 Qualified Stock Option Plan had been granted in violation of the terms of the 1969 plan by being granted to directors who were not also employees of the company. Therefore, options granted for 52,000 shares with an exercise price of $.125 per share were voided based upon this belief. On November 15, 1977, the Qualified Stock Option Plan was terminated. During 1980, the company determined that the grant of those options was not in violation of the plan and therefore, in August 1980, the company granted stock options for 52,000 shares to the directors whose options were voided and stock options for 4,000 shares to an employee who was unable to exercise options due to cancellation of the plan,

EXHIBIT 4 *(concluded)*

at fair market value at the time of the current grant, at which time they personally and unconditionally obligated themselves to pay the exercise price of the options within the five-year term of the options.

Information for the years ended October 31, 1980, and 1979, with respect to options granted is as follows:

shares outstanding, retroactive effect was given to all stock distributions as described in note E. Also, common stock equivalents are not antidilutive for any of the years.

Note G—Transactions with Related Parties
The company's operational facilities are rented on a year-to-year basis from the compa-

		Option Plan		Market Price	
	Number of Shares	Per Share	Total	Per Share	Total
Shares under option:					
October 31, 1979	12,000	$4.625	$ 55,500	$12.000	$ 144,000
October 31, 1980	77,000	$6.375	$490,875	$15.250	$1,174,250

At October 31, 1980, none of the above listed options had been exercised, with options for 7,000 shares still available for grant under the 1979 nonqualified stock option plan.

Note F—Earnings per Share
Earnings per share have been computed by dividing net earnings by the weighted average shares of common stock and common stock equivalents (common stock issuable upon exercise of the stock options) outstanding. In determining the weighted average number of common and common equivalent

ny's principal officers currently for approximately $132,000 annually.

In connection with the company's direct mail marketing programs, commissions are paid to another company controlled by a former officer of SafeCard. The commissions are based upon revenues derived from certain marketing programs and represent remuneration for the development and continuing assistance with such programs. Commissions paid to this officer's company were approximately $280,000 both in 1980 and 1979, and approximately $220,000 in 1978. The fee can be adjusted based on future revenues.

Note H—Unaudited Quarterly Financial Data
Quarter Ended

	January 31	April 30	July 31	October 31
1980:				
Revenues	$3,388,000	$3,720,000	$4,129,000	$4,900,000
Gross profit	$1,862,000	$2,010,000	$2,290,000	$2,114,000
Net earnings	$ 636,000	$ 754,000	$ 839,000	$ 827,000
Earnings per share (note F)	$ .24	$ .29	$ .32	$ .32
Weighted average number of common and common equivalent shares (note F) ...	2,596,400	2,599,624	2,600,144	2,625,213
1979*:				
Revenues	$3,027,000	$3,100,000	$3,222,000	$3,150,000
Gross profit	$1,278,000	$1,268,000	$1,543,000	$1,298,000
Net earnings	$ 475,000	$ 410,000	$ 515,000	$ 559,000
Earnings per share (note F)	$ .18	$ .16	$ .20	$ .22
Weighted average number of common and common equivalent shares (note F) ...	2,583,600	2,583,600	2,583,600	2,584,800

* The quarters ended January 31, April 30, and July 31, 1979, were adjusted from amounts as shown in the Form 10-Qs filed with the Securities and Exchange Commission due to expenses which should have been accrued in each quarter, but were erroneously omitted. The adjustments were not material to either quarter or to the year as a whole; therefore, no amendment was filed with the Securities and Exchange Commission.

Questions

1. Do you agree with SafeCard's accounting for marketing costs?[2] What accounting policy would you prefer?

2. Would you recommend the SafeCard stock as a "buy"?

---

[2] The following example may prove useful in understanding SafeCard's accounting for Hot-Line's marketing costs using a 10-year amortization period. Note that SafeCard reports to stockholders on an accrual basis, whereas for tax purposes it reports essentially on a cash basis. This is a conventional approach for suscriber businesses of this nature. The $12 Hot-Line revenue is amortized over the applicable year in the amount of approximately $1 per month. Marketing costs are deferred over a 10-year period employing a declining-balance method whereby 75 percent of these costs are amortized in the first 5 years.

Assume, for example, that the cost of acquiring 1,000 Hot-Line subscribers at $12 annually is $10,000 and the renewal rate is 80 percent. The amortization schedule would look something like this:

	Revenues	Amortization*
Year 1	$12,000	$2,300
Year 2	9,600	1,800
Year 3	7,700	1,400
Year 4	6,100	1,100
Year 5	4,900	900
Year 6, etc.	3,900, etc.	700, etc.

* $10,000 acquisition cost. Example does not include cost of service fulfillment.

CASE 18–4

A. G. Bartlett Corporation
Human Resources Accounting

The A. G. Bartlett Corporation had sales and earnings for 1985 of $25,310,588 and $700,222, respectively. For the 10 years ending with 1985, Bartlett's sales grew at a 20 percent compounded annual rate while earnings increased at a 21.5 percent rate.

Bartlett produced and marketed a broad line of leisure footwear and

---

This case was prepared by David Macey (under the direction of David F. Hawkins).

Copyright © 1970 by the President and Fellows of Harvard College

Harvard Business School case 171–027 (Rev. 1985)

related products. Its markets were characterized by intense price and style competition, which dictated that management have good internal controls. As part of its controls, Bartlett introduced in 1984, a "human asset accounting" concept.

The president's letter in the 1984 annual report stated under the subtitle "Organizational Assets":

> As managers, we are entrusted with the care of three types of assets: physicial assets, organizational assets, and customer loyalty assets. Each manager is responsible for effective utilization of these assets to create a profit for the organization while preserving the financial soundness of the business.
>
> If people are treated abusively, short-term profits will be derived at the expense of the company's organizational assets.
>
> Managers now work with accounting data which reflect the condition of physical assets and changes in these assets over a period of time. The assets of human resources and customer loyalty do not appear in dollar terms on the balance sheets. To employ effectively all three types of assets, and realize the objectives of A. G. Bartlett, equally reliable accounting instruments are required to reflect the condition of organizational assets and customer loyalty and changes in these assets over time.
>
> To fulfill these objectives we are now in the process of developing and installing a human resource accounting system to measure in dollar terms the organizational assets and changes in these assets over time.

In later sections of the 1984 report, "people—the human resources of the company" are referred to as that asset "without which all other assets become meaningless in terms of potential and future growth."

The initial development of this human asset accounting system was a joint effort by Bartlett and the Institute for Social Research.

Bartlett's commitment to human asset accounting was further articulated throughout its 1985 annual report:

> We set ambitious goals for profitable growth in 1985. We achieved these goals in the principal result areas of the business, namely, (1) to generate a profit on total resources employed, (2) to protect and improve the value of the financial, physical, organizational, and customer loyalty resources of the company, and (3) to manage profits to insure a sound financial position.
>
> The resources of the business are: (1) the financial resources available to the corporation; (2) the technological resources such as buildings, equipment, and production technology; (3) the human resources in terms of the skills and abilities possessed by the people who comprise the organization; (4) the proprietary resources such as corporate name, brand names, copyrights, and patents; (5) the information resources of the business which provide reliable data upon which to make timely decisions.

EXHIBIT 1
A. G. Bartlett Corporation and Subsidiaries,
Excerpts from 1986 Annual Report

Balance Sheet

	Financial and Human Resource	Financial Only
Assets		
Total current assets	$10,003,628	$10,003,628
Net property, plant, and equipment	1,770,717	1,770,717
Excess of purchase price of subsidiaries over net assets acquired	1,188,704	1,188,704
Net investments in human resources	986,094	—
Other assets	106,783	106,783
Total assets	$14,055,926	$13,069,832
Liabilities and Stockholders' Equity		
Total current liabilities	$ 5,715,708	$ 5,715,708
Long-term debt, excluding current installments	1,935,500	1,935,500
Deferred compensation	62,380	62,380
Deferred federal income taxes as a result of appropriation for human resources	493,047	—
Stockholders' equity:		
Capital stock	879,116	879,116
Additional capital in excess of par value	1,736,253	1,736,253
Retained earnings:		
Financial	2,740,875	2,740,875
Appropriation for human resources	493,047	—
Total stockholders' equity	5,849,291	5,356,244
Total liabilities and stockholders' equity	$14,055,926	$13,069,832

Statement of Income

	Financial and Human Resource	Financial Only
Net sales	$25,310,588	$25,310,588
Cost of sales	16,275,876	16,275,876
Gross profit	$ 9,034,712	$ 9,034,712
Selling, general, and administrative expenses	6,737,313	6,737,313
Operating income	$ 2,297,399	$ 2,297,399
Other deductions, net	953,177	953,177
Income before federal income taxes	$ 1,344,222	$ 1,344,222
Human resource expenses applicable to future periods	173,569	—
Adjusted income before federal income taxes	$ 1,517,791	$ 1,344,222
Federal income taxes	730,785	644,000
Net income	$ 787,006	$ 700,222

The information presented in this exhibit is provided only to illustrate the information value of human resource accounting for more effective internal management of the business. The figures included regarding investments and amortization of human resources are unaudited, and you are cautioned for purposes of evaluating the performance of the company to refer to the conven- *tional certified accounting data further on in this report.*

Human Resource Accounting
During the past year, work continued on the development of Bartlett's Human Resource Accounting System. The basic purpose of the system is to develop a method of measuring in dollar

EXHIBIT 1 *(continued)*

terms the changes that occur in the human resources of a business that conventional accounting does not currently consider.

Basic Concept

Management can be considered as the process of planning, organizing, leading, and controlling a complex mix of resources to accomplish the objectives of the organization. Those resources, we believe, are: physical resources of the company as represented by buildings and equipment, financial resources, and human resources which consist of the people who comprise the organization and proprietary resources which consist of trademarks, patents, and company name and reputation.

In order to determine more precisely the effectiveness of management's performance it is necessary to have information about the status of investments in the acquisition, maintenance, and utilization of all resources of the company.

Without such information, it is difficult for a company to know whether profit is being generated by converting a resource into cash or conversely whether suboptimal performance really has been generated by investments in developing the human resources which we expensed under conventional accounting practice.

Definition

Human resource accounting is an attempt to identify, quantify, and report investments made in resources of an organization that are not presently accounted for under conventional accounting practice. Basically, it is an information system that tells management what changes over time are occurring to the human resources of the business. It must be considered as an element of a total system of management—not as a separate "device" or "gimmick" to focus attention on human resources.

Objectives

Broadly, the Human Resource Accounting Information System is being designed to provide better answers to these kinds of questions: What is the quality of profit performance? Are sufficient human capabilities being acquired to achieve the objectives of the enterprise? Are they being developed adequately? To what degree are they being properly maintained? Are these capabilities being properly utilized by the organization?

As expressed in our 1985 annual report, our specific objectives in development of human resource accounting are . . . [see case for description].

Approach

The approach used has been to account for investments in securing and developing the organization's human resources. Outlay costs for recruiting, acquiring, training, familiarizing, and developing management personnel are accumulated and capitalized. In accordance with the approach conventional accounting employs for classification of an expenditure as an asset, only those outlays which have an expected value beyond the current accounting period deserve consideration as investments. Those outlays which are likely to be consumed within a 12-month period are properly classified as expense items. The investments in human resources are amortized over the expected useful period of the investment. The basic outlays in connection with acquiring and integrating new management people are amortized over their expected tenure with the company. Investments made for training or development are amortized over a much shorter period of time. The system now covers all management personnel at all locations of the corporation.

Research and development of the system began in late 1983. . . .

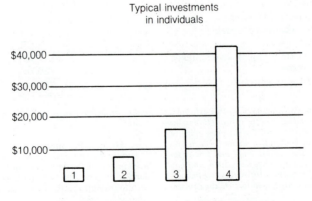

Typical investments
in individuals

1 - First line supervisor   3 - Middle manager
2 - Industrial engineer   4 - Top level manager

EXHIBIT 1 *(concluded)*

Applications

There are many potential applications for human resource accounting. Considering outlays for human resource investments which have a useful life over a number of years would have an impact upon the current year's revenue. Recognizing investments in human resources and their useful lives, losses resulting from improper maintenance of those resources can be shown in dollar terms. Estimating the useful lives of investments also provides a basis for planning for the orderly replacement of human capabilities as they expire, supplementing conventional manpower planning. Finally, recognizing investments in human resources will allow management to calculate dollar return on investment on a more comprehensive resource base for a particular profit center.

Summary

From the standpoint of management, knowledge of the human resource investments, maintenance, and returns is necessary for proper decision making and planning long-range corporate growth. As industry becomes increasingly technical and management becomes progressively more complex, we believe conventional accounting practice will come to recognize human resource accounting in financial reporting.

At this stage, the Human Resource Accounting System at A. G. Bartlett is best regarded as a potentially important tool of the overall management system. It is not an end in itself, and needs continuing refinement and development.

The 1985 report went on to define the basic objectives of Bartlett's human resource accounting system as being:

1. To provide Bartlett managers with specific feedback information on their performance in managing the organization resources and customer loyalty resources entrusted to their care so that they can make proper adjustments to their pattern of operations to correct adverse trends or further improve the condition of these resources.

2. To provide Bartlett managers with additional information pertaining to human resources to assist in their decision making.

3. To provide the organization with a more accurate accounting of its return on total resources employed, rather than just the physical resources, and to enable management to analyze how changes in the status of the resources employed affect the achievement of corporate objectives.

Bartlett clearly noted that the human resource accounting system was a "first pioneering step" and that it lacked refinement. Additionally, Bartlett stressed that, "The human resource capital accounts are used for internal informational purposes only and are not reflected, of course, in the financial data presented in this report."

The 1986 Bartlett annual report devoted 2 of its 24 pages to human resource accounting. (See Exhibit 1.) This material was introduced with a disclaimer which cautioned the reader that:

The figures included regarding investments and amortization of human resources are *unaudited* and you are cautioned for purposes of evaluating the performance of this company to refer to the *conventional certified* accounting data further on in this report.

Question

Comment on the efforts of A. G. Bartlett to measure in dollar terms the organizational assets and changes in these assets over time. What alternative measurement or disclosure approaches might the company have used to achieve the same end?

CHAPTER 19

Inventory Pricing and Analysis

Selection of a method for pricing inventories represents an important management decision. The procedure chosen will have a major impact on the measurement of net income and net working capital. Competent statement users always pay close attention to inventories, primarily because: they are a major asset of many firms, the management judgments and decisions that enter into their pricing can have a significant impact on financial results, and the state of a firm's inventories is often a good indicator of its economic health.

Inventory Pricing

Inventories include all tangible items held for sale or consumption in the normal course of business for which the company holds title, wherever they might be located. Typically, inventories can be placed in one of four categories: finished goods, goods in process, raw materials, and manufacturing supplies. There are several generally accepted methods for pricing inventories. The significant problems in inventory valuation result from the difficulties involved in allocating costs between periods and products, and the failure of selling prices and costs to move together.

Accounting Research Bulletin No. 43, chapter 4, sets forth the general principles applied to pricing of inventories of mercantile and manufacturing enterprises.

Periodic and Perpetual Inventory Systems

Inventory value is determined by multiplying the quantity of inventory on hand by the price per unit. There are two systems for determining inventory quantity: the periodic and the perpetual inventory systems. Irrespective of the system used, it is necessary periodically to inspect inventories physically.

The periodic inventory system involves a periodic determination of beginning inventory, purchases for the period, and ending inventory. These totals are determined by actual count. For these counts, the cost of goods sold may be determined by deduction. The basic formula is:

$$\text{Beginning inventories} + \text{Purchases} - \text{Ending inventories}$$
$$= \text{Cost of goods sold}$$

The perpetual inventory system involves keeping a running record of all the additions to and subtractions from the inventory.

Pricing Bases

Depending on the circumstances, the basis for pricing inventories may be cost; cost or market, whichever is lower; or selling price. The major objective underlying the selection of a pricing basis in a particular case should be the fairest determination of periodic income.

Cost Methods. Cost is the principal basis for pricing inventories. *Accounting Research Bulletin No. 43,* chapter 4, states:

> The primary basis for accounting for inventories is cost . . . as applied to inventories, cost means in principle the sum of the applicable expenditures and charges directly or indirectly incurred in bringing an article to its existing condition and location.

The inventory prices of manufacturing and merchandising companies reflect the different functions of these two classes of business activity. Manufacturing companies convert raw materials into finished goods. Consequently, their inventory prices reflect the cost of raw materials, direct labor, and factory overhead. Those costs associated with the product are referred to as product costs and are charged against revenues when the products are sold. All other costs, such as general administration and selling costs, are classified as period costs and are charged to the period in which they were incurred. Typically, a merchandising business does not incur conversion costs. As a result, its inventory prices are the prices it paid for the products it sells.

Every well-run business maintains some record of its costs. These costs may be collected and recorded on the basis of either individual jobs (a job cost system) or the various production processes (a process cost system). The costs assigned to the various finished and partially finished products may be predetermined standard costs or actual costs. If a standard cost system is used, the common practice is to assign any small difference between actual and standard costs to costs of good sold (COGS). If the variance is relatively large, however, some effort may be made to allocate the variance between the COGS and ending inventory accounts. In practice, a number of methods are used to allocate overhead costs to products. Most cost systems use a standard manufacturing overhead rate that allocates a fixed amount of overhead per unit to finished or partially finished goods, based on the amount of, say, direct labor dollars embodied in the product cost. Other common bases for allocating overhead are machine-hours and direct labor hours.

The exclusion of all factory overheads from inventory costs does not constitute an accepted accounting procedure for financial or tax accounting. Some argue that the inclusion of fixed factory overhead in inventory prices (and the cost of goods sold) is misleading, since it tends to make profit a function of production rather than sales: a buildup of inventory means more overhead will be charged to inventory and less to the current accounting period. These people advocate "direct costing," a procedure that includes in the product price only variable manufacturing costs. Fixed manufacturing costs are treated as period costs and are charged against income during the period in which they are incurred. Irrespective of the method used in financial reports, direct costing can be used for internal accounting purposes.

Often more than one product is produced from the same raw material. In the case of common products and by-products, raw material costs are typically allocated between the products on the basis of relative sales value, although various other methods are permissible as long as the results are not misleading. Often, for example, if the by-products represent a relatively minor portion of total production, the "by-product cost method" is used. Under this method, the by-product is initially valued at selling price less disposition costs. As a result, the profits and losses of the company are recorded on the sale of the primary product.

Inventory Methods. A number of generally acceptable methods based on historical costs are used to determine the price of inventories.

Illustration 19–1 will be used to demonstrate a number of these cost-based methods (how the actual unit costs were determined will be ignored in these examples).

ILLUSTRATION 19–1   ABC Company

	Units	Unit Cost	Total
Beginning inventory	2	$10	$20
Purchases:			
#1	1	11	11
#2	1	10	10
#3	1	12	12
#4	1	13	13
Cost of goods available for sale			$66
Total quantity available for sale	6		
Total sold during period	4		
Ending inventory	2		

Specific identification. The specific identification procedure associates the actual costs with the particular items in inventory. For example, if by inspection the ABC Company determined that its ending inventory consisted of purchases 1 and 3, the ending inventory would be valued at $23. Consequently, the cost of goods for the period would be $43 (total goods available for sale less ending inventory). While this method may relate revenues and costs directly, it is impractical for most businesses. It is sometimes used, however, for "big ticket" items, such as autos.

Last invoice price. The last invoice price method values the ending inventory at the most recent invoice price paid. Under this method, the two units in the ABC Company's ending inventory would be priced at $26 (2 × $13) and the cost of goods sold expense would be $40. For those companies with a rapid turnover of inventory and where older inventory items are used first, this method gives inventory prices that closely approximate those determined by the specific identification method. This method is not widely used.

Simple average. The simple average method prices the ending inventory as follows:

$$\frac{\text{Sum of invoice prices per unit}}{\text{Number of invoices}} \times \text{Number of units in ending inventory}$$

For ABC Company, this method would lead to an ending inventory value of $22.40 if the beginning inventory value per unit were included as an "invoice price." As a result, the cost of goods sold would be $43.60. The principal weakness of this procedure is that it gives equal weight to the invoice prices of large and small purchases. Like some of the other methods discussed in this section, however, it is used by small businesses because of its simplicity.

Weighted average. The weighted average method assigns to the ending inventory the average cost of the units available for sale during the period. The weighted average cost of ABC Company's ending inventory is $22, and the COGS expense for the period is $44:

Cost of goods available for sale	$66
Total units available for sale	6
Average cost	$11
Ending inventory price (2 units × $11)	22

Moving average. The moving average method computes the average unit price of the inventory after each purchase. The use of a moving average reduces the extent of the possible lag between inventory price and selling prices associated with the weighted average method. With a perpetual inventory system, the cost of goods sold of ABC Company is $42.22 and the value of the ending inventory is $23.78 (see Illustration 19–2).

ILLUSTRATION 19-2

	Physical Units			Dollar Costs		
Date	Additions To Stock	Reductions in Stock	Balance	Additions to Stock	Reductions in Stock	Balance
April 1...................	—	—	2	—	—	$20.00
6...................	1	—	3	$11	—	31.00
7...................	—	2	1	—	$20.66	10.34
15...................	1	—	2	10	—	10.34
16...................	1	—	3	12	—	32.34
25...................	—	2	1	—	21.56	10.78
27...................	1	—	2	13	—	23.78

First-in, first-out. The first-in, first-out (FIFO) method assigns to inventory the costs that reflect the most recent purchases. For ABC Company, the price of the ending inventory using the FIFO procedure is $25 (i.e., the sum of the costs of purchases 3 and 4). As a result, the COGS expense is $41.

Last-in, first-out. The last-in, first-out (LIFO) method assumes the most recent purchase costs are related to current revenues. As a result, the ending inventory reflects the oldest costs.

LIFO inventories consist of a series of "cost layers." The initial layer includes the quantities and related prices existing when LIFO was adopted. The ending inventory is the base cost layer plus the older layers of inventory required to equal the quantity of goods at the balance sheet date. For ABC Company, if LIFO had been adopted before the beginning of the period, the initial cost layer would be two units at $10 (i.e., the beginning inventory). The next layer would be purchase 1. Under the LIFO method, ABC's ending inventory determined by a periodic inventory system is $20 and the resulting COGS expense is $46.[1] Since unit reduction in inventory equaled purchases, the two units in the ending inventory are valued at the $20 shown for the two units in the beginning inventory. (In practice, LIFO inventory accounting is more complex than suggested by the ABC Company example. These complexities will be discussed later.)

A company can adopt the LIFO method for income tax purposes only if it also uses this method in its published financial statements. If ABC Company uses LIFO accounting, its taxable profits would be less than under FIFO, since the LIFO COGS would be higher ($46) than the FIFO figure ($41).

LIFO versus FIFO. The LIFO and FIFO methods are among the most popular inventory pricing procedures. In practice, each is considered an equally acceptable alternative. Their impact on working capital and net

---

[1] Illustration 19-2 shows that on April 7, ABC Company reduced its inventory to one unit, which is less than the LIFO layer of two units at the beginning of the year. The same thing occurred on April 25. Since the value of LIFO inventory is determined at year-end, if the depleted LIFO layers are replaced by year-end, the fact that the company "dipped into" its LIFO basis during the year has no impact on the cost of goods sold.

income, however, can differ significantly. For example, in the ABC situation, the LIFO procedure led to an ending inventory valued at $20, whereas the FIFO method resulted in an ending inventory valued at $25. The cost of goods sold for the period also reflected the different procedures: LIFO led to a COGS expense of $46, versus $41 with FIFO. The extent of the cost difference in this illustration should not be considered typical. It highlights, however, the relationship between the inventory pricing procedure, the inventory value, and the COGS expense.

The adoption of LIFO as an acceptable inventory method caused considerable controversy. The advocates of LIFO argued that this procedure stated the cost of goods sold in current dollars. As a consequence, they noted, cost and revenues would be matched in terms of relatively similar dollars, irrespective of the direction of the trend in prices. This result, the LIFO advocates argued, overcame a major weakness of FIFO, namely, that in periods of rising prices it leads to overstatement of profits, since a portion of these profits have to be used to replace the consumed inventories at higher costs. Similarly, in periods of falling prices, the LIFO proponents stated, FIFO leads to understatement of profits, since inventories produced or bought during an earlier period of higher prices are matched with current lower selling prices.

Those who opposed LIFO argued that it leads to an unrealistic balance sheet presentation of inventory. Except in some rare situations, LIFO does not correspond to the actual flow of goods, or necessarily result in an improved matching of costs and revenues. If a LIFO inventory consisting of very old cost layers were depleted, the LIFO opponents argued, the current profits would be misleading, since current revenues would be matched in part against the old, unrealistic costs.

While not necessarily agreeing that LIFO was a sound accounting method, a number of people became reconciled to LIFO because it represented a partial recognition of price-level changes for the purpose of determining income. Others accepted LIFO because of the tax advantage it gave users in periods of inflation. FIFO users may recognize these tax and income measurement advantages of LIFO, but still be reluctant to adopt it because of uncertainty about the impact on their stock prices of reporting lower profits under LIFO. The efficient-market theory suggests this concern is naive, on the grounds that the market sees through the LIFO-based profits to the underlying economic reality, which in periods of inflation is more favorable to LIFO companies, since they pay less taxes than FIFO companies. The results of specific research on this question are inconclusive.

Typically, LIFO companies do not use LIFO accounting for their overseas inventories, since in most foreign countries this accounting method is not available for tax purposes. In addition, only a part of the company's domestic inventories may be accounted for by the LIFO method. When more than one inventory method is used, the proportion of inventory accounted for by each principal method should be disclosed.

LIFO methodology.   LIFO inventory accounting can be applied to raw materials, finished goods, or some component of finished goods. It may be used to account for some inventories and not others. Or, it may be used to account for one item or a collection of items grouped into so-called dollar value pools. Pools are often formed around natural business unit inventories, product lines, or geographic locations.

ILLUSTRATION 19–3
Sample LIFO Calculation: Specific Identification Method

The Situation:

Time	Item	Quantity	Current Unit Cost	Total Current Cost
Beginning of year 1	A	2,000	$5.00	$10,000
(base year)	B	5,000	4.00	20,000
				$30,000
End of year 1	A	2,000	5.25	$10,500
	B	6,000	4.50	27,000
				$37,500
End of year 2	A	3,000	5.50	$16,500
	B	5,000	5.00	25,000
				$41,500
End of year 3	A	4,000	5.30	$21,200
	B	–0–	—	–0–
	C	4,000	4.00*	16,000
				$37,200

* Base year cost estimated at $3 per unit.

Specific Identification Method Illustration:

Time	Item	Quantity	Value		Total
End of year 1	A	2,000	$5.00		$10,000
	B	5,000	4.00	$20,000	
	Addition year 1	1,000	4.50	4,500	24,500
					$34,500
End of year 2	A	2,000	5.00	$10,000	
	Addition year 2	1,000	5.50	5,500	$15,500
		3,000			
	B	5,000	4.00		20,000
					$35,500
End of year 3	A	2,000	5.00	$10,000	
	Addition year 2	1,000	5.50	5,500	
	Addition year 3	1,000	5.30	5,300	$20,800
		4,000			
	C	4,000	4.00		16,000
					$36,800

There are two basic approaches to LIFO accounting, the specific identification method and the dollar value method.

Specific identification method. In the year for which LIFO is adopted, the beginning LIFO inventory is valued at cost and all units are combined to form the basic LIFO "layer."

Should the inventory at the end of the year exceed the beginning inventory, the additional inventory is priced at the current year's cost. This can be first purchase costs, last purchase costs, or the average for the year. Frequently, each purchase (or the average of a month's worth of purchases) is applied in order of acquisition under the inventory increase is accounted for in full. An average of the costs making up this increase is taken and treated as one LIFO layer.

If the year-end inventory is less than the beginning inventory, then the layers are reduced by the most recent acquisitions. Illustration 19–3 illustrates the specific identification method.

In practice, the specific identification method is used infrequently, except in firms that have only a few raw materials or manufactured goods. The ease and simplicity of its calculation are outweighed in most enterprises by the need to protect income from inflationary profits that could be brought about through inventory decreases, raw material substitutions, or product changes that charge low-priced LIFO layers of cost of goods sold in the year the inventory is reduced. The use of dollar value pools that incorporate a variety of items minimizes these problems.

Dollar value method. For each inventory pool formed, the cost of beginning inventory for every item in the pool is determined for the year LIFO is adopted. The sum of these costs is termed the "base-year cost" for that pool.

A number of dollar value methods are used for valuing inventories at the end of the first and subsequent years. The two most common are the double-extension method and the link-chain method. The latter uses a cumulative index of beginning and ending costs in each pool to value successive layers. It is not considered further here. The double-extension method is discussed below.

In the double-extension method, the year-end inventory pool is valued *(a)* at "current," year-end costs; and *(b)* at the cost it would have had (with its current composition) at the beginning of the base year. If an item was not in inventory in the base year, its base-year cost is estimated.

Each year's increment to the LIFO inventory is determined by:

a. Calculating the base-year cost of the total ending inventory in the pool;
b. Subtracting from this total the base-year cost of the inventory at the beginning of the year. The difference is a LIFO layer attributable to this year at base-level cost; and
c. Multiplying this current layer by the ratio of the current year's

ILLUSTRATION 19–4
Sample LIFO Calculation: Double-Extension Method

The Situation:

(Same as Illustration 19–3.)

Double-Extension Method:

	Total Base-Year Cost	Total Current Cost	Ratio B : A
Beginning of year 1	$30,000	$30,000	1.0000
End of year 1	34,000*	37,500	1.1029
End of year 2	35,000†	41,500	1.1857
End of year 3	32,000‡	37,200	1.1625

    * (2,000 × 5) + (6,000 × 4) = $10,000 + $24,000 = $34,000.
    † (3,000 × 5) + (5,000 × 4) = 15,000 + 20,000 = 35,000.
    ‡ (4,000 × 5) + (4,000 × 3) = 20,000 + 12,000 = 32,000.

	Total Base Cost	Ratio	Total LIFO Cost
End of year 1:			
Base-year inventory	$30,000	1.0000	$30,000
Layer no. 1	4,000	1.1029	4,412
	$34,000		$34,000
End of year 2:			
Base-year inventory	$30,000	1.0000	$30,000
Layer no. 1	4,000	1.1029	4,412
Layer no. 2	1,000	1.1857	1,186
	$35,000		$35,000
End of year 3:			
Base-year inventory	$30,000	1.0000	$30,000
Layer no. 1	2,000	1.1029	2,205
	$32,000		$32,205

cost to the base year's cost. This gives the LIFO layer in current dollars, and it is added to the beginning inventory.

Decrements to a LIFO inventory occur when the ending inventory in terms of base-year costs is less than the base-year cost of the beginning inventory. This decrement is removed from the most recent LIFO layers. Illustration 19–4 presents a double-extension inventory calculation.

The advantages of a dollar value method stem from the treatment of a number of inventory items as one pooled unit. In a LIFO pool, substitution of new materials for old ones or new products for discontinued ones does not necessarily result in the older costs being charged against sales since either permanent or temporary reduction in inventory of one item in the pool can be offset by an increase in others.

The disadvantages are clerical costs and the difficulty of double pricing every item in current and base-year terms. These are mitigated to some extent in the link-chain method, since only year-to-year price changes must be calculated.

Indexes can also be used on pool samples, although the samples in practice tend to include a substantial fraction of the pool.

Simplified LIFO. In 1982, the Internal Revenue Service (IRS) issued regulations to simplify the use of LIFO inventory methods for tax purposes. These rules, which were designed to reduce the cost of LIFO inventory accounting for small companies, permitted these companies to use a government price index in determining the carrying amounts of inventories under the dollar value LIFO method. This new IRS rule raised the issue of whether the simplified LIFO values were acceptable for financial reporting purposes. The FASB decided not to address this issue, thereby in essence allowing the tax approach to be used in financial reports unless its application led to a gross distortion of a company's experience.

Base stock. The base stock method, like the LIFO method, seeks to match current costs with current revenues. This method assumes that a business needs a minimum or basic inventory quantity to carry on normal operations. For example, if ABC Company needed an inventory of two units for normal operations, the two units would be regarded as the base stock. In a sense, it is argued, this base stock is similar to the company's fixed assets. If the company is to continue operations, the base stock must be preserved. Therefore, the argument continues, if the replacement cost of the minimum inventory rises, the increase in these costs should not be reflected in higher income. To avoid this effect, the base stock is assigned a cost well below current market.

The inventory in excess of the base stock can be valued by LIFO, FIFO, or some other method. Should a company cut into its base stock and intend to replace the deficient quantity later, a replacement provision is established equal to the difference between the base price and the current market price of the deficient units. When the units are replaced, they are replaced at the base price and the provision offset by the difference between their base price and actual cost.

The base stock method is generally accepted for financial accounting purposes. It is not approved for income tax purposes, however. Outside of some companies engaged in processing basic raw materials, this method is not widely used.

Cost or Market, Whichever Is Lower

A basic rule of accounting is that losses should be recorded as charges to income as soon as they are discovered. This rule takes precedence over the matching costs with revenue rule. So, any inventory losses should be recognized currently to the extent that they can be determined, and the cost of inventory in excess of its utility should be charged to income and not carried forward as an asset. The lower-of-cost-or-market rule applies to such situations and provides a guide to the proper accounting treatment. *Accounting Research Bulletin No. 43*, chapter 4, states:

> A departure from cost basis for pricing the inventory is *required* when the utility of goods is no longer as great as their cost. Where there is evidence that the utility of goods, in their disposal in the ordinary course of business, will be less than cost, whether due to physical deterioration, obsolescence, changes in price levels, or other causes, the difference should be recognized as a loss of the current period. This is generally accomplished by stating such goods at a lower level commonly designated as *market*.

The lower-of-cost-or-market rule is based on the assumption that costs and selling prices move together. Thus, a decrease in the replacement cost of an inventory item signals a potential selling price decline and a decline in utility of the inventory on hand. If the sales price does not decline and the inventory on hand will be sold at the normal margin, however, there will be no loss of utility. Conversely, if selling prices decline but the replacement cost does not, a lower than normal margin will be earned. This is also a signal that the utility of the inventory has decreased.

The word "cost" in the rule means the cost of replacing the inventory on hand by purchase in the open market or reproduction in the company's own factories. The purchase price includes all the costs of bringing the goods to their usual location. The reproduction cost includes all the direct and indirect costs associated with manufacturing the goods.

The term "market" has a specific technical meaning in the context of this rule. It is an indication of the utility of the inventory as measured by the relationship between replacement cost, selling price, and normal margin. As used in the rule, "market" also means current replacement cost, but with two provisions:

1. Market should not exceed realizable value (estimated selling price less costs of completion and disposal).
2. Market should not be less than net realizable value reduced by an allowance for an approximately normal profit margin. This figure is often referred to as the "market floor."

Thus, determining market requires comparing three values: replacement cost, net realizable value, and the market floor. If net realizable value is lower, it is market. If replacement cost is lower, it is market *unless* its use would result in a larger than normal profit margin; in that event, the market floor is market.

Illustration 19–5 shows how the lower-of-cost-or-market rule is applied.

Retail Method. The retail inventory method is used as an approximation of the cost-or-market method by retailers and others who keep their inventory records on a selling price basis. Application of this method requires that records be maintained of purchases from and returns to manufacturers,

ILLUSTRATION 19–5
Lower-of-Cost-or-Market Rule*

	Illus. 1	Illus. 2	Illus. 3	Illus. 4
Cost	$1.00†	$1.00	$1.00	$1.00
Replacement or reproduction cost	1.05	0.98†	0.99	0.94
Net realizable value	1.25	1.15	0.95†	1.20
Market floor: net realizable value less a normal profit	0.99	0.91	0.75	0.95†
Inventory write-down amount	0.00	0.02	0.05	0.05

Net realizable value and net realizable value less a normal profit are determined as follows:

	Illus. 1	Illus. 2	Illus. 3	Illus. 4
Selling price	$1.30	$1.20	$1.00	$1.25
Less: Cost of completion and disposal	0.05	0.05	0.05	0.05
Net realizable value	$1.25	$1.15	$0.95	$1.20
Normal profit (20% of selling price)	0.26	0.24	0.20	0.25
Net realizable value less a normal profit	$0.99	$0.91	$0.75	$0.95

* Philip L. Defliese, Kenneth P. Johnson, and Roderick K. MacLeod, *Montgomery's Auditing* (New York: The Ronald Press Co., 1975), p. 387.
† Represents the value to be used for inventory purposes.

showing cost and selling prices; and of customer sales and returns, showing selling prices. The cost of the ending inventory is calculated as follows:

1. Add the purchases during the period at cost to the opening inventory at cost.
2. Add the purchases at retail to the opening inventory at retail.
3. Subtract the first of these totals from the second. The difference is the so-called cumulative mark-on in dollars. Calculate this amount as a percentage of the total retail price of the goods available for sale during the period (determined in 2 above).
4. Subtract actual sales from the total retail price of goods available for sale to obtain computed inventory at retail.
5. Multiply the ending inventory at retail by the mark-on percentage (computed in 3 above) and subtract from inventory at retail to determine inventory at cost.

The retail method is widely used in the retail business, since it reduces the clerical work and permits cost to be omitted from price tags.

The following procedure is used to state inventories on a LIFO basis:

1. Inventory at retail value is calculated for all items in a department at inventory date.
2. The total department inventory at retail is reduced to a base-year value by applying the appropriate indexes published by the Bureau of Labor Statistics for this purpose. This base-level value is then separated into LIFO layers attributable to each year.

3. A layer is added if ending inventory is greater than beginning inventory. If it is less, the more recent layers in beginning inventory are moved to cost of goods sold.
4. Each layer in ending inventory is reduced to *cost* by using the average gross margin in that department appropriate to the year the layer was acquired.
5. The result is ending inventory at LIFO cost.

Selling Price. Another basis for pricing inventories is selling price. According to *Accounting Research Bulletin No. 43*, chapter 4:

> Only in exceptional cases may inventories properly be stated above cost. For example, precious metals having a fixed monetary value with no substantial cost of marketing may be stated at such monetary value; any other exceptions must be justified by inability to determine appropriate approximate cost, immediate marketability at quoted market price, and the characteristic of unit interchangeability. When goods are stated above cost, this fact should be fully disclosed.

If the selling price basis is used, the cost of disposition should be deducted. The principal arguments for the application of selling price basis are: first, the inventory is readily marketable at known market prices; and second, production is the critical business activity, rather than selling. In general, the inability to determine cost is the weakest argument for pricing inventories on a selling price basis.

Statement Presentation

Typically, inventories are shown in the current asset section of the balance sheet, immediately after accounts receivable. According to *Accounting Research Bulletin No. 43*, chapter 4:

> The basis of stating inventories must be consistently applied and should be disclosed in the financial statements; whenever a significant change is made therein, there should be disclosed the nature of the change and, if material, the effect on income.

Inventory Analysis

The inventory-turnover calculation is the basic financial analysis tool used to evaluate inventory management. It measures the number of times management's investment in inventory is turned over each year. As discussed in earlier notes, inventory turnover is measured by dividing the annual cost of sales by the average FIFO (or FIFO-equivalent) inventory for the period. The resulting turnover figure can then be converted to the average length of time an item spends in inventory by dividing the turnover rate into 365 days. The average age of the inventory is the turnover ratio expressed in days divided by 2. The brief inventory analysis discussion included in the earlier note should be read in conjunction with the inventory analysis presented here.

Another quantitative approach to analyzing inventories is to compute as percentages the relation of raw materials, work in process, and finished goods to total inventory. This calculation should be tracked over time. Any major shifts in the relationships should be noted and their causes identified and evaluated. For example, an increase in the finished goods percentage might indicate poor sales forecasting, a slowdown in customer orders, or a failure to react promptly to a downturn in business. The higher finished goods might also result from a change in manufacturing policy to reduce production costs by lengthening production runs, which then requires holding product in inventory in anticipation of future orders. Such a strategy may increase the company's capital needs and level of risk and should be closely monitored by statement analysts.

It is difficult to determine what the appropriate turnover ratio and distribution of inventory between raw materials, work in progress, and finished goods should be for a company. In general, a high turnover ratio is preferable to a low one, but if the turnover rate is too high, the company may be subject to stockouts or incur excessive production costs due to short production runs. Some clues as to how high or low an inventory turnover should be for a particular company, as well as the appropriate composition of its inventory, are the comparable ratios of other companies in the same industry, particularly the ratios of those companies with a reputation for having good management.

During periods of above-average inflation, it is important that statement users eliminate from the income of FIFO companies the so-called inventory profit, which is the difference between the replacement cost of the inventory items sold and their original cost. This portion of profits must be used in replacing the inventory sold in order to maintain inventory levels. In addition, on the balance sheet, statement users must restate the inventory of LIFO companies to its current value. This restatement is required to measure correctly the amount of capital committed to finance inventories.

The inventory notes and supplemental inflation disclosures are helpful in trying to reconcile the effect of the LIFO–FIFO choice on income and inventory values when examining a single company or comparing many companies. The data related to inventories can be used to adjust a LIFO company's income and inventory value to a FIFO basis. Similarly, the income of certain large FIFO companies that must publish supplemental inflation-adjusted data can be adjusted to a comparable LIFO basis. Here are the disclosure rules that make these analyses of the income statement and balance sheet effect of different inventory accounting possible:

    a.   When a company shifts from FIFO to LIFO accounting, the impact of the change on earnings in the year of change must be disclosed.

b. If a company already on LIFO for some of its inventories decides to extend the use of LIFO to other inventories, the effect of the LIFO extension on earnings must be disclosed.

c. LIFO companies must disclose in their notes to the financial statements for each period presented the difference between the LIFO and current cost values of their inventories. This disclosure, which is sometimes called the "LIFO reserve," is useful in two ways: first, this amount can be added to the LIFO inventory value shown on the face of the statement to obtain an approximation of the company's FIFO inventory value. Second, the change in LIFO reserve from one year to another is equivalent to the before-tax effect on earnings of using LIFO rather than FIFO accounting.

d. Sometimes LIFO companies at year-end dip into, or "invade," one of their LIFO inventory's old cost layers. Typically, this boosts earnings, since current revenues are matched with costs from a period when unit costs were considerably lower than the current replacement cost. The effect on earnings of LIFO layer invasions must be disclosed.

e. *Statement No. 33* requires the larger public companies to disclose the current cost of their inventories and related cost of goods sold. Thus, the FIFO companies that must comply with this rule will provide the data needed to restate their earnings to a LIFO basis. This can be accomplished by subtracting the current cost of goods sold from sales rather than the historical-cost FIFO figure. For all practical purposes, the income of most LIFO companies is already based on a current cost COGS valuation.

Inventory practices vary from company to company and involve management judgment. An auditor's opinion does not necessarily guarantee the figures are reliable.

Statement users must be wary of interim statement COGS figures. They may be little more than estimates based on the dubious assumption that the budgeted gross margin is being earned or that a LIFO company's management projection of year-end price levels is reliable. In addition, the percentage of manufacturing overhead costs management includes in interim and annual inventory (and cost of goods sold) can range from the bare minimum required for tax purposes to the maximum permitted by accounting rules. Statement users should always attempt to determine the costing practice used by the company being examined. A company that treats most of its manufacturing overhead as a period cost will tend to have more operating leverage than a company that classifies most of its manufacturing overhead as a product cost. Auditors are often present when year-end inventory is counted, but they do not always participate in counting all of the inventory. Also, they rely heavily on management representations that the inventory is salable. Under these conditions, a combination of an inept audit and a dishonest management can easily result in nonexistent, obsolete, damaged, and nonsalable inventory being recorded as good inventory and cost of goods sold being understated. It is almost impossible for the statement user to detect this type of fraud directly. Fortunately, in these situations there are usually enough "red flags" to alert the astute statement user that the company may be in trouble.

Often, the price movements of only a few of the cost elements in a LIFO company's cost of goods sold are responsible for the bulk of the inflation component of that expense item. For example, the price of copper drives the inflation component of an electrical manufacturer's LIFO COGS. Statement users should always identify the item that drives the LIFO-based costing and track its movements. The company's COGS and LIFO reserve should reflect these price changes. If they do not, either the company has changed the way it does business or the reader has detected a "red flag" suggesting closer examination of the company is warranted.

Companies with inventory problems sometimes attempt to hide their difficulties by shipping product to customers prematurely or extending generous credit terms to customers accepting early delivery. Accelerating sales may result in a book entry reducing inventory, but the so-called product sales should be regarded as the equivalent of moving inventory from the vendor's plant to the customers' plants. The vendor still has an inventory problem since the customer will not pay for the goods until the normal payment date. Statement users can detect this practice, which usually occurs near the end of the accounting period, by an unusual buildup of receivables.

Companies that manage inventories well usually do well in other aspects of management. The converse is true for companies that have poor inventory management. Statement users should respond favorably to companies that manage their inventories effectively. This is a critical management skill that can make a major contribution to the efficient use of capital and manufacturing facilities as well as to the effective execution of a company's product marketing program. Actions that lead to efficient inventory management include: short manufacturing cycles, integration of vendor and customer production plans, optimum inventory lot size scheduling, receipt of vendor shipments as close to use as possible, favorable vendor payment terms, infrequent stockouts, and reliable sales forecasts.

Summary

The valuation of inventories is critical to the periodic measurement of net working capital and net income. The importance of inventories is further reflected in the prominence this item receives in internal control systems and audit programs. There are many accepted procedures for valuing inventory, most of which are cost based. Management should select the inventory pricing method that leads to the fairest determination of periodic income. The accounting for inventories involves considerable controversy. Some argue that the number of acceptable accounting procedures should be reduced. Others contend that particular inventory methods are misleading. A number of people believe that the disclosure of inventories is inadequate. Clearly, this is an important area for all who prepare, audit, or use accounting statements.

CASE 19-1

GSC, Inc.
Adopting LIFO Inventory Valuation

In mid-January 1985, Terry O'Neil, controller of GSC, Inc., was examining the consequences of GSC's adopting a last-in, first-out (LIFO) method of valuing raw material. He was meeting the next afternoon with Gregory Spencer, president of GSC, and Chris Scott, GSC's auditor, to evaluate the impact of adopting LIFO on GSC's cash flow operating results and financial position. Terry was hopeful that the meeting would result in a decision so that he could get GSC's 1984 financial statements and the 1985 financial projections ready for his end-of-January meeting with the Shipman Bank & Trust Company—the holder of GSC's equipment mortgage and line-of-credit notes.

The Corporation

GSC, Inc., was formed in 1977 to manufacture a high-quality line of plastic-based kitchen and household accessories—spice racks, bookends, geometric shapes, and so on. These products are produced by taking Forclon, a chemical powder, and processing it in a fairly capital-intensive facility. The company has grown steadily, and in 1984 had an after-tax profit of $67,000 on sales of $1.7 million—Exhibits 1 and 2. For 1985, sales are estimated to be $2.4 million, and if expenses hold constant, such a sales volume will produce a pre-tax profit of $452,000 according to GSC's profit forecasting chart—Exhibit 3. This profit forecasting chart was based on the "contribution" reporting system that Greg Spencer and Terry O'Neil have used from the very beginning of their business. This system separates fixed and variable costs and reports the *contribution* to profit and fixed costs of both the manufacturing and selling activities—see Exhibit 1. GSC prepared expected, pro forma financial statements in the same contribution format each year and

This case was prepared by Neil C. Churchill.

Copyright © 1975 by the President and Fellows of Harvard College
Harvard Business School case 175–134 (Rev. 1985)

EXHIBIT 1

GSC, INC.
Statement of Operations
For the 12 Months Ending December 31, 1984

	Variable		Fixed	Total
	Dollars	Percent		
Sales	1,843,979			$1,843,979
Less: Sales discounts	70,919			70,919
Net sales	1,773,060	100.0		$1,773,060
Cost of sales:				
Materials	583,622			$ 583,622
Less: Increase in finished goods inventory ...	(37,599)			(37,599)
Raw materials in cost of sales	546,023	30.80		$ 546,023
Manufacturing expenses:				
Plant labor	110,592	6.24	$ 71,678	$ 182,270
Payroll taxes	6,177	0.35	5,052	11,229
Group health insurance			7,968	7,968
Utilities			39,242	39,242
Depreciation			268,326	268,326
Rental expense on land and building ...			55,161	55,161
Insurance and fire and casualty			23,073	23,073
Freight-out	62,728	3.54		62,728
Truck expense—out			15,191	15,191
Factory repairs			37,998	37,998
Factory supplies	25,267	1.42		25,267
Factory miscellaneous—administration ...			9,628	9,628
Cost of manufacturing	204,764	11.55	$533,317	$ 738,081
Less: Addition to finished goods inventory ...	3,800	.22	9,896	13,696
Manufacturing cost of goods sold	200,964	11.33	$523,421	$ 724,385
Cost of sales	746,987	42.13		$1,270,408
Gross contribution from manufacturing	1,026,073	57.87		$ 502,652
Selling and administrative expenses:				
Salaries			$ 90,186	$ 90,186
Commissions	76,627	4.32		76,627
Payroll taxes			5,899	5,899
Advertising and sales promotion			13,789	13,789
Auto expense			2,599	2,599
General taxes			11,739	11,739
Insurance—key man			3,252	3,252
Telephone and telegraph			10,770	10,770
Travel and entertaining			44,420	44,420
Professional services			15,967	15,967
Other expenses			22,621	22,621
Total selling and administrative expenses ...	76,627	4.32	$221,242	$ 297,869
Other income and expense:				
Interest expense			88,198	88,198
Total selling and administrative and other expenses ...	76,627	4.32	$309,440	$ 386,067
Net operating contribution	949,446	53.55		$ 116,585
Less: Fixed expense	832,861	46.97	$832,861	
Pre-tax profit	116,585	6.58		$ 116,585
Income tax				49,461
Net profit after tax				$ 67,124

EXHIBIT 2

GSC, INC.
Statement of Financial Position
December 31, 1984

Assets

Current assets:

Cash....................................	$ 10,713	
Accounts receivable net of reserve for doubtful accounts	245,867	
Notes receivable	16,517	
Other receivables	2,008	

Inventory:

Raw materials.............................	$157,081		
Finished goods............................	102,783	259,864	
Prepaid expenses		25,896	
Total current assets			$ 560,865

Property, plant, and equipment:

Leasehold additions and improvements	$ 22,929		
Machinery and equipment	2,123,434		
Office equipment	30,867		
Autos and trucks	21,766		
	$2,198,996		
Less: Reserve for depreciation	727,720		
Total property, plant, and equipment		1,471,276	
Total assets		$2,032,141	

Equities

Current liabilities:

Accounts payable	$ 307,907	
Notes payable to bank	120,000	
Accrued payroll and related taxes withheld	58,300	
Accrued expenses	17,876	
Federal income and state property taxes	53,728	
Total current liabilities	$ 557,811	
Long-term debt (less current portion)	952,472	
Total liabilities		$1,510,283

Stockholders' equity:

Cumulative preferred stock	$ 76,750	
Common stock...............................	41,890	
Paid-in surplus	35,089	
Retained earnings	368,129	
Total stockholders' equity		521,858
Total equities		$2,032,141

EXHIBIT 3
Break-Even Chart for the 12 Months Ending December 31, 1984 (in thousands)

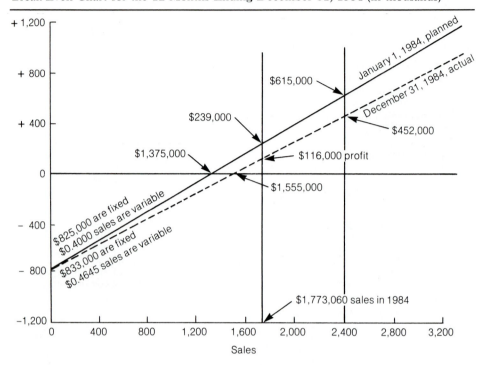

submitted them and the profit forecasting chart to the bank in January. The bank also receives financial statements on actual results at the end of each quarter. These same projected statements are used internally to monitor the progress of GSC.

Inventory Pricing

The raw material inventory was composed almost entirely of Forclon, and this material is an important component of GSC's costs—some 80 percent of the variable and 45 percent of the total manufacturing costs. GSC had experienced substantial price increases in 1984, and the cost of Forclon had risen from 23 cents a pound in early 1984 to 57 cents a pound in December. Currently it was 59 cents a pound and expected to remain close to this level for at least the first half of 1985. The rapid price increase in 1984 caused O'Neil and Scott to recommend looking at LIFO to save income taxes.

Scott proposed that GSC consider raw materials to be one LIFO "pool" and lump together the raw material inventory with the raw material component of finished goods. (There is, essentially, no work in process inventory.) To isolate this inventory pool, Scott prepared an inventory movement analysis in both physical and dollar terms—Exhibit 4—using the existing first-in, first-out inventory pricing system. Scott also prepared a summary of key financial ratios using FIFO—Exhibit 5—and gave both documents to O'Neil. O'Neil was now engaged in calculating the impact of LIFO and preparing a recommendation and the necessary supporting analyses for his meeting with Greg Spencer and Chris Scott the next day.

EXHIBIT 4
Raw Material Movement and Position during the Calendar Year Ending December 31, 1984

Beginning Inventory on January 1, 1984:

140,650 lbs. at $0.220		$ 30,943	
142,000 lbs. at 0.230		32,660	
282,650 lbs.			$ 63,603

January–March:

Purchased + 75,000 lbs. at .230 — $ +17,250
Used −303,040 lbs.

140,650 lbs. at 0.220	$ 30,943		
162,390 lbs. at 0.230	37,350	−68,293	−51,043
Balance 54,610 lbs.			$ 12,560

April–June:

Purchased +700,000 lbs.

100,000 lbs. at 0.230	$ 23,000		
200,000 lbs. at 0.295	59,000		
300,000 lbs. at 0.350	105,000		
100,000 lbs. at 0.375	37,500	$+224,500	

Used −488,170 lbs.

154,610 lbs. at 0.230	$ 35,560		
200,000 lbs. at 0.295	59,000		
133,560 lbs. at 0.350	45,746	−141,306	+83,194
Balance 266,440 lbs.			$ 95,754

July–September:

Purchased +350,000 lbs.

250,000 lbs. at 0.425	$106,250		
100,000 lbs. at 0.467	46,700	+152,950	

Used −403,230 lbs.

166,440 lbs. at 0.350	$ 58,254		
100,000 lbs. at 0.375	37,500		
136,790 lbs. at 0.425	58,136	−153,890	−940
Balance 213,210 lbs.			$ 94,814

October–December:

Purchased +520,000 lbs.

200,000 lbs. at 0.515	$103,000		
150,000 lbs. at 0.550	82,500		
170,000 lbs. at 0.570	96,900	$+282,400	

Used −453,790 lbs.

113,210 lbs. at 0.425	$ 48,114		
100,000 lbs. at 0.467	47,700		
200,000 lbs. at 0.515	103,000		
40,580 lbs. at 0.550	22,319	−220,133	+62,267
Balance 279,420 lbs.			$ 157,081

EXHIBIT 4 *(concluded)*

Ending Inventory Reconciliation

109,420 lbs. at 0.550	$ 60,181
170,000 lbs. at 0.570	96,900
279,420 lbs.	$157,081

Cost of Raw Materials Used

1st quarter	303,040 lbs.	$ 68,293
2d quarter	488,170 lbs.	141,306
3d quarter	403,230 lbs.	153,890
4th quarter	453,790 lbs.	220,133
	1,648,230 lbs.	$583,622

Raw materials in beginning finished goods inventory (82,020 lbs.)	18,040
Raw materials in goods available for sale (1,730,250 lbs.)	$601,662
Less: Raw materials in ending finished goods inventory (105,279)	55,639*
Cost of raw materials in sales (1,624,971)	$546,023

* 64,699 lbs. at 0.515	$33,320
40,580 lbs. at 0.550	22,319
105,279 lbs.	$55,639

EXHIBIT 5
Key Balances and Financial Ratios for the Calendar Year Ending December 31, 1984

	FIFO	LIFO
Ending raw material	$212,720	
In raw material inventory $157,081		
In finished goods 55,639		
Cost of raw materials used	$546,023	
Net operating contribution.............................	$949,446	
Pre-tax profit	$116,585	
Income tax expense...................................	$ 49,461	
Net profit after tax	$ 67,124	
Working capital	$ 3,054	
Current ratio	1.005/1	
Inventory turnover—raw material component	3.71	
Times interest earned	2.32	
Return of stockholders' equity (average)	0.14	
Implied growth rate (no dividends)	0.14	
"Cash flow" (net income and depreciation)	$335,450	

Questions

1. Calculate the beginning and ending inventories and the cost of materials in goods sold under the assumption that 1984 is the first year for GSC on a LIFO inventory basis.

2. Fill in the financial ratios on Exhibit 5 under LIFO. (Note, the combined state and federal income tax on the first $25,000 of income is 22 percent and is 48 percent on the remainder.)

3. What recommendation would you make, and what issues must be considered in preparing for your meeting with Spencer?

CASE 19-2

Chrysler Corporation
Switching from LIFO to FIFO

During 1970, Chrysler Corporation announced the following earnings for the first three quarters:

Date Reported	Quarter	Net Earnings (Loss) (in millions)
4/20/70 I		$(29.4)
7/16/70 II		8.1
10/19/70 III		1.1

On February 3, 1971, *The Wall Street Journal* published a detailed article concerning Chrysler's financial condition. Part of the article is reproduced below:

A year ago, Chrysler Corporation was in the midst of a massive retrenchment, aimed at moving back into the black and getting its financial house in order. In its efforts to prove its setback was temporary, the number

This case was prepared by Norman J. Bartczak.

three automaker left no stone unturned. It was clearly impatient to resume the growth pattern that made it one of the corporate stars of the 1960s.

John J. Riccardo, an aggressive, hard-nosed accountant, called the "flamethrower" by some critics, was installed as president and given full authority to reshuffle and whittle down the organization. To slash costs and "shorten the lines of communications," the brusque new president demoted some vice presidents and moved others laterally, wiping out whole layers of corporate bureaucracy. As many as 6,000 white-collar slots and at least one $100,000-a-year senior vice presidency disappeared.

At the same time, Chrysler sought to improve its shrunken working capital by cutting $100 million from its capital spending, reducing its quarterly dividend from 50 cents to 15 cents, and arranging $200 million of new financing.

By midsummer, Chairman Lynn Townsend, Chrysler's 51 year old boss and architect of its earlier growth, was boasting that the moves had pruned $150 million from costs and that the surgery was just about over. He indi-

EXHIBIT 1
Chrysler Corporation

		Stock Prices					
		Chrysler			S&P 500		
Date	Quarter	High	Low	Close	High	Low	Close
1969	I	$57.88	$49.50	$54.00	104.87	96.63	101.51
	II	$54.63	$44.88	$45.50	106.74	95.21	97.71
	III	$47.00	$35.50	$37.75	100.33	83.83	93.12
	IV	$42.50	$31.62	$34.38	99.23	88.62	92.06
1970	I	$35.75	$24.00	$27.75	94.25	84.42	89.63
	II	$28.63	$16.50	$18.00	90.70	68.61	72.72
	III	$28.13	$16.13	$26.88	84.57	70.69	84.30
	IV	$30.25	$23.63	$28.00	92.99	82.79	92.15
1971	I	$29.38	$24.50	$26.50	102.03	90.28	100.31
Date	Day						
2/03/71	Wednesday	$26.25	$25.38	$25.50	97.19	95.58	96.63
2/08/71	Monday	$27.13	$26.63	$27.00	98.04	96.13	97.45
2/09/71	Tuesday	$28.00	$26.75	$27.50	98.50	96.90	97.51
2/10/71	Wednesday	$28.25	$26.63	$28.25	97.97	96.23	97.39
2/11/71*	Thursday	$29.25	$28.50	$28.88	98.49	96.99	97.91
3/19/71	Friday	$28.25	$27.50	$27.63	101.74	100.35	101.01
3/22/71	Monday	$27.75	$27.33	$27.63	101.46	100.08	100.62
3/23/71	Tuesday	$27.00	$26.50	$26.75	101.06	99.62	100.28
4/02/71	Friday	$26.88	$26.63	$26.75	101.23	99.86	100.56
4/05/71	Monday	$27.75	$26.63	$27.75	101.41	99.88	100.79
4/06/71	Tuesday	$29.50	$29.00	$29.13	102.11	100.30	101.51
4/07/71*	Wednesday	$31.00	$29.25	$30.75	102.87	101.13	101.98
4/14/71	Wednesday	$30.50	$29.13	$30.38	104.01	102.28	103.37
4/15/71	Thursday	$31.13	$30.50	$30.63	104.40	102.76	103.52
4/19/71	Monday	$31.50	$30.75	$31.38	104.63	103.09	104.01
4/20/71	Tuesday	$32.25	$31.38	$31.63	104.58	103.06	103.61
4/21/71	Wednesday	$31.50	$30.88	$30.88	104.16	102.55	103.36
4/23/71	Friday	$33.38	$31.75	$33.00	104.63	102.79	104.05

* Volume leader on New York Stock Exchange.

EXHIBIT 2
Chrysler Corporation

Management of Chrysler
Executive Officers

Lynn A. Townsend, 51, Chairman of the Board

Mr. Townsend has been chief executive officer of Chrysler since April 9, 1966. He joined Chrysler in 1957 as comptroller. For 10 years prior to that time, he was with the accounting firm now named Touche Ross & Co., becoming a partner in 1952. At the time he joined Chrysler, Mr. Townsend was Touche Ross's partner-in-charge of the Chrysler audit. In 1958, Mr. Townsend was named group vice president—international operations. In 1960, he was elected administrative vice president and president in 1961. He became chairman of the board on January 1, 1967. He is a director of Manufacturers Hanover Trust Company.

Shares of Chrysler stock beneficially owned 52,631
Salaries and fees for 1970 .... $200,000
Salaries and fees for 1969 .... $200,000

V. E. Boyd, 58, Vice Chairman of the Board

Mr. Boyd joined Chrysler in 1962 as vice president and general sales manager. For nearly eight years prior to that time, he was associated with another automobile manufacturer in various sales capacities, the last of which was vice president of automotive sales. He began his career in 1931 in the automobile sales finance business. From 1937 to 1947, he held various sales positions with another automobile company, and from 1947 to 1954, he owned and operated automobile dealerships in Iowa and Nebraska. In 1963, he was named vice president and group executive—automotive sales, and in 1964, he was named group vice president—domestic automotive, with responsibility for all domestic automotive manufacturing and sales. He became president on January 1, 1967, and vice chairman of the board on January 8, 1970.

Shares of Chrysler stock beneficially owned 17,171
Salaries and fees for 1970 .... $175,000
Salaries and fees for 1969 .... $175,000

John J. Riccardo, 46, President

Mr. Riccardo joined Chrysler in 1959 as a financial staff executive on the international operations staff. Prior to that, he was employed by the accounting firm now known as Touche Ross & Co. At the time he joined Chrysler, Mr. Riccardo was Touche Ross's partner-in-charge of the Chrysler audit. In 1960, he was named general manager of the export-import division. In 1961, he was elected a vice president of Chrysler Canada, Ltd., and later served as executive vice president of that subsidiary until 1963 when he became general sales manager of the Dodge Car and Truck Division. In 1964, he also assumed additional responsibilities as assistant general manager of that division. He was appointed in 1965 as assistant general manager of the Chrysler-Plymouth Division. In 1966, he was named vice president—marketing staff. In January 1967, he became group vice president—domestic automotive, and in April 1967, he was put in charge of the U.S. and Canadian automotive group. He became president of Chrysler on January 9, 1970.

Shares of Chrysler stock beneficially owned 7,558
Salaries and fees for 1970 .... $166,667
Salaries and fees for 1969 .... $166,667

cated that the only thing left was for the results to start showing. "We think all the arrows are pointing up," he said.

Now that Chrysler's "recovery" is six months old, many financial analysts are disappointed. Some of the turnaround strategies and expectations haven't yet panned out. Meanwhile, new problems have cropped up and others have worsened. The firm's recovery is clearly behind schedule. And

some analysts fear emergency measures, designed to ease immediate problems, may have some detrimental long-range effects on the nation's sixth
biggest manufacturer. As if these problems weren't enough, yesterday
Chrysler narrowly averted a major crisis when it tentatively agreed to new
three-year contracts with some 10,000 white-collar workers after they
walked out.

Instead of rolling up an expected fourth quarter profit of $50 million
to $75 million, Chrysler earned $20 million or less. As a result, it will report,
probably Friday, that it broke even or posted a loss for all 1970—a worse
showing than 1969 and the poorest earnings year since Mr. Townsend took
charge in 1961. The first quarter is expected to be little better, and the
slow profit rebound may hurt Chrysler when it seeks new equity financing
it needs to fundamentally strengthen its financial position.[1]

On February 9, 1971, Chrysler Corporation released its Report to Shareholders for the year ended December 31, 1970 (see Exhibit 3). The report
began with the following "Message to Shareholders" from Chrysler's chairman, Lynn Townsend, and its president, John Riccardo:

To our shareholders:

Sales of Chrysler Corporation and consolidated subsidiaries throughout
the world in 1970 totaled $7.0 billion, compared with $7.1 billion in 1969.
Operations for the year resulted in a net loss of $7.6 million or $0.16 a
share, compared with net earnings of $99.0 million or $2.09 a share in
1969.

Net earnings for 1969 are restated to reflect a retroactive change in
the company's method of valuing inventories, from a LIFO (last-in, first-
out) to a FIFO (first-in, first-out) cost basis, as explained in the notes to
financial statements. The LIFO method reduces inventory values and earnings in periods of rising costs. The rate of inflation in costs in 1970 and
for the projected short-term future is so high that significant understatements of inventory values and earnings result. The use of the LIFO method
in 1970 would have reduced inventory amounts at December 31, 1970,
by approximately $150 million and did reduce inventory amounts reported
at December 31, 1969, by approximately $110 million. Also, the use of
the LIFO method in 1970 would have increased the loss for the year by
approximately $20.0 million, and its use in 1969 reduced the earnings as
reported for that year by $10.2 million. The other three U.S. automobile
manufacturers have consistently used the FIFO method. Therefore, the
reported loss for 1970 and the restated profit for 1969 are on a comparable
basis as to inventory valuation with the other three companies. Prior years'
earnings have been restated to make them comparable.

Results of operations for the first three quarters of 1970 were previously
reported on the LIFO method of valuing inventories. The restated results

---

[1] *The Wall Street Journal,* February 3, 1971, p. 16.

EXHIBIT 3
Chrysler Corporation

Edited Version of Chrysler's 1970 Annual Report[1]

CHRYSLER CORPORATION AND CONSOLIDATED SUBSIDIARIES
Consolidated Statement of Net Earnings
(Dollars in thousands, except per-share amounts)

Year Ended December 31	1970	Restated* 1969	Originally Reported† 1969	Originally Reported‡ 1968
Net sales	$6,999,676	$7,052,185	$7,052,185	$7,445,251
Equity in net earnings (loss) of unconsolidated subsidiaries	(6,210)	(6,286)	(6,286)	15,587
Other income and deductions	(19,963)	23,261	23,261	34,230
	$6,973,503	$7,069,160	$7,069,160	$7,495,069
Cost of products sold, other than items below	$6,103,251	$5,966,732	$5,988,332	$5,948,446
Depreciation of plant and equipment	176,758	170,306	170,306	186,573
Amortization of special tools	172,568	167,194	167,194	162,194
Selling and administrative expenses	386,042	431,706	431,706	415,810
Pension and retirement plans	121,406	114,578	114,578	119,376
Provision for incentive compensation plan	—			25,270
Interest on long-term debt	46,999	31,703	31,703	26,074
Taxes on income (credit)	(21,400)	91,700	80,300	321,200
	$6,985,624	$6,973,919	$6,984,119	$7,204,933
Net earnings (loss) including minority interest	$ (12,121)	$ 95,241	$ 85,041	$ 290,136
Minority interest in net loss of consolidated subsidiaries	4,518	3,730	3,730	593
Net earnings (loss)	$ (7,603)	$ 98,971	$ 88,771	$ 290,729
Net earnings (loss) a share	$(0.16)	$2.09	$1.87	$6.23

See notes to financial statements.

* Restated to reflect the change made in 1970 in accounting for inventories and to conform to 1970 classifications. The 1969 net earnings and net earnings a share, as previously reported, were $88.8 million and $1.87 respectively. See Inventories—Accounting Change note.

† In the Financial Review section of its 1969 annual report, Chrysler noted the following: "Chrysler's net earnings in the past two years were lower by $10.2 million or 22 cents a share for 1969 and $12.2 million or 26 cents a share for 1968 by using LIFO, compared with FIFO as used by other major automobile manufacturers."

‡ In the Financial Review section of its 1968 annual report, Chrysler noted the following: "In 1957, the company adopted the last-in, first-out (LIFO) method of valuing the domestic automotive and diversified products inventories under the provisions of LIFO Regulations of the Internal Revenue Code. Since that time, there has been an almost continuous inflationary trend. The use of the LIFO method during this period of increasing costs resulted in lower earnings and lower inventory carrying values than if the first-in, first-out (FIFO) method were used. Compared to the FIFO method (used by other major automobile manufacturers), Chrysler's net earnings in the past two years were lower by $12.2 million or 26 cents a share in 1968 and $2.5 million or 5 cents a share in 1967."

[1] Note: In its 1970 annual report, Chrysler reported 1970 figures and restated 1969 figures. Originally reported figures for 1969 and 1968 are included in the case for comparative purposes.

EXHIBIT 3 *(continued)*

CHRYSLER CORPORATION AND CONSOLIDATED SUBSIDIARIES
Consolidated Balance Sheet
(dollars in thousands)

Assets

December 31	1970	Restated* 1969	Originally Reported 1969	Originally Reported 1968
Current assets:				
Cash	$ 95,807	$ 78,768	$ 78,768	$ 94,735
Marketable securities—at cost and accrued interest	60,607	230,563	230,563	418,686
Accounts receivable (less allowance for doubtful accounts: 1970—$15,700; 1969—$13,400; 1968—$10,000)	438,853	477,881	477,881	546,848
Refundable United States taxes on income	80,000	—	—	—
Inventories (See Inventories—Accounting Change note)	1,390,681	1,335,198	1,225,194	996,196
Prepaid insurance, taxes, and other expenses	83,300	80,088	80,088	68,374
Income taxes allocable to the following year	17,416	27,186	83,680	85,234
Total current assets	$2,166,664	$2,229,684	$2,176,174	$2,210,073
Investment and other assets:				
Investments in and advances to associated companies outside the United States	$ 24,907	$ 15,497	$ 15,497	$ 16,182
Investments in and advances to unconsolidated subsidiaries	675,213	577,053	577,053	543,780
Income taxes allocable—noncurrent	22,302	32,465	32,465	23,223
Other noncurrent assets	44,972	55,815	55,815	54,385
Total investments and other assets	$ 767,394	$ 680,830	$ 680,830	$ 637,570
Property, plant, and equipment:				
Land, buildings, machinery, and equipment	$2,949,256	$2,825,624	$2,825,624	$2,507,731
Less: Accumulated depreciation	1,593,482	1,451,751	1,451,751	1,314,450
	$1,355,774	$1,373,873	$1,373,873	$1,193,281
Unamortized special tools	447,450	379,153	379,153	278,685
Net property, plant, and equipment	$1,803,224	$1,753,026	$1,753,026	$1,471,966
Cost of investments in consolidated subsidiaries in excess of equity	78,490	78,184	78,184	78,483
Total assets	$4,815,772	$4,741,724	$4,688,214	$4,398,092

See notes to financial statements.
* Restated to reflect the change made in 1970 in accounting for inventories.

EXHIBIT 3 (*continued*)

Liabilities and Shareholders' Investment

December 31	1970	Restated* 1969	Originally Reported 1969	Originally Reported 1968
Current liabilities:				
Accounts payable and accrued expenses	$1,095,984	$1,116,609	$1,116,609	$1,123,569
Short-term debt	374,186	477,442	477,442	134,437
Payments due within one year on long-term debt	34,573	39,825	39,825	32,290
Taxes on income	43,136	9,969	9,969	137,371
Total current liabilities	$1,547,879	$1,643,845	$1,643,845	$1,427,667
Other liabilities:				
Deferred incentive compensation	$ 2,727	$ 7,494	$ 7,494	$ 15,365
Other employee benefit plans	63,462	55,575	55,575	48,524
Deferred investment tax credit	21,775	25,598	25,598	23,927
Unrealized profits on sales to unconsolidated subsidiaries	49,280	47,336	47,336	38,177
Other noncurrent liabilities	68,733	89,871	89,871	106,758
Total other liabilities	$ 205,977	$ 225,874	$ 225,874	$ 232,751
Long-term debt:				
Notes and debentures payable	$ 671,053	$ 446,951	$ 466,951	$ 415,281
Convertible sinking fund debentures	119,999	119,999	119,999	119,999
Total long-term debt	$ 791,052	$ 586,950	$ 586,950	$ 535,280
International operations reserve	35,500	35,500	35,500	35,500
Minority interest in net assets of consolidated subsidiaries	79,743	95,149	95,149	100,570
Shareholders' investment:				
Represented by common stock-par value $6.25 a share:				
Authorized 80 million shares; issued and outstanding				
49,498,979 shares at December 31, 1970; 47,942,136 shares at				
December 31, 1969; and 46,989,688 shares at December 31, 1968	$ 309,369	$ 299,638	$ 299,638	$ 293,686
Additional paid-in capital	484,020	455,740	455,740	421,184
Net earnings retained for use in the business	1,362,232	1,399,028	1,345,518	1,351,454
Total shareholders' investment	$2,155,621	$2,154,406	$2,100,896	$2,066,324
Total liabilities and shareholders' investment	$4,815,772	$4,741,724	$4,688,214	$4,398,092

See notes to financial statements.
* Restated to reflect the change made in 1970 in accounting for inventories.

EXHIBIT 3 *(continued)*

CHRYSLER CORPORATION AND CONSOLIDATED SUBSIDIARIES
Consolidated Source and Application of Working Capital
(dollars in thousands)

Year Ended December 31	1970	Restated* 1969	Originally Reported 1969	Originally Reported 1968
Additions to working capital:				
From operations:				
Net earnings (loss)	$ (7,603)	$ 98,971	$ 88,771	$ 290,729
Depreciation	176,758	170,306	170,306	162,194
Amortization of special tools	172,568	167,194	167,194	186,573
Decrease (increase) in income taxes allocable—noncurrent	10,164	(9,243)	(9,243)	14,254
Proceeds from long-term borrowing	241,551	91,063	91,063	210,367
Proceeds from sale of common stock	38,012	40,507	40,507	34,176
Retirement of property, plant, and equipment	14,857	23,415	23,415	20,035
Total additions	$ 646,307	$ 582,213	$ 572,013	$ 918,328
Disposition of working capital:				
Cash dividends paid	$ 29,193	$ 94,707	$ 94,707	$ 93,342
Increase in investments and advances	107,570	32,587	32,587	111,045
Expenditures for property, plant, and equipment	173,793	374,534	374,534	217,026
Expenditures for special tools	241,746	271,762	271,762	204,730
Payments on long-term borrowing	37,449	39,392	39,392	35,272
Decrease in other liabilities	19,897	6,877	6,877	(13,531)
Other	3,713	2,231	2,231	27,234
Total dispositions	$ 613,361	$ 822,090	$ 822,090	$ 675,118
Increase (decrease) in working capital during the year	$ 32,946	$ (239,877)	$ (250,077)	$ 243,210
Changes in components of working capital:	*(Decrease) Increase in Working Capital*			
Cash	$ 17,039	$ (15,967)	$ (15,967)	$ (54)
Marketable securities	(169,956)	(188,123)	(188,123)	(5,854)
Accounts receivable	(39,028)	(68,967)	(68,967)	78,856
Refundable U.S. taxes on income	80,000	—	—	—
Inventories	55,483	250,958	228,998	167,307
Prepaid expenses	3,212	11,714	11,714	15,649
Income taxes allocable to the following year	(9,770)	(13,314)	(1,554)	18,186
Accounts payable and accrued expenses	20,625	6,960	6,960	(48,713)
Short-term debt	103,256	(343,005)	(343,005)	14,015
Payments due within one year on long-term debt	5,252	(7,535)	(7,535)	2,983
Taxes on income	(33,167)	127,402	127,402	835
Increase (decrease) in working capital during the year	$ 32,946	$ (239,877)	$ (250,077)	$ 243,210

See notes to financial statements.
* Restated to reflect the change made in 1970 in accounting for inventories and to conform to 1970 classifications.

EXHIBIT 3 *(continued)*

CHRYSLER CORPORATION AND CONSOLIDATED SUBSIDIARIES
Consolidated Statement of Additional Paid-In Capital
(dollars in thousands)

Year Ended December 31	1970	Restated* 1969	Originally Reported 1969	Originally Reported 1968
Balance at beginning of year	$ 455,739	$ 421,185	$ 421,185	$ 390,861
Excess of market price over par value of newly issued shares of common stock sold at the thrift-stock ownership programs (1,556,843 in 1970; 927,276 in 1969; 470,089 in 1968)	28,282	33,796	33,796	25,941
Excess of option price over par value of shares of common stock issued under the stock option plans (none in 1970; 25,172 in 1969; 146,236 in 1968)	—	758	758	4,383
Balance at end of year	$ 484,021	$ 455,739	$ 455,739	$ 421,185

Consolidated Statement of Net Earnings Retained for Use in the Business

Year Ended December 31	1970	Restated* 1969	Originally Reported 1969	Originally Reported 1968
Balance at beginning of year	$1,399,028	$1,351,454	$1,351,454	$1,154,067
Adjustment (for the years 1957 through 1968)		43,310		
As restated		$1,394,764		
Net earnings (loss)	(7,603)	98,971	88,771	290,729
Net earnings as restated	$1,391,425	$1,493,735	$1,440,225	$1,444,796
Cash dividends paid ($0.60 a share in 1970 and $2.00 a share in 1969 and 1968)	29,193	94,707	94,707	93,342
Balance at end of year	$1,362,232	$1,399,028	$1,345,518	$1,351,454

See notes to financial statements.
* Restated to reflect the change made in 1970 in accounting for inventories.

EXHIBIT 3 (continued)

CHRYSLER FINANCIAL CORPORATION AND CONSOLIDATED SUBSIDIARIES
Consolidated Balance Sheet
(dollars in thousands)

Editor's Note: Amounts may not add due to rounding.

December 31	1970	1969*
Assets:		
Cash	$ 135,000	$ 84,284
Marketable securities—at cost and accrued interest	1,234	1,470
Notes receivable (including amounts due after one year):		
Retail installment sale and lease financing	1,156,794	1,344,523
Wholesale	814,938	677,751
Commercial and other installment loans	69,417	63,341
	$2,041,150	$2,085,616
Less: Unearned income	88,589	102,899
Allowance for losses	21,054	23,699
Notes receivable—net	$1,931,506	$1,959,017
Accounts receivable	28,005	9,739
Collateral held for resale—at estimated realizable value	426	707
Prepaid expenses	14,531	7,007
Investments in and amounts due from unconsolidated subsidiaries and affiliated companies	40,836	53,190
Office furniture and equipment—at cost less accumulated depreciation	1,572	1,605
Total assets	$2,153,114	$2,117,022

EXHIBIT 3 (continued)

December 31	1970	1969*
Liabilities and Shareholders' Investment		
Liabilities:		
Notes payable, unsecured short-term	$1,503,826	$1,535,562
Long-term debt due within one year	6,765	5,327
Accounts payable and accrued expenses	32,012	24,116
Amounts due to affiliated companies	6,850	12,102
Income taxes payable	9,524	6,209
Income taxes deferred	12,209	13,072
Reserves withheld—dealers and other	24,500	23,320
Unamortized excess of the value of acquired net assets over purchase price	—	1,062
	$1,595,689	$1,620,773
Long-term debt:		
Notes payable, due at various dates to 1985	127,728	129,859
Subordinated notes payable, due at various dates to 1987	135,900	138,900
Shareholders' Investment:		
Preferred stock—par value $100 a share:		
Authorized, issued, and outstanding 400,000 shares	$ 40,000	$ 40,000
Common stock—par value $100 a share:		
Authorized, issued, and outstanding 250,000 shares	25,000	25,000
Additional paid-in capital	180,000	135,000
Net earnings retained for use in the business:		
Balance at beginning of year	27,489	12,123
Net earnings for the year	21,306	15,365
Balance at end of year	$ 48,795	$ 27,489
Total shareholders' investment	$ 293,795	$ 227,489
Total liabilities and shareholders' investment	$2,153,114	$2,117,022

See notes to balance sheet.

* Restated to conform to 1970 classifications.

EXHIBIT 3 *(continued)*

Notes to Financial Statements

Principles of Consolidation

The consolidated financial statements include the accounts of Chrysler Corporation and majority-owned and controlled subsidiaries except those engaged primarily in leasing, financing, insuring, retail selling, and realty activities. Investments in unconsolidated subsidiaries are carried at equity.

adjustment to inventory amounts will be taken into taxable income ratably over 20 years commencing January 1, 1971.

Taxes on Income

Taxes on income as shown in the consolidated statement of net earnings include the following (in millions of dollars):

	1970	1969	1968
Currently payable:			
United States taxes (credit)	$(81.8)	$50.0	$272.1
Other countries	44.3	36.3	54.5
Deferred taxes	16.1	(6.0)	(5.4)
As previously reported		80.3	321.2
Adjustments in deferred taxes for change in inventory valuation	—	11.4	13.6
Total taxes on income (credit)	$(21.4)	$91.7	$334.8

Inventories—Accounting Change

Inventories are stated at the lower of cost or market. For the period January 1, 1957, through December 31, 1969, the last-in, first-out (LIFO) method of inventory valuation had been used for approximately 60 percent of the consolidated inventory. The cost of the remaining 40 percent of inventories was determined using the first-in, first-out (FIFO) or average cost methods. Effective January 1, 1970, the FIFO method of inventory valuation has been adopted for inventories previously valued using the LIFO method. This results in a more uniform valuation method throughout the corporation and its consolidated subsidiaries and makes the financial statements with respect to inventory valuation comparable with those of the other United States automobile manufacturers. As a result of adopting FIFO in 1970, the net loss reported is less than it would have been on a LIFO basis by approximately $20 million, or $0.40 a share. Inventory amounts at December 31, 1968, 1969, and 1970, are stated higher by approximately $88 million, $110 million, and $150 million, respectively, than they would have been had the LIFO method been continued.

The corporation has retroactively adjusted financial statements of prior years for this change. Accordingly, the 1969 financial statements have been restated resulting in an increase in net earnings of $10.2 million, and net earnings retained for use in the business at December 31, 1969, and 1968, have been increased by $53.5 million and $43.3 million, respectively.

For United States income tax purposes, the

The provision for taxes on income for the year 1970 includes a credit of approximately $80 million resulting from the carryback of 1970 taxable losses to an earlier tax year as provided for in the U.S. Internal Revenue Code. Charges for currently payable taxes on income for subsidiaries outside the U.S. and for deferred taxes are also reflected in the net provision for taxes on income.

The change in inventory valuation resulted in a reduction in income taxes allocable to the following year of approximately $56 million at December 31, 1969.

Reduction in taxes resulting from the investment credit provisions of the Internal Revenue Code are being taken into income over the estimated lives of the related assets. The amounts of such credits which were reflected in net earnings were $6.3 million in 1970, $5.4 million in 1969, and $5.8 million in 1968.

Property, Plant, and Equipment

Property, plant, and equipment is carried substantially at cost less accumulated depreciation and amortization. Depreciation is generally provided on an accelerated basis. This has an effect of allocating proportionally greater amounts of cost to operations during the early, most productive years of the asset's life. Depreciation of property, plant, and equipment of Chrysler France, Chrysler Espana S.A., and Chrysler United Kingdom, Ltd., has been recorded on a straight-line basis. Amortization of the cost of special tooling is provided on a basis designed to allocate the costs to opera-

EXHIBIT 3 *(continued)*

tions during the years in which the tools are used in the productive process.

Debt and Debt Guarantees

In March 1970, the company sold to the public $100 million of 8⅞ percent sinking fund debentures with a final maturity in 1995 and $100 million of 8¾ percent notes due 1975. The proceeds were added to the general funds of the company and used to improve the company's working capital position. The reduction in short-term debt from $477.4 million at the end of 1969 to $374.2 million at December 31, 1970, reflects the drop in outstanding commercial paper of Chrysler Corporation. At the end of 1970, only $3.8 million in commercial paper was outstanding, compared with $250 million at the end of 1969 and a peak level of $439 million in March of 1970.

Total interest charges including interest on long-term debt were $107.4 million in 1970, $54.8 million in 1969, and $39.7 million in 1968.

The aggregate annual maturities and required prepayments of consolidated long-term debt are as follows for the years ending December 31: 1971—$34,572,552; 1972—$27,260,018; 1973—$36,326,877; 1974—$56,068,302; and 1975—$156,751,227.

Chrysler Corporation has guaranteed approximately $99 million of 6 percent notes due January 1, 1995, of Chrysler Realty Corporation. Chrysler Corporation and consolidated subsidiaries have also guaranteed other debt approximating $31 million principally of unconsolidated subsidiaries outside the United States. All outstanding long-term debt of Chrysler Overseas Capital Corporation is unconditionally guaranteed by Chrysler Corporation.

Cost of Investments in Consolidated Subsidiaries in Excess of Equity

The amount reflected in the consolidated financial statements represents the excess of cost of investments in consolidated subsidiaries over equities in net assets at dates of acquisition less amortization through December 31, 1965, at which point the corporation discontinued amortization of these costs.

International Operations

Net sales of subsidiaries operating outside the United States and Canada amounted to $1.7 billion for the year ended December 31, 1970, $1.6 billion for the year ended December 31, 1969, and $1.5 billion for the year ended December 31, 1968. Net losses of these subsidiaries were $7.9 million in 1970 compared with net earnings of $19 million in 1969 and $17.6 million in 1968. These results are after provisions for estimated United States taxes on unremitted net profits.

Pension and Retirement Plans

Chrysler Corporation and certain of its consolidated subsidiaries have pension and retirement plans covering substantially all of their employees. The total expense of these plans during 1970 was $121.4 million, which includes amortization of the unfunded prior service costs over periods not exceeding 30 years. The corporation's policy is to fund pension costs as accrued. Changes in the pension plans which will become effective in 1971 as a result of new collective bargaining agreements will increase the annual pension expense by approximately $48 million.

As of January 1, 1970, the actuarially computed value of the vested benefits for certain plans exceeds the total of those pension funds (at market value) by approximately $270 million. Pension funds for the other plans exceed the actuarially computed value of vested benefits. The value of vested benefits at December 31, 1970, has not yet been determined.

Incentive Compensation Plan

No awards of incentive compensation were made for 1969 or 1970.

Under a resolution adopted by the stockholders in 1929, amended in its entirety in 1956, and most recently amended in 1969 (called the Stockholders' Resolution), awards may be made only for those years in which the sum of (1) consolidated net earnings of the corporation and consolidated subsidiaries (as reported in the annual report to the stockholders) after taxes on income, (2) provision for incentive compensation, and (3) interest on long-term debt of the corporation exceeds 5½ percent of the sum of the shareholders' investment in the corporation and the long-term debt of the corporation. The total provision for awards in any year is limited to the lesser of 12 percent of such excess or the aggregate amount of all dividends declared on the common stock of the corporation during that year.

The Incentive Compensation Plan in effect for 1970 and subsequent years, established by the board of directors under authority granted to it by the Stockholders' Resolution, provides that awards be determined by a committee of directors, none of whom may be officers

EXHIBIT 3 *(continued)*

of the corporation or eligible to receive an award.

Common Stock

Of the authorized 80 million shares of common stock at December 31, 1970, 815,271 shares were reserved for the thrift-stock ownership programs, 1,558,942 shares for the stock option plans for salaried officers and key employees (65,942 shares for the 1952 stock option plan and 1,493,000 shares for the 1966 stock option plan), and 1,784,053 shares to cover conversion of debentures.

At January 1, 1970, options for 652,962 shares were outstanding. During 1970, options for 162,000 shares were granted, options for 200,020 shares were terminated, and no options were exercised. At December 31, 1970, options for 614,942 shares were outstanding at prices ranging from $22.38 to $69.50 a share, the average being $41.83. Options were granted at prices not less than 100 percent of market value at dates of grant. Options for 331,042 shares were exercisable at December 31, 1970.

Auditors' Opinion

Shareholders and Board of Directors
Chrysler Corporation

We have examined the accompanying consolidated balance sheet of Chrysler Corporation and consolidated subsidiaries as of December 31, 1970, and 1969, and the related statements of net earnings, net earnings retained for use in the business, additional paid-in capital, and source and application of working capital for the years then ended. Our ex-amination was made in accordance with generally accepted auditing standards, and accordingly included such tests of the accounting records and such other auditing procedures as we considered necessary in the circumstances. We performed similar examinations of the balance sheets of Chrysler Financial Corporation and consolidated subsidiaries and Chrysler Realty Corporation, and the related statements of net earnings, net earnings retained for use in the business, additional paid-in capital, and source and application of funds for the years then ended (not shown here).

In our opinion, the financial statements referred to above present fairly the financial position of Chrysler Corporation and consolidated subsidiaries, Chrysler Financial Corporation and consolidated subsidiaries, and Chrysler Realty Corporation at December 31, 1970, and 1969, the respective results of their operations and the source and application of funds for the years then ended, in conformity with generally accepted accounting principles applied on a basis consistent with that of the preceding year, after giving retroactive effect in the financial statements of Chrysler Corporation and consolidated subsidiaries to the change in inventory valuation, which we approve, described in the notes to financial statements.

TOUCHE ROSS & CO.
Certified Public Accountants
Detroit, Michigan
February 9, 1971

EXHIBIT 3 (concluded)

CHRYSLER CORPORATION AND CONSOLIDATED SUBSIDIARIES
Financial Statistics
(in millions of dollars)

	1970	1969	1968	1967	1966	1965	1964	1963	1962	1961
Operating Results:										
Passenger cars and trucks sold (in thousands of units)	2,459	2,447	2,624	2,252	2,134	2,077	1,807	1,519	892	802
Net sales	$ 7,000	7,052	7,445	6,213	5,650	5,300	4,287	3,505	2,378	2,127
Net earnings as previously reported	$	89	291	200	189	233	214	162	65	11
Effect of accounting change (note)		10	12	3	5	6	1	2	—	(2)
Net earnings (loss)	$ (8)	99	303	203	194	239	215	164	65	9
Net earnings a share as previously reported	$	1.87	6.23	4.35	4.16	5.44	5.50	4.23	1.74	.30
Effect of accounting change a share (note)		.22	.26	.06	.11	.15	.04	.05	.01	(.06)
Net earnings (loss) a share	$ (0.16)	2.09	6.49	4.41	4.27	5.59	5.54	4.28	1.75	.24
Average shares outstanding (in thousands)	48,693	47,391	46,680	46,038	45,449	42,870	38,901	38,203	37,564	37,233
Net earnings including minority interest as a percent of sales	(.2%)	1.4%	4.1%	3.3%	3.4%	4.5%	5.0%	4.7%	2.8%	0.4%
Cash dividends paid	$ 29	95	93	92	91	55	37	16	9	9
A share	$ .60	2.00	2.00	2.00	2.00	1.25	.96	.42	.24	.24
Common stock dividend							4%			
Expenditures for facilities other than special tools	$ 174	375	217	191	306	292	313	78	19	13
Depreciation	$ 177	170	162	153	130	102	74	59	55	67
Expenditures for special tools	$ 242	272	205	201	200	157	160	105	69	75
Amortization of special tools	$ 173	167	187	161	173	148	95	94	67	90
Financial Position—Year-End: (1961 through 1969 restated—note)										
Current assets	$ 2,167	2,230	2,253	1,967	1,495	1,503	1,303	1,390	1,021	906
Current liabilities	$ 1,548	1,644	1,428	1,397	1,022	937	879	798	438	386
Net current assets	$ 619	586	825	570	473	566	424	592	583	520
Property, plant, equipment, and tools— less accumulated depreciation	$ 1,803	1,753	1,472	1,407	1,282	1,067	871	556	399	439
Total assets	$ 4,816	4,742	4,441	3,980	3,177	2,958	2,438	2,139	1,539	1,414
Long-term debt	$ 791	587	535	360	216	224	242	256	238	250
Shareholders' investment	$ 2,156	2,154	2,110	1,866	1,730	1,606	1,139	937	784	725
Shares outstanding (in thousands)	49,499	47,942	46,990	46,373	45,755	45,220	39,184	38,600	37,600	37,449
Shareholders' investment a share	$ 43.55	44.94	44.90	40.24	37.80	35.49	29.08	24.26	20.85	19.36
Number of shareholders	204,329	174,066	159,970	179,749	195,805	140,708	112,724	77,020	77,750	80,231

Note—The net earnings for 1961 through 1969 have been restated to reflect the change from the LIFO (last-in, first-out) inventory valuation method to the FIFO (first-in, first-out) method effective January 1, 1970. The financial statistics have been restated accordingly.

on the FIFO method of valuing inventories for the four quarters of 1970 are as follows:

	Net Earnings (Loss) (millions)	Earnings (Loss) a Share
1st quarter	$(27.4)	$(0.57)
2d quarter	10.1	0.21
3d quarter	2.1	0.05
4th quarter	7.6	0.15
	$(7.6)	$(0.16)

Sales of the company's passenger cars, trucks, and tractors throughout the world during the year totaled 2,459,336 units, slightly above the 2,446,605 units sold in 1969. Unit sales outside the United States and Canada totaled 811,711 units, compared with 734,041 the previous year.

The United States economy during 1970 experienced a combination of inflation and recession, high unemployment, high interest rates, and restricted growth. Consumer confidence was weakened by economic and social problems at home, and by serious crises in the Middle East and Southeast Asia. A major strike in the automotive industry cut North American vehicle production and added to the consumer's lack of confidence. As a result, United States automobile industry sales for the year reached their lowest point since 1962.

The company's financial results for 1970 reflect these economic factors. There was a drop in North American factory sales of 64,939 cars and trucks. The shift in consumer demand toward smaller, less expensive automobiles which had been evident throughout 1969 also continued strongly through 1970, resulting in a less profitable product mix. In addition, costs increased heavily during the year and were not completely recovered in increased selling prices.[2]

In response to these pressures, the company made a number of important moves. Operating expense and capital expenditures underwent a thorough review and were substantially reduced. The company's corporate organization was realigned to produce a more direct system of operational controls for increased efficiency. The company took steps to improve the marketing and product programs for the short and the long term.

Sales outside the United States and Canada in 1970 were $1.7 billion or 25 percent of the company's total consolidated sales, compared with $1.6 billion or 22 percent of total sales in 1969. Many important markets overseas were affected by adverse business conditions, particularly rising labor and material costs and price, credit, and economic controls. In addition, widespread strikes throughout Great Britain seriously reduced production and sales. The company's mature investments overseas are returning

---

[2] During 1970, there was a shift in consumer demand to smaller and less expensive vehicles. Compacts accounted for 16.5 percent of all domestic sales in the U.S. market compared with 11.4 percent in 1969. Chrysler Corporation was in first place in the domestic segment of the compact market with 39.0 percent of all sales.

a profit, and maximum attention is concentrated on improving the operations of more recent investments including those in Great Britain, Spain, and Brazil.

As a result of these actions, and in spite of the depressed economy, Chrysler Corporation has operated at a profit for the nine-month period since April 1, 1970.

Net current assets totaled $619 million on December 31, 1970, compared with $586 million on the same date a year earlier. Shareholders' investment at year-end was $2,156 million or $44 a share. Expenditures for property, plant, and equipment, excluding special tools, totaled $174 million in 1970 and $375 million in 1969. Depreciation totaled $177 million in 1970 and $170 million in 1969. Expenditures for special tools amounted to $242 million in 1970 and $272 million for the year earlier. Amortization charges were $173 million in 1970 and $167 million in 1969.

In recent weeks, there have been some signs that the United States economy is regaining some momentum. Interest rates are going down and housing starts continue to increase. Industry retail sales were up 9.1 percent in January 1971 over the same period a year earlier. Chrysler Corporation passenger car sales were up 9.9 percent. The combination of improved consumer confidence, high levels of personal savings, and the general backlog of demand that built up during 1970 makes the outlook for the automotive industry encouraging for 1971.

We wish to thank our shareholders and customers for their loyalty to our products, and we extend our appreciation to our employees, dealers, and suppliers for their support during the past year.

John Riccardo
President

Lynn Townsend
Chairman

February 9, 1971

On March 12, 1971, Chrysler filed an 8-K[3] report with the Securities and Exchange Commission (SEC) which expanded on the change in inventory valuation method from LIFO to FIFO. According to the 8-K:

This change was made to provide a more uniform valuation method throughout the operations of Chrysler and makes its financial statements with respect to inventory valuation comparable with those of the other United States automobile manufacturers.

The change in the method of valuing inventories resulted in a reduction as of December 31, 1969, in the account Income Taxes Allocable to the

---

[3] A firm must file an 8-K report with the SEC within 15 days of the end of the month in which a material event affecting the firm occurs, e.g., an accounting change which will materially affect the firm's reported earnings.

Following Year of $56.5 million. For United States income tax purposes, the registrant retained the LIFO method of inventory valuation in 1970. The resulting differences between taxable earnings in 1970, based on the LIFO method of inventory valuation, and earnings set forth in the financial statements, based on the FIFO method, had the effect of further reducing Income Taxes Allocable to the Following Year by approximately $20 million at December 31, 1970. The adjustment to inventory amounts will be taken into taxable income ratably over 20 years commencing January 1, 1971.

As a result of the change in valuing inventories, the account Net Earnings Retained for Use in the Business was increased by $53.5 million as of December 31, 1969.

Background Information

Chrysler and the Automobile Industry

Chrysler Corporation and its domestic subsidiaries are engaged primarily in the manufacture, assembly, and sale in the United States of Plymouth, Dodge, Chrysler, and Imperial passenger cars, Dodge trucks, and related automotive parts and accessories. Foreign subsidiaries of Chrysler manufacture passenger cars and trucks and related parts and accessories most of which are sold outside the United States and some of which, principally Chrysler France and Chrysler United Kingdom, Ltd., passenger cars, are sold in the United States by a domestic subsidiary.

The automobile industry in the United States is highly competitive and is composed principally of four passenger car manufacturers, General Motors, Ford, Chrysler, and American Motors. New passenger cars are sold at retail primarily by dealers who are individually franchised by the manufacturer or a sales subsidiary of the manufacturer and who purchase cars, parts, and accessories from the manufacturer or the sales subsidiary for sale to their retail customers. Cars produced in the United States and Canada by the four passenger car manufacturers accounted for 85.2 percent (39.7 percent, 26.4 percent, 16.1 percent, and 3.0 percent, respectively) in 1970 and 88.7 percent (46.8 percent, 24.3 percent, 15.1 percent, and 2.5 percent respectively) in 1969 of all new passenger car registrations in the United states. Foreign imports accounted for most of the remaining registrations. The percentage of new passenger car registrations represented by foreign imports reached an all-time high of 14.7 percent in 1970; it was 7.3 percent, 9.3 percent, 10.5 percent, and 11.2 percent in the years 1966, 1967, 1968, and 1969, respectively.

Annual sales of the industry and of individual manufacturers within it have fluctuated widely over the years. This has been due to a number of factors. The purchase of an automobile is a deferrable item and the tendency of owners, when business conditions are adverse, is to keep their cars longer and postpone replacing them. When economic conditions appear more favorable, this tendency is reversed. In addition, it has been the practice of the industry to introduce new passenger car models annually, which requires substantial investments in styling, engineering, and special tooling. The degree of consumer acceptance of new models therefore can significantly affect sales and earnings. Other factors include the competition from other products and services for the consumers' dollars and competition of the foreign smaller car in the domestic market.

In the last quarter of 1970, a major strike at General Motors Corporation decreased North American vehicle production and as a result, United States automobile industry sales for the year reached their lowest point since 1962. GM's sales fell from $22.3 billion in 1969 to $18.8 billion in 1970. Net income declined even more precipitously from $1.7 billion in 1969 to $0.6 billion in 1970. Chrysler's problems paralleled those of GM and included unexpectedly low fourth-quarter sales which put pressure on working capital, especially cash. Chrysler's $7.6 million profit in the fourth quarter of 1970 was substantially less than the $20 million net profit that security analysts had been predicting. Typically, the fourth quarter was the profit-setting quarter for auto companies. Ford's successful introduction of the Pinto in the fourth quarter of 1970 helped it to stave off some of its competitors' problems. Sales at Ford increased in 1970 to $15.0 billion from $14.8 billion in 1969 and profits remained flat at $0.5 billion.

The following table provides five-year comparative information for: (1) number of cars sold from U.S. plants; (2) dollar sales volume of the "Big Three" auto manufacturers; and (3) net profits of the "Big Three" auto manufacturers:

Year	Thousands of Passenger Cars Sold			Total Sales (in billions)			Net Profits (in millions)		
	Chrysler	Industry	Percent of Industry	Chrysler	Ford	GM	Chrysler*	Ford	GM
1966	1,444	8,598	16.8	$5.7	$11.5	$20.2	$189	$621	$1,793
1967	1,366	7,437	18.4	$6.2	$12.2	$20.0	$200	$ 84	$1,627
1968	1,583	8,822	17.9	$7.4	$10.5	$22.8	$291	$626	$1,731
1969	1,393	8,224	16.9	$7.1	$14.8	$22.3	$ 89	$546	$1,710
1970	1,270	6,547	19.4	$7.0	$15.0	$18.8	$ (8)	$515	$ 609

* As originally reported on a LIFO basis except 1970 when Chrysler changed to FIFO.

U.S. Economy

The U.S. economy fell into a recession in 1970, and real gross national product (GNP) actually declined by 0.2 percent, for the entire year. This was the first "negative growth" in real GNP since 1958. During the 1960s, real GNP grew at an annual compounded rate of 4.4 percent.

Inflation (as measured by changes in the consumer price index) began to heat up during the latter half of the 1960s, rising from a mere 1.7 percent in 1965 to 5.4 percent by 1969 and 5.9 percent in 1970.

While recession and inflation rippled through the U.S. economy in 1970, the biggest financial shock occurred on June 21, 1970, when Penn Central Transportation Company, the nation's largest transportation company, filed for bankruptcy. In particular, the Penn Central bankruptcy raised havoc in the commercial paper market where Penn Central had defaulted on $82 million of outstanding commercial paper notes.

The immediate reaction of money market investors was an increased perception of the riskiness of the commercial paper market. Investors responded by shifting funds to other money market instruments and by investing in only very high-quality commercial paper. Some borrowing corporations, particularly those with profitability problems, faced a liquidity shortage because they were unable to continue obtaining short-term funds from investors. The actions of the Federal Reserve during June and July enabled and encouraged the commercial banks to supply credit to corporations confronted with the financial difficulties of the paper market. These actions restored stability to the commercial paper market by the end of July and prevented the development of a major liquidity crisis.

While the short-term effects were limited and controlled, the Penn Central default was one factor which tended to limit the subsequent growth of the commercial paper market. Credit quality, which had declined during the period of rapid growth, once again became an important concern of money market investors and seemed to become a formidable barrier to entry for potential borrowers. The emphasis on credit quality also seemed to force weaker credits to withdraw from the market.

The Penn Central failure and subsequent bankruptcies of other large U.S. companies, e.g., Four Seasons Nursing Homes, in 1970 raised serious concerns in the U.S. business community regarding the ability of the U.S. economy to resume its 1960s' growth trend. However, by the end of 1970, the U.S. economy appeared to be well positioned for recovery and most of the "doomsayers" retreated to the sidelines. Interest rates and inflation were moderating. By April 1971, the prime rate had fallen to 5.25 percent from a postwar high of 8.5 percent March 1970. Inflation was also subsiding and was expected to run approximately 4 percent for the entire year.

Chrysler in Early 1971

On March 22, 1971, the national credit office of Dun & Bradstreet eliminated its "prime" credit rating on the commercial paper of Chrysler Corporation and its chief financial units, Chrysler Financial Corporation and Chrysler Credit Canada, Ltd. Dun & Bradstreet assigned no rating to the commercial paper. An official of Dun & Bradstreet attributed the moves to Chrysler's "unimpressive operating results of 1969 and 1970."

On April 5, 1971, three working days after the close of the first quarter, Lynn Townsend announced estimated first-quarter profits of $10 million, or 20 cents a share, for Chrysler Corporation. This compared to a restated net loss of $27.4 million a year earlier. Mr. Townsend also reported record first-quarter sales of $1.8 billion, up 20 percent from $1.5 billion a year earlier. The quick release of the first-quarter results was widely interpreted in financial circles—and within Chrysler itself—as a move to counter the damaging impact on Chrysler's financial reputation of Dun & Bradstreet's removal of a credit rating for Chrysler's commercial paper.

According to an April 6, 1971, article in *The Wall Street Journal*, "Within Chrysler, some sources interpreted the early earnings release as an effort to influence the National Credit Office of Dun & Bradstreet, hopefully prompting it to restore its ratings on the commercial paper. (For companies the size of Chrysler, the only rating Dun & Bradstreet gives on commercial paper is 'prime.')"

On April 14, 1971, *The Wall Street Journal* published an article entitled "Hanover Trust Bank Defends Credit Status of its Client, Chrysler," excerpts of which follow:

> Rating or no rating, Chrysler Corporation is still creditworthy, according to Manufacturers Hanover Trust Company, chief banker for the big auto-maker.
>
> That's the assessment given to stockholders of Manufacturers Hanover Corporation at yesterday's annual meeting of the bank holding company.
>
> In an unusual defense of a customer, John F. McGillicuddy, president, told stockholders that Chrysler and its subsidiaries, Chrysler Financial Corporation and Chrysler Leasing Corporation, "have been and continue to be creditworthy customers of this bank." He said "our support of Chrysler" rests "on their ability to demonstrate, as we feel they have during these past months, their creditworthiness."
>
> Mr. McGillicuddy took pains to note that Chrysler recently released preliminary figures indicating the company "operated profitably during the first quarter of" this year. "We feel it is significant in that this represents the fourth consecutive profitable quarter for the corporation," he said.
>
> The executive stressed that neither Lynn Townsend, Chrysler chairman, or R. E. McNeill, Jr., a director of Chrysler and former chairman of the bank, participates in decisions "relating to extension of credit" by the bank to Chrysler. Both men are directors of Manufacturers Hanover.[4]

Chrysler Corporation held its annual meeting of stockholders on April 20, 1971. Chrysler's chairman, Lynn Townsend, began his remarks to the crowded meeting by stating that "We're sorry we had a bad 1970" but "we're coming out of it." According to the April 21, 1971, *Wall Street Journal:*

> At the meeting, Mr. Townsend, who was the architect of Chrysler's last resurgence a decade ago, didn't characterize the pace or expected extent of Chrysler's current recovery, which so far has disappointed some financial analysts. He said "we certainly aren't proud" of earnings of $10.8 million,

---

[4] *The Wall Street Journal*, April 14, 1971, p. 7.

or 22 cents a share, for the first quarter, except in the sense that a small profit was better than the year earlier's restated net loss of $27.4 million.

For all 1971, Mr. Townsend merely reiterated a forecast that Chrysler expects to show "a solid profit." But he then went on to say: "I define solid profit as sufficient earnings so that we aren't teetering on the brink of loss operations."

He held out the promise of a dividend increase, but was vague about when it might come. A year ago, Chrysler slashed its quarterly to 15 cents from 50 cents. "We don't like a 15 cent dividend," Mr. Townsend said. "We have also paid 30 percent to 45 percent" of earnings back to shareholders in dividends. "I would hope that as earnings develop, we could get to a better dividend."

In their speeches and answers to shareholder questions, Mr. Townsend and John J. Riccardo, president, stressed the long-range and short-term benefits expected from massive reorganizations and cost-cutting moves during the 18 months. Mr. Riccardo disclosed that one of the long-range steps includes programming "less frequent model changes," indicating that Chrysler is falling in line with an emerging industry pattern that may help to cut tooling expenses.

Mr. Townsend emphasized that Chrysler's financial position is "very solid." He noted that Standard & Poor's Corporation last week reaffirmed the single-A rating on the senior funded debt of Chrysler and its beleaguered sales finance subsidiary, while pinning a triple-A rating on the commercial paper of the sales finance unit. Since March 22, the commercial paper of Chrysler Financial has been under a cloud because the national credit office of Dun & Bradstreet, Inc., stripped it of its "prime" rating, citing Chrysler's unimpressive operating results in 1969 and 1970.

Mr. Townsend also reported a favorable development overseas. He said Chrysler U.K. posted "a profit in the first quarter of 1971" and its operations are "improving." Last year, the British operation was a prime contributor to a net loss of $7.9 million from overseas operations.[5]

Questions

1. Why did Chrysler change accounting methods?

2. How had Chrysler benefited from using LIFO prior to the switch to FIFO in 1970?

3. What was the actual and potential cash impact of the LIFO switch?

4. Approximate Chrysler's 1970 reported income for U.S. federal tax purposes. What does this figure imply? Can you reconcile this amount with the reported $7.6 million loss?

---

[5] *The Wall Street Journal*, April 21, 1971, p. 40.

CHAPTER 20

Analysis and Reporting of Intercorporate Investments and Business Combinations

Frequently, corporations acquire interests in other corporations ranging from a few shares of capital stock to 100 percent ownership. Sometimes, the assets or net assets, rather than the stock, are acquired. The reasons for these investments vary from temporary short-term investments of excess funds to permanent investments made to gain control of the acquired company. The accounting for these investments can vary depending on the amount of ownership acquired and the means used to acquire it. At the time these investments are announced, in order to understand the financial and income implications for investor company, experienced financial analysts prepare pro forma statements for the investor company reflecting the announced investment. This requires a good grasp of the accounting for intercorporate investments and business combinations.

The principal authoritative statements dealing with accounting for intercorporate investments and business combinations are: *Opinion No. 16*, "Business Combinations"; *Opinion No. 17*, "Intangible Assets"; *Opinion No. 18*, "Equity Method for Investments in Common Stock"; *Statement No. 12*, "Accounting for Certain Marketable Securities"; *Statement No. 38*, "Accounting for Preacquisition Contingencies of Purchased Enterprises"; and *Statement No. 58*, "Capitalization of Interest Costs in Financial Statements that Include Investments Accounted for by the Equity Method."

Initially, this chapter discusses the accounting for corporate investor holdings of common stock in other companies. It then covers the topic of business combinations.

Equity Investments

Opinion No. 18 requires the use of the equity method to account for all intercorporate investments involving stock, if the investment gives the in-

691

vestor the ability to exercise significant influence over the operating and financial policies of the investee company. This ability is presumed by the *Opinion* to exist for investments of 20 percent or more and is not presumed to exist for investments of less than 20 percent. Both presumptions may be overcome by predominant evidence to the contrary. Investments not qualifying for equity method accounting are reported using the cost method or as part of a portfolio of marketable equity securities.

Ownership Interests of Less than 20 Percent

Presentation of investments of less than 20 percent on the investor's balance sheet, and their effect upon current income, depends upon whether the investment is made for temporary, short-term reasons or for the purpose of creating some longer term relationship, and whether or not the securities involved are marketable.

Ownership interests of less than 20 percent are typically reported at cost or market, whichever is lower. Initially, the stock acquisition is recorded by charging an asset investment account for the investment cost, which includes the purchase price plus all incidental acquisition costs such as broker's commissions. Dividends received as a distribution of earnings subsequent to acquisition are recognized at the time of receipt as dividend income.

If marketable equity securities are involved, *Statement No. 12* requires that if the market value of the portfolio of marketable equity securities is below the portfolio cost at the balance sheet date, the portfolio should be written down to its market value. The amount by which the aggregate cost of the portfolio exceeds the market value is accounted for as a valuation allowance. That is, the portfolio is presented at cost less the valuation allowance in the balance sheet. If a company classifies some of its marketable securities as current and others as noncurrent, a separate determination of whether or not the portfolio's market value is less than its cost should be made for each of the current and noncurrent portfolios. If marketable equity securities are included in an unclassified balance sheet, the portfolio should be accounted for in the same way as a portfolio classified as a noncurrent asset.

Changes in the valuation allowance for a marketable equity security portfolio classified as a current asset must be included in the determination of net income in the period in which the change occurs. Accumulated changes in the valuation allowance for a marketable equity security portfolio included in the noncurrent assets should be included in the equity section of the balance sheet as an identifiable item. Should the market value of a current or noncurrent portfolio of marketable equity securities rise above the portfolio's cost and eliminate any previously recorded valuation allowance, no unrealized gain above the cost is recognized. Unrealized gains can only be recorded up to the amount of the valuation allowance.

If a security's current-noncurrent classification is changed, the security is transferred at the lower of its cost or market value at the transfer date. If the market value of the security is less than its cost, the market value becomes the new cost basis and the difference between the new and old cost basis is included in the determination of net income.

Ownership Interests of More than 20 Percent

Ownership interests of more than 20 percent are accounted for by the equity method on the statements of the investor company. These ownership interests can fall into a number of different categories. These categories determine whether or not the investment should be fully consolidated in consolidated statements and whether or not comprehensive tax allocation may be required when reporting the investor's share of the investee's undistributed earnings.

The acquisition of more than one half of the voting capital stock of a corporation creates a parent and subsidiary relationship. The company owning the controlling interest is the parent (or holding) company, and the controlled corporation is the subsidiary company. In this case, if the subsidiary qualifies for full consolidation (see Chapter 5), the investment will be reported on a fully consolidated basis in the consolidated statements of the investor company.

On the other hand, investments of 50 percent and less do not qualify for full consolidation. If they represent at least a 20 percent interest in the investee's voting stock, they are accounted for by the equity method on both the investor's parent company statement and the investor's consolidated statement. Ownership positions of more than 50 percent that do not qualify for full consolidation are also accounted for by the equity method.

As indicated in Chapter 14, a tax accrual for an investor's share of 50 percent or more in an investee's undistributed earnings accounted for by the equity method may or may not be required, depending on whether the undistributed profits are reinvested by the investee for an indefinite time. In contrast, tax accrual accounting is required for interests of less than 50 percent, irrespective of the investee's retained earnings policy.

Cost and Equity Methods Illustrated. An investor corporation records the acquisition of an equity interest in an investee by charging the cost of the stock purchased to an investment account. Cost is the cash price paid or the fair market value of the property exchanged. Subsequent to acquisition, the relationship with the subsidiary may be recorded by the parent using either (1) the cost method or (2) the equity method, depending on whether or not the equity method reporting criteria are met.

The *cost method* maintains the separate legal distinction between corporate entities. This method gives no recognition to the subsidiary company's earnings or losses in the parent's records. The investment account includes only the amounts invested in the investee by the investor corporation. Dividends from the subsidiary are credited to income at time of receipt.

After the initial acquisition cost has been entered in the parent's investment account, the *equity method* subsequently adds or subtracts from this amount the parent's proportional share of the changes in the subsidiary's retained earnings. The investment account increases as the parent's share of the subsidiary's reported earnings is credited to an income account. Dividends received from the subsidiary reduce the investment account. As a result of these entries, the investment account reflects initial cost plus or minus the parent's share of the change in the subsidiary's retained earnings subsequent to acquisition.

Illustration 20–1 summarizes the accounting entries in the parent's books applying the cost method and the equity method.

An investor's share of losses of an investee may equal or exceed the carrying amount of an investment accounted for by the equity method plus advances made by the investor. The investor ordinarily should discontinue applying the equity method when the investment (and net advances) is reduced to zero and should not provide for additional losses unless the investor has guaranteed obligations of the investee or is otherwise committed to provide further financial support for the investee. If the investee subsequently reports net income, the investor should resume applying the equity method only after its share of that net income equals the share of net losses not recognized during the period the equity method was suspended.

APB Opinion No. 18 noted that the difference between consolidation and the equity method lay in the details reported in the financial statements, not in the stockholders' equity and income determination goal. Therefore, the equity method should be applied in such a way as to produce the same stockholders' equity and net income as would be the case in consolidation. Accordingly, to achieve this result using the equity method, intercompany profits and losses should be eliminated from income until realized by the investor or investee as if the subsidiary, corporate joint venture, or investee company were consolidated. Similarly, when the cost of the investee company's investment is greater than its underlying equity in net assets, this difference should affect the determination of the amount of the investor's share of earnings or losses of the investee, as if it were a consolidated subsidiary. If the investee is unable to relate the difference to specific accounts, the difference should be considered goodwill and amortized over a period not to exceed 40 years.

Statement No. 58 added investments accounted for by the equity method to the list of assets qualifying for capitalization of consolidated interest cost as long as (1) the investee company has activities in progress necessary to commence its planned principal operations and (2) the investee's activities include the use of funds to acquire qualifying assets for its operations. The capitalized interest should be charged to consolidated income over an appropriate period such as the life of the related investee assets.

ILLUSTRATION 20-1
Cost and Equity Methods of Accounting for Intercorporate Investments

Transaction	Investor Owns Less than 20 Percent—Cost Method			Investor Owns More than 20 Percent—Equity Method		
a. Investor acquires part of investee company's stock for $200,000	a.	Investment .... Cash	200,000	200,000	a.	Investments .... Cash	200,000	200,000
b. Investee reports $40,000 earnings	b.	No entry			b.	Investments .... Income	32,000	32,000
c. Investee pays $20,000 in dividends	c.	Cash .... Dividend Income	3,800*	3,800	c.	Cash .... Investments	16,000	16,000†
d. Investee reports $20,000 loss	d.	No entry			d.	Income .... Investments	16,000	16,000†

* $20,000 × 0.19 (assumes 19 percent ownership).
† $20,000 × 0.80 (assumes 80 percent ownership).

Ability to Influence. Whether or not an investor has the ability to exercise significant influence over the operating and financial policies of an investee could be difficult to determine in practice. In order to achieve a reasonable degree of uniformity in the application of *Opinion No. 18,* The APB concluded that a direct or indirect investment of 20 percent or more in the voting stock of an investee should lead to the presumption that in the absence of contrary evidence, an investor has the ability to exercise a significant influence over an investee.

An investor's voting stock interest in an investee is based on the current outstanding stock held by stockholders who have voting privileges. Potential voting privileges which may become available to holders of securities of an investee are disregarded. Furthermore, an investor's share of the earnings or losses of an investee is based on the shares of common stock held by an investor, without recognition of securities of the investee which are designated as "common stock equivalents" under *APB Opinion No. 15.*

If, despite a holding of more than 20 percent of an investee's voting stock, an investor can present evidence suggesting that the presumption of ability to influence is not warranted, the investor can use the cost method to account for the investment. Such a situation may arise in the case of an investor company that owns more than 20 percent of an investee but for antitrust reasons has entered into an agreement with the government not to participate in the investee's affairs. Similarly, there are some examples of investor companies that have used the equity method to account for their investments in companies where their equity interest was less than 20 percent of the investee's voting stock. Usually in these cases, the investor controls the board of directors, despite the small stock holding.

Changes in Ownership Percentages

An investment in voting stock of an investee company may fall below the 20 percent level of ownership from sale of a portion of an investment by the investor, sale of additional stock by an investee, or other transactions, and the investor may thereby lose the ability to influence policy. An investor should discontinue accruing its share of the earnings or losses of the investee for an investment that no longer qualifies for the equity method. The earnings or losses that relate to the stock retained by the investor and were previously accrued should remain as a part of the carrying amount of the investment. The investment account should not be adjusted retroactively. However, in subsequent periods, dividends received by the investor which exceed the investor's share of earnings should be deducted from the carrying amount of the investment.

Alternatively, an investment in common stock of an investee that was previously accounted for by other than the equity method may qualify for use of the equity method of its level of ownership increases (i.e., acquisition of additional voting stock by the investor, acquisition or retirement of voting stock by the investee, or other transactions). When an investment qualifies for use of the equity method, the investor should adopt the equity method of accounting. The investment, results of operations (current and prior periods presented), and retained earnings of the investor should be adjusted retroactively in a manner consistent with the accounting for a step-by-step acquisition of a subsidiary.

Disclosure. Typically, when the investment in another company's common stock is significant relative to the investor's financial position and net income, the following disclosures are appropriate:

1. Financial statements of an investor should disclose parenthetically, in notes to financial statements, or in separate statements or schedules (1) the name of each investee and percentage of ownership of common stock, (2) the accounting policies of the investor with respect to investments in common stock, and (3) the difference, if any, between the amount at which an investment is carried and the amount of underlying equity in net assets, and the accounting treatment of the difference.

2. For those investments in common stock for which a quoted market price is available, the aggregate value of each identified investment based on the quoted market price usually should be disclosed. This disclosure is not required for investments in common stock of subsidiaries.

3. When investments in unconsolidated subsidiaries are, in the aggregate, material in relation to financial position or results of operations, summarized information as to assets, liabilities, and results of operations should be presented in the notes, or separate statements should be presented for such subsidiaries, either individually or in groups, as appropriate.

4. When investments in common stock of corporate joint ventures or other investments of 50 percent or less accounted for under the equity method are, in the aggregate, material in relation to the financial position or results of operations of an investor, it may be necessary for summarized information as to assets, liabilities, and results of operations of the investees to be presented in the notes or in separate statements, either individually or in groups, as appropriate.

5. Conversion of outstanding convertible securities, exercise of outstanding options and warrants, and other contingent issuances of an investee may have a significant effect on an investor's share of reported earnings or losses. Accordingly, material effects of possible conversions, exercises, or contingent issuances should be disclosed in notes to the financial statements of an investor.

Business Combinations: Two Approaches

A business combination occurs when two or more businesses are joined together as one entity to continue the same business activities each had carried on previously. Business combinations include all changes in corporate ownership that are termed mergers, purchases, consolidations, poolings, amalgamations, and acquisitions. The financial accounting issue raised in recording and reporting business combinations centers upon the valuation of the assets brought together in a business unit. The two methods used to record business combinations are (1) the purchase method and (2) the pooling of interests method.

Purchase Method

Under the purchase method of recording a business combination, the assets of the acquired entity are recorded at their fair market value on the books of the acquirer. This alternative treats the acquisition as if the dominant business had bought the net assets of another business and established a new cost basis for these acquired assets. All acquisitions of other companies, except those involving an exchange of common stock which meets all the restrictive conditions for a pooling of interests set forth in *Opinion No. 16*, must be recorded by the purchase method. (Those that meet these specific conditions *must* be accounted for by the pooling of interests method, as indicated later.)

Purchase Method Illustration. The accounting for purchases can be illustrated by a relatively simple example of a business combination.

Company A acquired Company B intending to continue the operations of both companies as a single unit. Company B's financial position at the date of acquisition was as follows:

	Book Value	Fair Market Value
Net current assets	$100,000	$100,000
Fixed assets	400,000	700,000
Total	$500,000	$800,000
Capital stock	$300,000	
Retained earnings	200,000	
Total	$500,000	

Company A paid $900,000 cash for Company B. The accounting entry in Company A's records is:

Dr. Net Current Assets	100,000	
Fixed Assets	700,000	
Excess of Purchase Price over Net Assets Acquired	100,000	
Cr. Cash		900,000

This transaction is clearly a purchase of Company B by Company A. The previous owners of Company B received cash and retained no ownership in the new business unit. Consequently, subsequent operations will be charged with depreciation based on fixed asset costs of $700,000, which is the fair market value of the assets acquired. The excess of the purchase price over the assets acquired is typically called goodwill. It is first recorded as an asset and subsequently charged to operations over a period of years not to exceed 40, as specified in *Opinion No. 17*. It is important to note that income from the acquired company will be included in Company A's accounts only from the date of acquisition, and Company B's retained earnings at acquisition are not carried over to Company A.

Pooling of Interests Method

Under the pooling of interests method, all assets of the newly combined group are valued at the same amounts at which they were previously carried in the accounts of the individual predecessor businesses. Underlying this alternative is the presumption that no new business entity has been created. Instead, it is assumed that ownership groups have merely contributed assets (or pooled resources) to carry on operations in an organization which is substantially a continuation of the preceding entities. Therefore, there is no reason to change asset values from those carried by the predecessor businesses.

Pooling of Interests Illustration. Using the example presented earlier, assume that Company A issued its own capital stock with a par value of $200,000 and a fair market value of $900,000 in payment for Company B, instead of paying $900,000 cash. In this transaction, the choice of the pooling of interests method can be strongly supported. The new entity is owned jointly by all stockholders of the previously separate corporations. The total assets and liabilities and retained earnings are undiminished and unchanged by the combinations. The stockholders of two corporations have merely pooled assets and liabilities and retained pro rata ownership in the new entity.

The combination would be entered on Company A's records as follows:

Dr.	Net Current Assets	100,000	
	Fixed Assets	400,000	
Cr.	Capital Stock		200,000
	Capital in Excess of Par Value		100,000
	Retained Earnings		200,000

It should be noted that subsequent operations of the combined companies will be charged with depreciation based upon the original $400,000 book value of Company B's fixed assets. Also, no goodwill is recognized and no related problems of subsequent amortization or write-off are encountered. Further, the retained earnings of Company B are carried over into the combination, and the paid-in capital accounts are adjusted to reflect any differences between the par value of Company B stock and the par value of stock issued by Company A.

Company A's statement of results of operations for the accounting period in which Company B was acquired will include the combined results of operations of the constituent interests for the entire annual accounting period in which the combination was effected.

Opinion No. 16, "Business Combinations"

The APB issued *Opinion No. 16,* "Business Combinations," to clarify criteria for using the purchase and pooling methods to account for business combinations. It concluded that both methods were acceptable in accounting for business combinations, but not as alternatives under the same conditions. A business combination meeting specified conditions *required* the pooling of interests method. All other combinations were *required* to use the purchase method.

Conditions Requiring Pooling Treatment

Pooling of interests was defined in *Opinion No. 16* as the presentation as a single interest of two or more common stockholder interests that were previously independent, and the combined rights and risks represented by those interests. The use of this method showed that the combining stockholder groups neither withdrew nor invested assets, but simply exchanged voting common stock in a ratio that determined their respective interests in the combined corporation.

The pooling of interests method could only be used if the transaction met all of the conditions specified in the opinion. In fact, if all of these conditions were met, the pooling of interests method had to be used. These basic conditions fall under three categories:

1. *With Respect to the Combining Companies*
   a. Each of the combining companies is autonomous and has not been a subsidiary or a division of another company within two years before the plan of combination is initiated.
   b. Each of the combining companies is independent of the other companies. (Independence existed if neither of the combining companies held as intercorporate investments more than 10 percent in total of the outstanding voting common stock of the other combining company.)

2. *With Respect to the Manner of Combining of Interests*
   a. The combination is effected in a single transaction or is completed in accordance with a specific plan within one year after the plan is initiated.
   b. A corporation offers and issues only common stock with rights identical to those of the majority of its outstanding voting common stock

in exchange for substantially all of the voting common stock interest of another company at the date the plan of combination is consummated.

c. None of the combining companies changes the equity interests of the voting common stock in contemplation of effecting the combination, either within two years before the plan of combination is initiated or between the dates the combination is initiated and consummated; changes in contemplation of effecting the combination may include distributions to stockholders and additional issuances, exchanges, and retirement of securities.

d. Each of the combining companies reacquires shares of voting common stock only for purposes other than business combinations, and no company reacquires more than a normal number of shares between the dates the plan of combination is initiated and consummated.

e. The ratio of the interest of an individual common stockholder to those of other common stockholders in a combining company remains the same as a result of the exchange of stock to effect the combination.

f. The voting rights to which the common stock ownership interests in the resulting combined corporation are entitled are exercisable by the stockholder; the stockholders are neither deprived nor restricted in exercising those rights for a period of years.

g. The combination is resolved at the date the plan is consummated, and no provision of the plan relating to the issue of securities or other considerations is pending.

3. *With Respect to the Absence of Planned Transactions*
    a. The combined corporation does not agree directly or indirectly to retire or reacquire all or part of the common stock issued to effect the combination.

    b. The combined corporation does not enter into other financial arrangements for the benefit of the former stockholders of a combining company, such as a guaranty of loans secured by stock issued in the combination which in effect negates the exchange of equity securities.

    c. The combined corporation does not intend or plan to dispose of a significant part of the assets of the combining companies within two years after the combination, other than disposals in the ordinary course of business of the formerly separate companies and to eliminate duplicated facilities of excess capacity.

The 90 Percent Test

The primary source of technical problems in applying these criteria is the definition of "substantially all of the voting common stock" which must be exchanged (see 2*b* above). The text of *Opinion No. 16* states that substantially all of the voting common stock means "90 percent or more." That is, at the date the combination is consummated, one of the combining companies (issuing corporation) issues voting common stock in exchange for at least 90 percent of the outstanding voting common stock of the other company (combining company).

For the purposes of computing the 90 percent figure, shares of the combining company are excluded if they were (1) acquired before and held by the issuing corporation and its subsidiaries at the date the plan of combination is initiated, regardless of the form of consideration; (2) acquired by the issuing corporation and its subsidiaries after the date the plan of combination is initiated other than by issuing its own voting common stock; or (3) outstanding after the date the combination is consummated.

An investment in the stock of the issuing corporation by a combining company may prevent a combination from meeting the 90 percent criterion, even though the investment of the combining company may not be more than 10 percent of the outstanding stock of the issuing corporation. To determine whether or not an investment by the company being acquired in the stock of the issuing corporation precludes use of the pooling method, this stock investment must be expressed as an equivalent number of shares of the combining company, because the 90 percent-of-shares-exchanged criterion is expressed in terms of shares of stock of the combining company. The procedure for this translation is shown in Illustration 20–2.

In a combination of more than two companies, the percentage of voting common stock is measured separately for each combining company.

Accounting Mechanics

The pooling of interests method requires that the recorded assets and liabilities of the separate companies be combined at their historical cost basis. However, since the separate companies may have recorded assets and liabilities under differing methods of accounting, it is permissible to adjust the amounts to the same basis of accounting if the change would otherwise have been appropriate for the separate company. Such a change in accounting method to make the accounts conform should be applied retroactively, and financial statements for prior periods should be restated.

The stockholders' equities are also combined as part of the pooling of interests, including the capital stock, capital in excess of par value, and retained earnings or deficits. If the par value of the total outstanding stock exceeds the capital stock of the separate combining companies, the excess is deducted first from contributed capital, then from retained earnings.

If treasury stock is used to effect a combination, this treasury stock should first be treated as retired, and the stock issued in the combination then treated as if it were previously unissued shares.

The treatment of stock of the combining companies held by another

ILLUSTRATION 20–2
Reduction of Shares Exchanged Due to Intercorporate Investment

Assume:

1. Company A (issuing company) agrees on March 31, 1985, to issue one share of A stock for each four shares of Company B.
2. Company B on March 31 has 100,000 shares of its own stock outstanding, and holds 2,000 shares of A as an investment.*
3. By March 31, 1986, Company A has issued 24,000 shares of its stock for 96,000 shares of B.

The required computation:

Shares of B exchanged for A	96,000
Shares of A held by B restated on basis of rate of exchange (2,000 shares of A @ 4:1)	8,000
Defined number of shares exchanged...............	88,000
Number of shares exchanged required for pooling	90,000

* The effect of the computation would be the same if B had purchased all or part of the 2,000 shares for cash after the combination plan had been initiated.

company depends on whether the holder is the issuing company or another combining company. If the investment of a combining company is in the common stock of the issuing company, it is, in effect, returned to the resulting combined corporation and should be treated as treasury stock. In contrast, an investment in the common stock of another combining company (not the issuing company) is an investment in stock that is exchanged in the combination for the common stock issued. This stock is in effect eliminated in the combination, and would be treated as retired stock.

Reporting Requirements

A corporation that uses the pooling of interests method of accounting for a combination should report results of operations for the period in which the combination occurs as though the companies had been combined as of the beginning of the period. Thus, the results of operations combine results of the separate companies from the beginning of the period to the date the combination is consummated, and represent combined operations from that date to the end of the period. The effects of intercompany transactions on current assets, liabilities, revenues, and cost of sales for the periods presented, and on retained earnings at the beginning of the periods presented, should be eliminated to the extent possible. The nature of any effects on earnings per share of nonrecurring intercompany transactions involving long-term assets and liabilities (such as fixed assets purchased before the combining date) need not be eliminated, but should be disclosed.

The combined corporation should disclose in notes to its financial statements the revenue, extraordinary items, and net income of each of the separate companies from the beginning of the perod to the date of combination. In addition, balance sheet and financial information presented for prior years should be restated on a combined basis to furnish comparative information. Such data should clearly indicate the nature of the information.

Expenses incurred in effecting a business combination accounted for as a pooling of interests should be deducted in determining the net income of the combined corporation for the period in which the expenses are incurred. These expenses include such items as registration fees and costs of furnishing information to stockholders.

Disclosure of Poolings

A combined corporation is required to disclose in its financial statements that a combination accounted for by the pooling of interests method has occurred during the period. The basis of the current presentation and restatements of prior periods may be disclosed in the financial statements by captions or by reference to the notes.

Notes to the financial statements of a combined corporation should disclose the following for the period in which a business combination occurs:

1. Name and brief description of the companies combined, except a corporation whose name is carried forward.
2. Description and number of shares of stock issued.
3. Details of the results of operations of the previously separate companies for the period before the combination was consummated that are included in the current combined income. The details should include revenue, extraordinary items, net income, other changes in stockholders' equity, and the amount of and manner of accounting for intercompany transactions.
4. Descriptions of the nature of any adjustments of net assets of the combining companies in order to adopt the same accounting practices, and of the effects of these changes on net income reported previously by the separate companies and now presented in comparative financial statements.
5. Details of an increase or decrease in retained earnings from changing the fiscal year of a combining company. The details should include at least revenue, expenses, extraordinary items, net income, and other changes in stockholders' equity for the period excluded from the reported results of operations.
6. Reconciliations of amounts of revenue and earnings previously reported by the corporation that issues the stock to effect the combination with the combined amounts currently presented in financial statements and summaries. A new corporation formed to effect a combination may instead disclose the earnings of separate companies which comprise combined earnings for the prior periods.

Business combinations consummated before the financial statements are issued, but which are either incomplete as of the date of the financial statements or initiated after that date, cannot be included in the statements of the prior period. However, the notes to the financial statements should disclose details of the effects of such combinations. The details should include revenue, net income, earnings per share, and the effects of anticipated changes in accounting methods as if the combination had been consummated at the date of the financial statements.

Purchase Accounting

The principal accounting issues to be decided in mergers required to be accounted for by the purchase method are:

1. Which company is the acquirer?
2. How much did the acquirer pay for the purchase?
3. What adjustments are required to the book values of the individual assets acquired and liabilities assumed so that these values on the acquirer's book reflect their net realizable value or fair market value?
4. How should any differences between the purchase price and those adjusted book values be handled in the accounts of the acquired?

Opinions No. 16 and *No. 17*, which were issued concurrently, discuss these issues.

Acquirer Characteristics. A corporation which distributes cash or other assets or incurs liabilities to obtain the assets or stock of another corporation is clearly the acquirer. In most cases involving exchanges of stock, the APB concluded that presumptive evidence of the acquiring corporation in combinations effected by an exchange of stock is obtained by identifying the former common stockholder interests which either retain or receive the larger portion of the voting rights in the combined corporation, unless other evidence clearly indicates that another corporation is the acquirer.

Purchase Price Determination. The responsibility for determining the purchase price rests with the acquiring company. The general principles governing this determination are:

1. Assets acquired by exchanging cash or other assets are recorded at cost, which is the amount of cash disbursed or the fair value of the assets distributed.
2. Assets acquired by assuming liabilities are recorded at cost, which is the present value of the amounts to be paid.
3. Assets acquired by issuing stock are recorded at the fair value of the stock or the fair value of the consideration given up for the stock.

The difficulty of determining the "fair value" of noncash assets or stock given up by the acquirer has led to the rule that their "cost may be determined either by the fair value of the consideration given or by the fair value of the property acquired, whichever is more clearly evident."

Book Value Adjustments. The acquiring company is responsible for making any required adjustment to the book values of assets acquired and liabilities assumed as a result of the purchase. *Opinion No. 16* presented some guidelines for this assignment of the purchase price. They are:

1. Marketable securities should be recorded at their current net realizable values.
2. The amounts shown for receivables should be the present value of amounts to be received, determined at appropriate current interest rates, less allowances for uncollectibility and collection costs, if necessary.
3. Inventories:
    a. Finished goods and merchandise should be recorded at their selling price less the sum of (1) cost of disposal and (2) a reasonable profit allowance for the selling effort of the acquiring corporation.
    b. Work in process must be valued at the estimated selling price of finished goods less the sum of (1) costs to complete, (2) costs of disposal, and (3) a reasonable profit allowance for the completing and selling effort of the acquiring corporation based on profit for similar finished goods.
    c. Raw materials have to be restated to their current replacement cost.
4. Plant and equipment *(a)* to be used must be stated at current replacement cost for similar capacity unless the expected future use of the assets indicates a lower value to the acquirer; *(b)* to be sold or held for later sale rather than used must be adjusted to its current net realizable value; and *(c)* to be used temporarily should be presented at its current net realizable value recognizing future depreciation for the expected period of use.
5. Intangible assets which can be identified and named, including contracts, patents, franchises, customer and supplier lists, and favorable leases, should be recorded at their appraised value.
6. Other assets, including land, natural resources, and nonmarketable securities, must be presented at their appraised value.
7. The amounts shown for accounts and notes payable, long-term debt, and other claims payable should be the present values of amounts to be paid determined at appropriate current interest rates.
8. Similarly, the amounts recorded for liabilities and accruals—for example, accruals for pension cost, warranties, vacation pay, deferred compensation—must be present value of amounts to be paid determined at appropriate current interest rates.

ILLUSTRATION 20-3
Implementation of *APB Opinion No. 16,* Purchase Accounting Using
Discounted Values

	Book Value	Basis of Valuation	Value for Purchase Accounting
Current assets:			
Cash	$ 10,000	Actual	$ 10,000
Accounts receivable (net)	90,000	Discounted 1 year @ 8%*	83,340
Fixed assets	400,000	Reproduction cost	700,000
	$500,000		$793,340
Accounts payable	$ 10,000	Actual	$ 10,000
Long-term debt	90,000	Five years @ 8%	61,290
	$100,000		$ 71,290
Net value of purchases	$400,000		$722,050

Net Charge against Income:

In year 1:	Income (accounts receivable, 90,000 − 83,340)	$6,660
	Expense (long-term debt)†	4,860
	Net credit to income	$1,800

* Assume, for the purposes of the example, that accounts receivable are due one year from this date (90,000 @ 0.926).

† Present value of debt @ 8 percent, payable in four years (90,000 @ 0.735) $66,150
Present value of debt @ 8 percent, payable in five years (90,000 @ 0.681) 61,290
Change in present value of debt . . . .$ 4,860

9. Other liabilities and commitments, including unfavorable leases, contracts, and commitments, and plant closing expense incident to the acquisition, should be recorded at the present value of amounts to be paid determined at appropriate current interest rates.

Additional rules are: an acquiring corporation should record periodically as a part of income the accrual of interest on assets and liabilities recorded at acquisition date at the discounted value of amounts to be received or paid (see Illustration 20–3). An acquiring corporation should not record as a separate asset the goodwill previously recorded by an acquired company and should not record deferred income taxes recorded by an acquired company before its acquisition. An acquiring corporation should reduce the acquired goodwill retroactively for the realized tax benefits of loss carry forwards of an acquired company not previously recorded by the acquiring corporation.

If unused investment tax credits of an acquired company are subsequently realized on the acquiring company's tax return, goodwill should be reduced by an equivalent amount until it is reduced to zero. Any remaining amount realized should be applied to reduce specific noncurrent assets. Any remaining amount realized should be recorded as a deferred credit and amortized to income over a period not to exceed 40 years.

Statement No. 38 requires that amounts be estimated and recorded as part of the purchase price allocation for contingencies of an acquired company that exist at the purchase date and are considered probable. Subsequently, any adjustments to these recorded amounts should be included in income when the appropriate adjustments are determined.

Goodwill

Goodwill purchased as a part of an acquisition must be amortized, according to *Opinion No. 17.* (Previously, the common practice was not to amortize goodwill.) The goodwill amortization can be based on anticipated loss in value if a logical basis can be determined. Otherwise, it must be amortized over a period not to exceed 40 years on a straight-line basis.

The Nature of Goodwill

It is difficult to give a precise definition of the nature of goodwill, since every business situation gives rise to a different mutation. However, in most situations it can be considered, in the technical sense, as simply being the cost paid for a business in excess of the fair market value of its net tangible and intangible assets and representing an expectation of earnings in excess of a normal return on these assets. It is only through such a transaction that goodwill can be recognized on the books of a company. Goodwill is an integral part of a business and cannot be regarded as an asset which is salable independent of the business.

"Negative Goodwill"

Sometimes companies are purchased for a price less than their book value. In these so-called bargain purchase cases, a "negative goodwill" or an "excess of book value of assets acquired over cost" item is created. If, after adjusting the book value of the assets acquired and liabilities assumed, the sum of the market or appraisal values of the assets acquired less liabilities still exceeds the purchase cost, the values assignable to noncurrent assets acquired (except marketable securities) should be reduced proportionately. Under *Opinion No. 16,* negative goodwill is prohibited unless such long-term assets are reduced to zero value. If such negative goodwill is then recorded, it must be amortized systematically as a credit to income over the period estimated to be benefitted, so long as the period is not in excess of 40 years. In addition, the method and period of amortization must be disclosed in the financial statements.

Goodwill Tax Consideration

Under the Internal Revenue Code, the cost of self-developed intangibles is deductible in the year paid or incurred, even though it may have a useful life extending beyond the taxable year. Such items are considered to be an ordinary and necessary expense of doing business. In contrast, the cost of a purchased intangible cannot be amortized for tax purposes unless it can be demonstrated that it has a limited life that can be estimated with reasonable accuracy. Under this provision, the purchase price of intangibles such as copyrights, patents, and other contracts of limited duration may be deducted from taxable income. However, purchased goodwill is expressly denied this treatment. The tax code assumes that the life of goodwill cannot be estimated reasonably. Consequently, the asset goodwill must, for tax purposes, be carried as an asset until the business giving rise to this item is sold. At that time, the tax basis of the business sold will be the market price paid originally for the business, which included goodwill.

Continuing Controversy

Over the years, the accounting for business combinations has been one of the most controversial problem areas in financial accounting. Most of the controversy centers on the legitimacy of pooling of interests accounting, the criteria for a pooling of interests, and the treatment of goodwill.

Some critics of business combination accounting maintain that business combinations in which a continuing entity survives are in essence purchase transactions and that the pooling of interests method is not appropriate in such combinations. Furthermore, they conclude that in those relatively rare combinations where no consistent company clearly emerges as the continuing entity, a new business has in effect been created. In these cases, the accounting should be similar to that for a new company: the assets and rights should be recorded at fair market value and no goodwill recognized. Based on these conclusions, they have recommended that the pooling of interests method be discontinued as an acceptable accounting practice.

Those holding this view argue that by treating as purchases most combinations that qualify for pooling of interests, financial statements would be more useful to investors. First, the fair market value of separate assets and property rights would be disclosed. Second, assigning fair market, rather than book, values to acquired assets would result in more realistic depreciation charges. Third, the amount paid for goodwill would be fully disclosed. Some go further and suggest that goodwill should be charged directly against the retained earnings of the acquiring corporation as an advance payment by the current stockholders for excess future earnings.

Others with similar views recommend that the pooling of interests concept be dropped and replaced by a "fair-value pooling" concept. They argue that the fair-value pooling treatment should be applied to those business combinations in which *(a)* the constituent combinations approximate each other in size; *(b)* it is difficult to determine which constituent acquired the other; and *(c)* the facts of the transaction clearly indicate that the combined entity is a new enterprise. All other combinations they would treat as purchases.

The fair-value pooling method proposed would record the assets of the new combined entity at their fair market value. Normally, because it is essentially a new enterprise, the combined entity would not begin operations with any retained earnings. However, if it was required to for legal or regulatory purpose, the combined entity may record as retained earnings that portion of the constituent companies' retained earnings that is legally available for dividends.

A number of accountants and business executives disagree with these conclusions. They argue that pooling of interests and purchase accounting are appropriate methods for accounting for business combinations and that many combinations are in effect pooling of interests. The challenge, they believe, is to identify the proper circumstances when each approach is appropriate.

Some accountants argue that combinations effected by cash are in substance different from those effected by stock, and a different method of accounting should be applied to each. Acquisitions for cash, they argue, should be treated as purchases, since one company gains control over the assets of another. An exchange of shares means that both groups of stockholders continue their ownership interest and genuine pooling of interests takes place, a fact which the accounting should reflect. While agreeing with this basic position, those who consider continuity of ownership interest as the key criterion for pooling believe purchase accounting is appropriate for combinations if either a material minority interest in a subsidiary company exists after acquisition of the subsidiary or if a material amount of preferred stock, either voting or nonvoting, has been used for the acquisition.

Others question the practicality of the fair-value pooling concept for combinations which in essence create "a new enterprise." In their opinion, the tests for determining whether or not a new enterprise has in fact been created are not clear and, hence, not operational.

The controversy over what is the appropriate accounting for business combinations continues. It is a high priority item for future addition to the FASB's agenda.

Financial Analysis

Intercorporate investment and business combination accounting creates many problems for statement users when evaluating companies individually or on a comparative basis. Some of these, such as the impact of the equity method's off-balance-sheet financing on debt-to-equity and coverage ratios, and the noncash nature of equity method earnings, have already been noted in Chapter 5. The comments below relate to these questions statement users should always ask when they encounter a business combination: What are the accounting implications of the acquisition terms and payments? Were these terms and payments developed in order to meet a specific accounting objective? How are future cash flows and past and future income streams influenced by the accounting and the acquisition terms and payments?

The accounting for business combinations can influence a company's current and future growth rate. Statement users must distinguish this source of growth. It may be a onetime earnings boost that can not be sustained by future operations. For example, a company with flat earnings acquiring another company with flat earnings for cash in a purchase transaction will include in its statements the acquiree's profits from the date of acquisition. The addition of these profits will cause the acquiring company's profits to rise relative to the period before acquisition. However, if the operating profits of both companies remain flat, the combined companies' profits will also be flat after the acquisition. Or, alternatively, an acquisition for stock of a company with a lower price-to-earnings ratio than the acquiring company, accounted for as a pooling of interests, will cause the acquiring company's earnings per share to rise. Again, unless the underlying operating earnings are rising, this earnings-per-share growth will be a onetime event. All too often, companies with weak underlying operations seeking growth through acquisitions find themselves so dependent on this source of growth that they increasingly acquire overpriced marginal companies to maintain their growth rate. Eventually, the weight of these marginal acquisitions causes the corporate structure to crumble. Statement users must be wary of such companies, particularly since their stock is often "hyped" by the promoter to maintain its price-to-earnings ratio to facilitate future acquisitions.

Pooling of interests accounting can change the acquiring company's past growth record, since the combining companies' past results are combined for accounting purposes as if the two companies had always been one. Statement users must be careful not to relate the acquiring company's past stock prices to the pooled results. The stock prices reflect the prepooling statements. In addition, the past pooling historical results may not be a good indicator of future growth rates. The acquired company's management might not be retained, and the combined companies may work less successfully together than they did as individual companies because of such factors as corporate culture differences.

Business combination accounting can also influence a company's future expenses and tax-related cash flows. Statement users must analyze this relationship carefully so as not to be misled by companies using business combination accounting to influence future operating performance at the expense of their potential cash flows. For example, the old book value and tax basis of a company acquired for stock in a pooling of interests deal become the acquirer's future costs. In contrast, if the same company had been acquired in a purchase transaction, the book value of many of the acquiree's assets and liabilities would be restated to their fair market value. These new values would be the acquiring company's future book and tax accounting values. Typically, in these situations, the acquired company's fixed assets are revalued upwards, creating more depreciation for book and tax purposes, which reduces the acquiring company's future profits and taxes. On the other hand, the acquiring company may decide not to be aggressive in allocating goodwill to assets that could raise its short-term expense level. It may prefer to leave as large a goodwill balance on its books as possible and minimize the annual goodwill charge by amortizing this amount over a 40-year period, which is probably considerably longer than the write-off period for, say, written-up fixed assets. This tactic may lead to higher short-term profits. It may also result in higher tax payments, since goodwill is nondeductible for tax purposes.

Goodwill is a difficult item for statement users to evaluate. It relates to the potential value to the acquirer of acquired entities that typically lose their identity once merged by the acquiring company into its consolidated statements. This makes it difficult for statement users to evaluate whether the goodwill balance is overstated, understated, or being amortized over a reasonable period of time. Unpleasant memories of unexpected goodwill write-downs have led many experienced statement users to favor companies that write off goodwill over relatively short periods of time, and to be suspicious of companies adopting 40-year write-off periods. Negative goodwill is seldom regarded as a positive income item since it has no positive cash flow attached to it and often arises from the purchase of troubled companies who must sell out for less than their net book value.

Combination accounting can be abused by unscrupulous managements to mislead unwary statement users. The best protection for statement users is to know the relevant accounting rules, carefully analyze the accounting results required by the acquisition deal, and be wary of managements that appear to be using combination accounting to puff up current results, rewriting history to imply greater future growth possibilities, and sacrificing future cash flow for improved bookkeeping results.

CASE 20-1

Williston International Industries
Purchase Accounting

On December 30, 1986, the Williston International board of directors voted to complete the acquisition as of December 30, 1986, of Erikson Machinery, a manufacturer and distributor of similar equipment to that sold by Williston.

Erikson was established by three brothers: Lionel Erikson, the founder, and currently the president, owned 60 percent of the common stock. Peter Erikson, currently vice president and treasurer, owned 25 percent. Of the remainder of the stock, 10 percent was held by Burger Erikson, the only son of Tor Erikson, the third brother, and Williston International held the rest. The two officers had previously agreed to exchange one share of $5 par-value Erikson stock for three shares Williston stock; Burger Erikson had refused to agree to the exchange.

Williston International Industries stock was traded over the counter. In late December, the average of bid and ask prices was $50.

Erikson stock had been purchased by Williston when the company was first established. Raymond Stevens, Williston's president at that time, had been a close friend of Lionel Erikson. After Mr. Stevens's death, Williston continued to hold the 5 percent stock interest in Erikson as an investment. There were no intercompany relationships or transactions.

The estimated financial statements of the Erikson Company at December 31, 1986, are presented in Exhibit 1, and of Williston in Exhibit 2.

Questions

1. Which treatment, pooling or purchase, is required? Does Burger Erikson's acquiesence make a difference? What other conditions might affect the purchase/pooling treatment?

2. Account for the acquisition of Erikson by Williston Company in 1986. Prepare a parent company and consolidated statement for the year.

This case was prepared by Mary Wehle.

Copyright © 1973 by the President and Fellows of Harvard College
Harvard Business School case 174–016 (Rev. 1985)

EXHIBIT 1

ERIKSON COMPANY
Income Statement
For the Year Ended December 31, 1986 (estimated)

Sales		$2,900,000
Cost of sales		1,900,000
		$1,000,000
Less: Selling expense	$250,000	
Administration	384,000	
Interest	6,000	640,000
		$ 360,000
Profit before taxes		
Taxes: Current	$170,000	
Deferred	10,000	180,000
		$ 180,000
Net income		173,000
Retained earnings, January 1, 1986		
Retained earnings, December 31, 1986		$ 353,000

ERIKSON COMPANY
Condensed Balance Sheet
Book and Appraisal Value (estimated)
December 31, 1986

		Book	Appraisal
Current assets:			
Cash		$ 35,000	$ 35,000
Marketable securities, at cost (market $350,000)		200,000	350,000
Accounts receivable (net)		178,000	175,000
Inventory		210,000	270,000
Total current assets		$623,000	$ 830,000
Long-term assets:			
Plant and equipment	$540,000		
Less: Accumulated depreciation	170,000	370,000	800,000
Total—book		$993,000	
Total assets—appraisal			$1,630,000
Current liabilities:			
Accounts payable		$ 50,000	$ 50,000
Accrued taxes		170,000	170,000
		$220,000	$ 220,000
Deferred taxes		120,000	120,000
Long-term debt, 6 percent, due 1990		100,000	63,000
			$ 183,000
Stockholders' Equity:			
Capital stock ($5 par)	$ 50,000		
Capital in excess of par value	150,000		
Retained earnings	353,000	$553,000	
Total—book		$993,000	
Total Liabilities—appraisal			$ 403,000

EXHIBIT 2

WILLISTON INTERNATIONAL INDUSTRIES, INC.
Condensed Balance Sheet
December 31, 1986
(in thousands)

Cash		$1,261
Marketable securities (at cost, market $500,000)		420
Inventory		1,100
Investments in subsidiaries at equity in net assets		949
Plant, property, and equipment	$2,476	
Less: Accumulated depreciation	226	2,250
Total assets		$5,980
Current liabilities		$ 470
Taxes payable		220
Long-term debt		500
Deferred taxes		190
		$1,380
Stockholders' equity:		
Common stock ($1 par)	$1,000	
Capital in excess of par value	500	
Retained earnings*	3,100	4,600
Total liabilities and stockholders' equity		$5,980

* Estimated after-tax net income for 1986, $ 1.1 million.

3. After completing Questions 1 and 2, assume that before closing the acquisition deal on December 30, 1986, the Williston board offered Burger Erikson the choice of either *(a)* a cash payment of $170 for each of his Erikson shares or *(b)* an exchange of stock based on 3.5 shares of Williston for each share of Erikson. How would the acceptance by Burger Erikson on December 30, 1986, of either of these offers effect the accounting treatment of the Erikson acquisition by Williston.

4. As the president of Williston, what accounting treatment would you prefer for this acquisition? (Assume you had an option and the facts are as presented in the case, except that Burger Erikson will accept the one-for-three exchange offer.)

CASE 20-2

Foster-Martin, Incorporated
Analysis of Criteria for Pooling of Interests Accounting

Foster-Martin, Inc., a manufacturer of television sets, intends to acquire all the outstanding stock of Comet Tube Company, a manufacturer of television tubes. It is expected that Foster-Martin will issue 175,000 shares of its capital stock in a nontaxable exchange for the net assets of Comet, which will be discontinued as a company and then operated as a division of Foster-Martin. The data in Exhibit 1 are taken from the financial statements of the companies at the close of the most recent fiscal year.

Foster-Martin has 457,500 shares of capital stock outstanding, of which 198,792 shares are owned directly or beneficially by Tom Foster and 118,400 are owned directly or beneficially by Lowell Martin. The remainder of the stock is widely held and is from time to time on the over-the-counter market.

Comet Tube Company was organized in 1975 by Messrs. Thomas and Hinchey, who own 75 and 25 percent of the company, respectively. The company has proved very profitable, net income after taxes having varied from 9 to 14 percent of sales in the past few years. Comet's product line will complement lines now manufactured by Foster-Martin, and the marketability of the Foster-Martin shares makes the transaction attractive to Thomas and Hinchey. Thomas and Hinchey have agreed not to dispose of any shares acquired in the transaction for a period of 12 months after its consummation.

All of the ownership interest in the original business will be represented in the surviving business. Mr. Thomas, who is now president of Comet, will continue as general manager of these operations and will also be placed on the Foster-Martin board of directors. Hinchey is now production manager of Comet and will continue in that capacity. Foster-Martin intends to sign employment contracts with both men.

This case was prepared by David F. Hawkins.
Harvard Business School case 171–237 (Rev. 1985)

EXHIBIT 1

Foster-Martin, Inc.	
Current assets	$2,100,000
Property, plant, and equipment (net)	2,399,000
Other assets	331,700
Current liabilities	852,700
Long-term debt	1,875,000
Capital stock	457,500
Retained earnings	1,645,500
Sales and other revenues	6,582,500
Net income before taxes	687,500
Net income after taxes	394,750
Recent market price	31

Comet Tube Company	
Current assets	$1,317,000
Current liabilities	750,000
Working capital	567,000
Fixed assets, net	574,000
Capital stock	175,000
Retained earnings	966,000
Sales	2,665,000
Other revenues	135,000
Net profit before taxes	775,000
Federal income tax	410,000

Questions

1. Does the case outlined above qualify as a pooling of interests? List the factors to be considered in determining whether a particular transaction is a pooling of interests or a purchase, and apply each of these factors to this case.

2. State whether your conclusion in 1 above would be changed by each of the following changes in facts, and why (changes should be considered individually and not cumulatively):

   a. Comet Tube Company is not liquidated after the acquisition; but because of certain local tax advantages, it is operated as a subsidiary.

   b. Thomas and Hinchey have indicated their intention to sell, shortly after the consummation of the transaction, 50,000 of the shares they acquire thereby and agree to hold the remainder for a period of 12 months.

   c. The 175,000 shares issued to Thomas and Hinchey are a special Class B common stock that differs from the common stock already outstanding only with respect to voting rights, which are $\frac{1}{10}$ that of the other common shares.

   d. Only 100,000 shares are issued to Thomas and Hinchey, and the remainder of the consideration for the transaction is paid in cash.

3. Assume that Foster-Martin, Inc., publishes an annual report containing comparative financial statements and a 10-year financial summary. If the transaction qualifies as a pooling of interests, what changes if any should be made in the prior year financial statements and the 10-year summary in the next annual report?

4. Assume that Foster-Martin acquired the capital stock of Comet Tube and contin-

ues to operate it as a subsidiary. How should the transactions be recorded on the books of Foster-Martin?

5. How should Foster-Martin account for the Comet acquisition if the company were acquired for $5.5 million cash?

CASE 20–3

Lawrence Paper Company
Accounting for Joint Ventures

In 1984, Facts Incorporated and Lehman Paper Corporation jointly formed the Lawrence Paper Company to build and operate a $31 million mill to produce high-quality machine-coated paper.

Under the terms of a long-term purchase contract, Facts and Lehman were each obligated to buy one half of the output of the Lawrence Paper Company.

In addition to an initial investment by Facts and Lehman in all of the common stock and some subordinated notes of Lawrence, the new company obtained financing by means of first mortgage bonds issued to four institutional investors. The latter source represented about 60 percent of the initial financing of the mill. The mortgage lenders viewed Facts's and Lehman's long-term purchase contracts with Lawrence as a form of security for the bonds.

The Lawrence Paper Company began operations in June 1986. A $29 million expansion program to add a second paper machine was announced in late 1986 and scheduled for completion by 1988. It was expected that nearly all of the funds for this expansion would be provided by institutional lenders.

This case was prepared by David F. Hawkins.

Facts Incorporated

Facts Incorporated published *Facts,* several other popular weekly magazines, and a number of trade journals. Early in 1984, Facts entered the book publishing business. Facts had a subsidiary which operated paper and board mills and timberlands in Oklahoma and a paperboard converter facility in South Carolina. Facts also owned several radio and television stations. In reporting the Lawrence joint venture to its stockholders, Facts Incorporated said:

> The company and Lehman Paper Corporation each owns 50 percent of the capital stock of Lawrence Paper Company (a corporation formed in January 1984, which is constructing a groundwood pulp and paper mill at Lawrence, Texas, at an estimated cost (including working capital) of approximately $31 million. Initially, the mill will contain one paper machine designed to produce approximately 78,000 tons of machine-coated printing paper annually. Lehman will manage the mill and supply its requirements of bleached chemical pulp. In addition to their stock ownership, the company and Lehman have made, and have agreed to make in the future, certain loans to Lawrence which will be evidenced by subordinated notes. At December 31, 1984, the total investment of the company and Lehman in the stock and notes of Lawrence amounted to $5 million and $3.5 million respectively, and, based on present estimates, the additional cash required from the company and Lehman for this purpose during 1985 will be approximately $2.6 million and $1.3 million, respectively. Lawrence has arranged for additional financing from four institutional investors in the maximum amount of $18.6 million first mortgage bonds. In the event that (1) funds required for certain purposes by Lawrence should exceed a specified amount, or (2) the corporation's "quick assets" (as defined) should be reduced below a specified amount, or (3) the mill should not be completed, or certain other conditions should not have been met, by stipulated dates, or (4) the corporation should determine not to complete such a mill, the company and Lehman are obligated on a 50–50 basis to purchase additional subordinated notes or to purchase the then outstanding first mortgage bonds of Lawrence and, under certain of the above-mentioned circumstances, to pay a termination fee to the purchasers of such bonds, as the case may be. The company is obligated under a long-term contract to purchase paper produced during 50 percent of the total available operating time of the paper machine or machines at the mill of Lawrence as well as to pay certain shutdown costs. Lehman is similarly obligated. The payments by the company and Lehman under such paper contracts are to be (1) amounts sufficient to enable Lawrence to recoup all costs, charges, and expenses (other than federal and state income taxes) properly includable in the determination of its net income and not attributable to periods of disability resulting from any act of God, fire, strike, or certain other causes, and (2) a fixed annual amount of $500,000 each as long as the mill contains only one paper machine.

Facts's annual report also indicated that the joint venture represented a hedge by Facts against anticipated shortages of the special paper used by Facts; the mill would supply one fifth of Facts's paper requirements; use the most modern equipment available; and was expected to operate at capacity.

The 1984 balance sheet of Facts showed stockholders' equity at $88 million, other liabilities at $46 million, long-term debt at $45 million, and current liabilities at $29 million.

Lehman Paper Corporation

Lehman Paper Corporation ranked as one of the world's largest paper companies.

In the president's covering letter for Lehman's 1984 annual report to stockholders, a brief reference was made to the plans for the new mill being built in conjunction with Facts Incorporated, noting that it would be completed some time in 1986. The following additional comments were included in the text of this same annual report in a section titled "Sales and Marketing":

> In anticipation of the high-quality output of the new mill under construction at Lawrence, Texas, we are developing new markets for the company's coated printing papers in the Midwest, South, and East. The Lawrence mill is owned jointly with Facts Incorporated, which will share its production with Lehman.

In a later section of the 1984 report, titled "Financial Review," the following description of the Lawrence Paper Company was presented:

> Lawrence common stock is owned 50 percent by Lehman and 50 percent by Facts Incorporated. During the year Lehman purchased 20,000 shares of common stock of this company at a cost of $2 million and made long-term advances of $1.5 million; Facts Incorporated also purchased 20,000 shares of common stock for $2 million and made long-term advances of $3 million. These advances will be secured by subordinated notes.
>
> It is contemplated that Lehman Paper will similarly advance an additional $1.3 million and Facts Incorporated an additional $2.6 million during 1985, and that Lawrence will sell approximately $18.6 million of 25-year, 8 percent first mortgage and collateral bonds to four institutional investors.

The 1984 balance sheet of Lehman reported the following: stockholders' equity, $378 million; long-term debt, $115 million; and current liabilities, $44 million.

In 1985, the explanation of the Lawrence financing was moved from the text of Lehman's annual report to a footnote to the financial statements. The amount reported to stockholders in 1985 as the investment in Lawrence was $4.8 million. The footnote read as follows:

> *Investments.* The investment in Lawrence Paper Company represents 20,000 shares of common stock (50 percent of the common stock outstand-

ing) at a cost of $2 million and long-term advances of $2.8 million. Lawrence is constructing a paper mill in Texas which will commence operation early in 1986. Lehman Paper Corporation will manage the mill and has contracts to purchase a portion of the output and to furnish certain amounts of pulp.

Lehman Paper Corporation has also made temporary advances of $1.5 million to Lawrence which will be repaid from the proceeds of the sale of bonds upon completion of the mill.

In 1986, the company's investment was reported at $4,605,000 and the footnote was similar to the 1985 footnote, except that it indicated the mill had begun operation in May 1986. The company's president, in his letter to stockholders, indicated that the mill was operating on a 24-hour, seven-day week schedule.

The president's letter also included the following comments:

> In the growing field of double-coated magazine papers, the new mill owned jointly with Facts Incorporated at Lawrence, Texas, should remain in a start-up status during much of 1987, the first full year of operations, as technological problems are smoothed out. Production and efficiency should steadily improve, and by the end of the year Lawrence paper should contribute to the rise in corporate sales volume, although the mill's high start-up costs will most probably offset any benefits to 1987 earnings.

Questions

1. How should Lehman and Facts account for their investment in the Lawrence Paper Company? Why?
2. How adequate is this method?
3. How should Lehman and Facts account for their long-term purchase contracts with Lawrence?
4. Do you believe the FASB should require full or partial consolidation of joint ventures?

CASE 20-4

Loews Corporation
Equity Method Accounting Change

Loews Corporation, formed in Delaware in November 1969, operates principally as a holding company controlling more than 100 wholly owned subsidiaries. Through its subsidiaries, Loews operates hotels, exhibits motion pictures through theater ownership, develops residential real estate, and manufactures and sells tobacco products. In addition, it manages a large portfolio of securities, primarily common stock. This case focuses on the financial accounting aspects of one of Loews's major intercorporate investments: the approximately 25 percent ownership investment in Wheeling-Pittsburgh Steel Corporation in fiscal year 1974.

Wheeling-Pittsburgh Steel Corporation Investment

Wheeling-Pittsburgh Steel Corporation is an integrated steel producer engaged in the manufacture of iron, steel ingot, semifinished, finished, and fabricated steel products. The industry is highly competitive, the giant of the industry of course being United States Steel Corporation. During 1974, Wheeling-Pittsburgh's steel production was approximately 3 percent of total industry production.

The president of Loews Corporation, Laurence Tisch, indicated in his address to the shareholders on November 19, 1974, that the "investment in Wheeling-Pittsburgh was prompted by the favorable long-term outlook for the basic business of Wheeling-Pittsburgh and by the record of achievement of its management."

In recent years, under the leadership of Robert E. Lauterbach, Wheeling-Pittsburgh has undertaken a plan of major plant additions and modernization. In early 1974, they announced a seven-year, $250 million capital expenditure program to develop "ownership" sources of low-cost raw materials, to construct a new battery of coke ovens in its Steubenville plant

This case was prepared by Dennis P. Frolin (under the direction of James F. Smith).

Copyright © 1975 by the President and Fellows of Harvard College
Harvard Business School case 176-089 (Rev. 1985)

EXHIBIT 1
Loews Corporation

WHEELING-PITTSBURGH STEEL CORPORATION
Five-Year Statistical Summary*
(thousands of dollars)

	1974	1973	1972	1971	1970
Revenues	1,043,715	763,815	609,707	530,057	525,715
Earnings before taxes	105,418	12,781	15,048	(3,988)	(6,223)
Provision for income taxes	32,000	6,120	6,898	(3,114)	(4,039)
Net earnings	73,418	6,661	8,150	(874)	(2,184)
EPS (common)	19.23	.98	1.39	(1.08)	(1.44)
Dividends declared (per common share)	.70	–0–	–0–	–0–	–0–
Stockholders' equity	313,857	245,933	242,303	237,010	240,954
Stock price:					
High	23¼	21⅝	24¼	20½	21⅝
Low.....................	13¼	10¼	15⅝	11½	9¾
Close	17¾	13	20⅜	17¾	11½
August 31	19¾	13⅛			

* Calendar years.

having an annual capacity near 1 million tons, and to carry out an extensive rebuilding and modernization program of its blast furnaces. Steel shipments, revenues, and net earnings reached record levels in 1973; and during 1974, revenues and net earnings skyrocketed (Exhibit 1).

Loews acquired 293,000 shares of Wheeling-Pittsburgh, approximately 8 percent of the common shares outstanding, during fiscal year 1973 for $4,236,000 and carried the holding as an "investment in securities, at cost" on its balance sheet. During fiscal 1974, Loews acquired an additional 634,000 shares of Wheeling-Pittsburgh for $10,156,000, so that as of August 31, 1974, Loews owned approximately 25.3 percent of Wheeling-Pittsburgh outstanding common stock. Loews thus controls a substantial block of voting shares of Wheeling-Pittsburgh, though it has no direct hand in managing its operations. For example, there are no officers or directors of Loews who are also officers or directors of Wheeling-Pittsburgh. The market value of these shares at August 31, 1974, was approximately $18,308,000.

Loews recorded its investment at cost, $14,392,000. Its equity in the net assets of Wheeling-Pittsburgh exceeded the cost by $58,571,000. Having acquired in excess of 20 percent of the voting stock of Wheeling-Pittsburgh, Loews began using in 1974 the equity method to account for this investment. The excess of net assets over cost is being amortized to income over a 12-year period.

Exhibit 2 includes excerpts from the Loews Corporation 1974 annual report relating to its Wheeling-Pittsburgh investment. Exhibits 3 and 4 present excerpts from the Loews Corporation's 1975 and 1976 annual reports.

EXHIBIT 2
Loews Corporation

LOEWS CORPORATION AND SUBSIDIARIES
Consolidated Balance Sheet

	August 31	
	1974	*1973*
Assets		
Current assets:		
Cash, including time deposits (1974, $10,640,000; 1973, $8,505,000)	$ 23,537,000	$ 21,314,000
Receivables—principally trade, less allowance for doubtful accounts and discounts (1974, $5,022,000; 1973, $2,919,000)	77,944,000	60,670,000
Inventories:		
Leaf tobacco	223,084,000	225,732,000
Manufactured stock	27,707,000	21,985,000
Materials, supplies, etc.	9,751,000	6,491,000
Real estate held for development and sale	57,302,000	47,112,000
Total current assets	$ 419,325,000	$ 383,304,000
Investments in securities:		
Associated company	$ 24,259,000	$ 4,236,000
Other	376,306,000	432,472,000
Total investments in securities	$ 400,565,000	$ 436,708,000
Total current assets and investments in securities	$ 819,890,000	$ 820,012,000
Investments and advances:		
Investments in and advances to unconsolidated companies	$ 4,165,000	$ 14,111,000
Mortgages and notes receivable (maturing through 2028 at interest rates ranging from 5% to 13%)	47,528,000	35,226,000
Land and other investments, at cost	23,365,000	19,652,000
Total investments and advances	$ 75,058,000	$ 68,989,000
Property, plant, and equipment, at cost:		
Land	$ 41,834,000	$ 41,994,000
Buildings and building equipment	154,880,000	154,053,000
Machinery and equipment	78,237,000	71,604,000
Leaseholds and leasehold improvements	11,322,000	10,969,000
Total	$286,273,000	$ 278,620,000
Less: Accumulated depreciation and amortization	92,881,000	85,821,000
Property, plant, and equipment—net	$ 193,392,000	$ 192,799,000
Other assets:		
Cost in excess of net assets acquired	$ 65,519,000	$ 67,115,000
Trademarks	100,033,000	100,033,000
Patents and licenses, less accumulated amortization (1974, $5,027,000; 1973, $179,000)	8,304,000	9,152,000
Prepaid expenses, deferred charges, etc.	11,682,000	10,002,000
Total other assets	$ 185,538,000	$ 186,302,000
Total assets	$1,273,878,000	$1,268,102,000

EXHIBIT 2 *(continued)*

	August 31	
	1974	*1973*
Liabilities and Shareholders' Equity		
Current liabilities:		
Short-term debt..	**$ 80,353,000**	$ 119,515,000
Accounts payable and accrued liabilities	**57,086,000**	51,929,000
Accrued taxes:		
Federal and foreign income taxes..................	**10,170,000**	5,243,000
Excise and other taxes	**22,316,000**	14,754,000
Current maturities of long-term debt, less unamortized discount	**8,914,000**	11,138,000
Total current liabilities	**$ 178,839,000**	$ 202,579,000
Long-term debt, less current maturities and unamortized discount:		
Senior debt	**$ 270,700,000**	$ 268,235,000
Subordinated debt	**371,932,000**	372,533,000
Long-term debt—net	**$ 642,632,000**	$ 640,768,000
Deferred credits and other liabilities:		
Deferred income taxes	**$ 17,011,000**	$ 17,316,000
Accrued employee benefits	**8,144,000**	6,738,000
Deferred credits and noncurrent liabilities	**3,617,000**	3,372,000
Total deferred credits and other liabilities	**$ 28,772,000**	$ 27,426,000
Shareholders' equity:		
Common stock, authorized 30 million shares of $1 par value; issued shares stated at par value	**$ 14,791,000**	$ 14,791,000
Additional paid-in capital	**116,522,000**	116,522,000
Earnings retained in the business	**345,003,000**	315,480,000
Total	**$ 476,316,000**	$ 446,793,000
Less: Common stock held in treasury, at cost (1974, 1,873,000 shares; 1973, 1,733,000 shares)	**52,681,000**	49,464,000
Total shareholders' equity	**$ 423,635,000**	$ 397,329,000
Total liabilities and shareholders' equity	**$1,273,878,000**	$1,268,102,000

EXHIBIT 2 *(continued)*

LOEWS CORPORATION AND SUBSIDIARIES
Statement of Consolidated Earnings and
Earnings Retained in the Business

	Year Ended August 31	
	1974	*1973*
Sales and operating revenues:		
Sales of manufactured products and revenues of theatre and hotel operations	$739,797,000	$714,021,000
Other revenues, principally rent and dividends	53,544,000	52,415,000
Total	$793,341,000	$766,436,000
Costs and expenses:		
Cost of sales and operating costs	$550,237,000	$505,655,000
Selling, advertising, and administrative	124,144,000	120,266,000
Depreciation and amortization	10,344,000	10,124,000
Interest and amortization of debenture discount and expense	58,579,000	51,796,000
Income taxes	14,158,000	27,363,000
Total	$757,462,000	$715,204,000
Earnings before security gains and equity in earnings of associated company	$ 35,879,000	$ 51,232,000
Security gains:		
Realized gains	$ 70,000	$ 17,213,000
Less: Applicable income taxes	44,000	5,328,000
Security gains—net	$ 26,000	$ 11,885,000
Equity in earnings of associated company	$ 9,379,000	–0–
Net earnings	$ 45,284,000	$ 63,117,000
Earnings retained in the business, beginning of year	315,480,000	269,541,000
Cash dividends (per share—$1.22 in 1974 and $1.21 in 1973)	(15,761,000)	(17,178,000)
Earnings retained in the business, end of year	$345,003,000	$315,480,000
Earnings per share—primary:		
Earnings before security gains and equity in earnings of associated company	$2.78	$3.61
Security gains—net		.84
Equity in earnings of associated company	.72	
Net earnings	$3.50	$4.45
Earnings per share—assuming full dilution:		
Earnings before security gains and equity in earnings of associated company	$2.73	$3.01
Security gains—net		.60
Equity in earnings of associated company	.60	
Net earnings	$3.33	$3.61

EXHIBIT 2 *(concluded)*

Notes to Consolidated Financial Statements

1. Investments in Securities:

Associated company—The company carries its investment in Wheeling-Pittsburgh Steel Corporation (Wheeling) at cost adjusted for the company's share of earnings and capital changes of Wheeling from dates of acquisition plus amortization of the excess of equity in net assets acquired over cost thereof. The company reports as earnings its proportionate share of Wheeling's earnings plus amortization of the excess of equity in net assets acquired over cost thereof and provides for appropriate deferred federal income taxes on the undistributed earnings so reported.

Other—Investments in other securities are carried at cost. The cost of securities sold is determined on the identified certificate or first-in, first-out method. The company has invested in securities in order to secure a return on funds it is holding for development and expansion opportunities. The company regularly and actively seeks development and acquisition opportunities which may require application of all or a portion of such funds. In view of the uncertainty as to when such opportunities may arise, the investment in securities has been classified as a noncurrent asset.

2. Investments in Securities

Associated company—At August 31, 1974, and 1973, the company held 927,000 and 293,000 shares, respectively, of the common stock of Wheeling, representing approximately 25.3 percent and 8.0 percent, respectively, of Wheeling's common shares outstanding at such dates. The company purchased 634,000 shares of Wheeling common stock for $10,156,000 during 1974 and 293,000 shares for $4,236,000 during 1973. At August 31, 1974, the quoted market value of the shares held was approximately $18,308,000 ($19.75 per share).

The company's equity in the net assets of Wheeling at August 31, 1974, exceeded the amount at which its investment was carried by $55,490,000. Such amount, representing the unamortized balance of the excess of equity in net assets acquired over cost thereof at the various dates the investment in Wheeling was acquired, is being amortized to income over a 12-year period (the approximate remaining life of Wheeling's fixed assets) beginning with the various dates of acquisition.

The company's equity in earnings of associated company comprises the following for 1974:

Equity in earnings	$6,786,000
Amortization of excess of equity in net assets acquired over cost thereof	3,081,000
Less: Applicable deferred federal income taxes	(488,000)
Total	$9,379,000

The equity in earnings of Wheeling included in the accompanying financial statements is based on Wheeling's unaudited financial statements for the period from Loews's initial investment through June 30, 1974. Net earnings as previously reported have not been restated since the effect on prior periods is not significant. No dividends had been declared on the common stock of Wheeling from the date of Loews's initial investment therein until August 28, 1974, at which time a dividend of $.35 per share was declared payable to holders of record as of September 12, 1974.

Unaudited net income applicable to common stockholders of Wheeling for the six months ended June 30, 1974 (the period during which Loews acquired a significant portion of its investment) was $24,674,000. Wheeling management announced on October 24, 1974, that, because of the high rate of inflation, they are considering adoption of the LIFO method of accounting for inventories to replace the current average cost method. Their decision is not expected to be reached until the end of calendar 1974.

Other—The quoted market value of other security investments aggregated approximately $281 million and $408 million at August 31, 1974, and 1973, respectively. In the opinion of management, the decline in market value at August 31, 1974, does not constitute a permanent impairment of these investments.

Securities with a quoted market value of approximately $11.5 million at August 31, 1974, are pledged as collateral in connection with the retirement plan covering hourly production employees and to secure other liabilities.

EXHIBIT 3
Loews Corporation, 1975 Annual Report

3. *Investments in Associated Companies*

Investments in associated companies consist of:

At December 31, 1975, the quoted market value of the investment in Wheeling was

| | December 31 | | August 31, |
	1975	1974	1974
Equity securities:			
Wheeling (25.2% owned by the company)............	$ 35,054,000	$ 35,554,000	$ 24,259,000
First Healthcare Corporation (100% owned by CNA)	7,072,000	26,289,000	
Healthco, Inc. (45.3% owned by CNA)	21,599,000	18,137,000	
Others	22,363,000	8,904,000	3,857,000
Notes	17,878,000	14,198,000	
Total	$103,966,000	$103,082,000	$ 28,116,000

The company's equity in the net assets of Wheeling at December 31, 1975, exceeded the amount at which its investment was carried by $48,704,000. Such amount, representing the unamortized balance of the excess of equity in net assets acquired over cost thereof (credit excess) at the various dates the investment in Wheeling was acquired, is being amortized to earnings over a 12-year period (the appxoximate remaining life of Wheeling's fixed assets) beginning with the various dates of acquisition.

$15,643,000. All other investees are closely held; however, in the opinion of management, the carrying value of such other investments is not in excess of their underlying value.

Data concerning the financial position and results of operations of the above companies and the company's equity in such operations are set forth below. Such data does not include the effect of purchase value adjustments (see note 1); however, the company's equity in operations includes the effect of such adjustments.

| | Year Ended December 31, 1975 | | December 31, 1975 | | December 31, 1974 | |
	Gross Revenues	Net Earnings (Loss)	Total Assets	Net Worth	Total Assets	Net Worth
			(in thousands)			
Wheeling	$ 836,686	$ 563	$675,537	$365,638	$722,361	$370,494
First Healthcare Corporation	33,113	(479)	25,050	8,682	59,285	28,299
Healthco, Inc.	173,000	5,000	107,334	58,016	96,470	50,681
Others*	29,840	(3,571)	113,455	35,474	113,739	24,902
Total	$1,072,639	$1,513	$921,376	$467,810	$991,855	$474,376

* Certain amounts included herein are unaudited.

EXHIBIT 3 *(concluded)*

Amounts credited to earnings and earnings retained in the business and cash dividends received by the company relating to the above investees are set forth below:

	Year Ended December 31, 1975	Four Months Ended December 31, 1974	Year Ended August 31, 1974
Credited to earnings:			
Equity in earnings (includes, in 1975, minority interest credit of $919,000)	$ 3,286,000	$ 7,487,000	$ 6,993,000
Amortization of credit excess	4,880,000	1,625,000	3,081,000
Provision for investment valuation	(3,660,000)		
Income taxes:			
Current	(709,000)	(24,000)	
Deferred	(1,309,000)	(513,000)	(492,000)
Total credited to earnings	$ 2,488,000	$ 8,575,000	$ 9,582,000
Credited to earnings retained in the business *(a)*:			
Equity in earnings		$ 2,922,000	
Deferred income taxes		(210,000)	
Total credited to earnings retained in the business		$ 2,712,000	
		$11,287,000	
Cash dividends	$ 1,142,000	$ 656,000	$ 66,000

a. The equity in earnings of Wheeling included in the accompanying financial statements for the three months ended September 30, 1974, and the month of December 1974 (credited to earnings in the statement of consolidated earnings) and the two months ended November 30, 1974 (credited to earnings retained in the business in the statement of consolidated shareholders' equity) is based on Wheeling's unaudited financial statements for the six months ended December 31, 1974. The equity in earnings for the two months ended November 30, 1974, was credited to earnings retained in the business to give effect to the company's change in its fiscal year-end and to adjust for the two-month lag in reporting its equity in Wheeling's earnings under its former August 31 fiscal year-end. The equity in earnings for the year ended August 31, 1974, is based on Wheeling's unaudited financial statements for the period from the company's initial investment through June 30, 1974.

EXHIBIT 4
Loews Corporation, 1976 Annual Report

4. *Investments in Associated Companies*

Investments in associated companies consist of:

the amount at which its investment was carried by $43,824,000. Such amount, represent-

	December 31	
	1976	1975
	(in thousands)	
Equity securities:		
Wheeling (25.2% owned by the company) (reclassified)		$ 35,054
First Healthcare Corporation (Sold in 1976 by CNA)		7,072
Healthco, Inc. (45.3% owned by CNA)	$23,180	21,599
Others	12,233	22,363
Notes	22,022	17,878
Total	$57,435	$103,966

The company's equity in the net assets of Wheeling at December 31, 1976, exceeded ing the unamortized balance of the excess of equity in net assets required over cost (credit

EXHIBIT 4 (continued)

excess) at the various dates the investment in Wheeling was acquired, was being amortized over a 12-year period (the approximate remaining life of Wheeling's fixed assets) beginning with the various dates of acquisition.

Management determined to reduce to market value as of December 31, 1976, the carrying value of the company's investment in Wheeling and to reflect this holding on the same basis as other investments in the company's investment portfolio. This determination was based on management's decision to no longer treat the Wheeling investment as a long-term holding. Accordingly, management considered it prudent to adjust the carrying value of the investment to the current market value ($17,150,000). The write down in carry-

ing value of the Wheeling investment, net of applicable taxes, amounted to $21,199,000 and reduced realized investment gains in the accompanying statement of consolidated earnings.

All other investees are closely held; however, in the opinion of management, the carrying value of such other investments is not in excess of their underlying value.

Data concerning the results of operations and financial position of the above companies and the company's equity in such operations are set forth below. Such data does not include the effect of purchase value adjustments (see note 1); however, the company's equity in operations includes the effect of such adjustments.

Years Ended December 31

	1976		1975	
	Gross Revenues	Net Earnings (Loss)	Gross Revenues	Net Earnings (Loss)
		(in thousands)		
Results of Operations				
Wheeling	$ 936,956	$ 3,237	$ 836,686	$ 563
First Healthcare Corporation (sold in 1976)	11,024	(97)	33,113	(479)
Healthco, Inc.	206,850	3,502	173,000	5,000
Others*	43,406	(2,100)	29,840	(3,571)
Total	$1,198,236	$ 4,542	$1,072,639	$1,513

December 31

	1976		1975	
	Total Assets	Shareholders' Equity	Total Assets	Shareholders' Equity
		(in thousands)		
Financial Position				
Wheeling (reclassified)			$675,537	$365,638
First Healthcare Corporation (sold in 1976)			25,050	8,682
Healthco, Inc.	$ 131,681	$ 61,744	107,334	58,016
Others*	40,531	19,337	113,455	35,474
Total	$ 172,212	$ 81,081	$921,376	$467,810

* Certain amounts included are unaudited.

EXHIBIT 4 *(concluded)*

Amounts credited to earnings and cash dividends received by the company from these investees are set forth below:

	Years Ended December 31	
	1976	1975
	(in thousands)	
Credited to earnings:		
Equity in earnings (losses) (includes, in 1976 and 1975, minotity interest credits of $507,000 and $919,000, respectively)	$ (1,481)	$ 3,286
Amortization of credit excess	4,880	4,880
Provision for investment valuation		(3,660)
Income taxes:		
Current...	(1)	(709)
Deferred...	381	(1,309)
Total credited to earnings	$ 3,779	$ 2,488
Cash dividends...	$ 15	$ 1,142

Questions

1. Reconcile Loews's 1974 accounting for its investment in Wheeling-Pittsburgh. DO NOT use the Wheeling-Pittsburgh data in Exhibit 1 of the case to reconcile Loews's accounting treatment of Wheeling-Pittsburgh. The data are not correct for this purpose. They have been restated for Wheeling-Pittsburgh's shift to LIFO accounting in November 1974. The case takes place prior to Wheeling-Pittsburgh shift to LIFO. Loews's recognition of its equity in Wheeling-Pittsburgh is as of June 30, 1974.

    The following is a breakdown of Wheeling-Pittsburgh's results as reported through June 30, 1974, i.e., prior to Wheeling-Pittsburgh's shift to LIFO in November 1974 (in thousands).

	Quarter Ended				Twelve Months Ended
	I 3/31/73	*II* 6/30/73	*III* 9/30/73	*IV* 12/31/73	12/31/73
Net sales	$178,814	$185,800	$190,812	$205,708	$761,134
Profit before tax	3,500	5,895	3,692	12,993	26,080
Income tax	872	1,525	954	3,405	6,756
Net income	$ 2,628	$ 4,370	$ 2,738	$ 9,588	$ 19,324
Preferred dividends	767	768	767	768	3,070
Net to common	$ 1,861	$ 3,602	$ 1,971	$ 8,820	$ 16,254
Common stockholders' equity	$275,667	$279,269	$281,240	$290,060	$290,060

	Quarter Ended		Six
	I	*II*	*Months Ended*
	3/31/74	*6/30/74*	*6/30/74*
Net sales	$212,659	$264,034	$476,693
Profit before tax....................	13,330	33,570	46,900
Income tax	4,930	15,761	20,691
Net income.......................	$ 8,400	$ 17,809	$ 26,209
Preferred dividends	767	768	1,535
Net to common	$ 7,633	$ 17,041	$ 24,674
Common stockholders' equity........	$297,693	$314,734	$314,734

2. Calculate Loews's 1974 return on the Wheeling-Pittsburgh investment. How important are the future operating results of Wheeling-Pittsburgh in the outcome of future ROI calculations?

3. How much profit would Wheeling-Pittsburgh have contributed to Loews's 1974 net income if the Wheeling-Pittsburgh investment had been treated as a marketable security accounted for using the *cost* method? What if the *market value* method was used?

4. Why do you think Loews decided in fiscal 1976 to no longer treat the company's investment in Wheeling-Pittsburgh as a "long-term holding" (see Exhibit 4)? The following data may help you in answering this question.

In January 1975, Loews switched its fiscal year-end from August 31 to December 31. For 1975, 1976, and 1977, Wheeling-Pittsburgh reported the following results to shareholders:

	Net Sales	Net Income to Common (millions)	Common Dividends	Share Price High	Low (per share)
1975:					
First quarter—3/31	$247.2	$ 10.4	$1.3	$28.00	$18.00
Second quarter—6/30	187.9	(1.3)	1.3	31.875	22.50
Third quarter—9/30	187.5	(14.4)	—	26.375	16.50
Fourth quarter—12/31	204.1	2.7	—	18.625	14.125
				Close	
Total	$826.7	$ (2.6)	$2.6	$16.875	
1976:					
First quarter—3/31	$231.0	$ (3.3)	—	$23.875	$16.625
Second quarter—6/30	256.7	4.4	—	23.00	19.00
Third quarter—9/30	249.9	2.6	—	22.00	16.75
Fourth quarter—12/31	193.7	(3.6)	—	18.625	16.00
				Close	
Total	$931.3	$ 0.1	$—	$18.50	
1977:					
First quarter—3/31	$210.9	$(19.6)	—	$20.00	$16.25
Second quarter—6/30	262.6	1.9	—	16.625	14.00
Third quarter—9/30	253.4	(4.6)	—	14.25	8.50
Fourth quarter—12/31	239.2	(4.9)	—	10.25	9.00
				Close	
Total	$966.1	$(27.2)	$—	$ 9.25	

5. Loews continued as of the end of 1981 to hold 25 percent (approximately 927,000 shares) of Wheeling-Pittsburgh's common stock. Wheeling-Pittsburgh has shown the following results for 1978, 1979, and 1980. Which method, i.e., the equity method; cost method; lower-of-cost-or-market method; market method, or some combination of methods; for valuing Loews's investment in Wheeling-Pittsburgh since 1974 seems most useful for estimating the value of Loews's common stock?

WHEELING-PITTSBURGH
As of December 31

	1978	1979	1980
		(in millions)	
Net sales	$1,161.6	$1,250.7	$1,100.1
Profit before taxes	23.4	59.6	9.1
Income tax expense (credit)	4.4	9.9	(5.6)
Net income (loss)	$ 19.0	$ 49.7	$ 14.7
Preferred dividends	4.7	3.5	3.6
Net to common	$ 14.3	$ 46.2	$ 11.1
Common dividends	—	$ 3.8	—
Common stockholders' equity	$ 297.7	$ 341.3	$ 353.3
Common share price:		*(per share)*	
High	$14.25	$24.00	$23.875
Low	$ 8.00	$11.125	$15.50
Close	$10.50	$17.125	$21.00

6. What suggestions do you have for improving the accounting rules for both business combinations and significant intercorporate investments?

PART SEVEN

Long-Term Financial Commitment Reporting and Analysis

CHAPTER 21

Long-Term Debt Reporting, Rating, and Analysis

For financial reporting purposes, long-term debt includes all creditor claims upon a company that are not payable within 12 months or the normal operating cycle, whichever is longer. These obligations include mortgage notes, bonds, installment payment contracts, and long-term notes. This chapter's accounting and analysis discussion focuses on those forms of long-term debt issued under formal agreements, such as bonds payable, which usually have at least a five-year term. The accounting and analysis for other forms of long-term debt are similar.

Characteristics of Long-Term Debt

Long-term debt issued by corporations to raise funds from credit sources represents a promise (1) to repay the sum of money at a specified future date and (2) to compensate the lender for the use of the lender's money through periodic interest payments. The basic conditions of the debt are printed on the face of the bond certificate. The full details of the contract between the company and the bondholders are contained in the bond indenture, which is held by a representative of the bondholder, who is known as the trustee under the indenture. In bankruptcy, the claims of the bondholders rank ahead of those of stockholders.

Long-term debt is issued in a variety of forms. It may be secured or unsecured; if unsecured, it is termed a debenture. Secured debt often takes its name from the character of the collateral pledged. For example, bonds secured by marketable securities are known as collateral trust bonds. Mortgage bonds or notes are secured by all or some of the fixed assets of the borrower. Securities backed by chattel mortgages may be called equipment trust certificates. Within the various categories of long-term debt, some

737

debt instruments, such as subordinated debentures, may rank lower than others in their claims upon the company's assets in bankruptcy.

There are also variations in the method and timing of the repayment of the principal amount of long-term debt. The basic bond is repayable in a lump sum at a specific future date. The sinking fund bond is a modification of this form. Its indenture requires the borrower to make periodic cash payments into a sinking fund. This cash, plus the accumulated interest on it, is used to retire the bonds at maturity. A more common type of sinking fund bond indenture calls for payments to a trustee, who uses the funds accumulated for making periodic bond retirements. This practice increases the probability that the lender will be repaid.

Serial bonds are another type of bond with provisions designed to reduce risk to the bondholders. These bonds are repayable in a series over the life of the issue instead of a single maturity date.

Callable bonds give the borrower the option, after a certain period of time, to redeem all or some of the debt prior to maturity for the payment of a specified call premium beyond the principal amount. The call provision gives the borrower greater flexibility in the design of his capital structure, in that as interest rates change he can replace old bonds with less expensive new ones.

Long-term debt indentures contain a number of provisions. Some provisions may restrict the dividend payments of the borrower. These restrictions often limit the use of additional short- or long-term debt, or require that the borrower stay within certain debt-to-equity and working capital ratio limits. Other provisions may include the right to convert the bonds to other securities, such as stock.

Typically, the borrower's obligations to pay interest is fixed. It is not conditional upon company earnings, except for income and participating bonds. The payment of interest on income bonds is conditional upon their earning income: if the income is not sufficient to pay interest, no payments need be made. The interest obligation may or may not be cumulative (i.e., unpaid interest from one year becomes a lien against future earnings). These bonds usually result from corporate reorganizations, when it is necessary to give old security holders a less desirable form of security so that new senior securities can be sold. Participating bonds entitle the holder to share in earnings with the stockholders in a pro rata or limited way, in addition to the bondholder's usual fixed interest.

In recent years, a number of new forms of debt securities have been issued. These include zero coupon bonds, variable interest rate bonds, and bonds convertible at the option of the issue into different financial instruments or, in some cases, the issuer's assets. A zero coupon bond does not pay periodic interest. Rather, it is issued at a deep discount from its face value, which is the amount the issuer promises to redeem the bond for at its maturity date. A variable interest rate bond, as its name implies, pays periodic interest that varies according to the current level of interest rates.

Registration

Bonds may be registered in one of three ways in the books of the issuer. Some are registered with respect to both principal and interest; that is, the name of the owner is recorded in the issuer's records, and checks for interest and principal payments are sent directly to the owner by the issuer. This protects the bondholder from losses or theft of certificates, since the transfer of ownership benefits can only be made effectively by changing the owner's name in the issuer's books. Other bonds are registered as to principal only. This protects the bondholder from loss or theft of principal. Interest is received by detaching, on the appropriate interest dates, coupons attached to the certificate and presenting them to a bank for deposit or collection. Bonds issued overseas are frequently not registered as to either interest or principal and are freely transferable. These are known as bearer bonds.

Financial Consideration

The long-term fund requirements of corporations are usually satisfied through the issuance of a combination of stocks and bonds and the retention of earnings. Compared to stocks, bonds have some attractive features. The interest payments are deductible as a business expense in determining taxable income, whereas dividends are not. The ownership interest is not diluted when bonds are issued. The earnings on the funds obtained through a bond issue may be greater than the related interest charge, with the result that the earnings per share of the stockholders increase since no additional equity shares are issued. This effect is called "financial leverage."

The major disadvantage of bonds is the fixed requirement to repay principal and to pay interest periodically. If a corporation fails to meet these obligations, the bondholders may assume control of the company or force it into bankruptcy.

Valuation

The price of a bond is the present value of its future stream of interest payments plus the present value of the maturity principal payment. The discount rate applied to these future payments is the investor's required rate of return for the class of bond acquired.

The most simple bond to value is a consol-type bond, which is a bond that never matures and pays interest at a fixed amount. Its value is the present value of an infinite series of equal interest payments, namely:

$$V = \frac{I}{K_r}$$

where:

$V = $ Price of the bond.

$I = $ Constant annual interest in dollars paid every year in perpetuity.

$K_r = $ Investor's required rate of return.

To illustrate, assume that the investor's required rate of return is 10 percent and the perpetual annual interest payment is $2 per year, paid at the end of each year. The value of this bond is $20 ($2 divided by .10).

For a bond with a specific maturity date, which most bonds have, the price of the bond today is:

$$V = \frac{I_1}{(1 + K_r)} + \frac{I_2}{(1 + K_r)} + \cdots + \frac{I_n + M_n}{(1 + K_r)^n}$$

where:

$V = $ Price of the bond.

$I = $ Annual interest paid in dollars.

$n = $ Number of years to maturity.

$M = $ Maturity principal payment.

$K_r = $ Investor's required rate of return.

To illustrate, assume a $1,000 bond has five years to mature. The annual interest payment is $80 and the investor's required rate of return is 8 percent. The price of the bond today is:

$$V = \frac{\$80}{(1 + .08)} + \frac{\$80}{(1 + .08)^2} + \frac{\$80}{(1 + .08)^3} + \frac{\$80}{(1 + .08)^4} + \frac{(\$80 + \$1000)}{(1 + .08)^5}$$

$$= \$74.07 + \$68.59 + \$63.51 + \$58.80 + \$735.03$$

$$= \$1000$$

or

$$V = \$80(.926)^1 + \$80(.857) + \$80(.794) + \$80(.735) + \$1080(.681)$$

$$= \$74.08 + \$68.56 + \$63.52 + \$58.80 + \$735.48$$

$$= \$1000.44$$

The price of a bond will respond to changes in interest rates. It is generally thought that the longer to the maturity time of any given security, the greater is the likelihood of a price change in response to a change in interest rates. For this reason, it is considered riskier to hold longer term securities; thus, they typically have higher yields or rates of return than do short-term bonds.

If the price of a bond is known, its yield to maturity is the discount

---

[1] Value in brackets is the present value of a dollar discounted at 8 percent received n years hence. (See Present Value Table A included at end of book.)

ILLUSTRATION 21–1

	Cash Flow	Times	Equals
Years	Item	PV Factor (12 Percent)*	Present Value
1–10	Annual interest payments, $100,000	5.650	$565,000
10	Repayment of principal, $1 million	0.322	322,000
Market value			$887,000

* See Tables A and B in Appendix. The PV factor 5.650 is the present value of an annuity of $1 per year for 10 years discounted to the present (Table B). The PV factor 0.322 is the present value of a dollar received 10 years hence discounted at 12 percent (Table A).

rate that, when applied to the future cash payments, gives a present value equal to the current price.

The Present Value Tables A and B in the Appendix of the book or the present value applications included in most hand-held calculators can also be used to approximate bond yields and bond prices. For example, assume the Viking Chemical Company issued $1 million worth of 10 percent, $1,000 principal bonds repayable in 10 years and the current market interest rate for comparable bonds was 12 percent, the company would receive $887,000 from the buyers of the bonds, or $887 per bond. Assuming interest is paid annually, this sum represents the present value of 10 annual payments of $100,000 plus payment of $1 million 10 years hence, all discounted at 12 percent. If a bondholder held the Viking bonds to maturity, the return on the investment of $887 per bond would be 12 percent. The computation of market value at issue is shown in Illustration 21–1.

The market price of a bond can vary during its life as the level of interest rates shifts or the quality of the company's credit changes. For example, assume that after five years pass, the market rate for bonds similar to the Viking Chemical Company's bonds falls to 8 percent very soon after the fifth interest payment. Since the Viking bond pays a 10 percent nominal rate, the market price for this issue of bonds will rise to $1,080,300, which is $1,080.30 per bond. Anyone buying the bonds in the market for this price would get a yield of 8 percent on this investment if the bonds were held over the remaining five years to maturity. Assuming annual interest payments, the present value calculations are shown in Illustration 21–2.

When bonds are bought between interest dates, the purchase price includes the accrued interest.

Investment Risk

All bonds have an investment risk associated with them. This risk can come from four sources: (1) *Default risk* arises from the possibility that the firm's future resources will be insufficient to meet part or all of the bond interest and principal payments. (2) *Interest rate risk* comes from possibilities that unexpected changes in interest rates will adversely affect the market value

ILLUSTRATION 21–2

Cash Flow		Times	Equals
Years	Item	PV Factor (8 Percent)*	Present Value
1–5	Annual interest payments, $100,000	3.993	$ 399,300
5	Repayment of principal, $1 million	0.681	681,000
Market value			$1,080,300

* See Tables A and B in Appendix. The PV factor 3.993 is the present value of an annuity of $1 per year for five years discounted to the present 8 percent (Table B). The PV factor 0.681 is the present value of a dollar received five years hence discounted at 8 percent (Table A).

of the bond. That is, a change in prevailing interest rates can affect the opportunity cost of holding a fixed interest security. (3) *Purchasing power risk* is the possibility of loss in real terms sustained by bondholders during inflationary periods when the purchasing power of money decreases. (4) *Marketability risk* relates to the ease with which the investor may dispose of the bond.

Although investments in U.S. government obligations involve some interest rate and purchasing power risks, they are generally described as risk-free investments, since the investor is certain that the issuer will make the required payments and a market will always exist for the bonds.

The required rate of return from a security is the minimum expected rate of return necessary to induce investors to buy or hold the security. The required rate is the sum of the riskless rate of interest (usually defined as the current yield on short-term U.S. Treasury securities) plus a risk premium. The investor's expected rate of return can be thought of as the rate of return in event of default times the probability of default, plus the promised yield to maturity at purchase, times 1 minus the default probability (see calculation below.) When this value is also the minimum rate of return required by the investor, this value less the riskless rate of return is the investor's risk premium for assuming this bond's risk of default. It is the probability portion of this concept that the bond ratings reflect, since an agency's rating indicates its assessment of the bond's relative default and marketability risks. The following equation describes the required rate of return for the investor:

$$K_r = R_f + \rho$$

where:

K_r = Investor's required rate of return.
R_f = Riskless rate of interest.
ρ = Risk premium.

The investor's required rate of return is always less than a bond's promised return at the time of purchase. At the time a bond is purchased, it promises a certain yield to maturity. This is the highest rate of return or yield that the investor can expect from this particular bond purchase. However, because there is some probability that any bond may default, the investor's expected or required rate of return from the bond purchase will be less than the maximum promised yield. Thus, when the required or expected yield is calculated as stated above, there is a difference between the maximum promised yield and the investor's expected or required rate of return. This difference is called the default premium.

This default premium plus the investor's required rate of return less the riskless interest rate is often referred to as the premium yield. To illustrate: assume that a bond's promised yield to maturity at purchase is 10 percent, the probability of default is 5 chances out of 100, and the rate of return in case of default is 0 percent. Thus, the investor's expected return is 9.5 percent, i.e., $[.10 \ (1 - .05)] + (.00 \times .05)$. If the investor's required rate of return is 9.5 percent, this bond is acceptable to the investor. Thus, in this case, the default premium is .5 percent (10 percent − 9.5 percent). If the riskless rate of return is 6 percent, the investor's risk premium is 3.5 percent (9.5 percent − 6.0 percent).

Rating Agencies

The two major bond-rating services are Moody's Investors Service, Inc., and Standard & Poor's Corporation. Moody's has been in existence for 68 years and Standard & Poor's for 53 years. These two companies rate public and private corporate bond issues, commercial paper, preferred stock, and some large debt offerings of foreign companies and government. Other rating agencies are Duff and Phelps, and Fitch's.

The information provided by the rating agencies is one of the factors that the marketplace uses to determine interest rates. Since many institutional investors can only own bonds above a certain rating, the rating also determines who will or will not buy the issue. If a rating is changed during the life of the bond, the change can lead to a change in its interest yield. A bond rating may also influence the value of a company's common equity, since some common stock rating services take bond ratings into account when they rate stocks.

A committee of the rating agency is responsible for ratings. Initially, in the case of corporate bonds, the company seeking a rating for a new issue makes a presentation to the rating agency. Some presentations take place at the issuer's headquarters because, when possible, the rating agency likes to see a company and its management in their own offices. Other presentations take place at the rating agency.

The agency expects to see at least the issuing company's top financial officer and a vice president, if not the chief executive officer. Besides supplying all of the relevant financial data, it is the duty of these top executives to "sell" their company. Occasionally, they bring slide presentations, movies, product samples, and scale models of operations. Most important, they must persuade the rating committee of the company in light of the prospective issue. Sometimes a representative of the agency visits the company. In addition, the following information is requested by the rating agency: preliminary prospectus or some written stipulation of the terms of the proposed issue, the most recent 10-K report filed with the SEC, five years of annual reports, quarterly statements since the last annual report, and sometimes pro forma balance sheets, income statements, and sources and uses of funds statements.

Based on these data, a bond analyst employed by the rating agency prepares a report on the company that measures the probability of trouble or loss for the investor, especially from default and poor marketability of the bonds. In this report, the analyst assesses the likelihood of earnings declining or turning negative; the likelihood of a company's survival during a recession period; the likelihood that the issuer will be able to repay the principal borrowed and pay the interest owed, and to do these two things at the times agreed upon. The analyst may suggest a rating to the rating committee.

Companies do not always agree with or accept the rating decisions, and all the agencies have provisions for appeals by a dissatisfied company. Approximately 2 percent of the appeals are upheld—usually because the company has offered additional information not made available at the original rating sessions.

The rating agencies charge a fee for rating a company's bonds. Many companies contract with the agencies to do a preliminary rating and then, depending on what it is, the company may or may not bring the issue to the marketplace.

Bond Ratings

A bond rating represents the likelihood that the debt issuer will pay principal and interest on time. For the most part, the higher a rating is, the lower is the required rate of return by investors. Illustration 21–3 lists the two agencies' principal ratings. Within most of these grades, the rating agencies also have degrees of rating indicated by plus or minus signs in the case of Moody's and 1, 2, and 3 by Standard & Poors.

Moody's has commented on their ratings and their significance as follows:

The quality of most bonds is not fixed and steady over a period of time . . . a change in rating may thus occur at any time in the case of an individual issue. Such rating change should serve notice that Moody's observes some alteration in the investment risks of the bond or that the previous rating did not fully reflect the quality of the bond as now seen.

Bonds carrying the same rating are not claimed to be of absolutely equal quality . . . the symbols cannot reflect the fine shadings of risks which actually exist . . . [ratings] have no value in forecasting the direction of future movements of market prices. Market price movements in bonds are influenced not only by the quality of individual issues but also by changes in money rates and general economic trends, as well as by the length of maturity, etc. During its life even the best quality bond may have wide price movements, although its high investment status remains unchanged.

Since rating involves a judgment about the future, on the one hand, and since they are used by investors as a means of protection, on the other, the effort is made when assigning ratings to look at "worst" potentialities in the "visible" future rather than solely at the past record and the status of the present. . . . They are not statistical ratings but an appraisal of long-term risks, such appraisal giving recognition to many nonstatistical factors.

The difference in risk associated with bonds of varying qualities is also reflected in the yield spreads. To illustrate this difference, at any one time the average industrial bond yields may be as follows:

Aaa....	8.35 percent	A......	9.00 percent
Aa.....	8.55 percent	Baa....	10.30 percent

The dividing line between what is considered to be an investment-grade bond and a noninvestment-grade bond is a rating equivalent to Standard & Poor's triple B. Anything higher is considered a relatively safe investment, while anything lower is not. Many unrated and less than investment quality bonds are referred to as "junk bonds." These bonds are popular investments because of their high yields and low default experience.

In published lists of ratings, Moody's rating generally precedes that of Standard & Poor's—i.e., for a triple A rated bond the listing would read "Aaa/AAA."

Rating Considerations

In general, five areas are examined in rating a bond:

1. The bond's indenture.
2. The issuer's asset protection.
3. Future earning power.
4. Financial resources.
5. Management.

Indenture

The indenture is the legal document stating the terms of the contract between the bondholder and the issuing company. The following questions are considered in examining the indenture:

1. Are there restrictions on any subsidiaries to issue their own debt? This is important since this debt would have priorities on the assets of the subsidiary in case of any default or bankruptcy.

ILLUSTRATION 21-3
Bond Ratings

Rating	Moody's	Rating	Standard & Poor's
Aaa	Bonds which are rated Aaa are judged to be of the best quality. They carry the smallest degree of investment risk and are generally referred to as "gilt edge." Interest payments are protected by a large or by an exceptionally stable margin and principal is secure. While the various protective elements are likely to change, such changes as can be visualized are most unlikely to impair the fundamentally strong position of such issues.	AAA	Bonds rated AAA are highest grade obligations. They possess the ultimate degree of protection as to principal and interest. Marketwise, they move with interest rates and hence provide the maximum safety on all counts.
Aa	Bonds which are rated Aa are judged to be of high quality by all standards. Together with the Aaa group they comprise what are generally known as high-grade bonds. They are rated lower than the best bonds because margins of protection may not be as large as in Aaa securities or fluctuation of protective elements may be of greater amplitude or there may be other elements present which make the long-term tasks appear somewhat larger than in Aaa securities.	AA	Bonds rated AA also qualify as high-grade obligations, and in the majority of instances differ from AAA issues only in small degree. Here, too, prices move with the long-term money market.
A	Bonds which are rated A possess many favorable investment attributes and are to be considered as upper medium-grade obligations. Factors giving security to principal and interest are considered adequate but elements may be present which suggest a susceptibility to impairment sometime in the future.	A	Bonds rated A are regarded as upper medium grade. They have considerable investment strength but are not entirely free from adverse effects of changes in economic and trade conditions. Interest and principal are regarded as safe. They predominantly reflect money rates in their market behavior, but to some extent, also economic conditions.
Baa	Bonds which are rated Baa are considered as medium-grade obligations, i.e., they are neither highly protected nor poorly secured. Interest payments and principal security appear adequate for the present, but certain protective elements may be lacking or may be characteristi-	BBB	The BBB or medium-grade category is borderline between definitely sound obligations and those where the speculative element begins to predominate. These bonds have adequate asset coverage and normally are protected by satisfactory earnings. Their susceptibility to chang-

cally unreliable over any great length of time. Such bonds lack outstanding investment characteristics and in fact have speculative characteristics as well.

Ba Bonds which are rated Ba are judged to have speculative elements; their future cannot be considered as well assured. Often the protection of interest and principal payments may be very moderate and thereby not well safeguarded during both good and bad times over the future. Uncertainty of position characterizes bonds in this class.

B Bonds which are rated B generally lack characteristics of the desirable investment. Assurance of interest and principal payments or of maintenance of other terms of the contract over any long period of time may be small.

Caa Bonds which are rated Caa are of poor standing. Such issues may be in default or there may be present elements of danger with respect to principal or interest.

Ca Bonds which are rated Ca represent obligations which are speculative in a high degree. Such issues are often in default or have other marked shortcomings.

C Bonds which are rated C are the lowest rated class of bonds, and issues so rated can be regarded as having extremely poor prospects of ever attaining any real investment standing.

---

ing conditions, particularly to depressions, necessitates constant watching. Marketwise, the bonds are more responsive to business and trade conditions than to interest rates. This group is the lowest which qualifies for commercial bank investment.

BB Bonds given a BB rating are regarded as lower medium-grade. They have only minor investment characteristics in the case of utilities; interest is earned consistently but by narrow margins. In the case of other types of obligors, charges are earned on average by a fair margin, but in poor periods deficit operations are possible.

B Bonds rated as low as B are speculative. Payment of interest cannot be assured under difficult economic conditions.

CCC/CC Bonds rated CCC are outright speculations, with the lower rating denoting the more speculative. Interest is paid, but continuation is questionable in periods of poor trade conditions. In the case of CC ratings the bonds may be on an income basis and the payment may be small.

C The rating of C is reserved for income bonds on which no interest is being paid.

DDD/DD/D All bonds rated DDD, DD, and D are in default, with the rating indicating the relative salvage value.

2. May the issuing company issue new debt which might subordinate the bonds now being rated or have a prior claim on the company's assets? Certain standards and key ratios should be met before a company should be able to issue additional debt.
3. Is a sinking fund required to help ensure repayment of principal to the bondholders? Such a requirement may require the issuer to retire a portion of the bond's principal before maturity. Or, alternatively, cash is paid by the issuer to a trustee prior to maturity. These funds are then used to retire the debt at maturity.
4. Is there a mortgage or lien on the company's income or assets?
5. Do the requirements of the indenture put too many constraints on the company? In other words, can the issuing company remain flexible enough to meet changing conditions?
6. Is the bond being issued a senior or subordinated debt? This is an important consideration to the bondholder, for in the event of bankruptcy and liquidation, senior debt will be repaid first.
7. What might be the impact of current and future regulations (e.g., ERISA, OSHA, etc.) on the claims of creditors and bondholders?

In most cases, the indenture will set out a financial framework within which the borrower must operate, defined by a minimum level of working capital, net worth, capitalization, liquidity, interest coverage, etc. Aside from considering the appropriateness of these constraints, the rating agency is concerned with indenture restrictions relating to intercompany and/or parent-subsidiary transactions. The entity being financed could, for example, be required to upstream profits or pay dividends which affect the ultimate security of the debt in question.

Increasingly, the structure of the indenture has been used as a creative tool for the issuer. For example, Standard & Poor's notes that the indenture can "separate out" the most liquid assets to be reserved for collateral against debt repayment, the objective of which is to further secure the issue and, hence, boost the rating and reduce the cost of the issue. This paper manipulation, however, could trigger a default on another obligation which could, in turn, result in default on the issue being rated. The bond rating agencies must, therefore, analyze the terms of the legal framework for their impact on the ultimate ability of the borrower to service and repay the lenders. With this in mind, the issuer should not be discouraged from developing support mechanisms in the indenture to enhance the company's ability to continue to raise money.

In summary, it must be noted that in determining the final rating, the indenture is far less important than the company's financial resources, earning power, asset protection, and management.

Asset Protection

In the event of default, bondholders look to the company's assets for protection from loss. Therefore, it is important to determine to what degree the debt of a company is covered by asset values. In addition to some key financial ratios, the following points are considered in assessing the degree of asset protection:

1. The composition of the company's working capital. The greater the proportion of liquid assets, the better is the position of the company.
2. The nature and value of inventories.
3. The status of a company's plant and equipment (age, efficiency, needed improvements, etc.).
4. Book value of assets and the adequacy of depreciation charges.
5. Leasing commitments and other obligations that might not appear on the face of the balance sheet.

The ratios often used to measure asset protection are:

$$1. \quad \frac{\text{Pro forma long-term debt}^2}{\text{Net property, plant, and equipment}}$$

$$2. \quad \frac{\text{Working capital}}{\text{Pro forma long-term debt}}$$

$$3. \quad \frac{\text{Pro forma long-term debt}}{\text{Equity}}$$

$$4. \quad \frac{\text{Net tangible assets}}{\text{Pro forma long-term debt}}$$

Future Earning Power

Investors would prefer to invest in a company that will be able to cover payment of debt from earnings rather than resort to liquidation of assets to cover it in the case of default. The following are considered in determining the issuer's future earning power:

1. The issuer's industry and its position in it.
2. The trends in the industry, such as market share, costs of operations, and tax and depreciation practices.
3. The adequacy of the issuer's financial controls.

In studying future earning power, the fixed charges coverage ratios are extremely important. They are designed to measure how adequately creditors can be protected by funds from operations in case a company incurs losses. The key coverage ratio is:

$$1. \quad \frac{\text{``Cash flow''}^3}{\text{Long-term debt (and short-term debt not being regularly retired)}}$$

---

[2] Existing debt plus proposed debt being rated.

[3] The funds from operations figure is frequently called "cash flow." This is misleading since this figure does not represent a flow of cash. It is a funds flow calculation, defined as a change in financial resources, which is made up of net income plus nonfund expenses less nonfund revenues.

The stability and continuation of the cash flow is assessed in evaluating long-term solvency. The more stable this cash flow is over time, the lower will be the interest coverage ratio that investors will accept.

Two additional ratios that measure the number of times earnings exceed annual interest obligations used in practice are:

$$2. \quad \frac{\text{Total interest charges and income before taxes}}{\text{Total interest charges}}$$

This is the most simple and most frequently used times-interest-earned ratio. If it is used to compute the coverage ratio for a senior debt issue, only the interest related to the senior debt is used in the denominator.

$$3. \quad \frac{\text{Total interest charges and adjusted net income}^4}{\text{Total interest charges}}$$

These ratios may be expanded to include other fixed charges incurred by a company, because failure to meet these obligations could also lead to insolvency. The "extra" fixed charges may include:

a. Sinking fund requirements. This fixed charge is not tax deductible. Therefore, it must be converted to a tax-deductible basis. This is accomplished by multiplying the sinking fund requirement by $1/(1 - \text{tax rate})$.

b. Noncancellable annual material purchase commitments.

c. Lease rentals. Usually one third of the total annual rentals is included in this adjustment. In the last two cases, if an expense amount is included in the denominator, it should be added to the numerator also.

Financial Resources

Cash and other working capital resources are examined so as to judge the ability of a company to withstand a dip in the economy or other adverse conditions and still be able to meet its debt payments. Asset quality and dividend and debt policies are also carefully examined. For example, an overly generous dividend may jeopardize a company's ability to protect itself financially in the future. The extent to which a company relies on external financing, both long- and short-term, may seriously affect future performance and ability to sustain itself against economic uncertainties. The following ratios are usually considered important by bond-rating agencies:

$$1. \quad \frac{\text{Working capital}}{\text{Pro forma long-term debt}}$$

---

[4] Adjusted as follows: add back minority interest; exclude equity in undistributed earnings of unconsolidated subsidiaries; and exclude nonrecurring items.

2. $\dfrac{\text{Working capital}}{\text{Net plant}}$

3. $\dfrac{\text{Adjusted net income and depreciation}}{\text{Current liabilities}}$

4. $\dfrac{\text{Cash and marketable securities and current receivables}}{\text{Current liabilities}}$

5. $\dfrac{\text{Cost of goods sold}}{\text{Average inventory during period}}$

6. $\dfrac{\text{Accounts receivable}}{(\text{Credit sales}/360)}$

Management

The rating agencies go beyond financial ratio analysis and look at the management of a company. Here their main concerns are the depth of management; management's philosophies, policies, and goals; and the quality of financial planning and projections. The rating agencies examine a company's acquisition policy and practice, particularly to see if the management is expanding into fields in which it has little expertise or knowledge. A company's research and development and its advertising practices are also compared to those of other companies in the same industry.

Other Ratios

Other common financial ratios may be used for the analysis and measurement of financial risk.

The financial leverage index measures the effect of financial leverage on the operating assets of a company. This effect is positive when the return on equity capital is greater than the return on total assets.

$$\text{Financial leverage index} = \frac{\text{Return on equity capital}^{[5]}}{\text{Return on total assets}^{[6]}}$$

Capital structure and long-term solvency are measured by the use of ratios and common-size analyses of balance sheets. The objective is to measure the risk inherent in a company's capital structure. The more debt there is, the greater are the fixed requirements to repay principal and meet periodic interest payments. This increases the risk of insolvency during periods of adverse conditions. The following ratios are used to examine this aspect of leverage:

---

[5] Return on equity capital = Net income *after* interest/Stockholders' equity.

[6] Return on total assets = Net income *before* interest/Total assets.

1. $\dfrac{\text{Equity capital}}{\text{Total liabilities}}$

A ratio greater than 1 to 1 indicates the owners have a greater financial interest in the company than do the creditors.

2. $\dfrac{\text{Equity capital}}{\text{Long-term debt}}$

The complement of this ratio is long-term debt/equity capital. It is sometimes used.

3. $\dfrac{\text{Equity capital}}{\text{Equity capital plus all liabilities}}$

This ratio reflects the extent to which equity capital is used to finance the assets of a company.

4. $\dfrac{\text{Long-term debt}}{\text{Equity capital plus all liabilities}}$

The proportion of total assets financed by debt is measured by this ratio.

5. $\dfrac{\text{Fixed assets}}{\text{Equity capital}}$

This ratio is used also to measure the extent to which fixed assets are financed by debt.

Industry-Related Rating Issues

In rating industrial bonds (i.e., corporate bonds of manufacturers, retailers, and the like), the agencies primarily look at the five key rating factors. The agencies also examine the issuer's preliminary prospectus, 10-K reports, annual reports for five years, quarterly statements since the last annual report, and pro forma financial statements.

The following ratio values are considered reliable approximations for a bond to *qualify* for the accompanying rating by Standard & Poor's. It is assumed that the values are similar for the rating of the other agencies.

	AAA	AA	A	BBB
$\dfrac{\text{Pro forma long-term debt}}{\text{Net property, plant, and equipment}}$	≤50%	same as AAA	≤75%	≤100%
$\dfrac{\text{Working capital}}{\text{Pro forma long-term debt}}$	≥1	same as AAA	=65–75%	=45–50%
$\dfrac{\text{Pro forma long-term debt}}{\text{Pro forma long-term debt + Equity}}$	≤25%	≤30%	≤35%	≤45%
$\dfrac{\text{Net tangible assets}}{\text{Pro forma long-term debt}}$	4:1 to 5:1	3.5:1 to 4:1	3:1 to 3.5:1	2.5:1 to 3:1

ILLUSTRATION 21–4
Illustrative Financial Ratios for Selected Industrial Debt Ratings

Moody's and S&P Rating	Number of Issues	Total Debt as a Percentage of Capitalization		Ratio of Earnings to Fixed Charges		Cash Flow as Percentage of Total Debt	
		Average	Range	Average	Range	Average	Range
AA/Aa	34	32	17–52	9.2	3.6–18.9	51	24– 98
AA/A or A/Aa	11	36	25–43	6.9	5.1– 9.7	38	23– 53
A/A	69	38	18–57	6.9	2.4–37.8	38	13–103
A/Baa or BBB/A	6	43	29–73	4.3	2.3– 8.1	34	22– 53
Baa/BBB	4	53	49–58	3.5	2.4– 4.5	27	17– 38

In attempting to assess a company's financial resources, the rating agencies look at the quality of current assets, dividend policy, and reliance on external financing. The industry is examined and the company's position within it is assessed when examining future earning power.

Here is some indication of the values earning power ratios are required to have in order to gain a particular rating:

	AAA	AA	A	BBB
$\dfrac{\text{Cash flow}}{\text{Long-term debt}}$	$\geq 75\%$	$\geq 45\%$	$\geq 35\%$	$\geq 25\%$
$\dfrac{\text{Income after taxes and interst charges}}{\text{Interest charges and rentals}}$	$7\text{–}8\times$	$4\text{–}5\times$	$\geq 3\times$	$\geq 2\times$

The rating agencies stress that ratios are not rigidly applied. For example, a company may have adequate asset protection according to the above ratios, but this may not be an indication that it is equally well protected in other areas. All five of the key rating factors must be carefully analyzed and a qualitative examination made for *each* factor, in addition to the quantitative financial analysis.

Illustration 21–4 shows that while the financial ratios for each rating category for both Moody's and Standard & Poor's have a "center of gravity," there is a substantial range around the mean. This reflects the many intangibles that enter into the rating process.

Utility Bonds

The same five factors used to analyze corporate industrial bonds are also used in rating the debt issues of utilities, although some factors are given more emphasis. One of the main differences is the indenture of utility bonds compared to that of the industrials. Most utility bonds are mortgage bonds. They are secured by special liens on assets and/or revenues of the issuing company, while most of the industrial issues are debentures, secured by the general credit of the issuer.

Usually the working capital/debt ratio is not considered important in assessing asset protection of a utility, because most do not pay back long-term debt with working capital. Also, utilities can safely carry more leverage than an industrial company, since the former are highly regulated and less subject to the income uncertainties that arise from competition.

Since utilities generally spend much more than they earn and must borrow frequently, their relationship with banks and their financial flexibility is carefully examined.

Because of inflation and the regulatory considerations in operating and financing a utility, future earnings may be affected in a very different way from that of other companies. The attitude of the regulatory commissions plays an important role, since so much depends on their willingness to grant rate relief when it is required to keep the utility financially sound.

Utilities are allowed to add a noncash credit to income to reflect the cost of the capital tied up in the construction of new facilities. This credit is called an allowance for funds used during construction (AFDC). The fixed charge coverage ratio is computed both before and after taxes and with and without this allowance. The more important ratio used is the one before taxes with the AFDC included in income.

Finance Bonds

Usually, the rating agencies do not rate the debt of finance companies with less than $25 million in equity capital or $35 million in capital funds. Capital funds are permanent, long-term financing represented by long-term debt, preferred stock, and net worth. The critical considerations that Standard and Poor's looks at fall into four categories: portfolio quality, income protection, capital structure, and management.

Insurance Bonds

In the process of analyzing insurance bonds, heavy emphasis is put on the quality of the company's assets and liabilities as well as value of loans to policyholders, since these companies have no control over the amounts policyholders borrow. The debt and equity positions of the company are another important consideration, as are the types of policies sold by the company. The rating companies also look carefully at the subsidiaries of the parent company.

Bank Holding Company Bonds

Rating agencies rate the debt issues of bank holding companies. Standard & Poor's has a computerized data base of some 100 statistical ratios it uses in the analysis of bank holding companies. These and the five key factors examined in rating other debt are used to rate bank holding company bonds.

Standard & Poor's has eight standards that a bank holding company must meet to become a candidate for its AAA debt rating.

1. The company must be in an important position in a significant market.
2. The company must be soundly capitalized.
3. The debt of the company must be sound relative to total capitalization.
4. The earnings should be sufficient in amount and growth relative to the amount of and growth of assets.
5. The assets and liabilities should be in balance and manageable.
6. The company and its subsidiaries must have adequate loan-loss reserves in relation to assets, plus a favorable record.
7. Quality and liquidity of assets relative to liabilities should be good.
8. Quality and reliability of management should be very high.

There are two areas to which bank holding company bond analysts pay particular attention. The first arises from the nature of bank holding companies, which have few income-producing assets within the holding company itself. Most of their productive assets are lodged in the subsidiaries, which raise debt capital directly from the public. Therefore, when analyzing a bank holding company's debt, attention must be paid to the capital and liquidity needs of the subsidiaries, the claims on the subsidiaries from their debt holders, and the nature of the parent's claim on the dividends of the subsidiaries.

The second area of particular interest is the holding company's use of double leverage. Double leverage occurs when the holding company transfers borrowed capital from itself to its subsidiaries in the form of an equity investment in the subsidiary. The subsidiary in turn uses this increase in its net worth to borrow additional debt. The extent of this practice is measured by the double leverage ratio, which is the relationship of the equity of the subsidiary to the parent's equity. This ratio is unique to this class of bond analysis.

Other Corporate Financing Vehicles

Some of the less common forms of fixed obligation issues, such as intermediate-term bonds, corporate notes, convertible bonds, preferred stock, private placements, and lease-related financing, are also rated.

Intermediate-Term Bonds. The maturity is usually anywhere from 5 to 10 years, the rate of interest being generally lower than long-term issues because the risk is less. Basically the same information required to rate a longer-term bond must be supplied by the issuer, and the ratings are done in the same way. Particular emphasis is placed on how the cash will be generated to pay off the issue, since payment is required within a relatively short period of time.

Corporate Notes. These are rated essentially in the same way as long-term bonds, exceptions being made in cases where the notes might be subordinated to a bond issue already outstanding or about to be issued. In this case, the note is generally rated one grade below the bond.

Convertible Debt. These bonds are convertible into common or preferred stock. Their prices are more volatile than longer term debt. They are rated in the same way as a longer term issue of the issuing company. No emphasis is placed on the fact that the debt can be converted into company stock.

Preferred Stock. Although this is an equity security, it is rated in much the same way as a bond would be, but the ratios used must be adjusted to take account of the stock's lower claim on assets and the after-tax nature of its dividend. Usually, the more debt that is outstanding, the lower will be the rating of the preferred stock, whose fixed dividend becomes less assured while the total fixed interest payments increase as the debt total increases.

Private Placements. As the word "private" implies, these issues are not made available to the general public. The interest paid is usually higher, but the issuing company does not have to make public its corporate financial information. The agencies rate very few of these securities, since the buyers usually have had experience with these bonds and can arrange for their own ratings.

Lease-Related Financing. This type of financing involves the issuance of debt to acquire an asset, which in turn is leased. The lease payments provide the source of cash to repay the debt. It is important for rating purposes that the lease payments provide for full payment of the related debt over the life of the lease. The terms of the lease are examined in much the same way as the indenture of a bond would be. The amount of equity put up by the lessor is also an important rating factor. The more equity that is contributed, the higher the rating is likely to be.

Commercial Paper

Companies issue commercial paper because it is usually less costly than borrowing from a bank, with an interest rate generally lower than a bank's prime rate. Commercial paper is short-term debt that is issued for not more than 270 days by corporations. It usually has a slightly higher rate of interest than Treasury bills. The proceeds from an offering must be used only for working capital purposes.

To rate commercial paper, the rating agencies require similar financial information to that requested when they rate a company's bonds. The analysis of this data is similar also, since the issuer must be able to pay back the debt out of cash flow in the near future. To obtain an acceptable rating, the coverage of debt must be adequate and the trend in earnings and cash flow should be upwards. In contrast to long-term debt ratings, emphasis is placed on the issuer's liquidity position, since the debt will have to be paid back in a relatively short period. Also, in order to receive one of the three acceptable ratings, a company must have a *minimum* rating of a triple B for its long-term senior debt, have access to at least two additional sources of funds, and demonstrate superior management. The ratio of total liabilities to common equity should be less than 1 to 1.

Commercial paper receives a different set of ratings. For example, Standard & Poor's uses six commercial paper ratings. However, an issuer will rarely accept anything lower than A-3, since there is no market for paper rated lower. The commercial paper ratings and the criteria which must be met to receive one of the three highest ratings are shown below. Formal definitions of A-1, A-2, and A-3 ratings have not been devised. The rating an issue receives depends on its strengths and weaknesses relative to the following Standard & Poor's commercial paper rating criteria.

1. Liquidity ratios must be sufficient to meet cash requirements. For industrial companies, these ratios include the quick ratio, current ratio, cash flow to current liabilities ratio, and cash flow to long-term debt ratio. For the acid or quick ratio, the issuing company is compared to others in the same industry. For the current ratio, Standard & Poor's usually prefers that current assets exceed current liabilities by at least 2 to 1; cash flow should be 40 percent of current liabilities, but must be at least 30 percent for an A rating. Cash flow should also be 40 percent of long-term debt but must be at least 30 percent.

2. If the issuing company has long-term senior debt outstanding, it should have a rating of at least A. If outstanding long-term senior debt is only rated BBB but the short-term outlook is extremely good, a company can qualify for one of the A ratings for its commercial paper.

3. The issuing company must have access to a minimum of two additional sources of external funding (i.e., bond market, banks, etc.).

4. Earnings and cash flow of the issuing company must be in an upward trend, except in unusual circumstances.

5. The issuing company should hold a strong position in a well-established industry.

6. Reliability and quality of management must not be subject to question.

Municipal Bonds

The SEC requires issuers of general obligation municipal bonds to submit to the underwriter of the issue such information as a breakdown of the issuer's debt, property valuations, tax-collection statements, census estimates, annual statements, economic conditions reports, and capital improvement programs. Depending on the municipality, other pieces of information are also required.

Debt structure is carefully scrutinized, both existing and proposed future debt, and measured in the following three ways: per capita debt, per capita debt to per capita income, and debt to total market valuations of taxable property. The question raised in this analysis is how much debt is already outstanding and how much more will need to be borrowed. In particular, the raters want to be assured that the cash from the debt issue will be used to finance what it is supposed to finance.

For revenue bonds, the issuing agent must supply information on the purpose of the issue (i.e., construction costs, dates, etc.), an engineer's report, past audits, the security that is backing the bond, in what other ways the property may be protected, and economic data (economic stability, estimated per capita market values of taxable property, income levels, and nature of local industry). Again, depending on the municipality and the project, other information may also be requested.

To qualify for at least a municipal bond rating of BBB, revenues must not be less than fixed charges. Some academic research done in the area of municipal bond ratings suggests that the ratings are influenced greatly by the following five variables: existing debt, assessed value, population, tax collection rate, and the state in which the issuer is located.

Accounting Practices

The principal controversy concerning accounting for bonds revolves around the handling of unamortized discount, issue costs, redemption premiums on bonds refunded, and debt restructuring.

Issuance of Bonds

When bonds are issued, they are recorded at their face value in the long-term liability account. Any difference between the proceeds of the sale and the face value of the bond is put into the liability account Bond Premium or the asset account Bond Discount. The premium or discount balance is then written off to the Bond Interest account over the life of the issue.

The accounting entry to record an issue of one thousand $1,000 bonds at their face value is:

```
Dr.  Cash .................................................  1,000,000
        Cr.  Bonds Payable ............................            1,000,000
```

If these bonds had been issued at a premium of $100,000, the entry would have been:

```
Dr.  Cash ..............................................  1,100,000
        Cr.  Bonds Payable ..............................              1,000,000
             Bond Premium ...............................                100,000
```

The accounting entry for a $100,000 discount is:

```
Dr.  Cash ..............................................    900,000
     Bond Discount .....................................    100,000
        Cr.  Bonds Payable .............................              1,000,000
```

The costs associated with issuing bonds include underwriting fees, taxes, printing, and engraving. These issuing costs are accounted for as a deferred cost and amortized over the life of the issue.

When there is more than one bond issue, each issue should be listed either separately on the balance sheet or in the notes. Fair disclosure requires that the interest rate, maturity date, collateral data amount, and the number of authorized and issued bonds be shown for each issue. Any convertibility and subordination of long-term debt should also be indicated. In addition, violations of any of the indenture stipulations should be disclosed.

Amortization of Bond Premium and Discount

There are two common methods for amortizing bond premium and discount items. The compound-interest method reduces the discount or premium by the amount needed to make the nominal interest expense equal to the effective rate of interest. *Opinion No. 21* requires this approach. The straight-line method may be used as a matter of convenience if the result is not materially different from the required method. It takes the discount or premium into the interest expense account over the life of the bond in equal amounts. This procedure results in an equal interest charge each period.

Illustration 21–5 demonstrates the compound-interest method, using a $1 million, five-year, 10 percent bond issued to yield 12 percent.

Using the amounts in Illustration 21–5 for each interest period, the first-year accounting entries for recording periodic interest payment and adjustment to the bond discount account are:

```
Dr.  Bond Interest Expense .............................    111,300
        Cr.  Cash ......................................                100,000
             Bond Discount .............................                 11,300
```

The entries for amortizing bond premium are similar, except the amortization charge is debited to the bond premium account.

ILLUSTRATION 21–5
Discount Amortization, Compound-Interest Method ($1 million five-year bonds, nominal rate 10 percent payable annually, sold at $927,500 to yield approximately 12 percent)

Interest Payment Periods	A Cash Interest Payment	B Effective Interest Expense (12 percent of E)	C Bond Discount Amortization (B − A)	D Unamortized Bond Discount Balance (D − C)	E Bond Carrying Value* − (PV of Future Interest + Principal Payments Discounted at 12 percent)
0	—	—	—	$72,500	$ 927,500
1	$100,000	$111,300	$11,300	61,200	939,700
2	100,000	112,764	12,764	48,436	952,200
3	100,000	114,264	14,264	34,172	996,000
4	100,000	115,920	15,920	18,252	982,300
5	100,000	118,252	18,252	—	1,000,000

* Carrying value on the balance sheet if the bond discount is treated as a valuation account rather than as an asset.

Extinguishment before Maturity

Corporations sometimes reacquire their debt securities through exercise of their call provision or by purchase in the open market. Bonds acquired by call are usually called at a periodic interest date, after paying and recognizing in the accounts the interest due for the period. Repurchase of debt securities occurs most frequently when interest rates rise and the market value of low nominal rate bonds declines. This provides the corporate issuer with the opportunity to reacquire these discounted debt obligations at less than their principal value. Once acquired, the debt security may be retired or used to satisfy sinking fund requirements.

The FASB in *Statement No. 4*, "Reporting Gains and Losses from Extinguishment of Debt," required that the gains and losses from the extinguishment of debt be classified as an extraordinary item. This conclusion does not apply to gains or losses from cash purchases of debt made to satisfy one year's sinking fund requirements. *Statement No. 64* permits these gains or losses to be recorded as ordinary income.

The reacquisition price of debt is the amount paid on early extinguishment, including any call premium and miscellaneous costs of reacquisition. If early extinguishment is achieved by a direct exchange of new securities, the reacquisition price is the total present value of the new securities.

To illustrate the accounting entries, assume that $100,000 par value of bonds with a related discount of $3,000 are retired after paying a call premium of $2,000. The entries to record the call and retirement are:

Dr.	Bonds Payable	100,000	
	Loss on Bond Extinguishment	5,000	
	Cr. Cash		102,000
	Bond Discount		3,000

For a similar issue that had originally been sold at a premium of $3,000, the accounting entries to record the call and retirement are:

```
Dr.  Bonds Payable .......................................  100,000
     Bond Premium ........................................    3,000
       Cr.  Cash ..........................................             102,000
            Gain on Bond Extinguishment ...................               1,000
```

Defeasance

The FASB permits recognizing gains from "in-substance defeasance" transactions involving taxable securities when a debtor irrevocably places sufficient qualifying assets in trust to use solely in satisfying that specific debtor's obligations. These transactions work as follows: A corporation establishes an irrevocable trust solely to discharge a long-term debt obligation. The trust is funded by the corporation with government securities bearing a higher interest rate than the corporate debt. Since the government securities' interest rate is higher than the corporate debt, the amount of government securities needed to fund future corporate debt obligations is less than the amount of the debt itself. If the debt being defeased is "old" debt, this difference in value is then recognized by the corporation as a current gain. If the debt has been incurred fairly recently, this gain must be amortized over the life of the new debt.

Troubled Debt Restructuring

For the purposes of accounting, a "troubled" debt restructuring implies that the creditor, for economic or legal reasons related to the debtor's financial difficulties, has granted a concession that it would not otherwise consider, such as a modification of the terms of the debt or accepting an equity interest in the debtor to satisfy a debt obligation.

A debtor that transfers its assets or an equity interest to a creditor in restructuring of troubled debt situations recognizes a gain to the extent that the carrying amount of the payable settled exceeds the fair value of the assets or equity interest transferred to the creditor.

If the terms of the debt agreement are modified in a troubled debt restructuring, the debtor accounts for the modification prospectively. The carrying amount of the payable remains unchanged unless the sum of the future cash payments exceeds the carrying amount of the payable. The new effective interest rate for computing interest expense is the discount rate that equates the present value of the debtor's restructured future cash payments with the carrying amount of the payable. If the sum of the future cash payments is less than the carrying amount of the payable, the carrying amount is reduced to the sum of the future cash payments, and all future payments are accounted for as reductions of the restructured payable. The reduction in value is recognized as a gain on restructuring of payables in the period of the restructuring.

Debtors must disclose in financial statements the nature of any debt restructuring.

Conversion

In order to make bonds more attractive to buyers, some issues give the bondholder the right under certain conditions to convert bonds into stock. The conversion terms can vary: the conversion ratio may specify a certain number of shares of stock to be issued for each bond, or it may simply indicate that stock of an equivalent par value to the bond's value may be issued. Sometimes the conversion right can be exercised only after a specific period of time.

When bonds are converted, the first step is to correct the current balances by recording any accrued interest and by adjusting, if necessary, the unamortized bond discount or premium accounts. The next step is to record the conversion. This can be done in one of two ways.

The first method records the conversion on a market value basis. The newly issued security is recorded at either its market value or the market value of the bonds, whichever is more readily determinable; the appropriate bonds payable account is reduced by the par value of the bonds converted; and any difference between par value of the bonds and the market value assigned to the new securities is reported as a gain or loss on conversion. This method assumes that the conversion terminates the bond transaction and begins a new one for the stock. Therefore, the relevant value associated with this transaction is the amount that would be received today if the bonds were sold, or if the stock was sold rather than exchanged. If the market values of the bonds and equity differ, the market value of the bonds is the preferred measure of the new equity created.

The alternative approach assumes that the original issue price of the bonds represented in large part a sum paid for the future delivery of stock. Therefore, when conversion occurs, the book value of the bonds should be transferred to the newly issued stock.

To illustrate, the Ronald Company offers bondholders 20 shares of $5 par value stock in exchange for each $1,000, 6 percent bond they hold. The market value of the stock is $60 per share, and of the bonds, $1,200 per bond. All accrued interest has been paid, and the balance of the unamortized premium account is equivalent to $20 per bond. Holders of 600 bonds exercise their conversion right. The accounting entries are:

Market Value Method (based on bonds' market value of $720,000)

Dr.	Bonds Payable (600 bonds @ $1,000)	600,000
	Bond Premium (600 × $20)	12,000
	Loss on Bond Conversion	108,000
	Cr. Common Stock (12,000 shares × $5 par value)	60,000
	Premium on Common Stock [600 × $1,200] −	
	$60,000	660,000

Book Value Method (based on bonds' book value of $612,000)

```
Dr.  Bonds Payable (600 bonds @ $1,000) ....................    600,000
     Bond Premium (600 × $20) ..............................     12,000
       Cr.  Common Stock (12,000 shares × $5 par value) .....              60,000
            Premium on Common Stock ($612,000 − $60,000) ..             552,000
```

The conversion of bonds into other bonds in the same company which are substantially the same, or into stock in accordance with the bond indenture, is considered by the Internal Revenue Service as a nontaxable transaction to the bondholder. All exchanges of bonds for other securities or property are taxable.

Debt Issued with Stock Warrants

The interest rate of bonds issued with warrants giving the bondholders the right to buy the issuer's common stock is typically lower than the rate for similar quality bonds without warrants. Therefore, the issuer is able to get a higher price for bonds by adding stock warrant features. This difference in the proceeds is in effect a payment by the bondholder for a future "call" on the stock of the issuer. The proceeds minus this amount can be considered as the imputed cost of the straight bond portion of the security.

In the case of convertible debt and debt issued with stock warrants where the debt must be converted to obtain the advantage of the warrants, the APB recommended in *Opinion No. 14* that no portion of the proceeds from the issuance be accounted for as attributable to the conversion feature. The APB noted that the inseparability of the debt and conversion feature was the primary difficulty, rather than the practical problems of valuing the conversion feature.

If the debt was issued with detachable stock warrants, the APB stated that the portion of the proceeds allocable to the warrants should be accounted for as a credit to paid-in capital. Since the face value of the debt obligation remains unchanged, the offsetting entry is to the discount or premium on debt accounts, depending upon the relationship between the proceeds of the issue and the face amount of the obligation. This has the effect of recording the discount or premium that would have been recorded if the issue had been sold as straight debt.

Warrants are often traded, and their fair market value can usually be determined by their market price at the issue date. This value is the basis for allocating the proceeds of the issue between the debt obligation and warrants. If no market exists for the warrants, the market value for the debt without warrants must be estimated.

Classification of Short-Term Debt Expected to Be Refinanced

For many years, corporations had a variety of ways to classify on their balance sheets short-term obligations that were expected to be refinanced on a long-term basis. For example, commercial paper, construction loans, or the currently maturing portion of long-term debt that was expected to be refinanced was sometimes classified as a current liability, a long-term liability, or as a class distinct from both the current and long-term liabilities. Those who classified these short-term obligations as something other than a current liability did so because satisfaction of the obligation was not expected to require the use of working capital during the ensuing fiscal year. Sometimes when annual reports were issued, the short-term obligations classified as noncurrent liabilities had not been refinanced, and the probability that the long-term refinancing would occur varied from not very likely to certain.

The FASB became disturbed by the variety of classification practices and the different levels of uncertainty associated with the probability of refinancing. Accordingly, it issued *Statement No. 6*, "Classification of Short-Term Obligations Expected to Be Refinanced," which specified that henceforth such obligations could be classified as noncurrent liabilities only if a company's intent to refinance its short-term obligation was supported by an ability to consummate the refinancing, demonstrated in either of the following ways. (1) After the date of an enterprise's balance sheet, but before the balance sheet is issued, a long-term obligation or equity security has been issued for the purpose of refinancing the short-term obligation on a long-term basis. Or, (2) before the balance sheet date, the company has entered into a financing agreement permitting the company to refinance the short-term obligation on a long-term basis on terms that are readily determinable. In addition, all of these conditions must be met: *(a)* The agreement does not expire during the 12 months (or operating cycle, if longer); and *(b)* during this period the agreement is noncancellable by the prospective lender, except for violation of a provision with which compliance is objectively determinable or measurable; *(c)* prior to the issuance of the statements, the agreement has not been violated and no information exists that suggests that it will be violated; and *(d)* the lender is financially capable of honoring the agreement.

Classification of Obligations that Are Callable

Many loans have provisions that if the borrower fails to meet certain requirements, such as a specified working capital level, the loan is callable by the lender immediately. When a company violates one of these covenants that makes a loan callable by the creditor, the loan should be reclassified as a short-term obligation unless the lender signs a written waiver of the call privilege for at least a year from the balance sheet date.

Inappropriate Interest Rates

In *Statement No. 21*, "Interest on Receivables and Payables," the APB set forth its views regarding the appropriate accounting when the face amount of a note does not reasonably represent the present value of the consideration given or received in the exchange. Such a transaction may occur when property is exchanged for a long-term, noninterest-bearing note, or for a note with artificially low interest.

In these circumstances, unless the note is recorded at its present value, the sales price and profit to the seller in the year of the transaction and the purchase price and cost to the buyer are misstated, and the interest income and interest expense in subsequent periods are also misstated. The present value of the note is determined by discounting all future payments at an imputed interest rate, which is the approximate rate that would have resulted if an independent borrower and an independent lender had negotiated a similar transaction under comparable terms and conditions with the option to pay cash upon purchase or to give a note in the amount of the purchase bearing the prevailing rate of interest to maturity. One guide to the appropriate rate is the prevailing rate for similar instruments of issuers with similar credit ratings.

The discount or premium resulting from the application of *Opinion No. 21* is not an asset or liability separable from the note that gives rise to it. Therefore, the discount or premium is reported in the balance sheet as a direct deduction from or addition to the face amount of the note.

The discount or premium is amortized and reported as interest in the income statement over the life of the note.

Transfers of Receivables with Recourse

It is a common business practice to sell accounts receivable to raise capital. Normally, the accounting for the sale is straightforward. The accounts receivable balance is reduced by the amount of receivables sold, the cash account is increased by cash received, and a gain or loss is recognized for the difference between the carrying amount of the receivables and the cash received.

The sale of receivables with recourse must be recorded as a borrowing rather than a sale if any one of the following criteria proposed by the FASB are not met:

a. The seller surrenders control of the future economic benefits of the receivables.
b. The seller's recourse obligation can be reasonably estimated.
c. The buyer cannot require the seller to repurchase the receivables, except under the recourse provisions.

Accounting Practices: The Buyer

Purchase of Bonds

Bonds may be bought at their face value or at a price which represents either a premium or discount from the face value. The accounting entries in the bondholder's books to record the purchase of bonds are:

```
Dr.  Investment in Bonds  ..............................................  xxx
      Cr.  Cash .............................................................       xxx
```

Interest Payments Received

When bonds are bought at their face value, the bondholder records the periodic interest received by a simple debit to Cash and credit to Interest Income. If the purchase involved a premium or discount and the bondholder intends to hold the bonds as a long-term investment, the accounting is more complex.

The carrying value of a bond bought at a discount gradually rises to par at maturity. Rather than wait until the maturity date to recognize all of this gain over cost, it is customary to record in the bondholder's accounts the increase as it accrues as part of his interest income. Thus, the interest income includes the interest payment received plus the change in the carrying value of the bond. The accounting entries are:

```
Dr.  Cash  ..................................................................  xxx
      Investment in Bonds  ...............................................  xxx
      Cr.  Bond Interest Income  ........................................       xxx
```

This treatment assumes that the discount is analogous to a prepayment of interest by the issuer. It also assumes that the bond will be held to maturity.

The carrying value of a bond purchased at a premium slowly declines to par at maturity. The accounting treatment for recognizing this change in carrying value is the reverse of the bond discount situation. However, the carrying value at any point in time should not be greater than the redemption value at the issuer's next optional redemption date. The accounting entries are:

```
Dr.  Cash  ..................................................................  xxx
      Cr.  Investment in Bonds  ........................................       xxx
           Bond Interest Income  ........................................       xxx
```

The change in the carrying value is the difference between the present value of future interest payments and the redemption payment at maturity at the current interest payment date, and the date of the prior interest payment. The discount rate used to compute these present values is the yield to maturity rate implicit in the purchase price. If the bondholder's balance sheet date does not match the interest payment date, the accrued interest to date is the difference between the carrying values at the two dates bounding the current accounting period.

To illustrate the calculation of change in carrying value, assume that $1 million of 10-year tax exempt bonds paying 5 percent annually is bought for $926,000 to yield 6 percent to maturity. Illustration 21–6 reflects the carrying value *after* one year. At the end of this year, the first annual interest payment of $50,000 is received.

ILLUSTRATION 21–6
Calculation of Carrying Value Change at End of Year 1

Years	Item	Times PV Factor (6 percent)	Equals Present Value
1–9	Annual interest payments, $50,000	6,802	$340,100
9	Principal repayment, $1,000,000	0.592	592,000
	Present value on first payment date		$932,100
	Present value at purchase date		926,000
	Change in bond investment		$ 6,100

The accounting entries to record interest income are:

```
Dr.  Cash ................................................. 50,000
     Investment in Bonds ...............................  6,100
         Cr.  Interest Income ..............................           56,100*
```

* More precise present value tables than those used in Appendix Tables A and B would have led to the following calculation:

```
Purchase price of bond ............................................... $926,399
Present value of bond at end of year 1 ...............................   938,983
Increase in bond value ...............................................  $  5,584
Nominal interest payment .............................................    50,000
Interest expense .....................................................  $ 55,584
```

Verification of interest expense: $926,399 × 6% = $55,584

A similar entry at the end of each period will result in a level effective rate of interest income being recognized on the carrying value of the bond. As the bond approaches maturity, the related interest income will slowly increase to reflect the increasing carrying value.

Alternatively, for convenience, investors often adjust the carrying value of their investment in bonds by an amount equal to the bond discount (or premium) divided by the number of interest periods to maturity. To determine interest income, this amount is added or deducted, depending on whether it relates to discount or premium, from the periodic interest payment received. This approach leads to the recognition of a level interest income item over the life of the bonds. However, since the carrying value is slowly increasing as maturity approaches, the effective rate of interest obtained by relating interest income to carrying value declines.

Changes in carrying value are not recognized when the issuer's financial condition casts doubt on the collection of par at maturity. Also, bonds held for short-term investments are carried at cost and are not typically adjusted for changes in carrying value. Such short-term investments are usually reported on the basis of the lower of cost or market, but unless a decline in market price is significant and appears to be permanent, the carrying value is seldom reduced to market. In all cases, the current market value should be disclosed parenthetically on the balance sheet.

The income tax regulations related to bonds are complicated. For income tax purposes, however, in most cases the investor reports as interest income the interest payments actually received or, as in the case of zero coupon bond, as the interest accrues. Upon disposal of the bonds, any difference between the amount received and the purchase price is reported as a taxable gain or loss. In general, the original purchaser will be taxed at ordinary rates on these gains up to the amount of the original discount at the bond's issue date. Other purchasers will pay capital gains rates on gains above their original purchase price. No gains or losses can be recognized before disposal.

Troubled Debt Restructuring

Statement No. 15's rules on troubled debt restructuring apply to lenders also.

A creditor receiving an equity interest in assets from a debtor in full satisfaction of a restructured troubled debt must account for the item received at its fair market value. Any excess of the recorded investment in the debt over the fair market value received is recorded as a loss in the period of restructuring to the extent it exceeds related loss provisions previously established.

The effects of a modification of the terms of a debt receivable are accounted for prospectively. The amount of the recorded investment in the receivable at the time of restructuring is adjusted only if it is less than the future cash proceeds specified by the new terms. The new effective interest rate is the discount rate that equates the new future cash receipts with the recorded investment in the receivable. If the undiscounted future cash flow is less than the amount of the recorded receivable investment before restructuring, the recorded receivable is reduced to the amount of the future cash flows, and the write-down is charged to current income. All future cash received is accounted for as a recovery of investment, and no interest income is recognized for the period between the restructuring and the maturity of the receivable.

Creditors should disclose the nature of any troubled debt restructuring.

Financial Analysis and Decision Models

In recent years, considerable research has been done on the role of data generated through financial analysis in statement users' decision-making processes. Much of this work has focused on the usefulness of financial data in predicting bankruptcy and bond ratings.

A number of researchers have attempted to predict bond ratings, simulate the rating-agency rating process, or predict bond rating changes by creating purely statistical models of rating agency decision-making activities. These researchers have developed models utilizing a limited number of variables while recognizing that in actual practice a multitude of quantitative and qualitative variables are examined by the rating agencies before a bond rating is assigned. Nevertheless, these studies suggest strongly that regardless of judgmental considerations, a reliable gauge of a potential agency rating can be determined from certain financial data.

These studies lead to several guideline conclusions for issuers and others interested in simple approaches to predicting bond ratings:

1. The variables that determine perhaps 50 to 70 percent of a bond rating are the following:
    *   Subordination status of issue;
    *   Size of issuer;
    *   Degree of financial leverage;
    *   Interest coverage adequacy; and
    *   Stability of issuer's dividends and earnings.
2. Variables such as asset protection, short-term liquidity, and marketability are probably less important.
3. Management, industry, general economic condition, future prospects, and other qualitative factors account for perhaps 30 to 50 percent of a bond rating.
4. Complicated extrapolations or transformations of financial and other data are probably not worth the effort and may even make communication of results more difficult.
5. Probably much of the financial ratio analysis that is used to help predict or determine bond ratings is redundant. One measure of size, leverage, profitability, or stability is probably enough. As long as a relatively standard definition of the variable is used, it may not matter which definition is chosen for analytical purposes.
6. High-quality bond ratings are typically associated with low earnings variability, a history of meeting obligations, good market acceptance, a preferred claim on assets, and a prudent leverage rate, which in turn implies a high fixed charges coverage ratio.

Models that employ financial data to predict *corporate insolvency or bankruptcy* due to severe financial and/or operational difficulties fall into two broad classes: univariate models that use a single variable to predict failure, and multivariate models with several variables used simultaneously in the prediction process.

The univariate approach research indicates that the financial ratios of failed firms differ from those of solvent firms, and that the nonliquid asset ratios are better predictors of failure than the liquid asset ratios. Furthermore, the nonliquid asset ratios that seem to be the best predictors of failure are the cash flow to total debt, net income to total assets, and total debt to total assets ratios. Cash flow is defined as net income plus depreciation, depletion, and amortization. In addition, the "mixed ratios," which are those with income or cash flow in the numerator and assets and liabilities in the denominator, are better predictors of failure than the short-term solvency ratios are. A list of the nonliquid and liquid ratios used in this research by one researcher, Beaver, are presented below:

List of Ratios Tested in Research

Nonliquid Asset Ratios

1. Cash flow to total debt.*
2. Net income to total assets.
3. Total debt to total assets.

Liquid Asset Ratios

Total asset group:
1. Current assets to total assets.
2. Quick assets to total assets.
3. Net working capital to total assets.
4. Cash to total assets.

Current department group:
1. Current assets to current debt (current ratio).
2. Quick assets to current debt (quick ratio).
3. Cash to current debt.

Net sales or turnover group:
1. Current assets to sales.
2. Quick assets to sales.
3. Net working capital to sales.
4. Cash to sales.

---

* Total debt includes all liabilities plus preferred stock.

The multivariate approach research predicts a quantitative measure of solvency status. Scores below a critical level indicate a firm is very likely to slip from the nonfailed to failed firm category. The score is derived from a linear combination, developed through mathematical techniques, of some characteristics that best discriminate between failed and nonfailed firms.

For example, one researcher, Altman, that used this approach developed the following discriminant function for small manufacturing firms:

$$Z = 0.012X_1 + 0.014X_2 + 0.033X_3 + 0.006X_4 + 0.010X_5$$

where:

$X_1 =$ Working capital/total assets (a liquidity measure).
$X_2 =$ Retained earnings/total assets (a measure for reinvested earnings).
$X_3 =$ Earnings before interest and taxes/total assets (a profitability measure).
$X_4 =$ Market value of equity/book value of total liabilities (a measure for the firm's financial structure or leverage).
$X_5 =$ Sales/total assets (a measure for the sales-generating ability of the firm's assets).

The ratios are expressed in absolute terms, for example, a working capital to asset ratio of 10 percent is noted at 10.0, and a sales to total asset ratio of 2.0, or 200 percent, is noted as 200.0.

A Z score below 1.81 indicates potential bankruptcy. A score above 2.99 suggests a company will remain viable. And, scores between 1.81 and 2.99 indicate a gray area where a firm may or may not be approaching bankruptcy.

The variables included in a successful prediction equation may not be the most significant for predicting bankruptcy when measured independently (as in the univariate research). For instance, the equation above was derived by testing 22 potential variables. Among these variables, X_5 was the least significant when measured individually. However, the multivariate approach derives the most successful prediction equation for replicating the interactions among the variables. This is the principal difference between the multivariate and univariate models.

The Bottom Line

Real cash flow and the ability to obtain cash is the "bottom line" of most analyses focusing on a company's financial viability.

The importance of cash to a company's viability supersedes all other considerations. Those responsible for assessing a company's ability to meet its maturing financial obligations should never lose sight of this fact.

CASE 21-1

Pace Corporation
Accounting for Bonds

On June 30, 1978, Pace Corporation issued 11 percent, convertible first mortgage 10-year bonds having a maturity value of $3 million. The bonds were issued at a price to yield 10 percent.

The Pace bonds were dated June 30, 1978, and required semiannual interest payments. They were redeemable after June 30, 1983, and before June 30, 1985, at 104; thereafter until maturity they were redeemable at 102. They were also convertible into Pace $10 par value common stock according to the following schedule:

Before June 30, 1983: 60 shares of common stock for each $1,000 bond.
July 1, 1983, to June 30, 1986: 50 shares of common stock for each $1,000 bond.
After June 30, 1986: 40 shares of common stock for each $1,000 bond.

The following transactions occurred in connection with Pace's bonds.

July 1, 1984: Bonds having a maturity value of $500,000 were converted into common stock.
December 30, 1985: Bonds having a maturity value of $500,000 were reacquired by Pace Corporation by purchase on the market at 99¼ and accrued interest. The reacquired bonds were canceled immediately.
June 30, 1986. Pace Corporation called the remaining bonds for redemption. In order to obtain the cash necessary for the redemption and for business expansion, a $4 million issue of 20-year, 8 percent sinking fund debenture bonds were issued at a price to yield 8 percent. The new bonds were dated June 30, 1986, and also called for semiannual interest payments.

Harvard Business School case 166–003 (Rev. 1985)

Questions

1. Determine the amount of the proceeds from the June 30, 1978, bond issue. Illustrate the December 31, 1978, balance sheet disclosure(s) related to this indebtedness. (Use tables at the end of Question 4.)

2. Determine the amount of "interest expense" to be deducted in arriving at the net income for the year ending December 31, 1979.

3. Describe the balance sheet and income statement effects of the July 1, 1984, conversion, including dollar amounts involved.

4. Describe the balance sheet and income statement effects of the June 30, 1986, redemption, including dollar amounts involved.

Present Value of $1

Periods	3 Percent	3.5 Percent	4.0 Percent	4.5 Percent	5.0 Percent	5.5 Percent
10	0.744	0.709	0.676	0.644	0.614	0.585
20	0.554	0.503	0.456	0.415	0.377	0.343
40	0.307	0.253	0.258	0.172	0.142	0.117

Present Value of $1 per Period

Periods	3 Percent	3.5 Percent	4.0 Percent	4.5 Percent	5.0 Percent	5.5 Percent
10	8.530	8.317	8.111	7.913	7.222	7.538
20	14.877	14.212	13.590	13.008	12.462	11.950
40	23.115	21.355	19.793	18.402	17.159	16.046

CASE 21-2

Prentice Stevens, Inc.
Rating Industrial Debt

Prentice Stevens, Inc., a leading investment banking firm, was negotiating bond underwritings with five of its clients: Orion, Inc., Midwest Mining

This case was prepared by David F. Hawkins.

Copyright © 1985 by the President and Fellows of Harvard College
Harvard Business School case 186–133

EXHIBIT 1
Prentice Stevens, Inc.

Orion, Inc.

Orion, Inc., is a multinational diversified manufacturer of consumer and industrial products. More than 90 percent of its operations are in four basic industries: chemicals and coatings, pulp and paper, foods, and consumer products, including typewriters and appliances. The company's long-term debt consists of the following: a subsidiary 25-year, 5½ percent, unsecured sinking fund debenture; three 20-year sinking fund debentures at 5¾ percent, 7¼ percent, and 9¼ percent, respectively, secured only by the creditworthiness of the company; some 5½ percent convertible subordinated debentures; and other miscellaneous subsidiary debt and lease obligations. The various indentures restrict the company from incurring further senior debt unless immediately thereafter, consolidated net tangible assets will be at least 250 percent of consolidated senior funded debt and 200 percent of consolidated funded debt. Indentures also restrict the company from paying cash dividends or acquiring stock after a certain date in excess of consolidated net income and net proceeds from stock sale after such date, plus a specified amount.

The company proposes to issue a $50 million 20-year, 10 percent sinking fund debenture. The sinking fund requirement, which is designed to retire 91 percent of the issue prior to maturity, begins six years from the issue date and will retire annually not less than $3,250,000 and not more than $6.5 million of the principal.

Selected Accounts (thousands of dollars)	1976	1975	1974	1973	1972
Net sales	$1,331,897	$1,287,454	$1,202,248	$ 980,281	$ 917,817
Cost of goods sold	968,179	956,550	876,106	708,946	671,894
Selling and administrative expenses	291,816	269,898	264,270	227,481	215,141
Gross income	71,079	61,061	60,870	43,278	31,066
Interest on long-term debt	15,173	12,722	9,848	10,452	11,802
Other interest	2,225	6,270	3,173	1,541	1,673
Provisions for all taxes	25,170	16,828	22,503	13,786	7,964
Net income	30,395	27,886	27,646	18,299	10,327
Dividends	$ 6,182	$ 4,579	$ 3,892	$ 915	—
Depreciation	38,168	33,055	30,334	27,210	23,845
Cash and temporary investments	$ 45,077	$ 21,009	$ 6,640	$ 9,391	$ 17,164
Notes and accounts receivable (net)	171,358	169,664	189,024	152,931	134,315
Products, materials, supplies	240,372	214,034	213,353	177,975	160,586
Total current assets	$ 465,993	$ 415,777	$ 425,908	$ 356,560	$ 328,330
Land, buildings, machinery and equipment	518,281	507,831	433,712	400,194	369,100
Less: Depreciation reserve	266,989	248,952	226,475	212,832	192,262
Other assets and deferred charges	22,805	29,422	13,538	8,785	3,181
Intangibles					5,518
Total assets	$ 740,090	$ 704,078	$ 646,683	$ 552,707	$ 515,149
Total current liabilities	$ 178,140	$ 164,146	$ 193,941	$ 126,619	$ 104,033
Long-term debt	210,389	214,472	152,906	149,439	162,024
Debt of foreign subsidiaries	—	—	—	—	—
Minority interest	—	—	—	—	—
Deferred taxes	12,751	11,586	16,583	17,158	13,457
Common stock (par $5)	45,809	45,784	45,782	45,782	45,753
Capital surplus	111,377	111,351	111,349	111,349	111,321
Retained earnings	156,457	132,244	108,937	85,183	67,799
Total stockholders' equity	313,643	289,379	266,068	242,314	224,873
Reacquired shares	—	—	—	—	—
Total	$ 740,090	$ 704,078	$ 646,683	$ 552,707	$ 515,149
No. common shares at year-end	9,161,885	9,156,885	9,156,485	9,156,485	9,150,640
Lease expenses	$ 53,800				
Pro forma long-term debt / Net property, plant, and equipment	1.04	.82	.74	.80	.92
Working capital / Pro forma long-term debt	1.11	1.17	1.52	1.54	1.38
Pro forma long-term debt / Equity	.83	.74	.58	.62	.72
Net tangible assets / Pro forma long-term debt	2.75	3.15	4.14	3.64	3.13
Cash flow / Long-term debt	.326	.284	.379	.305	.148
Total interest charges + income before tax / Total interest charges	4.09	3.22	4.68	3.61	2.31

EXHIBIT 2
Prentice Stevens, Inc.

Midwest Mining Company

Incorporated in 1922, Midwest Mining Company manufactures refractory products which are heat-resistant clay and basic mineral products whose prime function is to provide structure of or linings of facilities where high temperatures are required. These products are used by major customers in the steel, glass, nonferrous metals, rock products, ceramics, waste disposal, and petroleum industries to contain high temperature processes and reactions. They have subsidiaries worldwide.

Long-term debt currently consists of the following: domestic banks, revolving credit —$36 million; foreign banks, notes payable,

8.8 percent average interest—$17,690,000; construction loan—$13.7 million; other mortgages and notes payable, average interest 5.1 percent—$4,573,000; capitalized leases, 5.6 percent average interest—$1,605,000. Loan agreements with various banks and insurance companies provide that the company maintain certain levels of working capital, limit total liabilities, capital expenditures, and foreign investments and restrict payment of dividends. The company proposes to issue a $25 million, 30-year, 10 percent unsecured debenture for which no sinking fund is provided.

Selected Accounts
(thousands of dollars)

	1976	1975	1974	1973	1972
Net sales	$ 326,589	$ 329,023	$ 320,098	$ 228,229	$ 179,402
Cost of goods sold	315,863	317,292	303,096	221,298	177,292
Selling and administrative expenses }					
Gross income	10,726	11,731	17,002	6,931	2,110
Interest on long-term debt }	7,746	4,815	3,898	4,553	2,453
Other interest }					
Provisions for all taxes	1,984	5,976	7,308	2,070	1,811
Net income	893	9,271	10,125	6,202	(2,508)
Dividends	$ 670	$ 1,431	$ 832	$ 340	$ 145
Depreciation	12,038	9,984	8,246	8,982	8,483
Cash and temporary investments	$ 7,362	$ 8,268	$ 9,089	$ 11,537	$ 10,259
Notes and accounts receivable (net)	62,523	49,400	69,442	44,021	36,816
Products, materials, supplies	79,343	73,522	60,298	45,133	38,628
Total current assets	$ 151,782	$ 134,440	$ 140,962	$ 102,956	$ 87,834
Land, buildings, machinery, and equipment	276,615	246,404	207,541	201,677	193,340
Less: Depreciation reserve	144,247	135,419	128,181	131,075	125,062
Other assets and deferred charges	12,464	10,461	10,795	7,698	13,293
Intangibles	—	—	—	—	—
Total assets	$ 296,614	$ 255,886	$ 231,117	$ 181,256	$ 169,405
Total current liabilities	$ 86,376	$ 65,972	$ 68,333	$ 43,864	$ 38,534
Long-term debt	66,616	48,452	29,859	22,732	22,152
Debt of foreign subsidiaries	—	—	—	—	—
Minority interest	—	—	—	333	301
Deferred taxes	6,165	7,435	4,095	1,810	2,510
Common stock (par $5)	19,020	19,020	19,020	19,020	19,020
Capital surplus	18,485	18,485	18,485	18,485	18,485
Retained earnings	70,426	70,133	63,386	52,053	45,806
Total stockholders' equity	108,204	108,572	102,374	91,262	85,314
Reacquired shares	—	—	—	—	—
Total	$ 296,614	$ 255,886	$ 231,117	$ 181,256	$ 169,405
No. common shares at year-end	3,804,009	3,804,009	3,804,009	3,804,009	3,804,009
Lease expenses	$ 1,560				
Pro forma long-term debt / Net property, plant, and equipment	.69	.44	.38	.32	.32
Working capital / Pro forma long-term debt	.71	1.41	2.43	2.60	2.23
Pro forma long-term debt / Equity	.85	.45	.29	.25	.26
Net tangible assets / Pro forma long-term debt	3.24	5.28	7.74	7.97	7.65
Cash flow / Long-term debt	.194	.397	.615	.668	.496
Total interest charges + Income before tax / Total interest charges	1.38	2.44	4.36	1.52	.86

EXHIBIT 3
Prentice Stevens, Inc.

Simmons Corporation

Simmons Corporation is a multinational company engaged primarily in the manufacture and distribution of cosmetics and fragrances; it is the market leader in cosmetics and fragrances sold at retail. As of December 31, 1976, the company had outstanding a $21,223,000, 4¾ percent Eurodollar subsidiary convertible debenture and a $50 million unsecured, 4¾ percent convertible subordinated debenture. The company has agreed to certain restrictions provided by indentures, which to date have been met, on levels of working capital, dividend payments, debt ratio, acquisition of its own stock, and creation of liens on or sales and leasebacks of certain properties in connection with the notes and the company's revolving credit agreement with its banks.

The company wishes to issue a $100 million, 10-year, 8.45 percent debenture. There is no provision for a sinking fund and the issue is secured only by the creditworthiness of the company. Restrictions are similar to those described above. The proceeds will be added to working capital to be available for general corporate purposes.

Selected Accounts (thousands of dollars)	1976	1975	1974	1973	1972
Net sales	$ 955,600	$ 775,614	$ 635,263	$ 522,351	$ 451,833
Cost of goods sold	349,544	282,356	234,392	190,305	163,015
Selling and administrative expenses	431,599	357,556	300,410	246,358	219,596
Gross income	187,015	146,351	113,052	95,926	75,132
Interest on long-term debt	10,760	8,565	3,301	3,035	2,935
Other interest	9,379	9,532	10,671	6,199	5,400
Provisions for all taxes	71,933	56,641	44,943	38,338	28,179
Net income	81,473	64,254	54,005	46,729	39,830
Dividends	$ 23,757	$ 18,720	$ 16,735	$ 13,942	$ 13,028
Depreciation	11,532	9,306	8,003	6,849	6,105
Cash and temporary investments	$ 268,452	$ 245,988	$ 108,312	$ 105,911	$ 81,766
Notes and accounts receivable (net)	165,254	154,978	149,729	140,804	128,471
Products, materials, supplies	180,625	166,063	177,519	118,378	106,639
Total current assets	$ 640,249	$ 591,287	$ 456,388	$ 374,599	$ 325,582
Land, buildings, machinery, and equipment	202,294	153,258	134,997	110,832	104,578
Less: Depreciation reserve	63,647	52,587	43,129	31,518	27,937
Other assets and deferred charges	14,792	19,482	17,686	17,127	18,714
Intangibles	79,953	57,008	46,377	40,800	41,647
Total assets	$ 873,641	$ 768,448	$ 612,319	$ 511,840	$ 462,584
Total current liabilities	$ 230,462	$ 177,739	$ 182,473	$ 125,202	$ 107,233
Long-term debt	182,430	183,227	96,910	109,208	116,567
Debt of foreign subsidiaries	—	—	—	—	—
Minority interest	—	—	—	—	—
Deferred taxes	4,530	4,700	4,893	4,228	2,916
Common stock (par $1)	30,154	14,960	14,244	13,293	13,166
Capital surplus	72,301	77,729	69,282	60,242	52,838
Retained earnings	355,776	301,704	247,128	202,228	173,504
Total stockholders' equity	458,231	394,393	330,654	275,763	239,508
Reacquired shares	2,012	2,611	2,611	2,561	3,640
Total	$ 873,641	$ 768,448	$ 612,319	$ 511,840	$ 462,584
No. common shares at year-end	30,054,873	29,781,302	29,531,766	28,115,274	27,787,386
Lease expenses	$ 14,724				
Pro forma long-term debt / Net property, plant, and equipment	2.04	1.82	1.05	1.38	1.52
Working capital	1.45	2.26	2.83	2.28	1.87
Pro forma long-term debt / Pro forma long-term debt / Equity	.616	.465	.293	.396	.487
Net tangible assets	2.81	3.88	5.84	4.31	3.61
Pro forma long-term debt / Cash flow	.510	.401	.640	.491	.394
Long-term debt / Total interest charges + Income before tax / Total interest charges	9.29	8.10	8.09	10.4	9.01

EXHIBIT 4
Prentice Stevens, Inc.

Sunshine Foods, Inc.

Sunshine Foods, a multinational company engaged primarily in the manufacture or processing and distribution of various lines of food products, directly owns a large number of plants. The company already has three sinking fund debentures outstanding at 4⅜ percent, 6⅞ percent, and 8⅜ percent, respectively, secured by the creditworthiness of the company. The indentures require that the company may not mortgage or pledge any property without equally securing the debentures, and the company may not merge into another corporation if its property would be subject to a mortgage without equally securing its debentures.

Sunshine Foods has been in business for 54 years and has a strong management. The company is one of the industry leaders and its products are known and respected for high standards of quality. It proposes to issue a $100 million, 30-year, 7.60 percent sinking fund debenture, secured in the same manner as the existing debentures. The annual sinking fund requirement is $5 million of principal, retiring 95 percent of the issue prior to maturity. The proceeds of this issue will be used to reduce short-term debt and for general corporate purposes.

Selected Accounts

(thousands of dollars)	1976	1975	1974	1973	1972
Net sales	$ 4,976,643	$ 4,857,378	$ 4,471,427	$ 3,601,534	$ 3,196,789
Cost of goods sold	3,990,939	3,920,605	3,647,233	2,827,058	2,457,717
Selling and administrative expenses	691,762	649,994	613,596	569,930	541,790
Gross income	306,850	304,307	225,556	216,932	207,872
Interest on long-term debt	15,854	16,794	14,318	8,872	8,388
Other interest	9,751	15,246	24,962	8,085	3,441
Provisions for all taxes	142,386	128,678	82,222	94,443	95,408
Net income	135,650	139,551	94,627	103,428	88,335
Dividends	$ 58,919	$ 53,305	$ 52,160	$ 49,330	$ 49,741
Depreciation	$ 57,821	$ 52,376	$ 49,150	$ 46,690	43,727
Cash and temporary investments	37,301	33,482	36,240	33,987	68,012
Notes and accounts receivable (net)	310,654	304,690	300,666	260,978	207,592
Products, materials, supplies	763,353	706,624	793,045	558,612	464,269
Total current assets	$ 1,111,308	$ 1,044,796	$ 1,129,951	$ 853,576	$ 739,873
Other assets	56,006	12,215	8,219	8,987	8,320
Land, buildings, machinery, and equipment	1,123,432	1,062,628	977,601	914,008	892,562
Less: Depreciation reserve	517,837	478,699	453,208	434,395	433,087
Prepaid expenses and deferred charges	15,047	11,444	13,509	13,178	11,186
Intangibles	33,848	34,133	34,366	35,544	27,319
Total assets	$ 1,821,854	$ 1,686,517	$ 1,710,438	$ 1,390,897	$ 1,245,193
Total current liabilities	$ 518,201	$ 485,557	$ 582,443	$ 410,839	$ 313,974
Long-term debt	217,697	215,533	237,474	138,610	130,765
Debt of foreign subsidiaries	3,060	—	—	4,408	4,700
Minority interest	2,979	2,831	2,430	2,298	2,060
Deferred taxes	44,798	32,299	26,575	19,717	17,504
Common stock (par $2.50)	73,628	73,628	73,628	73,628	73,585
Capital surplus	49,337	49,324	49,910	49,958	49,543
Retained earnings	952,682	885,951	799,706	757,239	703,142
Total stockholders' equity	1,085,647	1,008,903	923,244	880,826	826,270
Reacquired shares	69,741	70,427	73,232	73,162	57,526
Total	$ 1,821,854	$ 1,686,517	$ 1,710,438	$ 1,390,897	$ 1,245,193
No. common shares at year-end	27,800,258	27,784,009	27,717,615	27,719,643	28,045,696
$\dfrac{\text{Pro forma long-term debt}}{\text{Net property, plant, and equipment}}$	.52	.37	.45	.28	.29
$\dfrac{\text{Working capital}}{\text{Pro forma long-term debt}}$	1.87	2.59	2.31	3.19	3.26
$\dfrac{\text{Pro forma long-term debt}}{\text{Equity}}$	.293	.214	.257	.157	.158
$\dfrac{\text{Net tangible assets}}{\text{Pro forma long-term debt}}$	5.63	7.67	7.06	9.78	9.31
$\dfrac{\text{Cash flow}}{\text{Long-term debt}}$	.609	.890	.605	1.08	1.01
$\dfrac{\text{Total interest charges + Income before tax}}{\text{Total interest charges}}$	12.0	9.5	5.7	12.8	17.6

EXHIBIT 5
Prentice Stevens, Inc.

Beekhus Industrials Company

Beekhus Industrials is a 73-year-old company with two foreign subsidiaries. It is the world's largest manufacturer of vulcanized fibre and the 13th largest steel company in the United States. The company is engaged primarily in the production of steel, a highly competitive industry.

The company has a 25-year, 5 percent, unsecured sinking fund subordinated debenture outstanding, as well as $9 million, ¼ percent above prime, revolving credit notes and a $975,000 industrial development lease at varying rates. Among the restrictions imposed by the company's debt agreements, payment of cash dividends, purchase redemption, or retirement of Beekhus capital stock, the steel company's capital stock, or of any subordinated indebtedness is limited to an aggregate amount not to exceed $30 million plus 60 percent of aggregate consolidated net earnings of the company.

It proposes to issue a $50 million, 30-year, 10% sinking fund debenture. The sinking fund would commence 20 years from the issue date, retiring by redemption the lesser of 2½ percent of outstanding debentures on the October 1 before each November 14 or $1,250,000. In addition, the company must make cash sinking fund payments during the last five years to retire by redemption the lesser of 5 percent of outstanding debentures each year or $2 million.

Selected Accounts (thousands of dollars)	1976	1975	1974	1973	1972
Net sales	$ 443,682	$ 323,948	$ 517,908	$ 379,486	$ 326,840
Cost of goods sold	383,377	277,178	380,290	324,491	281,385
Selling and administrative expenses	25,539	20,215	23,661	16,189	13,203
Gross income	21,400	14,678	102,131	27,374	21,260
Interest on long-term debt	4,851	3,343	3,052	2,672	2,449
Other interest	7,293	7,375	7,521	6,686	6,950
Provisions for all taxes	4,074	2,319	46,839	9,649	4,042
Net income	12,870	7,011	47,203	12,132	8,761
Dividends	$ 21,695	$ 13,923	$ 6,335	$ —	$ —
Depreciation	13,366	11,877	11,826	11,432	10,992
Cash and temporary investments	$ 23,501	$ 44,151	$ 102,562	$ 24,058	$ 4,950
Notes and accounts receivable (net)	54,858	44,166	47,522	48,165	45,082
Products, materials, supplies	72,938	75,926	69,956	53,134	59,507
Total current assets	$ 153,388	$ 166,247	$ 223,886	$ 127,108	$ 111,168
Land, buildings, machinery and equipment	304,321	289,420	283,501	266,668	260,324
Less: Depreciation reserve	164,453	154,687	152,545	143,722	137,858
Other assets and deferred charges	58,134	12,402	3,936	2,138	2,386
Intangibles	—	—	—	—	—
Total assets	$ 351,390	$ 313,382	$ 358,778	$ 252,192	$ 236,020
Total current liabilities	$ 81,274	$ 64,038	$ 107,090	$ 59,156	$ 48,857
Long-term debt	103,930	95,007	91,510	83,652	82,768
Debt of foreign subsidiaries	—	—	—	—	—
Minority interest	25,432	25,618	25,750	18,713	17,404
Deferred taxes	13,891	11,993	21,317	13,598	12,319
Common stock (par $1)	906	6,284	1,609	1,630	1,257
Capital surplus	62,592	34,655	23,896	26,778	27,809
Retained earnings	58,602	68,997	75,909	35,041	30,024
Total stockholders' equity	122,100	109,936	101,414	63,449	59,090
Reacquired shares	—	—	—	—	—
Total	$ 351,390	$ 313,382	$ 358,778	$ 252,192	$ 236,020
No. common shares at year-end	13,311,510	12,183,761	11,649,464	14,375,425	12,319,293
Lease expenses	$ 4,763				
$\dfrac{\text{Pro forma long-term debt}}{\text{Net property, plant, and equipment}}$	1.10	70.5	69.9	68.0	67.6
$\dfrac{\text{Working capital}}{\text{Pro forma long-term debt}}$	.47	1.08	1.28	.81	.75
$\dfrac{\text{Pro forma long-term debt}}{\text{Equity}}$	1.26	.864	.902	1.32	1.40
$\dfrac{\text{Net tangible assets}}{\text{Pro forma long-term debt}}$	2.28	3.30	3.92	3.01	2.85
$\dfrac{\text{Cash flow}}{\text{Long-term debt}}$	.252	.199	.569	.282	.239
$\dfrac{\text{Total interest charges} + \text{Income before tax}}{\text{Total interest charges}}$	1.76	1.37	9.66	2.93	2.26

Company, Simmons Corporation, Sunshine Foods, Inc., and Beekhus Industrial Company. Summary sheets prepared for the executive committee presenting each company's business, existing debt, the nature of its proposed issue, selected balance sheet data, and key financial ratios are presented in Exhibits 1–5. The final piece of information to be added to each summary sheet before being presented to the committee is the anticipated bond rating the issue might receive from the major rating agencies.

Questions

1. Rank the five cases in order of the quality of their long-term debt (highest at top of list).

2. What debt rating would you assign to each of the five companies' long-term debt? (Use Moody's classification scheme.)

CASE 21-3

Bishop Industries, Inc.
Predicting Bankruptcy

On March 18, 1970, Michael Frye met with his boss, Gerry Bloomfield, to discuss the possibility of adding the stock of Bishop Industries to their firm's investment portfolio. Their firm, Turnaround Investment Ventures (TIV), was a small New York–based investment service specializing in assessing turnaround situations. As an initial screen for turnaround candidates, TIV used a computer program which monitored the financial performance of companies that were in loss positions or had suffered substantial earnings setbacks. Companies which met a set of quantitative criteria were printed out and sent to the appropriate TIV analyst to be considered for further detailed analysis.

This case was prepared by Norman J. Bartczak.

One of the criteria of the computer program was known as the "Z-Score Screen." This screen used a set of weighted ratios from a model developed by Professor Edward Altman to ascertain the "bankruptcy profile" of a firm (see Chapter 21 for a description of the Altman model).

Using balance sheet items as of the end of the period and the closing share price, Michael Frye obtained the following Z-scores for Bishop Industries, Inc., for the fiscal years ended October 31, 1966, 1967, 1968, and 1969.

End of Fiscal Year	Z-Score
1966	3.71
1967	3.16
1968	0.75
1969	0.84

Although Bishop's Z-Score was still in the "bankruptcy zone" at the end of fiscal 1969, Mr. Frye wondered if the slight increase in the Z-Score might be signaling the beginning of a turnaround. Mr. Frye noted that in July 1969, Bishop had recruited a new president, Alec Faberman from Revlon, Inc. Also, during 1969 operating losses had been reduced by $4.6 million from those reported in fiscal 1968. Mr. Frye noted further that on July 29, 1969, Bishop Industries completed an $8.8 million refinancing transaction. The financing package included: (1) the sale of $3 million of 7 percent, 12-year secured notes with warrants to purchase 800,000 shares to a group of four insurance companies; and (2) $3 million in equity capital through the private sale of 1 million common shares, at a price below market value, to several funds, corporations, and private investors. Two million, eight hundred thousand dollars of the package represented revision and consolidation of existing senior indebtedness. In addition, the transaction relieved Bishop of the obligation of making amortization payments during the next three and one half years on its present senior and subordinated long-term debt. Finally, Mr. Frye knew that other cosmetics companies, in general, appeared to be rather highly valued by the marketplace. He had before him the following price-earnings ratio information for the two largest cosmetics companies and the Standard & Poor's 425 Industrials:

	S&P 425 Industrials		Avon		Revlon	
Year	High	Low	High	Low	High	Low
1965	17.9	15.7	45.5	30.9	16.7	12.2
1966	17.1	13.3	46.6	34.4	16.8	10.5
1967	18.9	15.2	65.7	33.5	25.4	13.5
1968	19.2	15.4	60.4	44.3	28.3	21.6
1969	19.0	16.0	60.1	42.9	34.4	23.7

P/E Ratios

Company Background

Bishop Industries, Inc., was incorporated in New York in January 1962 as Hazel Bishop, Inc., as the result of a consolidation of Hazel Bishop, Inc. (incorporated November 12, 1948) and Lanolin Plus, Inc. (incorporated May 18, 1953). It changed its name from Hazel Bishop, Inc., to Bishop Industries, Inc., in May 1967.

Until 1968, the years subsequent to the consolidation with Lanolin Plus proved to be moderately successful for Bishop. It advertised its products heavily on television and became associated with such well-known television series as "This Is Your Life." Bishop's sales grew by approximately 10 percent compounded annually from 1962 through 1967. However, its net income was relatively volatile over this period; $19,000 in 1962; $416,000 in 1963; $1,654,000 in 1964; $136,000 loss in 1965; $1,011,000 in 1966; and $192,000 in 1967. Bishop's stock price mirrored this volatility and ranged as follows: $13.63–$4.75 in 1962; $6.13–$3.75 in 1963; $12.13–$4.25 in 1964; $11.75–$6.63 in 1965; $9.88–$5.88 in 1966; and $18.13–$7.25 in 1967.

Fiscal 1968 was a disastrous year for Bishop Industries. On sales of $24.5 million, down 26 percent from 1967, Bishop incurred a net loss of $7.6 million. Industry sources were puzzled at the dramatic downturn in Bishop's fortunes. Bishop explained its 1968 results to its shareholders as follows:

To Our Shareholders:

It is in the nature of a highly competitive consumer industry, such as ours, that success depends on the coordination of product development and manufacturing, marketing, and financial planning. Whenever these functions fail to mesh perfectly, adverse effects on sales and profits are inevitable.

When it became evident during the past year that Bishop Industries was suffering from severe setbacks of this nature, your board made a full appraisal of the apparent causes and began remedial steps to counteract them.

Our examination revealed that Bishop's product line was excellent and that we had every reason to be optimistic about new products being developed in our research laboratories. But it also disclosed severe weaknesses in our past marketing program and policies as well as inadequate capital funds and resources to maintain and expand production and distribution needs.

The financial results in this report reflect these fears with surprising, though disappointing precision. The overall loss of $7,605,378, after tax credit of $771,628, can be traced in large part to a decline in sales from $33,052,406 in 1967 to $24,466,643 in 1968, with no compensating reduction in the cost of sales or overhead.

More than one quarter of the loss, or about $2 million, resulted from merchandise inventory being reevaluated in relation to its ultimate salability as well as additional reserves and write-offs. And while it is best, in such cases, to accept the consequences of such drastic write-offs, it is important at the same time to buttress this step with a fresh look at the marketing program.

With these facts at hand, your board of directors began to realign the company's management in several channels—notably in financial and sales planning. In this program, it received substantial encouragement by Realty Equities Corporation of New York, a broadly diversified company listed on the American Stock Exchange.

The company's financial position was strengthened by the acquisition by REC in November 1968 of 375,000 shares of Bishop common stock in exchange for 125,000 shares of REC common stock. The exchange ratio has since been renegotiated to provide for the issuance of a total of 500,000 shares of Bishop common stock of which 125,000 are subject to approval by our shareholders. Moreover, our directors have granted REC a 10-year option, subject to shareholders' approval, to purchase an additional 200,000 shares of Bishop common stock at $14 per share.

Strengthened in this way, your board of directors obtained the financial, management, and administrative counseling of A. Sam Gittlin, who is highly regarded in business and banking circles and has a proven record in administrative and financial management. Subsequently, on January 30, 1969, Mr. Gittlin was elected vice chairman of the board and chief executive officer of our company. As chief executive, he succeeds Morton Edell, the former president who retired but will be available if needed as a consultant.

At the same time, the board elected Martin Brody and William C. Jaus to be directors, filling vacancies left by the resignations of Mr. Edell, Charles Green, and Milton J. Lesnik. Both Mr. Brody and Mr. Jaus have broad experience as chief executives of consumer-oriented industries. Mr. Brody is chairman and president of Restaurant Associates Industries, Inc., and Mr. Jaus is president of the Foods Division of Dolly Madison Industries, Inc.

The new management team was recently augmented by the appointments of Richard Barnett and Richard Van Vliet. Mr. Barnett, who was appointed executive vice president for marketing and sales, has established an enviable record with Rayette-Faberge, where he was vice president, Alberto-Culver Company and International Latex Corporation. Mr. Van Vliet, who was previously associated with the Bristol-Myers Company's controller's division, was named controller and assistant treasurer.

At the time Realty Equities acquired its Bishop shares, its management stated that it was making the investment as part of its own diversification program as well as to strengthen Bishop's financial management. To implement this plan, your board was pleased last December to elect three executives of Realty Equities as directors. They are Morris Karp, president, Jerome Deutsch, executive vice president, and Alan H. Franklin, vice president.

The management changes, which have been and will be combined with newly instituted cost and production controls, coordinated and imaginative marketing policies, and management's studied determination to recast the company's financial structure, augur well for the future of Bishop Industries and its products. In addition, an extensive program has been instituted to tighten our production cost controls, to reduce overhead substantially, to reduce inventories and relate marketing programs to profit controls, all of which will serve to improve the company's performance. As, over the coming 12 months, the company eliminates some of its unprofitable product lines, we can look forward to a narrowing gap between overall sales volume, which may decline, and financial results from operations, which should rise.

In view of all this, I trust you share with our new management and directors the conviction that Bishop Industries has taken on a new vitality which should reflect itself in substantial growth and profitability in the years ahead.

Sincerely,

Wilbur E. Dewell
Chairman of the Board

On June 9, 1969, Bishop Industries reported the following interim results for the quarter and six months ended April 30, 1969:

	1969	1968
	(dollars in thousands)	
Quarter April 30:		
Sales	$3,173.3	$7,766.5
Net loss	442.1	607.7
Six months:		
Sales	$6,903.8	$14,916.0
Net loss	1,285.2	870.0

At the annual shareholders' meeting on June 26, 1969, shareholders approved an increase of Realty Equities Corporation's ownership of Bishop to 20 percent from 16.3 percent. As part of the agreement and in return for Bishop stock, Realty arranged a $1 million short-term bank loan to Bishop.

Bishop holders also approved a new stock option plan that offered 50,000 Bishop shares to A. Sam Gittlin, chief executive officer of Bishop, and 2,000 shares each to Martin Brody and William C. Jaus, new Bishop directors, at a price of $3 a share. The day before the meeting, Bishop common closed at $6.75 on the American Stock Exchange. It closed at $6.625 on June 27, 1969. According to Bishop's proxy statement, the reason for the plan was to encourage certain new employees to "become more personally involved in its success" and to encourage them to remain with Bishop.

On July 14, 1969, Bishop announced the election of Alec R. Faberman as president and chief executive officer. Mr. Faberman succeeded A. Sam Gittlin as chief executive officer. Mr. Gittlin continued as chairman of Bishop.

Mr. Faberman was recruited from Revlon, Inc., where he had worked for 19 years, during which time he held the positions of vice president and controller, vice president and general manager—operations, and, most recently, group vice president—subsidiaries.

Under the terms of an employee agreement with Bishop, until October 31, 1969, Bishop agreed to pay Mr. Faberman a salary at the rate of $80,000 per year. From November 1, 1969, through October 31, 1970, his salary rate would be $95,000 per year. In addition, Bishop agreed to pay Mr. Faberman a bonus of 2 percent of net pre-tax profits from operations ("pre-tax profits") up to $2 million, plus 1½ percent up to the next $2 million, 1 percent up to the next $2 million, and ½ percent of any pre-tax profits in excess of $6 million for the fiscal year ended October 31, 1970. For fiscal years ending October 31, 1971, 1972, 1973, and 1974, Mr. Faberman's salary would be $100,000 per year. In addition, he would receive a bonus of 2½ percent of pre-tax profits up to $2 million for the fiscal year ended during each of those years, plus 2 percent of pre-tax profits up to the next $2 million, 1½ percent up to the next $2 million, 1 percent up to the next $2 million, and ½ percent of any pre-tax profits in excess of $8 million.

Mr. Faberman was also given a stock option to purchase 50,000 shares of Bishop's common stock at a price of $0.10 per share subject to certain restrictions. Mr. Faberman exercised this option in September 1969 and paid $5,000 for 50,000 shares of Bishop's common.

As mentioned previously, on July 29, 1969, Bishop announced the completion of an $8.8 million refinancing transaction.

On September 15, 1969, Bishop reported the following interim results:

	1969	1968
	(dollars in thousands)	
Quarter July 31:		
Sales	$2,645.8	$ 4,957.2
Net loss	566.0	1,817.1
Nine months:		
Sales	$9,549.6	$19,873.6
Net loss	1,851.2	2,687.4

On March 4, 1970, Bishop reported the following results for the fiscal year ended 1969 and for the first quarter ended January 31, 1970:

	1969	1968
	(dollars in thousands)	
Year ended October 31:		
Sales	$12,277.3	$24,466.6
Loss	3,445.3	8,377.0
Tax credit	—	771.6
Net loss	3,445.3	7,605.4
Quarter ended January 31:		
Sales	$ 3,250.0	$ 3,730.5
Net loss	380.0	843.0

EXHIBIT 1
Bishop Industries, Inc.

Board of Directors and Stock Price Information

Board of Directors

Name	Principal Occupation	Bishop Common Stock Beneficially Owned: March 1, 1970
Leo Betisch	Consultant	109
Martin Brody	Chairman of the board, Restaurant Associates Industries, Inc., New York, N.Y.	100
Wilbur E. Dewell	Owner, Wilbur E. Dewell Associates, Foreign and Domestic Marketing Consultants, Fairfield, Connecticut	800
Alec R. Faberman	President and chief executive officer of Bishop	50,000
Justin N. Feldman	Partner, Poletti, Freidin, Prashker, Feldman, & Gartner, Attorneys, New York, N.Y.	100
Alan N. Franklin	Vice president, Realty Equities Corporation of New York	(1)
A. Sam Gittlin	Chairman of the board of Bishop; chairman, Barrington Industries, Inc.	(1)
William C. Jaus	Group vice president, Dolly Madison Industries, Inc., Philadelphia, Pennsylvania	2,100
Morris Karp	President, Realty Equities Corporation of New York	(1)

(1) Realty Equities Corporation of New York, of which Messrs, Franklin, Gittlin, and Karp are directors and/or officers, owns 883,334 shares of Bishop's common stock.

Stock Price

	Bishop Industries			Realty Equities		
	High	Low	Close	High	Low	Close
1968: Quarter ended:						
March 31	$15.75	$ 8.625	$ 9.375	$22.00	$10.00	$17.00
June 30	13.25	9.25	11.75	28.125	15.75	24.50
September 30	13.125	9.25	11.875	32.75	24.625	31.00
December 31	15.00	11.00	13.125	37.75	29.625	32.50
1969: Quarter ended:						
March 31	14.625	7.75	9.00	35.00	27.125	30.125
June 30	10.25	6.50	6.75	30.50	19.50	21.00
September 30	7.625	5.25	6.00	22.25	14.00	14.25
December 31	8.325	5.325	5.875	16.50	9.50	10.25
1970: Period ended:						
March 18	7.75	5.25	6.00	12.625	9.25	10.125

EXHIBIT 2
Bishop Industries, Inc.

BISHOP INDUSTRIES, INC., AND SUBSIDIARIES
Selected Excerpts from 1969 Annual Report
Eight-Year Financial Summary

Fiscal Year-End October 31	1969	1968	1967	1966	1965	1964	1963	1962
Income:								
Net sales	$12,277	$24,467	$33,052	$31,085	$27,964	$28,065	$23,214	$20,478
Earnings (loss) before interest and taxes	(2,596)	(7,508)	767	2,309	150	2,488	744	133
Interest expense	897	637	415	398	411	429	328	114
Net earnings (loss)	(3,445)	(7,605)	192	1,011	(136)	1,654	416	19
Retained earnings (deficit)	(9,131)	(5,685)	1,920	2,472	2,002	2,125	551	135
Earnings (loss) per share	($1.23)	($3.85)	$0.10	$0.52	($0.07)	$0.85	$0.21	$.01
Financial position:								
Current assets	$ 8,694	$11,074	$17,677	$14,163	$13,960	$12,423	$10,387	$10,185
Current liabilities	4,515	10,192	9,135	4,779	5,906	9,307	6,547	6,881
Working capital	4,179	882	8,542	9,384	8,054	3,116	3,840	3,304
Plant and equipment, net	2,635	2,927	2,692	2,125	2,054	2,050	2,114	2,434
Total assets	16,291	18,522	22,162	17,383	17,274	15,714	13,028	13,295
Long-term debt	9,365	5,949	6,066	5,839	6,123	1,193	1,258	1,486
Stockholders' equity	2,355	2,296	6,961	6,765	5,245	5,214	5,223	4,927
Common shares outstanding at year-end	3,602,791	2,347,791	1,962,795	1,962,257	1,962,257	1,942,787	1,942,787	1,951,440
Common stockholders at year-end	10,853	10,401	9,949	9,589	10,524	11,600	13,250	14,254
Employees at year-end	345	550	710	670	504	443	451	530
Closing stock price—October 31	$ 7.000	$13.000	$12.875	$ 6.000	$ 8.750	$ 9.875	NA	NA
Year-end price rate—December 31	8.500%	6.250%	6.000%	6.000%	5.000%	5.000%	5.000%	5.000%

EXHIBIT 2 *(continued)*

Dear Shareholder:

The fiscal year ended October 31, 1969, was one of consolidation of company facilities and operations, reassessment and repositioning of corporate sales and marketing strategy, as well as recruitment of a new management team at Bishop Industries. As noted in the previous annual report, A. Sam Gittlin was elected chief executive officer (and subsequently board chairman) of Bishop on January 30, 1969. He immediately instituted a twofold program to strengthen the company's weakened financial position, namely availing the company quickly of every possible economy that could prudently be employed with no injury to the future and recasting the company's financial structure. Both of these goals were met.

These planned economies were instrumental in reducing our operating losses by approximately $4.6 million from those sustained in the preceding fiscal year. The refinancing and recasting, completed July 29, was in the amount of $8,780,000 and resulted in the infusion of approximately $2.5 million of new working capital after repaying short-term obligations, including satisfaction of bank loans. Additionally, Bishop was relieved of making amortization payments during the next three and one-half years on its present senior and subordinated notes.

In order to maximize the impact of the new financial structure and develop meaningful programs as a foundation for profitable future growth, the board directed the recruitment of a president with a proven record of accomplishment in the consumer package goods industry, preferably in cosmetics. On July 14, I was elected to that position.

At this time, there were certain new priorities which had to be established and certain goals which had to be met. The most important priority concerned the development of new relationships with our suppliers; the most urgent goal was reestablishment of our position at the store level. The company was successful in accomplishing both, aided by creditor confidence in new management and the knowledge that Bishop products enjoyed wide consumer acceptance.

Concurrently, the company decided to increase significantly the depth of its top management team, placing special emphasis on sales and marketing experience as well as research and development talent, since these are the heart of our business. We have also strengthened the company's financial and operational divisions, emphasizing tighter controls and improved decision-making procedures. Great efforts are still being made to reduce costs throughout the company while maintaining or upgrading the efficiency of operations and rendering the best possible service to Bishop's customers.

We have recruited a group of new executives and special consultants representing a century of experience in the cosmetic and package goods field. These people are young, aggressive, and ambitious, and they bring to our company the expertise required to move us forward. All members of the new Bishop team, including the president, have held important positions in well-known companies. They have joined us because they are dedicated to and confident of the revival of a new and exciting Bishop, whose future will be secured by orderly growth and profit-oriented operations.

Within several months, a nationwide network for sales and distribution of our products, sorely lacking in recent years, was developed. This network is being subjected daily to reassessment and improvement. Our products are steadily gaining greater consumer acceptance. Of equal importance is the growing confidence shown in Bishop Industries itself by retail buyers and distributors of cosmetics and toiletries in every branch of the trade. The company is pressing vigorously toward its goals through a policy of service reliability, resourceful marketing methods, active research and development of new products, and new, exciting packaging designs for both existing and emerging product lines.

The company is now determined to bring to the trade and consumer the highest quality and fashion in cosmetics. Our current product lines, especially the new Hazel Bishop and Lanolin Plus labels, plagued by poor shelf space in the past few years, are being actively extended and completed. Our Lanolin Plus line of products, now enjoying wide acclaim, will shortly become a complete cosmetic line in every sense of the word and hopefully will appear on the shelves of every major outlet in America.

Plus White toothpaste has just been selected for use by the U.S. Olympic team through 1972 and a new package and marketing program was designed to capitalize fully on this opportunity. Our RD natural hair coloring restorer for men will receive new advertising support and serve as the foundation of a complete new RD family of hair products

EXHIBIT 2 *(continued)*

and related cosmetics and toiletries for men. Our Fabulous Fakes collection is being expanded rapidly into a sophisticated and complete label of its own, to include many items in the nail enamel, nail care, and treatment lines. Moreover, Bishop has ready for marketing or on the drawing boards a large number of new products of similar type, including items for Lilly Daché, Angelique, and International Club for Men—products for which we envision early and successful market penetration. Some of these products are pictured on the facing page.

We think the progress manifested this year will benefit our shareholders, whose personal endorsements and continued purchases of our products have been of great help. To better inform our stockholders, we are including in this report for the first time a consolidated statement of source and application of funds.

Sincerely,

Alec R. Faberman
President

EXHIBIT 2 (*continued*)

BISHOP INDUSTRIES, INC., AND SUBSIDIARIES
Consolidated Balance Sheets
October 31, 1969, 1968, 1967, 1966, and 1965

Assets	1969	1968	1967	1966	1965
Current assets:					
Cash	$ 1,295,274	$ 153,826	$ 1,062,257	$ 1,300,974	$ 1,102,712
Short-term investments, at cost (approximates market)	600,000	—	—	500,000	—
Receivables, less allowances for doubtful accounts, sales returns, and discounts, 1969, $825,000; 1968, $721,000; 1967, $523,000; 1966,$278,000; 1965, $298,000 (note 2)	2,573,449	3,180,357	6,475,439	6,036,844	5,964,774
Federal income taxes refundable	—	771,628	—	—	796,030
Inventories (notes 2 and 3)	4,023,158	6,584,697	9,522,598	6,033,012	5,761,635
Prepaid expenses	202,139	383,111	616,410	291,814	334,734
Total current assets	$ 8,694,020	$11,073,619	$17,676,704	$14,162,644	$13,959,885
Investment in common stock of Realty Equities Corporation (notes 2 and 4)	3,050,000	3,050,000	—	—	—
Plant and equipment, at cost (notes 2 and 5)	3,971,096	4,336,751	3,798,347	3,053,364	2,832,924
Less: Accumulated depreciation	1,336,220	1,409,909	1,106,119	927,973	778,761
Plant and equipment, net	$ 2,634,876	$ 2,926,842	$ 2,692,228	$ 2,125,391	$ 2,054,163
Investment in excess of net assets of purchased subsidiary, at amortized cost (note 1)	—	366,410	366,410	—	—
Trade names and other intangibles, at amortized cost (notes 2 and 6)	416,529	—	—	—	—
Unamortized debt discount and issue expenses (note 8)	449,875	561,097	776,504	418,335	453,874
Deferred charges and other assets (notes 1 and 11)	667,023	396,220	428,702	461,184	182,792
	378,824	147,500	221,585	215,555	623,217
Total assets	$16,291,147	$18,521,688	$22,162,133	$17,383,109	$17,273,931

EXHIBIT 2 *(continued)*

Liabilities	1969	1968	1967	1966	1965
Current liabilities:					
Current maturities of long-term liabilities	$ 115,043	$ 511,045	$ 296,188	$ 283,962	$ 69,680
Trade payables:					
Notes	1,257,352	366,329	5,564,120	3,182,102	3,234,282
Accounts	2,131,352	4,967,547	1,981,573		1,750,000
Loans payable, principally to banks	97,288	3,037,817			
Accrued liabilities	914,128	1,308,974	1,292,884	1,312,891	851,755
Total current liabilities	$ 4,515,163	$10,191,712	$ 9,134,765	$ 4,778,955	$ 5,905,717
Long-term liabilities, less current maturities:					
Notes payable to institutional lenders (note 8):					
Senior notes, 7%	5,782,500	2,540,000	2,770,000	3,000,000	3,000,000
Subordinated notes, 6½%	2,000,000	1,867,000	2,000,000	2,000,000	2,000,000
Mortgages payable, 6% to 6¾%	1,105,355	1,163,781	1,021,236	839,231	1,123,194
Other notes payable, noninterest bearing and at rates 5% to 9%	477,621	377,863	274,967	—	—
Total long-term liabilities	$ 9,365,476	$ 5,948,644	$ 6,066,203	$ 5,839,231	$ 6,123,194
Deferred royalty income	55,773	85,329	—	—	—
Commitments and contingent liabilities (note 9)					
Stockholders' Equity					
Preferred stock, par value $1 per share, authorized 200,000 shares; none issued					
Common stock, par value $.10 per share, authorized 5 million shares; issued, 1969, 3,616,201 shares; 1968, 2,361,201 shares; 1967, 1,976,205 shares; 1966 1,900,196 shares; 1965, 1,827,627 shares (notes 4, 8, 10 and 11)	361,621	236,121	197,621	190,020	182,763
Additional paid-in capital	11,184,206	7,805,723	4,904,007	4,162,966	3,120,314
Retained earnings (deficit)	(9,130,747)	(5,685,496)	1,919,882	2,472,282	2,002,288
	$ 2,415,080	$ 2,356,348	$ 7,021,510	$ 6,825,268	$ 5,305,365
Less: Treasury common stock, 13,410 shares, at cost	60,345	60,345	60,345	60,345	60,345
Total stockholders' equity	$ 2,354,735	$ 2,296,003	$ 6,961,165	$ 6,764,923	$ 5,245,020
Total liabilities and stockholders' equity	$16,291,147	$18,521,688	$22,162,133	$17,383,109	$17,273,931

See notes to financial statements.

EXHIBIT 2 *(continued)*

BISHOP INDUSTRIES, INC., AND SUBSIDIARIES
Consolidated Statements of Operations
For the Years Ended October 31, 1969, 1968, 1967, 1966, and 1965

	1969	1968	1967	1966	1965
Sales	$13,939,126	$28,770,764	$36,629,184	Not reported	$27,963,108
Less: Sales returns and allowances	1,661,843	4,304,121	3,576,778	Not reported	15,139,340
Net sales	$12,277,283	$24,466,643	$33,052,406	$31,084,567	$27,963,108
Cost of goods sold	8,016,862	17,507,289	17,908,964	16,632,955	15,139,340
Gross margin	$ 4,260,421	$ 6,959,354	$15,143,442	$14,451,612	$12,823,768
Advertising, promotional, selling, and administrative expenses	6,700,111	13,882,973	13,889,595	11,712,896	12,244,121
	$(2,439,690)	$(6,923,619)	$ 1,253,847	$ 2,738,716	$ 579,647
Other deductions (income):					
Discounts allowed	226,219	414,901	540,966	548,779	490,020
Interest expense	896,678	637,486	415,175	398,005	410,832
Other, net	(69,730)	168,887	(54,255)	(118,701)	(60,416)
	$ 1,053,167	$ 1,221,274	$ 901,886	$ 828,083	$ 840,436
Earnings (loss) before provision for federal income taxes	(3,492,857)	(8,144,893)	351,961	1,910,633	(260,789)
Provision (credit) for federal income taxes:					
Provision for taxes	—	—	160,000	900,000	—
Prior years' provision no longer required	(47,606)	—	—	—	—
Tax credit arising from carryback of tax losses	—	(771,628)	—	—	(125,179)
Deferred tax benefits written off	—	232,113	—	—	—
Net earnings (loss)	$(3,445,251)	$(7,605,378)	$ 191,961	$ 1,010,633	$ (135,610)
Net earnings (loss) per share	$(1.23)	$(3.85)	$0.10	$0.52	$(0.07)

See notes to financial statements.

EXHIBIT 2 *(continued)*

BISHOP INDUSTRIES, INC., AND SUBSIDIARIES
Consolidated Statement of Source and Application of Funds
For the Year Ended October 31, 1969

Working capital at beginning of year			$ 881,907
Source of funds:			
Net proceeds from sale of common stock		$3,098,858	
Net proceeds from issuance of senior notes		2,870,197	
Issuance of long-term notes in payment of trade accounts payable		405,621	
Deferment of amortization of senior and subordinated notes		363,000	
Other, net		35,049	
Total funds provided			6,772,725
			$7,654,632
Application of funds:			
Net loss		$3,445,251	
Depreciation	$185,950		
Amortization of intangible assets and deferred items	227,238	(413,188)	
		$3,032,063	
Portion of long-term liabilities transferred to current liabilities		98,116	
Purchase of trade names, trademarks, and contract rights		258,382	
Deferred product development costs incurred		87,214	
Total funds applied			3,475,775
Working capital at end of year			$4,178,857

See notes to financial statements.

To the Stockholders and
Board of Directors of
Bishop Industries, Inc.:

We have examined the consoldiated balance sheet of Bishop Industries, Inc., and Subsidiaries as of October 31, 1969, the related consolidated statements of operations, stockholders' equity, and source and application of funds for the year then ended. Our examination was made in accordance with generally accepted auditing standards, and accordingly included such tests of the accounting records and such other auditing procedures as we considered necessary in the circumstances. It is not the general practice of certain customers to confirm balances of accounts receivable from them; however, we have satisfied ourselves as to such receivables by means of other auditing procedures. We previously examined and reported upon the consolidated financial statements for the year 1968.

In our opinion, subject to the effect, if any, of the contingency referred to in note 4, the aforementioned statements present fairly the consolidated financial position of Bishop Industries, Inc., and Subsidiaries at October 31, 1969, and 1968, and the consolidated results of their operations for the years then ended, and the consolidated source and application of funds for the year ended October 31, 1969, in conformity with generally accepted accounting principles applied on a consistent basis.

Newark, New Jersey
March 6, 1970 (except as to note 8,
as to which the date is March 17, 1970)

LYBRAND, ROSS BROS., &
MONTGOMERY

EXHIBIT 2 (continued)

BISHOP INDUSTRIES, INC., AND SUBSIDIARIES
Consolidated Statements or Stockholders' Equity
For the Years Ended October 31, 1969, 1968, 1967, 1966, and 1965

	Common Stock	Additional Paid-In Capital	Retained Earnings (Deficit)	Treasury Common Stock	Total Stockholders' Equity
Balance, November 1, 1965	$182,763	$ 3,120,314	$ 2,002,288	$(60,345)	$ 5,245,020
Net earnings			1,010,633		1,010,633
4% stock dividend paid in January, 1967 (72,569 shares)	7,257	533,382	(540,639)		
Amount attributable to warrants to purchase common stock issued to holders of long-term notes		320,000			320,000
Tax benefit resulting from abandonment of trade names written off by Lanolin Plus, Inc., prior to its merger into the company		206,630			206,630
Other		(17,360)			(17,360)
Balance, November 1, 1966	$190,020	$ 4,162,966	$ 2,472,282	$(60,345)	$ 6,764,923
Net earnings			191,961		191,961
4% stock dividend paid in January, 1968 (75,493 shares)	7,549	736,812	(744,361)		
Exercise of stock options (520 shares)	52	4,229			4,281
Balance, November 1, 1967	$197,621	$ 4,904,007	$ 1,919,882	$(60,345)	$ 6,961,165
Net loss			(7,605,378)		(7,605,378)
Issuance of 385,000 shares in exchange for 125,000 shares of common stock of Realty Equities Corporation (note 4)	38,500	3,011,500			3,050,000
Deferred federal income tax benefits written off		(109,784)			(109,784)
Balance, October 31, 1968	$236,121	$ 7,805,723	$(5,685,496)	$(60,345)	$ 2,296,003
Net loss			(3,445,251)		(3,445,251)
Issuance of 125,000 shares as additional consideration in exchange for 125,000 shares of common stock of Realty Equities Corporation and applicable costs (note 4)	12,500	(22,680)			(10,180)
Net proceeds from sale in July 1969 of 1 million shares (45,000 additional shares issued as compensation for brokerage services)	104,500	2,989,358			3,093,858
Issuance of 35,000 shares in connection with an agreement covering the acquisition of a purchased subsidiary (note 1)	3,500	99,310			102,810
Portion of proceeds from sale of senior notes allocated to warrants issued (note 8)		167,495			167,495
Discounted market value of 50,000 shares sold under Restricted Stock Purchase Plan (note 11)	5,000	145,000			150,000
Balance, October 31, 1969	$361,621	$11,184,206	$(9,130,747)	$(60,345)	$ 2,354,735

See notes to financial statements.

EXHIBIT 2 *(continued)*

Bishop Industries, Inc., and Subsidiaries
Notes to Consolidated Financial Statements

*1. Principles of Consolidation and Changes
in Accounting Policy:*

The consolidated financial statements include the accounts of the company and its active

3. Inventories

Inventories which are stated at the lower of cost (first-in, first-out) or market comprise the following:

	1969	1968	1967	1966	1965
Finished goods and work in process	$2,337,222	$4,974,351	$6,218,868	$3,897,929	$3,539
Raw and component materials	3,435,936	3,610,346	3,303,730	2,135,083	2,222
	$5,773,158	$8,584,697	$9,522,598	$6,033,012	$5,761
Less: Valuation reserve	1,750,000	2,000,000	Not separately disclosed		
Inventories, net	$4,023,158	$6,584,697	$9,522,598	$6,033,012	$5,761

subsidiaries, all of which are wholly owned. All significant intercompany transactions have been eliminated.

Under the terms of an amendment to an agreement covering the acquisition in May 1967 of a subsidiary, Marshall Imports, the company issued in August 1969, 35,000 shares of its common stock for release from all obligations under such acquisition agreement. The discounted market value of the shares issued was added to the cost of investment in excess of net assets of this purchased subsidiary. As of November 1, 1968, the company adopted the policy of amortizing such excess by ratable charges to income over a period of 10 years. Previously, this account was not amortized. The effect of this change was to increase the net loss for 1969 by $46,300 ($.02 per share).

Also, as of November 1, 1968, the company adopted the policy of deferring certain costs incurred in connection with the development of its products. Previously, such costs had been charged to income as incurred. Deferred product development costs are being amortized over three years. As a result of this change, the net loss for 1969 was decreased by $72,700 ($.03 per share).

2. Assets Pledged as Collateral:

Assets pledged as collateral for the senior notes comprise all receivables and inventories (and the proceeds from these items), 125,000 shares of common stock of Realty Equities Corporation and all trademarks and trade names of the company and related rights. Land and buildings with a cost of $2,253,000 are pledged as collateral for mortgages payable.

4. Exchange of Stock and Stock Option:

Under the terms of an agreement dated October 31, 1968 (amended in March 1969) with Realty Equities Corporation of New York, the company exchanged 500,000 shares of its common stock (375,000 shares in 1968 and 125,000 shares in 1969) for 125,000 shares of Realty Equities' common stock. An additional 10,000 shares of the company's common stock were issued in 1968 in payment of the related brokerage fee. The 125,000 shares of Realty Equities' stock were recorded as an investment at the aggregate market price of such shares at the time of the exchange negotiations, less a 20 percent discount and estimated registration costs, as such shares were registered at no cost to the company. The discounted market value of the shares issued for the brokerage fee was recorded as an additional cost of the investment in Realty Equities' stock. Under the terms (as amended) of the exchange agreement, a 10-year option was granted to Realty Equities to purchase 200,000 shares of the company's common stock at $14 per share.

The Realty Equities' common stock is pledged with the institutional lenders as collateral for long-term notes payable (see note 8). The lenders may at their election, with certain restrictions, sell this stock and apply the proceeds to the payment of the notes. Based on the per-share market price of Realty Equities' common stock on March 6, 1970, the indicated market value of the company's investment in such stock amounted to approximately $1 million. At October 31, 1969, such stock investment is shown at its original re-

EXHIBIT 2 *(continued)*

corded amount since the company considers the decline in the market value of these shares, which it acquired as a long-term investment, to be temporary and neither the company nor, absent special circumstances, the lenders, have any present intention to sell such stock. No provision for any contingent loss which may be sustained in connection with this investment has been made in the accompanying financial statements.

5. Plant and Equipment and Depreciation Policy:

Plant and equipment comprise the following:

7. Federal Income Taxes:

At October 31, 1969, unused carryforward losses approximating $7,430,000 (which excludes a $1,750,000 inventory valuation reserve) and $392,000 were available to reduce possible future U.S. and Canadian taxable income, respectively. The U.S. losses expire $3,960,000 in 1973 and $3,470,000 in 1974. The Canadian losses expire $233,000 in 1973 and $159,000 in 1974. Also, at October 31, 1969, the company and its subsidiaries had approximately $77,000 of investment credit carryforwards, which expire during the next six fiscal years, available to reduce possible future U.S. income taxes.

	1969	1968	1967	1966	1965
Land	$ 470,125	$ 470,125	$ 359,455	$ 359,455	$ 359,455
Buildings, equipment, and improvements	1,783,033	1,782,610	1,551,605		
Machinery and equipment	1,134,521	1,221,032	1,010,605	2,693,909	2,473,469
Office furniture, fixtures, and equipment	508,254	605,705	599,828		
Leasehold improvements	75,163	257,279	276,854		
	$3,971,096	$4,336,751	$3,798,347	$3,053,364	$2,832,924

The provision for depreciation, determined by the straight-line method, amounted to approximately $186,000, $230,000, $182,000, $150,000, and $137,000 for 1969, 1968, 1967, 1966, and 1965, respectively. In addition, provision was made in 1968 for approximately $110,000 estimated obsolescence applicable to equipment and leasehold improvements at four beauty salons which were disposed of during 1969.

6. Trade Names and Amortization Policy:

The costs of certain trade names and contract rights are being amortized by the straight-line method over their estimated useful lives of five years. At October 31, 1969, trade names, trademarks, and contract rights carried at an aggregate cost of $259,000, which are considered to have an unlimited life, are not being amortized. Provision for amortization amounted to approximately $69,000, $98,800, $36,400, $40,000, and $30,000 for 1969, 1968, 1967, 1966, and 1965 respectively. (See note 14).

The Appellate Division of the U.S. Treasury Department has upheld the company's position and has reversed previously asserted tax deficiencies for the years 1963 and 1964 plus related interest. Taxable years 1965 through 1967 have been examined by the Internal Revenue Service with no resulting additional tax liability proposed.

In 1968, $232,000 of deferred tax benefits arising from allowances for sales returns and discounts were charged to income since realization was not assured.

8. Notes Payable to Institutional Lenders:

On July 29, 1969, the company borrowed $3,012,500 by issuance of additional principal amount of senior notes and warrants to purchase shares of common stock. In addition, the interest rate of the then outstanding senior notes was increased and the repayment terms and covenants of such senior notes and the subordinated notes were revised. At October 31, 1969, such notes payable to institutional lenders aggregated $7,782,500. The notes are

EXHIBIT 2 *(continued)*

payable in aggregate annual installments as follows:

1970 .... $	—
1971	—
1972	—
1973	908,500
1974	775,500
1975	775,500
1976	775,500
1977	775,500
1978	775,500
1979	775,500
1980	775,500
1981	775,500
1982	133,000
1983	537,000
	$7,782,500

The terms of the notes require maintenance at all times of consolidated net working capital of not less than $5 million, consolidated net worth (as defined) of $3 million, and consolidated net worth (as defined) plus subordinated debt of $5 million. Current indebtedness for loans from banks or commercial factors must not exceed $2 million and indebtedness for loans from others must not exceed $1.5 million at any time. Restrictions are also placed on cash dividends and the purchase or redemption of stock is limited to 25 percent of consolidated net earnings subsequent to October 31, 1969.

On March 17, 1970, the institutional lenders and the company entered into an agreement which amended the notes and established the following requirements: (1) Sale by the company to Realty Equities Corporation (or others) of securities (junior subordinated debt, preferred stock, or common stock) for not less than $1 million by August 31, 1970, and (2) minimum consolidated net working capital of $3.5 million, minimum net worth (as defined) of $1.5 million, and minimum net worth (as defined) plus subordinated debt of $3.5 million until the date of the aforementioned sale of securities or by August 31, 1970, whichever first occurs. Thereafter, each of the foregoing requirements are increased by $1 million to November 1, 1970, whereupon the former requirements in effect at October 31, 1969, become applicable. Net worth (as defined) is to include the junior subordinated debt which may be outstanding.

The institutional lenders have unconditionally and irrevocably waived the working capital and net worth conditions of default,

which conditions existed as of October 31, 1969, and to March 17, 1970. At October 31, 1969, net working capital amounted to $4,179,000, net worth (as defined) was $2,193,000, and net worth (as defined) plus subordinated debt aggregated $4,193,000. The lenders had previously waived their right to declare the principal amount of notes to be due and payable with respect to the conditions of default which existed under terms of the original notes which were replaced or amended in July 1969.

Warrants to purchase 891,429 shares common stock were outstanding at October 31, 1969. The warrants were issued to the institutional lenders in connection with the issuance of the long-term notes and are exercisable in respect to (a) 800,000 shares at $4 per share to June 1, 1974, and at $5 per share thereafter to June 1, 1979, and (b) 91,429 shares at $10.50 per share at any time up to May 15, 1975. The portion of the proceeds of the notes attributable to the warrants was treated as debt discount and is being amortized in equal installments over the term of the notes.

9. Commitments and Contingencies:
The company and its subsidiaries are obligated as lessees under various leases for operating and warehouse facilities and equipment. Aggregate rentals under all leases (exclusive of property taxes and related expenses) amounted to approximately $461,000 for 1969 and $642,000 for 1968. With respect to property leases expiring more than three years after October 31, 1969 (including a facility subleased to others at the company's cost of $15,000 annually to 1980), rentals aggregate approximately $60,000 on an annual basis and $530,000 over the lives of such long-term leases.

Under the terms of a license agreement, the company is obligated to pay minimum royalties of $50,000 annually for a period of 10 years beginning with November 1, 1969, for the manufacture of licensed products.

The company has agreed to use its best efforts to file a registration statement under the Securities Act of 1933 at its expense by April 30, 1970. The company will not receive any of the proceeds from such registration.

A claim has been asserted against the company for advertising services and costs which the claimant alleges were incurred on behalf of the company. Counsel is of the opinion that the company has a meritorious defense to this claim. The company believes that the disposition of this matter will not have a material

EXHIBIT 2 *(concluded)*

effect on consolidated financial position and no provision has been made with respect to such contingent liability.

10. Stock Options:

At October 31, 1969, options to purchase shares of common stock were outstanding under Employee Stock Option Plans approved by the stockholders in 1960, 1962, and 1965. The options were granted at either 95 percent or 100 percent of the market price on the date of grant. The options become exercisable in installments during the three years following the date of grant and generally expire five years after grant. During 1969, options were granted to 33,500 shares at market prices ranging from $5.63 to $12.94 per share, and options for 56,626 shares were canceled or terminated. No options were exercised during the year. At October 31, 1969, there were 29,556 shares under option at prices ranging from $5.63 to $15.75 per share (of which 4,181 shares were exercisable) and 27,768 shares were reserved for future grants.

See note 4 for information with respect to a stock option for 200,000 shares granted to Realty Equities Corporation. Options to purchase 32,448 shares at $5.43 per share, which were outstanding at October 31, 1968, under 1964 agreements with former officers, terminated in February 1969.

11. Restricted Stock Purchase Plan:

In June 1969, the stockholders approved a Restricted Stock Purchase Plan under which a total of 150,000 shares of common stock may be offered, until June 30, 1979, to key employees, officers, and directors of the company and its subsidiaries. The prices at which shares may be sold under the plan may not be less than the par value of the shares as determined over the five trading days preceding the offer. Restrictions as to the sale or disposition of shares sold under the plan lapse, in general, over a period of four years following the date of sale.

In August 1969, 50,000 shares were sold under this plan to an officer at par value. The excess ($145,000) of the discounted market value at the date of the sale over the sale price has been recorded as deferred compensation and is being charged ratably to income over the period from the date of the sale to the dates on which the restrictions lapse.

12. Retirement Plan:

The company has a noncontributory, trusteed retirement plan for eligible salaried employees. The plan provides for annual retirement benefits at normal retirement age 65 based on average annual compensation in excess of certain social security coverage for years of credited service and also provides for the payment of death benefits. The provision for pension costs charged to operations, which have not been funded, amounted to approximately $75,000, $80,200, $67,200, $56,500, and $30,200 for 1969, 1968, 1967, 1966, and 1965, respectively. At October 31, 1969, the unfunded reserve liability was estimated to be $179,000. The portion applicable to past service costs is being amortized over a 20-year period.

13. Per-Share Data:

Net earnings (loss) per share was computed using the weighted average number of shares outstanding during each year (1969, 2,804,406 shares; 1968, 1,976,205 shares; 1967, 1,-962,387 shares; 1966, 1,962,257 shares; 1965, 1,952,522 shares). Outstanding warrants and stock options to purchase common stock have not been considered in computing net earnings (loss) per share since no dilution would result from their exercise.

14. Subsequent Events:

On November 3, 1969, the company acquired at a cost of $500,000 an option from a wholly owned subsidiary of Realty Equities Corporation to purchase for $1 million all of the stock of its subsidiary. The company elected not to exercise this option and the $500,000 was returned to the company during February 1970, with interest at the rate of 12 percent per annum.

Subsequent to October 31, 1969, the company decided to reconvey trademarks which it originally acquired for a maximum conditional obligation of $300,000. The unpaid balance of this obligation ($266,200) will be satisfied by such reconveyance or unilateral termination. Retroactive effect has been given to such termination in the October 1969 consolidated balance sheet and accordingly, $33,800 has been charged to operations for 1969.

Bishop's annual report to shareholders for fiscal 1969 was issued on March 17, 1970 (see Exhibit 2).

Questions

1. Would you recommend that Turnaround Investment Ventures buy the Bishop stock? Why?
2. How useful was the Altman Z-Score in your decision?
3. If you believe that Bishop is heading for bankruptcy, how long from March 1970 do you think it will be before the company files for bankruptcy?

CHAPTER 22

Lease Accounting and Analysis

Leases are used to finance the use of assets. This chapter discusses the accounting by lessees and lessors for long-term personal and property leases. It does not cover leverage leases and lease agreements involving natural resources principally because of their complex and varied nature.

FASB Statement No. 13 and its various amendments and interpretations deal with the accounting for leases. *Statement No. 13* defines a lease as "an agreement conveying the right to use property, plant, or equipment (land and/or depreciable assets) for a stated period of time." The *Statement* covers agreements that meet this definition, even though they are not identified as leases, such as a heat supply contract for nuclear fuel, which under current accounting rules is treated as a depreciable asset. The *Statement* does not apply to rights to explore for or to exploit natural resources, nor does it apply to licensing agreements.

The FASB's approach to lease accounting is based on the belief that *(a)* the characteristic of the leasing transaction should determine the appropriate lessee and lessor accounting and *(b)* and accounting for a lease by both parties to the lease should be similar. Those who opposed the board's position argued that the nature of the lessee's and lessor's businesses was often sufficiently different to warrant different accounting treatment by the two parties.

User Questions

The ability to analyze lease accounting and lease arrangements is a critical financial analysis skill. Many of the unpleasant earnings surprises that investors experience result from companies using lease accounting that does not reflect the realities of the situation. The key lease-related questions statement users need to answer are:

1. Does the lease accounting accurately reflect the economic and business substance of the lease?

2. What are the cash flow implications of the lease arrangement to the lessee and lessor?
3. How does the lessor's pattern of periodic income differ from the related cash inflows?
4. What is the probability that the lessee may default on its lease payments or the lessor fail to meet the lease obligations? What are the consequences of default?
5. What is the real nature of the lease-related assets and liabilities recognized and not recognized on the financial statements?
6. To what extent have lease accounting rules influenced the lease deal? How might possible lease accounting rule changes affect this type of lease arrangement?
7. What role does on- and off-balance-sheet lease financing play in the company's total capital structure, policy, and plans? Is this a prudent use of leasing?
8. Are the lessor's revenue recognition rules realistic for sales accomplished through lease financing arrangements?
9. What happens to the lease-related assets and obligations in the event of the lessee or lessor experiencing financial difficulties?
10. What is the probability that the lessee will extend the lease beyond the initial term? What impact will this have on the lessee and lessor?
11. What residual values will revert to the lessor at the end of the lease term? Are these valuable?

To answer these questions in a meaningful way requires that statement users understand lease accounting, diligently read the details of the lease arrangement, carefully project lease-related cash flows, penetrate the form of the lease to identify its substance, and appreciate the executory contract status of lease agreements.

Leasing Practice

A lease agreement conveys the right to use property in return for a series of specified future rental payments over a definite period.

There are a great many different leasing agreements in practice. A typical lease contract contains provisions covering the following areas:

1. The duration of the lease, which can run from a few hours to the expected economic life of the asset.
2. The options open, if any, to renew the lease or purchase the property at the end of the lease's term. In some cases, these renewal or purchase options can be exercised for a nominal consideration.
3. The duties of the lessor to service the leased property. The service duties may range from none to complete maintenance.

4. The restrictions, if any, on the lessee's business activities, such as paying dividends or entering new bank loans.
5. The penalties for early termination of the lease. Often, the cost of termination is the lessor's unrecovered costs plus a penalty payment.
6. The consequences of default. Usually, the lease agreement requires the lessee to pay immediately all future payments in the event of default. However, in practice this provision may be difficult to enforce since the lessor has an obligation to attempt to mitigate any losses.
7. The obligation of the lessor to provide the lessee with "quiet enjoyment" of the leased property.

There are a number of advantages and disadvantages to leasing assets. One of the advantages claimed by leasing companies is that certain lease obligations do not have to be listed among a company's liabilities, whereas loan obligations must be recorded. Consequently, by financing asset acquisitions with leases of this type, rather than borrowing, a company can report a better debt-equity ratio. Some of the other advantages cited by leasing companies include: shifting the risk of ownership, such as technological obsolescence, onto the lessor; freeing of lessee capital to finance working capital needs; possible tax advantages in certain cases that make leasing cheaper on an after-tax basis than owning; and 100 percent financing.

Typically, the cost of a lease is slightly higher than the cost of a direct borrowing to finance acquisition of an asset. However, in some cases, because of the tax treatment of leased assets, the lessor may be willing to lease at a cost lower than the lessee's marginal borrowing rate. For example, the availability to the lessor of depreciation write-offs may make the after-tax return from leasing higher than the return from straight loans. In return for these tax advantages, the lessor may give the lessee a lease at a cost that is less than the lessee's debt cost.

Lessee's Statements

The principal lessee accounting question raised by leasing is: Are assets and liabilities created on the lessee's books by entering an agreement to lease property on a rental basis?

The FASB concluded in *Statement No. 13* that any lease agreement that substantially transfers all of the benefits and risks of ownership to the lessee should be accounted for as an acquisition of an asset and the incurrence of an obligation. Such leases are called "capital leases." All other leases are regarded as rentals and are called "operating leases." In these cases, no asset or related liability need be shown on the lessee's balance sheet, and the rental payments are charged to operations as they become payable.

Capital Leases. Statement No. 13 requires that leases meeting any *one* of the following four criteria be accounted for as "capital leases":

1. Title is transferred to the lessee by the end of the lease term.[1]
2. The lease contains a bargain purchase option.[2]
3. The least term is at least 75 percent of the leased property's estimated economic life.[3]
4. The present value of the minimum lease payments[4] is 90 percent or more of the fair value of the leased property[5] less any related investment tax credit retained by the lessor. (If the beginning of the lease term falls within at least 25 percent of the total estimated economic life of the leased property, including earlier years of use, this criterion need not be used for the purpose of classifying the lease.)

A capital lease is recorded initially by the lessee as an asset (capital lease asset) and a liability (obligation under capital lease). The amount of the asset and liability is the present value of the rental and other minimum lease payments or the fair value of the leased property. The present value discount rate is the interest rate implicit in the lease, if the lessee knows this implicit rate and it is less than the lessee's incremental borrowing rate. If these two conditions are not met, the lessee's incremental borrowing rate should be used. The capitalized amounts are then accounted for like any other asset that is amortized and interest-bearing debt that is reduced over its term. That is, the asset is amortized in a manner consistent with the lessee's normal depreciation policy over the lease term or, if the lease meets the first or second of the capital lease criteria listed above, over the leased asset's estimated economic life. The interest expense on the re-

---

[1] The lease term is the fixed noncancelable term of the lease plus all periods, if any, covered by bargain renewal options but not extending beyond the date a bargain purchase option becomes exercisable.

A bargain renewal option is a provision that allows the lessee, at the lessee's option, to renew the lease for a rental that at the inception of the lease is expected to be substantially less than the fair rental of the property at the date the option becomes exercisable.

[2] A bargain purchase option is a provision that allows the lessee, at the lessee's option, to acquire the leased asset for a price that at the inception of the lease is expected to be substantially less than the fair market value of the property at the date the option becomes exercisable.

[3] The estimated economic life is the estimated remaining useful life of the leased property with the purpose for which it was intended at the inception of the lease, without limitation by the term of the lease.

[4] The minimum lease payment includes: (1) the minimum rental payments over the lease term, excluding estimated executory costs, such as maintenance costs; (2) any guarantee of the residual value at the expiration of the lease term; (3) any payment required for failure to renew or extend the lease at the expiration of the lease term; and (4) the payment called for by a bargain purchase option. If the lease contains a bargain purchase option, only the rental payments plus the bargain purchase option would be included in the minimum payment computation.

[5] The fair value of the leased asset is the price at which the property could be sold.

corded liability is recognized in proportion to the remaining unpaid balance of the obligation.

Illustration 22–1 presents the balance sheet classification for capital leases required by *Statement No. 13.*

As noted above, when capitalized lease obligations are recorded on the face of financial statements, an asset account, Leased Property under Capital Leases, and a liability account, Obligations under Capital Leases, are shown. Subsequently, as the leased property right is "consumed" and the rental payments made, the two balance sheet accounts are reduced. The asset account is amortized in the same manner as owned property is depreciated. This treatment recognizes the fact that depreciation schedules reflect the characteristics of the property, not the means used to finance its acquisition. The liability account is extinguished by the principal repayment amount implicit in the rental payment. The remaining portion of the rental payment is charged to the income statement as an interest expense.

Typically, rental payments are level. Therefore, in the case of long-term leases, the liability account would be extinguished slowly at first, since the bulk of the rental payment would be interest on the unpaid balance of the obligation. Toward the end of the lease, the opposite would occur, because the unpaid balance and related interest charges would be smaller.

Operating Leases. Leases that do not meet any of the four capital lease criteria listed above are classified as "operating leases." No related assets or liabilities are recorded at the time the lessee enters into such lease agreements, and the rentals for these leases are charged to operations as they become payable. Should the rental payments be unequal amounts over the lease term, the rental expense should be recognized on the straight-line basis, unless some other systematic method that reflects the benefits derived from the leased asset is more appropriate.

Accounting Entries. To illustrate the accounting entries by a lessee, assume that the lessee signs a 10-year lease payable in annual amounts of

ILLUSTRATION 22–1

LAMBERT DIVERSIFIED PRODUCTS, INC.						
Balance Sheet						
	December 31				*December 31*	
	1986	*1985*			*1986*	*1985*
Assets			**Liabilities**			
Leased property under capital leases less accumulated amortization	XXX	XXX	Current: Obligations under capital leases		XXX	XXX
			Long-term: Obligations under capital leases		XXX	XXX

$1,000. The implicit pre-tax interest rate of the lease financing is 10 percent.

If the transaction is regarded as an operating lease, the lessee simply records the rental payment for the lease as an expense at the time of payment:

```
Dr.  Equipment Rental Expense ...................................  1,000
     Cr.  Cash ................................................          1,000
```

If the lease obligation is a capital lease, the following entries would be made to recognize an asset and a related liability at the time the lease was signed by the lessee:

```
Dr.  Capital Lease—Equipment ...................................  6,145
     Cr.  Obligation under Capital Lease...........................          6,145
```

To recognize the present value of future lease obligations (in this case, $1,000 a year for 10 years discounted at 10 percent per year,[6] the first rental payment would be recorded as follows:

```
Dr.  Obligation under Capital Lease ...............................  385
     Interest Expense (10 percent of $6,145) .......................  615
     Cr.  Cash ..................................................          1,000
```

An additional entry each year should be made to recognize the amortization of the Capital Lease—Equipment asset.

```
Dr.  Amortization Expense—Equipment (10 percent of $6,145) ..........  615
     Cr.  Accumulated Amortization—Equipment .....................          615
```

The Accumulated Amortization—Equipment account is shown on the balance sheet as a contra account to the Capital Lease—Equipment account.

The following year, the interest expense would be less, since the balance of the rental obligation had been reduced by $385 during the first year. The second-year entries are:

```
Dr.  Obligation under Capital Lease ...............................  424
     Interest Expense (10 percent of $6,145 − $385) .................  576
     Cr.  Cash ..................................................          1,000
```

---

[6] The present value of a stream of payments or receipts is the amount that would have to be invested today to generate that cash flow at a given rate of interest. For example, $6,145 invested today at 10 percent would return $1,000 per year for 10 years to the investor. At the end of that time, the investment would be recouped and the return would be 10 percent. Thus, the present value of $1,000 per year for 10 years discounted at 10 percent is $6,145. Present value tables that can be used to make this calculation are included in Appendixes A and B.

If the lease rental included executory costs, such as maintenance and real estate taxes paid by the lessor, these amounts would be deducted from the gross rental for the purpose of making the present value capital lease calculation. Only the net rental is capitalized. In this illustration, there are no executory costs. If executory costs are included in the lease rental, a separate accounting entry is made to reflect these costs annually as they are paid. The entry is:

```
Lease Executory Cost Expense ....................................  XXX
     Cash ......................................................          XXX
```

In subsequent years, more of the $1,000 lease payment will go toward reducing the balance of the obligation under capital leases as the annual interest on the declining balance of this account gets smaller. At the end of the lease period, the capital lease obligation liability account will be reduced to zero by the last lease payment.

Over the life of the lease, the amortization and interest expenses will be equal to the total net lease rental payments. Thus, the total cost of a lease is the same irrespective of whether it is classified as a capital or operating lease. However, the sum of the annual lease-related interest expense and asset amortization charges for a capital lease will be greater than the annual rental expense for an operating lease in the early years of a lease term. In the later years of the lease, the reverse is true.

The lessee disclosure requirements are summarized in Illustration 22–2.

Lessor's Statements

The accounting for leases on the lessor's statements raises several problems: the allocation of the rental revenues and costs to the appropriate accounting periods; the allocation of lease acquisition, operating, and closing costs in a manner that is systematic, fair, and consistent with the revenue recognition method; and the appropriate description and classification of leased assets in the balance sheet.

Statement No. 13 classifies leases from the lessor's point of view in three categories, namely: direct financing leases, sales-type leases, and operating leases. The accounting for each category is different.

Criteria.   A lease that satisfies *one* of the four lessee capital lease criteria is classified from the point of view of the lessor by *Statement No. 13* as being either a direct financing or a sales-type lease, provided it also meets *both* of these criteria:

1. Collectibility of the payments required from the lessee is reasonably predictable.
2. No important uncertainties surround the amount of costs yet to be incurred by the lessor under the lease.[7]

A lease meeting the two criteria listed above is classified as a sales-type lease when the fair value of the leased property is different from its carrying amount. Otherwise, it is classified as a direct financing lease. Leases that do not meet these two criteria are classified as operating leases.

---

[7] Important uncertainties might include commitments by the lessor to guarantee performance of the leased property in a manner more extensive than the typical product warranty or to effectively protect the lessee from obsolescence of the leased property. However, it is not intended that the necessity of estimating executory expenses such as insurance, maintenance, and taxes to be paid by the lessor shall constitute an important uncertainty.

ILLUSTRATION 22–2
Lessee Disclosure Requirements

Disclosure	Disclosure Applicable to			Disclosure Required for		
	Capital Leases	Noncancelable Operating Leases of More than One Year	All Operating Leases	Each Balance Sheet Presented	Latest Balance Sheet Presented	Each Income Statement Presented
1. General description of lessee's leasing activities, including:						
a. Basis for determining contingent rentals.	X	X	X			
b. Existence and terms of renewal or purchase options and escalation clauses.	X	X	X			
c. Dividend or other restrictions.	X	X	X			
2. Gross amount of assets in the aggregate and by major property categories.	X			X		
3. Amount of accumulated amortization in total.	X			X		
4. Separate disclosure of amortization unless it is included in depreciation expense and that fact disclosed.	X					X
5. Minimum future lease payments in the aggregate and for each of the five succeeding fiscal years.	X	X			X	
6. Amount of aggregate future minimum lease payments representing:						
a. Executory costs.	X				X	
b. Imputed interest to reduce to present value.	X				X	
7. Total of minimum future rentals due from noncancelable subleases.	X	X			X	
8. Total contingent rentals actually incurred.	X					X
9. Rental expense with separate amounts for minimum and contingent rentals and sublease rental income.			X			X

ILLUSTRATION 22–3
Operating Method

Year	Lease Payments Received (a)	Sum-of-the-Years' Digits		Straight-Line Depreciation	
		Depreciation Expense (b)	Gross Profit or Loss (c) = (a) − (b)	Depreciation Expense (d)	Gross Profit or Loss (e) = (a) − (d)
1	$ 2,700	$ 3,167	$ (467)	$ 1,900	$ 800
2	2,700	2,533	167	1,900	800
3	2,700	1,900	800	1,900	800
4	2,700	1,267	1,433	1,900	800
5	2,700	633	2,067	1,900	800
6	100	100	0	100	0
7	100	100	0	100	0
8	100	100	0	100	0
9	100	100	0	100	0
10	100	100	0	100	0
Total	$14,000	$10,000	$4,000	$10,000	$4,000

Sales-type leases normally arise in situations where a manufacturer uses leases as a means of marketing products. Direct financing leases usually result when the lessor's primary mission is to finance the acquisition of property by a lessee.

Operating Leases. The accounting for operating leases by lessors is fairly straightforward. It recognizes revenue as each rental receipt is received. Costs related to the leased asset, such as depreciation and executory costs, like maintenance, are expensed as incurred. Thus, the lease profit is the difference between the lease rentals received and the related depreciation and executory costs. Under the operating lease method, the leased asset is shown as an asset, less its accumulated depreciation. No receivable recognizing the lessee's future obligation to pay rental is recorded.

Illustration 22–3 illustrates the operating method with different depreciation schedules. The illustration assumes that equipment costing the lessor $10,000 is leased for a five-year period with 60 noncancelable monthly payments of $225 each. The unguaranteed residual value is zero. At the end of five years, the lessee has the option of renewing for one year at a time for a nominal annual rental of $100. In the illustration, it is assumed that five renewal payments are received and at the end of 10 years, the equipment is abandoned by the lessor. The total payments for the 10 years is thus $14,000, and the lessor's total gross profit is $4,000. Assuming 95 percent of the equipment cost is amortized during the initial term of the lease, the question is: How much of the $4,000 gross profit should be recognized each year? Columns (c) and (e) of Illustration 22–3 show how the annual gross profit (or loss) varies with the depreciation method selected.

ILLUSTRATION 22–4
Financing Method

Year	Months in Year*	Gross Profit
1	60–49	$1,251
2	48–37	975
3	36–25	700
4	24–13	425
5	12–1	149
6	0	100
7	0	100
8	0	100
9	0	100
10	0	100
Total		$4,000

* The sum of 60 months' digits is 1,830. During the first year, the sum of the 49th through the 60th month is 654/1,830, so 35.7 percent of the income is recognized during the first year.

Direct Financing Leases. When a lease falls in the direct financing category, the lessor's net investment in the lease is recorded as an asset on the lessor's balance sheet. The net investment consists of the sum of the minimum lease payments and the unguaranteed residual value, if any, less the unearned lease income. Unearned income is determined by subtracting the cost or carrying value of the leased property from the gross investment. Unearned income is amortized over the lease term so as to produce a constant periodic rate of return on the net investment.

Illustration 22–4 shows the application of this financing method to the example presented above. In Illustration 22–4, the deferred gross income is recognized over the initial lease period on the sum-of-the-months'-digits basis.[8] This technique approximates more refined interest calculations. The income over the renewal periods is equal to the option period payments of $100 per year.

Accounting Entries. Using the same example as Illustration 22–3, which assumes that a company purchases an asset for $10,000 and then leases it, the operating method recognizes the income as the cash is received from the $2,700 annual lease rental charge. The leased asset owned by

---

[8] Rather than actually working out what the unpaid principal amounts to each month, which would require splitting each lease payment into an interest portion and a principal repayment portion, the total amount of gross profit is simply spread over the life of the lease on a declining scale. The method is called "sum-of-the-months'-digits," or sometimes the "rule of 78." Some banks use it for their consumer installment loans; a 12-month loan has 78 months' digits, and during the first month the bank recognizes 12/78 of the total interest charge. This is a reasonable approximation to the result obtained by using a more accurate method based on compound interest, even though it does tend to recognize income slightly earlier than a true compound-interest-based method.

the lessor is depreciated in this case on a straight-line basis of $1,900 per year. The gross profit is the difference between these amounts.

```
Dr.  Cash ...............................................  2,700
     Cr.  Rental Income .........................................          2,700

Dr.  Depreciation Expense .......................................  1,900
     Cr.  Allowance for Depreciation .............................          1,900
```

Based on the gross profit schedule in Illustration 22–4 and the aggregate lease payments and asset cost in Illustration 22–3, the direct financing method recognizes at the time the lease is signed the following asset and liability accounts:

```
Dr.  Lease Payments Receivable ...............................  14,000
     Cr.  Deferred Profit on Leasing.............................          4,000
          Cost of Leased Asset ..................................          10,000
```

The profit is recognized as each $2,700 payment is received:

```
Dr.  Cash ...............................................  2,700
     Cr.  Lease Payments Receivable .............................          2,700

Dr.  Deferred Profit on Leasing ..................................  1,251
     Cr.  Current Profit on Leasing ..............................          1,251
```

The amount of the last entry is the first-year sum-of-the-months'-digits figure shown in Illustration 22–4.

Therefore, at the end of the first year, the receivable from leasing would be $11,300 and the remaining deferred profit $2,749 ($4,000 − 1,250). At the end of the second year, the lease receivable would be $8,600 ($11,300 − 2,700) and the deferred profit account $1,774 ($2,749 − 975).

Sales-Type Leases. As part of their regular marketing programs, a number of manufacturers are willing to lease, rather than sell, their products to customers. In these cases, the manufacturer receives the normal manufacturing profit margin as well as a return on the lease financing. Depending on the circumstances, the manufacturing profit on leased assets should be recognized either at the time the lease agreement is signed or over the lease period.

According to *Statement No. 13*, if a deal qualifies as a sales-type lease, it should be accounted for by the lessor as follows. The present value of the minimum lease payments receivable from the lessee is reported as sales. The carrying amount of the leased property plus any initial direct costs, less the present value of any unguaranteed residual value, is charged to cost of sales. The difference between the sales and cost of sales amounts is the seller's gross profit. The financing aspect of the sales-type leases is then accounted for similarly to a direct financing lease.

A manufacturer using leasing as a marketing aid under the lease conditions illustrated in Illustrations 22–3 and 22–4 might have the following breakdown for a $10,000 sale on a 10-year lease contract basis of a product that cost the manufacturer $8,000 to produce:

```
Cost ..........................$ 8,000
Manufacturing profit ...........  2,000
Selling price .................$10,000
Deferred leasing profit .........  4,000
Lease payments receivable.....$14,000
```

If the sales-type lease conditions listed above were met, the $2,000 profit from manufacturing would be recognized immediately, and the financing profit from leasing the equipment would be recognized over the life of the lease.

Under the *direct financing method* to calculate the periodic income, the accounting entries would be:

1. Immediate (to recognize manufacturing profit):

```
Dr.  Lease Payments Receivable ............................  14,000
     Cr.  Sales .............................................          10,000
          Deferred Profit on Leasing ........................           4,000

Dr.  Cost of Goods Sold......................................   8,000
     Cr.  Inventory...........................................           8,000
```

2. As the first payment is received (to recognize leasing revenue using the sum-of-the-years'-digits method):

```
Dr.  Cash....................................................   2,700
     Cr.  Lease Payments Receivable ........................           2,700

Dr.  Deferred Profit on Leasing .............................   1,251
     Cr.  Current Profit .....................................           1,251
```

The subsequent leasing profit entries would follow the schedule shown in Illustration 22–4. If there is substantial risk in the lease, recognition under the *operating method* would be required. The accounting entries would be the same as for Illustration 22–3, except the depreciation expense would be based on the manufacturer's cost of $8,000, not the $10,000 basis used in Illustration 22–3.

Initial Direct Costs. Leasing costs such as commissions and legal fees can be directly associated with consummating particular leases. In the case of direct financing leases, these costs are charged against income as incurred, and a portion of the unearned income equal to the initial direct costs is recognized as income in the same period. Initial direct costs associated with sales-type leases are included in the cost of goods sold. Initial direct costs related to operating leases are deferred and allocated over the lease term in proportion to the recognition of rental income.

Lessor Disclosure. The following information with respect to leases should be disclosed in the lessor's financial statements:

For sales-type and direct financing leases:

1. These three components of net investment in sales-type and direct financing leases as of the date of each balance sheet presented:
   a. Future minimum lease payments to be received, with separate deduction for (i) amounts representing executory costs included in the minimum lease payments; and (ii) the accumulated allowance for uncollectible minimum lease payments receivable.
   b. The unguaranteed residual values accruing to the benefit of the lessor.
   c. Unearned income.
2. Future minimum payments to be received for each of the five succeeding fiscal years as of the date of the latest balance sheet presented.
3. The amount of unearned income included in income to offset initial direct costs charged against income for each period for which an income statement is presented (for direct financing leases only).
4. Total contingent rentals included in income for each period for which an income statement is presented.

For operating leases:

1. The cost or carrying amount, if different, of property on lease or held for leasing, separately, by major classes of property according to nature or function, and the amount of accumulated depreciation in total as of the date of the latest balance sheet presented.
2. Minimum future rentals on noncancelable leases as of the date of the latest balance sheet presented, in the aggregate and for each of the five succeeding fiscal years.
3. Total contingent rentals included in income for each period for which an income statement is presented.

For leases of either type, a general description of the lessor's arrangements should be included.

Related Parties

Leases between related parties should be classified in accordance with *Statement No. 13's* capital and operating lease criteria in the separate financial statements of related parties. In cases where the terms of the lease agreement have been significantly affected by the fact the lessee and lessor are related, the accounting classification should reflect the economic substance of the agreement rather than its legal form. In consolidated statements or financial statements in which an investment in an investee is accounted for on the equity basis, any profit or loss on lease transactions with a related party should be eliminated. A subsidiary whose principal business is leasing assets to its parent or other affiliated entities should be consolidated.

Leases Involving Real Estate

The FASB in *Statement No. 13* divided leases involving real estate into four categories: (1) leases involving land only; (2) leases involving land and buildings; (3) leases involving real estate and equipment; and (4) leases involving only part of a building or building complex.

A lease involving land only would be classified as a capital lease if it contained a bargain purchase option or transferred the land to the lessee at the end of the lease term. All other leases involving land only would be classified as operating leases. A land-only capital lease would not be amortized, since the assumption is that the lessee would acquire the land. A lessor could account for a capital land-only lease as a direct financing or sales-type lease if the lessor criteria for this treatment were met.

A lease involving land and buildings which transfers the lease assets to the lessee at the end of the lease term or provides for a bargain purchase should be broken into two parts—a land capital lease and a building capital lease. The division of the capitalized value of the total lease between its two parts should be based on the relative values of the land and the buildings. In this situation, only the building capital lease should be amortized. The lessor would account for this lease as a single lease.

Other leases involving both land and buildings would be classified as capital or operating leases according to the appropriate criteria. If the land's value is less than 25 percent of the total property's value and capital lease criteria other than the bargain purchase or transfer of ownership criteria are met, both the lessee and lessor would treat the lease as a single lease, and the lessee would amortize the entire capitalized amount over the estimated economic life of the building. If the value of the land is 25 percent or more of the total property's fair value, both the lessor and lessee should divide the lease into a land lease and a building lease. However, in these circumstances, the land lease should always be classified as an operating lease.

The equipment portion of a lease involving both real estate and equipment should be accounted for separately from the real estate by both the lessee and lessor.

In general, if the leased property is part of a building or building complex, both the lessee and lessor should classify and account for the lease according to the method proposed for leases involving land and buildings.

Sale and Leaseback

The sale and leaseback is a financing device whereby the owner of a property sells it and simultaneously leases it back from the buyer. The lease portion of the transaction presents no accounting problem; it is treated like any other lease. A seller lessee accounting problem arises when there is a gain or loss on the sale of the asset, however.

Statement No. 13 treats a sale and leaseback as a single transaction. It requires seller-lessees to classify leases arising from sale-and-leaseback transactions as capital or operating leases. In either case, any loss on the sale should be recognized as such at the time of the sale. Gains are deferred. The actual treatment of this deferred gain depends on the lessee's classification of the lease. If it meets any one of the criteria for a capital lease, any gain on the sale of the leaseback property must be deferred and amortized over the lease term in proportion to the amortization of the capital lease asset. The deferred gain is presented on the balance sheet as a deduction from the capital lease asset. When the lease is an operating lease, any gain on the sale of the asset is amortized in proportion to the rental payments over the time the asset is expected to be used.

If the lease meets the bargain purchase or asset transfer criteria for a capital lease, the purchaser-lessor should record the transaction as a purchase and a direct financing lease; otherwise, the purchaser-lessor should record the transaction as a purchase and an operating lease.

The Controversy

Prior to *Statement No. 13*, lessees did not usually list lease property rights and rental obligations on their balance sheets. The Accounting Principles Board approved this practice, principally because it viewed leases as being similar to executory contracts. According to *APB Opinion No. 5*, which *Statement No. 13* replaced:

> It seems clear that leases covering merely the right to use property in exchange for future rental payments do not create an equity in the property and are thus nothing more than executory contracts requiring continuing performance on the part of both the lessor and the lessee for the full period covered by the leases. The question of whether assets and liabilities should be recorded in connection with leases of this type is, therefore, part of the larger issue of whether the rights and obligations that exist under executory contracts in general (e.g., purchase commitments and employment contracts) give rise to assets and liabilities which should be recorded.
>
> The rights and obligations related to unperformed portions of executory contracts are not recognized as assets and liabilities in financial statements under generally accepted accounting principles as presently understood. Generally accepted accounting principles require the disclosure of rights and obligations under executory contracts in separate schedules or notes to the financial statements if the omission of this information would tend to make the financial statement misleading. The rights and obligations under leases which convey merely the right to use property, without an equity in the property accruing to the lessee, fall into the category of pertinent

information which should be disclosed in schedules or notes rather than by recording assets and liabilities in the financial statements.

This reasoning is used by some to argue against the FASB's *Statement No. 13*. In addition, others object to the FASB *Statement's* position on capital leases in lessee balance sheets for some of the following reasons: the rental obligation does not represent a liability to repay borrowed funds; it is simply a commitment for future rent expenses; the legal rights of the lessor are different from those of lenders in bankruptcy. Others argue that the right to use leased property is not the same as ownership, and hence the lease right is not an asset. According to this point of view, assets are rights acquired irrevocably, whereas a lease provides for services yet to be rendered and which may not be performed.

Those who support the recording on lessee financial statements of capital lease rights and obligations claim that leasing is a form of financing with more similarities to conventional debt financing than to executory contracts. The proponents of lease capitalization claim that the lessor essentially completes the lessor's part of the agreement when the lessor delivers the leased property. Consequently, the lease agreement is different from the typical executory contract, since no significant future service is to be performed by the lessor. In addition, those supporting capitalization claim that the lessee is committed to making a series of fixed cash payments which reduce the lessee's ability to meet similar obligations to other creditors. Accounting, they point out, is interested in presenting a useful report of the company's financial condition. Given this purpose, they consider it indefensible to omit a significant asset and liability from the balance sheet.

Two points of view concerning a lease arrangement underlie *Statement No. 13*. These two concepts, to certain aspects of which some FASB members gave greater weight than to others, are:

1. The important characteristic of a lease is the transfer for its term of possession and control of use of property by the lessor to the lessee, subject to any restrictions in the lease. As a result of the transfer, the lessee has acquired a resource representing the potential service to be obtained from using the property. The lessee has agreed to pay for that resource through periodic payments. Financial statements should report as assets the resources being used in the business and as obligations the agreement to pay for them.

The lessor has relinquished service potential inherent in the property. He has disposed of a resource at a price. Financial statements should report the result of substituting one resource for another.

A lease is different from some take-or-pay contracts and other kinds of executory contracts where neither party has performed, that is, where neither property nor service has been transferred.

In viewing the transfer of service potential and the concurrent contractual agreement for the payment and receipt of cash as the essential elements to be recorded in accounting for leases, it is acknowledged that those essential elements are present in most lease arrangements. It is recognized, however, that only in limited circumstances have lessees accounted for the results of lease arrangements in a manner that reflects those essential elements. The adoption of the (classification) criteria (for capital leases) together with the disclosures required represent, under this view, a practical advance in recognizing in financial statements the essential nature of the resources of lessees and lessors and the obligations of lessees.

2. A lease that transfers substantially all of the benefits and risks incident to ownership of property should be accounted for as an acquisition of a tangible asset by the lessee and as a sale or financing by the lessor. All other leases are in substance executory contracts and should be accounted for in a manner consistent with that accorded other executory contracts, namely, as operating leases.

It is recognized that all noncancelable leases convey some portion of the benefits and risks incident to the property. However, it is only in those leases that transfer all, or a sufficiently large portion, of the benefits and risks, that the economic effect on the parties closely approaches that of an installment purchase. It is that economic effect, and that alone, which justifies the classification of some leases as capital leases by the lessee and as sales-type or direct financing leases by the lessor.

The classification criteria set forth are viewed in this concept as appropriate for the identification of those leases in which substantially all of the benefits and risks have been transferred to the lessee. The fact that the lease term need be for only 75 percent of the economic life of the property or that the lessor may retain a residual value of up to 25 percent is not inconsistent with the concept of "substantially all."

Financial Analysis

In most financial analyses, capital leases and many operating leases—particularly those that involve assets that are critical to the firm's operations or have long lease terms—are regarded as a form of debt. The lessee is the borrower and the lessor the creditor. As a result, lease payments are included in fixed charges–coverage ratios and lease obligations are regarded as part of the debt component of the debt-equity ratio. Because the lease payment includes two elements, an interest charge and a principal repayment typically, only a third of the total rentals is included in interest-coverage ratios. Also, since lessors have an obligation to mitigate their damages should a lessee default, some analysts exclude as much as two thirds of the lease obligations from the debt portion of the debt-equity ratio calculation.

Financial analysts should always be wary of the use of leases to finance sales or to avoid recording debt on the balance sheet. Some manufacturer-lessor companies using leasing to finance the sale of their products deliberately write the terms of their leases to ensure that sales accounting is required. This is accomplished by including what appear to be bargain renewal options in the lease agreement. In these cases, the analyst should focus on the question: Will the lessee renew? If the answer is no, or there is doubt in the analyst's mind, the analyst should restate the company's statements to reflect sales made through operating lease arrangements. Typically, the company's earnings will be significantly lower and will probably better reflect the actual situation. Similarly, in order to avoid reporting additional debt on their balance sheets, some lessees arrange with their lessors to structure the form of their lease agreements in such a way that the lease is classified as an operating lease when in substance it is a capital lease. All off-balance-sheet lease financing should be closely scrutinized to see if in fact it is in essence a form of debt.

Unsatisfactory Situation

The parallel accounting for leases by lessees and lessors that the FASB believed flowed from its concept of a lease transaction was a break with past lease accounting practices. Today, there are many who believe that the FASB should reexamine its position on lease accounting. They claim lease accounting rules are too complex and often encourage lessees to enter into uneconomical operating lease arrangements to avoid capitalizing their lease obligations. Also, there is a widespread suspicion that loopholes in the rules allow lease agreements to be written in such a way that their legal form satisfies the operating lease criteria, although in substance they are capital leases. Statement users must be alert to this accounting manipulation.

Draxson Industries
Accounting for Sale and Leasebacks and Lessee's Lease Commitments

In May 1980, the newly elected president of Draxson Industries was reviewing the presentation of the company's lease transactions in the 1980 financial statements. Draxson Industries sold supplies and equipment to the commercial dry-cleaning and laundry industries.

The Company

In 1979, sales and net income reached all-time highs of $16.4 million and $343,000, respectively. Stockholders' equity at the close of that year totaled $2.6 million.

Operations of the company had always been profitable. In the 10-year period from 1970 to 1979, net income had ranged from 9 to 22.8 percent of shareholders' equity at the beginning of the year. Book value per share of stock had climbed from $2.68 to $10.54 during the same period. A 10-year summary of selected operating and financial information is shown in Exhibit 1.

From its earliest years, Draxson Industries sought to build a reputation for offering its customers a full line of high-quality equipment and operating supplies. The dry-cleaning and laundry industries in the nationwide market looked to Draxson leadership in the development of new equipment, accessories, and specialized consumable supplies.

The company acted primarily as a national distributor for a number of relatively small manufacturers and as exclusive representative for others in limited geographic areas. About 90 percent of the products sold by Draxson were manufactured by others. The balance, consisting of replacement parts for standard laundry and dry-cleaning equipment such as belts, padded

This case was prepared by F. R. Madera (under the direction of David F. Hawkins).

Copyright © 1965 by the President and Fellows of Harvard College

Harvard Business School case 110–163 (Rev. 1985)

EXHIBIT 1

Ten-Year Summary (figures in thousands of dollars except percentages and per-share figures)

	1979	1978	1977	1976	1975	1974	1973	1972	1971	1970
Operations:										
Net sales	16,418	15,222	13,056	11,659	10,516	10,099	9,340	7,711	6,246	5,379
Income before federal income tax	750	539	507	286	246	375	402	308	183	188
Percentage of sales	4.3%	3.5%	3.9%	2.5%	2.3%	3.7%	4.3%	4.0%	3.0%	3.5%
Net income to shareholders	343*	259	240	134	118	178	183	145	90	77
Percentage of sales	2.1%	1.7%	1.9%	1.1%	1.1%	1.8%	1.9%	1.9%	1.4%	1.4%
Per share	$1.39	$1.16	$1.09	$0.60	$0.53	$0.80	$0.82	$0.65	$0.41	$0.34
Dividends paid in cash	94	14	7	2	2	15	—	15	15	15
Financial position:										
Current assets	4,633	4,423	3,490	2,915	2,742	2,634	2,345	1,978	1,566	1,278
Current liabilities	1,988	2,289	1,415	1,282	1,201	1,164	1,156	995	865	647
Working capital	2,645	2,134	2,075	1,633	1,541	1,470	1,189	983	701	631
Current ratio	2.3	1.9	2.5	2.3	2.3	2.3	2.0	2.0	1.8	1.9
Long-term debt	371	424	472	262	390	428	315	441	186	178
Shareholders' equity	2,605	2,036	1,852	1,552	1,420	1,305	1,127	801	672	597
Percentage of net income to share-holders' equity at beginning of year	16.8%	14.0%	15.5%	9.6%	9.0%	15.8%	22.8%	21.6%	15.0%	14.3%
Book value per share†	$10.54	$9.16	$8.33	$6.99	$6.39	$5.87	$5.07	$3.61	$3.02	$2.68

* Does not include income tax refund of 23 cents per share.
† Based on 247,000 shares outstanding at December 31, 1979, and 222,000 shares outstanding in 1978 and prior years.

rollers, and chemically treated press covers, were manufactured in the company's Philadelphia plant.

Following the death of the company's president and principal stockholder, the management of the company changed. The new management embarked upon an aggressive expansion program. Existing branches were strengthened by adding sales personnel and increasing inventories. The company's geographic sales coverage became nationwide as branches were established in new cities.

Funds for Draxson's expansion program had been obtained from several sources. The largest part of increased working capital requirements was internally generated. Minimum dividends were paid to stockholders during the expansion period. Capital stock sold to several members of the new management team provided about $100,000. The balance was obtained by borrowing on long-term notes, which were refinanced late in 1977. In 1979, the company's working capital position was improved by the sale of 25,000 additional shares of capital stock to the general public. At the close of 1979, Draxson's stock was held by about 600 stockholders.

Draxson's Lease Activities

Since its incorporation, the company had signed a number of lease agreements involving real estate. In 1980, a sale-and-leaseback arrangement was used to acquire a building to house the New York branch. Also in 1980, management was considering the leasing of automobiles needed in company operations.

Real Estate Leases. Draxson leased all of the physical facilities used in operations. When the home office and plant space requirements exceeded its Philadelphia building, the company sold its plant and moved into leased property.

Branch operations had always been conducted in leased facilities. In most cases, new branches were established in very low-rent districts under three- to five-year leases. After sufficient sales volume was obtained, the branches were moved to larger and better buildings. At the close of 1979, all of Draxson's operations except the New York branch were housed in fairly new, modern buildings. A schedule of the company's real estate leases is shown in Exhibit 2.

Draxson's management had subscribed to a principle of leasing real estate to conserve working capital for inventory and accounts receivable expansion. Early in 1979, the company's treasurer said,

> We have always leased, but I would be inclined to say that leasing is not an industry practice. Many of our competitors, I know, own their own buildings, but this may well be one of the reasons that they have failed to expand from more than one or two locations.
>
> All our leases are negotiated at the best possible price to the company.

EXHIBIT 2
Real Estate Leases at May 28, 1980

	Philadel- phia	New York	Chicago	Cleve- land	Atlanta	Kansas City	Dallas	Los Angeles	Seattle
Date of lease	5-1-78	11-1-70	2-1-76	5-1-77	10-1-79	9-1-77	7-1-79	4-1-78	8-1-77
Length of lease	20 yrs.*	10 yrs.	25 yrs.	10 yrs.	5 yrs.	5 yrs.	10 yrs.§	10 yrs.	5 yrs.
Probable life of property (from date of lease)	50 yrs.	30 yrs.	30 yrs.	50 yrs.	30 yrs.	20 yrs.	50 yrs.	50 yrs.	20 yrs.
Option to buy at a nominal price?	No	No	No	No	No	No	No	No	No
Cancellation provisions	None	None	None	None	None	None	None	None	None
Amount of annual rental	$45,400*	†	$18,000	$13,900	$9,600	$3,600	$12,600	$13,500	$5,800
Other payments by lessee?									
Taxes	Yes	No‡	No	No‡	No‡	No	No‡	Yes	No
Insurance	Yes	No‡	No	No	No	No	No	Yes	No
Maintenance	Yes	Yes	Yes	Yes	Yes	Yes	Yes	Yes	Yes
Heat	Yes	Yes	No	Yes	Yes	Yes	Yes	Yes	Yes
Light	Yes	Yes	Yes	Yes	Yes	Yes	Yes	Yes	Yes

* Plus four five-year renewal options with annual rentals of $24,100, $22,900, $22,900, and $22,900, respectively.
† $39,700 for first five years and $40,700 for second five years.
‡ Payments required by lessee equal to increases over the initial base year of the lease.
§ Plus two five-year renewal options.

We do not know exactly what percentage of net income the lessor receives on his investment, but we assume it to be in the 6 to 10 percent range, depending on current interest rates and the lessor's tax status. As our annual report for 1979 indicates, we earned 16.8 percent on our shareholders' money, using it for trading purposes.

No attempt has been made to compare the cost of leasing either with long-term debt or equity capital. These are studies that probably should have been made, but I doubt that they would have seriously altered the company's leasing program. Any method of obtaining equity or long-term capital immediately requires some extra strings on management. This is a factor that we are reluctant to assume, especially when any resultant savings is hit by high income tax rates and earnings at present are satisfactory.

Planned Sale and Leaseback. For a number of years, Draxson had been planning to move its New York City branch to better facilities in a more desirable location. The lease on the New York premises was to terminate November 1, 1979.

After exhausting all efforts to find suitable existing space, arrangements were completed early in 1980 to obtain required facilities through a sale-and-leaseback transaction. Unimproved land was purchased at a cost of $300,000. A contract had been signed with a New York contractor for the construction of a one-story building on the site. Interim financing had been obtained from the company's Philadelphia bank. The building scheduled for completion early in September 1981 was to cost $500,000, including all financing and related costs. The completed building, together with the land, was to be sold to the Old Quaker Life Insurance Company of Philadelphia for $750,000 and immediately leased by Draxson for a period of 25 years at a monthly lease rental of $4,500. The lease provided that Draxson would pay all costs of maintaining the property as well as periodic amounts equal to the property taxes and insurance costs. At the expiration of the lease, Draxson was to have the option of purchasing the property for $250,000. It was estimated that the steel and masonry building would have a physical life of 40 years.

Automobile Leasing. In May 1980, management of Draxson Industries was considering the adoption of a policy of providing automobiles for certain key sales personnel in all branches. Currently, company-owned automobiles were used only by executives at Philadelphia. Under the contemplated plans, a fleet of about 20 automobiles would be leased from a national firm of automotive equipment lessors. The plan, if adopted, would probably be effected later in 1980 when 1981 model autos became available.

Approximate costs were available, although the lessor had not submitted his detailed proposals. Under a typical lease arrangement, the lessor would provide new autos at the estimated fleet cost price of about $3,500 for periods of two years. In addition to a monthly payment of $100 per unit, the lessee would pay an annual charge for insurance, taxes, and licensing, depending upon the location of the auto's use. The lessee would, of course, pay all costs of operation and normal maintenance. The leases would be noncancelable. If Draxon did not lease the cars, it planned to borrow short-term funds at 6 percent from a local bank to finance the purchase.

London Subsidiary. In late 1979, the Draxon management decided to expand their business overseas. Their plan was to acquire a well-established British company in the same field as Draxon. In February 1980, Draxon located a desirable company and entered into negotiations for its acquisition. The British company's two owners were willing to sell their business to Draxon for Draxon stock. However, for tax and cash flow reasons they wanted Draxon to lease, rather than buy, the company's buildings. The two owners would also retain title to the company's land assets. In May 1980, Draxon was considering a proposed 25-year noncancelable net lease which called for an annual rental of $30,000. The estimated remaining economic life of the building was 30 years. The proposed lease included a five-year renewal option at a $15,000 rental. The lease did not include a provision for Draxon to acquire the property, since the two owners wished to transfer the ownership of the land and building to their heirs as part of an estate tax planning scheme. Draxon's management tentatively had concluded that this lease arrangement was acceptable. Draxon intended to borrow from English banks the funds needed to finance the working capital of its new English subsidiary. The current interest rate for long-term corporate debt in England was 8 percent.

Questions

1. How should Draxon account on the face of its 1980 financial statements for its existing and contemplated leases?
2. How should the sale and leaseback of the New York property be reflected in the 1980 statements?

CASE 22-2

Crime Control, Inc.
Lessor Accounting for Sales

On October 14, 1983, Crime Control, Inc., issued the following press release:

FOR IMMEDIATE RELEASE

INDIANAPOLIS, IND., Oct. 14, 1983—Crime Control, Inc. (NASDAQ: CRIM), announced today that as a result of Radio Shack's proposed plan to institute its own in-house security alarm systems, replacing in the future the service Crime Control provides, that Radio Shack has indicated it does not presently plan to exercise its "bargain renewal options" under the approximately 2500 leases in effect between the companies.

According to James W. Clark, Jr., chairman of the board and president, "Crime Control and Radio Shack are attempting to determine the best course of action for both companies. Negotiations have commenced to determine if Radio Shack wishes to purchase our equipment or continue to lease it through existing contracts that expire from 1985 through 1988. Crime Control may be required to write off the effect of the three-year renewal period; however, in the event of a sale of the systems to Radio Shack, the net investment in the leases would be written off against the proceeds received from Radio Shack."

Mr. Clark added, "Crime Control has its equipment in 2500 company-owned Radio Shack stores. Presently, Radio Shack represents approximately 9 percent of Crime Control's monthly recurring billing, but amounts to only 2–3 percent of total annual revenues. This number is expected to decrease to 5 percent of monthly recurring billing and 1 percent of total annual revenues upon completion of the proposed Alarmex acquisition scheduled to close in 1983. In the meantime, we are confident that the possible loss of this business will not have a significant effect on Crime Control's future earnings."

The stock market reacted very unfavorably to Crime Control's press release. On volume of 316,200 shares, Crime Control's common stock closed at $18 per share on October 14, off $3.25 (15.3 percent) from its close of $21.25 on October 13. The stock continued to drift downward subsequent

This case was prepared by Norman J. Bartczak.

to the October 14 announcement, closing at a 1983 low of $13.75 a share on October 27.

On October 27, 1983, Crime Control issued the following press release containing its estimate of the economic effect of Radio Shack's action:

FOR IMMEDIATE RELEASE

INDIANAPOLIS, IND., Oct. 27, 1983—Crime Control, Inc. (NASDAQ: CRIM), announced today that due to Radio Shack's intention of not renewing its three-year bargain renewal options under their alarm system leases with the Company, Crime Control has revised their earnings estimates for the year ended December 31, 1983.

According to James W. Clark, Jr., chairman of the board and president, "If Radio Shack elects to purchase the alarm systems presently in use, the unusual and nonrecurring charge may be immaterial. However, if they do not purchase the equipment, Crime Control's earnings for 1983 will be adversely effected [sic] by approximately $.30 per share. [Prior to the Radio Shack action, Crime Control had been projecting earnings per share of $1.28 for all of 1983, and net income of $4.3 million on revenues of $41.0 million.] This would result in Crime Control reporting earnings of approximately $1 per share for 1983, an increase of 25 percent over 1982 earnings of $.80 per share."

Mr. Clark concluded, "Our previous estimates for 1984 of $80 million in total revenues and $2 earnings per share remain unchanged."

On November 15, 1983, Crime Control issued its third-quarter report to shareholders (Exhibit 1), announcing record revenues and earnings for the company. On volume of 37,600 shares, Crime Control's stock closed at $14.50 per share on November 15, up $.25 from its close on November 14.

Company Background

Crime Control, Inc. (CCI) was incorporated under the laws of the State of Indiana on December 30, 1977, CCI designs, installs, services, and monitors from a remote location electronic security systems used primarily to protect businesses against burglaries and fires. Upon receiving an alarm signal, CCI's monitoring personnel summon the appropriate police or fire department and notify the customer. CCI's systems sometimes are also used to monitor such conditions as electric power interruptions, freezer temperature suitability, water pressure adequacy, and flooding. CCI also markets closed circuit television systems, card access systems, remote environmental control systems for buildings, and medical emergency alert systems.

CCI specifies and procures, but does not manufacture, the components of its systems and has no plans to engage in such manufacturing. Some system assembling of the various components is typically conducted by CCI's installation personnel.

A substantial majority of CCI's systems are leased by commercial enterprises, typically retail establishments. The remainder are leased or have been sold, mainly to residential and governmental customers. Substantially all users of CCI's systems are required to contract for both monitoring and maintenance. CCI's security system aggreements normally combine a lease of the alarm system (or a portion of the system) with an agreement for monitoring and report services. The minimum term for "sales-type" leases its typically a fixed noncancelable term of five years with three-year bargain renewal periods, while the minimum term for CCI's "operating" leases is typically three years. In the case of commercial and other lease customers, CCI generally retains ownership of all alarm system equipment and can thereby retain certain tax benefits.

Leasing Policies

As a result of its acquisition in mid-1983 of Houston-based McCane-Sondock Protection Systems, Inc., CCI currently has a mix of approximately 50 percent operating leases and 50 percent sales-type capital leases. This represents a significant shift from CCI's previous mix of 10 percent operating leases and 90 percent capital leases. According to CCI, "this shift will continue with its pending Alarmex acquisition." However, CCI also points out that "the capitalization of leases will remain a major measure of company growth as 'capital lease sales' are reported in the financial statements. Most new customers' system leases are reported as sales with all costs reflected against the sales revenue. Therefore, sales figures are an accurate pulse that measure true growth."

Under the operating lease method of accounting the amounts billed to lessees are recorded as revenue as earned and the cost of the equipment is depreciated over 10 years. According to CCI, this will result in a steady stream of contractual revenues being reflected as "service and monitoring fees" which, based upon the present level of operating leases, will amount to approximately $8 million in the next 12 months. In 1986, CCI's leases which were accounted for as sales-type leases in 1978 will become operating leases if they are renewed by the lessees. In each subsequent year, the sales-type capital leases entered into eight years earlier, if renewed, will also become operating leases.

CCI normally requires customers leasing systems to enter into a lease for a term of at least five years (60 months), with a "bargain renewal" option for at least one additional three-year (36-month) period. The renewal period is a bargain renewal in part because the initial rental rate for each renewal period will be at least 10 percent less than the rate at the expiration of the preceding term. According to CCI, it "is required to account for these long-term leases as 'sales-type' leases under the 'capital lease' method of accounting since the lease term exceeds 75 percent of the estimated economic life of the equipment (10 years). That method of accounting attempts

EXHIBIT 1
Crime Control, Inc.

Third-Quarter 1983 Report to Shareholders

	Nine-Month Periods Ended September 30		Three-Month Periods Ended September 30	
	1983	1982	1983	1982
Revenues:				
Equipment sales—lease	$16,071,766	$10,769,020	$ 5,552,450	$3,811,850
Equipment sales—direct	1,034,943	856,002	518,697	314,058
Service and monitoring fees on sales-type leases	1,781,467	1,042,562	665,976	409,077
Interest earned on sales-type leases	3,436,406	2,712,881	1,314,938	1,014,197
Monitoring fees on operating leases	3,587,515	288,575	2,152,775	154,392
Other	914,021	624,709	560,232	151,880
	$26,826,118	$16,293,749	$10,765,068	$5,855,454
Expenses:				
Cost of equipment sold	$ 2,094,913	$ 2,200,075	$ 908,315	$ 756,800
Salaries and wages	6,946,166	3,692,844	2,862,160	1,434,393
Administrative and general	6,001,797	2,993,830	2,809,044	1,049,232
Provision for doubtful accounts	1,404,771	1,094,338	60,657	461,462
Taxes, other than on income	625,142	297,565	271,045	97,270
Interest	2,918,759	2,309,868	1,107,126	716,934
Depreciation	648,253	305,474	279,836	117,339
Amortization of intangible assets	934,216	539,539	286,214	191,244
	$21,574,017	$13,433,533	$ 8,584,397	$4,824,674
Income before provision for income taxes	$ 5,252,101	$ 2,860,216	$ 2,180,671	$1,030,780
Provision for income taxes—deferred	2,298,000	887,000	954,000	320,000
Net income	$ 2,954,101	$ 1,973,216	$ 1,226,671	$ 710,780
Earnings per share	$.95	$.74	$.34	$.26

I am honored to have been elected chairman of the board and president of Crime Control on October 4, 1983. It gives me great pleasure to report our third-quarter results for 1983 which show record revenues and earnings.

Revenues for the three months ended September 30, 1983, were up by 84 percent to $10,765,068 compared to $5,855,454 for the same period in 1982. Net income increased by 73 percent to $1,226,671 or $.34 per share versus $710,780 or $.26 per share for the same period a year ago.

The nine-month results in 1983 also showed new record levels with revenues of $26,826,118 (up 65 percent) and net income of $2,954,101 (up 50 percent) compared to $16,293,749 and $1,973,216, respectively, for the same period in 1982. Earnings per share were $.95 for the nine months in 1983 compared to $.74 in 1982, with weighted average shares outstanding increased significantly by the 1,210,000 share offering of common stock on July 21, 1983.

Your company experienced strong retail sales growth from its Houston, Texas, market in the third quarter. We expect this trend to continue in subsequent quarters.

Negotiations with Radio Shack regarding the sale of the alarm systems leased from

Crime Control are continuing and are expected to conclude during the fourth quarter. Therefore, the effect of the previously announced nonrecurring charge (resulting from Radio Shack's intention not to renew its bargain renewal options under its leases with Crime Control) has not been recorded in the third quarter.

The Alarmex acquisition is on schedule for an early December closing. The purchase of Alarmex represents our first entry into the California/West Coast market which is one of the three primary growth areas targeted by Crime Control, along with Texas and Florida.

As we enter into our second Five-Year Plan, the outlook has never been better for continued growth and greater profitability.

We appreciate your loyalty and continued support.

James W. Clark, Jr.
Chairman and President

	September 30, 1983	December 31, 1982
Assets:		
Cash and temporary cash investments	$ 6,221,891	$ 5,716,571
Net investment in sales-type leases	39,212,764	26,082,236
Nonnegotiable certificate of deposit	3,200,000	4,000,000
Inventory	2,253,507	1,369,021
Property and equipment, net	6,485,510	2,114,656
Purchased rights to customer lists, net	6,478,346	4,117,386
Excess of purchase price over fair value of acquired assets	10,607,480	—
Other	4,163,300	2,045,128
	$78,622,798	$45,444,998
Liabilities:		
Notes payable	$12,821,478	$ 4,170,698
Convertible subordinated debentures	20,000,000	20,000,000
Notes payable—shareholders	3,200,000	4,000,000
Deferred income taxes	3,694,000	1,396,000
Other	2,667,212	1,892,315
	$42,382,690	$31,459,013
Shareholders' equity:		
Common stock, $1 par value, 15 million and 5 million shares authorized, respectively	$ 4,009,414	$ 2,798,868
Additional paid-in capital	27,104,199	9,014,723
Retained earnings	5,126,495	2,172,394
	$36,240,108	$13,985,985
	$78,622,798	$45,444,998

to reflect the economic reality of certain leases which, in part because of the length of their term relative to the useful economic life of the equipment, more closely resemble sales than leases."

Under the sales-type capital lease method of accounting, the aggregate payments due under a long-term lease (including the bargain renewal period) are deemed to consist of a "sales price," interest on such sales price (as if the "sale" were financed by CCI), and monthly provisions for service and monitoring payments. In accordance with this method of accounting, CCI records as revenue from the "lease sale," at the inception of the lease, an amount equivalent to the "sales price" of its systems, which consists of the present value of the aggregate payments attributable to such system due over the 96 months of the lease. This is calculated by aggregating the present value of the 96 monthly installments (net of estimated costs of servicing and monitoring), each discounted at the rate implicit in the lease (which normally has approximated 2 percent over the prevailing prime rate as of the inception of the lease). Once the present value is recognized as revenue, the amount recorded is unaffected by any subsequent change in the prime rate. The balance of the payments under the lease contract (net of servicing and monitoring costs) not immediately recognized is recorded as unearned interest and recognized as interest income monthly over the life of the lease. For example, if the implicit rate were 13 percent, approximately 63 percent of the aggregate rentals (net of servicing and monitoring costs) would be recorded at the inception of the lease, with the remainder being recorded over the term of the lease. If the implicit rate were less than 13 percent, a greater portion of the aggregate net rentals would be recorded at the inception of the lease and, conversely, if the implicit rate were greater than 13 percent, more of the aggregate net rentals would be recorded over the term of the lease. The portion of the lease payments representing income for servicing and monitoring the system is recognized as revenue monthly over the term of the lease contract. All direct costs of the system, including cost of goods sold and selling and installation expenses (but excluding financing costs), are expensed at the time of reporting the lease sale. Although CCI's long-term leases are accounted for as sales-type leases, no sale of the equipment is involved and CCI retains ownership of all systems subject to such leases, thereby also availing itself of the tax benefits and residual values related to the equipment.

The following hypothetical example illustrates the impact (before indirect expenses) of a typical sales-type lease transaction at the inception of the lease, assuming a $600 installation fee, a $60 monthly lease payment of which $10 per month is allocated to the executory costs related to service and monitoring, a 96-month lease term (initial 60-month term plus 36-month bargain renewal period), a residual value of the leased property of $100, an implicit interest rate of 13 percent and direct expenses of $1,800. All direct costs of the system, including cost of goods sold and all selling and

Balance sheet (impact at lease inception):

Cash (installation fee)			$ 600
Total minimum lease payments receivable (96 months at $60 per month)	$ 5,760		
Amounts allocated to service and monitoring (96 months at $10 per month)	(960)		
Minimum lease payments receivable	$ 4,800		
Allowance for doubtful accounts (1.25 percent of the total minimum lease payments receivable)	(72)		
Net minimum lease payments receivable		$ 4,728	
Estimated residual value of leased property *(b)*		100	
Unearned interest income *(c)*:			
Equipment portion *(a)*	$(1,793)		
Residual value portion *(b)*	(64)		
		(1,857)	
Net investment in sales-type lease			2,971
Accounts payable (direct expenses)			(1,800)
Addition to net assets before indirect expenses			$ 1,771

Income statement (impact at lease inception):

Installation fee	$ 600		
Present value of $4,800 minimum lease payments *(a)*	3,007		
Equipment sales lease		$ 3,607	
Reduction of cost of equipment sold (present value of the $100 residual value of leased property) *(b)*		36	
Provision for doubtful accounts		(72)	
Income before expenses			$ 3,571
Direct expenses.......................................			1,800
Income before indirect expenses			$ 1,771

(a) "Minimum lease payments receivable" ($4,800) has a present value of $3,007 calculated by discounting at 13 percent (1.08 percent per month) on an "annuity due" basis (payments due at the beginning of each month). The difference between $4,800 and $3,007 is the financing cost ($1,793) of the equipment portion of the lease to the subscriber and unearned interest income to CCI.

(b) The present value, discounted at 13 percent annual interest (calculated monthly as above), of the $100 estimated residual value of the leased equipment is $36. The difference between $100 and $36 is also unearned interest income to CCI.

(c) "Unearned interest income" is recognized monthly to produce a constant periodic rate of return on the "net investment in the sales-type lease."

installation expenses, but excluding financing costs, are expensed at the time of recognizing each lease sale.

CCI attempts to recover increases in financing costs, maintenance, and other expenses through periodic increases in lease charges. Although CCI is generally permitted under the terms of its leasing and service agreements to make such increases, customers have the right to cancel their agreements in lieu of accepting such increases. The installation charges that generally would be incurred by a customer in changing companies tend to discourage such cancellations, as long as CCI's service has been satisfactory. Although CCI has experienced cancellations in response to rate increase notices, to date such cancellations have been minimal. CCI currently provides an allowance for doubtful accounts of 1.25 percent of its lease contract receivables. In the event of a default or cancellation by a lessee, CCI writes off the remaining net investment in the lease against the allowance.

Acquisitions

According to CCI,

Acquisitions are an integral part of CCI's growth strategy. CCI is continually evaluating possible acquisition candidates as a means of economically expanding into new market areas and increasing its business in existing markets. Acquisitions in geographic areas targeted as new regional centers expand CCI's potential customer base, facilitate its marketing efforts to new subscribers in the area, and allow CCI to service such customers more quickly and profitably than in an area where CCI has no start-up base. Following such an acquisition, CCI will typically increase the sales force. Subsequent acquisitions in the same area are also desirable, principally because they result in lower operating costs per customer due to the economies of scale inherent in greater utilization of the monitoring and servicing capability of the central station. In the future, CCI also intends to expand into areas not targeted as new regional centers through the acquisition of numerous small alarm companies located throughout the country. CCI believes that, because the protective service industry historically has been fragmented, there are numerous attractive candidates available.

Through December 31, 1982, CCI acquired certain assets and customer lists of 12 companies in the central station alarm business. Following each acquisition, CCI salesmen called upon the acquired company's customers to convert them to CCI's standard long-term lease contract. By one year after an acquisition, usually 70 percent to 85 percent of the acquired customers have executed long-term contracts.

From January 1, 1983, through November 15, 1983, CCI made the following acquisitions:

Company	Location	Date Acquired	Acquisition Price	Monthly Billings
Crimefighters Systems	Ft. Lauderdale	March 21, 1983	$ 297,000	$ 10,000
Alarm Engineers, Inc.	Houston, Texas	May 2, 1983	3,645,000	120,000
McCane-Sondock Protection Systems	Houston, Texas	June 7, 1983	16,000,000	670,000

CCI currently plans to follow its previous practice and convert the customers of Crimefighter Systems and Alarm Engineers to long-term contracts. However, CCI does not presently intend to convert the existing customers of McCane-Sondock, or the customers obtained in future acquisitions, to long-term contracts. As was noted earlier, CCI expects that this change in practice will substantially increase its base of operting leases that generate level recurring revenues over their terms.

CCI expects to close the acquisition of Alarmex, a West Coast firm, for $21.4 million in cash in December. Alarmex has $17 million in annual revenues and pre-tax income of $5.2 million. Its 11 operating locations serve 23,000 accounts in California, Nevada, Washington, and Texas. At present, CCI expects to finance the bulk of the Alarmex purchase from the remaining funds available to it from its $30 million revolving bank credit. The acquisition of Alarmex will increase CCI's accounts to 49,000 from its present 26,000.

Competition

Much of the protective service industry has historically been fragmented with numerous small companies competing for customers in local areas. In addition, several major firms such as American District Telegraph (ADT), Wells Fargo Alarm Services (owned by Borg-Warner), Holmes Protection, and Honeywell, Inc. (which together presently service more than 50 percent of the security market), offer security systems to customers located throughout the country. CCI must thus compete not only with local alarm businesses present in its markets but also with larger national companies, many of which charge less for their systems than CCI charges. However, CCI believes that its marketing efforts and the quality of its systems make it one of the predominant competitors in each of its primary market areas.

Although technological advances have not historically been a significant competitive factor, the protective alarm industry may be susceptible to changes in technology which could adversely affect CCI's competitive ability. Furthermore, none of CCI's systems is covered by patents (which is not unusual in the protective alarm industry) and the technology utilized in CCI's systems is available to competitors. Nevertheless, CCI believes that it can continue to compete favorably. Because CCI purchases all the component devices used in its systems, it believes it can upgrade its systems as new technology emerges and becomes available through existing or new vendors. Moreover, CCI's existing customers have either purchased their systems outright or, more frequently, leased such systems for a long-term period, thus placing much of the risk of obsolescence on customers.

The total market for private security equipment and services is estimated to be about $15 billion for 1983. Predicasts, Inc., a Cleveland-based research firm, has estimated the market to grow between 10 percent and 15 percent a year for the next 10 years, suggesting a tripling of the market by the early 1990s.

Management and Stock Ownership

Directors and Executive Officers

Name	Position	As of 12/31/82 Remuneration	At 6/30/83 Shares Owned
Donald R. Gray Age—37	Consultant (a)	$206,500	1,074,605 (a)
James W. Bowman Age—39	Director and vice president—technical operations	100,000	689,065
James W. Clark, Jr. Age—31	Director, chairman of the board, and president (b)	100,000	163,830 (a)
E. Davis Coots Age—39	Director and secretary, partner—Coots, Henke, & Wheeler	N/A	525
John W. Biddinger Age—43	Director, president—Biddinger Investment Capital Corporation	125,000 (c)	5,500
Joseph Shaeffer Age—41	Vice president—national sales	154,632 (d)	N/A
James Walker Age—33	Vice president—operations	88,424	N/A
J. Jeffry Berty Age—29	Controller and chief accounting officer	<50,000	N/A

(a) Until October 4, 1983, Mr. Gray was chairman of the board and president. On or about October 4, 1983, Mr. Gray sold 202,868 shares to Mr. Clark and granted Mr. Clark an option to purchase 405,737 of Mr. Gray's shares until October 3, 1985. In addition, Mr. Gray granted Mr. Clark a proxy to vote 210,000 of Mr. Gray's shares. These transactions, along with similar transactions between Mr. Bowman and Mr. Clark, give Mr. Clark control over approximately 35 percent of CCI's common stock.

(b) Until October 4, 1983, Mr. Clark was vice president—finance, treasurer (principal financial officer), and assistant secretary.

(c) Represents consulting fees paid to Mr. Biddinger.

(d) Mr. Shaeffer is compensated on a commission basis.

EXHIBIT 2
Crime Control, Inc.
Selected Excerpts from 1982 Annual Report

Selected Financial Data

	Years Ended December 31				
	1982	1981	1980	1979	1978
Revenues	$22,756,586	$14,671,120	$5,838,116	$2,882,746	$ 685,631
Income before provision for federal income taxes	3,568,394	2,011,311	1,649,310	867,673	159,275
Net Income (a)	2,172,394	1,392,311	926,310	508,673	97,275
Net income per share (a) (b)	$.80	$.70	$.46	$.25	$.05
Weighted average shares outstanding (b)	2,729,679	2,000,000	2,000,000	2,000,000	2,000,000
Total assets	45,444,998	25,427,255	9,777,314	3,709,176	611,061
Debt obligations	28,170,698	18,602,277	6,529,007	2,491,047	393,197
Total liabilities	31,459,013	20,711,872	7,073,242	2,654,414	485,972
Shareholders' equity	13,985,985	4,715,383	2,704,072	1,054,762	125,089

(a) A pro forma provision for federal income tax has been deducted as if the company had been a taxable corporation for the years 1979 through 1981, during which it was a Subchapter S corporation.

(b) Reflects the 2,000-for-1 stock split effected December 14, 1981.

EXHIBIT 2 *(continued)*

To our shareholders:

In just five years, Crime Control ranks among the fastest growing companies in the expanding security alarm industry. From 500 customers and total assets of $100,000 in 1978, Crime Control has grown to over 12,000 customers in 48 states and Puerto Rico and total assets of $45 million at year-end 1982. For the year ended December 31, 1982, Crime Control reported a revenue increase of 55 percent, rising to $22.8 million from $14.7 million. Net income for the year climbed to $2.2 million, equals to $.80 per share, compared to $1.4 million, equal to $.70 per share in 1981. Per-share figures include a 35 percent increase in common shares outstanding for 1982.

While revenues and income from operations posted strong gains, net income was affected by fourth-quarter adjustments. The primary adjustment was a higher provision for federal income tax in 1982 which resulted in an $.11 per-share reduction.

Acquisitions

While maintaining our growth through internal expansion, Crime Control also strengthened its external growth through its successful acquisition program. During 1982, the company acquired three companies in South Florida and two in Washington, D.C.–Baltimore. These acquisitions increased our market penetration and the addition of those companies furthers economies of scale and more efficient operations.

In March 1983, Crime Control announced one more acquisition in Fort Lauderdale, Florida, and set the stage for our initial entrance into the important Texas market by agreeing to acquire Alarm Engineers, Inc., one of the five largest alarm service companies in Houston. While Alarm Engineers represents the first of several planned acquisitions in Houston, we intend to establish a regional operational center there to monitor customers throughout the state of Texas. Our philosophy is to enter a market and establish Crime Control as the leading alarm company within that area in a period of two to three years.

Balance Sheet Strengthened

In addition to our initial public offering last year of $7.25 million, we completed a $20 million public placement of convertible debentures in November of 1982. At year-end, we had negotiated a line of credit for up to $30 million with a new group of banks. We are relying on this new line of credit to add greater flexibility to our acquisition program and allow us to finance the strong increase we are expecting in the leased sales of our equipment in our major markets.

During the year, we also reduced our debt-to-equity ratio to 1.73 to 1, compared to 3.10 to 1 in 1981. At the same time, book value per share increased 118 percent to $5.12 compared to $2.35 a year ago.

Looking Ahead

Major goals were achieved in 1982, but management expects 1983 to be the greatest year in Crime Control's history.

We expect that our customer base will double resulting in increased revenues.

Our planned regional center in Houston is expected to be firmly established and ready to provide a solid foundation for future growth throughout the state of Texas. Internal promotion and external recruiting are expected to strengthen the management team and insure the depth of management necessary to handle our anticipated future growth. Crime Control is planning a nationwide network of working affiliates of approximately 200 independent security businesses. And finally, we are pleased to report that the financial resources are in place to finance our planned growth for 1983.

Respectfully submitted,

Donald R. Gray
President

EXHIBIT 2 *(continued)*

Statement of Financial Position,
December 31, 1980, 1981, 1982

	1982	*1981*	*1980*
Assets			
Cash and temporary cash investments, at cost which approximates market (note 4)	$ 5,716,571	$ 1,208,051	$1,045,900
Net investment in sales-type leases (note 3)	26,082,236	14,101,116	5,591,852
Accounts receivable	677,820	963,780	465,300
Nonnegotiable certificates of deposit (note 7)	4,000,000	4,000,000	
Inventory (note 1)	1,369,021	1,083,554	374,600
Property and equipment, net (note 5)	2,114,656	1,384,554	881,530
Purchased rights to customer lists, net	4,117,386	2,294,225	1,405,700
Unamortized debt expense (note 6)	1,040,382	—	
Deferred charge, costs incurred on stock offering (note 9)		342,432	
Other assets	326,926	49,543	12,100
Total assets	$45,444,998	$25,427,255	$9,777,314
Liabilities			
Accounts payable—trade	$ 747,754	$ 901,727	$ 341,900
Accounts payable—other	183,136	269,536	
Accrued interest and other expenses	961,425	938,332	202,200
Notes payable (note 6)	4,170,698	14,602,277	6,529,000
Convertible subordinated debentures (note 6)	20,000,000	—	
Notes payable—shareholders (note 7)	4,000,000	4,000,000	
Deferred income taxes	1,396,000	—	
Total liabilities	$31,459,013	$20,711,872	$7,073,242
Shareholders' Equity			
Common stock, no par value, stated value $1 per share, 5 million shares authorized; issued and outstanding—2,798,868 shares in 1982, 2 million shares in 1981 and 1980 (note 9)	$ 2,798,868	$ 11,160	$ 11,100
Additional paid-in capital	9,014,723	4,704,223	1,418,600
Retained earnings (note 9)	2,172,394	—	1,274,200
Total shareholders' equity	$13,985,985	$ 4,715,383	$2,704,072
Total liabilities and shareholders' equity	$45,444,998	$25,427,255	$9,777,314

Statement of Income
Years Ended December 31, 1980, 1981, 1982

	1982	*1981*	*1980*
Revenues			
Equipment sales—lease	$15,148,186	$10,311,476	$4,354,852
Equipment sales—direct	1,020,362	958,456	342,449
Service and monitoring fees	2,107,214	1,943,620	594,234
Interest earned on leases	3,571,040	1,436,573	524,311
Other, including $775,778 interest income on temporary cash investments in 1982	909,784	20,995	22,270
	$22,756,586	$14,671,120	$5,838,116

EXHIBIT 2 *(continued)*

Statement of Income
Years Ended December 31, 1980, 1981, 1982

	1982	*1981*	*1980*
Expenses:			
Cost of equipment sold	$ 2,954,977	$ 2,569,900	$ 878,199
Salaries and wages	5,654,615	3,830,023	1,219,014
Administrative and general	3,941,100	2,654,000	1,067,107
Provision for doubtful accounts	1,453,354	560,167	110,680
Taxes, other than on income	504,364	269,426	78,326
Interest	3,403,097	1,938,694	566,091
Depreciation	489,561	290,363	136,531
Amortization of purchased rights to customer lists ...	787,124	547,236	132,858
	$19,188,192	$12,659,809	$4,188,806
Income before provision for income taxes	$ 3,568,394	$ 2,011,311	$1,649,310
Provision for income taxes—deferred	1,396,000	—	—
Net income	$ 2,172,394	$ 2,011,311	$1,649,310
Provision for income taxes—pro forma		619,000	723,000
Pro forma net income		$ 1,392,311	$ 926,310
Earnings per share	$.80	$.70	$.46

Statement of Changes in Shareholders' Equity
1980, 1981, 1982

	Common Stock		Additional Paid-In Capital	Retained Earnings
	Shares Issued	Amount		
Balance at January 1, 1980	1,000	$ 11,160	$ 618,654	$ 424,948
Cash dividends paid	—	—	—	(800,000)
Contribution by shareholders	—	—	800,000	—
Net income	—	—	—	1,649,310
Balance at December 31, 1980	1,000	$ 11,160	$1,418,654	$1,274,258
Net income	—	—	—	2,011,311
2,000-for-1 stock split (note 9)	1,999,000	—	—	
Transfer of retained earnings balance to additional paid-in capital (note 9)	—	—	3,285,569	(3,285,569)
Balance at December 31, 1981	2,000,000	$ 11,160	$4,704,223	—
Net income	—	—	—	$2,172,394
Shares sold to the public, net of expenses	725,000	725,000	5,413,656	—
Shares issued upon conversion of Wackenhut note (note 2)	38,766	38,766	248,734	—
Shares issued to acquire Security Engineering, Inc. (note 2)	35,102	35,102	636,950	—
Adjustment to reflect $1 per share stated value of common stock	—	1,988,840	(1,988,840)	
Balance at December 31, 1982	2,798,868	$2,798,868	$9,014,723	$2,172,394

EXHIBIT 2 *(continued)*

Statement of Changes in Financial Position
Years Ended December 31, 1980, 1981, 1982

	1982	*1981*	*1980*
Source of Funds:			
Net income	$ 2,172,394	$ 2,011,311	$ 1,649,310
Items not requiring (providing) funds in the current period:			
Increase in sales-type leases	(13,434,474)	(9,075,431)	(3,471,194)
Provision for doubtful accounts	1,453,354	560,167	110,680
Depreciation and amortization	1,276,685	837,599	269,389
Deferred income taxes	1,396,000	—	—
Other	2,673	(3,449)	1,605
Total used in operations	$(7,133,368)	$(5,669,803)	$(1,440,210)
Net proceeds from subordinated convertible debenture offering	18,951,284	—	—
Net proceeds from public equity offering	6,138,656	—	—
Increase in notes payable		8,073,270	4,037,960
Increase in notes payable-shareholders		4,000,000	—
Additional capital contributed by shareholders		—	800,000
Common shares issued in acquisition	672,052	—	—
Common shares issued upon conversion of Wackenhut note	287,500	—	—
Decrease in accounts receivable	285,960	—	—
Increase in accounts payable and accrued liabilities	(130,880)	1,295,824	380,868
Other, net	3,473	(14,572)	70,392
	$19,074,677	$ 7,684,719	$ 3,849,010
Application of Funds:			
Decrease in notes payable, net of new borrowings of $10,892,910	$10,431,579	—	—
Purchase of nonnegotiable certificate of deposit . .		$ 4,000,000	—
Purchase of rights to customer lists	2,610,285	1,435,734	$ 1,299,721
Purchase of property and equipment	1,238,826	879,609	732,211
Cash dividends paid		—	800,000
Increase in accounts receivable		498,459	337,242
Increase in inventory	285,467	708,865	140,581
	$14,566,157	$ 7,522,667	$ 3,309,755
Increase in cash and temporary cash investments	$ 4,508,520	$ 162,052	$ 539,255

Notes to Financial Statements

1. Summary of Significant Accounting Policies:

Crime Control, Inc. (the company) provides electronic alarm systems, including service and monitoring, to commerical and residential customers.

Sales-type leases:

Sales-type lease receivables include equipment sales, service, and monitoring and are generally due in monthly or quarterly installments over a term of five years with a bargain renewal option for an additional three years. The bargain renewal option allows the lessee

the option to renew at 10 percent less than the rental rate in effect at the expiration of the initial lease term. The company believes there is reasonable assurance that its customers will exercise the bargain renewal option based upon the scheduled rent reduction, an industry average customer life of 10 to 13 years, and the "penalty" the customer would incur in the form of an installation fee to change to different equipment. The leases have been accounted for as sales-type leases under the provisions of *Statement of Financial Accounting Standards (SFAS) No. 13* since the lease term exceeds 75 percent of the estimated economic life of the equipment (10 years).

Income recognition:

Income is recognized on equipment sales when the equipment is delivered and installed. Income from service and monitoring is recognized as income on a straight-line basis over the term of the contract. Unearned interest income on lease contracts receivable is amortized to income over the lease term so as to produce a constant periodic rate of return on the net investment in the lease.

Operating leases:

Rentals and monitoring fees relating to operating leases, generally related to companies acquired, are recorded as billed. Such customers are generally billed monthly.

Inventory:

The inventory of equipment held for sale or lease and related repair parts is stated at the lower cost (first-in, first-out method) or market.

Property and equipment:

Property and equipment are recorded at cost. Depreciation is computed on the straight-line method over the estimated useful lives as follows:

Vehicles	3 years
Furniture and equipment and computer equipment	5–10 years
Purchased alarm systems	8 years

Leasehold improvements are amortized over the lease term (five years).

The cost, less related accumulated depreciation, of purchased alarm systems under contracts converted to sales-type leases is charged to cost of equipment sold at the date of conversion. The cost of systems remaining under operating leases is depreciated on the straight-line method over the remaining estimated useful lives of the equipment.

Purchased rights to customer lists:

The excess of cost of purchased alarm system companies over the fair value of the tangible assets acquired is ascribed to the unexpired portion of existing lease contracts and the customer list. Such costs are amortized over 96 months. The company uses the sum-of-the-years'-digits method during the initial two-year period during which many of the custom-

ers are expected to be converted to long-term, sales-type leases, and the straight-line method thereafter. The accumulated amortization was $1,531,316, $744,192, and $196,956 at December 31, 1982, 1981, and 1980, respectively.

Bonus arrangements:

The company has no established bonus or incentive compensation plans. The board of directors awarded a discretionary bonus of $50,000 in 1981.

Federal and state income taxes:

During 1981 and 1980, the company was not subject to income taxes because of an election under Subchapter S of the Internal Revenue Code. Under Subchapter S, the shareholders consented to the inclusion of the effects of the company's operations in their own federal and state income tax returns. The provision for income taxes—pro forma is the approximate expense which would have been incurred in 1981 and 1980 assuming the company had no Subchapter S election.

Deferred income taxes are provided on income and expenses recognized in different periods for financial reporting purposes than for income tax purposes. Deferred income tax results principally from the reporting of the sales-type leases as operating leases for tax purposes.

Earnings per share:

Earnings per share is computed based on net income for 1982 and pro forma net income for 1981 and 1980 using the weighted average number of common and common equivalent shares outstanding after adjustment for the 1981 stock split (see note 9). Common stock equivalents result from dilutive stock options and warrants computed using the treasury stock method and shares contingently issuable related to an acquisition described in note 2. The number of shares used was 2,729,679 for 1982 and 2 million for 1981 and 1980. Fully diluted earnings per share assumes conversion of the convertible debentures, but is not significantly different and is therefore not separately reported.

2. Acquisitions:

During 1980, the company expanded its customer base through the acquisition of certain assets of two alarm system companies. In May 1980, certain assets (primarily a customer list plus inventory and equipment at Miami, Flo-

EXHIBIT 2 *(continued)*

rida) were purchased from Farrey's Wholesale Hardware, Inc., for cash ($71,000) and a 6 percent, $200,930 note (present value of $127,612 with interest imputed at 21 percent. In November 1980, the assets of Alarm Services Corporation, doing business as Beltway Alarm Services Company (Beltway), an alarm system company located near Washington, D.C., were purchased for $1.3 million cash and a $1,136,452 note including interest at 6 percent (present value of $704,118 with interest imputed at 18 percent).

During 1981, the company acquired certain assets of two additional alarm system companies, both of which had been operated as divisions of larger corporations. In March 1981, the company purchased the customer list and some other assets of Seaboard Service System, Ltd. (Seaboard), a division of Peoples Drug Stores, Incorporated, located near Washington, D.C., for $300,000 in cash and a $450,000 note including interest at 6 percent (present value of $377,792 with interest imputed at 17.5 percent). The note was repaid in February 1982 from the proceeds of the public stock offering. In July 1981, the assets of the Miami Alarms Division of Wackenhut Electronic Systems Corporation (Wackenhut) were purchased for $500,000 cash, a $600,000, 15 percent promissory note and a $575,000, 6 percent convertible promissory note. Wackenhut exercised its option following the company's public stock offering to convert one half of the principal amount of the $575,000 note into 38,766 shares of common stock and to receive the remainder in cash.

In January 1982, the company acquired certain assets and rights to its customer list from D. J. Enterprises, Inc. (doing business as Bur-tell II), for cash ($440,000) and a deferred payment of $110,000, including interest at 9 percent due in February 1983. The company is negotiating an adjustment to the final settlement of the purchase price due to termination of purchased customers. The $110,000 deferred payment is not expected to be required and therefore has not been recorded as a liability. The majority of the $440,000 has been allocated to purchased rights to customers lists with the balance allocated to installed alarm equipment. Any further adjustment in the purchase price will be added to or subtracted from purchased rights to customer lists.

In June 1982, the company acquired certain assets of Security Controls, Inc., a McLean, Virginia, alarm company, for approximately $400,000 in cash. The company filed suit against the seller for breach of certain terms of the acquisition contract and in March 1983 agreed to accept $25,000 as full settlement of the dispute. The adjustment will reduce the purchased rights to customer lists to which the majority of the purchase price was assigned.

On August 2, 1982, the company acquired certain assets of Security Engineering, Inc., a central station alarm business in the Fort Lauderdale, Florida, area. The purchase price, which is subject to adjustment, was payable in cash ($300,000 at the closing and $200,000 on the adjustment date 14 months after the closing) and by issuing 35,102 shares of common stock having a market value $14.25 per share. In addition, the company is obligated to pay additional cash or issue additional shares of common stock if, during the 90-day period commencing August 2, 1984, the highest average of the mean between the closing bid and asked prices of the company's common stock for any five consecutive trading days during such period is not at least $19.25 per share. The purchase price ($1,153,169) includes the common stock at the contingent price of $19.25 per share and is net of imputed interest of $22,544 on the $200,000 deferred payment.

In December 1982, the company acquired certain assets of North American Security Systems, Inc. (NASS), a central station alarm company in the Fort Lauderdale, Florida, area. The purchase price, which is subject to downward adjustment, was payable in cash ($430,000 at the closing and $37,000 on the adjustment date 10 months after closing). The purchase price was primarily allocated to purchased rights to customer lists.

Also in December 1982, the company acquired certain assets of Burglar Alarm Systems, Inc. (BAS), a central station alarm and monitoring business in the Fort Lauderdale, Florida, area. The purchase price, which is subject to adjustment, was payable in cash ($590,000 at the closing). The purchase price was primarily allocated to purchased rights to customer lists.

The purchase price of each of the above acquisitions, discounted in certain circumstances at the prevailing interest rate at the time of acquisition to reflect the present value of the notes payable, exceeded the fair value of the tangible assets acquired as follows:

EXHIBIT 2 *(continued)*

Selling Entity	Adjusted Purchase Price	Fair Value of Tangible Assets	Amount Allocated to Value of Purchased Rights to Customer Lists
Farrey's	$ 198,612	$ 50,380	$ 148,232
Beltway	2,004,118	848,605	1,155,513
Seaboard	677,792	21,800	655,992
Wackenhut	1,553,795	709,625	844,170
Bur-tell II	439,340	93,343	345,997
Security Controls	400,000	95,395	304,605
Security Engineering	1,153,169	224,000	929,169
NASS	466,748	100,150	366,598
BAS	711,097	68,250	642,847

All of the above acquisitions have been accounted for by the purchase method and, accordingly, results of operations have been included in the statements of income since the respective dates of acquisition.

If Wackenhut (the significant 1981 acquisition) had been acquired on January 1, 1980, and had been included in the results of operations for 1980, along with the pro forma results of Beltway as if Beltway had been acquired on January 1, 1980, the unaudited pro forma results would have been:

Revenues	$8,921,000
Net income	243,000
Net income per share	.12

If Bur-tell II, Security Engineering, and NASS had been acquired on January 1, 1981, and had been included in the results of operations for 1981, along with the pro forma results of Wackenhut as if it had been acquired on January 1, 1981, the results would have been:

Revenues	$17,155,000
Net income	668,000
Net income per share	.34

If Security Engineering and NASS had been acquired on January 1, 1982, and had been included in the results of operations for 1982, the unaudited pro forma results would have been:

Revenues	$23,253,000
Net income	1,983,000
Net income per share	.73

In management's opinion, the pro forma financial information is not necessarily indicative of the results that would have occurred or of future results of operations of the combined companies. Net income and net income per share are reduced in 1981 and 1980 by a pro forma provision for income taxes (see note 1).

The effect of the Farrey's Wholesale Hardware, Inc., results cannot be determined because the assets acquired represented a division without separate financial statements, and subsequent to the acquisition of the alarm division, all financial records of the company were destroyed in a fire in an area affected by the May 1980 riots in Miami, Florida. Based on the limited information available, management does not believe the effect of the Farrey's acquisition, if known, would be material to the company. The results of operations of Seaboard, Security Controls, and BAS are not material to the company; therefore the pro forma results do not give effect to the operations of these companies.

3. Net Investment in Sales-Type Leases:
The net investment in sales-type leases consists of the following:

	1982	1981	1980
Total minimum lease payments receivable	$56,652,947	$32,460,161	$12,814,727
Amounts allocated to service and monitoring	(11,788,453)	(6,387,817)	(2,861,869)
Minimum lease payments receivable	$44,864,494	$26,072,344	$ 9,952,858
Allowance for doubtful accounts	(570,000)	(325,000)	(130,000)
Net minimum lease payments receivable	$44,294,494	$25,747,344	$ 9,822,858
Estimated residual value of leased property	1,024,600	559,000	180,000
Unearned income	(19,236,858)	(12,205,228)	(4,411,006)
	$26,082,236	$14,101,116	$ 5,591,852

EXHIBIT 2 *(continued)*

Uncollectible accounts charged to the allowance in 1982, 1981, and 1980 were $1,208,354, $365,167, and $20,680, respectively.

Interest, ranging from 12 percent to 22 percent, has been imputed on lease receivables based on an amount normally approximating 2 percent in excess of the prime lending rate at the inception of the respective leases which management believes approxi-

ments include noninterest bearing compensating balances held by lenders pursuant to certain loan agreements of $75,000, $480,000, and $95,000 at December 31, 1982, 1981, and 1980, respectively.

5. Property and Equipment:

Property and equipment consist of the following:

	1982	1981	1980
Vehicles	$ 589,772	$ 578,543	$ 294,110
Leasehold improvements	253,609	9,106	—
Computer equipment	664,674	145,826	51,700
Furniture and equipment	1,128,737	810,738	475,720
Purchased alarm systems on operating leases	370,300	273,300	250,000
	$3,007,092	$1,817,513	$1,071,530
Accumulated depreciation	892,436	432,959	190,000
	$2,114,656	$1,384,554	$ 881,530

mates the implicit interest rate based on the creditworthiness of the lessees. In each of the next five years, approximately $7.3 million of the $56.6 million total minimum lease payments receivable matures with the balance of $20.1 million due after five years.

The residual value of the leased equipment is based on its estimated fair value at the end of the lease term.

The company has one major customer which accounted for revenues of $4,817,000, $2,985,000, and $1,060,000 in 1982, 1981, and 1980, respectively.

4. Cash and Temporary Cash Investments:

Temporary cash investments of $4,297,701 at December 31, 1982, represent money market funds earning interest at 8.4 percent. Temporary cash investments of $1 million at December 31, 1981, and $900,000 at December 31, 1980, represent repurchase agreements earning interest at 10.5 percent and 15.5 percent, respectively. Cash and temporary cash invest-

Furniture and equipment and computer equipment include gross assets acquired under capitalized leases of $485,351 at December 31, 1982; the related amount of accumulated depreciation was $48,535. Amounts at December 31, 1981, and 1980, were insignificant.

6. Debentures and Notes Payable:

In 1982, the company issued $20 million in convertible subordinated debentures due November 1, 1997, with interest payable semiannually at 10 percent. The debentures can be converted to common stock at a price of $18 per share or redeemed at the option of the company at a range of prices from 110 percent in 1984 to par value in 1996. If not earlier converted or redeemed, the debentures will require sinking fund payments of $2 million each year beginning November 1, 1988.

The cost of issuing the debentures has been deferred and is amortized to interest expense over the expected life of the debentures.

Other notes payable are as follows:

EXHIBIT 2 *(continued)*

	1982	1981	1980
Lease loans, collateralized by certain sales-type leases (paid in December 1982 with the debenture proceeds)	$ —	$ 3,898,109	$1,488,624
Equipment loans, (including $463,739 in 1982 related to capitalized leases) collateralized by equipment, payable in monthly installments of $18,242, including interest at rates ranging from 12% to 20%, with maturities from January 1983 to July 1987	781,814	656,015	282,050
Acquisition loans, payable to former owners of purchased companies with interest, or for certain notes imputed interest, at rates ranging from 13.5% to 21%	1,457,077	2,538,243	1,066,652
Line of credit for $9 million originally expiring in April, 1987, collateralized by certain lease receivables and equipment. The line was partially paid with proceeds from the debentures in December 1982 and replaced by a new line of credit in January 1983. See note 13......................	1,931,807	6,035,391	2,065,299
Payable to a bank, repaid January 1982 and 1981, respectively	—	1,000,000	900,000
Other, originally payable from January 1982 to June 1986 with interest ranging from prime plus 2% to prime plus 2½%, paid in 1982 with proceeds of the equity offering	—	474,519	726,382
	$4,170,698	**$14,602,277**	**$6,529,007**

The acquisition loans are generally collateralized by the assets purchased, and substantially all the notes are guaranteed by certain corporate officers. Certain lines of credit also require compensating balances as described in note 4.

The principal portion of notes payable due in the next five years is as follows:

Due	Amount
1983	$2,692,000
1984	572,000
1985	446,000
1986	203,000
1987	172,000
	$4,085,000
After five years	86,000
	$4,171,000

Information relating to lines of credit and certain lease loans is as follows:

capital stock, incurrence of certain indebtedness, and advances to officers and stockholders without the consent of the lenders.

7. Related Party Transactions and Commitments:

On December 31, 1981, the principal shareholders of the company loaned the company $4 million. The amount is payable in annual installments of $800,000 with interest at prime plus one half of 1 percent commencing January 1983. The note may be repaid before maturity at the option of the company or upon demand by the principal shareholders. A nonnegotiable certificate of deposit of the same amount (earning interest at 2½ percent below the prime rate, currently 9 percent) is collateral to the loan and will be redeemed in amounts equal to the note payments required. The shareholders have also pledged their shares of the company stock as collateral.

	1982	1981	1980
Average aggregate amount outstanding during the period	**$10,371,873**	$5,613,965	$570,000
Maximum amount outstanding at any month end ...	**11,681,253**	8,770,311	840,000
Weighted average interest rate during the period ...	**18.0%**	22.0%	19.9%

The loan agreements restrict payment of cash dividends, issuance and retirement of

The company previously rented its home office building from an officer of the company

EXHIBIT 2 *(continued)*

on a month-to-month basis. Related rent expense totaled $6,000, $6,000, and $5,000 for the years ended December 31, 1982, 1981, and 1980, respectively. The company leases its Beltsville, Maryland, and Virginia offices from a former officer of the company under a five-year lease expiring October 1985, requiring monthly payments of $5,128.

Minimum rentals on noncancellable operating leases for the next five years are as follows at December 31, 1982:

Year	Amount
1983	$232,016
1984	232,825
1985	228,970
1986	193,496
1987	100,760
	$988,067

In April 1982, the company entered into a lease agreement with an unrelated lessor for a new home office and central station monitoring facility. Rent payments include a minimum annual payment of $90,360 plus the company's proportionate share of the utilities, taxes, and other operating expenses of the building. The lease expires in 1987.

Total rent expense for all facilities and equipment was $373,065, $201,693, and $40,421 for years 1982, 1981, and 1980, respectively.

8. Income Taxes:

The following is a reconciliation of income taxes calculated at the federal statutory rate to the provisions for income taxes (pro forma for 1981 and 1980):

	1982	1981	1980
Provisions for taxes on income at statutory rate	**$1,641,000**	$925,000	$759,000
Investment tax credit (accounted for on the flow-through method)	**(320,000)**	(287,000)	(17,000)
Other	**75,000**	(19,000)	(19,000)
	$1,396,000	$619,000	$723,000

The election under Subchapter S of the Internal Revenue Code was automatically terminated retroactive to January 1, 1982, by the public offering on January 29, 1982. If the company had been a taxable corporation for the years 1979 to 1981, deferred income taxes at December 31, 1981, would approximate $2,160,000 resulting from the reporting of lease income on the operating method for income tax return purposes and the capital lease method for financial reporting purposes. The reversal of this timing difference will result in a provision for income taxes, and currently payable income taxes, greater than that at customary income tax rates in the absence of sufficient originating timing differences. The tax losses passed through to the shareholders for the years 1979, 1980, and 1981 (which would have been available as a corporate net operating loss carryover if not for the Subchapter S election) totaled approximately $6 million.

The company has net operating loss carryforwards of $4,572,000 at December 31, 1982, which expires as follows: $72,000—1993, $4.5 million—1997. The company also has a $320,000 investment tax credit carryforward which expires in 1992. The utilization of such carryforwards would be recorded as an increase in deferred income taxes.

9. Shareholders' Equity:

In December 1981, the company increased its authorized common stock to 5 million shares and declared a 2,000-for-1 stock split. All per-share amounts have been retroactively restated to give effect to the split.

Pursuant to the rules of the Securities and Exchange Commission regarding termination of a Subchapter S election, all retained earnings accumulated to December 31, 1981, have been transferred to additional paid-in capital.

In December 1981, the stockholders of the company approved an Employee Stock Purchase Plan for which 100,000 shares have been reserved. The plan provides all full-time employees, except beneficial holders of 5 percent or more of the company's stock, an opportunity to purchase common stock at 90 percent of fair market value. Purchases are limited to a percentage of annual compensation. No shares have been purchased under the plan.

At the same time, the stockholders ap-

EXHIBIT 2 *(continued)*

proved an Incentive Stock Option Plan for which an additional 100,000 shares have been reserved. Options may be granted to any employee, except persons who would directly or indirectly own more than 5 percent of the company's common stocks subject to certain limitations as to amount, and become exercisable proportionally over 6 years with an expiration date no later than 10 years from date of grant. On October 1, 1982, options to purchase 63,000 shares at $12.25 were granted; options are exercisable ⅓ in October 1984 and proportionally thereafter.

On February 5, 1982, the company received approximately $6.2 million, net of underwriting and other expenses, from the proceeds of a public offering of 725,000 shares of common stock. In connection with the public offering, the company sold to Thomson McKinnon Securities, Inc., five-year stock purchase warrants for 72,500 shares of common stock. The warrants can be exercised beginning on January 29, 1983, at a price of $10.70 per share. The exercise price increases by $0.70 per year thereafter.

10. Compensated Absences:

During 1982, the company initiated a vacation pay policy. *SFAS No. 43* requires that the cost of benefits such as vacations be accrued as earned. The company has expensed vacation costs as paid. Due to personnel retained at acquired companies and other factors, the amount of the accrual is not reasonably estimatable and, accordingly, the company has not accrued the liability at December 31, 1982. In 1983, management anticipates such an accrual can be estimated and will decrease net income by the cumulative effect of the accrual at December 31, 1983. The amount is not expected to be material.

11. Fourth-Quarter Results:

Fourth-quarter earnings in 1982 were decreased by a change in the annual effective tax rate to 39 percent for the year from the estimated tax rate of 31 percent used for the first nine months. The effect of this change was to decrease net income per share by approximately $0.9 through September 30, 1982, and a total of $.11 for the full year. Also, in January 1983, the company reached an agreement with Indiana Bell Telephone Company in settlement of litigation between the companies. The company has paid $100,000 ($.02 per share), which was accrued during the fourth quarter, to settle the suit.

Management believes that other fourth-quarter adjustments, if properly recorded in prior quarters, would have reduced net income per share through September 30, 1982, by approximately $.03, primarily related to inventory and interest expense adjustments.

12. Contingencies:

On January 19, 1982, the company was served with notice of a complaint alleging unauthorized use of the name "Crime Control, Inc." in the State of Maryland. The suit seeks to enjoin the company from the use of that name in Maryland and seeks an unspecified amount of compensatory and punitive damages. Management intends to vigorously contest the suit and believes that any liability resulting therefrom will not be material to the company's operations or financial condition as a whole.

13. Subsequent Events:

In January 1983, the company completed a new revolving credit and term loan agreement as of December 31, 1982, with seven participating banks for up to $30 million. The agreement provides for the company to pay interest only on the revolving credit loans to June 30, 1984, at which time they may be converted into four-year term loans. Under the terms of the agreement, the company is required to maintain specified levels of net worth, debt-to-equity ratios, and working capital. The agreement calls for interest on the revolving loans at the rate of 1 percent above prime, 1½ percent above prime on the term loans, and fees of one quarter of 1 percent on the total commitment plus one half of 1 percent on the unused commitment. Borrowings under the agreement may be prepaid without premium or penalty. The loan is collateralized by certain lease contracts, equipment, other personal property, and insurance policies on certain officers. The loan agreement requires the maintenance of compensating cash balances equal to the sum of 10 percent of the commitment under the line of credit during the commitment period and 10 percent of the aggregate principal amount of the term loans thereafter.

On March 14, 1983, the company entered into an agreement to acquire certain assets of Alarm Engineers, Inc., a Houston, Texas, alarm company for approximately $3.5 million in cash, 60 percent at closing (expected to be in April 1983) with the remainder placed in escrow to be paid within 10 months.

On March 21, 1983, the company acquired certain assets of Crimefighter Systems, Inc., a Southeastern Florida alarm company,

EXHIBIT 2 *(concluded)*

for approximately $300,000 (approximately $150,000 in cash at closing and approximately $150,000 payable in March 1984), the allocation of which has not been determined.

The company also entered into an agreement on March 25, 1983, to acquire all of the common stock of another alarm service company in Houston for an aggregate of approximately $16 million in cash. Completion of this acquisition is subject to an audit of the financial statements of the Houston company, an appraisal of their assets and the availability of adequate funds to complete the transaction.

Board of Directors and Shareholders
CRIME CONTROL, INC.
Indianapolis, Indiana

We have examined the balance sheets of Crime Control, Inc., as of December 31, 1982, 1981, and 1980, and the related statements of income, changes in shareholders' equity, and changes in financial position for the years then ended. Our examinations were made in accordance with generally accepted auditing standards and, accordingly, included such tests of the accounting records and such other auditing procedures as we considered necessary in the circumstances.

In our opinion, the financial statements referred to above present fairly the financial position of Crime Control, Inc., at December 31, 1982, 1981, and 1980, and the results of its operations and changes in its financial position for the years then ended, in conformity with generally accepted accounting principles applied on a consistent basis.

Coopers & Lybrand
Indianapolis, Indiana
March 15, 1983, except as to note 13 the date of which is March 25, 1983

Questions

1. Do you agree with Crime Control's use of "capital lease" accounting?

2. Why is Crime Control changing its mix of leases between capital and operating leases?

3. What do you think is Crime Control's potential as an equity investment as of November 15, 1983?

CHAPTER 23

Pension Cost Accounting and Analysis

A pension plan is an arrangement whereby a company provides for retired employees' benefits that can be determined in advance. The major accounting controversy centers on how to measure the charge of the cost of these plans to income and how to report the employee's pension obligation. Other related issues involve accounting for changes in the actuarial assumptions, appreciaiton of pension fund assets, and revisions to the plan.

Pension costs are an important cost of doing business. Except in rare cases, when a company commits itself to pay pensions to its employees upon their retirement, that cost may be expected to continue as long as the company has employees. Employers use pension plans as part of their personnel policies to attract, motivate, and hold better qualified workers and executives. This is motivated in large part by the tax inducements offered to employers by the federal government to encourage them to set up "qualified" pension plans. The Employee Retirement Income Security Act (ERISA) protects employees covered by private pension plans.

For many years, the accounting for pension plans was governed by *APB Opinion No. 8.* In this *Opinion,* the APB decided that pension costs, including the related administration expense, should be accounted for on an accural basis, which assumes that the employee will continue to provide benefits. This was a break from past practice, in which some major companies recognized pension costs only to the extent if cash payments were made to pensioners or to a pension trust fund.

In 1985, the FASB issued a proposed *Statement* to supersede its earlier employer pension accounting pronouncements. This *Statement* would:

1. Standardize the method for measuring net periodic pension expense among companies using each company's actual pension benefit formula and the actual future service period of those employees covered by the plan;
2. Require immediate recognition of a pension liability by companies

whose accumulated pension benefit obligation is greater than the fair value of the pension plan assets; and

3.   Greatly expand employee pension disclosure requirements.

All of the proposed pension accounting rules, except the liability requirement, would be effective for fiscal years beginning after December 15, 1986. The liability rule would go into effect for fiscal years beginning after December 15, 1988. Early application is encouraged, and restatement of any previously issued financial statement is not permitted. Because of this restriction, statement users comparing financial statements issued before and after a company adopts the new *Statement* must know both the old and new rules to make correct use of the data.

The disclosure of an employer's postretirement health care and life insurance benefit payments and obligations is covered by *Statement No. 81.*

Pension Plans

A full understanding of pension cost accounting and the analytical issues related to it requires an appreciation of the actuarial valuation techniques, funding instruments, agencies, and methods involved in determining the financial provisions for pension benefits. Therefore, the discussion of pension cost accounting and analysis is preceded by a brief description of pension plans.

The three most popular types of corporate pension plans are defined contribution plans, profit sharing plans, and defined benefit plans. An employer may maintain a single-employer pension plan or participate in a multiemployer plan, to which two or more unrelated employers contribute. Some companies use more than one type of pension plan to satisfy their pension obligations.

A defined contribution plan provides for each participant an individual account to which the employer is obligated to make periodic contributions. The employee's ultimate pension payments depend solely on the amount contributed to the account and the gains or losses earned. The employer is only liable for contributions to the plan, not for benefits payable to the retired employees.

A profit sharing plan is similar to a defined contribution plan. As its name implies, the employer agrees to assign a portion of the company's profits to the employee's pension fund. The amount contributed may or may not be set by formula.

A defined benefit pension plan specifies that the employer will provide to each retired employee a specified pension payment, usually based on factors such as age, years of service, and salary.

Unless specified otherwise, this chapter deals with single-employer defined benefit pension plan accounting and analysis.

Valuation

Actuarial valuation is the process of determining the amounts needed to finance a pension plan. This process relies on three principal concepts. First, the valuation is for a closed group of employees. Second, the ultimate cost of the plan is primarily the present value, as of the valuation date, of the expected future benefit payments. Third, the valuation is merely an approximation, because of uncertainties inherent in the actuarial assumptions underlying the calculations. After it is determined, the valuation of a pension plan is sometimes separated into two portions: *(a)* retroactive pension costs or benefits assigned on account of services rendered in years prior to the inception or current modification of the pension plan;[1] and *(b)* pension benefits or costs based on service after its inception or current modification.[2] In making the actuarial valuation, however, these costs are not considered separately.

Assumptions

When they estimate the cost of pension plans, actuaries must make a number of difficult assumptions regarding uncertain future events. For example, they have to make estimates of the expected rate of return on the pension fund, the fund's administrative expenses, and the amounts and timing of future benefits. The future benefit estimates, in turn, may involve estimates of future employee compensation levels, cost-of-living indexes, mortality rates (both before and after retirement), retirement ages, employee turnover, vesting privileges, and social security benefits.

Clearly, it is most unlikely that the actuarial assumptions will occur as projected, so it is necessary to review and change the actuarial assumptions from time to time. If the original assumptions turn out to have been optimistic, there will be an actuarial deficiency.

The net adjustment for actuarial gains and losses is handled by actuaries in one of two ways when revising valuations and contribution patterns. The so-called immediate method applies a net actuarial gain to reduce the employer's next contribution. This method is not used for net losses. The spread method spreads a net gain or loss over present and expected future contributions. Some actuaries use the immediate method for handling net gains and the spread method for losses.

---

[1] *Opinion No. 8* refers to these costs as "past service costs" whereas the proposed FASB *Statement* uses the term "prior service costs," which in *Opinion No. 8* is used to describe a slightly different concept. For the purposes of this chapter we will assume the two terms are synonymous.

[2] *Opinion No. 8* uses the term "normal cost" to describe these benefits. The proposed FASB *Statement* refers to this item as the "service cost component" of the net periodic pension cost. Again, for the purposes of this chapter we will assume these are synonymous terms.

Benefit Formulas

The three most popular formulas for determining employee pension payments are the flat benefit, career-average-pay, and final pay formulas. Flat benefit formulas base benefits on a fixed amount per year of service. A career-average-pay formula bases benefits on the employee's compensation over the entire period of service with the employer. Final pay formulas base employee benefits on the employee's compensation over a specified number of years near the end of that employee's service period, or else on the period of highest compensation.

Funding Instruments and Agencies

Typically, employers make some financial provision for the current and future benefits they are obligated to pay under their pension plans. Among a variety of funding instruments, the most popular are contracts with life insurance companies (insured plans) and trust agreements (trust fund plans).

Insured plans cover a number of possible arrangements. For example, individual policies providing death and retirement benefits may be issued to a trustee for each employee. A similar arrangement is a group annuity contract issued to the employer. Both of these arrangements specify the premiums and benefits.

Other popular insured funding arrangements are deposit administration contracts and immediate participation guarantee contracts. Essentially, both of these plans require the employer to open an account with an insurance company and to make regular contributions to this account. The insurance company agrees to add interest to the account at a specified rate. When the employee retires, the insurance company issues an annuity providing the stipulated benefits and the annuity premium is withdrawn from the employer's account.

Trust fund plans require the employer's contributions to be made to a trustee who invests the funds and pays retirement benefits according to the terms of the trust agreement. Trustees may be an individual, a bank, or a group of individuals. The terms of trust agreements may give the trustee full power to select investments, or the trustee may be subject to general direction by the employer.

Employee Retirement Income Security Act

The Employee Retirement Income Security Act (ERISA) prohibits pension plans from establishing eligibility requirements of more than one year of service or an age greater than 25, whichever is later. Employers are also required to fund annually the full cost for current benefit accruals and to amortize past service benefit liabilities over 30 to 40 years. Another section of the law establishes minimum vesting standards and creates an insurance program funded by employers to cover vested benefits. In addition, the law imposes a liability on the employer to reimburse this fund for any insurance benefits that are paid if the company's plan fails. The amount of this liability is limited to 30 percent of the employer's net worth. ERISA also sets regulatory reporting standards for employers and pension trusts.

Income Tax Considerations

Most pension plans are designed so that the employer contributions are deductible for tax purposes during the year contributed. There are several other tax aspects which should be noted. First, the tax treatment of pension costs follows cash, rather than accrual, accounting. Second, the earnings of qualified trust plans are tax free. Third, employer contributions to the fund are not taxable income to employees until distributed as retirement benefits.

Pension Accounting

Opinion No. 8, "Accounting for the Cost of Pension Plans," required the accrual approach to pension accounting. The FASB's proposed *Statement* retains this basis.

The following accounting entries illustrate the accrual approach to accounting for pension costs. Assume a *new* pension plan with a first-year cost of $100,000 and a retroactive benefit cost of $300,000.

1. At the time the plan is established, no accounting entry is made to record the retroactive benefit cost.
2. After the first year, the actuarially determined payment that should be made to the fund is $100,000.

Dr. Pension Expense	100,000	
Cr. Pension Payment Liability		100,000

3. The company makes an actual cash payment of $50,000 to the pension fund. (The company intends to fund the remaining $50,000 sometime during the next accounting period.)

Dr. Pension Payment Liability	50,000	
Cr. Cash		50,000

It is important to note that no entry is made in the company's books to record the retroactive cost at the time the plan is established. Also, the pension expense was recorded as $100,000, even though only $50,000 cash was paid to the pension fund in the current accounting period. The difference between the expense and the cash payment was recorded as a pension liability. If the full $100,000 pension cost had been funded in the same period as the expense was recorded, no pension liability would have shown on the employer's statements.

Under *Opinion No. 8,* the only way a company could report a pension liability or asset on the face of its balance sheet was to under- or overfund its recorded pension expense. The proposed FASB *Statement* retains this feature, but adds to it the requirement to record unfunded total pension obligations as liabilities.

Opinion No. 8

While drafting *Opinion No. 8,* the APB encountered considerable disagreement as to the appropriate definition of pension costs. Most members agreed that the annual pension cost should include the actuarial present value of benefits earned by employees during the period. The principal difference in members' views concerned the accounting for retroactive benefits arising at the time a plan was adopted or amended.

In order to substantially narrow the difference in accounting for the cost of pension plans, the APB expressed its requirements in terms of a minimum method based on a normal-cost-plus-interest concept, and a maximum method based on the concept of amortization of past or retroactive service cost. One result of this conclusion is that under *Opinion No. 8,* any period may be selected for the amortization of past service cost, as long as the total annual provision falls between the minimum and maximum. The proposed FASB *Statement* rejected the minimum-maximum approach and the free choice of retroactive benefit cost amortization periods.

Opinion No. 8 defines the minimum and maximum methods as follows:

Minimum method: The total of normal cost[3] and an assumed interest charge on unfunded retroactive service cost.

Maximum method: The sum of normal cost, 10 percent of retroactive benefits arising at the time the plan was adopted until fully amortized, 10 percent of any increases or decreases in retroactive benefit costs arising from amendments of an existing plan until fully amortized, and an assumed interest charge on the difference between cumulative amounts expensed and cumulative amounts funded.

Some companies can make substantial reductions in their annual pension expense when investment gains are realized by the pension fund, when the estimated future earnings rate of the fund is increased, or accumulated appreciation in pension fund investments is recognized in the actuarial valuation. All of these events are "actuarial gains." The APB concluded in *Opinion No. 8* that actuarial gains and, in like manner, actuarial losses "should be given effect in the provision for pension cost in a consistent manner that reflects the long-range nature of pension cost." The recommended way to accomplish this was to "spread" or "average" actuarial gains and losses over a period of years.

---

[3] Defined by *Opinion No. 8* as the annual cost assigned, under the actuarial cost method in use, to years subsequent to the inception of a pension plan or to a particular valuation date.

Opinion No. 8 succeeded in eliminating wide fluctuation in the annual pension costs of companies. However, many accounting commentators wanted to see the differences in current practice still further reduced. The FASB was responsive to these critics when it issued its 1985 proposal.

New Approach

The FASB's proposed *Statement* would have the greatest impact on corporations with underfunded, single-employer, defined benefit pension plans. These companies may have to record a pension liability equivalent to their pension underfunding on their corporate balance sheet. Employers who participate in multiemployer defined benefit plans or sponsor profit sharing and defined contribution plans would continue to use their current pension accounting methods, but their required pension disclosures would be expanded. The new accounting per se would not change cash flows; however, some employers are expected to change their funding and pension investment policies on the basis of the new accounting. It was anticipated that the new accounting would encourage employers to fund their plans up to the required minimum to avoid recording a corporate liability, and to favor insurance contracts over securities as pension fund investments.

Key Terms

The proposed pension *Statement* introduces four new terms that financial statement users, accountants, and managers must appreciate before they can understand the new pension accounting rules. These terms are:

1. *Net periodic pension cost:* the account recognized in an employer's financial statements as the cost of the pension plan for a period. The *Statement* uses the term "net periodic pension cost" instead of the current term "pension expense" because part of the cost recognized in a period may be capitalized along with other costs as part of an asset such as inventory.
2. *Fair value of plan assets:* the amount that a pension plan could reasonably expect to receive for its investments in a current exchange between a willing buyer and a willing seller, that is, other than in a forced liquidation sale. This is the method used to value the pension plan assets.
3. *Accumulated benefit obligation:* the actuarial present value of vested and nonvested benefits attributed by the pension benefit formula to service to date, and to *current* and *past* compensation, if applicable. The accumulated benefit obligation is considered by the FASB as representative of a pension plan's obligation should the plan cease to exist.
4. *Projected benefit obligation:* the actuarial present value of all bene-

fits attributed by the pension benefit formula to employee service rendered to date using *current* and *past* compensation and assumptions as to *future* compensation if the company's pension benefit formula is based on such future compensation levels.[4] If a company's pension benefit formula does not incorporate assumptions about future compensation,[5] the accumulated benefit obligation and the projected obligation have the same value.

It is important to be aware of the distinction between the latter two terms, because net periodic pension cost is based in part on the projected benefit obligation, and pension liability calculations incorporate the accumulated benefit obligation.

Fundamental Aspects Retained

The FASB's new pension proposal is based upon three fundamental concepts underlying *Opinion No. 8* pension accounting. These are:

1. *Net cost.* There is one pension cost and it aggregates at least three elements: (a) the compensation cost of pension benefits promised employees, (b) the interest cost resulting from the deferred payment of those benefits, and (c) the results of investing in assets to fund the promised benefits.
2. *Delayed recognition.* Certain changes in the pension obligation and plan assets are not recognized as they occur but are gradually and systematically spread over subsequent periods.
3. *Offsetting.* The plan assets and obligations can be netted against each other since the employer has considerable control over these items and the substantial risks and rewards associated with them are in large part borne by the employer.

These three aspects are peculiar to pension accounting and, in many respects, are in conflict with the accounting principles applied elsewhere in corporate financial reports. They have, however, widespread general acceptance, and most corporate issuers of financial statements believe the FASB was sensible to retain these concepts as the foundation for its new pension accounting rules.

Three Proposed Changes

The FASB's pension proposal seeks to retain the fundamental framework described above with three changes. These are:

1. A standardized method for measuring net periodic pension cost by recognizing the compensation cost of a pension over the employ-

---

[4] Such as in final pay, or career-average-pay pension plans.
[5] Such as flat benefit or nonpay-related pension plans.

ee's approximate service period and by relating that cost more directly to the terms of the plan.

2. The immediate recognition of a liability (the so-called minimum liability) in certain circumstances when the accumulated benefit obligation exceeds the fair value of the plan assets, although it would continue to delay recognition of the related charge to net periodic pension cost.

3. Expanded disclosures providing more current pension information than was incorporated under *Opinion No. 8* in the notes to financial statements.

These changes were made to improve the comparability and clarity of pension accounting. They would also result in pension data that reflect a particular company's circumstances better than the existing rules in *Opinion No. 8.*

It is important to note that the above changes do not provide for the recording of a pension asset by the employer in any circumstances when the fair value of the plan assets exceeds the accumulated benefit obligation. The FASB invited comments on this position and, depending on the responses it receives, may at a later date in overfunded situations make provision for recording under certain circumstances an employer pension asset.

Another important point to note is that the potential pension liability calculation is based on the accumulated benefit obligation, not the projected benefit obligation. This means that companies with final-pay-related plans would not take into account future assumptions about employee compensation when measuring their pension liability.

The accounting for pension plans of U.S. corporations abroad would have to conform to the new rules.

Minimum Liability

The FASB's proposal goes beyond the basic accrual accounting requirement of *Opinion No. 8.* It would require some companies to record an additional minimum liability based on the status of their pension plan assets and obligations. The proposed *Statement* says:

> If the accumulated benefit obligation exceeds the fair value of plan assets and either *(a)* a net asset has been recognized as prepaid pension cost or *(b)* the net liability already recognized as unfunded accrued pension cost is less than that excess, the employer shall recognize an additional amount so that the resulting liability is equal to the unfunded accumulated obligation.

If an employer records an additional liability pursuant to the above rule, an equal amount would have to be recognized as an intangible asset, provided that the intangible asset recognized was not greater than the amount of unrecognized prior service costs.[6] If an additional liability required to be recognized exceeds unrecognized prior service costs, that excess would be recorded as a reduction of owners' equity.

Accounting Illustration

To illustrate the new approach to pension liability accounting, assume the following:

   a.   A company's net periodic pension cost is $100,000. It funds $50,000 of this cost. The resulting accounting entries based on accrual accounting are:

Dr.	Net Periodic Pension Cost (to record the expense) $100,000	
	Cr. Cash (to reduce cash)......................	$50,000
	Unfunded Accrued Pension Cost (liability created by underpayment)	$50,000

   b.   The company has a $560,000 accumulated pension obligation and the fair value of its plan assets is $500,000. The company's unrecognized prior service cost is $5,000. To bring the balance sheet pension liability up to the $60,000 difference between the accumulated benefit obligation ($560,000) and the plan assets ($500,000), and to record the intangible asset (which can be no more than the unrecognized prior service cost ($5,000)) and the adjustment to owners' equity, the accounting entries are:

Dr.	Intangible (to record the intangible asset).............................. $5,000	
	Owners' Equity (to reduce owners' equity) $5,000	
	Cr. Additional Pension Liability (to bring the total pension liability up to $60,000)............................	$10,000

The employer's intangible asset, pension liability, and owners' equity balances would be adjusted at the end of each accounting period to reflect the current status of the accumulated benefit obligation, plan assets, unrecognized prior service cost, and unfunded accrued pension cost balances. These balance sheet adjustments would not directly enter into the computation of net periodic pension cost. Also, because of valuation changes in the elements entering into the liability calculation, the liability might disappear from the balance sheet in one period and reappear in another.

---

[6] Retroactive benefits granted in plan amendments that have not yet been recognized as part of net periodic pension cost.

Net Periodic Pension Cost

A company's net periodic pension cost under the board's proposal would be the net of these five components:

1. *Service cost.* This component is the actuarial present value of benefits attributed by the pension benefit formula to services rendered by employees during the accounting period. The service cost is based on accrual accounting and is unaffected by the funded status of the plan.

2. *Interest cost.* Measuring the projected benefit obligation as a discounted present value requires accrual of an interest cost over time at rates equal to the assumed discount rate. The interest cost component is equivalent to the increase in the projected benefit obligation due to the passage of time during the accounting period. Since this component of cost is based on the projected benefit obligation, it incorporates assumptions about future salary levels if the pension benefit formula incorporates future salaries. The interest rate is the rate used to discount the future pension obligations.

3. *Return on plan assets.* This component of net periodic pension cost reduces the net cost by the assumed investment income from the plan assets based on assumed rates of return equal to the discount rate used to measure the projected benefit obligation. This is an actuarial calculation and is not based on the plan's actual returns. Actual returns in excess of or less than those assumed are treated as gains or losses.

4. *Amortization of unrecognized net gain or loss.* As a minimum, amortization of the unrecognized cumulative net gain or loss resulting from a change in either the projected benefit obligation or the plan assets (because of experience different from that assumed or a change in actuarial assumptions) is included as a component of net periodic pension cost if, as of the beginning of the year, that unrecognized net gain or loss exceeds 10 percent of the projected benefit obligation or the fair value of plan assets, whichever is greater. If amortization is required, the minimum amortization[7] is the excess over the 10 percent test divided by the service period of the active employees expected to receive benefits under the plan. The amortization of any unrecognized net gain or loss may either increase or decrease the net periodic pension cost.

5. *Amortization of unrecognized prior service costs.* The cost of pro-

---

[7] If the plan has primarily inactive participants, the average remaining life expectancy should be used as the amortization period. The proposal permits alternative systematic methods of amortization as long as the periodic amortized amount is greater than the minimum calculated by using the average remaining service lives (or life expectancy, if appropriate) approach.

viding retroactive benefits (that is, prior service cost) arising at the initiation or amendment of a plan are amortized over time rather than at the time of the plan's initiation or amendment. The cost of retroactive benefits is the increase in the projected benefit obligation at the date of the amendment.[8] This cost is amortized by assigning an equal amount to each future period of service of each employee active at the date of the plan's initiation or amendment who is expected to receive benefits under the plan.

Transition Calculation

At the beginning of the period in which the proposed *Statement* is first applied, most corporations would have an unrecognized prior service cost. It would be equal to the difference between the following two amounts, irrespective of whether it is an unrecognized net obligation or net asset: (a) the projected benefit obligation, and (b) plan assets plus previously recognized unfunded accrued pension cost (or minus previously recognized prepaid pension cost). This unrecognized prior service cost would be amortized over the projected future service life of active employees expected to receive benefits under the plan at the time the new accounting was adopted.

Disclosure Requirements

The disclosure requirements of the board's plan go far beyond what was previously required. The proposal would require corporations with single-employer defined benefit plans to provide a detailed description of the plan, a listing of the five components of net periodic pension cost, the net periodic pension cost as a percentage of total payroll, an explanation of the net change in the fair value of plan assets, and a reconciliation of the funded status of the plan with the amounts shown on the employer's balance sheet. In addition, the proposal requires disclosures of the weighted average discount rate and rate of compensation increases assumed.

Other Plans

The proposal does not plan to change the accounting for annuity contract funded pension plans, defined contribution plans, or multiemployer plans.[9] Typically, the net periodic pension cost of these plans is the actuarially

---

[8] A plan amendment can reduce, rather than increase, the projected benefit obligation. Such a reduction is used to reduce any existing unrecognized prior service cost, and the excess, if any, is amortized on the same basis as the cost of benefit increases.

[9] To the extent that benefits are covered by annuity contracts, they are excluded from the projected benefit obligation and the accumulated benefit obligation. Annuity contracts are also excluded from plan assets.

determined payment required to meet the employer's periodic funding obligations. Under the FASB proposal, the disclosure required for these plans will be expanded.

Management Actions and Investment Considerations

Since the balance sheet requirements of the proposed *Statement* would not go into effect until late 1989, management has a window through which to assess the proposed pension accounting, take action to mitigate its immediate undesirable impact, and reset its long-range pension program strategy.

It was anticipated that companies with underfunded pension plans would continue to raise their discount rates[10]; buy high-yielding annuities and/or bonds to fund their known retiree or close-to-retiree obligations; and to change their actuarial assumptions. Their goal is to reduce, if not eliminate, their underfunding and reduce future pension costs and pension funding cash flows. Other companies might change their plans from a defined benefit to a defined contribution or profit sharing plan and let the employees handle the problem of benefits.

Companies with overfunded situations may well elect, as many have for various reasons, to recapture the overfunded assets. The new accounting would do little to discourage this action, particularly if a company with a low discount rate can raise the discount rate and recapture even more cash. The FASB has proposed that the gain from recapturing overfunded assets be included in income during the recapture period.

Postretirement Benefits

In addition to pension payments, many employers provide postretirement health care and life insurance benefits to employees. Most companies account for these costs on a cash basis and do not fund these obligations. Only a handful of employers use accrual accounting and fund part of this obligation.

Statement No. 81 requires the following disclosures about an employer's domestic and foreign employee postretirement health care and life insurance benefits:

1. A description of the benefits provided and the employee groups covered.
2. A description of the employer's current accounting and funding policies for these benefits.
3. The cost of those benefits recognized for the period.

---

[10] The FASB proposal requires companies to use discount rates that reflect the rates at which pension benefits could be effectively settled, such as the rates implicit in current pricing of annuity contracts. Companies using discount rates lower than these rates will have to increase their discount rates.

The unfunded nature of this corporate obligation is a concern to many employees, unions, and legislators. They are fearful that companies experiencing difficulties may renege on their postretirement benefit promises. It is anticipated that the emerging pressure to force some minimum level of funding of postretirement benefit obligations will grow.

Pension Plan Accounting

Statement No. 35 sets forth the accounting and disclosure requirements for defined benefit pension plans. The primary objective of the *Statement* is to provide financial information that is useful in assessing the plan's present and future ability to pay benefits when due. Accordingly, the *Statement* requires that annual plan statements include:

1. The net assets available for benefits presented on an accrual basis at fair value.
2. The changes in the net assets since the last statement.
3. The actuarial present value of accumulated plan benefits based on employees' history of pay and service and other appropriate factors as of either the beginning of the year or the statement date.

Financial Analysis

The analysis of net periodic pension cost and pension obligations is difficult for statement users. The subject is complex; much of the information needed to evaluate the appropriateness of a company's pension policies is not disclosed, and the actuarial assumptions vary greatly between companies. Nevertheless, statement users must do the best they can with the data available, since management's pension accounting and funding can significantly influence the level and quality of earnings and cash flows.

There is considerable controversy as to how statement users should view underfunded pension plans. Many regard the underfunding as a form of off-balance-sheet financing. While accepting this concept, others note that the company's principal obligation is to ensure that its retirees receive their benefits, and full funding of pension obligations is seldom needed to meet this responsibility. Also, they argue, a corporation may be able to earn more on the funds not contributed by using them in its business than the plan could earn on its employer contribution. This improves the workers' current and future position. Another point of view accepts these positions, but notes that there are ERISA, employee, and union pressures for full funding.

All of these opinions are valid. Accordingly, prudent statement users regard unfunded pension obligations as a form of off-balance-sheet financing, with less financial risk attached to it than, say, the level of financial risk associated with off-balance-sheet captive finance subsidiary debt. As a result, some analysts include a consideration of some portion of unfunded pension obligations in their appraisal of the adequacy of debt-equity ratios.

The relative degree of financial risk that analysts should attach to unfunded pension obligations can be measured by comparing the unfunded obligation with the owners' equity in the company. The higher this ratio of unfunded obligation to owners' equity, the greater the financial risk. In addition, the higher the percentage the unfunded vested obligation is of this total unfunded obligation, the greater is the level of financial risk, since vested benefits are pension benefits that accrue to an employee irrespective of whether the employee continues in the service of the employer.

Most managements are aware of these user points of view and, after weighing them, seem to prefer to fund their pension obligations fully in order to avoid criticism as well as potential future funding problems. Consequently, many statement users regard an underfunded pension plan as a red flag: if management is unable to fund fully, there must be some unfavorable reason why it cannot.

Statement users should always pay close attention to the discount rate applied to reduce the future pension obligations to their present value (the assumed earning rate on plan assets). This figure, which can vary significantly between companies, plays a material role in the measurement of both the pension obligation and net pension cost. A high earnings discount rate that is not guaranteed by nature of the plan assets should be regarded as a red flag. It suggests management may be using an unrealistic discount rate to reduce artificially its pension obligation and cost. Similarly, an upward shift in the discount rate may be a red flag, since managements tend to prefer to use conservative discount rates, even though the plan's actual earnings rate may be higher.

The actuarial assumptions made by management are also critical in measuring the pension obligations and net periodic pension costs. Conservative assumptions increase these and add to earnings quality. Liberal assumptions reduce these two items and should be regarded as red flags. Unfortunately, statement users find it difficult to obtain and interpret the actuarial assumptions management has used.

Some pension plans are overfunded. Statement users regard this overfunding as a potential source of capital for the employer corporation. In recent years, many companies have either recaptured portions of this excess or cited it as justification to reduce their annual funding. In some leveraged buyouts, the acquiring group has used such excess funding to finance part of its acquisition price. In order to recapture the excess, the employer company must terminate the existing plan, fund the vested employee's interest, and establish a new plan. The after-tax value of the excess funding recaptured is an addition to profits and owners' equity.

Less than Ideal

The FASB believed it would be conceptually appropriate and preferable to recognize a net pension liability or asset measured as the difference between the projected benefit obligation and plan assets, either with no delay in recognition of gains or losses, or perhaps with gains or losses re-flected currently in comprehensive income but not in earnings. However, the board concluded this approach would be too great a change from current *Opinion No. 8* practice to be adopted at the present time. In the light of this practical consideration, the board concluded that the provision of its proposed *Statement* as a whole represented an improvement in financial reporting. The board's decision was probably the correct one to make under the circumstances. Statement users, however, should remember that the securities markets respond to economic realities, whether or not they are captured by accounting presentations, and the board's preferred, conceptu-ally sounder view is closer to the economic reality of pension obligations and costs than its compromise solution. Accordingly, statement users should always recast, to the extent possible, accounting statements incorporating the compromise pension accounting to reflect the preferred pension ac-counting.

CASE 23-1

Summit Manufacturing Company
Accounting for Pension Costs

Peter Berol, the chief executive officer of Summit Manufacturing Company, a small machine tool manufacturer, was concerned with the impact of a proposed change in pension accounting on the company's balance sheet. In the recent past, the company had contributed more cash to the pension plan than it had recorded as its pension expense. This had resulted in a prepaid pension cost asset being recorded in 1982 and 1983. In 1984, because of unexpected liquidity problems, the annual contribution to the plan was cut drastically. This action eliminated the pension prepayment asset. To get a better understanding of the potential impact of the new pension accounting, Berol decided to have his administrative assistant, Joe Lyons, recompute the company's 1981–84 pension cost and balance sheet presentations using the FASB's proposed pension accounting. He explained the proposal to Lyons and instructed him as follows:

> Joe, I don't think we are going to like the FASB's proposed new pension accounting rules. I plan to write a comment letter to the FASB, but before I do that I want you to give me an estimate of how the proposal might impact us. I asked our consulting actuary to pull together some data related to our pension costs, plan funding, and plan assets and liabilities for the last four years (Exhibit 1). I want you to use this data to reconstruct what our 1981–84 pension reporting would have looked like if we had followed the FASB's proposal.
>
> I want you to assume we made the transition from the old to the new accounting at the beginning of 1981. According to our actuary, our initial unfunded obligation would have been $1.1 million. That's the difference between our projected benefit obligation of $2 million and the $900,000 fair market value of our assets at that date. According to the proposal, this $1.1 million would be considered our initial unrecognized prior service cost. Our actuary calculated that the amortization rate would be 100/1,050

This case was prepared by David F. Hawkins.

Copyright © 1985 by the President and Fellows of Harvard College
Harvard Business School case 186–082

EXHIBIT 1

SUMMIT MANUFACTURING COMPANY
Selected Pension Cost and Plan Data, 1981–84
(in thousands)

	For Year Ended December 31			
	1981	*1982*	*1983*	*1984*
Plan assets and obligations:				
Plan assets	$1,165	$1,505	$1,622	$1,517
Accumulated benefit obligation	1,254	1,628	1,616	1,554
Projected benefit obligation	1,879	2,442	2,424	2,331
Unfunded accumulated benefits	89	123	—	37
Overfunded accumulated benefits	—	—	6	—
Net plan gain or (loss)	251	312	(67)	37
Other data:				
Annual contribution to plan	334	385	467	180
Periodic service cost	100	106	181	157

	For Year Beginning January 1			
	1981	*1982*	*1983*	*1984*
Plan assets and obligation:				
Projected benefit obligation	$2,000	$1,879	$2,442	$2,424
Plan assets (at market).......................	900	1,165	1,505	1,622
"Corridor"*	200	188	244	242

* Ten percent of the greater of projected benefit obligation or plan assets.

in the first year, 95/1,050 in the second year, 90/1,050 in the third year, and 85/1,050 in 1985. The estimated transition unrecognized service cost for our 1982 plan amendment is $750,000. It would be amortized using the same schedule. That is, 100/1,050 in 1982, and so forth. Under the old accounting rules, we wrote our prior service cost off over 30 years, but our actuary tells me we would not be able to do this anymore. We have to use a remaining-service-period-based amortization schedule. To keep things simple, I think our actuary's schedule is based on the assumption that we had 100 employees covered by the plan at the transition date and, of the original 100, 5 were expected to depart each year.

Let me explain a few of the items on the schedule I gave you (Exhibit 1). The plan assets and accumulated benefit obligation numbers are the actual figures we published in the annual report following *FASB Statements Nos. 35 and 36.* They may not be exactly the same as they would be under the proposal, but they are close enough. The obligation is based on past and current salaries.

The projected benefit obligation is a figure our actuary gives us every year. It reflects the fact we have a final-pay plan. As you may recall, this figure is not published in our annual report. Incidentally, I wonder if we should publish it? I noticed General Electric published their obligation taking salary progression into account. General Electric has very smart management. I was interested in their comments on what they consider their true pension liability to be. I made a copy of their pension note; here it is (Exhibit 2). I'd like your comments on whether or not we should consider including a similar note in our 1985 annual report. Of course, when we have to follow the board's proposal, we will be required to disclose this figure.

The next two lines—underfunded and overfunded accumulated benefits—are self-evident.

The net plan gain or loss line is the net change in the plan's asset balance and the projected benefit obligation that is due to such things as change in fair value and actuarial assumption.

Our actual annual contributions to the plan are shown next. Our policy is to fund the plan on the last day of the fiscal year.

The periodic service cost data are the present value of benefits attributed by our plan to employee service during the period. We used the actual "normal" cost numbers we experienced between 1981 and 1984 for this element of net periodic pension cost.

EXHIBIT 2
Summit Manufacturing Company

1984 General Electric Annual Pension Note

Note 3: Pensions and other Retiree Benefits
General Electric and its consolidated affiliates sponsor a number of pension plans. The costs of these plans were $603 million in 1984, $643 million in 1983, and $570 million in 1982.

tematic basis which does not give undue weight to short-term market fluctuations.

A comparison of the present value of pension plan benefits with carrying value of trust assets is shown in the table below.

General Electric Pension Plan December 31 (in millions)	1984	1983	1982
Present value of accumulated benefits recognizing projected future compensation and service	$ 11,116	$10,604	$ 9,800
Carrying value of trust assets	9,704	8,590	7,477
Unfunded liability	$ 1,412	$ 2,014	$ 2,323
Persons receiving pensions at year-end	103,800	97,800	91,500

General Electric Pension Plan (the "pension plan") is the most significant pension plan and substantially all employees in the United States are participants. The projected unit credit method, which recognizes the effect of future compensation and service of employees, is used to determine trust funding and pension cost. Changes in pension benefits allocable to previous service of employees (prior-service liabilities) are amortized to pension costs over 20 years. Gains and losses which occur because actual experience differs from amounts assumed are amortized over 15 years.

Pension plan benefits are funded through the General Electric Pension Trust (the "trust"). The "carrying value" of investments is amortized cost plus recognition of appreciation in the common stock portfolio on a sys-

The funding program and company cost determination for the pension plan use 7.5 percent as the estimated rate of future trust income, except for the effect in 1984 of a dedicated portfolio. This fixed-income portfolio, consisting of securities backed by the U.S. Treasury, has been dedicated to the payment of certain future pension benefits. The value of trust assets at the end of 1984 includes $824 million for this portfolio. The rate of return on the dedicated portfolio (13.4 percent) was a factor in determining the present value of plan benefits.

If the dedication had not occurred, the present value of benefits at the end of 1984 would have been $580 million greater. The dedication reduced 1984 pension costs by $28 million. Amortization of continued favorable

EXHIBIT 2 *(continued)*

trust income experience also reduced pension costs. Pension cost as a percentage of compensation was 6.9 percent in 1984 (8.1 percent in 1983 and 7.1 percent in 1982).

Condensed financial statements for the General Electric Pension Trust, which are not consolidated with those of the company, follow.

A calculation and disclosure of the present value of accumulated plan benefits is required by *Statement of Financial Accounting Standards No. 36 (SFAS 36).* The *SFAS 36* benefit amounts shown on the next page differ from the data shown earlier in this note for the General Electric Pension Plan because they are based only on compensation and ser-

General Electric Pension Trust

Net Assets at Current Value, December 31 (millions)	1984	1983	1982
U.S. government obligations and guarantees	$ 2,238	$2,004	$1,580
Corporate bonds and notes	1,076	1,037	1,144
Real estate and mortgages	1,976	1,341	1,053
Common stocks and other equity securities	5,782	5,180	4,247
	$11,072	$9,562	$8,024
Cash and short-term investments	145	256	270
Other assets—net	133	68	146
Net assets	$11,350	$9,886	$8,440

Change in Net Assets at Current Value for the Year (millions)	1984	1983	1982
Net assets at January 1	$ 9,886	$8,440	$6,579
Company contributions	503	545	470
Employee contributions	101	87	102
Investment income	931	857	796
Benefits paid	(421)	(376)	(331)
Unrecognized portion of change in current value	350	333	824
Net assets at December 31	$11,350	$9,886	$8,440

Investment income of the trust, including systematic recognition of common stock appreciation, as a percentage of the average carrying value of the portfolio was 10.3 percent in 1984, 10.8 percent in 1983, and 11.6 percent in 1982.

The General Electric Supplementary Pension Plan, an unfunded plan providing supplementary retirement benefits primarily to long-service professional and managerial employees in the United States, is another significant plan. Changes in prior-service liabilities along with other gains and losses are amortized over a period of 20 years. Current service costs and amortization are charged to costs currently and are recorded as company liabilities.

vice to date (i.e., they exclude the expected effect of future compensation and service) and because benefits applicable to the Supplementary Plan are included. In addition, the table shows the current value of trust assets plus accruals. General Electric believes funding comparisons for the pension plan shown earlier in this note are more realistic because the benefit amounts include the expected effect of future compensation and service, and because trust assets are valued on a basis which minimizes the impact of short-term market fluctuations. The interest rate assumptions used in determining the present value of benefits are the same as discussed previously for the pension plan.

EXHIBIT 2 *(concluded)*

General Electric Pension Plan and Supplementary Pension Plan December 31 (millions)	1984	1983	1982
SFAS 36 estimated present value of accumulated plan benefits:			
Vested benefits	$ 8,331	$ 7,939	$7,160
Nonvested benefits	709	557	528
Total accumulated benefits	$ 9,040	$ 8,496	$7,688
Current value of trust assets plus accruals	$11,695	$10,172	$8,682

Retiree health care and life insurance benefits. General Electric and its affiliates have a number of plans providing retiree health care and life insurance benefits. The cost of the principal U.S. plans was $138 million in 1984.

Generally, employees who retire or terminate after qualifying for optional early retirement under the General Electric Pension Plan are eligible to participate in retiree health care and life insurance benefit plans. Health care benefits for medical and dental expenses incurred by eligible retirees under age 65 and eligible dependents are included in company costs as covered expenses are actually incurred. For eligible retirees and spouses over age 65, scheduled hospital benefits which supplement Medicare and scheduled prescription drug benefits are provided, and the present value of future benefits is funded or accrued by the company and included in company costs in the year the retiree becomes eligible for benefits. The present value of life insurance benefits for eligible retirees is funded and included in company costs in the year of retirement.

The bottom portion of the schedule (Exhibit 1) contains the data, along with the net plan gain and loss figures I mentioned earlier, needed to compute the minimum amortization of our unrecognized net gain or loss related to plan assets and obligations. The average remaining service period you should use for amortization purposes is 10.5 years. Remember, it is only the cumulative unrecognized net gain at the beginning of the year in excess of the so-called "corridor" that is amortized. Since the proposal assumes the cumulative unrecognized net gain is zero at the beginning of the transition year, there would be no amortization of gain in 1981. I believe our actuary said that the minimum amount of the cumulative unrecognized net gain amortized in 1982 would have been about $6,000.[1]

The discount rate we use to calculate the present value of pension obligations is 9 percent. This is also the assumed earnings rate on the plan assets. Our actuary told me that to approximate the interest cost on projected benefit obligations and the return on investment elements of the net peri-

---

[1] Cumulative unrecognized gain as of the beginning of the period $251,000
Less: "Corridor" 187,900
$ 63,100
Times: Average service period (years) 10.5
Minimum amortization of gain .... $ 6,010

odic pension cost, we can apply our 9 percent rate to the beginning balances of those two accounts. For example, the 1981 interest cost component would be $180,000, which is 9 percent of the beginning $2 million projected benefit obligation. Similarly, 1981 investment return element is about $81,000, which is 9 percent of the beginning-of-year plan asset balance.

Incidentally, the future compensation rate increase assumed in the projected benefit obligation is 6 percent.

Questions

1. Complete Joe Lyons' assignment. Recast the 1981–84 pension data to conform to the FASB's proposed pension accounting to replace *Opinion No. 8.* Assume 1981 is the transition year. Show the accounting entries you made to record your pro forma 1981–84 pension costs and liabilities using the FASB's proposed rules.

2. How do you think the actuary computed the unrecognized prior service and net plan gain amortization rates?

3. In the light of your pro forma data, how might the following data influence the way the company computes and accounts for pension costs in the future? Should the FASB's proposal be accepted?

Summit Manufacturing, Inc.

	Discount Rate	Increase in Future Compensation Levels
Weighted average assumed rate used	9 percent	6 percent
(Decrease) increase in project benefit obligation that would result from using a rate 1 percent higher................	$(340,000)	$180,000
(Decrease) increase in net periodic pension cost that would result from using a rate 1 percent higher................	$(50,000)	$ 30,000

4. Do you agree with the views expressed in the General Electric 1984 pension note? Should Summit adopt a similar disclosure in its 1985 annual report?

PART EIGHT

Stockholders' Equity Reporting and Analysis

CHAPTER 24

Equity Capital Transactions and Analysis

The owners' equity or net worth section of the balance sheet shows the accumulated investment of the owners of the corporation, the stockholders. The stockholders' investment may be "direct," through purchase of common or preferred stock, or "indirect," through the corporation's retention of earnings which might have been paid out to stockholders. Net worth represents the "book" or residual value of the corporation; this residual is the assets less the liabilities. The net worth section of the balance sheet discloses the sources and nature of equity capital, including the types of stock authorized and outstanding and any statutory or contractual limitations.

To use this data effectively, the reader of the report must understand the accounting, legal, and financial distinctions between the various accounts that make up the equity section. Statement users who are aware of these distinctions are not likely to make the common mistake of treating the owners' equity section of the balance sheet as a single account. This error can be costly, particularly when several classes of common stock are involved with very different voting rights and claims on residual assets; when management has engaged in extensive stock buyback transactions; or when generous stock dividends have been declared. Under these circumstances, a detailed analysis of owners' equity is required to appreciate the relative rights of the class of stock of interest to the analyst, the relationship between stock buyback transactions and reported return on equity and earnings per share, and the changes in the retained earnings account that may affect adversely a company's ability to pay cash dividends. In addition, statement users need to understand owners' equity accounting in order to know how to compute and interpret the common financial statistic "book value per share."

Owners' Equity

The stockholders' investment in the corporation is represented by either common or preferred stock. More than one type of each kind of stock may be issued. If there is more than one class of stockholder, the equity interest of each class should be disclosed fully in either the financial statements or the accompanying footnotes. Accounting treats both classes of stock in a similar fashion.

Owners of preferred stock have certain privileges ahead of the common stockholders, such as a preference in dividends or liquidation. Preferred stock dividends are usually fixed in amount and can be noncumulative or cumulative; usually no dividend can be paid on the common stock until preferred dividends previously earned but not declared are paid. Preferred shares may be classified as participating. That is, the owners can participate in dividend distribution with the common shareholders once a specified level of dividends has been paid to the common shareholders. In liquidation, after the claims of creditors have been settled, preferred stockholders have a preferred fixed claim on assets relative to the common stockholders. Typically, preferred stock does not carry voting rights. Most preferred stock is redeemable under certain conditions, at the corporation's option, at a specified price schedule which usually includes a special redemption premium. Sometimes preferred stockholders are granted the privilege of converting their stock into shares of common stock. The conversion ratio and conditions vary from issue to issue, but the intent of the company is usually the same: to make the preferred stock more attractive to potential purchasers.

Common stock represents the residual ownership interest in a company after recognizing the preferred stockholders' preferred position. Common stockholders elect directors, share in the profits of the business after preferred dividends are paid, and in liquidation share in the residual assets of the company after the claims of all creditors and preferred stockholders have been settled. Often, common stockholders have the option to purchase any new common shares issued by their company in proportion to their holdings. This is called a "preemptive" right.

The common stockholders' investment in a company is typically shown in three parts:

1. Capital stock.
2. Capital in excess of par value.[1]
3. Retained earnings.

The capital stock account shows the par or stated value of the common shares issued. It is customary to disclose the number of shares authorized by the board of directors for the company, the number issued, and the number owned by the company as treasury stock, if any. The par value of a share bears no relationship to actual value. It is simply the amount

---

[1] Alternative names for this account found in older balance sheets are: "other contributed capital," "paid-in surplus," and "capital surplus." The term "surplus" is discouraged because of the misleading inferences naive readers of financial statements may draw from its use. Even today, however, accountants and business executives in conversations will use for the sake of convenience the term "capital surplus" rather than the preferred, but longer, caption "capital in excess of par value."

engraved on the face of the stock certificate. This practice satisfies a legal requirement and indicates the limit of the stockholders' liability for the debts of the company. To limit legal liability and lessen certain stock transfer taxes, the par value is usually arbitrarily set as low as possible. Some states permit companies to issue no-par stock. In these cases, the no-par stock is assigned an arbitrary value and recorded on the books at this stated value, which is usually very low.

Typically, shares are issued at a price in excess of their par or stated value. In these cases, the excess amount is shown in the capital in excess of par value account. In addition, the value of any capital the company received which did not involve issuing shares, such as donated assets, is included in this account. Other transactions which are described later that could affect the capital in excess of par values account include: treasury stock transactions, stock dividends, and stock splits. The adjustments to the capital in excess of par value account associated with accounting for "pooling of interests" has been discussed previously in Chapter 20.

The accounting entries for a new stock issue are fairly straightforward. For example, assume the Lawson Corporation issued at a price of $25 per share 10,000 new common shares with a par value of $5 per share. The underwriting costs were $15,000. Consequently, the net proceeds to the company from the issue were $235,000. The accounting entries are:

```
Dr.  Cash ................................................  235,000
    Cr.  Capital Stock .......................................          50,000
         Capital in Excess of Par Value  .......................         185,000
```

None of these transactions, including the underwriting costs, affect net income. The preferred practice is to show the increase in the capital accounts net of the direct underwriting costs associated with the stock issue and paid to noncompany-related entities.

Retained earnings represents the accumulated earnings of the company less dividends. It also includes the cumulative effect of any special credits and charges, such as prior period income adjustments, not included in the income computation. If there is no capital in excess of par value available, the retained earnings account may properly be charged with those items normally absorbed by the capital in excess of par value account. Also, under some circumstances, such as the declaration of a stock dividend, a portion of the retained earnings account may be transferred to the capital accounts. It is not considered good practice to add to retained earnings the net worth increments created by reappraisal of assets. These increments should be clearly segregated from retained earnings and their source indicated by an appropriate account title.

Treasury Stock

Treasury stock is a company's own stock which has been issued and subsequently reacquired by the company but not yet retired formally. Treasury stock is shown as a deduction at cost from capital, rather than as an asset, since legally a company can only reacquire its own stock with unrestricted capital. Treasury stock does not have voting privileges and does not enter into the computation of earnings per share.

When treasury stock is retired, the capital account is reduced by the stock's par or stated value. The number of shares authorized remains unchanged, but the number of shares issued is reduced by the number of shares of stock retired. Any difference between the retired treasury stock's cost and the amount charged to the capital account is deducted from the capital in excess of par value account applicable to the retired class of shares. If the capital in excess of par value account is inadequate to absorb the full excess of cost over par value, any remaining excess is charged to retained earnings.

When treasury stock is resold, the capital in excess of par value account is adjusted to reflect any difference between the stock's cost and selling price. Losses on sales of treasury stock in excess of cumulative net gains from sales or retirements of the same class of stock are charged to retained earnings. As far as accounting is concerned, such transactions do not give rise to corporate profits or losses.

Dividends

Dividends are the pro rata distribution to stockholders of retained earnings. They can be in the form of cash, stock, or property. Generally, corporations can only declare dividends out of earnings, although some state laws and corporate agreements permit the declaration of dividends from sources other than earnings.

The board of directors' declaration of dividends in cash or property legally binds the company to pay the dividends, unless the stockholders rescind the decision. Therefore, at the time dividends in cash or property are declared, retained earnings is charged with the dividend amount and a current liability account, Dividends Payable, is established. When the dividends are distributed, the liability account is reduced accordingly. Typically, when property is distributed as dividends, the retained earnings account is reduced by the book value of the property.

Sometimes the directors of a company may segregate in a separate account in the owners' equity section of the balance sheet a portion of the retained earnings account and label it as being a restricted or appropriated reserve. This practice indicates that the reserved amount is not legally available for distribution to stockholders as dividends until the restrictions are removed. When the conditions leading to the segregation of retained earnings no longer exist, the reserve should be eliminated and credited to retained earnings directly. Even if no special reserve is created, any restrictions of retained earnings as to dividend distributions should be fully disclosed in footnotes or parenthetical notation.

Ordinarily, dividends are not paid on treasury stock.

Stock Dividends and Splits

Stock dividends and splits are treated differently for accounting purposes, although they are generally regarded as being essentially the same from the financial point of view, since in either case they leave the shareholders' proportional share of owners' equity unchanged.

Accounting Research Bulletin No. 43 distinguishes between stock dividends and stock splits as follows. A stock dividend "is prompted mainly by a desire to give the recipient shareholders some ostensibly separate evidence of a part of their respective interests in accumulated corporate earnings without distribution of cash or other property which the board of directors deems necessary or desirable to retain in the business." In contrast, a stock split-up "is prompted mainly by a desire to increase the number of outstanding shares for the purpose of effecting a reduction in their unit market price and, thereby, of obtaining wider distribution and improved marketability of the shares."

Accounting practice and the Internal Revenue Service do not regard a stock dividend or split as income to the recipient. The rationale for this position was cited in *Eisner* v. *Macomber* (252 U.S. 189), wherein it was held that stock dividends are not income under the 16th Amendment. The court ruled:

> A stock dividend really takes nothing from the property of the corporation and adds nothing to the interests of the stockholders. Its property is not diminished and their interests are not increased . . . the proportional interest of each shareholder remains the same. The only change is in the evidence which represents that interest, the new shares and the original shares together representing the same proportional interests that the original shares represented before the issue of the new ones.
>
> Since a shareholder's interest in the corporation remains unchanged by a stock dividend or split-up except as to the number of share units constituting such interest, the cost of the shares previously held should be allocated equitably to the total shares held after receipt of the stock dividend or split-up. When any shares are later disposed of, a gain or loss should be determined on the basis of the adjusted cost per share

Nevertheless, accounting practice does treat a stock dividend on the books of the issuing company as if it were a dividend to the recipient, principally because many recipients appear to regard it as such. *ARB No. 43* states:

> A stock dividend does not, in fact, give rise to any change whatsoever in either the corporation's assets or its respective shareholders' proportionate interest therein. However, it cannot fail to be recognized that, merely as a consequence of the expressed purpose of the transaction and its characterization as a *dividend* in related notices to shareholders and the public at large, many recipients of stock dividends look upon them as distributions of corporate earnings and usually in an amount equivalent to the fair value of the additional shares received. Furthermore, it is to be presumed that such views of recipients are materially strengthened in those instances

which are by far the most numerous, where the issuances are so small in comparison with the shares previously outstanding that they do not have any apparent effect upon the share market price and, consequently, the market value of the shares previously held remains substantially unchanged.

The Committee on Accounting Procedure (CAP) believed that where these circumstances existed, the company must "in the public interest" account for the transaction by transferring from retained earnings to the permanent equity capital accounts (i.e., the capital stock and capital in excess of par values accounts) an amount equal to the "fair value" of the additional shares issued. For example, to account for the issuance of 10,000 shares with a par value of $5 and fair value of $25 as a stock dividend, the following entries would be required.

```
Dr.  Retained Earnings ......................................  250,000
     Cr.  Capital Stock ........................................              50,000
          Capital in Excess of Par Value  ........................          200,000
```

Unless this approach was used, the CAP believed "the amount of earnings which the shareholder may believe to have been distributed to him will be left, except to the extent otherwise dictated by legal requirements, in earned surplus subject to possible further similar stock issuances or cash distributions."[2]

Where the number of additional shares issued as a stock dividend was so great that it had, or might reasonably be expected to have, the effect of materially reducing the market value per share, the CAP believed there was no likelihood of dividend income implications or possible other constructions that stockholders might attribute to stock dividends. In these circumstances, the nature of the transaction clearly indicates it is a stock split. Consequently, the CAP did not require retained earnings to be capitalized, except to the extent required by law. For example, assume a company split its stock two for one, issued 100,000 new shares, and reduced its par value per common share from $5.00 to $2.50. Under these circumstances, no accounting entries would be required. The capital stock account would remain unchanged. However, the notes to the capital section of the balance sheet would now show twice as many authorized and outstanding shares as before the split, and a par value per share of half the original value. Now, assume the company did not reduce its par value per share. In order to reflect the $500,000 increase in par value of the stock issued, the following entries would be required:

```
Dr.  Retained Earnings ......................................  500,000
     Cr.  Capital Stock ........................................              500,000
```

---

[2] The accounting for stock dividends recommended by the CAP will in most cases result in capitalization of retained earnings in an amount in excess of that called for by the laws of the state of incorporation. Such laws usually require capitalization of the par value of the shares issued. However, these legal requirements are minimum requirements and do not prevent the capitalization of a larger amount.

In addition, when the circumstances indicated that a stock split had occurred, the CAP required that use of the word "dividend" should be avoided in related corporate resolutions, notices, and announcements. In cases where legal requirements prevented this, the CAP required that the transaction be described as a "split-up effected in the form of a dividend."

The problem of resolving at what point a stock dividend becomes so big as to constitute a stock split was resolved by *ARB No. 43* as follows:

> Obviously, the point at which the relative size of the additional shares issued becomes large enough to materially influence the unit market price of the stock will vary with individual companies and under differing market conditions and, hence, no single percentage can be laid down as a standard for determining when capitalization of earned surplus in excess of legal requirements is called for and when it is not. However, on the basis of a review of market action in the case of shares of a number of companies having relatively recent stock distributions, it would appear that there would be few instances involving the issuance of additional shares of less than, say, 20 percent or 25 percent of the number previously outstanding where the effect would not be such as to call for the procedure [described for accounting for stock dividends].

ARB No. 43 does not indicate the appropriate date for determining the fair market value of stock dividends. Typically, the declaration date is used, although in practice the ex-dividend and payment dates have also been used.

Noncompensatory Plans to Issue Stock to Employees

Many companies have implemented stock purchase plans to encourage employee ownership of the company's shares by allowing the employee to purchase shares at prices slightly below the current market price. The hope is that the share ownership will lead to a better relationship between the employee and the company. The primary interest of such plans is not to compensate employees.

In *Opinion No. 25*, "Accounting for Stock Issued to Employees," the APB concluded that employer corporations need not recognize any element of compensation expense for employees who acquire stock through such noncompensatory plans as long as the plan had at least four criteria, namely: (1) substantially all full-time employees, after meeting limited employment qualifications, can participate; (2) the stock is offered to eligible employees equally or based on a uniform percentage of salary or wages; (3) the time permitted for exercise of an option or purchase right is limited to a reasonable period; and (4) the discount from the market price of the stock is no greater than would be reasonable in an offer of stock to stockholders. Any employee stock acquisition plan or agreement that does not possess these four characteristics is classified for accounting purposes as a compensatory plan.

Compensatory Stock Option and Purchase Plans

To compensate managers and to increase their interest in their company's activities, companies sometimes issue nontransferable rights to managers on a selective basis which entitle them to buy a stated number of shares of stock at a specific price during some limited time period. These plans do not have the characteristics of noncompensatory plans.

If the fair market value of a stock option is more than the option price at the time the option is granted, any gain the recipient realizes at the time the option is exercised may be taxed as ordinary income. Consequently, the option price is usually close to the market price at the time the right is granted.

The hope of those granting stock options is that the managers receiving them will exert such efforts that the price of the company's stock will rise above the option price. If this expectation is realized, the stock option recipient regards the increase in value of the stock purchase right as additional compensation.

For a number of years, there was considerable accounting controversy as to how to measure such compensation and over what period to expense it. For example: On January 1, 1985, John Lester, the president of a publicly owned company, is granted the right to purchase 10,000 shares of the company's $5 par-value stock at a price of $10 per share. The earliest time he can exercise this right is December 1, 1985. His right expires on December 31, 1988. The market price of this stock on January 1, 1985, was $12 per share. By December 31, 1985, the price had reached $20 per share. On January 25, 1988, John Lester exercised his right and was issued 10,000 shares at $10 per share. The current market price was $35 per share.

To ignore the compensation element of these events would lead to an overstatement of the company's income and an understatement of John Lester's cost of services. The problem is how to measure the compensation. Is it the difference between the grant price and the market price at the grant date? The difference between the grant price and the market price at the time the option is exercised? Or, the difference between the grant price and the price of the stock when the grantee sells it?

Opinion No. 25 concluded that in the case of compensatory plans, such as the John Lester one cited above, compensation for services should be measured by the difference between the quoted market price of the stock and the amount, if any, the employee is required to pay at the measurement date, which is the first date that both the number of shares an individual employee is entitled to receive and the option price are known. If a quoted market price is unavailable, then an estimate of the market value must be made.

The measurement date in the John Lester example is the grant date. Also, since the market value of the optioned stock at that date is $12 per share and the option price is $10 per share, compensation must be recognized.

If compensation is involved in a stock option plan, the amount of the compensation should be charged to income in some reasonable manner consistent with the facts of the situation in the period during which the employee's services are rendered. Sometimes the stock option plan states that the employee can exercise the option only if the employee agrees to stay with the company for a specified period of time. In this case, it is reasonable to charge the compensation to income during this specified period. The offset to the income charge should be a credit to the Accumulated Credit under Stock Option Plan account which is shown in the owners' equity section of the balance sheet. When the stock option is exercised, the credit item is eliminated.

Using the John Lester example, the accounting entries would be:

a. When the option was granted:

Dr. Additional Compensation	20,000	
Cr. Accumulated Credit under Stock Option Plan*		20,000

b. When the option was exercised:

Dr. Cash	100,000	
Accumulated Credit under Stock Option Plan	20,000	
Cr. Common Stock, $5 par value		50,000
Capital in Excess of Par Value		70,000

Issuance of 10,000 shares at $10 per share pursuant to stock option plan.

---

* 10,000 shares times the difference between the option price and the price at the grant date.

If a stock option is not exercised because an employee fails to meet all of his obligations, any related accrued compensation expense should be adjusted by decreasing compensation expense in the period of forfeiture. If an option is not exercised before its expiration date, a similar accounting entry is made. In both cases, the related accumulated credit is added to owners' equity.

Should a company obtain a tax benefit under an employee stock option plan, the amount of the tax benefit allocated to income should be limited to the tax benefit related to the compensation cost recognized in income for accounting purposes. The balance of the tax benefit, if any, should be considered as a capital transaction.

Since *APB Opinion No. 25* was issued, there have been several more important pronouncements dealing with compensatory stock plans. *FASB Interpretation No. 38* deals specifically with the accounting for stock option, purchase, and award plans involving so-called junior stock, a separate class of stock issued to certain employees at favorable prices that is subordinate to the employer company's regular common stock but is convertible into common stock if specific future events occur. The compensation measurement date for these plans is the date on which the number of shares of regular common stock that an employee is entitled to receive in exchange for the junior stock is known. The compensation element is the difference between the price paid by the employee for the junior stock and the price of the regular common stock at the measurement date.

In an earlier *Interpretation (No. 28)* dealing with stock appreciation rights and other variable stock option and award plans, the FASB decided the compensation element relating to such variable plans should be measured at the end of each period as the amount by which the quoted market value of the shares of the employer's stock covered by the grant exceeds the option price or value specified under the plan. A stock appreciation right is an award to an employee entitling the employee to receive cash, stock, or a combination of cash and stock in an amount equivalent to any excess in the market value of a stated number of shares of the employer company's stock over a stated price. The compensation element of such plans is accrued as a charge to expense over the periods the employee performs the related services. Changes in the quoted market value are reflected as an adjustment to accrued compensation and compensation expense in the periods in which changes occur until the date the number of shares and purchase price are both known. The accounting for stock appreciation rights is also discussed in Chapter 13.

The board's specification of a measurement date other than the date of grant or award in these two *Interpretations* raised questions as to the validity of the approach used in *Opinion No. 25* to account for compensatory stock plans. As a result, the FASB decided to add accounting for stock compensation plans to its agenda.

Sometimes corporations loan money to officers to acquire the company's common stock. Under SEC rules, the unpaid balance of these loans is reported as a deduction from owners' equity.

Convertible Securities

A number of companies have issued bonds and other debt obligations which have future implications for the shareholders' equity accounts because they either are convertible into stock or carry detachable warrants to purchase stock. Chapter 21 indicated the appropriate accounting for these conversion privileges and warrants.

Owners' Equity Analysis

The analysis of shareholders' equity typically focuses on the determination of book value, which is equivalent to owners' equity with or without certain adjustments. Many financial authors relegate book value to a low level of importance (or even meaningless statistic) in the hierarchy of financial ratio data. This is a mistake since there are many practical applications where book value plays an important role. In these situations, determining book value is merely a straightforward exercise. The question of what book value figure is relevant depends on the analyst's purpose. Also, in the case of complex capital structure situations, there may be controversy over the appropriate way to calculate the relevant figure.

In companies with simple capital structures, book value is equal to owners' equity. If there is preferred stock outstanding, however, the common stockholders' book value is equal to owners' equity less the preferred stock. If preferred stock dividends are in arrears, these are excluded from book value. The preferred stock value used in making this calculation is its liquidation value. This may be different from its par value or call value. If more than one class of common stock is outstanding, book value should be allocated to each class in accordance with the rules governing that class's preference in liquidation.

As its name implies, book value per share is equal to book value divided by the number of common shares outstanding at the end of the accounting period. Typically, common stock equivalents used in computing earnings per share are not included in this calculation. Some analysts argue it would be more conservative to include the per-share value of dilutive senior convertible debt issues, options, and warrants in the book value per share calculation. They would also adjust book value for any capital additions assumed to arise from debt conversions. This approach is not popular because it seems to have no practical significance.

Typically, the book value of a firm is equivalent to its owners' equity as determined by generally accepted accounting principles. In certain cases, this figure may be adjusted. For example, in some situations a distinction is made between book value and tangible book value, which is owners' equity after eliminating intangible assets from the asset side of the basic accounting equation (owners' equity = assets − liabilities). Tangible book value is of interest to creditors concerned with estimating collateral values represented by "hard" assets that may have some value in liquidation. Sometimes in loan covenants all or a portion of the deferred tax liability is considered equivalent to equity and as such is included in the definition of owners' equity for determining permissible debt-to-equity ratio limits. In liquidation analysis, book value is usually based upon the estimated liquidation values of a company's assets and liabilities, rather than their balance sheet values. Accounting book values are frequently adjusted to a market value equivalent in selling situations, when the company's accounting book value is significantly below its book value based on the current market cost or replacement value of its assets, including such items as trademarks, patents, and liabilities, such as contingencies, that may not be listed on the balance sheet.

Comparisons of company book values can be misleading unless certain adjustments are made for differences in accounting policies and real values. Conservative accounting practices such as accelerated depreciation, LIFO inventory accounting, and rapid amortization of intangibles tend to depress book values relative to those of companies using more liberal accounting methods. Accounting adjustments, such as adding back LIFO reserves to inventory, should be made when comparing book values of companies with different approaches to accounting. In the case of some companies, there may also be a significant difference betweeen the book and market values of assets that enter into the book value calculation. This quality difference must be considered in making intercompany book value comparisons.

Rarely will the book value of a company be equivalent to its market value as a going concern, in liquidation or for collateral purposes. For this reason, book value is often regarded as having little value. Despite this, book value figures are used in a variety of different situations. Many private companies, in the absence of a market-determined stock price, use book value per share as the equivalent of their stock's value for pricing shares for buy-back agreements, stock option awards, and estimate valuation purposes. Some utility regulators use book value as a basis for determining allowable rates of return. Stock prices are often quoted as a multiple of book value, as a way to communicate the relative value of stocks. Book value is also used frequently in defining debt convenants. Finally, many business acquisition agreements include provisions for purchase price adjustments if the book value of the acquired company is less than a certain figure after any adjustments that may be required to its assets and liabilities based on the postacquisition audit.

Beyond using the owners' equity section to compute book value, this section of the balance sheet should be examined for such things as possible debt covenant violations; accounting adjustments that did not go through income, such as transaction gains or losses and accounting changes; changes in the relative standing of different classes of equity holders; restrictions on dividend payments; possible dilution from holders of convertible debt, options, and warrants; and possible value to others in liquidation, merger, or acquisition.

The effect of stock buybacks on equity should be analyzed carefully. A stock buyback can increase a company's return on equity and earnings per share. These improvements may hide a deteriorating operating situation. In the absence of future buybacks, the improved return on equity will deteriorate over time, and the gain in earnings per share will not persist beyond a few years. In stock buyback situations, analysts should always compute the company's key ratios before and after the buyback effect for the year of the buyback and for several years thereafter.

CASE 24-1

Kemp Foods Corporation
Accounting for Owners' Equity

"Here's the entire mess," said Ed McCowan, as papers of various sizes and colors fluttered from the large manila envelope and spread over the desk of Dan Conner, CPA.

I bought 40 shares of Kemp Foods common last year in May. Since then I've received proxy statements, notices of stock splits, stock certificates, quarterly financial statements, and a few dividend checks. When this thick annual report came in yesterday's mail, I called you. I knew what to do with those little dividend checks, but to tell the truth I don't know what the rest of this means. I thought the annual report would explain things, but I don't see any relationship between my 40 shares and the big numbers and big words in the report.

If that wasn't enough, this morning I read in the paper that Kemp expects to borrow $3 million for 15 years at 10 percent. The deal is expected to close in the next 30 days. The company anticipates using its cash to buy back in the open market 100,000 shares at approximately $30 per share. What will this do to my stock? How does this impact the company?

"It appears that you saved everything, Ed." said Dan Conner. "Let's see if we can list things as they happened from the beginning." He made these notes on a desk pad as he selected papers from the assortment before him:

May 5, 1984, bought 40 common at 38 plus commission	$1,539.60
July 20, 1984, received cash dividends, 40 at 25 cents	10.00
Oct. 20, 1984, received cash dividends, 40 at 25 cents	10.00
Oct. 25, 1984, received 2 shares, common stock dividend	
Jan. 20, 1985, received cash dividends, 42 at 25 cents	10.50
Mar. 15, 1985, received 21 shares, 3 for 2 stock split	
Apr. 20, 1985, received cash dividends, 63 at 20 cents	12.60

This case was prepared by F. R. Madera under the direction of David F. Hawkins. Copyright © 1965 by the President and Fellows of Harvard College Harvard Business School case 110–101 (Rev. 1985)

EXHIBIT 1

KEMP FOODS CORPORATION
Comparative Balance Sheets
April 30, 1985, and 1984

	1985	1984
Assets		
Current assets:		
Cash	$ 996,020	$ 1,124,588
Receivables (net)	5,076,894	5,084,087
Inventories, at the lower of cost (FIFO basis)		
or market	10,440,509	8,708,578
Total current assets	$16,513,423	$14,917,253
Prepaid expenses	133,434	230,002
Plant and equipment:		
Land	$ 290,349	$ 346,319
Buildings and leasehold improvements	4,200,760	4,719,515
Machinery and equipment	3,916,508	4,275,927
Automotive equipment	601,393	586,030
Construction in progress	2,033,324	—
	$11,042,334	$ 9,927,791
Less: Accumulated depreciation and amortization	5,038,251	4,532,968
Net plant and equipment	$ 6,004,083	$ 5,394,823
Total assets	$22,650,940	$20,542,078
Liabilities and Stockholders' Equity		
Current liabilities:		
Bank loans	$ 2,192,500	$ 1,350,000
Current maturities of long-term debt	170,790	163,478
Accounts payable and accrued liabilities	2,187,440	1,770,026
Income taxes	1,014,527	936,889
Dividends payable	126,811	102,554
Total current liabilities	$ 5,692,068	$ 4,322,947
Long-term debt, noncurrent portion	3,660,223	3,831,013
Deferred income taxes and other expenses	273,850	174,225
	$ 9,626,141	$ 8,328,185
Stockholders' equity:		
Cumulative 4% preferred stock, par value $100;		
authorized 15,000 shares, issued 8,995		
shares less 198 shares in treasury	$ 879,700	
Common stock, par value $5; authorized		(See Exhibit 2)
1 million shares, issued 590,552 shares,		
(4,482 shares in treasury, see below)	2,952,760	
Capital in excess of par value	2,853,702	
Retained earnings:		
Reserve for plant expansion	1,466,676	
Unappropriated*	4,997,457	
	$13,150,295	
Less: Treasury stock, common (4,482 shares at cost)	125,496	
Total stockholders' equity	$13,024,799	12,213,893
Total liabilities and stockholders' equity	$22,650,940	$20,542,078

*Under terms of the long-term debt agreement, $2,330,808 of retained earnings at April 30, 1985, is restricted against payment of cash dividends on or purchase of common stock.

"Now, let's look at the quotations in today's *Wall Street Journal* and see how you've made out over the past year. Here it is on the Pacific Coast Exchange. The June 10 closing price was 28½. Now we'll look at the April 30, 1985, annual report together and see what it tells us."

This case concerns corporate financial reporting for changes in shareholders' equity and its meaning to the investor.

The Company

Kemp Foods Corporation was established in Illinois in 1967 to acquire and operate three small vegetable canning plants. Operations were expanded to include canning of fruits and frozen fruit processing. The growth of these newer activities in the late 1970s was responsible for transfer of company headquarters to California. In 1985, the company had 15 canning and processing plants throughout the Midwest and on the West Coast.

Kemp's operations had always been profitable. Earnings per share of common reached a historic high of $2.27 in the fiscal year ended April 30, 1985. Net income for the year was $1.3 million on sales of almost $59 million. Stockholders' equity at April 30, 1985, exceeded $13 million. The company's comparative balance sheets at the close of the two most recent years are shown in Exhibit 1. An analysis of common stock, paid-in surplus, and retained earnings is shown in Exhibit 2.

Most of the funds needed to finance the company's growth had been provided internally. Modest cash dividends had been paid quarterly without interruption since 1976, when the common stock was split three for one. In 1972, after a public offering of preferred and common stock, a policy of supplementing the regular cash dividends with stock dividends to common stockholders was adopted. Five percent stock dividends were declared in each year thereafter except for 1975 and 1976, when stock dividends were 20 percent and 10 percent respectively. The 4 percent preferred stock was gradually being retired as it became available in the market at an attractive price. Some funds had been obtained by the use of long-term debt, and future expansion was to be financed more extensively in this way.

The price of Kemp Foods' common stock had risen steadily since the mid-1970s. For example, the price had ranged from a low of 12¾ to a high of 18⅝ in the year 1979 and reached an all time high of 43½ in 1984.

Questions

1. Evaluate Ed McCowan's investment at June 10, 1985.
2. Examine the stockholders' equity section of Kemp Foods' balance sheet to:
   a. Determine how each item was originally created.
   b. Explain changes during the year ended April 30, 1985.

EXHIBIT 2

Common Stock, Paid-In Surplus, and Retained Earnings for the Year Ended April 30, 1985

	Common Stock		Capital in Excess of Par Value	Retained Earnings	
				Reserve for Plant Exp.	Unappro-priated
	Shares	Par Value			
Balance at May 1, 1984	375,130	$1,875,650	$3,197,277	$3,500,000	$2,742,831
Add:					
Net income for the year	—	—	—	—	1,376,871
Gain on sale of 600 shares common treasury stock	—	—	17,716	—	—
Discount on 245 shares of preferred stock purchased	—	—	4,003	—	—
Reduction in reserve for plant expansion	—	—	—	(2,033,324)	2,033,324
Total	375,130	$1,875,650	$3,218,996	$1,466,676	$6,153,026
Add or (deduct):					
Transfer to common stock in connection with 3 for 2 stock split	196,690	983,450	(983,450)	—	—
Cash dividends:					
Preferred ($4 per share)	—	—	—	—	(35,386)
Common ($0.95 per share)	—	—	—	—	(408,367)
5% stock dividend, recorded at fair market value of $38 per share	18,732	93,660	618,156	—	(711,816)
Balance at April 30, 1985	590,552	$2,952,760	$2,853,702	$1,466,676	$4,997,457

3. Contrast Kemp's methods of reporting preferred treasury stock and common treasury stock.

4. What is the effect of Kemp's acquisition of treasury stock upon investor McCowan's holdings?

5. Suggest improvements Kemp might make in reporting stockholders' equity information on its balance sheet.

6. How does the issuance of stock options to the management change the company's net worth accounts at *(a)* date of issuance, *(b)* date the options are first exercisable, and *(c)* date exercised? Assume options to buy 2,000 shares are first exercisable in 1985. (These were issued originally at a price equal to the then current market price of 20.) What would be the accounting entry for these options if they were exercised during 1985, when the market price of Kemp stock was 26? How did the company originally account for the granting of these options?

7. How will the proposed 100,000 share purchase impact Kemp's balance sheet, income statement, and key ratios? Use 1985 data to illustrate your answer. What might be the impact on McCowan's investment if he holds onto his Kemp stock?

PART NINE

Special Reporting and Analysis Problems

CHAPTER 25

Foreign Operations Accounting and Analysis

Multinational corporations operate a number of currencies. Typically, their overseas subsidiaries maintain their accounting records in the local currency. For equity method accounting and consolidation purposes, these different currency statements must be restated to a common currency, which for United States–controlled multinationals in the U.S. dollar.

The process of translation expresses in dollars the foreign currency-denominated financial measurements of a company. *No actual conversion* of assets or liabilities from one currency to another takes place. If the exchange rate between the dollar and the local foreign currency changes, this accounting procedure can give rise to an unrealized dollar translation adjustment, which can be either a gain or loss. Realized exchange gains or losses can also result from the *actual* conversion of foreign currency or the settlement of a receivable or payable denominated in a foreign currency at a rate different from that when the item was recorded.

FASB Statement No. 52, "Foreign Currency Translation," established the accounting and reporting standards for translating statements from one currency to another. This *Statement* also governs the reporting of foreign currency transactions and certain forward contracts, such as hedges.

Statement users must understand the various approaches to incorporating the financial statements of foreign operations in the consolidated statements presented to U.S. stockholders. Depending on the accounting method used, exchange rate shifts may have very different impacts on the earnings and ratios of the consolidated entity. If the statement user does not have a good grasp of foreign currency translation accounting, the statement user will not appreciate the interplay between accounting methods, exchange rate shifts, and financial statement values. Also, meaningful comparisons between companies using different accounting approaches will be more difficult to make, and erroneous conclusions based on ratio analysis and reported income may be reached.

It is difficult to determine exactly how exchange rate movements will impact a company's financial statements and cash flows. Nevertheless, analysts must form opinions as to the general direction and approximate dollar impact. Beyond the financial statement consideration, analysts must also be able to identify the operating and financial actions a company might take to mitigate adverse consequences and to take advantage of opportunities created by exchange rate changes. When evaluating overseas entities' statements, analysts must also develop an appreciation of the political, legal, and environmental factors that can influence the flow of cash from the overseas operations to their U.S. parent as well as shape the future development of the company's overseas opportunities.

Exchange Rate

The exchange rate is the amount of one country's currency that equals one unit of another country's. For example, A$1 (Australian) is equivalent to U.S.$.85. Conversely, one would have to pay A$1.18 to purchase U.S.$1.00. Since each country has its own currency, there is a multiplicity of exchange rates. The rates for the major countries involved in international trade are published daily in leading newspapers.

At any moment, more than one exchange rate may exist between two currencies. For example, the "spot," or immediate currency delivery rate is usually different from the forward rate for delivery in, say, 90 days. Sometimes, countries use different rates for financing different types of goods and services. Also, in some cases, a black market rate may exist alongside the official government rate.

The supply and demand for foreign currencies is influenced by international movements involving goods, services, and investments, as well as currency speculation. For example, when United States residents export goods or services, they receive payment in U.S. dollars. To obtain these dollars, the foreign importers must exchange some of their currency. Thus, U.S. exports increase the supply of foreign currency and the demand for U.S. dollars in the foreign exchange market. The reverse situation exists when U.S. residents import goods or services.

In a free market, the exchange rate for a given currency will tend to stablize at the point where the supply and demand for that currency are in balance. This balance can be influenced by a variety of factors. Since a country's exports and imports often reflect its internal cost-price structure, changes in the domestic purchasing power of different currencies may influence their relative exchange rates. The exchange in free markets is also influenced by the fact that not all imports and exports are bought on price alone. For example, consumer preferences for certain imports and inelastic demand situations can complicate the adjustment mechanism. If any discrepancies between foreign exchange markets exist, arbitrage by foreign currency traders will soon eliminate them.

The major trading countries support a worldwide system of exchange rates that permits rates to fluctuate freely. To minimize the possibility that freely fluctuating rates could cause distortions in a country's balance of payments and internal economy, governments use a number of devices that increase the supply or decrease the demand for their currencies to keep their exchange rates fairly stable and at a desired level. These include selling or adding to foreign exchange reserves, establishing foreign exchange controls, imposing import controls, subsidizing exports, and reducing or expanding foreign aid programs.

Restrictions on the free exchange of currencies can lead to a currency being overvalued. In these cases, it becomes desirable to shift funds from the overvalued currency to the more normally valued ones. To halt this flight from the overvalued ("soft") currency to the normally valued ("hard") currencies, its government can declare the soft currency inconvertible, or not subject to exchange. Countries can make their currencies inconvertible for all people; for residents but not foreigners; for some but not all other currencies; or for certain types of transactions only.

At times, governments with serious adverse balance of payments problems are unable to maintain their currency's exchange rate. The classic solution to this problem is to let the currency devalue. It is hoped that this step will improve the balance of trade by making it more expensive for citizens to import goods and less expensive for foreigners to buy exports. Successful devaluation requires an increase in exports and, since local prices of imported goods will rise, an anti-inflationary domestic fiscal policy must be instituted. Since trade is only one part of the international payments system, however, currency speculation, foreign investments, and military aid may also affect the payments balance.

Translation of Statements

To include the local currency-denominated financial statements of foreign operations of U.S. companies in the U.S. dollar consolidated statements prepared for the parent's stockholders, it is necessary to express the overseas subsidiary's statements in their U.S. dollar equivalent, determined in accordance with generally accepted accounting principles. No actual cash changes hands in this process. It is simply a worksheet adjustment. For example, to convert the balance sheet account Cash in Australian dollars to U.S. dollars, the cash balance on the Australian statement is multiplied by $.85, since A$1 equals U.S.$.85.

As explained later, some items in the foreign currency-denominated financial statements will be restated to dollars uing the exchange rate at the time of the transaction giving rise to the item, and others will be restated using the exchange rate as of the balance sheet date. If there has been a change in the exchange rate, when each item is converted to U.S. dollars the statements will probably be out of balance. The balancing item is a translation adjustment gain or loss. This gain or loss can arise only from the process of translation.

Once each of the items on the right-hand side of the following equation has been converted from local currency to U.S. dollars, the translation adjustment gain or loss can be computed as follows:

$$\text{Translation adjustment gains or losses} = \text{Assets} - (\text{Liabilities} + \text{Beginning net worth} + \text{Profit} - \text{Dividends})$$

If the answer is a negative amount, then a translation loss has occurred. Depending on the circumstances, it must be deducted, either directly or through the income statement, from the owners' equity portion of the right-hand side of the balance sheet to bring the right and left sides into balance. That will occur if after translation:

$$\text{Assets} < (\text{Liabilities} + \text{Beginning net worth} + \text{Profit} - \text{Dividends})$$

Conversely, if the translated assets are greater than the translated right-hand side of the equation, a translation adjustment gain will occur.

The way to translate each of the items in the equation from local currency to U.S. dollars is specified in *Statement No. 52.*

Statement No. 52

The FASB's objective in releasing *Statement No. 52* was to set foreign currency translation standards that *(a)* provide information that is generally compatible with the expected economic effects of an exchange rate change on a company's cash flow and owners' equity and *(b)* reflect in consolidated statements the financial results and relationships as measured in the primary currency in which each entity included in the consolidated results conducts its business.

The *Statement* refers to the primary currency in which an entity does business as its functional currency. The designation of each foreign entity's functional currency is an important management decision. It determines the method used to translate the foreign currency-denominated financial statements into U.S. dollars and the disposition of any translation adjustment gain or loss.

The board's functional currency and economic effects goals are the foundation on which *Statement No. 52* rests. Depending on how a company's situation is assessed in terms of these two objectives, the effect of translation on the consolidated statements can vary significantly. For example, if the operating unit's local currency is designated as its functional currency, the current-rate method (see below) is used to translate the statements to dollars and any translation adjustments are direct adjustments to owners' equity. Alternatively, if the U.S. dollar is considered the unit's functional currency, the remeasurement method (see below) is used to convert the foreign currency statements into their dollar equivalents. In this case, any remeasurement adjustments are included in the determination of income.

The current-rate and remeasurement approaches[1] to translation outlined in the *Statement* reflect the board's conclusions about how its two translation accounting goals can best be met:

- The effect of changing currency prices on the carrying amounts of all foreign assets and liabilities should be recorded currently after recognizing situational differences.
- The economic effects of exchange rate changes on an overseas operating unit that is relatively self-contained and integrated within a foreign country relate primarily to the net investment in that unit. Translation adjustment gains or losses that arise from consolidating such foreign operations do not change the parent's cash flows. Consequently, in these cases, the current-rate translation method should be used; the local currency should be designated as the functional currency; and translation adjustments should not be included in the consolidated U.S. dollar-denominated income, but rather be made directly to owners' equity.
- The economic effects of an exchange rate shift on a foreign operation that is essentially an extension of the parent's domestic operations relate primarily to individual assets and liabilities and affect the parent's cash flow directly. Accordingly, the functional currency of such a business should be the U.S. dollar; the remeasurement approach should be used to translate; and translation adjustments should be included in net income.

Functional Currency

A foreign entity's functional currency is the currency of the main country in which the entity operates. Normally, that is the currency of the country in which the business generates and spends cash.

As indicated above, the local currency should be the functional currency for operations that are relatively self-contained and integrated within a particular foreign country. Alternatively, the board concluded that the U.S. dollar should be the functional currency for overseas businesses that are primarily a direct extension or integrated component of the parent company's operations.

In practice, determining the functional currency of an operation can

---

[1] *Statement No. 52* draws a technical distinction between translation and remeasurement. Translation is the process of expressing a company's functional currency statements in the reporting currency. Remeasurement is the process for measuring in the functional currency financial statements stated in another currency. If the functional and reporting currency are both the U.S. dollar, the remeasured statement is equivalent to the translated statement.

be difficult. Many operations do not clearly fall into one or the other of the two operating situations described by the board. To assist managements in making functional currency determinations, the board identified a number of economic facts to consider. These are listed in Illustration 25–1. The considerations listed indicate whether the functional currency should be the local currency or the parent company's currency. The board did not assign any priorities to these indicators. Also, if management regards factors other than those listed by the board as relevant to the functional currency decision, they can be considered also.

The functional currency determination need not be made on a legal-entity basis. It may be made on an operation-by-operation basis. For example, an entity may have distinct, self-contained operations in several countries, and each may have its own functional currency. In some cases, the facts may indicate that a company's functional currency is the currency of a foreign country other than the one in which the entity is located.[2]

Once an entity's functional currency has been determined, the designa-

ILLUSTRATION 25–1
Functional Currency Indicators

Indicator	Foreign Currency	Parent's Currency
Cash flow	Cash flows related to the foreign entity's individual assets and liabilities are primarily in the foreign currency and do not directly affect the parent company's cash flows.	Cash flows related to the foreign entity's individual assets and liabilties directly affect the parent's cash flows on a current basis and are generally available for remittance to the parent company.
Sales price	Sales prices for the foreign entity's products are not primarily responsive on a short-term basis to changes in exchange rates but are determined more by local competition or local government regulation.	Sales prices for the foreign entity's products are primarily responsive on a short-term basis to changes in exchange rates; for example, sales prices are determined more by worldwide competition or by international prices.
Sales market	There is an active local sales market for the foreign entity's products, although there may also be significant amounts of exports.	The sales market is mostly in the parent's country, or sales contracts are denominated in the parent's currency.

---

[2] If the foreign entity's functional currency is a currency other than the U.S. dollar or the entity's reporting currency, a two-step translation process is used. First, the remeasurement process is used to remeasure the reporting currency statements in their functional currency equivalent. Then, these functional currency statements are translated into U.S. dollars using the current-rate method, and any translation adjustment gain or loss resulting from this second step is included in owners' equity.

ILLUSTRATION 25–1 *(concluded)*

Indicator	Foreign Currency	Parent's Currency
Expenses	Labor, materials, and other costs for the foreign entity's products or services are primarily local costs, even though there may be some imports.	Labor, materials, and other costs for the foreign entity's products or services, on a continuing basis, are primarily costs for components obtained from the country in which the parent company is located.
Financing	Financing is primarily denominated in foreign currency, and funds generated by the foreign entity's operations are sufficient to service existing and normally expected debt obligations.	Financing is primarily from the parent or other dollar-denominated obligations, or funds generated by the foreign entity's operations are not sufficient to service existing and normally expected debt obligations without the infusion of additional funds from the parent company. Infusion of funds from the parent for expansion is not a factor, provided funds generated by the foreign entity's expanded operations are expected to be sufficient to service that additional financing.
Intercompany transactions and arrangements	There is a low volume of intercompany transactions, and the relationship between the operations of the foreign entity and the parent company is not extensive. The foreign entity's operations may rely on the parent's or affiliates' competitive advantages, however, such as patents and trademarks.	There is a high volume of intercompany transactions and the relationship between the operations of the foreign entity and the parent company is extensive. In addition, the parent's currency generally would be the functional currency if the foreign entity were a device or shell corporation for holding investments, obligations, intangible assets, etc., that could readily be carried on the parent's or an affiliate's books.

tion should be used consistently, unless significant changes in the entity's economic circumstances suggest clearly that another currency should be designated.

Current-Rate Method

As its name suggests, the current-rate method uses the current exchange rate to translate all elements of financial statements, except owners' equity. For assets or liabilities, the exchange rate at the balance sheet date is used.

Income statement items are translated at the exchange rate at the time they are recognized for income determination purposes. A distinctive feature of the current-rate method is that translation adjustments are made directly to owners' equity.

The current-rate method is used when the functional currency is other than the U.S. dollar.

In practice, companies translate recurring revenue and expense items at the average exchange rate for the period. This is a less expensive approach than attempting to translate each transaction at the exchange rate on the transaction day. If a significant transaction occurs, however, such as a material gain on the sale of an asset, the transaction date exchange rate should be used for translation purposes.

The cumulative translation adjustments included directly in equity under the current-rate method are reported under that title, "Equity Adjustments from Foreign Currency Translation." Companies must keep track of the sources of the amounts carried in this account, because if an entity, or part of an entity, responsible for a portion of the accumulated translation adjustment is sold or liquidated, the related translation adjustment is included in the computation of the gain or loss on the transaction.

An Illustration: Overseas Incorporated

Illustration 25–2 presents the worksheet for translating a foreign subsidiary's local currency balance sheet and income statement into dollars using the current-rate method. Later, in Illustration 25–4, the same foreign currency statements are used to illustrate the remeasurement method.

The example assumes the company started business on January 1, 1985; plant is bought at the beginning of the year; sales, purchases of raw materials, and expenses are spread evenly throughout the year; inventory is priced at its average cost for the year (relevant only for Illustration 25–4); plant is depreciated on a straight-line basis over 10 years; and no dividends are paid. On January 1, 1985, the exchange rate was four local units to U.S.$1. During the year, the currency steadily devalued relative to the dollar so that on December 31, the exchange rate was eight local units to U.S.$1. The average rate for the year was six local units to the U.S. dollar.

The rate for translating Overseas Incorporated's capital stock in Illustration 25–2 is four local currency units to the dollar. Thus, the dollar equivalent of these local currency balances in this account can be obtained by multiplying the foreign currency balance by 0.25 (1 U.S. dollar/4 local currency units). Since the exchange rate changed evenly throughout the year, a factor of 0.167 (1 U.S. dollar/6 local currency units) can be used to translate the revenues and expenses that occurred evenly throughout the year. On the last day of the year, the exchange rate is eight local currency units to the dollar. Consequently, a factor of 0.125 (1 U.S. dollar/8 local currency units)

ILLUSTRATION 25–2
Foreign Statement Translation Example Using Current-Rate Method—
Overseas Incorporated

	1985 Financial Statements (local currency)	Translation Factors	1985 Financial Statements (U.S. dollars)*
Assets			
Cash and receivables	40	.125	5
Inventory	32	.125	4
Plant	80	.125	10
Less: Accumulated depreciation	(8)	.125	(1)
Total assets	144		18
Liabilities			
Current liabilities	56	.125	7
Long-term debt	24	.125	3
Total liabilities	80		10
Owners' Equity			
Capital stock	20	.25	5
Beginning retained earnings	0	—	0
Plus net income	44	(see below)	7
		Equity adjustment from currency translation (plug, 18–22)	(4)
Total liabilities and owners' equity	144		18
Income Statement			
Sales	401	.167	67
Less: Cost of sales	196	.167	33
Gross margin	205	.167	34
Depreciation	8	.167	1
Other expenses	153	.167	26
Net income	44		7

* Rounded to nearest dollar.

can be used to convert those year-end balance sheet accounts that must be translated at the balance sheet date exchange rate.

When Overseas Incorporated's foreign currency statements are translated into U.S. dollars, the balance sheet translation process leads to a translation adjustment loss of four U.S. dollars, since the company had an excess of translated liabilities and owners' equity ($22) over translated assets ($18). Because the current-rate method is used, the translation adjustment loss is not included in the income statements. It is shown only on the translated statements as an adjustment to owners' equity.

The board believes that for reasonably self-contained foreign operations, the translated financial statements of the parent company should carry over to the consolidated dollar statements the local currency statement's profit or loss position and financial relationships, such as the current ratio and gross margin percentage. As shown in Illustration 25–2, the current rate achieves this goal mechanically by *(a)* multiplying the local currency amounts by a constant factor equivalent to the current exchange rate between the local currency and the dollar and *(b)* including translation adjustments, if any, in owners' equity.

Remeasurement

The remeasurement process is used whenever an entity's functional currency is other than its local currency. When the U.S. dollar is the functional currency, the remeasurement process is used to restate the overseas entity's local currency-denominated financial statements in U.S. dollars.

The remeasurement process is similar to the current-rate method except for these important differences:

a. The remeasurement adjustment is included in net income.

b. Certain nonmonetary balance sheet and related income statement accounts are remeasured using historical exchange rates (if exchange rate at the time of the transaction giving use to the asset or liability). Illustration 25–3 lists those accounts that are remeasured using historical exchange rates.

ILLUSTRATION 25–3
Selected Accounts Remeasured Using Historical Exchange Rates

Balance Sheet Items

Marketable securities carried at cost
  Equity securities
  Debt securities not intended to be held until maturity
Inventories carried at cost
Prepaid expenses such as insurance, advertising, and rent
Property, plant, and equipment
Accumulated depreciation on property, plant, and equipment
Patents, trademarks, licenses, and formulas
Goodwill
Other intangible assets
Deferred charges and credits, except deferred income taxes and unamortized policy acquisition
  costs for life insurance companies
Deferred income
Common stock
Preferred stock carried at issuance price

Income Statement Items

Cost of goods sold
Depreciation of property, plant, and equipment
Amortization of intangible items such as goodwill, patents, licenses, etc.
Amortization of deferred charges or credits, except deferred income taxes and policy acquisition
  costs for life insurance companies

An Illustration: Overseas Incorporated

The remeasurement process is demonstrated in Illustration 25–4, using the same Overseas Incorporated data previously presented in Illustration 25–2. The principal differences between the remeasurement and current-rate examples are:

a.   The remeasurement process uses a historical exchange rate to restate inventory, plant, accumulated depreciation, cost of sales, and

ILLUSTRATION 25–4
Foreign Statement Remeasurement Example—Overseas Incorporated

	1985 Financial Statements (local currency)	Translation Factors	1985 Financial Statements (U.S. dollars)*
Assets			
Cash and receivables	40	.125	5
Inventory	32	.167	4
Plant................................	80	.25	20
Less: Accumulated depreciation	(8)	.25	(2)
Total assets	144		27
Liabilities			
Current liabilities.....................	56	.125	7
Long-term debt.......................	24	.125	3
Total liabilities	80		
Owners' Equity			
Capital	20	.25	5
Beginning retained earnings	0	—	0
Plus net income	44	Income before remeasurement or loss (see below)	6
			21
		Remeasurement exchange gain (plug, 27–21)	6
Total liabilities and owners' equity	144		27
Income Statement			
Sales	401	.167	67
Less: Cost of sales	196	.167	33
Gross margin	205		34
Depreciation	8	.25	2
Other expenses	153	.167	26
Net income	44	Income before remeasurement exchange gains or losses	6
		Remeasurement exchange gain	6
		Net income	12

* Rounded to nearest dollar.

depreciation, whereas the current-rate method translates these three balance sheet items at the balance sheet date exchange rate and the two expense items at the average rate for the period to which the expense items apply.

b. The remeasurement process includes the remeasurement exchange gain in the determination of net income, whereas the foreign currency translation loss arising from the current-rate method is a direct adjustment to owners' equity.

Since Overseas Incorporated's reporting currency is the same as its functional currency, remeasurement is equivalent to translation.

Highly Inflationary Economies

Statement No. 52 requires that the financial statements of overseas entities in highly inflationary economies be remeasured using the parent's reporting currency as their functional currency, which in the case of U.S. parent corporation is the U.S. dollar. A highly inflationary economy is defined as one that has a cumulative three-year inflation rate of approximately 100 percent or more. This definition should be applied with judgment.

The FASB adopted its special rule for entities operating in highly inflationary economies because the use of the current-rate method to translate assets and liabilities in such economies might produce unrealistic results. For example, assume a subsidiary in a highly inflationary economy acquired a building on January 1, 1985, for the local currency equivalent of U.S.$2 million. During the year, the local currency devalued 100 percent against the dollar and the local annual inflation rate was 100 percent. If the building asset valued in local currency were translated into U.S. dollars using the year-end exchange rate, its carrying value on the consolidated U.S. dollar statements would be reduced from the beginning-of-year value of U.S.$2 million to U.S.$1 million because of the devaluation of the local currency. This result is unrealistic, since the value of the building in local currency probably doubled because of inflation. As a result, its actual U.S. dollar equivalent value may still be approximately U.S.$2 million.

In addition, using the current-rate method to translate the local currency depreciation expense for the building would result in decreasing dollar equivalents as the local currency devalued. Using the historical exchange rate, as required by the remeasurement process, to remeasure the local-currency cost of the building and related depreciation stabilizes the dollar equivalents.

The FASB decision to require financial statements of foreign entities in highly inflationary economies to be remeasured using the reporting currency reflects the board's view that a currency that has largely lost its utility as a store of value cannot be a functional unit of measurement. While the board's solution to the problem of unstable units of measurement is not completely satisfactory, it is a pragmatic solution that reduces potential inflationary distortions without introducing general price-level accounting into the basic financial statements.

Write-Downs

The application of the lower-of-cost-or-market rule involves special consideration for foreign entities that maintain their accounting records in a currency other than their functional currency. For example, even when the local currency reports do not require a write-down, an inventory write-down may be required in the functional currency statements if, after remeasurement, cost is more than market in the functional currency. The opposite could also occur. An inventory write-down recorded in the local currency statements might be reversed in the functional currency statements if the functional currency market exceeds the remeasurement cost. Similarly, write-downs recorded in the local currency statements of other assets, such as plant, may have to be reversed in the remeasurement process if the functional currency sales price exceeds the remeasurement cost.

Foreign Currency Transactions

A foreign currency transaction is a transaction involving a currency other than the entity's functional currency. It may be a transaction of the parent, of the subsidiary, or of both.

At the time of a foreign currency transaction, the transaction should be measured and recorded in the functional currency of the recording company using the exchange rate on that day. At each subsequent balance sheet date, the recorded foreign currency transaction balances should be adjusted to their current functional currency equivalent using the balance sheet date exchange rate. Any adjustments resulting from this procedure are made directly to the current income of the foreign entity. After translation, these foreign currency transaction gains and losses of a subsidiary can in turn give rise to consolidated statement gains or losses.

The general rule applies to all foreign currency transactions except certain intercompany currency accounts and hedging transactions.

Intercompany Balances

Exchange adjustments to intercompany balances meeting the foreign currency transaction test that could be considered as long-term investments by the parent in the foreign entity, thereby not affecting cash flow, are made directly to owners' equity, rather than to current income. Typically, intercompany balances whose settlement date is not planned or anticipated in the foreseeable future fall into this long-term investment category.

Forward Exchange Contracts

A forward exchange contract is an agreement to exchange currency of different countries at an agreed rate on a future settlement date. This future rate is known as the forward rate. Typically, this rate is different from the spot rate at the contract date. The spot rate is the exchange rate for immediate exchange of different currencies. At any time, a forward rate may be at a premium or discount to the spot rate. For example, a company agrees to exchange U.S.$10,000 for 80,000 French francs 12 months hence. The forward rate is U.S.$.125 per franc. At the time the contract is negotiated, the spot rate is nine francs per dollar, or U.S.$.111. Because the forward rate is greater than the spot rate, the contract has a premium of U.S.$1,120 [F80,000 × ($.125 − $.111)]. If the forward rate were less than the spot rate, the contract would have a discount.

Companies enter into forward exchange contracts for a variety of reasons. These range from protecting from exchange fluctuations accounts receivables denominated in foreign currencies arising from export sales to pure currency speculation.

The accounting for forward exchange contracts intended as hedges is determined by management's economic intentions when it enters into a contract. The gain or loss on a hedging contract is computed by multiplying the foreign currency amount of the contract by the difference between the spot rate on the measurement date (i.e., the balance sheet date or the settlement date), and the spot rate on the contract date (or the last measurement date). For example, if the French franc spot rate at the balance sheet date was U.S.$.120 and the franc spot rate at the earlier contract date was U.S.$.111, the unrealized gain at the balance sheet date for an open F100,000 forward exchange contract would be U.S.$900 [F100,000 × (.120 − .111)]. If this contract is hedging a F100,000 account payable, the U.S.$900 gain would be offset by a similar loss on the payable, which would now require U.S.$900 more to be spent to acquire the francs needed to pay the debt.

If a forward exchange contract hedges a firm foreign currency commitment, the gain or loss is deferred and included in the basis of the foreign currency transaction when it is recorded. If the contract hedges a net investment in a foreign entity, the gain or loss is treated as an adjustment to the translation component of stockholders' equity at the end of the reporting period. In either case, the discount or premium may be amortized to income over the life of the contract or accounted for in the same way as the gain or loss on the contract. If the forward contract hedges other than a firm foreign currency commitment or a net investment in a foreign entity, the gain or loss is included in income currently and the premium or discount is amortized to income over the life of the contract.

Gains or losses on forward exchange contracts entered into for purposes of currency speculation are included in income currently. No separate accounting recognition is given to discounts and premiums. They are included as part of the exchange gain or loss and recognized currently. The contract's gain or loss is computed by multiplying the foreign currency amount of the forward contract by the difference between the forward rate available for the remaining period of the contract and the contracted rate (or the rate last used to measure a gain or loss for an earlier period). For example, assume that the contracted forward rate for a F100,000 forward exchange contract entered into earlier is U.S.$.125 and the current forward rate for a similar contract is U.S.$.130. The speculator's gain in this case is $500 [F100,000 ($.130 − $.125)].

Hedging transactions can take a variety of forms other than forward exchange contracts. *Statement No. 52* recognizes this fact. The only requirement is that the accounting for these alternative hedges reflect the economic intent.

Since management has considerable latitude in designating hedging transactions, cash balances, receivables, and borrowings denominated in a foreign currency can be hedges. Intercompany foreign currency transactions can also be hedges, but only when the account is a foreign currency transaction of only one of the entities.

Measurement and Motivation

The business decisions managers of overseas entities make in response to exchange rate shifts may be biased by the internal accounting method used to measure their profit performance.

Typically, American companies measure the performance of their overseas operating units in U.S. dollars. They want to encourage the overseas managers to make decisions that enhance the dollar value of the U.S. shareholders' interests. A few companies use the overseas unit's local currency profit to measure overseas managers. This can be a misleading indication of managerial performance. For example, rising local currency profits may be inadequate to offset local currency devaluation relative to the dollar. As a result, the contribution of the overseas unit to consolidated dollar results may be declining, while the overseas managers may be rewarded for higher local profits.

Not all companies use the same approach to measure the U.S. dollar profit performance of their overseas managers. Many use the identical *Statement No. 52* accounting for both internal and external accounting purposes. Some use a modified version of this *Statement*. Others use methods that depart significantly from the required external reporting standard. The selection of the appropriate internal measurement for overseas managers depends on the scope of the overseas managers' authority over balance sheet items, the company's overseas operating and financial objectives, and the cost of maintaining alternative accounting systems for foreign operations.

Before *Statement No. 52,* translation gains and losses were usually included in the performance measurement of overseas managers with balance sheet responsibilities. The FASB's adoption of *Statement No. 52* complicated this aspect of performance measurement. Depending on whether the local unit's functional currency is another foreign currency, the U.S. dollar, or the local currency, translation gains or losses may or may not be included in the local unit's income.

The current-rate method's exclusion of the translation gain or loss from income when the local currency is the functional currency may reduce the overseas managers' incentive to manage balance sheet accounts to minimize translation losses and maximize translation gains. In these cases, a departure from *Statement No. 52* accounting may be considered. The inclusion of translation gains and losses in income for internal measurement purposes may overcome in part this disincentive. Since the current-rate method's base for computing the translation gain or loss is the overseas unit's net assets (i.e., total assets less total liabilities), as long as the unit has a positive net asset position equivalent to owners' equity, it will be exposed to translation gains and losses stemming from exchange rate shifts. In this situation, it is difficult for the overseas manager to influence the translation gain or loss figures, since an asset balance equivalent of owners' equity cannot easily be changed in the short run.

The foreign manager's incentive to manage balance sheet accounts is higher when the U.S. dollar or some currency other than the local one is the functional currency. In this case, the remeasurement process requires that the balance sheet adjustments resulting from exchange rate shifts be included in income. These gains or losses are a function of both the entity's net monetary asset position and the direction of the exchange rate shift. If the local currency is devaluing against the dollar, the local manager is encouraged to restructure the entity's balance sheet to have an excess of monetary liabilities, such as bank debt and accounts payable, over monetary assets, such as cash and accounts receivable. In this situation, a net monetary liability balance generates remeasurement gains, since the net monetary liability is equivalent to fewer dollars because of devaluation.

In contrast, if the local currency were appreciating, the local manager would be biased toward having an excess of monetary assets over monetary liabilities so as to generate remeasurement gains. These gains are the increase in the dollar equivalent value of the net monetary assets resulting from the upward revaluation of the local currency.

Irrespective of whether the current-rate or remeasurement method is used, a devaluation of the local currency relative to the dollar reduces the dollar equivalent of the local currency profits. This reduction can motivate the local managers to raise prices. This may be difficult to do, because competitors who measure their profits in the local currency will not be under the same pressure.[3] The reverse is true if the local currency appreciates against the U.S. dollar.

Some companies reduce their exposure to translation and remeasurement losses and profit reductions due to local currency devaluation by hedging all or part of their exposed portion. This can be expensive. To reduce their cost, some companies hedge only the net monetary asset exposure of those overseas entities whose functional currency is the dollar. The net asset exposure of those entities whose functional currency is the local currency is of less concern, since their translation losses are excluded from income.

Regardless of how the overseas manager is measured or what generally accepted accounting principles governing foreign currency translation are in force, someone in the organization must be responsible for seeing that the economic value of the U.S. stockholders' investment is protected against adverse exchange rate shifts and fully enhanced by favorable currency movements. This requires continuous planning, expert knowledge of world economics and currency movements, and an aggressive approach to financial management on a worldwide basis. It is not an easy task.

Statement Analysis

Currency exchange rate shifts are critical to the economic value of companies whose profitability is very dependent on their overseas operations, such as the major U.S. pharmaceutical companies. In these situations, the principal purpose of statement analysis is often to gain insight into how past and anticipated changes in exchange rates impact the actual and perceived economic value of these companies, particularly as it is reflected in their stock prices.

The principal analytical challenge facing those examining the financial statements of multinational corporations is to estimate how exchange rate shifts will influence operating income before considering remeasurement and translation adjustments. Determining the direction of the change is easy. If the U.S. dollar strengthens against a foreign entity's local currency,

---

[3] Another complicating factor for the local manager of a U.S. foreign entity is that the local competitors may be using accounting principles different from those followed by the U.S. company and its overseas subsidiaries. The local company may be free to set up and draw down reserves at will, reappraise assets, reflect inflation, not consolidate subsidiaries, not allocate taxes, write assets off quickly, and follow other accounting practices not sanctioned in the United States of America. Statement users looking at non-U.S. corporations should always be conscious of the fact that the statements most probably were prepared using unfamiliar accounting principles. Knowing the accounting principles followed is essential to correctly interpreting these statements and understanding how the accounting may influence the foreign managers' behavior.

the dollar equivalent of the overseas company's local currency profits declines. The opposite occurs when the dollar weakens.

Estimating the amount of the change is considerably more difficult. It can seldom be done with a high degree of accuracy or confidence. The geographical segment data showing the source of profits by geographical regions may be helpful in this task. First, it can be used to determine how material the foreign operations are to the consolidated entity's financial results. This determination can be made by expressing the segment data related to overseas operations as a percentage of total sales, income, and assets. Second, if the analyst knows how the U.S. dollar has moved against the currencies of these regions included in the overseas segments or the currency of the country within each segment providing the majority of the segment's profit, a rough estimate of the impact of exchange rate shifts can be made.

In making this assessment, the analyst must remember several things. First, the quality of the overseas earnings may differ from the domestic income. Questions such as these should be asked: Is the income earned in expanding markets? How diverse are the sources of this income? How is income affected by local inflation? Second, the overseas management may react to the exchange rate shift by raising local prices to offset local currency devaluation or shifting profits to areas where the dollar is weakening against the local currency. Therefore, a complete analysis also requires an appreciation of management's responses to shifting exchange rates.

The choice of the functional currency can influence many of the common financial ratios of multinational companies. If the functional currency is the U.S. dollar, some overseas assets and liabilities are remeasured using historical exchange rates. The use of different rates in the remeasurement process can change the underlying local currency ratios of companies with extensive overseas property, plant, and equipment investments and slow-moving inventories. For example, the assets will be remeasured using old rates. Sales will be remeasured using current rates. If the sales in local currency are steady and the local currency is appreciating relative to the dollar, the remeasured asset turnover rates will improve. The pretranslation local currency ratios of companies whose functional currency is not the parent's reporting currency are not influenced by the translation process when converted to a dollar basis, since the current rate is used to translate all of the income statement, asset, and liability values.

Translation and remeasurement adjustments reflect the impact of changing exchange rates on owners' equity. Whether or not for valuation purposes these should be included in income is a controversial issue. *Statement No. 52* tried to resolve this debate by the use of the functional currency concept. Most security analysts appear to accept the board's economic rationale underlying this concept. They include remeasurement adjustments in income and exclude translation adjustments from income. Nevertheless, while doing this they are mindful of the fact that stockholders are better off when translation adjustment gains occur and worse off when translation adjustment losses are incurred. How this awareness enters, if at all, into the equity valuation process is unclear at this time.

Income earned overseas may not be freely available for U.S. stockholders or the financing of U.S. operations. An appraisal of foreign operations should always include an assessment of the ability of the foreign companies to repatriate earnings to their U.S. parent and affiliates. Overseas income that is unavailable to the parent is of lower quality than income generated in the United States. The repatriation of income may be limited by managerial policies, such as a decision to finance overseas operations exclusively with overseas earnings, or legal and political factors, such as currency restrictions. Also, sometimes companies are reluctant to repatriate their foreign earnings because they have not accrued U.S. taxes on these earnings. If repatriated, some U.S. tax may have to be paid on the earnings and a related tax expense recorded. Finally, statement users should also be aware that overseas earnings may be repatriated in forms other than dividends, such as through the payment of accounts payable incorporating generous profit margins due to the parent for goods and services rendered.

Statement No. 52 was adopted by most companies in 1982. Prior to that time, foreign currency accounting was governed by *Statement No. 8.* In general, *Statement No. 8* required all corporations to use a translation method similar to *Statement No. 52's* remeasurement method. As a result, translation gains or losses were included in income. Reviewers of a company's history should be aware of this fact when statements issued prior to 1982 are included in their analysis.

Statement No. 52 is still a controversial approach to accounting for overseas operations. There are many who disagree with its underlying rationale and reject its functional currency concept. However, to keep this controversy in perspective it is useful to remember the comment made by a senior financial officer of a major U.S. corporation upon reading *Statement No. 52* for the first time. "This is the worst translation method I have ever seen, except for every other one."

CASE 25-1

Turner Machinery International

Turner Machinery International, a U.S. multinational corporation, sold advanced computer-controlled production equipment on a worldwide basis. The company had small manufacturing facilities and sales offices in a number of foreign countries. Thomas Matthews, the corporate financial vice president, was faced with the task of revising the company's accounting for overseas activities to conform to the recently issued *FASB Statement No. 52.* Matthews was sure that for all of the company's subsidiaries other than the West German subsidiary, the local currency should be designated as the functional currency for the reporting entity. He was unsure what the West German subsidiary's functional currency should be. To help resolve his dilemma, he decided to ask his assistant, Jim Taylor, to prepare pro forma statements for the West German subsidiary using the deutsche mark and the U.S. dollar as the functional currency. Accordingly, Matthews instructed Taylor as follows:

> I don't know what to do. Our West German subsidiary's functional currency could be the deutsche mark or the U.S. dollar. The subsidiary does a lot of business in West Germany as well as the rest of Europe for itself. In addition, it acts as a foreign sales branch for some of our U.S. divisions. It takes orders for them, bills and collects directly from their European customers, and provides a local warehouse service to facilitate prompt delivery of the U.S. divisions' products. Also, it manufactures a critical subassembly that is shipped to our U.S. and Latin American plants. Both of these activities contribute important profits.
>
> I have not pushed the numbers yet, but, depending on which way I go, intuitively I know under *Statement No. 52* the functional currency choice will make a major difference to the susidiary's 1981 financial statements.
>
> Here is the deutsche mark actual December 31, 1980, balance sheet (Exhibit 1), the projected December 31, 1981, balance sheet (Exhibit 2), and our budgeted 1981 income statement (Exhibit 3). I want you to express

This case was prepared by David F. Hawkins.

Copyright © 1985 by the President and Fellows of Harvard College
Harvard Business School case 185–063

EXHIBIT 1

TURNER MACHINERY INTERNATIONAL
West German Subsidiary's Statement of Financial Position
December 31, 1980

	Deutsche Marks	Functional U.S. Dollar		Functional Deutsche Mark	
		Exchange Rate*	U.S. Dollars	Exchange Rate*	U.S. Dollars
Assets					
Current assets:					
Cash	DM 575,000		$		$
Certificate of deposit	1,960,784				
Accounts receivable	1,685,000				
Inventories	1,600,000				
Total current assets	5,820,784				
Property and equipment	2,250,000				
Less: Accumulated depreciation	260,000				
Property and equipment (net)	1,990,000				
Total assets	DM 7,810,784		$		$
Liabilities and Stockholders' Equity					
Current liabilities:					
Accounts payable	DM 1,745,625		$		$
Due to parent	2,941,176				
Total current liabilities	4,686,801				
Long-term debt	2,000,000				
Deferred income taxes	45,000				
Stockholders' equity:					
Capital stock	600,000				
Paid-in capital	200,000				
Retained earnings	278,983				
Equity adjustment from translation					
Total stockholders' equity	1,078,983				
Total liabilities and stockholders' equity	DM 7,810,784		$		$

* Deutsche mark–U.S. dollar rate (i.e., DM1 = U.S.$.51) times deutsche mark amounts equals U.S. dollars (i.e., cash DM 757,000 × U.S.$.51 = U.S.$293,250).

EXHIBIT 2

TURNER MACHINERY INTERNATIONAL
West German Subsidiary's Statement of Financial Position
December 31, 1981

	Deutsche Marks	Functional U.S. Dollar		Functional Deutsche Mark	
		Exchange Rate	U.S. Dollars	Exchange Rate	U.S. Dollars
Assets					
Current assets:					
Cash	DM 530,000		$		$
Certificate of deposit	2,222,222				
Accounts receivable	1,400,000				
Inventories	1,500,000				
Prepaid expenses	75,000				
Total current assets	5,727,222				
Property and equipment	2,400,000				
Less: Accumulated depreciation	410,000				
Property and equipment (net)	1,990,000				
Total assets	DM 7,717,222		$		$
Liabilities and Stockholders' Equity					
Current liabilities:					
Accounts payable	DM 1,570,000		$		$
Due to parent	3,333,333				
Total current liabilities	4,903,333				
Long-term debt	1,600,000				
Deferred income taxes	60,000				
Stockholders' equity:					
Capital stock	600,000				
Paid-in capital	200,000				
Retained earnings	353,889				
Equity and adjustment from translation					
Total stockholders' equity	1,153,889				
Total liabilities and stockholders' equity	DM 7,717,222		$		$

EXHIBIT 3

TURNER MACHINERY INTERNATIONAL
West German Subsidiary's Statement of Income
1981

	Deutsche Marks	Functional U.S. Dollar		Functional Deutsche Mark	
		Exchange Rate	U.S. Dollars	Exchange Rate	U.S. Dollars
Sales	DM 7,800,000		$		$
Other income	31,250				
	7,831,250				
Costs and expenses:					
Cost of goods sold	6,200,000				
General and administrative	650,000				
Depreciation	150,000				
Interest	220,000				
	7,220,000				
Gross profit	611,250				
Transaction gain (loss)	(130,719)				
Income before income taxes	480,531				
Income taxes:					
Current	290,625				
Deferred	15,000				
	305,625				
Net income	174,906				
Retained earnings at beginning of year	278,983				
	453,889				
Less: Dividends paid	100,000				
Retained earnings at end of year	DM 353,889		$		$

these deutsche mark statements in their U.S. dollar equivalents using *Statement No. 52*, under two conditions. First, assume that the U.S. dollar is the functional currency. Second, assume we take the deutsche mark as the functional currency. The international accounting section can give you all the data you will need.

Following Matthews' instructions, Taylor met with the head of the international accounting section. Here are the notes Taylor took during that meeting:

1. The year-end exchange rates are: Actual 1980, DM1.96 = U.S.$1 (or DM1 = U.S.$.51); projected 1981, DM2.22 = U.S.$1 (or DM1 = U.S.$.45).

2. The projected average 1981 exchange rate is DM2.19 = U.S.$1 (DM1 = U.S.$.457).

3. The exchange rate at September 30, 1978, the date capital stock and long-term debt were issued and the initial property and equipment were acquired, was DM1.89 = U.S.$1 (DM1 = U.S.$.529).

4. The average exchange rate during the production period for 1980 year-end inventory was DM1.87 = U.S.$1 (DM1 = U.S.$.534). The company uses FIFO inventory accounting.

5. The 1980 and 1981 certificate-of-deposit and due-to-parent items are U.S. dollar-denominated instruments with U.S. dollar values of $1 million and $1.5 million, respectively. The net impact of the DM130,719 loss exchange rate change on these items is recorded in the transaction gain (loss) account listed on the subsidiary's local currency 1981 income statement before remeasurement and/or translation into U.S. dollars.

6. In the year of change, when the local currency is the functional currency, the retained earnings on the 1980 year-end dollar statement should be the same figure computed according to *Statement No. 8*. This can be approximated by assuming the DM45,000 deferred income taxes balance on the 1980 year-end balance sheet is remeasured and translated at the current rate (i.e., DM1 = U.S.$.51) when converting to U.S. dollars. (*Statement No. 8* used a historical rate to translate this item.) This simplifying assumption will make the remeasured 1980 deutsche mark balance sheet (assuming the U.S. dollar is the functional currency) approximately the same U.S. dollar balance sheet that would result from using *Statement No. 8*. Therefore, for the purposes of this analysis, the 1980 year-end dollar retained earnings will be the same under both functional currency assumptions. Of course, this figure is also the beginning 1981 retained earnings.

7. The projected exchange rate at June 30, 1981, is DM2.41 = U.S.$1 (DM1 = U.S.$.415), the date prepaid expenses are projected to

be incurred, additional property and equipment purchased, and dividends declared.

8. The West German subsidiary's 1981 cost of goods sold in deutsche marks was calculated as follows:

Inventories at January 1, 1981	DM1,600,000
Cost of 1981 production	6,100,000
	DM7,700,000
Less inventories at December 31, 1981	1,500,000
Cost of 1981 goods sold	DM6,200,000

The 1981 production is schedule to be spread evenly throughout the year. The estimated exchange rate for the last quarter of 1981 is DM2.30 = U.S.$1 (DM1 = U.S.$.435).

9. The 1981 DM150,000 depreciation expense included DM10,000 related to depreciable assets purchased on June 30, 1981 (see note 7, above).

10. Use the *related earnings* account as "plug" numbers (i.e., the number needed to balance the statement) when remeasuring the 1980 and 1981 deutsche mark balance sheets into U.S. dollars under the assumption that the U.S. dollar is the functional currency.

11. Use the *transaction gain* (loss) account line in the 1981 income statement as a "plug" number when remeasuring the 1981 deutsche mark income statements assuming the dollar is the functional currency.

12. All of the items on the 1981 dollar statement of income and retained earnings can be computed directly when the local currency is designated as the functional currency.

13. Use the equity-adjustment-from-translation line in the 1981 U.S. dollar balance sheet (assuming the deutsche mark is the functional currency) as a "plug" number.

Questions

1. How did the DM130,719 transaction loss arise (see Exhibit 3)? Show how this loss was calculated.

2. Complete Exhibits 1, 2, and 3.

3. What differences does the choice of functional currency make in the West Germany subsidiary's dollar statement results? How do these results differ from the subsidiary's ratios and performance when measured in deutsche marks?

4. What is the 1981 addition to the translation adjustment to stockholders' equity when the deutsche mark is the functional currency?

5. Can you explain the components of the following "plug" numbers?

    a. the 1980 year-end equity adjustment from translation, assuming the local currency is the functional currency.

    b. The 1981 transaction gain (loss) account, assuming the U.S. dollar is the functional currency.

    c. The 1981 equity-adjustment-from-translation line in the 1981 balance sheet, assuming the local currency is the functional currency.

6. Turner Machinery International is forecasting that the dollar will appreciate relative to the deutsche mark. Describe what the impact on the West German subsidiary's 1981 statements would be of a dollar devaluation relative to the deutsche mark during 1981.

CHAPTER 26

Business Segment Disclosure and Analysis

A number of publicly traded companies have diversified into more than one industry as well as expanded their operations overseas, principally through acquisitions and mergers. To help statement users understand these diversified companies better, *FASB Statement No. 14*, "Financial Reporting for Segments of a Business Enterprise," requires that diversified companies in their annual financial statements disclosure supplemental financial information related to their principal industry segments, different country operations, export sales, and major customers. For each reported industry segment and geographical grouping, the diversified company must disclose sales, operating profit or loss, and the carrying amount of identifiable assets. These requirements do not apply to nonpublic companies.

While the segment data available to analysts is skimpy, it is nevertheless very useful for developing an understanding of how a business generates its sales, earns its income, and spends its capital. It can also reveal the impact of changes in the value of the dollar relative to other currencies in a multinational business. Proficient segment analysis involves identifying changes in the segment mix over time, appraising the segment results against comparable industry trends, and determining how a particular company's segment diversification affects its level of operating and financial leverage and risk. To interpret segment disclosure data in a meaningful manner, analysts must be aware of various ways these data are prepared, the potential shortcomings of the data, and the accounting rules governing these required disclosures. The challenge of segment analysis is to do a lot with a little data. This requires going beyond the data presented to perform an analysis that gives that analyst an edge over rivals.

Diversification Trend

The modern diversification movement has been characterized by the joining together of domestic and foreign companies operating in unrelated or only slightly related industries. This type of expansion is in contrast with earlier patterns of corporate growth which involved companies in domestic markets either integrating vertically to distribute and supply their own products or integrating horizontally to enter related businesses.

The principal corporate reasons for diversification are:

1. To minimize economic instability resulting from cyclical market factors or overreliance on a single product line or geographic area.
2. To acquire new products, technological know-how, and management skills more cheaply and with less risk through acquisition than internal development would allow.
3. To expand into nonrelated businesses so as to avoid antitrust laws that restrict horizontal and vertical growth.
4. To take advantage of the opportunity provided by mergers to boost earnings and sales through the "pooling of interests" and increase growth rates through purchase accounting treatments of acquisitions.

The principal disclosure issues raised by business diversification are:

1. Are there any circumstances under which the issuers of financial data should report the results of operations on some basis other than total company figures?
2. If so, what, and how should they be reported?

Investment Analysis

The identification of industry segment and geographical financial data is essential for proper appraisal for investment purposes of the past performance and future risk and prospects of diversified companies. For example, if only total company data is examined, the fact that a company was losing money in one segment might be missed by an investor, since the loss would be combined with other segments' profits in the company's total profit figure. Also, the relative importance of the diverse segments of the business changed over time. Without specific knowledge about the separate parts of the business, investors can not judge how these changes affected the stability or risk associated with the total enterprise.

Statement No. 14

The FASB believes that segment information permits statement users to make better appraisals of a corporation's past performance and future prospects and risks than they could using total enterprise data. The FASB's *Statement* requires that annual financial statements which purport to be in accordance with generally accepted accounting principles include data related to the enterprise's operations in different industries and regions on a worldwide basis, major customers, and export sales. The auditor's report covers these disclosures. The required information may be presented in the body of the financial statements with appropriate explanations in the notes, entirely in the notes, or in a separate schedule included as an integral part of the financial statements.

Industry Segments

Statement No. 14 defines an industry segment as a "component of an enterprise engaged in providing a product or service or a group of related products and services primarily to unaffiliated customers (i.e., customers outside of the enterprise) for a profit."

A reportable segment is "an industry segment or a group of two or more industry segments for which information is required" to be reported by the *Statement.*

The *Statement* suggests that in grouping products or services to form a reportable segment, the three-digit Standard Industrial Classification system (SIC)[1] and the Enterprise Standard Industrial Classification system (ESIC) may be helpful. However, the *Statement* recognizes that these classification schemes may not be suitable in all cases and that management judgment should be used to determine the appropriate segments. The *Statement* suggests that the following criteria should be considered in making the reportable segment decision:

a. *The nature of the product.* Related products or services have similar purposes or end uses. Thus, they may be expected to have similar rates of profitability, similar degrees of risk, and similar opportunity for growth.

b. *The nature of the production process.* Sharing of common or interchangeable production or sales facilities, equipment, labor force, or service group or use of the same or similar basic raw materials may suggest that products or services are related. Likewise, similar degrees of labor intensiveness or similar degrees of capital intensiveness may indicate a relationship among products or services.

c. *Markets and marketing methods.* Similarity of geographic marketing areas, types of customers, or marketing methods may indicate

---

[1] There are over 400 three-digit industry groups. For example, the two-digit "machinery, except electrical" group includes the following three-digit groups:

1. Engines and turbines.
2. Farm and garden machinery and equipment.
3. Construction, mining, and materials handling machinery and equipment.
4. Metalworking machinery and equipment.
5. Special industry machinery, except metalworking machinery.
6. General industry machinery and equipment.
7. Office, computing, and accounting machines.
8. Refrigeration and service industry machinery.
9. Miscellaneous machinery, except electrical.

a relationship among products or services. For instance, the use of a common or interchangeable sales force may suggest a relationship among products or services. The sensitivity of the market to price changes and to changes in general economic conditions may also indicate whether products or services are related or unrelated.

Essentially, the test as to whether a segment is significant and reportable is whether or not it accounts for 10 percent of the combined enterprise's sales to unaffiliated customers and intersegment sales, segment profits (excluding industry segments incurring losses), or identifiable assets.[2] In addition, the total reportable industry segment information presented must meet an overall test. At least 75 percent of the sales to unaffiliated customers of all industry segments must be represented by the defined reportable industry segments. If the aggregated defined reportable segments do not meet this test, then additional reportable segments should be identified until the 75 percent test is met. *Statement No. 14* indicates that if defined reportable segments exceed 10 in number and the test is still not satisfied, it may be appropriate to combine certain segments into broader industry categories to meet the 75 percent test while still maintaining a workable number of defined reportable segments.

For each reportable segment, the following information is required: revenue, operating profit or loss, and identifiable assets. Illustration 26–1 presents an example of the disclosure required by the *Statement* for each reportable segment. The note accompanying this disclosure should include a description of the segments, a definition of the accounts, a description of the methods used to derive the data, and any comments that may be needed to make the data useful. The information related to the company's sales to major customers may also be presented in this note.

Segment revenue is defined to include sales to unaffiliated customers and intersegment sales accounted for on the basis used by the enterprise to price intersegment sales or transfers. As shown in Illustration 26–1, separate disclosure is required for intersegment sales and sales to unaffiliated customers. Intraindustry segment transactions should be eliminated.

The operating profit or loss line on Illustration 26–1 is computed by subtracting from each industry segment's revenue the costs and expenses that can be directly related to that industry segment's revenue plus other operating costs and expenses which can be allocated to it on some reasonable basis.

The *Statement* specifically states that none of the following items is to be added or deducted in computing the operating profit or loss of an industry segment:

Revenue earned at the corporate level and not derived from the operations of any industry segment; general corporate expenses; domestic and

---

[2] Thus, if over 90 percent of a company's revenues, profits, and assets relate to a single industry segment, industry segment disclosure is not required beyond the aggregate information presented in the financial statements.

ILLUSTRATION 26–1

Information about the Company's Operations in Different Industries for the Year Ended December 31, 1985

	Specialty Textiles	Glass Containers	Information Technology	Other	Eliminations	Consolidated
Sales to unaffiliated customers	$1,000	$2,000	$1,500	$ 200		$ 4,700
Intersegment sales	200		500		$(700)	
Total revenue	$1,200	$2,000	$2,000	$ 200	$(700)	$ 4,700
Operating profit	$ 300	$ 290	$ 600	$ 50	$ (40)	$ 1,200
Equity in net income of Ranco						100
Expenses of central administrative office						(100)
Interest expense						(200)
Income from continuing operations before income taxes						$ 1,000
Identifiable assets at December 31, 1985	$2,400	$4,050	$6,000	$1,000	$ (50)	$13,400
Assets employed at the company's central administrative office						1,600
Total assets at December 31, 1985						$15,000

foreign income taxes; equity in income or loss from unconsolidated subsidiaries and other unconsolidated investees; gain or loss on discontinued operations; extraordinary items; minority interest; and the cumulative effect of a change in accounting principles.

"Identifiable assets" include those tangible and intangible assets that can be directly associated with or reasonably allocated to an industry segment.

Unconsolidated subsidiaries and investments in joint ventures should be accounted for by the equity method. Disclosure of the investee's products and services is required.

Statement No. 14 requires that the industry segment revenue be reconciled to the consolidated revenue; the industry segment operating profit and loss be reconciled to consolidated pre tax income; and the identifiable assets of the industry segments be reconciled to the total consolidated assets.

The note accompanying the segment data should also disclose for each reportable segment the related depreciation, capital expenditures, equity method income and investments, and impact of any accounting changes.

The segment data should also be commented upon in the Management Discussion and Analysis section of the annual report.

Country Operations

Business environments can vary significantly from country to country. Operations in different countries can entail different types and degrees of risk, rates of profitability, and opportunities for growth. Because of these differences, the FASB in *Statement No. 14* requires that the annual financial statements of corporations should include information about their significant operations in different countries or groups of countries. Illustration 26–2 presents an example of the required foreign operations disclosure. These financial data and related notes are similar to those presented for the industry segments.

As a minimum, separate information should be presented for both the aggregate foreign and domestic operations. If the company has significant operations in individual countries or groups of countries whose business environments differ, the foreign operations should be further disaggregated by groups of countries or, if significant, individual countries. *Statement No. 14* does not recommend any particular approach to grouping foreign operations. Factors to be considered are geographical proximity, economic and political affinity, and the nature and degree of interrelationship of the enterprise's operations in various countries.

Major Customers and Export Sales

Irrespective of whether or not a company must report information about its operations in different industries or countries, *Statement No. 14* (as

ILLUSTRATION 26–2

Information about the Company's Operations in Different Countries for the Year Ended December 31, 1985

	United States	Western Europe	Latin America	Elimi- nations	Consolidated
Sales to unaffiliated customers	$3,000	$1,000	$ 700		$ 4,700
Intercountry sales within the company	1,000			$(1,000)	
Total revenue	$4,000	$1,000	$ 700	$(1,000)	$ 4,700
Operating profit	$ 900	$ 400	$ 100	$ (200)	$ 1,200
Equity issued income of Ranco					100
Expense of central administrative office					(100)
Interest expense					(200)
Income from continuing operations before income taxes					$ 1,000
Working capital at December 31, 1985	$2,400	$ 800	$ 500	$ (150)	$ 3,600
Property, plant, and equipment	$6,200	$3,800	$2,100		$12,100
Less: Accumulated depreciation	1,900	1,100	500		3,500
Net at December 31, 1985	$4,300	$2,700	$1,600		$ 8,600
Identifiable assets at December 31, 1985	$7,700	$3,400	$2,450	$ (150)	$13,400
Assets employed at the company's central administrative office					1,600
Total assets at December 31, 1985					$15,000

amended by *Statement No. 30*) requires that when a company's total business or reportable segment significantly depends on a single customer or a few customers, the relative importance of the customer(s) should be explained in the financial statements. The rule is that the amount of sales to an individual company, domestic government, or foreign government must be disclosed when the sales are 10 percent or more of the company's revenues. In addition, disclosure should be made in the financial statements of significant revenue derived from export sales from the company's home country to unaffiliated foreign customers. If significant, this information should be reported by country or groups of countries to which the exports are made.

Oil and Gas Reserves

Oil- and gas-producing companies and diversified companies with significant activities in these businesses are required by *Statement No. 25* to disclose their reserve quantities, costs incurred, and capitalized costs.

Investor Surveys

Surveys of financial analysts and investment advisors conducted as part of the continuing research effort to determine what constitutes useful segment disclosure indicate that the dominant investment objective is a maximum return in the long run from a combination of dividends and capital appreciation. The company characteristics considered most important in achieving this goal are growth potential, managerial ability, and profitability, in that order. The most useful measures of profitability are return on owners' equity, return on total assets, and net income as a percentage of sales. The preferred indicators of managerial ability are growth of the company, return on owners' equity, and the personal reputation of key personnel. The growth potential of a company is best indicated by the growth of its major markets, rate of growth in earnings per share, and research and development expenditures.

In the case of diversified companies, there is widespread agreement that it is necessary to appraise the major segments of a business on an industry-by-industry basis before considering them in combination, particularly where the sales and profits of different segments are affected differently by economic conditions.

Information concerning business segments that analysts consider most useful is: contribution, net income and operating income, sales or gross revenues, and total or net assets devoted to the operations of the component. Most analysts apparently do not feel it is necessary for the independent auditor's opinion to cover these data. A large number of analysts have expressed a desire for a standard approach to defining reporting components on some product basis, such as the Standard Industrial Classification.

The minimum point at which it becomes necessary to report separately for a component, in the opinion of most analysts surveyed, is when it accounts for between 10 percent and 14 percent of whatever base the analyst eventually selects as being the most relevant for understanding the company. Some of the bases suggested are: sales, net income, assets employed, net income before allocation of common costs, and total expenses. The analyst surveys also indicate the number of components reported upon should not exceed 11, in most cases.

Corporate Viewpoint

The response of companies to the exposure draft of *Statement No. 14* indicated that most managements support the basic concept of full and fair disclosure. However, many of them have expressed a strong conviction that the content and format of segment disclosure should be on a voluntary basis and appropriate to the company's interests. Forced disclosure of profits and revenues by business segments, they argued, might be:

1. Harmful, since it could be used against the company by customers, competitors, labor unions, and governmental agencies.
2. Misleading, if it led to uniform rules for reporting the results of operations by segments that did not permit the reports to reflect the unique characteristics of a company.
3. Misinterpreted, because the public could not appreciate the limitations of the somewhat arbitrary basis for most cost allocations.

It is clear from surveys that most companies collect data for management purposes on the basis of organizational units. However, this is done in a variety of ways for different management control purposes.

Companies seem to be split almost equally between those with a close relationship between organizational units and product lines and those with little relationship between organizational units and product lines. The majority of companies prepare fairly complete income statements and balance sheets by organizational units, whereas the remainder prepare partial income statements and balance sheets of one sort or another for organizational units. Typically, the amount of information collected by product lines is significantly less than that available for organizational units.

Common Costs

A difficult problem in trying to determine the profits of business segments is how to handle common or joint costs, those that are jointly shared by more than one business segment. For example, the headquarters accounting staff may keep the accounts for each of the company's components. The costs of this department are common to all of the company's operations. There is usually no clearly discernible way to associate these costs with the particular parts of a business. They must be allocated on some reasonable, but nevertheless arbitrary, basis if they are assigned to other parts of the business.

While most companies allocate all of their noninventory common costs to business segments, some companies do not, principally because they consider that some costs cannot be charged to segments on any reasonable basis.

Irrespective of the degree to which common costs are allocated, a variety of cost allocation bases are used. Some companies spread common costs on the basis of segment sales or profit before common noninventory cost allocations. Others use component asset or investment as the basis. Some allocate noninventory common costs on the basis of specific segment expense items, whereas others do it through negotiations with the managers of the operation affected by the allocations. Some use a basis combining several of these methods. In addition, many companies use more than one method for allocating costs among the different components of their company.

Profit Contribution

One way to minimize the subjective element that enters into segment reporting through the allocating of joint costs is to report the profitability of segments before joint costs are allocated. This so-called profit contribution approach divides costs into two categories: those directly attributable to a single unit and those that do not relate directly to a single unit. The profit contribution of the reporting segment is the difference between the revenues of the unit or product and the costs directly attributable to it.

A profit contribution approach to segment disclosure was initially proposed by the FASB in its exposure draft of *Statement No. 14.* It was eliminated as a requirement from the final draft. However, if a company wishes to disclose this figure, it is free to do so.

Profit contribution is the contribution a unit makes to covering the company's total common costs. If the total defined profit of all the segments is greater than the total common costs, the company will be profitable. The relationship between segment-defined profit and company profit varies from industry to industry, depending on the mix of common and direct costs. For example, common costs such as advertising represent a higher proportion of total costs for companies dealing with consumer products than for manufacturers of industrial goods, such as machine tool companies. Consequently, the profit contribution as a percentage of sales for these two business categories will differ.

A number of questions have been raised concerning the usefulness of profit contribution. Will readers understand the limitations of this figure? Will they recognize, for example, that the relationship between assets employed and profit contribution is in many cases meaningless? Will readers try to make their own joint cost allocations, based on an inadequate appreciation of the situation? What are the dangers for management in publishing this figure? For example, the defined profit for a segment will be higher than its profits after joint cost allocations. Will customers use this defined profit as an argument for reduced prices? Will labor unions use it, rather than the total company profit, as a basis for justifying wage increases?

Partly to avoid some of these possibilities, the FASB decided that operating profit, which is profit contribution less certain allocated costs, should be the basis for segment profitability disclosure.

Transfer Prices

Transfer prices are prices charged for goods and services that are transferred between units in the same company. The transfer price is revenue to the selling unit and a cost to the buying unit. These prices are not subjected to the pressures of arm's-length bargaining that exist in the marketplace, and hence lack the objectivity usually associated with sales to those outside the company. The costs and revenues created by these internal transfers are eliminated in the preparation of consolidated statements, since the transfers are offsetting within the corporate entity. In segment reports, however, these transfers are not eliminated. Thus, the sales and costs of the individual segments may total more than those reported for the entire company on a consolidated basis.

A variety of transfer pricing practices exist in practice, often in the same company. Transfer prices range from the equivalent of market prices to direct costs. Some companies base prices on established pricing formulas. Others leave the establishment of the price of internally transferred products or services to negotiations between the units involved.

A number of factors influence the setting of transfer prices. In some situations, the prices of goods moved into states that levy taxes on inventories are deliberately set at a low value in order to minimize taxes. Some companies use their transfer price system as a management control device. The pricing approach used will vary with the different motivational objectives top management hopes to achieve through its control system. Transfer prices between foreign and domestic operations are sometimes used as a device to repatriate cash from foreign operations, rather than through cash dividends which may be restricted by exchange controls.

Reporting Bases

There are a number of different possible ways a diversified company could be divided for reporting purposes. These include:

1. Legal entities.
2. Organizational units.
3. Type of customer.
4. Geographical distribution of activities.
5. Product categories, or industry groupings.

In many cases, there will be a close relationship among some of these bases. For instance, a legal entity may be identical to an organizational unit or to a product line. The rest of this chapter examines the appropriateness of these segments for reporting to public investors. The issue raised is: Can one basis be applied effectively and fairly to all companies?

Some of the respondents to the investor surveys mentioned earlier suggested that legal entity should be the basis for segment disclosure. This approach was rejected by the FASB. Typically, the *legal entities* through which a company operates often bear little relationship to the operating structure of the company. Some companies maintain separate corporate entities to hold property, to meet state legal requirements, to protect company names, or to lease property to other entities within the corporate structure. In such cases, corporate operations are often conducted without regard for these legal subdivisions. Also, unless required by law, financial statements are seldom prepared for these operationally insignificant entities. Many argue that to ask coporations to prepare statements for such entities would be an unreasonable requirement.

Since most companies maintain fairly detailed records by *organizational divisions,* it has been suggested this segment might be an appropriate basis for reporting purposes.

For most companies, organizational data is readily available and could be put in a form suitable for publication at little additional cost. However, several considerations may make this kind of data irrelevant for security investment decisions. For example, the organization of most diversified companies is constantly in a state of flux as they take on new companies. This makes year-to-year comparisons difficult. Sometimes the activities of divisions are closely related to each other, as they are in vertically integrated companies. In these cases, it may be misleading to split their common activity into parts based on divisions. Another argument against using divisional bases for reporting is that the divisional organization may reflect historical patterns of doing business, rather than the current realities. In some companies, the availability of talented executives may determine how the divisional units are structured. Then, there is always the questionability of uninformed investors' ability to use data prepared for managers who have considerable knowledge about the industries involved, the reasons for divisional structure, and the limitations of the data.

The risk of diversified companies depends in large measure on the *type of customer* they serve. One important breakdown of a business for investment appraisal purposes is between government and civilian business. Another is between ultimate consumers; middlemen, such as wholesalers and jobbers; and those who add value to purchased items, such as manufacturers. Dealings with each of these customer categories have different risk and profit characteristics. For example, the margins on government business are often less than on civilian business. Also, the risk of a sudden cutback in the level of expenditures is considered higher than for nongovernment sales. In addition, the things a company must do to be successful vary somewhat by the kinds of customers it serves. *FASB Statement No. 14* recognizes that knowledge of key customers is useful to statement users.

Companies seem to be able to generate reports of revenues by type of customer fairly readily. However, very few companies keep records of profitability by customer, and to require them to do so might impose a burden upon them.

Investors are often interested in the *geographical distribution* of a company's business, since this is a variable that may affect the risk and profit characteristics of a company. The economic fortunes of regions change, and the extent to which a company has facilities and markets in these regions will affect its future prospects. Most companies split their financial records between foreign and domestic operations. Thus, these figures can be made available to investors with little additional effort. Few companies, however, keep records by regions within the United States or the foreign countries in which they operate. Consequently, to give regional data to investors requires recasting the accounting data. This involves extra costs.

The FASB apparently believes that geographical data is worth the extra cost, since it has required a regional breakdown of consolidated results on a worldwide basis.

Product or industry categories seem to be the most frequently suggested basis for segment reporting. This is the basic approach required by the FASB. Clearly, it is of interest to investors to know how much each of the broadly defined product categories of a company contributes to its success. For example, it makes a considerable difference to investors if the success of a diversified company with computer, typewriter, business machine, and office furniture products is due mainly to its computer or its office furniture products, principally because a higher price-earnings multiplier may be applied to the earnings of computer-oriented companies than to those of office furniture companies.

While *Statement No. 14* presents some guidelines, there is little agreement on what constitutes a product line. Also, there are many practical problems in establishing an all-inclusive, well-defined list of product categories which could be uniformly used by all corporations. Some companies, particularly diversified companies, view their product lines very broadly. Others see their product lines in narrow terms. One company selling canned foods may simply view itself as being in the food business. Another company in the same business may regard its product lines as being canned fish, canned meats, and canned soups. It may go even further and break these categories down by different trademarks or container size.

The product lines of some companies tend to blend together. For example, it may be difficult for a company that makes soaps, detergents, window cleaners, waxes, and polishes to draw a clear distinction between the cleaning compounds and polishing products, particularly as some products both clean and wax.

Two other problems are encountered in trying to define a set of product lines as a common basis for component reporting. First, some products are used in other products. For instance, a diversified company may make printed wire circuit boards which it and its customers use in computers, communications equipment, television sets, and satellites. In this case, it is not clear to what product category the circuit boards belong. Second, product innovation is widespread and frequent in our economy. This creates a problem in that any set of established product categories may well become obsolete in a relatively short period of time.

Reporting segments of a business by *industry groupings* is similar in approach to product line reporting, except that categories are broader. It also has many of the same problems: there is no common agreement as to what constitutes an industry; industries tend not to be discrete; and they are constantly changing as new products and markets are created and old ones disappear.

Different Views

No one basis appears to be universally acceptable for defining segment-reporting categories. However, elements of all the possibilities discussed (with perhaps the exception of legal entities) can be appropriate in some cases. The FASB recognizes this reality and has adopted a flexible solution which leaves it up to each corporation to use the basis most appropriate to its specific case.

Those who doubt management's ability to be objective in such matters are dissatisfied with this latter approach. To make it operational, they suggest defining concrete minimum reporting requirements using some uniform system applicable to all corporations. In addition, others believe that the authority for determining the number of reporting units and the kind of data disclosed should rest with the independent auditor rather than management. Also, any departure from the minimum guidelines would have to be justified by management and the company's independent auditors. Even those who take this position, however, agree that the bases for disclosure should be broadly defined. Also, they concede that the base selected should most probably be related to markets, products, or industry, which, when broadly defined, are very similar in meaning.

Others who agree that investors probably need segment data are concerned that segment reporting encourages the misuse of accounting statements by investors, unions, and government agencies. In addition, they argue, to pile the vagaries of segment reporting on top of the existing uncertainties of financial reporting only makes the corporate reporting system more chaotic and less useful.

Analytical Value and Techniques

Segment reporting is an established corporate reporting requirement. Even with the detailed guidelines set forth in *Statement 14,* statement users must be wary of how they use such data. It can be very misleading unless the statement user has a firm grasp of the definition of the reporting bases, the nature of joint cost allocations, the methods used to price intercompany transfers, and the appropriateness of these items to the company and its industry. Also, because management has flexibility to define its own segments, the segment data of one company may be of little use in making comparisons with the segment data of other companies. Also, studies of segment data over time may be difficult as management changes segment definitions to reflect changes in the nature of the business.

The goal of segment analysis is to appreciate better the operating and financial risk of the company, the sources of its profits, and its future prospects. With above limitations in mind, the analyst can use segment data to enhance a company analysis in these ways:

1. Identify the historical relationship between intracompany and external sales by segments to see if the segments are becoming more or less dependent on external customers for its sales.
2. Compute the relative contribution to total company sales and profits of each segment's noncompany sales and profits, to identify shifts in the relative importance of segments.
3. Use an index number or compound growth rate analysis over time to identify and compare the growth rates of segments, sales, and profits, and the sources of changes in the total company's growth rates.
4. Calculate the operating profit percentage margin and operating profit return on assets for each segment to identify the relative profitability of segments and the relationship to total company profitability over time.
5. Compute the trends in each segment's total assets using an index number and absolute annual dollar change approaches to understand better the capital allocation decisions of management and the capital requirements of each segment and the total company.
6. Compare the relative percentage distribution of assets by segments over time to appreciate the changing character of the company's asset base.
7. Use index number, absolute annual dollar changes, annual percentage distribution, and capital expenditure to depreciation expense ratio-type analyses to gain a better understanding of the company's distribution of expenditures for property, plant, and equipment by segments so as to identify which segments are being favored, the capital expenditure requirements of each segment, the adequacy of the capital expenditures by segments, and the sources of the total company's capital expenditure needs.
8. Calculate asset turnover ratios for each segment to determine how efficiently each segment's assets are utilized and the various segments' impact on total company asset utilization efficiency.

9. Combine the asset turnover, operating profit margin, and return on asset calculations to identify how turnover and margin performance influence each segment's return on assets and to explain the influence of segments on changes in the total company's return on assets.
10. Prepare similar calculations to those described above using the geographic segment data to gain insights into such areas as the company's geographic strategy, source of profits, asset utilization, exchange rate exposure, and country risk.

The above ratio-type data should be evaluated and tested against management's stated goals, strategies, and its own analysis of segment results. In addition, it should be related to the various segments' relevant industry trends and forecast, exchange rate trends and predictions, general domestic and foreign economic conditions, industry and product life cycle stages, as well as relevant domestic and foreign political developments to determine the past and prospective influence of these environmental factors on segment and total company performance, requirements, challenges, and opportunities.

The text of many annual reports is organized by segments. These segment narrative reviews should be read in conjunction with the segment financial results and discussions included in the notes to the financial statements. In addition, analysts should review the segment-related discussions included in the annual 10-K and quarterly 10-Q SEC company filing. These materials tend to be more frank and objective than the more optimistic presentations usually included in the text of annual reports.

The major customer and industry disclosures should never be neglected. The condition of these customers and industries may determine in large measure the future condition of the reporting company. Always check the financial condition, operating results, and prospects of these major customers, as well as the prospects of the critical industries served by the company.

More than any other area of financial analysis, segment analysis requires the analyst to reach out beyond the present data to other sources. The astute analysts know this and by doing so hope to gain an edge over rivals who are less competent, energetic, and diligent. To appreciate segment data fully requires an understanding of the relevant segments, industry, geographical environment, and operating characteristics. Seldom is sufficient insight in these areas provided by management in its periodic reports.

CASE 26-1

Liberty Investment Management
Business Segment Data Disclosure

Anne Bright, a food analyst for Liberty Investment Management, a pension fund management firm, was assigned the task of analyzing the business segment data in the 1984 Quaker Oats Company's annual report. Here are some excerpts from the conversation in which Ms. Bright's supervisor, Joan Bennett, the director of research, gave her the assignment:

> Anne, Quaker Oats' management announced that the company had achieved the highest return on equity in its history. Management even included a Du Pont analysis to show how they did it. Here it is *(Exhibit 1)*. I want you tell me how the various business segments might have contributed to the company's success.

EXHIBIT 1
Liberty Investment Management

Quaker Oats' Return on Equity from Continuing Operations, 1979–1984						
Fiscal Years	*1979*	*1980*	*1981*	*1982*	*1983*	*1984*
Asset turnover	1.65	1.78	1.71	1.76	1.78	2.04
Return on sales	× 4.37%	4.14%	4.18%	4.38%	4.41%	4.03%
Return on assets	= 7.21%	7.37%	7.15%	7.71%	7.85%	8.22%
Leverage factor	× 2.20	2.25	2.33%	2.36	2.31	2.41
Return on equity	= 15.9 %	16.6 %	16.7 %	18.2 %	18.1 %	19.8 %

I am impressed with several aspects of the report. First, in the introduction, the management clearly stated their financial and operating objectives *(Exhibit 2)*. Second, on the cover, management showed how it viewed the major segments and where each was expected to go in the future. This was communicated by a chart depicting each of Quaker's four lines

This case was prepared by David F. Hawkins.

Copyright © 1985 by the President and Fellows of Harvard College
Harvard Business School case 186–115

EXHIBIT 2
Liberty Investment Management

Quaker Oats' Financial Objectives and Operating Strategies
Returns and Growth: A Balance

In last year's annual report, the message was,
"We're doing what we said we would."
We still are. This fiscal 1984 annual report reviews our progress
this year in detail and provides insight
into future directions.

Our mission, as always,
is to maximize return on investment for Quaker shareholders,
both today and consistently in future years.
The method is to balance these two major objectives
—our number one and number two financial objectives—
return on investment and growth.

Financial Objectives	*Operating Strategies*
1.	1.
Improve return on equity to 19+ percent over time.	Be a leading marketer of strong consumer brands of goods and services.
2.	2.
Achieve "real" earnings growth averaging 5 percent per year over time.	Achieve profitable, better-than-average real volume growth in worldwide grocery and toy businesses.
3.	3.
Increase Quaker's dividend consistent with earnings growth in "real" terms.	Improve profitability of low-return businesses or divest.
4.	4.
Maintain a strong financial position as represented by Quaker's current bond and commercial paper ratings.	Establish a meaningful position in specialty retailing businesses which will enhance overall corporate growth.

The prime financial goal of a corporation must be to enhance the value of the investment for its shareholders. The investor is looking for returns in the form of dividends and appreciation of the stock while the company maintains its financial strength. It is with this in mind that Quaker has enunciated its financial objectives.

Our financial objectives provide the benchmark for measuring our progress toward achieving our financial goals.

Our actions of the past year were consistent with our operating strategies.

The acquisition of Stokely-Van Camp, the recovery at Fisher-Price, and the aggressive new product activity by U.S. Grocery will contribute to profitable, better-than-average, real growth in the grocery and toy businesses (strategy 2) while maintaining Quaker's position as leading marketer of strong consumer brands (strategy 1). The Eyelab acquisition will enable us to build a stronger position in specialty retailing (Strategy 4). In addition, we closed the sale of our Chemicals Division (strategy 3).

EXHIBIT 3
Liberty Investment Management

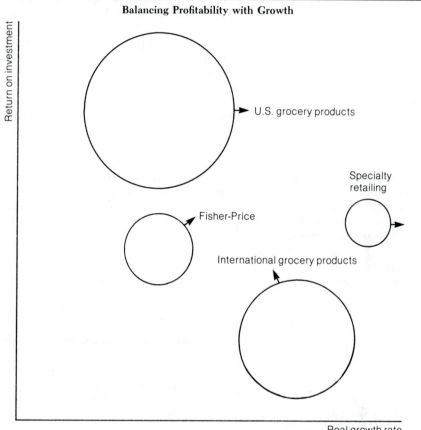

Balancing Profitability with Growth

Return on investment

U.S. grocery products

Specialty retailing

Fisher-Price

International grocery products

Real growth rate

of business[1] in relative size based on sales plotted on real growth and return on investment axes. The chart also indicates where each business had been and where management believed each is going in the future *(Exhibit 3)*.

[1] The segments and their principal product lines are:

United States Grocery Products—ready-to-eat and hot cereals; snacks; mixes, syrups, and corn products; frozen pizza and breakfast products; canned chili; dry, semimoist, and canned dog foods; semimoist and canned cat foods; pork and beans; beverages; and institutional and food service products.

International Grocery Products—food and pet food products in Canada, Europe, Latin America, and the Pacific; and household products in Latin America and the Pacific.

Fisher-Price—crib and playpen, preschool, audio-visual, dolls, trucks, action figures, plush toys, arts and crafts, construction sets, juvenile furnishings, educational software, and children's apparel.

Specialty Retailing—mail-order crafts; retail and mail-order specialty tools and gifts; retail and mail-order men's and women's clothing; retail prescription and nonprescription eyewear products.

Third, the report's text and financials present an unusual amount of segment and product data *(Exhibit 4)*. The real-growth and return-on-investment chart presentation is repeated for each major business segment.

Quaker was featured recently in a *Fortune* article. Its thrust was that under Mr. Smithberg, Quaker Oats' chairman and chief executive officer, the once sleepy cereal company, founded in 1891, was introducing glitzy new products, whittling costs, and managing finances adroitly. The article also noted that the food-processing industry was only growing at a mere 2 percent a year. Smithberg is described as a master marketer. No doubt that's one of the major reasons Quaker's advertising and merchandising expenditures for its existing businesses have gone from $212 million in 1979 to $573 million in 1984.

Questions

1. Complete Anne Bright's assignment. How have the various business segments contributed to the company's record 1984 return on equity? How has the management changed the character and mix of the company's various business segments since 1979? Does the segment data support management's appraisal of the company's achievements and prospects?

EXHIBIT 4
Liberty Investment Management: Selected Excerpts from Quaker Oats' 1984 Annual Report

Financial Highlights

(Millions of dollars except share and percent data)

Year Ended June 30	1984	1983	Percent Change
From continuing operations:			
Net sales	$3,344.1	$2,611.3	28.1%
Operating income	326.0	286.1	13.9%
Income after taxes	138.7	119.3	16.3%
Return on average common equity	19.8%	18.1%	
Per common share:			
Income from continuing operations	$ 6.71	$ 5.83	15.1%
Dividends declared	$ 2.20	$ 2.00	10.0%
Book value	$ 35.57	$ 32.07	10.9%
Common stock:			
Common shareholders' equity	$ 720.1	$ 639.4	12.6%
Average number of common shares outstanding (in thousands)	20,103	19,752	1.8%
Number of shareholders	26,785	27,943	(4.1)%
Capital expenditures	$ 120.1	$ 124.2	(3.3)%

Letter to Shareholders

To Our Shareholders and Employees:

This was a year in which Quaker made substantial progress towards reaching our corporate objectives. We are pleased to report that our fiscal 1984 results show the highest return on equity in company history, and double-digit "real" earnings growth. This performance was led by excellent volume gains in our U.S. grocery products business, aided by a host of successful new product introductions and the largest acquisition in our history, Stokely-Van Camp. Our results also reflect the strong recovery of Fisher-Price's domestic business from last year's depressed levels. Strength in these areas more than made up for weakness in our edible oils business in It-

EXHIBIT 4 *(continued)*

aly, which was the major cause of an overall earnings decline in our international grocery products business.

Here Are the Highlights:

- Earnings per share from continuing operations reached $6.71 per share, 15 percent better than last year's figure. When the effect of inflation is subtracted, "real" earnings growth was 11 percent. Contributing to this advance were earnings of $.65 cents a share from the newly acquired Stokely-Van Camp operations and a $.19 per share gain on a debt-for-debt exchange.

- Return on shareholders' equity for the year reached a record high of 19.8 percent, compared to 18.1 percent last year.

- Sales increased 28 percent to $3.34 billion.

- The company raised the annual dividend on its common stock by 10 percent, to $2.20 per share, for fiscal 1984, our 17th consecutive year of dividend increases.

- Early in the fiscal year, Quaker completed the largest acquisition in our history, Stokely-Van Camp, Inc. By year-end, all Stokely-Van Camp operations had been successfully integrated into the company.

- Our U.S. grocery products business introduced the largest number of new products in company history.

- Fisher-Price recovered from depressed fiscal 1983 results, benefiting from an excellent Christmas buying season, strong order volume for its 1984 toy line, and reduced costs.

- In November, the company acquired Eyelab, a specialty retailer of eyewear, based in New York and New Jersey.

- This spring, we completed the sale of our Chemicals Division for $45.3 million in cash and securities.

Summary of the Year's Activities

U.S. Grocery Products. Sales for the year totaled $1.7 billion, 37 percent better than last year's performance, with the Stokely business contributing $288 million. Total operating income was $210.9 million, a major improvement over the prior year, boosted by $32.2 million in operating income from Stokely. Excluding Stokely, operating income was $178.7 million, down modestly from last year. Our overall operating income growth was re-strained by our planned, substantial increase in advertising and marketing expenditures to support the greatest number of new product introductions in our history and to extend the franchise of *Gatorade* thirst quencher.

Excluding Stokely-Van Camp, "real" growth in sales totaled 10 percent, representing unit volume growth as well as a shift to more profitable items in the mix of products we sold. Unit volume rose 3 percent without Stokely, reflecting exceptional gains in grain-based snacks aided by the introduction of *Quaker Granola Dipps* bars and two new flavors in our highly successful *Quaker* Chewy Granola Bar line. Unit volume gains also came from food service, Instant *Quaker* Oatmeal, *Aunt Jemima* syrups, our dry dog food brands, frozen breakfast items, and ready-to-eat cereals. Both *Gatorade* thirst quencher and *Van Camp's* pork and beans, acquired with Stokely, achieved better-than-expected volumes during their first year as part of Quaker.

International Grocery Products. Sales rose 3 percent to $905 million, while operating income declined 21 percent to $46.9 million. The decline resulted mainly from a major shortfall in our corn oil business in Italy, but also included $6.6 million in nonrecurring charges related to the restructuring of our European and Pacific operations. The United Kingdom, Brazil, and the Benelux countries showed solid operating income and volume gains. Our Latin American businesses performed well in a difficult economic environment, thanks to tight management of working capital and fixed investment.

Fisher-Price. The division improved significantly over last year, with sales of $383 million, up 14 percent, and operating income of $43.6 million, a 47 percent gain. Reduced manufacturing and overhead costs worldwide complemented very strong U.S. and Canadian sales. New product introductions were particularly successful, led by the *Fisher-Price* child's camera. During the year, Fisher-Price also entered three nontoy areas—juvenile furnishings, educational computer software for children, and children's clothing, the last two through licensing agreements. While Fisher-Price's European business has not yet experienced the improvement of the domestic area, the same strategies which contributed to the recovery in the U.S. business are being applied in Europe.

Specialty Retailing. The Specialty Retailing Group recorded sales of $157 million, a 22 percent gain, and operating income of $16.8 million, 6 percent above last year. Operating income in fiscal 1983 included a favora-

EXHIBIT 4 *(continued)*

ble $1.8 million prior-year inventory adjustment at Jos. A Bank Clothiers. Sales were bolstered by the Eyelab acquisition, the acceleration of new store openings for Jos. A. Bank Clothiers and Brookstone and a particularly strong recovery at Herrschners. Operating income was adversely affected by increased expenditures associated with the opening of the new Brookstone and Jos. A. Bank stores.

Financial

In December, the company issued a new, zero-rate installment note in exchange for two outstanding issues of private placement debt. This debt-for-debt exchange provided a one-time, pre-tax gain of $5.7 million, or $.19 per share after taxes. Net financing costs—the net total of interest expense and foreign exchange gains or losses—rose $1.6 million. Interest expense for the year was $59.9 million, or $18 million above last year, due to higher levels of domestic borrowing related to the Stokely acquisition and higher interest rates in Latin America. The higher interest expense in Latin America was offset by foreign exchange gains of $9 million.

A Perspective on Quaker

As we have stated on the inside cover of this report, we believe that Quaker will maximize value for its shareholders by achieving a balance between consistent, competitive returns on investment from year to year and solid, profitable growth over the long term. The balance we seek is embodied in the financial objectives and operating strategies which we have been consistently communicating over the last four years and which appear on the inside cover of this report. Our financial objectives provide the benchmark for measuring our progress towards the balance between returns and growth. Our operating strategies outline the steps we will take to make that progress. This year the Stokely-Van Camp acquisition, the Fisher-Price recovery and U.S. Grocery's new product activity all will contribute to profitable, above-average, "real" growth in our grocery and toy businesses, while maintaining Quaker's position as a leading marketer of strong consumer brands. Our acquisition of Eyelab will help us grow in the highly profitable specialty retailing business while the sale of our Chemicals Division was consistent with our strategy of divesting low-return businesses.

In the future, we will continue to emphasize investments in U.S. Grocery Products and Specialty Retailing, supporting a steady stream of new products and accelerated store openings, respectively. We will also continue

to grow through acquisition, as in the case of Stokely-Van Camp and Eyelab. We expect Fisher-Price to continue its profitable growth, with the new diversified businesses, such as juvenile furnishings and licensing ventures, making an increasingly important contribution. Given the great expansion in International Grocery Products over the last few years and the state of many foreign economies, we will focus on improving International's profitability, through capital controls and improved overheads, while supporting aggressive marketing programs in opportunity areas.

September 9, 1984

William D. Smithburg
Chairman and Chief Executive Officer

Frank J. Morgan
President and Chief Operating Officer

Six-Year Analysis

Sales

Over the last five years, Quaker sales from existing businesses have increased annually at a compound rate of 13.7 percent. When we adjust for inflation using the GNP deflator, sales grew at a compound rate of 6 percent per year.

Sales for U.S. Grocery Products grew at an annual rate of 14.9 percent over the last five years, aided by the fiscal 1984 acquisition of Stokely-Van Camp, new product introductions, price increases, and the favorable effect on sales of selling proportionately more value-added products. Excluding Stokely-Van Camp, sales grew annually at 11 percent in nominal terms (not adjusted for price increases).

For International Grocery Products, sales increased at an average rate of 12 percent for the period fiscal 1979 through fiscal 1984, aided by acquisitions, internal new product development, and substantial unit volume growth, offset by unfavorable translation of local currency sales into U.S. dollars as the U.S. dollar has strengthened in value over the last few years.

Fisher-Price's sales increased at a lesser rate than the grocery areas from fiscal 1979 through fiscal 1984, reflecting, in large part, the softness of the U.S. toy market during fiscal 1983 and the continuing problems of weak

EXHIBIT 4 *(continued)*

economic conditions and unfavorable currency translation in European toy markets. However, Fisher-Price has shown a strong rebound in fiscal 1984 from the depressed level in fiscal 1983.

Specialty Retailing's sales totaled $157 million in fiscal 1984, up dramatically from a small base of $18.1 million in fiscal 1979, due to several acquisitions and, more recently, an acceleration in retail store expansion. In fiscal 1984, the acquisition of Eyelab added $7 million (seven months' sales) to the group's sales.

Operating Income

Operating income from existing businesses increased at a compound annual rate of 14 percent from fiscal 1979 to fiscal 1984. Adjusting for inflation, operating income from existing businesses grew 7 percent per year, compounded.

Over the last five years, operating income growth has been particularly strong for U.S. Grocery Products. Excluding Stokely-Van Camp, the base business showed a compound operating income gain of 13 percent per year. This growth has been achieved through improved product mix and by steadily reducing our overheads as a percent of sales, with compound annual price increases of about 7 percent.

Operating income growth for International Grocery Products has been 7.2 percent

Advertising and Merchandising Expenditures (A&M)

Marketing investment is necessary to build and maintain our consumer franchises. In fiscal 1984, overall A&M from existing businesses increased 32 percent, or $140 million, to $574 million. Most of this increase occurred in U.S. Grocery Products. The numerous new product entries in U.S. Grocery Products lifted its expenditures, excluding Stokely-Van Camp, 28 percent, or $66 million, to $305 million.

While these expenditures constrain profit growth initially, they support the development of strong, long-lived brand franchises which will provide growth and returns for shareholders over the long term. Since fiscal 1979, A&M has increased 22 percent per year, compounded, and now represents approximately 18 percent of sales from existing businesses, from a fiscal 1979 level of 13 percent of sales.

Capital Expenditures

Capital investment is also essential for future growth. In fiscal 1984, capital spending totaled $118.4 million. These expenditures primarily supported our three largest lines of business; in fact, more than 90 percent of the fiscal 1984 expenditures were in the worldwide grocery and toy businesses and over half of the total was devoted to U.S. Grocery alone.

Fiscal Year	C.G.R.*	*1984*	*1983*	*1982*	*1981*	*1980*	*1979*
				(dollars in millions)			
Sales	14.9%	**$1,719.7**	$1,258.9	$1,197.1	$1,056.6	$944.0	$858.1
Operating Income	16.6%	**$ 210.9**	$ 183.8	$ 142.5	$ 129.1	$106.1	$ 98.0
Identifiable assets	16.4%	**$ 769.8**	$ 483.8	$ 457.6	$ 450.2	$395.3	$361.5
Return on sales		12.3%	14.6%	11.9%	12.2%	11.2%	11.4%
Return on assets		33.6%	39.0%	31.4%	30.5%	28.0%	28.2%

* Five-year compound growth rates.

per year, compounded, over the last five years. While acquisitions and internal expansion of the businesses have contributed growth, unfavorable currency translation, weak economies worldwide over the past several years, and fiscal 1984's Italian operating income decline have limited our progress.

Fisher-Price's operating income growth of 6.4 percent per year, compounded, over the last five years reflects the earnings difficulty experienced in fiscal 1983. Fiscal 1984 operating income reflected a strong recovery over fiscal 1983.

Starting from a small base of $2.2 million of operating income in fiscal 1979, and again, aided by acquisitions, Specialty Retailing operating income has grown to $16.8 million in fiscal 1984.

U.S. Grocery Products

U.S. Grocery Products is Quaker's largest business segment. This fiscal year it accounted for 54.3 percent of Quaker's sales and 66.3 percent of Quaker's operating income from existing businesses. U.S. Grocery Products employs assets totaling $769.8 million, 47 percent of total identifiable assets from existing businesses. U.S. Grocery Products is also Quaker's most profitable business segment. Over the last six years, the return on assets (operating income as a percent of average identifiable assets) has averaged 32 percent, and the return on sales (operating income as a percent of sales) has averaged 12 percent.

While for each business segment, U.S. Grocery Products, International Grocery Products, Fisher-Price, and Specialty Retailing, we

EXHIBIT 4 *(continued)*

show the return on sales and assets, these returns are not directly comparable among segments because of differing business dynamics and because they are computed on a historical cost, not current cost, basis. However, the trend of these returns is important and indicates the recent progress of each segment.

Fiscal 1984 Progress

Sales up 37 percent:
This fiscal year, sales for U.S. Grocery Products reached $1,719.7 million, a 37 percent increase over last year. Stokely-Van Camp, which was acquired during fiscal 1984, had sales of $288.3 million included in U.S. Grocery Products sales and accounted for about two thirds of the increase. Excluding Stokely, sales increased 14 percent, with price increases accounting for about 4 percent of the gain. The remaining 10 percent increase in sales, therefore, was a "real" gain, reflecting both unit volume growth and a favorable shift in the mix of products sold.

Operating Income up 15 percent:
Operating income rose 15 percent to $210.9 million. Stokely-Van Camp contributed $32.2 million to U.S. Grocery Products' operating income. Excluding Stokely-Van Camp, operating income of $178.7 million was down modestly from last year, reflecting the 28 percent planned increase in advertising and merchandising expenditures which supported the largest number of new product introductions in Quaker's history. Excluding Stokely-Van Camp, the anticipated incremental marketing investment totaled $66 million and represents an investment in future growth.

Returns remain solid:
Return on sales (operating income as a percent of sales) remained strong at 12.3 percent, despite record levels of advertising and merchandising expenditures which are expected to be maintained during our current and projected period of very aggressive new product

activity. The return on sales hit a record level in fiscal 1983, when commodity costs were low and new product activity was just beginning to accelerate.

The operating income return on assets (operating income as a percent of average assets) at 33.6 percent in fiscal 1984 is strong, although below last year's return for the same reasons noted above.

"Real" Growth Trends

As noted, excluding Stokely-Van Camp, real growth in sales in fiscal 1984 totaled 10 percent, representing both unit volume growth and the favorable shift in the mix of products sold. Excluding Stokely-Van Camp, overall unit volume was up 3 percent, reflecting gains in the snacks, hot and ready-to-eat cereals, food service, syrup, frozen breakfast, and dry dog food categories. The Stokely-Van Camp products also increased unit volume year-to-year in fiscal 1984. Categories declining in tonnage this year included pancake, pizza, corn products, and canned and semimoist pet foods. Market shares increased in the majority of product categories.

Quaker has achieved significant unit volume gains in "growth" categories, which include instant oatmeal, ready-to-eat cereals, granola snacks, dry dog food, and food service. Over the last five years, growth categories advanced from 34 percent of total volume to 48 percent. Compound growth in these categories was 7.1 percent per year over that period. In addition, products in these categories tend to offer greater value to the consumer and typically carry above-average margins.

"Mature" categories, usually characterized by stable or declining unit volume and high return on investment, include standard oats, mixes, syrup, corn goods, frozen foods, and canned and semimoist pet foods. Tonnage in mature categories has declined 4.6 percent per year from fiscal 1979 to 1984, and went from 66 percent to 52 percent of our total

U.S. Grocery Products: Unit Volume Growth, "Mature" versus "Growth" Categories, F79–F84

	Percent of Total U.S. Grocery Products Tonnage		5-Year Compound Growth Rates
	Fiscal 1979	Fiscal 1984	
Mature Categories	66%	52%	−4.6%
Growth Categories	34%	48%	+7.1%

Mature: Standard oats; mixes, syrup and corn goods; frozen foods; canned and semimoist pet foods; chili.
Growth: Instant Oatmeal; ready-to-eat cereals; snacks, dry dog food; food service.

EXHIBIT 4 *(continued)*

volume. That decrease mainly reflects industry declines in canned and semimoist pet food and also reflects the impact on tonnage of the relatively heavy weight of the canned products. However, despite the volume loss for mature categories, their profitability did increase over the same period.

Since the Stokely businesses were acquired in fiscal 1984, they are not included in this discussion. In future calculations, *Gatorade* thirst quencher will be included as a growth category and *Van Camp's* products will be included in the mature categories.

Net unit volume has been flat over the last five years because of declines in mature categories which have represented more than half of the total tonnage. However, by continuing our emphasis on investment in growth categories in the future, we believe we can achieve overall unit volume gains similar to those achieved this fiscal year.

Unit volume is only one measure of real growth. Real growth can also be derived by

selling more value-added products. This is the favorable effect of a shift in product mix which accounted for approximately 7 percent of the fiscal 1984 sales gain. A good example of this is evident in the hot cereals category. Quaker generates more sales dollars per pound of Instant *Quaker* Oatmeal than regular oatmeal. Since Instant *Quaker* Oatmeal grows faster in unit volume than regular *Quaker* Oats, overall dollar sales for the hot cereals category, excluding price increases, have increased at a faster rate than overall hot cereals unit volume.

Over the past five years, sales have increased 11 percent per year, compounded (excluding Stokely-Van Camp). As noted, unit volume growth was flat over this period and price increases averaged 7 percent per year. Thus, real sales have increased 4 percent per year.

Real growth is also reflected in operating income gains. Operating income growth is derived from gross margin improvement, af-

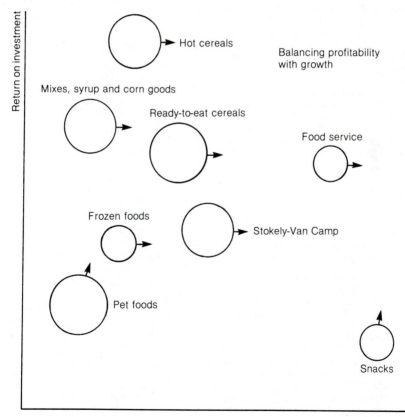

EXHIBIT 4 (continued)

fected by real growth in sales, from both unit volume and product mix, and favorable commodity costs. It is also derived from product productivity improvements, which means that overhead costs decline as a percent of sales. At the same time, an increase in marketing investment as a percent of sales can inhibit growth in operating income.

This year's operating income growth for U.S. Grocery Products was totally due to the contribution of Stokely-Van Camp, otherwise restrained by the planned increase in marketing expenditures. However, over the past five years (excluding Stokely-Van Camp), U.S. Grocery operating income growth averaged 13 percent per year. Since price increases accounted for about 7 percent each year on average, real growth in operating income was approximately 6 percent per year, mainly due to a combination of gross margin and productivity improvements which more than offset higher marketing investment as a percent of sales.

Balancing Return on Investment with Growth

Volume, mix, and productivity improvements are fundamental to U.S. Grocery's strategy to build growth while maintaining good returns. The chart on page 9 illustrates each of U.S. Grocery Product's categories in terms of their relative returns on invested capital and real growth rates. As the chart indicates, U.S. Grocery is comprised of a number of very profitable categories, such as hot cereals, corn goods, and mixes, which have good returns on investment but are not growth categories. At the same time, higher growth, but with initially lower returns while marketing investments are made in initial years, will be derived from new product categories, such as grain-based snacks. Growth in U.S. Grocery has been, and will continue to be, achieved by identifying segments of opportunity and effectively developing and marketing new products to fill these needs.

New Product Activity

The level of new product activity in snacks, hot and ready-to-eat cereals, and pet foods this year represents the beginning of a steady stream of new products to meet consumer needs in profitable growth segments of the grocery business. This requires investments in research and development, advertising and merchandising, and capital expenditures.

For fiscal 1984, advertising and merchandising expenditures (including Stokely-Van Camp) rose over 47 percent. Excluding Stokely, advertising and merchandising ex-

penditures were up 28 percent. These marketing investments must be made when the products are initially introduced in order to generate interest by consumers to try the new brands. In fiscal 1984, the timing of these introductions was such that the majority of the marketing spending occurred in the second and third quarters. This quarterly variation in marketing spending for new products will vary from year-to-year depending on the timing of new product introductions and any related seasonality.

Capital expenditures in support of U.S. Grocery growth objectives increased 18 percent to $69 million and represented about half of the company's capital spending. A major expansion program for grain-based snack production at our Shiremanstown, Pennsylvania, plant was completed in June of this year.

Foods Division

Quaker's largest single profit center, the Foods Division, increased sales 46 percent in fiscal 1984, with the Stokely-Van Camp acquisition alone increasing sales by 33 percent.

Hot Cereals

Quaker's oldest and best known products, hot cereals, include Old Fashioned and Quick *Quaker* Oats and Instant *Quaker* Oatmeal. Quaker has the number-one market share position of the hot cereals category, and hot cereals is Quaker's most profitable business. Growth in the hot cereals category has been achieved by steady growth in Instant *Quaker* Oatmeals. Unit volume growth in Instant Oatmeal has been about 6 percent per year, compounded, over the last five years. Furthermore, Instant *Quaker* Oatmeal has dollar sales in excess of the combined sales of Old Fashioned and Quick *Quaker* Oats. This growth has been the result of positioning Instant Oatmeal as a hot, ready-to-eat cereal and introducing a series of successful flavor variations. This year, increased unit volume and market share in hot cereals are due to the excellent results in our instant oatmeals business. This comes primarily from the success of our newest Instant *Quaker* Oatmeal, Peaches and Cream, and from the increased contents of our packages from 8 packets of Instant Oatmeal to 10. For regular *Quaker* Oats, volume is sensitive to weather—temperature in particular—and fiscal 1984 tonnage declined modestly because of an unusually warm fall in 1983.

Ready-to-Eat Cereals

Quaker's ready-to-eat cereal volume increased modestly in fiscal 1984. Total market

EXHIBIT 4 *(continued)*

Fiscal Years	C.G.R.*	1984	1983	1982	1981	1980	1979
				(sales in millions of dollars)			
Hot cereals	12.9%	$ 219.6	$194.2	$183.9	$158.5	$136.3	$119.5
Ready-to-eat cereals ..	13.3%	280.7	258.5	235.2	204.0	171.3	150.6
Mixes, syrup, and corn goods	6.4%	195.7	197.7	199.0	187.7	152.7	143.3
Snacks	n/a	125.8	61.1	23.0	—	—	—
Stokely-Van Camp	n/a	288.3	—	—	—	—	—
Frozen foods	5.6%	104.0	104.0	99.3	89.9	89.7	79.2
Other foods	9.5%	79.6	69.5	74.4	70.0	59.6	50.6
Total Foods Division ..	19.0%	$1,293.7	$885.0	$814.8	$710.1	$609.6	$543.2

* Five-year compound growth rates.

share was about the same as a year ago. Ready-to-eat cereals represent a key area for profitable growth for Quaker.

We have continued to support our established brands, *Cap'n Crunch, Life,* and *Quaker* 100% Natural cereals. These three key brands maintained their strong market positions in fiscal 1984, with volume gains evident for *Cap'n Crunch* and *Life* cereals. Volume of *Quaker* 100% Natural cereal was off slightly after several years in a row of above-average gains. *Life* cereal continues to be the leading nutritional ready-to-eat cereal. Supporting *Life* cereal in fiscal 1984 was the May introduction of *Raisin Life.* The *Cap'n Crunch* cereal franchise, the leading children's presweet cereal, was expanded this year by the introduction of *Choco Crunch* cereal.

Volume declined sharply for *Quaker Halfsies* cereal, introduced in fiscal 1983 as the first children's cereal sweetened with aspartame. The decline was caused in part by adverse publicity regarding the use of aspartame, but more importantly, by the growing attraction of other types of cereal for children, especially licensed cereals. Volume for *Quaker* Corn Bran cereal also declined as consumers continued to evidence a waning interest in bran cereals. A new advertising campaign at the end of fiscal 1984, with the message that *Quaker* Corn Bran is better tasting, produced encouraging results.

Near the end of fiscal 1984, Quaker announced its first entry in licensed ready-to-eat cereals with *Mr. T* cereal, based on the very popular television personality. The Mr. T cartoon character is the star of one of the leading children's television shows and is extremely well liked by children and mothers. The licensed cereal category represents 17 percent of the presweet cereal segment and is one of the fastest growing categories of the ready-to-eat cereal market.

Mixes, Syrup, and Corn Products

Quaker's pancake mixes and syrups are marketed under the *Aunt Jemima* brand name. Quaker's pie crust mix and other mixes are marketed under the *Flako* name. Corn products, which include regular and instant grits, yellow and white cornmeal, and tortilla flour, are sold under the *Quaker* and *Aunt Jemima* brands. These categories represent excellent businesses for Quaker, with growth limited to new specialty products.

For fiscal 1984, pancake volume was off, due to industry declines. However, we improved our strong number-one market share position.

Quaker's syrup category showed a strong tonnage gain. *Aunt Jemima Lite* Syrup, introduced in fiscal 1981 and continuing to have strong growth, is an example of how innovation can create growth in a mature category. During fiscal 1984, we improved our number-two market share position.

Corn products volume declined in fiscal 1984 for two reasons. First, consumers switched to flour because of its significant price advantage over corn products given the effect of last year's drought coupled with government programs that reduced corn supplies. In addition, our price increases in January, reflecting dramatically higher corn costs, were not followed by the competition. Prices were subsequently rolled back in response to both competitive pressures and in anticipation of lower corn prices, with favorable unit volume results. Despite a modest decline in market share, we maintained our number-one market share position in fiscal 1984.

Grain-Based Snacks

The growth in the grain-based snack market reflects contemporary consumer interest in convenient, more healthful snacking. The grain-based snack market is one of the fastest growing food categories and now represents

EXHIBIT 4 *(continued)*

$350 million in grocery store sales. Quaker has been participating in this market growth. In fiscal 1984, volume gains were dramatic, and we improved our share of the market significantly.

Quaker entered this market in fiscal 1982 with the regional introduction of *Quaker* Chewy Granola Bars, available in four flavors. In fiscal 1983, *Quaker* Chewy Granola Bars achieved national distribution in grocery stores. As of April of this year, individually wrapped *Quaker* Chewy Granola Bars are available nationally through confectionery distribution, such as candy counters and vending machines. Also, during fiscal 1984, Quaker introduced two new flavors of *Quaker* Chewy Granola Bars, Chunky Nut & Raisin and Peanut Butter & Chocolate Chip. And, subsequent to year-end, yet another new flavor was introduced, Chocolate, Graham & Marshmallow, "the great taste of S'mores."

In fiscal 1984, Quaker introduced an entirely new granola snack, *Granola Dipps*, a moist and chewy granola bar dipped in real milk chocolate. As of April, this product was available nationally in four flavors. This is Quaker's second new product line in the snacks category. It has been extremely successful in its early stages and will help achieve our strategy to be the leader in the grain-based snack category.

In just three years, Quaker has captured almost 40 percent of the granola snack market and has built over a $100 million growing business. This growth has been supported by advertising, merchandising, and capital expenditures. In fiscal 1984, Quaker expanded its production facilities at Shiremanstown, Pennsylvania, for grain-based snack products. The start-up of this facility in June went smoothly and exceeded expectations.

Stokely-Van Camp

Quaker's acquisition of Stokely-Van Camp in fiscal 1984 significantly increased the size of Quaker's U.S. Foods Division, with a sales contribution of $288.3 million. The two best known brands, *Van Camp's* beans and *Gatorade* thirst quencher, represented our primary interest in acquiring Stokely-Van Camp.

Van Camp's is the country's leading brand of canned dry beans, primarily Pork'n Beans, as well as specialty products such as *Beanee Weenee* and dark red kidney beans. Canned dry beans is a mature category with approximately $465 million in retail sales, and *Van Camp's* products represent about one third of this market. Fiscal 1984 sales for *Van Camp's* beans (11 months) were approximately $165 million. Van Camp's represents a profitable, stable business for Quaker. Volume for Van Camp's was up slightly compared to last year.

Gatorade thirst quencher is a profitable, well-recognized brand, with excellent growth potential. *Gatorade* is a unique, scientifically formulated thirst quencher, available in three flavors, in liquid and powdered form, which replenishes lost fluids and restores the body's natural chemical balance following exercise. Fiscal 1984 sales (11 months) were approximately $120 million. For fiscal 1984, exceptional unit volume gains were aided by a hot August and Quaker's initial marketing efforts in the spring of 1984.

We plan to extend the *Gatorade* franchise both geographically and demographically. Since the warmer months of April through September represent the peak period of consumption, *Gatorade's* first national ad campaign was started in May, with a major effort during television coverage of the summer Olympics.

Although we acquired Stokely-Van Camp, Inc., our interest is in *Gatorade* and *Van Camp's* products. Only the results of these products are included in U.S. Grocery Products' results. During fiscal 1984, we sold Stokely's small Purity Mills and Pomona Products businesses which, combined, had approximately $16 million in sales. We are currently concentrating our efforts on divesting the Industrial Products Division, with $158 million in sales, which makes edible oils and specialty chemicals. These other Stokely businesses, sold, or to be sold, are included in the "Sales and Operating Income by Industry Segment" table for fiscal 1984 in the line captioned "Other."

In addition, to reduce operating costs, the closing of the Stokely-Van Camp processing plant in Lawrence, Kansas, and a can manufacturing facility in Newport, Tennessee, were announced in the fourth quarter of fiscal 1984. Production at both operations will be consolidated into existing facilities in Indianapolis at significant cost savings.

In total, the continuing integration of Stokely has been very successful. Shortly after the acquisition, Stokely orders were being processed by Quaker's U.S. Grocery organization, and marketing, manufacturing, purchasing, and quality assurance had been integrated with Quaker's Foods Division. Since January 1, sales have been handled by Quaker's direct sales force, which was increased in size to permit better coverage of both exist-

EXHIBIT 4 *(continued)*

ing Quaker and the new Stokely businesses, at costs significantly less than for Stokely's previous outside broker sales force. In addition, the use of Quaker's sales force capitalizes on Quaker's reputation with the trade.

Frozen Foods

Quaker's frozen foods line consists of frozen waffles, french toast, and pancake batter, marketed under the *Aunt Jemima* brand, and *Celeste* frozen pizza. Unit volume for *Celeste* frozen pizza declined in fiscal 1984, due to heavy marketing spending by competitors in the premium segment where *Celeste* pizza has a leading market share. Market share for *Celeste* pizza in fiscal 1984 was in line with historical levels. *Aunt Jemima* frozen breakfast products' unit volume increased for the third year in a row, and its number-one market share position improved.

Both *Celeste* frozen pizza and *Aunt Jemima* frozen breakfast products produced good returns in fiscal 1984. We are striving to strengthen our share in the frozen food business while maintaining these returns. To realize growth opportunities, we will be developing new products and improving existing items.

Other Foods

Quaker markets *Wolf* Brand Chili, a regional brand sold primarily in the Southwest. *Wolf*

Quaker. The Food Service Division, with fiscal 1984 sales of $121 million, continued to show significant profitable-growth this year.

Food Service consists of four product groups, as follows: (1) the Bakery Group, consisting mainly of biscuits, crackers, and related products; (2) the Quaker base business, including ready-to-eat cereals, mixes, *Wolf* Brand Chili, frozen products, and more recently, *Gatorade* thirst quencher; (3) specialty products, involving distribution of products like *Knott's Berry Farm* jelly and jams and *Pace* Picante sauces; and (4) *Ardmore Farms* products, consisting of portion-control citrus and fruit juices.

The Food Service Division's continuing strategy for growth is based on initially establishing a strong foothold in this large and fragmented market with Quaker's well-known consumer brands and then expanding sales with new products and new categories of products to a broader consumer base. Internally developed products, new product categories, license agreements, and further acquisitions are expected to contribute to growth. Ardmore Farms, the first acquisition by Food Service which took place in fiscal 1982, has been extremely successful and had had good volume, sales, and operating income increases.

Pet Foods Division

(sales in millions of dollars)

Fiscal Years	C.G.R.*	1984	1983	1982	1981	1980	1979
Sales	2.0%	$305.0	$277.4	$319.2	$297.9	$292.8	$276.2

* Five-year compound growth rate.

Brand Chili had an exceptional year, with volume up over 10 percent.

In addition, Quaker sells processed grains and cereals to industrial customers.

Food Service Division

Quaker's pet food products include a broad line of dog and cat foods. Marketed under the *Ken-L Ration* brand name, the dog food line consists of dry, semimoist, and canned products. Marketed under the *Puss'n Boots* brand name, the cat food line consists of semimoist and canned products.

(sales in millions of dollars)

Fiscal Years	C.G.R.*	1984	1983	1982	1981	1980	1979
Sales	25.6%	$121.0	$96.5	$63.1	$48.6	$41.6	$38.7

* Five-year compound growth rate.

With the continuing growth of away-from-home food consumption, the food service field represents an attractive growth area for

Overall volume for pet food was flat in fiscal 1984, after a decline the prior year. The dry dog segment showed a healthy volume

EXHIBIT 4 *(continued)*

increase and an improved market share position, reflecting the successful restaging last fall of *Kibbles 'n Bits 'n Bits 'n Bits* and *Love Me Tender Chunks.*

The pet foods business represents a large category in which Quaker plans to defend its share aggressively, while improving profitability. This strategy includes supporting key brands in the profitable and growing dry dog food segment and introducing new products in fast-growing specialty niche areas. This strategy has led to the successful restaging of Quaker's dry dog food products and to the entry into the cat treat market in fiscal 1984 with *Puss 'n Boots Pounce.* Further supporting this strategy, at the end of fiscal 1984, two more new products were announced. The first was *Puppy Kibbles 'n Bits,* which builds on the strong brand franchise of regular *Kibbles 'n Bits 'n Bits 'n Bits* and is in an important growing segment of the dry dog food market. The second new product was *Snausages,* a highly palatable premium treat for dogs. Premium dog snacks are one of the fastest-growing niches of the dog food category.

The canned and semimoist dog food segments are mature industry categories. Quaker's volume declined in both segments in fiscal 1984, although these businesses continue to make good income contributions. To support Quaker's position in the important canned dog food segment, late in fiscal 1984, a major product improvement was announced on *Ken-L Ration* canned dog food. This product upgrade is being supported by increased marketing expenditures.

International Grocery Products

Fiscal 1984 Progress
Sales up 3 percent:
Sales of $905 million were up 3 percent over last year, aided by full-year sales of the major European pet food acquisition made in mid-fiscal 1983. The increase in sales did not fully reflect the volume advances, due to continuing weakness of foreign currencies.

Operating income down 21 percent:
Operating income of $46.9 million declined by 21 percent. The primary reason for the decrease was the earnings decline in our Italian corn oil business. In addition, the operating income decline included $6.6 million in nonrecurring charges relating to a restructuring of both the European and Pacific operations.

Returns decline:
Both return on sales and return on assets declined due to the magnitude of the problem with the Italian business.

Unit Volume Trends
Volume advanced 10 percent. This increase was aided by the comparison of a full year's volume in fiscal 1984 of Quaker's major European pet food acquisition versus one-half year in fiscal 1983, and strong volume gains in the United Kingdom and Brazil. The improvement was hindered by a sharp volume decline in Italian oils. Over the last five years, International Grocery Products has had substantial unit volume gains, averaging 13 percent per year. For the future, our volume targets are more moderate, on the order of 5 to 10 percent growth per year, and greater emphasis is being placed on returns.

Fiscal Year	C.G.R.*	1984	1983	(dollars in millions) 1982	1981	1980	1979
Sales	12.0%	**$905.0**	$877.6	$869.9	$845.1	$726.4	$513.8
Operating income .	˙7.2%	**$ 46.9**	$ 59.1	$ 52.1	$ 49.5	$ 37.2	$ 33.2
Identifiable assets .	11.8%	**$459.0**	$482.5	$432.6	$409.8	$348.7	$262.8
Return on sales ...		**5.2%**	6.7%	6.0%	5.9%	5.1%	6.5%
Return on assets ..		**10.0%**	12.9%	12.4%	13.1%	12.2%	14.5%

* Five-year compound growth rates.

International Grocery Products is Quaker's second largest business segment, representing 28.6 percent of sales in fiscal 1984 and 14.7 percent of operating income. This segment employs assets totaling $459 million, 28 percent of total identifiable assets from existing businesses. In fiscal 1984, the operating income return on average assets was 10 percent, and the operating income return on sales was 5.2 percent.

Balancing Return on Investment with Growth
The chart on the right illustrates by geographic area the strategic direction for International Grocery Products in terms of growth and return on invested capital.

In Europe, we have had rapid growth, with volume increasing by 18 percent, compounded, over the last five years and sales advancing by 16 percent per year. Quaker has

EXHIBIT 4 *(continued)*

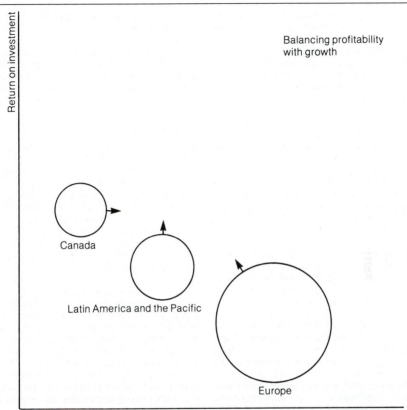

established a number-two market share position on the Continent in growth niches, such as pet foods and ready-to-eat cereals. In pet foods, we made a major acquisition in fiscal 1983 to solidify our number-two position in the European consumer pet food market. With adequate manufacturing capacity in place, we are consolidating that position and growing with the market. At the same time, we are putting greater emphasis on returns by concentrating on improving the cost structure and better resource management.

In Latin America, our strategy is to continue a trend of improving returns by reduc-

of low investment strategies), and by concentrating marketing support on key income-generating product categories. This is vital in the current economic environment. In the Pacific Region, which represents a small area for Quaker, our strategy is to focus on improving returns.

For Quaker Canada, one of Quaker's larger subsidiaries outside the U.S., which has good returns, the strategy will focus on maintaining returns, while increasing volume growth through new product development.

Europe

(sales in millions of dollars)

Fiscal Years	C.G.R.*	1984	1983	1982	1981	1980	1979
Sales	15.7%	**$552.4**	$511.9	$450.1	$449.3	$412.7	$266.0

* Five-year compound growth rates.

ing invested capital (basically through strict working capital control and implementation

Quaker's European Grocery sales are about evenly divided between pet foods and human

EXHIBIT 4 *(continued)*

foods. Despite sharp volume declines in Italian oils, volume for Europe was up nicely. This increase was aided by the major European pet food acquisition in mid-fiscal 1983 and by strong volume gains in the United Kingdom. All European subsidiaries, except in Italy, contributed to the volume increase.

Our Italian subsidiary, Chiari & Forti, produces an edible corn oil positioned as a healthful oil that typically sells at a lower price than olive oil. However, due to market conditions during fiscal 1984, these prices were at parity. Chiari & Forti's earnings fell as consumers switched from corn oil to olive oil. Chiari & Forti, which in terms of fiscal 1983 revenue and earnings was Quaker's largest business outside the United States, was modestly unprofitable in fiscal 1984, compared to a $12 million operating income contribution in fiscal 1983.

A major objective for fiscal 1985 is to recover the market position and profitability. We expect Chiari & Forti will be profitable again in fiscal 1985. However, profitability likely will be significantly below the peak level of fiscal 1983.

Also in Italy, early this fiscal year, Quaker acquired a small distributor of imported premium food products, Sorba, S.p.A. Products include caviar, French champagne, and smoked salmon.

In France and Germany, where our businesses are primarily pet foods, results were below expectations. In Germany, where the 1983 pet foods acquisition improved our market share position against a tough major competitor, this resulted from expected competi-

Performance of the United Kingdom business was well ahead of last year, with a strong increase in operating income continuing a major turnaround of several years' duration. A favorable response to the relaunch of *Felix* cat food and a very good hot cereals season, aided by the fiscal 1983 acquisition of *Scott's* Oats, contributed to the improved results.

Latin America and Pacific

Quaker has leading brands and market share positions in hot cereals, corn goods, grain-based beverages, chocolate products, sardines, and scouring pads in various Latin American countries. The three major countries in the region for Quaker are Brazil, Colombia, and Mexico, which together represent over three quarters of Quaker's fiscal 1984 Latin American sales and unit volume. In fiscal 1984, operating income increased significantly despite a sales decline of 7.5 percent related to currency devaluations and only a marginal increase in unit volume. The sales shortfall occurred in Venezuela and Mexico. In Venezuela, unit volume was about even with last year; however, due to the effect of the maxi-devaluation of the currency, the same unit volume in fiscal 1984 translated into much lower dollar sales. In Mexico, unit volume and sales dollars declined due to the recession that followed the maxi-devaluation of the currency in fiscal 1983. The consumer's loss of purchasing power affected the demand for nonessential items, such as Quaker's Mexican chocolate products.

Latin America

Fiscal Years	C.G.R.*	*1984*	*1983*	*1982*	*1981*	*1980*	*1979*
				(sales in millions of dollars)			
Sales	6.9%	**$226.8**	$245.1	$303.2	$292.9	$219.7	$162.8

* Five-year compound growth rate.

tive response, while in France, a weak economy hindered results. Excluding a write-off, operating income in France was up and our market share improved, while in Germany we remained modestly unprofitable.

In the Benelux countries, results were very good, with volume, sales, and operating income increasing for both human and pet foods. With the major European pet food acquisition, Quaker has the leading market share in pet foods in Holland. Cereal volume showed strong gains, due to continued success of *Cruesli* (similar to *Quaker* 100% Natural cereal), introduced in Holland in fiscal 1982.

However, the income decline caused by the Mexican and Venezuelan sales shortfall was more than offset by improvements in Brazil. The Brazilian business had an excellent year with favorable volume comparisons across all product lines, which include cereals, *Toddy* beverages, and *Coqueiro* sardines. An investment in a new freezer system, completed in fiscal 1982, reduced the problem of occasional shortages of fish.

In Colombia, earnings were down somewhat versus a year ago, due to increased competitive action in the steel wool market, which hindered the results of *Bon Bril* scouring pads.

EXHIBIT 4 *(continued)*

Quaker Colombia's other businesses performed as expected.

In the Pacific Region, where our businesses are relatively small, operating income, excluding nonrecurring charges, was off modestly from a year ago. Australia and Taiwan are the two major Pacific region countries where Quaker manufacturing facilities are located. In Australia, Quaker has leading market share positions in frozen pastry, hot cereals, and semimoist dog food. Frozen pastry showed a good volume increase in fiscal 1984, while pet food volumes declined significantly, and hot cereals were off due to unseasonably mild weather. In Taiwan, Quaker completed its first full year of production and sales of baby cereal from its new plant. The plant started up in March of the prior fiscal year and is in the early stages of a long-term venture.

Fisher-Price is Quaker's third largest business segment. This fiscal year it accounted for 12.1 percent of Quaker's sales and 13.7 percent of Quaker's operating income. Fisher-Price employs assets totaling $318.1 million, 19.4 percent of total identifiable assets from existing businesses. In fiscal 1984, the operating income return on average assets was 14 percent, and the return on sales (operating income as a percent of sales) was 11.4 percent.

Fiscal 1984 Progress

Sales up 14 percent:
Sales reached $383.4 million, a 14 percent increase over the depressed level of fiscal 1983. U.S. sales rebounded to a record high of $282.4 million, driven by the best December in our history. International sales remained soft, due to a number of factors, including weak European economies and currencies.

Canada

		(sales in millions of dollars)					
Fiscal Years	C.G.R.*	1984	1983	1982	1981	1980	1979
Sales	8.2%	**$125.8**	$120.6	$116.6	$102.9	$94.0	$85.0

* Five-year compound growth rate.

Quaker-Canada had strong performance in fiscal 1984, with sales up 4 percent, despite a two-and-a-half-month strike which halted production at our Peterborough, Ontario, plant. Operating income was slightly below a year ago.

Pet foods represents about half of Canada's total sales, with hot and ready-to-eat cereals, snacks, mixes, syrups, and food service making up the balance. In fiscal 1984, unit volume declined modestly, due to the strike and softness in pet foods.

Quaker Chewy Granola Bars were introduced nationally in Canada in fiscal 1984, and results have exceeded expectations. Production of *Quaker* Chewy Granola Bars began in April of fiscal 1984 at Quaker-Canada's Peterborough, Ontario, plant.

Operating income up 47 percent:
Operating income climbed to $43.6 million, a more than 47 percent improvement over the depressed level of fiscal 1983. The major factors were strong sales in the U.S. and Canada, spurred by economic recoveries and a return to basic toys, and reduced manufacturing and overhead costs worldwide.

Improving returns:
Operating income return on sales improved 2.6 points to 11.4 percent, in spite of essentially flat selling prices and a more than 25 percent increase in advertising and merchandising spending. As a result of improving return on sales and tighter asset management, we achieved over a 4 point gain in return on assets (operating income as a percent of average identifiable assets), which was 14 percent for fiscal 1984.

Fisher-Price

		(dollars in millions)					
Fiscal Year	C.G.R.*	1984	1983	1982	1981	1980	1979
U.S. Sales	8.3%	**$282.4**	$232.1	$261.2	$250.4	$259.4	$189.2
International sales ...	3.0%	**$101.0**	$103.8	$112.1	$116.4	$104.5	$ 87.1
Total sales	6.8%	**$383.4**	$335.9	$373.3	$366.8	$363.9	$276.3
Operating income ...	6.4%	**$ 43.6**	$ 29.6	$ 50.0	$ 46.0	$ 50.3	$ 31.9
Identifiable assets ...	6.0%	**$318.1**	$305.8	$315.4	$296.2	$305.4	$237.2
Return on sales		**11.4%**	8.8%	13.4%	12.5%	13.8%	11.5%
Return on assets		**14.0%**	9.5%	16.4%	15.3%	18.5%	14.7%

* Five-year compound growth rates.

EXHIBIT 4 *(continued)*

Real Growth

Since one quarter to a third of the toy line each year represents new toys, all with different price points, and other toys are discontinued, it is virtually impossible to measure unit volume growth. In addition, for the international business it can be misleading to use dollar sales growth, either nominal or adjusted for inflation, as a measure of real growth because dollar sales include the effect of currency translation. For the U.S. business (both toys and diversified products), however, nominal sales less average price increases is the best measure of real growth.

Over the past five years, nominal U.S. sales growth was 8 percent, compounded, with prices increasing at a compound rate of about 7 percent per year. Thus, real sales growth has been 1 percent per year during this period, which includes the depressed fiscal 1983 results. However, sales growth for fiscal 1984 rebounded to a "real" rate of about 20 per-

cent. Similarly, operating income has not increased in real terms over the last five years (again, including the depressed results in fiscal 1983); however, for fiscal 1984, "real" operating income growth was over 40 percent.

With the encouraging progress made in fiscal 1984, looking ahead, we believe 5 percent real growth in both sales and operating income is a reasonable target.

Balancing Return on Investment with Growth

Continued improvement in fiscal 1984 financial trends is at the heart of Fisher-Price's objectives and plans for the future. We aim to build value for Quaker's shareholders by achieving the optimal balance between real growth and return on investment. That means getting consistent volume and income growth overall, while improving returns.

The chart below illustrates Fisher-Price Europe, Fisher-Price U.S. and Canada, and

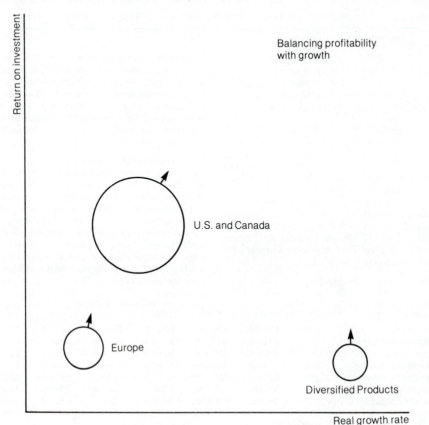

EXHIBIT 4 *(continued)*

the Diversified Products area in terms of their relative return on investment and growth potential. As the chart indicates, in Europe we must significantly improve our returns, while in the U.S. and Canada we must build on the progress made in fiscal 1984. Diversified Products, a new area for Fisher-Price, is in a developmental stage, and returns will improve as the businesses in that area mature. Fisher-Price will continue to grow by strengthening its share of the preschool toy market, furthering expansion into toys for school-age children, and diversifying into non-toy areas.

U.S. Business

Approximately 75 percent of Fisher-Price's sales are in the United States. Two thirds of these sales are for infant and preschool children. In fiscal 1984, Fisher-Price strengthened its preeminent position in the infant and preschool market. The division continues to have an excellent consumer franchise, especially with parents, based on its longstanding reputation for play value, product safety, durability, and dollar value.

Fisher-Price has continued to grow through expansion into older age categories, which now represent one third of Fisher-Price U.S. sales. Older age categories include (in descending order of sales dollars) audiovisual toys, building systems, arts and crafts, and adventure people. In the audiovisual category, one of the most exciting toys introduced this year for the 1984 Christmas season is the *Fisher-Price* camera. It's a Kodak camera on the inside, with a durable Fisher-Price designed exterior, that makes picture taking for youngsters easy and fun. It is already sold out to the retail trade. Last year, Quaker entered the building set category for school-age children with *Construx*, which continued to be popular this year. For the 1984 Christmas season, Fisher-Price extended the *Construx* line by introducing several new construction sets with space themes.

Fisher-Price's new toy line for fiscal 1985 is one of the strongest ever. In addition to the *Fisher-Price* camera and *Construx* building sets for older children, Fisher-Price strengthened its preschool line with a number of new toys, including *Fisher-Price* roller skates and a new zoo playset. The new line received a very good response from the trade at the Toy Fair in February, and orders for the 1984 Christmas season are exceptionally strong.

As we look to the new toy year, we are optimistic that the progress Fisher-Price U.S. made in fiscal 1984 will continue.

International Businesses

Approximately 25 percent of Fisher-Price's sales are international, chiefly from Canada and Europe, with a small amount from Australian sales and worldwide exports. Trends in the Canadian business parallel the excellent recovery of the U.S. business. The Canadian business had a strong fiscal 1984. In Europe, recoveries in profitability and volume growth have not yet occurred, and we have addressed that in several ways.

To improve profitability, we have increased our operating efficiency through centralizing distribution and sales company administration wherever possible. Also, with our plant expansion in England, we are sourcing 95 percent of our finished goods in Europe compared to 50 percent five years ago. This increases profitability and reduces currency exposure.

To stimulate growth in Europe, we have implemented the strategy for infant and preschool toys that worked so well for the U.S. An aggressive program of selective price rollbacks plus advertising and merchandising spending increases have been put in place. In addition, to grow, we have introduced new categories, audiovisual toys for older age children and a doll line especially developed for the European market.

Diversified Products

Fisher-Price made its first entry into nontoy areas in fiscal 1984 with a line of 19 items of juvenile furnishings, including a high chair and changing table. It is a logical extension of Fisher-Price's existing business, since juvenile furnishings are purchased by parents who are familiar with Fisher-Price's reputation for quality, durability, and value. This reputation is an advantage in the juvenile furnishings market, which is very fragmented and where little brand recognition currently exists.

Licensing provides another good opportunity to expand the *Fisher-Price* brand name in areas in which vertical integration poses unacceptable business risk in relation to returns. In fiscal 1984, we licensed our name for the manufacture of children's clothing and educational computer software.

Under an agreement with The Activity Center, Inc., of New York City, Fisher-Price is directing the design, development, quality control, and advertising of durable, high-quality, color-coordinated clothes for children

EXHIBIT 4 *(continued)*

wearing size 12 months to size seven. The playwear concept has been in development for two years, and market research with mothers indicates the clothing line offers functional and long-lasting garments at a reasonable cost. The Activity Center, Inc., will oversee the manufacturing and the distribution of the clothing.

Spinnaker Software of Cambridge, Massachusetts, one of the computer industry's leaders in producing high-quality educational software, will produce, market, and distribute educational software under the *Fisher-Price* brand name. The software, which is designed for children ages 3 to 12, assists children in math, language, creativity, learning skills, and computer literacy. As is the case with juvenile apparel, Fisher-Price will evaluate and approve all products and advertising using its name.

These ventures are currently a very small portion of Fisher-Price but represent an area for future growth. In addition, licensing agreements such as these offer us a good opportunity to increase operating income with virtually no increase in capital spending—which will help us improve our returns while incurring minimal risk.

Specialty Retailing

Over the past six years, as the Specialty Retailing Group has evolved from being exclusively mail-order to a stronger retailing focus, the increased investment in new retail stores has produced a decreasing, though still very attractive, return on assets. This change in focus is the reason for the name change to Specialty Retailing.

Fiscal 1984 Progress
Sales up 22 percent:
In fiscal 1984, total sales increased from $128.6 million to $157 million, an increase of 22 percent.

Operating income advanced 6 percent:
Operating income in the year went from $15.8 million to $16.8 million, a 6 percent increase. However, operating income in fiscal 1983 included a favorable $1.8 million prior-year inventory adjustment for Jos. A. Bank. Excluding this adjustment, operating income was up 20 percent.

Returns remain high:
The businesses comprising this group are characterized by good rates of return. Although in fiscal 1984 the operating income return on sales and the return on assets declined, mainly due to the prior-year inventory

Fiscal Year	C.G.R.*	(dollars in millions)					
		1984	1983	1982	1981	1980	1979
Sales	54.0%	**$157.0**	$128.6	$117.8	$55.4	$47.9	$18.1
Operating income . .	50.2%	**$ 16.8**	$ 15.8	$ 11.6	$ 5.5	$ 4.8	$ 2.2
Identifiable assets . .	89.9%	**$ 91.4**	$ 65.2	$ 52.2	$14.4	$12.5	$ 3.7
Return on sales . . .		**10.7%**	12.3%	9.8%	9.9%	10.0%	12.2%
Return on assets . .		**21.5%**	26.9%	34.8%	40.9%	59.3%	56.4%

* Five-year compound growth rates.

Specialty Retailing is the new name for Quaker's direct-to-consumer group. The smallest of Quaker's four lines of business, Specialty Retailing is composed of four companies: Jos. A. Bank Clothiers, Brookstone, Herrschners, and Eyelab. For fiscal 1984, the group accounted for 5 percent of Quaker's sales and 5.3 percent of Quaker's operating income. The group employs assets totaling $91.4 million, 5.6 percent of total identifiable assets for existing businesses. In fiscal 1984, the operating income return on assets was 21.5 percent, and the operating income return on sales was 10.7 percent.

adjustment at Jos. A. Bank, both remained strong.

Balancing Return on Investment with Growth
The chart on page 951 illustrates Quaker's four specialty retailing businesses in terms of their relative profitability and growth potential. As shown, Jos. A. Bank, Brookstone, and Eyelab are expected to contribute high growth and, in general, maintain good returns in the future. While Herrschners, being entirely a mail-order business in a more mature market category, grows at a much slower rate,

EXHIBIT 4 *(continued)*

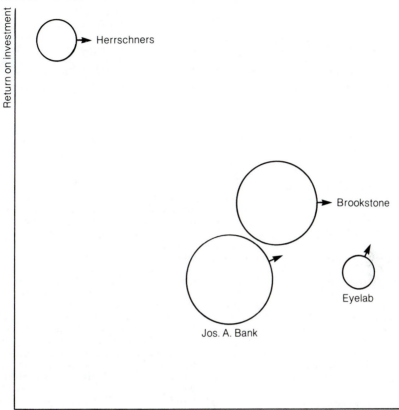

it is expected to continue to contribute historically high returns and a steadily increasing stream of income. Although operating income from Specialty Retailing was up only modestly (without considering the prior-year inventory adjustment at Jos. A. Bank) in fiscal 1984, a higher rate of growth than any other Quaker business, both in nominal and real terms, should result in an increasing contribution to Quaker's sales and operating income over time.

Jos. A. Bank Clothiers

Jos. A. Bank Clothiers is a retail and direct-mail marketer of traditional men's and women's apparel and accessories. It is the largest of the four businesses, contributing over 50 percent of Speciality Retailing sales. Sales for the year increased by 17 percent. The increase is attributed to a combination of slightly higher same-store sales and the opening of four new stores during the year. At the end of fiscal 1984, Bank had 19 stores in the following locations: Atlanta, Georgia; Baltimore, Maryland (3); Birmingham, Alabama; Boston, Massachusetts; Charlotte, North Carolina; Chicago, Illinois (2); Dallas, Texas; Denver, Colorado; Detroit, Michigan; Houston, Texas; Philadelphia, Pennsylvania (2); Richmond, Virginia; and Washington, D.C. (3). Plans call for continued growth through new-store expansion.

Catalog sales were down modestly as compared to the previous year, due to out-of-stock problems last fall and attrition to new retail stores. The mail-order portion, which is less than 20 percent of the business, is becoming smaller as retail store openings increase.

Operating income for Jos. A. Bank was down versus a year ago due to the comparison

EXHIBIT 4 *(continued)*

against fiscal 1983 results, (which included a favorable $1.8 million prior-year inventory adjustment), weakness in the women's apparel line, and difficulties in the availability of certain merchandise items. However, excluding the inventory adjustment, operating income was even with last year.

Brookstone

Brookstone is a marketer of hard-to-find tools and housewares sold through mail-order catalogs and retail stores. With about 25 percent of sales, Brookstone is the second largest business in the Specialty Retailing Group. For fiscal 1984, sales were up 24 percent, due to a combination of a healthy increase in same-store sales and sales from the six new stores opened during the year.

Tool catalog sales, which represent slightly less than half of the company's sales, were flat for the fiscal year due to lower response rates than in previous years resulting, in part, from attrition to new Brookstone stores and catalogs. During the year, Brookstone introduced two new catalogs, *Weathertamers,* featuring energy-saving items, and *Yard and Garden,* an offshoot of the tool catalog, which offers special gardening tools. These catalogs were introduced at test levels of circulation, and the response rate has met expectations. In addition, sales from the *Homewares* catalog, introduced in fiscal 1983, were up sharply because of increased circulation.

Increases in overhead expenses associated with anticipated new store openings, as well as disappointing tool catalog response rates, held operating income about even with a year ago.

The majority of the future growth for Brookstone will come from an acceleration of retail store openings. With six new stores opened and one closed during fiscal 1984, Brookstone had 20 stores as of June 30 in the following locations: Atlanta, Georgia (2); Baltimore, Maryland; Boston, Massachusetts (2); Chicago, Illinois; Costa Mesa, California; Dallas, Texas; Manchester, New Hampshire; Minneapolis, Minnesota (2); New York, New York; Peterborough, New Hampshire; Philadelphia, Pennsylvania (2); Pittsburgh, Pennsylvania; Stamford, Connecticut; and Washington, D.C. (3). Subsequent to year-end, Brookstone opened three additional stores in the following locations: Short Hills, New Jersey; Paramus, New Jersey; and Los Angeles, California.

Herrschners

Herrschners is the number-one mail-order marketer of needle crafts in the United States

and Canada. It is a highly profitable, mature business. Fiscal 1984 was a very successful year for Herrschners. Although a small company, its sales for the past year moved up solidly, and operating income was up sharply from a weak fiscal 1983. Herrschners, which is sensitive to the economy, benefited in fiscal 1984 from the economic recovery. In addition, the company's position was strengthened in fiscal 1984 by the shutdown of one of Herrschners' major competitors. Herrschners made a strong contribution to Quaker's Specialty Retailing Group's operating income.

Eyelab

Eyelab, the most recent addition to the Specialty Retailing Group, is an eyewear department store chain, selling prescription and nonprescription products. The acquisition of Eyelab is consistent with one of Quaker's key operating strategies—to establish a meaningful position in specialty retailing in order to enhance overall corporate growth. With the Eyelab acquisition, Quaker intends to achieve both real growth and maintain good returns.

The business was started in 1980 and is representative of a new concept of marketing eyewear products. Each Eyelab store has separate departments for men, women, and children, and offers a selection of over 10,000 frames. Additionally, the stores contain processing laboratories that can fill almost all prescriptions in less than two hours. At the time of the acquisition, there were four Eyelab stores with annual sales of approximately $10 million. As of June 30, there were seven stores in the following locations: Carle Place, New York; East Brunswick, New Jersey; Hicksville, New York; Paramus, New Jersey; Rockville, Maryland; Springfield, New Jersey; and Totowa, New Jersey. Growth for Eyelab will result from an acceleration of store openings during the coming years and from growth in the market for eyewear.

The eyewear market itself is growing, and optical department stores like Eyelab are expected to participate in an ever-increasing share of the market by reason of the selection, value, and service they offer. In addition, existing demographic trends indicate that the eyewear market will experience significant real growth during the 1980s, and 1990s, as the population ages. Also, with glasses becoming a fashion accessory, many people own several pairs to fit different occasions.

Eyelab's sales and operating income, while reasonably strong for fiscal 1984, are a small percentage of the group's total.

EXHIBIT 4 *(continued)*

THE QUAKER OATS COMPANY AND SUBSIDIARES

Eleven-Year Selected Financial Data

(millions of dollars except share and percent data)

Year Ended June 30(a) *Financial Statistics (b)*	*5-Year Compound Growth Rate*	*10-Year Compound Growth Rate*	***1984***	*1983*	*1982*	*1981*	*1980*	*1979*	*1978*	*1977*	*1976*	*1975*	*1974*
Current ratio			**1.5**	1.5	1.5	1.5	1.6	1.8	1.8	2.0	2.0	2.4	1.8
Working capital	4.8%	5.6%	**$ 316.8**	$ 261.9	$ 266.6	$ 252.4	$ 265.9	$ 250.7	$ 223.1	$ 233.2	$ 215.5	$ 208.7	$ 184.5
Working capital turnover *(c)*			**11.6**	9.9	9.9	9.2	8.5	7.5	6.6	6.4	6.5	6.6	6.8
Property, plant, and equipment—net	7.6%	8.6%	**$ 730.6**	$ 616.3	$ 618.4	$ 633.3	$ 572.8	$ 507.4	$ 458.0	$ 406.7	$ 373.6	$ 358.2	$ 319.3
Depreciation expense	15.6%	11.7%	**$ 70.0**	$ 52.3	$ 46.3	$ 42.3	$ 37.1	$ 33.9	$ 30.2	$ 29.0	$ 30.4	$ 27.4	$ 23.1
Total assets	9.8%	8.8%	**$ 1,806.8**	$ 1,463.7	$ 1,476.7	$1,454.1	$1,334.2	$1,131.5	$1,008.8	$ 924.3	$ 854.9	$ 765.1	$ 776.4
Long-term debt	4.9%	1.6%	**$ 200.1**	$ 152.8	$ 162.2	$ 165.2	$ 151.7	$ 157.5	$ 159.4	$ 151.8	$ 148.7	$ 158.3	$ 171.4
Redeemable preference stock			**$ 38.5**	$ 41.3	$ 45.4	$ 46.7	$ 50.0	$ 50.0	$ 50.0	$ 50.0	$ 50.0	$ 50.0	$ —
Common shareholders' equity	7.0%	7.9%	**$ 720.1**	$ 639.4	$ 630.5	$ 612.6	$ 582.9	$ 513.6	$ 461.5	$ 434.3	$ 386.0	$ 350.1	$ 335.2
Book value per common share	6.5%	8.2%	**$ 35.57**	$ 32.07	$ 32.17	$ 31.98	$ 28.85	$ 25.94	$ 23.13	$ 20.75	$ 18.62	$ 16.91	$ 16.19
Return on average common shareholders' equity			**19.8%**	18.1%	18.2%	16.7%	16.6%	15.9%	15.3%	16.8%	12.1%	6.4%	11.6%
Gross profit as a percent of sales			**38.0%**	39.6%	36.6%	34.2%	33.8%	33.9%	33.7%	32.1%	31.2%	25.2%	25.4%
Advertising and merchandising as a percent of sales			**17.2%**	16.6%	14.7%	13.8%	12.7%	12.3%	11.7%	10.3%	9.8%	8.5%	6.7%
Research and development as a percent of sales			**.9%**	1.0%	1.0%	1.0%	.9%	1.0%	1.2%	1.0%	1.1%	1.1%	1.2%
Income as a percent of sales			**4.1%**	4.6%	4.6%	4.4%	4.4%	4.6%	4.9%	5.1%	3.6%	1.8%	3.3%
Long-term debt ratio *(d)*			**20.9%**	18.3%	19.4%	20.0%	19.3%	21.8%	23.8%	23.9%	25.1%	28.0%	33.4%
Total debt ratio *(e)*			**35.5%**	33.5%	34.1%	36.8%	33.1%	30.7%	33.0%	30.9%	30.8%	31.5%	45.9%
Common dividends as a percent of income available for common			**32.9%**	34.3%	31.2%	32.0%	30.8%	30.7%	31.2%	27.7%	39.2%	75.5%	42.2%
Number of common shareholders			**26,785**	27,943	29,552	30,418	30,818	31,567	31,853	31,830	24,747	25,064	22,320
Number of employees worldwide			**28,400**	25,200	26,000	30,900	31,400	31,400	29,600	27,800	23,900	25,100	25,400
Market price range of common stock—High			**$ 64⅝**	$ 51¾	$ 43½	$ 37¾	$ 34½	$ 27½	$ 26	$ 27¾	$ 28⅜	$ 24⅜	$ 39⅞
—Low			**$ 42¾**	$ 35¼	$ 31¼	$ 25⅞	$ 23½	$ 22	$ 20	$ 20⅞	$ 15	$ 11	$ 19¾

(a) Financial data presented, where appropriate, reflects pro forma amounts assuming retroactive application of the fiscal 1979 accounting change for investment tax credit.

(b) Income-related statistics have been restated to exclude the results of Chemicals, U.S. Games, and Restaurants, which are reported as discontinued operations. Balance sheets and related statistics for fiscal 1983 and prior years have not been restated for these discontinued businesses.

(c) Net sales divided by average working capital.

(d) Long-term debt divided by long-term debt plus total equity including redeemable preference stock.

(e) Total debt divided by total debt plus total equity including redeemable preference stock.

EXHIBIT 4 *(continued)*

THE QUAKER OATS COMPANY AND SUBSIDIARIES

Consolidated Statement of Income

	(millions of dollars except share data)		
Year Ended June 30	**1984**	1983	1982
Net sales	**$3,344.1**	$2,611.3	$2,576.2
Cost of goods sold	**2,073.1**	1,576.3	1,634.4
Gross profit..............................	**1,271.0**	1,035.0	941.8
Selling, general, and			
administrative expenses	**952.9**	758.7	689.5
Interest expense—net	**59.9**	41.9	45.9
Other (income) expense	**(1.9)**	14.5	(.5)
Income from continuing operations			
before income taxes	**260.1**	219.9	206.9
Provision for income taxes	**121.4**	100.6	89.6
Income from continuing operations	**138.7**	119.3	117.3
Discontinued operations—			
(Loss) from operations—net			
of income taxes	**—**	(7.0)	—
(Loss) on disposal—net			
of income taxes	**—**	(55.5)	(20.4)
Total (loss) from discontinued operations	**—**	(62.5)	(20.4)
Net income..............................	**138.7**	56.8	96.9
Preference dividends	**3.9**	4.1	4.3
Net income available for common	**$ 134.8**	$ 52.7	$ 92.6
Per common share:			
Income from continuing operations	**$ 6.71**	$ 5.83	$ 5.81
(Loss) from discontinued operations	**—**	(.35)	—
(Loss) on disposal.......................	**—**	(2.82)	(1.05)
Net income..............................	**$ 6.71**	$ 2.66	$ 4.76
Dividends declared	**$ 2.20**	$ 2.00	$ 1.80
Average number of common shares			
outstanding (in thousands)	**20,103**	19,752	19,455

See accompanying notes to consolidated financial statements.

EXHIBIT 4 *(continued)*

THE QUAKER OATS COMPANY AND SUBSIDIARIES

Consolidated Statement of Changes in Financial Position

	(millions of dollars)		
Year Ended June 30	**1984**	*1983*	*1982*
Operations:			
Income from continuing operations:	**$ 138.7**	$ 119.3	$ 117.3
Depreciation and amortization	**74.2**	55.1	49.3
Deferred income taxes and other items	**60.3**	22.2	16.8
Total from continuing operations	**$ 273.2**	$ 196.6	$ 183.4
(Loss) from discontinued operations	**—**	(54.7)	(14.5)
Reclassification of noncurrent assets to other current assets	**—**	45.1	—
Decrease (increase) in receivables	**(123.6)**	1.8	(23.2)
Decrease (increase) in inventories	**(70.5)**	58.5	(28.2)
Decrease (increase) in other current assets	**55.7**	(42.2)	(2.1)
Increase (decrease) in trade accounts payable	**56.1**	(7.4)	7.2
Increase (decrease) in other current liabilities	**39.6**	6.7	27.9
Effect of exchange rate changes	**(10.6)**	(6.2)	(8.5)
Other—net	**22.4**	2.1	(6.2)
Funds from operations	**$ 242.3**	$ 200.3	$ 135.8
Cash dividends declared	**(48.3)**	(43.6)	(39.6)
Investing activities:			
Additions to properties	**(120.1)**	(126.0)	(119.3)
Cost of acquisitions, excluding working capital	**(94.1)**	(32.1)	(26.8)
Decrease (increase) in long-term receivables and investments	**2.9**	4.4	(5.3)
Disposals of property, plant, and equipment	**13.4**	9.5	47.6
	$(197.9)	$(144.2)	$(103.8)
Financing activities:			
Net increase (decrease) in short-term debt............................	**26.9**	1.9	(29.6)
Proceeds from new long-term debt	**119.4**	9.3	25.3
Retirement of long-term debt	**(112.9)**	(15.4)	(29.4)
Issuance of common treasury stock	**12.3**	10.1	13.7
Purchase of treasury stock (common and preference)	**(2.7)**	(3.8)	(1.2)
	$ 43.0	$ 2.1	$ (21.2)
Net increase (decrease) in cash and marketable securities	**$ 39.1**	$ 14.6	$ (28.8)

See accompanying notes to consolidated financial statements.

EXHIBIT 4 *(continued)*

THE QUAKER OATS COMPANY AND SUBSIDIARIES

Sales and Operating Income by Industry Segment (a)

(millions of dollars except share data)

Year Ended June 30	Sales							Operating Income						
	Five-Year Compound Growth Rate	1984	1983	1982(b)	1981(b)	1980(b)	1979(b)	Five-Year Compound Growth Rate	1984	1983	1982(b)	1981(b)	1980(b)	1979(b)
U.S. Grocery Products	14.9%	$1,719.7	$1,258.9	$1,197.1	$1,056.6	$ 944.0	$ 858.1	16.6%	$210.9	$183.8	$142.5	$129.1	$106.1	$ 98.0
International Grocery Products	12.0%	905.0	877.6	869.9	845.1	726.4	513.8	7.2%	46.9	59.1	52.1	49.5	37.2	33.2
Fisher-Price	6.8%	383.4	335.9	373.3	366.8	363.9	276.3	6.4%	43.6	29.6	50.0	46.0	50.3	31.9
Specialty Retailing	54.0%	157.0	128.6	117.8	55.4	47.9	18.1	50.2%	16.8	15.8	11.6	5.5	4.8	2.2
Total existing businesses	13.7%	3,165.1	2,601.0	2,558.1	2,323.9	2,082.2	1,666.3	14.0%	318.2	288.3	256.2	230.1	198.4	165.3
Other (c)	n.a.	179.0	10.3	18.1	61.2	111.4	101.1	n.a.	7.8	(2.2)	4.9	1.9	7.6	8.3
Total sales and operating income	13.6%	$3,344.1	$2,611.3	$2,576.2	$2,385.1	$2,193.6	$1,767.4	13.4%	326.0	286.1	261.1	232.0	206.0	173.6
Less: General corporate expenses								9.6%	15.0	16.9	7.3	12.1	11.5	9.5
Interest expense—net								34.5%	59.9	41.9	45.9	31.9	24.8	13.6
Foreign exchange (gain) loss—net								n.a.	(9.0)	7.4	1.0	.8	(1.9)	4.9
Income from continuing operations before income taxes								12.3%	260.1	219.9	206.9	187.2	171.6	145.6
Provision for income taxes								13.8%	121.4	100.6	89.6	82.9	76.0	63.5
Income from continuing operations								11.1%	$138.7	$119.3	$117.3	$104.3	$ 95.6	$ 82.1
Income from continuing operations per common share								11.5%	$ 6.71	$ 5.83	$ 5.81	$ 4.96	$ 4.51	$ 3.89

n.a. = not applicable.

(a) Sales between industry segments were not material and are not separately set forth.

(b) Restated to exclude the Restaurant, Chemicals, and U.S. Games business segments which are reported as discontinued operations.

(c) Fiscal 1984 includes the operations of Stokely-Van Camp which were sold or are to be sold, fiscal 1983 and earlier years include the Mexican toy operations sold in fiscal 1983, and fiscal 1981 and earlier years include Burry and Needlecraft which were sold in fiscal 1981.

EXHIBIT 4 *(continued)*

THE QUAKER OATS COMPANY AND SUBSIDIARIES

Industry Segment Information
(millions of dollars)

	Identifiable Assets				Capital Expenditures				Depreciation and Amortization			
	1984	*1983*	*1982*	*1981*	*1984*	*1983*	*1982*	*1981*	*1984*	*1983*	*1982*	*1981*
U.S. Grocery Products	$ 769.8	$ 483.8	$ 457.6	$ 450.2	$ 68.5	$ 58.2	$ 30.1	$ 41.2	$ 33.4	$ 23.0	$ 21.5	$ 19.1
International Grocery Products	459.0	482.5	432.6	409.8	29.1	45.2	60.0	58.7	21.1	17.6	14.4	13.9
Fisher-Price	318.1	305.8	315.4	296.2	13.7	17.1	21.3	21.2	12.9	12.5	11.5	9.6
Specialty Retailing	91.4	65.2	52.2	14.4	7.1	3.5	2.1	1.6	2.8	1.9	1.6	.5
Total existing businesses	$1,638.3	$1,337.3	$1,257.8	$1,170.6	$118.4	$124.0	$113.5	$122.7	$ 70.2	$ 55.0	$ 49.0	$ 43.1
Other *(a)*	34.3	—	12.8	20.1	1.7	.2	.6	4.1	4.0	.1	.3	1.6
Corporate *(b)*	134.2	126.4	206.1	263.4	—	—	—	—	—	—	—	—
Total consolidated	$1,806.8	$1,463.7	$1,476.7	$1,454.1	$120.1	$124.2	$114.1	$126.8	$ 74.2	$ 55.1	$ 49.3	$ 44.7

THE QUAKER OATS COMPANY AND SUBSIDIARIES

Geographic Area Information
(millions of dollars)

	Sales (c)				Operating Income				Identifiable Assets			
	1984	*1983*	*1982*	*1981*	*1984*	*1983*	*1982*	*1981*	*1984*	*1983*	*1982*	*1981*
United States	$2,164.0	$1,623.5	$1,580.7	$1,367.2	$249.5	$210.6	$183.7	$163.0	$1,113.1	$ 783.6	$ 748.7	$ 694.7
Canada	160.3	151.3	148.3	135.6	12.4	10.7	8.7	7.2	60.0	58.8	52.3	53.1
Europe	614.4	581.0	525.8	533.0	22.0	34.8	30.5	31.6	325.3	346.7	282.2	252.4
Latin America and Pacific	226.4	245.2	303.3	288.1	34.3	32.2	33.3	28.3	139.9	148.2	174.6	170.4
Total existing businesses	$3,165.1	$2,601.0	$2,558.1	$2,323.9	$318.2	$288.3	$256.2	$230.1	$1,638.3	$1,337.3	$1,257.8	$1,170.6
Other *(a)*	179.0	10.3	18.1	61.2	7.8	(2.2)	4.9	1.9	34.3	—	12.8	20.1
Corporate *(b)*	—	—	—	—	—	—	—	—	134.2	126.4	206.1	263.4
Total consolidated	$3,344.1	$2,611.3	$2,576.2	$2,385.1	$326.0	$286.1	$261.1	$232.0	$1,806.8	$1,463.7	$1,476.7	$1,454.1

(a) Fiscal 1984 includes the operations of Stokely-Van Camp which were sold or are to be sold, fiscal 1983 and earlier years include the Mexican toy operations sold in fiscal 1983, and fiscal 1981 includes Burry and Needlecraft which were sold in fiscal 1981.

(b) Corporate identifiable assets include the net assets of discontinued operations, corporate cash and marketable securities, and miscellaneous receivables and investments.

(c) Represents sales to unaffiliated customers only; sales between geographic segments are not material.

EXHIBIT 4 (continued)

Note 2: Acquisitions and Dispositions

Acquisitions. During the first quarter of fiscal 1984, the company acquired Stokely-Van Camp, Inc., pursuant to a tender offer. The tendered shares, combined with shares acquired previously and also those purchased under agreements with certain Stokely-Van Camp shareholders, resulted in Quaker's owning 77 percent of Stokely-Van Camp common stock. All remaining shares were acquired pursuant to a merger which was approved by Stokely-Van Camp shareholders in September 1983 and became effective on October 31, 1983. The purchase price was approximately $238 million. Results of operations have been consolidated since the acquisition date.

Presented below are the consolidated results as reported for fiscal 1984 compared to pro forma combined results of Quaker and Stokely-Van Camp, Inc., for fiscal 1983. Fiscal 1984, as reported, is indicative of a full year of combined operations, since 11 months of Stokely results since acquisition are included in consolidated Quaker reporting. The pro forma combined results for fiscal 1983 assumes the acquisition had occurred at July 1, 1982. The pro forma data was prepared making those adjustments necessary due to the revaluation of the acquired assets of Stokely-Van Camp, Inc., and certain other adjustments required as a result of the acquisition. The adjustments do not include nonrecurring expenses which resulted directly from the acquisition.

timore, a marketer of traditional men's and women's clothing and accessories. The results of operations for these businesses have been consolidated since their respective dates of acquisition. Pro forma data is not presented because the effect on consolidated results is not material. During the last three fiscal years, the company made several other acquisitions, none of which had a significant effect on consolidated results. The excess of cost over net assets of acquired businesses for all acquisitions was $57.4 million in fiscal 1984, $2.5 million in fiscal 1983 and $19 million in fiscal 1982.

Discontinued Operations. During fiscal 1983, the company recorded write-offs related to its decision to sell the chemicals business segment and to discontinue the operations of its U.S. Games video-game cartridge business segment. The reserve for the loss on disposal (net of income tax benefit of $44.3 million) was $55.5 million, or $2.82 per share. The loss from operations for these two businesses for the period July 1, 1982, to March 31, 1983 (net of income tax benefit of $6.7 million) was $7 million. As of June 30, 1983, the remaining net assets and liabilities of these businesses were reclassified on the consolidated balance sheet to the caption "Other current assets," net of the loss reserve. The items reclassified consisted primarily of fixed assets, inventory, and receivables. During 1984, the chemicals business was sold for cash, notes, and preferred stock of approximately $45.3 million.

	(millions of dollars except share data)	
	F-84 as Reported	F-83 Pro Forma Combined
Revenue	$3,344.1	$2,994.5
Income from continuing operations	138.7	126.2
Net income	138.7	63.7
Per common share:		
Income from continuing operations	$ 6.71	$ 6.15
Net income	$ 6.71	$ 2.98

In November 1983, the company acquired, in a purchase transaction, Eyelab, Inc., a retailer of prescription and nonprescription eyewear products. In February 1983, the company acquired, in a purchase transaction, the European pet food business of the Ralston Purina Company. In September 1982, the company purchased the assets and the oats business of Scott's Oats, Great Britain. In July 1981, the company acquired, in a purchase transaction, Jos. A. Bank Clothiers, Inc., of Bal-

In fiscal 1982, the company entered into an agreement to sell substantially all of the assets of the Restaurant Division. The aftertax loss on the sale amounted to $20.4 million (net of income tax benefits of $15.9 million), or $1.05 per share.

The consolidated statement of income has been restated for all years presented to report the results of discontinued operations separately from continuing operations. Where considered appropriate, income-related notes

EXHIBIT 4 *(continued)*

were restated to exclude amounts for discontinued operations. Prior-year balance sheets and related notes were not restated. Sales applicable to discontinued operations, prior to the recording of the write-offs, were $78.7 million in fiscal 1983 and $212.2 million in 1982.

The reserve for losses (pre-tax) on discontinued operations is as follows:

(millions of dollars)	1984	1983	1982
Balance at beginning of year	$62.5	$ 5.8	$ —
Additions	—	99.8	36.3
Deductions for businesses sold	(27.6)	—	(29.5)
Charges against related reserves	(15.4)	(43.1)	(1.0)
Balance at end of year	$19.5	$62.5	$ 5.8

During the last three fiscal years, the company made several other dispositions, none of which had a significant effect on consolidated results.

Additional 10-K Information

U.S. Grocery Products Description

Through Quaker's U.S. Grocery business, the company is a major participant in the competitive packaged foods industry in the United States. Quaker is the leading manufacturer in the U.S. of hot cereals, pancake mixes, cornmeal, hominy grits, canned dry beans, and among the five largest manufacturers of grain-based snacks, ready-to-eat cereals, frozen pizza, syrup, and pet foods. Quaker's grocery products are purchased by consumers through a wide range of food distributors. Quaker maintains a full-time sales force and has distribution centers throughout the country, each of which carries an inventory of most of the company's grocery products. In addition, Quaker markets a line of 375 items for the food service market, including *Quaker* hot and ready-to-eat cereals, mixes, *Wolf* Brand Chili, *Aunt Jemima* frozen breakfast products, *Ardmore Farms* portion-control frozen fruit juices, *Gatorade* thirst quencher, and *Burry-Lu* cookies and crackers.

Raw Materials

The raw materials used in manufacturing include oats, wheat, soy products, corn, rice, sweeteners, almonds, raisins, beef, shortening, meat by-products, dry beans, and fish, as well as a variety of packaging materials. While most of these products are purchased on the open market, Quaker purchases commodity futures contracts, when considered appropriate, in order to assure supply at reasonable prices. This practice has tended to limit the impact of volatile commodity prices. Energy

availability is important in maintaining production, and costs have been stable for the past 18 months. Supplies of all raw materials have been adequate and continuous.

International Grocery Products Description

Quaker's International Grocery Products business is broadly diversified, both geographically and by product line. Internationally, Quaker participates in the foods, pet foods, and household products markets. Quaker both manufactures and markets these products in Argentina, Australia, Brazil, Canada, Colombia, Denmark, the United Kingdom, France, Germany, Italy, Mexico, Taiwan, The Netherlands, Uruguay, and Venezuela. The company also markets products in most countries of the free world. Quaker is the leading hot cereals producer in many countries and has other leading market positions for products in a number of countries, including the following: the leading producer of edible seed oils in Italy; the leading producer of beverage chocolate and chocolate candy in Mexico; the leading sardine processor in Brazil; the leading honey company in The Netherlands; the leading scouring pad manufacturer in Colombia; and the second largest pet food company in Continental Europe.

Raw Materials

Raw materials used by the international grocery business are basically the same as in the grocery business in the U.S. but also include corn oil, sardines, cacao beans, and steel wire. Supplies of all raw materials have been adequate and continuous.

Fisher-Price Description

Fisher-Price is one of the major manufacturers in the highly competitive U.S. toy industry. Fisher-Price also has a substantial international business, manufacturing and selling toys in the United Kingdom and Belgium, and operating sales companies in Canada, Germany, France, Italy, Spain, and Australia. Fisher-Price has the leading market position in infant and preschool toys worldwide. The company also manufactures and markets juvenile furnishings in the U.S. For the entire industry,

EXHIBIT 4 *(concluded)*

retail sales of toys are highly seasonal, with most retail sales occurring within the October–December period because of Christmas demand. Extended payment terms are customary, and this increases the need for short-term financing. However, Fisher-Price has early-order programs available, which are now customary in the industry, and which smooth out its production and sales throughout the year.

Raw Materials

Although Fisher-Price is producing toys and juvenile furnishings using a broad range of materials, plastic remains the principal raw material. Plastic resins rose modestly in price during fiscal 1984 and remain in adequate supply.

Specialty Retailing

Quaker's Specialty Retailing Group consists of Jos. A. Bank Clothiers, Inc., Brookstone Company, Inc.; Herrschners, Inc., and Eyelab, Inc. Jos. A. Bank manufactures and markets men's and women's apparel and accessories through retail outlets and mail-order catalogs. Brookstone markets specialty tools and housewares through mail-order catalogs and retail outlets. Herrschners is a mail-order marketer of needlecraft goods. Eyelab markets prescription and nonprescription eyewear products through retail stores.

Raw Materials

Jos. A. Bank purchases various fabrics from suppliers, which are used to manufacture clothing. The company generally has not had difficulties in obtaining fabric and supplies from manufacturers. No significant fluctuations occurred in the cost of fabric purchased by Jos. A. Bank during fiscal 1984.

CHAPTER 27

Interim Period Reporting and Analysis

Publicly traded companies publish quarterly for their stockholders and file with the SEC unaudited data related to their activities for the past quarter and the year to date. The APB in *Opinion No. 28* set forth the basic guidelines for preparing these interim reports. Most of the issues involved in interim reporting are the same as those encountered in annual reporting. However, a number of reporting practices are peculiar to interim reporting. This chapter concentrates on these latter issues.

The same financial analysis techniques that statement users apply to annual statements can be used to interpret interim reports. The difficulty in applying these techniques is that the financial data presented in interim reports is condensed, not explained in detail by accompanying notes, unaudited, and very dependent on management judgments. As a result, the statement user often has less confidence in the results of his or her analysis of interim reports than in the conclusions drawn from analysis of annual statements.

To overcome some of the limitations of interim reports, statement users should always refer to the company's last annual report to refresh their understanding of the company's accounting principles, construct their own detailed current period and year-to-date funds statements using the balance sheet data most companies present, examine past fourth-quarter adjustments to gain an appreciation of the reliability of management judgments, and, finally, use interim period data cautiously.

Illustration 27–1 presents an example of comparative income statements presented in an interim report.

SEC Requirements

The SEC requirements covered three topics: the content of the quarterly SEC filings, the disclosure of quarterly data in annual reports, and the relationship of the independent public accountant to the quarterly data.

ILLUSTRATION 27–1

HAMPTON METALS COMPANY, INC.
Consolidated Statement of Earnings
(dollars and shares in thousands)

	Nine Months Ended April 30		Three Months Ended April 30	
	1986	1985†	1986	1985*
Steel products	$ 86,249	$ 69,372	$26,520	$25,113
Plastic products and machinery	54,553	45,382	17,345	14,385
Aluminum, zinc, and brass products	36,887	45,430	11,669	17,459
Miscellaneous products	27,406	26,779	10,105	9,520
Net sales	$205,095	$186,963	$65,639	$66,477
Cost of products sold	$171,710	$155,736	$53,001	$55,764
Selling and administrative expenses	14,944	13,753	5,223	4,784
Interest expense	2,103	2,197	594	762
Other deductions and credits—net	(185)	(598)	67	(308)
	$188,572	$171,088	$58,885	$61,002
Earnings before income taxes	$ 16,523	$ 15,875	$ 6,754	$ 5,475
Federal and state income taxes	8,350	7,300	3,400	2,500
Net earnings	$ 8,173	$ 8,575	$ 3,354	$ 2,975
Depreciation and amortization	$ 6,024	$ 4,920	$ 1,910	$ 1,720
Average number of shares outstanding	4,002	3,888	4,002	4,002
Earnings per share	$ 2.04	$ 2.21	$ 0.84	$ 0.74

* Earnings before taxes, net earnings have been restated from amounts previously reported to reflect the change to the LIFO method of valuing inventories during fiscal 1985.
† Subtract the final year-end amount.

The SEC quarterly reports must include a condensed income statement, balance sheet, and funds flow statement; a narrative analysis of the results of operations; the approval of any accounting change by the filing company's independent public accountant; and the signature of the company's chief financial or accounting officer. In addition, management is encouraged to make whatever additional financial disclosures it believes are appropriate. A statement must also be included that the financial data have been reviewed in accordance with professional standards by a CPA.

The SEC requires disclosure in a note to the annual financial statements of net sales, gross profit (net sales less costs and expenses associated directly with or allocated to products sold or services rendered), income before extraordinary items and cumulative effect of a change in accounting, per-share data based upon such income, and net income for each quarter within the fiscal periods for which income statements are presented. Where this note is part of audited financial statements, it may be designated as "unaudited," but the release recognizes that auditors will be associated with the data.

Certain companies, such as those with limited trading interest in their stock, are exempt from these quarterly and annual report requirements.

Inherent Problem

The determination of the results of operations for periods of less than a full year presents inherent difficulties for the management trying to prepare a meaningful statement and the investor seeking to use the interim data.

The most common difficulty is that information for any period less than a full year may have limited usefulness because the reporting period is too short to reflect adequately the nature of a company's business. For example, the revenues of some businesses fluctuate widely among interim periods because of seasonal or random factors. In other businesses, heavy fixed costs incurred in one interim period may benefit another period. In other situations, costs and expenses related to a full year's activities may be incurred at infrequent intervals throughout the year. In this case, costs may be allocated to products in process or to the interim periods to avoid distorting the interim results.

Another reporting problem inherent in interim reporting is that in the limited time available, it is impractical to develop the complete information needed to present the report. As a result, many costs and expenses are estimated in interim reports. For example, it may not be practical to perform extensive reviews of individual inventory items, costs on individual long-term contracts, and precise income tax calculations. As a result, the interim data are tentative, and subsequent refinement or corrections of these estimates may distort the results of operations of later interim periods. Similarly, the effects of disposal of a segment of a business and extraordinary, unusual, or infrequently occurring events and transactions will often be more pronounced on the results of operations for an interim period than they will be on results for the annual period.

Fundamental Accounting Issue: Interim Reporting Objective

There is considerable controversy as to what the principal objective should be for interim financial reporting. *Opinion No. 28* settled on one of the two major contending objectives, but some of its recommendations seem more consistent with the rejected alternative than the one adopted.

The two principal alternative objectives follow from their proposers' views of the nature of the interim period. One group believes that each interim period should be viewed as the basic accounting period. (This approach is called the "independent theory.") In contrast, those who propose the alternative objective maintain that each interim period should be viewed as an integral part of the annual period (the so-called "dependent theory").

Basic Accounting Period

Those who support the basic accounting period position tend to think of an accounting period as such, irrespective of its length, and to believe that the events and transactions of each accounting period should be reported. From this position, they conclude that the results of operations for each interim period should be determined in essentially the same manner as if the interim period were an annual accounting period. Under this view, deferrals, accruals, and estimations at the end of each interim period would be determined by following essentially the same principles and judgments that the company applies to annual reports. For example, if an expenditure was expensed in the annual statement, it should be expensed in any interim report, irrespective of the amount of the expenditure and its relationship to the annual amount or the revenues of other interim periods within this year.

Integral Part of Annual Period

Those who hold that interim financial data are an integral part of the annual period believe they are essential to provide investors with timely information on the progress the enterprise is making toward its annual results of operations. Therefore, the usefulness of interim data rests on the predictive relationship that it has to the annual period results. Thus, each interim period should be regarded as an integral part of the annual period rather than a discrete period standing on its own.

Under this view, deferrals, accruals, and estimations at the end of each interim period are affected by judgments made then as to the results of operations for the balance of the annual period. Thus, for example, a portion of an estimated annual expenditure that might be expensed for the entire annual period might be accrued or deferred at the end of an interim period as management allocates the estimated annual expense between interim periods on a basis that reflects time, sales volume, or production activity.

Opinion No. 28 and Other Authoritative Statements

Opinion No. 28 adopted the integral part point of view based on the dependent theory. The *Opinion* recognized that, in general, each interim report should be based on the accounting policies used in the preparation of the latest annual statements, unless some accounting policies have been changed in the current year. However, it went on to conclude that certain modifications of these annual report practices may be required in interim reports so that the reported results may correspond better to the results of operations for the annual period.

Interim Reporting Guidelines

Opinion No. 28 recommended a number of guidelines for the preparation of interim statements. The principal emphasis was on the matching of costs and revenues, the reporting of extraordinary items and the disposal of a business, and disclosure requirements. Here is a summary of the *Opinion's* recommendations.

Revenues. Revenues earned during an interim period should be recognized on the same basis as followed for the full year. For example, if the revenue from long-term contracts is accounted for under the percentage-of-completion method in annual statements, the same approach should be used in interim reports. If future losses on such contracts become evident during an interim period, the projected losses should be recognized in full in the interim period, however.

Product Costs. Costs that are associated directly with or allocated to the products and services sold are called product costs. These costs for both annual and interim reporting purposes should be charged to the period in which the related revenue is recognized. Examples of product costs include material costs, direct production wages and related fringe benefits, variable manufacturing overheads, warranty expenses, and similar expenses whose total level tends to vary with or relate closely to business volume.

Most product costs are included in the income statement as an element of the cost-of-goods-sold figure. This item in interim reports should be regarded as a very tentative expression of the expense, since the inventory valuation procedures used to measure it are typically based on perpetual inventory records and estimates of future inventory replenishment costs, rather than physical counts and actual prices. Inventory records are seldom accurate; and the future cost estimates of executives are seldom correct due to random factors, a desire to be conservative, a need to inflate current profits, or poor forecasting information and skills.

For interim reporting purposes, companies should generally use the same inventory pricing methods as those followed to determine annual results. However, some exceptions may be appropriate for interim reporting. For example, some companies use estimated gross profit rates to determine the cost of goods sold during interim periods. Under this procedure, management simply assumes a margin percentage—usually the margin achieved in prior annual periods or budgeted for the current annual period—and applies it to the sales of the period to determine the period's dollar gross margin. This approach in times of inflation can produce misleading results if a company does not keep close track of its cost increases and is slow to raise prices.

Other companies that use the LIFO method may, at an interim date, encounter a temporary liquidation of the LIFO base period inventories which are expected to be replaced by the end of the annual period. If these base period costs are allowed to flow through to the income statement, profits would be inflated and not representative of the annual results.

In such cases, the inventory at the interim reporting date should not give effect to the LIFO liquidation. The cost of sales for the interim reporting period should conclude the expected cost of replacement of the liquidated LIFO base. Again, in periods of inflation or commodity shortages, this estimate is difficult to make, since commodity prices are impossible to forecast.

Many companies use standard cost accounting systems for determining inventory and product costs. These companies should generally follow the same procedure in reporting purchase price, wage rate, usage, or efficiency variances from standard cost at the end of the interim period as followed at the end of the fiscal year. However, if the cost variances associated with an interim period are planned and are expected to be absorbed by the end of the annual period, they may be deferred and not recognized in the interim period in which they occur. The decision as to what is "planned" and "unplanned" rests with the reporting management.

Whether to apply the lower-of-cost-or-market rule in reporting inventories for interim periods also requires judgment on management's part. If a company has inventory losses from market price declines at an interim period date, the loss should be recognized in the interim period in which it occurs if management believes the loss is permanent. On the other hand, if a market decline at an interim date can reasonably be expected to be restored in the current fiscal year, the temporary decline need not be recognized at the interim date. Should management decide to recognize an inventory loss in one interim period and if the market price later recovers in the same fiscal year, the gain can be recognized in the later interim period in which it occurs.

Other Costs. All businesses have costs and expenses that are not allocated or associated directly with product and service revenues. These other costs include such items as advertising expenditures, vacation pay, maintenance costs, and property taxes. According to *Opinion No. 28,* these other costs may be expensed as incurred *or* allocated among interim periods based on an estimate of time expired, benefit received, or other activity associated with the period. In line with its overall objective for interim statements, the *Opinion* expressed a preference for allocating these other costs between periods, but it did not preclude the option to expense as incurred.

To guide management in interim accounting for cost and expenses other than product costs, the APB set forth these standards:

1. Procedures adopted for assigning specific expense items to an interim period should be consistent with the bases followed by the company for that item in reporting results of operations at an annual reporting date.
2. When a specific cost item charged to expense for annual reporting purposes benefits more than one interim period, the item may be allocated as an expense between those interim periods that benefit from the expenditure.
3. Costs and expenditures incurred in an interim period that cannot

be identified with the activities or benefits of other interim periods should be charged to the interim period in which they are incurred.

4. Costs should not be assigned arbitrarily to an interim period.
5. Gains and losses that arise in any interim period similar to any that would not be deferred at year-end should not be deferred to later interim periods within the same year.

Opinion No. 28 presents a number of examples of the preferred accounting for costs other than product costs. Here are some of these examples:

Many companies schedule their major repair work during the annual plant vacation shutdown period, typically in the summer months. These repairs benefit the whole year's operations and relate to the use of the plant during the year. In these cases, it is appropriate to estimate the cost of these repairs at the beginning of the year and then allocate the cost over the entire year for interim reporting purposes. This means that prior to the actual repair work, a portion of the expenditure may be charged to each interim period on an accrual basis. This is achieved through a debit to the repair expense account and a credit to a reserve for repair expenditure, which is a liability account. When the anticipated expenditure is made, the reserve is charged. Any excess expenditures above the reserve amount is deferred. Then, over the year's remaining interim periods, the difference between the actual repair expenditure and the amount of the accumulated reserve (an asset called deferred repair expense) is amortized by a debit to expense and credit to the deferred asset account, according to the allocation basis adopted at the beginning of the year.

Quantity discounts are often allowed customers based upon annual sales volume. In order to relate this discount to the sales of each interim period, an amount for anticipated year-end discounts should be charged to each interim period based on the relationship between interim period sales to customers and customers' estimated annual sales and discounts.

The accounting entry to record anticipated discounts at the time sales are made is:

```
Dr.  Discounts and Allowances ........................................  xxx
     Cr.  Reserve for Discounts and Allowances ........................       xxx
```

Later, as discounts are earned by customers, the reserve for allowances is eliminated and any discounts in excess of this reserve are charged to sales over the remaining portion of the annual period.

Property taxes, interest, and rents are usually payable as of a certain day. Typically, these costs are accrued or deferred at annual reporting dates to record a full year's charge.[1] Similar procedures should be adopted at each interim reporting date to provide for an appropriate cost in each period.

---

[1] Interim statements presume that the interim report user is familiar with the company's annual report accounting policies, which were disclosed in the latest annual report.

Advertising expenditures may benefit more than one interim period. If this is clearly the case, the advertising costs may be deferred and charged over the beneficial interim periods.

In some sales programs, it is necessary to stock dealers with products before launching an advertising program. If a subsequent advertising program is clearly implicit in the sales arrangement, the anticipated program costs may be accrued and assigned to interim periods in relation to sales recorded prior to the time the advertising service is rendered.

The amounts of certain costs and expenses are frequently subjected to year-end adjustments, even though they can be reasonably approximated at interim dates. Examples of such items include inventory shrinkage, allowance for quantity discounts, and discretionary year-end bonuses. To the extent possible, year-end adjustments should be estimated at the beginning of the year and the estimated costs assigned to interim periods so that the interim periods bear a reasonable portion of the anticipated annual amount.

The quality of the accounting practices companies follow to report their nonproduct costs, such as year-end bonuses, in interim statements vary considerably from company to company. For example, interim period accrual or deferral accounting for nonproduct costs usually requires management to estimate the annual expenditures for these costs in advance. This estimate may be influenced by how difficult it is for management to report its desired level of interim profits. If management is having trouble reaching its interim profit goal, it may be tempted to underestimate the annual expenditure and thus reduce the amount to be charged to the interim periods. The hope is that things will turn out better by year-end and annual profits will be high enough to absorb the undercharge without anyone detecting what was done in the interim reports. Alternatively, if management is making more than its interim profits goal, the estimated annual expenditures may be overestimated so as to build up the interim period expenses. This will bring profits down to the desired amount and provide a profit cushion should business take a turn for the worse by year-end. Again, since the annual estimate is not disclosed, the statement user finds it hard to establish how management is over- or underestimating to manage interim profits.

Opinion No. 28 recommends that the tax rate applied to each interim period's pre-tax income for determining tax expense should be the best estimate of the effective tax rate expected to be applied to the full fiscal year's pre-tax profits. This requires that the interim period rate reflect anticipated investment tax credits, foreign tax rates, capital gains rates, and other similar tax planning alternatives. Since a management estimate is required to implement the *Opinion's* recommendation, the quality of the estimate may vary depending on (a) the company's ability to reach its interim profit goals and (b) management's willingness to use accounting techniques to raise or lower its interim profits.

FASB Interpretation No. 18, "Accounting for Income Taxes in Interim

Periods," explains the application of *Opinion No. 28's* general rule for computing interim income taxes for a variety of specific situations.

Extraordinary and Unusual Items. Immaterial extraordinary items can be included as part of the calculation of income before extraordinary items. In the case of interim reports, a question arises as to whether the interim period profit before extraordinary items or the estimated annual profit before extraordinary items should be the basis on which to measure materiality. *Opinion No. 28* recommends that the year-end profit estimate be used.[2] Thus, an extraordinary item that is very material relative to interim earnings results, but immaterial relative to the annual profit estimate, may be included in the interim period's income before extraordinary items. To let the statement reader be made aware of the inclusion of such items in income, the *Opinion* recommends that all "unusual" events and items be disclosed.

The effects of disposal of a segment of a business should be reported separately in interim statements.

Other kinds of events that should be disclosed to provide the statement user with a proper understanding of interim financial reports include unusual seasonal reports and business combinations that for accounting purposes are treated as poolings of interests and business acquisitions.

Extraordinary items, gains, or losses from a business segment disposal and unusual or infrequently occurring items should not be prorated over the balance of the fiscal year.

Accounting Changes

In general, if a company changes its interim or annual accounting practices, policies, or estimates in an interim period, the change should be reported according to the provisions of *Opinion No. 20.*[3]

The FASB modified this APB *Opinion* when it published *Statement No. 3*, "Reporting Accounting changes in Interim Financial Statements." According to this FASB *Statement,* if a cumulative-effect-type accounting change is made, such as a switch from FIFO to LIFO inventory accounting, during the first interim period of an enterprise's fiscal year, the cumulative effect of the change on retained earnings at the beginning of that fiscal year should be included in net income of the first interim period (and in last-12-months-to-date financial reports that include that first interim period).

If a cumulative-effect-type accounting change is made in other than the first interim period of an enterprise's fiscal year, no cumulative effect

---

[2] The year-end profit estimate is the suggested test of materiality for all interim statement items.

[3] Discussed in Chapter 12.

of the change should be included in net income of the period of change. Instead, financial information for the prechange interim periods of the fiscal year in which the change is made should be restated by applying the newly adopted accounting principle to those periods. The cumulative effect of the change on retained earnings at the beginning of that fiscal year should be included in restated net income of the first interim period of the fiscal year in which the change is made (and in any year-to-date or last-12-months-to-date financial reports that include the first interim period). Whenever financial information that includes those prechange interim periods is presented, it should appear on the restated basis.

Currency Exchange Rates

The effect of currency exchange rate shift should be recorded in the interim accounting period when the change occurs.

Seasonal Business

The revenues of certain businesses are subjected to material seasonal variations. *Opinion No. 28* suggests that to avoid the possibility that the interim reports of these companies could be interpreted by statement users as indicative of the annual results, the interim reports should disclose the seasonal nature of the business. In addition, it recommends that seasonal businesses consider supplementing their interim reports with information for 12-month periods ending at the interim date on a comparative basis for the current and preceding year.

Prior Interim Period Adjustments

FASB Statement No. 16, "Prior Period Adjustments," deals with the treatment in interim reports of prior interim period adjustments. These are adjustments that *(a)* relate directly to business activities of specific prior interim periods of the current fiscal year; and *(b)* could not be reasonably estimated prior to the current interim period, but become reasonably estimable in the current interim period.

   If the prior interim period adjustments become known in any period other than the first interim period, that portion related to the current period should be included in the current period's income. Prior interim periods of the current fiscal year should be restated to include the portion of the item that is directly related to each period. If a portion of the item relates to prior fiscal years, that portion should be included in the first interim period of the current fiscal year.

Role and Limitations

Often by the time a company's annual data are available, its stock price has already anticipated them many months earlier. This discounting is in large measure influenced by the interim period reports that precede the annual reporting date. As a result, there are many who believe that interim financial data are more important to the securities market than annual period data.

Fundamental investors use interim data in two ways. Some use them to predict the annual results. Others use them to check to see if the reporting company is on a track which will validate the investor's prior prediction of its annual results.

While statement users use interim data in this fashion, they should not lose sight of three facts that will limit the usefulness of these disclosures. First, because of the shortness of the period, interim data are less reliable than annual data as a measure of corporate health. Second, despite the SEC requirements, the interim disclosures are meager. Third, managements can—and do—create interim earnings through accounting judgments in order to meet statement users' expectations.

Another problem that may limit the usefulness of the first two interim reports of each year is the interim reporting strategy many managements have typically followed in the past. Some managements like to understate their first- and second-quarter results so that (1) they can keep some profits in reserve should problems occur later in the year, and (2) they can finish with a strong fourth quarter. If companies have followed this strategy in the past, they may be able to top the previous year's first-two-quarter results by simply not understating current results as they may have done in prior years. In these cases, any improvement over last year would not be real progress, but just the result of a change in interim reporting strategy.

CASE 27-1

Craftsland International
Interim Financial Reporting Policy

Craftsland International is a multinational diversified U.S. company whose stock is publicly traded. In 1982, Craftsland had become known as a "growth" stock. During this same period, a number of major institutional investment funds had acquired large holdings of the stock, and the stock's price had risen rapidly.

Craftsland was about to issue its first-quarter 1983 financial statements to shareholders. The company's quarterly statements to shareholders included a condensed income statement and balance sheet following presentation instructions outlined by the Securities and Exchange Commission [SEC] for filing quarterly report 10-Q to the SEC. An auditor's opinion was not included since an independent audit was not required when issuing quarterly reports. Also, unless a change had been made in accounting principles, no footnotes were provided. Besides the financial statements, Craftsland's quarterly reports included a brief discussion and analysis of operations by management. Craftsland's first-quarter 1979 report to shareholders is shown in Exhibit 1.

The following board of directors' discussion of the first-quarter 1983 statements for Craftsland International took place in early April 1983. The statements were due to be released later in the month:

> *Lawrence (vice president, finance):* The figures for the first quarter don't look good. However, I believe we have it in our power to push them over the same period results for last year, if we want to do so.
>
> *Franklin (outside director):* What do you mean by that?
>
> *Lawrence:* Let me explain. Last year, we earned 52 cents per share for the first quarter, which was the best we had ever done to date for that period. This year, we have only 47 cents per share, before any adjustments to my accounting decisions that you may wish to make.

This case was prepared by Norman J. Bartczak.

Copyright © 1981 by the President and Fellows of Harvard College
Harvard Business School case 181–086

EXHIBIT 1

CRAFTSLAND INTERNATIONAL AND CONSOLIDATED SUBSIDIARIES
Consolidated Condensed Statements of Income

	Three Months Ended March 31	
	1982	1981*
	(thousands of dollars, except per-share data)	
Net sales	$19,920	$15,380
Cost of goods sold	15,274	11,733
Gross profit	4,646	3,647
Selling and administrative expenses	2,968	2,377
Other expenses	117	141
Income before taxes	1,561	1,129
Income taxes	714	511
Net income	$ 847	$ 618
Earnings per share	$0.52	$0.46

* Restated for poolings of interests.

Consolidated Condensed Balance Sheet

	March 31	
	1982	1981*
	(thousands of dollars)	
Assets		
Cash and marketable securities	$ 2,233	$ 1,140
Accounts receivable	15,581	13,324
Inventories	17,385	13,491
Other current assets	1,632	2,070
Total current assets	$36,831	$30,025
Property, plant, and equipment, net	9,631	8,351
Other assets	5,952	5,376
Total	$52,414	$43,752
Liabilities and Shareholders' Equity		
Accounts payable	$ 6,882	$ 4,846
Notes payable	4,650	3,933
Other liabilities	7,252	4,001
Total current liabilities	$18,784	$12,780
Long-term debt	8,318	8,892
Other noncurrent liabilities	1,548	1,686
Shareholders' equity	23,764	20,394
Total	$52,414	$43,752

* Restated for poolings of interests.

(In reporting its first quarter 1982 results to the Securities and Exchange Commission on Form 10-Q, Craftsland supplied the same income statement and balance sheet it issued to shareholders, and a condensed version of the management letter to shareholders discussing the results of operations. In addition, on its Form 10-Q, Craftsland included the following condensed statement of changes in financial position, two footnotes, and a limited review letter from its auditors.)

EXHIBIT 1 *(concluded)*

CRAFTSLAND INTERNATIONAL AND CONSOLIDATED SUBSIDIARIES
Consolidated Condensed Statement of Changes in Financial Position

	Three Months Ended March 31	
	1982	1981*
	(thousands of dollars)	
Source of funds:		
From operations	$1161	$ 867
Increase in long-term debt..................	412	208
Other—net	92	36
	$1665	$1111
Application of funds:		
Property, plant, and equipment, net	$ 425	$ 460
Reduction in long-term debt	457	20
Increase in working capital	783	631
	$1665	$1111

* Restated for poolings of interests.

1. The accompanying unaudited consolidated condensed financial statements have been prepared in accordance with the instructions to Form 10-Q and therefore do not include all information and footnotes necessary for a fair presentation of financial position and results of operations in conformity with generally accepted accounting principles. In the opinion of management, the consolidated condensed financial statements reflect all adjustments necessary to a fair statement of the financial results for the interim periods.

2. Smith, Jones and Company, Independent Certified Public Accountants, have performed a limited review of the unaudited consolidated condensed financial statements as of and for the three months ended March 31, 1982, in accordance with standards established by the American Insititute of Certified Public Accountants. All adjustments or additional disclosures proposed by them have been effected in the data presented. Their report is attached.

SMITH, JONES & CO.
Certified Public Accountants
1 Plaza Boulevard
New York, New York 10022

The Board of Directors
Craftsland International

We have made a limited review, in accordance with standards established by the American Institute of Certified Public Accountants, of the consolidated condensed balance sheet of Craftsland International as of March 31, 1982, and the related consolidated condensed statements of income and changes in financial position for the three months then ended. Since we did not make an audit, we express no opinion on the statements referred to above. To comply with the requirements of the Securities and Exchange

Commission, we confirm the company's representation concerning proposed adjustments and disclosures included in the accompanying Form 10-Q for the three months ended March 31, 1982, in accordance with related instruction K.

SMITH, JONES & CO.

New York, New York
April 27, 1982

EXHIBIT 2
Craftsland International

Excerpts from Craftsland International's 1982 First-Quarter
Report: Title, "Growth Through Diversification"

Management's Discussion and Analysis of Operations

To Our Shareholders, Customers, and Employees:

The record sales and earnings of this quarter exceed any first quarter in Craftsland's history. In fact, sales and earnings are exceeded only by the fourth quarter of the preceding year.

Consolidated net income of Craftsland International for the three-month period ended March 31, 1982, was up 30 percent to $847,000, equal to 52 cents a share. This compared to $618,000, equal to 46 cents a share, in the first quarter last year.

Consolidated sales for the first three months of this year reached an all-time high of $19,920,000, an increase of 30 percent from $15,380,000 in the same period last year. Costs increased in line with our increased sales volume.

This growth represents both a continuation of the basic demand factors of Craftsland's products and a responsiveness to Craftsland's new program of diversification through acquisition. Our three principal operating sectors, Consumer Products, Paper Products, and Industrial Systems, all showed consistent performance throughout the quarter, the growth due to our successful worldwide search for compatible and reinforcing acquisitions.

As the cover of this quarterly report indicates, your management is committed to "growth through diversification." We expect that this strategy will enable Craftsland to sustain its current growth.

David X. Morris
President and Chief Executive Officer

April 29, 1982

Morris (president): Frankly, I think it is imperative that we report a good first quarter. Last year, our earnings were a record high and our fourth quarter was extremely strong. In fact, it was out best quarter ever . . .

Powers (outside director): Yes, I know. But didn't we pull a lot of income into the last quarter from this year to get those results? For example, we cut advertising, accelerated foreign dividend receipts, picked up DISC[1] tax savings for the first time, deferred maintenance, accelerated equipment installation to get the investment tax credit, recognized income on advanced shipments . . . It seems to me that what we did was to "rob Peter to pay Paul." Now we have to pay the price.

Morris: I admit we pushed a bit, but the fact is, the stock market reacted

---

[1] Prior to 1985, corporations exported through domestic international sales corporations (DISCs). These were special corporations permitted by the tax code to encourage exports. DISCs were required to pay taxes immediately on only part of their profits. The payment of taxes on the remainder of the profits was deferred as long as the untaxed profits were used for export purposes. Should these profits subsequently be used for nonexport purposes, the deferred tax payment became payable. Prior to 1982, for book purposes, internationals accrued these potential taxes. In 1982, the company adopted "flow-through" tax accounting for its DISC taxes (i.e., only recorded the taxes actually paid). This practice was permitted. In 1985, this tax code eliminated DISCs. They were replaced by FSCs (Foreign Sales Corporations). A portion of the taxes due on a FSC's export profits was permanently forgiven.

favorably to our strong finish to last year and our stock price has really started to climb. In fact, since mid-January our price-earnings ratio has gone from 21 times to 24 times this year's estimated earnings, which the market estimates will be higher than last year. I don't think we can afford to lose this stock price momentum.

Lawrence: I am convinced that if we report earnings for this quarter that are not substantially above last year's first-quarter results, we will see our price-earnings ratio decline. This is a very "nervous" stock market we are in. The Dow is high, but it is subject to wide fluctuations on a daily basis.

Braun (vice president, marketing): Why are the first-quarter earnings less than last year? What are the causes and dollar value? What options do we have? I for one want to keep the stock's price-earnings ratio up.

Lawrence: Here is an analysis of the differences between this year and last year: First, because we deferred maintenance on a worldwide basis from last year to this year, our first-quarter maintenance costs are up by 2 cents a share over last year. Also, since the first quarter is normally the heaviest maintenance month of the year, we have an extra 2 cents per share charge above what the average will be for the next three quarters, which have fairly equal maintenance expenditures. I have charged the extra 4 cents maintenance to the first quarter.

Second, our DISC tax deferrals in this quarter ran at the rate of 3 cents per share. This is our peak export period. It is over one third of the year's projected DISC tax saving of 8 cents, which we can flow through to income. Last year's fourth quarter was the first time we had material DISC tax savings. In that case, we credited all of the savings to that quarter's income. Now, I believe we should spread our DISC tax savings equally over the full year on a quarter by quarter basis. So, I picked up 2 cents for this quarter and deferred 1 cent. Actually the DISC tax impact on earnings is a "plus" from last year at this time.

Braun: Do we have to spread the benefit?

Lawrence: No. We can pick up the DISC earnings as earned. However, I felt "spreading" was the preferred approach.

Powers: It all depends on how you define "preferred."

Lawrence: Next, we have the costs of relocating the Southern Paper Sioux Springs offices. These came to 3 cents a share. Actually, we had planned to do that last year but put it off because we didn't want to hurt last year's earnings. I included all of that cost in the first quarter.

Morris: I talked to Bill [Lawrence] about these charges which are depressing earnings and he tells me that it is good accounting to recognize costs and defer revenues. I suspect he is correct, but do we necessarily have to do this for interim reports?

Bill, you have some more items don't you?

Lawrence: Yes. This first quarter includes a dividend of 4 cents per share we got from our Brazilian subsidiary in March. Since we account for this subsidiary on the cost basis, we only pick up income from it as it is received in dividends in the United States.

Morris: Last February, I felt we were having earnings problems, so I put extra pressure on Brazil to repatriate some dividends. As you know, they were held up by legal problems from getting these funds to us last year.

Cohen (vice president, personnel): What do the dividends from overseas cost-basis investments look like this year?

Morris: Well I think we can get about 10 cents per share's worth in the last quarter, but between now and then I am not very hopeful. Incidently, 10 cents is all we budgeted for from foreign dividends this year.

Frankly, while domestic and export sales and profits are on track from regular operations, our overseas operations are down. In fact, that is the principle reason for our problems. In particular, the new Italian company, Grazini, which we picked up late last year and included in the consolidated results on a pooling of interests basis, is a real "lemon." I have to admit we were in a big hurry to acquire it. We wanted its full-year profits to be included in the full year's results. As you know, its profits were up some 200 percent over the previous year.

Peter [Pike], why don't you explain the situation to us.

Pike (vice president, international): Well, the company is still delivering operating profits, but its inventories and receivables turned out to be overstated. Once our internal auditors got in last January and examined what we had bought, they found a lot of obsolete and damaged inventories. Also, the receivables' bad debt reserves were too low. In addition, some equipment was still carried on the books, but it couldn't be found. Then some more equipment should be written off. It is junk.

All this amounts to a 6 cents per share write-off . . .

Lawrence: I charged it to operating income.

Morris: Of course, we have a law suit in the Italian courts against the Grazini brothers to recover these amounts.

Braun: What do you think our chances are of collecting?

Morris: Very slim. However, I thought it was worth the effort. Maybe to protect their name they may settle out of court. They are not dishonest. They're just poor bookkeepers.

Outside of the Grazini problem, I expect our foreign operations will deliver their budgeted share of this year's earnings per share by December 31.

Braun: Bill [Lawrence], how did you charge the major advertising program we had in March?

Lawrence: I figured we spent about 2 cents a share above our average monthly budget. The principal cost was the "unusual" TV show and related radio and paper advertising. All of this was charged to March.

Braun: The benefits will come in April, May, and June, won't they? In fact, so far this month our sales are up just as we planned. It seems to me that—to quote you from an earlier meeting—"proper matching of costs and revenues" should require us to defer this "extra" 2 cents per share to the second quarter.

Morris: What about investment tax credit benefits?

Lawrence: Well, you'll recall we pushed the installation of qualified property from the first quarter of this year into the fourth quarter of last year. As a result, we only have a 1-cent-per-share benefit in the first quarter of this year, which we flow through to earnings. Our projected credits for the year are worth 12 cents per share. This is fairly certain, as most of the orders for the property have been placed and the delivery schedules call for the property to be installed by year-end.

Morris: Can we pull some of these into the first quarter? After all, if we don't, our effective tax rate will be different than for the year as a whole.

Lawrence: I'm not sure. If we did that, we would have to take a second look at our DISC tax benefits accounting also.

Morris: Are our projected DISC benefits as sure as our projected ITC benefits?

Lawrence: They're fairly sure, but not as certain as the ITC benefits.

There are two more items I wanted to mention. First, I have picked up in the first quarter one third of the third-quarter advertising costs related to this year's special fall campaign. I'll pick up another third in each of the next two quarters. This special program, which is in addition to our normal advertising costs, is going to cost about 6 cents per share above our regular advertising costs, which are run fairly evenly throughout the year.

Second, due to the change in the dollar relative to many overseas currencies, we had an exchange gain of 4 cents per share. I did not include this in the first-quarter results. In my opinion, by year-end we could end up with currency losses. So, I feel it is wise to defer this gain as a possible offset against future losses.

Morris: Thank you, Bill [Lawrence].

Well, here's our problem. The security analysts are predicting we will make nearly 60 cents for the first quarter. We don't have that kind of performance now. However, I feel that if we don't report 60 cents, our price-earnings ratio will drop. If this happens, I am fearful that our merger negotiations with Apex in Cleveland and Contrelli in Italy will collapse or not produce the earnings-per-share impact we expected. We need the earnings of both of these companies and at least one more merger to meet our forecasted profits for this year. As I reported to the finance committee last month, these two mergers under negotiation will be for our stock and will be accounted for as a pooling of interests. . . . The Apex price-earnings ratio based on our offering price is 20 times this year's projected earnings . . . The Contrelli family are interested in us because they feel we are a growth stock. . . .

Well, gentlemen, what do you think we should do?

A summary of Craftsland's quarterly income statements for 1982 as originally reported to shareholders at the end of each quarter is presented below. In addition, a summary of Craftsland's quarterly income statements for 1982 as adjusted for 1982 poolings of interests and presented in a footnote in Craftsland's 1982 annual report is presented below:

	1982 Quarterly Income Statements as Originally Reported			
	March 31	*June 30*	*September 30*	*December 31*
Net sales	$19,920	$20,230	$23,704	$26,511
Income before taxes	1,561	1,540	1,742	2,121
Provision for taxes	714	673	789	889
Net income	847	867	953	1,232
Earnings per share	$ 0.52	$ 0.53	$ 0.58	$ 0.70

	1982 Quarterly Income Statements as Adjusted for Poolings of Interests and Presented in the 1982 Annual Report			
	March 31	*June 30*	*September 30*	*December 31*
Net sales	$20,682	$23,873	$24,617	$26,511
Income before taxes	1,694	1,825	1,992	2,121
Provision for taxes	779	897	925	889
Net income	915	928	1,067	1,232
Earnings per share	$ 0.52	$ 0.53	$ 0.61	$ 0.70

Questions

1. What do you think is Craftsland's first-quarter 1983 earnings per share?

2. What first-quarter 1983 earnings-per-share figure should management report to the public? Why?

3. What can you learn from an analysis of Craftsland's 1982 first-quarter interim report and a comparison of the 1982 quarterly results as originally reported and restated for poolings of interests?

CHAPTER 28

Recognition and Evaluation of Contingencies

The note to financial statements that deals with contingencies is one of the most troublesome notes for statement users to interpret and evaluate. For the purposes of contingency accounting and disclosure, a contingency is defined as an existing condition, situation, or set of circumstances involving uncertainty as to the possible gain or loss to an enterprise that will ulitmately be resolved when one or more future events occur or fail to occur. The resolution of the uncertainty may confirm the acquisition of an asset or reduction of a liability, or the loss or impairment of an asset or incurrence of a liability. The accounting for contingencies is covered by *FASB Statement No. 5.*

The accounting process requires many estimates in accounting for ongoing and recurring business activities. In most cases, the uncertainty inherent in these estimates does not necessarily give rise to a contingency as that term is used in *Statement No. 5*. For example, depreciation accounting requires that estimates be made to allocate the known cost of an asset over the period of use by the enterprise. The fact that an estimate is involved does not make depreciation a contingency, since the eventual expiration of the asset is not uncertain. Also, accrued amounts that represent estimates of amounts owed for services received but not yet billed are not contingencies, since there is nothing uncertain about the fact that obligations have been incurred.

Statement No. 5 presents these examples of loss contingencies: collectibility of receivables; warranty obligations; risk of loss or damage of enterprise property by fire, explosion, or other hazards; threat of expropriation of assets; pending or threatening litigation; actual or possible claims and assessments; risk of loss from catastrophes assumed by property and casualty insurance companies; guarantees of indebtedness of others; obligation of commercial banks under standby letters of credit; and agreements to repurchase receivables (or to repurchase the related property) that have been sold. In these examples, the likelihood that a future event or events will confirm the loss or impairment of an asset or incurrence of a liability can range from probable to remote.

Statement No. 5

Statement No. 5 established new standards for financial accounting and disclosure for loss contingencies and reconfirmed the accounting for gain contingencies previously expressed in *ARB No. 50* issued by the Committee on Accounting Procedure.

The key provisions of *Statement No. 5* are:

1. An estimated loss from a loss contingency shall be accrued by a charge to income only if *both* of the folowing conditions are met:
   a. Information available prior to the issuance of the financial statements indicates that it is probable[1] that an asset had been impaired or a liability had been incurred at the end of the most recent accounting period for which statements are being presented. Implicit in this condition is the expectation that one or more future events will probably occur that confirm the fact of the loss.
   b. The amount of the loss can be reasonably estimated.
   If these two criteria are met, an accrual must be made.
2. Contingency gains usually are not recorded prior to realization, but may be disclosed in the notes prior to realization.
3. Reserves are not permitted for catastrophe losses, general or unspecified business risks, and self-insurance, except for some self-insurance for employee-compensation-related costs which are excluded from the scope of *Statement No. 5.*
4. Disclosure sufficient to "not make the statements misleading" should be made of the nature and estimated loss for both accrued loss contingencies and loss contingencies that are not accrued, but represent at least a reasonable possibility of a loss.
5. Classification of a portion of retained earnings as "appropriated" for loss contingencies is permitted as long as it is shown within the stockholders' equity section of the balance sheet, but losses cannot be charged to an appropriation of retained earnings, and no part of such appropriation can be transferred to income.

---

[1] *Statement No. 5* defines the terms "probable," "reasonably possible," and "remote" as follows:

Probable. The future event or events are likely to occur.

Reasonably possible. The chance of the future event or events occurring is more than remote but less than likely.

Remote. The chance of the future event or events occurring is slight.

It is important to note that a loss contingency can only be accrued if the two specific conditions mentioned earlier, 1.*a* and *b*, are met. According to the FASB:

> The purpose of those conditions is to require accrual of losses when they are reasonably estimable and relate to the current or a prior period. The requirement that the loss be reasonably estimable is intended to prevent accrual in the financial statements of amounts so uncertain as to impair the integrity of those statements. The board has concluded that disclosure is preferable to accrual when a reasonable estimate of loss cannot be made. Further, even losses that are reasonably estimable should not be accrued if it is not probable that an asset has been impaired or a liability has been incurred at the date of an enterprise's financial statements because those losses relate to a future period rather than the current or a prior period. Attribution of a loss to events or activities of the current or prior periods is an element of asset impairment or liability incurrence.

Later, the FASB in *Interpretation No. 14* clarified how to deal with situations where the first condition, 1.*a* above, has been met and a range of loss can be reasonably estimated, but no single amount within the range appears at the time to be a better estimate than any other amount within the range. In these cases, the board decided the minimum amount in the range should be accrued.

Loss Contingencies Subsequent to the Balance Sheet Date

Information concerning a loss contingency which becomes known subsequent to the date of the financial statements, but before their issuance, may satisfy the two accrual criteria. Whether or not this post-financial statement date information requires accrual of a loss contingency as of the statement date depends on when the related asset was impaired or liability was incurred. If the post-statement date information indicates that events leading to the loss occurred or were in process during the period preceding the financial statement date, then an accrual for a loss contingency should be made at the financial statement date. If the event giving rise to the contingency loss occurred after the financial statement date, no accrual at the balance sheet date should be made. However, disclosure of this post-financial statement event is required if nondisclosure would make the financial statements misleading.

Accounts Receivable and Warranty Obligations

The FASB believed that the uncollectibility of receivables and product warranties constituted contingencies and as such are within the scope of *Statement No. 5*.

Accordingly, potential losses from uncollectible receivables must be accrued at the time of sale when both of the contingency loss accrual criteria have been met. These criteria may be considered in relation to individual receivables or to groups of similar types of receivables. If the reasonable estimation criterion cannot be satisfied, it is doubtful if the sale or accrual method of income recognition is appropriate. Therefore, consideration should be given to using the installment method, the cost recovery method, or some other appropriate method for income recognition.

Similarly, if the two accrual criteria are met, losses from warranty obligations must be accrued at the time of sale. The criteria can be applied to either individual sales or groups of similar sales made with warranties. If accrual is precluded because the reasonable estimate criterion cannot be met, consideration should be given to delaying the recognition of the sale until the warranty period expires or the contingency criteria can be satisfied.

Self-Insurance

Some businesses choose not to purchase insurance against the risk of loss that may result from injury to others, damage to the property of others, or business interruption. Exposure to future risks of this kind creates a contingency. However, the FASB concluded that mere exposure to risks of these types does not mean that an asset has been impaired or a liability has been incurred in the current or some prior period. As a result, the accrual of a loss contingency is not warranted.

Some companies do not carry insurance against the risk of future loss or damage to its property by fire, explosion, or other hazards. The occurrence of these events is random, and until they occur no asset has been impaired or a liability incurred. Therefore, it is inappropriate to accrue for this type of contingency loss prior to its occurrence.

Litigation, Claims, and Assessments

Statement No. 5 states that the following factors, among others, must be considered in determining whether accrual and/or disclosure is required with respect to pending or threatened litigation and actual or possible claims and assessments:

a. The period in which the underlying cause of the pending or threatened litigation or of the actual or possible claim or assessment occurred.
b. The degree of probability of an unfavorable outcome.
c. The ability to make a reasonable estimate of the amount of loss.

An accrual may be appropriate for litigation, claims, or assessments whose underlying cause occurred before the date of the financial statement and where an unfavorable outcome is probable and a reasonable estimate can be made of the loss. In the case of unasserted claims and assessments, a judgment must first be made as to whether the assertion of a claim is probable. If such a claim is probable, an accrual can be made if an unfavorable outcome is probable and the amount of the loss can be reasonably estimated. If there are several aspects of litigation, each of which gives rise to a possible claim, then the accrual criteria should be applied to each possible claim to determine whether an accrual should be made for any part of the claim.

Threat of Expropriation

Statement No. 5 defines the threat of expropriation of assets as a contingency. Thus, the two accrual criterion must be met before an accrual for the loss can be made. The imminence of an expropriation may be indicated by a public or private declaration of intent by a government to expropriate assets of the enterprise or actual expropriation of assets of other enterprises.

Catastrophe Losses

At the time a property and casualty insurance company issues an insurance policy covering the risk of property loss from catastrophes, a contingency arises. *Statement No. 5* prohibits property and casualty insurance companies from accruing estimated losses related to future catastrophes, since over the short run, the actuarial predictions of the rate of occurrence and the amounts of loss "are subject to substantial deviations."

Indirect Guarantees of Indebtedness

Indirect guarantees and other similar loss contingencies where the possibility of loss may be remote should be disclosed. The disclosure should include the nature and amount of the guarantee.

Items Not Affected

Statement No. 5 excludes from its scope the following items, which are covered by other decisions of the FASB and its predecessors: pension costs; deferred compensation contracts; capital stock issued to employees; other related employee costs, such as group insurance, vacation pay, workmen's compensation, and disability benefits; net losses on long-term construction-type contracts; and write-down of carrying amount of operating assets because of questionable recovery of cost.

Contingency Gains

Examples of contingencies that may result in the acquisition of assets, or in gains, are claims against others for patent infringements, price redetermination upward, and claims for reimbursement under condemnation proceedings. Contingencies of this type which may result in gains should not be reflected in the accounts since to do so might be to recognize revenue prior to its realization. Adequate disclosure should be made of gain contingencies, however.

Objections

The FASB received a number of objections to its accounting for contingencies proposal. One objection was that it was a retreat from conservatism. The FASB did not agree that this was the case, since its proposal did not require virtual certainty before an accrual. In the absence of a probable occurrence of the contingency event and a reasonable estimate of the loss, the FASB believed accrual for unlikely events and uncertain amounts impaired the integrity of financial statements.

Another objection was that the matching concept required that estimated losses from certain types of contingencies that irregularly occur over a long period of time should be accrued in each accounting period. The FASB noted that the matching concept associated costs with revenues on a cause-and-effect basis and as such did not support the objection raised.

Other opponents claimed the new rules would lead to greater earnings volatility, which would lead to lower equity prices. The FASB felt that the use of accounting reserves to reduce inherent earnings volatility was misleading. In order to reduce earnings volatility, some critics of the FASB recommendations claimed, companies would be forced to purchase unnecessary insurance to cover contingencies.

The FASB recognized that insurance reduces or eliminates risks. In contrast, accounting reserves do not reduce risks. Accordingly, the FASB rejected the contention that the use of accounting reserves could be an alternative to insurance against risk. The FASB believed it could not sanction the use of an accounting procedure to create the illusion of protection from risk when, in fact, protection does not exist. Furthermore, the FASB argued that earnings fluctuations are inherent in risk retention and they should be reported as they occur.

Accounting Entries

When a company accrues an estimated loss for a contingency, this is reported by making (1) a charge to income prior to the occurrence of the event that is expected to resolve the uncertainty and (2) a related credit entry to a contingency reserve for a similar amount, which is listed among the liability accounts. Then, when the event occurs that confirms the loss, the reserve is used to absorb the loss. If appropriate, a provision for the related tax effect of the actual loss is also made at the time the anticipated loss is accrued. For example, assume a company anticipated that it may have to pay $100,000 damages as the result of a claim brought against the company in the courts. In the period in which the management becomes aware of this possibility, it will charge the anticipated $100,000 loss, less the related tax effect, to income and set up a $100,000 litigation reserve as a liability. In a later accounting period, when a court decision confirms the loss and the successful litigant is paid, the actual loss is charged to the balance sheet contingency reserve and cash is reduced by a similar amount. If the amount of the claim in less than the related reserve, the excess reserve in credited to income. If the claim paid is greater than the reserve, the excess is charged to income.

The accounting entries to establish the reserve and the related deferred tax asset[2] are:

Dr.	Litigation Expense	100,000	
	Cr. Litigation Reserve		100,000
Dr.	Deferred Taxes	50,000	
	Cr. Tax Expense		50,000

The entries to record the payment of the $100,000 litigation loss are:

Dr.	Litigation Reserve	100,000	
	Cr. Cash		100,000
Dr.	Taxes Payable	50,000	
	Cr. Deferred Taxes		50,000

It is important to note that the accrual for accounting purposes of a loss related to a contingency does not create or set aside funds which can be used to lessen the possible financial impact of the loss. The creation of a contingency reserve by a charge to income is simply an accounting provision. The accrual, in and of itself, provides no financial protection that is not available in the absence of the accrual.

Financial Analysis

Because of the uncertainty involved, financial statement analysts find it difficult to predict, interpret, and evaluate corporate contingencies. Another complicating factor is that the statement user does not have access to sufficient data to form an independent appraisal of the management judgments that underlie their accounting treatment of contingencies. Usually, the best that statement users can do is to form gross assessments of the reasonableness of management's judgments based on available public information related to the causes of the contingency and its impact on others, if any; the analysts' own understanding of the situation gained by analysis of current and past statements; and the statement users' confidence in management based upon its exercise of judgment in other situations.

Fortunately, in most situations the statement user is somewhat protected

---

[2] A deferred tax asset is created because the loss is recognized for book purposes only. The loss can not be deducted for tax purposes until it is actually incurred.

against poor management judgment by the tendency of managers aware of the necessity to record major contingency losses to over-reserve for anticipated losses. Their motivation is to avoid future surprises and to create possible future "earnings banks" should the anticipated loss be less than the reserved amount. If this happens, management simply eliminates the excess reserve and related deferred tax assets, and credits the net amount to income.

In contrast, statement users are less protected by managers' motivation when management must simply disclose a potential contingency loss. In these cases, the tendency of management is either to delay disclosure in the hope that things will improve, or if required to disclose, to minimize the potential adverse impact. In these cases statement users usually must go to information sources beyond the financial reports, such as court records and trade journals, to obtain the information required to assess the situation more accurately.

As noted earlier, it is important for statement users to remember that creation of a reserve for a contingency loss and the recognition of the related expense does not create a fund to pay for the loss, reduce the risk associated with the contingency's occurrence and adverse impact, eliminate the need to take action to deal with the situation, or create a taxable loss. Financial resources must still be found to fund any cash losses created by the contingency. The contingency event's related probabilities are independent of the accounting treatment. Management must still deal administratively with the problem, although the recording of the reserve may make this task easier since it can be done without concern for its impact on future earnings per share. Finally, the tax code only allows a contingency loss to be deducted for tax purposes when the actual loss has been incurred. As a result, statement users should always remember that the tax treatment of the loss is uncertain at the time a contingency loss reserve is established, since it is dependent on the extent of the estimated actual loss and the company's overall tax status at that time.

Frequently, companies report significant profit gains in the period following the accounting recognition of a contingency loss, and management proclaims that the company's situation has turned around. This can be an illusion. It does not represent the actual situation, since the actual contingency losses may be occurring during this period and they are being charged to the reserve rather than income. The improved profits do not signal better times. To avoid falling into the trap of believing management's optimistic interpretations, statement users should keep track of contingency loss reserves established in earlier periods and use this knowledge to put current earnings into their proper perspective. Finally, in those situations, management may reverse unused reserves resulting from earlier over-reserving to give an added boost to the apparent profit recovery. This is a cashless profit source that should be valued at zero and regarded as low-quality earnings.

The announcement that a company is recording a contingency reserve often comes as a surprise to many statement users. Because of the nature of many contingencies, such as a loss from a fire, this is understandable. However, many others can be anticipated through normal financial analysis techniques. For example, a massive write-off of uncollectible accounts receivable might be expected when a company's accounts receivable to sales ratio deteriorates significantly. Similarly, losses due to the company's being called upon to make good on the guarantee of the indebtedness of another company in financial difficulties might be anticipated if a financial analysis of the borrower's statements indicates it is experiencing increasing financial difficulties. Statement users wishing to minimize accounting surprises should always ask themselves as they review the results of their financial analyses, "Are there any indications that a material loss contingency might have to be recognized in the near future?"

CASE 28-1

International Industries, Inc.
Accounting for Contingencies

This case presents selected excerpts from two meetings of the audit committee of International Industries, Inc.

The first meeting occurred in April 1985 when the audit committee of International Industries, a multinational conglomerate met to discuss the implications for the company's accounting policies of possibly a more rigorous application of *Statement No. 5,* "Accounting for Contingencies." This action was the direct result of a request by the firm's new auditors to reconsider the firm's contingency accounting policy. International's fiscal year begins on July 1.

The second meeting took place in August 1985 to discuss the implication for the 1985, and possibly 1986, fiscal year financial results of some events that had occurred subsequent to the close of the 1985 fiscal year, but before the financial statements for the year had been issued.

During the last decade, the company earnings per share had grown at a 15 percent per year rate with little year-to-year variation from this trend. Management was proud of this record, particularly since it had been achieved during inflationary and recessionary periods. Management wished to continue this growth rate and to satisfy what it perceived to be a preference of investors for a stable pattern of earnings, which management believed indicated less uncertainty or risk than fluctuating earnings. In turn, the management believed that a 15 percent growth rate with a low variability of the expected return would enhance the company's price-earnings ratio and minimize the amplitude of the swings in the company's stock price relative to changes in the market's average price as measured by such indices as the S&P 400. In management's opinion, a stock with these characteristics was useful for convincing the owners of private companies to merge with International. During the last few years, such acquisitions

This case was prepared by David F. Hawkins.

Copyright © 1976 by the President and Fellows of Harvard College

Harvard Business School case 117–032 (Rev. 1985)

had been an important source of International's earnings growth. In addition, the company planned to issue subordinated convertible debentures as soon as security market conditions were favorable to such an issue. Management believed International's earnings characteristics would make this issue attractive to investors and at the same time allow the company to pay a low interest rate and set the conversion price well above the current price of the company's equity stock.

The audit committee consisted of three outside directors: Frank Noonan, the chairman; Louis Athos; and Harold Farrow. None of its members had financial backgrounds. Frank Noonan was a retired army general. Louis Athos owned an export-import firm. He was a close friend of the International president, Joseph Patterson. Harold Farrow was a substantial International stockholder. Two years earlier, International had acquired his company. At that time, Farrow had withdrawn from the management of his company.

One of the functions of International's audit committee was to report to the board of directors on the appropriateness of the company's financial reporting practices. As part of this responsibility, the committee participated with management in setting the company's financial reporting policies.

International estimated 1985 net income was $150 million. The company's net assets were approximately $1 billion.

April Meeting

The following dialogue represents selected excerpts from the April 1985 audit committee meeting.

> *Noonan (chairman, audit committee):* Our new independent auditors have raised a number of questions regarding our application of *Statement No. 5.* Subsequently, I asked the financial office to prepare a list of the company's current accounting for contingencies practices. At this meeting, I think we should discuss what changes the audit committee believes should be made in these practices. I have asked Joe [Patterson, the company president] and Peter [Kelly, the company's financial vice president] to sit in on this meeting. They can supply us with whatever additional data we need to form our conclusions.
>
> The first item on my list is possible accounts receivables losses from bad debts. Currently we accrue for these losses based on our past experience, the experience of other companies in the same business, and our appraisal of our customer's financial condition. So far, from the total company point of view, our actual write-off experience has been very close to the projection underlying our accruals. I do not think we need to change our policy on accounting for losses related to collectibility of receivables.
>
> *Athos (member of the audit committee):* How has our experience been for groups of similar receivables rather than for the company as a whole?

Noonan: As you might expect, there are many variations. However, I couldn't locate any group of receivables where actual experience suggests that our loss reserves are not reasonable estimates.

Farrow (member of audit committee): What about those Plastic Division receivables we discussed last month? As I recall, the division had some $50 million of outstanding receivables and some 50 percent of them are overdue, most of which are with smaller companies. In the past, we seemed to have a good feel for the credit risks in this business, but I don't think that is true anymore. The oil crisis and inflation during the 1970s and the current recession in our industry have adversely changed the economics of many of our customer's businesses and the demand for their end products. The recession has hit the smaller companies very hard. Let's be frank. We raised the bad debt reserve on these receivables from 2 to 4 percent of receivables but we don't really know if that is adequate. I heard that Tempo (the major competition of the Plastic Division) has a 7 percent reserve. Personally, I think that is a more realistic figure.

Kelly (financial vice president): You're right, but when I prepared the figures for Frank [Noonan], I included the Plastic Division receivables in with the total Chemical Group's receivables. When you consider that the group's receivables are slightly over $150 million, the problems you raise with the Plastic Division receivables become immaterial.

Farrow: I guess from that perspective you are correct.

Patterson (president): While on the subject of the Plastic Division, you might be interested to know that at yesterday's executive committee meeting I got approval of my plan to increase our share of the plastic market by offering on a very aggressive basis more generous credit terms for our products. The small- to medium-sized companies need financial help. We will use our financial strength to tie them to us through long-term purchase contracts under which they will pay us the amount due for each shipment as follows: 25 percent 30 days after delivery, 25 percent 60 days after delivery, 25 percent 90 days after delivery, and the remainder within 120 days of delivery. The normal terms of credit are 1 percent 10, net 30 days.

We are prepared to invest $30 million in this effort. This is a large sum and there is no doubt that this approach to building market share carries some financial risk, but I think the gamble will pay off. However, just to be on the safe side I plan to establish a bad debt reserve equal to 5 percent of the receivables created by this marketing plan.

Noonan: That sounds prudent.

The next item on my list is losses related to warranty obligations. Currently, we have not been accruing for this contingency. The practice has been to charge warranty costs as incurred. This practice has been justified in the past because the amounts involved were immaterial and the difference between cost and accrual accounting was not very great. The company has had a study underway since last January looking into the question of whether International should begin accruing for warranty obligations as recommended by our CPAs. Peter [Kelly], what is the status of that study?

Kelly: As you will recall, the proposal to consider accruing warranty costs came from my office for several reasons. First, warranty costs were becoming very substantial. Second, they were beginning to vary considerably from our budgeted figures. This in turn made it harder to manage earnings. My proposed solution was to switch to the accrual approach. In this way, we could smooth out the recognition of this cost item over the years.

The study group has not reached any conclusions yet. However, I know that the warranty costs for this fiscal year will be $2.5 million higher than budgeted. We don't seem to have a very good handle on this cost item.

Noonan: I think we should defer any discussion on this item until the study group's report is completed. Let's move on.

The next item is our exposure to significant catastrophe losses in our Property Insurance Group (a property and casualty insurance company in which International held a 40 percent equity interest). As you may recall, *Statement No. 5* does not permit companies like Property to accrue for losses in anticipation of catastrophe losses. To protect itself against significant losses, Property has been buying considerable amounts of reinsurance. The finance committee (of International) believes this strategy is getting too expensive. The committee asked me to let them know how the audit committee feels about letting Property retain a little more risk, which would reduce their reinsurance premiums. I told the committee chairman this was not an audit committee matter. They would have to handle that "hot potato" on their own.

Farrow: I agree with you, but let me just make one comment. I think that the FASB decision on catastrophe reserves for insurance companies was a mistake. In my opinion catastrophes are certain to occur and as such are not contingencies. Also, on the basis of experience and the application of appropriate statistical techniques, I have got to believe that catastrophe losses can be predicted over the long term with reasonable accuracy. Then, some portion of the premium is intended to cover losses that usually occur infrequently and at intervals longer than both the terms of the policies in force and the financial accounting and reporting period. As a result, it seems to me that proper matching of costs and revenues requires that catastrophe losses should be accrued when the revenue is recognized—or at least a portion of the premiums should be deferred beyond the terms of the policies in force to periods in which the catastrophes occur—to match catastrophe losses with the related revenues.

Patterson: I agree with you, but the FASB didn't find those arguments persuasive. The FASB decision on catastrophe reserves is fact. We must live with it. However, I do have some concerns: First, irregularly occurring catastrophes will cause erratic variations in earnings. This runs counter to our whole earnings strategy. Second, Property Insurance was a prime insurer that did not buy very much reinsurance to protect itself against catastrophe losses before *No.* 5. It used the substantial catastrophe reserve that it built up to absorb these losses. As I recall, the size of this reserve was one of the reasons we bought into the company. Now, to keep earnings stable the company has to buy much more reinsurance than it did pre-*No.* 5. These premiums hurt the company's cash flow. However, it is necessary to do this in order to make the risk characteristics of its earnings stream comparable to those of casualty companies that reinsure. Thus, the FASB accounting decision forced us to purchase reinsurance. That was wrong.

Kelly: One more small point. Reinsurance premiums reduce income before the catastrophe occurs. Thus, if you buy reinsurance or accrue for a catastrophe loss, the effect on income is the same—income is reduced prior to the catastrophe. I can't see why paying a premium makes a difference in the accounting that is allowed.

Noonan: As you will recall, the FASB decision means that the insurance premiums paid by International for protection against the loss of its property by fire, explosion, or similar hazards increased. It wasn't only Property that was impacted. We had to extend our insurance coverage to include all of those risks that formerly we self-insured against. This was wrong also. I hope the FASB will reexamine this position.

Noonan: Let's move on to the litigation loss reserves. In the past, we have accumulated a reserve for litigation losses. No additions were made to the reserve last year, but additions were made in every prior year for the last 10 years.

Athos: Was the reserve set up with specific litigation in mind?

Kelly: No. You could think of it as a general-type reserve. Our auditors think the reserve should be reversed as it does not relate to any specific litigation. I've put our old auditors off for years, but now our new auditors are insisting it be reversed.

Athos: What have been our charges to the reserve in recent years?

Kelly: There have been no material charges over the last two years. Three years ago, we made a $1.2 million charge to it to settle out of court a patent infringement claim. Today the balance of the reserve is $10 million.

Athos: What litigation are we involved in now, and what is its status?

Patterson: We have three major litigation problems at present. A number of female employees in one of our subsidiaries have joined together and are suing us on behalf of themselves and other women employees for $5 million. They claim the company's promotion practices have discriminated against women. They want to be paid the differences between the wages they believe they would have received if they had been promoted on the same basis as men and what they now get. The suit was filed in January of this year. At this time, our legal counsel is unable to express an opinion that the outcome will be favorable to International. Should we lose, it is hard to determine what the ultimate settlement will be. This type of litigation is fairly new.

The second suit is a claim against us for failure to perform on a major glass division contract to install all of the windows in a new 50-story office tower. The project's completion was delayed for nearly a year due to our inability to solve some glass technology and installation engineering problems that arose when the windows kept blowing out. This suit was filed over a year ago. It is for $10 million in damages. The plaintiff is claiming for the cost of lost rentals, lost tenants, and damages done to surrounding property.

Our lawyers advised us to settle out of court as they believe the plaintiff will be successful. Also, the glass division's marketing department did not want to have a court trial. They thought it would be bad publicity. I agreed. So, I instructed our counsel to enter into negotiations. So far we have agreed to pay $1 million for lost rentals. The other claims are still being negotiated. It seems most likely that the lost tenants' claim will be settled for about $1 million, but we have no idea at this time what the figure will be for the damage to surrounding property. That is somewhat dependent on the outcome of suits by surrounding property owners for damages against the tower owners. We are not involved in those suits, but the tower owners feel that we are the cause of any losses that they may have.

The third suit is not in litigation. At the time of the patent infringement problem I mentioned earlier, we discovered that our chemical division may inadvertently be violating some other patents held by others. These patent holders have not given any indication that they are aware of our possible infringement of their patent. If they should ever sue it would be for a large sum, which I estimate in the range of $15 million to $25 million. Of course, our chemical engineers have been busy trying to develop alternatives to these patents, but so far we have not been able to make a breakthrough. In the meantime, we have had to continue using these patented processes since they are critical to our chemical division's operations.

Farrow: What do you think are the chances that we might get sued?

Patterson: I have no idea. However, our patent lawyers tell me that if we get sued, our chances of a favorable outcome are not good. Based on their assessment of the possible claimants, similar cases, and our use of the patented process, they believe an out-of-court settlement in the order of $5 million to $10 million might be possible.

Farrow: Well, I think we ought to continue to have a litigation reserve. If these litigation losses occur, it would play havoc with our earnings stream.

Kelly: I agree with you, but given our CPA's position and *Statement No. 5*, I don't think that this will be so easy to do. . . .

August Meeting

In early August 1985, the audit committee met to review with International's senior management two events involving possible contingency losses that had occurred since the end of the company's fiscal year (June 30, 1985).

Since the company's 1985 statements had not yet been published, there was a question as to whether or not the 1985 results should reflect these subsequent events.

The first event was the possible expropriation of the company's assets in a Latin American country. Sections of the audit committee discussion related to this agenda item are presented below:

Patterson: President Cruz has just announced that his government intends to nationalize the country's mining industry. Presumably this will include our mining subsidiary, International Mining S.A., and its related transportation subsidiary, International Transportation S.A. Ever since President Cruz took over power last March with the army's backing, we have been expecting such an announcement, since the nationalization of this country's raw material resources and communications network was a central part of his party's political platform. In early May, when the government took over the local telephone company, which was a subsidiary of a U.S. company, it became clear that Cruz meant what he said.

Noonan: Do you expect any losses?

Patterson: Yes. Cruz indicated that the government would issue government 30-year bonds bearing a 3 percent interest rate as compensation for the physical properties of the expropriated companies. Compensation would be based on the tangible asset's book value. The finance department estimates we would have a loss somewhere between $15 million and $17 million, after taking into account insurance coverage, the intangible assets that would have to be written off, and the real value of the bonds.

Athos: This turn of events should require us in fiscal 1986, when the expropriation occurs, to write off our losses.

Kelly: Well, there is another possibility. It might be argued that our assets were impaired when President Cruz took over the government and that his recent expropriation announcement was simply additional evidence with respect to conditions that existed before June 30, 1985. This interpretation might require us to charge the loss in 1985 fiscal year.

I am meeting tomorrow with our auditors to discuss this matter . . .

The second event involving a potential contingency loss was the unexpected announcement in late July by one of the Plastic Division's largest customers that it was filing for bankruptcy. This customer owed International $3.4 million. Based on materials filed with the bankruptcy court, International's lawyers believed that the company would recover no more than 5 percent of the amount owed. Here are excerpts from the audit committee's meeting related to this event:

Noonan: How did we let this customer get so much credit from us?

Patterson: Well, our new marketing approach using trade credit was very effective. This particular customer was buying all of its plastic requirements from us.

Athos: Did you know they were in financial trouble when you offered them our new terms last April?

Patterson: No. However, since the bankruptcy announcement I have gone back and looked at the company's December 31, 1984, financial statements. They clearly indicated a bankruptcy was likely, since the company was in trouble with the senior lender's covenants and the days of trade credit used were way out of proportion to industry averages. I asked our credit people how they let this happen. They indicated that prior to our new credit terms program this customer bought very little from us, so no credit analysis had been made. Then, once the new program was offered to them, they bought over $4 million of plastics from us in the period between April and June 30. This rapid build up of business caught the credit staff by surprise. Then, I suspect marketing was not anxious to push for a credit check, since the Plastic Division and Chemical Group were having trouble making their profit goal. This was profitable business. Our contribution margin was close to 50 percent.

As a result of my inquiries into how these sales were made, I will be making some personnel changes in the Chemical Group and Plastic Division.

Noonan: What was the status of the plastic customer receivables as of June 30?

Patterson: The balance was about $65 million of which $30 million were on the new marketing program terms.

Questions

1. How should International account for contingency losses in fiscal years 1985 and 1986?

2. Do you agree with the comments related to contingency loss reserves expressed in the case?

PART TEN

Comprehensive Financial Reporting and Analysis Review Cases

PART TEN

Comprehensive Financial reporting and Analysis Review Cases

REVIEW CASE 1

Limited Editions, Inc.
Establishing a Financial Reporting Strategy for a New Business

If you haven't learned to love it by 1989, we'll buy it back at the original price.

The above statement appeared as the prominent headline in a Limited Editions, Inc., advertisement placed in a monthly magazine catering to a select, high-income readership. Its intent is to announce the company's new porcelain figurine, "Foxes in Spring," which would be offered in limited quantities at a price of $2,000. Limited Editions' idea is to offer literally "a beautiful investment opportunity" with capital gains potential to a wealthy investor. By guaranteeing that production would be limited, the figurines could immediately attain status similar to an antique.

The guarantee offered by Limited was quite simple:

Subject to being in its original condition, we guarantee to repurchase any of our "Foxes in Spring" figurines at the original price of $2,000 at any time after five years from the date of purchase.[1]

The guarantee was not restricted to the original purchaser and hence was transferable from one party to another. The only other return provision allowed a purchaser to receive an 80 percent refund of the purchase price if the figurine was returned within three months from the date of purchase.

The figurines are offered for sale in only one extremely reputable store in each of 10 large American cities. These stores were individually identified in the advertisement. Each of the 10 was provided with one "Foxes in Spring" figurine to be used for display. It was informally understood that Limited Editions would not ask for the return of the figurine. The stores otherwise have no inventory. When a customer signs a "subscription re-

---

This case was prepared by Dennis P. Frolin.

Copyright © 1975 by the President and Fellows of Harvard College
Harvard Business School case 176–083 (Rev. 1985)

[1] As printed in the advertisement.

quest," the store forwards it to Limited. The "subscription" was an indication of interest but carried no contractual obligation on the part of the buyer. Limited would fill the subscription by shipping directly to the customer. Upon notification of shipment, the retail store would then bill the customer. Upon collection, the store deducted its 10 percent commission and forwarded the net amount of $1,800 to Limited. If a figurine was returned in the first three months, Limited simply sent an 80 percent refund ($1,600) to the customer. Limited did not request a refund of the 10 percent sales commission from the retail store.

Production of "Foxes in Spring" was strictly limited to 500 pieces. The design of the figurine and the mold from which it would be produced were created by an artist for a fee of $50,000. This fee was paid in 1984. Production was contracted out to a reputable company which agreed to run batches of 100 pieces upon instructions from Limited. When a batch was produced, each figurine was then hand painted and finished by skilled workers. Due to the extremely high-quality standards demanded by Limited, producing, painting, and finishing the first batches expectedly required substantially more cost than the later batches. Production cost data is summarized in Exhibit 2.

Limited Editions was incorporated as a separate legal entity in June 1984. The initial common stock was sold for $10,000. The corporation is 50 percent owned by a small, diversified, over-the-counter company engaged in a variety of businesses and 50 percent owned by a small number of self-proclaimed "venture capitalists" who play no active role in managing the company. The "venture capitalists" readily admit that their interest in Limited Editions, Inc., was in part nurtured by the widely publicized success stories of companies like The Franklin Mint[2] that have capitalized on the public's recent interest in "collector items" as an investment hedge against inflation. Both the management and owners of Limited Editions hope to build the company into a leader in this new, unexploited figurine market. Encouraged by the apparent success of the company's first figurine, management was already laying detailed plans for a number of fugure offerings.

Design and production began in July 1984; promotion in September; and sales in October. The bulk of 1984 sales appeared to be related to the year-end Christmas season. Of the 290 figurines shipped to customers in 1984, 100 were to shareholders (or members of their families), or to management employees (or members of their families). Since these sales were not made through a retail dealer, the full $2,000 purchase price was received in cash by Limited Editions. Of the 190 pieces shipped to nonrelated parties, cash had been received by year-end from the retailer for

---

[2] The Franklin Mint, traded on the New York Stock Exchange, is recognized as one of the leading producers of limited edition collectibles. Its issues include commemorative and art medals in silver and gold, sculptures in pewter and bronze, deluxe leather-bound books, and works of art in fine crystal.

EXHIBIT 1
Unit Data for 1984

	1984
Figurines produced	400
Figurine subscriptions received	320
Figurines shipped	290
Figurines sent to retailers for display	10
Figurines returned	0
Figurines in inventory	100
Figurines for which cash was collected by December 31, 1984	240
Figurines for which cash was not collected by December 31, 1984	50

EXHIBIT 2
Batch Production Data

Batch	Date	Units	Cost
1......	July 1984	100	$40,000
2......	September 1984	100	30,000
3......	October 1984	100	20,000
4......	December 1984*	100	10,000
5......	March 1985†	100	10,000

* Paid in January 1985.
† As of December 31, 1984, Limited Editions was not really sure what the last batch of 100 figures would cost. The $10,000 ultimately paid would have been a reasonable estimate as of December 31, 1984.

140 pieces; 50 pieces were uncollected; none of the 190 pieces were returned in 1984 but 20 of them were returned in 1985, some after the three-month return period had expired. Each of the 20 customers promptly received a $1,600 cash refund.

Exhibit 1 summarizes the relevant unit data for 1984. Promotional and advertising costs of $20,000 were paid in 1984. Limited planned to do no further advertising of "Foxes in Spring" in 1985. General and administrative expenses for 1984 were $30,000, and all these expenses were paid in cash before year-end.

Questions

1. Select in your opinion the best package of financial accounting policies for Limited Editions, Inc. You should not feel constrained by GAAP rules.

2. Defend your choices of financial accounting policies. The best way to defend your choices is *(a)* list what criteria are relevant in selecting an accounting alternative, *(b)* list the alternatives, and *(c)* analyze how well each alternative meets the various criteria.

3. Prepare Limited Editions, Inc., 1984 financial statements consistent with your choices in Question 1. (Assume that Limited will use *cash basis* accounting for federal income taxes and a 50 percent tax rate.)

REVIEW CASE 2

Texas Land and Royalty Company
Evaluation of a Corporate Financial Reporting Policy

On June 1, 1986, Peter Small, a faculty member of an eastern business school, interviewed Phillip Lord, financial vice president of Texas Land and Royalty Company. During their interview, they discussed Texas Land and Royalty's policies regarding the recognition of income from the company's various activities.

Texas Land and Royalty Company

The Texas Land and Royalty Company was founded in 1888 to develop certain Texas real estate holdings. Over the years, this land and royalty company became involved, through a series of wholly owned subsidiary companies, in a number of activites related to agriculture, real estate, and oil (see Exhibit 1).

Initially, the company bred calves and range-fattened steers. Later, around 1903, the company created a water utility subsidiary to build an extensive irrigation system on the company's property. Subsequently, cotton was raised on this irrigated land by both the company and tenant farmers, who turned over part of their harvest to the company as rent. Both the company and the tenant farmers purchased their water from the company-owned water utility.

In 1938, oil was discovered on the Texas Land and Royalty properties. During World War II, the company leased its oil lands to a number of major oil companies who proceeded to develop the leases. In return, Texas Land and Royalty received a royalty on every barrel of oil extracted from its land. During the war and early postwar years, the company built up large cash reserves from these oil royalties. During 1985, oil royalties accounted for some 10 percent of the company's revenues.

This case was prepared by David F. Hawkins.

Copyright © 1964 by the President and Fellows of Harvard College
Harvard Business School case 109–013 (Rev. 1985)

EXHIBIT 1
Corporate Relationships

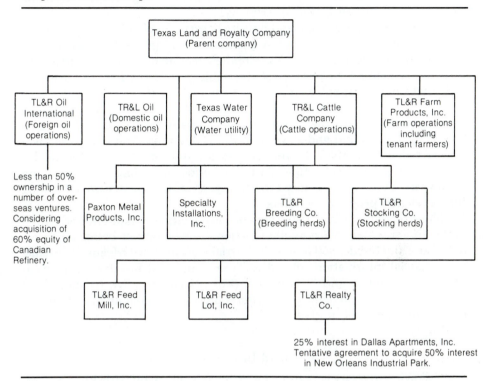

Beginning in 1950, the company began to expand its operations. First, the company built a feed mill and acquired some feed lots in northeast Texas. The output of the feed mill was sold on the feed lots and used to fatten the company's beef cattle just prior to sale. In addition, the company contracted to fatten in its feed lots the cattle of other cattle companies.

Next, in 1958, Texas Land and Royalty acquired two manufacturing companies. The first company, Paxton Metal Products, sold small component parts to the capital goods industry. The second company, Specialty Installations, Inc., custom built and installed large machinery installations, such as complete automobile body production lines. Both these companies were wholly owned subsidiaries. In 1975, they accounted for about 18 percent of the company assets and 8 percent of its profits.

In 1984, Texas Land and Royalty expanded its oil activities by entering into several agreements with major oil companies to explore and develop oil concessions in Canada and South America. Recently, one of these ventures had discovered oil in commercial quantities in northern Canada. In all of these joint ventures, Texas Land and Royalty held less than a 50 percent interest. In June 1986, the company was considering the acquisition of a 60 percent interest in a proposed Canadian refining company to refine the newly discovered Canadian crude oil.

During 1984, Texas Land and Royalty became involved in the residential real estate business. The company purchased a 25 percent equity interest in a newly formed real estate development company, Dallas Apartments, Inc. (the remaining 75 percent of the equity was owned by two national real estate development companies). After making this investment, Texas Land and Royalty entered into a sale and option agreement with Dallas Apartments to sell to the development company certain parcels of land owned by Texas Land and Royalty in the Dallas area. The first parcel was transferred during 1985. In return, Texas Land and Royalty received a note for $4 million, collectible during a period extending to a maximum of 10 years. These collections were contingent on Dallas Apartments selling the developed property to others.

More recently, Texas Land and Royalty Company had entered into a tentative agreement with another national development company to acquire land and build a $50 million industrial park in New Orleans, Louisiana.

Financial information related to Texas Land and Royalty Company is shown in Exhibit 2 and 3. Exhibit 2 presents comparative balance sheet data for the years 1984 and 1985. Exhibit 3 presents profit and loss information during this same period.

Lord Interview

The following are excerpts from Peter Small's interview with Phillip Lord:

Lord: As I understand it, you are interested in the policies Texas Land and Royalty follows with respect to the recognition of income from its various operations.

Small: Well, why don't you tell me about your company's consolidation policy? This policy, I believe, is relevant to all the topics I plan to discuss.

Lord: Our policy is simple. We consolidate the operations of all companies in which we have at least a 50 percent equity interest.

Small: I have another general question: What do you think the stockholders of Texas Land and Royalty are primarily interested in? Current earnings or long-term capital appreciation?

Lord: Because we are the kind of company we are, asset values ought to be the most important consideration of our investors. Certainly our company policy is to develop future earning power. And, in an important respect, our assets represent the current value of these future earnings. Of course, this value is only significant when you produce the earnings. Nevertheless, the assets we hold currently determine to a large extent the future prospects for appreciation of our stockholders' investment.

EXHIBIT 2

TEXAS LAND AND ROYALTY COMPANY
Consolidated Balance Sheet
December 31, 1984, and 1985
(in thousands)

	1985	1984
Assets		
Current assets		
Cash	$ 2,402	$ 2,316
Accounts receivable	11,000	10,012
Inventories (note 1)	18,269	17,889
Other current assets	2,275	1,783
Total current assets	$33,946	$32,000
Investment and loans to associated companies	4,000	3,200
Marketable securities (note 2)	14,100	12,600
Property, plant, and equipment (note 3):		
Land	$ 8,233	$ 8,483
Buildings	24,005	23,912
Machinery and equipment	21,293	20,665
Leaseholds	5,143	4,922
Land improvement	9,201	8,436
	$67,875	$66,418
Less: Accumulated depreciation, depletion, and amortization	20,005	18,967
Net property, plant, and equipment	$47,870	$47,451
Total assets	$99,916	$95,251
Liabilities		
Current liabilities:		
Federal and state income taxes	$ 4,601	$ 4,991
Accounts payable	3,500	3,406
Accrued property taxes	1,401	1,296
Other current liabilities	2,264	3,090
Total current liabilities	$11,766	$12,783
Long-term debt	2,600	6,600
Deferred profit (note 4)	3,750	—
Capital stock (note 5)	20,000	20,000
Retained earnings	61,800	55,868
Total liabilities	$99,916	$95,251

The accompanying Notes to Financial Statements selected by the case writer are an integral part of these statements (see Exhibit 3).

We feel that by all odds, the most significant factor determining the value of the company is the earnings that it produces. The assets derive their value essentially from their earning power. The assets otherwise are of value only as a matter of ultimate liquidation. Therefore, we feel, as management, our primary function is to generate further earning capacity from the assets which we now have.

The foregoing is not to say that it might not be desirable to give share owners a more accurate or better informed opinion concerning the value of the assets of the company as related to current market.

EXHIBIT 3

TEXAS LAND AND ROYALTY COMPANY
Consolidated Income Statement
Years Ended December 31, 1984, and 1985
(in thousands)

	1985	1984	1983
Revenues:			
Sales, royalties, and rent	$93,968	$92,111	$90,001
Interest and other revenues	1,846	1,202	1,200
Total revenue	$95,814	$93,313	$91,201
Expenses:			
Costs and operating expenses	$71,426	$70,001	$69,402
Oil and mineral exploration	4,204	3,906	3,201
Selling, administrative, and general	7,016	6,847	6,007
Federal and state taxes	4,236	4,001	3,950
Total expenses.....................................	$86,882	$84,755	$82,560
Net income	$ 8,932	$ 8,558	$ 8,641
Less: Dividends	3,000	3,000	3,000
Amount transferred to retained earnings..................	$ 5,932	$ 5,558	$ 5,641

The accompanying Notes to Financial Statements selected by the case writer are an integral part of these statements:

Note 1: Inventories as of December 31, were as follows:

	1985	1984
Manufacturing:		
Raw material and work in process	$ 3,211	$3,004
Finished goods	4,122	4,006
Cattle:		
Market herd..................................	5,267	5,331
Breeding herd	3,621	3,100
Farm produce	1,233	1,640
Other inventories	815	808
Total	$18,269	$17,889

Note 2: Marketable securities are stated at cost, adjusted for amortization of premium or discount. On December 31, the market value of these securities amounted to $15,120,000 in 1985 and $13.3 million in 1984.

Note 3: All property, plant, and equipment is stated at cost. The company uses straight-line depreciation. A number of the company's fixed assets still in use are fully depreciated. They have been removed from the fixed asset accounts. The company uses the flow-through method to record investment tax credits. No discovery value has been assigned to the oil reserves related to the company's holdings in Texas. The cost of improvements to real property and of machinery and other equipment is being charged to operations in equal annual installments over their respective useful lives. For financial statement purposes, intangible drilling costs are capitalized and charged to operations on a unit-of-production basis. In determination of taxable income, these costs are deducted in the year incurred.

Note 4: In 1984, the company purchased an interest in the Dallas Apartments, Inc. At the same time, the company entered into a sale and option agreement with that company relating to some of Texas Land and Royalty's land in Dallas. During 1985, certain parcels of land were transferred under this agreement. In payment, the company received a note for $4 million collectible during a period extending to a maximum of 10 years. The profit from this sale was deferred and is being taken into income, subject to applicable taxes, as collections are received.

Note 5: Under the company's incentive stock option plan, options at prices no less than 95 percent of market value at date of grant are held by 10 key employees and officers. These options amount to less than 2 percent of the outstanding stock held by the company's 6,052 shareholders.

There is serious distortion in our balance sheet when viewed in terms of present worth. I think it can very well be argued that share owners deserve to have further information concerning present worth of the assets of the company. This, however, should not be construed as meaning that the management considers this to be a significant factor in determining the market value of the stock.

Small: If you don't mind, I'd like now to talk about specific aspects of your operations. Why don't we begin with the manufacturing operations?

Lord: Fine. That's a fairly straightforward situation. We treat Paxton Metal products as a regular manufacturing company. We are essentially producing to orders, and we recognize income as of the date we invoice the customer. Most of the orders are small, and the production cycle is short. Few items are produced for inventory.

Small: Does Paxton Metals ever get involved in situations involving progress payments?

Lord: Occasionally Paxton gets into progress payment situations. They usually involve government contracts. However, because these progress payments contracts are so rare and involve small amounts of money, typically we expense the costs of these projects as incurred and treat the progress payments as income when received.

Small: You said "few items are produced for inventory." Does this mean some items are produced for inventory?

Lord: Yes. One of Paxton's biggest customers is the appliance industry. Each year, Paxton supplies component parts to the appliance manufacturers. We build up large inventories of these items during our slow production months because we know we have *almost* assured sales. This practice smooths out our production cycle and helps us to avoid laying off our workers.

Small: When do you recognize the income from these sales to the appliance manufacturers?

Lord: When we ship and invoice the items. This is consistent with Paxton's general policy with respect to income recognition.

Small: I see, but what about Specialty Installations, Inc.?

Lord: That's a completely different kind of operation. Specialty Installations makes and installs a few large custom machine installations each year. These contracts typically involve progress payments, large sums of money, and take many, many months to complete.

In this case, we pick up the profits as we accumulate the costs on each job. We take into revenue the percentage of the contract's total selling price to the contract's total expected costs times the accumulated costs. We follow this policy to avoid great distortions in income from year to year.

Small: Are there ever sales between Paxton Metals and Specialty Installations?

Lord: Sometimes, but these profits are washed out in consolidation.

Small: Could we now turn to your real estate operations?

Lord: Surely.

Small: As I understand it, most of the land Texas Land and Royalty Company owns was acquired before 1890. Also, this land is carried on the books at its original cost. Is this correct?

Lord: Yes. Our land is shown on the balance sheet at some $8 million.

Small: Do you think the stockholders would be more interested in knowing the appreciation in the value of this land, year by year, rather than just its historical cost?

Also, wouldn't the balance sheet be a more meaningful document if the land was shown at, say, its current market value and in current-value dollars? After all, the consumer price index has risen from, say, 25 in 1890 to something over 300 today.

Similarly, don't you think the annual increase or decrease in the value of the land should be recorded as some form of income?

Lord: Now you're putting me on the hot seat. Frankly, I have no idea of the value of our land, before or after federal taxes. There are parts of our holdings we could sell for $200,000 or more an acre. Whereas, there are other parcels we couldn't give away.

Also, there is another complication. We use our land primarily for cattle and farming operations. Now, if we began selling our land off in the fashion of a dealer in real estate, we would have to pay ordinary income taxes on the gain. We intend to remain in the farming and cattle business, so we are locked into holding our land. Under these conditions I am not sure it makes sense to talk about "market values. . . ."

In many respects, the balance sheet is one of the world's most misleading documents. Therefore, it is important for people to understand what its limitations are. Certainly, it doesn't show economic values. Yet, if we tried to portray current market values or price-level-adjusted values, I think we might well destroy the continuity of the balance sheet, which I believe is important.

I will readily agree that assets are seldom, if ever, worth in market terms the values shown on the balance sheet. But would these figures be any more meaningful if I inserted your estimate of the market value for the historic cost? Perhaps we could have a professional geologist estimate each year the value of our oil reserves. Yet, from experience, I know that professional geologists change their minds about the characteristics of a field and amount of recoverable oil. Of course, we do include an SEC/FASB mandated value of our proven oil and gas reserves in our annual report. This is an artificial calculation using unrealistic discount rates. It is not current values. Also, we do show the assessed values of our land as part of our *Statement No. 33* current cost disclosure.

Small: Is that value separated out as a single item?

Lord: No. What I try to do is produce an honest income statement which gives a reasonable picture of earnings based on conservative accounting practices.

Small: I notice you use the flow-through method to record investment credits.

Lord: Yes. It may not be the most conservative approach, but we believe these credits come and go with each administration and it is wrong to show them in income when you are not receiving new credits anymore. If you used the deferral method and credits are no longer available under the tax code, statement users might think you are still getting these credits. This could be misleading.

Small: Are you using many fully depreciated assets?

Lord: Yes. As you might imagine, with a company as old as ours, this is not unusual.

Small: Do you include any inflation-adjusted depreciation for these assets in your *Statement No. 33* disclosure?

Lord: No. It's not required.

Small: Recently, you sold some land to Dallas Apartments, Inc. How do you propose to handle the profit on that sale?

Lord: First of all, let me say that this was a nonrecurring sale of property no longer economically employed in our business. It should be an extraordinary item for GAAP reporting, but it is not under the rules.

Now, as to how we propose to recognize the profits. Basically, after applicable taxes are deducted, we will defer the $3,750,000 profit on this sale and take it into income as collections are made.

Incidentally, we have loaned Dallas Apartments some $2 million. We will recognize the interest on this loan as it accrues, because it will be interest income from a nonconsolidated associated company.

Small: Talking about investments, I notice you have some marketable securities listed as long-term assets. Why do you report these at original cost rather than current market value?

Lord: As you probably noticed, we do give the market values of these securities in the footnotes to our financial statements. However, to answer your question, we are not holding these securities for speculation. We are not a mutual fund. These securities are like our cash balances; they are simply liquid resources that we need to hold in order to efficiently operate our cattle and our farming business. Also, their market value is above cost.

Small: You mentioned the farm operations—what policies do you follow here for the recognition of income?

Lord: In practice, this presents few problems. For instance, our policy is to recognize profit at the time the cotton crop is baled. We have a known market for the crop at that time.

Most of our farm income is derived from our share-rental agreements. That is, when our tenants pick their cotton crop, we get credit for one bale out of every four they press. The bales are not physically separated, they all go to market together. In fact, the cotton of the tenant farmers and the company is all sold through the same outlets.

At year-end, about seven eighths of the crop is harvested. For practical reasons, we don't try to accrue the income on the unharvested crop.

Small: Is cotton the only crop you raise?

Lord: No. Currently we are developing some citrus groves on one of our properties. We are deferring some of the costs of these groves until they bear commercial quantities of fruit. This should take about three to five years.

Also, we grow some barley, which we sell to the feed mill. This profit is washed out in consolidation.

Small: What is the policy with respect to your cattle operations?

Lord: Our cattle operations are decentralized. We have three breeding ranches, four stocker ranches, and a feed lot.

Small: What is the difference between these three types of operations?

Lord: At the breeding ranch, we breed and raise calves. The breeding herd can be regarded as a fixed asset. The calves are then moved to the stocker ranches and fed on range grass until the cattle obtain a weight of about 600 pounds. This takes about 15 months. Then the cattle are transferred to the feed lot. After about 120 days in the feed lot on a concentrated high-protein diet, the cattle reach weights of 1,000 pounds or more and are ready for slaughter.

Each of these operations is managed as a separate unit with a profit and loss responsibility. A breeding ranch manager may sell to one of our stocker ranches or to buyers outside the company, depending on prices. The same company policy applies to the stocker ranches. In line with this policy, we transfer cattle from one inventory to another, say, stocker inventory to the feed lot inventory, at market price.

Small: I gather a known current market price exists for cattle at each stage of their development from breeding ranch to feed lot.

Lord: Yes. From the overall company point of view, our policy with respect to cattle is to recognize profits at the time of sale to persons outside the company. Thus, when a stocking manager moves his cattle to our feed lot, the profit we credit to the stocker is for internal management purposes only. This profit is eliminated in consolidation. However, should a stocking manager sell to an outsider, that profits is recognized for external reporting purposes.

Small: Why do you use the "outside sale" criterion as the basis for recognizing income from cattle operations?

Lord: I think it is prudent. Also, our various herds are so large—about 200,000 cattle in all—that it would be a tremendous problem to come up with a reliable income figure based on the herd's appreciation and depreciation in value based on changes in market prices.

Incidentally, you may be interested in our inventory pricing policies. Except for our breeding herd and company-produced farm products, inventories are stated at the lower of cost or market. The breeding herd is carried at cost less accumulated depreciation. The company-produced farm products are stated at their market value at the time of harvest or market at year-end, whichever is lower.

All inventories are costed on a first-in, first-out and specific identification basis.

Small: That's interesting. You said earlier you had a feed mill operation. . . .

Lord: Yes. This is truly an integrated operation. The feed lot uses the barley grown on our own land irrigated by our own water utility. Let me take you through the whole operation.

When the water utility sells water to the company, the utility recognizes the profit. It is required to do this for utility regulation purposes. We in turn recognize the full utility price as part of the cost of producing barley. Insofar as the profit of the utility is included in our barley costs, the profits from intracompany transfers of water are not eliminated. There is always a slight time lag, however, since the costs of the barley not harvested at the end of the year are deferred, not expensed. These amounts are not material. Therefore, we don't worry.

Now, the barley is transferred to the feed mill at market price. This profit gets washed out in consolidation. However, we do recognize and report as part of our annual profit the feed mill's profit from the sale of feed to our feed lots. We do this for two reasons. First, we regard our feed mill and feed yard as two distinct profit centers. Second, the feed cost is an important ingredient in the formula for determining what is owed to us by those outside the company for whom we fatten cattle.

Let me explain. We sell feed to those outsiders who place cattle in our feed lots under two types of arrangements. First, we might sell grain by the ton. Second, we might sell an increase of so many pounds weight on the animals.

Under both of these arrangements, we are prepared to finance the outsider's purchase of both cattle and grain. As security, we hold the title to his cattle when they are placed in the lot. We also agree to handle the sale of the fattened cattle.

In return, we charge the outsider the cost of the feed plus an interest charge on our captial invested in his animals and feed. These interests costs are accrued.

For parent company financial reporting purposes, the milling profit is recognized when the feed is sold to the feed lot, irrespective of whether or not the feed is given to company- or outsider-owned cattle. The cost of feed is then incorporated in the deferred costs related to the cattle operation. These deferrals are expensed when the cattle are sold.

All of these sales of feed to the lots are made at market price.

Small: Can we now turn to your oil operations?

Lord: We have two types of oil operations: domestic and foreign. Domestically, our oil revenues are the royalties we receive from our leased oil lands. The lessees pay us a royalty based on the number of barrels of oil they extract. We recognize the income at the time the oil is extracted. Now, internationally, because we own less than 50 percent of the companies involved, we plan not to consolidate these operations. Rather, we will recognize the income from these operations when dividends are received in the United States.

Small: Why?

Lord: Primarily because of the risks involved. The political climate of the countries touched by our Latin American ventures is very unstable. In particular, the threat of nationalization is always present in the international oil business. Also, there are numerous currency exchange restrictions which make it difficult to repatriate all of your current earnings.

Small: Is this true of Canada? It is a fairly stable country, isn't it?

Lord: You have a point there. Because of the relatively stable political picture, I will have to recognize the Canadian refinery income as earned.

Small: If you go ahead with the New Orleans industrial park venture, how will you account for its income?

Lord: If we go into this deal, we will have a 50 percent equity. Like most real estate ventures, this will be heavily leveraged. I think we plan to use about 90 percent debt and 10 percent equity. We will use the equity method to account for this venture.

Small: I notice you have an overfunded pension plan. In fact, your plan assets have a market value in excess of $15 million over your plan's vested liabilities. Have you given any thought to recapturing that excess?

Lord: No. We are conservative. We use a 5 percent discount rate. Also, the liability figure you refer to includes an 8 percent salary progression assumption. . . .

Questions

1. Evaluate the corporate reporting policy of Texas Land and Royalty Company. Do you believe the company's financial statements "fairly" report the financial condition of the company and its results of operations?

2. If Texas Land and Royalty Company was free to choose its own accounting policies (i.e., not constrained by generally accepted accounting principles), how do you think it should report its financial condition and results of operations?

REVIEW CASE 3

SCM Corporation
Quality of Earnings and Financial Analysis

In September 1978, Tom Jensen, the portfolio manager for Statewide Insurance, met with Charles Graham, one of Statewide's newly hired financial analysts, to discuss the latest financial statements of SCM Corporation. The following conversation ensued:

Graham: Tom, I've been scanning the 1978 financials of SCM and I think we may want to consider them for our portfolio. According to the President's Letter (Exhibit 1), "fiscal 1978 was the fifth consecutive record year for SCM Corporation. Sales, net income, earnings per share, and dividends were all at record levels." What do you think?

Jensen: Well Chuck, I've been tracking SCM's stock for a while and I'm not sure. SCM's P/E ratio has hovered between 4 and 5 since 1974 compared to around 8 for the market. In addition, the stock has been selling at about a 50 percent discount from its book value even though SCM has shown consistently improving profits over the past few years. I wonder how SCM has achieved its earnings growth. Why don't you give me a report on the quality of SCM's earnings before we evaluate SCM for our portfolio?

Graham: What do you mean by "the quality of SCM's earnings?"

Jensen: Simply an evaluation of the accounting policies and techniques that SCM is using to arrive at its earnings numbers. As you know, the more liberal accounting policies a company uses, the sooner it recognizes revenues and profits and/or the more nonoperational items tend to "assist" earnings. However, a company with liberal accounting policies is often subject to relatively volatile earnings swings if economic conditions turn bad or if it can't continue to utilize certain events, like the sale of property, etc., to smooth earnings.

Jensen: I notice here in the President's Letter (Exhibit 1) that Mr. Elicker expressed some disappointment with the results for fiscal 1978, even though they were at record highs. He states that:

This case was prepared by Norman J. Bartczak.

Copyright © 1980 by the President and Fellows of Harvard College

Harvard Business School case 181–069 (Rev. 8/82)

EXHIBIT 1
SCM Corporation

President's Letter

To the Shareholders:

Fiscal 1978 was the fifth consecutive record year for SCM Corporation. Sales, net income, earnings per share, and dividends were all at record levels.

Last year's other major accomplishments included: an increased dividend; strategically important acquisitions in typewriters, coatings and resins, and foods; increased research and development expenditures; attainment of a higher portion of sales and margin contribution from new products; elimination of losses from business equipment; and a successful jury verdict in the trial of the lawsuit against Xerox Corporation.

Nevertheless, the year had its disappointments. While a few of our businesses did well and had record operating income, others were beset by a series of internal and external problems that resulted in modest to sizable declines in operating income. Operating income, perhaps the best indicator of how well our overall business fared, was down 19 percent last year.

For the year, net income increased slightly to $37.6 million, or $4.03 a share, up from $37.4 million, or $4.01 a share, for fiscal 1977. Sales increased 10 percent to $1.51 billion, from $1.38 billion the previous year.

Fiscal 1978 net income was a record despite the decline in operation income because of two factors. First, net income included several favorable nonrecurring items including better than anticipated results on disposition of our European copier operations. Second, the effective tax rate for fiscal 1978 was only 27 percent due mainly to investment tax credits for additions to fixed assets that went into production during the year. The effective tax rate for fiscal 1977 was 46 percent.

Here are some highlights of fiscal 1978.

- Operating income for Chemicals was down 85 percent, with more than half the decline due to a loss in inorganic chemcials, particularly titanium dioxide, our largest selling chemcial product. In addition, profits for Organic Chemicals were down.
- Glidden Coatings and Resins had its second consecutive record year and was the leading contributor to SCM's profits.
- Operating income for Paper Products was off somewhat despite an improvement in the forms business. The pulp and

paper industry worldwide appears to be recovering from a three-year slump that has particularly affected pulp.
- Durkee Foods' operating income declined 42 percent. Most of this was in edible oil refining operations and was a result of reduced demand and lower margins brought about by sharp fluctuations in raw materials prices, principally in the first fiscal quarter.
- Typewriters and appliances had its second record year. Smith-Corona typewriters increased sales in all model categories; operating income for Proctor-Silex appliances was the best since it merged with SCM.
- Business Equipment's operating income was $4.5 million compared to a loss in the previous year, with about $1.1 million of this attributable to domestic operations and the balance reflecting foreign exchange gains and the nonrecurring item mentioned earlier.

We had expected that second-half results last year would benefit from expansions in chemicals and pulp. This additional capacity did not go into production on schedule and, when it did, technical problems restricted output.

Capital expenditures were $62.6 million last year, down from $66.1 million in 1977. For the last several years, chemicals and paper products have received approximately half of all capital expenditures. Major capital expenditure projects in fiscal 1978 included the completion of expansion programs at the Jackson, Alabama, pulp mill and the Ashtabula, Ohio, titanium dioxide plant. Funds were also spent on an expansion of organic chemicals facilities and the Coatings and Resins and Foods research center outside Cleveland. Acquisitions accounted for about $8 million of total capital spending.

In accordance with our policy of paying out approximately 25 percent of earnings, in June the board of directors voted to increase the quarterly cash dividend 2½ cents a share to 27½ cents, an annual rate of $1.10. This was the fifth increase in the cash dividend in the past five years and reflects continued confidence in prospects for improved earnings and cash flow in the future.

Progress has been made in our antitrust

EXHIBIT 1 *(concluded)*

lawsuit against Xerox Corporation. In August, a federal court jury awarded SCM a total of $37.3 million in damages which would be trebled under federal antitrust law. While we recognize that there will be further proceedings in this matter, we look forward with confidence to an ultimately favorable resolution.

An improvement in some of our businesses began during the fourth quarter, and this trend should continue into fiscal 1979. Substantial gains are possible next year in Foods and Chemicals, the two businesses which had the sharpest declines in operating profits last year. Coatings and Resins and Typewriters and Appliances did well last year, but we expect them to do somewhat better in fiscal 1979. Paper Products should also improve.

On balance at this time, the outlook for fiscal 1979 is promising. Operating earnings should increase. The size of the increase will depend in large measure on the general health of the U.S. economy.

Paul H. Elicker
President and Chief Executive Officer
August 18,1978

While a few of our businesses did well and had record operating income, others were beset by a series of internal and external problems that resulted in modest to sizable declines in operating income. Operating income, perhaps the best indicator of how well our overall business fared, was down 19 percent last year.

Here's a copy of SCM's 1978 10-K (Exhibit 2). Why don't you go through it and analyze SCM's operating income. Focus on SCM's accounting policies and/or any unusual events which may have helped or hindered SCM's operating results. Make any adjustments you think might be necessary to provide a better indication of SCM's operating income for 1977 and 1978.

Questions

1. Do SCM's financial statements indicate that SCM has turned around?

2. Focus on Footnote 5—Income Taxes. What strikes you about SCM's income taxes from 1974 through 1978 relative to SCM's pre-tax income for the same period?

3. Other items to consider are:
   a. Footnote 8—Retirement Plans.
   b. Footnote 9—Supplemental Compensation Plans.
   c. Footnote 15—Quarterly Results.

4. Estimate SCM's earnings per share in 1977 and 1978 on what you consider to be an "operational" basis. For simplicity, use 10 million as the number of shares outstanding for 1977 and 1978.

5. In 1975, SCM reported an increase in primary earnings per share of $.02. In 1978, SCM again reported an increase in primary earnings per share of $.02. What kind of "signal," if any, do you think SCM sent to the market by reporting these $.02 increases? Do you think SCM could have reported an earnings per

share *decrease* of $.02 in each of these years? What "signal" do you think SCM would have sent to the market if it reported primary earnings per share down by $.02 in either 1975 or 1978? How do you think the market would have reacted?

6. What would you look for in SCM's future financial statements as evidence that SCM had turned around?

EXHIBIT 2
SCM Corporation

SCM Corporation 1978 Form 10-K, as Filed with the Securities and Exchange Commission September 28, 1978

SECURITIES AND EXCHANGE COMMISSION
Washington, D.C. 20549

FORM 10-K
Annual Report Pursuant to Section 13 or 15(d) of
the Securities Exchange Act of 1934
For the Fiscal Year Ended June 30, 1978
Commission File Number 1-3143

SCM Corporation
(Exact name of registrant as specified in its charter)

New York	**15-0451820**
(State or other jurisdiction of incorporation or organization)	(I.R.S. employer identification number)
299 Park Avenue, New York, New York	**10017**
(Address of principal executive offices)	(Zip code)

(212) 752-2700
(Telephone)

Securities Registered Pursuant to Section 12(b) *of the Act:*

Title of Each Class	Name of Each Exchange on which Registered
Common Stock, par value $5 per share........................	New York Stock Exchange Pacific Stock Exchange
5½% sinking fund debentures due 1980–1984	New York Stock Exchange
5¾% sinking fund debentures due 1980–1987	New York Stock Exchange
7¼% sinking fund debentures due 1980–1988	New York Stock Exchange
9¼% sinking fund debentures due 1980–1990	New York Stock Exchange
10% sinking fund debentures due 1982–1996	New York Stock Exchange
5½% convertible subordinated debentures due 1980–1988	New York Stock Exchange
5¼% convertible subordinated debentures due 1980–1989	New York Stock Exchange

Securities Registered Pursuant to Section 12(g) *of the Act:*
None
(Title of Class)

Indicate by check mark whether the registrant (1) has filed all reports required to be filed by Section 13 or 15(d) of the Securities Exchange Act of 1934 during the preceding 12 months (or for such shorter period that the registrant was required to file such reports), and (2) has been subject to such filing requirements for the past 90 days. Yes √. No. . . .

Indicate the number of shares outstanding of each of the issuer's classes of common stock, as of the close of the period covered by this report.

Class	Outstanding at June 30, 1978
Common stock, par value $5 per share	9,211,596 shares

Item 1. Business

SCM Corporation's ("SCM" or the "company") operations are grouped into six seg-

EXHIBIT 2 *(continued)*

ments: Chemcials, Coatings and Resins, Paper Products, Foods, Typewriters and Appliances, and Business Equipment. Businesses which are not included in one of these groupings are not material to the company and are grouped under Other.

Business Segments

The detail of SCM's net sales, income from operations, total assets, depreciation expense, and capital expenditures by segment for the five years ended June 30, 1978, are set forth in the following table.

| | Year Ended June 30 | | | | |
	1978	1977	1976	1975	1974
			(amounts in thousands)		
Net sales:					
Chemicals	$ 190,467	$ 179,355	$ 155,882	$ 122,159	$ 116,745
Coatings and Resins	402,194	381,639	362,995	332,754	312,013
Paper Products	184,659	168,630	161,747	165,673	141,096
Foods	390,453	347,602	320,292	342,951	289,224
Typewriters and Appliances	273,081	228,703	216,035	181,101	203,079
Business Equipment	60,007	62,449	107,069	121,967	124,633
Other	28,758	29,468	28,641	35,011	30,579
	$1,529,619	$1,397,846	$1,352,661	$1,301,616	$1,217,369
Eliminations*(a)*	(20,312)	(20,202)	(20,764)	(14,162)	(15,121)
Total	$1,509,307	$1,377,644	$1,331,897	$1,287,454	$1,202,248
Income (loss) from operations:					
Chemicals	$ 2,195	$ 14,712	$ 12,277	$ 11,283	$ 13,375
Coatings and Resins	32,303	28,414	23,057	17,090	26,314
Paper Products	19,130	22,576	25,215	41,658	25,531
Foods	11,918	20,374	16,991	7,988	2,675
Typewriters and Appliances	26,498	22,345	16,486	8,846	18,898
Business Equipment	4,519	(2,059)	(9,738)	(15,747)	(12,468)
Other	3,766	4,841	3,328	2,475	1,094
	$ 100,329	$ 111,203	$ 87,616	$ 73,593	$ 75,419
Corporate expense	(27,552)	(20,868)	(13,814)	(11,784)	(12,247)
Total	$ 72,777	$ 90,335	$ 73,802	$ 61,809	$ 63,172
Total assets:					
Chemicals	$ 187,639	$ 182,893	$ 169,782	$ 148,660	$ 90,374
Coatings and Resins	230,681	211,941	212,524	187,544	192,596
Paper Products	98,822	83,454	69,814	54,696	58,714
Foods	140,774	136,758	110,025	104,402	111,975
Typewriters and Appliances	163,750	131,265	129,888	120,859	110,303
Business Equipment	12,295	12,141	37,552	75,527	68,018
Other	10,637	9,467	10,505	12,390	14,703
Total	$ 844,598	$ 767,919	$ 740,090	$ 704,078	$ 646,683
Depreciation expense:					
Chemicals	$ 9,962	$ 7,202	$ 6,619	$ 5,353	$ 3,574
Coatings and Resins	4,486	3,389	3,908	3,655	3,720
Paper Products	4,320	3,516	3,383	2,878	3,206
Foods	2,914	2,645	2,562	2,882	2,425
Typewriters and Appliances	5,909	6,002	5,951	5,231	4,516
Business Equipment	2,143	7,644	15,147	12,257	12,182
Other	709	634	598	799	711
Total	$ 30,443	$ 31,032	$ 38,168	$ 33,055	$ 30,334
Capital expenditures:					
Chemicals	$ 17,500	$ 21,016	$ 10,550	$ 36,787	$ 7,549
Coatings and Resins	13,896	10,693	10,100	4,719	5,202
Paper Products	13,280	17,403	7,834	5,986	13,191
Foods	5,855	9,308	2,101	2,614	3,883
Typewriters and Appliances	11,704	5,591	5,080	11,247	9,894
Business Equipment	56	1,318	2,420	25,005	18,368
Other	259	789	617	781	1,051
Total	$ 62,550	$ 66,118	$ 38,702	$ 87,139	$ 59,138

(a) Represents primarily sales of titanium dioxide by the Chemicals segment to the Coatings and Resins and Paper Products segments.

EXHIBIT 2 *(continued)*

Item 2. Summary of Operations.
Statements of Consolidated Income

The following statements of consolidated income of SCM Corporation and subsidiary companies for the five years ended June 30, 1978, have been examined by Deloitte Haskins & Sells, independent certified public ac-countants, whose opinion with respect thereto appears elsewhere in this filing. These statements should be read in conjunction with the notes immediately following and the other consolidated financial statements and notes to financial statements included elsewhere in this filing.

	Year Ended June 30				
	1978	1977	1976	1975	1974
	(dollar amounts in thousands except per-share amounts)				
Net sales	$1,509,307	$1,377,644	$1,331,897	$1,287,454	$1,202,248
Cost of sales(b)	1,128,947	1,000,579	968,179	956,550	876,106
Gross profit	380,360	377,065	363,718	330,904	326,142
Selling, administrative, and research expenses	307,583	286,730	289,916	269,095	262,970
Income from operations	72,777	90,335	73,802	61,809	63,172
Other (income) expense, net	(215)	1,130	823	(55)	1,002
Interest:					
Long-term debt	15,903	16,642	15,173	12,722	9,848
Other	6,684	4,622	3,467	6,901	3,470
Income	(1,117)	(1,404)	(1,242)	(631)	(297)
Total	21,470	19,860	17,398	18,992	13,021
Income before income taxes	51,522	69,345	55,581	42,872	49,149
Income taxes	13,942	31,933	25,186	14,986	21,503
Net income	$ 37,580	$ 37,412	$ 30,395	$ 27,886	$ 27,646
Per share of common stock:					
Net income(a)	$4.03	$4.01	$3.30	$3.04	$3.02
Net income assuming full dilution(a)	$3.75	$3.70	$3.04	$2.83	$2.81
Cash dividends	$1.025	$ .85	$.675	$ .50	$.425
Weighted average number of shares(a):					
Primary	9,318,477	9,318,750	9,213,394	9,173,395	9,159,220
Assuming full dilution	10,389,299	10,495,217	10,489,254	10,406,188	10,375,135

Notes to Statements of Consolidated Income

(a) Net income per share has been computed by dividing net income by the weighted average number of common and common equivalent shares outstanding during the year. Common equivalent shares are the shares assumed issued through exercise of outstanding stock options bearing an exercise price lower than the average market price during the period. The number of such equivalent shares has been reduced to reflect the assumption that proceeds of such options would be used by SCM to reacquire its common shares.

Net income per share assuming full dilution has been computed based on the assumption that convertible debt obligations were converted and all dilutive outstanding stock options were exercised as of the beginning of the fiscal year.

(b) The opening and closing inventories used to determine the cost of sales were as follows: June 30, 1978—$278,891,000; 1977—$270,915,000; 1976—$240,372,000; 1975—$214,034,000; 1974—$213,353,000; 1973—$177,975,000.

As of June 30, 1978, approximately 17 percent of SCM's total inventories were priced on the last-in, first-out (LIFO) method. Had all inventories currently on LIFO been priced on a first-in, first-out (FIFO) basis, inventories would have been approximately $18.5 million higher at June 30, 1978, and $17.6 million higher at June 30, 1977.

Management's Discussion and Analysis of the Statements of Consolidated Income
Fiscal 1978 Compared to Fiscal 1977

Net sales for fiscal 1978 increased 9.6 percent from fiscal 1977. Most of this increase was from Typewriters and Appliances and Foods. Typewriters and Appliances had increased sales because of higher volume in all major products, including a new appliance, and because of the addition of typewriters manufactured at the Glasgow, Scotland, plant

EXHIBIT 2 *(continued)*

purchased during the year. Higher Foods sales resulted from increased edible oils prices and increased volume in consumer foods. Sales of Coatings and Resins, Paper Products, and Chemicals also increased, mainly because of higher unit volume. Coatings and Resins was also aided by higher prices.

Fiscal 1978 operating income decreased 19.4 percent from the prior year principally because of a loss in Chemicals' titanium dioxide operation and severe fluctuations in the prices for edible oils used in Foods. Operating income from Paper Products also decreased because the effect of lower pulp prices more than offset higher profits in business forms. Decreased operating income in Chemicals, Foods, and Paper Products was partly offset by improvements in Business Equipment, Typewriters and Appliances, and Coatings and Resins. Business Equipment was profitable, following several years of losses, because of reduced depreciation charges and better than anticipated results on disposition of the European copier operations. The increase in operating income of Typewriters and Appliances was primarily due to increased sales of appliances and the portable typewriters produced in the United States and Singapore. The improvement in operating income from Coatings and Resins reflects reduced foreign exchange losses as well as gains on the sale of two Latin American paint plants.

Corporate expense includes the cost of SCM's lawsuit against Xerox Corporation, which was $10.3 million in fiscal 1978 compared to $7.0 million in fiscal 1977.

Though pre-tax income declined 25.7 percent, net income for fiscal 1978 increased slightly to $37.6 million because of the low tax rate. The tax rate of 27.1 percent, down from 46.0 percent in fiscal 1977, reflected high investment tax credits and better than anticipated tax benefits from the disposition of the European copier operations.

Fiscal 1977 Compared to Fiscal 1976

In fiscal 1977, net sales increased 3.4 percent from fiscal 1976. Increases in Foods, Chemicals, and Coatings and Resins resulted from both increased physical volume and higher selling prices. The gain in Typewriters and Appliances was primarily due to improved sales of top-of-the-line typewriters. There was a moderate increase in sales of Paper Products as gains in paper and business forms offset a decrease in pulp sales. Business Equipment sales decreased as a result of ex-

cluding the European copier operations which were in the process of disposition. If Euorpean copier sales and sales from the disposed Coatings and Resins operation in Germany had been excluded from both years, fiscal 1977 sales would have increased 8.0 percent rather than 3.4 percent from fiscal 1976.

Operating income for fiscal 1977 increased 22.4 percent from the prior year as all lines of business except Paper Products had improved operating results. The largest improvements in operating income were in Typewriters and Appliances and Coatings and Resins. The increase in Typewriters and Appliances came from an improved mix of higher margin products in typewriters and improved performance of Proctor-Silex appliances. Although affected by substantial foreign exchange losses, Coatings and Resins had increased profits because of higher gross margins. Operating income of Foods increased primarily due to increased volume in spices. Chemicals' operating income increased as the effect of improved demand for organic chemicals more than offset decreased margins in inorganic chemicals. Operating income from Paper Products declined because of a combination of weak prices for pulp and increased manufacturing costs. The Business Equipment loss was reduced substantially because depreciation and obsolescence charges decreased to $7.6 million in fiscal 1977 from $18.3 million in fiscal 1976.

Corporate expense increased in fiscal 1977 principally because of increased cost of SCM's lawsuit against Xerox Corporation.

Interest expense was $19.9 million, up from $17.4 million in 1976, as a result of higher interest rates and an increase in total borrowings.

For additional information concerning the company and its performance for fiscal 1978, 1977, and 1976, reference is made to Item 1—Business, Notes to the Statements of Consolidated Income and Notes to Financial Statements.

Executive Officers of the Registrant

Executive officers are elected at a meeting of the board of directors on the date of the annual meeting of shareholders and hold office until the next such board meeting or until their successors are appointed. Executive officers are listed on the next page, and each has been employed by SCM or its subsidiaries for more than five years.

EXHIBIT 2 *(continued)*

Name	Age	Principal Occupation	First Elected
James Balph	49	Vice president	1972
George F. Burns	58	Vice president; president of the Consumer Products Division, and director	1963
William V. Cawley	47	Vice president and treasurer	1968
Robert E. Dorfmeyer	62	Vice president; president of the Foods Division	1976
Herbert H. Egli	48	Vice president—finance and controller	1970
Paul H. Elicker	55	President, chief executive officer, and director	1957
Victor E. Feuerherd	53	Vice president	1973
George E. Hall	53	Senior vice president— administration and director	1963
William D. Kinsell	59	Vice president; president of the Coatings and Resins Division	1976
Ernest J. Klimczak	54	Vice president; president of Allied Paper, Inc.	1973
Paul W. Neidhardt	61	Senior vice president; senior division president; and director	1967
William L. Rodich	61	Vice president; president of the Chemical/Metallurgical Division	1975
Edward J. Romay	57	Vice president	1976
Richard Sexton	49	Vice president, general counsel, and secretary	1972
Gerard F. Stoddard	44	Vice president	1973

Board of Directors

Name	Year Elected	Principal Occupation	Shares of SCM Common Owned
Robert O. Bass†	1975	President, Borg-Warner Corporation	500
Richard C. Bond*‡	1967	President, board of trustees, John Wanamaker Philadelphia, Inc.	100
John T. Booth	1965	Executive vice president, Blyth Eastman Dillon and Co.	500
George F. Burns	1968	Vice president of SCM; president, Consumer Products Division	4,221
Lewis H. Durland	1956	Chairman, First National Bank and Trust Company of Ithaca, New York	1,508
Paul H. Elicker*	1964	President and chief executive officer of SCM	11,600
George E. Hall*	1965	Senior vice president— administration of SCM	5,547
George D. Kennedy*†‡	1971	President, International Minerals and Chemical Corporation	100

EXHIBIT 2 *(continued)*

Name	Year Elected	Principal Occupation	Shares of SCM Common Owned
Paul W. Neidhardt*	1967	Senior vice president of SCM; senior division president	3,495
Crocker Nevin*†‡	1967	Investment banker, Drexel Burnham and Company, Inc.	118
William W. Quinn‡	1970	President, Quinn Associates, management consultants	122
Robert A. Schoellhorn	1977	President, Abbott Laboratories	200
E. Everett Smith†	1973	Of counsel, McKinsey and Company	100

* Member of Executive Committee.
† Member of audit committee.
‡ Member of compensation committee.

Remuneration of Highest Paid Officers and Directors

Name	Age	Position	Aggregate Remuneration (a)
George F. Burns	58	Vice president; president of the Consumer Products Division, and director	$ 226,186
Paul H. Elicker	55	President, chief executive officer, and director	$ 403,441
George E. Hall	53	Senior vice president—administration and director	$ 265,643
Paul W. Neidhardt	61	Senior vice president, senior division president, and director	$ 251,614
All 24 directors and officers as a group			$2,705,543

(a) This amount includes salaries, incentive compensation awards, directors' fees, and other renumeration (see footnote 9, "Supplemental Compensation Plans").

Financial Statements
SCM CORPORATION AND SUBSIDIARY COMPANIES
Consolidated Balance Sheets

	June 30, 1978		June 30, 1977	
	(amount in thousands)			
Assets				
Current assets:				
Cash (note 11)		$ 8,879		$ 9,038
Marketable securities (at cost which approximates market value)		1,219		2,569
Accounts receivable	$216,798		$182,988	
Less: Allowance for doubtful accounts	7,249	209,549	6,156	176,832
Inventories (note 1):				
Raw materials and work in process	$134,653		$122,903	
Finished goods	144,238	278,891	148,012	270,915
Deferred income taxes (notes 1 and 5)		6,077		3,226
Prepaid expenses		9,936		7,785
Total current assets		$514,551		$470,365
Property, plant, and equipment—at cost (notes 1 and 3)	$584,018		$539,706	
Less: Accumulated depreciation	279,487	304,531	260,844	278,862
Other assets (note 4)		25,516		18,692
Total		$844,598		$767,919

EXHIBIT 2 *(continued)*

	June 30, 1978		June 30, 1977	
		(amount in thousands)		
Liabilities and Shareholders' Equity				
Current liabilities:				
Loans payable (note 11)		$ 63,949		$ 30,261
Accounts payable		77,284		55,964
Accrued liabilities:				
Salaries, wages, and commissions	$ 20,794		$ 17,176	
Pension	14,000		12,600	
Taxes, other than income taxes	10,578		10,714	
Interest	6,084		5,422	
Other	37,484	88,940	41,250	87,162
United States and foreign income taxes (notes 1 and 5)		1,771		8,920
Long-term debt payments due within one year		3,406		3,600
Total current liabilities		$235,350		$185,907
Long-term debt (note 6)		189,620		201,163
Deferred income taxes (notes 1 and 5)		23,660		15,938
Other liabilities		23,834		21,262
Shareholders' equity (note 7):				
Common stock, $5 par value				
Authorized: 15 million shares				
Oustanding: June 30, 1978—9,211,596 shares				
June 30, 1977—9,196,384 shares	$ 46,058		$ 45,982	
Additional paid-in capital	111,872		111,604	
Retained earnings (note 6)	214,204	372,134	186,063	343,649
Total		$844,598		$767,919

See accompanying notes to financial statements.

SCM CORPORATION AND SUBSIDIARY COMPANIES
Statements of Changes in Consolidated Financial Position
For the Five Years Ended June 30, 1978

	1978	1977	1976	1975	1974
			(amounts in thousands)		
Sources:					
Operations:					
Net income	$37,580	$ 37,412	$ 30,395	$ 27,886	$ 27,646
Add expenses not requiring working capital:					
Depreciation	30,443	31,032	38,168	33,055	30,334
Deferred income taxes—noncurrent	7,722	3,187	1,165	(4,997)	(575)
Other, net	2,549	1,295	8,148	7,114	1,802
Working capital provided by operations	$ 78,294	$ 72,926	$ 77,876	$ 63,058	$ 59,207
Long-term debt and lease obligations	1,202	68	53,236	72,741	10,000
Disposals of property, plant, and equipment	6,438	7,516	4,022	2,442	8,920
Decrease (increase) in working capital	5,257	3,395	(36,222)	(19,664)	(2,026)
Total	$91,191	$ 83,905	$ 98,912	$118,577	$ 76,110
Applications:					
Additions to property, plant, and equipment	$ 62,550	$ 66,118	$ 38,702	$ 87,139	$ 59,138
Reduction of long-term debt	12,745	9,294	57,319	11,175	6,533
Cash dividends	9,439	7,806	6,182	4,579	3,892
Other changes in noncurrent items	6,457	687	(3,291)	15,684	6,547
Total	$ 91,191	$ 83,905	$ 98,912	$118,577	$ 76,110
Changes in working capital:					
Current assets:					
Cash and marketable securities	$ (1,509)	$(33,470)	$ 24,068	$ 14,369	$ (2,751)
Accounts receivable—net	32,717	5,474	1,694	(19,360)	36,093
Inventories	7,976	30,543	26,338	681	35,378
Deferred income taxes	2,851	1,021	(4,432)	(7,223)	643
Prepaid expenses	2,151	804	2,548	1,402	(15)
Change in current assets	$ 44,186	$ 4,372	$ 50,216	$ (10,131)	$ 69,348

EXHIBIT 2 *(continued)*

	1978	1977	1976	1975	1974
			(amounts in thousands)		
Current liabilities:					
Loans payable	$(33,688)	$(17,753)	$ 8,042	$ 14,693	$(27,545)
Accounts payable	(21,320)	5,015	(5,671)	10,408	(14,820)
Accrued liabilities	(1,778)	2,287	(11,531)	(720)	(20,079)
United States and foreign income taxes	7,149	4,180	(10,077)	9,556	(3,205)
Long-term debt payments due within one year	194	(1,496)	5,243	(4,142)	(1,673)
Change in current liabilities	$(49,443)	$ (7,767)	$(13,994)	$ 29,795	$(67,322)
Increase (decrease) in working capital	$ (5,257)	$ (3,395)	$ 36,222	$ 19,664	$ 2,026

See accompanying notes to financial statements.

Opinion of Independent Certified Public Accountants

SCM Corporation:

We have examined the consolidated financial statements and schedules of SCM Corporation and subsidiary companies ("SCM") as listed in item 13(a) of your Annual Report (Form 10-K) to the Securities and Exchange Commission for the fiscal year ended June 30, 1978. Our examinations were made in accordance with generally accepted auditing standards and, accordingly, included such tests of the accounting records and such other auditing procedures as we considered necessary in the circumstances.

As further discussed in note 14 to the financial statements, in July and August, 1978, a federal court jury rendered verdicts which may or may not ultimately result in substantial payments to SCM.

In our opinion, such consolidated financial statements present fairly the financial position of SCM at June 30, 1978, and 1977, and the results of its operations and the changes in its financial position for each of the five years in the period ended June 30, 1978, in conformity with generally accepted accounting principles applied on a consistent basis; and the schedules, when considered in relation to the basic consolidated financial statements, present fairly in all material respects the information shown therein.

DELOITTE HASKINS & SELLS

New York, New York
August 16, 1978

Notes to Financial Statements

1. Accounting Policies

Principles of consolidation: The consolidated financial statements include the accounts of all wholly owned and majority-owned subsidiaries. Investments in minority-owned affiliates and joint ventures, included in other assets, are adjusted to recognize SCM's share of their income or losses where the investment is 20 percent or more.

Inventories: Inventories are generally priced at the lower of average cost or market, except for inventories of pulp, paper, and the raw material content of edible oils which are priced at the lower of last-in, first-out (LIFO) cost or market.

Property, plant, and equipment: Depreciation is provided on a straight-line basis at rates based on estimated useful lives. At the time properties are retired or disposed of, the property and related accumulated depreciation accounts are relieved of the applicable amounts, and any profit or loss is included in operating income.

Maintenance and repairs: Routine maintenance and repairs are charged against operations as incurred. Expenditures that materially increase capacities or extend useful lives are capitalized.

Income taxes: Income taxes are provided for in the year transactions affect net income regardless of when such transactions are recognized for tax purposes. The tax effect of timing differences is accounted for as deferred taxes. Provision is also made for income taxes on undistributed earnings of foreign subsidiaries not considered to be permanently invested. Investment tax credits are included

EXHIBIT 2 *(continued)*

as reductions of income tax expense in the year such credits become deductible.

Retirement plans: SCM has several retirement plans that provide pensions for substantially all of its employees. Pension plan provisions include normal cost, interest on unfunded prior service liabilities, and amortization of actuarial gains or losses including prior service costs arising from plan amendments. Contributions to pension funds are made when actuarial computations prescribe such funding.

2. Foreign Operations

The effect of subsidiary operations outside the United States and its possessions on consolidated net sales, net income (loss), and total assets, for the five years ended June 30, 1978, was:

Fiscal Year	Net Sales	Net Income (Loss) (amounts in thousands)	Total Assets
1978	$182,781	$ 7,330	$158,540
1977	165,140	388	119,792
1976	213,078	2,463	135,054
1975	197,706	(3,099)	128,395
1974	176,857	5,611	120,867

The increase in net income of these operations in fiscal 1978 reflects better than anticipated results on the disposition of European copier operations, gains on the sale of two Coatings and Resins facilities which were replaced, and a reduction of foreign exchange losses.

Total assets of these operations increased during fiscal 1978 principally because of the purchase of a typewriter plant in Glasglow, Scotland, and the completion of a new Coatings and Resins plant in Brazil.

SCM's management believes that the risk of doing business in the foreign countries in which SCM operates (i.e., government policies, high social welfare costs, currency fluctuations, and different tax structures) is somewhat greater than the risk of doing business domestically.

3. Property, Plant, and Equipment

The cost of property, plant, and equipment consists of:

	June 30, 1978	June 30, 1977
	(amounts in thousands)	
Land	$ 21,836	$ 23,026
Buildings	128,216	123,127
Machinery and other equipment	433,966	393,553
Total	$584,018	$539,706

SCM provides depreciation based on estimated useful lives as follows: buildings, 20 to 50 years; machinery and other equipment, 3 to 25 years.

The company has undertaken a program to install new chemical equipment at its Baltimore chloride process plant which incorporates certain aspects of the technology currently utilized at the company's Ashtabula, Ohio, facility. As a result of this program, the company has accelerated the depreciation of the technology and equipment being replaced to coincide with its remaining useful life.

4. Other Assets

As of June 30, 1978, and 1977, other assets includes production rights, patents, and other intangibles of $11 million and $1.4 million; investments in unconsolidated affiliates and joint ventures of $5.8 million and $4.8 million; and long-term receivables of $5.7 million and $6.3 million. The increase in production rights, patents, and other intangibles during 1978 was related principally to the acquisition of a typewriter plant in Glasgow, Scotland.

5. Income Taxes

Income taxes consists of:

	Year Ended June 30				
	1978	1977	1976	1975	1974
			(amounts in thousands)		
Current:					
United States	$12,787	$26,937	$14,210	$10,271	$20,292
Investment credit	(8,016)	(3,052)	(1,884)	(2,645)	(2,300)
Foreign..	2,931	3,108	5,363	4,331	3,292
State and local	1,369	2,774	1,900	803	1,300
Total current	$ 9,071	$29,767	$19,589	$12,760	$22,584

EXHIBIT 2 *(continued)*

	1978	1977	1976	1975	1975
			(amounts in thousands)		
Deferred:					
United States	$ 6,251	$ 1,890	$ 5,144	$ 2,562	$ (1,237)
Foreign	(1,380)	276	453	(336)	156
Total deferred	$ 4,871	$ 2,166	$ 5,597	$ 2,226	$ (1,081)
Total income tax expenses	$13,942	$31,933	$25,186	$14,986	$21,503
Reconciliation of effective tax rate:					
Statutory U.S. income tax rate	48.0%	48.0%	48.0%	48.0%	48.0%
Investment credit	(15.6)	(4.4)	(3.4)	(6.2)	(4.7)
DISC benefit	(2.0)	(1.2)	(.9)	(4.6)	(2.1)
Foreign operations	(4.5)	1.9	(.2)	(.7)	.3
Other, net	1.2	1.7	1.8	(1.5)	2.3
Effective tax rate	27.1%	46.0%	45.3%	35.0%	43.8%
Deferred taxes result from timing differences relative to:					
Business realignment	$ 2,535	$ (117)	$ (482)	$ (253)	$ (491)
Inventory valuations	147	1,113	1,023	111	1,460
Foreign operations	2,377	(522)	2,466	(879)	—
Depreciation	2,577	4,447	1,446	1,585	99
Other, net	(2,765)	(2,755)	1,144	1,662	(2,149)
Total deferred taxes	$ 4,871	$ 2,166	$ 5,597	$ 2,226	$ (1,081)

Year Ended June 30

At June 30, 1978, provision for income taxes has not been made on $50 million of undistributed earnings of subsidiaries and joint ventures since these earnings are considered to be permanently invested.

6. Long-Term Debt

At June 30, 1978, and 1977, long-term debt due after one year consisted of the following:

	1978	1977
	(amounts in thousands)	
5½% sinking fund debentures due 1980–1984	$ 6,175	$ 8,700
5¾% sinking fund debentures due 1980–1987	11,469	12,168
7¼% sinking fund debentures due 1980–1988	12,495	14,000
9¼% sinking fund debentures due 1980–1990	26,250	28,000
10% sinking fund debentures due 1982–1996	50,000	50,000
8⅞% note (Pollution Control Revenue Bonds) due 1991–2000	17,000	17,000
Lease obligation (6% Environmental Improvement Revenue Bonds, due 1984–1993)	10,000	10,000
Other loans from 4% to 14%	8,477	9,091
5½% convertible subordinated debentures due 1980–1988	34,106	37,948
5¼% convertible subordinated debentures due 1980–1989	13,648	14,256
Total long-term debt	$189,620	$201,163

Approximate long-term debt maturities, including the current portion of long-term debt, during the next five years will be: 1979—$3.4 million; 1980—$5.6 million; 1981—$9.8 million; 1982—$12.8 million; 1983—$12.7 million.

Under the most restrictive provisions of the indentures related to long-term debt, retained earnings of $93.6 million were available at June 30, 1978, for declaration of cash dividends.

7. Capital Stock

A summary of shares of common stock reserved at June 30, 1978, and 1977 follows:

	1978	1977
Reserved for issuance under stock option plans	402,689	417,901
Reserved for issuance upon conversion of:		
5½% subordinated debentures due 1980–1988	733,313	815,919
5¼% subordinated debentures due 1980–1989	293,190	306,251

Under the provisions of SCM's Stock Option Plans, options to purchase shares of SCM common stock have been granted to officers and key employees.

A summary of options that became exercisable and options during each of the five years ended June 30, 1978, and the shares under option at June 30, 1978, and 1977, follows:

EXHIBIT 2 *(continued)*

	Number of Shares	Option Price Range per Share	Option Price Total	Fair Market Value Range per Share	Fair Market Value Total
Options that became exerciseable:					
Years ended June 30,					
1978	12,100	$11.50 to 21.88	$ 197,000	$15.50 to 24.00*(a)*	$ 224,000
1977	14,540	8.75 to 17.00	214,000	19.13 to 23.88*(a)*	328,000
1976	275,322	8.75 to 16.75	3,122,000	10.50 to 13.13*(a)*	3,033,000
1975	24,200	8.75 to 18.50	354,000	8.50 to 11.63*(a)*	207,000
1974	80,050	12.00 to 20.38	1,245,000	8.88 to 13.63*(a)*	954,000
Options exercised:					
Years ended June 30,					
1978	15,212	8.75 to 16.75	176,000	16.75 to 24.75*(b)*	321,000
1977	34,499	8.75 to 16.75	399,000	16.63 to 24.63*(b)*	706,000
1976	5,000	8.75 to 11.38	51,000	10.75 to 17.75*(b)*	82,000
1975	400	8.75	4,000	11.25 to 12.13*(b)*	5,000
1974	None				
Shares under options at June 30,					
1978 (granted 1973–1978)	313,106	8.75 to 21.88	3,822,000	8.75 to 21.88*(c)*	3,837,000
1977 (granted 1973–1977)	324,118	8.75 to 21.88	3,867,000	8.75 to 21.88*(c)*	3,883,000

(a) At dates options became exercisable.
(b) At dates options were exercised.
(c) At dates options were granted.

The exercise price of the options is not less than the fair market value of the stock at the date of grant, except for the "tandem options" which were granted at the lower of market price on the date of grant or the exercise price of the basic option to which they are related. Options become exercisable in cumulative installments of 40 percent, 40 percent, and 20 percent, respectively, on the first, second, and third anniversaries of the date of grant. When options are exercised, the excess of the option price over the par value of the shares issued is credited to additional paid-in capital.

During 1978 and 1977, nonqualified options to purchase 17,500 and 2,000 shares, respectively, were granted. Also during 1977, qualified options to purchase 1,000 shares were granted. No qualified options were granted during 1978.

In addition to common shares, the authorized capital stock of SCM includes 500,000 shares of preferred stock, par value $50, none of which is outstanding.

8. Retirement Plan

Pension expense, including interest on unfunded prior service liabilities and, in 1976, a provision for vested benefits, was approximately $15 million in 1978, $14 million in 1977, $15 million in 1976, $13 million in 1975, and $12.5 million in 1974. Unfunded prior service liabilities decreased to approximately $75 million at June 30, 1978, from $85 million at June 30, 1977, because of a change in actuarial assumptions, which also decreased pension expense for 1978 by approximately $1.3 million. The actuarially computed value of vested benefits exceeded the total of the trust fund assets and the consolidated balance sheet accruals by approximately $31 million and $22 million at June 30, 1978, and 1977, respectively.

9. Supplemental Compensation Plans

SCM has two shareholder-approved supplemental compensation plans. The Incentive Compensation Plan for Key Employees provides for awards of supplemental compensation to officers and key employees who have made an outstanding contribution to SCM's business. The Long-Term Performance Award Plan, adopted in fiscal 1977, provides for awards of supplemental compensation, which may, at the discretion of the board of directors, be payable in cash or common stock, based on the attainment of preestablished cumulative earnings objectives over three-year periods. The amount charged against operations for these plans, pursuant to the limitations set forth therein, was $1,873,000 in 1978, $2,046,000 in 1977, $1,273,000 in 1976, $1,065,000 in 1975, and $1,245,000 in 1974.

EXHIBIT 2 *(continued)*

10. Foreign Exchange

Operations were charged with pre-tax foreign exchange losses of $2.8 million in 1978, $6 million in 1977, $1.8 million in 1976, and $1.7 million in 1975. Foreign exchange losses charged against operations in fiscal 1974 were immaterial.

11. Credit Lines and Compensating Balances

The maximum short-term borrowing outstanding at any month-end during the year was $71.8 million at May 31, 1978. SCM's unsecured short-term credit lines at June 30, 1978, totaled $89.4 million of which $63.9 million was outstanding. The average short-term borrowing outstanding during the fiscal year was $43.3 million, most of which represented foreign borrowings at interest rates higher than those of the United States. The average interest rate for such borrowings, calculated by dividing total interest by the average amount outstanding, was 13.3 percent.

The average interest rate for short-term borrowings outstanding at June 30, 1978, was 12.6 percent without giving effect to compensating balances. SCM has informally agreed to maintain compensating balances, generally based on 10 percent of credit lines available. At any given date, cash is not restricted by compensating balance agreements.

12. Leases

Rental expense under operating leases, net of sublease income, was $25.9 million, $27.2 million, $26.6 million, $24.6 million, and $20.8 million for the years ended June 30, 1978, 1977, 1976, 1975, and 1974, respectively. Future minimum rental commitments at June 30, 1978, reduced by total sublease income of $12.6 million, are: 1979—$14 million; 1980—$12.2 million; 1981—$10.8 million; 1982—$9.6 million; 1983—$8.4 million; total thereafter—$45.6 million. These future commitments include a $15 million capital lease obligation which, if capitalized in accordance with *Financial Accounting Standard No. 13*, would have had an immaterial effect on assets, liabilities, and net income.

13. Supplementary Income Statement Information

	Year Ended June 30				
	1978	1977	1976	1975	1974
			(amounts in thousands)		
Maintenance and repairs	$45,581	$42,793	$36,342	$34,441	$28,287
Depreciation of property, plant, and equipment	30,443	31,032	38,168	33,055	30,334
Taxes, other than income taxes ...	31,344	32,446	30,567	27,563	25,222
Advertising costs	27,977	26,579	29,675	25,347	26,186
Research and development costs .	19,700	16,500	14,000	19,005	18,897

Depreciation of property, plant, and equipment for 1976 includes approximately $2.5 million of additional depreciation which resulted from a reduction of the depreciable lives of plain paper copiers. The charges for amortization of intangible assets and royalties are not shown because they are less than 1 percent of sales. Rental expense for the five years ended June 30, 1978, is included in note 12.

14. Litigation

In July 1973, SCM filed suit in federal court charging Xerox Corporation with unlawful monopolization and restraint of trade in the office copier business. The trial began in June 1977, and in July and August 1978, jury verdicts were rendered which could result in payments to SCM of up to $112 million plus reasonable attorneys' fees and costs, before applicable income taxes. As all or part of the verdicts could be set aside in further proceedings, no amounts have been reflected in SCM's financial statements with respect to such payments.

15. Quarterly Results (Unaudited)

Unaudited financial results by quarter for the fiscal years ended June 30, 1978, and 1977, are summarized below.

EXHIBIT 2 *(continued)*

					Earnings per Share	
Fiscal Quarter	Net Sales	Gross Profit	Income Taxes	Net Income	Net Income	Assuming Full Dilution
		(in thousands, except per-share amounts)				
1978—First	$ 365,393	$ 96,100	$ 8,936	$10,281	$1.10	$1.02
Second .	359,513	92,493	2,591	6,985	.75	.70
Third	365,791	86,524	(1,993)	5,103	.55	.53
Fourth ..	418,610	105,243	4,408	15,211	1.63	1.50
Total ..	$1,509,307	$380,360	$13,942	$37,580	$4.03	$3.75
1977—First	$ 335,629	$103,711	$10,183	$11,161	$1.20	$1.10
Second .	337,607	87,611	6,965	8,503	.91	.84
Third	339,384	86,977	6,048	6,355	.68	.65
Fourth ..	365,024	98,766	8,737	11,393	1.22	1.11
Total ..	$1,377,644	$377,065	$31,933	$37,412	$4.01	$3.70

Net income for the fiscal 1978 first quarter includes approximately $1.5 million or $.16 per share from the sale of a facility and the favorable settlement of litigation on a disputed utility rate.

Results and tax benefits on the disposal of the European copier operations were better than anticipated, contributing net income of $2.8 million or $.30 per share in fiscal 1978—$1.8 million or $.19 per share in the third quarter and the balance in the second and fourth quarters.

Estimates of the effective tax rate for fiscal 1978 were adjusted quarterly to reflect changes in the anticipated level of operating income and investment tax credits.

Results for the first quarter of fiscal 1977 reflect a net charge of $1.7 million or $.18 per share, the estimated loss on disposition of SCM's European copier operations and certain other European operations.

16. Replacement Cost (unaudited; abridged by Casewriter)

		Property, Plant, and Equipment			
	Inventories	Cost	Net	Depreciation Expense	Cost of Sales*
June 30, 1978: (in thousands)					
Historical cost for which estimated replacement cost data is provided........................	$278,891	$ 532,682	$285,892	$29,377	$1,090,885
Estimated replacement cost	$302,896	$1,013,392	$464,009	$50,302	$1,092,692
June 30, 1977: (in thousands)					
Historical cost for which estimated replacement cost data is provided........................	$258,001	$ 439,469	$216,455	$23,678	$ 917,574
Estimated replacement cost	$285,183	$ 858,259	$381,903	$46,618	$ 929,685

* Excluding depreciation expense.

EXHIBIT 2 *(continued)*

17. Schedules

Schedule V
Property, Plant, and Equipment
For the Two Years Ended June 30, 1978
(amounts in thousands)

Column A	Column B	Column C	Column D	Column F
	Balance at Beginning	Additions		Balance at End of
Classification	of Year	at Cost	Retirements	Year
For the year ended June 30, 1978:				
Land and land improvements	$ 23,026	$ 1,136	$ 2,326	$ 21,836
Buildings	123,127	10,532	5,443	128,216
Machinery and other equipment	393,553	50,882	10,469	433,966
Total	$539,706	$62,550	$18,238	$584,018
For the year ended June 30, 1977:				
Land and land improvements	$ 22,130	$ 1,580	$ 684	$ 23,026
Buildings	119,525	10,870	7,268	123,127
Machinery and other equipment	376,626	53,668	36,741	393,553
Total	$518,281	$66,118	$44,693	$539,706

Schedule VI
Accumulated Depreciation of Property, Plant, and Equipment
For the Two Years Ended June 30, 1978
(amounts in thousands)

Column A	Column B	Column C	Column D	Column F
		Additions		
	Balance at	Charged to		Balance at
	Beginning	Costs and		End of
Description	of Year	Expenses	Retirements	Year
For the year ended June 30, 1978:				
Land improvements	$ 3,924	$ 644	$ 742	$ 3,826
Buildings	46,635	3,410	1,499	48,546
Machinery and other equipment	210,285	26,389	9,559	227,115
Total	$260,844	$30,443	$11,800	$279,487
For the year ended June 30, 1977:				
Land improvements	$ 3,636	$ 426	$ 138	$ 3,924
Buildings	47,487	3,174	4,026	46,635
Machinery and other equipment	215,866	27,432	33,013	210,285
Total	$266,989	$31,032	$37,177	$260,844

EXHIBIT 2 *(concluded)*

Schedule XII
Reserves
For the Two Years Ended June 30, 1978
(amounts in thousands)

Column A	Column B	Column C Additions	Column D	Column E
Description	Balance at Beginning of Year	Charged to Costs and Expenses	Deductions (1)	Balance at End of Year
Reserves deducted from assets to which they apply:				
For the year ended June 30, 1978:				
Reserves for doubtful accounts receivable	$6,156	$2,234	$1,141	$7,249
For the year ended June 30, 1977:				
Reserves for doubtful accounts receivable	$7,542	$1,249	$2,635	$6,156

(1) Deductions include uncollectible accounts written off, net of recoveries, and the net effect of discounts and allowances.

APPENDIX

Present Value Tables

TABLE A: Present Value of $1 Table A shows the present value of $1 received *n* years hence at *i* annual rate of return on the original investment. For example, to find the amount that would have to be invested today (the "present value") to receive $1 10 years hence if the annual rate of return earned was 10 percent, follow these steps: First, go across the top of the table to the 10 percent column. Next, go down this column until the 10 years line is reached. The factor 0.386 is found at this location in the table. This factor indicates that an investment of approximately 38 cents today at 10 percent annual interest will grow to $1 in 10 years.

Years Hence	1%	2%	4%	6%	8%	10%	12%	14%	15%	16%	18%	20%	22%	24%	25%	26%	28%	30%	35%	40%	45%	50%
1	.990	.980	.962	.943	.926	.909	.893	.877	.870	.862	.847	.833	.820	.806	.800	.794	.781	.769	.741	.714	.690	.667
2	.980	.961	.925	.890	.857	.826	.797	.769	.756	.743	.718	.694	.672	.650	.640	.630	.610	.592	.549	.510	.476	.444
3	.971	.942	.889	.840	.794	.751	.712	.675	.658	.641	.609	.579	.551	.524	.512	.500	.477	.455	.406	.364	.328	.296
4	.961	.924	.855	.792	.735	.683	.636	.592	.572	.552	.516	.482	.451	.423	.410	.397	.373	.350	.301	.260	.226	.198
5	.951	.906	.822	.747	.681	.621	.567	.519	.497	.476	.437	.402	.370	.341	.328	.315	.291	.269	.223	.186	.156	.132
6	.942	.888	.790	.705	.630	.564	.507	.456	.432	.410	.370	.335	.303	.275	.262	.250	.227	.207	.165	.133	.108	.088
7	.933	.871	.760	.665	.583	.513	.452	.400	.376	.354	.314	.279	.249	.222	.210	.198	.178	.159	.122	.095	.074	.059
8	.923	.853	.731	.627	.540	.467	.404	.351	.327	.305	.266	.233	.204	.179	.168	.157	.139	.123	.091	.068	.051	.039
9	.914	.837	.703	.592	.500	.424	.361	.308	.284	.263	.225	.194	.167	.144	.134	.125	.108	.094	.067	.048	.035	.026
10	.905	.820	.676	.558	.463	.386	.322	.270	.247	.227	.191	.162	.137	.116	.107	.099	.085	.073	.050	.035	.024	.017
11	.896	.804	.650	.527	.429	.350	.287	.237	.215	.195	.162	.135	.112	.094	.086	.079	.066	.056	.037	.025	.017	.012
12	.887	.788	.625	.497	.397	.319	.257	.208	.187	.168	.137	.112	.092	.076	.069	.062	.052	.043	.027	.018	.012	.008
13	.879	.773	.601	.469	.368	.290	.229	.182	.163	.145	.116	.093	.075	.061	.055	.050	.040	.033	.020	.013	.008	.005
14	.870	.758	.577	.442	.340	.263	.205	.160	.141	.125	.099	.078	.062	.049	.044	.039	.032	.025	.015	.009	.006	.003
15	.861	.743	.555	.417	.315	.239	.183	.140	.123	.108	.084	.065	.051	.040	.035	.031	.025	.020	.011	.006	.004	.002
16	.853	.728	.534	.394	.292	.218	.163	.123	.107	.093	.071	.054	.042	.032	.028	.025	.019	.015	.008	.005	.003	.002
17	.844	.714	.513	.371	.270	.198	.146	.108	.093	.080	.060	.045	.034	.026	.023	.020	.015	.012	.006	.003	.002	.001
18	.836	.700	.494	.350	.250	.180	.130	.095	.081	.069	.051	.038	.028	.021	.018	.016	.012	.009	.005	.002	.001	.001
19	.828	.686	.475	.331	.232	.164	.116	.083	.070	.060	.043	.031	.023	.017	.014	.012	.009	.007	.003	.002	.001	
20	.820	.673	.456	.312	.215	.149	.104	.073	.061	.051	.037	.026	.019	.014	.012	.010	.007	.005	.002	.001	.001	
21	.811	.660	.439	.294	.199	.135	.093	.064	.053	.044	.031	.022	.015	.011	.009	.008	.006	.004	.002	.001		
22	.803	.647	.422	.278	.184	.123	.083	.056	.046	.038	.026	.018	.013	.009	.007	.006	.004	.003	.001	.001		
23	.795	.634	.406	.262	.170	.112	.074	.049	.040	.033	.022	.015	.010	.007	.006	.005	.003	.002	.001			
24	.788	.622	.390	.247	.158	.102	.066	.043	.035	.028	.019	.013	.008	.006	.005	.004	.003	.002	.001			
25	.780	.610	.375	.233	.146	.092	.059	.038	.030	.024	.016	.010	.007	.005	.004	.003	.002	.001	.001			
26	.772	.598	.361	.220	.135	.084	.053	.033	.026	.021	.014	.009	.006	.004	.003	.002	.002	.001				
27	.764	.586	.347	.207	.125	.076	.047	.029	.023	.018	.011	.007	.005	.003	.002	.002	.001	.001				
28	.757	.574	.333	.196	.116	.069	.042	.026	.020	.016	.010	.006	.004	.002	.002	.002	.001	.001				
29	.749	.563	.321	.185	.107	.063	.037	.022	.017	.014	.008	.005	.003	.002	.002	.001	.001	.001				
30	.742	.552	.308	.174	.099	.057	.033	.020	.015	.012	.007	.004	.003	.002	.001	.001	.001	.001				
40	.672	.453	.208	.097	.046	.022	.011	.005	.004	.003	.001	.001										
50	.608	.372	.141	.054	.021	.009	.003	.001	.001	.001												

TABLE B: Present Value of $1 Received Annually for n Years Table B shows the present value of $1 received annually for each of the next n years if i annual rate of return is earned on the remaining balance of the original investment throughout this period. For example, to find the amount needed to be invested today to receive $1 for each of the next 20 years if 10 percent can be earned on the investment, follow these steps: First, go across the top of the table in the 10 percent column. Next, go down the column to the 20 years line. The factor 8.514 is shown at this spot. This factor tells us that a 10 percent investment of $8.51 today will return to the investor $1 for each of the next 20 years. At the end of that time, the investor will have recovered all of his original investment plus a return of 10 percent. Therefore the present value of $1 per year for 20 years discounted at 10 percent is $8.51.

Years (n)	1%	2%	4%	6%	8%	10%	12%	14%	15%	16%	18%	20%	22%	24%	25%	26%	28%	30%	35%	40%	45%	50%
1	0.990	0.980	0.962	0.943	0.926	0.909	0.893	0.877	0.870	0.862	0.847	0.833	0.820	0.806	0.800	0.794	0.781	0.769	0.741	0.714	0.690	0.667
2	1.970	1.942	1.886	1.833	1.783	1.736	1.690	1.647	1.626	1.605	1.566	1.528	1.492	1.457	1.440	1.424	1.392	1.361	1.289	1.224	1.165	1.111
3	2.941	2.884	2.775	2.673	2.577	2.487	2.402	2.322	2.283	2.246	2.174	2.106	2.042	1.981	1.952	1.923	1.868	1.816	1.696	1.589	1.493	1.407
4	3.902	3.808	3.630	3.465	3.312	3.170	3.037	2.914	2.855	2.798	2.690	2.589	2.494	2.404	2.362	2.320	2.241	2.166	1.997	1.849	1.720	1.605
5	4.853	4.713	4.452	4.212	3.993	3.791	3.605	3.433	3.352	3.274	3.127	2.991	2.864	2.745	2.689	2.635	2.532	2.436	2.220	2.035	1.876	1.737
6	5.795	5.601	5.242	4.917	4.623	4.355	4.111	3.889	3.784	3.685	3.498	3.326	3.167	3.020	2.951	2.885	2.759	2.643	2.385	2.168	1.983	1.824
7	6.728	6.472	6.002	5.582	5.206	4.868	4.564	4.288	4.160	4.039	3.812	3.605	3.416	3.242	3.161	3.083	2.937	2.802	2.508	2.263	2.057	1.883
8	7.652	7.325	6.733	6.210	5.747	5.335	4.968	4.639	4.487	4.344	4.078	3.837	3.619	3.421	3.329	3.241	3.076	2.925	2.598	2.331	2.108	1.922
9	8.566	8.162	7.435	6.802	6.247	5.759	5.328	4.946	4.772	4.607	4.303	4.031	3.786	3.566	3.463	3.366	3.184	3.019	2.665	2.379	2.144	1.948
10	9.471	8.983	8.111	7.360	6.710	6.145	5.650	5.216	5.019	4.833	4.494	4.192	3.923	3.682	3.571	3.465	3.269	3.092	2.715	2.414	2.168	1.965
11	10.368	9.787	8.760	7.887	7.139	6.495	5.938	5.453	5.234	5.029	4.656	4.327	4.035	3.776	3.656	3.544	3.335	3.147	2.752	2.438	2.185	1.977
12	11.255	10.575	9.385	8.384	7.536	6.814	6.194	5.660	5.421	5.197	4.793	4.439	4.127	3.851	3.725	3.606	3.387	3.190	2.779	2.456	2.196	1.985
13	12.134	11.343	9.986	8.853	7.904	7.103	6.424	5.842	5.583	5.342	4.910	4.533	4.203	3.912	3.780	3.656	3.427	3.223	2.799	2.468	2.204	1.990
14	13.004	12.106	10.563	9.295	8.244	7.367	6.628	6.002	5.724	5.468	5.008	4.611	4.265	3.962	3.824	3.695	3.459	3.249	2.814	2.477	2.210	1.993
15	13.865	12.849	11.118	9.712	8.559	7.606	6.811	6.142	5.847	5.575	5.092	4.675	4.315	4.001	3.859	3.726	3.483	3.268	2.825	2.484	2.214	1.995
16	14.718	13.578	11.652	10.106	8.851	7.824	6.974	6.265	5.954	5.669	5.162	4.730	4.357	4.033	3.887	3.751	3.503	3.283	2.834	2.489	2.216	1.997
17	15.562	14.292	12.166	10.477	9.122	8.022	7.120	6.373	6.047	5.749	5.222	4.775	4.391	4.059	3.910	3.771	3.518	3.295	2.840	2.492	2.218	1.998
18	16.398	14.992	12.659	10.828	9.372	8.201	7.250	6.467	6.128	5.818	5.273	4.812	4.419	4.080	3.928	3.786	3.529	3.304	2.844	2.494	2.219	1.999
19	17.226	15.678	13.134	11.158	9.604	8.365	7.366	6.550	6.198	5.877	5.316	4.844	4.442	4.097	3.942	3.799	3.539	3.311	2.848	2.496	2.220	1.999
20	18.046	16.351	13.590	11.470	9.818	8.514	7.469	6.623	6.259	5.929	5.353	4.870	4.460	4.110	3.954	3.808	3.546	3.316	2.850	2.497	2.221	1.999
21	18.857	17.011	14.029	11.764	10.017	8.649	7.562	6.687	6.312	5.973	5.384	4.891	4.476	4.121	3.963	3.816	3.551	3.320	2.852	2.498	2.221	2.000
22	19.660	17.658	14.451	12.042	10.201	8.772	7.645	6.743	6.359	6.011	5.410	4.909	4.488	4.130	3.970	3.822	3.556	3.323	2.853	2.498	2.222	2.000
23	20.456	18.292	14.857	12.303	10.371	8.883	7.718	6.792	6.399	6.044	5.432	4.925	4.499	4.137	3.976	3.827	3.559	3.325	2.854	2.499	2.222	2.000
24	21.243	18.914	15.247	12.550	10.529	8.985	7.784	6.835	6.434	6.073	5.451	4.937	4.507	4.143	3.981	3.831	3.562	3.327	2.855	2.499	2.222	2.000
25	22.023	19.523	15.622	12.783	10.675	9.077	7.843	6.873	6.464	6.097	5.467	4.948	4.514	4.147	3.985	3.834	3.564	3.329	2.856	2.499	2.222	2.000
26	22.795	20.121	15.983	13.003	10.810	9.161	7.896	6.906	6.491	6.118	5.480	4.956	4.520	4.151	3.988	3.837	3.566	3.330	2.856	2.500	2.222	2.000
27	23.560	20.707	16.330	13.211	10.935	9.237	7.943	6.935	6.514	6.136	5.492	4.964	4.524	4.154	3.990	3.839	3.567	3.331	2.856	2.500	2.222	2.000
28	24.316	21.281	16.663	13.406	11.051	9.307	7.984	6.961	6.534	6.152	5.502	4.970	4.528	4.157	3.992	3.840	3.568	3.331	2.857	2.500	2.222	2.000
29	25.066	21.844	16.984	13.591	11.158	9.370	8.022	6.983	6.551	6.166	5.510	4.975	4.531	4.159	3.994	3.841	3.569	3.332	2.857	2.500	2.222	2.000
30	25.808	22.396	17.292	13.765	11.258	9.427	8.055	7.003	6.566	6.177	5.517	4.979	4.534	4.160	3.995	3.842	3.569	3.332	2.857	2.500	2.222	2.000
40	32.835	27.355	19.793	15.046	11.925	9.779	8.244	7.105	6.642	6.234	5.548	4.997	4.544	4.166	3.999	3.846	3.571	3.333	2.857	2.500	2.222	2.000
50	39.196	31.424	21.482	15.762	12.234	9.915	8.304	7.133	6.661	6.246	5.554	4.999	4.545	4.167	4.000	3.846	3.571	3.333	2.857	2.500	2.222	2.000

SOURCE: From tables computed by Jerome Bracken and Charles J. Christenson. Copyright © 1961 by the President and Fellows of Harvard College. Used by permission.

INDEXES

CASE INDEX

SUBJECT INDEX

*This book has been set VideoComp in 10 and 9 point
Gael, leaded 2 points. Part titles and chapter numbers
are 24 point Spectra Light. Part numbers are 32 point
Spectra Light and chapter titles are 18 point Spectra
Light. The size of the type page is 29 by 49½ picas.*